About the author

Respected wine critic and vigneron James Halliday AM has a career that spans 50 years, but he is most widely known for his witty and informative writing about wine. As one of the founders of Brokenwood in the Hunter Valley and thereafter of Coldstream Hills in the Yarra Valley, James is an unmatched authority on every aspect of the wine industry, from the planting and pruning of vines through to the creation and marketing of the finished product. His winemaking has led him to sojourns in Bordeaux and Burgundy, and he had a long career as a wine judge in Australia and overseas. In 1995 he received the wine industry's ultimate accolade, the Maurice O'Shea Award. In 2010 James was made a Member of the Order of Australia for his services to the wine industry. Between 1960 and 1988 he was also a lawyer and partner of a large Sydney/Melbourne law firm.

James has written or contributed to nearly 80 books on wine since he began writing in 1970. His books have been translated into Mandarin, Japanese, French, German, Danish, Icelandic and Polish, and have been published in the United Kingdom and the United States, as well as in Australia. He is the author of *Varietal Wines*, *James Halliday's Wine Atlas of Australia*, *The Australian Wine Encyclopedia* and *A Life in Wine*.

EXPAND YOUR WINE KNOWLEDGE WITH A HALLIDAY WINE COMPANION SUBSCRIPTION

SAVE $20 ON AN ANNUAL MEMBERSHIP*

- ACCESS MORE THAN 140,000 TASTING NOTES
- MANAGE YOUR WINE COLLECTION WITH THE VIRTUAL CELLAR
- ENJOY SIX ISSUES OF HALLIDAY MAGAZINE A YEAR

SUBSCRIBE NOW AT

winecompanion.com.au

ENTER COUPON CODE **COMPANION21**
AT CHECKOUT

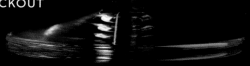

Halliday
WINE COMPANION

THE BESTSELLING AND DEFINITIVE GUIDE TO AUSTRALIAN WINE

ESTABLISHED 1986 – WINECOMPANION.COM.AU

2021

Hardie Grant

BOOKS

Wine zones and regions of Australia

NEW SOUTH WALES		
WINE ZONE	WINE REGION	
Big Rivers (A)	Murray Darling	1
	Perricoota	2
	Riverina	3
	Swan Hill	4
Central Ranges (B)	Cowra	5
	Mudgee	6
	Orange	7
Hunter Valley (C)	Hunter	8
	Upper Hunter	9
Northern Rivers (D)	Hastings River	10
Northern Slopes (E)	New England	11
South Coast (F)	Shoalhaven Coast	12
	Southern Highlands	13
Southern New South Wales (G)	Canberra District	14
	Gundagai	15
	Hilltops	16
	Tumbarumba	17
Western Plains (H)		

SOUTH AUSTRALIA		
WINE ZONE	WINE REGION	
Adelaide Super Zone includes Mount Lofty Ranges, Fleurieu and Barossa wine regions		
Barossa	Barossa Valley	18
	Eden Valley	19
Fleurieu (J)	Currency Creek	20
	Kangaroo Island	21
	Langhorne Creek	22
	McLaren Vale	23
	Southern Fleurieu	24
Mount Lofty Ranges	Adelaide Hills	25
	Adelaide Plains	26
	Clare Valley	27
Far North (K)	Southern Flinders Ranges	28
Limestone Coast (L)	Coonawarra	29
	Mount Benson	30
	Mount Gambier	31
	Padthaway	32
	Robe	33
	Wrattonbully	34
Lower Murray (M)	Riverland	35
The Peninsulas (N)	Southern Eyre Peninsula*	36

VICTORIA		
WINE ZONE	WINE REGION	
Central Victoria (P)	Bendigo	37
	Goulburn Valley	38
	Heathcote	39
	Strathbogie Ranges	40
Gippsland (Q)	Upper Goulburn	41
	Alpine Valleys	42
North East Victoria (R)	Beechworth	43
	Glenrowan	44
	King Valley	45
	Rutherglen	46
North West Victoria (S)	Murray Darling	47
	Swan Hill	48
Port Phillip (T)	Geelong	49
	Macedon Ranges	50
	Mornington Peninsula	51
	Sunbury	52
	Yarra Valley	53
Western Victoria (U)	Ballarat*	54
	Grampians	55
	Henty	56
	Pyrenees	57

* For more information see page 50.

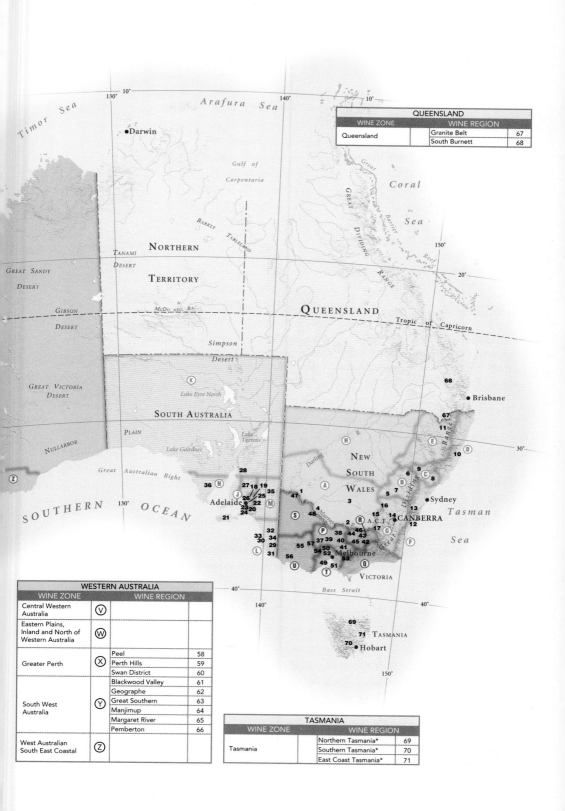

QUEENSLAND		
WINE ZONE	WINE REGION	
Queensland	Granite Belt	67
	South Burnett	68

WESTERN AUSTRALIA			
WINE ZONE		WINE REGION	
Central Western Australia	Ⓥ		
Eastern Plains, Inland and North of Western Australia	Ⓦ		
Greater Perth	Ⓧ	Peel	58
		Perth Hills	59
		Swan District	60
South West Australia	Ⓨ	Blackwood Valley	61
		Geographe	62
		Great Southern	63
		Manjimup	64
		Margaret River	65
		Pemberton	66
West Australian South East Coastal	Ⓩ		

TASMANIA		
WINE ZONE	WINE REGION	
Tasmania	Northern Tasmania*	69
	Southern Tasmania*	70
	East Coast Tasmania*	71

Published in 2020 by Hardie Grant Books,
an imprint of Hardie Grant Publishing

Hardie Grant Books (Melbourne)
Building 1, 658 Church Street
Richmond, Victoria 3121

Hardie Grant Books (London)
5th & 6th Floors
52–54 Southwark Street
London SE1 1UN

hardiegrantbooks.com

The *Australian Wine Companion* is a joint venture between James Halliday and
Explore Australia Pty Ltd.

The map in this publication incorporates data copyright © Commonwealth of
Australia (Geoscience Australia) 2004. Geoscience Australia has not evaluated
the data as altered and incorporated within this publication and therefore gives
no warranty regarding accuracy, completeness, currency or suitability for any
particular purpose.

Australian wine zones and wine regions data copyright © Australian Wine
and Brandy Corporation, April 2005

ISBN 978 1 74379 644 3
VINTAGE CELLARS EDITION 978 1 74379 709 9

10 9 8 7 6 5 4 3 2 1

Cover design by Pidgeon Ward
Illustration by Andrew Murray
Typeset by Megan Ellis
Author photograph by Julian Kingma
Printed by McPherson's Printing Group, Maryborough, Victoria

Contents

Introduction

My introduction to the 2010 edition of the *Wine Companion* was written as Australia's wine producers continued to grapple with overproduction – caused by the reversal of the dizzy rise in exports (and production) over the first seven years of the new millennium. Common wisdom was that we needed to permanently remove 46 500ha, or 400 000t, to balance supply and demand. Nature intervened: after a bumper 2009 crop, 2010 fell dramatically to the smallest harvest of the following nine vintages. On the sales side, China spent $164 million importing our wines.

By the 2015 edition, the obstinately overvalued AUD (oscillating around 93 cents of the USD) was the centre of frustration. But for the 2018 edition, I was able to open with the words: 'Australian wine is in a good place right now. The green shoots of a few years ago are now leaves, flowers and grapes.' The exchange rate had fallen substantially, China's imports had soared to $360 million, and the harvest was spot on the 2009–2014 average of 1.76 million tonnes.

In the year preceding the 2020 edition, China and Hong Kong spent over $1.1 billion on Australian wine, the value exceeding that of the US, UK and Canada combined. Chinese tourism was flying, with education of Chinese students one of Australia's largest exports.

In the 12 months to March 2020, wine exports to China rose by 13% to $1.2 billion, but who knows when that figure will be exceeded. As this 2021 edition goes to print in June 2020, Australia's exports to China are in the political vortex of our overall trade relations and have been identified by China as a target in its sights. Exports will fall, the only questions by how much and for how long.

I haven't even mentioned COVID-19, but it has been brutal in its impact on small to medium-sized wineries, the vast majority reliant on tourism for the bulk of their sales income. When a household name such as Rocky O'Callaghan sends a signed letter to everyone on Rockford's mailing list encouraging them to buy more, you realise how far, wide and deep the COVID-19 impact has penetrated the wine business.

I might have started this introduction reporting on the worst season ever for grape growing across the entire country, which I cover in detail for the vintage snapshot on pages 58–62. It was a deadly cocktail of full-on drought as the growing season got underway, then extreme heat and windy conditions that badly affected flowering and fruit-set. Of course, this also fanned the flames of the never-ending bushfires that devoured vineyards, farm equipment and wineries (the tragedy of Kangaroo Island a soul-searing example); the ensuing smoke taint ruined such red grapes that withstood all that had gone before.

As the spectre of COVID-19 becomes less daunting, I implore those who read these words to plan visits – the longer, the better – to the ever-changing beauty of Australia's 63 wine regions. Those small to medium-sized wineries, many family owned and run, are seeking to free themselves from the vinous crucifix so many bear, and a quick look at the vintage charts on pages 56–7 will tell you there is a feast to be had with the wines of 2019.

How to use this book

Before I launch into my normal explanation of the way the *Wine Companion* works, I need to lay out the groundwork for a one-off major change with this year's winery ratings. If you read my snapshot of the weather conditions leading up to, during and immediately after the harvest on pages 58–62, you will realise this was a freakishly terrible vintage. Drought and bad weather during flowering decimated the yields in every region of Australia, previously unheard of. Bushfires burnt vineyards, wineries and houses, leaving smoke taint in their wake. Then COVID-19 struck, devastating the cellar door and restaurant trade, followed by the abrupt termination of most exports to China. For all these reasons, no winery's rating has been reduced this year.

Wineries

Henschke   ★★★★★

1428 Keyneton Road, Keyneton, SA 5353 **Region** Eden Valley
T (08) 8564 8223 **www**.henschke.com.au **Open** Mon–Sat 9–4.30
Winemaker Stephen Henschke **Est.** 1868 **Dozens** 30 000 **Vyds** 109ha
Henschke is the foremost medium-sized wine producer in Australia. Stephen and Prue Henschke have taken a crown jewel and polished it to an even greater brilliance. In this 2021 edition of the *Wine Companion*, it has a staggering six wines with 97–99 points, and a further 13 with 95–96 points. Year on year they have quietly added labels for single vineyards, single varieties or blends. The wines hail from the Eden Valley (the majority), the Barossa Valley or the Adelaide Hills. There's a compelling logic and focus – no excursions to McLaren Vale, Coonawarra, etc. There are now four wines from the Hill of Grace Vineyard: the icon itself, Hill of Roses (also shiraz), Hill of Peace (semillon) and Hill of Faith (mataro); the last two are only made in exceptional years. Recognition as Winery of the Year is arguably long overdue. Exports to all major markets.

Henschke

The producer name appearing on the front label is used throughout the book.

★★★★★

Under normal circumstances, I look at the ratings for this and the previous two years; if the wines tasted this year justify a higher rating than last year, that higher rating is given. If, on the other hand, the wines are of lesser quality, I take into account the track record over the past two years (or longer where the winery is well known) and make a judgement call on whether it should retain its ranking or be given a lesser one. In what I call the mercy rating, in most instances a demotion is no more than half a star. Where no wines are submitted by a well-rated winery with a track record of providing samples, I may use my discretion to roll over last year's rating. However, as noted above, this year no winery's rating was reduced.

While there are (only) 1165 wineries profiled in this edition, there are more than 2800 wineries to be found on www.winecompanion.com.au.

The number at the end of each rating below notes the number of wineries in that category in this year's edition, but the percentage is that of the total number of wineries in the *Wine Companion* database at the time of going to print. Two caveats: first, I retain a discretionary right to depart from the normal criteria; second, the basis of the ratings are best understood on the website, where all wine ratings appear.

Some may think my ratings are too generous, but just over half (59.1%) of the 'active' wineries in our database are given ratings in this book, spread across the eight ratings categories. Moreover, if I were to reduce the number of wineries in each category by (say) 50%, the relative ranking would not change, other than a massive increase in the NR category, providing no useful guidance for the reader.

★★★★★   Outstanding winery regularly producing wines of exemplary quality and typicity. Will have at least two wines rated at 95 points or above, and has had a 5-star rating for the previous two years. 273 wineries, 9.7%

    Where the winery name itself is printed in red, it is a winery generally acknowledged to have had a long track record of excellence in the context of its region – truly the best of the best. 102 wineries, 3.6%

★★★★★   Outstanding winery capable of producing wines of very high quality, and did so this year. Also will usually have at least two wines rated at 95 points or above. 285 wineries, 10.1%

★★★★☆   Excellent winery able to produce wines of high to very high quality, knocking on the door of a 5-star rating. Will normally have one wine rated at 95 points or above, and two (or more) at 90 and above, others 87–89. 199 wineries, 7%

★★★★   Very good producer of wines with class and character. Will have two (or more) wines rated at 90 points and above (or possibly one at 95 and above). 221 wineries, 7.8%

★★★☆   A solid, usually reliable maker of good, sometimes very good wines. Will have one wine at 90 points and above, others 86–89. 52 wineries, 1.8%

★★★   A typically good winery, but often has a few lesser wines. Will have wines at 86–89 points. 31 wineries, 1.1%

NR   The NR rating mainly appears on www.winecompanion.com.au. The rating is given in a range of circumstances: where there have been no tastings in the 12-month period; where there have been tastings but with no wines scoring more than 88 points; or where the tastings have, for one reason or another, proved not to fairly reflect the reputation of a winery with a track record of success. NR wineries in the book are generally new wineries with no wine entries. 3 wineries, 50.1%

The vine leaf symbol indicates the 59 wineries that are new entries in this year's *Wine Companion*.

1428 Keyneton Road, Keyneton, SA 5353 **T** (08) 8564 8223

Contact details are usually those of the winery and cellar door, but in a few instances may simply be a postal address; this occurs when the wine is made at another winery or wineries, and is sold only through the website and/or retail.

Region Eden Valley

A full list of zones, regions and subregions appears on pages 50–3. Occasionally you will see 'various', meaning the wine is made from purchased grapes from a number of regions, often for a winery without a vineyard of its own.

www.henschke.com.au

An important reference point, normally containing material not found (for space reasons) in this book.

Open Mon–Sat 9–4.30

Although a winery might be listed as not open or only open on weekends, many may in fact be prepared to open by appointment. A telephone call will establish whether this is possible or not. For space reasons we have simplified the open hours listed; where the hours vary each day or for holidays, we simply refer the reader to the website.

Winemaker Stephen Henschke

In all but the smallest producers, the winemaker is simply the head of a team; there may be many executive winemakers actually responsible for specific wines in the medium to large companies (80 000 dozens and upwards). Once again, space constraints mean usually only one or two winemakers are named, even if they are part of a larger team.

Est. 1868

Keep in mind that some makers consider the year in which they purchased the land to be the year of establishment, others the year in which they first planted grapes, others the year they first made wine, and so on. There may also be minor complications where there has been a change of ownership or break in production.

Dozens 30 000

This figure (representing the number of 9-litre/12-bottle cases produced each year) is merely an indication of the size of the operation. Some winery entries do not feature a production figure: this is either because the winery (principally, but not exclusively, the large companies) regards this information as confidential.

Vyds 109ha

Shows the hectares of vineyard/s owned by the winery.

Henschke is the foremost medium-sized wine producer in Australia. Stephen and Prue Henschke have taken a crown jewel and polished it to an even greater brilliance. In this 2021 edition of the *Wine Companion*, it has a staggering six wines with 97–99 points, and a further 13 with 95–96 points …

The summary is surely self-explanatory, except that I have tried to vary the subjects I discuss in this part of the winery entry.

Tasting notes

Hill of Grace 2015 Henschke says the '15 vintage provided stunning and elegant Eden Valley shiraz with extraordinary flavours, purity of fruit and acid balance. And indeed that's a fair description of this medium-bodied Hill of Grace. The colour is still bright, clear crimson-purple, and the beautifully balanced fruit flavours are vibrantly fresh. It would be easy to underestimate the likely longevity of this wine. One of the all-time greats. Vino-Lok. 14.5% alc. **Rating** 99 **To** 2045 $865

There has been a progressive adoption of the 100-point system in wine shows and in reviews by other commentators. The majority follow the system outlined below, and which I used in precisely this form in the *Wine Companion 2021*. Space constraints mean that only 4063 notes are printed in full in this book, with points, drink-to dates and prices included for a further 4056 wines. Tasting notes for wines 95 points and over are printed in red. Tasting notes for all wines receiving 84 points or above appear on www.winecompanion.com.au. See also page 25.

Points	Medal		Rating
97–99	GOLD		**Exceptional.** Wines that have won a major trophy/ trophies in important wine shows, or are of that standard.
95–96	GOLD		**Outstanding.** Wines of gold medal standard, usually with a great pedigree.
94	SILVER		Wines on the cusp of gold medal status, virtually indistinguishable from those wines receiving 95 points.
90–93	SILVER		**Highly recommended.** Wines of silver medal standard, wines of great quality, style and character, and worthy of a place in any cellar.
89	BRONZE		**Recommended.** Wines on the cusp of silver medal standard, the difference purely a judgement call.
86–88	BRONZE		Wines of bronze medal standard; well produced, flavoursome wines, usually not requiring cellaring.
84–85			**Acceptable.** Wines of good commercial quality, free from significant fault.
80–83			**Over to you.** Everyday wines without much character and/or somewhat faulty.
75–79			**Not recommended.** Wines with one or more significant winemaking faults.
✪			**Special value.** Wines considered to offer special value for money within the context of their glass symbol status.

Hill of Grace 2015

The tasting note opens with the vintage of the wine tasted.

Henschke says the '15 vintage provided stunning and elegant Eden Valley shiraz with extraordinary flavours … Vino-Lok. 14.5% alc. **Rating 99 To 2045 $865**

This tasting note will have been made within the 12 months prior to publication. Even that is a long time, and during the life of this book the wine will almost certainly change. More than this, remember the tasting is a highly subjective and imperfect art.

The initials CM, JF, JP, NG or SC appearing at the end of a tasting note signify that Campbell Mattinson, Jane Faulkner, Jeni Port, Ned Goodwin or Steven Creber tasted the wine and provided the tasting note and rating. Short biographies for each member of the tasting team can be found on page 63.

Vino-Lok

This is the closure used for this particular wine. The closures in use for the wines tasted are (in descending order): screwcap 86.2% (last year 87.9%), one-piece natural cork 6.8% (last year 6.5%), Diam 4.4% (last year 4.1%). The remaining 2.6% (in approximate order of importance) are Crown Seal, Vino-Lok, ProCork, Zork and Twin Top. I believe the percentage of screwcap-closed wines will continue to rise for red wines; 96.1% of white wines tasted were screwcapped, leaving little room for any further increase. If the bottle is not a standard 750ml, its size will also be included here.

14.5 % alc.

This piece of information is in one sense self-explanatory. What is less obvious is the increasing concern of many Australian winemakers about the rise in levels of alcohol, and much research and practical experimentation (for example picking earlier, or higher fermentation temperatures in open fermenters) is occurring. Reverse osmosis and yeast selection are two of the options available to decrease higher than desirable alcohol levels. Recent changes to domestic and export labelling mean the stated alcohol will be within a maximum of 0.5% difference to that obtained by analysis.

To 2045

Rather than give a span of drinking years, I have simply provided a (conservative) 'drink to' date. Modern winemaking is such that, even if a wine has 10 or 20 years of future during which it will gain greater complexity, it can be enjoyed at any time over the intervening months and years.

$865

I use the price provided by the winery. It should be regarded as a guide, particularly if purchased retail.

Winery of the Year

Henschke

Henschke is the foremost medium-sized winery in Australia, and its recognition as Winery of the Year is long overdue. Whether you consider the winery's history, the number and quality of its present wines, or its future, the answer is the same: it has no equal.

Stephen is the fifth generation of the Henschke family, and he and wife Prue along with their three children – sixth-generation Johann, Justine and Andreas – are variously involved in the business. Stephen and Prue have taken the irreplaceable vineyard that is the jewel in the crown of a flourishing family business, polished it, and steadily built a complex and compelling suite of estate-owned and local-grower-supplied wines of consistently flawless quality.

Stephen's father, Cyril, was the visionary who turned around what was a quiet producer of bulk shiraz from the Hill of Grace vineyard. Cyril purchased and bottled shiraz from Colin Angas's 16ha 40-year-old Mount Edelstone shiraz vineyard from 1952. Hill of Grace was sold into jugs, bottles or whatever vessel customers provided until it, too, was bottled from 1958.

In 1978, Stephen became assistant winemaker, and he and Cyril made the winery's first Cabernet Sauvignon. Cyril's death in the following year saw the wine named after him. It was also in that year the wine received the trophy for best Burgundy (!) at the Royal Adelaide Wine Show.

Stephen and Prue have purchased two further properties at Lenswood in the Adelaide Hills. These vineyards have all given birth to labels, as have wines made from contract growers in the Barossa (nine wines between 1996 and 2017) and the addition of Hill of Roses (shiraz), Hill of Faith (mataro) and Hill of Peace (semillon) from parts of the Hill of Grace vineyard.

Stephen is the winemaker, Prue the viticulturist behind the magnificent array of wines profiled in this edition of the *Wine Companion*. They are headed by six wines with 97–99 points, four with 96 points and nine with 95, then ten with 90–94 points.

There are no tricks of equipment or practice in the winery, just attention to detail. For many years now they have been using organic/biodynamic practices in the vineyards, though the Henschkes have not sought certification. Quite apart from the application of the bio sprays and compounds, no herbicides or insecticides are used. Prue has added her own signature with a continuous thick layer of straw mulch running along each row, enhancing worm and microbial activity and preventing loss of moisture. Great wine made in the vineyard? Absolutely.

Previous Winery of the Year recipients were Paringa Estate (2007), Balnaves of Coonawarra (2008), Brookland Valley (2009), Tyrrell's (2010), Larry Cherubino Wines (2011), Port Phillip Estate/Kooyong (2012), Kilikanoon (2013), Penfolds (2014), Hentley Farm Wines (2015), Tahbilk (2016), Mount Pleasant (2017), Mount Mary (2018), Seville Estate (2019) and Jim Barry Wines (2020).

Winemaker of the Year

Brett Grocke

Brett Grocke made his first appearance in the 2010 edition of the *Wine Companion* with three wines from the first vintage of Eperosa in 2005. His income came through Grocke Viticulture, a one-man business providing technical and consulting services to owners of vineyards spread across the Barossa Valley, Eden Valley, Adelaide Hills, Riverland, Langhorne Creek and Hindmarsh Valley.

His tertiary education began at the University of Adelaide, graduating in 1996 with a Bachelor of Applied Science (Exercise and Sport Science), excelling at golf and hockey. His focus tightened with a Graduate Diploma in Viticulture from the same university, secured in 2000. For five years he built his consulting practice, accumulating insights that can't be taught at university. His first vintage was completed in the corner of a shed in Tanunda with a hand-operated basket press, the wine moved by gravity. (I remember my first vintage in 1973 with the utmost clarity – it was much the same, except that I was one of three, not solo like Brett.)

Brett embarked on what turned out to be an eight-year search for a small vineyard with mature shiraz. He was particularly interested in the Krondorf region, where his father had sold his substantial vineyard holdings in the early '90s.

In June 2013 the Magnolia Vineyard came onto the market for the first time in over 150 years. It had been farmed by the Yates family since the 1850s, with shiraz first planted in 1896, followed by grenache in 1900, semillon in 1941, '71 and '75, and more shiraz in 1965, '96, 2010 and '17. The vineyard is in Vine Vale, the crucible of much of the earliest Barossa Valley plantings. The soil is alluvial sand, metres deep, the vineyard protected from western afternoon sun by a small gum-lined hill.

Only two months later a 6.2ha property on Krondorf Road came on the market, with 4.1ha of grenache planted in 1903. In an agreement that could only be struck in the Barossa, Brett and Rocky O'Callaghan formed a 50/50% partnership to buy the property, with a loan agreement sufficient to also provide funds for Eperosa's first winery, with an ultra-low footprint and maximum sustainability.

Brett has also been able to buy grenache from the 1858 Stonegarden Vineyard in the Eden Valley, and joined with the Light Regional Council to buy the grapes from a single row of ancient shiraz vines that once formed a boundary row of a vineyard now covered with houses.

So, you might ask, why does all this make Brett the Winemaker of the Year? Of the 56 wines he has made since 2005, 33 have received 95 or more points. He is a fiercely committed and proud sixth-generation Barossan vigneron/winemaker; as he explains, 'Eperosa has evolved from my interest in unique vineyards and great wine. My desire is to create wine from a soil up perspective, and stay true to the premise that exceptional wine is born from great fruit.'

Previous Winemaker of the Year recipients were Robert Diletti (2015), Peter Fraser (2016), Sarah Crowe (2017), Paul Hotker (2018), Julian Langworthy (2019) and Vanya Cullen (2020).

Wine of the Year

Brokenwood Graveyard Vineyard Hunter Valley Shiraz 2018

At the risk of oversimplification, the Hunter Valley has three soil types. The best (especially for red wines) is found on the scattered hillsides of friable red volcanic soils: free draining, yet with good water retention capacity. Next is the sandy soil of the wandering beds of creeks that once used to flow water: the consistency allows vine roots to penetrate deep in their search for hidden moisture; the bond between great semillon and sandy alluvial soils is very powerful. The third and most common soil type is acidic clay that needs constant cajoling to provide a modest crop of grapes. It is home to shiraz, the most ubiquitous red variety, accounting for two-thirds of the total red crop in the Hunter Valley.

I was one of three Sydney lawyers – now the only survivor – who embarked on a plan to establish a small Hunter Valley vineyard in the late 1960s. After several years, we found a 4ha block of acidic clay on which we planted shiraz and established Brokenwood. In 1978 we purchased an adjacent 16ha vineyard planted by Hungerford Hill mainly to shiraz on the selfsame nondescript soil.

In 1983, Iain Riggs AM was headhunted to become Brokenwood's first qualified winemaker, with his track record of making trophy-winning chardonnay in McLaren Vale being the deal-maker. Iain's wisdom has been the rock on which one of Australia's best small to medium-sized wineries has been built, Graveyard Shiraz its flag-bearer. How can this be, I hear you ask, if the soil is so deficient? Cover crops, gypsum and trace elements have played a continuous role in improving the structure of the soil. The 50-plus-year-old vines have been handled with kid gloves; any that die are replaced by an 18-month-old cane from a vine on one or other side, its tip buried in the soil, which then establishes its own root system.

The grapes are hand-picked and sorted, destemmed, not crushed, open-fermented with cultured yeast, hand-plunged, then have four days' cold soak run off to barrel, and are finally matured in used French puncheons. There are 500 dozen made, and only when the season permits. None were made 1992 (two-year drought), 2008, 2012, 2015, 2016 (rain) or 2020 (smoke taint). 2018 followed 2017's lead, each devoid of rain, allowing winemakers to choose the picking date, not a date imposed by the weather. The result was the best wines since the golden year of 1965.

After I had decided that this Graveyard was the Wine of the Year, Iain announced he was retiring on 30 June 2020, but he will remain on the board of directors.

Previous Wine of the Year recipients were Bass Phillip Reserve Pinot Noir 2010 (2014), Xanadu Stevens Road Cabernet Sauvignon 2011 (2015), Serrat Shiraz Viognier 2014 (2016), Best's Thomson Family Shiraz 2014 (2017), Henschke Hill of Grace 2012 (2018), Duke's Vineyard Magpie Hill Reserve Riesling 2017 (2019) and Yangarra Estate Vineyard High Sands McLaren Vale Grenache 2016 (2020).

Best Value Winery

Best's Wines

Many years ago, a basic algorithm was created that took into account the price of each wine being reviewed for the *Wine Companion* and the points it received to automatically add a 'special value' rosette at the end of its tasting note. It took out of play an emotional reaction that caused me to write 'good value' or 'great value' as part of a tasting note. Viewed in isolation, these words were reasonable; the problem was that they were influenced by a whole host of things that could impinge on the fairness or otherwise of the remarks. Shortly put, it wasn't consistent. The system was in play long before the band of tasters for the *Wine Companion* came on board; had it not been, the need for the algorithm would have been even more acute. Whatever one may think of the system, it has never led to complaints by winemakers or consumers.

You may say that the Best Value Winery should be that which collects the highest number of rosettes, or the highest strike rate. Both are important, but in this case there are yet other important factors that should be taken into account, and this year's winner has loads of them.

Best's Wines has a 154-year history with only two families involved, the current Thomson family for exactly 100 years, with the business having been established by Henry Best in 1868.

It has 1.2ha of pinot meunier planted in 1867, with 141 vines of pinot noir randomly interplanted at the same time. These are respectively the oldest plantings of the two varieties in the world, as phylloxera destroyed those in France (Burgundy and Champagne) and elsewhere in Europe. Best's pinot meunier was part of generic red blends until a large crop in 1967 led to its vinification as a single variety – a practice only then gaining traction in Australia. The fact that the currently available 2019 vintage is only $100 is fantastic, unbeatable value.

Ben Thomson and his father, Viv, would also likely point to the $25 price tag for the core range of 2019 Riesling, 2019 Pinot Noir, 2018 Shiraz, 2018 Cabernet Sauvignon and 2019 Dolcetto, all given 95 points by either Jane Faulkner or me. I haven't attempted a forensic search but can't remember a five-core-varietal band coming up so consistently.

The secret is the Grampians climate (and soils). The red wines in particular have cool-grown finesse, length and freshness draped over warm-grown structure, the varietal flavours speaking with utmost clarity. If I wanted to grow medium-bodied red wines with a 30-year future, I'd head to the Grampians.

Previous Best Value Winery recipients were Hoddles Creek Estate (2015), West Cape Howe (2016), Larry Cherubino Wines (2017), Grosset (2018), Provenance (2019) and Domaine Naturaliste (2020).

Best New Winery

Varney Wines

Alan Varney was 18 when he left home in 1998 to backpack around the world, with no fixed timeline or destination. Things changed the following year when he met wife-to-be Kathrin. 'I chased her to her hometown of Berlin,' he says, 'and from that base I started tasting my way through the world of wine.' Back in Australia with Kathrin, he obtained a degree in oenology from Melbourne University and worked vintages in Central Victoria.

After their two sons were born, Alan and Kathrin decided to move to South Australia, where Alan worked with Orlando Wines and Longview Vineyard in the Adelaide Hills. A fill-in vintage at d'Arenberg turned into an 11-year stay as he grew into a senior winemaking position. He's also fitted in vintages in California, New York and most recently Portugal, in 2017 – the same year he established Varney Wines.

He has built strong relationships with local growers; many are lasting friends – and trusted suppliers of grenache, mourvedre, shiraz, touriga, nebbiolo, cabernet sauvignon, fiano, semillon and chardonnay. All the grapes come from special vineyards in McLaren Vale and the Adelaide Hills (plus one small parcel from Langhorne Creek).

There's no vinification process outside Alan's experience, but equally there's no predetermined pathway. The choices are intuitive: whole bunch, whole berry, extended cold soak, carbonic maceration, indigenous/wild yeast, submerged cap, foot treading, extended post-ferment maceration – whatever the fruit calls for.

New oak, however, is off the agenda, as is fining and filtration. Likewise, few of the wines exceed 14% alcohol. Add in the environmentally sensitive winery and the picture starts to take shape. The Entrada trio of Verdelho, Rose of Grenache and GMT (Grenache Mourvedre Touriga) are made in a drink-now style inspired by Alan's vintage in the small Portuguese town of Entradas. The common theme of these wines is brightness and freshness of the varietal fruit expression, coupled with effortless balance and length. There are 250 dozen made of each wine.

The volume of the four Essentials wines run from 33 to 160 dozen, the prices $28 to $35. They share the balance and freshness of the Entrada wines, the reds with no overt tannins or oak. All the wines are medium-bodied and supple. They will develop with time in bottle, gaining added complexity.

Previous Best New Winery recipients were Rob Dolan Wines (2014), Flowstone (2015), Bicknell fc (2016), Bondar Wines (2017), Dappled (2018), Mewstone (2019) and Shy Susan (2020).

Ten of the best new wineries

Each one of these wineries making its debut in the *Wine Companion* has earned a five-star rating. They are thus the leaders of the 59 new wineries in this edition, although a number of other first-up wineries also achieved five stars. The ultimate selection criteria included the number of wines earning 95 points or above, and also value for money. Without disparaging selections in prior years, this was a hot field, with some fascinating careers ahead for many. Varney Wines is Best New Winery and accordingly heads the list; the remaining wineries are in alphabetical order.

Varney Wines McLaren Vale

BEST NEW WINERY

The story of Varney Wines appears opposite, plus further details are of course given in the winery entry on pages 696–97.

Apogee Northern Tasmania

This, one assumes, is the final personal adventure of Dr Andrew Pirie AM, who obtained his doctorate in viticulture from the University of Sydney for a detailed study of the Tasmanian climate, which led to the establishment of Pipers Brook Vineyard in 1974. He founded Apogee in 2007, with a 2ha site in Pipers River, the wheel turning full circle with its mix of sparkling and table wines.

bakkheia Geographe

bakkheia is the left-field venture of Michael and Ilonka Edwards, with prior occupations as disparate as navy clearance diver (he) and Vogue fashion/lifestyle/food magazines (she). The name references bacchanalian frenzies occasioned by the consumption of vast amounts of wine. The other feature is an unusual membership scheme.

Blewitt Springs Wine Co McLaren Vale

Phil Tabor found his Adelaide design engineering business the subject of a bidding war between two suitors, the deal completed at the top of the market. With no need to work, he participated in his first vintage in McLaren Vale in 2013 purely out of curiosity. Duly hooked, and with the help of well-known winemaker Phil Christiansen, he purchased Blewitt Springs Wine Co in 2015 with 7.3ha of mature shiraz, with the self-designed and -built winery opening in 2017.

Marion's Vineyard Northern Tasmania

The Marion's Vineyard story would provide a great subject for an *Australian Story* documentary – or a modern-day opera – with family success initially achieved in California, then carried on to the planting of a beautiful vineyard on the banks of the Tamar River by Marion and Mark Semmens. Daughter Cynthea made wine around the world before returning with husband David in 2010, opening a new chapter in the story.

Max & Me Eden Valley

Max was the German Shepherd x whippet saved by Phil Lehmann from the RSPCA pound, and it was Max who introduced Phil to his canine-loving wife-to-be during a visit to the Barossa. The passage of time sees Sarah raising their two children and managing direct wine sales.

Mulline Geelong

The winery name takes in those of winemaker Ben Mullen and business partner Ben Hine. Mullen has covered much ground since graduating from Adelaide University's oenology degree in 2012, working at Domaine Dujac (France) in 2013 and Craggy Range (New Zealand) in '15, then back to Australia, filling in time at Yarra Yering, Oakridge, Torbreck and Leeuwin Estate, before Clyde Park '17-18. Hine is a lawyer with prior involvement in hospitality and runs the business side of the winery.

Ox Hardy McLaren Vale

The family line of Ox (Andrew) Hardy stretches back to his great-great-grandfather Thomas Hardy, a giant in the 19th-century wine fabric of South Australia. The Upper Tintara Vineyard was purchased by Thomas in 1871 and expanded with shiraz in 1891. These are the ancestor vines of today, producing shiraz of exceptional depth and intensity.

Paralian Wines McLaren Vale/Adelaide Hills

By the time Charlie Seppelt and Skye Salter established Paralian (meaning someone who lives by the sea) in 2018, they had accumulated 46 vintages working for others in Australia and France. Wanderings over, they chose McLaren Vale – Blewitt Springs in particular – in which to make their permanent home. You can be sure future vintages will be equally as good as those of today.

Wren Estate Heathcote

Owner/winemaker Michael Wren was a Flying Winemaker across multiple continents before joining Esporao, one of Portugal's leading wineries. He was particularly struck by the use of stone lagares: the large, shallow (knee-deep) fermenters that facilitate foot treading or stomping of red varieties, resulting in wines of great colour and richness with a soft palate. He found a 14.5ha vineyard planted in 2002 to multiple clones (and rootstocks) of shiraz, and makes individual block wines using replica lagares with great results.

Ten of the best value wineries

This is an eclectic group of wineries, united by the mouth-watering prices they put on their wines, be it $15 or $150 a bottle. Some are newcomers; others have many decades in the business, none more so than Best's Wines, the leader of the pack. It accordingly heads the list; the remaining wineries are in alphabetical order.

Best's Wines Grampians

BEST VALUE WINERY

The story of Best's Wines appears on pages 17 and 108–9. Of its 10 wines in this *Wine Companion*, eight were between 95 and 97 points, all with value rosettes. Great history doesn't have to be expensive, especially the case with the old-vine pinot meunier.

Bleasdale Vineyards Langhorne Creek

Ten of Bleasdale Vineyard's wines in this *Wine Companion* received over 95 points, all with value rosettes: a potent example of Langhorne Creek's ability to produce lovely wines at a modest price, from estate vineyards that have been significantly upgraded in recent years. The Adelaide Hills wines are also part of a forward-looking strategy.

Deep Woods Estate Margaret River

It may seem strange that Deep Woods Estate should be in this group, but virtually every one of its 15 entries in the *Wine Companion 2021* has a value rosette. It's why the empire Peter Fogarty built is certain to continue its eye-watering growth: you can be assured prices return a sufficient profit to generate self-funded development. It also helps that Julian Langworthy was Winemaker of the Year in the *Wine Companion 2019*.

Flowstone Wines Margaret River

All of the 10 wines submitted from Flowstone appear in this *Wine Companion*, nine with a value rosette, and four with 97 points. This former Best New Winery is laying claim to best winery, not just best value. It is also striking that its Queen of the Earth Sauvignon Blanc should be in the 97-point leader group. Flowstone's attention to detail is typified by the appealing label designs and the fact that the labels themselves are made from 81% limestone, the remainder bonding resin.

Forest Hill Vineyard Great Southern

The value all Forest Hill's wines offer is exceptional, the style that of old money – another prime example of consistently extraordinary value. Six wines pointed between 96 (three), 97 (two) and 98 (one) laid an irrefutable claim to inclusion near the top of the totem pole. Forest Hill has the early days of the Great Southern in its DNA.

Hahndorf Hill Winery **Adelaide Hills**

Hahndorf Hill writes the book on gruner veltliner, using sophisticated winemaking techniques to do so. The result is unfailing value. Seven of its wines scored 95 or 96 points, only one with a price exceeding $29. Major success in all the wine shows Hahndorf Hill enters is up there with the very best. The cellar door is in the South Australian Tourism Hall of Fame.

Head Wines **Barossa Valley**

Alex Head's pathway was unusual – a degree in biochemistry from Sydney University, then experience in fine wine stores, importers and an auction house – but explains why he is making such elegant wines. Of the 12 wines submitted, two received 97 points, four 96 points and three 95 points. His field of play is the tapestry of differing sites in the Barossa Valley, and their interaction with shiraz. The inspiration has come from the Côte-Rôtie in the Northern Rhône Valley.

Medhurst **Yarra Valley**

The sense of humour of former CEO of Southcorp, Ross Wilson, and the urbane make-up of winemaker Simon Steele are a unique recipe for success. Seven of the eight Medhurst wines submitted scored between 95 and 97 points, and all seven received a value rosette. There is a quiet elegance to all of the wines. The winery, recessed into the hillside, was recognised for its excellence in the Victorian Architecture Awards.

Mewstone Wines **Southern Tasmania**

The winery address of 11 Flowerpot Jetty Road, Flowerpot might suggest this is just a whimsical venture, but production of 4000 dozen tells a different story. Best New Winery in the *Wine Companion 2019*, Mewstone is now one of the best value wineries. Second label Hughes & Hughes also holds its place on quality (as well as price).

New Era Vineyards **Adelaide Hills**

New Era was taking all the right steps to become an unqualified success when its vineyard was lost to a bushfire in December 2019: a vicious blow that could never have been foreseen. It's bittersweet that six wines appearing in this year's *Wine Companion* received 95 or 96 points, all six with the value rosette.

Ten dark horses

To qualify for this award, each winery has to have received a 5-star rating for the first time and a history of at least four lesser ratings. Yarran is Dark Horse of the Year and accordingly heads the list; the remainder are in alphabetical order.

Yarran Wines Riverina

DARK HORSE OF THE YEAR

Sam Brewer was raised by grapegrowing parents John and Lorraine, and when he completed his wine degree at Charles Sturt University, the family celebrated by taking a tonne of shiraz and fermenting it in a stainless-steel milk vat. Since then production has risen and grape sources (including Heathcote) have broadened as Sam has put beyond doubt his winemaking skills. It is doubly appropriate that one of the wines securing the Dark Horse accolade should be an estate-grown Riverina Shiraz selling for $15. If that is your price limit, Yarran gives you the best-quality wines, both white and red. Yarran's track record suggests this award is no flash in the pan.

Barwon Ridge Wines Geelong

Barwon Ridge kept to itself after its establishment in 1999, making a single *Wine Companion* appearance in the 2010 edition, coming back in '17. Winemaking at Leura Park is part of the reason for the rating rise since '18, now 5 stars. Considerable work has seen the return of the original shrub and tree vegetation; the birds approve as the grapes ripen, but the Ansons are happy with the trade-off. The wines are all vegan.

Ceres Bridge Estate Geelong

Challon and Patricia Murdock decided to use the DIY approach when they planted 1.8ha of chardonnay in 1996 – and saw 50% of the vines die. In 2000 they planted 1.1ha of pinot noir, which had to be replanted in '01. Stoically, they planted shiraz, nebbiolo, sauvignon blanc, viognier, tempranillo and pinot gris, and hit pay dirt in 2018. Scott Ireland and Sam Vogel make the wines, hence the quality.

Ellis Wines Heathcote

Heathcote's 50-million-year-old vivid red Cambrian soils (derived from weathered greenstone) have a proven track record with shiraz, and this is the focus of the substantial estate plantings dating back to 1999. Bryan and Joy Ellis were happy to sell their crop to high profile wineries such as Taltarni, Domaine Chandon and Heathcote Winery, but were doubly rewarded when they decided to keep part of the production for their own wine. In 2019, their 2016 Premium Shiraz won a gold medal at the Royal Melbourne Wine Awards, and was in a taste-off for the Best Victorian Shiraz. The 2018 Viognier won a gold medal and trophy at the Heathcote Wine Show '19.

Pindarie Barossa Valley

Owners Tony Brooks and Wendy Allan met at Roseworthy College in 1985, Tony a sixth-generation farmer studying agriculture, New Zealand–born Wendy studying viticulture. Tony went overseas for years, managing sheep feedlots in Saudi Arabia, Turkey and Jordan. Wendy spent 12 years with Penfolds, rising to become a senior viticulturist, working vintages and assessing viticulture in California, Israel, Italy, Germany, France, Portugal, Spain and Chile along the way. Since 2014, Pindarie has received 4.5 stars five times and so was overdue for 5 stars, which it earned in fine style this year with two wines on 97 points and one with 95.

RiverBank Estate Swan Valley

An unusual journey, disappearing from the *Wine Companion* between 2009 and 2020. It burst back onto the scene in '17 when purchased by the three members of the Lembo family, highly successful wedding/event operators in Perth. They lured the highly talented Digby Leddin from Lamont's Winery; after two decades of service there, he was seeking a new challenge – and rose to it with showers of awards in '19.

Sutton Grange Winery Bendigo

A casual lunch on the property with Alec Epis, AFL legend, and Stuart Anderson, 50-year wine industry veteran and founder of Balgownie Estate, encouraged Peter Sidwell, Melbourne businessman and racehorse owner, to plant 12ha of vines as a minor diversification. There are two labels, Fairbank (the 19th-century name of the property) and the small-volume Estate range. The arrival of Melanie Chester, a former Len Evans Tutorial scholar, has seen good wines become even better.

Traviarti Beechworth

After 15 years in the fine wine business in Melbourne, both as buyers and thereafter in sales and marketing, Simon Grant and Helen Murray began the search for a suitable place to grow and make nebbiolo, chardonnay and tempranillo. They found a place in 2011, sufficient for a 0.43ha vineyard and a tiny onsite winery. With a second vineyard recently planted to nebbiolo and barbera, production will upscale from the present 650 dozen.

Wangolina Mount Benson

This is the darkest of all the dark horses, having been content with a terse two-line winery summary in the *Wine Companion* that in no way did justice to owner/winemaker Anita Goode or her wines. Wangolina did not submit wines for the 2014, '15 and '18 editions, and came within a whisker of doing so this year. Which would have been a pity, because things are happening at Wangolina, Anita (currently with purple hair) making admirable wines, including Gruner Veltliner (95 points) and excellent Mount Benson Semillon and Syrah (also 95 points).

Wine x Sam Strathbogie Ranges

Since 1991, Sam Plunkett and Bron Dunwoode have moved backwards and forwards from small to large operations in the Strathbogie Ranges. They bounced in and out of the *Wine Companion* but since the 2018 edition have earned 4 or 4.5 stars, breaking through to 5 this year after catching the eye of Jeni Port. They also attracted the attention of Naked Wines, and hey presto, production leapt to 70 000 dozen, the grapes largely supplied by contract growers.

Best of the best by variety

As per usual, the number of wines in each group is limited. The varietal categories are the same as in prior years, as is the link of each wine with its region or subregion. The rating cut-off point reflects the strength of the particular varietal category. The wine names have been shortened, but still enable the exact wine to be identified in the tasting notes for the winery in question. These are the best of the 8987 wines included in this edition.

Riesling

The Great Southern region – including its subregions of Mount Barker, Porongurup and Frankland River – is the most prolific scorer, with six wines. The Clare and Eden valleys tie for second place with two wines each, hardly surprising. The remaining wines fall under the head of 'usual suspects', Henty with a long track record of success.

Rating	Wine	Region
98	Seppelt Drumborg Vineyard 2019	Henty
98	Forest Hill Vineyard Block 1 2019	Mount Barker
98	Duke's Vineyard Magpie Hill Reserve 2019	Porongurup
97	Clonakilla 2019	Canberra District
97	Tim Adams Skilly Ridge 2018	Clare Valley
97	Woodvale Cellar Release Skilly 2011	Clare Valley
97	Dandelion Wonderland of the Eden Valley 2019	Eden Valley
97	Poonawatta The Eden 2019	Eden Valley
97	Frankland Estate Poison Hill 2019	Frankland River
97	Larry Cherubino Cherubino 2019	Great Southern
97	ATR Hard Hill Road Writer's Block 2018	Great Western
97	Forest Hill Vineyard Block 2 2018	Mount Barker
97	Abbey Creek Vineyard 2018	Porongurup

Chardonnay

Margaret River and Adelaide Hills emerge at the top of this category, the styles of their wines radically different but ever reliable. Leeuwin Estate has always been my choice as Australia's best maker of chardonnay, its wine a mixture of purity and intensity, with length and balance underwriting its greatness. And it never misses the mark.

Rating	Wine	Region
99	Penfolds Bin 144 Yattarna 2017	Cool climate blend
99	Leeuwin Estate Art Series 2016	Margaret River
99	Leeuwin Estate Art Series 2017	Margaret River
98	Shaw + Smith Lenswood Vineyard 2017	Adelaide Hills
98	Shaw + Smith M3 2018	Adelaide Hills
98	Giaconda Estate Vineyard 2017	Beechworth
98	Giaconda Estate Vineyard 2016	Beechworth
98	Singlefile The Vivienne 2017	Denmark
98	Clyde Park Vineyard Single Block C 2019	Geelong

98	Vasse Felix Heytesbury 2018	Margaret River
98	Tolpuddle Vineyard 2018	Tasmania
98	Giant Steps 2019	Yarra Valley
98	Hoddles Creek Estate Road Block 2017	Yarra Valley
98	Mount Mary 2018	Yarra Valley

97 **Adelaide Hills** Bird in Hand TED Edward Andrew 2017, Bondar 2018, Murdoch Hill The Rocket Limited Release 2019, Tapanappa Tiers Vineyard Piccadilly Valley 2018, The Lane Vineyard Reginald Germein Single Vineyard 2017 **Beechworth** Fighting Gully Road 2018 **Geelong** Clyde Park Vineyard Single Block B3 2019, Lethbridge Allegra 2017, Mulline Single Vineyard Portarlington Chardonnay 2019 **Margaret River** Brookland Valley Limited Release Reserve 2018, Cape Mentelle 2017, Credaro Family Estate 1000 Crowns 2018, Cullen Kevin John Legacy Series Fruit Day 2016, Deep Woods Estate Reserve 2018, Domaine Naturaliste Artus 2018, Evans & Tate Redbrook Reserve 2014, Evoi 2018, Evoi Reserve 2018, Flowstone 2017, Flowstone Queen of the Earth 2017, Howard Park 2018, Moss Wood Wilyabrup 2018, Nocturne Tassell Park Vineyard 2018, Robert Oatley Margaret River The Pennant 2018, Thompson Estate 2018, Wise Eagle Bay 2018, Xanadu Reserve 2018 **Mornington Peninsula** Eldridge Estate of Red Hill Wendy 2018 **Tasmania** Bay of Fires 2018, Delamere Block 3 2016, Gala Estate Black Label 2018, Marion's Vineyard 2018, Mewstone D'Entrecasteaux Channel 2018, Sailor Seeks Horse 2017 **Yarra Valley** Coldstream Hills Reserve 2019, Dappled Les Verges Single Vineyard 2018, Medhurst Reserve 2018, Oakridge 864 Single Block Release Aqueduct Block Henk Vineyard 2018, Rochford Premier Single Vineyard 2019, Toolangi F Block Yarra Valley Chardonnay 2019

Semillon

As ever, the Hunter Valley has a vice-like grip on this globally unique bond. Brokenwood salutes the retirement of long-serving CEO and chief winemaker Iain Riggs with a double achievement: the ILR Semillon and Graveyard Shiraz both with 99 points in the *Wine Companion 2021*.

Rating	Wine	Region
99	Brokenwood ILR Reserve 2014	Hunter Valley
98	Drayton's Family Susanne 2013	Hunter Valley
97	RidgeView Museum Release Generations Reserve 2009	Hunter Valley
97	Thomas Braemore Cellar Reserve 2014	Hunter Valley
97	Tyrrell's Museum Release Vat 1 2015	Hunter Valley
96	Peter Lehmann Margaret 2013	Barossa Valley
96	Briar Ridge Vineyard Cellar Reserve Dairy Hill Single Vineyard 2011	Hunter Valley
96	Comyns & Co Single Vineyard Casuarina 2019	Hunter Valley
96	De Iuliis 2019	Hunter Valley
96	De Iuliis Single Vineyard 2019	Hunter Valley
96	First Creek Oakey Creek Single Vineyard 2019	Hunter Valley
96	First Creek Single Vineyard Murphys 2017	Hunter Valley
96	Keith Tulloch Field of Mars Block 2A 2017	Hunter Valley
96	Margan Family Aged Release 2014	Hunter Valley
96	Meerea Park Terracotta Individual Vineyard 2013	Hunter Valley
96	Pepper Tree Museum Release Single Vineyard Reserve Alluvius 2009	Hunter Valley
96	Vinden Estate Somerset Vineyard 2019	Hunter Valley
96	Calabria Family Museum Release Three Bridges Reserve 2012	Riverina

Sauvignon blanc

While the points are tightly bunched, quality sauvignon blanc can flourish in a wide range of climates if the winemaker enjoys the task of building controlled complexity.

Rating	Wine	Region
97	Flowstone Queen of the Earth 2018	Margaret River
96	Michael Hall Piccadilly and Lenswood 2019	Adelaide Hills
96	Sidewood Estate Mappinga Fume Blanc 2018	Adelaide Hills
96	Mulline Single Vineyard Bannockburn Fume Blanc 2019	Geelong
96	Domaine Naturaliste Sauvage 2017	Margaret River
96	Terre à Terre Down to Earth 2019	Wrattonbully
95	**Adelaide Hills** Bleasdale 2019, Shaw + Smith 2019 **Canberra District** Poachers Vineyard 2019 **Coonawarra** Katnook Estate 2019 **Great Southern** Cherubino Beautiful South White Wine 2018, Singlefile Small Batch Release Barrel Ferment Fume Blanc 2018 **Margaret River** Deep Woods Estate 2019, Flowstone 2018, Higher Plane Fume Blanc 2019, House of Cards Three Card Monte Single Vineyard 2019, Howard Park 2019, Stella Bella 2019 **Mount Barker** Singlefile Single Vineyard Fume Blanc 2019, West Cape Howe 2019 **Orange** Ross Hill Pinnacle Series Griffin Road Vineyard 2018 **Tasmania** Freycinet Wineglass Bay 2018 **Wrattonbully** Terre à Terre Crayeres Vineyard 2017, Terre à Terre Crayeres Vineyard 2018 **Yarra Valley** Gembrook Hill 2018, Mayer Empire of Dirt 2019	

Semillon sauvignon blends

Lay down your glasses. It's all over. Margaret River is the champion, emulating the Hunter Valley's grip on unoaked semillon. These are great wines for spring and summer, with or without food.

Rating	Wine	Region
96	Hay Shed Hill Block 1 Semillon Sauvignon Blanc 2018	Margaret River
96	Stella Bella Suckfizzle Sauvignon Blanc Semillon 2018	Margaret River
96	Xanadu DJL Sauvignon Blanc Semillon 2019	Margaret River
95	Coates The Semillon Sauvignon Blanc 2019	Adelaide Hills
95	Juniper Crossing Semillon Sauvignon Blanc 2019	Margaret River
95	Juniper Estate Aquitaine Blanc 2018	Margaret River
95	Oates Ends Sauvignon Blanc Semillon 2019	Margaret River
95	Pierro L.T.C. 2019	Margaret River
95	Rosily Vineyard Semillon Sauvignon Blanc 2019	Margaret River
95	Snake + Herring Perfect Day Sauvignon Blanc Semillon 2018	Margaret River
95	Stella Bella Semillon Sauvignon Blanc 2019	Margaret River
95	Thompson Estate SSB Semillon Sauvignon Blanc 2019	Margaret River
95	Vasse Felix Sauvignon Blanc Semillon 2018	Margaret River
95	Windance Sauvignon Blanc Semillon 2019	Margaret River
95	Mount Mary Triolet 2018	Yarra Valley

Other white varieties and blends

A group of wines that place little or no reliance on oak to build complexity and length.

Rating	Wine	Region
97	Yalumba The Virgilius Viognier 2018	Eden Valley
97	Crittenden Estate Cri de Coeur Savagnin 2015	Mornington Peninsula

97	Moores Hill Estate Pinot Gris 2019	Tasmania
97	Stargazer Tupelo 2019	Tasmania
96	Hahndorf Hill Pinot Grigio 2019	Adelaide Hills
96	Hahndorf Hill GRU Gruner Veltliner 2018	Adelaide Hills
96	Hahndorf Hill Reserve Gruner Veltliner 2017	Adelaide Hills
96	Ten Minutes by Tractor 10X Pinot Gris 2017	Mornington Peninsula
96	Holm Oak Arneis 2019	Tasmania
96	Ben Haines Volta Brackets Marsanne 2018	Yarra Valley

Sparkling white and rose

Tasmania is no surprise – we shall see an ever-growing percentage of sparkling wines from the state, quality going alongside regional origin.

Rating	Wine	Region
99	House of Arras EJ Carr Late Disgorged 2005	Tasmania
98	House of Arras Rose 2009	Tasmania
97	Terre à Terre Daosa Blanc de Blancs 2015	Adelaide Hills
97	Chandon Cellar Release Winemaker's Selection Rose 2013	Yarra Valley

Sparkling red

Shiraz provides by far the best base for sparkling red wines.

Rating	Wine	Region
95	St Hallett Black Sparkling Shiraz NV	Barossa
95	Peter Lehmann Black Queen Sparkling Shiraz 2014	Barossa Valley
95	Teusner MC Sparkling Shiraz 2013	Barossa Valley
95	Ashton Hills Vineyard Sparkling Shiraz 2013	Clare Valley
95	Grampians Estate Rutherford Sparkling Shiraz 2017	Grampians

Sweet

Riesling has the game by its whiskers – it achieves intensity of flavour without loss of varietal character and, again, without a witches' brew of ultra-sweet cordial flavours. In their different ways, these wines are world class, but still struggle for recognition.

Rating	Wine	Region
99	Lethbridge Botrytis Riesling TBA 2018	Henty
98	Riposte Museum Release Reserve Noble Traminer 2011	Adelaide Hills
97	Pressing Matters R69 Riesling 2019	Tasmania
97	Delatite Catherine's Block Reserve 2019	Upper Goulburn

Rose

Many consumers don't treat rose as seriously as it deserves. It really is a happy hunting ground these days, as winemakers across the country look at each other's efforts and become thoroughly intrigued by what is possible. A great match for Asian food, the prices ridiculously low.

Rating	Wine	Region
96	Abbey Vale Premium RSV 2019	Margaret River
96	Nocturne Carbunup SR Sangiovese Nebbiolo Rose 2019	Margaret River
96	tripe.Iscariot Aspic Grenache Rose 2019	Margaret River

95   **Adelaide Hills** Hahndorf Hill Hills Rose 2019 **Barossa Valley** Schwarz Wine Company Rose 2019, Turkey Flat Rose 2019, Whistler Rose 2019 **Coonawarra** Pepper Tree Limited Release Rose 2019 **Eden Valley** Blue Rock Vineyard Series Pinot Noir Rose 2019 **Heathcote** Kennedy Pink Hills Rose 2019 **McLaren Vale** Cockfighter's Ghost Single Vineyard Sangiovese Rose 2019, SC Pannell Koomilya JC Block Shiraz 2019, Sherrah Grenache Rose 2019, Thomas St Vincent Blewitt Springs Fleurieu Provencale Rose 2018, Varney Entrada Rose of Grenache 2019, Wirra Wirra Mrs Wigley Rose 2019 **Margaret River** Deep Woods Estate Harmony Rose 2019, La Kooki Rose Blonde 2019, Stella Bella Skuttlebutt Rose 2019, Victory Point River Rose 2019 **Nagambie Lakes** Tahbilk Grenache Mourvedre Rose 2019 **Orange** Rose by Rowlee 2019 **Tasmania** Delamere Hurlo's Rose 2017, Delamere Rose 2019, Gala Estate White Label Pinot Rose 2018, Pipers Brook Vineyard Rose 2019, Small Island Patsie's Blush Rose 2019, Tasmanian Vintners Pinot Noir Rose 2018 **Yarra Valley** De Bortoli Vinoque Nebbiolo Rose 2019, Medhurst Estate Vineyard Rose 2019, One Block Moonlit Forest Light Chilled Red 'Carter' Rose 2018

Pinot noir

Put these treasures alongside Burgundies at twice the price and they won't yield any ground. Yet the journey still has a long way to go, with new clones slotting in alongside MV6, an old clone unique to Australia. The average age of vines is also rising – the oldest are now over 40 years old. The ratings (including those for the 97–point wines) give you a roadmap for all the best regions other than the king: Tasmania.

Rating	Wine	Region
99	Bannockburn Serre 2017	Geelong
99	Bass Phillip Reserve 2017	Gippsland
99	Bay of Fires 2018	Tasmania
99	Sinapius Vineyard The Enclave Single Vineyard Close Planted 2017	Tasmania
98	Robin Brockett Fenwick Vineyard 2017	Geelong
98	Bass Phillip Issan Vineyard 2017	Gippsland
98	Bass Phillip Premium 2017	Gippsland
98	Hoddles Creek Estate DML 2018	Mornington Peninsula
98	Dawson & James 2016	Tasmania
98	Giant Steps Nocton Vineyard 2018	Tasmania
98	Home Hill Estate 2018	Tasmania
98	Home Hill Kelly's Reserve 2018	Tasmania
98	Shy Susan 2018	Tasmania
98	Mount Mary 2018	Yarra Valley
98	Rochford Terre Single Vineyard 2019	Yarra Valley

97   **Adelaide Hills** Ashton Hills Vineyard Reserve 2018 **Beechworth** Giaconda Estate Vineyard 2017 **Geelong** Banks Road Soho Road Vineyard Barrique Eight 2017, Banks Road Will's Selection 2017, Clyde Park Vineyard Single Block D 2019, Clyde Park Vineyard Single Block F College Bannockburn 2019, Farrside by Farr Geelong 2018, Scotchmans Hill Cornelius Norfolk Vineyard 2017 **Gippsland** Bass Phillip Crown Prince 2017 **Henty** The Story R. Lane 2018 **Mornington Peninsula** Handpicked Capella Vineyard 2018, Hurley Vineyard Garamond Balnarring 2018, Paringa Estate The Paringa Single Vineyard 2018, Stonier Reserve 2019, Yabby Lake Vineyard Single Vineyard 2018 **Tasmania** Josef Chromy Block 17 2014, Mewstone Hughes & Hughes 2018, Sinapius Vineyard La Clairiere Single Vineyard Close Planted 2017, Tamar Ridge Single Block 2017, Tertini 2018, Tolpuddle Vineyard 2018 **Yarra Valley** Coldstream Hills Reserve 2019, Helen's Hill Estate The Smuggler Single Clone 2017, Rochford Premier Single Vineyard 2019, Yarra Yering 2018

Shiraz

The sheer weight of numbers – the utter dominance of shiraz – is reflected in the 116 wines listed here. Shiraz is the unchallenged market leader in both domestic and export markets, and the best wines are simply getting better year on year.

Rating	Wine	Region
99	Schild Estate Moorooroo 2017	Barossa Valley
99	Penfolds Bin 95 Grange 2015	Blend
99	Henschke Hill of Grace 2015	Eden Valley
99	Mount Langi Ghiran Langi 2018	Grampians
99	Brokenwood Graveyard Vineyard 2018	Hunter Valley
99	Bekkers Syrah 2018	McLaren Vale
99	Ox Hardy 1891 Ancestor Vines Upper Tintara Vineyard 2008	McLaren Vale
99	Yangarra Estate Vineyard Ironheart 2017	McLaren Vale
98	Pike & Joyce L'optimiste 2018	Adelaide Hills
98	Cimicky Grand Reserve 2017	Barossa Valley
98	Eperosa Magnolia 1896 2017	Barossa Valley
98	Eperosa L.R.C. Shiraz 2017	Barossa Valley
98	Hemera Estate JDR 2017	Barossa Valley
98	Kalleske Johann Georg Old Vine Single Vineyard 2017	Barossa Valley
98	Maverick Ahrens' Creek 2017	Barossa Valley
98	Penfolds Bin 798 RWT 2017	Barossa Valley
98	Turkey Flat The Ancestor 2016	Barossa Valley
98	Giaconda Warner Vineyard 2016	Beechworth
98	Dandelion Red Queen 2017	Eden Valley
98	Henschke Hill of Roses 2016	Eden Valley
98	Kellermeister The Meister 2017	Eden Valley
98	Mount Pleasant 1946 Vines Rosehill Vineyard 2018	Hunter Valley
98	Mount Pleasant 1965 Vines Rosehill Vineyard 2018	Hunter Valley
98	Tyrrell's Old Patch 2018	Hunter Valley
98	Hickinbotham Clarendon Vineyard Brooks Road 2018	McLaren Vale
98	Oliver's Taranga HJ 2017	McLaren Vale
98	Ox Hardy Slate Fermented 2018	McLaren Vale
98	Yangarra Estate Vineyard King's Wood 2018	McLaren Vale
98	Windance 2018	Margaret River

97   **Adelaide Hills** Shaw + Smith Balhannah Vineyard 2016, Sidewood Estate Ironstone Barrels The Tyre Fitter Syrah 2018 **Barossa** Bethany East Grounds 2017, Henschke Tappa Pass Vineyard Selection 2017, St Hallett Blackwell 2017, St Hallett Old Block 2016, Yalumba The Octavius Old Vine Shiraz 2017 **Barossa Valley** Eisenstone Dimchurch vd. Ebenezer 2018, Eisenstone Greenock 2017, Head The Brunette Moppa 2017, Head The Redhead Menglers Hill 2018, Hemera Estate Limited Release Home Block 2017, Hentley Farm Clos Otto 2017, Hentley Farm Museum Release The Beauty 2015, John Duval Eligo The Barossa 2017, John Duval Entity 2018, Kalleske Eduard Old Vine 2017, Kellermeister Black Sash 2017, Kilikanoon Kavel's Flock 2016, Peter Lehmann Masterson 2015, Pindarie Black Hinge Reserve 2017, Pindarie Western Ridge 2018, Smidge Magic Dirt Greenock 2016, Soul Growers Gobell Single Vineyard 2018, Soul Growers Hampel Single Vineyard 2018, Soul Growers Hoffmann Single Vineyard 2018, Torbreck The Factor 2016, Utopos 2017 **Beechworth** Giaconda Estate Vineyard 2016, Piano Piano Henry's Block 2017 **Bendigo** Sutton Grange Estate Syrah 2018 **Canberra District** Clonakilla O'Riada 2018 **Clare Valley** Pikes The E.W.P. 2017

Coonawarra Brand's Laira Stentiford's Old Vines 2016, Wynns Michael Limited Release 2016 **Eden Valley** Flaxman Estate 2017, Henschke Mount Edelstone 2016, Henschke The Wheelwright Vineyard 2016, Hutton Vale Farm 2016, Maverick Trial Hill 2017, Max & Me Boongarrie Vineyard 2017, Max & Me Boongarrie Vineyard Whole Bunch Syrah 2017, Poonawatta Museum Release The 1880 2010, Poonawatta Museum Release The Cuttings 2010, Smidge Magic Dirt Menglers Hill Shiraz 2016, Woods Crampton Frances & Nicole Old Vine Single Vineyard 2017 **Geelong** By Farr 2018, Mulline Single Vineyard Bannockburn Syrah 2019 **Glenrowan** Baileys of Glenrowan Varley Organic 2019 **Grampians** Seppelt St Peters 2018, The Story R. Lane Westgate Vineyard Syrah 2017 **Heathcote** Ellis Premium 2016 **Hilltops** R. Paulazzo G-0501 2017 **Hunter Valley** Capercaillie The Ghillie 2018, First Creek 2017, Margan Family Aged Release 2014, Mount Pleasant Mountain C Light Bodied Dry Red 2018, Mount Pleasant Mountain D Full Bodied Dry Red 2018, Tyrrell's 4 Acres 2018 **Langhorne Creek** Bleasdale The Powder Monkey Single Vineyard 2015 **McLaren Vale** Bondar Violet Hour 2018, Brini Estate Limited Release Sebastian Single Vineyard 2012, Brokenwood Wade Block 2 Vineyard 2018, Dune Desert Sands 2018, Fox Creek Old Vine 2018, Gemtree Obsidian 2018, Geoff Merrill Henley 2012, Kay Brothers Amery Block 6 2017, Mr Riggs Wine Company 2017, Ox Hardy 1891 Ancestor Vines Upper Tintara Vineyard 2010, Paralian Springs Hill Vineyard 2019, Primo Estate Joseph Angel Gully 2017, Sherrah Reserve 2018, Wines by Geoff Hardy Pertaringa Yeoman 2017 **Margaret River** Cape Mentelle Two Vineyards 2016 **Mornington Peninsula** Portsea Estate Estate Syrah 2017 **Mount Barker** Forest Hill Vineyard Block 9 2018, X by Xabregas Terence Syrah 2018 **Porongurup** Duke's Vineyard Magpie Hill Reserve 2018 **Pyrenees** DogRock Degraves Road Single Vineyard 2018, Summerfield Jo 2018, Taltarni Estate 2016 **Yarra Valley** De Bortoli Section A8 Syrah 2018, Oakridge 864 Single Block Release Close Planted Block Oakridge Vineyard Syrah 2018, Seville Estate Dr McMahon 2017, Seville Estate Old Vine Reserve 2018, Yarra Yering Carrodus 2018

Grenache and blends

This category brings grenache and its siblings into the frame, either as a variety or as a two- or three-way blend. I am hugely excited by the changing approach to grenache, particularly by appropriate vineyard management and a clear vision of the winemaking style. The result of this approach has been, and will continue to be, more elegant, perfumed versions of the varieties. McLaren Vale is presently the chief custodian, but it shouldn't rest on its laurels and assume that others can't play the same game – because they can.

Rating	Wine	Region
99	Brothers at War Single Vineyard Grenache 2018	Barossa Valley
99	Yangarra Estate Vineyard High Sands Grenache 2017	McLaren Vale
99	Serrat Grenache Noir 2019	Yarra Valley
98	Kellermeister Rocamora Ancestor Vine Stonegarden Vineyard Grenache 2018	Eden Valley
98	Chalk Hill Alpha Crucis Old Vine Grenache 2018	McLaren Vale
98	Chapel Hill 1897 Vines Grenache 2018	McLaren Vale
97	Eperosa Krondorf Grenache 2017	Barossa Valley
97	Hentley Farm H Block Shiraz Cabernet 2017	Barossa Valley
97	Turkey Flat Grenache 2018	Barossa Valley
97	Z Rustica Grenache 2019	Barossa Valley
97	Eperosa Stonegarden 1858 Grenache 2017	Eden Valley
97	Thistledown Advance Release Mengler Hill Grenache 2019	Eden Valley
97	Bekkers Grenache 2018	McLaren Vale

97	SC Pannell Old McDonald Grenache 2018	McLaren Vale
97	SC Pannell Smart Clarendon Grenache 2018	McLaren Vale
97	Two Hands Twelftree Moritz Road Blewitt Springs Grenache 2017	McLaren Vale
97	Varney GSM 2017	McLaren Vale
97	Mount Mary Marli Russell RP2 2018	Yarra Valley
97	Yarra Yering Light Dry Red Pinot Shiraz 2019	Yarra Valley

Shiraz viognier

Shiraz viognier is now an accepted wine in its own right. The malleability of shiraz in the context of climate and terroir in no way diminished by the inclusion of 5% (plus or minus) of co-fermented viognier. This group may be small, but it represents the output of three of Australia's best winemakers.

Rating	Wine	Region
98	Serrat Yarra Valley Shiraz Viognier 2019	Yarra Valley
97	Spinifex La Maline 2018	Barossa Valley
97	Clonakilla Shiraz Viognier 2018	Canberra District

Cabernet sauvignon

This is a line-up of very fine cabernets, Margaret River doing its usual thing and McLaren Vale the surprise performer. McLaren Vale has long been recognised as a dependable provider of wines with good varietal expression (thanks to its water-cooled climate), and it underlined that ability here in no uncertain fashion.

Rating	Wine	Region
99	SC Pannell Koomilya CP Block 2016	McLaren Vale
99	Wines by Geoff Hardy Pertaringa Tipsy Hill Single Vineyard 2017	McLaren Vale
99	Moss Wood Wilyabrup 2016	Margaret River
98	Wynns John Riddoch Limited Release 2016	Coonawarra
98	Houghton Jack Mann Single Vineyard 2017	Frankland River
98	Cloudburst 2017	Margaret River
98	Cullen Vanya Flower Day 2017	Margaret River
98	Cullen Vanya Wilyabrup 2016	Margaret River
98	Houghton Gladstones 2017	Margaret River
98	West Cape Howe King Billy 2014	Mount Barker
98	Duke's Vineyard Magpie Hill Reserve 2018	Porongurup
97	**Barossa** Cimicky Grand Reserve 2017 **Barossa Valley** Maverick Ahrens' Creek 2017, Soul Growers Limb Single Vineyard 2018 **Coonawarra** Patrick Grande Reserve 2012 **Eden Valley** Henschke Cyril Henschke 2016 **Langhorne Creek** Ballycroft Small Berry New French Oak 2016 **McLaren Vale** Hickinbotham Clarendon Vineyard Trueman 2018 **Margaret River** Deep Woods Estate Reserve 2017, Deep Woods Estate Yallingup Grand Selection Single Vineyard 2017, Devil's Lair 2018, Evoi Reserve 2018, Flowstone Queen of the Earth 2016, Fraser Gallop Estate Parterre Wilyabrup 2016, Hay Shed Hill Block 2 2017, Houghton Wisdom 2017, Jilyara of Wilyabrup The Williams' Block 2018, Leeuwin Estate Art Series 2016, Nocturne Sheoak Vineyard 2018, tripe.Iscariot Stygian Bloom 2018, Wise Eagle Bay Wilyabrup 2017, Xanadu Reserve 2017 **Margaret River/Mount Barker** Howard Park Abercrombie 2017 **Mount Barker** Rosenthal The Collector 2018 **Yarra Valley** Squitchy Lane Vineyard 2018, Yarra Yering Carrodus 2018

Cabernet and family

Margaret River provided more wines for this bracket than any other region, but it didn't have it all its own way.

Rating	Wine	Region
99	Hickinbotham Clarendon Vineyard The Peake Cabernet Shiraz 2018	McLaren Vale
99	Mount Mary Quintet 2018	Yarra Valley
97	St Hugo Barossa Coonawarra Cabernet Shiraz 2017	Barossa/Coonawarra
97	Penfolds Bin 389 Cabernet Shiraz 2017	SA Blend
97	Hickinbotham Clarendon Vineyard The Revivalist Merlot 2018	McLaren Vale
97	Howard Park ASW Cabernet Sauvignon Shiraz 2017	Margaret River
97	Cloudburst Malbec 2017	Margaret River
97	McHenry Hohnen Rolling Stone 2016	Margaret River
97	Vasse Felix Tom Cullity Cabernet Sauvignon Malbec 2016	Margaret River
97	Duke's Vineyard The Morrissey 2018	Porongurup

Other red varieties and blends

There's no predicting what will come in this always small group of very special wines.

Rating	Wine	Region
98	Mayer Nebbiolo 2019	Yarra Valley
97	Hayes Family Vineyard Series Primrose Vineyard Mataro 2019	Barossa Valley
97	John Duval Annexus Mataro 2017	Barossa Valley
97	John Duval Annexus Mataro 2018	Barossa Valley
97	Fighting Gully Road Black Label La Longa Sangiovese 2017	Beechworth
97	Traviarti Nebbiolo 2018	Beechworth
97	Best's Old Vine Pinot Meunier 2019	Great Western
97	Clairault Cellar Release Petit Verdot 2014	Margaret River

Fortified

The points speak for themselves. These are unique to Australia in terms of their age, their complexity, their intensity and their varietal make up. They arguably represent the best value of all given the cost of production, notably in the amount of working capital tied up for decades.

Rating	Wine	Region
100	Seppeltsfield 100 Year Old Para Liqueur 1920	Barossa Valley
99	All Saints Estate Museum Rutherglen Muscadelle NV	Rutherglen
99	All Saints Estate Museum Rutherglen Muscat NV	Rutherglen
99	Morris Old Premium Rare Topaque NV	Rutherglen
98	Grant Burge 40 Year Old Super Rare Fortified Tawny NV	Barossa Valley
98	Baileys of Glenrowan Winemakers Selection Rare Old Muscat NV	Glenrowan
98	Patritti McLaren Vale Rare Old Fortified Chardonnay NV	McLaren Vale
98	Campbells Merchant Prince Rare Muscat NV	Rutherglen
98	Chambers Rosewood Rare Rutherglen Muscadelle NV	Rutherglen
98	Morris Old Premium Rare Liqueur Rutherglen Muscat NV	Rutherglen

Best wineries of the regions

The nomination of the best wineries of the regions has evolved into a three-level classification (further explained on page 10). At the very top are the wineries with their names and stars printed in red; these have been generally recognised for having a long track record of excellence – truly the best of the best. Next are wineries with their stars (but not their names) printed in red, which have had a consistent record of excellence for at least the last three years. Those wineries with black stars have achieved excellence this year (and sometimes longer).

ADELAIDE HILLS

Anderson Hill ★★★★★
Anvers ★★★★★
Ashton Hills Vineyard ★★★★★
Bird in Hand ★★★★★
BK Wines ★★★★★
Casa Freschi ★★★★★
Catlin Wines ★★★★★
Coates Wines ★★★★★
Coulter Wines ★★★★★
Deviation Road ★★★★★
Elderslie ★★★★★
Geoff Weaver ★★★★★
Golding Wines ★★★★★
Guthrie Wines ★★★★★
Hahndorf Hill Winery ★★★★★
Howard Vineyard ★★★★★
Karrawatta ★★★★★
La Linea ★★★★★
La Prova ★★★★★
Lobethal Road Wines ★★★★★
Longview Vineyard ★★★★★
Main & Cherry ★★★★★
Mike Press Wines ★★★★★
Mt Lofty Ranges Vineyard ★★★★★
Murdoch Hill ★★★★★
New Era Vineyards ★★★★★
Ngeringa ★★★★★
Ochota Barrels ★★★★★
Petaluma ★★★★★
Pike & Joyce ★★★★★
Riposte ★★★★★
Saint and Scholar ★★★★★
Shaw + Smith ★★★★★
Sidewood Estate ★★★★★
Tapanappa ★★★★★
The Lane Vineyard ★★★★★

Tomich Wines ★★★★★
Turon Wines ★★★★★
View Road Wines ★★★★★

ADELAIDE ZONE

Heirloom Vineyards ★★★★★
Hewitson ★★★★★
Nick Haselgrove Wines ★★★★★
Patritti Wines ★★★★★
Penfolds Magill Estate ★★★★★

ALBANY

Wignalls Wines ★★★★★

ALPINE VALLEYS

Billy Button Wines ★★★★★
Bush Track Wines ★★★★★
Mayford Wines ★★★★★

BALLARAT

Mitchell Harris Wines ★★★★★
Tomboy Hill ★★★★★

BAROSSA VALLEY

1847 | Chateau Yaldara ★★★★★
Artisans of the Barossa ★★★★★
Atze's Corner Wines ★★★★★
Ballycroft Vineyard & Cellars ★★★★★
Bethany Wines ★★★★★
Brothers at War ★★★★★
Burge Family Winemakers ★★★★★
Charles Melton ★★★★★
Chateau Tanunda ★★★★★
Cimicky Wines ★★★★★
David Franz ★★★★★
Dorrien Estate ★★★★★
Dutschke Wines ★★★★★
Eisenstone ★★★★★

Elderton ★★★★★
Eperosa ★★★★★
First Drop Wines ★★★★★
Gibson ★★★★★
Glaetzer Wines ★★★★★
Glen Eldon Wines ★★★★★
Grant Burge ★★★★★
Hare's Chase ★★★★★
Hart of the Barossa ★★★★★
Hayes Family Wines ★★★★★
Head Wines ★★★★★
Hemera Estate ★★★★★
Hentley Farm Wines ★★★★★
John Duval Wines ★★★★★
Kaesler Wines ★★★★★
Kalleske ★★★★★
Kellermeister ★★★★★
Landhaus Estate ★★★★★
Langmeil Winery ★★★★★
Love Over Gold ★★★★★
Magpie Estate ★★★★★
Massena Vineyards ★★★★★
Maverick Wines ★★★★★
Paulmara Estates ★★★★★
Penfolds ★★★★★
Peter Lehmann ★★★★★
Pindarie ★★★★★
Purple Hands Wines ★★★★★
Rockford ★★★★★
Rolf Binder ★★★★★
St Hallett ★★★★★
St Hugo ★★★★★
Saltram ★★★★★
Schild Estate Wines ★★★★★
Schubert Estate ★★★★★
Schwarz Wine Company ★★★★★
Seppeltsfield ★★★★★
Sons of Eden ★★★★★
Soul Growers ★★★★★
Spinifex ★★★★★
Teusner ★★★★★
Thorn-Clarke Wines ★★★★★
Tim Smith Wines ★★★★★
Torbreck Vintners ★★★★★
Turkey Flat ★★★★★
Two Hands Wines ★★★★★
Utopos ★★★★★
Vindana Wines ★★★★★
Whistler Wines ★★★★★
Wolf Blass ★★★★★
Woods Crampton ★★★★★

Yelland & Papps ★★★★★
Z Wine ★★★★★

BEECHWORTH

A. Rodda Wines ★★★★★
Castagna ★★★★★
Domenica Wines ★★★★★
Fighting Gully Road ★★★★★
Giaconda ★★★★★
Golden Ball ★★★★★
Indigo Vineyard ★★★★★
Piano Piano ★★★★★
Savaterre ★★★★★
Serengale Vineyard ★★★★★
Traviarti ★★★★★
Vignerons Schmolzer & Brown ★★★★★

BENDIGO

Balgownie Estate ★★★★★
Sandhurst Ridge ★★★★★
Sutton Grange Winery ★★★★★

BLACKWOOD VALLEY

Dickinson Estate ★★★★★
Nannup Ridge Estate ★★★★★

CANBERRA DISTRICT

Clonakilla ★★★★★
Eden Road Wines ★★★★★
Helm ★★★★★
Lake George Winery ★★★★★
Lark Hill ★★★★★
McKellar Ridge Wines ★★★★★
Mount Majura Vineyard ★★★★★
Nick O'Leary Wines ★★★★★
Poachers Vineyard ★★★★★
Ravensworth ★★★★★

CENTRAL VICTORIA ZONE

Mount Terrible ★★★★★

CLARE VALLEY

Atlas Wines ★★★★★
Clos Clare ★★★★★
Grosset ★★★★★
Jaeschke's Hill River Clare Estate
  ★★★★★
Jeanneret Wines ★★★★★
Jim Barry Wines ★★★★★
Kilikanoon Wines ★★★★★
Knappstein ★★★★★

Leasingham ★★★★★
Liz Heidenreich Wines ★★★★★
Mount Horrocks ★★★★★
O'Leary Walker Wines ★★★★★
Naked Run Wines ★★★★★
Paulett Wines ★★★★★
Pikes ★★★★★
Rieslingfreak ★★★★★
Shut the Gate Wines ★★★★★
Steve Wiblin's Erin Eyes ★★★★★
Sussex Squire ★★★★★
Taylors ★★★★★
Tim Adams ★★★★★
Vickery Wines ★★★★★
Wendouree ★★★★★
Wilson Vineyard ★★★★★
Woodvale ★★★★★

COONAWARRA

Balnaves of Coonawarra ★★★★★
Brand's Laira Coonawarra ★★★★★
Highbank ★★★★★
Katnook ★★★★★
Leconfield ★★★★★
Majella ★★★★★
Parker Coonawarra Estate ★★★★★
Patrick of Coonawarra ★★★★★
Penley Estate ★★★★★
Redman ★★★★★
Wynns Coonawarra Estate ★★★★★
Zema Estate ★★★★★

DENMARK

Harewood Estate ★★★★★
Silverstream Wines ★★★★★
The Lake House Denmark ★★★★★

EDEN VALLEY

Flaxman Wines ★★★★★
Forbes & Forbes ★★★★★
Gatt Wines ★★★★★
Heathvale ★★★★★
Heggies Vineyard ★★★★★
Henschke ★★★★★
Hutton Vale Farm ★★★★★
Irvine ★★★★★
Leo Buring ★★★★★
Max & Me ★★★★★
Mountadam ★★★★★
Pewsey Vale Vineyard ★★★★★
Poonawatta ★★★★★

Stage Door Wine Co ★★★★★
Torzi Matthews Vintners ★★★★★
Yalumba ★★★★★

FRANKLAND RIVER

Alkoomi ★★★★★
Ferngrove ★★★★★
Frankland Estate ★★★★★
Swinney ★★★★★

GEELONG

Austin's Wines ★★★★★
Banks Road ★★★★★
Bannockburn Vineyards ★★★★★
Barrgowan Vineyard ★★★★★
Barwon Ridge Wines ★★★★★
Bellbrae Estate ★★★★★
Brown Magpie Wines ★★★★★
Ceres Bridge Estate ★★★★★
Clyde Park Vineyard ★★★★★
Dinny Goonan ★★★★★
Farr | Farr Rising ★★★★★
Lethbridge Wines ★★★★★
McGlashan's Wallington Estate ★★★★★
Mulline ★★★★★
Oakdene ★★★★★
Paradise IV ★★★★★
Provenance Wines ★★★★★
Robin Brockett Wines ★★★★★
Scotchmans Hill ★★★★★
Shadowfax ★★★★★
Spence ★★★★★
Yes said the Seal ★★★★★

GEOGRAPHE

bakkheia ★★★★★
Capel Vale ★★★★★
Iron Cloud Wines ★★★★★
Willow Bridge Estate ★★★★★

GIPPSLAND

Bass Phillip ★★★★★
Lightfoot & Sons ★★★★★
Narkoojee ★★★★★

GLENROWAN

Baileys of Glenrowan ★★★★★

GRAMPIANS

ATR Wines ★★★★★
Best's Wines ★★★★★
Fallen Giants ★★★★★

Grampians Estate ★★★★★
Montara ★★★★★
Mount Langi Ghiran Vineyards
    ★★★★★
Seppelt ★★★★★
SubRosa ★★★★★
The Story Wines ★★★★★

GRANITE BELT

Boireann ★★★★★
Heritage Estate ★★★★★

GREAT SOUTHERN

Byron & Harold ★★★★★
Castelli Estate ★★★★★
Forest Hill Vineyard ★★★★★
Kings Landing ★★★★★
Marchand & Burch ★★★★★
Plan B Wines ★★★★★
Rockcliffe ★★★★★
Rosenthal Wines ★★★★★
Singlefile Wines ★★★★★
Staniford Wine Co ★★★★★
Trevelen Farm ★★★★★
Willoughby Park ★★★★★

GREAT WESTERN

Black & Ginger ★★★★★

GUNDAGAI

Nick Spencer Wines ★★★★★

HEATHCOTE

Bull Lane Wine Company ★★★★★
Domaine Asmara ★★★★★
Ellis Wines ★★★★★
Heathcote Estate ★★★★★
Jasper Hill ★★★★★
Kennedy ★★★★★
Munari Wines ★★★★★
Occam's Razor | Lo Stesso ★★★★★
Paul Osicka ★★★★★
Sanguine Estate ★★★★★
Tar & Roses ★★★★★
Tellurian ★★★★★
Vinea Marson ★★★★★
Wren Estate ★★★★★

HENTY

Basalt Wines ★★★★★
Crawford River Wines ★★★★★

Jackson Brooke ★★★★★

HILLTOPS

Freeman Vineyards ★★★★★
Moppity Vineyards ★★★★★

HUNTER VALLEY

Audrey Wilkinson ★★★★★
Bimbadgen ★★★★★
Briar Ridge Vineyard ★★★★★
Brokenwood ★★★★★
Capercaillie Wines ★★★★★
Carillion Wines ★★★★★
Cockfighter's Ghost | Poole's Rock
    ★★★★★
De Iuliis ★★★★★
First Creek Wines ★★★★★
Gartelmann Wines ★★★★★
Glenguin Estate ★★★★★
Gundog Estate ★★★★★
Hart & Hunter ★★★★★
Keith Tulloch Wine ★★★★★
Lake's Folly ★★★★★
Leogate Estate Wines ★★★★★
McLeish Estate ★★★★★
Margan Family ★★★★★
Meerea Park ★★★★★
Mount Pleasant ★★★★★
Mount View Estate ★★★★★
Pepper Tree Wines ★★★★★
RidgeView Wines ★★★★★
Silkman Wines ★★★★★
Stomp Wine ★★★★★
Thomas Wines ★★★★★
Tinklers Vineyard ★★★★★
Tulloch ★★★★★
Tyrrell's Wines ★★★★★
Vinden Estate ★★★★★
Whispering Brook ★★★★★

KANGAROO ISLAND

The Islander Estate Vineyards ★★★★★

KING VALLEY

Brown Brothers ★★★★★
Dal Zotto Wines ★★★★★
Pizzini ★★★★★
Wood Park ★★★★★

LANGHORNE CREEK

Bleasdale Vineyards ★★★★★

Bremerton Wines ★★★★★
Lake Breeze Wines ★★★★★

MACEDON RANGES

Bindi Wine Growers ★★★★★
Curly Flat ★★★★★
Granite Hills ★★★★★
Hanging Rock Winery ★★★★★
Lane's End Vineyard ★★★★★
Passing Clouds ★★★★★

MCLAREN VALE

Aphelion Wine ★★★★★
Battle of Bosworth ★★★★★
Bekkers ★★★★★
Blewitt Springs Wine Co ★★★★★
Bondar Wines ★★★★★
Cape Barren Wines ★★★★★
Chalk Hill ★★★★★
Chapel Hill ★★★★★
Cooter & Cooter ★★★★★
Coriole ★★★★★
cradle of hills ★★★★★
d'Arenberg ★★★★★
Dabblebrook Wines ★★★★★
Dodgy Brothers ★★★★★
DOWIE DOOLE ★★★★★
Dune Wine ★★★★★
Fox Creek Wines ★★★★★
Gemtree Wines ★★★★★
Geoff Merrill Wines ★★★★★
Hardys ★★★★★
Haselgrove Wines ★★★★★
Heartwines ★★★★★
Hedonist Wines ★★★★★
Hickinbotham Clarendon Vineyard
     ★★★★★
Hither & Yon ★★★★★
Hugh Hamilton Wines ★★★★★
Jarressa Estate Wines ★★★★★
Kangarilla Road Vineyard ★★★★★
Kay Brothers Amery Vineyards
     ★★★★★
Longline Wines ★★★★★
Loonie Wine Co ★★★★★
Mitolo Wines ★★★★★
Mr Riggs Wine Company ★★★★★
Oliver's Taranga Vineyards ★★★★★
Ox Hardy ★★★★★
Paralian Wines ★★★★★
Paxton ★★★★★
Penny's Hill ★★★★★

Pirramimma ★★★★★
Primo Estate ★★★★★
Reynella ★★★★★
Richard Hamilton ★★★★★
Rudderless ★★★★★
Samuel's Gorge ★★★★★
SC Pannell ★★★★★
Serafino Wines ★★★★★
Sherrah Wines ★★★★★
Shingleback ★★★★★
Shirvington ★★★★★
Shottesbrooke ★★★★★
Smidge Wines ★★★★★
Thomas St Vincent ★★★★★
Three Dark Horses ★★★★★
Ulithorne ★★★★★
Varney Wines ★★★★★
Vigena Wines ★★★★★
Wirra Wirra ★★★★★
Yangarra Estate Vineyard ★★★★★
Zerella Wines ★★★★★
Zonte's Footstep ★★★★★

MANJIMUP

Peos Estate ★★★★★

MARGARET RIVER

Amelia Park Wines ★★★★★
Aravina Estate ★★★★★
Arlewood Estate ★★★★★
Brash Vineyard ★★★★★
Brookland Valley ★★★★★
Brown Hill Estate ★★★★★
Cape Mentelle ★★★★★
Cape Naturaliste Vineyard ★★★★★
Churchview Estate ★★★★★
Clairault | Streicker Wines ★★★★★
Cloudburst ★★★★★
Credaro Family Estate ★★★★★
Cullen Wines ★★★★★
Deep Woods Estate ★★★★★
Devil's Lair ★★★★★
Domaine Naturaliste ★★★★★
Driftwood Estate ★★★★★
Evans & Tate ★★★★★
Evoi Wines ★★★★★
Fermoy Estate ★★★★★
Firetail ★★★★★
Flametree ★★★★★
Flowstone Wines ★★★★★
Flying Fish Cove ★★★★★
Forester Estate ★★★★★

Fraser Gallop Estate ★★★★★
Grace Farm ★★★★★
Happs ★★★★★
Hay Shed Hill Wines ★★★★★
Heydon Estate ★★★★★
Higher Plane ★★★★★
House of Cards ★★★★★
Howard Park ★★★★★
Jilyara of Wilyabrup ★★★★★
Juniper ★★★★★
La Kooki Wines ★★★★★
Leeuwin Estate ★★★★★
Lenton Brae Wines ★★★★★
McHenry Hohnen Vintners ★★★★★
Moss Wood ★★★★★
Mr Barval Fine Wines ★★★★★
Nocturne Wines ★★★★★
Oates Ends ★★★★★
Palmer Wines ★★★★★
Peccavi Wines ★★★★★
Pierro ★★★★★
Robert Oatley Margaret River ★★★★★
Sandalford ★★★★★
Stella Bella Wines ★★★★★
Thompson Estate ★★★★★
tripe.Iscariot ★★★★★
Trove Estate ★★★★★
Twinwoods Estate ★★★★★
Umamu Estate ★★★★★
Vasse Felix ★★★★★
Victory Point Wines ★★★★★
Voyager Estate ★★★★★
Walsh & Sons ★★★★★
Wills Domain ★★★★★
Windance Wines ★★★★★
Windows Estate ★★★★★
Wise Wine ★★★★★
Woodlands ★★★★★
Woody Nook ★★★★★
Xanadu Wines ★★★★★

MORNINGTON PENINSULA

Allies Wines ★★★★★
Circe Wines ★★★★★
Crittenden Estate ★★★★★
Dexter Wines ★★★★★
Eldridge Estate of Red Hill ★★★★★
Elgee Park ★★★★★
Foxeys Hangout ★★★★★
Garagiste ★★★★★
Hurley Vineyard ★★★★★
Jones Road ★★★★★

Kooyong ★★★★★
Main Ridge Estate ★★★★★
Merricks Estate ★★★★★
Montalto ★★★★★
Moorooduc Estate ★★★★★
Paradigm Hill ★★★★★
Paringa Estate ★★★★★
Port Phillip Estate ★★★★★
Portsea Estate ★★★★★
Principia ★★★★★
Quealy Winemakers ★★★★★
Scorpo Wines ★★★★★
Stonier Wines ★★★★★
Ten Minutes by Tractor ★★★★★
Trofeo Estate ★★★★★
Tuck's ★★★★★
Willow Creek Vineyard ★★★★★
Yabby Lake Vineyard ★★★★★

MOUNT BARKER

Gilberts ★★★★★
Plantagenet ★★★★★
Poacher's Ridge Vineyard ★★★★★
Terra Riche ★★★★★
3 Drops ★★★★★
Towerhill Estate ★★★★★
West Cape Howe Wines ★★★★★
Xabregas ★★★★★

MOUNT BENSON

Mount Benson Estate ★★★★★
Wangolina ★★★★★

MOUNT LOFTY RANGES ZONE

Michael Hall Wines ★★★★★

MUDGEE

Craigmoor | Montrose ★★★★★
Huntington Estate ★★★★★
Robert Stein Vineyard ★★★★★

NAGAMBIE LAKES

Box Grove Vineyard ★★★★★
Mitchelton ★★★★★
Tahbilk ★★★★★

NORTH EAST VICTORIA ZONE

Eldorado Road ★★★★★

ORANGE

Gilbert Family Wines ★★★★★
Nashdale Lane Wines ★★★★★

Patina ★★★★★
Philip Shaw Wines ★★★★★
Printhie Wines ★★★★★
Rikard Wines ★★★★★
Ross Hill Wines ★★★★★
Swinging Bridge ★★★★★

PEMBERTON
Bellarmine Wines ★★★★★

PERTH HILLS
Millbrook Winery ★★★★★

PORONGURUP
Abbey Creek Vineyard ★★★★★
Castle Rock Estate ★★★★★
Duke's Vineyard ★★★★★

PYRENEES
Blue Pyrenees Estate ★★★★★
Dalwhinnie ★★★★★
DogRock Winery ★★★★★
Mount Avoca ★★★★★
Summerfield ★★★★★
Taltarni ★★★★★

QUEENSLAND ZONE
Witches Falls Winery ★★★★★

RIVERINA
Calabria Family Wines ★★★★★
De Bortoli ★★★★★
Lillypilly Estate ★★★★★
McWilliam's ★★★★★
Michel Marie ★★★★★
R. Paulazzo ★★★★★
Yarran Wines ★★★★★

RIVERLAND
Ricca Terra ★★★★★

RUTHERGLEN
All Saints Estate ★★★★★
Anderson ★★★★★
Buller Wines ★★★★★
Campbells ★★★★★
Chambers Rosewood ★★★★★
Morris ★★★★★
St Leonards Vineyard ★★★★★
Stanton & Killeen Wines ★★★★★

SHOALHAVEN COAST
Coolangatta Estate ★★★★★

SOUTH AUSTRALIA
Angove Family Winemakers ★★★★★
Dandelion Vineyards ★★★★★
Thistledown Wines ★★★★★
Wines by Geoff Hardy ★★★★★

SOUTH WEST AUSTRALIA ZONE
Kerrigan + Berry ★★★★★
Snake + Herring ★★★★★

SOUTHERN FLEURIEU
Salomon Estate ★★★★★

SOUTHERN HIGHLANDS
Centennial Vineyards ★★★★★
Tertini Wines ★★★★★

STRATHBOGIE RANGES
Fowles Wine ★★★★★
Wine x Sam ★★★★★

SUNBURY
Craiglee ★★★★★
Galli Estate ★★★★★
The Hairy Arm ★★★★★

SWAN DISTRICT
Mandoon Estate ★★★★★

SWAN VALLEY
Corymbia ★★★★★
Faber Vineyard ★★★★★
Houghton ★★★★★
John Kosovich Wines ★★★★★
RiverBank Estate ★★★★★
Sittella Wines ★★★★★
Upper Reach ★★★★★

TASMANIA
Alex Russell Wines ★★★★★
Apogee ★★★★★
Barringwood ★★★★★
Bay of Fires ★★★★★
Bream Creek ★★★★★
Chatto ★★★★★
Clover Hill ★★★★★
Dalrymple Vineyards ★★★★★
Dawson & James ★★★★★
Delamere Vineyards ★★★★★
Domaine A ★★★★★
Dr Edge ★★★★★
Freycinet ★★★★★

Gala Estate ★★★★★
Ghost Rock Vineyard ★★★★★
Holm Oak ★★★★★
Home Hill ★★★★★
House of Arras ★★★★★
Jansz Tasmania ★★★★★
Josef Chromy Wines ★★★★★
Marion's Vineyard ★★★★★
Meadowbank Wines ★★★★★
Mewstone Wines ★★★★★
Milton Vineyard ★★★★★
Moores Hill Estate ★★★★★
Moorilla Estate ★★★★★
Pipers Brook Vineyard ★★★★★
Pooley Wines ★★★★★
Pressing Matters ★★★★★
Riversdale Estate ★★★★★
Sailor Seeks Horse ★★★★★
Shy Susan Wines ★★★★★
Sinapius Vineyard ★★★★★
Small Island Wines ★★★★★
Stargazer Wine ★★★★★
Stefano Lubiana ★★★★★
Stoney Rise ★★★★★
Tamar Ridge | Pirie ★★★★★
Tasmanian Vintners ★★★★★
Tolpuddle Vineyard ★★★★★

TUMBARUMBA

Coppabella of Tumbarumba ★★★★★

UPPER GOULBURN

Delatite ★★★★★
Kensington Wines ★★★★★

VARIOUS

Handpicked Wines ★★★★★
Ministry of Clouds ★★★★★
Sentio Wines ★★★★★
Stonefish ★★★★★

WESTERN AUSTRALIA

Larry Cherubino Wines ★★★★★

WESTERN VICTORIA ZONE

Norton Estate ★★★★★

WRATTONBULLY

Terre à Terre ★★★★★

YARRA VALLEY

B Minor ★★★★★
Ben Haines Wine ★★★★★

Bicknell fc ★★★★★
Bird on a Wire Wines ★★★★★
Chandon Australia ★★★★★
Coldstream Hills ★★★★★
Dappled Wine ★★★★★
DCB Wine ★★★★★
De Bortoli ★★★★★
Denton Viewhill Vineyard ★★★★★
Dominique Portet ★★★★★
Fetherston Vintners ★★★★★
First Foot Forward ★★★★★
Gembrook Hill ★★★★★
Giant Steps ★★★★★
Greenstone Vineyards ★★★★★
Hillcrest Vineyard ★★★★★
Hoddles Creek Estate ★★★★★
Journey Wines ★★★★★
Kellybrook ★★★★★
Mac Forbes ★★★★★
Mandala ★★★★★
Many Hands Winery ★★★★★
Mayer ★★★★★
Medhurst ★★★★★
Mount Mary ★★★★★
Oakridge Wines ★★★★★
One Block ★★★★★
Payne's Rise ★★★★★
Punch ★★★★★
Punt Road ★★★★★
Rob Dolan Wines ★★★★★
Rochford Wines ★★★★★
Santarossa Wine Company ★★★★★
Santolin Wines ★★★★★
Serrat ★★★★★
Seville Estate ★★★★★
Soumah ★★★★★
Squitchy Lane Vineyard ★★★★★
Stefani Estate ★★★★★
Sutherland Estate ★★★★★
Tarrahill. ★★★★★
TarraWarra Estate ★★★★★
The Wanderer ★★★★★
Thick as Thieves Wines ★★★★★
Tokar Estate ★★★★★
Toolangi Vineyards ★★★★★
Wantirna Estate ★★★★★
Warramate ★★★★★
Yarra Edge ★★★★★
Yarra Yering ★★★★★
Yarrabank ★★★★★
Yering Station ★★★★★
Yeringberg ★★★★★

Australian vine plantings

There is much talk these days about 'alternative varieties', and with some misgivings on my part, I shall adopt it and its counterpart, 'traditional varieties'. Indeed, it makes sense to discuss traditional varieties first, because I need to place all varieties within an Australian context. The traditional varieties have been split into first and second divisions not based on quality, but because of drastic disparities in tonnage. The order of the alternative varieties is based on an arbitrary split between red and white varieties, and is thereafter alphabetical. Comparison figures for 2008 are not included for the alternative varieties because many of them weren't even around 10 years ago.

Jancis Robinson MW et al. explore 1368 varieties being grown somewhere on earth today; I am sure she would readily admit that list is in a state of flux, with new varieties being identified, others found to be genetically identical, some cuckoos pretending to be identical when they are not, and still others given place names and wearing those with pride. Then you have four founding varieties as common as pinot or as left field as tribidrag (the latter the same as primitivo and zinfandel). Gouais blanc is another founding father dating back hundreds of years, but also grown in the WH Chambers vineyard in Rutherglen, pronounced 'gooey' by patriarch Bill Chambers and planted (or replanted) after phylloxera. And so into the breach.

Traditional varieties

FIRST DIVISION

Variety	2009 tonnes	2019 tonnes	2019 value (million)
Shiraz	394070	374511	$337.28
Chardonnay	384185	318908	$148.05
Cabernet sauvignon	248451	227000	$192.06

Shiraz takes pride of place. More was grown in 2019 than chardonnay, albeit by a relatively narrow margin until you take into account the value of the crop, twice that of chardonnay. Shiraz came to Australia in 1832 via the vast Busby collection of varieties; the cuttings were taken from the hill of Hermitage on 10 December 1831. Another 140 or so years were to pass before vignerons in other parts of the world realised the quality of shiraz, Max Schubert being its messiah.

As more and more regions in a multitude of countries found that shiraz grew well, cropped well and was forgiving of shortcomings in both the vineyard and winery, the rush to plant it began – and continues to this day. There is, however, one region that has the history, terroir and old vines that will never be equalled by any other region. It is the Barossa Valley, which has an Old Vine Charter that says it all. 'Old Vine' must be equal or greater than 35 years of age; 'Survivor Vine', 70; 'Centenarian Vine', unsurprisingly, 100 years; and 'Ancestor Vine', an incredible 125 years of age.

There are many reasons for the premium price shiraz commands, first and foremost its impact on the Chinese market, where history is valued to an extent not matched in any other place or region. Next, Australian shiraz is competing with cabernet sauvignon à la Bordeaux, both wines typically medium to full-bodied. As the Chinese market becomes more knowledgeable about the way wine is treated in Western markets, so will their demand for medium-bodied wines increase.

Shiraz has a 150-year history in Australia, **chardonnay** little more than 40 years. Australians have been on a sharp learning curve about chardonnay. It captured the previously non-existent UK market for Australian wine in the latter part of the 1980s. It was buttercup yellow, the fruit in a yellow peach/tropical spectrum, and it needed every bit of that fruit to stand up to the cheap American oak chips and planks ladled into it.

It was the small(ish) family wineries in climates such as Margaret River and the Yarra Valley that, beginning in the 1990s, started the still-continuing changes in the way chardonnay is made. The major focus has been on reducing the oak used in both fermentation and maturation of the wine. Specifically, barrel sizes have doubled from barrique (225l) to puncheon (500l) or larger, heavy toasting has been banished, and lees stirring has become strictly optional. One could write a book on the vinification of chardonnay, but this isn't the place. Suffice it to say that elegant, fine, fruit-focused and long wines are the desired outcome at the present.

Max Schubert made one Grange using **cabernet sauvignon** but abandoned the idea because there wasn't enough grown in South Australia in the early 1960s. Some started to appear in the early 1970s from Coonawarra (Mildara made its famous 1963 Cabernet Sauvignon aka Peppermint Pattie, but subsequent vintages failed to excite). Coonawarra remained the go-to destination until the mid-1980s, but thereafter Margaret River and the Great Southern of Western Australia have moved into first place, something that mightily displeases the Coonawarra vignerons. Wynns Coonawarra Estate, which saved the region's life in the early 1950s, has kept the flame burning.

SECOND DIVISION

Variety	2009 tonnes	2019 tonnes	2019 value (million)
Pinot noir	31 310	42 583	$43.74
Pinot gris	26 200	63 087	$39.64
Sauvignon blanc	63 638	80 990	$46.12
Riesling	39 620	21 055	$19.09
Semillon	81 851	48 269	$19.73

Personal prejudices fly high, wide and handsome here, but **pinot noir** is not only one of Europe's oldest varieties (registering more than 1000 clones/biotypes) and a great-grandchild of shiraz and cabernet sauvignon (by different genetic pathways) – it also makes the most ravishing wine known to humans or angels.

That is the good news. The bad news is the temperamental nature of the variety, demanding the perfect site, the most fastidious and sensitive upbringing in the winery, and constant prayer to the wine gods. The dress circle of regions around Melbourne, Tasmania, and dots here and there from the east coast, the south coast and the south of Western Australia can bring tears of joy or despair at will.

Pinot gris is a variety made in heaven for winemakers happy to work with high yields and level residual sugar in the wine as a substitute for (diluted) true fruit flavour. The consumer doesn't object because the wine is seldom expensive.

It is easy to sneer at **sauvignon blanc**, the curl of the lip engendered by the knowledge that both North and South Island (Marlborough the fulcrum between the two) make dramatically flavoured sauvignon blanc at a fraction of the price of its Australian sibling. This may or may not remind consumers of the ability of Margaret River (and other south western regions) to make high quality blends of semillon sauvignon blanc: the percentages the choice of the winemaker, barrel ferment likewise optional, but exceptional money par for the course.

The choice between **riesling** and **semillon** may well depend on the answer to the question whether you were born in Adelaide (hence riesling) or Sydney (semillon). In truth these varieties bring the same benefits to the consumer: fresh, crisp and lively in their youth, gradually moving into honeyed lemon toast with age, and every point along the development path guaranteed by the arrival of screwcaps.

Alternative varieties

RED

Variety	2019 tonnes	2019 growers	2019 hectares	2019 value (million)
Barbera	551	101	104	$0.36
Cabernet franc	1057	395	552	$1.30
Dolcetto	1202	43	154	$0.63
Durif	10603	133	417	$7.36
Gamay	–	22	15	–
Lagrein	192	29	17	$0.23
Montepulciano	697	26	49	$0.69
Mourvedre	5304	274	729	$4.52
Nero d'Avola	867	19	33	$1.15
Pinot meunier	851	60	50	$1.29
Tempranillo	5386	333	712	$5.59

Barbera came to Australia over 50 years ago, but hasn't caught the eye of Italophiles. **Cabernet franc** is the parent of cabernet sauvignon, merlot and carmenere. Prized in Margaret River as a blend component with cabernet sauvignon. **Dolcetto** is dotted through small holdings in the Hunter Valley, Barossa Valley and cooler regions in Victoria and South Australia. Light-bodied wines with fresh cherry fruits. **Durif** is here to stay, its tonnage up from 4142t in 2010. It obtained its substantial footprint in North East Victoria, making ultra-full-bodied wines, and was then taken to the Riverland where irrigation-fed crops provide a win–win situation with large yields of deeply coloured wines and an abundance of fruit/tannin flavours. **Gamay** hasn't yet hit the statistical basket, but there's enough happening in the Yarra Valley and Mornington Peninsula to ensure it will do so soon enough. Supple, juicy red berry–fruited wines don't need pinot noir in a blend. **Lagrein**, for DNA hounds, is a nephew/niece of dureza (a parent of shiraz), a grandchild of pinot noir, and a cousin of shiraz. Its deep crimson-purple colour and intense confit black/forest fruit flavours mean slow development in bottle. **Montepulciano** is doubtless assisted by its Italian links, and it seems likely the plantings are increasing, even if slowly. A workhorse in Italy, which has over 95% of the world's 34660ha plantings. **Mourvedre** is, or has been until recently, known as mataro, and esparte in Great Western. It's usually blended with other Rhône varieties, contributing colour and tannins. **Nero d'Avola** is a trendy variety in Australia, and a cornerstone in Sicily. Its cherry/raspberry/strawberry flavours are very attractive. **Pinot meunier** has snuck in the side door of still table wine, having been previously limited to use in sparkling wines. To my surprise (and that of others) it can make a lovely wine. **Tempranillo** is akin to mourvedre and durif when production is the sole measure. However, it has proved its worth in regions spread far and wide, with red and black cherry the flavour drivers.

WHITE

Variety	2019 tonnes	2019 growers	2019 hectares	2019 value (million)
Fiano	2791	50	88	$2.00
Marsanne	1275	111	192	$0.60
Muscadelle	291	45	82	$0.32
Prosecco	8894	–	–	$7.43
Verdelho	7333	383	1339	$3.59
Vermentino	1747	80	93	$0.99
Viognier	5799	515	1194	$3.03

Fiano is the wild child of the newest arrivals and is surely here to prosper, with an innate texture described by Jancis Robinson as 'rich, waxy, strongly flavoured, fashionable Southern Italian'. On the evidence to date, it performs in both warm and cool Australian regions, and doesn't need barrel fermentation or maturation to give off its best. **Marsanne** has made a home away from home for itself in the Nagambie Lakes, with Tahbilk having one of the largest plantings in the world. It has many similarities to semillon, crisp in its youth, with lemon zest acidity, gaining depth and texture with age. **Muscadelle** was traditionally called tokay in Australia, that usage now banned by the wine agreement with the EU. It's almost entirely used to make one of the two great fortified wines of North East Victoria, its importance measured by its quality, not quantity. **Prosecco** is the runaway train, of little statistical importance in 2010. Its sudden rise to importance here has also occurred in the US, with the UK as one of the major markets for a wine that is pleasant but bordering on neutral. **Verdelho** has the world as its oyster, for it is only here that winemakers and consumers agree that gentle fruit salad flavours are worth pursuing. **Vermentino** is one of the most widely planted new-generation alternative varieties. Its vibrant acidity and full range of citrus flavours provide a wine that can be made in a wide variety of growing season climates. **Viognier** is unquestionably responsible for making totally delicious medium-bodied red wine when included in the fermentation of shiraz, using somewhere between 3% and 7%. Making a mono-varietal viognier that will attract discerning palates is extremely difficult.

Varietal wine styles and regions

For better or worse, there simply has to be concerted action to highlight the link between regions, varieties and wine styles. It's not a question of creating the links: they are already there, and have been in existence for periods as short as 20 years or as long as 150 years. So here you will find abbreviated summaries of those regional styles (in turn reflected in the Best of the Best lists commencing on page xx).

Riesling

Riesling's link with the **Eden Valley** dates back at least to when Joseph Gilbert planted his Pewsey Vale vineyard, and the grape quickly made its way to the nearby **Clare Valley**. These two regions stood above all others for well over 100 years, producing wines that shared many flavour and texture characteristics: lime (a little more obvious in the Eden Valley), apple, talc and mineral, lightly browned toasty notes emerging with five to 10 years' bottle age. Within the last 20 or so years, the subregions of Western Australia's **Great Southern** have established a deserved reputation for finely structured, elegant rieslings with wonderful length, sometimes shy when young, bursting into song after five years. The subregions are (in alphabetical order) **Albany, Denmark, Frankland River, Mount Barker** and **Porongurup. Canberra** is up with the best and **Tasmania**, too, produces high class rieslings, notable for their purity and intensity courtesy of their high natural acidity. Finally, there is the small and very cool region of **Henty** (once referred to as Drumborg), its exceptional rieslings sharing many things in common with those of Tasmania.

Chardonnay

This infinitely flexible grape is grown and vinified in all 63 regions, and accounts for half of Australia's white wine grapes and wine. Incredibly, before 1970 it was all but unknown, hiding its promise here and there (**Mudgee** was one such place) under a cloak of anonymity. It was in Mudgee and the **Hunter Valley** that the first wines labelled chardonnay were made in 1971 (by Craigmoor and Tyrrell's). Its bold yellow colour, peaches and cream flavour and vanilla oak was unlike anything that had gone before and was accepted by domestic and export markets with equal enthusiasm. When exports took off into the stratosphere between 1985 and '95, one half of Brand Australia was cheerful and cheap oak-chipped chardonnay grown in the **Riverina** and **Riverland**. By coincidence, over the same period chardonnay from the emerging cool-climate regions was starting to appear in limited quantities, its flavour and structure radically different to the warm-grown, high-cropped wine. Another 10 years on, and by 2005–6 the wine surplus was starting to build rapidly, with demand for chardonnay much less than its production. As attention swung from chardonnay to sauvignon blanc, the situation became dire. Lost in the heat of battle were supremely elegant wines from most cool regions, **Margaret River** and **Yarra Valley** the leaders of the large band. Constant refinement of the style, and the adoption of the screwcap, puts these wines at the forefront of the gradually succeeding battle to re-engage consumers here and abroad with what are world class wines.

Semillon

There is a Siamese-twin relationship between semillon and the **Hunter Valley**, which has been producing a wine style like no other in the world for well over 100 years. The humid and very warm climate (best coupled with sandy soils not common in the region) results in wines that have a median alcohol level of 10.5% and no residual sugar, are cold-fermented in stainless steel and bottled within three months of vintage. They are devoid of colour and have only the barest hints of grass, herb and mineral wrapped around a core of acidity. Over the next five to 10 years they develop a glowing green-gold colour, a suite of grass and citrus fruit surrounded by buttered toast and honey notes. As with rieslings, screwcaps have added decades to their cellaring life. The **Adelaide Hills** and **Margaret River** produce entirely different semillon, more structured and weighty, its alcohol 13–14%, and as often as not blended with sauvignon blanc, barrel fermentation of part or all common. Finally, there is a cuckoo in the nest: Peter Lehmann in the **Barossa/Eden Valley** has adapted Hunter Valley practices, picking early, fermenting in steel, bottling early, and holding the top wine for five years before release – and succeeding brilliantly.

Sauvignon blanc

Two regions, the **Adelaide Hills** and **Margaret River**, stood in front of all others until recently joined by **Orange**; these three produce Australia's best sauvignon blanc, wines with real structure and authority. It is a matter of record that Marlborough sauvignon blanc accounts for one-third of Australia's white wine sales; all one can do is say that the basic Marlborough style is very different, and look back at what happened with Australian chardonnay. Margaret River also offers complex blends of sauvignon blanc and semillon in widely varying proportions, and with varying degrees of oak fermentation.

Sparkling

The pattern is eerily similar to that of pinot noir: **Tasmania** now and in the future the keeper of the Holy Grail, the **Port Phillip** zone the centre of activity on the mainland.

Pinot noir

The promiscuity of shiraz (particularly) and cabernet sauvignon is in sharp contrast to the puritanical rectitude of pinot noir. One sin of omission or commission and the door slams shut, leaving the bewildered winemaker on the outside. **Tasmania** is the El Dorado for the variety, and the best is still to come with better clones, older vines and greater exploration of the multitudinous mesoclimates that Tasmania has to offer. While it is north of Central Otago (New Zealand), its vineyards are all air conditioned by the Southern Ocean and Tasman Sea, and it stands toe-to-toe with Central Otago in its ability to make deeply coloured, profound pinot with all the length one could ask for. Once on the mainland, Victoria's Port Phillip zone, encompassing **Geelong, Macedon Ranges, Sunbury, Mornington Peninsula** and **Yarra Valley**, is the epicentre of Australian pinot noir, **Henty** a small outpost. The sheer number of high quality, elegant wines produced by dozens of makers in those regions put the **Adelaide Hills** and **Porongurup** (also capable of producing quality pinot) into the shade.

Shiraz

Shiraz, like chardonnay, is by far the most important red variety and, again like chardonnay, is tremendously flexible in its ability to adapt to virtually any combination of climate and soil/terroir. Unlike chardonnay, a recent arrival, shiraz was the most important red variety throughout the 19th and 20th centuries. Its ancestral homes were the **Barossa Valley, the Clare Valley, McLaren Vale** and the **Hunter Valley**, and it still leads in those regions. With the exception of the Hunter Valley, it was as important in making fortified wine as table wine over the period 1850–1950, aided and abetted by grenache and mourvedre (mataro). In New South Wales, the **Hilltops** and **Canberra District** are producing elegant, cool-grown wines that usually conceal their power (especially when co-fermented with viognier) but not their silky length. Further north, but at a higher altitude, **Orange** is also producing fine, fragrant and spicy wines. All the other New South Wales regions are capable of producing good shiraz of seriously good character and quality; shiraz ripens comfortably but quite late in the season. Polished, sophisticated wines are the result. Victoria has a cornucopia of regions at the cooler end of the spectrum; the coolest (though not too cool for comfort) are the **Yarra Valley, Mornington Peninsula, Sunbury** and **Geelong**, all producing fragrant, spicy medium-bodied wines. **Bendigo, Heathcote, Grampians** and **Pyrenees**, more or less running east–west across the centre of Victoria, are producing some of the most exciting medium-bodied shirazs in Australia, each with its own terroir stamp, but all combining generosity and elegance. In Western Australia, **Great Southern** and three of its five subregions, **Frankland River, Mount Barker** and **Porongurup**, are making magical shirazs, fragrant and spicy, fleshy yet strongly structured. **Margaret River** has been a relatively late mover, but it, too, is producing wines with exemplary varietal definition and finesse.

Cabernet sauvignon

The tough-skinned cabernet sauvignon can be, and is, grown in all regions, but it struggles in the coolest (notably **Tasmania**) and loses desirable varietal definition in the warmer regions, especially in warmer vintages. Shiraz can cope with alcohol levels in excess of 14.5%, cabernet can't. In South Australia, **Coonawarra** stands supreme, its climate (though not its soil) strikingly similar to that of Bordeaux, the main difference lower rainfall. Perfectly detailed cabernets are the result, with no need of shiraz or merlot to fill in the mid-palate, although some excellent blends are made. **Langhorne Creek** (a little warmer) and **McLaren Vale** (warmer still) have similar maritime climates, doubtless the reason McLaren Vale manages to deal with the warmth of its summer–autumn weather. The **Eden Valley** is the most reliable of the inner regions, the other principal regions dependent on a cool summer. From South Australia to Western Australia, where **Margaret River**, with its extreme maritime climate shaped by the warm Indian Ocean, stands tall. It is also Australia's foremost producer of cabernet merlot et al. in the Bordeaux mix. The texture and structure of both the straight varietal and the blend is regal, often to the point of austerity when the wines are young, but the sheer power of this underlying fruit provides the balance and guarantees the future development of the wines over a conservative 20 years, especially if screwcapped. The **Great Southern** subregions of **Frankland River** and **Mount Barker** share a continental climate that is somewhat cooler than Margaret River's, and has a greater diurnal temperature range. Here cabernet has an incisive, dark berry character and firm but usually fine tannins – not demanding merlot, though a touch of it and/or malbec can be beneficial. It is grown successfully through the centre and south of Victoria, but is often overshadowed by shiraz. In the past 20 years it has ceased to be a problem child and become a favourite son of the **Yarra Valley**; the forward move of vintage dates has been the key to the change.

Fortified

Rutherglen and **Glenrowan** are the two (and only) regions that produce immensely complex, long barrel-aged muscat and muscadelle, the latter called tokay for more than a century, now renamed topaque. These wines have no equal in the world, Spain's Malaga nearest in terms of lusciousness, but nowhere near as complex. The other producer of a wine without parallel is Seppeltsfield in the **Barossa Valley**, which each year releases an explosively rich and intense tawny liqueur style that is 100% 100 years old.

Australia's geographical indications

The process of formally mapping Australia's wine regions is all but complete, though it will never come to an outright halt – for one thing, climate change is lurking in the wings.

The division into states, zones, regions and subregions follows; those regions or subregions marked with an asterisk are not yet registered, and may never be, but are in common usage. The bizarre Hunter Valley GI map now has Hunter Valley as a zone, Hunter as the region and the sprawling Upper Hunter as a subregion along with Pokolbin (small and disputed by some locals). Another recent official change has been the registration of Mount Gambier as a Region in the Limestone Coast zone. I am still in front of the game with Tasmania, dividing it into Northern, Southern and East Coast. In a similar vein, I have included Ballarat (with 18 wineries) and the Southern Eyre Peninsula (two wineries).

AUSTRALIA		
State/zone	Region	Subregion
Australia South Eastern Australia* (incorporates the whole of the states of NSW, Vic and Tas, and only part of Qld and SA)		

NEW SOUTH WALES		
State/zone	Region	Subregion
Big Rivers	Murray Darling Perricoota Riverina Swan Hill	
Central Ranges	Cowra Mudgee Orange	
Hunter Valley	Hunter	Broke Fordwich Pokolbin Upper Hunter Valley
Northern Rivers	Hastings River	
Northern Slopes	New England Australia	
South Coast	Shoalhaven Coast Southern Highlands	

NEW SOUTH WALES		
State/zone	**Region**	**Subregion**
Southern New South Wales	Canberra District Gundagai Hilltops Tumbarumba	
Western Plains		

SOUTH AUSTRALIA		
State/zone	**Region**	**Subregion**
Adelaide (super zone, includes Mount Lofty Ranges, Fleurieu and Barossa)		
Barossa	Barossa Valley Eden Valley	High Eden
Far North	Southern Flinders Ranges	
Fleurieu	Currency Creek Kangaroo Island Langhorne Creek McLaren Vale Southern Fleurieu	
Limestone Coast	Coonawarra Mount Benson Mount Gambier Padthaway Robe Wrattonbully	
Lower Murray	Riverland	
Mount Lofty Ranges	Adelaide Hills Adelaide Plains Clare Valley	Lenswood Piccadilly Valley Polish Hill River* Watervale*
The Peninsulas	Southern Eyre Peninsula*	

VICTORIA		
State/zone	**Region**	**Subregion**
Central Victoria	Bendigo Goulburn Valley Heathcote Strathbogie Ranges Upper Goulburn	Nagambie Lakes
Gippsland		

VICTORIA		
State/zone	**Region**	**Subregion**
North East Victoria	Alpine Valleys Beechworth Glenrowan King Valley Rutherglen	
North West Victoria	Murray Darling Swan Hill	
Port Phillip	Geelong Macedon Ranges Mornington Peninsula Sunbury Yarra Valley	
Western Victoria	Ballarat* Grampians Henty Pyrenees	Great Western

WESTERN AUSTRALIA		
State/zone	**Region**	**Subregion**
Central Western Australia		
Eastern Plains, Inland and North of Western Australia		
Greater Perth	Peel Perth Hills Swan District	Swan Valley
South West Australia	Blackwood Valley Geographe Great Southern Manjimup Margaret River Pemberton	Albany Denmark Frankland River Mount Barker Porongurup
West Australian South East Coastal		

QUEENSLAND		
State/zone	**Region**	**Subregion**
Queensland	Granite Belt South Burnett	

TASMANIA		
State/zone	**Region**	**Subregion**
Tasmania	Northern Tasmania* Southern Tasmania* East Coast Tasmania*	

AUSTRALIAN CAPITAL TERRITORY

NORTHERN TERRITORY

Wine and food or food and wine?

It all depends on your starting point: there are conventional matches for overseas classics, such as caviar (Champagne), fresh foie gras (sauternes, riesling or rose) and new season Italian white truffles (any medium-bodied red). Here the food flavour is all important, the wine merely incidental.

At the other extreme come 50-year-old classic red wines: Grange, or Grand Cru Burgundy, or First Growth Bordeaux, or a Maurice O'Shea Mount Pleasant Shiraz. Here the food is, or should be, merely a low-key foil, but at the same time must be of high quality.

In the Australian context I believe not enough attention is paid to the time of year, which – particularly in the southern states – is or should be a major determinant in the choice of both food and wine. And so I shall present my suggestions in this way, always bearing in mind how many ways there are to skin a cat (but not serve it).

Spring

Sparkling
Oysters, cold crustacea, tapas, any cold hors d'oeuvres

Young riesling
Cold salads, sashimi

Gewurztraminer
Asian cuisine

Young semillon
Antipasto, vegetable terrine

Pinot gris
Crab cakes, whitebait

Verdelho, chenin blanc
Cold smoked chicken, gravlax

Mature chardonnay
Grilled chicken, chicken pasta, turkey, pheasant

Rose
Caesar salad, trout mousse

Young pinot noir
Seared kangaroo fillet, grilled quail

Merlot
Pastrami, warm smoked chicken

Cool-climate medium-bodied cabernet sauvignon
Rack of baby lamb

Light to medium-bodied cool-climate shiraz
Rare eye fillet of beef

Young botrytised wines
Fresh fruits, cake

Summer

Chilled fino
Cold consommé

Semillon (2–3 years)
Gazpacho

Riesling (2–3 years)
Seared tuna

Young barrel-fermented semillon sauvignon blanc
Seafood or vegetable tempura

Young off-dry riesling
Prosciutto & melon/pear

Cool-climate chardonnay
Abalone, lobster, Chinese-style prawns

Semillon or riesling (10 years)
Braised pork neck

Mature chardonnay (5+ years)
Braised rabbit

Off-dry rose
Chilled fresh fruit

Young light-bodied pinot noir
Grilled salmon

Aged pinot noir (5+ years)
Coq au vin, wild duck

Young grenache/sangiovese
Osso bucco

Hunter Valley shiraz (5–10 years)
Beef spare ribs

Sangiovese
Saltimbocca, roast poussin

Medium-bodied cabernet sauvignon (5 years)
Barbecued butterfly leg of lamb

Mature chardonnay
Smoked eel, smoked roe

All wines
Parmigiana

Autumn

Amontillado
Warm consommé

Barrel-fermented mature whites
Smoked roe, bouillabaisse

Complex mature chardonnay
Sweetbreads, brains

Aged marsanne or semillon (10 years)
Seafood risotto, Lebanese

Grenache
Grilled calf's liver, roast kid, lamb or pig's kidneys

Mature Margaret River cabernet merlot
Lamb fillet, roast leg of lamb with garlic and herbs

Cool-climate merlot
Lamb loin chops

Fully aged riesling
Chargrilled eggplant, stuffed capsicum

Mature grenache/Rhône blends
Moroccan lamb

Rich, full-bodied Heathcote shiraz
Beef casserole

Southern Victorian pinot noir
Peking duck

Young muscat
Plum pudding

Winter

Dry oloroso sherry
Full-flavoured hors d'oeuvres

Sparkling Burgundy
Borscht, wild mushroom risotto

Viognier
Pea and ham soup

Aged semillon (10+ years)
Vichyssoise (hot)

Sauvignon blanc
Coquilles St Jacques (pan-fried scallops)

Chardonnay (10+ years)
Cassoulet

Semillon sauvignon blanc (2–4 years)
Seafood pasta

Tasmanian pinot noir
Squab, duck breast

Mature pinot noir
Mushroom ragout, ravioli

Mature cool-grown shiraz viognier
Pot-au-feu

Grampians shiraz (10 years)
Chargrilled rump steak

Full-bodied Barossa shiraz (15–20 years)
Venison, kangaroo fillet

Coonawarra cabernet sauvignon
Braised lamb shanks/shoulder

Muscat (rare)
Chocolate-based desserts

Topaque (rare)
Creme brûlée

Vintage fortified shiraz
Dried fruits, salty cheese

Australian vintage charts

Each number represents a mark out of 10 for the quality of vintages in each region.

 Red wine   White wine   Fortified

NSW

Hunter Valley
2016	2017	2018	2019
6	8	9	8
7	9	8	9

Mudgee
2016	2017	2018	2019
8	7	9	7
9	6	8	7

Orange
2016	2017	2018	2019
8	7	9	8
7	8	8	9

Canberra District
2016	2017	2018	2019
9	9	9	9
9	8	8	9

Hilltops
2016	2017	2018	2019
9	9	9	9
8	7	8	8

Southern Highlands
2016	2017	2018	2019
8	6	8	7
8	6	8	8

Tumbarumba
2016	2017	2018	2019
8	9	9	8
9	8	9	8

Riverina/Griffith
2016	2017	2018	2019
7	8	8	8
7	8	8	8

Shoalhaven
2016	2017	2018	2019
8	7	8	7
8	8	8	8

SA

Barossa Valley
2016	2017	2018	2019
8	7	9	9
7	8	7	7

Eden Valley
2016	2017	2018	2019
8	7	9	9
9	10	9	9

Clare Valley
2016	2017	2018	2019
8	8	7	8
9	9	7	9

Adelaide Hills
2016	2017	2018	2019
8	8	8	9
7	9	7	8

McLaren Vale
2016	2017	2018	2019
8	9	8	8
7	8	7	7

Southern Fleurieu
2016	2017	2018	2019
8	9	10	8
8	8	8	7

Langhorne Creek
2016	2017	2018	2019
9	8	9	9
7	7	7	7

Kangaroo Island
2016	2017	2018	2019
9	8	9	8
9	9	9	9

Adelaide Plains
2016	2017	2018	2019
9	8	–	–
8	8	–	–

Coonawarra
2016	2017	2018	2019
9	7	9	10
8	9	8	8

Wrattonbully
2016	2017	2018	2019
10	9	9	10
10	9	9	10

Padthaway
2016	2017	2018	2019
–	8	–	10
–	8	–	9

Mount Benson & Robe
2016	2017	2018	2019
8	7	9	8
9	9	9	9

Riverland
2016	2017	2018	2019
8	7	8	8
7	8	8	8

VIC

Yarra Valley
2016	2017	2018	2019
7	8	7	9
7	8	7	8

Mornington Peninsula
2016	2017	2018	2019
8	8	9	8
7	9	8	9

Geelong
2016	2017	2018	2019
7	8	8	10
8	7	7	8

Macedon Ranges
2016	2017	2018	2019
8	7	9	8
9	8	7	7

Sunbury
2016	2017	2018	2019
7	–	–	7
7	–	–	8

Gippsland
2016	2017	2018	2019
8	9	9	9
8	9	9	9

	2016	2017	2018	2019
Bendigo	8	8	8	9
	8	7	8	8
Heathcote	9	7	8	9
	8	7	7	6
Grampians	6	9	8	9
	7	8	8	9
Pyrenees	7	8	10	8
	8	8	8	8
Henty	10	5	10	9
	10	8	10	8
Beechworth	8	7	8	8
	8	7	8	9
Nagambie Lakes	8	8	9	9
	9	7	7	7
Upper Goulburn	8	7	9	8
	9	9	8	9
Strathbogie Ranges	7	7	9	8
	7	7	9	8
King Valley	7	8	9	9
	8	10	9	7
Alpine Valleys	6	9	9	7
	6	10	10	9

	2016	2017	2018	2019
Glenrowan	8	7	8	9
	9	7	7	7
Rutherglen	7	6	9	8
	9	6	9	8
Murray Darling	7	7	7	8
	8	8	8	8

WA

	2016	2017	2018	2019
Margaret River	9	8	9	8
	9	8	9	9
Great Southern	8	7	10	8
	9	9	9	8
Manjimup	6	7	8	7
	7	8	9	8
Pemberton	8	7	9	10
	9	9	9	9
Geographe	8	8	8	8
	8	8	8	8
Perth Hills	9	9	8	8
	8	9	9	7
Swan Valley	6	6	9	8
	7	7	8	10

QLD

	2016	2017	2018	2019
Granite Belt	8	6	10	8
	7	9	9	8
South Burnett	–	8	9	9
	–	8	9	8

TAS

	2016	2017	2018	2019
Northern Tasmania	8	8	8	9
	8	7	8	9
Southern Tasmania	8	9	8	9
	8	9	9	8

Australian vintage 2020: a snapshot

This was a year which most vignerons would prefer to forget. Only Western Australia had a relatively successful 12 months, with Pemberton, Manjimup and Geographe as unlikely champions. Margaret River and Great Southern were protected from birds (thanks to massive flowering of Marri trees); the quality there was high but yields very low. Moving east, New South Wales produced precious little grapes, every one of its regions with no meaningful crop. Smoke taint coupled with drought in the first half of the year, then came rain in the second half. The Hunter Valley, Canberra District and Mudgee made no red wines full stop. South Australia's 13 regions all had small crops, with smoke taint and fires the coup de grace on Kangaroo Island. Victoria's 19 regions all had a vintage in two halves: wind and heat up to December, which decimated flowering and fruit-set, then a mild and calm second half that arrived too late. As in many parts of eastern Australia, some very good wines will emerge, but yields are generally deplorable. Queensland's Granite Belt was crucified by unrelenting drought; at the country's other extreme, Tasmania's north, east and south also had to deal with dry conditions (irrigating before bud burst) and miserable yields.

New South Wales

The **Hunter Valley** was one of the all-too-many regions that suffered blow after blow. First up was lack of winter/spring rain, followed by full-scale drought (October to December received a total of 15mm) coupled with extreme heat. The last three days of December were over 41°C; January dealt out 12 days over 35°C; patch rain achieving nothing. The final blow was smoke taint, which resulted in the total destruction of the shiraz (and other red grapes). A token rose here and there was par for the course. **Mudgee** might have fared better, but in the end smoke taint destroyed the red varietal harvest. The higher elevation of **Orange** could have mitigated the drought (a 20% drop), but again smoke destroyed the red wines-to-be, with small amounts of riesling and sauvignon blanc (if whole-bunch pressed) a token result. The **Canberra District** was headlined with brutal courage by Tim Kirk of Clonakilla announcing on 18 February that the winery would not make any wine from any vineyard in New South Wales this year. Other Canberra District wineries told the same mournful story. The silver lining was the high quality wine from 2018 and 2019 that Clonakilla and many others will be selling over the next 18 months. **Hilltops** had full-on drought through the growing season until some rain at the end of March – too late to achieve much. Drought plus very low yields of doubtful quality meant most wineries didn't pick any red grapes. The **Southern Highlands** was a write-off thanks to smoke, as was the case in **Tumbarumba**. **Shoalhaven Coast** lurched between extremely dry conditions from October to January (accompanied by high December temperatures), and then the wettest February on record, before smoke taint hammered the last nail in the coffin. In the **Riverina**, drought, fire, rain and COVID-19 combined at various stages of the growing season. December was hotter than normal, but the rest of the season was cool, harvest 7–10 days later than 2019. Rain required quick action. Chardonnay, sauvignon blanc and (what else than) shiraz performed best.

SOUTH AUSTRALIA

Barossa Valley's growing season rainfall was even lower than 2018, down 50% on average. Temperatures were cooler and drier than long-term average, and yields down 60–70%. Riesling and very aromatic grenache are the standouts. The **Clare Valley** was in drought, and this, coupled with poor set, resulted in the lowest yields in the last 40 years. Riesling is the one success – the tiny bunches of red wines with high tannins seem inescapable. **Eden Valley** in drought conditions had very low yields, but warm conditions (a strange contrast to the Barossa and Clare Valleys) resulted in excellent quality across the board. **McLaren Vale** experienced spots of bizarre frost here and there, fruit-set drawn out except for a short but vicious heat spike. Consequentially, shiraz and cabernet yields were at an abysmal all-time low, yet grenache and petit verdot were close to normal, and overall quality was high, grenache a star. The **Adelaide Hills** felt like a Punch and Judy show, with disastrous bushfires in parts, smoke damage in others, and yet no impact elsewhere. Overall, yields were way below long-term average. Quality for the wines that made it to bottle will be exceptional, with a bedrock of high natural acidity and pristine varietal flavours. **Coonawarra** started the growing season three weeks later than long-term average, but frosts came nonetheless, and cool, humid weather during flowering ultimately led to poor fruit-set. Yields were very low, similar to 2002, with small, thick-skinned berries, the red wines with vibrant colours and fine tannins. **Langhorne Creek**'s rainfall was very low through winter and spring until two days over 38°C in late November caused major damage to flowering. A calm, cool summer followed, but the damage was done: yields miserable, picking costs sky-high. Ironically, the quality is excellent, cabernet sauvignon leading the way. **Wrattonbully** had an unusually dry growing season, the weather cooler than normal, disrupting flowering, but leaving the fruit with perfect acidity and balanced varietal fruit flavours. **Padthaway** had a very good time of it, the only quibble being lower yields than those of the previous year. The cool weather up to flowering continued through to harvest, with no rain events to upset ripening or picking. Shiraz, cabernet sauvignon, sauvignon blanc and chardonnay stood out with good natural acidity, and exceptional colour and balanced flavours in the red wines. **Kangaroo Island** attracted nationwide evening news with the fierce bushfires that devastated 45% of the island's surface. These fires destroyed the largest and most important winemaker's vineyard, house, shearing shed, irrigation pumps, water tanks, bird nets and all equipment except the tractor. The Islander Estate winery itself was saved, and with it all the wine from the 2019 vintage and before. **Mount Benson** and **Robe**, two adjacent regions in the Limestone Coast Zone, suffered less than most, with no smoke taint a huge relief. But red grape varieties were 60% down, white varieties 30% down. The **Riverland** will be remembered for the wonderful depth and brightness of the colour. Shiraz and merlot joined hands with sweet spicy flavours and mouth-watering tannins. Chardonnay, sauvignon blanc and pinot gris continued the good things in small parcels, but shiraz will be the best variety, though yields are significantly down.

Victoria

The **Yarra Valley** rejoiced with good August/September rainfall before wild variations in maximum temperatures — a very mild season following a very hot November — meaning slow ripening after a late bud burst. That said, nails were chewed to the quick by weeks of smoke from the Hunter Valley, replaced by smoke from Gippsland. Incredibly, smoke taint tests came back zero, leading to retest after retest: zero. Old smoke, you see. Yields were pathetically low, with tiny bunches, fruit quality high to very high. The **Mornington Peninsula** had above-average rainfall, and an exceptionally windy spring decimated flowering and led to tiny bunch weights and yields. Pinot noir will be the standout. **Geelong** experienced one problem after another. Good winter rain resulted in even bud burst that was smashed by a frost in late September, effectively starting the growing season again, only to be followed by cold, windy conditions that reduced the potential crop by 50% (chardonnay most affected). Hot weather either side of Christmas came next, then bursts of unwelcome rain and smoke that seemed to be the last straw, until the old smoke/new smoke conundrum was understood. **Gippsland** was happier than many, yields down but not dramatically, courtesy of cool wet weather during flowering, the cool summer/autumn spreading harvest dates and reducing intake pressure. The **Grampians** enjoyed dam-filling winter/spring rainfall, then moderate swings between very cool and warm from February through March. Yields were low except for chardonnay and pinot noir. Overall quality was high with good natural acidity and vibrant fruit intensity. Smoke taint destroyed the **Alpine Valleys** vintage. **King Valley** experienced early smoke (pre-veraison) that had no impact. The season had ups and downs, resulting in smaller and lighter bunches decreasing yield, but ultimately gave rise to very good fruit quality, prosecco the star. No wine was made in many **Beechworth** wineries due to fire damage and smoke taint, the cruelest cut being the ideal weather that might have produced a great vintage. **Upper Goulburn** followed the pattern of very low yields for all varieties due to poor weather during flowering and summer heat spikes, thereafter with perfect weather through February and March, the quality described as extraordinarily good. **Henty** suffered three separate episodes of black frost, then windy conditions through flowering and on through the growing season. Yields were low except for semillon, an absolute star (in a region where riesling is normally the winner). Smoke was never an issue. **Ballarat** was smashed by frost in late September, by cold and windy conditions during flowering, by hot weather either side of December, and by rain during the tiny harvest. **Macedon Ranges** avoided smoke but not adverse cold weather during flowering. Yields were very low across all varieties, but the cooler growing season has resulted in very good chardonnay and pinot noir. **Nagambie Lakes** had the alternating hot and cool days that affected many parts of Central Victoria. No bushfires or smoke to contend with, but the windy November/December badly affected flowering and fruit-set. Much reduced intake will be offset by the quality of crisp riesling and marsanne and deeply coloured and flavoured shiraz and cabernet sauvignon. **Strathbogie Ranges** had one of the driest years on record, yet apart from a few days of heat, it was a very mild growing season, the most notable feature the extremely low yields — and a few days of rain in mid-harvest. **Bendigo** was a tale of two halves. Dry, windy and cold conditions before Christmas led to poor fruit-set and ultimately reduced yield to 50% of normal. The second half was mild, and rain fell when needed. Both red and white varieties fared well, the quality good. In **Heathcote** the continuing drought allied with a number of days over 35°C. The result was exceptionally low yields, culminating in dark, concentrated shiraz needing attention to detail. The **Pyrenees** had a similar story – good winter rain, then not a drop more. The heat of early summer was followed by very cool, dry conditions, the ensuing yields very low, the quality of cabernet sauvignon excellent. **Glenrowan** and **Rutherglen** both reported yields down 30% on normal due to drought and heat impact, smoke still a question mark, and durif the best performer. **Murray Darling** had almost no rain up to vintage, but hot and dusty conditions in November and December impacted on flowering, leading to low yields of very good quality thanks to ideal conditions from January to March.

Western Australia

Margaret River had low rainfall and warmer than average temperatures in spring, continuing into summer. Isolated rain and hail patches exacerbated an overall pattern of small bunches coupled with low berry weight. The standout was cabernet sauvignon, with physiologically ripe tannins and balanced acidity, although chardonnay was described by one prominent grower as having 'incredible purity and clarity'. A massive Marri flowering reduced bird pressure to zero, and the low rainfall meant minimal mildew issues. An early vintage variously described as very good to excellent quality. The **Great Southern** had the driest winter and spring for over 100 years, and the dry conditions carried on in summer until rain events in late January/early February proved to be a godsend, refreshing the vines and not impeding harvest. Yields were 50–60% down, and the mild weather resulted in rapid ripening. This required rapid response in picking, but with appropriate management high quality grapes were harvested. **Manjimup** had good winter rain, but as spring arrived the rain stopped and temperatures rose, reaching low- to mid-30s, and rapid ripening resulted in the earliest harvest on record. Yet riesling, chardonnay, pinot noir and shiraz stood out in a harvest of very good quality. **Pemberton** had adequate winter/spring rainfall to fill the dams, along with comparatively mild growing conditions through the entire season with no disease or bird pressure. Low yields were of excellent quality, riesling and pinot noir the standouts. **Geographe** had the hottest December days ever, accompanied by the driest December since 2008, conditions that continued through summer. The yields were low, but no bushfires or birds meant the grapes were in perfect condition across all varieties, with purity of varietal fruit, bright and fresh flavours and deep colours. **Swan Valley** had average spring rainfall and above-average temperatures, which resulted in rapid growth and the earliest vintage experienced by many growers. Heatwaves in December preceded veraison and had little or no impact. Yields were down 20% in a vintage of excellent quality, particularly chenin blanc and semillon. **Perth Hills** had low to moderate spring rain, then extremely dry weather through summer, and autumn was bone-dry. Shiraz was the star of a vintage of likewise excellent quality.

Tasmania

East Coast Tasmania went into the growing season in the grip of drought, after the third year in a row of dry winter. On 8 September, 72mm of rain filled depleted water storages and breathed life into vines as bud burst followed. The coolest vintage since 2006 allied with wind during flowering saw yields down 30–40%. The silver lining came in the form of small berry and bunch sizes, resulting in pinot noir with remarkable intensity of colour and flavour. Chardonnay, riesling and sauvignon blanc are all very good. Growers in **Southern Tasmania** went into the season with no rain since the previous year's dry finish, many irrigating before bud burst. Spring brought no relief: dry, windy conditions impacted on fruit-set and slowed growth for a very late yet low yielding year. The quality of chardonnay for sparkling wines and pinot noir for table wines both look to be outstanding. **Northern Tasmania** had good late winter rainfall, but the cool and windy conditions resulted in a lot of hen and chicken in the bunches, and yield was down 30% in a late harvest. Quality will be well above average.

Queensland

Granite Belt didn't have to deal with bushfires or smoke, despite the extreme drought continuing through the growing season. If you didn't have a bore, buying water via tankers was the only way to provide enough moisture for the vegetative growth necessary to ripen the crop of tiny berries. Fiano and tempranillo did best, as did one winery's merlot. **South Burnett** had some early spring rainfall, but was then dry and warm until well after harvest; like the Granite Belt, bore water was vital for a crop. A low yield, the standouts being viognier, verdelho and tempranillo.

The tasting team

James Halliday

Head of tasting (see page 1).

Campbell Mattinson

Campbell is an award-winning journalist, author, editor and publisher.
He has been a key reviewer for the *Wine Companion* for many years, is the
publisher of the WINEFRONT website and the author of *The Big Red
Wine Book* and *The Wine Hunter*.

Jane Faulkner

Jane is a respected journalist with more than 25 years' experience. She
has a special interest in Italian and alternative varieties, chairs several
wine shows and is chief of judges for the Australian Alternative Varieties
Wine Show. Aside from her love of wine, Jane is an avid traveller and
zealous environmentalist.

Jeni Port

Jeni is a wine writer and judge. She was the longest-serving wine writer
on *The Age* newspaper (30 years), is deputy chair of the Wine List of the
Year Awards for both Australia and China, and was a founding board
member of the Australian Women In Wine Awards. Her numerous awards
include the 2018 Wine Communicators of Australia Legend of the Vine.

Ned Goodwin MW

Ned has worn many hats, including show judge, dux of the Len Evans
Tutorial, sommelier, educator, TV host, wine buyer, consultant, critic and
writer. Born in London, raised in Australia, educated in France and Japan,
and with continued business across Asia, his varied international experience
brings a fresh perspective to the *Wine Companion* tasting team.

Steven Creber

Steven started out as a winemaker in the Yarra Valley in the 1970s. Over
the next decade he worked in north-east Victoria, the Barossa Valley and
Coonawarra. He retired from a 20-odd year career with Dan Murphy's as
a taster, buyer and writer in 2012. He's since returned to the Yarra Valley,
consulting to and writing for a number of wine businesses.

Acknowledgements

Each year the outgoing *Wine Companion* takes with it 90% of the content it contains. Every tasting note migrates permanently to the website. Every winery is sent a reminder to check their contact information, winemaker, vineyard plantings, production and summary material. The content for the new edition is proofread twice over the course of the year, the all-important tasting notes receiving special attention. The assembled content is checked again as the book begins to take shape, ensuring that the introduction and winery entries and index fill exactly 776 pages, not a page more nor a page less since 2013. And so, to those whose loyalty makes the book as it is.

Paula Grey has been minder-in-chief since 1991, her accumulated experience and wisdom central to the completion of each year's edition. She is the voice of the *Wine Companion*, dealing with emails and phone calls, placating those with problems who initially believe they needed to speak to me, finishing the conversation when that need has evaporated. She knows more about the assembly of this book than anyone else, either here in my office or at Hardie Grant. And it is she who interprets my handwritten tasting notes.

Beth Anthony spends months upon months receiving and unpacking boxes of wine, checking each box to determine whether the list included accords with the contents. Next she checks our database to ascertain whether the wine has already been tasted; if not, she enters it, and tags every bottle as it is allocated to a tasting group along with another 50 or so bottles. She prints tasting sheets with the name of the wine, its vintage, alcohol and RRP. If the winery has provided background vinification notes, they will be appended to the tasting sheet. A day's tasting is progressively placed on the table, grouped by variety, and Beth then opens each bottle and pours each tasting sample in its glass (Riedel Ouverture Magnum). Beth has been doing this for 20 years. She has a sixth sense of any irregularity and a remarkable memory of prior vintages. Although Beth continued working throughout her cancer battle, during (and since) Beth's illness, her indefatigable sister Jake Keymer came on board as a casual worker, having previously stewarded for me on weekends when I was tasting 6–7 days a week.

Then there are the members of the tasting team – Campbell Mattinson, Jane Faulkner, Jeni Port, Ned Goodwin and Steven Creber – who share the load during the long months, working their way through half of the almost 9000 wines assessed this year. My thanks for your dedication to a job that may seem like fun, and can be anything but.

At Hardie Grant, my thanks to Jacinta Hardie Grant, general manager of HGX, who has taken on much of the Halliday responsibility from father-in-law Sandy Grant; to Roxy Ryan, managing director of Hardie Grant Books; publishing director Jane Willson; and project editor Emily Hart. Then, most importantly, to editor Alison Proietto, who had to deal with the arcane language of grapegrowing and winemaking, as well as the cross-referencing of never-ending facts and figures within each winery's entry. And to Megan Ellis, whose magic wand in typesetting these pages in the blink of an eye continues to amaze me.

Finally, I thank the wineries who sent their wines. Without them, there'd be no *Wine Companion*.

Australian wineries and wines

A. Rodda Wines

★★★★★

PO Box 589, Beechworth, Vic 3747 **Region** Beechworth
T 0400 350 135 **www**.aroddawines.com.au **Open** Not
Winemaker Adrian Rodda **Est.** 2010 **Dozens** 800 **Vyds** 2ha
Adrian Rodda has been winemaking since 1998. Originally working with David Bicknell at
Oakridge, he was involved in the development of the superb Oakridge 864 Chardonnay, his
final contribution to 864 coming in 2009. At the start of '10 he and wife Christie, a doctor,
moved to Beechworth and co-lease Smiths Vineyard with Mark Walpole of Fighting Gully
Road. Smiths Vineyard, planted to chardonnay in 1978, is a veritable jewel.

ŸŸŸŸŸ Willow Lake Vineyard Yarra Valley Chardonnay 2019 A fine, almost slender
chardonnay with wood smoke and custard powder characters drifting through
white peach and nectarine. There's a vanilla note on the finish and a touch of
oatmeal. But the truth is that this presents as a unified front, every step watched
and considered. Screwcap. 13% alc. **Rating** 95 **To** 2032 CM
Beechworth Cuvee de Chez 2018 Cabernet sauvignon 58%, merlot 18%,
petit verdot 9%, cabernet franc 8%, malbec 7%. Beautifully fruited, fragrant and
structured. It's medium in weight with currant and plum flavours aplenty, violet-
like highlights and a combination of anise and redcurrant through the finish. Most
impressive. Screwcap. 14% alc. **Rating** 95 **To** 2030 CM
Smiths Vineyard Beechworth Chardonnay 2019 A fine wine with white
flower, almond, nashi pear and white peach flavours shooting elegantly through
the palate. It's playing its cards pretty close to its chest at this early stage but it has
line and length in spades. Screwcap. 13% alc. **Rating** 94 **To** 2029 CM
Baxendale Vineyard Whitlands Chardonnay 2019 Taut and textural but
there's plenty of energy here and it has the flavour to match. Apple, nectarine and
peach flavours with flashes of cedar, custard and wood smoke. It's a wine with
pure, long lines. Screwcap. 13.5% alc. **Rating** 94 **To** 2029 CM
Aquila Audax Vineyard Beechworth Tempranillo 2018 Coffee grounds,
chicory, peppercorns, cola and ripe black cherry. It's attractively fruited but, unlike
many a tempranillo, it's not too fruit-sweet and manages to play many savoury
cards. There's a positive firmness and dryness to the finish; it feels polished,
structured and complete. Screwcap. 14% alc. **Rating** 94 **To** 2029 CM

Abbey Creek Vineyard

★★★★★

2388 Porongurup Road, Porongurup, WA 6324 **Region** Porongurup
T (08) 9853 1044 **www**.abbeycreek.com.au **Open** By appt
Winemaker Castle Rock Estate (Robert Diletti) **Est.** 1990 **Dozens** 1000 **Vyds** 1.6ha
This is the family business of Mike and Mary Dilworth. The name comes from a winter creek
that runs alongside the vineyard and a view of The Abbey in the Stirling Range. The vineyard
is split between pinot noir, riesling and sauvignon blanc. The rieslings have had significant
show success for a number of years.

ŸŸŸŸŸ Porongurup Riesling 2018 A great example of riesling from Porongurup, a
Great Southern subregion that produces riesling of exquisite focus and balance
effortlessly. Citrus blossom leads with ultimate precision to the mouth-watering
flavours of the palate, the balance achieved between acidity and fruit is perfect, the
length prodigious. Screwcap. 12% alc. **Rating** 97 **To** 2032 $25 ✪

ŸŸŸŸŸ Museum Release Porongurup Riesling 2011 **Rating** 93 **To** 2025 $40 JF
Porongurup Pinot Noir 2018 **Rating** 90 **To** 2027 $30 JF

 Abbey Vale

★★★★☆

1071 Wildwood Road, Yallingup Hills, WA 6282 **Region** Margaret River
T (08) 9755 2121 **www**.abbeyvalewines.com.au **Open** Wed–Sun 10–5
Winemaker Ben Roodhouse, Julian Langworthy **Est.** 2016 **Dozens** 2000 **Vyds** 17ha

Situated in the north of the Margaret River region, the Abbey Vale vineyards were established in 1985 by the McKay family. The highest quality fruit comes from the original plantings of chardonnay, shiraz and cabernet sauvignon. The picturesque cellar door offers a range of local produce and artisan cheeses to accompany the wines, and overlooks a large dam that provides visitors with one of the most sublime views in the region.

ΨΨΨΨ Premium RSV Margaret River Rose 2019 Merlot and shiraz, fermented separately at moderate temperatures to promote complexity and nuance while retaining what is a truly beautiful pale magenta colour. The palate is equally compelling, rose petals and pomegranate. Screwcap. 13% alc. **Rating** 96 To 2022 $25 ✪

Premium RSV Margaret River Shiraz 2018 Estate-grown, 15 months in new and used oak, then a barrel selection. Ticks all the boxes. Blackberry fruit and almost silky tannins to the fore in this skilfully made, medium to full-bodied Margaret River shiraz. Screwcap. 14.5% alc. **Rating** 94 To 2038 $25 ✪

After Hours Wine   ★★★★

455 North Jindong Road, Carbunup, WA 6285 **Region** Margaret River
T 0438 737 587 **www**.afterhourswine.com.au **Open** Fri–Mon 10–4 or by appt
Winemaker Phil Potter **Est.** 2006 **Dozens** 3000 **Vyds** 8.6ha
In 2005 Warwick and Cherylyn Mathews acquired the long-established Hopelands Vineyard, planted to cabernet sauvignon (2.6ha), shiraz (1.6ha), merlot, semillon, sauvignon blanc and chardonnay (1.1ha each). The first wine was made in '06, after which they decided to completely rework the vineyard. The vines were retrained, with a consequent reduction in yield and rise in wine quality and value. Exports to China.

ΨΨΨΨΨ Oliver Margaret River Shiraz 2018 A medium to full-bodied shiraz with black fruits and tannins competing for space, but no resolution one way or another. Screwcap. 14.5% alc. **Rating** 90 To 2032 $30

ΨΨΨΨ P.J. Margaret River Cabernet Sauvignon 2017 Rating 89 To 2025 $30

 # Alcorso Wines   ★★★★

38B Sunderland Street, Moonah, Tas 7009 **Region** Tasmania
T 0428 379 877 **www**.alcorsowines.com **Open** Not
Winemaker Julian Alcorso **Est.** 2011 **Dozens** 600
In 2011 Julian Alcorso embarked on a five-year project to make pinot noir and riesling that would be marketed by Tasmanian owned and based Fine Drop Wines, owned by Ryan O'Malley. The current vintage (as at April 2020) is '12, but with '13, '14 and '15 made and bottled, will be released sequentially over the next three years. This allowed Julian to retire from active winemaking and simply keep in quarterly touch with Ryan. The closure of the tourist industry because of Covid-19 has made economic life exceedingly difficult, but once it is reopened, this route to market will resume, slowly but surely.

ΨΨΨΨΨ Riesling 2012 Bright quartz–green; astonishingly youthful, so much so you wonder whether it will behave like Peter Pan, never fully developing. After much thought, I've decided this is irrelevant as you taste the wine for the first time. Screwcap. 12.4% alc. **Rating** 95 To 2022 $55

ΨΨΨΨΨ Pinot Noir 2012 Rating 90 To 2027 $110

 # Alex Russell Wines   ★★★★★

1866 Pipers River Road, Lower Turners Marsh, Tas 7267 **Region** Northern Tasmania
T 0400 684 614 **www**.alexrussellwines.com.au **Open** Not
Winemaker Alex Russell **Est.** 2014 **Dozens** 1200 **Vyds** 14ha
Alex Russell's story brings back memories of Steve and Monique Lubiana's 1990 move from the family winery in the Riverland to Tasmania's Derwent River to make high quality sparkling wine. Alex studied viticulture at La Trobe Bundoora. After finishing that degree he

moved to Mildura to take on a technical role. He then enrolled in wine science at Charles Sturt University, made wine at Zilzie (2008) and then at Angove Family Winemakers, where he was introduced to the Riverland Vine Improvement Committee (RVIC). He volunteered as experimental winemaker for RVIC and was exposed to everything from albarino to zinfandel, while still working for Angove. After establishing RVIC's Cirami Estate brand he moved on in '14 to establish his own winery in a leased shed in Renmark, making 17 different varietal wines. That business continues notwithstanding his move to Tasmania, simply because the Riverland vintage is largely finished before that of Tasmania starts. Exports to the EU.

ƥƥƥƥƥ **Cazadora Pipers River Riesling 2019** The grapes were harvested at 5°C in the early morning in late Apr, destemmed, after 4 hours tipped directed into the press, the juice cold-settled, racked and warmed for tank fermentation at 13°–14°C for 20 days. Super penetrating and intense, citrus and high tensile acidity in unrelenting warfare. Long future. Screwcap. 11% alc. **Rating** 95 **To** 2029 $35 ☺
Cazadora Pipers River Pinot Noir 2018 The machine harvester was set to allow whole and barely crushed berries through to the fermenter; 7 days on skins, fermented at low temperatures. Very good colour. Damson and blood plum aromas, then a racy array of red fruits including wild strawberry, pomegranate and red cherry. Screwcap. 13% alc. **Rating** 95 **To** 2030 $45
Son of a Bull Tasmania Riesling 2019 Machine-harvested in the early morning, crushed and destemmed to tank, 6 hours skin contact, cold-settled, racked and warmed for fermentation at 15°C. Very much more accessible now thanks to its higher alcohol. Screwcap. 12% alc. **Rating** 94 **To** 2027 $25 ☺

ƥƥƥƥƟ **Cazadora Pipers River Gewurztraminer 2019 Rating** 91 **To** 2023 $35
Son of a Bull Tasmania Pinot Noir 2019 Rating 91 **To** 2029 $28
Alejandro Riverland Tempranillo 2018 Rating 90 **To** 2023 $23

Alkoomi ★★★★★

Wingebellup Road, Frankland River, WA 6396 **Region** Frankland River
T (08) 9855 2229 **www**.alkoomiwines.com.au **Open** 7 days 10–5
Winemaker Andrew Cherry **Est.** 1971 **Dozens** 80 000 **Vyds** 164ha
Established in 1971 by Merv and Judy Lange, Alkoomi has grown from a single hectare to one of WA's largest family-owned and operated wineries. Now owned by daughter Sandy Hallett and her husband Rod, Alkoomi is continuing the tradition of producing high quality wines which showcase the Frankland River region. Alkoomi is actively reducing its environmental footprint; future plans will see the introduction of new varietals. Alkoomi operates cellar doors in Albany and at the winery. Exports to all major markets.

ƥƥƥƥƥ **Black Label Frankland River Shiraz 2018** Matured in French oak for 12 months. Savoury spice and licorice aromas build a framework for the full-bodied blackberry/black cherry fruit at the centre of the wine, tannins joining in on the finish. Great vintage, top class wine. Screwcap. 14.5% alc. **Rating** 96 **To** 2038 $28 ☺
Black Label Frankland River Shiraz 2017 Estate-grown, matured in French oak (20% new) for 12 months. The aromas and flavours are on the same page for this elegant, medium-bodied wine; red fruits and spices joining the undertow of black fruits. Screwcap. 14.5% alc. **Rating** 95 **To** 2032 $28 ☺
Black Label Frankland River Cabernet Sauvignon 2018 From 9 small blocks ex estate vineyards, picked over 2 weeks, matured for 14 months in French oak (20% new). A full-bodied, statuesque cabernet at the dawn of what will be a very long life. Cassis, tapenade and dark chocolate all contribute. Screwcap. 14% alc. **Rating** 95 **To** 2038 $30 ☺
Blackbutt 2014 The more flamboyant of the 3 vintages I was lucky enough to taste side by side. This is a meld of cabernet (67.4%), malbec (16.8%), the rest franc. Rounder, denser, richer and altogether riper. And yet despite the higher alcohol, the fruit tones on this are arguably the more savoury; the tannins polished and managed impeccably. The overall impression, the most Bordeaux-like: leaf, bouquet

garni, cassis and clove, swathed in a sage-soused tannic fold, accentuated by classy oak. Long and enveloping. Screwcap. Rating 95 To 2035 $62 NG

Black Label Frankland River Riesling 2019 Estate-grown. Minerally acidity provides the backbone and overall structure for a wine that will flourish in bottle over the next 5–10 years. Screwcap. 12.5% alc. Rating 94 To 2029 $30 ✪

Blackbutt 2013 Cabernet (58.8%), malbec (29.9%), along with dollops of cabernet franc and merlot respectively. This is delicious, with the malbec providing the filling in cabernet's doughnut. Rounder and more finely tuned than the '12. Cooler, too. Suave. Cassis a waft of leaf, graphite and pencil shavings. This is a sophisticated and highly savoury red, exuding class and great promise, with tannins ever so slightly drying. Screwcap. Rating 94 To 2030 $62 NG

ΨΨΨΨΨ **White Label Shiraz 2018** Rating 93 To 2030 $18 ✪
Blackbutt 2012 Rating 93 To 2027 $62 NG
Black Label Sauvignon Blanc 2019 Rating 92 To 2022 $28
Black Label Sauvignon Blanc 2018 Rating 92 To 2022 $28
White Label Cabernet Merlot 2018 Rating 92 To 2030 $18 ✪
White Label Riesling 2019 Rating 91 To 2025 $18 ✪
White Label Chardonnay 2019 Rating 91 To 2025 $18 NG ✪
Jarrah Shiraz 2013 Rating 90 To 2024 $45 NG
White Label Cabernet Merlot 2017 Rating 90 To 2025 $18 ✪

All Saints Estate ★★★★★

All Saints Road, Wahgunyah, Vic 3687 **Region** Rutherglen
T 1800 021 621 **www**.allsaintswine.com.au **Open** Sun–Fri 10–5, Sat 10–5.30
Winemaker Nick Brown, Chloe Earl **Est.** 1864 **Dozens** 25 000 **Vyds** 47.9ha
The winery rating reflects the fortified wines, including the unique releases of Museum Muscat and Muscadelle, each with an average age of more than 100 years (and table wines). The one-hat Terrace Restaurant makes this a must-stop for any visitor to North East Victoria, as does the National Trust–listed property with its towering castle centrepiece. All Saints and St Leonards are owned and managed by fourth-generation Brown family members Eliza, Angela and Nick. Eliza is an energetic and highly intelligent leader, wise beyond her years, and highly regarded by the wine industry. The Brown family celebrated the winery's 150th anniversary in 2014. Exports to the US, the Philippines, Hong Kong and China.

ΨΨΨΨΨ **Museum Rutherglen Muscadelle NV** Intensity, complexity and quality are beyond measure and words. James Halliday's note in the *Wine Companion 2020* says it all: 'Its concentration and searing intensity are such that you want to physically bite the wine. Amid the fireworks and white-light display there is a certain calm of the so-fine spirit, the sweet/sour flavours of ancient balsamic vinegar amazing.' 375ml. Vino-Lok. Rating 99 $1000 CM

Museum Rutherglen Muscat NV The full biscuit if ever there was one. The concentration of flavour here is immense to say the least, and while of course it's warm with alcohol, inherent to both the style and the concept, it's remarkable how the density of flavour essentially buries the alcohol in its big warm arms. In a word: monumental. In two: life affirming. 500ml. Rating 99 $1000 CM

Grand Rutherglen Tawny NV Stunning concentration of flavour, and both the balance and complexity to match. It's quite alarmingly good. Burnt toffee, raisin, rancio and sweet tea flavours put on a wonderful show. It goes on with it, and then some, on the finish as well. Vino-Lok. 18% alc. Rating 97 $75 CM ✪

ΨΨΨΨΨ **Rare Rutherglen Muscadelle NV** The green olive hue to this wine's pools of brown is an experience in itself. It starts and finishes with butterscotch – slippery texture – but in between there's a world of spice, dried fruits, honey and more. Mind-blowing. 375ml. Vino-Lok. 18% alc. Rating 96 $120 CM

Grand Rutherglen Muscat NV This boasts tremendous intensity; its treacle, chocolate, honey and raisin characters lifted by inherent rancio. This is luscious to say the least but most impressively it also soars on from the finish. Vino-Lok. 18% alc. Rating 96 $75 CM ✪

Classic Rutherglen Muscadelle NV Seriously good. Terrific intensity of butterscotch, green olive, burnt toffee and rancio flavours. It all follows through on the finish. Bowls you over with both its concentration of flavour and sheer quality. 375ml. Vino-Lok. 19% alc. **Rating** 95 $40 CM

Grand Rutherglen Muscadelle NV Concentration of flavour is excellent as you'd expect but the range and complexity is another level again. This is a river as wide as it is deep. Intense raisin, tobacco, prune, butterscotch and toast flavours put on a charismatic display. Semblances of dusty dried herbs enter the fray. It's quite excellent. Vino-Lok. 19% alc. **Rating** 95 $75 CM

Pierre 2017 51% cabernet sauvignon, 24% merlot, 25% cabernet franc. Matured in French oak (28% new). It has both control and oomph. It's run with flavour and it spreads through the finish. We're in excellent territory here. Currants, cloves, wood smoke, dried herbs and a sweet vanillan character. It's built for the future but it's so well balanced that you could easily drink it now. Screwcap. 14.1% alc. **Rating** 94 To 2034 $40 CM

Family Cellar Durif 2016 It's a malty, licorice red with baked plum, prune and saltbush characters pushing it straight into full-bodied territory. There's ample tannin here but fruit flavour swamps straight on through. It has very good shape in the mouth, despite its overdone/overcooked nature, and certainly packs plenty into the glass. Screwcap. 14.5% alc. **Rating** 94 To 2039 $75 CM

ŸŸŸŸ♀ **Family Cellar Shiraz 2016** Rating 93 To 2034 $75 CM
Rutherglen Muscadelle NV Rating 93 $26 CM ✪
Classic Rutherglen Muscat NV Rating 93 $40 CM
Rosa 2019 Rating 92 To 2022 $32 CM
Shiraz 2018 Rating 92 To 2028 $32 CM
Durif 2017 Rating 91 To 2027 $32 CM
Riesling 2019 Rating 90 To 2024 $26 CM
Marsanne 2018 Rating 90 To 2023 $26 CM
Sangiovese Cabernet 2019 Rating 90 To 2025 $30 CM

Allegiance Wines   ★★★★☆

Scenic Court, Alstonville, NSW 2477 **Region** Various
T 0434 561 718 **www.**allegiancewines.com.au **Open** Not
Winemaker Contract **Est.** 2009 **Dozens** 40 000
When Tim Cox established Allegiance Wines in 2009 he had the decided advantage of having worked in the Australian wine industry across many facets for almost 30 years. He worked on both the sales and marketing side, and also on the supplier side with Southcorp. He started Cox Wine Merchants to act as distributor for Moppity Vineyards, and successfully partnered with Moppity for over 5 years. This is a virtual wine business, owning neither vineyards nor winery, and having wines made for the business or purchased as cleanskins or as bulk wine. Exports to NZ, Hong Kong and China.

ŸŸŸŸŸ **The Artisan Coonawarra Cabernet Sauvignon 2018** 30+yo vines. French oak (25% new). Strong gum leaf characters before a generous serve of blackcurrant rolls in. Tannin, flavour and flow. Fresh and more-ish but well structured. Screwcap. 14.5% alc. **Rating** 94 To 2032 $40 CM

ŸŸŸŸ♀ **Unity Margaret River Chardonnay 2019** Rating 93 To 2025 $60 CM
The Artisan Reserve McLaren Vale Shiraz 2017 Rating 92 To 2030 $60 CM
The Artisan Trident Margaret River Cabernets 2016 Rating 92 To 2030 $40 CM
Vortex Miscela Rosso 2017 Rating 92 To 2026 $30 CM
Unity Yarra Valley Chardonnay 2018 Rating 91 To 2026 $60 CM
Unity Barossa Valley Shiraz 2018 Rating 91 To 2027 $100 CM
The Artisan Barossa Valley Malbec 2018 Rating 91 To 2025 $40 CM
Fullylove Tumbarumba Chardonnay 2019 Rating 90 To 2024 $25 CM

Vortex Melange Rouge 2016 Rating 90 To 2027 $30 CM
The Artisan McLaren Vale Barbera 2017 Rating 90 To 2024 $40 CM

Allies Wines ★★★★★

4 Evans Street, Somers, Vic 3927 **Region** Mornington Peninsula
T 0412 111 587 **www**.allies.com.au **Open** By appt
Winemaker David Chapman **Est.** 2003 **Dozens** 1000 **Vyds** 3.1ha
A former chef and sommelier, David Chapman began Allies in 2003 while working at
Moorooduc Estate. He makes pinot noir, emphasising the diversity of the Mornington
Peninsula by making a number of wines sourced from different districts. David spends much
of his time in the vineyard, working to ensure well exposed and positioned bunches achieve
ripe, pure flavours and supple tannins. His winemaking focuses on simple techniques that
retain concentration and character: no added yeasts, and no fining or filtration. Production of
Allies wines is small and will probably remain that way, given that any expansion will limit the
number of vines David can personally tend. Exports to Hong Kong.

ŸŸŸŸ Assemblage Chardonnay 2019 An exceptional light to gently mid-weighted
wine boasting a steely resolve of pungent mineral at its heart. Long across the
palate. Oatmeal, stone fruits and impeccably appointed high quality oak seams find
confluence with maritime acidity, all guiding the fray. Merricks and Tuerong fruit:
the light and the dark. An assemblage of beauty and mettle. Screwcap. Rating 95
To 2027 $30 NG ○

ŸŸŸŸ Merricks Pinot Noir 2018 Rating 93 To 2025 $42 NG
Assemblage Pinot Noir 2019 Rating 91 To 2024 $30 NG

Allinda ★★★★

119 Lorimers Lane, Dixons Creek, Vic 3775 **Region** Yarra Valley
T 0432 346 540 **www**.allindawinery.com.au **Open** Not
Winemaker Al Fencaros, Jeff Bashford **Est.** 1991 **Dozens** 7000 **Vyds** 3.5ha
Winemaker Al Fencaros has a Bachelor of Wine Science (CSU) and was formerly employed
by De Bortoli in the Yarra Valley. Al's grandparents made wine in Hungary and Serbia, and
Al's father continued to make wine after migrating to Australia in the early 1960s. The
vineyard is now 29 years old, and is managed without the use of chemical fertilisers, herbicides
or pesticides. The Allinda wines are produced onsite; all except the Shiraz (from Heathcote)
are estate-grown. Limited retail distribution in Melbourne and Sydney. Exports to China.

ŸŸŸŸŸ Limited Release Yarra Valley Cabernets 2017 Fine wine with a fine future.
Blackcurrant and mulberry flavours team with spearmint, wood smoke and briary
tobacco before turning dry and tannic through the finish. There's a slip of red
licorice here, a menthol note, a little chocolate. The thing is that everything seems
well integrated; nothing is overplayed. It has good persistence, too. Screwcap.
13% alc. Rating 94 To 2032 $35 CM

ŸŸŸŸ Limited Release Yarra Valley Syrah 2018 Rating 93 To 2028 $35 CM
Heathcote Shiraz 2018 Rating 93 To 2029 $29 CM
Limited Release Yarra Valley Pinot Noir 2018 Rating 91 To 2026 $35 CM

Altamont Wine Studio

c/- 15 Spring Valley Road, Piccadilly, SA 5151 **Region** Adelaide Hills
T 0448 047 888 **www**.altamontwinestudio.com **Open** Not
Winemaker Michael Sawyer **Est.** 2012 **Dozens** 800
Michael Sawyer and Michael Morrissey are now the sole owners of Altamont. Wine was
not produced in 2015 or '16, but after a few wines were made in '17, Altamont was back
in full production from the '18 vintage. The wines are made at Tapanappa, and include
chardonnay (Lenswood), pinot gris and pinot noir (Piccadilly) and shiraz (Nairne). Exports to
Malaysia, Singapore, Japan and Hong Kong.

🍷🍷🍷🍷🍷 **Balhannah Adelaide Hills Pinot Gris 2019** Chilled before whole-bunch pressing direct to used French oak for a slow ferment on full solids. The vinification has given the wine context and complexity – well above average. Screwcap. 13% alc. **Rating** 91 **To** 2027 $24
Lenswood Adelaide Hills Chardonnay 2019 Hand-picked, chilled for 16 hours, whole-bunch pressed to used French oak, a slow 15-day ferment on full solids, matured for 6 months. Skinnier than expected, unsweetened lemon first up and last down. Screwcap. 13% alc. **Rating** 90 **To** 2024 $24

🍷🍷🍷🍷 **Shining Rock Adelaide Hills Sangiovese 2019 Rating** 89 **To** 2023 $25

Amadio Wines

461 Payneham Road, Felixstow, SA 5070 **Region** Adelaide Hills/Kangaroo Island
T (08) 8337 5144 **www**.amadiowines.com **Open** Wed–Sun 10–5.30
Winemaker Danniel Amadio **Est.** 2004 **Dozens** 50000 **Vyds** 126ha
Danniel Amadio says he has followed in the footsteps of his Italian grandfather, selling wine from his cellar (cantina) direct to the consumer. Amadio Wines has substantial vineyards, primarily in the Adelaide Hills and Barossa Valley. They also source contract-grown grapes from Clare Valley, McLaren Vale and Langhorne Creek, with a strong suite of Italian varieties. The Kangaroo Island Trading Company wines are produced with fifth-generation islanders Michael and Rosie Florance from their Cygnet River vineyard; there is a second cellar door in the main street of Kingscote. Exports to the UK, the US, Canada, Denmark, Russia, India, Indonesia, South Korea, Singapore, Hong Kong and China.

🍷🍷🍷🍷🍷 **Kangaroo Island Trading Company Shiraz 2016** Estate-grown, matured for 17 months in a mix of American and French oak. Has retained exceptional depth and hue, the wild blackberry flavours of remarkable structure and intensity. Screwcap. 14.5% alc. **Rating** 95 **To** 2031 $39
Heritage Selection Adelaide Hills Sagrantino 2017 Many of the Australian sagrantinos I have tasted have been scrawny things. Olivers, Heathvale and Chalmers are notable exceptions and join this wine that offers a sweet (grape, not residual sugar) array of spicy cherry flavours, supported by soft tannins and a fresh finish. Cork. 14.5% alc. **Rating** 94 **To** 2029 $45

🍷🍷🍷🍷🍷 **Heritage Selection Adelaide Hills Montepulciano 2017 Rating** 92 **To** 2024 $45 SC

🍇 Amarco Wine Group

28 Jenke Road, Marananga, SA 5355 **Region** Barossa Valley
T 0433 256 669 **Open** By appt
Winemaker Tom White, Amarco Rohan **Est.** 2017 **Dozens** 500 **Vyds** 10ha
The following background comes direct from the Rohan family. Make of it what you will, but the quality of the wines is good. "Rohan Family series wine is proudly produced from Amarco wine group, which bases on Barossa Valley. The Rohan family worked for South Australia wine industry since 1996, naming their own brand on 2017. Rohan family, dedicates to produce wine as a dreamer, use their wine making skill to create fancy juicy taste in order to break the old tradition. Also, as a walker, catering for Australia wine lovers, Rohans insist to use ultimate fruit in Barossa Valley for achieving their dreams in a very close future." Exports to East Asia, Hong Kong and China.

🍷🍷🍷🍷🍷 **Rohan Family Dreamer Barossa Valley Cabernet Sauvignon Shiraz Merlot 2017** Hand-picked, the components vinified separately, variously matured in French or American oak. Dense crimson-purple. Plenty of core fruit, but also powder puff/chocolate aromas and flavours. Clever work in the winery. Cork. 15% alc. **Rating** 93 **To** 2037 $70
Rohan Family Walker Barossa Valley Shiraz 2017 From a single vineyard at Marananga, open-fermented, 24 months in French and American oak. Well made; its display of sweetly juicy black fruits filling the senses, not interrupted by tannins. Cork. 15% alc. **Rating** 90 **To** 2027 $70

Amelia Park Wines ★★★★★

3857 Caves Road, Wilyabrup, WA 6280 **Region** Margaret River
T (08) 9755 6747 **www.**ameliaparkwines.com.au **Open** 7 days 10–5
Winemaker Jeremy Gordon **Est.** 2009 **Dozens** 25 000 **Vyds** 9.6ha
Jeremy Gordon's winemaking career started with Evans & Tate, and Houghton thereafter, before he moved to the eastern states to broaden his experience. He returned to Margaret River, and after several years he and wife Daniela founded Amelia Park Wines with business partner Peter Walsh. Amelia Park initially relied on contract-grown grapes, but in 2013 purchased the Moss Brothers site in Wilyabrup, allowing the construction of a new winery and cellar door. Exports to the UK, the US, Canada, India, the Philippines, Singapore, Thailand and China.

🍷🍷🍷🍷 Margaret River Cabernet Merlot 2018 A bigger Bordeaux family is here, not only is this wine led by cabernet sauvignon and merlot but malbec and petit verdot also appear. They form a complex and exciting wine. It is warm and inviting with typical Margaret River terroir notes of eucalyptus, Aussie bush, bay leaf, allsorts/licorice confection, spice and ripe black fruits. Plush and seamless, it has enjoyed its 12 months in French oak and been all the better for the experience. Screwcap. 14.5% alc. **Rating** 96 **To** 2033 $33 JP ❂
Reserve Margaret River Chardonnay 2018 Makes a gracious Margaret River entrance with expressive rock pool, saline, white peach, melon and fresh-cut grapefruit. The reserve mantle is well earned. Crunchy acidity cuts a swathe through luscious fruit in this wine. It's almost lean by Margaret River standards, giving it plenty of room to grow. Screwcap. 13.5% alc. **Rating** 95 **To** 2031 $65 JP

🍷🍷🍷🍷 Frankland River Shiraz 2018 **Rating** 93 **To** 2032 $33 JP
Reserve Margaret River Cabernet Sauvignon 2017 **Rating** 93 **To** 2030 $65 JP
Margaret River Chardonnay 2019 **Rating** 92 **To** 2028 $33 JP
Margaret River Malbec 2018 **Rating** 91 **To** 2026 JP

Amherst Winery ★★★★

285 Talbot-Avoca Road, Amherst, Vic 3371 **Region** Pyrenees
T 0400 380 382 **www.**amherstwinery.com **Open** W'ends & public hols 11–5
Winemaker Luke Jones, Andrew Koerner (Consultant) **Est.** 1989 **Dozens** 1500 **Vyds** 5ha
In 1989 Norman and Elizabeth Jones planted vines on a property with an extraordinarily rich history, commemorated by the name Dunn's Paddock. Samuel Knowles was a convict who arrived in Van Diemen's Land in 1838. He endured continuous punishment until he fled to SA in 1846. He changed his name to Dunn and in 1851 married 18-year-old Mary Taaffe. They walked to Amherst, pushing a wheelbarrow carrying their belongings. The original lease title is in his name. In January 2013 Norman and Elizabeth's son Luke and his wife Rachel acquired the Amherst Winery business; Luke has a wine marketing diploma and a diploma in wine technology. Exports to China.

🍷🍷🍷🍷 Walter Collings Pyrenees Shiraz 2016 The earliest vintage in regional history. This is in an altogether different league, although the culture of staves continues: 3 years in 50% new. Pulpy. Grapey. Jubilantly lilac floral, although a bit treacly across boysenberry and mulberry fruit flavours. A gentle skein of acidity tidies it up somewhat. Screwcap. **Rating** 92 **To** 2025 $50 NG
Pyrenees Pinot Noir 2018 A warm place for pinot, this manages to shake down plenty of morello cherry notes and root spice, melding them with vanillan French oak (12 months) in celebration of a forward, eminently approachable pinot, tapered by a gentle astringency. Screwcap. **Rating** 91 **To** 2024 $25 NG

🍷🍷🍷 Chinese Gardens Cabernet Sauvignon 2017 **Rating** 89 **To** 2025 $28 NG

Amour Wines

69 Bruce Road, Orange, NSW 2800 **Region** Orange
T 0423 240 720 **www**.amourwines.com.au **Open** By appt
Winemaker Matt Eades **Est.** 2014 **Dozens** 300 **Vyds** 2.4ha
Like others before him, Matt Eades embarked on a career in insurance and law, but the lure of wine was too strong to be held at bay. It all began in 1997 with his first visit to a nearby wine region. In 2009 he enrolled in the Charles Sturt oenology degree, graduating in '13. His first vintage was in the Yarra Valley in '10, making his first wines from Beechworth shiraz in '12 and '13. Together with wife Katie, he has adopted Orange as their principal home base.

🍷🍷🍷🍷🍷 **Orange Shiraz 2017** Hand-picked, open-fermented with wild yeast, 19 months in 25% new French oak. Abundant red fruit, spice and pepper on the bouquet, and more of the same on the palate; the oak certainly part of the picture but well integrated. Quite rich and ripe in flavour in the context of cool-climate shiraz, but framed by fine and lightly astringent tannins which run long on the finish. Screwcap. 13.5% alc. **Rating** 94 **To** 2027 $50 SC

🍷🍷🍷🍷🍷 **Orange Chardonnay 2018 Rating** 92 **To** 2023 $42 SC

Anderson

★★★★★

1619 Chiltern Road, Rutherglen, Vic 3685 **Region** Rutherglen
T (02) 6032 8111 **www**.andersonwinery.com.au **Open** 7 days 10–5
Winemaker Howard Anderson, Christobelle Anderson **Est.** 1992 **Dozens** 2000
Vyds 8.8ha
Having notched up a winemaking career spanning over 55 years, including a stint at Seppelt (Great Western), Howard Anderson and family started their own winery, initially with a particular focus on sparkling wine but now extending across all table wine styles. Daughter Christobelle graduated from the University of Adelaide in 2003 with first class honours, and has worked in Alsace, Champagne and Burgundy either side of joining her father full-time in '05. The original estate plantings of shiraz, durif and petit verdot (6ha) have been expanded with tempranillo, saperavi, brown muscat, chenin blanc and viognier.

🍷🍷🍷🍷🍷 **Grand Muscat NV** Really interesting. Texturally less arresting than the Classic, but deeply coloured through to olive on the rim. The mouthfeel has more room to move, as it were, with excellent rancio and acidity. Spices of every shape, size and colour; the length and aftertaste compelling. Vino-Lok. 18% alc. Rating 95 $60
Cellar Block Shiraz 2014 Hand-picked, matured for 12 months in new and 1yo French barrels, the wine released as a 5yo. The oak is still prominent, but doesn't subvert the wild blackberry and pepper varietal fruit flavours, nor the overall elegance of the wine. Screwcap. 14.5% alc. **Rating** 94 **To** 2034 $40
Storyteller Basket Press Durif 2014 Two gold medals from the Australian Small Makers Wine Show '17 and '18 for this self-described mid-range durif set the scene. It's only 14% alc., but it has drive and full-bodied shape, and is clearly durif. Screwcap. **Rating** 94 **To** 2029 $33

🍷🍷🍷🍷🍷 **Classic Muscat NV Rating** 92 $30
Verrier Basket Press Durif Shiraz 2014 Rating 91 **To** 2029 $33
Cellar Block Durif 2014 Rating 90 **To** 2029 $45

Anderson Hill

407 Croft Road, Lenswood, SA 5240 **Region** Adelaide Hills
T 0407 070 295 **www**.andersonhill.com.au **Open** Wed–Sun & public hols 11–5
Winemaker Ben Anderson, Turon White **Est.** 1994 **Dozens** 4000 **Vyds** 9ha
Ben and Clare Anderson planted their vineyard in 1994. A substantial part of the grape production is sold (Hardys and Penfolds have been top-end purchasers of the chardonnay), but enough is retained to produce their wines. The cellar door has panoramic views, making the venue popular for functions. Exports to Norway and China.

ŸŸŸŸŸ Single Vineyard Reserve Lenswood Shiraz 2018 A barrel selection. Spicy and peppery with a touch of florals, yet this is no wallflower. It has the fruit density, richness and volume to contain the oak, firm tannins and everything in-between. Cork. 14.5% alc. **Rating** 95 **To** 2032 $95 JF

O Series Lenswood Shiraz 2018 Deep dark purple hue. Wafts of exotic spices mingling with black plums and unobtrusive charry oak, more a seasoning than anything else. Full-bodied, rich with ribbons of velvety tannins. Impressive. Cork. 14.5% alc. **Rating** 95 **To** 2030 $40 JF

ŸŸŸŸŸ Single Vineyard Reserve Lenswood Pinot Noir 2018 **Rating** 93 **To** 2027 $80 JF

Art Series Three Pears Chardonnay 2018 **Rating** 90 **To** 2024 $30 JF

Andrew Peace Wines   ★★★★

Murray Valley Highway, Piangil, Vic 3597 **Region** Swan Hill
T (03) 5030 5291 www.apwines.com **Open** Mon–Fri 8–5, Sat 12–4
Winemaker Andrew Peace, David King **Est.** 1995 **Dozens** 180 000 **Vyds** 270ha
The Peace family has been a major Swan Hill grapegrower since 1980, moving into winemaking with the opening of a $3 million winery in '96. Varieties planted include chardonnay, colombard, grenache, malbec, mataro, merlot, pinot gris, riesling, sangiovese, sauvignon blanc, semillon, tempranillo and viognier. The planting of sagrantino is the largest of only a few such plantings in Australia. Exports to all major markets.

ŸŸŸŸŸ Australia Felix Swan Hill Sagrantino 2017 While I like the concentration of fruit and vibrancy of this vintage, I prefer the earthy grounded nature of the '16. Lots of blue fruits here, with spice, anise and minty eucalyptus-clad oak tannins that are drying, rather than guiding and invigorating. I can imagine the cooperage used. Screwcap. **Rating** 93 **To** 2030 $45 NG

Australia Felix Swan Hill Sagrantino 2016 Andrew Peace boasts the largest plantings of this sturdy, densely coloured and prodigiously structured Italian indigene. And very good it is too, boding for a bright future in this dry land. I could drink this over so much warm-climate shiraz. Why? Because it has a spleen of ferruginous tannins that imbue a sophisticated savouriness, drawing one in for the next glass. Moreover, despite weight and concentration, the wine feels poised and light in the best sense, drawing on its tannic mettle to placate the fruit in the name of drinkability. Think the dry structural focus of Italy, with some Aussie fruit. Screwcap. **Rating** 93 **To** 2025 $45 NG

Australia Felix Premium Barrel Reserve Wrattonbully Cabernet Shiraz 2017 A rich, atavistic expression reminiscent of days of yore. Black and blue fruit references, licorice backstrap and pillars of piney, minty oak-driven tannins. A nostalgic ride. A delicious sinful one. Screwcap. **Rating** 91 **To** 2029 $28 NG

Cellar Release Muscat NV A grapey and spicy muscat, celebrating the variety's youthful joyousness. Turkish delight, date, lychee and orange blossom. In the context of Aussie expressions, this is on the lighter side and is good, slightly chilled, as an apero. Screwcap. **Rating** 91 $18 NG ✪

Empress Joanna Vineyard Wrattonbully Cabernet Sauvignon 2018 This is a solid, fully loaded cabernet, spooling cassis, damson plum and mocha oak scents across a thread of finely wrought saline tannins. At this price, one can't ask for much more. Screwcap. 14% alc. **Rating** 90 **To** 2025 $19 NG ✪

Full Moon Swan Hill Durif 2018 A vivid purple. A dense red that manages to mitigate the ferocious tannins of the variety with pulpy riffs on violet, dark cherry and boysenberry. Nicely extracted. Nicely played. Screwcap. 13.5% alc. **Rating** 90 **To** 2024 $20 NG ✪

Angas Plains Estate

317 Angas Plains Road, Langhorne Creek, SA 5255 **Region** Langhorne Creek
T (08) 8537 3159 **www**.angasplainswines.com.au **Open** 7 days 11–5
Winemaker Peter Douglas **Est.** 1994 **Dozens** 3000 **Vyds** 15.2ha

In 1994 Phillip and Judy Cross began the Angas Plains Estate plantings, first with cabernet sauvignon, second shiraz and third a small block of chardonnay predominantly used as a sparkling base. The location on ancient Angas River floodplains, together with cooling evening breezes from the local Lake Alexandrina, proved ideally suited to the red varieties. Skilled contract winemaking has resulted in some excellent wines from the estate-grown shiraz and cabernet sauvignon. Exports to Singapore, Hong Kong and China.

ŸŸŸŸŸ **Emily Cross Langhorne Creek Shiraz 2016** Plum and Asian spice aromas, with the clang of French and American oaky edges (12 months) softening to a comforting maltiness. These will be sublimated by the crescendo of warmth, density and extract in time. Full, but shaping up nicely. The finish is rewardingly long. Cork. **Rating** 94 **To** 2031 $40 NG

ŸŸŸŸŸ **Emily Cross Langhorne Creek Shiraz 2018 Rating** 93 **To** 2035 $40 NG
PJs Cabernet Sauvignon 2018 Rating 92 **To** 2030 $25 NG ✪
Langhorne Creek Tempranillo 2018 Rating 92 **To** 2026 $22 NG ✪
Langhorne Creek Lagrein 2018 Rating 92 **To** 2024 $22 NG ✪
PJs Shiraz 2018 Rating 91 **To** 2030 $26 NG

Angove Family Winemakers

Bookmark Avenue, Renmark, SA 5341 **Region** South Australia
T (08) 8580 3100 **www**.angove.com.au **Open** Mon–Fri 10–5, Sat 10–4, Sun 10–3
Winemaker Tony Ingle, Paul Kernich, Ben Horley, Marco Ripa **Est.** 1886
Dozens 1 million **Vyds** 480ha

Founded in 1886, Angove Family Winemakers is one of Australia's most successful wine businesses – a fifth generation family company with a tradition of excellence and an eye for the future. Angove wines includes The Medhyk, Warboys Vineyard, Family Crest, Alternatus, Organics, Nine Vines and Long Row brands. The McLaren Vale cellar door is nestled in the family's certified organic and biodynamic Warboys Vineyard on Chalk Hill Road, the Renmark cellar door (home of the St Agnes Distillery) in Bookmark Avenue. In early 2019 Angove acquired the 12.7ha Angel Gully Vineyard in Clarendon from Primo Estate, and will rename the vineyard Angels Rise. Angove is committed to remaining privately owned and believes remaining in family hands enables the company to be master of its own destiny. Exports to all major markets.

ŸŸŸŸŸ **Warboys Vineyard McLaren Vale Shiraz 2017** Estate-grown, hand-picked and sorted, matured in used French puncheons for 10 months. A super fragrant bouquet opens proceedings for a wine that embraces region and variety without discrimination. The ensuing balance a given. The fruits range across plum and berry with a touch of chocolate, and the tannins are fine and soft. Screwcap. 14% alc. **Rating** 96 **To** 2032 $44 ✪

ŸŸŸŸŸ **Alternatus McLaren Vale Tempranillo 2018 Rating** 92 **To** 2023 $23 ✪
Alternatus McLaren Vale Fiano 2019 Rating 90 **To** 2021 $23

Angullong Wines

★★★★

Victoria Street, Millthorpe, NSW 2798 **Region** Orange
T (02) 6366 4300 **www**.angullong.com.au **Open** 7 days 11–5
Winemaker Jon Reynolds, Drew Tuckwell, Ravri Donkin **Est.** 1998 **Dozens** 20 000
Vyds 216.7ha

The Crossing family (Bill and Hatty, and third generation James and Ben) has owned a 2000ha sheep and cattle station for over half a century. Located 40km south of Orange, overlooking the Belubula Valley, more than 200ha of vines have been planted. In all there are 15 varieties, with shiraz, cabernet sauvignon and merlot leading the way. Most of the production is sold. Exports to Germany and China.

🍷🍷🍷🍷 **Orange Pinot Grigio 2019** Trophy for Best Pinot Grigio/Pinot Gris Australian Highland Wine Show '19. Pear, apple, snow pea and citrus skin and pith combine in a flavour fest of grigio/gris. Screwcap. 13.5% alc. **Rating** 93 **To** 2022 $22 ✪
Fossil Hill Paddock Blend White 2018 This is the best white of the range. A bit Ralph Lauren, but the meld of marsanne (68%) and vermentino (32%) works really well. Tatami, stone fruit, Meyer lemon and some nutty lees reel off length, poise and crunchy drinkability. Lovely flow and substantial intrigue to this. Screwcap. **Rating** 93 **To** 2024 $26 NG ✪
Crossing Reserve Orange Cabernet Sauvignon 2016 Dry-grown and, according to the tech sheet, 'low yielding'. This is a fine, fully fledged ripe cabernet, paradoxically soaring well above the cool-climate boundaries. Blackcurrant; vanillan, mocha, cedar tannins; and a brushing of verdant herb. Slick and salubrious with fine ageing potential. Screwcap. **Rating** 92 **To** 2030 $48 NG
Orange Sauvignon Blanc 2019 Angullong made the reputation for Orange's sauvignon blancs on the dual proposition of clear-cut varietal character and low-price value. Its bouquet is scented with tropical fruits, the palate following suit. Screwcap. 12.5% alc. **Rating** 91 **To** 2020 $22 ✪
Fossil Hill Chardonnay 2018 Smart oak, extended lees handling resplendent with stirring and a sure approach across fermentation, has resulted in a mid-weighted chardonnay brimming with stone fruit scents, candied citrus zest and a kernel of creaminess at its core. Screwcap. **Rating** 91 **To** 2026 $26 NG
Crossing Reserve Shiraz 2016 This is a slick, detailed wine. Ample cool-climate personality is embedded across clove-soused peppery acidity, giving drive and a little length. But the wine lacks texture and structure. Black fruit references, spice, salami scents and oak, sure. Screwcap. **Rating** 91 **To** 2026 $48 NG
Orange Chardonnay 2018 Fermented cool in tank, with the pressings handled in large-format wood; then blended. And it works well. Vibrant scents of nectarine, white peach and curd. Some oatmeal, toasted nuts and nougat too, serving as a creamy kernel. Mid-weighted, highly flavoured and fresh. Screwcap. **Rating** 90 **To** 2023 $22 NG
Orange Cabernet Sauvignon 2016 It presents an even flow of fruit flavour and it does so in uncomplicated fashion. It's an attractive red wine. Berries, anise and chocolate notes with a drift of dried herbs. It's all neatly laid out. Screwcap. 14.5% alc. **Rating** 90 **To** 2024 $22 CM

Annie's Lane

Level 8, 161 Collins Street, Melbourne, Vic 3000 (postal) **Region** Clare Valley
T (03) 8533 3000 **www**.annieslane.com.au **Open** Not
Winemaker Tom Shanahan **Est.** 1851 **Dozens** NFP
Annie's Lane is the Clare Valley brand of TWE. The name comes from Annie Wayman, a turn-of-the-century local identity. The wines consistently over-deliver against their price points. Copper Trail is the flagship release, and there are some other very worthy cellar door and on-premise wines.

Anvers

633 Razorback Road, Kangarilla, SA 5157 **Region** Adelaide Hills
T (08) 7079 8691 **www**.anvers.com.au **Open** Sun 11–5
Winemaker Kym Milne MW **Est.** 1998 **Dozens** 10000 **Vyds** 24.5ha
Myriam and Wayne Keoghan's principal vineyard is in the Adelaide Hills at Kangarilla (16ha of cabernet sauvignon, shiraz, chardonnay, sauvignon blanc and viognier); the second (97-year-old) vineyard is at McLaren Vale (shiraz, grenache and cabernet sauvignon). Winemaker Kym Milne has experience gained across many of the wine-producing countries in both northern and southern hemispheres. Exports to the UK and other major markets.

ŶŶŶŶŶ **The Giant Langhorne Creek Shiraz Cabernet Sauvignon 2012** The Giant
is made from 95yo shiraz and 45yo estate vines, matured in French and American
oak. It's only medium to full-bodied, and has been made with undoubtedly high
quality fruit singing the song of a pure blend. Its line and length are impeccable.
Cork. 14.5% alc. **Rating** 96 **To** 2037 $250

20 Years Old Rare Tawny NV Bright, clear colour, consistent with age. Viscous
and rich, it has Christmas cake and all the spices needed. The finish is long, and
there is no bite from the spirit. Authentic style. Remarkably, in '13 the wine won
the Perpetual Trophy for Best Australian Fortified Tawny at the Rutherglen Wine
Show. Cork. 19% alc. **Rating** 96 $60 ✪

WMK Adelaide Hills Shiraz 2017 Only 150 dozen made. Matured for
12 months in French oak. Radiates the cool vintage and the Adelaide Hills with
its foresty/spicy/peppery nuances to black fruits. The tannins are precise; firm, but
not too much so. Cork. 14.5% alc. **Rating** 95 **To** 2033 $55

ŶŶŶŶŶ **Kingsway Adelaide Hills Shiraz 2018 Rating** 93 **To** 2033 $30
Single Vineyard Adelaide Hills Syrah 2018 Rating 91 **To** 2021 $25
Brabo Clare Valley Riesling 2019 Rating 90 **To** 2026 $15 ✪

Aphelion Wine   ★★★★★

18 St Andrews Terrace, Willunga, SA 5172 **Region** McLaren Vale
T 0404 390 840 **www**.aphelionwine.com.au **Open** Not
Winemaker Rob Mack **Est.** 2014 **Dozens** 2500
Aphelion Wine is akin to a miniature painting done with single-hair paintbrushes. When
you consider the credentials of winemaker Rob Mack, supported by co-founder wife Louise
Rhodes Mack, great oaks come to mind. Rob has accumulated two degrees (first Accounting
and Management in 2007, then the Bachelor of Wine Science from CSU in '16). He scaled
the heights of direct marketing as wine buyer and planner (June '10–Jan '13) for Laithwaites
Wine People, and spent the next 18 months as production manager for Direct Wines in
McLaren Vale. Woven through this has been significant employment with five wineries, four
in McLaren Vale, which he obviously knows well. Rob was voted Young Gun of Wine '18.
Exports to the UK, the US and Hong Kong.

ŶŶŶŶŶ **Pir Blewitt Springs Chenin Blanc 2019** Fermented partly in tank and barrel,
the latter portion under the aegis of ambient yeast with regular stirring. This is a
very fine chenin. Texturally detailed, impeccably poised and intense with red apple
flavours etched with a pungent flintiness. This evinces authority while going down
easily. A complex wine of purity, precision and little fuss, hailing from a single
50yo vineyard. Screwcap. **Rating** 95 **To** 2025 $30 NG ✪

The Confluence McLaren Vale Grenache 2019 This is just ripe enough,
noting the tendency in these parts to pick earlier to retain freshness. This has
a majority whole-berry ferment, old vines and a judicious seasoning (30%) of
whole-bunch for herbal complexity and tannic build. Yet the overall impression is
one of imminent drinkability. Slurpy, even. A compote of red berry notes, bitter
orange and cranberry. The finish is long and juicy, with a granular sandy edginess.
A delicious wine. Screwcap. **Rating** 95 **To** 2025 $35 NG ✪

Rapture 2018 Class is embedded in the tannins: fine-grained, sandy and taut.
The quality oak is nestled in effortlessly, galvanising notes of raspberry bonbon,
lavender, scrub, bergamot and cranberry. The wines here are dialled back of
late, with a suggestion of earlier picked components threaded across the range.
50% mataro, 38% grenache, 12% shiraz. Cork. **Rating** 95 **To** 2028 $60 NG

The Tendance McLaren Vale Shiraz 2018 A mesh of 2 pickings – one early
and one later – across 2 separate vineyards. Some snazzy Dominique Laurent oak
treatment embellishes. There is a sheen of violet, dark cherry, blue fruit references
and salumi coating any angles in a plush velour of pleasure. A crowd pleaser. Slick
gear. Screwcap. **Rating** 94 **To** 2032 $35 NG

Emergent Mataro 2018 I believe that this noble variety, together with grenache
and southern Italian indigenes, are the future of Australian viticulture. They are

neither thirsty, early ripening, nor effete; in essence, well suited to the torrid dry conditions of this land. This rich red was sourced from 3 vineyards across cooler and warmer zones: Blewitt, Willunga and Sellicks, with the warmer Willunga material fermented as 50% whole-bunch. The result is a ferrous beam of chinotto, dark cherry and dried herb laying down a patina of pleasure with a clench of reductive tension. Screwcap. **Rating** 94 **To** 2028 $35 NG

🍷🍷🍷🍷🍷 **Affinity GMS 2019** Rating 92 **To** 2026 $35 NG
Sagaro 2019 Rating 92 **To** 2022 $28 NG

 # Apogee ★★★★★

1083 Golconda Road, Lebrina, Tas 7254 **Region** Northern Tasmania
T (02) 6395 6358 **www**.apogeetasmania.com **Open** By appt Nov–Jan Wed–Sun 11–4.30
Winemaker Dr Andrew Pirie **Est.** 2007 **Dozens** 1000 **Vyds** 2ha
Andrew Pirie (or Dr Andrew Pirie AM) has stood tall among those viticulturists and winemakers who have sought to understand and exploit Tasmania's terroir and climate over the past 40 years. He is as far removed from soap box oratory as it is possible to be, quietly spoken and humble. His vision 48 years ago – longer still on some measures – saw the establishment of Pipers Brook Vineyard in 1974, using the detailed studies of Tasmania's regional climates in '72. In '77 he became the first (and last) person to complete study for his doctorate in viticulture from the University of Sydney. While making some of the best table wines to come from Tasmania in the last quarter of the 20th century, his focus shifted to sparkling wine in '99. In 2007 he acquired a 2ha site near Lebrina in the Pipers River district, planting pinot noir (62%), chardonnay (16%) and pinot meunier (2%) for sparkling wine, and pinot gris (20%) for table wine. Apogee's historic farm cottage is now an intimate cellar door where (by appointment) visitors can observe a hand disgorging demonstration. Pinot gris and pinot noir are also made under the Alto label.

🍷🍷🍷🍷🍷 **Alto Pinot Noir 2018** Clone 777, wild-fermented, matured in French barriques. Deep, bright crimson-purple. A highly aromatic bouquet with red berries/cherries. The palate is an exercise in purity, bright yet with flesh and effortless length. A truly lovely pinot. Screwcap. 12.8% alc. **Rating** 96 **To** 2028 $65 ✪
Deluxe Brut 2014 The pale pink-bronze hue points to pinot noir and pinot meunier, but there's also pinot gris as well as chardonnay on the loose. The extra time this wine has had, and the (possible) touch of pinot gris have served to loosen it up into a textured and balanced wine with nutty/toasty nuances. Diam. 12% alc. **Rating** 96 $63 ✪
Deluxe Brut 2015 A pinot noir, chardonnay, pinot meunier base wine; the remainder of the info on the postage stamp-sized label illegible without a microscope. Given Andrew Pirie's background, it is certain it has spent at least 3 years on yeast lees (traditional method) and that the dosage is low. The length of the palate is admirable. Diam. 12% alc. **Rating** 95 $63
Deluxe Sparkling Rose 2016 Traditional method. The base wine was 75% pinot noir, the balance evenly split between chardonnay and pinot meunier. Whole-bunch pressed with some soaking of the skins to pick up colour ex the skins of the pinot noir; 25% fermented in an old oak cask. Rich flavours. Diam. 12% alc. **Rating** 95 $75

🍷🍷🍷🍷🍷 **Alto Pinot Gris 2019** Rating 93 **To** 2024 $45
Alto Pinot Gris 2018 Rating 91 **To** 2027 $45
Alto Pinot Gris 2016 Rating 91 **To** 2027

Arakoon ★★★☆

7/229 Main Road, McLaren Vale, SA 5171 **Region** McLaren Vale
T 0434 338 180 **www**.arakoonwines.com.au **Open** By appt
Winemaker Raymond Jones **Est.** 1999 **Dozens** 3000 **Vyds** 3.5ha
Ray and Patrik Jones' first venture into wine came to nothing: a 1990 proposal for a film about the Australian wine industry with myself as anchorman. In '99 they took the plunge

into making their own wine and exporting it, along with the wines of others. As the quality of the wines has improved, so has the originally zany labelling been replaced with simple but elegant labels. Exports to Sweden, Denmark, Germany, Singapore, Malaysia and China.

🍷🍷🍷🍷🍷 **McLaren Vale Cabernet Sauvignon 2016** Open-fermented, extended maceration, matured in French and American oak. It is, as promised, full-bodied, with a generous swag of tannins (it is cabernet, after all) to accompany the black fruits and bay leaf flavours. Screwcap. 14% alc. **Rating** 91 **To** 2030 $20 ✪

🍷🍷🍷🍷 **McLaren Vale Viognier 2017 Rating** 89 **To** 2023 $14 ✪

Aravina Estate ★★★★★

61 Thornton Road, Yallingup, WA 6282 **Region** Margaret River
T (08) 9750 1111 **www**.aravinaestate.com **Open** 7 days 10–5
Winemaker Ryan Aggiss **Est.** 2010 **Dozens** 10 000 **Vyds** 28ha
In 2010 Steve Tobin and family acquired the winery and vineyard of Amberley Estate from Accolade, but not the Amberley brand. Steve turned the property into a multifaceted business with a host of attractions including a restaurant and wedding venue.

🍷🍷🍷🍷🍷 **Wildwood Ridge Reserve Margaret River Chardonnay 2018** Gingin clone, hand-picked, chilled overnight, whole-bunch pressed to French oak (36% new), matured for 11 months. Elegant, vibrant and totally enjoyable now or over the next 3–5 years. The fruit definition is right on the money. Screwcap. 12.5% alc. **Rating** 95 **To** 2028 $60
Single Vineyard Margaret River Shiraz 2018 Matured for 19 months in French oak (25% new). '18 was a great red wine vintage, and this is a high quality medium to full-bodied wine; the bouquet throwing a confetti of spices and black pepper in the air, the palate gathering all this and more with part juicy, part structured flavours and mouthfeel. Screwcap. 13.5% alc. **Rating** 95 **To** 2038 $35 ✪
Wildwood Ridge Reserve Margaret River Malbec 2018 Matured in 2yo oak. A single barrel selected for this inaugural release. Deep purple colour. Rich, mouthfilling plum/dark berry fruit flavours, very good balance. Seems impossible only one barrel was selected. Screwcap. 13.5% alc. **Rating** 94 **To** 2033 $45

🍷🍷🍷🍷🍷 **Limited Release Margaret River Tempranillo 2018 Rating** 93 **To** 2025 $35
Single Vineyard Block 4 Chenin Blanc 2018 Rating 92 **To** 2029 $35
The 'A' Collection Chenin Blanc 2019 Rating 90 **To** 2026 $25
Wildwood Ridge Reserve Margaret River Cabernet Sauvignon 2017
Rating 90 **To** 2027 $65

Arlewood Estate ★★★★★

679 Calgardup Road West, Forest Grove, WA 6286 **Region** Margaret River
T (08) 9757 6676 **www**.arlewood.com.au **Open** Thurs–Mon 11–5 or by appt
Winemaker Stuart Pym **Est.** 1988 **Dozens** 3500 **Vyds** 6.08ha
The antecedents of today's Arlewood shifted several times; they might interest a PhD researcher, but – with one exception – have no relevance to today's business. That exception was the 1999 planting of the vineyard by the (then) Xanadu winemaker Jurg Muggli. Garry Gossatti purchased the run-down, close-planted vineyard in 2008, and lived in the onsite house from '08–12, driving to Perth one day per week for his extensive hospitality/hotel business (which paid Arlewood's bills). His involvement in the resurrection of the vineyard was hands-on, and the cool site in the south of Margaret River was, and remains, his obsession. He now drives down every weekend from Perth to talk to viticulturist Russell Oates and contract winemaker Stuart Pym, clearly believing that the owner's footsteps make the best fertiliser. Exports to the UK, Malaysia, Hong Kong and China.

🍷🍷🍷🍷🍷 **Margaret River Chardonnay 2018** Not shy in coming forward with its creamy, buttery, nutty flavours and an infusion of melon, stone fruit and lemon curd. While it satisfies because it has richness and plumpness via fruit and oak inputs, the bright acidity puts a zip on it running away. Screwcap. 13.5% alc. **Rating** 95 **To** 2028 $35 JF

ㅅㅅㅅㅅㅅ **Margaret River Cabernet Sauvignon 2017 Rating** 93 **To** 2032 $40 JF
Villaggio The Fume Blanc 2019 Rating 92 **To** 2024 $22 JF ✪

Arlo Vintners   ★★★★

8 Jones Road, Rutherglen, Vic 3685 **Region** Rutherglen
T 0431 037 752 **www**.arlovintners.com **Open** Not
Winemaker Dan Bettio, Lennie Lister **Est.** 2016 **Dozens** 400 **Vyds** 2.5ha
If you are thinking about starting a small winery from scratch, you must have a business plan. Dan Bettio and Lennie Lister are the owners of Arlo Vintners, each with over 20 years experience working in wine, chiefly in North East Victoria. Their plan is close to a template for others to adopt. Its credo is to select vineyards with something special about the region and adopt small-batch winemaking to produce 100 dozen bottles of each of their wines. They intend to open a cellar door in Rutherglen, the beating heart of North East Victoria.

ㅅㅅㅅㅅㅅ **Old Vine Shiraz 2016** All the dark fruit flavour you could wish for but with ample savoury spice. Indeed, floral nuances give this a distinctly pretty edge. Tannin churns, oak balances, peppercorn notes swing through. It's in fine shape at every turn. Screwcap. 14.4% alc. **Rating** 94 **To** 2030 $36 CM
Durif 2016 It has all the density of dark berried flavour that you'd want and expect but it's prettied up by floral notes and boasts quite impeccable balance. Tannin hasn't been held back, but it sits beautifully in the wine; indeed everything here is immaculate. Screwcap. 14.6% alc. **Rating** 94 **To** 2028 $29 CM ✪

ㅅㅅㅅㅅㅅ **Cabernet Petit Verdot 2016 Rating** 93 **To** 2027 $29 CM
Rose 2017 Rating 92 **To** 2020 $24 CM ✪

Artis Wines   ★★★★☆

7 Flora Street, Stepney, SA 5069 **Region** Clare Valey/Adelaide Hills
T 0418 802 495 **www**.artiswines.com.au **Open** Not
Winemaker Andrew Miller **Est.** 2016 **Dozens** 400
What do you do after decades working for one of the largest wine groups in Australia? You start your own very small wine business making 400 dozen bottles of Clare Valley Riesling and Adelaide Hills Shiraz. And in doing so, you call upon your experience gained over the years working in France, Spain, the US, NZ, Argentina and Portugal, coupled with travel to many more wine regions.

ㅅㅅㅅㅅㅅ **Single Vineyard Adelaide Hills Gruner Veltliner 2019** Slow, steady ferment and then matured in oak for 7 months. Satiny texture with stone fruit, overt spice and earthy flavours. It has weight but it also has energy and everything pushes convincingly through the finish. Ticks many boxes. Screwcap. 13.4% alc. **Rating** 95 **To** 2024 $37 CM
Single Vineyard Adelaide Hills Chardonnay 2018 Sun-filled fruit flavour and the toasty/malty oak to match, though the finish manages to exhibit a good deal of elegance. Peach, steel, nashi pear and lactose flavours add plenty of flesh to the palate. You're on pretty good ground here. Screwcap. 13.4% alc. **Rating** 94 **To** 2026 $45 CM

ㅅㅅㅅㅅㅅ **Single Vineyard Adelaide Hills Syrah 2018 Rating** 93 **To** 2026 $45 CM

Artisans of the Barossa   ★★★★★

Vino Lokal, 64 Murray Street, Tanunda, SA 5352 **Region** Barossa Valley
T (08) 8563 3935 **www**.artisansofbarossa.com **Open** Sun–Wed 12–6, Thurs–Sat 12–10
Winemaker Various **Est.** 2005 **Dozens** 3000
The Artisans of the Barossa is a group of winemakers that share a like-minded approach to winemaking and enjoyment of wine. They are Hobbs of Barossa Ranges, Schwarz Wine

Company, John Duval Wines, Sons of Eden and Spinifex. Each is highly successful in its own business, but relishes the opportunity of coming together to build on their collective winemaking skills and experience, knowledge of the vineyard landscape and their connections through the local wine community. The Artisans wines are made from grapes grown in the Barossa Valley, the Eden Valley, or both. Exports to Malaysia, Singapore and China.

ŸŸŸŸŸ **Jason Schwarz Light Pass Shiraz 2018** Named in honour of Colonel Light who discovered the break in the hills leading from the Barossa Valley to the Eden Valley. Medium-bodied. Literally flows along the supple palate, unfolding black fruits then spices allied with fine, balanced tannins. No hint of alcohol heat, instead a splash of red fruit. Screwcap. 14.5% alc. **Rating** 96 **To** 2040
Greg Hobbs Keyneton Shiraz 2018 An immediately delicious bouquet and palate; blackberry and plum fruit, ripe tannins in perfect balance. Length and focus are part of an indissoluble whole, but with the grace of a medium-bodied shiraz. Screwcap. 15% alc. **Rating** 96 **To** 2040
John Duval Ebenezer Shiraz 2018 The grapes were grown by viticultural master John Scholz in the driest and warmest part of the Barossa Valley, cool nights due to the vineyard's 290–305m elevation and east–west row orientation. This wine has a pulsating bouquet. The palate laden with blackberry and stewed plum flavours; plus dark chocolate added for good measure. The ripe tannins leave it until the last moment to appear. Screwcap. 14.5% alc. **Rating** 96 **To** 2040
Peter Schell High Eden Shiraz 2018 Dry-grown 20yo east-facing vines at 500m above sea level; two-thirds destemmed; the balance whole bunch with 14 days on skins, matured in a single used 600l French demi-muid. Particularly fresh and elegant red and black fruits on the palate with fine, persistent, tannins carrying a savoury message. Screwcap. 13.3% alc. **Rating** 95 **To** 2038
Corey Ryan & Simon Cowham Angaston Shiraz 2018 40% of the fruit was whole bunch and hand-plunged for 25 days, pressed to French hogsheads (45% new) for 15 months maturation. A powerful, evocative wine. Its spicy/peppery notes coupled with a long, zesty, red berry–accented palate with detailed tannins providing both texture and structure. Screwcap. 14.5% alc. **Rating** 95 **To** 2040
John Lienert Gomersal Shiraz 2018 The wine is powerful and very focused, but is unexpectedly light on its feet thanks to mouth-watering juicy fruit flavours that coexist with the tannins. Screwcap. 14.5% alc. **Rating** 95 **To** 2038

ŸŸŸŸŸ **Barrel Blend Shiraz 2017 Rating** 92 **To** 2032 $28

Artwine ★★★★

72 Bird in Hand Road, Woodside, SA 5244 **Region** Adelaide Hills/Clare Valley
T 0411 422 450 **www**.artwine.com.au **Open** 7 days 11–5
Winemaker Contract **Est.** 1997 **Dozens** 10000 **Vyds** 21ha
Owned by Judy and Glen Kelly, Artwine has three vineyards. Two are in Clare Valley: one on Springfarm Road, Clare; the other on Sawmill Road, Sevenhill. The third vineyard is in the Adelaide Hills at Woodside, which houses their cellar door. Artwine currently has 15 varieties planted. The Clare Valley vineyards have tempranillo, shiraz, riesling, pinot gris, cabernet sauvignon, fiano, graciano, grenache, montepulciano, viognier and cabernet franc. The Adelaide Hills vineyard has prosecco, pinot noir, merlot and albarino.

ŸŸŸŸŸ **Madame V Viognier 2018** Machine-harvested, cool-fermented. No issue with the vinification, just with the variety. It's an upper class viognier. Screwcap. 12.5% alc. **Rating** 90 **To** 2020 $25
The Real Thing Albarino 2019 Interesting. The Adelaide Hills has given the wine a juicy citrus grip. Screwcap. 12.5% alc. **Rating** 90 **To** 2022 $30
The Grace Graciano 2016 Only a single maturation phase here. Likewise, drink sooner than later. Screwcap. 14% alc. **Rating** 90 **To** 2020 $32

ŸŸŸŸ **Wicked Stepmother Fiano 2019 Rating** 89 **To** 2021 $40
Grumpy Old Man Grenache 2018 Rating 89 **To** 2025 $40
Leave Your Hat On Montepulciano 2016 Rating 89 **To** 2009 $40

Arundel Farm Estate ★★★

321 Arundel Road, Keilor, Vic 3036 **Region** Sunbury
T (03) 9338 9987 **www**.arundelfarmestate.com.au **Open** Fri 11–3, w'ends 11–4
Winemaker Mark Matthews, Claude Ceccomancini **Est.** 1984 **Dozens** 1000 **Vyds** 7.4ha
The first stage of the vineyard in 1984 was 0.8ha of shiraz and cabernet sauvignon. Rick
Kinzbrunner of Giaconda made the first vintage in '88 and for some years thereafter, but the
enterprise lapsed until it was revived with new plantings in '96 and 2000. Today it is planted
solely to shiraz and viognier. In October '11 Claude and Sandra Ceccomancini acquired the
business and appointed Mark Matthews as winemaker. Exports to China.

♥♥♥♥ **Reserve Sunbury Shiraz 2018** Hand-picked from the original block planted
in '84, 50% whole bunches placed on top of the crushed and destemmed portion,
the tank then sealed for 10 days, then opened for maceration/fermentation for a
further 10 days, matured for 14 months in old French oak. Good colour, but there
is aberrant acid on the prowl. Pity, a lot of work (and thought). Diam. 14% alc.
Rating 89 **To** 2027 $40

Ashbrook Estate

379 Tom Cullity Drive, Wilyabrup, WA 6280 **Region** Margaret River
T (08) 9755 6262 **www**.ashbrookwines.com.au **Open** 7 days 10–5
Winemaker Catherine Edwards, Brian Devitt **Est.** 1975 **Dozens** 12 500 **Vyds** 17.4ha
This fastidious producer of consistently excellent estate-grown table wines shuns publicity
and is less well known than is deserved, selling much of its wine through the cellar
door and to a loyal mailing list clientele. It is very much a family affair: Brian Devitt is at
the helm, winemaking is by his daughter Catherine, and viticulture by son Richard (also a
qualified winemaker). Exports to the US, Canada, Germany, Indonesia, Japan, Singapore, Hong
Kong and China.

♥♥♥♥♥ **Reserve Margaret River Chardonnay 2016** Fermented in French barriques
for 8 months. This is a rich, almost luscious wine; exuding aromas and flavours
of expensive oak, poached peach and pear with a drizzle of creamed honey –
impressive within a certain style. Drinking at its best now while it retains its
freshness. Screwcap. 13.5% alc. **Rating** 95 **To** 2023 $65 SC
Margaret River Cabernet Sauvignon 2017 Aged in French oak (20% new)
for 18 months. Small portions of petit verdot, cabernet franc and merlot in the
blend. Distinctively varietal and regional. Aromas of blackcurrant, redcurrant and
bay leaf are framed by cedary oak; the palate perfectly weighted with beautifully
fine and supple tannins. Screwcap. 13.5% alc. **Rating** 95 **To** 2030 $35 SC ✪

♥♥♥♥♡ **Gold Label Margaret River Riesling 2019** **Rating** 93 **To** 2030 $27 SC ✪
Margaret River Chardonnay 2018 **Rating** 93 **To** 2025 $35 SC
Margaret River Verdelho 2019 **Rating** 93 **To** 2024 $27 SC ✪
Margaret River Shiraz 2017 **Rating** 93 **To** 2027 $32 SC
Margaret River Petit Verdot 2017 **Rating** 93 **To** 2027 $45 SC
Margaret River Semillon 2019 **Rating** 92 **To** 2030 $27 SC
Margaret River Sauvignon Blanc 2019 **Rating** 91 **To** 2022 $27 SC

Ashton Hills Vineyard

126 Tregarthen Road, Ashton, SA 5137 **Region** Adelaide Hills
T (08) 8390 1243 **www**.ashtonhills.com.au **Open** Fri–Mon 11–5
Winemaker Stephen George, Paul Smith **Est.** 1982 **Dozens** 3000 **Vyds** 3ha
Stephen George made Ashton Hills one of the great producers of pinot noir in Australia,
and by some distance the best in the Adelaide Hills. With no family succession in place, he
sold the business to Wirra Wirra in April 2015. (It had been rumoured for some time that
he was considering such a move, so when it was announced, there was a sigh of relief that it
should pass to a business such as Wirra Wirra, with undoubted commitment to retaining the
extraordinary quality of the wines.) Stephen will continue to live in the house on the property,
and provide ongoing consulting advice. Exports to the US, Hong Kong and China.

ɪɪɪɪɪ **Reserve Pinot Noir 2018** 70% 38yo D5V12 and 10% each of 777, Martini and MV6 clones (the clonal make-up varying each year); fermented with 30% whole berries, matured in French oak (50% new, normally 30%) for 10 months. Striking wine. The fruit impact deals with the oak. Extreme length. Screwcap. 14.5% alc. **Rating** 97 **To** 2030 $85 ☉

ɪɪɪɪɪ **Estate Riesling 2019** Sourced from 8 rows (1200 vines) planted by Stephen George in '82. As ever, very intense and layered. No tricks to the vinification, making the task of elbowing out great pinot noir all the more impressive. A truly lovely wine – exceptional. Screwcap. 12.5% alc. **Rating** 96 **To** 2034 $35 ☉

Piccadilly Valley Chardonnay 2019 It's downright unreasonable that Ashton Hills, with its over-large tennis court vineyard in the Piccadilly Valley, should be able to make stunning pinot noirs (Reserve, Estate and varietal, contract-grown), chardonnay and a riesling to die for. This Chardonnay is matured for 9 months in new and used French oak. Screwcap. 12.5% alc. **Rating** 95 **To** 2032

Estate Pinot Noir 2018 50% Martini clones, 20% each D5V12 and 777 and 10% MV6; fermented with 30% whole bunches and matured in 1–3yo French oak for 10 months. The similarities to the Reserve are greater than the differences. This is elegant and very long, the oak absorbed, the whole bunch adding a savoury twist. Red fruits lead, purity follows. Screwcap. 14.5% alc. **Rating** 95 **To** 2028 $55

Clare Valley Sparkling Shiraz 2013 One of the very best Australian sparkling reds, the base wine ex Wendouree. Rich, deep and supple. Poached plum fruit plus a touch of spice. Will flourish with time in bottle. Diam. 14% alc. **Rating** 95 $50

ɪɪɪɪ **Piccadilly Valley Pinot Noir 2018 Rating** 89 **To** 2024 $35

Atlas Wines   ★★★★★

PO Box 458, Clare, SA 5453 **Region** Clare Valley
T 0419 847 491 www.atlaswines.com **Open** Not
Winemaker Adam Barton **Est.** 2008 **Dozens** 8000 **Vyds** 24ha
Before establishing Atlas Wines, owner and winemaker Adam Barton had an extensive winemaking career: in McLaren Vale, the Barossa Valley, Coonawarra, the iconic Bonny Doon Vineyard in California and at Reillys Wines in the Clare Valley. He has 6ha of shiraz and 2ha of cabernet sauvignon grown on a stony ridge on the eastern slopes of the region, and sources small batches from other distinguished sites in the Clare and Barossa valleys. The quality of the wines is extraordinarily good and consistent. Exports to the UK, the US and China.

ɪɪɪɪɪ **516° Barossa Valley Shiraz 2017** Sporting a new label but no change to the wine. Fruit sourced from a single vineyard of old vines (age not specified) at Kalimna. It's fabulous. Silky texture, tannins velvety and savoury. The drive is long and it feels effortless. It offers a complete flavour package of dark plums, juniper berries, roasted coffee beans and baking spices. Screwcap. 14.5% alc. **Rating** 95 **To** 2030 $45 JF

429° Clare Valley Shiraz 2017 The darkest ruby hue entices. So too the ripe plum flavours, all spicy with licorice and even a umami soy-sauce character that's appealing. It's full-bodied with a sheen across the palate meeting up with textural tannins somewhat bolstered by 15% new French oak hogsheads/puncheons. Everything in place. Screwcap. 14.5% alc. **Rating** 95 **To** 2030 $45 JF

Clare Valley Grenache 2018 Fom 80yo vines in Leasingham, wild fermented, then aged in used French hogsheads for 5 months. It has all the charm of the variety with its raspberry and spiced cherry flavours and flecks of fresh herbs too. Thankfully, it has a lovely savoury aspect and dryness as opposed to lots of sweet flavour. Lighter framed, sandy tannins and drinkability stamped all over. Screwcap. 14% alc. **Rating** 95 **To** 2026 $28 JF ☉

ɪɪɪɪ♀ **Clare Valley Shiraz 2017 Rating** 93 **To** 2028 $28 JF
Adelaide Hills Chardonnay 2019 Rating 92 **To** 2026 $30 JF

ATR Wines

103 Hard Hill Road, Armstrong, Vic 3377 **Region** Grampians
T 0457 922 400 **www.**atrwines.com.au **Open** Thurs–Sun & public hols 1–5
Winemaker Adam Richardson **Est.** 2005 **Dozens** 4000 **Vyds** 7.6ha
Perth-born Adam Richardson began his winemaking career in 1995, working for Normans, d'Arenberg and Oakridge along the way. He has held senior winemaking roles, ultimately with TWE America before moving back to Australia with wife Eva and children in late 2015. In '05 he had put down roots in the Grampians region, establishing a vineyard with old shiraz clones from the 19th century and riesling, extending the plantings with tannat, nebbiolo, durif and viognier. The wines are exceptionally good, no surprise given his experience and the quality of the vineyard. He has also set up a wine consultancy business, drawing on experience that is matched by few consultants in Australia. Exports to Europe.

🍷🍷🍷🍷 **Hard Hill Road Writer's Block Great Western Riesling 2018** Now here's a riesling that immediately captures all the taster's senses, clearing a path for the intense lime/lemon flavours that follow. The wine increases its tactile power on the finish and very long aftertaste. The writer is Adam Richardson's wife Eva, who no longer has writer's block. Screwcap. 12% alc. **Rating** 97 **To** 2032 $38 ✪

🍷🍷🍷🍷 **Chockstone Grampians Riesling 2019** Other than gentle pressing and low extraction, there's nothing special about the vinification, leaving the pure fruit of the cool Grampians climate to work its magic. There's a softness to the flavours that coexist with the low pH and minerally acidity; Meyer lemon and lime with tropical nuances. Screwcap. 12% alc. **Rating** 95 **To** 2029 $22 ✪
Chockstone Grampians Shiraz 2018 The deep, dark colour semaphores a wine not to be taken lightly. The bouquet emanates spiced black cherry, pepper, licorice; the black cherry also joining in on the palate. Despite its richness and complexity, the wine stays within the boundaries of medium-bodied; the lack of overt phenolic extraction or alcohol heat are keys to its elegance. Screwcap. 14.5% alc. **Rating** 95 **To** 2038 $28 ✪
Chockstone Grampians Rose 2019 A 4-variety blend, all vinified separately. Shiraz and durif are drained after 2–4 hours on skins, nebbiolo and tannat are kept on skins for 24 hours before draining; blended after fermentation, held in tank for 3 months. It is a multifaceted rose, the red berry flavour set given texture and structure, 10g/l of residual sugar lost in the wash. The price is as mouth-watering as the wine. Screwcap. 13.5% alc. **Rating** 94 **To** 2023 $22 ✪

🍷🍷🍷🍷 **Grower Series Ludvigsen Shiraz 2017** **Rating** 93 **To** 2027 SC
Grower Series Leeke Shiraz 2017 **Rating** 93 **To** 2027 SC
Grower Series Dakis Great Western Shiraz 2017 **Rating** 93 **To** 2027 SC
Chockstone Grampians Pinot Gris 2019 **Rating** 92 **To** 2024 $22 ✪
Grower Series Toomey Shiraz 2017 **Rating** 92 **To** 2027 SC
Grower Series Morris Shiraz 2017 **Rating** 91 **To** 2027 SC

Attwoods Wines

45 Attwoods Road, Scotsburn, Vic 3352 **Region** Ballarat
T 0407 906 849 **www.**attwoodswines.com.au **Open** Not
Winemaker Troy Walsh **Est.** 2010 **Dozens** 650 **Vyds** 2ha
Australian-born and educated winemaker and owner Troy Walsh began his journey into wine as a sommelier in London for 12 years (1990–2002), working his way up to some of the most exalted restaurants. In '10 he began following the Flying Winemaker path of vintages in Australia and France each year. He also quickly ran his colours up the mast by focusing on pinot noir and chardonnay in Burgundy and Geelong. The wineries he worked with here and in France all used whole-bunch fermentation as a significant part of the vinification process, and he uses the practice to a greater or lesser degree in most of his wines. Initially all of the grapes were contract-grown, and Troy continues to purchase grapes from two vineyards near Bannockburn. In '10 Troy and wife Jane purchased an 18ha property 20km south of Ballarat, and moved the family from Melbourne, establishing a 1.5ha ultra-high

density (1m × 1.2m spacing) planting of pinot noir (MV6, 777 and Pommard) and 0.5ha of chardonnay. Attwoods also leases a 27yo vineyard at Garibaldi planted to 0.5ha each of pinot noir and chardonnay.

Atze's Corner Wines   ★★★★★

451 Research Road, Nuriootpa, SA 5355 **Region** Barossa Valley
T 0407 621 989 www.atzes.com **Open** Fri–Sat 1–sunset, Sun & public hols 12–5.30
Winemaker Andrew Kalleske **Est.** 2005 **Dozens** 2500 **Vyds** 30ha
The seemingly numerous members of the Kalleske family have widespread involvement in grapegrowing and winemaking in the Barossa Valley. This venture is that of Andrew Kalleske, son of John and Barb. In 1975 they purchased the Atze Vineyard, which included a small block of shiraz planted in '12, but with additional plantings along the way, including more shiraz in '51. Andrew purchases some grapes from the family vineyard. It has 20ha of shiraz, with small amounts of mataro, petit verdot, grenache, cabernet, tempranillo, viognier, petite sirah, graciano, montepulciano, vermentino and aglianico. The wines are all estate-grown and made onsite. The new cellar door opened in 2019, designed to enjoy the the sunset over the 100+-year-old vineyard. Exports to South Korea, Hong Kong and China.

🍷🍷🍷🍷🍷 Bachelor Barossa Valley Shiraz 2018 Matured for 18 months in French oak (10% new), the remainder used French and American hogsheads. A wine of freakish intensity and power drawn from black fruits, not oak and not alcohol. Screwcap. 14.8% alc. **Rating** 95 **To** 2048 $35 ✪

Eddies Old Vine Barossa Valley Shiraz 2017 This vineyard was planted in 1912, '51 and '75. The wine offers a tapestry of flavours and mouth-watering spices and cedar (from 25% new French and American oak). The old vines and the vintage have stared the oak down, giving satsuma plum, dark chocolate and black fruits room to claim equality. Cork. 15% alc. **Rating** 95 **To** 2042 $60

Boehm's Black Single Vineyard Barossa Valley Shiraz 2017 I absolutely agree with Andrew Kalleske's improbable description of the wine as 'elegant and polished' for a Barossa Valley shiraz with 15% alcohol. The answer to the paradox is the '17 vintage and the quality of the tannins it invested in the wine. Screwcap. **Rating** 95 **To** 2037 $60

Forgotten Hero Barossa Valley Shiraz 2016 It's had 14 days extended maceration before transfer to French hogsheads (100% new) for 20 months maturation. All good stuff, except there's too much oak for the fruit to escape and express itself. Time will undoubtedly help. Cork. 15.5% alc. **Rating** 94 **To** 2032 $120

🍷🍷🍷🍷♀ Wild Rose Barossa Valley Rose 2018 **Rating** 90 **To** 2020 $25

Audrey Wilkinson   ★★★★★

750 De Beyers Road, Pokolbin, NSW 2320 **Region** Hunter Valley
T (02) 4998 1866 www.audreywilkinson.com.au **Open** 7 days 10–5
Winemaker Xanthe Hatcher **Est.** 1866 **Dozens** NFP **Vyds** 35.33ha
Audrey Wilkinson is one of the most historic and beautiful properties in the Hunter Valley, known for its stunning views and pristine vineyards. It was the first vineyard planted in Pokolbin, in 1866. The property was acquired in 2004 by the late Brian Agnew and has been owned and operated by his family since. The wines, made predominantly from estate-grown grapes, are released in three tiers: Audrey Wilkinson Series, Winemakers Selection and Reserve, the latter only available from the cellar door. Exports to the US, Canada, the UK, Finland and the Czech Republic.

🍷🍷🍷🍷🍷 The Ridge Hunter Valley Semillon 2019 Made from the best fruit from old vines on the western ridge of The Ridge vineyard. It's an eye-catching quartz-like green-gold colour in the glass, and you could say that sets the scene for the wine itself. Aromas and flavours are mostly in the lemon and green apple spectrum with an underlying minerally quality, and a slatey acidity that pulls it long on the finish. Screwcap. 11.5% alc. **Rating** 95 **To** 2024 $45 SC

The Lake Hunter Valley Shiraz 2018 Grown on the old vine Lake block on the estate vineyard, 15% whole-bunch fermented, matured in French puncheons. Lots of gamey, savoury, earthy regional character on the bouquet, but the red berry fruit is the anchor. It's generously built in Hunter terms, ripe and flavoursome, but the palate length and tannin are the outstanding features. Screwcap. 14.5% alc. Rating 95 To 2043 $120 SC

Winemakers Selection Hunter Valley Semillon 2019 A selection of the best parcels from the vintage. Citrus, lemongrass and green herb aromas as expected, but pebbly; minerally notes are equally prominent. This vintage seems a little richer and more forward on the palate than usual, and the acidity a little softer. That said, it maintains its high quality and is only going to become more interesting with time. Screwcap. 11.5% alc. **Rating** 94 **To** 2035 $30 SC ✪

Winemakers Selection Hunter Valley Tempranillo 2019 From the older vines on the estate vineyard. It has the full collection of every type of cherry under the sun diffused into a light stream of delicately shaped and textured light-bodied wine. Screwcap. 13.5% alc. **Rating** 94 **To** 2029 $40

ΨΨΨΨΨ **Winemakers Selection Chardonnay 2019** Rating 93 To 2028 $35
The Oakdale Chardonnay 2019 Rating 93 To 2027 $45
Semillon 2019 Rating 92 To 2029 $23 SC ✪
Winemakers Selection Malbec 2018 Rating 90 To 2028 $65 SC

🍇 Auld Family Wines ★★★★

26 Sydenham Road, Norwood, SA 5067 **Region** Barossa Valley
T 0433 079 202 **www**.auldfamilywines.com **Open** Not
Winemaker Sam Auld, Simon Adams **Est.** 2018 **Dozens** 5000
The Barossa-based Auld family has been centrally involved with wine for six generations; the most recent, Jock and Sam Auld, have founded this new brand. They rightly celebrate their family history, starting with Patrick Auld, who arrived in SA in 1842, purchased 147ha of land at Magill adjacent to Captain Penfold, and began planting in '45, achieving fame for Auldana's wines. Second generation William Patrick Auld in '88 commenced a wine and spirit business in Adelaide named WP Auld and Sons. Today's wines are branded The William Patrick, Strawbridge and Wilberforce – the last not the name of a family member, but a horse. Patrick Auld was a member of the expedition led by John McDouall Stuart that crossed Australia from south to north for the first time. He (Auld) rode his horse – named Wilberforce – which lived for 37 years. Exports to Vietnam, Taiwan and China.

ΨΨΨΨΨ **Strawbridge Langhorne Creek Cabernet Sauvignon 2016** Hand-picked and sorted, open-fermented, 14 days on skins, vigorously pumped over at the peak of fermentation, matured in French hogsheads for 12 months. Langhorne Creek can be relied on to produce shiraz and cabernet sauvignon full of flavour but without strong tannins or alcohol impeding the course of the fruit's passage across and along the palate. Screwcap. 14% alc. **Rating** 94 **To** 2036 $42

ΨΨΨΨΨ **William Patrick Barossa Shiraz 2016** Rating 93 To 2036 $50
Wilberforce Eden Valley Riesling 2019 Rating 92 To 2039 $35
Strawbridge Barossa Shiraz 2017 Rating 90 To 2037 $42

Austin's Wines ★★★★★

870 Steiglitz Road, Sutherlands Creek, Vic 3331 **Region** Geelong
T (03) 5281 1799 **www**.austinswines.com.au **Open** By appt
Winemaker John Durham, Duncan Lowe **Est.** 1982 **Dozens** 25 000 **Vyds** 60ha
Pamela and Richard Austin have quietly built their business from a tiny base, and it has flourished. The vineyard has been progressively extended to over 60ha. Son Scott (with a varied but successful career outside the wine industry) took over management and ownership in 2008. The quality of the wines is admirable. Exports to the UK, Canada, Hong Kong, Japan and China.

♟♟♟♟♀ **6Ft6 Geelong Rose 2019** Perfumed with florals and spice; flavoured with red berries, watermelon and lemony acidity. The palate races along yet it has enough texture to keep one's interest well into the second pour. Screwcap. 13.5% alc. **Rating** 92 **To** 2021 $25 JF ✿

Moorabool Valley Geelong Shiraz 2018 This is not shy in coming forward with boisterous flavours. And yet it appeals. Reductive meaty notes injected into the damson plum and black cherries, Middle Eastern spices there too. Full-bodied, stern with vice-like tannins and very drying on the finish. Screwcap. 14.5% alc. **Rating** 91 **To** 2028 $45 JF

Moorabool Valley Geelong Riesling 2019 It has a certain charm with its lime/lemon zest and juiciness, all tangy and tart with freshly grated green apple. Best now. Screwcap. 11.5% alc. **Rating** 90 **To** 2026 $32 JF

Moorabool Valley Geelong Chardonnay 2018 Given the vintage conditions, this has come together well. Oak driving some of the palate weight and flavour. Savouriness comes through with grilled nuts and creamy, honeyed flavours tamed by the lemony acid line. Screwcap. 12.6% alc. **Rating** 90 **To** 2025 $45 JF

Moorabool Valley Geelong Pinot Noir 2018 An austere style with spiced rhubarb, humus and bracken to the fore. Tight, lean palate with the acidity pronounced, and so is the oak. Definitely needs a rich dish as a dining partner. Screwcap. 12.5% alc. **Rating** 90 **To** 2027 $45 JF

♟♟♟♟ **6Ft6 Geelong Sauvignon Blanc 2019 Rating** 89 **To** 2021 $25 JF

Aylesbury Estate   ★★★★☆

72 Ratcliffe Road, Ferguson, WA 6236 **Region** Geographe
T 0427 922 755 **www.aylesburyestate.com.au Open** Not
Winemaker Luke Eckersley, Damian Hutton **Est.** 2015 **Dozens** 4800 **Vyds** 13ha
Ryan and Narelle Gibbs (and family) are the sixth generation of the pioneering Gibbs family in the Ferguson Valley. When the family first arrived in 1883, they named the farm Aylesbury, after the town in England whence they came. For generations the family ran cattle on the 200ha property, but in 1998 it was decided to plant 4.2ha of cabernet sauvignon as a diversification of the business. Merlot (2.5ha) followed in 2001, and sauvignon blanc (1.6ha) in '04. In '08 Ryan and Narelle took over ownership and management of the business from Ryan's father, selling the grapes until '15, when the first Aylesbury Estate wines were made. Exports to China.

♟♟♟♟♀ **Q05 Gamay 2019** How can one not love this? A scream of mottled red berry fruits, anise and biar, crammed across gently scratchy tannins and bright acidity. Drink in large draughts! Screwcap. **Rating** 92 **To** 2022 $32 NG

The Pater Series Ferguson Valley Cabernet Sauvignon 2017 A bumptious, fully flared expression of Aussie cabernet: mint, sage, cassis, black olive and a smudge of vanillan oak. Full of flavour. Screwcap. **Rating** 92 **To** 2027 $50 NG

Q05 Arneis 2019 Nashi pear gelato and tangy, talcy acidity. Mid-weighted and vibrant. A delicious dry white wine, offering ample versatility at the table. Screwcap. **Rating** 91 **To** 2022 $32 NG

Waterfall Gully Ferguson Valley Cabernet Sauvignon 2018 Mint, cassis and dried sage splayed across a green bean tannic spectrum. A medium-bodied, savoury expression that is firmly of place. Screwcap. **Rating** 91 **To** 2025 $23 NG ✿

Waterfall Gully Ferguson Valley Merlot 2018 A conflation of mint, red and blackcurrant and gently astringent tannins, following 10 months in French oak (20% new). Screwcap. **Rating** 90 **To** 2023 $23 NG

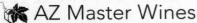 # AZ Master Wines   ★★★

2/16 Wareham Street, Springvale, Vic 3171 (postal) **Region** Various
T 0456 789 116 **www.azwines.com.au Open** Not
Winemaker Various Contract **Est.** 2006 **Dozens** 50 000

Awei Lin began sourcing wine in 2006, and exporting with Gapsted Wines in '08. The growth of the business led him to join forces with Zhiming Yi in '15. Derek Fitzgerald, Russell Burns and Richard Langford make the Barossa Valley wines (processed at Elderton, Cooper Burns and Lambert Estate). Oliver Crawford makes the Cabernet Sauvignon (a blend of Coonawarra and Limestone Coast grapes) and Peter Douglas makes the 100% Coonawarra wines at DiGiorgio, the barrels stored there and at Hollicks. Cellar doors are planned for all regions, the first in the Barossa Valley. Exports to China.

ΨΨΨΨ **005 Eden Valley Riesling 2019** Soft, light-bodied, but balanced. Easy consumption, very good for Chinese food. Screwcap. 11% alc. **Rating** 89 To 2022 $25

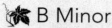 # B Minor

100 Long Gully Road, Healesville, Vic 3777 **Region** Victoria
T 0417 083 645 **www**.bminor.com.au **Open** Not
Winemaker Ben Haines **Est. Dozens** 10000
B Minor was originally a small, artisan wine brand created in 2010 by Ben Haines Wine focusing on producing fresh, creative wines specifically targeting on-premise and specialty retail venues in the US and Australia. In '19, Ben created a new business and a new life for B Minor, keeping the spirit of exploration and taking it to a far broader audience. B Minor challenges the notion that wine made on a large scale has to be industrial. The mission is to create an international brand delivering fresh, balanced and expressive wines of excellent value. Exports to the US and Asia.

ΨΨΨΨΨ **Grampians Shiraz 2018** From a single vineyard at Great Western planted with Best's old clone. Hand-picked, wild-fermented with 10% whole bunches/90% whole berries, matured for 18 months in French barriques (10% new). Good grapes, good vintage, good region, good winemaking. Ticks all the boxes. Screwcap. 14% alc. **Rating** 96 To 2038 $30 ✪

Great Western Cabernet Sauvignon 2018 Hand-picked from 3 vineyards, 33% partly crushed, 21 days on skins in total, matured for 14 months in French barriques (10% new). This is a very, very good cabernet, with pure blackcurrant cassis fruit held in the embrace of fine-spun tannins and a hint of oak. Bargain+. Screwcap. 14% alc. **Rating** 96 To 2038 $30 ✪

Yarra Valley Viognier 2019 Very early picking has worked well, with sufficient varietal expression and length without any of the oily phenolics that later picked viognier can suffer. Fermentation continued for 6 weeks, and no SO_2 was added until after a further 4 weeks, thereafter on gross lees without stirring for 8 months, not fined or filtered. Quite an effort. Screwcap. 11.3% alc. **Rating** 94 To 2024 $25 ✪

ΨΨΨΨΨ Victoria Shiraz 2017 **Rating** 90 To 2023 $15 ✪

BackVintage Wines

2/177 Sailors Bay Road, Northbridge, NSW 2063 **Region** Various
T (02) 9967 9880 **www**.backvintage.com.au **Open** Mon–Fri 9–5
Winemaker Julian Todd, Nick Bulleid MW, Mike Farmilo (Contract) **Est.** 2003
Dozens 10000
BackVintage Wines does not own vineyards or a winery. Says Nick Bulleid, 'We buy grapes, manage the fermentation and subsequent maturation. We also blend bulk wine sourced from some of the best winemakers throughout Australia.' The value for money offered by these wines is self-evident and quite remarkable.

ΨΨΨΨΨ **Old Vine Grenache Shiraz 2017** Old blocks of vines, including 60yo grenache, contributed to this 53/47% blend. Not bad for a $13 wine! An astounding level of complex winemaking, revealing itself in one smart and very tasty young wine. The emphasis is on the quality of the fruit, which reveals tangy raspberry, red plum and dark chocolate wrapped in a medium-bodied youngster with a deceptively long finish. Bravo! Screwcap. 14% alc. **Rating** 95 To 2032 JP ✪

ŶŶŶŶŶ **Eden Valley Shiraz 2017** Rating 92 To 2030 $20 JP ✪
Barossa Reserve Cabernet Shiraz 2016 Rating 90 $20 JP ✪

Bailey Wine Co ★★★★☆

PO Box 368, Penola, SA 5277 **Region** Coonawarra
T 0417 818 539 **www.**baileywineco.com **Open** Not
Winemaker Tim Bailey **Est.** 2015 **Dozens** 750
After two decades living and working in Coonawarra, Tim Bailey decided to take a busman's
holiday by establishing his own small wine business. Tim worked at Leconfield for 21 years,
and has also worked in the Sonoma Valley of California, travelling through the Napa Valley
as well as France. Tim has a simple philosophy: 'Find great growers in the regions and let the
vineyard shine through in the bottle.' Thus he sources Clare Valley riesling, Grampians shiraz,
Adelaide Hills chardonnay and Coonawarra cabernet sauvignon. Exports to China.

ŶŶŶŶŶ **Mount Gambier Pinot Noir Rose 2019** Picked early, pressed with a
Champagne cycle, the juice settled, then fermented with 2 different yeasts in used
hogsheads, matured for 4 months. Very pale pink. The flavours are of forest fruits/
wild strawberries with an overall citrussy acidity. Serious rose. Screwcap. 12% alc.
Rating 90 $22

Baileys of Glenrowan ★★★★★

779 Taminick Gap Road, Glenrowan, Vic 3675 **Region** Glenrowan
T (03) 5766 1600 **www.**baileysofglenrowan.com.au **Open** 7 days 10–5
Winemaker Paul Dahlenburg **Est.** 1870 **Dozens** 15 000 **Vyds** 144ha
Since 1998 the utterly committed Paul Dahlenburg has been in charge of Baileys and has
overseen an expansion in the vineyard and the construction of a 2000t capacity winery.
The cellar door has a heritage museum, winery viewing deck, contemporary art gallery and
landscaped grounds preserving much of the heritage value. Baileys has also picked up the pace
with its muscat and topaque, reintroducing the Winemakers Selection at the top of the tree,
while continuing the larger volume Founder series. In December 2017 Casella Family brands
purchased the brand and the Glenrowan property from TWE.

ŶŶŶŶŶ **Winemakers Selection Rare Old Muscat NV** A walnut-mahogany colour
with a ruby shimmer. Exotic Middle Eastern spices, fennel seeds and pomander
infuse molasses and brandy-soaked sultanas. It's complex and layered, yet bright,
unsullied and beguiling. 375ml. Vino-Lok. 17.5% alc. Rating 98 $75 JF ✪
Varley Organic Shiraz 2019 A selection of the best shiraz, and made only in
exceptional vintages, goes into the flagship wine honouring the company's first
winemaker, Varley Bailey. He'd be proud of this with its refinement and detail.
Perfectly composed with a joyous combination of red fruits, blueberries and a
sprinkling of spice, but it is the palate that sings: a fine acid line, svelte tannins and
length like no tomorrow. Screwcap. 14% alc. Rating 97 To 2042 $75 JF ✪
Winemakers Selection Rare Old Topaque NV From the moment this
is poured with its alluring rich mahogany and olive green hue, it's obvious
something special awaits. It doesn't disappoint. The richness of lime jellies and
butterscotch, chocolate and baking spices are all aligned perfectly, as is the palate.
Luscious, smooth as silk and beautifully composed. It is as fresh as it is complex.
Bravo. 375ml. Vino-Lok. 17.5% alc. Rating 97 $75 JF ✪

ŶŶŶŶŶ **1920s Block Shiraz 2019** While it has the excitement of youth, this is already
proving to be something special. It has plenty of class plus a core of succulent
fruit. Distinct lithe tannins are key to this, as is the pulsing line of acidity gliding
across a medium-weighted frame. Wow. Screwcap. 14.5% alc. Rating 96 To 2035
$45 JF ✪
VP 140 Touriga Nacional Tinta Barroca Tinta Cao 2018 The focus is using
Portuguese varieties – touriga nacional, tinta barroca and tinta cao to craft this
vintage fortified. Precocious in its youth with a flush of dark purple fruit, wine

gum lollies and flecks of dry herbs. The spirit is integrated, tannins aplenty and the best years ahead of it. Screwcap. 18.2% alc. **Rating** 95 $30 JF ✪

Organic Shiraz 2019 What a turnaround from the '18 vintage — Baileys has backed off big time with extraction and oak to a more vibrant, even subtle, style. This is electrifying. Crunchy red fruit, spicy and tangy, medium-bodied with tensile tannins and an exuberance not seen before. Screwcap. 13.8% alc. **Rating** 95 **To** 2029 $27 JF ✪

1920s Block Shiraz 2017 Impressive from start to finish. Dark fruits, hint of fruitcake and loads of baking spices. It's ripe for sure but the glorious tannins, all velvety and plush, just skate on through the full-bodied palate. Screwcap. 15.5% alc. **Rating** 95 **To** 2030 $45 JF

Durif 2019 From the '19 vintage, all Baileys table wines are certified organic. It also represents a shift in the winemaking, just backing off a bit, allowing the fruit to shine more, as is the case here. Made with whole-berries in the ferment giving the wine such vibrancy. It's also spicy, juicy, medium-bodied with neatly pitched tannins and delicious. A durif to savour and drink. Screwcap. 13.5% alc. **Rating** 95 **To** 2028 $27 JF ✪

Organic Small Batch Series Nero d'Avola 2019 Text book. It's floral and flirty, juicy and tangy with vibrant cherry and pips. Raspberry-like acidity plus soft tannins of an Italian persuasion. Screwcap. 13.3% alc. **Rating** 95 **To** 2024 $20 JF ✪

Founder Series Classic Topaque NV This sings with youth and life, with a tangy lemon acidity keeping in check all the rich, gorgeous flavours. Think fruitcake, strong lapsang souchong tea, lime marmalade and more. Pleasingly sweet and seamless in its composure. Vino-Lok. 17% alc. **Rating** 95 $30 JF ✪

Founder Series Classic Muscat NV This is so heady and divine, it's possible to swoon in anticipation. A flight of fragrance from lavender, Mr Lincoln roses to raisins in toffee and Pontefract licorice. Acidity tempers the sweetness and results in an ethereal impression. Vino-Lok. 17% alc. **Rating** 95 $30 JF ✪

Shiraz 2017 Firmly in ripe and plush territory with a fair whack of oak, but it holds its own thanks to a core of briary fruit, licorice and poached plums dusted with cocoa. Full-bodied, cuddly with ample tannins and warming on the finish. A winter wine. Screwcap. 15.1% alc. **Rating** 94 **To** 2028 $27 JF ✪

🍷🍷🍷🍷🍷 **Organic Small Batch Series Rose 2019** **Rating** 93 **To** 2021 $20 JF ✪
Organic Small Batch Series Fiano 2019 **Rating** 90 **To** 2022 $20 JF ✪
Durif 2017 **Rating** 90 **To** 2027 $27 JF

Baillieu   ★★★☆

32 Tubbarubba Road, Merricks North, Vic 3926 **Region** Mornington Peninsula
T (03) 5989 7622 **www.**baillieuvineyard.com.au **Open** At Merricks General Wine Store
Winemaker Geraldine McFaul **Est.** 1999 **Dozens** 2400 **Vyds** 9.2ha
Charlie and Samantha Baillieu have re-established the former Foxwood Vineyard, growing chardonnay, viognier, pinot gris, pinot noir and shiraz. The north-facing vineyard is part of the 64ha Bulldog Run property owned by the Baillieus, and is immaculately maintained. The refurbished Merricks General Wine Store is a combined bistro/providore/cellar door.

🍷🍷🍷🍷🍷 **Mornington Peninsula Chardonnay 2018** Whole-bunch pressed, settled in tank, fermented in French barriques (20% new), 20% mlf. Attractive wine. A neat balance between fruit, oak and acidity. Peach, nectarine and grapefruit link seamlessly; the oak subliminal, the acidity balanced. Screwcap. 13.2% alc. **Rating** 92 **To** 2028 $35

🍷🍷🍷🍷 **Mornington Peninsula Pinot Noir 2018** **Rating** 89 **To** 2022 $40
Mornington Peninsula Vintage Brut 2017 **Rating** 89 $35

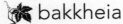 # bakkheia

 ★★★★★

2718 Ferguson Road, Lowden, WA 6240 **Region** Geographe
T (08) 9732 1394 **www.**bakkheia.com.au **Open** By appt
Winemaker Michael Edwards **Est.** 2006 **Dozens** 1000 **Vyds** 3ha

This is the retirement venture of Michael and Ilonka Edwards. Michael had 25 years as a clearance diver with the Australian Navy, and then pursued a career in the marine industry. Ilonka had a long-term involvement in the Vogue fashion/food/lifestyle magazines while based in Sydney. They found their way to the Preston Valley in the Geographe region of WA in 2005 and purchased a property that had a patch of cabernet sauvignon planted in 1999. They now have 3ha of grenache, mourvedre, graciano, tempranillo, cabernet sauvignon, shiraz and malbec; purchasing chardonnay and sauvignon blanc from a neighbour. They have an unusual approach to marketing, starting with the winery name linked to the Roman words for Bacchus and bacchanalian frenzies induced by wine, lots of wine. When the time came to make and sell wine, rather than sell through liquor stores, they set up a membership system. Exports to Singapore.

ΨΨΨΨΨ **The Wonderful Miss Gerry Preston Valley Grenache 2018** A gorgeous grenache (aged 6 months in used French oak) that retains its juicy fruit vibrancy, yet stays firmly in savoury territory. Heady with wafts of musk, mint/menthol, licorice and an alluring aroma of damp soil after a morning summer rain. A core of sweet fruit across the medium-bodied palate is tempered by textured tannins. Screwcap. 14.3% alc. **Rating** 95 **To** 2025 $32 JF ✪

Tripartite Preston Valley Grenache Shiraz Mourvedre 2018 A split between 50% grenache, 33% shiraz and 17% mourvedre, and a very successful one at that. Excellent dark ruby hue. Some meaty reduction mingling with dark fruit, licorice and warm earth – a promise of a savoury infused wine, not a fruit bomb. Full-bodied, well pitched tannins and persistence. What a bargain. Screwcap. 14.5% alc. **Rating** 95 **To** 2029 $25 JF ✪

Priapus Preston Valley Cabernet Sauvignon 2016 An elegant cabernet sauvignon that has the right amount of cassis, blueberry and leafy freshness stamping it varietally. Seamlessly composed, medium-bodied and refined. Savoury, earthy tones plus exotic spices, soy sauce and licorice, and lovely, grainy tannins. Drinking superbly now. Won the trophy for best cabernet at the Geographe Wine Show '18. Screwcap. 14.3% alc. **Rating** 95 **To** 2026 $32 JF ✪

Aequitas Preston Valley Tempranillo 2018 Geographe is the unsung hero of varieties such as tempranillo. Of course, dedication is needed for a result such as this. A core of perfect fruit, doused in baking spices, a touch of mint and jamon-like small goods. Medium-weighted with stealthy tannins and a minerally led acid line. Super wine. Screwcap. 14.3% alc. **Rating** 95 **To** 2028 $26 JF ✪

United & Undaunted Preston Valley Mourvedre 2017 A balanced amalgam of gravelly yet ripe tannins, tangy and tart red fruits, baking spices, prosciutto, boot polish and dried herbs. Such a satisfying drink but alas, just 60 dozen produced. Screwcap. 14.2% alc. **Rating** 95 **To** 2023 $26 JF ✪

ΨΨΨΨΨ **Chardonnay 2018 Rating** 93 **To** 2024 $26 JF ✪
Reserve Chardonnay 2018 Rating 92 **To** 2024 $32 JF
H&B Reserva Single Vineyard Garnacha 2018 Rating 92 **To** 2026 $35 JF
Cojones Muy Grandes Rose 2019 Rating 90 **To** 2021 $20 JF ✪
Cojones Muy Grandes Rose 2018 Rating 90 **To** 2020 $20 JF ✪
Tripartite Grenache Shiraz Mourvedre 2016 Rating 90 **To** 2026 $25 JF

Balgownie Estate

★★★★★

Hermitage Road, Maiden Gully, Vic 3551 **Region** Bendigo
T (03) 5449 6222 **www.**balgownieestatewines.com.au **Open** 7 days 11–5
Winemaker Tony Winspear **Est.** 1969 **Dozens** 10 000 **Vyds** 35.28ha

Balgownie Estate is the senior citizen of Bendigo, its original vineyard plantings now 50 years old. The estate also has a cellar door in the Yarra Valley (Yarra Glen), where operations fit in neatly with the Bendigo wines. Balgownie has the largest vineyard-based resort in the Yarra Valley, with over 65 rooms and a limited number of spa suites. In April 2016 Chinese Interactive China Cultural Technology Investments purchased the Balgownie Bendigo and Yarra Valley operations for $29 million. Exports to the UK, the US, Canada, Fiji, Hong Kong, Singapore, China and NZ.

ΨΨΨΨΨ **Museum Release Bendigo Chardonnay 2012** The very cool season provided perfect fruit. Whole-bunch pressed, matured for 11 months on lees with batonnage in French barriques (30% new). Six gold medals and a trophy. It's vibrantly fresh and delicious with white peach and white nectarine on the long, lingering palate. Screwcap. 13.5% alc. **Rating** 96 **To** 2025 $85
Rock Block Bendigo Shiraz 2017 East–west row orientation. It is true that it has a firmer structure and texture, but not to excess, the tannins not harsh or abrasive. All up, this is my preferred wine in the shiraz lineup. Screwcap. 14.5% alc. **Rating** 96 **To** 2037 $65 ✪
Centre Block Bendigo Shiraz 2017 Vines planted '69. Hand-picked, 20% whole bunch, 25% whole berry, 1.5% viognier 'addition'; open-fermented, 24 days on skins, 12 months in French oak (30% new). A good wine, worthy of the label of bygone years. Screwcap. 14% alc. **Rating** 95 **To** 2037 $65
Railway Block Bendigo Shiraz 2017 Hand-picked, 30% whole bunch, 30% whole berry, 2% viognier; open-fermented, matured for 12 months in French oak (25% new). This has a certain get-up-and-go mouthfeel, although the flavour wheel doesn't change much. Screwcap. 14% alc. **Rating** 95 **To** 2032 $65
Bendigo Cabernet Sauvignon 2017 40yo vines. Open-fermented, 18 days on skins, matured for 18 months in French barriques (30% new). The cool vintage gave the wine effortless and pure cabernet structure, the length further aided by firm tannins. Will be very long-lived. Screwcap. 14% alc. **Rating** 95 **To** 2047 $45

ΨΨΨΨΨ **Yarra Valley Chardonnay 2018 Rating** 91 $45
Black Label Bendigo Shiraz 2018 Rating 90 **To** 2028 $25

Ballandean Estate Wines   ★★★★

Sundown Road, Ballandean, Qld 4382 **Region** Granite Belt
T (07) 4684 1226 **www.**ballandeanestate.com **Open** 7 days 9–5
Winemaker Dylan Rhymer, Angelo Puglisi **Est.** 1970 **Dozens** 12 000 **Vyds** 34.2ha
A rock of ages in the Granite Belt, owned by the ever-cheerful and charming Angelo Puglisi and wife Mary. Mary has introduced a gourmet food gallery at the cellar door, featuring foods produced by local food artisans as well as Greedy Me gourmet products made by Mary herself. Ballandean Estate can't always escape the unpredictable climate of the Granite Belt. Exports to Singapore, Taiwan and China.

ΨΨΨΨΨ **Opera Block Granite Belt Shiraz 2017** Estate-grown, hand-picked. Said to be whole-bunch pressed which is, of course, wrong; matured for 14 months in used French oak. The wine is brightly coloured and fresh, with red fruits to the fore on the medium-bodied palate. ProCork. 13.8% alc. **Rating** 92 **To** 2027 $32
Granite Belt Malvasia 2019 Succeeds brilliantly. Screwcap. 12% alc. **Rating** 90 **To** 2022 $30
Granite Belt Sinatlis 2017 A saperavi/durif blend, matured in used French oak for 14 months; part of a Strange Bird promotion started years ago. Given the alcohol and the varieties, it's amazing that this is medium-bodied. ProCork. 15.4% alc. **Rating** 90 **To** 2027 $42
Granite Belt Nebbiolo 2017 Has almost none of the fearsome tannins and acidity for which nebbiolo is best known. The colour is light and still primary red – no tawny hints at all. Will match any Italian dish. ProCork. 12.4% alc. **Rating** 90 **To** 2027 $42

Ballycroft Vineyard & Cellars

1 Adelaide Road, Greenock, SA 5360 **Region** Barossa Valley
T 0488 638 488 **www**.ballycroft.com **Open By** appt 7 days 11–4
Winemaker Joseph Evans **Est.** 2005 **Dozens** 600 **Vyds** 4ha

This micro-business is owned by Joseph and Sue Evans. Joe's life on the land started in 1984; he later obtained a viticulture degree from Roseworthy. Between '92 and '99 he worked in various capacities at Rockford Wines, and then at Greenock Creek Wines. Joe and Sue are a two-person band, so would-be visitors to the cellar door would be wise to make an appointment for a personal tasting with one of them. Groups of up to eight people are welcome.

🍷🍷🍷🍷🍷 **Small Berry New French Oak Langhorne Creek Cabernet Sauvignon 2016** A prodigiously rich and intoxicating wine, literally and metaphorically. Comprised largely of pressings, this is a svelte ride of piercing blackcurrant flavours. The oak is but an echo, buried in the morass. A smooth sheath of cocoa, vanilla, graphite and black plum, splayed across milk chocolate tannins that melt while drinking. A smooth operator with little shame but plenty of cheek and glory. Cork. 15.1% alc. **Rating** 97 **To** 2034 $99 NG ✪

🍷🍷🍷🍷🍷 **Small Berry French Oak Greenock Barossa Valley Shiraz 2017** This corpulent red was aged in shaved older French wood for 28 months. The result is bold and sumptuous. The cedar oak tannins serve as a welcome guide to a gushing stream of blue to dark fruit references, lilac, anise, bitter chocolate and mace. This is inimitably Barossa. As avuncular and warming, as it is polished and contemporary. Screwcap. 14.9% alc. **Rating** 95 **To** 2032 $49 NG

Small Berry Greenock Barossa Valley Durif 2017 Durif can pack a wallop of flavour meshed to firm, implacable tannins. Their management often makes or breaks a wine, particularly when crafted as a full-bodied expression. Here, deft extraction, the choice of oak and length of elevage (28 months in shaved American) proves a winning approach. Burly and firm, sure. But suave, classy and long; the persistence of blueberry, violet and crushed rock scents, compelling. A delicious wine. Screwcap. 15.2% alc. **Rating** 95 **To** 2025 $39 NG

Small Berry American Oak Greenock Barossa Valley Shiraz 2017 A stylistic approach, syncing with the vanilla-coconut brittle scents of the wood. Otherwise, a cavalcade of black fruit allusions, licorice blackstrap, smoked meat and five-spice. Dense and thick, a bourbon riff across the finish. Over-the-top for some, sheer hedonistic delight for others. Screwcap. 15.6% alc. **Rating** 94 **To** 2029 $49 NG

🍷🍷🍷🍷🍷 **Small Berry Langhorne Creek Montepulciano 2019 Rating** 92 **To** 2023 $25 NG ✪

Small Berry Barossa Valley Mataro 2018 Rating 91 **To** 2028 $35 NG

Balnaves of Coonawarra

15517 Riddoch Highway, Coonawarra, SA 5263 **Region** Coonawarra
T (08) 8737 2946 **www**.balnaves.com.au **Open** Mon–Fri 9–5, w'ends 11.30–4.30
Winemaker Pete Bissell **Est.** 1975 **Dozens** 10 000 **Vyds** 74.33ha

Grapegrower, viticultural consultant and vigneron, Doug Balnaves has over 70ha of high quality estate vineyards. The wines are invariably excellent, often outstanding; notable for their supple mouthfeel, varietal integrity, balance and length – the tannins are always fine and ripe, the oak subtle and perfectly integrated. Coonawarra at its best. Exports to the UK, the US, Canada, Indonesia, South Korea and China.

🍷🍷🍷🍷🍷 **Cabernet Merlot 2017** A smooth outcome courtesy of nicely textural merlot fruit boasting the prettiest florals. Strikingly dense purple-garnet hue. Bright juniper berry, cassis notes with the aforementioned roses, violets, potpourri. Melds nicely on the palate with tight-grained oak and highlights of garden mint. Screwcap. 14% alc. **Rating** 95 **To** 2038 JP

The Blend 2016 60% merlot, 34% cabernet sauvignon, 5% cabernet franc and 1% petit verdot. Changes under the bonnet have made one of Australia's best value Bordeaux blends even better with new clones of cabernet and merlot. Perfectly balanced and weighted cassis, bay leaf, blackcurrant and cedary oak all playing a role. Screwcap. 14.5% alc. Rating 95 To 2036 $20 ✪

Cabernet Sauvignon 2017 A sleek little number by any reckoning, with plenty of character. Lifted aromas with Coonawarra regional mint, cassis, black cherry. Smooth entry all the way. Love the heightened spice content and bitter chocolate. Grainy tannins to close, touch of leather. It's got the lot. Screwcap. 14% alc. Rating 95 To 2041 JP

ŸŸŸŸŸ **Entav Clone Cabernet Sauvignon Merlot Petit Verdot 2018** Rating 93 To 2028 JP
The Blend 2017 Rating 93 To 2027 $20 JP ✪
Chardonnay 2018 Rating 92 To 2030 $35 JP
Shiraz 2018 Rating 90 To 2026 JP

Bangor Estate   ★★★★

20 Blackman Bay Road, Dunalley, Tas 7177 **Region** Southern Tasmania
T 0418 594 362 **www.bangorshed.com.au Open** 7 days 10–5
Winemaker Tasmanian Vintners **Est.** 2010 **Dozens** 2000 **Vyds** 4ha
Bangor Estate's story starts in 1830, when John Dunbabin, convicted of horse stealing, was transported to Van Diemen's Land. Through sheer hard work he earned his freedom and bought his own land, paving the way for five generations of farming at Bangor. Today it is a 6200ha property on the Forestier Peninsula in one of the most southerly parts of Tasmania, with 5100ha of native forest, grasslands and wetlands, and 35km of coastline. Both Matt and Vanessa Dunbabin have PhDs in plant ecology and plant nutrition, putting beyond question their ability to protect this wonderful property – until 2000ha were burnt in the 2013 bushfires that devastated their local town of Dunalley and surrounding areas. They established a cellar door in partnership with Tom and Alice Gray from Fulham Acquaculture, also badly affected by the fires. Hence the Bangor Vineyard Shed was born. The vineyard is planted to 1.5ha each of pinot noir and pinot gris, and 1ha of chardonnay. A host of very well made and sensibly prices wines mark a welcome return to the *Companion*.

ŸŸŸŸŸ **Abel Tasman Pinot Noir 2017** Fragrant, spice-laden pinot noir of poise and charm. Good territory here. Fresh and stewed cherries, garden herbs, ripe fruit but with tang and undergrowth. Smoky tannin curls through the finish. Beautifully balanced and finished. Screwcap. 13.7% alc. Rating 95 To 2028 $48 CM
1830 Chardonnay 2017 It carries its usual (generous) load of varietal flavour but this release is also flinty, spicy and complex. It's a very good wine. Lively, well fruited and sweet-oaked but with more than a little X-factor. Screwcap. 12% alc. Rating 94 To 2026 $40 CM
Jimmy's Hill Pinot Gris 2018 It bristles with flavour and at all points along the palate, it feels convincing. Stone fruit, nashi pear, apple and mineral characters come sparked with spice. More than a few fireworks. Screwcap. 14.2% alc. Rating 94 To 2022 $32 CM
Abel Tasman Pinot Noir 2016 A wine of undergrowth, mouthfeel, shape and length. It feels unforced, but there's an array of flavours on offer here and the inherent structure to have it feeling neat and controlled. Good growing and making on display. Every time you pick up the glass you notice something different. Screwcap. 13.7% alc. Rating 94 To 2028 $48 CM

ŸŸŸŸŸ **Lagoon Bay Riesling 2018** Rating 93 To 2027 $36 CM
Jimmy's Hill Reserve Pinot Gris 2018 Rating 93 To 2022 $45 CM
Tasmania Riesling 2019 Rating 92 To 2026 CM
Jimmy's Hill Pinot Gris 2019 Rating 92 To 2023 $32 CM
Maria Rose 2019 Rating 92 To 2022 $36 CM
Methode Traditionelle Vintage 2015 Rating 92 $48 CM

1830 Chardonnay 2018 Rating 91 To 2025 $40 CM
Captain Spotswood Tasmania Pinot Noir 2018 Rating 91 To 2025
$34 CM

Banks Road ★★★★★

600 Banks Road, Marcus Hill, Vic 3222 **Region** Geelong
T (03) 5258 3777 **www.**banksroad.com.au **Open** Fri–Sun 11–5
Winemaker William Derham **Est.** 2001 **Dozens** 2000 **Vyds** 6ha
Banks Road is a family-owned and operated winery on the Bellarine Peninsula. The estate vineyard is adopting biodynamic principles, eliminating the use of insecticides and moving to eliminate the use of all chemicals on the land. The winery not only processes the Banks Road grapes, but also makes wine for other small producers in the area. All in all, an impressive business.

ΨΨΨΨΨ Will's Selection Bellarine Peninsula Pinot Noir 2017 A best barrel selection with an extra 6 months maturation in French oak (50% new). Riddled with spices and fruits on the vibrant bouquet and extra long palate; the '17 vintage also in on the act. Screwcap. 13.6% alc. Rating 97 To 2030 $50 ✪
Soho Road Vineyard Barrique Eight Bellarine Peninsula Pinot Noir 2017 From the oldest vines on the Peninsula, planted '78. A first selection ex ferment to new French oak, then a further selection of a second barrel. Excellent colour. The most powerful and complex of the 4 Banks Road pinots, its sails full of new and secondary flavours. Screwcap. 13.2% alc. Rating 97 To 2034 $75 ✪

ΨΨΨΨΨ Soho Road Vineyard Bellarine Peninsula Pinot Noir 2017 40yo vines, hand-picked; 20% whole bunch, 80% whole berry, 12 months in French oak. A comparatively pure and elegant bouquet is promptly followed by a feisty palate merging plum/cherry fruit with spicy/savoury nuances and a lingering finish. Screwcap. 13.2% alc. Rating 96 To 2032 $40 ✪
Soho Road Vineyard Bellarine Peninsula Chardonnay 2017 40yo estate vines, hand-picked; wild-fermented in French oak (35% new), 35% mlf, matured for 18 months. The '17 vintage speaks loud and clear, grapefruit holding hands with white peach and apple. Long finish and very good balance. Screwcap. 13.2% alc. Rating 95 To 2027 $40
Bellarine Pinot Noir 2017 MV6, 114 and 115 clones; 10–15% whole bunch, 20% cold soak, wild ferment, 10 months in French oak (30% new). Holding its hue well. A cocktail of exotic spices on the bouquet, the palate focusing more on purple fruits, but it's the juicy/slippery fruit that give the wine its birthmark. Screwcap. 13.6% alc. Rating 95 To 2032 $35 ✪
CS Wine Co Heathcote Shiraz 2018 Selectiv'-harvested, 16 days on skins, 30% new oak. Deep crimson-purple; flush with velvety dark berry fruits, soft tannins and satsuma plum. Mouthfeel and length are its raison d'être. Screwcap. 13.5% alc. Rating 94 To 2038 $28 ✪

ΨΨΨΨ♀ Bellarine Chardonnay 2016 Rating 93 To 2024 $33
Bellarine Shiraz 2017 Rating 93 To 2027 $33
Rice Vineyard Grampians Shiraz 2015 Rating 93 To 2030 $30
Bellarine Sauvignon Blanc 2018 Rating 91 To 2022 $24

Bannockburn Vineyards ★★★★★

92 Kelly Lane, Bannockburn, Vic 3331 (postal) **Region** Geelong
T (03) 5281 1363 **www.**bannockburnvineyards.com **Open** By appt
Winemaker Matthew Holmes **Est.** 1974 **Dozens** 6000 **Vyds** 21.2ha
The late Stuart Hooper had a deep love for the wines of Burgundy, and was able to drink the best. When he established Bannockburn, it was inevitable that pinot noir and chardonnay would form the major part of the plantings, with lesser amounts of riesling, sauvignon blanc, cabernet sauvignon, shiraz and merlot. Bannockburn is still owned by members of the Hooper

family, who continue to respect Stuart's strong belief in making wines that reflect the flavours of the vineyard. Exports to Canada, Singapore, Japan, Hong Kong and China.

♟♟♟♟♟ **Serre 2017** Close-planted MV6 planted in '84 and '86. Vinified separately: one batch whole bunch; the other destemmed, pressed to French hogsheads (20% new), matured for 12 months before blending. The perfumed bouquet of red berries, rose petals and spice leads into a wondrously fine, elegant and long palate. It is the product of many things, including the great southern Victorian '17 vintage. Screwcap. 12.5% alc. **Rating** 99 **To** 2037 $97 ❂

♟♟♟♟♟ **Geelong Chardonnay 2018** Good winter/spring rain, then dry through summer. Whole-bunch pressed, wild-fermented in French barriques and puncheons (20% new). Beautiful length and shape to the blend of white peach and grapefruit flavours. Screwcap. 13.5% alc. **Rating** 96 **To** 2028 $67 ❂
Geelong Pinot Noir 2018 Predominantly clone MV6, plus 114, 115 and 777 planted '76, '97 and '07. The batches were wild-fermented with 20% whole bunches, matured for 12 months in French hogsheads (30% new). Plum, cherry, bright acidity and fine, persistent tannins will bring pleasure at any time along the development trail. Screwcap. 13% alc. **Rating** 96 **To** 2033 $67 ❂
Geelong Shiraz 2016 Single PT clone planted 1990. Perfect weather in 2016. Wild-fermented on skins for 2 weeks with 20% whole bunches, pressed to French hogsheads (20% new), bottled Aug '17. Harmonious, elegant, yet also complex; olive, pepper and plum. Screwcap. 13% alc. **Rating** 95 **To** 2031 $46

♟♟♟♟♀ **Geelong Riesling 2019 Rating** 93 **To** 2034 $32

Barmah Park Wines   ★★★☆

945 Moorooduc Road, Moorooduc, Vic 3933 **Region** Mornington Peninsula
T (03) 5978 8049 **www.**barmahparkwines.com.au **Open** Wed–Sun 10–5
Winemaker Richard McIntyre, Jeremy Magyar, Han Tao Lau **Est.** 2000 **Dozens** 5000
Vyds 2.75ha
Barmah Park has plantings of pinot gris and pinot noir (using clones MV6 and G5V15), the first wines made in 2003. The restaurant overlooks the vines and offers breakfast and lunch, as well as dinner on Friday and Saturday evenings. Exports to Asia.

♟♟♟♟♀ **Cape Schanck Reserve Heathcote Shiraz 2018** From a 30yo vineyard; aged for a minimum of 12 months in new and older French and American oak. Shows a more light-weighted side of Heathcote shiraz. Regional earthiness comes through, and the red berry fruit is ripe, but the palate is soft and the tannin quite gentle. Cork. 14.3% alc. **Rating** 91 **To** 2030 $60 SC

♟♟♟♟ **Cape Schanck Mornington Chardonnay 2016 Rating** 89 **To** 2023 $50 SC

Barnyard1978   ★★★★

12 Canal Rocks Road, Yallingup, WA 6282 **Region** Margaret River
T (08) 9755 2548 **www.**barnyard1978.com.au **Open** 7 days 10.30–5
Winemaker Todd Payne **Est.** 1978 **Dozens** 1250 **Vyds** 4ha
The then Sienna Estate made the first plantings in 1978, but under the new ownership of Raminta and Egidijus Rusilas, a five-year restoration program of the somewhat neglected vineyard, plus new plantings, has paid dividends. So, too, has the opening of a restaurant with two separate tasting decks for different times of day – winner of an award by the Master Builders Association of Western Australia for its low environmental impact construction.

♟♟♟♟♀ **Margaret River Sauvignon Blanc Semillon 2018** 52% sauvignon, 40% semillon and a splash of chardonnay, presumably for a bit of mouthfeel. Hand-picked at this price. Spicy herbs like galangal and lemongrass; tonic, talc and a blazing riff of gooseberry. This hits all the right notes. Some barrel influence toning and conferring a whiff of complexity. Screwcap. **Rating** 90 **To** 2022 $24 NG

Margaret River Chardonnay 2018 The stamp of the Gingin clone and its redolent notes of peaches and cream are apparent. Mid-weighted, nicely layered by quality oak (40% new; 7 months) and a chord of saline acidity. Offers sturdy value. Screwcap. **Rating** 90 **To** 2024 $30 NG

♟♟♟♟ **Aged Release Margaret River Cabernet Sauvignon Cabernet Franc 2014** Rating 89 To 2022 $28 NG

Barossa Boy Wines ★★★★

161 Murray Street, Tanunda, SA 5382 **Region** Barossa Valley
T (08) 8563 7550 **www.**barossaboywines.com.au **Open** Mon–Fri 10–4, Sat 10–1
Winemaker Trent Burge **Est.** 2016 **Dozens** 3500
Sixth generation Barossan, Trent Burge is the son of Grant and Helen Burge, and a self-styled country boy who liked nothing better than exploring the family's 356ha of vineyards spread across the Barossa on his motorbike. Cricket intervened, taking him to England on a cricket club program each English summer, returning to Australia each English winter to work as a cellar hand and earn enough to sustain himself for the following six months. The endless summers ceased in 2006 when he joined the Grant Burge wine business full-time, learning every facet of winemaking and marketing. In February '16 Accolade acquired the Grant Burge business, making it inevitable that Trent would strike out on his own. The slick website, the high quality labelling and packaging of his Barossa Boy Wines bear witness to his experience in marketing. He says his grapes come from vineyards in special sites across the Barossa and Eden valleys, and it's a fair bet the family vineyards play a large role in that. In '17 he and wife Jessica welcomed their first child, the seventh generation now in place. Exports to the UK.

♟♟♟♟♟ **Lifeblood Shiraz 2017** Cedary, mocha characters are prominent on the bouquet with dark plummy fruit sitting in the background and earthy regional characters coming through. Depth and intensity of flavour are developing on the palate, but the tannin is a challenge at present. Diam. 14% alc. **Rating** 93 **To** 2032 $80 SC
Cheeky Tilly Riesling 2019 The back label discloses Eden Valley as the region, that origin underlined by Meyer lemon flavours and bright acidity. Screwcap. 12% alc. **Rating** 92 **To** 2030 $30
Double Trouble Shiraz Cabernet Sauvignon 2017 Raspberry licorice comes to mind as I smell this wine, and the red-fruited theme continues on the bouquet and palate, with both sweet and woody spice notes in the mix. It's medium-bodied and quite approachable; ripe but not jammy, and the tannin is really only obvious on the finish. Screwcap. 14% alc. **Rating** 90 **To** 2025 $30 SC

♟♟♟♟ **Little Tacker Grenache Shiraz Mataro 2017** Rating 89 To 2023 $30 SC

Barrgowan Vineyard ★★★★★

30 Pax Parade, Curlewis, Vic 3222 **Region** Geelong
T (03) 5250 3861 **www.**barrgowanvineyard.com.au **Open** By appt
Winemaker Dick Simonsen **Est.** 1998 **Dozens** 150 **Vyds** 0.5ha
Dick and Dib (Elizabeth) Simonsen began planting their shiraz (with five clones) in 1994, intending to make wine for their own consumption. With all clones in full production, the Simonsens make a maximum of 200 dozen and accordingly release small quantities of shiraz, which sell out quickly. The vines are hand-pruned, the grapes hand-picked, the must basket-pressed, and all wine movements are by gravity. The quality is exemplary.

♟♟♟♟♟ **Simonsens Bellarine Peninsula Shiraz 2018** A pleasant enough mid-weight red with cool-climate accents of violet, iodine and blueberry given tension by some peaty reduction. Plenty of mid-palate, but not quite the drive of freshness to provide the length. Cork. **Rating** 90 **To** 2023 $35 NG

Barringwood

60 Gillams Road, Lower Barrington, Tas 7306 **Region** Northern Tasmania
T 0416 017 475 **www.**barringwood.com.au **Open** Not
Winemaker Josef Chromy Wines (Jeremy Dineen) **Est.** 1993 **Dozens** 3000 **Vyds** 5ha
Barringwood has been producing elegant wines from the ultra-cool climate of northwest
Tasmania for over 20 years, the vines planted in 1993. The vineyard is perched on a steep
north-facing slope (overlooking the Don valley across to Bass Strait), with one of the longest
growing seasons in Tasmania allowing the grapes time to develop complexity while retaining
acidity. Vanessa and Neil Bagot were captivated by the property and purchased Barringwood
in 2012. They have developed two new vineyards at Cranbrook and Evandale, with further
plantings planned.

ŶŶŶŶŶ Chardonnay 2018 Hand-picked, whole-bunch pressed direct to used French
      barriques, only free-run 500l/t used, wild-fermented, matured for 10 months with
      stirring (no mlf). Takes off like an express train as it races across and along the
      palate. Screwcap. 13.5% alc. **Rating** 95 **To** 2026 $36
      Mill Block Pinot Noir 2017 Clones 114, 155, D5V12 and 777; wild-fermented
      with 15% whole bunches, matured in French oak (20% new) for 9 months. The
      impact of the whole bunches, superior fruit and the length all come to the cause
      of the wine, as does its terroir. Screwcap. 12.5% alc. **Rating** 95 **To** 2023 $60

ŶŶŶŶŶ Classic Cuvee 2016 **Rating** 93 $48
      Pinot Gris 2019 **Rating** 92 **To** 2025 $34
      Methode Traditionelle Cuvee NV **Rating** 92 $32

Barristers Block

141 Onkaparinga Valley Road, Woodside, SA 5244 **Region** Adelaide Hills
T (08) 8389 7706 **www.**barristersblock.com.au **Open** 7 days 10.30–5
Winemaker Anthony Pearce, Peter Leske **Est.** 2004 **Dozens** 7000 **Vyds** 18.5ha
Owner Jan Siemelink-Allen has over 20 years in the industry, first as a grapegrower of 10ha
of cabernet sauvignon and shiraz in Wrattonbully, then as a wine producer from that region.
In 2006 she and her family purchased an 8ha vineyard planted to sauvignon blanc and pinot
noir near Woodside in the Adelaide Hills. Exports to the UK, Germany, Vietnam, Malaysia,
South Korea, Hong Kong, Singapore and China.

ŶŶŶŶŶ Limited Release Wrattonbully Cabernet Sauvignon 2017 Estate-grown,
      hand-picked, matured for 18 months in French hogsheads. Wrattonbully at its best:
      silky smooth and supple; cassis fruit, almost juicy. Screwcap. 13.8% alc. **Rating** 94
      To 2030 $34

ŶŶŶŶŶ Limited Release Aston Adelaide Hills Fiano 2019 **Rating** 92 **To** 2022 $27
      JP Wrattonbully Shiraz 2016 **Rating** 92 **To** 2029 $89
      Limited Release The Bully Wrattonbully Shiraz 2017 **Rating** 90 **To** 2023 $34

Barton Jones Wines

39 Upper Capel Road, Donnybrook, WA 6239 **Region** Geographe
T 0409 831 926 **www.**bartonjoneswines.com.au **Open** W'ends 11–4
Winemaker Contract **Est.** 1978 **Dozens** 2000 **Vyds** 3ha
Barton Jones has 3ha of semillon, chenin blanc, shiraz and cabernet sauvignon from 1978 – the
vines are some of the oldest in the region. The vineyard and cellar door are on gentle north-
facing slopes, with extensive views over the Donnybrook area.

ŶŶŶŶŶ The Shilly Shally Chenin Blanc 2016 Hand-picked after severe crop thinning,
      fermented in used French oak, matured for 9 months. The twitch of acidity on
      the finish should underwrite the complexity that will develop over the years to
      come. Chenin is a dark horse. Screwcap. 12.8% alc. **Rating** 94 **To** 2026 $25 ❂

ŶŶŶŶŶ The Bigwig Margaret River Shiraz 2016 **Rating** 92 **To** 2031 $28
      The Box Seat Semillon 2016 **Rating** 91 **To** 2027 $25

Barwang

Barwang Road, Young, NSW 2594 (postal) **Region** Hilltops
T (02) 9722 1200 **www**.mcwilliams.com.au **Open** Not
Winemaker Russell Cody, Andrew Higgins **Est.** 1969 **Dozens** NFP **Vyds** 100ha
Peter Robertson pioneered viticulture in the Young area when he planted vines in 1969 as part of a diversification program for his 400ha grazing property. When McWilliam's acquired Barwang in '89, the vineyard amounted to 13ha; today the plantings are 100ha. The label also takes in 100% Tumbarumba wines, as well as Hilltops/Tumbarumba blends. Exports to Asia.

🍷🍷🍷🍷🍷 **Hilltops Shiraz 2019** It's slight in that it doesn't have much volume but the most has been made of what's here. The red-berried fruit is supple, the tannin is fine, the texture bounces between juicy and silken and the overall balance is spot on. Screwcap. 14% alc. **Rating** 91 **To** 2025 CM

Barwon Ridge Wines ★★★★★

50 McMullans Road, Barrabool, Vic 3221 **Region** Geelong
T 0418 324 632 **www**.barwonridge.com.au **Open** W'ends, public hols & by appt
Winemaker Jack Rabbit Vineyard (Nyall Condon) **Est.** 1999 **Dozens** 900 **Vyds** 3.6ha
In 1999 Geoff and Joan Anson planted chardonnay, shiraz and marsanne at Barwon Ridge, the vines growing slowly (if at all) in the limestone soil. The vineyard nestles in the Barrabool Hills, just to the west of Geelong. Geoff and Joan focus on producing premium fruit; the vineyard is now planted to pinot noir, pinot meunier, shiraz, cabernet sauvignon, marsanne and chardonnay. The wines are made at Leura Park. The vineyard is part of the re-emergence of winemaking in the Barrabool Hills, after the area's first boom from the 1840s to the '80s. The well written website contains a wealth of information about the history of the region.

🍷🍷🍷🍷🍷 **Chardonnay 2017** Whole-bunch pressed to new and used French oak for wild fermentation and 7 months maturation. This is a high class chardonnay making light of the passage of 3 years. Pink grapefruit and white peach do the talking; lees stirring and mlf adding complexity. Screwcap. 13% alc. **Rating** 96 **To** 2032 $29 ✪
Shiraz 2017 Hand-picked, fermented with some whole bunches, plunged daily, matured for 18 months in French oak (25% new). Vibrant and medium-bodied, with a flavour wheel of red fruits seasoned by spice and pepper notes. Screwcap. 13.1% alc. **Rating** 95 **To** 2032 $38
Rose 2018 Shiraz pressed and removed from skins, fermented in used oak, crossflow-filtered. A very good rose with much more flavour than most, yet light on its feet with fresh cleansing acidity. Rose petals and spice fill the floral bouquet. Screwcap. 12.2% alc. **Rating** 94 **To** 2021 $25 ✪

🍷🍷🍷🍷🍷 **Marsanne 2017 Rating** 92 **To** 2027 $29
Fortified Shiraz 2017 Rating 90 $25

Basalt Wines ★★★★★

1131 Princes Highway, Killarney, Vic 3283 **Region** Henty
T 0429 682 251 **www**.basaltwines.com **Open** 7 days 10–5
Winemaker Scott Ireland **Est.** 2002 **Dozens** 800 **Vyds** 2.8ha
Shane and Ali Clancey have turned a former potato paddock into a small, but very successful, wine business. In 2002 Shane began planting a multi-clone pinot noir vineyard, plus a small planting of tempranillo. Basalt Wines' grape intake is supplemented by a Drumborg vineyard, including 0.4ha of 26yo MV6 pinot noir and, even more importantly, riesling of the highest quality. Shane is viticulturist, assistant winemaker, wholesaler and runs the cellar door, and Ali is involved in various parts of the business, including the small flock of babydoll sheep which graze next to the winery.

🍷🍷🍷🍷🍷 **Great Ocean Road Riesling 2019** It's a joyous riesling with purity as its bedrock and perfume laid on top. Red apples, limes and associated florals put on an utterly seductive display in the most uncomplicated of ways. Screwcap. 11.8% alc. **Rating** 94 **To** 2032 $29 CM ✪

The Bream King Tempranillo 2018 Sits firmly in the savoury camp with confidence. It's an undergrowthy tempranillo: twiggy, clovey, a little peppery, too. The fruit flavours are ripe but cool, forest berry territory, while cedar wood oak is modest but well applied. The overall set of this wine makes you think that it will mature handsomely. Screwcap. 13.4% alc. **Rating** 94 **To** 2030 $42 CM

Drumborg Chardonnay 2018 Rating 92 **To** 2028 $29 CM
Great Ocean Road Pinot Noir 2018 Rating 92 **To** 2026 $38 CM

Bass Phillip   ★★★★★

Tosch's Road, Leongatha South, Vic 3953 **Region** Gippsland
T (03) 5664 3341 **www.**bassphillip.com **Open** By appt
Winemaker Phillip Jones **Est.** 1979 **Dozens** 1500
Phillip Jones handcrafted tiny quantities of superlative pinot noir which, at its best, had no equal in Australia. Painstaking site selection, ultra-close vine spacing and the very, very cool climate of South Gippsland are the keys to the magic of Bass Phillip and its eerily Burgundian pinots. One of Australia's greatest small producers, they are heading down a new path after Jones announced that he sold the assets (winery, stock and 14ha of vineyards) to a syndicate led by Burgundian winemaker Jean-Marie Fourrier (who has known Jones for 14 years) and two Singaporeans who already have lucrative wine businesses. The price hasn't been disclosed, but Jones had set a hefty price tag for those who have previously thought it would be a nice business to own.

Reserve Pinot Noir 2017 Surely Australia's greatest maker of pinot noir. This comes from a single, small plot in the original vineyard, made in micro quantities only when the vintage is of appropriate quality. It is as supremely long as it is complex and supple. It will prosper for decades, revealing new facets. ProCork. 14.2% alc. **Rating** 99 **To** 2037 $675
Premium Pinot Noir 2017 This wine is all about the peacock's tail and the lingering aftertaste. The bouquet is perfumed and very complex, wandering from earth to shrub and tree with tangy herbal earthy flavours and aromas. On retasting, red fruits have made their appearance, the flavours lustrous and lingering. ProCork. 14.3% alc. **Rating** 98 **To** 2037 $240
Issan Vineyard Pinot Noir 2017 This vineyard was planted by Phillip Jones in '94 and has served its apprenticeship well; now all the indicia of mature vines. The bouquet is lush and complex with berries of earth and tree, tracing ribbons of flavours flowing comfortably past oak and tannins that would make a Burgundian smile. A star in the lineup. ProCork. 14.4% alc. **Rating** 98 **To** 2037 $90 ✪
Estate Pinot Noir 2017 Excellent colour, deep but clear. It signals the arrival of fragrant small berry fruits, from cherry to blackberry, the palate bringing the full suite of pinot aromas and flavours. If this were the top wine of the portfolio you would be wholly satisfied. ProCork. 14.5% alc. **Rating** 97 **To** 2032 $90

Crown Prince Pinot Noir 2017 One of the entry level wines in the portfolio, vinified under the influence of the moon, the planets and the earth. It is awesomely powerful and daunting. Earthy, savoury notes abound throughout, but it's the bouquet that draws you back again and again, echoed by the zesty, spice-ridden finish and aftertaste. ProCork. 14% alc. **Rating** 96 **To** 2032 $65 ✪
Bin 17K Backyard Pinot Noir 2017 Although the alcohol suggests otherwise, it has green/stemmy flavours that aren't attractive. Two hours later it is a very different story, suggesting double decanting – normally a blasphemy for pinot. ProCork. 14.6% alc. **Rating** 94 **To** 2027 $92
Gamay 2017 To everyone's surprise, Len Evans planted gamay at his house in the Hunter Valley. Despite the red volcanic soil, he found it impossible to do anything other than make a dry red wine of no great distinction. This is much more than that, although it does need more time to spread its wings. ProCork. 13.7% alc. **Rating** 94 **To** 2032 $55

Bass River Winery

1835 Dalyston Glen Forbes Road, Glen Forbes, Vic 3990 **Region** Gippsland
T (03) 5678 8252 **www.**bassriverwinery.com **Open** Thurs–Tues 9–5
Winemaker Pasquale Butera, Frank Butera **Est.** 1999 **Dozens** 1500 **Vyds** 4ha
The Butera family has established 1ha each of pinot noir and chardonnay and 2ha split equally to riesling, sauvignon blanc, pinot gris and merlot. Both the winemaking and viticulture are handled by the father and son team of Pasquale and Frank. The small production is principally sold through the cellar door, with some retailers and restaurants in the South Gippsland area. Exports to Singapore.

1835 Gippsland Pinot Noir 2018 Hand-picked, fermented with 80% whole berry/20% whole bunch, 20 days on skins, gravity fed to the underground cellar, matured for 11 months in French oak (20% new). Light but bright and clear colour. It's elegant and fresh, with red fruits and wisps of green/mint flavours. Can't fault the winemaking; the (minor) issue stems from the vineyard and ripeness. Screwcap. 13% alc. **Rating** 94 **To** 2028 $50

1835 Chardonnay 2018 Rating 92 **To** 2023 $40
1835 Vintage Brut Chardonnay Pinot Noir 2016 Rating 92 $40
1835 Iced Riesling 2017 Rating 92 $30
Single Vineyard Riesling 2019 Rating 90 **To** 2025 $25
Single Vineyard Sauvignon Blanc 2019 Rating 90 **To** 2022 $25
Single Vineyard Field Blend 2018 Rating 90 **To** 2021 $22

Battle of Bosworth ★★★★★

92 Gaffney Road, Willunga, SA 5172 **Region** McLaren Vale
T (08) 8556 2441 **www.**battleofbosworth.com.au **Open** 7 days 11–5
Winemaker Joch Bosworth **Est.** 1996 **Dozens** 15000 **Vyds** 80ha
Owned and run by Joch Bosworth (viticulture and winemaking) and partner Louise Hemsley-Smith (sales and marketing), this winery takes its name from the battle that ended the War of the Roses, fought on Bosworth Field in 1485. The vineyards were established in the early 1970s in the foothills of the Mt Lofty Ranges. The vines are fully certified A-grade organic. The label depicts the yellow soursob (*Oxalis pes-caprae*), whose growth habits make it an ideal weapon for battling weeds in organic viticulture. Shiraz, cabernet sauvignon and chardonnay account for 75% of the plantings. The Spring Seed Wine Co wines are made from estate vineyards. Exports to the UK, the US, Canada, Sweden, Norway, Belgium, Hong Kong and Japan.

Chanticleer McLaren Vale Shiraz 2017 No information supplied regarding winemaking, but this is an organic, single vineyard. The wine is polished yet refined in its own way. Savoury tannins have a velvety plushness, fruit really succulent and spicy, and the palate is full-bodied but not unwieldy. Screwcap. 14.5% alc. **Rating** 95 **To** 2030 $45 JF
Braden's McLaren Vale Shiraz 2017 Fabulous inky purple and the pleasure doesn't stop with its colour. The fruit in this is gorgeous – intense flavours infused with baking spices and clove/cedary oak. Yet it remains buoyant with almost sweet tannins. Impressive. Screwcap. 14.5% alc. **Rating** 95 **To** 2032 $45 JF

Puritan McLaren Vale Shiraz 2019 Rating 92 **To** 2022 $22 JF ✪
Heretic 2018 Rating 90 **To** 2025 $28 JF

Bay of Fires

40 Baxters Road, Pipers River, Tas 7252 **Region** Northern Tasmania
T (03) 6382 7622 **www.**bayoffireswines.com.au **Open** Mon–Fri 11–4, w'ends 10–4
Winemaker Penny Jones **Est.** 2001 **Dozens** NFP
Hardys purchased its first grapes from Tasmania in 1994 with the aim of further developing and refining its sparkling wines, a process that quickly gave birth to House of Arras (see separate entry). The next stage was the inclusion of various parcels of chardonnay from

Tasmania in the 1998 Eileen Hardy, then the development in 2001 of the Bay of Fires brand. Bay of Fires has had outstanding success with its table wines: pinot noir was obvious, the other wines typically of gold medal standard. Exports to the US, Asia and NZ.

ŸŸŸŸŸ Pinot Noir 2018 From the East Coast and Derwent Valley. Hand-picked, wild ferment, matured in French oak (29% new) from the best Burgundian coopers. This is a pinot I would happily fill my cellar with. It is only medium-bodied but it's gloriously long and elegant, the tannins superfine yet building the aftertaste. Screwcap. 13.5% alc. **Rating** 99 **To** 2030 $61 ❂
Chardonnay 2018 Clones I10V5, P58 and B124. Selectiv'-harvested, pressed, barrel-fermented (36% new), matured for 9 months. Tasmania is a happy hunting ground for first class chardonnay, marrying varietal flavour, finesse, length and great balance. White peach/grapefruit is all you need to know. Screwcap. 13.5% alc. **Rating** 97 **To** 2032 $58 ❂

ŸŸŸŸŸ Eddystone Point Pinot Gris 2019 Aromas of autumnal fruits coupled with some lightly phenolic, skinsy characters present a faithful representation of the variety on the bouquet; and the palate follows through with the flavours and mouthfeel to seal the deal. Obviously high quality fruit skilfully handled. Screwcap. 14% alc. **Rating** 94 **To** 2024 $32 SC

ŸŸŸŸŸ Eddystone Point Chardonnay 2018 **Rating** 93 **To** 2025 $32 SC
Eddystone Point Pinot Noir 2018 **Rating** 93 **To** 2025 $32 SC
Eddystone Point Sauvignon Blanc 2019 **Rating** 90 **To** 2022 $32 SC

Bay of Shoals Wines   ★★★★☆

49 Cordes Road, Kingscote, Kangaroo Island, SA 5223 **Region** Kangaroo Island
T (08) 8553 0289 **www.**bayofshoalswines.com.au **Open** 7 days 11–5
Winemaker Kelvin Budarick **Est.** 1994 **Dozens** 5000 **Vyds** 15ha
John Willoughby's vineyard overlooks the Bay of Shoals, which is the northern boundary of Kingscote, Kangaroo Island's main town. Planting of the vineyard began in 1994 and it now comprises riesling, sauvignon blanc, savagnin, pinot gris, pinot noir, cabernet sauvignon and shiraz. In addition, 460 olive trees have been planted to produce table olives.

ŸŸŸŸŸ Kangaroo Island Savagnin 2019 Savagnin is genetically identical to traminer, and the floral/spice/orange blossom bouquet is the opening stanza. The palate adds sweet stone fruit, citrus and honey to the pot. This is a particularly good example of savagnin/traminer/gewurztraminer. Screwcap. 12.5% alc. **Rating** 95 **To** 2023 $25 ❂
Kangaroo Island Rose 2019 Made from merlot harvested in the early morning, 5 hours skin contact. Pale but bright magenta. The 25-day ferment was stopped with 8g/l residual sugar, the acidity of 6.7g/l enough to balance the sweetness to the point where it wouldn't be recognised as anything more than fruit. Screwcap. 12% alc. **Rating** 94 **To** 2021 $25 ❂

ŸŸŸŸŸ Kangaroo Island Sauvignon Blanc 2019 **Rating** 92 **To** 2021 $25 ❂
Kangaroo Island Pinot Gris 2019 **Rating** 91 **To** 2022 $25
Kangaroo Island Riesling 2019 **Rating** 90 **To** 2027 $28
Kangaroo Island Arinto 2019 **Rating** 90 $28

Beautiful Isle Wines   ★★★★☆

2 Upper McEwans Road, Legana, Tas 7277 **Region** Northern Tasmania
T 0418 379 548 **www.**beautifulislewines.com **Open** Wed–Mon 10–5
Winemaker Cynthea Semmens, Devid Feldheim **Est.** 2013 **Dozens** 5000
Owners and winemakers Cynthea Semmens and David Feldheim established this business as a vinous lovechild after their permanent return to Tasmania (see Marion's Vineyard entry). The Beautiful Isle brand name was that used by the founder of the apple orchard in 1880, but the name and design of the striking labels had fallen out of copyright and trademark. The apple shed on the Marion's Vineyard housed boxes full of the labels that had been used

by negociants who purchased the fruit, put the labels on the apple boxes and crates, and sent them to the mainland for export to England. The cellar door opened in 2017, the bottles bearing designs taken from the heyday of the apple growing, and Beautiful Isle Wines became a financial stepping stone for the ultimate resolution of the ownership of Marion's Vineyard.

🏆🏆🏆🏆🏆 **Peacock Pinot Noir 2018** Four clones, multiple ferments, 15% whole bunch, 10% new French oak. Fragrant bouquet, red and purple fruit; fine texture/structure. The main theme is forest fruit, with a subtext of savoury tannins. Absolutely on top of the game. Screwcap. 13.4% alc. **Rating** 95 **To** 2028 $29 ✪

🏆🏆🏆🏆🏆 **Cabernet Sauvignon 2015 Rating** 93 **To** 2025 $29
Red Delicious 2017 Rating 93 **To** 2025 $25 ✪
Peacock Rose 2019 Rating 90 **To** 2021 $25
Peacock Vintage Rose 2016 Rating 90 $50

Bekkers ★★★★★

212 Seaview Road, McLaren Vale, SA 5171 **Region** McLaren Vale
T 0408 807 568 **www.bekkerswine.com Open** Thurs–Sat 10–4 or by appt
Winemaker Emmanuelle Bekkers, Toby Bekkers **Est.** 2010 **Dozens** 1000 **Vyds** 5.5ha
This brings together two high-performing, highly experienced and highly credentialled business and life partners. Toby Bekkers graduated with an honours degree in applied science in agriculture from the University of Adelaide, and over the ensuing years has had broad-ranging responsibilities as general manager of Paxton Wines in McLaren Vale, and as a leading exponent of organic and biodynamic viticulture. Emmanuelle Beckkers was born in Bandol in the south of France, and gained two university degrees, in biochemistry and oenology, before working for the Hardys in the south of France, which led her to Australia and a wide-ranging career, including Chalk Hill. Exports to the UK, Canada, France and China.

🏆🏆🏆🏆🏆 **McLaren Vale Syrah 2018** Hand-picked, the vinification very gentle to avoid extraction of aggressive tannins, matured in French puncheons (58% new) on lees with minimal additions until Dec '19. A truly great McLaren Vale syrah; as smooth as velvet, yet with layer upon layer of purple and black fruits that are hypnotic in their perfection. Screwcap. 14% alc. **Rating** 99 **To** 2043 $110 ✪
McLaren Vale Grenache 2018 Picked 1, 10 and 23 Mar; each parcel wild yeast–open fermented separately with 10% whole bunches, the remainder destemmed, 5–6 days cold soak, matured in French puncheons. Bright, clear colour. Medium-bodied, exceptional balance, spicy red/purple berries, fine tannins and a very long finish. Screwcap. 14.5% alc. **Rating** 97 **To** 2045 $80 ✪

🏆🏆🏆🏆🏆 **McLaren Vale Syrah Grenache 2018** A 64/36% blend from multiple parcels spread across 6 vineyards; vinified separately, 15% whole bunch grenache, 30% whole bunch syrah, 5–16 days cold soak, wild fermentation, basket-pressed to used oak. Deeply coloured. Medium to full-bodied – noticeably more full-bodied than the Grenache – with black fruits. Screwcap. 14% alc. **Rating** 96 **To** 2043 $80

Beklyn Wines ★★★☆

PO Box 802, Goolwa, SA 5214 **Region** Fleurieu
T 0405 189 363 **www.beklynwines.com Open** Not
Winemaker Mark Shaw, Rebekah Shaw **Est.** 2016 **Dozens** 600 **Vyds** 20ha
Mark and Rebekah Shaw's wine journey began while working in vineyards in McLaren Vale in 1994. In 2002 they built their first home in Currency Creek on the Fleurieu Peninsula. They planted 10ha of shiraz, and have recently planted another 10ha. Their first wine ('16) was from purchased grapes from three vineyards in McLaren Vale, but in the future grapes from their estate plantings will be used. The pattern of grape growing and selling part of the production and using the remainder to make their own wines is a sensible approach. 'Beklyn' means 'pretty brook', derived from the passage of water flowing through the estate.

Bell & Gong ★★★★

Valleyfield Vineyard, 873 Illawarra Road, Longford, Tas 7301 **Region** Northern Tasmania
T 0417 423 889 **www.**bellandgong.com **Open** Thurs–Mon 10–3
Winemaker Tasmanian Vintners **Est.** 2013 **Dozens** 1200 **Vyds** 1.7ha

Simon and Frances Stewart were told it wasn't possible to grow vines in the cracking clay subsoils of Longford, but went ahead anyway and now have 5000 vines of clones Pinot Fin (sic), Pommard and Abel in production. At the moment they source riesling and sauvignon blanc, but intend to plant a hectare of chardonnay. The cellar door, opened in 2017, is a moveable feast: depending on the weather it may be in the garden, at tables along the verandah or, in winter, in their country kitchen or dining room – the latter doubling as the cellar because it's the coldest room in the house. The name of their business comes from Simon's time as a master mariner and a one-time requirement for a ship setting anchor in a fog: a bell sounded rapidly for 5 seconds in the bow, then a gong sounded rapidly for 5 seconds in the stern.

ΨΨΨΨ **Riesling 2018** From the Coal River Valley. Cold-fermented, deliberate retention of 6.34g/l residual sugar to balance the Tasmanian acidity. The desired balance is there, but the fruit tension isn't as urgent as I would like. Perhaps it's starting its journey to layered complexity. Screwcap. 12.5% alc. **Rating** 94 To 2028 $30 **○**

ΨΨΨΨ **Sauvignon Blanc 2019** **Rating** 92 To 2022 $30
Pinot Noir 2018 **Rating** 92 To 2028 $48

Bellarmine Wines ★★★★★

1 Balyan Retreat, Pemberton, WA 6260 **Region** Pemberton
T 0409 687 772 **www.**bellarmine.com.au **Open** By appt
Winemaker Dr Diane Miller **Est.** 2000 **Dozens** 5000 **Vyds** 20.2ha

This vineyard is owned by German residents Dr Willi and Gudrun Schumacher. Long-term wine lovers, the Schumachers decided to establish a vineyard and winery of their own, using Australia partly because of its stable political climate. The vineyard is planted to merlot, pinot noir, chardonnay, shiraz, riesling, sauvignon blanc and petit verdot. Exports to the UK, the US, Germany and China.

ΨΨΨΨ **Pemberton Riesling Half-dry 2019** Such is the balance that you don't notice the sweetness. It's there, but masked by crisp acidity and the sorbet zest of the fruit. Easy to miss the quality of this delicious wine. Screwcap. 12% alc. **Rating** 95 $26 **○**

Pemberton Riesling Select 2019 A blossom and musk bouquet is the portal for a complex wine of depth and length. A classic each-way proposition, balance and fruit integrity the keys. Screwcap. 10.5% alc. **Rating** 95 To 2029 $26 **○**

Pemberton Riesling Dry 2019 The bouquet offers floral notes first up, moving quickly to lime and lemon blossom, with a surge of minerality drawing saliva from the mouth while extending the length of what is a very good riesling. Screwcap. 13.5% alc. **Rating** 94 To 2033 $26 **○**

ΨΨΨΨ **Pemberton Sauvignon Blanc 2019** **Rating** 92 To 2021 $20 **○**

Bellbrae Estate ★★★★★

520 Great Ocean Road, Bellbrae, Vic 3228 **Region** Geelong
T (03) 5264 8480 **www.**bellbraeestate.com.au **Open** See website
Winemaker David Crawford **Est.** 1999 **Dozens** 3000 **Vyds** 7ha

The Surf Coast area of Geelong enjoys a slightly milder climate overall than other areas of the Geelong viticultural region. Being so close to Bass Strait, Bellbrae Estate experiences a maritime influence that reduces the risk of frost in spring and provides more even temperature ranges during summer – ideal growing conditions for producing elegant wines that retain their natural acidity. Wines are released under the Bellbrae Estate and Longboard labels.

ŸŸŸŸŸ **Bells Geelong Syrah 2018** Hand-picked, open-fermented, matured in French barriques (50% new) for 14 months on fine lees. A very attractive cool-climate shiraz with fragrant red and blue fruit aromas; the medium-bodied palate a juicy and exact follow on. Screwcap. 13.5% alc. **Rating** 95 **To** 2033 $42

Bells Geelong Syrah 2017 Hand-picked, crushed and destemmed, open-fermented, pressed to French barriques (50% new, 50% 1yo) for 14 months. Has the restraint of '17 writ large with spice as much as red fruits providing the flavour base, superfine tannins part of what comes naturally. Screwcap. 13.5% alc. **Rating** 95 **To** 2032 $42

Longboard Geelong Pinot Noir 2018 Clones MV6, 777 and 114; 30% whole bunch fermentation and maceration, matured for 12 months in 1–3yo French barriques. Packs a punch with dark berries/stewed plums, spices and ripe tannins. Obviously picked when ripe, not too late. Its best years are in front of it. Screwcap. 13.5% alc. **Rating** 94 **To** 2030 $27 ✪

ŸŸŸŸŸ **Boobs Geelong Chardonnay 2018 Rating** 92 **To** 2025 $40
Longboard Geelong Shiraz 2018 Rating 92 **To** 2025 $25 ✪

Ben Haines Wine ★★★★★

342 Rae Street, Fitzroy North, Vic 3068 (postal) **Region** Yarra Valley
T 0417 083 645 **www.**benhaineswine.com **Open** Not
Winemaker Ben Haines **Est.** 2010 **Dozens** 4000
Ben Haines graduated from the University of Adelaide in 1999 with a degree in viticulture, waiting a couple of years (immersing himself in music) before focusing on his wine career. An early interest in terroir led to a deliberate choice of gaining experience in diverse regions including the Yarra Valley, McLaren Vale, Adelaide Hills, Langhorne Creek, Tasmania and Central Victoria, as well as time in the US and France. His services as a contract winemaker are in high demand, and his name pops up all over the place. Exports to the US and Asia.

ŸŸŸŸŸ **Volta Brackets Marsanne 2018** Fermented (wild) in neutral 500l puncheons over 3 months. Rested on gross lees for 20 months. Bottled unfined and unfiltered. It walks completely to its own beat, but it's also a wonderful expression of the variety. It smells and tastes strongly of sweet roasted almonds though it's also minerally, smoky, honeyed and ripped with stone fruit–like flavour. It's grippy and dry to finish, sweetened by oak too, but it manages to push out long through the aftertaste. It's quite something. Cork. 11.8% alc. **Rating** 96 **To** 2027 $45 CM ✪

Firelights Grampians Syrah 2017 It's a beautiful wine. Built on acidity and refreshing for it, but the quality is in its intricate, detailed, complex length. It tastes of graphite, black cherry, cloves, boysenberry and fennel, and while it's only medium in weight it has plenty of razzle-dazzle; its fruit is bright and perfumed but this wine's more savoury aspect really puts on a show. Diam. 12.5% alc. **Rating** 96 **To** 2036 $75 CM ✪

Grampians Shiraz 2019 100% whole bunches, fermented wild, bottled unfined and unfiltered. It's had a lot of love and attention put into it and it shows. It presents a wide array of peppery/bunchy/herbal flavours, but it's also svelte and textural and the fruit, well, it's ripe and ready to seduce. It's a fresh, complex, well structured wine of substance. Screwcap. 13% alc. **Rating** 95 **To** 2036 $30 CM ✪

Yarra Valley Chardonnay 2019 From a vineyard at Gruyere planted in '86. It's taut and controlled with very good concentration of fruit and just enough oak to give it some emphasis. Nectarine, white peach, oatmeal and citrus flavours come dusted with nougat and vanilla. Its future looks bright. Screwcap. 12% alc. **Rating** 94 **To** 2026 $28 CM ✪

Yarra Valley Shiraz 2019 Walnut and black cherry flavours move confidently through the palate. Whole bunch influence is clear, but it's a wine with many tricks up its sleeve: ripe fruit, appropriate oak, excellent balance and texture among them. Screwcap. 13.5% alc. **Rating** 94 **To** 2035 $30 CM ✪

ΨΨΨΨϘ Yarra Valley Pinot Noir 2019 Rating 93 To 2028 $35 CM
Avondrust Yarra Valley Pinot Noir 2019 Rating 93 To 2030 $50 CM
Dirty Franc 2019 Rating 90 $40 CM

Ben Murray Wines   ★★★★☆

PO Box 781, Tanunda, SA 5352 **Region** Barossa Valley
T 0438 824 493 www.benmurraywines.com **Open** By appt
Winemaker Dan Eggleton **Est.** 2016 **Dozens** 800 **Vyds** 1ha
Ben Murray doesn't exist, but owners Dan Eggleton and Craig Thompson do. Each has had
years of experience in various facets of the wine business. Dan brings 20 years working for
businesses ranging from major corporates to boutique enterprises. Craig brings a 1ha old vine
grenache vineyard at Lyndoch into the venture, plus experience as a wine importer. The one
thing they specifically have in common is a love of drinking wine.

ΨΨΨΨΨ Marananga Barossa Valley Shiraz 2017 Hand-picked, crushed, 25 days on
skins, the cap worked throughout, matured in new and used French and American
barriques for 18 months. Penetrating and rich; black fruits, bramble and black
pepper. This is a wine that will be around for some time. Screwcap. 14.5% alc.
Rating 95 To 2037 $55
Casa Rossa Vineyard Anima Reserve Barossa Valley Grenache 2017
The vineyard has been tended by the same family for half a century, the wine
naturally grown and naturally made. Hand-picked, whole berries wild-fermented,
new and old oak, neither fined nor filtered. This is a lovely Barossa grenache with
bright, clear colour, slipping in some fine-grained tannins among the cherry fruits.
Screwcap. 14.5% alc. Rating 94 To 2027 $30 ✪

ΨΨΨΨ Marananga Barossa Valley Rose 2019 Rating 89 To 2021 $19 ✪
Marananga Barossa Valley Grenache 2017 Rating 89 To 2024 $20

Bended Knee Vineyard   ★★★★

PO Box 334, Buninyong, Vic 3357 **Region** Ballarat
T (03) 5341 8437 www.bendedknee.com.au **Open** Not
Winemaker Peter Roche **Est.** 1999 **Dozens** 250 **Vyds** 1.25ha
Peter and Pauline Roche have 0.5ha each of chardonnay and pinot noir planted at
moderately high density, and 0.25ha of ultra-close-planted pinot noir at the equivalent of
9000 vines/ha. Here four clones have been used: 114, 115, G5V15 and 777. The Roches say,
'We are committed to sustainable viticulture and aim to leave the planet in better shape than
we found it'. Ducks, guinea fowl and chooks are vineyard custodians, and all vine canopy
management is done by hand, including pruning and picking. Although production is tiny,
Bended Knee wines can be found at some of Melbourne's best restaurants.

ΨΨΨΨϘ Chardonnay 2018 100 dozen made. 25% new oak, fermented wild. Bell clear
pear, apple and stone fruit flavours with a bright spot of citrussy acidity on the
finish. Good carry, flavour and ripeness within an elegant, slender context. It's in a
good drinking place right now. Screwcap. 12.7% alc. Rating 93 To 2024 $40 CM
Pinot Noir 2017 100 dozen made. A most attractive wine. Perfumed, fruit-
forward and vibrant, but with a round of undergrowthy complexity. Beet,
strawberry, cedar wood and sweet-spice notes have this in an excellent drinking
place. Screwcap. 13.8% alc. Rating 93 To 2025 $40 CM

Beresford Wines   ★★★★

252 Blewitt Springs Road, McLaren Flat, SA 5171 **Region** McLaren Vale
T (08) 8383 0362 www.beresfordwines.com.au **Open** 7 days 10–5
Winemaker Chris Dix **Est.** 1985 **Dozens** 9000 **Vyds** 28ha
This is a sister company to Step Rd Winery in Langhorne Creek, owned and run by VOK
Beverages. The estate plantings are shiraz (13ha), cabernet sauvignon (9.3ha), grenache (3ha)
and chardonnay (2.7ha), but they account for only a part of the production. Some of the

wines offer excellent value. Exports to the UK, Germany, Denmark, Poland, Singapore, Hong Kong and China.

ΨΨΨΨΨ **Estate McLaren Vale Cabernet Sauvignon 2017** Dusty and leaf-strewn, but with a generous core of sweet, curranty fruit. Honeyed oak plays a role too, as do saltbush and licorice. It threatens to go over the top but never does; it offers a seamless glide of ripe flavour. Screwcap. 14% alc. **Rating** 93 **To** 2029 CM
Limited Release McLaren Vale Cabernet Sauvignon 2017 Bay leaves soaked in Ribena, red licorice coated in vanillan cream. It's not sophisticated, but it's plush, smooth, sweet and generous. Screwcap. **Rating** 93 **To** 2030 CM
Estate McLaren Vale Shiraz 2017 A little too sweet and warm for its own good, but it does punch out red licorice and dense plum flavours in good volume. Violet, musk and stressed herb characters round out a capable, if not compelling, red wine. Screwcap. 14.7% alc. **Rating** 92 **To** 2020 CM
Limited Release McLaren Vale Shiraz 2017 Heavy with oak, firm with tannin, bold of fruit. Redcurrant and sweet mulberry/rhubarb flavours slide creamily through the mouth, oak spice and toast trailing behind. Oak wins out over fruit in the end, but there's little denying its smooth appeal. Screwcap. **Rating** 92 **To** 2029 CM
Grand Reserve McLaren Vale Shiraz 2017 Machine-harvested and open-fermented before going into a mix of French (70%) and American oak. It's all choc-mint and deep plum until the finish where green-edged oak and jangly acidity take over. The nose has a marshmallow-like suggestion of sweetness and the mid-palate pours it on, but the finish is hard to defend. Screwcap. **Rating** 90 **To** 2032 $120 CM
Classic McLaren Vale Cabernet Sauvignon 2017 The inherent sternness of cabernet gives this sweet-fruited red just enough shape to keep it tidy. It's a wash of curranty fruit, a smidgen of resiny oak in support. It's uncomplicated, but it works well enough. Screwcap. 14% alc. **Rating** 90 **To** 2026 CM

ΨΨΨΨ **Classic McLaren Vale Chardonnay 2018** **Rating** 89 **To** 2025 $28
McLaren Vale Rose 2019 **Rating** 89 **To** 2021 $25 CM

Berton Vineyards ★★★★

55 Mirrool Avenue, Yenda, NSW 2681 **Region** Riverina
T (02) 6968 1600 **www**.bertonvineyards.com.au **Open** Mon–Fri 10–4, Sat 11–4
Winemaker James Ceccato, Bill Gumbleton, Glen Snaidero **Est.** 2001 **Dozens** 1.2 million **Vyds** 32.14ha
The Berton Vineyards partners – Bob and Cherie Berton, James Ceccato and Jamie Bennett – have almost 100 years' combined experience in winemaking, viticulture, finance, production and marketing. The 30ha property in the Eden Valley was acquired in 1996 and the vines planted. Wines are released under various labels: Berton Vineyards (Reserve, Winemakers Reserve, Metal Label), Foundstone, Outback Jack and Head Over Heels. Exports to the UK, the US, Sweden, Norway, Russia, Japan and China.

ΨΨΨΨΨ **Reserve Coonawarra Cabernet Sauvignon 2017** Enticing dark ruby hue. A range of regional flavours from blackberries and licorice mints to freshly cut herbs. In the medium-bodied spectrum, yet firm. Green walnut–like tannins add some heft. Screwcap. 14.5% alc. **Rating** 90 **To** 2028 $20 JF ✪

Best's Wines ★★★★★

111 Best's Road, Great Western, Vic 3377 **Region** Grampians
T (03) 5356 2250 **www**.bestswines.com **Open** Mon–Sat 10–5, Sun 11–4
Winemaker Justin Purser **Est.** 1866 **Dozens** 25 000 **Vyds** 34.2ha
Best's winery and vineyards are among Australia's best kept secrets. Indeed the vineyards, with vines dating back to 1866, have secrets that may never be revealed: for example, one of the vines planted in the Nursery Block has defied identification and is thought to exist nowhere else in the world. Part of the cellars too, go back to the same era, constructed by

butcher-turned-winemaker Henry Best and his family. The Thomson family has owned the property since 1920, with Ben, the fifth generation, having taken over management from father Viv. Best's consistently produces elegant, supple wines; the Bin No. 0 is a classic, the Thomson Family Shiraz (largely from vines planted in 1867) is magnificent. Very occasionally a pinot meunier (with 15% pinot noir) is made solely from 1868 plantings of those two varieties; there is no other pinot meunier of this vine age made anywhere else in the world. Justin Purser brings with him a remarkable CV with extensive experience in Australia, NZ and Burgundy. In the *Wine Companion 2017* Best's was awarded the mantle of Wine of the Year from a field of almost 9000 wines; this year they are Best Value Winery. Exports to the US, Canada, Singapore, Japan, Hong Kong and China.

Old Vine Great Western Pinot Meunier 2019 It's one thing to have seriously old vines, planted in 1868, and quite another to have them metamorphose into a contemporary wine full of harmony and balance. Well here it is in all its beauty. Heady with florals aplenty, an array of Middle Eastern spices and mint with a delicacy on the palate, yet there's substance and detail too. A wine of finesse and elegance. Screwcap. 13% alc. **Rating** 97 **To** 2039 $100 JF ✪

Foudre Ferment Great Western Riesling 2019 Vines planted '78 and '98, harvested by the sophisticated Opti grape sorter-destemmer, 4 hours in the Opti before pressing, thence to a 7yo foudre for fermentation and maturation on lees. You'd better pay attention as you take your first sip – this is not your grandma's riesling. Unsweetened lime sorbet. Screwcap. 11% alc. **Rating** 96 **To** 2030 $35 ✪

LSV Great Western Shiraz 2018 Opti-harvested, whole-berry fermentation with 15% whole bunches and 2% viognier. A rich, layered, hedonistic wine; fruits of forest/forest floor with both blackberry and raspberry on display. The balance of tannins, oak and fruit is evidenced by the wine (and its show success). Screwcap. 14.5% alc. **Rating** 96 **To** 2042 $35 ✪

Great Western Riesling 2019 Whole-bunch pressed to stainless steel for cold fermentation, stopped with 7g/l residual sugar. Gold medal Melbourne Wine Awards '19, top gold Victorian Wine Show '19. It has the intense lime zest and pith flavours that I find irresistible. Bright acidity glides alongside the fruit. Screwcap. 11% alc. **Rating** 95 **To** 2035 $25 ✪

Great Western Pinot Noir 2019 Under Justin Purser's guidance, pinot noir constantly excels and morphs beautifully. This crackles with pleasure and the 50% whole bunches in the fermentation add sapidity as much as stemmy, albeit ripe, flavours. Cherries and pips, star anise and menthol; a palate that's light and bright with supple tannins and tangy citrussy acidity. Absurdly priced – as in a bargain. Screwcap. 12.5% alc. **Rating** 95 **To** 2028 $25 JF ✪

Bin No. 1 Great Western Shiraz 2018 Picked by hand and by Opti sorter/harvester, whole-berry fermentation with 5% whole bunches. Wine show success is no surprise. Typical Great Western wine with high quality intensity, focus and length to its spicy/peppery black forest floor fruits, at only 14% alcohol. Screwcap. **Rating** 95 **To** 2038 $25 ✪

Great Western Cabernet Sauvignon 2018 Includes 10% merlot, cabernet franc and shiraz, matured for 12 months in old vats or French hogsheads. A cascade of silver medals. This is a potent and precisely vinified wine of great length. Screwcap. 14.5% alc. **Rating** 95 **To** 2038 $25 ✪

Great Western Nursery Block Dry Red 2019 The mother of all blends with vines originally planted in 1868; comprising about 20 different red varieties, some still unidentified although the back label mentions Bad Bearer, Rough Leaf, and 'the underrated Pinot Dru' (aka cabernet sauvignon apparently). There's a vibrancy here with cassis, juniper, lavender and an earthy, heady fragrance. Tangy, juicy across the lighter framed palate, pliant tannins though. Just delicious drinking with a story to tell. Screwcap. 12% alc. **Rating** 95 **To** 2029 $45 JF

Great Western Dolcetto 2019 Expect a wave of florals led by lavender, with fresh herbs and eucalyptus infusing the dark plums. It's buoyant and bright across the palate but don't be fooled, plenty of fine-sandpaper tannins shaping this. Spot on. 13% alc. **Rating** 95 **To** 2024 $25 JF ✪

Great Western Pinot Meunier Pinot Noir 2019 This just starts out gently with its cherries, kirsch and rose essence aromas. A touch of woodsy spice and spearmint comes to the fore. It's an intriguing wine; it's not showy yet it has a light layering of flavour and succulence with subtle tannins. A wine for today. Screwcap. 13.5% alc. **Rating** 94 **To** 2028 $45 JF

♟♟♟♟♟ **Great Western Sparkling Shiraz 2016 Rating** 91 $35

Bethany Wines   ★★★★★

378 Bethany Road, Tanunda, SA 5352 **Region** Barossa
T (08) 8563 2086 **www**.bethany.com.au **Open** Mon–Sat 10–5, Sun 1–5
Winemaker Alex MacClelland **Est.** 1981 **Dozens** 18 000 **Vyds** 38ha
The Schrapel family has been growing grapes in the Barossa Valley for over 140 years. Their winery is nestled high on a hillside on the site of an old bluestone quarry. Geoff and Rob Schrapel produce a range of consistently well made and attractively packaged wines. Bethany has vineyards in the Barossa and Eden valleys. Exports to all major markets.

♟♟♟♟♟ **East Grounds Barossa Shiraz 2017** From the estate's highest vineyard block situated on the eastern ridge of the Barossa foothills. Quite a lovely example of shiraz grown in a temperate climate. It's medium-bodied, the bouquet full of spice, red fruits, rose petals and cherry blossom characters all translating straight to the long, supple palate. Tannins and oak are part of the backdrop, simply providing the finish of the wine. Screwcap. 14% alc. **Rating** 97 **To** 2042 $48 ✪

♟♟♟♟♟ **Blue Quarry Single Vineyard Eden Valley Riesling 2019** Steps taken to pick early from the cool site of the vineyard – and the result is a wine full of Rose's lime juice and a squeeze of lemon. Seriously good riesling. Drink whenever, young or old. Screwcap. 10.5% alc. **Rating** 96 **To** 2030 $40 ✪
GR Reserve Barossa Valley Shiraz 2018 Matured in barrel for 10 months, 56% new French, 44% American. Full-bodied and needing more time for the oak to stop impeding the rich flavours of the plum and blackberry fruits. The requisite balance is there. Cork. 14.5% alc. **Rating** 95 **To** 2038 $125
GR Reserve Barossa Valley Shiraz 2017 From 2 vineyards that shone in the cool conditions. Generous use (70%) of new French and American oak is usual practice for Bethany, likewise 18 months maturation. The elegant, fresh, medium-bodied palate is a reflection of the cool, dry vintage. Some may wonder where the wine is headed; the answer decades away, or drink tonight – such is the magic of the vintage. Cork. 14.5% alc. **Rating** 95 **To** 2037 $125
LE Barossa Shiraz 2017 Sourced predominantly from a single Eden Valley vineyard. This is a slightly bolder version of the GR Reserve, but has been vinified with restraint from start to finish; part crushed and part whole-berry fermentation, matured in 38% new French and American oak for 18 months. Cork. 14.5% alc. **Rating** 95 **To** 2042 $75
Blue Quarry Barrel Select Barossa Valley Shiraz 2017 Part destemmed whole berries, part crushed and destemmed, matured for 18 months in new and used oak. The '17 vintage has been used with skill; black and purple fruits with a precisely judged framework of tannins. Screwcap. 14.5% alc. **Rating** 95 **To** 2037 $45
Blue Quarry Single Vineyard Barossa Valley Cabernet Sauvignon 2017 Most crushed and pressed but some whole berries, matured in French oak, some new. Excellent, deep colour; '17 was a glorious vintage for Barossa Valley cabernet, the cool conditions and slow ripening allowing good vineyards to produce blackcurrant supported by black olive and cedary oak, with a tannin profile of high quality cabernet. Screwcap. 14.5% alc. **Rating** 95 **To** 2042 $45
Museum Release Reserve Eden Valley Riesling 2011 The Schrapel family hit the bullseye when it decided to leave a touch of residual sugar to balance the high acidity of this wine. It's all about balance, not depth or exotic tastes. It's a lovely wine. Screwcap. 11% alc. **Rating** 94 **To** 2031 $40

Blue Quarry Single Vineyard Eden Valley Chardonnay 2018 Night-harvested from the Batten Vineyard, crushed and pressed in the early morning, the partly clarified juice taken to barrel for fermentation, one barrel undergoing mlf. The palate tells you this was a smart decision, as does the laboratory result of 7.1g/l of acidity. It's light on its feet; white peach, citrus/grapefruit and Granny Smith apple flavours all on parade. Screwcap. 12.5% alc. **Rating** 94 **To** 2028 $40
First Village Barossa Valley Rose 2019 52% mataro, 48% grenache; the latter pressed directly to stainless steel for ferment, the mataro fermented in stainless steel and used hogsheads, blended and bottled after 2 months. A dry rose of real character and quality, flavour and texture. Screwcap. 12.5% alc. **Rating** 94 **To** 2021
First Village Barossa Valley Shiraz 2017 Very attractive label design picking up the history of Bethany with a vintage of exceptional quality. It provides a mix of spiced red and black fruits, a soupcon of oak and a dazzling lightness as it travels along the palate. Drink with enthusiasm and no delay. Screwcap. 14.5% alc. **Rating** 94 **To** 2029 $25 ✪
First Village Barossa Valley GSM 2018 Rich and full-bodied. The blend thoroughly synergistic, the fruit flavours tracking red, purple and black, the mouthfeel velvety and long. Great value. Screwcap. 14.5% alc. **Rating** 94 **To** 2030 $25 ✪

ⵣⵣⵣⵣⵣ **First Village Eden Valley Riesling 2019** Rating 93 To 2030 $25 ✪
First Village Barossa Valley Grenache 2017 Rating 92 To 2028 $25 ✪
First Village Barossa Valley Grenache 2018 Rating 90 To 2026 $25

Between the Vines   ★★★

452 Longwood Road, Longwood, SA 5153 **Region** Adelaide Hills
T 0403 933 767 **www**.betweenthevines.com.au **Open** W'ends & public hols 12–5
Winemaker Matt Jackman, Simon Greenleaf **Est.** 2013 **Dozens** 400 **Vyds** 2.1ha
The estate vineyard (2.1ha of chardonnay) was planted in 1995, and purchased by Stewart and Laura Moodie in 2006. The vineyard is fully managed by Stewart and Laura, who do all the spraying/netting/wire lifting, pruning, fruit and shoot thinning; Laura having undertaken a year-long viticulture course. They employ backpackers for labour where needed, and only bring in professional teams for the harvest. In '13, the Moodies grafted 0.2ha of the chardonnay to tempranillo and created the Between the Vines brand, bottling small quantities of pinot noir and tempranillo under their label. Matt Jackman makes the wine in consultation with the Moodies (Simon Greenleaf makes the sparkling wines).

ⵣⵣⵣⵣ **Single Vineyard Langhorne Creek Tempranillo 2019** The regional stamp is strong and inviting. A ripe style with cherry cola, freshly rolled tobacco, woodsy spices and musk. It's robust and sweetly-fruited across the palate, with firm tannins. Take this to a bbq. Screwcap. 13.5% alc. **Rating** 89 **To** 2023 $22 JF

Bicknell fc   ★★★★★

41 St Margarets Road, Healesville, Vic 3777 **Region** Yarra Valley
T 0488 678 427 **www**.bicknellfc.com **Open** Not
Winemaker David Bicknell **Est.** 2011 **Dozens** 7600 **Vyds** 2.5ha
This is the busman's holiday for Oakridge chief winemaker David Bicknell and partner Nicky Harris (viticulturist). It is focused purely on chardonnay and pinot noir, with no present intention of broadening the range nor, indeed, the volume of production. Since 2014 all the grapes have come from Val Stewart's close-planted vineyard at Gladysdale, planted in 1988. The partners have leased this vineyard, which will become the total focus of their business. Since 2015 the wines have been labelled Applecross, the name of the highest mountain pass in Scotland, a place that David Bicknell's father was very fond of.

ⵣⵣⵣⵣⵣ **Applecross Yarra Valley Chardonnay 2018** Hand-picked, chilled, whole-bunch pressed direct to French puncheons for wild ferment over 3 weeks, SO_2 the only addition, no stirring, no mlf. It has hastened slowly to its release in

early '21. White peach/pink grapefruit/apple are the baseline flavours. Screwcap.
13.6% alc. **Rating** 95 **To** 2028 $50

Applecross Yarra Valley Pinot Noir 2018 Destemmed whole-berry ferment,
19 days on skins including cold soak and post-ferment settling. Brilliantly clear,
bright colour. David Bicknell runs a tight ship, the minimal message of the
fermenting must resulting in a pure, perfumed, light-bodied pinot with years in
front of it. For the purist. Screwcap. 13.1% alc. **Rating** 95 **To** 2028 $50

Big Easy Radio

11 Stonehouse Lane, Aldinga, SA 5773 **Region** McLaren Vale
T 0437 159 858 **www**.bigeasyradio.com **Open** Not
Winemaker Matt Head **Est.** 2017 **Dozens** 4000 **Vyds** 4ha
Matt Head has ventured far and wide to bring challenging blends (varietal and regional)
together in triumph. Moreover, these (most attractive, if left field) wines are all very
competitively priced. Exports to Denmark and Japan.

**Funtime Fountain McLaren Vale The Montepulciano & The Sangiovese
2018** As the back label quips, 'An end to the overspend'. Indeed! This represents
exceptional value, feeling like a riper Italian idiom by virtue of the dry, moreish,
structural authority. Black fruits, sour cherry and strewn herb. Highly versatile at
the table. Screwcap. **Rating** 95 **To** 2024 NG

Cosmic-Antennae Tempranillo 2018 Rating 93 **To** 2023 NG
Forget Babylon Touriga Malbec 2018 Rating 92 **To** 2024 $30 NG
Drink the Sun Rose 2019 Rating 91 **To** 2020 NG

Bigibila Wines

85 Polleters Road, Moonambel, Vic 3478 **Region** Pyrenees
T 0425 739 319 **www**.bigibila.com **Open** Fri–Mon 11–5
Winemaker Contract **Est.** 1994 **Dozens** 3000 **Vyds** 12.5ha
Peter Bicknell planted shiraz, cabernet sauvignon, cabernet franc and merlot in 1994; the
first vintage was in 2002 under the original name of Polleters. Jillian Henderson joined
the company in '14 and together they planted new varieties, built a winery and increased
production. Peter and Jillian make rich, powerful estate-grown wines using sustainable farming
and low impact winemaking practises. 'Bigibila' means echidna in the Gamilaraay language,
spoken by the Gamilaroi people. Exports to Canada and China.

Shiraz 2018 Open-fermented, 10% whole bunch, matured in American oak
(25% new) for 18 months. Inky purple. Very full-bodied, with all the dials of
fruit, oak and tannins turned up to maximum. Screwcap. 15.3% alc. **Rating** 89
To 2023 $30

Wyatt's Shiraz 2018 Oh dear. Instead of turning the dials down, they have
been set even higher: alcohol increased, new American oak increased to 30%,
maturation 20 months. I was a rabbit caught in the headlights when I chronicled
these changes and tasted the wine. For those seeking the ultimate in full-bodied
style. Screwcap. 15.8% alc. **Rating** 89 **To** 2028 $40

Bike & Barrel

PO Box 167, Myrtleford, Vic 3736 **Region** Alpine Valleys
T 0409 971 235 **Open** Not
Winemaker Jo Marsh, Daniel Balzer **Est.** 2013 **Dozens** 280 **Vyds** 1.5ha
Brian and Linda Lewis split their vineyard and wine interests in two. One part is a
10ha commercial vineyard, established on undulating free-draining slopes above the valley
floor, mainly supplying local wineries with chardonnay, prosecco, pinot noir and tempranillo.
For Bike & Barrel they have 1.5ha of pinotage, fiano, schioppettino and refosco dal
peduncolo rosso.

ΨΨΨΨΨ **Alpine Valleys Chardonnay 2017** It's a little bit flinty, it's a little bit funky, with a lot of flavour packed in between. Full of ripe stone fruit, lemon balm and curd with some oak spice and creamy-nutty leesy notes too. It's quite luscious and rich, but not at all heavy thanks to fresh acidity. A very satisfying rendition crafted by Jo Marsh. Screwcap. 12.8% alc. Rating 95 To 2025 $28 JF ☻

ΨΨΨΨΨ **Alpine Valleys Fiano 2017** Rating 93 To 2022 $24 JF☻
Slaughteryard Creek Alpine Valleys Pinot Noir 2018 Rating 90 To 2023 $28 JF
Slaughteryard Creek Alpine Valleys Pinot Noir 2015 Rating 90 To 2021 $30
House Block Alpine Valleys Schioppettino 2015 Rating 90 To 2020 $ CM

Bilgavia Wines   ★★★

PO Box 246, Singleton, NSW 2330 **Region** Hunter Valley
T (02) 6574 5314 **Open** Not
Winemaker Michael McManus **Est.** 2003 **Dozens** NFP **Vyds** 17.87ha
Leona and Phil Gunter purchased Parsons Creek Farm in 2011. It covers 200ha of prime alluvial and loam land, but also terra rossa soil for the shiraz, chardonnay, semillon and verdelho plantings. The farm has a magnificent homestead, a well kept vineyard and a thoroughbred horse facility. Most of the grapes are sold, with sufficient quantity retained for the Bilgavia label.

ΨΨΨΨ **Hunter Valley Chardonnay 2012** The wine is remarkably fresh, almost to a point. You would be expecting textural and flavour complexity here, but there is none. You might be forgiven for thinking this is one for the cellar, but you may be surprised when, another 5 years down the track, the wine has not moved from youth to maturity. Screwcap. 12.5% alc. **Rating** 89 To 2025 $28

Billy Button Wines   ★★★★★

11 Camp Street, Bright, Vic 3741 **Region** Alpine Valleys
T 0418 559 344 **www.**billybuttonwines.com.au **Open** Thurs–Sun 12–6
Winemaker Jo Marsh **Est.** 2014 **Dozens** 5000
Jo Marsh makes light of the numerous awards she won during her studies for her Degree in Agricultural Science (Oenology) at the University of Adelaide. She then won a contested position in Southcorp's Graduate Recruitment Program; she was appointed assistant winemaker at Seppelt Great Western in 2003. By '08 she had been promoted to acting senior winemaker, responsible for all wines made onsite. After Seppelt, she became winemaker at Feathertop, and after two happy years decided to step out on her own in '14. She has set up a grower network in the Alpine Valleys and makes a string of excellent wines. Billy Button also shares a cellar door with Bush Track Wines in the heart of Myrtleford.

ΨΨΨΨΨ **Silver Xenica Alpine Valleys Chardonnay 2018** This label is for Jo Marsh's pick of the favourite parcel of white fruit from the vintage – something that really stood out. In '18 it was a very classy chardonnay. Expect creamed honey, a touch of brioche and melted butter, ginger and oak spice; all reined in by a line of fine acidity. It's also incredibly long and persistent on the finish. Screwcap. 13% alc. Rating 96 To 2028 $40 JF ☻
The Classic Alpine Valleys Chardonnay 2018 Great to see chardonnay from this region stamping its class. Here it's dabbed with lemon balm, a hint of lavender, ginger tea; it then builds with creamed honey, delicious lemon pudding and curd. Satisfying with plenty of flavour, but it's not a big wine. Retains a fine shape thanks to a neat acid line. Screwcap. 13% alc. Rating 95 To 2028 $32 JF ☻
King Valley Alpine Valleys Rosso 2018 If a delicious, lighter framed red is the order of the day (or night), here it is. Yet there's substance in the mix, too. Full of tangy juicy fruit, earthy tones, Italian herbs; grainy tannins with a bright acid line and flourish on the finish. Screwcap. 14% alc. Rating 95 To 2022 $22 JF ☻
The Affable Alpine Valleys Barbera 2018 There's a plushness, a juiciness and lots of Italian flavours working across the medium-bodied palate, making this

the best barbera to date from Billy Button. In the taste profile are wood smoke and cherry pips, blackberry essence plus fleshy fruit; the crisp acidity keeps it all buoyant. Screwcap. 13.5% alc. **Rating** 95 To 2025 $32 JF ✪

The Renegade Alpine Valleys Refosco 2018 A deceptive wine, it sneaks up then explodes with flavour and definition. Teetering on medium-bodied with blackberries on the cusp of ripeness, Alpine herbs, pine needle coolness and a taut acid line coupled with raw silk-like tannins to close. Screwcap. 13.5% alc. **Rating** 95 To 2024 $32 JF ✪

The Clandestine Alpine Valleys Schioppettino 2018 This is a scintillating variety with its perfume of violets, pepper and red fruits, yet with more savouriness on the palate. It's by no means rich or sweet, in fact quite linear with very subtle tannins; the driving force is its Alpine-fresh acidity. Screwcap. 13.5% alc. **Rating** 95 To 2022 $32 JF ✪

ToToToToTo **The Torment Riesling 2019 Rating** 93 To 2029 $27 JF ✪
The Groovy Gruner Veltliner 2019 Rating 93 To 2024 $27 JF ✪
The Alluring Tempranillo 2018 Rating 93 To 2026 $32 JF
The Happy Gewurztraminer 2019 Rating 92 To 2024 $27 JF
The Mysterious Malvasia 2018 Rating 92 To 2023 $27 JF
The Little Rascal Arneis 2019 Rating 91 To 2021 $27 JF
The Chameleon Pinot Gris 2019 Rating 90 To 2024 $27 JF
The Demure Pinot Blanc 2019 Rating 90 To 2023 $27 JF
Alpine Valleys King Valley Rosato 2019 Rating 90 To 2021 $20 JF ✪
The Rustic Sangiovese 2018 Rating 90 To 2023 $32 JF

Bimbadgen   ★★★★★

790 McDonalds Road, Pokolbin, NSW 2320 **Region** Hunter Valley
T (02) 4998 4600 **www.**bimbadgen.com.au **Open** Fri–Sat 10–7, Sun–Thurs 10–5
Winemaker Richard Done, Mark Smith **Est.** 1968 **Dozens** 30 000 **Vyds** 26ha
Bimbadgen's Palmers Lane vineyard was planted in 1968 and the McDonalds Road vineyard shortly thereafter. Both sites provide old vine semillon, shiraz and chardonnay. Since assuming ownership in '97, the Lee family has applied the same level of care and attention to cultivating Bimbadgen as they have to other properties in their portfolio. The small but impressive production is consumed largely by the owner's luxury hotel assets, with limited quantities available in the Sydney market. Exports to the UK, Switzerland, Germany, the Netherlands, Japan, Taiwan and China.

ToToToToTo **Signature McDonalds Road Vineyard Semillon 2019** Crushed, destemmed and settled in stainless steel. Cultured yeast, cool ferment. A classic young Hunter semillon of spring blossom, apple, lemon pith, nougat. It's a lovely wine in the mouth, soft and succulent with fine texture and excellent balance. Will age a treat. Screwcap. 11.5% alc. **Rating** 95 To 2038 $35 JP ✪

Signature Hunter Valley Semillon 2019 Pale straw. Signature represents the best parcels of fruit from any vintage and this young semillon was sourced from a block on Bimbadgen's Palmers Lane vineyard. One for the cellar, with penetrating lemon-lime intensity. Zingy to the max with lively acidity. It's biding its time but the balance, already obvious, bodes well for a long and prosperous life. Screwcap. 10.5% alc. **Rating** 95 To 2037 $50 JP

Museum Release Signature Hunter Valley Semillon 2014 For those who wonder what happens to those zesty young Hunter semillons once they have celebrated a few birthdays, here is the answer. That simple lemony-fruit aroma of youth takes on a complex bouquet of beeswax and honeysuckle. The wine grows deeper, richer in flavour and longer; and that juvenile body of before is transformed into an attractive adult. Spot on. Screwcap. 12% alc. **Rating** 95 To 2035 $50 JP

Museum Release Signature Palmers Lane Hunter Valley Semillon 2014 Lemon curd, coriander, fennel and toast offer a rousing start. Classic aged Aussie semillon characters here that are just so enticing and once they hit the palate, they go on and on. Soft acidity is deceptive. There is plenty left in the tank. Drink some now, keep some for later. Screwcap. 12% alc. **Rating** 95 **To** 2027 $50 JP

McDonalds Road Hunter Valley Shiraz 2018 Crushed into stainless steel fermenters, regular pumpovers for colour and tannin extraction before pressed into French barriques, 12 months maturation. Beautifully lifted and expressive aromas. Fine-edged and packed with chocolate-covered plums, licorice blackstrap, ginger. It runs free in the mouth until pursued and brought to ground by savoury tannins. Screwcap. 14.3% alc. **Rating** 95 **To** 2036 $45 JP

Signature Hunter Valley Shiraz 2018 Fruit crushed into stainless steel, regular pumpovers for colour and tannin extraction. Pressed into French barriques, matured for 16 months. Old vines – planted in '68 and '70 – show how it's done with powerful, concentrated fruit qualities shining through. Cinnamon, cardamom, acacia, Italian espresso, panforte. Comes together nicely on the palate, but still a little taut. Screwcap. 14.5% alc. **Rating** 95 **To** 2041 $75 JP

Palmers Lane Hunter Valley Semillon 2019 Bimbadgen keeps things pretty simple in its winemaking approach to semillon: crushed, destemmed, cool fermentation in stainless steel with neutral yeast. It's less-is-more winemaking that results in a purity of flavour profile: classic lemon drops, apple, pear skin and quince and super bright acid cut. It's everything you need. Screwcap. 10.9% alc. **Rating** 94 **To** 2027 $35 JP

♥♥♥♥♡ **Palmers Lane Chardonnay 2019** Rating 92 **To** 2027 $35 JP
McDonalds Road Chardonnay 2019 Rating 92 **To** 2027 $35 JP
Vermentino 2019 Rating 92 **To** 2025 $25 JP ◎

Bindi Wine Growers   ★★★★★

343 Melton Road, Gisborne, Vic 3437 (postal) **Region** Macedon Ranges
T (03) 5428 2564 **www.**bindiwines.com.au **Open** Not
Winemaker Michael Dhillon, Stuart Anderson (Consultant) **Est.** 1988 **Dozens** 2000
Vyds 6ha

One of the icons of Macedon. The Chardonnay is top-shelf, the Pinot Noir as remarkable (albeit in a very different idiom) as Bass Phillip, Giaconda or any of the other tiny-production, icon wines. The addition of Heathcote-sourced shiraz under the Pyrette label confirms Bindi as one of the greatest small producers in Australia. Exports to the UK, the US and other major markets.

Bird in Hand   ★★★★★

Bird in Hand Road, Woodside, SA 5244 **Region** Adelaide Hills
T (08) 8389 9488 **www.**birdinhand.com.au **Open** Mon–Fri 10–5, w'ends 11–5
Winemaker Kym Milne MW, Dylan Lee, Matteo Malagese **Est.** 1997 **Dozens** 120000
Vyds 29ha

This family-owned business takes its name from a gold mine that prospered nearby during the 19th century. Andrew Nugent and winemaking director Kym Milne (MW) work together to produce estate wines of high quality. Sustainable initiatives in the vineyard include fertilisers and fungicides being derived from organic sources, and herbicide use has been drastically reduced, with future use moving to zero. The wines are released in four tiers: Tribute Series, Nest Egg, Bird in Hand and Two in the Bush. Exports to all major markets.

♥♥♥♥♥ **TED Edward Andrew Adelaide Hills Chardonnay 2017** Represents the most exceptional barrels of chardonnay made in the outstanding '17 vintage. It is a wine of restraint and finesse: white peach, Granny Smith apple and citrus singing the melody; barrel ferment characters the chorus. Will be long lived. Screwcap. 13% alc. **Rating** 97 **To** 2030 $150 ◎

♥♥♥♥♥ **Nest Egg Adelaide Hills Shiraz 2015** Matured in French oak for over 18 months. This is a delicious, smooth as silk, high quality cool-grown shiraz. Quite fascinating. Screwcap. 14.5% alc. **Rating** 96 **To** 2035 $99

Marie Elizabeth Adelaide Hills Cabernet Sauvignon 2013 Deeply coloured. Has all the hallmarks of top class cabernet sauvignon: blackcurrant to the fore, accompanied by nuances of black olive and sage; typical cabernet tannins run through the length of the palate, their role to support, not challenge, the fruit. The balance between the French oak resulting from 24 months maturation and the opulent fruit is nigh on perfect. A long future awaits those with patience. Screwcap. 14.5% alc. **Rating** 96 **To** 2043 $375

Adelaide Hills Merlot 2018 Very good colour. Has more structure and texture than most Australian merlots, but doesn't become heavy-footed as a result. Its fruit flavour spectrum from red to purple doesn't lose direction; the length and finish convincing. Screwcap. 14% alc. **Rating** 95 **To** 2029 $40

Pinot Grigio 2019 Nice grigio, complex but not overblown. The white-striped cylindrical bottle sends a subliminal message of a wine with generous nashi pear/ citrus/apple flavours. Vino-Lok. 12.5% alc. **Rating** 94 **To** 2022 $32

♚♚♚♚♚ **Adelaide Hills Arneis 2019 Rating** 92 **To** 2023 $32

Bird on a Wire Wines

51 Symons Street, Healesville, Vic 3777 (postal) **Region** Yarra Valley
T 0439 045 000 **www.**birdonawirewines.com.au **Open** Not
Winemaker Caroline Mooney **Est.** 2008 **Dozens** 850
This is the full-time business of winemaker Caroline Mooney. She grew up in the Yarra Valley and has had (other full-time) winemaking jobs in the valley for over 10 years. The focus is on small, single vineyard sites owned by growers committed to producing outstanding grapes. Having worked at the legendary Domaine Jean-Louis Chave in the 2006 vintage, she has a special interest in shiraz and marsanne, both grown from distinct sites on a single vineyard in the Yarra Glen area. Exports to the UK.

♚♚♚♚♚ **Yarra Valley Chardonnay 2017** It's from the Willowlake vineyard in the Upper Yarra and it's in a beautiful drinking place. It has flesh and flavour, excellent thrust and the length to match. Chalk, honeysuckle and loads of stone fruit. The press release suggests barbecued scallops as an accompaniment; it sounds terrific. Lovely wine. Screwcap. 13.1% alc. **Rating** 95 **To** 2026 $45 CM

Yarra Valley Syrah 2016 33% whole bunches and 15% new French oak. Grown on a vineyard at Yarra Glen. It's a nutty, peppery, twiggy shiraz with excellent, plush texture and sure delivery of cherry-plum fruit flavour. It's medium in weight and has everything balanced just so. Honey-soy characters hover about the nose; cedar wood adds polish to the palate. There's a lot to like about this. Screwcap. 14.2% alc. **Rating** 95 **To** 2030 $45 CM

♚♚♚♚♚ **Yarra Valley Marsanne 2015 Rating** 90 **To** 2023 $35 CM

BK Wines

Knotts Hill, Basket Range, SA 5138 **Region** Adelaide Hills
T 0410 124 674 **www.**bkwines.com.au **Open** By appt
Winemaker Brendon Keys **Est.** 2007 **Dozens** 4000
BK Wines is owned by NZ-born Brendon Keys and wife Kirsty. Brendon has packed a great deal into the past decade. He bounced between Australia and NZ before working in California with the well known Paul Hobbs; he then helped Paul set up a winery in Argentina. Brendon's tag-line is 'Wines made with love, not money', and he has not hesitated to confound the normal rules of engagement in winemaking. If he isn't remembered for this, the labels for his wines should do the trick. Exports to Canada, Norway, Italy, France, Cambodia, South Korea, NZ, Japan, Singapore, Hong Kong and China.

♚♚♚♚♚ **Archer Beau Single Barrel Piccadilly Valley Adelaide Hills Chardonnay 2017** This is a superb wine that balances a reductive mineral pungency with a laissez-faire oxidative riff. Dried hay, quince, camomile and curry powder notes, similar to a fine Jura. The acidity, though, far more relaxed. Juicy, layered and very

long. Pulse and flow. No hard angles. Effortless and extremely delicious. Cork.
Rating 96 To 2025 $110 NG
**Swaby Single Vineyard Piccadilly Valley Adelaide Hills Chardonnay
2019** Fermented wild in 1 and 2yo barrels, where it spent 10 months with regular
stirring. The result is an intense, richly flavoured wine that belies its lowish alcohol
with a billow of dried fig, tatami and mineral. Forceful and energetic across the
palate to virtually sublimate any obvious fruit references, aside from the feel of ripe
extract. A textural totem. Cork. Rating 95 To 2027 $60 NG

ΨΨΨΨΨ **Ramato Adelaide Hills Pinot Gris 2019** Rating 93 To 2023 $32 NG
Ovum Single Vineyard Lenswood Adelaide Hills Pinot Gris 2019
Rating 93 To 2024 $37 NG
**Waning Crescent Single Vineyard Mt Barker Summit Adelaide Hills
Syrah 2019** Rating 93 To 2024 NG
**One Ball Single Vineyard Kenton Valley Adelaide Hills Chardonnay
2019** Rating 92 To 2024 $38 NG
Skin n' Bones Single Vineyard Lenswood Adelaide Hills Pinot Noir 2019
Rating 92 To 2025 $37 NG
Gower Single Vineyard Lenswood Adelaide Hills Pinot Noir 2019
Rating 92 To 2027 $60 NG
Remy Single Barrel Lenswood Adelaide Hills Pinot Noir 2017 Rating 92
To 2024 $110 NG

Black & Ginger   ★★★★★

563 Sugarloaf Road, Rhymney, Vic 3374 **Region** Great Western
T 0409 964 855 **www.**blackandginger.com.au **Open** Not
Winemaker Hadyn Black **Est.** 2015 **Dozens** 400
This is the venture of two friends who met in 2002 after attending the same high school.
Haydn Black is cellar hand and winemaker, working in the Great Western region. Darcy
Naunton (ginger) is an entrepreneur in Melbourne. Their common interest in wine saw
them take a great leap in 2015 and buy 1t of shiraz from the renowned Malakoff Vineyard
in the Pyrenees, with further vintages following. Haydn and partner Lucy Joyce purchased a
rundown vineyard in Great Western in late '16, naming the wine Lily's Block after Haydn's
mother, who did much of the pruning and picking but unfortunately passed away before
tasting the wine.

ΨΨΨΨΨ **Malakoff Vineyard Pyrenees Shiraz 2018** 50% whole-bunch ferment,
3% viognier; 13 days on skins, 18 months in barrel (15% new). Juicy black cherry
and plum glide across the palate imparting flavour in harmony with all the
winemaker additions. The Malakoff Vineyard can produce superb fruit. Screwcap.
14.5% alc. Rating 95 To 2040 $45

ΨΨΨΨΨ **Arrawatta Vineyard Grenache Nouveau 2019** Rating 93 To 2021 $25 ❂
Miss Piggy Orange Muscat & Riesling 2019 Rating 90 To 2022 $25

BlackJack Vineyards   ★★★★☆

3379 Harmony Way, Harcourt, Vic 3453 **Region** Bendigo
T (03) 5474 2355 **www.**blackjackwines.com.au **Open** W'ends & some public hols 11–5
Winemaker Ian McKenzie, Ken Pollock **Est.** 1987 **Dozens** 3000 **Vyds** 6ha
Established by the McKenzie and Pollock families on the site of an old apple and pear orchard
in the Harcourt Valley, BlackJack is best known for some very good shirazs. Despite some
tough vintage conditions, BlackJack has managed to produce supremely honest, full-flavoured
and powerful wines, all with an edge of elegance. Exports to China.

ΨΨΨΨΨ **Mr Ramoy 2016** The first vintage of this blend of equal amounts from the
original shiraz block, the cabernet block and Block 6 shiraz. Crushed and
fermented separately in new French puncheons, sealed after fermentation, and
kept on skins for another 6 weeks, blended and returned to the same puncheons

for 22 months maturation. It might have been a disaster, but has come through
with flying colours; ornate, detailed and many-splendoured. Screwcap. 14.5% alc.
Rating 95 To 2036 $75

ŸŸŸŸŸ Block 6 Bendigo Shiraz 2017 Rating 92 To 2032 $38
Chortle's Edge Shiraz 2017 Rating 90 To 2027 $22
Bendigo Cabernet Merlot 2016 Rating 90 To 2026 $28

Bleasdale Vineyards ★★★★★

1640 Langhorne Creek Road, Langhorne Creek, SA 5255 **Region** Langhorne Creek
T (08) 8537 4000 **www**.bleasdale.com.au **Open** Mon–Sun 10–5
Winemaker Paul Hotker, Matt Laube **Est.** 1850 **Dozens** NFP **Vyds** 45ha
This is one of the most historic wineries in Australia; in 2015 it celebrated 165 years of
continuous winemaking by the direct descendants of the founding Potts family. Not so long
before the start of the 21st century, its vineyards were flooded every winter by diversion of the
Bremer River, which provided moisture throughout the dry, cool, growing season. In the new
millennium, every drop of water is counted. The vineyards have been significantly upgraded
and refocused: shiraz accounts for 45% of plantings, supported by seven other proven varieties.
Bleasdale has completely revamped its labels and packaging, and has headed to the Adelaide
Hills for sauvignon blanc, pinot gris and chardonnay under the direction of gifted winemaker
(and viticulturist) Paul Hotker. Exports to all major markets.

ŸŸŸŸŸ The Powder Monkey Single Vineyard Langhorne Creek Shiraz 2015
Matured in French oak (27% new) for 12 months. Gold medal Melbourne Wine
Awards '16. Previously tasted Jan '17; has held its colour well – and all of its other
features. In its youth I wrote, 'It is very concentrated and powerful, but there's
no sign of a midriff bulge. The fruits are all black, both berry and cherry, the oak
and tannins built into the very fabric of the wine.' Screwcap. 14% alc. **Rating** 97
To 2035 $69 ✪

ŸŸŸŸŸ The Iron Duke Langhorne Creek Cabernet Sauvignon 2018 It will be
some time before this sees the light of day – release date July '21 – yet it is already
showing its class. Blackberries dipped in dark chocolate, a sprinkling of baking
spices, violets and eucalyptus. In a medium-bodied mode, with slinky tannins and
a lingering finish. It will impress even more in time. Screwcap. 14% alc. **Rating** 96
To 2035 $69 JF ✪
Adelaide Hills Riesling 2019 The overall impact is juicy and refreshing, yet
there is a delicacy and focus from the seductive array of perfectly ripened fruit
that doesn't relax its grip on the long finish and aftertaste of the palate. Screwcap.
12% alc. **Rating** 95 To 2030 $29 ✪
Adelaide Hills Sauvignon Blanc 2019 On point for the variety in this region.
Lime and lemon juice – plus zest – mix it up with some feijoa and fresh herbs,
notably basil. Crisp sorbet-like acidity and a lingering finish make this an excellent
drink. Screwcap. 12.5% alc. **Rating** 95 To 2022 $22 JF ✪
Generations Langhorne Creek Shiraz 2018 It starts with a waft of meaty
reduction before florals, licorice and Middle Eastern spices take over. There's more.
Black plums, charry oak and a savoury overlay with plush tannins and a certain
vivacity. Appeals now, but will further reward those with patience. Screwcap.
14% alc. **Rating** 95 To 2035 $35 JF ✪
The Powder Monkey Single Vineyard Langhorne Creek Shiraz 2018
This is a sleeper – not due for release until Jul '21. Laden with dark fruit, an
assortment of baking spices and very silky smooth tannins working across the
full-bodied palate. While aged 1 year in French puncheons (20% new) might not
read as much, it comes across as more: charry, sweet and meaty. Screwcap. 14% alc.
Rating 95 To 2034 $69 JF
Wellington Road Langhorne Creek Shiraz Cabernet 2018 While shiraz
sits at 52%, cabernet initially struts its stuff more assertively with cassis, blackberry
essence and mint-choc flavours. Medium-bodied and even across the palate thanks
largely to its fine tannins. Screwcap. 14% alc. **Rating** 95 To 2030 $32 JF ✪

Frank Potts 2018 The aromas soar with violets, blackberries and exotic spices, although the medium-bodied palate is somewhat reticent. Tannins are neatly poised, however there's a slight edge to the oak; this has already found its groove. Screwcap. 14% alc. **Rating** 95 **To** 2028 $35 JF ✪

Langhorne Creek Cabernet Franc 2019 The suggestion is to slightly chill this juicy cabernet franc because it's made in an early drinking style best enjoyed as a spring–summer red. Well, it's delicious and easily enjoyed in autumn–winter too. Spicy red berries flecked with aniseed and, while it is lighter framed, tannins hold sway giving a grainy texture and some oomph to the finish. Screwcap. 13% alc. **Rating** 95 **To** 2023 $30 JF ✪

Generations Langhorne Creek Malbec 2018 Immediately impressive with its youthful purple-black hue. Laden with blackberry essence, plump plums, sweet licorice and more umami flavours of iodine and seaweed. It's fuller bodied but quite contained, with ribbons of velvety tannins and a flourish on the finish. The surprise is its approachability now, yet will continue to reward for quite some time. Screwcap. 14% alc. **Rating** 95 **To** 2032 $35 JF ✪

♟♟♟♟♟ **Adelaide Hills Chardonnay 2019 Rating** 93 **To** 2027 $30 JF
Second Innings Malbec 2018 Rating 93 **To** 2028 $22 JF✪
Adelaide Hills Pinot Gris 2019 Rating 92 **To** 2022 $22✪
Bremerview Langhorne Creek Shiraz 2018 Rating 92 **To** 2026 $22 JF✪
Langhorne Creek Grenache 2019 Rating 92 **To** 2026 $30 JF
Broad-Side Langhorne Creek Shiraz Cabernet Sauvignon Malbec 2018
Rating 91 **To** 2027 $22 JF✪
Mulberry Tree Langhorne Creek Cabernet Sauvignon 2018 Rating 91
To 2028 $22 JF✪
Potts' Catch Langhorne Creek Verdelho 2019 Rating 90 **To** 2024 $22 JF
Wellington Road Langhorne Creek GSM 2018 Rating 90 **To** 2027 $32 JF

🍇 Blewitt Springs Wine Co ★★★★★

477 Blewitt Springs Road, Blewitt Springs, SA 5171 **Region** McLaren Vale
T 0402 106 240 **www.**blewittspringswineco.com.au **Open** By appt
Winemaker Phil Tabor **Est.** 2017 **Dozens** 500 **Vyds** 7.3ha
It's impossible to do justice to the fast-moving complexity of Phil and Nina Tabor's Blewitt Springs Estate in the confines of this summary. Briefly, Phil's design engineering business in Adelaide became the subject of a bidding war between two suitors in 2008; the deal completed at the top of the market. In '13 he worked his first vintage in McLaren Vale and found a mentor in the well known Phil Christiansen. In '15 he purchased the 40ha Blewitt Springs Estate Vineyard, with 7.3ha of shiraz planted in three blocks in 1998, 2005 and '08. First he designed and built the 40t winery, completed in time for the bumper vintage of '17. He had agreed to sell 30t, assuming it would leave him with 8–10t, and swapped/purchased grenache and hatfuls of other varieties. In fact, he was left with 26t, the fermenters full to overflowing. Things returned to normal and 80% of the fruit is sold each year. Concurrently he had begun the cellar door building, renovated a stone bungalow and begun a new house for Nina and him to live in, leaving the bungalow as a luxury B&B. Phil is a hands-on operator and has every intention of doing much of the winemaking and viticulture himself. He has made space in the winery for other winemakers to make one-off wine, and he has learnt by seeing what (and why) they do. The key, however, is his belief in cool fermentation of his red wines, and he won't be changing that.

♟♟♟♟♟ **Reserve Shiraz 2017** '17 and Blewitt Springs are a potential force, with intense black and purple fruits creating the agenda timeline for a wine of great regional typicity, dark chocolate contributing the full stop. The vinification for all the Blewitt Springs wines is virtually identical. Screwcap. 14.6% alc. **Rating** 95 **To** 2040 $50

McLaren Vale Shiraz 2017 From the estate vineyard at Blewitt Springs on 750 million-year-old soils. Cold-soaked, cool-fermented, matured in old French and American oak for 18 months. The finish is lively and textured, black cherry dipped in dark chocolate. Screwcap. 14.6% alc. **Rating** 95 **To** 2037 $28 ✪

McLaren Vale Grenache 2017 Cold-soaked, 2 weeks on skins, matured in used American oak for 12 months. The spicy, savoury, lively aromas and flavours are in high relief. Screwcap. 14.6% alc. **Rating** 95 **To** 2027 $28 ○

🏆🏆🏆🏆🏆 McLaren Vale Grenache 2018 **Rating** 93 **To** 2028 $28
McLaren Vale Barbera 2016 **Rating** 90 **To** 2026 $28

Bloodwood ★★★★☆

231 Griffin Road, Orange, NSW 2800 **Region** Orange
T (02) 6362 5631 **www**.bloodwood.biz **Open** By appt
Winemaker Stephen Doyle **Est.** 1983 **Dozens** 4000 **Vyds** 8.43ha
Rhonda and Stephen Doyle are two of the pioneers of the Orange district; 2013 marked Bloodwood's 30th anniversary. The estate vineyards (chardonnay, riesling, merlot, cabernet sauvignon, shiraz, cabernet franc and malbec) are planted at an elevation of 810–860m, which provides a reliably cool climate. The wines are sold mainly through the cellar door and by an energetic, humorous and informatively run mailing list. Bloodwood has an impressive track record across the full gamut of wine styles, especially riesling; all of the wines have a particular elegance and grace. Very much part of the high quality reputation of Orange. Exports to Malaysia.

🏆🏆🏆🏆🏆 Shiraz 2017 Hand-picked and sorted in the vineyard, destemmed whole berries, cold-soaked, open-fermented hand-plunged, pressed to French hogsheads (25% new) (immersion bent) for 24 months maturation. Cool-grown flavours leap out of the glass with warm spices, pepper, bramble, forest floor and a complex, savoury palate. A lovely, elegant, medium-bodied wine picked at the exact moment for the best outcome. Screwcap. 13.8% alc. **Rating** 95 **To** 2032 $34 ○
Pinot Noir 2018 MV6 (50% of the total), 777, 114 and 115 clones; hand-picked and sorted in the vineyard. Fermentation was initiated when 777 was ready, then co-fermented and pressed to new French barriques and hogsheads, matured for 5 months. Improbably, the wine isn't smothered in oak, but it (oak) certainly provides a warm doona. Screwcap. 13.7% alc. **Rating** 94 **To** 2029 $35

🏆🏆🏆🏆🏆 Chirac 2009 **Rating** 92 $50
Riesling 2019 **Rating** 91 **To** 2024 $27
Schubert 2018 **Rating** 91 **To** 2025 $35
Big Men in Tights 2019 **Rating** 91 **To** 2021 $22 ○

Blue Gables ★★★★☆

100 Lanigan Road, Maffra West Upper, Vic 3859 **Region** Gippsland
T (03) 5148 0372 **www**.bluegables.com.au **Open** By appt w'ends 10–5
Winemaker Alastair Butt, Mal Stewart (sparkling) **Est.** 2004 **Dozens** 1800 **Vyds** 3.7ha
Blue Gables is the culmination of a long-held dream for chemical engineer Alistair and journalist wife Catherine Hicks. They purchased 8ha of a north-facing hillside slope from Catherine's father's dairy farm and built a two-storey gabled roof farmhouse, hence the name. This small vineyard, nestled high above the Macalister Irrigation District in East Gippsland, was established in 2004 with the planting of the first vines, and continued in '05 with 0.8ha each of sauvignon blanc, pinot gris and shiraz and 0.4ha of chardonnay. The wines have had significant success in the Gippsland and Victorian wines shows.

🏆🏆🏆🏆🏆 KT Reserve Shiraz 2018 This is a fine shiraz that bridles the tension and floral notes of more contemporary styles, while offering a warmer mid-palate boasting blue fruit allusions and tapenade; a riff of pepper grind acidity pulls it all long to a satisfying finish. Screwcap. **Rating** 93 **To** 2028 $65 NG
Gippsland Rose 2019 A translucent light coral hue shows promise. This mid-weighted rose was crafted from straight pinot gris, imparting berry sap and plenty of crunch. Almost saline on the finish, in the best sense. Screwcap. **Rating** 92 **To** 2020 $28 NG

Hanratty Hill Eastern Gippsland Shiraz 2018 This is a charming, plump, medium-bodied shiraz that exudes a warmth seldom seen in cooler sites this far south. Crafted with a meld of French and American oak, the latter conferring a toasty ampleur, there is ripe blue and boysenberry fruits, a whiff of vanilla pod and a finely tuned carriage of granular tannins pulling the flavours to good length. Screwcap. **Rating** 92 **To** 2026 $35 NG

Eastern Gippsland Pinot Gris 2019 A solid gris with resonant, dutifully ripe flavours of nashi pear and baked apple pie. The acidity is a little shrill on the back end, but there is enough stuffing to the middle of this weighty gris to handle it. A versatile wine at the table. Screwcap. **Rating** 91 **To** 2022 $30 NG

Jesse Eastern Gippsland Chardonnay 2018 The endeavours to confer tension through reductive handling result in a strong struck-match aroma that carries through to the palate. This, conversely, is ample and reminiscent of dried straw, oatmeal and stone fruit flavours. A wine that is a bit knees and elbows in its youth. Perhaps patience will reward. Screwcap. **Rating** 90 **To** 2024 $30 NG

Blue Pyrenees Estate ★★★★★

Vinoca Road, Avoca, Vic 3467 **Region** Pyrenees
T (03) 5465 1111 **www.**bluepyrenees.com.au **Open** 7 days 11–5
Winemaker Andrew Koerner, Chris Smales **Est.** 1963 **Dozens** 60 000 **Vyds** 149ha
Forty years after Remy Cointreau established Blue Pyrenees Estate (then known as Chateau Remy), the business was sold to a small group of Sydney businessmen. Former Rosemount senior winemaker Andrew Koerner heads the winery team. The core of the business is the very large estate plantings, most decades old, but with newer arrivals, including viognier. Blue Pyrenees has a number of programs designed to protect the environment and reduce its carbon footprint. Blue Pyrenees Estate has been purchased by Glenlofty Wines, forming the largest producer in the Pyrenees. Exports to Asia, primarily China.

ᵞᵞᵞᵞᵞ **Richardson Shiraz 2017** 25–40yo vines, destemmed, 20% whole bunches, 3 weeks on skins, 24 months in French and American oak (50% new). Medium to full-bodied. More elegance courtesy of the vintage and the response of the winemaking team. Shiraz fruit leads the way, tannins unusually subdued. Big tick. It is also remarkable how the oak has been taken on board. Diam. 14.5% alc. **Rating** 95 **To** 2037 $60

ᵞᵞᵞᵞᵞ **Section One Shiraz 2017 Rating** 91 **To** 2037 $44
Estate Red 2017 Rating 91 **To** 2032 $45
Luna Methode Traditionelle Chardonnay Pinot Noir NV Rating 91 $28
Exclusive Release Viognier 2019 Rating 90 **To** 2021 $28
Richardson Cabernet Sauvignon 2017 Rating 90 **To** 2022 $60
Richardson Reserve Cabernet Sauvignon 2013 Rating 90 **To** 2030 $150
Methode Traditionnelle Midnight Cuvee 2016 Rating 90 $36

Blue Rock Wines ★★★★☆

PO Box 692, Williamstown, SA 5351 **Region** Eden Valley
T 0419 817 017 **www.**bluerockwines.com.au **Open** Not
Winemaker Zissis Zachopoulos **Est.** 2005 **Dozens** 4000 **Vyds** 15ha
This is the venture of the brothers Zachopoulos: Nicholas, Michael and Zissis, the last with a double degree in viticulture and wine science from CSU. Michael and Nicholas manage the 104ha property, situated in the Eden Valley at an elevation of 475m. Most blocks are north-facing, the slopes providing frost protection with their natural air drainage; the soils likewise rich and free-draining. The vineyards have been planted so far to mainstream varieties, with an ongoing planting program including tempranillo, pinot gris, pinot noir, grenache and mataro. Most of the 450–500t production is the subject of a sales agreement with Grant Burge, but 75t are retained each year to make the Blue Rock wines.

ᵞᵞᵞᵞᵞ **Eden Valley Vineyard Series Pinot Noir Rose 2019** Among the darker, candy pink roses going around. It pulses with cranberry, plum, strawberry and apple blossom aromas and flavours. Fine and linear. Keen acidity is key to its high appeal. Screwcap. 12.5% alc. **Rating** 95 To 2025 $17 JP ❂

🍷🍷🍷🍷🍷 **The Christopher Barossa Shiraz Cabernet 2016** Rating 93 To 2032 $55 JP
Pantelis Barossa Cabernet Sauvignon 2015 Rating 90 To 2028 $50 JP

Boat O'Craigo   ★★★★☆

458 Maroondah Highway, Healesville, Vic 3777 **Region** Yarra Valley
T (03) 5962 6899 **www**.boatocraigo.com.au **Open** Fri–Sun 10.30–5.30
Winemaker Rob Dolan (Contract) **Est.** 1998 **Dozens** 3000 **Vyds** 21.63ha
Boat O'Craigo is a second-generation family business established by Steve and Margaret Graham in 1998 with the planting of a vineyard at Kangaroo Ground. The elevated site was planted with shiraz, cabernet sauvignon, grenache and viognier. The first vintage was in 2003. A second vineyard in Healesville, purchased in '03, is home to the cellar door. It is bounded by the Graceburn Creek and Black Spur Ranges, with plantings of pinot noir, chardonnay, gewurztraminer, gruner veltliner, pinot gris and sauvignon blanc. Since '15 Travers, Steve and Margaret's eldest son, has run the business. Boat O'Craigo was awarded Dark Horse of the Year in the *Wine Companion 2018*. Exports to Hong Kong and China.

🍷🍷🍷🍷🍷 **Black Cameron Single Vineyard Yarra Valley Shiraz 2018** This just sits right. Comfortable without it being overwhelming. A delicate combination of cherries, pepper and woodsy spices. Medium-bodied with supple, fine-grained tannins and an invitation to pour now. Screwcap. 13.5% alc. **Rating** 95 To 2028 $32 JF ❂

🍷🍷🍷🍷🍷 **Black Spur Single Vineyard Yarra Valley Sauvignon Blanc 2019** Rating 92 To 2022 $24 JF ❂
Reserve Yarra Valley Chardonnay 2017 Rating 90 To 2026 $45 JF
Braveheart Single Vineyard Yarra Valley Cabernet Sauvignon 2018 Rating 90 To 2028 $32 JF

Bochara Wines   ★★★★

1099 Glenelg Highway, Hamilton, Vic 3300 **Region** Henty
T (03) 5571 9309 **www**.bocharawines.com.au **Open** Fri–Sun 11–5 or by appt
Winemaker Martin Slocombe **Est.** 1998 **Dozens** 1000 **Vyds** 2.2ha
Planted in 1998, the 2.2ha vineyard includes sauvignon blanc (1ha), pinot noir (0.8ha) and gewurztraminer (0.4ha); varieties all well suited to the cold and sometimes temperamental Henty climate. The winery's tiny scale means that all operations are done by hand, with wines made onsite by owners Martin Slocombe and Kylie McIntyre. The wines are sold from the rustic cottage at the vineyard, and in restaurants and retailers across south western Victoria. The Belle Époque label design is taken from a 1901 poster advertising farming land at Bochara.

🍷🍷🍷🍷🍷 **Pinot Noir 2018** Hand-picked and open-fermented, aged in French oak. Ripe aromas, plums and cherries; notes of leaf mulch and oak providing further dimension. Full-flavoured but not heavy; some sweetness to the fruit with very light tannin; acidity seemingly providing the backbone. Surprisingly forward drinking from this cool region. Screwcap. 12.8% alc. **Rating** 92 To 2028 $31 SC
Picnic Train Rose 2018 Pinot noir crushed, pressed, juice settled and racked; a portion finishing ferment in used French barriques. Extended lees contact in tank component. Attractive bouquet typical of this variety in rose style, with strawberry aromas prominent and other red berries in the mix. Good mouthfeel; fruit sweetness well balanced with fresh acidity, and a tangy finish. Screwcap. 12.5% alc. **Rating** 91 To 2022 $26 SC

🍷🍷🍷🍷 **Sauvignon Blanc 2018** Rating 89 To 2022 $26 SC

Boireann

26 Donnellys Castle Road, The Summit, Qld 4377 **Region** Granite Belt
T (07) 4683 2194 **www**.boireannwinery.com.au **Open** Fri–Mon 10–4
Winemaker Brad Rowe **Est.** 1998 **Dozens** 1000 **Vyds** 1.6ha

Boireann is set among the great granite boulders and trees that are so much a part of the Granite Belt. The vineyard is planted to 11 varieties, including four that make the Lurnea, a Bordeaux blend; shiraz and viognier; grenache and mourvedre for a Rhône blend; and a straight merlot. Tannat, pinot noir (French) and sangiovese, barbera and nebbiolo (Italian) make up the viticultural League of Nations. Peter and Therese Stark sold the business in 2017 but worked closely with new managers Brad Rowe and wife Metz; Brad made his first wines in 2018. Exports to Hong Kong and China.

ŸŸŸŸŸ **Granite Belt Shiraz Viognier 2018** 550 bottles made. 10% viognier. Old Block Shiraz. It's a complex, smoky, spicy shiraz with cherry, game and especially plum flavours curling persuasively through the mouth. Viognier is noticeable and yet swept entirely along by the plushness of shiraz. Although this wine has ample flavour and exquisitely ripe tannin, its quality is almost entirely due to its out-of-the-ordinary complexity. Every time you bring it to your mouth you notice something different. Screwcap. 13.6% alc. **Rating** 95 To 2030 $65 CM
Granite Belt Cabernet Sauvignon 2018 Excellent depth of flavour and the structure to match. The quality is clear. Boysenberry, wood smoke, redcurrant and cedar wood flavours come whispered with fresh tobacco. Impressive. Screwcap. 14.6% alc. **Rating** 95 To 2032 $35 CM ✪
Granite Belt Shiraz 2018 Game, mulch and general spice notes lend a distinctly savoury edge. This is particularly complex and dry, though there's also very good concentration of fruit and plenty of foresty herb notes. A wine of presence. When you drink this wine you enter its world. Screwcap. 13.2% alc. **Rating** 94 To 2032 $35 CM
Granite Belt Tannat 2018 It's a strikingly dry, serious red with cherry, chicory and fresh leather flavours cut through with both apple-like acidity and sheets of earth-shot tannin. It's well fruited and absolutely savoury. Intriguing wine. Screwcap. 13.7% alc. **Rating** 94 To 2029 $35 CM

ŸŸŸŸŸ **La Cima Granite Belt Sangiovese 2018** Rating 93 To 2027 $35 CM
The Lurnea 2018 Rating 92 To 2029 $35 CM
La Cima Rosso 2018 Rating 92 To 2026 $40 CM
La Cima Granite Belt Nebbiolo 2018 Rating 91 To 2025 $40 CM
Granite Belt Mourvedre 2018 Rating 91 To 2027 $35 CM
La Cima Granite Belt Barbera 2018 Rating 90 To 2023 $35 CM

Bondar Wines

Rayner Vineyard, 24 Twentyeight Road, McLaren Vale, SA 5171 **Region** McLaren Vale
T 0147 888 553 **www**.bondarwines.com.au **Open** By appt
Winemaker Andre Bondar **Est.** 2013 **Dozens** 3000 **Vyds** 13.5ha

Husband and wife Andre Bondar and Selina Kelly began a deliberately unhurried journey in 2009, which culminated in the purchase of the celebrated Rayner Vineyard post-vintage '13. Andre had been a winemaker at Nepenthe wines for 7 years, and Selina had recently completed a law degree but was already disillusioned about the legal landscape. They changed focus and began to look for a vineyard capable of producing great shiraz. The Rayner Vineyard had all the answers: a ridge bisecting the land, Blewitt Springs sand on the eastern side; and the Seaview, heavier clay loam soils over limestone on the western side. The vineyard has been substantially reworked and includes 10ha of shiraz, with smaller amounts of grenache, mataro, touriga, carignan, cinsaut and counoise. Exports to the UK, the US and China.

ŸŸŸŸŸ **Adelaide Hills Chardonnay 2018** Hand-picked, single vineyard, 405 dozen made. A complex wine, but there's no suggestion of its fruit being compromised by winemaker's thumbprints. It has perfect balance and a freshness to the white peach, melon and grapefruit flavours. The finish and aftertaste are the high points of a high class wine. Screwcap. 12.5% alc. **Rating** 97 **To** 2032 $35 ✪

Violet Hour McLaren Vale Shiraz 2018 The fabulous deep violet colour wasn't the inspiration for the name of the wine, but the glove fits. It is medium to full-bodied, overflowing with flavour, yet has a studied elegance. Oak and tannins provide texture and structure, but not to the point of distraction. Screwcap. 14.1% alc. **Rating** 97 **To** 2038 $28 ✪

ΨΨΨΨΨ **Rayner Vineyard Shiraz 2018** Shimmering mid-ruby, almost lilac. This is slick. Polished and yet far from the overtly manipulated wines so often the scar on the warm-climate vine scape. Floral. Boysenberry pie in a glass. Sexy vanillan oak clads the seams. Peppery acidity tows the tail. Long and seamless. Screwcap. **Rating** 95 **To** 2027 $45 NG

Mataro 2018 Hand-picked sans additions, this delicious wine hails from the warm flats of Wilunga. Prime turf for this physiologically ferrous and late ripening variety to strut it's heavy riffs: charcuterie, anise, damson plum, fecund strawberry, white pepper and a twine of dried herb. Very good with a tannic grind growing in the glass. Screwcap. **Rating** 95 **To** 2027 $32 NG ✪

Fiano 2019 Hand-picked at dawn, fermented in ceramic eggs. Here it is again, fiano is a white wine with its own inbuilt characteristic of producing its own texture and structure – oak not needed, nor included. Really attractive wine, great value. Screwcap. 13% alc. **Rating** 94 **To** 2022 $28 ✪

McLaren Vale Grenache Cinsault Rose 2019 Salmon-pink. The voluminously scented bouquet, with a handful of spice added for good measure, is replicated on the vibrantly fresh and flavoursome palate. Classic anywhere, any time proposition, but with serious intent. Screwcap. 13% alc. **Rating** 94 **To** 2021 $24 ✪

ΨΨΨΨΨ **Rayner Vineyard Grenache 2019 Rating** 92 **To** 2024 $38 NG
Junto McLaren Vale GSM 2019 Rating 92 **To** 2024 $28 NG

Boroka   ★★★★

PO Box 242, Warragul, Vic 3820 **Region** Various
T (03) 5623 3391 **www**.boroka.com.au **Open** Not
Winemaker Hamish Seabrook **Est.** 1968 **Dozens** 500
The Boroka of today bears no resemblance to that of the late 1960s and '70s, when its activities were centred on the foothills of the Grampians in western Victoria. David McCracken received support from Viv Thomson of Best's and its then winemaker Trevor Mast. While the McCracken family moved from Great Western, and these days reside elsewhere, the connection with the region has been maintained through Hamish Seabrook, who not only makes the Boroka wines, but was a winemaker for Best's before moving to the Barossa Valley, where he now lives and works. He sources grapes and wines from various parts of SA and Victoria for the Boroka brand. Exports to China.

ΨΨΨΨΨ **The Pinnacle Coonawarra Cabernet Sauvignon 2015** Machine-harvested, open-fermented, matured in French oak (30% new) for 24 months. Powerful and rich, with layers of blackcurrant, mulberry and tannins, the latter woven throughout the palate and will sustain the wine for many years to come. Looks like Pete Bissell may have made the wine. Diam. 15% alc. **Rating** 95 **To** 2035 $42

ΨΨΨΨΨ **Crackerjack Shiraz 2016 Rating** 92 **To** 2029 $48

Boston Bay Wines   ★★★☆

Lincoln Highway, Port Lincoln, SA 5606 **Region** Southern Eyre Peninsula
T (08) 8684 3600 **www**.bostonbaywines.com.au **Open** 7 days 12–4
Winemaker David O'Leary, Nick Walker **Est.** 1984 **Dozens** 2200 **Vyds** 6.95ha
A tourist-oriented operation that has extended the viticultural map in SA. Situated on the same latitude as Adelaide, it overlooks the Spencer Gulf at the southern tip of the Eyre Peninsula. Proprietors Graham and Mary Ford say, 'It is the only vineyard in the world to offer frequent sightings of whales at play in the waters at its foot'.

ԱԱԱԱՉ **Riesling 2019** Pronounced lime juice and other citrus aromas on the bouquet with some floral notes, all of which provides clear and attractive varietal definition. Flavoursome and soft on the palate, although the lively acidity kicks in on the finish. Drink it while it's fresh and youthful. Screwcap. 12% alc. **Rating** 90 **To** 2024 $24 SC

ԱԱԱԱ **Merlot 2017** **Rating** 89 **To** 2024 $24 SC

Bourke & Travers ★★★★

PO Box 457, Clare, SA 5453 **Region** Clare Valley
T 0400 745 057 **www**.bourkeandtravers.com **Open** Not
Winemaker David Travers, Michael Corbett **Est.** 1998 **Dozens** 250 **Vyds** 6ha
Owner David Travers' family has been continuously farming in Australia for 157 years. In the 1870s David's great-grandfather, Nicholas Travers, established a vineyard south of Leasingham, between what is now Kilikanoon and O'Leary Walker. However, his son Paul left to establish a large sheep and grazing property near Port Lincoln. Paul's son Gerald (David's father) retains these properties today; David is heavily involved in their operation. He (David) established Bourke & Travers on Armagh Creek in 1996 and planted the first grapes (shiraz) in '98. The Bourke in the brand comes from David's mother's maiden name. The wine portfolio has been increased with a Syrah Rose, a single vineyard Grenache and the introduction of 25% whole-bunch fermentation in the Shiraz. Only one wine was submitted for the *Wine Companion 2021*, David Travers taking the opportunity to age his wines.

ԱԱԱԱԱ **Single Vineyard Clare Valley Shiraz 2018** Hand-picked, matured in used large-format oak. It's medium-bodied, black fruits dotted with splashes of red; both flavour and structure having impeccable balance. Screwcap. 13.8% alc. **Rating** 94 **To** 2030 $40

Bowen Estate ★★★★☆

15459 Riddoch Highway, Coonawarra, SA 5263 **Region** Coonawarra
T (08) 8737 2229 **www**.bowenestate.com.au **Open** Mon–Fri 10–5, w'ends 10–4
Winemaker Emma Bowen **Est.** 1972 **Dozens** 12 000 **Vyds** 33ha
Regional veteran Doug Bowen presides over one of Coonawarra's landmarks, but he has handed over full winemaking responsibility to daughter Emma, 'retiring' to the position of viticulturist. In May 2015 Bowen Estate celebrated its 40th vintage with a tasting of 24 wines (Shiraz and Cabernet Sauvignon) from 1975 to 2014. Exports to the UK, the Maldives, Sri Lanka, Singapore, China, Japan and NZ.

ԱԱԱԱԱ **Coonawarra Cabernet Sauvignon 2018** Deep crimson-purple. It is full of rich fruit, yet not extractive or alcoholic, simply full-bodied with a perfect marriage of fruit, oak and tannins. Bowen has had its ups and downs – this is definitely up. Screwcap. 14.5% alc. **Rating** 95 **To** 2038 $34
Coonawarra Shiraz 2018 Rich and complex; layers of blackberry and satsuma plum reflecting an outstanding vintage. A long life ahead for those who are patient. Screwcap. 14.5% alc. **Rating** 94 **To** 2038 $34

Bowman's Run ★★★★

1305 Beechworth-Wodonga Road, Wooragee, Vic 3747 **Region** Beechworth
T (03) 5728 7318 **Open** By appt
Winemaker Daniel Balzer **Est.** 1989 **Dozens** 200 **Vyds** 1ha
Struan and Fran Robertson have cabernet sauvignon, riesling and small plots of shiraz and traminer dating back to 1989. The tiny winery is part of a larger general agricultural holding.

ԱԱԱԱՉ **Beechworth Cabernet Sauvignon Shiraz 2016** Bright crimson-purple colour sets the scene for a light to medium-bodied blend, cassis and red fruits providing a juicy mouthfeel of harmonious fruit flavours. Screwcap. 13.8% alc. **Rating** 92 **To** 2029 $30

Jessie's Rock Beechworth Rose 2019 Brilliant pink-magenta. No info on the grapes used, but that barely matters. It's fresh, crisp and dry; length and balance there for the taking. A very good rose for all seasons. Screwcap. 12.5% alc. **Rating** 90 **To** 2021 $25

Box Grove Vineyard ★★★★★

955 Avenel-Nagambie Road, Tabilk, Vic 3607 **Region** Nagambie Lakes
T 0409 210 015 **www**.boxgrovevineyard.com.au **Open** By appt
Winemaker Sarah Gough **Est.** 1995 **Dozens** 2500 **Vyds** 28.25ha
This is the venture of the Gough family, with industry veteran (and daughter) Sarah Gough managing the vineyard, winemaking and marketing. Having started with 10ha each of shiraz and cabernet sauvignon under contract to Brown Brothers, Sarah decided to switch the focus of the business to what could loosely be called 'Mediterranean varieties'. These days shiraz and prosecco are the main varieties, with smaller plantings of pinot gris, primitivo, vermentino, roussanne, sousao, grenache, nebbiolo, negroamaro, mourvedre and viognier. Osteria (an Italian word meaning a place that serves wine and food) hosts tastings and meals prepared by visiting Melbourne chefs, by appointment. Exports to the UK and China.

🍷🍷🍷🍷🍷 **Shiraz Roussanne 2017** The shiraz (97%) and roussanne (3%) were grown side by side, picked and fermented together, matured in new and old French barriques. This is a fragrant and lively light to medium-bodied wine; the finish long and clean. Elegant with a capital E. Screwcap. 14.1% alc. **Rating** 95 **To** 2023 $35 ❂
Roussanne 2018 Part wild-fermented in used French oak, part in stainless steel, matured on light lees for 15 months, stirred every 6 weeks. It has all come together very well: enticing colour and flavours of ripe pink grapefruit and melon. Screwcap. 14% alc. **Rating** 94 **To** 2023 $35

🍷🍷🍷🍷🍷 **Pinot Gris 2019 Rating** 90 **To** 2021 $28
Vermentino 2019 Rating 90 **To** 2020 $28
Primitivo 2018 Rating 90 **To** 2024 $39
Late Harvest Viognier 2019 Rating 90 **To** 2022 $28

Boydell's ★★★★☆

65 Allyn River Road, East Gresford, NSW 2317 **Region** Hunter Valley
T (02) 4938 9661 **www**.boydells.com.au **Open** Not
Winemaker First Creek (Liz Silkman) **Est.** 2016 **Dozens** NFP **Vyds** 7ha
Jane and Daniel Maroulis own and operate two businesses on an 80ha property at East Gresford. First is a combined vineyard and luxury accommodation (Boydell's Escape) in a large African safari tent that has attracted much praise in lifestyle/travel media; second is the breeding of cattle. The vineyard is planted to verdelho (2ha), chardonnay (newly planted, 2ha), shiraz (1.5ha), merlot (1ha) and pinot noir (0.5ha). Having the wines made by Liz Silkman at First Creek Winemakers was a very wise decision. The name of the winery refers to Charles Boydell, who first took up the land in 1826.

🍷🍷🍷🍷🍷 **Reserve Hunter Valley Chardonnay 2019** Peachy, buttery, creamy cashew flavours and texture flow into, through and around each other. Ready now. Screwcap. 12.3% alc. **Rating** 93 **To** 2022 $45

🍷🍷🍷🍷 **Hunter Valley Verdelho 2019 Rating** 89 **To** 2020 $25

Brand & Sons – Coonawarra ★★★★

PO Box 18, Coonawarra, SA 5263 **Region** Coonawarra
T 0488 771 046 **www**.brandandsons.com.au **Open** Not
Winemaker Sam Brand **Est.** 2000 **Dozens** 2000 **Vyds** 37ha
The Brand family story starts with the arrival of Eric Brand in Coonawarra in 1950. He married Nancy Redman and purchased a 24ha block from the Redman family, relinquishing his job as a baker and becoming a grapegrower. It was not until '66 that the first Brand's Laira

wine was made. The family sold 50% of the Brand's Laira winery in '94 to McWilliam's, Jim Brand staying on as chief winemaker until he died in 2005. Sam Brand is the fourth generation of this family, which has played a major role in Coonawarra for over 50 years. Exports to the US, Canada, Singapore, Hong Kong and China.

ΨΨΨΨΨ **Icon Cabernet Sauvignon 2016** Crushed and destemmed, open-fermented, the juice bled off to increase concentration of the fruit, matured in French oak (65% new) for 22 months. The colour is slightly turbid, and the run-off was essential. Cork. 14.5% alc. **Rating** 90 **To** 2029

Brand's Laira Coonawarra ★★★★★

14860 Riddoch Highway, Coonawarra, SA 5263 **Region** Coonawarra
T (08) 8736 3260 **www.**brandslaira.com **Open** Mon–Fri 9–4.30, w'ends & public hols 11–4
Winemaker Peter Weinberg, Amy Blackburn **Est.** 1966 **Dozens** NFP **Vyds** 278ha
Three days before Christmas 2015, Casella Family Brands received an early present when it purchased Brand's Laira from McWilliam's. Over the years McWilliam's had moved from 50% to 100% ownership of Brand's and thereafter it purchased an additional 100ha of vineyards (taking Brand's to its present 278ha) and had expanded both the size, and the quality, of the winery. Exports to select markets.

ΨΨΨΨΨ **Stentiford's Old Vines Shiraz 2016** The back label says the vines were planted by Captain Stentiford in 1893, and the length and focus of the wine in the mouth speaks eloquently of very old vines. The structure and texture, coupled with the dark fruits, are the keys to the wine's quality, though not making oak and tannins irrelevant. Screwcap. 14% alc. **Rating** 97 **To** 2046

ΨΨΨΨΨ **One Seven One Cabernet Sauvignon 2016** High quality Coonawarra cabernet at the helm. Deep colour. Intense blackcurrant and mulberry fruit and firm but not aggressive tannins. Oak is not mentioned in the dispatches, but is present in what is a high quality wine. Screwcap. 14.5% alc. **Rating** 95 **To** 2041

ΨΨΨΨΨ **1968 Vines Cabernet Sauvignon 2016 Rating** 91 **To** 2031 $40
August Tide Red Blend 2016 Rating 90 **To** 2025 SC
August Tide Red Blend 2014 Rating 90 **To** 2029 $25

Brangayne of Orange ★★★★

837 Pinnacle Road, Orange, NSW 2800 **Region** Orange
T (02) 6365 3229 **www.**brangayne.com **Open** Mon–Fri 11–4, Sat 11–5
Winemaker Simon Gilbert, Will Gilbert **Est.** 1994 **Dozens** 3500 **Vyds** 25.7ha
The Hoskins family (formerly orchardists) moved into grapegrowing in 1994 and have progressively established high quality vineyards. Brangayne produces good wines across all mainstream varieties ranging, remarkably, from pinot noir to cabernet sauvignon. It sells a substantial part of its crop to other winemakers. Exports to China.

ΨΨΨΨΨ **Isolde Reserve Chardonnay 2018** It takes time for this to unfurl. It reveals gentle lemon blossom and ginger spice. It's not a big wine; just enough stone fruit and oak spice to warrant another look. Screwcap. 13.3% alc. **Rating** 90 **To** 2026 $30 JF
Merlot 2018 Vibrant purple hue for a merlot. Fresh and lively with its cooling plums, spice and garrigue. It needs time to settle as the oak feels raw and the acidity puckering. Screwcap. 14% alc. **Rating** 90 **To** 2027 $35 JF

ΨΨΨΨ **Riesling 2019 Rating** 89 $22 JF

Brash Vineyard ★★★★★

PO Box 455, Yallingup, WA 6282 **Region** Margaret River
T 0448 448 840 **www.**brashvineyard.com.au **Open** Not
Winemaker Bruce Dukes (Contract) **Est.** 2000 **Dozens** 1500 **Vyds** 18ha

Brash Vineyard was established in 1998 as Woodside Valley Estate. While most of the grapes were sold to other Margaret River producers, cabernet sauvignon, shiraz, chardonnay and merlot were made, and in '09 the Cabernet Sauvignon and the Shiraz earned the winery a 5-star rating. It is now owned by Chris and Anne Carter (managing partners, who live and work onsite), Brian and Anne McGuinness, and Rik and Jenny Nitert. The vineyard is now mature and produces high quality fruit.

YYYYY **Single Vineyard Margaret River Chardonnay 2018** Estate-grown, hand-picked, fermented and matured for 9 months in a mix of new and used French oak. Still as fresh as a daisy, with grapefruit prominent on the long finish. Classy chardonnay. Screwcap. 13.6% alc. **Rating** 95 **To** 2025 $35 ✪
Brash Road Vineyard Single Vineyard Margaret River Sauvignon Blanc 2019 Clear quartz. An attractive wine with a tropical fest of aromas and flavours, the length paying tribute to a totally delicious sauvignon blanc. Screwcap. 12.4% alc. **Rating** 94 **To** 2022 $23 ✪
Single Vineyard Margaret River Cabernet Sauvignon 2017 Estate-grown, 2.6t/acre, matured for 16 months in new and used French oak. Medium-bodied. Elegant from start to the long finish and aftertaste. Screwcap. 14.2% alc. **Rating** 94 **To** 2030 $40

YYYYY **Single Vineyard Margaret River Shiraz 2017** Rating 92 To 2032 $35
Single Vineyard Margaret River Cabernet Sauvignon 2016 Rating 92 **To** 2029 $40

Brave Goose Vineyard ★★★★

PO Box 852, Seymour, Vic 3660 **Region** Central Victoria
T 0417 553 225 **www**.bravegoosevineyard.com.au **Open** By appt
Winemaker Nina Stocker **Est.** 1988 **Dozens** 1000 **Vyds** 6.5ha
The Brave Goose Vineyard was planted in 1988 by former chairman of the Grape & Wine Research and Development Corporation, Dr John Stocker and wife Joanne. In '87 they found a property on the inside of the Great Dividing Range, near Tallarook, with north-facing slopes and shallow, weathered ironstone soils. They established 2.5ha each of shiraz and cabernet sauvignon, and 0.5ha each of merlot, viognier and gamay; but made only small amounts under the Brave Goose label. The brave goose in question was the sole survivor of a flock put into the vineyard to repel cockatoos and foxes. Two decades on, Jo and John handed the reins of the operation to their winemaker daughter Nina and son-in-law John Day.

YYYYY **Central Victoria Shiraz 2017** Hand-picked, chilled, wild-fermented with 10% whole bunch, matured for 12 months in 2yo French oak. All the right steps for a medium-bodied shiraz. Blackberry and black cherry are couched in supple tannins, oak a reprise. Screwcap. 14% alc. **Rating** 94 **To** 2032 $28 ✪
Cabernet Sauvignon 2018 Includes 10% merlot and 5% malbec. Destemmed, small open fermenters, 15 days post-ferment maceration, matured for 18 months in 2yo French oak, not fined. Full crimson-purple hue; a rich medium to full-bodied cabernet that is all about fruit, not tannins. Almost creamy cassis, good line and length, ditto balance, admirable control of alcohol and tannins. Screwcap. 14% alc. **Rating** 94 **To** 2033 $28 ✪

YYYYY **Viognier 2018** Rating 90 To 2022 $28

Bream Creek ★★★★★

Marion Bay Road, Bream Creek, Tas 7175 **Region** Southern Tasmania
T 0419 363 714 **www**.breamcreekvineyard.com.au **Open** Not
Winemaker Pat Colombo **Est.** 1974 **Dozens** 6500 **Vyds** 7.6ha
Until 1990 the Bream Creek fruit was sold to Moorilla Estate, but since then the winery has been independently owned and managed by Fred Peacock, legendary for the care he bestows on the vines under his direction. Fred's skills have seen an increase in production and outstanding wine quality across the range, headed by the Pinot Noir. The list of trophies and medals won is extensive. Fred's expertise as a consultant is in constant demand. Exports to China.

♟♟♟♟♟ **Old Vine Reserve Riesling 2019** Vinous. Long. Powerful and yet so delicate. Akin to a penumbra of yellow: grapefruit, quince and lemon. A smoky whiff and salinity, too. The fleck of residual sugar sublimated by the greater whole to the point of palpable dryness. Real thrust and parry between fruit and structure here. Very fine. **Rating** 96 **To** 2031 $48 NG ✪

Pinot Noir 2017 First tasted Jan '19, then late Sept '19 in the company (inter alia) of the Bass Phillip wines from the '17 vintage, and it stood proud. Less intoxicatingly powerful, but pure and fragrant; the palate supple and exceptionally long. Fully deserves its string of trophies. Great value. Screwcap. 13.5% alc. **Rating** 96 **To** 2032 $42 ✪

Riesling 2019 This address' rieslings are benchmark. Talc, bath salts, lemon scents and whiff of gentle lime without anything pushed to brittle acid levels. This wine skims the cheeks, gently punctuating the effortless flow with flecks of mineral energy. Screwcap. **Rating** 95 **To** 2029 $31 NG ✪

Reserve Chardonnay 2017 Highly impressive. Creamy and stone fruit-rich, yet linear, wild-yeast pungent, pebbly and mineral. Cool-climate salient, yet the intensity of tangerine, dried mango, toasted hazelnut, curd and apricot scents suggests a botrytic whiff. Meursault-like. Riveting vinosity, thrust of fruit and parry of energy. Delicious wine. Screwcap. **Rating** 95 **To** 2025 $48 NG

Late Disgorged 2005 A blend of 58% chardonnay and the rest, pinot noir. A brooding wine of incredible depth and complexity. Founded on an extended period on lees, well in excess of a decade; it billows across the mouth as a plume of creamy nourishment. Toasty and rich, the bead of fizz is relentless, serving as a carriage for notes of honeysuckle, orange blossom, ginger and brioche. This rivals a very fine Champagne, without the febrile acidity. **Rating** 95 $75 NG

♟♟♟♟♟ **Pinot Noir 2018 Rating** 93 **To** 2025 $42 NG
Late Picked Schonburger 2018 Rating 93 **To** 2024 $31 NG
Sauvignon Blanc 2019 Rating 92 **To** 2022 $31 NG
Chardonnay 2018 Rating 92 **To** 2026 $36 NG
Pinot Grigio 2019 Rating 92 **To** 2022 $31 NG
Pinot Rose 2019 Rating 91 **To** 2022 $31 NG
Cabernet Merlot 2018 Rating 91 **To** 2026 $36 NG
Schonburger 2019 Rating 90 **To** 2021 $31 NG

Bremerton Wines   ★★★★★

Strathalbyn Road, Langhorne Creek, SA 5255 **Region** Langhorne Creek
T (08) 8537 3093 **www.**bremerton.com.au **Open** 7 days 10–5
Winemaker Rebecca Willson **Est.** 1988 **Dozens** 30 000 **Vyds** 120ha
Bremerton has been producing wines since 1988. Rebecca Willson (chief winemaker) and Lucy Willson (marketing manager) are the first sisters in Australia to manage and run a winery. With 120ha of premium vineyards (80% of which goes into their own labels), they grow cabernet sauvignon, shiraz, verdelho, chardonnay, sauvignon blanc, malbec, merlot, fiano, graciano and petit verdot. Exports to most major markets.

♟♟♟♟♟ **Batonnage Langhorne Creek Chardonnay 2018** Maturation in French oak barriques for 12 months with batonnage has a following and it's easy to see why. It keeps to a citrus line – lemon zest and pink grapefruit pith – then detours into grilled nuts and almond meal, finishing with a leesy, creamy mouthfilling magnetism and juicy fruit acidity. Seduction is complete. Screwcap. 12.5% alc. **Rating** 95 **To** 2028 $32 JP ✪

Special Release Langhorne Creek Fiano 2019 The white Sicilian is a rising star in this part of SA. It shows its class through and through with clean fruit, focused acidity balanced by a resounding smooth mouthfeel and length. Nashi pear, Golden Delicious apple, lemon peel and an almond/ground pistachio nuttiness that adds crunch. Good drinking. Screwcap. 12.5% alc. **Rating** 95 **To** 2029 $24 JP ✪

Old Adam Langhorne Creek Shiraz 2017 Old Adam is representative of some of the best quality shiraz produced at Bremerton. It is both complex and yet down to earth in a typical Langhorne Creek way, with layers of ripe, blackberry fruit and dark chocolate in the lead. Black olive tapenade savoury aroma notes mix with sour cherry cola. Concentrated fruit power with balanced mocha oak and focussed tannins build on the palate. A wine still in the building process. Do not disturb. Diam. 14.5% alc. **Rating** 95 **To** 2034 $56 JP

B.O.V. 2016 60% shiraz, 40% cabernet sauvignon. Only 4 barrels were selected for BOV. How seductive, how dangerously drinkable now, but the best is yet to come. Intense black fruits, licorice and chocolate notes wind their way around gently expressive oak. Big impact wine but never excessive, it floods the mouth with flavour, in balance with oak and velvety tannins all the way. Diam. 14.5% alc. **Rating** 95 **To** 2034 $85 JP

Special Release Langhorne Creek Grenache 2019 The decision to not blend this parcel of grenache and to present it as a stand alone wine was wise. It has personality to burn. Lifted, intense perfume of raspberry cordial, stewed plums, chocolate-covered cherries and star anise. Concentrated fruit burrows deep into the palate and just keeps going. Certainly opens your mind to the grape and its possibilities, if you needed convincing, that is. Screwcap. 14.5% alc. **Rating** 95 **To** 2028 $24 JP ✪

Batonnage Langhorne Creek Shiraz Malbec 2018 Fermented and matured in French oak for 16 months, the malbec lees-stirred (batonnage). Lees stirring can be a tannin tamer, hence the softness in this wine. It helps emphasise the fruit, in all of its blackberry, black cherry, spicy plumminess. Smooth across the palate, fine in tannin and bursting with intensity, it's so good now. Ageing ability will be interesting to see. Screwcap. 14.5% alc. **Rating** 94 **To** 2030 $32 JP

Special Release Tempranillo Graciano 2018 55/45% tempranillo/graciano. The Spanish blend highlights the connection these two grapes share. They are made for each other. Fragrant wine of herbs and spices, sour cherries, bitter chocolate and tempranillo's signature red licorice. Impressively tannin-taut, but with enough release for the black and red fruits to star. A faint hint of savouriness to close. Screwcap. 14% alc. **Rating** 94 **To** 2028 $24 JP ✪

🍷🍷🍷🍷🍷 **Special Release Vermentino 2019 Rating** 93 **To** 2025 $24 JP ✪
Special Release Mourvedre 2018 Rating 93 **To** 2026 $24 JP ✪
Special Release Grenache 2019 Rating 92 **To** 2024 $24 JP ✪
Special Release Malbec 2018 Rating 92 **To** 2025 $24 JP ✪
Racy Rose 2019 Rating 91 **To** 2024 $18 JP ✪
Special Release Shiraz 2019 Rating 91 **To** 2023 $24 JP
Mollie & Merle Verdelho 2019 Rating 90 **To** 2024 $18 JP ✪
Special Release Vermentino 2018 Rating 90 **To** 2024 $24 JP
Tamblyn Cabernet Shiraz Malbec Merlot 2018 Rating 90 **To** 2026 $18 JP ✪
Special Release Petit Verdot 2018 Rating 90 **To** 2033 $24 JP
Special Release Lagrein 2017 Rating 90 **To** 2031 $24 JP

Briar Ridge Vineyard   ★★★★★

Mount View Road, Mount View, NSW 2325 **Region** Hunter Valley
T (02) 4990 3670 **www**.briarridge.com.au **Open** 7 days 10–5
Winemaker Alex Beckett, Gwyneth Olsen (Consultant) **Est.** 1972 **Dozens** 9500
Vyds 39ha

Semillon and shiraz have been the most consistent performers. Underlying the suitability of these varieties to the Hunter Valley, Briar Ridge has been a model of stability, and has the comfort of substantial estate vineyards from which it is able to select the best grapes. It also has not hesitated to venture into other regions, notably Orange. Alex Beckett has taken over winemaking duties from Gwyn Olsen (Gwyn remains as a consultant). Exports to the UK, Europe and Canada.

🍷🍷🍷🍷🍷 Dairy Hill Single Vineyard Semillon Museum Release 2011 Quite a few re-release cellar/museum wines are strutting across middle-age. In this instance, early middle-age! Showcasing scents of buttered toast, lemon oil and curd that patience bestows. It takes a while to be sure. Featherweight, almost ethereal; belying a crunchy, beguiling intensity. The acidity – juicy, slate-like and saliva-sucking – readying one for the next sip. Screwcap. **Rating** 96 **To** 2030 $80 NG

Dairy Hill Single Vineyard Hunter Valley Semillon 2019 In the epicentre of the '19 vintage – a happy hunting ground for semillon. In what I term 'modern style', the wine has an extra volume of citrus fruit on the bouquet and the mid-palate, pulled smartly into balance by minerally acidity. Screwcap. 12.3% alc. **Rating** 95 **To** 2034 $35 ✪

Stockhausen Hunter Valley Semillon 2019 A superlative '19, densely packed with the vintage's forceful dry extract while maintaining a strong fealty to regional type, with a featherweight strut across the palate boding well for a long, bright future. Balletic and finely tuned. Lemongrass, barley water, quince and candied citrus zest are thrust long by a chalky waft of acidity. Screwcap. **Rating** 95 **To** 2034 NG

Dairy Hill Single Vineyard Hunter Valley Shiraz 2018 Matured in French puncheons. Has made the most of the exceptional vintage with black fruits, spice and light colour woven through each other. French oak provides the bond for long-term maturation. Screwcap. 14.1% alc. **Rating** 95 **To** 2038 $60

Stockhausen Hunter Valley Shiraz 2018 A glossy ruby to crimson hue. A pulpy, gently reductive and modern interpretation of the mid-weighted and savoury Hunter style. Blueberry, iodine, licorice, a smudge of tapenade and ample florals. Soaring aromatics! Best, though, are the building tannins. Growing with air across the gums, they placate the fruit while setting a tone for a fine future. Screwcap. **Rating** 95 **To** 2032 NG

Cellar Reserve Karl Stockhausen Signature Series Shiraz 2011 Mid-ruby. Aromas of saddle leather, boot polish and sarsaparilla, mingle with dark cherry. Lapsang too. Moreish tannins are far from drying. Having spent 16 months in 10% new French wood, I suggest that the fruit and structural attributes will find even greater harmony down a short track. This is old-school. Avuncular. But with plenty of regional soul. Screwcap. **Rating** 95 **To** 2025 $85 NG

Museum Release Dairy Hill Vineyard Hunter Valley Shiraz 2009 Crafted by the sensitive hand of winemaker Mark Wood, this is archetypal Hunter. Leather-crusted tannins, firm, dusty and pliant, set the stage. The fruit, aged into a mottled melody of dried Asian plum, tea and spices, is savoury and delicious. The finish, woodsy and spindly, is still vibrant, however my bets are on an earlier term drinking window. This said, the wine grows in the glass nicely and I may well be wrong. **Rating** 95 **To** 2023 $110 NG

ŶŶŶŶŶ **Fume Sauvignon Blanc Semillon 2019** Rating 93 To 2025 $23 NG ✪
Briar Hill Hunter Valley Chardonnay 2018 Rating 92 To 2030 $35
Hunter Valley Albarino 2019 Rating 92 To 2022 $28 NG
Old Vines Hunter Valley Shiraz 2017 Rating 92 To 2024 $25 NG ✪
Cold Soaked Cabernet Sauvignon 2017 Rating 92 To 2024 $25 NG ✪
Early Harvest Hunter Valley Semillon 2019 Rating 91 To 2025 $23 NG ✪
Stockhausen Hunter Valley Chardonnay 2018 Rating 91 To 2023 $28 NG
Limited Release Orange Cabernet Sauvignon 2017 Rating 90 To 2025 $25 NG

Brini Estate Wines   ★★★★☆

698 Blewitt Springs Road, McLaren Vale, SA 5171 **Region** McLaren Vale
T (08) 8383 0080 **www.**briniwines.com.au **Open** By appt
Winemaker Adam Hooper (Contract) **Est.** 2000 **Dozens** 8000 **Vyds** 16.4ha
The Brini family has been growing grapes in the Blewitt Springs area of McLaren Vale since 1953. In 2000 John and Marcello Brini established Brini Estate Wines to vinify a portion of the grape production (up to that time it had been sold to companies such as Penfolds,

Rosemount Estate and d'Arenberg). The flagship Limited Release Shiraz is produced from dry-grown vines planted in 1947, the other wines from dry-grown vines planted in '64. Exports to Vietnam and China.

🍷🍷🍷🍷🍷 **Limited Release Sebastian Single Vineyard McLaren Vale Shiraz 2012** First tasted Mar '16 and it's still vibrant; the colour still primary and bright, the aromas and flavours in unison with blackberry and blueberry fruit given a lick of regional chocolate. It is a gloriously fresh wine from a great vintage, and has a future measured in decades, not years. Blewitt Springs at its best. Screwcap. 14.5% alc. **Rating** 97 **To** 2042 $55 ❂

🍷🍷🍷🍷🍷 **Koota Gra McLaren Vale Grenache Mourvedre Shiraz 2016** A 58/28/14% blend from old vines at Blewitt Springs. Still holding bright crimson hue and clarity. Fresh red fruits are sustained by superfine tannins. Delicious wine at any price. Screwcap. 14.5% alc. **Rating** 94 **To** 2022 $18 ❂

🍷🍷🍷🍷🍷 **Christian McLaren Vale Shiraz 2015 Rating** 93 **To** 2026 $45 JF
Blewitt Springs McLaren Vale Shiraz 2017 Rating 90 **To** 2027 $24 JF
Sebastian McLaren Vale Shiraz 2017 Rating 90 **To** 2026 $32 JF
Estate McLaren Vale Grenache Shiraz 2017 Rating 90 **To** 2026 $24 JF
Estate McLaren Vale Merlot 2017 Rating 90 **To** 2026 $24 JF

Brokenwood ★★★★★

401–427 McDonalds Road, Pokolbin, NSW 2321 **Region** Hunter Valley
T (02) 4998 7559 **www.**brokenwood.com.au **Open** Mon–Sat 9.30–5, Sun 10–5
Winemaker Iain Riggs, Stuart Hordern **Est.** 1970 **Dozens** 100 000 **Vyds** 64ha
A fashionable winery producing consistently excellent wines. Its big-selling Hunter Semillon provides the volume to balance the limited quantities of the flagships ILR Semillon and Graveyard Shiraz. Brokenwood purchased the Graveyard Vineyard from Hungerford Hill in 1978 and has been working to totally rehabilitate the vineyard. It's been a vine by vine exercise, with a degree of experimentation of rootstocks and clonal material from other, even older vineyards. There is also a range of wines coming from regions including Beechworth (a major resource is the Indigo Vineyard), Orange, Central Ranges, McLaren Vale, Cowra and elsewhere. In 2017 Iain Riggs celebrated his 35th vintage at the helm of Brokenwood, offering a unique mix of winemaking skills, management of a diverse business and an unerring ability to keep Brokenwood's high profile fresh and newsworthy. He also contributed a great deal to various wine industry organisations. In May 2020 Iain announced his retirement, effective 30 June '20, but he will remain on the board of directors and consult on any issue where his experience will assist. Exports to all major markets.

🍷🍷🍷🍷🍷 **ILR Reserve Hunter Valley Semillon 2014** Pale straw-green; an extraordinary colour for an extraordinary wine. A fragrant bouquet introduces a palate that has the best of all worlds: lemon, lemon curd, beeswax and fruit spice with no hint of the searing acidity Hunter Valley semillon can throw at the unwary. Here it is perfectly (and naturally) balanced. A worthy companion to the sublime Graveyard Shiraz '18. Screwcap. 11.5% alc. **Rating** 99 **To** 2034 $100 ❂
Graveyard Vineyard Hunter Valley Shiraz 2018 A single block of mainly 50yo vines was hand-picked, destemmed, open-fermented, 8–19 days on skins, matured in French oak of various shapes and sizes. Excellent colour through to the rim. Take a bottle with you to drink with Maurice O'Shea and he'll be ecstatic. It's supple, perfectly balanced, a pure expression of a quirky vineyard that has been the work of Iain Riggs for 4 decades; '18 was a great vintage, and he nailed it. *Wine Companion 2021* Wine of the Year. Screwcap. 13.5% alc. **Rating** 99 **To** 2058 $350
Wade Block 2 Vineyard McLaren Vale Shiraz 2018 30yo vines, machine-harvested, crushed and destemmed, open-fermented, 7–9 days on skins, matured in French barriques, puncheons and a 2700l cask (28% new). Full-bodied and wastes no time in laying out the reasons why you should buy it. It has a complex web of

blackberry and satsuma plum fruits, licorice and dark chocolate and cedary oak. Raise your glasses and enjoy. Screwcap. 14% alc. **Rating** 97 **To** 2043 $75 ✪

ΨΨΨΨΨ **Hunter Valley Semillon 2019** Has a little bit extra to the fruit line. While still speaking to classic lemon-accented aromas and flavours, there is an extra edge of lemon/passionfruit sorbet. The drinking window will remain open for as long as you wish. Screwcap. 11% alc. **Rating** 95 **To** 2039 $28 ✪
Indigo Vineyard Beechworth Chardonnay 2019 Hand-picked, whole-bunch pressed, wild-fermented in French barriques and puncheons (30% new), matured for 7–8 months. A more powerful bouquet and more drive on the intense palate build on foundations of grapefruit and white peach fruit, sparkling acidity to close. Screwcap. 13% alc. **Rating** 95 **To** 2031 $66
Forest Edge Vineyard Orange Chardonnay 2019 Various clones, identical vinification to its Indigo Vineyard Beechworth sibling. A high quality chardonnay with an array of white peach and Granny Smith apple, and good length. Screwcap. 13% alc. **Rating** 94 **To** 2029 $66
Verona Vineyard Hunter Valley Shiraz 2018 20yo vines, hand-picked, cultured yeast, 10 days on skins, matured in used French oak. Rich and complex, but has none of the finesse that makes Graveyard so great. It will richly reward a minimum 10 years in the cellar; preferably more, for the hackles of its tannins to smooth down. Screwcap. 14% alc. **Rating** 94 **To** 2040 $100
Wildwood Road Margaret River Cabernet Sauvignon 2018 Crushed and destemmed, matured in French barriques and puncheons (29% new). A fragrant, medium-bodied wine; purity, balance and length its calling cards. Superfine tannins are also on the money. Screwcap. 14% alc. **Rating** 94 **To** 2038 $100

ΨΨΨΨΨ **Beechworth Nebbiolo Rosato 2019** **Rating** 93 **To** 2021 $30
Hunter Valley Shiraz 2018 **Rating** 91 **To** 2029 $50
McLaren Vale Cabernet Sauvignon Merlot 2017 **Rating** 90 **To** 2027 $36

Bromley Wines   ★★★☆

PO Box 571, Drysdale, Vic 3222 **Region** Geelong
T 0487 505 367 **www**.bromleywines.com.au **Open** Not
Winemaker Darren Burke **Est.** 2010 **Dozens** 300
In his previous life Darren Burke worked as an intensive care nurse in Australia and the UK, but at the age of 30 he fell to the allure of wine and enrolled in the Bachelor of Applied Science (Oenology) at the University of Adelaide. Thereafter he became graduate winemaker at Orlando, then at Alkoomi Wines, fitting in a vintage in Chianti. With successful vintages in 2005 and '06 completed, and the impending birth of his and wife Tammy's first child, the couple moved back to the east coast. There Darren worked at several wineries on the Bellarine Peninsula before taking up his winemaking post at Leura Park Estate. Darren says, 'The essence of Bromley is family. All our wines carry names drawn from our family history. Family is about flesh and blood, sweat and tears, love and laughter.' Exports to Singapore.

ΨΨΨΨ **Harrison Vineyard Bellarine Pinot Noir 2018** A profoundly spicy bouquet, but backs off somewhat on the palate; not easy to decide whether this is due to the hands-off fermentation approach, or lowish alcohol. Screwcap. 13% alc. **Rating** 89 **To** 2023 $35
Murray Vineyard Bellarine Pinot Noir 2018 A similar back-to-front approach to its sibling (except no whole bunches); once 50% of the fermentable sugar occurred, the wine was plunged daily, at dryness followed by 18 days of maceration, pressed to used French oak for 10 months maturation. The low intervention approach is a challenge. Screwcap. 13% alc. **Rating** 89 **To** 2023 $36

Brook Eden Vineyard   ★★★★

167 Adams Road, Lebrina, Tas 7254 **Region** Northern Tasmania
T (03) 6395 6244 **www**.brookeden.com.au **Open** Sept–May 7 days 11–5
Winemaker Fran Austin **Est.** 1988 **Dozens** 1000 **Vyds** 2.1ha

At 41° south and an altitude of 160m, Brook Eden is one of the coolest sites in Tasmania and represents 'viticulture on the edge'. While the plantings remain small (1ha pinot noir, 0.8ha chardonnay and 0.3ha pinot gris), yield has been significantly reduced, resulting in earlier picking and better quality grapes.

🍷🍷🍷🍷🍷 **Pinot Nero 2017** It's a nutty, tangy pinot noir with twig, wood smoke and undergrowth elements and enough foresty fruit flavours to keep it all moving. It's lightish and certainly built on acidity, but it's also complex and sustained. It will develop well. Screwcap. 12.9% alc. **Rating** 94 **To** 2027 $42 CM
Pinot Nero 2016 A smoky, peppery, slightly gamey pinot with herb, twig and spice notes flaying about and tangy, berried fruit as the underpinning. Reduction (slight) has been put to positive effect and the finish has a sinewy, well structured feel. It's a complex amalgam, as they say in the classics. Screwcap. 13.5% alc. **Rating** 94 **To** 2027 $42 CM

🍷🍷🍷🍷🍷 **Chardonnay 2017 Rating** 93 **To** 2025 CM
Pinot Grigio 2016 Rating 91 **To** 2022 CM

Brookland Valley ★★★★★

Caves Road, Wilyabrup, WA 6280 **Region** Margaret River
T (08) 9755 6042 **www**.brooklandvalley.com.au **Open** Oct–May 7 days 11–5, June–Sept 7 days 11–4
Winemaker Courtney Treacher **Est.** 1984 **Dozens** NFP
Brookland Valley has an idyllic setting, plus its cafe and Gallery of Wine Arts, which houses an eclectic collection of wine, food-related art and wine accessories. After acquiring a 50% share of Brookland Valley in 1997, Hardys moved to full ownership in 2004 and it is now part of Accolade Wines. The quality, value for money and consistency of the wines are exemplary.

🍷🍷🍷🍷🍷 **Limited Release Reserve Margaret River Chardonnay 2018** Hand-picked, whole-bunch pressed, wild-yeast fermentation in French oak (40% new), matured for 10 months. The impact of oak is less than expected, indirectly pointing to selection of the best fruit from the estate vineyard. It has the same balance as that of its sibling. Screwcap. 13.5% alc. **Rating** 97 **To** 2028 $77 ✪

🍷🍷🍷🍷🍷 **Estate Margaret River Chardonnay 2018** Hand-picked, whole-bunch pressed, wild-yeast fermented and matured in French oak (35% new) for 9 months. Elegant, fine and very long in the mouth. White peach, melon and pink grapefruit are all in play. The fruit/oak balance works very well. Screwcap. 13.5% alc. **Rating** 95 **To** 2025 $49

Brookwood Estate ★★★★

Treeton Road, Cowaramup, WA 6284 **Region** Margaret River
T (08) 9755 5604 **www**.brookwood.com.au **Open** 7 days 11–5
Winemaker Peter Stanlake **Est.** 1996 **Dozens** 4500 **Vyds** 6.1ha
Trevor and Lyn Mann have a mature vineyard consisting of 1.3ha each of semillon, sauvignon blanc and shiraz; 1.2ha of chenin blanc and 1ha of cabernet sauvignon. Exports to Germany and China.

Brothers at War ★★★★★

16 Gramp Avenue, Angaston, SA 5353 **Region** Barossa
T 0405 631 889 **www**.brothersatwar.com.au **Open** Not
Winemaker Angus Wardlaw **Est.** 2014 **Dozens** 2800
David Wardlaw was one of the bastions of the Barossa Valley in the second half of the 20th century, working alongside greats such as Peter Lehmann, John Vickery, Jim Irvine and Wolf Blass. For son Angus Wardlaw, a life in wine was inevitable, working first (in 2009) at Dorrien Estate and after four years starting at Kirrihill Wines in the Clare Valley. He has a love for all things Eden Valley. His brother Sam Wardlaw, with a love of all things Barossa, started in the production side of the business when he worked for Premium Wine Bottlers until '09,

when he was employed by Andrew Seppelt at Murray Street Vineyards, spending the next six years there. Matt Carter's role is mysterious; while he started as a cellar hand at Colonial Wine for a couple of vintages, he has since moved into civil construction, currently running large infrastructure projects but returning from time-to-time to drink plenty of the Brothers at War wines. Exports to China.

ΨΨΨΨΨ **Single Vineyard Barossa Valley Grenache 2018** From the 150+yo vines of the celebrated Stonegarden Vineyard in the Eden Valley; 50% whole bunches, 50% whole berries wild-fermented, matured in used French puncheons for 12 months. Beautifully articulated to throw all of the vibrant and pure varietal fruit on full display. A particular feature are the finish and aftertaste, aspects seldom commented on with grenache. Cork. 13.8% alc. **Rating** 99 **To** 2038 $80 ✪

ΨΨΨΨΨ **Single Vineyard Old Vine Barossa Valley Syrah 2017** 80yo vines, 30% whole bunch, 70% whole berry, 3 weeks on skins, matured for 18 months in French oak (50% new). A perfect study in old vine elegance and harmony; the grapes picked when ripe, not overripe. Great pair (with its shiraz sibling) deserving high praise. Disfigured cork. 14.2% alc. **Rating** 96 **To** 2032 $80

Single Vineyard Old Vine Barossa Valley Shiraz 2017 20% whole bunch, 80% whole berry, matured in French oak (50% new) for 18 months. Super elegant, yet also powerful, with a spicy/savoury mouth-watering edge to the palate and its long finish. Irregular interior of the bottle neck. Disfigured the cork. 14.2% alc. **Rating** 96 **To** 2032 $80

Single Vineyard Eden Valley Mataro 2018 80+yo vines from the Pendee Farm vineyard in the Eden Valley. Wild-fermented with 20% whole bunches, 80% destemmed, plunged for 14 days, pressed to French hogsheads for 12 months maturation. Shows what old mataro vines can do if the grapes are respected and the winery skilled. Cork. 13.5% alc. **Rating** 96 **To** 2038 $80

Nothing in Common Eden Valley Riesling 2019 From 60yo vines near the township of Eden Valley. A wine stacked with varietal character and a sense of place, the lemon and lime fruits frocked with crisp acidity. I'd be happy to drink it tonight, pondering on the back label suggestion that 'it will benefit from delicate cellaring'. Screwcap. 11% alc. **Rating** 94 **To** 2034 $35

I'm Always Right Eden Valley Cabernet Sauvignon 2018 From a vineyard near the Eden Valley township. A strong, unflinching savoury cabernet with a seasoning of bay leaf and black olive tapenade over a medium-bodied, well structured varietal fruit base. Screwcap. 14% alc. **Rating** 94 **To** 2033 $35

ΨΨΨΨΨ **Fist Fight Barossa Shiraz 2018 Rating** 90 **To** 2033 $35

Brown Brothers   ★★★★★

Milawa-Bobinawarrah Road, Milawa, Vic 3678 **Region** King Valley
T (03) 5720 5500 **www.**brownbrothers.com.au **Open** 7 days 9–5
Winemaker Joel Tilbrook, Cate Looney, Geoff Alexander, Katherine Brown,
Tom Canning, Simon McMillan **Est.** 1885 **Dozens** Over 1 million **Vyds** 520ha
Draws upon a considerable number of vineyards spread throughout a range of site climates – from very warm to very cool. An expansion into Heathcote added significantly to its armoury. In 2010 Brown Brothers took a momentous step, acquiring Tasmania's Tamar Ridge for $32.5 million. In May '16 it acquired Innocent Bystander and stock from Giant Steps, and with it a physical presence in the Yarra Valley. The premium quality varietal wines to one side, Brown Brothers has gained two substantial labels: Innocent Bystander Moscato and Innocent Bystander Prosecco. It is known for the diversity of varieties with which it works, and the wines represent good value for money. Deservedly one of the most successful family wineries – its cellar door receives the greatest number of visitors in Australia. A founding member of Australia's First Families of Wine. Exports to all major markets.

ΨΨΨΨΨ **Patricia Pinot Noir Chardonnay 2012** An 80/20% blend from the high altitude Whitlands Plateau. Straw, with some colour from time on tirage. Granny Smith apple, citrus and melon; a complex and composed wine with depth of flavour and a lightly creamy texture with a long, refined, dry finish. Cork. 12% alc. Rating 96 $47 ○

Patricia Chardonnay 2018 Patricia never ceases to be anything less than exciting drinking. Since the move by Brown Brothers into Tasmania, it has gained a slightly different, cooler and finer flavour base. That said, the '18 vintage presents a rich, evocative Chardonnay of preserved lemon, ginger biscuit, white peach, lemon rind, honeyed spice. There is generosity without being heavy. Bad day? Here is the antidote. Screwcap. Rating 95 To 2030 $45 JP

Patricia Cabernet Sauvignon 2016 A multi-regional exploration of what it means to be a modern Victorian cabernet sauvignon; from the lashings of toasty oak, intense bold blackberry, licorice blackstrap and plum to the peppery intrigue. Lots of flavour marching along a lovely tannic backbone and the finish fines off nicely with persistence. Screwcap. Rating 95 To 2040 $62 JP

Patricia Noble Riesling 2015 Hand-picked, botrytis-affected. A style that has won and continues to win major awards, placing it among Australia's best dessert white wines. Brilliant deep gold. Resonates throughout with golden syrup, apricot, citrus blossom and orange peel. Thick and sticky, clings to the sides of the mouth and won't let go. Toffee, nutty, caramel goes long on the finish. Luscious and clean. Screwcap. 10.5% alc. Rating 95 To 2035 $37 JP

Patricia Shiraz 2016 Moves to a slightly different Patricia beat, a definite meaty/savoury expression compared to the previous vintage. Aromas of smoky, toasty, cedary oak, bbq sauce to the fore. Here, the solid fruit is one thing but the treatment it has received is another, taking it into high-end territory with enhanced savoury tannins, black fruits, hyper spice. Built from the bottom up, built to last. Give it plenty of time. Screwcap. Rating 94 To 2040 $62 JP

Methode Traditionelle King Valley Pinot Noir Chardonnay Pinot Meunier NV A blend of 57% pinot noir, 33% chardonnay and 10% pinot meunier; all parcels whole-bunch pressed, 2 years on lees prior to disgorgement. Excellent balance and length, with the contrasting fruit flavours complexed by the time on lees. Can't be faulted. Cork. 12.5% alc. Rating 94 $25 ○

Sparkling Brut Rose NV 80/20% Victoria/Tumbarumba. Super clean, fruit-driven sparkling with subtle creamy yeast overtones that can't put a foot wrong. The producer is one assured sparkling maker who knows what drinkers want. Dusty cherry, pomegranate. The bead is strong, acidity cuts through well and the strawberry-crush flavour is so tasty. Cork. 12.5% alc. Rating 94 $25 JP ○

ＹＹＹＹＹ Limited Release Single Vineyard King Valley Gamay 2019 Rating 93 To 2026 $25 JP ○
1889 King Valley Chardonnay 2019 Rating 92 To 2030 $19 JP ○
Origins Series Tempranillo 2018 Rating 92 To 2032 $19 JP ○
Limited Release Fiano 2019 Rating 91 To 2027 $25 JP
Origins Series Victoria Rose 2019 Rating 91 To 2025 $19 JP ○
Victoria Moscato 2019 Rating 91 $17 JP ○
Ten Acres Heathcote Shiraz 2018 Rating 90 To 2037 $30 JP

Brown Hill Estate ★★★★★

925 Rosa Brook Road, Rosa Brook, WA 6285 **Region** Margaret River
T (08) 9757 4003 **www.**brownhillestate.com.au **Open** 7 days 10–5
Winemaker Nathan Bailey **Est.** 1995 **Dozens** 3000 **Vyds** 22ha
The Bailey family is involved in all stages of wine production, with minimum outside help. Their stated aim is to produce top quality wines at affordable prices, via uncompromising viticultural practices emphasising low yields. They have shiraz and cabernet sauvignon (8ha each), semillon, sauvignon blanc and merlot (2ha each). The quality of the best wines in the portfolio is very good.

ＹＹＹＹＹ Perseverance Signature Range Margaret River Cabernet Merlot 2017
Neither the back label nor the detailed page of info supplied specify the blend percentages. Hand-picked and sorted, crushed separately; the merlot

open-fermented, the cabernet in tank; matured in French oak (40% new) before blending. An elegantly constructed wine: medium-bodied, fine tannins, olive and herb sidelights to cassis at the centre. Screwcap. 14% alc. **Rating** 95 **To** 2032 $70

Ivanhoe Reserve Margaret River Cabernet Sauvignon 2017 Estate-grown, hand-picked and sorted, matured for 18 months in new and used French barriques. A stalky Margaret River cabernet with the structure and tannin texture of the fruit to repay cellaring. The winemaker's thumbprint is kept under control, cassis and cabernet tannin left to do their own thing. Screwcap. 14% alc. **Rating** 95 **To** 2036 $40

Golden Horseshoe Reserve Margaret River Chardonnay 2018 Hand-picked, chilled, whole-bunch pressed, fermented in new and 1yo French barriques. This has good mouthfeel and varietal expression, the oak surprisingly well behaved. It is still youthful, with room to grow and prosper. Screwcap. 13.5% alc. **Rating** 94 **To** 2024 $38

Fimiston Reserve Margaret River Shiraz 2017 Hand-picked and sorted, destemmed then crushed; part of the must drained off to finish fermentation in French barriques, the remainder pressed to tank; the parcels blended and matured for 18 months in French barriques (35% new). While only medium-bodied, the blackberry and plum fruit has a sprinkle of spices. Screwcap. 14% alc. **Rating** 94 **To** 2042 $40

♟♟♟♟♟ **Trafalgar Cabernet Merlot 2018** Rating 92 To 2028 $27
Hannans Cabernet Sauvignon 2018 Rating 92 To 2028 $27
Lakeview Sauvignon Blanc Semillon 2019 Rating 90 To 2022 $25
Croesus Reserve Merlot 2017 Rating 90 To 2030 $40
Great Boulder Signature Range Cabernet Shiraz Merlot Malbec 2017 Rating 90 To 2032 $45
Oroya Reserve Malbec 2018 Rating 90 To 2030 $45

Brown Magpie Wines ★★★★★

125 Larcombes Road, Modewarre, Vic 3240 **Region** Geelong
T (03) 5266 2147 **www.**brownmagpiewines.com **Open** Jan 7 days 11–4, Nov–Apr w'ends 11–4
Winemaker Loretta Breheny, Shane Breheny, Daniel Greene **Est.** 2000 **Dozens** 5000 **Vyds** 9ha
Shane and Loretta Breheny's 20ha property is situated predominantly on a gentle, north-facing slope, with cypress trees on the western and southern borders providing protection against the wind. Vines were planted over 2001–02, with pinot noir (4ha) taking the lion's share, followed by pinot gris and shiraz (2.4ha each) and 0.1ha each of chardonnay and sauvignon blanc. Viticulture is Loretta's love; winemaking (and wine) is Shane's.

♟♟♟♟♟ Modewarre Mud Reserve Single Vineyard Geelong Shiraz 2016
A selection of the 2 best barrels from the vintage, aged for 26 months in French oak. Despite the warm year, this is unequivocally cool-climate shiraz in essence, with peppery spice, dry twig and pipe tobacco aromas combining with black fruit and cedary oak on the bouquet. Medium-bodied but full-flavoured. Time will add another level of complexity. Screwcap. 14% alc. Rating 95 To 2032 $60 SC

Paraparap Reserve Single Vineyard Geelong Pinot Noir 2016 Several clones (mainly MV6), some whole bunch, and fermented in a combination of different vessels with varying maceration times. Pinot at the full-bodied end of the spectrum, loaded with ripe red fruit and enough oak to make its presence felt without dominating. This vineyard will produce more elegant wines than this, but the quality is undoubted. Screwcap. 13.6% alc. **Rating** 94 **To** 2026 $60 SC

Single Vineyard Geelong Shiraz 2016 Hand-picked, some whole bunch and some whole berries in the ferment, 16 months in French oak. Gamey and earthy is the first impression on the bouquet, the varietal aromas of dark fruit, pepper and woody spice emerging with time in the glass. It's ripe and almost luscious on the palate, but its origins from a cool region are clear. There's plenty here to get you involved. Screwcap. 13.5% alc. **Rating** 94 **To** 2028 $38 SC

🍷🍷🍷🍷♀ Single Vineyard Geelong Pinot Noir 2016 Rating 93 To 2026 $38 SC
Single Vineyard Geelong Pinot Gris 2018 Rating 92 To 2023 $29 SC
Single Vineyard Geelong Pinot Grigio 2018 Rating 92 To 2021 $29 SC
Late Harvest Single Vineyard Geelong Botrytis Pinot Gris 2017
Rating 92 To 2024 $29 SC

Bull Lane Wine Company ★★★★★

PO Box 77, Heathcote, Vic 3523 **Region** Heathcote
T 0427 970 041 **www**.bulllane.com.au **Open** Not
Winemaker Simon Osicka **Est.** 2013 **Dozens** 500
After a successful career as a winemaker with what is now TWE, Simon Osicka, together
with viticulturist partner Alison Phillips, returned to the eponymous family winery just within
the eastern boundary of the Heathcote region in 2010. Spurred on by a decade of drought
impacting on the 60-year-old dry-grown vineyard, and a desire to create another style of
shiraz, Simon and Alison spent considerable time visiting Heathcote vineyards with access to
water in the lead-up to the '10 vintage. After the weather gods gave up their tricks of '11,
Bull Lane was in business. Exports to Denmark and China.

🍷🍷🍷🍷🍷 Heathcote Marsanne Roussanne 2019 A blend of 86% marsanne,
14% roussanne. Grapes were harvested separately but processed together; pressed
and juice sent to large-format seasoned French barrels, partial mlf, lees stirring.
Winemaker Simon Osicka has great hopes for marsanne roussanne becoming
Heathcote's standout white wine. Inviting aromas of spring blossom, honeysuckle,
jasmine and pear skin. Marsanne can have a fatness that needs to be controlled to
bring out its best. Here, it is used to build texture and a degree of richness on the
palate with roussanne contributing the acidity and structure. Intense and layered
with age on its side. Screwcap. 13.5% alc. **Rating** 95 To 2028 $27 JP
Heathcote Shiraz 2018 Sourced from the east-facing slope of the Mt Camel
Range. Hand-picked, fermented in 1t pots with 10% whole berries, 3 weeks on
skins, maturation in seasoned French hogsheads. In its 7th vintage and fulfilling the
winemaker's intention to make a 'complex, flavoursome and balanced' expression
of shiraz, the wine is also beautifully restrained. Generous and flowing with
aromas of lush black fruits, blood plums and turned earth with high spice notes.
Excellent balance. Screwcap. 14.5% alc. **Rating** 95 To 2028 $27 JP

Buller Wines ★★★★★

2804 Federation Way, Rutherglen, Vic 3685 **Region** Rutherglen
T (02) 6032 9660 **www**.bullerwines.com.au **Open** 7 days 10–5
Winemaker Dave Whyte **Est.** 1921 **Dozens** 10 000 **Vyds** 32ha
In 2013, after 92 years of ownership and management by the Buller family, the business was
purchased by Gerald and Mary Judd, a well known local couple and family with extensive
roots in the northeast. They are hands-on in the business and have overseen investment in the
cellar, storage, operations and, importantly, vineyards. Exports to all major markets.

🍷🍷🍷🍷 Balladeer Rutherglen Durif 2018 Open-fermented, hand-plunged, extended
maceration, matured in American and French hogsheads for 12 months. Full-
bodied, as one would expect, but is surprisingly supple. Whether this is a good
thing is an open question, but it sets the glass half full. Screwcap. 14% alc.
Rating 89 To 2026 $29

Bunkers Margaret River Wines ★★★★

1142 Kaloorup Road, Kaloorup, WA 6280 **Region** Margaret River
T (08) 9368 4555 **www**.bunkerswines.com.au **Open** Not
Winemaker Severine Logan **Est.** 2010 **Dozens** 5500 **Vyds** 34ha
Over the past 20+ years, Mike Calneggia has had his fingers in innumerable Margaret River
viticultural pies. He has watched some ventures succeed, and others fail. And while Bunkers

Wines (owned by Mike and Sally Calneggia) is only a small part of his viticultural undertakings, it has been carefully targeted from the word go. It has the six mainstream varieties (cabernet, semillon, merlot, chardonnay, sauvignon blanc and shiraz) joined by rising star, tempranillo, in the warm and relatively fertile northern part of the Margaret River. Severine Logan is winemaker and Murray Edmonds the viticulturist (Murray ex Evans & Tate). Mike and daughter Amy are responsible for sales and marketing. They say, 'The world of wine is full of serious people making serious wines for an ever-decreasing serious market ... Bunkers wines have been created to put the "F" word back into wine: "FUN", that is.' Exports to China.

ŶŶŶŶ♀ **Lefthanders Sauvignon Blanc Semillon 2019** The 'left hander' is a particularly dangerous surf break in Margaret River. Drinkability is the only dangerous aspect of this 64/36% blend; sauvignon gently tropical, semillon the tent pegs. Will flourish with more bottle age. Screwcap. 12.5% alc. **Rating** 92 To 2022 $20 ○

Honeycombs Chardonnay 2018 Honeycomb is a clean surf break. Night-harvested, fermented and matured in oak. The wine is driven by its melon and white peach fruit, its length building on retasting. Screwcap. 12.5% alc. **Rating** 91 To 2028 $20 ○

Bunnamagoo Estate

603 Henry Lawson Drive, Mudgee, NSW 2850 **Region** Mudgee
T 1300 304 707 **www.**bunnamagoowines.com.au **Open** 7 days 10–4
Winemaker Robert Black **Est.** 1995 **Dozens** 100 000 **Vyds** 108ha
Bunnamagoo Estate (on one of the first land grants in the region) is situated near the historic town of Rockley. A 6ha vineyard planted to chardonnay, merlot and cabernet sauvignon has been established by Paspaley Pearls. The winery and cellar door are located at the much larger (and warmer) Eurunderee Vineyard (102ha) at Mudgee. Exports to the UK, Singapore, Fiji, Papua New Guinea, Indonesia, Hong Kong and China.

ŶŶŶŶŶ **Pinot Gris 2019** A variety that is increasingly being made very well in Australia. This is no exception. Baked apple spice segues to pear gelato and quince. The flow of fruit is offset by textural warmth imparted by wild fermentation in older French wood. A trickle of gentle acidity and chew. A relaxed gris reminiscent of an Alsatian expression. Screwcap. **Rating** 94 To 2024 $22 NG ○

ŶŶŶŶ♀ **1827 Hand-picked Chardonnay 2018 Rating** 93 To 2026 NG
Chardonnay 2018 Rating 92 To 2025 NG
Rose 2019 Rating 91 To 2020 NG
Blanc de Blanc 2015 Rating 90 $50 NG

Burge Family Winemakers

1312 Barossa Way, Lyndoch, SA 5351 **Region** Barossa Valley
T (08) 8524 4644 **www.**burgefamily.com.au **Open** Thurs–Mon 10–5
Winemaker Derek Fitzgerald **Est.** 1928 **Dozens** 10 000 **Vyds** 10ha
In 2013 Burge Family Winemakers – an icon producer of exceptionally rich, lush and concentrated Barossa red wines – marked 85 years of continuous winemaking by three generations of the family. Burge Family was purchased by the Wilsford Group in November '18; the legacy of the Burge Family will be preserved with no change in wine style. Derek Fitzgerald has stepped into Rick Burge's shoes, having made wine in the Barossa for 14 years. Exports to Hong Kong and China.

ŶŶŶŶŶ **Draycott Barossa Valley Shiraz 2018** 50yo vines, hand-picked, wild yeast–open fermented, 14 days on skins, matured for 20 months in French oak (50% new). Full of blackberry fruit: part fresh, part jam. Spice also appears on the bouquet and palate. Cellaring will be rewarded. Screwcap. **Rating** 95 To 2038 $60

Garnacha Dry Grown Barossa Valley Grenache 2016 One of the Barossa Valley's signature grenache styles à la winemaker Rick Burge, who brings a touch of European sophistication to the grape mixed with Aussie boldness. Perfumed and

floral – violets are a standout. Savoury black fruits, a touch potpourri, a whisper of licorice. Fine tannins meld seamlessly on the palate. To do justice, let it breathe. Screwcap. 14.7% alc. **Rating** 95 **To** 2027 JP
Clochmerle GSR 2018 Grenache, shiraz, roussanne, tinta cao and souzao. It's got the suggestion of a bits and pieces blend, but it works very well indeed. The Rhône varieties knit together in a medium-bodied, fresh stream of spicy fruits; the finish fresh and vibrant. It's a steal. Screwcap. **Rating** 95 **To** 2028 $25 ✪
Eden Valley Riesling 2019 Mature vines are the key to a high quality Eden Valley riesling. Citrus/green apple fruit extends through the long palate and lingering aftertaste. Screwcap. 11.5% alc. **Rating** 94 **To** 2034 $27 ✪

♟♟♟♟♙ **Shiraz 2018** Rating 93 **To** 2030 $40
Tempranillo 2019 Rating 92 **To** 2029 $25 ✪
Olive Hill Old Vine Barossa Valley Semillon 2019 Rating 90 **To** 2021 $27

Burke & Wills Winery ★★★★

3155 Burke & Wills Track, Mia Mia, Vic 3444 **Region** Heathcote
T (03) 5425 5400 **www**.wineandmusic.net **Open** By appt
Winemaker Andrew Pattison, Robert Ellis **Est.** 2003 **Dozens** 1200 **Vyds** 1.6ha
After 18 years at Lancefield Winery in the Macedon Ranges, Andrew Pattison moved his operation a few kilometres north in 2004 to set up Burke & Wills Winery at the southern edge of the Heathcote region. The vineyards at Mia Mia comprise 0.6ha of shiraz, 0.6ha of Bordeaux varieties (cabernet sauvignon, petit verdot, merlot and malbec) and 0.4ha of gewurztraminer. He still sources a small amount of Macedon Ranges fruit from his former vineyard; additional grapes are contract-grown in Heathcote. In '17 the winery won the inaugural Premier's Award for Best Victorian Wine with the '15 Vat 1 Shiraz.

♟♟♟♟♟ **Vat 2 American Oak Heathcote Shiraz 2015** Crushed and destemmed, 5 days cold soak, plunged during 5-day ferment, settled for 3 weeks, matured for 16 months in used American hogsheads. Full-bodied, but not clumsy; plum and blackberry fruit holding sway, the oak not intrusive, the tannins soft. Screwcap. 14.5% alc. **Rating** 94 **To** 2035 $28 ✪
Mia Mia Heathcote Planter's Blend 2016 A blend of all the varieties planted in the vineyard: shiraz, petit verdot, merlot, malbec and cabernet sauvignon. Matured in new and used French barriques. This is really attractive; fresh, well balanced. The best value by far from Burke & Wills. Screwcap. 13.5% alc. **Rating** 94 **To** 2036 $25 ✪

♟♟♟♟ **Gewurztraminer 2019** Rating 89 **To** 2022 $28

Bush Track Wines ★★★★★

161 Myrtle Street, Myrtleford, Vic 3737 **Region** Alpine Valleys
T 0409 572 712 **www**.bushtrackwines.com.au **Open** Thurs 11–6, Fri–Sat 11–7, Sun 11–6
Winemaker Jo Marsh, Eleana Anderson **Est.** 1987 **Dozens** 550 **Vyds** 9.65ha
Bob and Helen McNamara established the vineyard in 1987, planting 5.53ha of shiraz with 11 different clones, 2ha of chardonnay, 1.72ha of cabernet sauvignon and 0.4ha of sangiovese. They have made small volumes of wines since 2006. Improvement in vineyard practices and the services of Jo Marsh (Billy Button Wines) and Eleana Anderson (Mayford Wines) should secure the future of Bush Track Wines.

♟♟♟♟♟ **Alpine Valleys Chardonnay 2018** At first this is all about restraint, a seemingly gentle wine with soft acidity. Yet there is flavour with creamed honey and lemon curd with more savoury inputs. It sits right. Nothing is forced. It is long, pure and a pleasure to drink. Screwcap. 12.5% alc. **Rating** 96 **To** 2026 $28 JF ✪
Ovens Valley Shiraz 2018 A lovely, elegant style that's fragrant with florals, licorice and woodsy spices. It's well composed and medium-bodied with a core of juicy fruit tempered by finely grained tannins. And while there's a vibrancy, it also lingers long on the finish. Screwcap. 14.5% alc. **Rating** 95 **To** 2028 $30 JF ✪

ㅜㅜㅜㅜㅇ Conmara Ovens Valley Shiraz 2017 Rating 93 To 2030 $50 JF
Alpine Valleys Sangiovese Cabernet 2018 Rating 92 To 2027 $30 JF

Byrne Vineyards ★★★★☆

PO Box 15, Kent Town BC, SA 5071 **Region** South Australia
T (08) 8132 0022 **www.**byrnevineyards.com.au **Open** Not
Winemaker Peter Gajewski, Phil Reedman MW **Est.** 1963 **Dozens** 126 400 **Vyds** 235ha
The Byrne family has been involved in the SA wine industry for three generations, with
vineyards in the Clare Valley and Riverland. Wine styles include vine-dried, field blends,
vegan-friendly wines and regional wines. Exports to the UK, the US, Canada, Germany,
Denmark, Sweden, Norway, the Netherlands, Poland, Russia, NZ, Japan and China.

ㅜㅜㅜㅜㅜ Calcannia Cellar Reserve Clare Valley Grenache 2016 Centurion vines
hand-picked and fully destemmed to yield a dense grenache with real – yes, you
read it correctly in this age of lolly water – tannins. Plied with used American
and French oak, this builds across the mouth nicely, scattering dark berry flavours,
orange rind scents, cranberry and briar in its wake. Pliant, fibrous tannins. Savoury
and delicious. Screwcap. **Rating** 94 To 2024 $49 NG
Antiquarian Clare Valley Sangiovese 2016 There is good winemaking and
an inherent understanding of the dry structural focus of Italy's great grapes, here.
Medium to full-bodied, highly attractive sangiovese. Red to dark mottled fruit,
sarsaparilla, bitter chocolate and a plume of frisky, nicely edgy tannins laced with
dried herb towing it all long. Impressive. Screwcap. **Rating** 94 To 2024 $49 NG

ㅜㅜㅜㅜㅇ Antiquarian Clare Valley Pinot Noir Shiraz 2018 Rating 92 To 2028
$59 NG
Antiquarian Barossa Shiraz 2017 Rating 92 To 2029 $59 NG
Antiquarian Clare Valley Shiraz 2017 Rating 92 To 2029 $59 NG
Flavabom Field White 2018 Rating 91 To 2023 $25 NG
Antiquarian Clare Valley Cabernet Sauvignon 2018 Rating 90 To 2027
$28 NG

Byron & Harold ★★★★★

57 River Way, Walter Point, WA 6152 (postal) **Region** Great Southern/Margaret River
T 0402 010 352 **www.**byronandharold.com.au **Open** Not
Winemaker Kate Morgan **Est.** 2011 **Dozens** 36 000 **Vyds** 34ha
The owners of Byron & Harold make a formidable partnership, covering every aspect of
winemaking, sales, marketing, business management and administration. Paul Byron and
Ralph (Harold) Dunning together have more than 65 years of experience in the Australian
wine trade, working at top levels for some of the most admired wineries and wine distribution
companies. Andrew Lane, also an owner, worked for 20 years in the tourism industry,
including in a senior role with Tourism Australia, leading to the formation of the Wine
Tourism Export Council. More recently he developed the family vineyard (Wandering Lane).
Exports to the UK, Canada, China and NZ.

ㅜㅜㅜㅜㅜ The Partners Great Southern Riesling 2019 This and its Rose & Thorns
sibling have been identically vinified, but this has significantly greater presence,
starting with the bouquet, which has a powder puff note to the dominant citrus.
The palate picks up the pace further with Meyer lemon, grapefruit and lime.
Screwcap. 12% alc. **Rating** 96 To 2034 $40 ☻
The Partners Great Southern Cabernet Sauvignon 2018 Crushed and
destemmed, 25 days on skins, matured in French oak (50% new) for 18 months.
A decidedly complex bouquet and a palate that brings more of the same. There's
a spicy piquancy to the cassis fruit, and a cedary framework ex the oak. Screwcap.
14.5% alc. **Rating** 96 To 2040 $60 ☻
Rose & Thorns Great Southern Riesling 2019 A fragrant citrus blossom
bouquet leads into a riesling that's all about elegance and finesse, the winemaker's

footprint nowhere to be seen. Its day will come around 5 years hence, and continue thereafter. Screwcap. 12% alc. **Rating** 95 **To** 2034 $28 ❂

The Protocol Margaret River Chardonnay 2018 Identical vinification to The Partners, but this had 35% new French oak. No funk/reduction here, and the intense fruit of white peach, grapefruit and nectarine carries the long palate with ease. Screwcap. 12.5% alc. **Rating** 95 **To** 2030 $50

The Protocol Margaret River Shiraz 2018 Matured for 18 months in French oak (25% new). Shiraz is no longer a stranger in Margaret River, nor even a poor cousin of cabernet. This wine is a happy midpoint between cool and warm-grown shiraz, with an inviting bouquet and palate of cherry on lees and warm spicy notes. The oak is positive, tannins doing their job without aggression. Screwcap. 14.5% alc. **Rating** 95 **To** 2038 $50

Gravity Margaret River Cabernet Sauvignon 2018 Machine-harvested, crushed and destemmed, 10–33 days on skins, matured for 18 months in French oak (29% new). A very well made cabernet, supple and medium-bodied. The fruit and oak are as one, albeit the blackcurrant fruit will emerge on top if there's ever a fight. As it is, a sheer pleasure. Screwcap. 14.8% alc. **Rating** 95 **To** 2038 $40

Rags to Riches Margaret River Cabernet Sauvignon 2017 Includes 14% Great Southern cabernet and 13% merlot. A well conceived and carried out blend with blackcurrant, black olive and bay leaf influences. Most importantly, it has depth and a backbone of tannins. Screwcap. 14% alc. **Rating** 95 **To** 2032 $28 ❂

The Partners Great Southern Chardonnay 2018 Destemmed whole berries, wild-fermented, 9 months in French oak (55% new). A complex, slightly funky bouquet. Is reduction a good or bad thing? It's a personal choice. Screwcap. 14% alc. **Rating** 94 **To** 2028 $50

The Protocol Margaret River Cabernet Sauvignon 2018 Destemmed whole-berry fermentation; part open, part static; 10–35 days on skins, matured in French oak (43% new) for 18 months. The oak is high quality but it's too much for the fruit now. Time will most probably sort it out. Screwcap. 14.8% alc. **Rating** 94 **To** 2038 $50

♟♟♟♟♟ **The Partners Great Southern Pinot Noir 2018** Rating 93 To 2027 $50
Wandering Lane Great Southern Riesling 2018 Rating 91 To 2028 $15 ❂
The Partners Great Southern Pinot Noir 2017 Rating 90 To 2025 $50
First Mark Great Southern Cabernet Sauvignon 2017 Rating 90 To 2029 $28

Calabria Family Wines ★★★★★

1283 Brayne Road, Griffith, NSW 2680 **Region** Riverina/Barossa Valley
T (02) 6969 0800 **www**.calabriawines.com.au **Open** Mon–Fri 8.30–5, w'ends 10–4
Winemaker Bill Calabria, Emma Norbiato, Tony Steffania, Jeremy Nascimben, Sam Mittiga **Est.** 1945 **Dozens** NFP **Vyds** 100ha

Calabria Family Wines (until 2014 known as Westend Estate) has successfully lifted both the quality and the packaging of its wines. Its 3 Bridges range is anchored on estate vineyards. The operation is moving with the times, increasing its plantings of durif and introducing aglianico, nero d'Avola and St Macaire (once grown in Bordeaux, and on the verge of extinction, this 2ha is the largest planting in the world). Equally importantly, it is casting its net over the Barossa Valley, Hilltops and King Valley premium regions, taking this one step further by acquiring a vineyard in the Barossa Valley (Corner Light Pass Road/Magnolia Road, Vine Vale) and opening a cellar door/restaurant. Exports to the UK, the US and other major markets including China.

♟♟♟♟♟ **Museum Release Three Bridges Reserve Semillon 2012** Wow! Why have we been drinking so many sweet semillons from Riverina when the region is clearly able to also present aged, dry semillons such as this? It's a simply stunning wine and still with a long road ahead. Brioche and buttered toast notes mingle with honeysuckle, apple blossom and an intense lemon zestiness. Young (yes, 8 years young!), fresh with great balance and vigorous acidity; this is a beauty. Screwcap. 13% alc. **Rating** 96 **To** 2030 $30 JP ✪

Calabria Bros. Eden Valley Riesling 2019 Showing all the style of a classic Eden Valley riesling and a joy to drink. Bursts with citrus blossom, jasmine, lantana and lime cordial. Compact and taut with that fine Eden Valley line and length, the juicy riesling fruit is the star. And it's just starting out. Screwcap. 11.5% alc. **Rating** 95 **To** 2033 $20 JP ✪

Saint Petri Barossa Valley Grenache Shiraz Mataro 2018 Named after a local Barossa church, Saint Petri pays homage to the original settlers of the region. It's a generous and fruit-led wine typical of the Barossa and made with enviable restraint by Emma Norbiato. Spiced-up aromas of black cherry, raspberry pastille, chocolate and gingerbread with white pepper. Smooth, seamless and almost endless; the pace quickens on the palate and fruit flavours intensify with smooth tannins through to the end. ProCork. 14.5% alc. **Rating** 95 **To** 2034 $90 JP

Calabria Private Bin Riverina Montepulciano 2018 Bill Calabria and winemaker Emma Norbiato moved into Italian varieties a while back and each year their knowledge and aptitude for these alternative grapes grows impressively. Montepulciano is a case in point. It's solid and serious red wine at a $15 price tag. Incredible. Deep red-garnet. Blackberry, black cherry, potpourri, earth, dried herbs with a thread of rocky road chocolate running loose. Merges beautifully on the palate with black and red cherry intensity, chocolate-coated cranberry and licorice blackstrap. Outstanding value. Screwcap. 14% alc. **Rating** 95 **To** 2026 $15 JP ✪

Francesco Show Reserve Grand Tawny NV So good, in every sense, to have a quality winemaker pursuing a tawny from the Barossa. It is the great fortified of the region and we are seeing less and less produced. Its age (Grand is 11–20 years in average age) is evident immediately in the olive-edged walnut-brown colour. Super concentrated aromas of raisin, prune, toffee, peanut brittle. Rich, sweet and persistent with spice, licorice, fruitcake and clean spirit; it lingers on and on. Superb. 500ml. Screwcap. 19% alc. **Rating** 95 $45 JP

Alternato Shiraz Durif Nero d'Avola Montepulciano 2017 Co-fermented, 50% whole bunches, a mix of tank (30%) and barrel (70%) maturation. These cocktail blends often fall flat, but not here. It is vibrantly fresh and juicy, red fruits to the fore. Screwcap. 14% alc. **Rating** 94 **To** 2027 $30 ✪

3 Bridges Barossa Valley Grenache 2018 Grenache and Calabria are proving to be a good fit producing some well composed and elegant examples. Winemaker Emma Norbiato resists the temptation to go bold with Barossa fruit and seeks another more temperate road, one made to highlight the grape's pretty florals, violets, confectionery and fresh, macerated cherries and spice. It is medium-bodied, laced with savoury tannins and the right mix of fruit versus oak. Screwcap. 14.5% alc. **Rating** 94 **To** 2027 $25 JP ✪

3 Bridges Cabernet Sauvignon 2018 Purple-garnet. Nori, black bean sauce, pretty cabernet florals, blackcurrant, sage. It's a complex start and more follows with the delivery of a gentle power, malleable tannins and expressive blackberry, chocolate, spice, Aussie bush flavours. So much to love at such an attractive price point. Screwcap. 14% alc. **Rating** 94 **To** 2030 $25 JP ✪

Three Bridges Mourvedre 2018 Mourvedre brings solid tannin support and intense blackcurrant fruit flavour and spice to the party, all of which are celebrated here, together with some extra touches. Cassis, blood plums; leafy with floral sweetness. A wildness on the palate, of bush berries and herbs; rosemary and thyme are a real feature together with grainy tannins. An individual in its entirety, handled with sensitivity. Screwcap. 14.5% alc. **Rating** 94 **To** 2034 $35 JP

🍷🍷🍷🍷🍷 **Pierre d'Amour Shiraz 2017** **Rating** 93 **To** 2026 $20 JP ✪
Saint Petri Barossa Valley Shiraz Carignan 2018 **Rating** 93 **To** 2029 $90 JP
Reserve Barossa Valley Cabernet Sauvignon 2017 **Rating** 93 **To** 2032 $50
3 Bridges Botrytis Semillon 2017 **Rating** 93 **To** 2024 $25 JP ✪
3 Bridges Limited Release Durif 2009 **Rating** 92 **To** 2026 $60 JP
3 Bridges Chardonnay 2018 **Rating** 91 **To** 2026 $25 JP

3 Bridges Durif 2018 Rating 91 To 2028 $25 JP
Calabria Bros. Eden Valley Riesling 2018 Rating 90 To 2025 $20 ✪
Pierre d'Amour Rose 2019 Rating 90 To 2024 $20 JP ✪
Cool Climate Series Hilltops Shiraz 2017 Rating 90 To 2025 $15 ✪
Calabria Brothers Old Vine Barossa Valley Shiraz 2016 Rating 90 To 2031
$30 JP
3 Bridges Barossa Valley Grenache 2017 Rating 90 To 2025 $25
Calabria Private Bin Nero d'Avola 2018 Rating 90 To 2024 $15 JP ✪

Caledonia Australis | Mount Macleod   ★★★★

PO Box 626, North Melbourne, Vic 3051 **Region** Gippsland
T (03) 9329 5372 **www**.southgippslandwinecompany.com **Open** Not
Winemaker Mark Matthews **Est.** 1995 **Dozens** 4500 **Vyds** 16.18ha
Mark and Marianna Matthews acquired Caledonia Australis in 2009. Mark is a winemaker with
vintages in numerous wine regions around the world. He works as a winemaking teacher and
also runs a contract winemaking business. Marianna has experience with major fast-moving
consumer goods brands globally. The Matthews have converted the main chardonnay block
to certified organic and are rehabilitating around 8ha of wetlands with the local catchment
authority. Exports to Canada and Japan.

🍷🍷🍷🍷🍷 **Caledonia Australis Gippsland Pinot Noir 2018** The acidity is palpably
natural and juicy; the fruit, harvested on the earlier side, its foil. Structural checks!
Tomatillo, rhubarb and persimmon scents meander to sour cherry. 15% whole
bunch, 20% barrel fermentation and 18 months in older neutral oak following a
polyglot of micro-harvests, all to facilitate textural intrigue, rather than the stamp
of wood and winemaking. Lots of love manifest in a swiggable pinot. All sass and
crunch. Screwcap. **Rating** 92 **To** 2024 $32 NG
Mount Macleod Umbra Method Ancestral Blanc de Blanc 2015 Certified
organic, this has a lot of lees age, offering imminent pleasure across glazed
stone fruits and plenty of curd to creamed cashew and nougatine-filled leesy
nourishment. Cork. **Rating** 90 NG

Calneggia Family Vineyards Estate   ★★★

1142 Kaloorup Road, Kaloorup, WA 6280 **Region** Margaret River
T (08) 9368 4555 **www**.cfvwine.com.au **Open** Not
Winemaker Severine Logan **Est.** 2010 **Dozens** 1500 **Vyds** 34ha
The Calneggia family has owned vineyards and been involved in wine in the Margaret
River region for over 25 years. The family owns several premium vineyards and labels across
the region including Rosabrook, Bunkers, Bramble Lane, Brian Fletcher Signature Wines and
now their first Calneggia Family Vineyards Estate wines.

Campbells   ★★★★★

4603 Murray Valley Highway, Rutherglen, Vic 3685 **Region** Rutherglen
T (02) 6033 6000 **www**.campbellswines.com.au **Open** Mon–Sat 9–5, Sun 10–5
Winemaker Julie Campbell **Est.** 1870 **Dozens** 36 000 **Vyds** 72ha
Campbells has a long and rich history, with five generations of the family making wine for
over 150 years. There were difficult times: phylloxera's arrival in the Bobbie Burns Vineyard
in 1898; the Depression of the 1930s; and premature deaths. But the Scottish blood of founder
John Campbell has ensured that the business has not only survived, but quietly flourished.
Indeed, there have been spectacular successes in unexpected quarters (white table wines,
especially riesling) and expected success with muscat and topaque. Scores of 99 points from
Robert Parker and 100 points from *Wine Spectator* put Campbells in a special position. The
death of Colin Campbell has seen fifth generation Julie Campbell assume the role of head
winemaker, fourth generation Malcolm continuing to be responsible for viticulture. The other
four members of the fifth generation all working in the business are well equipped to move

up the ladder when the time comes. A founding member of Australia's First Families of Wine. Exports to the UK, the US, China and other major markets.

ŸŸŸŸŸ **Merchant Prince Rare Muscat NV** With base wines from before most of us were born, consider yourself to be drinking liquid history. This is a world class fortified with extraordinary concentration and richness, yet blessed, through the blender's art, with refinement, vitality. Walkers salted caramels, burnt fig, nougat aromas with Turkish delight and so much more. Luscious and intense with licorice blackstrap, plum pudding, grilled walnuts unwinding through the mouth, clean and going on and on. 375ml. Screwcap. 18% alc. **Rating** 98 $140 JP ✪

Isabella Rare Rutherglen Topaque NV Such richness and concentration! You will rarely experience anything more complex and thought-provoking. Drinking Isabella is an intellectual exercise: imagine the earliest parcels of muscadelle laid down to create the solera, with decades of quiet ageing. Deep mahogany hue. Butterscotch, dried fruits, caramel, malt biscuits and aromatic spirit. A slow burst of potent, lush fruit with mocha, roasted coffee bean, grilled nuts, licorice blackstrap. Wow! 375ml. Screwcap. 18% alc. **Rating** 97 $140 JP ✪

ŸŸŸŸŸ **Grand Rutherglen Topaque NV** Not every producer can build a complex solera system, it takes generations. Neither can every producer understand the blending complexities involved, nor the freshness and balance required to make a great fortified. This is a fortified masterclass in a glass. A superb wine with lifted aromatics, freshness of spirit and so much intensity of flavour courtesy of winemaker patience and aged muscadelle. 375ml. Screwcap. 17.5% alc. **Rating** 96 $70 JP ✪

Classic Rutherglen Topaque NV The second tier Classic range of fortifieds is where most of us shop. Accordingly, it tends to sing the sweetest and the loudest with obvious complexity. Among the nutty, burnt butter and caramel there is a solid sweetness, but the injection of citrus really livens things up. The flavour is further brightened with fresh, clean, neutral spirit. 500ml. Screwcap. 17.5% alc. **Rating** 95 $40 JP

Classic Rutherglen Muscat NV Oh, what sweet bliss! Elegant, intense and ethereal in the glass. Medium amber. Roasted almond, lemon peel, fig and toffee meet potpourri. No shortage of power or intensity on the palate, revealing brandy soaked raisins, lemon drops and licorice with Italian panforte and, of course, roasted nuts. Wood age characters meld with the freshest, most neutral spirit to deliver a clean pair of heels. Average age 6–10 years. Screwcap. 17.5% alc. **Rating** 95 $40 JP

Grand Rutherglen Muscat NV The colour is so much darker, the aromas more intense and the presence in the glass is a thing of beauty. Average age for the Grand fortified classification is 11–19 years. Walnut brown with an olive tinge. So intense, so intoxicating with layer upon layer of molasses, dark chocolate, coffee bean, nougat and orange peel. Neutral spirit helps accentuate and refresh. An Australian icon done proud. Screwcap. 17.5% alc. **Rating** 95 $70 JP

Bobbie Burns Rutherglen Shiraz 2017 Always good value, Bobbie Burns has legions of fans. A generous, expressive wine with a solid, quality fruit base. It offers some arresting spice, dark chocolate and dense black fruit aromas. Packs a lot of character on the palate, the oak (sweet, vanilla) and supple tannins and a touch of Aussie bush and mint, enough to make an ex-pat jump on the next plane. A load of class. Screwcap. 14.5% alc. **Rating** 94 **To** 2028 $23 JP ✪

Limited Release Rutherglen Durif 2017 I have no idea why durif should not be viewed as friendly and as inviting as shiraz. In the hands of a sympathetic maker, those pesky tannins purr. Big in colour and personality, with lifted aromatics of cherry, stewed plums, spice, musk. Succulent palate with confident display of toasty oak and well managed tannins. So much for being a rustic red, far from it. Meet the elegant durif. Screwcap. 14% alc. **Rating** 94 **To** 2032 $28 JP ✪

Rutherglen Muscat NV Freshness is the keyword here, together with a depth of complexity that goes beyond the price tag. Sultana, dried currants, prune, fig smothered in leatherwood honey and toffee. The basic age of the solera is young, but it manages both depth and persistence, with coffee grounds and vanillan oak and a clean, fresh grapey finish. Screwcap. 17.5% alc. **Rating** 94 $22 JP ❂

ㅇㅇㅇㅇ♀ The Sixties Block 2018 Rating 93 To 2025 $28 JP
Rutherglen Topaque NV Rating 93 $22 JP ❂
Limited Release Rutherglen Roussanne 2018 Rating 92 To 2026 $25 JP ❂
Marsanne Roussanne Viognier 2019 Rating 92 $28 JP

Cape Barren Wines ★★★★★

PO Box 738, North Adelaide, SA 5006 **Region** McLaren Vale
T (08) 8267 3292 **www**.capebarrenwines.com **Open** By appt
Winemaker Rob Dundon **Est.** 1999 **Dozens** 17000 **Vyds** 16.5ha
Cape Barren was founded in 1999 by Peter Matthew. He sold the business in late 2009 to Rob Dundon and Tom Adams, who together have amassed in excess of 50 years' experience in winemaking, viticulture and international sales. The wines, including shiraz and grenache, are sourced from dry-grown vines between 70 and 125 years old. Chardonnay, sauvignon blanc and gruner veltliner are sourced from the Adelaide Hills. Exports to the US, Canada, Switzerland, NZ, China and other markets across Asia.

ㅇㅇㅇㅇㅇ Old Vine Reserve McLaren Vale Shiraz 2017 Made from 48–75yo vines; one-third completed fermentation in new French hogsheads, the remainder in used oak. This approach has worked wonders, adding texture and spicy/savoury nuances to the black fruits. Blewitt Springs and the '17 vintage have done the rest. Cork. 14.5% alc. **Rating** 96 To 2031 $48 ❂
Old Vine McLaren Vale Grenache 2018 Made from 20% 65yo Blewitt Springs vines, 80% 84yo McLaren Vale vines; each parcel vinified differently, but unified by maturation for 6 months in used French hogsheads before blending. It has delicious red fruits on the bouquet and palate alike, the wine no more than medium-bodied. Screwcap. 14.5% alc. **Rating** 95 To 2038 $35 ❂
Native Goose McLaren Vale Shiraz 2018 Sourced from 3 vineyards 45–70yo, crushed separately, 8 days on skins in upright static fermenters, twice-daily pumpovers, run off skins at 2° baume. It's medium-bodied, reflecting the freshness of the fruit and its pliable texture. Oak and tannins both do what is expected of them. Screwcap. 14.5% alc. **Rating** 94 To 2033 $26 ❂

ㅇㅇㅇㅇ♀ Native Goose Single Vineyard Adelaide Hills Chardonnay 2018
Rating 91 To 2027 $26
Native Goose McLaren Vale GSM 2018 Rating 90 To 2028 $26
McLaren Vale Cabernet Sauvignon Merlot Cabernet Franc 2018
Rating 90 To 2025 $18 ❂

Cape Bernier Vineyard ★★★★☆

230 Bream Creek Road, Bream Creek, Tas 7175 **Region** Southern Tasmania
T (03) 6253 5443 **www**.capebernier.com.au **Open** By appt
Winemaker Frogmore Creek (Alain Rousseau) **Est.** 1999 **Dozens** 1800 **Vyds** 4ha
Andrew and Jenny Sinclair took over from founder Alastair Christie in 2014. The vineyard plantings consist of 2ha of pinot noir (including three Dijon clones), 1.4ha of chardonnay and 0.6ha of pinot gris on a north-facing slope with spectacular views of Marion Bay. The property is one of several in the region that are changing from dairy and beef cattle to wine production and tourism. Exports to Singapore.

ㅇㅇㅇㅇㅇ Chardonnay 2018 Estate-grown, matured for 9 months in French oak. A little bottle age has allowed the wine to open its wings with a display of stone fruits led by ripe white nectarine and white peach, the acidity no issue whatsoever. Chardonnay can be a reluctant bride in Tasmania, but this is almost at the altar. Screwcap. 14% alc. **Rating** 95 To 2028 $42

ㅇㅇㅇㅇ♀ Haphazard Pinot Gris 2019 Rating 93 To 2022 $30

Cape Grace Wines

281 Fifty One Road, Cowaramup, WA 6284 **Region** Margaret River
T (08) 9755 5669 **www**.capegracewines.com.au **Open** 7 days 10–5
Winemaker Dylan Arvidson, Mark Messenger (Consultant) **Est.** 1996 **Dozens** 2000
Vyds 6.25ha

Cape Grace can trace its history back to 1875, when timber baron MC Davies settled at
Karridale, building the Leeuwin lighthouse and founding the township of Margaret River;
120 years later, Robert and Karen Karri-Davies planted their vineyard to chardonnay,
shiraz and cabernet sauvignon, with smaller amounts of cabernet franc, malbec and chenin
blanc. Robert is a self-taught viticulturist; Karen has over 15 years of international sales and
marketing experience in the hospitality industry. Winemaking is carried out on the property;
consultant Mark Messenger is a veteran of the Margaret River region. Exports to Singapore
and China.

ŶŶŶŶŶ **Reserve Margaret River Chardonnay 2018** Hand-picked, whole-bunch
pressed, wild-fermented in French oak (60% new) from 3 coopers, no mlf,
matured for 10 months. Has great intensity and length, especially on the finish and
aftertaste. No reduction. Screwcap. 12.9% alc. **Rating** 95 **To** 2028 $68
Margaret River Chardonnay 2018 Identical vinification to the Reserve except
75% mlf and 45% new oak. A touch of funky reduction on the bouquet, the
palate direct and still very fresh, with white peach and grapefruit driving through
to the finish. Screwcap. 12.9% alc. **Rating** 94 **To** 2026 $38

ŶŶŶŶŶ **Basket Pressed Cabernet Sauvignon 2017 Rating** 93 **To** 2032 $55
Basket Pressed Malbec 2018 Rating 91 **To** 2025 $40

Cape Jaffa Wines

459 Limestone Coast Road, Mount Benson via Robe, SA 5276 **Region** Mount Benson
T (08) 8768 5053 **www**.capejaffawines.com.au **Open** 7 days 10–5
Winemaker Anna Hooper, Derek Hooper **Est.** 1993 **Dozens** 10 000 **Vyds** 22.86ha

Cape Jaffa was the first of the Mount Benson wineries. Cape Jaffa's fully certified biodynamic
vineyard provides 50% of production, with additional fruit sourced from a certified biodynamic
grower in Wrattonbully. Having received the Advantage SA Regional Award in '09, '10 and
'11 for its sustainable initiatives in the Limestone Coast, Cape Jaffa is a Hall of Fame inductee.
Exports to the UK, Canada, Thailand, the Philippines, Hong Kong, Singapore and China.

ŶŶŶŶŶ **Epic Drop Wrattonbully Mount Benson Shiraz 2018** A blend of
50% Mount Benson, 40% Wrattonbully and 10% '19 Mount Benson shiraz. Aged
in 17% new and 83% 1yo French oak for 15 months. There's a silky smooth feel
about this wine, but depth and complexity make it more than just that. Blackberry,
licorice, and sweet spice aromas and flavours are at the core, with dark chocolate at
the edges. For now or later. Screwcap. 14.5% alc. **Rating** 95 **To** 2033 $29 SC ❂

ŶŶŶŶŶ **En Soleil Wrattonbully Pinot Gris 2019 Rating** 93 **To** 2023 $27 SC ❂
Upwelling Limestone Coast Cabernet Sauvignon 2017 Rating 93
To 2029 $29 SC
Limestone Coast Rose 2019 Rating 91 **To** 2022 $20 SC ❂
Limestone Coast Sauvignon Blanc 2019 Rating 90 **To** 2022 $20 SC ❂
Limestone Coast Shiraz 2018 Rating 90 **To** 2025 $20 SC ❂

Cape Mentelle

331 Wallcliffe Road, Margaret River, WA 6285 **Region** Margaret River
T (08) 9757 0888 **www**.capementelle.com.au **Open** 7 days 10–5
Winemaker Frederique Perrin Parker, Coralie Lewis, David Johnson, Ben Cane
Est. 1970 **Dozens** 80 000 **Vyds** 145ha

Part of the LVMH (Louis Vuitton Möet Hennessy) group. Cape Mentelle is firing on all
cylinders; the winemaking team is fully capitalising on the extensive and largely mature
vineyards, which obviate the need for contract-grown fruit. It is hard to say which of the wines

is best; the ranking varies from year to year. That said, Cabernet Sauvignon leads the portfolio, which includes Sauvignon Blanc Semillon, Chardonnay, Shiraz and Zinfandel. Exports to all major markets.

ŸŸŸŸŸ **Margaret River Chardonnay 2017** Hand-picked, whole-bunch pressed, wild-fermented. Gleaming straw-green. It takes a millisecond for its flavour mass to reach every corner of the mouth. Has gained further complexity since first tasted in Mar '19, with a twist of grapefruit zest joining white fleshed stone fruit. Screwcap. 14.5% alc. **Rating** 97 **To** 2030 $49 ✪

Two Vineyards Margaret River Shiraz 2016 A blend of parcels from the Trinders Vineyard (great power and depth) and the Chapman Brook Vineyard (nuanced, fine, floral characters); 50–70 days on skins; 21 months in French (80%) and American (20%) oak, 50% new oak overall. A powerful, layered shiraz of great length and balance. The fruit flavours are in the black spectrum, the tannins firm but ripe. Cork. 14% alc. **Rating** 97 **To** 2046 $98 ✪

ŸŸŸŸŸ **Margaret River Zinfandel 2017** Zinfandel's complex path from Bordeaux to the Napa Valley and thence to Margaret River, is a tale in itself. It's not an easy variety to grow, nor make, and Cape Mentelle has consistently been the best in Australia. Screwcap. 14.9% alc. **Rating** 95 **To** 2027 $60

Margaret River Rose 2018 The very complex blend of shiraz, grenache, tempranillo, zinfandel, mourvedre and viognier is matched by the full range of vinification techniques variously including direct pressing to barrel, cold soak and saignee across the batches. There's every reason why this and similar high quality roses should be the wine style of choice for BYO Chinese/Asian restaurants. Screwcap. 13.5% alc. **Rating** 94 **To** 2020 $28 ✪

ŸŸŸŸŸ **Trinders Margaret River Cabernet Merlot 2017** Rating 92 **To** 2032 $31

Cape Naturaliste Vineyard   ★★★★★

1 Coley Road (off Caves Road), Yallingup, WA 6282 **Region** Margaret River
T (08) 9755 2538 **www.**capenaturalistevineyard.com.au **Open** 7 days 10.30–5
Winemaker Bruce Dukes, Craig Brent-White **Est.** 1997 **Dozens** 5400 **Vyds** 10.7ha
Cape Naturaliste Vineyard has a long and varied history going back 150 years, when it was a coaching inn for travellers journeying between Perth and Margaret River. Later it became a dairy farm and in 1970 a mining company purchased it, intending to extract nearby mineral sands. The government stepped in and declared the area a national park, whereafter (in '80) Craig Brent-White purchased the property. Bruce Dukes joined Craig as winemaker, initially responsible for the white wines, before red wines were added to the roster. The vineyard is planted to cabernet sauvignon, shiraz, merlot, semillon and sauvignon blanc, and is run on an organic/biodynamic basis with little or no irrigation.

ŸŸŸŸŸ **Torpedo Rocks Reserve Single Vineyard Margaret River Shiraz 2016** Hand-picked, matured for 18 months in 90% French oak, 10% American; every barrel tasted for inclusion (or not). A delicious medium–bodied palate; fruit, oak and tannin seamlessly joined, albeit with a cherry and blackberry medley. King of the Castle. Screwcap. 13.8% alc. **Rating** 95 **To** 2036 $60

Torpedo Rocks Single Vineyard Margaret River Merlot 2016 Includes 13% malbec, matured for 18 months in French barriques. The Bordelais would immediately recognise (and appreciate) this medium–bodied wine with its earthy/ black olive undertones to blackcurrant fruit. Screwcap. 13.5% alc. **Rating** 95 **To** 2030 $40

Torpedo Rocks Reserve Single Vineyard Margaret River Cabernet Malbec 2016 A 91/9% blend, matured for 18 months in French barriques; a barrel selection resulting in only 125 dozen bottles made. This deserves attention and the right food – it's not just 'let's have a glass' stuff. Screwcap. 13.8% alc. **Rating** 95 **To** 2036 $60

Torpedo Rocks Single Vineyard Margaret River Malbec 2017 Hand-picked, matured for 18 months in French barriques. Malbec and cabernet franc are the 2 red Bordeaux varieties that escape the eastern side of Australia (with the exception of Langhorne Creek and Wendouree in the Clare Valley). This is round, medium-bodied, relatively soft and with plum on the mid-palate, thence the finish. Screwcap. 14.4% alc. **Rating** 94 **To** 2032 $40

ΨΨΨΨΨ **Margaret River Semillon Sauvignon Blanc 2019** Rating 91 To 2022 $20 ✪
Margaret River Sauvignon Blanc 2019 Rating 90 To 2022 $20 ✪

Capel Vale ★★★★★

118 Mallokup Road, Capel, WA 6271 **Region** Geographe
T (08) 9727 1986 **www**.capelvale.com **Open** 7 days 10–4
Winemaker Daniel Hetherington **Est.** 1974 **Dozens** 50000 **Vyds** 90ha
Established by Perth-based medical practitioner Dr Peter Pratten and wife Elizabeth in 1974. The first vineyard adjacent to the winery was planted on the banks of the quiet waters of Capel River. The viticultural empire has since expanded, spreading across Geographe (15ha), Mount Barker (15ha), Pemberton (28ha) and Margaret River (32ha). There are four tiers in the Capel Vale portfolio: Debut (varietals), Regional Series, Black Label Margaret River Chardonnay and Cabernet Sauvignon and, at the top, the Single Vineyard Wines. Exports to all major markets.

ΨΨΨΨΨ **Single Vineyard Series Whispering Hill Mount Barker Riesling 2019**
A masterclass in its purity of varietal expression. Citrus blossom and a waft of spice on the bouquet, then a mouth-watering display of crushed lime leaf, unsweetened lemon and green apple sorbet. Life-sustaining acidity is the first and last sensation in the mouth. Screwcap. 11.5% alc. **Rating** 96 **To** 2030 $40 ✪
Black Label Margaret River Cabernet Sauvignon 2018 The best parcel of fruit ex the Scholar Vineyard, then a best barrel selection. An attractive, medium-bodied wine; juicy blackcurrant/cassis fruit, supple tannins, very good length and balance. From the great '18 vintage. Screwcap. 14% alc. **Rating** 95 **To** 2038 $50
Single Vineyard Series Whispering Hill Mount Barker Shiraz 2018 The best fruit from Whispering Hill, nearly all from the smallest block at the top of the hill; matured in French oak. High quality plum/black cherry fruit clasped by French oak. Screwcap. 14% alc. **Rating** 94 **To** 2033 $90

ΨΨΨΨΨ **Regional Series Mount Barker Riesling 2019** Rating 92 To 2029 $27

Capercaillie Wines ★★★★★

4 Londons Road, Lovedale, NSW 2325 **Region** Hunter Valley
T (02) 4990 2904 **www**.capercailliewines.com.au **Open** 7 days 10–4.30
Winemaker Lance Mikisch **Est.** 1995 **Dozens** 5000 **Vyds** 8ha
A successful winery in terms of the quality of its wines, as well as their reach outwards from the Hunter Valley. The Capercaillie wines have generous flavour. Its fruit sources are spread across southeastern Australia, although the portfolio includes wines that are 100% Hunter Valley. Exports to China.

ΨΨΨΨΨ **The Ghillie 2018** Hand-picked; fermentation completed in French oak. Very good deep colour. This is perfectly vinified, featuring the great vintage in a 14% alcohol frame. It is supremely elegant, with gently dark fruits that will weather over decades, regional characters slowly overtaking varietal fruit. It will be a long journey with pleasure at every point along the way. Screwcap. **Rating** 97 **To** 2043 $70 ✪

ΨΨΨΨΨ **The Clan 2018** A blend of 75% Hunter Valley cabernet, 25% estate-grown petit verdot; 14 months in French hogsheads. It is the first vintage of The Clan to be 100% Hunter Valley. It is a luscious wine, full of juicy cassis fruit. Screwcap. 14% alc. **Rating** 96 **To** 2048 $70 ✪

ΨΨΨΨΨ **Hunter Valley Chardonnay 2019** Rating 92 To 2024 $35
Hunter Valley Chambourcin 2018 Rating 92 To 2024 $35

Hunter Valley Gewurztraminer 2019 Rating 90 To 2022 $28
The Ghillie 2017 Rating 90 To 2037
Hunter Valley Petit Verdot 2018 Rating 90 To 2024 $35

Capital Wines   ★★★★☆

13 Gladstone Street, Hall, ACT 2618 **Region** Canberra District
T (02) 6230 2022 **www**.capitalwines.com.au **Open** Thurs–Mon 11–4
Winemaker Andrew McEwin, Phil Scott **Est.** 1986 **Dozens** 3500 **Vyds** 5ha
In early 2020, Bill Mason and Colin and Kay Andrews of Jirra at Jeir Station acquired Capital
Wines from Andrew and Marion McEwin. The cellar door in Hall, less than 15 minutes
from the heart of the national capital, features the Capital Wines range, Kosciuszko
wines from Tumbarumba (owned by Bill Mason and family) and the Jirra at Jeir Station wines
from Murrumbateman. Jeir Station, halfway between Hall and Murrumbateman, supplies
much of the fruit for the Capital wines.

🍷🍷🍷🍷 **The Ambassador Tempranillo 2016** Matured in French oak for 6 months.
A faithful rendition of the tempranillo grape in all of its dark-fruited intensity and
savouriness. Red licorice, black cherry, dried herbs and chocolate are open and
enticing aromas. Warm and rounded on the palate, it's inviting with a host of
black and blue and gentle savoury notes and supple tannins. Screwcap. 13.8% alc.
Rating 93 **To** 2025 $27 JP ✪
The Backbencher Canberra District Merlot 2017 Matured in French
oak for 18 months. Lively aromatics, violets, lantana, raspberry leaf, red and blue
berries, chocolate buds. A strong-bodied example of the grape combining cool-
climate veracity, namely pepper-infused firm tannins, with lifted merlot prettiness.
Screwcap. 14.1% alc. **Rating** 90 **To** 2026 $27 JP

🍷🍷🍷🍷 **The Ambassador Tempranillo 2017** **Rating** 89 **To** 2024 $27 JP

Carillion Wines   ★★★★★

749 Mount View Road, Mount View, NSW 2325 **Region** Hunter Valley
T (02) 4990 7535 **www**.carillionwines.com.au **Open** Thurs–Mon 10–5
Winemaker Andrew Ling **Est.** 2000 **Dozens** 6000 **Vyds** 148ha
In 2000 the Davis family decided to select certain parcels of fruit from their 28ha Davis
Family Vineyard in the Hunter Valley, along with the family's other vineyards in Orange (the
30ha Carillion Vineyard) and Wrattonbully (the 90ha Stonefields Vineyard), to make wines
that are a true expression of their location. To best reflect this strong emphasis on terroir,
the resulting wines were categorised into three labels, named after their respective vineyards.
In recent years Tim Davis has taken over the reins from his father John, and brought these
selected brands under the Carillion banner. He also launched the Lovable Rogue range of
wines, which highlight his keen interest in alternative grape varieties (particularly Italian), as
well as exploring innovative and experimental winemaking methods.

🍷🍷🍷🍷 **Origins GM198 Clone Orange Riesling 2019** The clone is a selection from
Alsace, grown here at an elevation of 800m. The heady bouquet and the ripe
citrus and apple palate are 100% true to the clone as grown in Alsace. Striking.
Screwcap. 11.8% alc. **Rating** 95 **To** 2030 $30 ✪
Aged Release Tallavera Grove Hunter Valley Semillon 2011 This
showcases Hunter's majesty that is, whatever you think of these febrile
lightweighted whites, hugely reliant on patience. Only now is this starting to
forage the lemon drop, curd, buttered toast, marmalade, quince and truffle scents;
all embedded in the better wines of the region; '11 was a very fine vintage.
Screwcap. **Rating** 95 **To** 2030 NG
Origins Fenestella Hunter Valley Shiraz 2018 A contemporary take on
Hunter shiraz, flouting violet, bacon back, blueberry and iodine scents as if the
wine was from somewhere far cooler. Mid-weighted, pulpy and grape spiced.
Classy French oak mows in the seams. Gently. This is very good. Screwcap.
Rating 95 **To** 2030 NG

Single Barrel Hunter Valley Sagrantino 2018 Sagrantino is among the most phenolically endowed red varieties on the planet, yet despite the pliancy (detailed and moreish) and the phalanx of red and dark fruit allusions brushed with wood smoke, tomato skin and sandalwood, there is an innate elegance to this. It is not heavy. The oak embellishes, serving as a passage to a long flow of flavour and textural intrigue. This is very good. The region might want to plant more sturdy Italian material with this showing. Cork. **Rating** 95 **To** 2026 $70 NG

Single Barrel Orange Chardonnay 2018 A Meursault strut with toasted hazelnut, nougat, peach and oak-embellished complexity; sensitively appointed and beautifully integrated. Very intense, with the extract streamlined but billowing across the cheeks all at once, making one reach for the next sip. The feel to this is more Californian: buxom but fresh enough despite the relatively soft acidity. Cork. **Rating** 94 **To** 2024 $70 NG

Lovable Rogue Skin Contact Vermentino 2019 Fermented wild with an extended period on skins to confer structure, while leaching aromas of Golden Delicious apple, quince, green almonds and fennel. This is delicious. Hard to spit. Despite its inherent nobility as one of the top few Italian white grape varieties, its stretch in Australia is forlorn. This changes the paradigm. Screwcap. **Rating** 94 **To** 2023 NG

Origins Block 22 Wrattonbully Cabernet Sauvignon 2017 Hand-picked from vines planted on a limestone shelf just below the surface. Cassis is the central theme for a lively medium-bodied palate; supple and long. The wine reflects the cool vintage with extra fragrance, freshness and restrained alcohol. Screwcap. 14% alc. **Rating** 94 **To** 2037 $50

ΨΨΨΨΨ **Origins Old Grafts Hunter Valley Semillon 2019** Rating 93 To 2028 NG
Lovable Rogue Lees Stirred Hunter Valley Fiano 2019 Rating 92 To 2021 $30 NG
Orange Pinot Gris 2019 Rating 91 To 2020 NG
The Feldspars Orange Shiraz 2018 Rating 91 To 2024 $50 NG
Expressions Hunter Valley Orange Shiraz Pinot Noir 2018 Rating 91 To 2022 $25 NG
Orange Cabernet Sauvignon 2018 Rating 91 To 2027 NG
Loveable Rogue Funky Ferment Verduzzo 2019 Rating 90 To 2022 NG
Expressions Orange Pinot Noir Rose 2019 Rating 90 To 2020 $25
Davis Premium Vineyards Rogue Series Moon Child Orange Aglianico 2018 Rating 90 To 2023 $30 NG
Lovable Rogue Foot Stomped Hunter Valley Sagrantino 2018 Rating 90 $30 NG

Carlei Estate | Carlei Green Vineyards ★★★★

1 Alber Road, Upper Beaconsfield, Vic 3808 **Region** Yarra Valley/Heathcote
T (03) 5944 4599 **www**.carlei.com.au **Open** W'ends 11–6
Winemaker Sergio Carlei **Est.** 1994 **Dozens** 10 000 **Vyds** 2.25ha
Sergio Carlei has come a long way, graduating from home winemaking in a suburban garage to his own (commercial) winery in Upper Beaconsfield; Carlei Estate falls just within the boundaries of the Yarra Valley. Along the way Carlei acquired a Bachelor of Wine Science from CSU, and established a vineyard with organic and biodynamic accreditation adjacent to the Upper Beaconsfield winery, plus 7ha in Heathcote. Contract winemaking services are now a major part of the business. Exports to the US, Singapore and China.

ΨΨΨΨ **Green Vineyards Upper Goulburn Cabernet Sauvignon 2016** Hand-picked, destemmed, no crushing, 24 days skin contact, 23 months in French oak (10% new). Good colour; possible volatile acidity forces the tannins through the palate. Diam. 14% alc. **Rating** 89 **To** 2029 $33

Casa Freschi

159 Ridge Road, Ashton, SA 5137 **Region** Adelaide Hills/Langhorne Creek
T 0409 364 569 **www**.casafreschi.com.au **Open** By appt
Winemaker David Freschi **Est.** 1998 **Dozens** 2000 **Vyds** 7.55ha
Casa Freschi is a small, quality-obsessed vigneron, currently producing single vineyard wines from two vineyards (in the Adelaide Hills and in Langhorne Creek). David Freschi's parents, Attilio and Rosa, planted 2.5ha of cabernet sauvignon, shiraz and malbec in 1972 in Langhorne Creek. David expanded the plantings with 2ha of close-planted nebbiolo in '99. The pursuit of a white wine vineyard led David to the Adelaide Hills. In '03 he purchased a 3.2ha site at 580m in Ashton and planted chardonnay, pinot gris, riesling and gewurztraminer at 8000 vines/ha, all grown using organic principles. The wines are made at the gravity-fed micro-winery built in '07. Exports to the UK, Singapore, the Philippines and Japan.

ŸŸŸŸŸ **La Signorina 2019** A field blend of 44% riesling, 37% gewurztraminer and a splash of gris; all hand harvested before wild fermentation in French barriques, sans fining or filtration. Organic, sure, but more intuitive; more hands-off. Bravo! This is Alsace on steroids. Far better than so much wine from there. Apple, spice, quince, grape, lychee and yet, despite the aromatic fireworks, this mid-weighted beauty is more about textural detail flowing long while etching flavours into every crevice across the palate. A wonderful wine. Screwcap. **Rating** 95 **To** 2023 $32 NG ✪
Profondo Old Vines 2017 A blend of 75% cabernet and 25% shiraz; fermented naturally, 28 months in used French barriques. This is classy, rich but supple. Powerful, but light of touch across the palate, the tannins nicely polymerised and mocha-creamy. Delicate poise is demonstrated across a plume of truffled black fruits, violet, anise and sage. A fine drink, with my bets on earlier to mid-term enjoyment. Cork. **Rating** 94 **To** 2027 $70 NG

ŸŸŸŸŸ **Ragazzi Adelaide Hills Chardonnay 2018 Rating** 93 **To** 2025 $28 SC
Ragazzi Adelaide Hills Pinot Grigio 2019 Rating 92 **To** 2022 $28 NG
La Signora 2017 Rating 92 **To** 2025 $45 SC
Ragazzi Langhorne Creek Nebbiolo 2017 Rating 92 **To** 2024 $28 SC
Langhorne Creek Syrah 2017 Rating 91 **To** 2026 $55 NG
Langhorne Creek Nebbiolo 2017 Rating 91 **To** 2027 $70 NG
Adelaide Hills Chardonnay 2018 Rating 90 **To** 2024 $55 NG
La Signorina 2016 Rating 90 **To** 2022 $35 SC
Langhorne Creek Malbec 2017 Rating 90 **To** 2027 $55 NG

Casella

Wakely Road, Yenda, NSW 2681 **Region** Riverina
T (02) 6961 3000 **www**.casellafamilybrands.com **Open** Not
Winemaker Alan Kennett, Frank Mallamace **Est.** 1969 **Dozens** 12.5 million **Vyds** 3000ha
The fairytale success story for Casella, gifted the opportunity to establish yellow tail as a world brand overnight by Southcorp withdrawing the distribution of (inter alia) its best selling Lindemans Bin 65 Chardonnay in the US, is now almost ancient history. yellow tail will remain the engine room for Casella well into the future, but it has now moved decisively to build a portfolio of premium and ultra-premium wines through its acquisition of Peter Lehmann in 2014; and then Brand's Laira winery, cellar door and the use of the brand name from McWilliam's in '15 – McWilliam's had invested much time and money in expanding both the vineyards and the winery. The Peter Lehmann and Brand's Laira brands will transform the future shape of Casella's business. In December '17 Casella Family Brands purchased Baileys of Glenrowan. The fact that Casella now has over 3000ha of vineyards spread across Australia is a case of putting its money where its mouth is. It is second only to Treasury Wine Estates in export sales (by value), followed by Pernod Ricard and Accolade. Exports to all major markets.

ŸŸŸŸŸ **1919 Cabernet Sauvignon 2016** Bright garnet. Looking, smelling and tasting younger and brighter than its 4 years would otherwise indicate; perhaps the result of some judicious multi-regional blending within SA. Aussie bush aromas with blackberry, clove, cigar box and smoky toast. Good cabernet touchstones, especially the dried herbs and spice. Structured and balanced, rich and textured. Screwcap. 14.5% alc. **Rating** 95 **To** 2036 $100 JP

ΨΨΨΨΨ **1919 Shiraz 2016 Rating** 92 **To** 2036 $100 JP
1919 Shiraz 2015 Rating 92 **To** 2036 $100 JP
1919 Cabernet Sauvignon 2015 Rating 92 **To** 2035 $100 JP
Three Vintners Cabernet Sauvignon 2018 Rating 90 **To** 2025 $16 JP ✪

Cassegrain Wines ★★★★

764 Fernbank Creek Road, Port Macquarie, NSW 2444 **Region** Hastings River
T (02) 6582 8377 **www**.cassegrainwines.com.au **Open** Mon–Fri 9–5, w'ends 10–5
Winemaker John Cassegrain (Chief), Alex Cassegrain (Senior) **Est.** 1980 **Dozens** 50 000
Vyds 34.9ha
Cassegrain has continued to evolve and develop. It still draws on the original Hastings River vineyard of 4.9ha, where the most important varieties are semillon, verdelho and chambourcin, with pinot noir and cabernet sauvignon making up the numbers. However, Cassegrain also part-owns and manages Richfield Vineyard in the New England region, with 30ha of chardonnay, verdelho, semillon, shiraz, merlot, cabernet sauvignon and ruby cabernet. Grapes are also purchased from Tumbarumba, Orange, Hilltops, Mudgee and the Hunter Valley. Exports to Japan, China and other major markets.

ΨΨΨΨΨ **Aged Release Edition Noir Central Ranges Semillon 2015** Assuming this is a museum release, it has held up well. Lanolin, quince marmalade and buttered toast, with candied citrus zest echoing across a vibrant line of cool Central Ranges' acidity. Plenty of gas in the tank, but nice drinking now. Screwcap. 12% alc. **Rating** 91 **To** 2025 $32 NG
Edition Noir Pinot Vierge 2019 The estate's ode to the contemporary code of crafting gris with some skin inflection, imparting a mottled pink to onion skin hue, together with scents of woodsy red berry fruits and crunchy seams of freshness. A highly versatile wine. Best thought of as a richer rose and/or a lighter red. Screwcap. 14.5% alc. **Rating** 91 **To** 2021 $33 NG
Fromenteau Reserve Chardonnay 2018 High quality vanilla pod oak guides riffs of nectarine, mandarin and white peach across a chord of flinty mineral and tangy acidity; a kernel of nuts and nougatine at the core. Mid-weighted. Just. Fresh and dutifully vibrant. Screwcap. 13% alc. **Rating** 90 **To** 2024 $50 NG
Reserve Falerne 2017 A classic Bordeaux blend of cabernet and merlot. This feels far more mid-weighted and savoury than the 14.5% alcohol suggests. Cassis, a whiff of spearmint, mulch, dried tobacco and graphite. The tannins splay broad, but keep it poised. This is a nice drink. **Rating** 90 **To** 2024 $55 NG
Sparkling Chambourcin NV A disease-resistant hybrid capable of production in a subtropical climate, this was crafted traditionally with a second fermentation in bottle. A fine savoury nose segues to notes of tomato bush, brambly red berries and soy. The finish is nicely frothy, joyous and of good length. Cork. **Rating** 90 $32 NG

ΨΨΨΨ **Edition Noir Semillon 2018 Rating** 89 **To** 2024 $28 NG
Edition Noir Semillon 2017 Rating 89 **To** 2027 $28 NG
Shiraz 2018 Rating 89 **To** 2024 $25 NG
Edition Noir de Solere 2018 Rating 89 **To** 2022 $35 NG

Castagna ★★★★★

88 Ressom Lane, Beechworth, Vic 3747 **Region** Beechworth
T (03) 5728 2888 **www**.castagna.com.au **Open** By appt
Winemaker Julian Castagna, Adam Castagna **Est.** 1997 **Dozens** 1800 **Vyds** 4ha
Julian Castagna is an erudite and totally committed disciple of biodynamic grapegrowing and winemaking. While he acknowledges that at least part of the belief in biodynamics has to be intuitive, he also seeks to understand how the principles and practices enunciated by Rudolf

Steiner in 1924 actually work. He purchased two egg-shaped, food-grade concrete tanks, each holding 900l. They are, he says, 'the most perfect shape in physics', and in the winery they reduce pressure on the lees and deposit the lees over a larger surface area, which, he believes, will eliminate the need for batonnage. His son Adam is responsible for the 400 dozen or so of Adam's Rib made each year, complementing the production of Castagna. Exports to the UK, France, Spain, Denmark, South Korea, Hong Kong, China and Japan.

♀♀♀♀♀ **Growers Selection Harlequin 2016** Straw into amber. Nutty and spicy with flavour and texture in spades. It's a blend of assorted white varieties, all of which received skin contact. Layer after layer of flavour. Skin contact/orange wines need to be your thing, but this is a very good example. Diam. 13.5% alc. **Rating** 94 To 2022 $40 CM

Un Segreto Beechworth Sangiovese Shiraz 2016 One of those wines that smells good even as you swallow it. It's lavender-like and blueberried, with suede leather, black cherry and woodsy spice notes rippling through a beautiful spread of flavour-infused tannin and convincing length. It's not by any stretch a big wine; it neither wants to be, nor needs to be. It takes prettiness and gives it gravity. Diam. 13.5% alc. **Rating** 94 To 2026 $75 CM

♀♀♀♀♀ **Growers Selection Chardonnay 2017** Rating 93 To 2024 $50 CM
Adam's Rib The White 2017 Rating 93 To 2023 $40 CM
Allegro 2018 Rating 93 To 2022 $32 CM
La Chiave Beechworth Sangiovese 2016 Rating 93 To 2025 $75 CM
Growers Selection King Valley Savagnin 2018 Rating 92 To 2022 $40 CM
Adam's Rib The Red 2016 Rating 92 To 2025 $40 CM
Beechworth Chenin Blanc 2018 Rating 91 To 2023 $55 CM
Growers Selection Quisbianco 2018 Rating 90 To 2021 $40 CM
Sauvage Beechworth Shiraz 2016 Rating 90 To 2023 $40 CM

Castelli Estate   ★★★★★

380 Mount Shadforth Road, Denmark, WA 6333 **Region** Great Southern
T (08) 9364 0400 **www**.castelliestate.com.au **Open** By appt
Winemaker Mike Garland **Est.** 2007 **Dozens** 10 000
Castelli Estate will cause many small winery owners to go green with envy. When Sam Castelli purchased the property in late 2004, he was intending simply to use it as a family holiday destination. But because there was a partly constructed winery he decided to complete the building work and simply lock the doors. However, wine was in his blood courtesy of his father, who owned a small vineyard in Italy's south. The temptation was too much and in '07 the winery was commissioned. Fruit is sourced from some of the best sites in WA: Frankland River, Mount Barker, Pemberton and Porongurup. Exports to the US, South Korea, Singapore, Japan and China.

♀♀♀♀♀ **Il Liris Rouge 2017** Cabernet sauvignon (60%), shiraz (35%), malbec (5%). Lashings of sweet berried fruit and a sure serve of smoky cedar wood oak. It could easily get out of control but it doesn't, it remains mannered and surefooted as it unveils complexity after complexity. It's a beautiful red. Vino-Lok. 14.7% alc. **Rating** 96 To 2040 $75 CM ✪

Il Liris Chardonnay 2018 You have to enjoy struck-match characters because there's a good deal of them here but the fruit still manages to carry the day. This is an impressive wine. Alive with stone fruit and still bursting to impress through the finish. Vino-Lok. 13% alc. **Rating** 95 To 2028 $70 CM

Pemberton Chardonnay 2018 Matchstick characters make their presence felt, but the intensity of flavour, and all-round complexity are most definitely upper echelon. This chardonnay has power, class and persistence. It's smoky and reductive, but it's charged with quality ripe fruit and it's strung on pure acid lines. Beautiful. Screwcap. 13.7% alc. **Rating** 95 To 2028 $34 CM ✪

Denmark Pinot Noir 2017 Largely clones 114 and 777, matured in 1800l foudres. Superb colour. Good varietal expression on both the aromatic bouquet and intense palate. There's a lot happening here, with satsuma plum and dark cherry flavours bolstered by positive tannin and oak influences. Exceptional development potential. Screwcap. 13.8% alc. **Rating** 95 **To** 2027 $34 ✪

Empirica Frankland River Tempranillo 2018 The flow, the balance, the texture: this is tempranillo on song. If you like this variety then you really need some of this. Sheets of fine tannin, a bed of red-berried fruit, a whisper of dried herbs. It's not a big wine but it doesn't need to be. Screwcap. 14% alc. **Rating** 95 **To** 2029 $44 CM

Great Southern Riesling 2019 Intensity of flavour is served both pure and soft. This is a riesling to tuck into and (thoroughly) enjoy. Citrus flavours of various descriptions work their magic. There's a suggestion of fruit sweetness but it's a dry style/wine. Lovely. Screwcap. 12.4% alc. **Rating** 94 **To** 2028 $27 CM ✪

Denmark Pinot Noir 2018 Sweet, smoky oak and complex, undergrowthy fruit combine to excellent effect here. It's both fragrant and structural though most importantly its spice-strewn flavour profile is at its peak as it fans out on the finish. Screwcap. 14.1% alc. **Rating** 94 **To** 2030 $34 CM

Empirica Uno Denmark Pinot Noir 2018 Juicy length, inbuilt complexity, ripe tannin and a good deal of seduction. Maybe there's a little alcohol warmth but the quality of this wine more than carries the day. Cranberries, cherry, earth, sweet spices, wood smoke notes and more. Very good. Diam. 14.5% alc. **Rating** 94 **To** 2031 $70 CM

ŸŸŸŸŸ **Empirica Frankland River Syrah 2018** **Rating** 93 **To** 2028 $38 CM
Empirica Uvaggio 2017 **Rating** 93 **To** 2025 $34
The Sum Riesling 2019 **Rating** 92 **To** 2027 $19 CM ✪
The Sum Riesling 2018 **Rating** 92 **To** 2028 $19 ✪
Empirica Fiore Del Campo 2018 **Rating** 92 **To** 2022 $26
Margaret River Cabernet Merlot 2018 **Rating** 91 **To** 2027 $22 CM ✪
Great Southern Shiraz Malbec 2017 **Rating** 90 **To** 2023 $22
The Sum Cabernet Sauvignon 2018 **Rating** 90 **To** 2026 $19 CM ✪

Castle Rock Estate ★★★★★

2660 Porongurup Road, Porongurup, WA 6324 **Region** Porongurup
T (08) 9853 1035 **www**.castlerockestate.com.au **Open** 7 days 10–5
Winemaker Robert Diletti **Est.** 1983 **Dozens** 4500 **Vyds** 11.2ha
An exceptionally beautifully sited vineyard (riesling, pinot noir, chardonnay, sauvignon blanc, cabernet sauvignon and merlot), winery and cellar door on a 55ha property with sweeping vistas of the Porongurup Range, operated by the Diletti family. The standard of viticulture is very high, and the vineyard itself is ideally situated. The two-level winery, set on a natural slope, maximises gravity flow. The rieslings have always been elegant and have handsomely repaid time in bottle; the Pinot Noir is the most consistent performer in the region; the Shiraz is a great cool-climate example; and Chardonnay has joined a thoroughly impressive quartet, elegance the common link. Rob Diletti's excellent palate and sensitive winemaking mark Castle Rock as one of the superstars of WA. Exports to China.

ŸŸŸŸŸ **Porongurup Riesling 2019** Excellent flow, weight, flavour and length. Purity is arguably the key but aromatics and texture are also of real note here. Flavour, it just sings on. Screwcap. 12% alc. **Rating** 96 **To** 2034 $25 CM ✪

A&W Porongurup Riesling 2018 A riesling with texture, flavour and elegance. The way its citrussy, slatey flavours slip through the mouth is quite something. Screwcap. 12% alc. **Rating** 96 **To** 2030 $35 CM ✪

Porongurup Pinot Noir 2018 Fantastic array of scents and flavours. Spices, flowers, berries and woodsy herbs. A curl of smoky tannin. Excellent linger to the finish. Nothing feels pushed. Not especially powerful, but it keeps going long after it has every right not to. Screwcap. 13.5% alc. **Rating** 95 **To** 2030 $37 CM

Diletti Chardonnay 2017 Varietal character in spades. It might weigh in at relatively low alcohol, but grilled peach, custard powder and sweet cedar wood flavours put on a thoroughly convincing, not to mention flavoursome, display. Beautiful mouthfeel. Screwcap. 12% alc. **Rating** 94 **To** 2025 $30 CM ✪

Porongurup Shiraz 2017 Medium-bodied in a beautiful way. Clove, peppercorn, plum and black cherry flavours sweep through the palate in satiny style. There's barely a kink nor a ruffle. It has a clear savoury, gently meaty edge and it's all the better for it. Price is better than reasonable. Screwcap. 13.5% alc. **Rating** 94 **To** 2029 $30 CM ○

ΨΨΨΨ **Porongurup Sauvignon Blanc 2019 Rating** 91 **To** 2021 $20 CM ○

Catherine Vale Vineyard   ★★★☆

656 Milbrodale Road, Fordwich, NSW 2330 **Region** Hunter Valley
T (02) 6579 1334 **www**.catherinevalewines.com.au **Open** Fri 11–3, w'ends & public hols 10–5
Winemaker Daniel Binet **Est.** 1993 **Dozens** 500 **Vyds** 4.45ha
Wendy Lawson has taken over management of Catherine Vale Vineyard for the foreseeable future, after the death of Bill in Jan 2016. Bill taught at Knox Grammar School for 28 of his 36-year teaching career. After that, Bill and Wendy continued for 20 years in the Hunter Valley and the communities around Broke. This retirement venture is now 21yo with the lion's share of the vineyard planted to chardonnay and semillon, with smaller amounts of verdelho, arneis, dolcetto and barbera. The Lawsons planted the latter three varieties after visiting the Piedmont region in Italy, pioneering the move to these varieties in the Hunter. In '12 Wendy received an OAM for her work in tourism, the environment and viticulture.

ΨΨΨΨ **Semillon 2018** Semillon with some body. It's driven by citrus and slate-like characters, though there's a gentle (positive) waxiness to the texture. It's only just entering a good drinking zone. Screwcap. 9.5% alc. **Rating** 91 **To** 2027 $20 CM ○

ΨΨΨΨ **Barbera 2017 Rating** 89 **To** 2023 $28 CM

Catlin Wines   ★★★★★

39B Sydney Road, Nairne, SA 5252 **Region** Adelaide Hills
T 0411 326 384 **www**.catlinwines.com.au **Open** Not
Winemaker Darryl Catlin **Est.** 2013 **Dozens** 2000
Darryl Catlin grew up in the Barossa Valley with vineyards as his playground, picking bushvine grenache for pocket money as a child. Stints with Saltram, the Australian Bottling Company and Vintner Imports followed in his 20s, before he moved on to gain retail experience at Adelaide's Royal Oak Cellar, London's Oddbins and McKay's Macquarie Cellars. Next, he studied for a winemaking degree while working at Adelaide's East End Cellars. Then followed a number of years at Shaw + Smith, rising from cellar hand to winemaker, finishing in 2012 and establishing his own business the following year. Exports to the UK and China.

ΨΨΨΨΨ **Pudding and Pie Adelaide Hills Pinot Noir 2017** From a single vineyard in Hahndorf. Hand-picked, wild-fermented in small batches with some whole-bunch inclusion, matured in French oak for 9 months. A lovely wine, profiting from the cool vintage. Has elegance, finesse and length. Screwcap. 12.5% alc. **Rating** 95 **To** 2032 $28 ○

Sorella Single Vineyard Adelaide Hills Montepulciano 2016 This deeply coloured wine takes no prisoners – it doesn't need to. This is an iron fist in a velvet glove. Its power doesn't emanate from a high alcohol jab to the solar plexus or sock-it-to-them tannins; what it does have is all of those characteristics within a swathe of strangely comforting black and purple fruits. Screwcap. 14% alc. **Rating** 95 **To** 2041 $28 ○

Glenco Single Vineyard Adelaide Hills Shiraz 2016 The single vineyard is at Macclesfield. Picked in several passes; fermented in small batches, some with whole bunches retained, most crushed/destemmed; matured for 11 months in French oak. Cherry/berry fruit, whole-bunch spice and fine tannins all contribute. Screwcap. 14% alc. **Rating** 94 **To** 2036 $28 ○

ŸŸŸŸŸ GB's Adelaide Hills Montepulciano Rose 2019 Rating 93 To 2024 $20 ✪
Pudding and Pie Adelaide Hills Pinot Noir 2019 Rating 91 To 2029 $28
EXP #3 Loose Goose Gruner Veltliner 2019 Rating 90 To 2020 $28
EXP #2 Hellagrud Gruner Veltliner 2019 Rating 90 To 2020 $28
The Gellert Adelaide Hills Gamay 2019 Rating 90 To 2029 $28

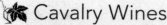 Cavalry Wines ★★★☆

PO Box 193, Nagambie, Vic 3608 **Region** Heathcote
T 0411 114 958 **www**.cavalrywines.com **Open** Not
Winemaker Adam Foster **Est.** 2016 **Dozens** 700 **Vyds** 9.6ha
The vineyard was planted in the 1960s with 5.8ha of shiraz, 2.7ha of cabernet sauvignon and a field blend of chardonnay, verdelho and riesling. (There was very little planted in Australia at that time.) The first owner made a little wine for his personal use, but most of the grape production was used to make excellent grappa, although history doesn't relate how it made its way to market. More recently the grapes were sold to other wineries, and a major part continues to be sold. The current owners are Peter Nash, previously an insurance underwriter, and Josephine Hands, a former teacher. Ardent wine lovers with a history of small investments in wine, their next step in retirement was to become vignerons – and to put the property in trust for their grandchildren. They say that they gave their winery its name because it shares three boundaries with the Australian Army.

ŸŸŸŸŸ **Christine Heathcote Cabernet Shiraz 2017** This is the best of the Cavalry wines. There is a hint of regional mint alongside the dark fruits, but it doesn't distract. Screwcap. 13.5% alc. **Rating** 90 **To** 2027 $43

ŸŸŸŸ **Rosaria Premium Heathcote Shiraz 2017** Rating 89 To 2022 $54

Caviste ★★★★

4/80 Hobsons Road, Kensington, Vic 3031 (postal) **Region** Victoria
T 0417 946 276 **www**.cavistewines.com **Open** Not
Winemaker David Manning **Est.** 2016 **Dozens** 315
Hobart-born (1967) David Manning packed a lifetime of experience in hospitality before jumping into the perils of winemaking. A job promotion led him to Perth, but in '96, tired of the long hours of hospitality management, he commenced working as a casual at Houghton's cellar door. Nine years later, having risen to manager of on-premise sales and marketing, he secured a similar position with Negociants, albeit with a far greater and varied portfolio taking in imported wines as well as domestic. Three years later he moved to Melbourne for Negociants and completed an agricultural science degree, majoring in winemaking/viticulture. In '17 he left Negociants and commenced a permanent position with the winemaking team at Ten Minutes by Tractor in January '18. Caviste, his own micro-brand, dates back to '16; there are no plans for a winery or cellar door, simply a desire to increase the quality of the wines.

ŸŸŸŸŸ **Yarra Valley Syrah 2019** Hand-picked, the grapes arriving at the winery in great condition. Destemmed; after 11 days on skins pressed to used French hogsheads. Red fruits rule the day on the palate, albeit with some cool-grown spicy, flowery notes. Overall balance and length are impressive. Screwcap. 13.6% alc. **Rating** 92 $25 ✪
Mornington Peninsula Pinot Gris 2019 Hand-picked, 75% whole-bunch pressed to used barriques, 25% fermented on skins with plunging for 19 days extracting colour (the wine is indeed pink) and phenolics. Treated as a red wine to top barrels and blend back to the finished wine. Dry finish. A lot of work for 50 dozen bottles. Screwcap. 13.7% alc. **Rating** 90 **To** 2021 $25
Mornington Peninsula Pinot Noir 2019 Given the condition of the grapes that 'arrived at the winery somewhat dehydrated with obvious signs of sunburn and some shrivel', the winemaking was very expertly handled. Hand-sorting, cold soak and 35% whole bunch saw the retention of natural acidity, the wine's saving grace. Screwcap. 14.5% alc. **Rating** 90 **To** 2023 $32

Yarra Valley Syrah 2018 Hand-picked fruit was in great condition. Mostly destemmed, with a small component of whole berry briefly cold-soaked, a 13-day ferment (skin contact) then pressed to French hogsheads (20% new) for maturation. Rich and satisfying; the only question is whether it is too rich. Screwcap. 14% alc. **Rating** 90 **To** 2025 $25

Centennial Vineyards ★★★★★

'Woodside', 252 Centennial Road, Bowral, NSW 2576 **Region** Southern Highlands
T (02) 4861 8722 **www**.centennial.net.au **Open** 7 days 10–5
Winemaker Tony Cosgriff **Est.** 2002 **Dozens** 10 000 **Vyds** 28.65ha
Centennial Vineyards, jointly owned by wine professional John Large and investor Mark Dowling, covers 133ha of beautiful grazing land, with the vineyard planted to pinot noir (7.13ha), chardonnay (6.76ha), pinot gris (4.06ha) and smaller amounts of riesling, pinot meunier, albarino, tempranillo, gruner veltliner and gewurztraminer. Centennial purchased the 8.2ha Bridge Creek Vineyard in Orange to meet the challenge of the Southern Highlands' capricious weather. Exports to the UK, the US, Denmark, Singapore, China and South Korea.

🍷🍷🍷🍷🍷 **Road Block 116 Riesling 2019** It starts out a little subdued with a hint of lemon blossom and a zesty lime juice freshness across the tight palate. It does start to give more – some texture, some grip – with a dry finish. Overall moreish and satisfying. Screwcap. 11% alc. **Rating** 95 **To** 2029 $26 JF ❂
Winery Block Tempranillo 2018 A very appealing, lighter framed rendition more-or-less in a joven style. A lovely mix of cherries and pomegranate, tart cranberries and loads of red musk/licorice, yet plenty of savoury delight too. Crunchy acidity and lots of it, with textural, decisive tannins closing in. Screwcap. 13.5% alc. **Rating** 95 **To** 2026 $28 JF ❂

🍷🍷🍷🍷🍷 **Winery Block Pinot Grigio 2019** Rating 93 To 2023 $26 JF ❂
Limited Blanc de Blancs NV Rating 93 $40 JF
Barrel Select Sparkling Shiraz NV Rating 93 $29 JF
Road Block 1012 Riesling 2019 Rating 91 To 2027 $26 JF
Brut Traditionelle NV Rating 91 $35 JF
House Block Gewurztraminer 2019 Rating 90 To 2022 $29 JF
Reserve Single Vineyard Chardonnay 2018 Rating 90 To 2028 $33 JF
Reserve Single Vineyard Pinot Gris 2018 Rating 90 To 2022 $33 JF
Reserve Pinot Noir Rose 2019 Rating 90 To 2021 $28 JF
Reserve Single Vineyard Pinot Noir 2018 Rating 90 To 2024 $35 JF
Dolce Classico Corvina Rondinella 2018 Rating 90 To 2022 $39 JF

Ceres Bridge Estate ★★★★★

84 Merrawarp Road, Stonehaven, Vic 3221 **Region** Geelong
T (03) 5271 1212 **www**.ceresbridge.com.au **Open** By appt
Winemaker Scott Ireland, Sam Vogel **Est.** 1996 **Dozens** 400 **Vyds** 7.4ha
Challon and Patricia Murdock began the long, slow and very frustrating process of establishing their vineyard in 1996. They planted 1.8ha of chardonnay in that year, but 50% of the vines died. They persevered by planting 1.1ha of pinot noir in 2000, and replanting in '01. In '05 they signified their intention to become serious by planting shiraz, nebbiolo, sauvignon blanc, viognier, tempranillo and pinot grigio. The vines are now mature; the pinot noir, chardonnay and shiraz cementing this year's 5-star rating.

🍷🍷🍷🍷🍷 **Paper Mill Chardonnay 2018** A wistful, thoughtful chardonnay still marking time, but this lovely will be consumed way too young because it demands it. Low-yielding fruit has concentrated the goodness: grilled grapefruit, lemon curd, fig, almond, oatmeal. It will continue to meld and improve. One to watch. Screwcap. 13.5% alc. **Rating** 95 **To** 2031 $30 JP ❂
Paper Mill Pinot Noir 2018 The Barwon Valley at the foot of the Barrabool Hills is a relatively new district, capable of producing wines with almost effortless

balance and the brightest of fruit flavours. Luminous cherry red. Macerated raspberry, cranberry, fresh cherry, lavender, violets. A driving palate with red fruits the propellant; slim and purposeful with powder-fine tannin. Screwcap. 13.5% alc. **Rating** 95 **To** 2027 $30 JP ✪

Paper Mill Shiraz 2018 Hand-picked, crushed, destemmed, inoculated yeast ferment, barrel age in French oak for 12 months. This is one smart wine. Deep purple-garnet. Arresting pomegranate, blueberry, black cherry fruits mingle with black olive savouriness, thyme and brown spice. It's a smooth operator with plushness and concentration. In perfect balance. Screwcap. 13.5% alc. **Rating** 95 **To** 2030 $30 JP ✪

Chain of Ponds

c/- 83 Pioneer Road, Angas Plains, SA 5255 (postal) **Region** Adelaide Hills
T (08) 8537 0600 **www.chainofponds.com.au Open** Not
Winemaker Greg Clack **Est.** 1985 **Dozens** 20 000

It is years since the Chain of Ponds brand was separated from its then 200ha of estate vineyards, which were among the largest in the Adelaide Hills. It does, however, have long-term contracts with major growers. Prior to the 2015 vintage, Greg Clack came onboard as full-time chief winemaker. In May '16 Chain of Ponds closed its cellar door and moved to Project Wine's small-batch processing facility at Langhorne Creek, completing its withdrawal from the Adelaide Hills other than the grape purchasing contracts. Exports to the UK, the US, Canada, Singapore, Hong Kong, the Philippines, Japan and China.

🍷🍷🍷🍷🍷 **Stopover Single Vineyard Adelaide Hills Barbera 2018** Hand-picked, destemmed into small open fermenters, 3 days cold soak, plunged twice daily, 10 days on skins, pressed to French oak (30% new) to complete primary and mlf, matured for 9 months. Juicy red fruits, supple mouthfeel. Lovely stuff, the tannins like a silken gauze. Screwcap. 13.5% alc. **Rating** 95 **To** 2033 $35 ✪

Black Thursday Adelaide Hills Sauvignon Blanc 2019 Has the multifaceted sauvignon blanc style that Greg Clack has used to build more complexity to tank-fermented sauvignon blanc rather than a barrel-fermented one. There is 4% semillon, the components picked in a wide swathe of baumes. Good wine. Screwcap. 12.5% alc. **Rating** 94 **To** 2023 $20 ✪

Ledge Single Vineyard Adelaide Hills Shiraz 2018 A full-bodied shiraz that stops within inches of over-extraction – carefully managed, not dumb luck. Black fruit is dominant with tar, blackberry, licorice and pepper all on display. The time it spent in used French hogsheads was exactly right. Screwcap. 14% alc. **Rating** 94 **To** 2033 $35

Amadeus Single Vineyard Adelaide Hills Cabernet Sauvignon 2018 Destemmed, 2 days cold soak, open-fermented with rack and return, 30% drained off, matured in French oak (40% new) for 15 months; includes 3% shiraz. A full-bodied, rich and complex cabernet with its natural substrate of ripe tannins. Screwcap. 14.5% alc. **Rating** 94 **To** 2038 $35

🍷🍷🍷🍷🍷 **Corkscrew Road Single Vineyard Adelaide Hills Chardonnay 2018**
Rating 93 **To** 2028 $35
Morning Star Single Vineyard Adelaide Hills Pinot Noir 2018 **Rating** 93 **To** 2028 $35
Innocence Adelaide Hills Pinot Noir Rose 2019 **Rating** 92 **To** 2021 $20 ✪
Grave's Gate Adelaide Hills Syrah 2018 **Rating** 92 **To** 2028 $20 ✪
Novello Semillon Sauvignon Blanc 2019 **Rating** 91 **To** 2024 $16 ✪
Diva Adelaide Hills Chardonnay Pinot Noir NV **Rating** 90 $20 ✪

Chalk Hill

58 Field Street, McLaren Vale, SA 5171 **Region** McLaren Vale
T (08) 8323 6400 **www.chalkhill.com.au Open** Not
Winemaker Renae Hirsch **Est.** 1973 **Dozens** 20 000 **Vyds** 89ha

The growth of Chalk Hill has accelerated after passing from parents John and Diana Harvey to grapegrowing sons Jock and Tom. Both are heavily involved in wine industry affairs. Further acquisitions mean the vineyards now span each district of McLaren Vale, planted to both the exotic (savagnin, barbera and sangiovese) and mainstream (shiraz, cabernet sauvignon, grenache, chardonnay and cabernet franc). The Alpha Crucis series is especially praiseworthy. Exports to most markets; exports to the US under the Alpha Crucis label, to Canada under the Wits End label.

🍷🍷🍷🍷🍷 **Alpha Crucis Old Vine McLaren Vale Grenache 2018** Sourced primarily from 80yo bushvines in Blewitt Springs. The colour is light and clear, the highly fragrant red berry/bramble bouquet no less inviting. When the palate unfolds its celestial wings, the quality of the shimmering red berries and polished tannins strike home. Screwcap. 14% alc. **Rating** 98 **To** 2038 $50 ✪

🍷🍷🍷🍷🍷 **Alpha Crucis Adelaide Hills Chardonnay 2018** 75% of the grapes came from one of the highest vineyards in the Piccadilly Valley. I'm not convinced by the bouquet, but the palate is a different story – white peach and citrussy delicacy sweeping the cobwebs away. Screwcap. 13% alc. **Rating** 96 **To** 2030 $50 ✪
Alpha Crucis Titan McLaren Vale Cabernet Sauvignon 2018 From 2 vineyards, 25yo and 50yo; vinified separately, 15 months in French oak (25% new). A first class cabernet from a warm vintage. Screwcap. 14.5% alc. **Rating** 96 **To** 2038 $35 ✪
Alpha Crucis McLaren Vale Shiraz 2018 Very deep colour is no surprise. Black fruits, licorice, bitter chocolate and French oak aromas and flavours. The tannins are more obvious than those of its siblings, but so is the depth of fruit. It will almost certainly leave its siblings thrashing around in its wake 5 years hence. Screwcap. 14.5% alc. **Rating** 95 **To** 2043 $85
McLaren Vale Shiraz 2018 Six parcels from 3 estate vineyards; vinified separately in new and used French oak. Complex and satisfying, medium to full-bodied black fruit allsorts and a (forgiven) whisper of excess oak. Screwcap. 14.5% alc. **Rating** 95 **To** 2037 $28 ✪
Alpha Crucis McLaren Vale Syrah 2018 A vibrant mix of red and black fruits framed by integrated oak and fine tannins. Elegant wine. Screwcap. 14% alc. **Rating** 95 **To** 2033 $50
McLaren Vale Barbera 2018 Open-fermented and matured in largely used French oak. Barbera can be dull and boring, but not this wine. It paints the mouth with juicy red fruits that are complete in themselves. Screwcap. 14% alc. **Rating** 95 **To** 2027 $28 ✪

🍷🍷🍷🍷🍷 **McLaren Vale Grenache Tempranillo 2018** **Rating** 92 **To** 2028 $26
Luna McLaren Vale Shiraz 2018 **Rating** 91 **To** 2026 $20✪

Chalmers   ★★★★☆

118 Third Street, Merbein, Vic 3505 **Region** Heathcote
T 0400 261 932 **www.chalmers.com.au Open** Not
Winemaker Bart van Olphen, Tennille Chalmers, Kim Chalmers **Est.** 1989
Dozens 10 000 **Vyds** 27ha
Following the 2008 sale of their very large vineyard and vine nursery propagation business, the Chalmers family has refocused its wine businesses. All fruit comes from the 80ha property on Mt Camel Range in Heathcote, which provides the grapes for the individual variety, single vineyard Chalmers range (Vermentino, Fiano, Greco, Lambrusco, Rosato, Nero d'Avola, Sagrantino and Aglianico). The entry-level Montevecchio label features blends and more approachable styles. A second vineyard at Merbein is a contract grapegrower, but also has a small nursery block housing the Chalmers' clonal selections. In '13 a program of micro-vinification of the rarer, and hitherto unutilised, varieties from the Nursery Block was introduced. In '17 a new winery was commissioned in time for most of that year's vintage, and from '18 all winemaking was carried out at Merbein. Exports to the UK and Japan.

♥♥♥♥♡ **Lambrusco 2018** Because it's dry, it has no mid-palate structure. Between a rock and a hard place. Hand-picked, traditional method, 9 months on lees, 4g/l dosage. Points for the serious approach. Crown seal. 11% alc. **Rating** 90 $43

Chambers Rosewood   ★★★★★

Barkly Street, Rutherglen, Vic 3685 **Region** Rutherglen
T (02) 6032 8641 **www.**chambersrosewood.com.au **Open** Mon–Sat 9–5, Sun 10–5
Winemaker Stephen Chambers **Est.** 1858 **Dozens** 5000 **Vyds** 50ha
Chambers' Rare Muscat and Rare Muscadelle (previously Topaque or Tokay) are the greatest of all in the Rutherglen firmament and should be treated as national treasures; the other wines in the hierarchy also magnificent. Stephen Chambers (sixth generation) comes into the role as winemaker, but father Bill is seldom far away. Exports to the UK, the US, Canada, Belgium, Denmark, China and NZ.

♥♥♥♥♥ **Rare Rutherglen Muscadelle NV** Almost opaque across a hue of molasses and mahogany grand piano shades. Mind-boggling just how old the average component in this prodigious blend must be; surely a centurion. Date, cinnamon, tomatillo. A Moroccan souk. Ethereal. Nutty rancio for lift and joy. Imperious, this. Rather than a dessert wine, I strongly suggest this elixir as a meditational sipper. Undoubtedly among the smattering of truly world class wines from this country. **Rating** 98 $250 NG

♥♥♥♥♥ **Grand Rutherglen Muscat NV** A dense mahogany hue, suggesting prodigious age across the blend of wines contributing to this kaleidoscope of textures, aromas and flavour. Cedar, varnish, grape, spice, date rosewater, given life by a rancio walnut tang. Immense. Exotic. Paradoxically, savoury. **Rating** 96 $55 NG ✪
Old Vine Rutherglen Muscadelle NV Muscadelle kicks around Sauternes and the south-west of France before reaching its fortified apogee here, in Rutherglen. Mahogany. Date, fig, molasses, orange zest; not rancio depth as yet, but fresher for it. I love the underlying lemon curd lift of Muscadelle; despite the decadence, there is always freshness. Screwcap. **Rating** 95 $30 NG ✪
Old Vine Rutherglen Muscat NV A shift to older wines: older base average and longer time in wood than the generic regional expression. A mahogany hue. Date, dried fig and the whiff of the Moroccan souk coming into play: dried apricot, ginger, cardamom and turmeric. This tier is stellar value. Screwcap. **Rating** 95 $25 NG ✪

♥♥♥♥♡ **Rutherglen Muscat NV Rating** 92 $22 NG ✪
Rutherglen Muscadelle NV Rating 91 $22 NG ✪
Rutherglen Gouais 2008 Rating 90 To 2021 $20 ✪
Rutherglen Durif 2017 Rating 90 To 2027 $20 NG ✪

Chandon Australia   ★★★★★

727 Maroondah Highway, Coldstream, Vic 3770 **Region** Yarra Valley
T (03) 9738 9200 **www.**chandon.com.au **Open** 7 days 10.30–4.30
Winemaker Dan Buckle, Glenn Thompson, Adam Keath **Est.** 1986 **Dozens** NFP
Vyds 184ha
Established by Möet & Chandon, this is one of the two most important wine facilities in the Yarra Valley; the tasting room has a national and international reputation, having won a number of major tourism awards in recent years. The sparkling wine product range has evolved with the 1994 acquisition of a substantial vineyard in the cool Strathbogie Ranges and the 2014 purchase of the high-altitude vineyard established by Brown Brothers. These supplement the large intake from the Yarra Valley at various altitudes. Under the leadership of Dan Buckle the high quality standards have been maintained. Exports to Japan, Thailand, Indonesia, Singapore, South Korea, Malaysia, Vietnam, the Philippines, Taiwan and Hong Kong.

♥♥♥♥♥ **Cellar Release Winemaker's Selection Rose 2013** The palest of pale roses is in another hemisphere from Chandon's NV Brut Rose. It comes from the

Yarra Valley, Whitlands Plateau and Strathbogie Ranges. It has a heady perfumed bouquet with violets and spice, the palate of ultimate elegance and effortless length. Diam. 12.5% alc. **Rating** 97 $64 ✪

ŸŸŸŸŸ **Methode Traditionelle Vintage Brut 2015** Over 36 months on lees, disgorged July '18; from estate vineyards at Coldstream, Whitlands and Strathbogie. The interaction of cold-climate sites and varieties gives rise to flavours ranging between grapefruit, green apple, almonds and marzipan. Compelling complexity and length. Cork. 12.5% alc. **Rating** 95 $42
Limited Edition Upper Yarra Valley Cuvee 205 2015 Made from 74.7% chardonnay, 23% pinot noir and 2.3% pinot meunier. The bouquet is strikingly similar to poached pears, cream and cinnamon; the palate sticking tightly to this theme, its acidity balanced by the dosage of 6g/l. It spent over 48 months on yeast lees, all adding to the undoubted complexity. Diam. 12.5% alc. **Rating** 95 $59
Limited Edition Whitlands Plateau Vintage Blanc de Blancs 2015 Kept in stainless steel or bottle throughout its elevage, with no oak. It is pure chardonnay in the sense of its reservoir of flavours of white flowers, grapefruit, Granny Smith apple and spice. Diam. 12.5% alc. **Rating** 94 $42

ŸŸŸŸŸ **Vintage Yarra Valley Cuvee 2016** Rating 93 $39
Vintage Blanc de Noirs 2015 Rating 92 $39
Brut Rose NV Rating 92 $25 ✪
Methode Traditionelle Brut NV Rating 90 $25

Chapel Hill   ★★★★★

1 Chapel Hill Road, McLaren Vale, SA 5171 **Region** McLaren Vale
T (08) 8323 8429 **www**.chapelhillwine.com.au **Open** 7 days 11–5
Winemaker Michael Fragos, Bryn Richards **Est.** 1973 **Dozens** 70000 **Vyds** 44ha
A leading medium-sized winery in McLaren Vale. In late 2019 the business was purchased from the Swiss Thomas Schmidheiny group – which owns the respected Cuvaison winery in California and vineyards in Switzerland and Argentina – by Endeavour Drinks (part of the Woolworths group). Wine quality is unfailingly excellent. The production comes from estate plantings of shiraz, cabernet sauvignon, chardonnay, verdelho, savagnin, sangiovese and merlot, plus contract-grown grapes. The red wines are not filtered or fined, and there are no tannin or enzyme additions, just SO_2 – natural red wines. Exports to all major markets.

ŸŸŸŸŸ **1897 Vines McLaren Vale Grenache 2018** Hand-picked from a single block planted in 1897. Destemmed, open-fermented, gentle hand-plunging, the small thick-skinned berries given a 12-day ferment and matured in used French puncheons for 13 months. A very high quality wine. Traditional grenache at its greatest; the palate at once velvety and spicy, ripe tannins expertly managed. Length, balance and purity. Screwcap. 14.5% alc. **Rating** 98 To 2048 $65 ✪

ŸŸŸŸŸ **Road Block McLaren Vale Shiraz 2018** Matured in French hogsheads (18% new) for 20 months. Michael Fragos is a master of McLaren Vale shiraz, delivering a strong sense of place. Generosity is at its heart; sweet black fruit and high spice with, in this case, a pomegranate exotic touch. So smooth in mouthfeel and concentrated in fruit quality, with a mouth-watering, cranberry juiciness to close. Screwcap. 14.5% alc. **Rating** 96 To 2033 $65 JP ✪
Gorge Block McLaren Vale Cabernet Sauvignon 2018 Matured in French oak hogsheads (20% new) for 20 months. A rare-ish Vale cabernet expression with a mineral-led fineness and structure which gives rise to cool lines and a super long finish. Red and blue fruits infused with licorice and spice, there's also an attractive spearmint/mint quality. And white pepper. Indeed, this could be mistaken for a cool-climate super spiced-up cabernet with bare traces of oak. And the finish goes and goes. Screwcap. 14.5% alc. **Rating** 96 To 2030 $65 JP ✪
The Vicar McLaren Vale Shiraz 2018 Matured in French oak hogsheads (25% new) for 21 months. There is a certain style to The Vicar that one might call dark and inky. Brooding, too. Maybe it's the role of oak, maybe it's in the

sourcing of fruit from Chapel Hill's best growers, or in the hands and mind of the winemaker, but it's one intense drinking experience. Black throughout, licorice, the full spice rack and Vale savoury earth. Pronounced tannins are there for the journey ahead. Screwcap. 14.5% alc. **Rating 95 To** 2038 $75 JP

House Block McLaren Vale Shiraz 2018 Matured in French oak hogsheads (18% new) for 20 months. Chapel Hill is a shiraz specialist making multiple styles from the one region. House Block fits nicely into the friendly shiraz category, it's so easy to get to know. Upfront fruit power all the way charged by blackberries, licorice, black olive savouriness and dark chocolate. Warm toasty oak caps off an archetypal Aussie shiraz. Screwcap. 14.5% alc. **Rating 95 To** 2028 $65 JP

McLaren Vale Shiraz 2018 An impressive embodiment of the classic Vale shiraz: rich, concentrated and enduring in appeal. Vibrant purple colour. Mass of blackberries and currants, mulberry, brown spice and barbecued game meats. The subtlety of the savouriness offers an intriguing note, as does the prune and smoked goods. There's a lot happening here. Something for every shiraz drinker. Screwcap. 14.5% alc. **Rating 94 To** 2035 $33 JP

ΨΨΨΨΨ **Bush Vine McLaren Vale Grenache 2018 Rating** 93 **To** 2030 $30
McLaren Vale Cabernet Sauvignon 2017 Rating 93 **To** 2029 $30
The Vinedresser Cabernet Sauvignon 2017 Rating 93 **To** 2029 $25 ✪
Adelaide Sangiovese Rose 2019 Rating 92 **To** 2022 $18 ✪
The Parson McLaren Vale Shiraz 2018 Rating 92 **To** 2025 $18 ✪
The Parson McLaren Vale Grenache Shiraz Mourvedre 2019 Rating 92 **To** 2025 $18 JP ✪
McLaren Vale Mourvedre 2018 Rating 92 **To** 2029 $28 JP
Home Grown McLaren Vale Shiraz 2018 Rating 90 **To** 2029 $28
The Vinedresser McLaren Vale Shiraz 2018 Rating 90 **To** 2026 $26 JP
McLaren Vale Shiraz Mourvedre 2018 Rating 90 **To** 2028 $28

Charles Melton   ★★★★★

Krondorf Road, Tanunda, SA 5352 **Region** Barossa Valley
T (08) 8563 3606 **www.**charlesmeltonwines.com.au **Open** 7 days 11–5
Winemaker Charlie Melton, Krys Smith **Est.** 1984 **Dozens** 12000 **Vyds** 32.6ha
Charlie Melton, one of the Barossa Valley's great characters, with wife Virginia by his side, makes some of the most eagerly sought à la mode wines in Australia. There are 7ha of estate vineyards at Lyndoch, 9ha at Krondorf and 1.6ha at Light Pass; the lion's share shiraz and grenache, and a small planting of cabernet sauvignon. An additional 30ha property was purchased in High Eden, with 10ha of shiraz planted in 2009 and a 5ha field of grenache, shiraz, mataro, carignan, cinsaut, picpoul and bourboulenc planted in '10. The expanded volume has had no adverse effect on the quality of the rich, supple and harmonious wines. Exports to all major markets.

ΨΨΨΨΨ **Voices of Angels Adelaide Hills Shiraz 2016** The highlight of the '16 Charles Melton reds. As usual a splash of riesling goes into this as it grows on the same site and up to 15% whole-bunches in the ferment. While this is concentrated and deep – a considerable 29 months in French barrels – it has vivacity too. Spiced red fruits; firm tannins that are neatly pitched; clearly oak a player but behaving. Screwcap. 14.5% alc. **Rating 95 To** 2028 $86 JF

The Kirche Barossa Shiraz Cabernet Sauvignon 2017 A 70/30 split that forms a rich, concentrated yet vibrant whole. Wafts of cassis and plums, fruitcake and baking spices. Full-bodied with determined tannins, neatly pitched and ready to cellar. Screwcap. 14.5% alc. **Rating 95 To** 2035 $45 JF

Sotto di Ferro PX NV It takes skill and patience to make this style of wine. Perfect grapes, a maximum of 8 bunches strung together and suspended in a hanging shed to dry for 8 weeks. The precious drops of nectar pressed to 60l casks and left there for 4 years. It morphs into a dark amber elixir, sweet and luscious with a hint of aged balsamic vinegar – rich and molasses-like and wonderfully fresh. Screwcap. 11.5% alc. **Rating 95 To** 2021 $70 JF

♀♀♀♀♀ **The Father In Law Barossa Shiraz 2017** Rating 91 To 2028 $28 JF
Rose of Virginia 2019 Rating 90 To 2021 $28 JF
La Belle Mere 2017 Rating 90 To 2027 $28 JF

Chateau Tanunda   ★★★★★

9 Basedow Road, Tanunda, SA 5352 **Region** Barossa Valley
T (08) 8563 3888 **www**.chateautanunda.com **Open** 7 days 10–5
Winemaker Neville Rowe **Est.** 1890 **Dozens** 150 000 **Vyds** 100ha
This is one of the most historically significant winery buildings in the Barossa Valley, built from bluestone quarried at nearby Bethany in the late 1880s. It has been restored by John Geber and family, and a new small-batch basket press has been installed. Chateau Tanunda owns almost 100ha of vineyards in Bethany, Eden Valley, Tanunda and Vine Vale, with additional fruit sourced from a group of 30 growers covering the panoply of Barossa districts. The wines are made from hand-picked grapes, basket-pressed and are neither fined nor filtered. There is an emphasis on single vineyard and single district wines under the Terroirs of the Barossa label. The impressive building houses the cellar door, the Grand Cellar (with over 300 barrels of wine) and the Barossa Small Winemakers Centre, offering wines from boutique winemakers. The arrival of John's daughter, Michelle Geber, in 2018 has nothing to do with nepotism and everything to do with her exceptional talent; her CV covers every aspect of wine and wine business. Exports to all major markets.

♀♀♀♀♀ **50 Year Old Vines Barossa Cabernet Sauvignon 2017** From vines in the heart of Bethany; small open fermenters, matured in French oak for 18 months. It's the great '17 vintage that makes this wine stand out, the cool season more suited to cabernet than any other red variety in the Barossa Valley. Screwcap. 14.5% alc. **Rating** 96 **To** 2047 $80

150 Year Old Vines Barossa 1858 Field Blend 2016 The field blend is of interplanted grenache, mourvedre and malbec. The clear, crimson colour is a good omen and the wine is indeed very good. There is a balance between plum, blackberry and black cherry within a framework of French oak and tannins. It's only medium-bodied, but its balance should ensure a long future, the only uncertainty the cork. 14.9% alc. **Rating** 96 **To** 2040 $500

150 Year Old Vines Barossa Semillon 2019 From a single vineyard in Light Pass; hand-picked and sorted, fermented in stainless steel before 7 months maturation in used French oak. There's no question at all about the power and length of the wine, nor its varietal expression. Screwcap. 12% alc. **Rating** 95 **To** 2028 $60

Terroirs of the Barossa Greenock Shiraz 2017 From the western ridge, the vineyard with rich red and brown clay soils. Interesting texture, more light and shade. Plum fruit. The least apparent alcohol heat. Cork. 15% alc. **Rating** 95 **To** 2032 $55

The Everest Barossa Shiraz 2016 Bottle no 769/1200. The absolute pinnacle of winemaking at Chateau Tanunda from specific low-yielding blocks. Open-fermented, 10 days on skins, plunged, 18 months in French and American oak. Opaque; dense crystallised fruit dipped in dark chocolate. A winner if served with cognac and coffee. Cork. 15% alc. **Rating** 95 **To** 2036 $295

The Chateau Single Vineyard Barossa Cabernet Sauvignon 2018 A lurch back in time to 15% alcohol. Yes, it's got unlimited flavour, but it's so sad – this vineyard owned by Chateau Tanunda must have offered some lovely grapes at 14%. They did select 36 rows, and it has soft, savoury bay leaf/tapenade nuances to accompany blackcurrant fruit flavours. Full-bodied, but balanced. Cork. **Rating** 95 **To** 2038 $38

The Chateau Bethanian Single Vineyard Barossa Valley Shiraz 2017 From 22 acres of sandy loam around the Bethany hamlet, 18 months in a mix of new and used oak. Full-bodied in The Chateau style. Diam. 15.5% alc. **Rating** 94 **To** 2030 $38

Terroirs of the Barossa Eden Valley Shiraz 2017 Less outright heat and more texture. Fine tannins, yet firm in its texture. Cork. 15.5% alc. **Rating** 94 To 2032 $55

Terroirs of the Barossa Marananga Shiraz 2017 From the northwest quadrant. Always been there, but the district has only recently gained respect, particularly as the producer of the Barossa Valley's most powerful wines. Jam, black forest, oak, licorice, dark chocolate. Gets away from the alcohol heat with ease. Cork. 15.5% alc. **Rating** 94 To 2032 $55

The Everest Old Vine Barossa Grenache 2016 From a small parcel of 100yo dry-grown bushvines. Hand-picked and sorted into a 1t open fermenter. Basket-pressed before 18 months maturation in used French oak. Ultra-traditional full-bodied wine endowed with ample supply of heat. Cork. 15% alc. **Rating** 94 To 2026 $295

Grand Barossa Grenache Shiraz Mourvedre 2018 A 67/22/11% blend; matured for 18 months in new and used French oak. Partial whole-bunch fermentation for the grenache, all the components vinified in small batches. Rich, full-flavoured, but not overdone. Good value. Screwcap. 15% alc. **Rating** 94 To 2028 $25 ✪

ΨΨΨΨ♀ **50 Year Old Vines Barossa Shiraz 2017** Rating 93 To 2029 $80
50 Year Old Vines Barossa Shiraz 2016 Rating 93 To 2032 $80
Grand Barossa Cabernet Sauvignon 2018 Rating 93 To 2028 $25 ✪
Terroirs of the Barossa Ebenezer Shiraz 2017 Rating 92 To 2030 $55
Grand Barossa Dry Riesling 2019 Rating 91 To 2024 $25

Chatto   ★★★★★

68 Dillons Hill Road, Glaziers Bay, Tas 7109 **Region** Southern Tasmania
T (03) 6114 2050 **www**.chattowines.com **Open** Not
Winemaker Jim Chatto **Est.** 2000 **Dozens** 1000 **Vyds** 1.5ha
Jim Chatto is recognised as having one of the very best palates in Australia, and has proved to be an outstanding winemaker. He and wife Daisy long wanted to get a small Tasmanian pinot business up and running but, having moved to the Hunter Valley in 2000, it took six years to find a site that satisfied all of the criteria Jim considers ideal. It is a warm, well drained site in one of the coolest parts of Tasmania, looking out over Glaziers Bay. So far they have planted eight clones of pinot noir, with a spacing of 5000 vines/ha. This will be a busman's holiday for some years to come following Jim's appointment as chief winemaker for Mount Pleasant and Pipers Brook. The '19 crop was lost to bushfire smoke taint, but the many Tasmanian vigneron friends of the Chatto family have come to the rescue, and while there will be no Isle Black Label Pinot Noir (estate-based), there will be sufficient Tasmanian-grown pinot noir and chardonnay to cope with demand.

ΨΨΨΨΨ Mania Pinot Noir 2018 Hand-picked and sorted, matured in French puncheons (10% new) for 10 months. Superb clarity to the crimson colour announces a very expressive, very pure array of red fruits backed up by superfine tannins. Exceptional wine at this price. Screwcap. 13.6% alc. Rating 96 To 2030 $30 ✪

Chrismont   ★★★★☆

251 Upper King River Road, Cheshunt, Vic 3678 **Region** King Valley
T (03) 5729 8220 **www**.chrismont.com.au **Open** 7 days 10–5
Winemaker Warren Proft **Est.** 1980 **Dozens** 25 000 **Vyds** 100ha
Arnie and Jo Pizzini's substantial vineyards in the Cheshunt and Whitfield areas of the upper King Valley have been planted to riesling, chardonnay, pinot gris, merlot, barbera, sagrantino, marzemino, arneis, prosecco, fiano, petit manseng, tempranillo, sangiovese and nebbiolo. The La Zona range ties in the Italian heritage of the Pizzinis and is part of the intense interest in all things Italian. In January 2016 the Chrismont Cellar Door, Restaurant and Larder was opened. As well as a 7-day cellar door, the development can seat up to 300 guests and is designed to host weddings, corporate events, business conferences and group celebrations. A feature is the

'floating' deck over the vineyard, which can seat up to 150 people and has floor-to-ceiling glass looking out over the Black Ranges and King Valley landscape. Exports to the Philippines, Malaysia and Singapore.

ŶŶŶŶŶ **King Valley Pinot Gris 2017** This is good. Really good with heady aromas of jasmine and honeysuckle met with complex flavours of baked spiced apples, poached pears and ginger spice. It's also textural with creamed honey. Overall it is luscious but far from heavy, instead, the finish lingers. Screwcap. 13.5% alc. Rating 95 To 2024 $26 JF ✪

ŶŶŶŶŶ **King Valley Riesling 2019** Rating 93 To 2028 $19 JF ✪
La Zona King Valley Sagrantino 2016 Rating 93 To 2026 $30 JF
La Zona Oro Dolce King Valley Late Harvest Arneis 2018 Rating 93 To 2022 $25 JF ✪
La Zona King Valley Sangiovese 2017 Rating 92 To 2024 $27 JF
La Zona King Valley Barbera 2017 Rating 92 To 2026 $27 JF
La Zona King Valley Nero d'Avola 2018 Rating 92 To 2023 $30 JF
King Valley Chardonnay 2018 Rating 90 To 2026 $26 JF
La Zona King Valley Arneis 2018 Rating 90 To 2021 $22 JF
La Zona King Valley Prosecco NV Rating 90 $22 JF

Churchview Estate ★★★★★

8 Gale Road, Metricup, WA 6280 **Region** Margaret River
T (08) 9755 7200 **www**.churchview.com.au **Open** Mon–Sat 10–5
Winemaker Dave Longden **Est.** 1998 **Dozens** 45 000 **Vyds** 59ha
The Fokkema family, headed by Spike Fokkema, immigrated from the Netherlands in the 1950s. Business success in the following decades led to the acquisition of the 100ha Churchview Estate in '97 and to the progressive establishment of substantial vineyards (planted to 16 varieties), managed organically. Exports to all major markets.

ŶŶŶŶŶ **The Bartondale Margaret River Cabernet Sauvignon 2018** Margaret River makes it all seem so simple: 94% cabernet, 6% malbec; picked on the correct day, 14 days on skins then pressed to French barrels (70% new) for mlf, 12 months in oak prior to blending. Luscious cassis is gently trimmed by fine-grained tannins and cedary oak. Screwcap. 14.5% alc. Rating 95 To 2038
St Johns Limited Release Margaret River Zinfandel 2018 Hand-picked to retain a whole-berry fermentation with 10 days on skins, pressed to American oak (40% new) to finish fermentation, racked off lees and returned to the same oak for 12 months maturation. The oak is very obvious on the bouquet, but the palate is another thing with a vibrant, long and spicy backdrop to the red fruits. Screwcap. 15% alc. Rating 95 To 2028
St Johns Limited Release Margaret River Cabernet Malbec Petit Verdot Merlot 2018 A 50/25/13/12% blend; the varieties vinified in various ways and kept separate until blending and bottling, 40% matured in new French oak. In the outcome, the medium to full-bodied fruit holds sway over the oak. Screwcap. 14.5% alc. Rating 94 To 2038

ŶŶŶŶŶ **The Bartondale Margaret River Shiraz 2018** Rating 93 To 2033
St Johns Limited Release Margaret River Shiraz Viognier 2018 Rating 91 To 2030
The Bartondale Margaret River Chardonnay 2018 Rating 90 To 2023

Cimicky Wines ★★★★★

100 Hermann Thumm Drive, Lyndoch, SA 5351 **Region** Barossa Valley
T (08) 8524 4025 **www**.cimickywines.com.au **Open** By appt
Winemaker Charles Cimicky, Sam Kurtz, Andrew Aldridge **Est.** 1972 **Dozens** 15 000 **Vyds** 14.42ha

The Cimicky property was originally settled in Lyndoch in 1842 by early German pioneers. Karl Cimicky purchased the property in 1970, expanding the vineyards and building the imposing Tuscan-style winery, which he named Karlsburg. When Karl retired in the '80s, his son Charles Cimicky and partner Jennie took over the business. The winery was completely refitted and, despite historically keeping an ultra-low profile, they produced a range of highly acclaimed red wines. In 2018 Charles and Jennie sold the business to the Hermann Thumm Drive Property Partnership.

🍷🍷🍷🍷🍷 **Grand Reserve Barossa Valley Shiraz 2017** Blend of 95% from the Barossa Valley, 5% Eden Valley; matured for 2 years in 60% French/40% American oak (50% new); this wine a barrel selection. A pretty remarkable wine, the intensity of the luscious blackberry/plum fruit easily accounts for the new oak. Diam. 14.5% alc. **Rating** 98 **To** 2047 $400

Grand Reserve Barossa Cabernet Sauvignon 2017 From the finest estate blocks: 53% Barossa Valley, 47% Eden Valley. Open-fermented, matured for 2 years in French hogsheads (50% new); this wine a barrel selection. A full-bodied cabernet of very high quality, revelling in the cool vintage and Eden Valley; supple mouthfeel, cassis flavours. Diam. 14.5% alc. **Rating** 97 **To** 2040 $400

🍷🍷🍷🍷🍷 **Reserve Barossa Valley Cabernet Sauvignon 2016** Matured for 2 years in new and used French hogsheads. Very good cabernet; medium to full-bodied; the fruit/oak balance is good, as is the length. Diam. 14.5% alc. **Rating** 95 **To** 2040 $100

Reserve Barossa Valley Shiraz 2017 Open-fermented, not fined or filtered, matured for 2 years in 25% new American and 8% new French oak. Full-bodied overall, but would have been better if the percentages had been reversed. Screwcap. 14.8% alc. **Rating** 94 **To** 2037 $100

Trumps Barossa Valley Shiraz 2017 Part contract-grown, part from the estate; matured in used oak for 18 months. An attractive medium-bodied wine that shows the '17 vintage to full advantage. Screwcap. 14.5% alc. **Rating** 94 **To** 2032 $27 ✪

🍷🍷🍷🍷🍷 **Autograph Barossa Valley Shiraz 2016 Rating** 90 **To** 2034 $45

Circe Wines   ★★★★★

PO Box 22, Red Hill, Vic 3937 **Region** Mornington Peninsula
T 0417 328 142 **www.**circewines.com.au **Open** Not
Winemaker Dan Buckle **Est.** 2010 **Dozens** 800 **Vyds** 2.9ha
Circe was a seductress and minor goddess of intoxicants in Homer's *Odyssey*. Circe Wines is the partnership of winemaker Dan Buckle and marketer Aaron Drummond, very much a weekend and holiday venture, inspired by their mutual love of pinot noir. They have a long-term lease of a vineyard in Hillcrest Road, not far from Paringa Estate. Dan says, 'It is not far from the Lieu-dit "Buckle" Vineyard my dad planted in the 1980s'. Circe has 1.2ha of vines, half chardonnay and half MV6 pinot noir. They have also planted 1.7ha of pinot noir (MV6, Abel, 777, D2V5 and Bests' Old Clone) at a vineyard in William Road, Red Hill. Dan Buckle's real job is chief winemaker at Chandon Australia. Exports to the UK.

🍷🍷🍷🍷🍷 **Hillcrest Road Vineyard Mornington Peninsula Pinot Noir 2018** From a 0.8ha vineyard of MV6 planted '93, sorted on the vine by the removal of all but 1 bunch per cane. Open-fermented, 100% whole bunch, kept under CO_2 for 10 days carbonic maceration, 8 days fermentation and maceration, then fermentation finished in oak (20% new). A rich, resonant pinot with a bracelet of fine-spun tannins. Screwcap. 13.5% alc. **Rating** 96 **To** 2033 $70 ✪

Single Vineyard Blanc de Blancs 2014 Traditional method, it looks as if it spent some years on tirage. It is very well made (no surprise), elegance its middle name, with the white fruit flower combination operating throughout. Perfect dosage. Diam. 12.5% alc. **Rating** 95 $60

Mornington Peninsula Pinot Noir 2018 Thinned to 1 bunch per shoot, hand-picked, 30% partial whole bunch 'à la Coldstream Hills '97', 30% whole bunch and pigeage and a mix of whole bunch and crushed ferments with the same attention to detail. The difference is seemingly of clone 115 planted in '14. This is a light-bodied version of its MV6 sibling. Screwcap. 13.5% alc. **Rating** 94 **To** 2028 $40

♥♥♥♥♡ **Mornington Peninsula Pinot Noir 2017 Rating** 90 **To** 2023 $40

Clairault | Streicker Wines   ★★★★★
3277 Caves Road, Wilyabrup, WA 6280 **Region** Margaret River
T (08) 9755 6225 **www**.clairaultstreicker.com.au **Open** 7 days 10–5
Winemaker Bruce Dukes **Est.** 1976 **Dozens** 15 000 **Vyds** 113ha
This multifaceted business is owned by New York resident John Streicker. It began in 2002 when he purchased the Yallingup Protea Farm and vineyards. This was followed by the purchase of the Ironstone Vineyard in '03 and then the Bridgeland Vineyard. The Ironstone Vineyard is one of the oldest vineyards in Wilyabrup. In April '12 Streicker acquired Clairault, bringing a further 40ha of estate vines, including 12ha now over 40 years old. The two brands are effectively run as one venture. A large part of the grape production is sold to winemakers in the region. Exports to the US, Canada, Norway, Dubai, Malaysia, Singapore, Hong Kong and China.

♥♥♥♥♥ **Clairault Cellar Release Margaret River Petit Verdot 2014** This rich, luxuriant wine has aged beautifully to early middle age, with plenty more in store. A glossy mid-ruby. Aromas of graphite, pencil lead, blood plum, mulberry and cedar are pixelated by juicy acidity and impeccably honed granular tannins. Coffee-bean-mocha flavours linger long, yet they are a conflation of well judged extraction, the right riff of oak and optimally ripe fruit. Nothing excessive here. Bravo! Screwcap. **Rating** 97 **To** 2024 $30 NG ✪

♥♥♥♥♥ **Streicker Ironstone Block Old Vine Margaret River Cabernet Sauvignon 2016** Gently crushed, to the point that the berries just split, without gleaning excessive astringency. Pumped over for 18 days, 3 times per day. The sort of extraction regime more should adopt. A whiplash of cassis, black olive, bouquet garni and clove. Compelling intensity here, with gravelly graphite tannins keeping it all on the straight and narrow. This rich red will provide riveting drinking in maturity. Screwcap. **Rating** 96 **To** 2033 $60 NG ✪

Streicker Ironstone Block Old Vine Margaret River Chardonnay 2018 This is sumptuous chardonnay. From the heart of Wilyabrup, this was barrel-fermented and aged for 9 months. A portion underwent malolactic conversion. Peaches and cream. A luxuriant core of creamed cashew and praline, with vanilla pod oak sewing the seams. Screwcap. **Rating** 95 **To** 2027 $50 NG

Clairault Estate Margaret River Cabernet Sauvignon 2016 A pleasure to taste a wine that is firmly of its turf. Bouquet garni, lead and pencil shavings intermingle with blackcurrant, sage and mint. Oak guides the flavours long while providing a bit of cedar bristle across the seams. This will settle across the long life ahead. Very fine, pointed, graphite-complex. Compellingly long and highly regional. Screwcap. **Rating** 95 **To** 2032 $60 NG

Streicker Methode Traditionelle Blanc de Blancs 2015 This ambitious fizz spent 30 months on lees which, to be frank, is just long enough. While there is the salty tang of maritime acidity driving the wine long, it is not high enough to cope with more yeast-embellishment. Well judged! Brioche, lanolin and lots of praline scents mingle with stone fruit allusions and a whiff of jasmine. This is a very good sparkling. Rich, but fresh. Poised and authoritative. Cork. **Rating** 95 $45 NG

Streicker Bridgeland Block Fume Blanc 2018 Hand-picked, cold-crushed and barrel-fermented (33% new oak), remaining in barrel for 9 months. Oak threads a loom of complexity with sauvignon otherwise seldom seen: lanolin, lemon drop, spearmint, redcurrant and greengage, woven across a quilt of mineral detail and crunch with a seam of great length and calm. Nothing tangy or sour. A very good wine auguring well for mid-term ageing. Screwcap. **Rating** 94 **To** 2027 $30 NG ✪

🍷🍷🍷🍷⚲ **Clairault Estate Chardonnay 2018** Rating 93 To 2027 $45 NG
Clairault Cabernet Sauvignon 2018 Rating 93 To 2028 $30 NG
Clairault Halley & Lex Margaret River Cabernet Sauvignon 2017
Rating 93 To 2030 $18 ✪
Clairault Cabernet Sauvignon Merlot 2018 Rating 92 To 2026 NG
Clairault Sauvignon Blanc Semillon 2019 Rating 91 To 2022 $22 NG ✪
Clairault Chardonnay 2018 Rating 91 To 2024 $28 NG
Clairault Halley & Lex Sauvignon Blanc 2018 Rating 90 To 2021 $18 ✪

Clare Wine Co ★★★

PO Box 852, Nuriootpa, SA 5355 **Region** Clare Valley
T (08) 8562 4488 **www**.clarewineco.com.au **Open** Not
Winemaker Reid Bosward, Stephen Dew **Est.** 2008 **Dozens** 5000 **Vyds** 36ha
An affiliate of Kaesler Wines, its primary focus is on exports. Its vines are predominantly given over to shiraz and cabernet sauvignon. It also has riesling and semillon, but no chardonnay, which is presumably purchased from other Clare Valley growers. Exports to Malaysia, Singapore, Hong Kong and China.

Clarnette & Ludvigsen Wines ★★★★☆

270 Westgate Road, Armstrong, Vic 3377 **Region** Grampians
T 0409 083 833 **www**.clarnette-ludvigsen.com.au **Open** By appt
Winemaker Leigh Clarnette **Est.** 2003 **Dozens** 400 **Vyds** 15.5ha
Winemaker Leigh Clarnette and viticulturist Kym Ludvigsen's career paths crossed in late 1993 when both were working for Seppelt; Kym with a 14ha vineyard in the heart of the Grampians, all but 1ha of chardonnay, 0.5ha of viognier and 0.25ha of riesling planted to rare clones of shiraz, sourced from old plantings in the Great Western area. They met again in 2005 when both were employed by Taltarni. The premature death of Kym in '13 was widely reported, in no small measure due to his (unpaid) service on wine industry bodies. With next generations on both sides, the plans are to continue the business. Exports to China.

🍷🍷🍷🍷🍷 **Grampians Riesling 2019** Following a relatively cool extended fermentation, this was settled clear. The result: a lemon straw hue jittering to notes of grapefruit pulp, green apple, Rose's lime and talc. Vivid, but the winning quotient is the mellifluous meld of juicy natural acidity, streamlined flow of fruit and long gentle finish. A delicious riesling. Screwcap. Rating 95 To 2027 $23 NG ✪

🍷🍷🍷🍷⚲ **Reserve Grampians Shiraz 2017** Rating 93 To 2026 $65 NG
Le Grampian Chardonnay 2018 Rating 92 To 2024 NG
Grampians Sangiovese Rose 2019 Rating 92 To 2021 $23 NG ✪
Grampians Tempranillo 2019 Rating 90 To 2024 $28 NG

Claymore Wines ★★★★☆

7145 Horrocks Way, Leasingham, SA 5452 **Region** Clare Valley
T (08) 8843 0200 **www**.claymorewines.com.au **Open** Mon–Sat 10–5, Sun 11–4
Winemaker Nathan Norman **Est.** 1998 **Dozens** 35 000 **Vyds** 50ha
Claymore Wines is the venture of Anura Nitchingham, a medical professional who imagined this would lead the way to early retirement (which, of course, it did not). The starting date depends on which event you take first: the purchase of the 4ha vineyard at Leasingham in 1991 (with 70-year-old grenache, riesling and shiraz); the purchase of a 16ha block at Penwortham in '96, and planted to shiraz, merlot and grenache; making the first wines '97; or when the first releases came onto the market in '98. The labels are inspired by U2, Pink Floyd, Prince and Lou Reed. Exports to the UK, Canada, Denmark, Malaysia, Singapore, Taiwan, Hong Kong and China.

🍷🍷🍷🍷🍷 **Superstition Reserve Clare Valley Riesling 2019** Aromas of crisp green apple and slatey minerality combine with touches of honey and straw on the bouquet, precursors of things to come. In the mouth it's quite full and textural as young riesling goes, the fresh sweet-fruited flavours building in layers as it moves along the palate. That slatey minerality of the bouquet is reprised on the finish which is taut and long. Screwcap. 11.9% alc. **Rating** 95 To 2034 $32 SC ✪

ŶŶŶŶŶ **Joshua Tree Watervale Riesling 2019 Rating** 93 To 2029 $22 SC ✪
Dark Side of the Moon Shiraz 2018 Rating 93 To 2028 $25 SC ✪
London Calling Cabernet Malbec 2018 Rating 92 To 2025 $32 SC

Clonakilla ★★★★★

Crisps Lane, Murrumbateman, NSW 2582 **Region** Canberra District
T (02) 6227 5877 **www**.clonakilla.com.au **Open** Mon–Fri 11–4, w'ends 10–5
Winemaker Tim Kirk, Bryan Martin **Est.** 1971 **Dozens** 20 000 **Vyds** 14ha
The indefatigable Tim Kirk, with an inexhaustible thirst for knowledge, is the winemaker and manager of this family winery founded by his father, scientist Dr John Kirk. It is not at all surprising that the quality of the wines is exceptional, especially the Shiraz Viognier, which has paved the way for numerous others but remains the icon. Demand for the wines outstrips supply, even with the 1998 acquisition of an adjoining 20ha property by Tim and wife Lara Kirk, planted to shiraz and viognier. In 2007 the Kirk family purchased another adjoining property, planting of another 1.8ha of shiraz, plus 0.4ha of grenache, mourvedre and cinsaut. Exports to all major markets.

ŶŶŶŶŶ **Canberra District Riesling 2019** There's some colour pick-up that seems earlier than normal, perhaps due to the dry conditions through winter and spring, and the wine was slow out of the blocks. Then 110cm of rain fell in Jan, changing everything for the better. The awe-inspiring Canberra District comes on song as its hymn of intense citrus/mineral takes control. Very high quality. Screwcap. 12% alc. **Rating** 97 To 2039 $35 ✪
O'Riada Canberra District Shiraz 2018 A wild ride in the vineyard with a hail storm reducing an already small drought-affected crop. From this point through to harvest the weather was perfect. So is the colour, deep but crystal clear, blind tasting a tiara of spices and cracked pepper, the fruit supple and precisely balanced by oak and tannins. Screwcap. 14.5% alc. **Rating** 97 To 2040 $40 ✪
Shiraz Viognier 2018 Hand-picked and sorted, fermented with 28% whole bunches and 6% viognier. Fragrant to the point of perfumed aromas of spices, rose petals and red fruit blossom. The palate is, as ever, very complex, with spice berries sewn together in a necklace of tannins. The length is all one could wish for. Screwcap. 14% alc. **Rating** 97 To 2038 $120 ✪

ŶŶŶŶŶ **Murrumbateman Syrah 2018** Whole berries fermented warm by native yeasts, 1 month maceration time on skins and 2 years in French puncheons. By any measure, an extraordinary Australian shiraz sourced from 600m in elevation with fruit so elegant: red-berried and aromatic and gentle in savoury spice. You could write a book about the tannins, teased out through extended maceration time, and so, so fine. Screwcap. 14% alc. **Rating** 96 To 2031 $130 JP
Tumbarumba Chardonnay 2019 From a warm vintage, which in Tumbarumba terms means it's still on the cool side of things. A striking linear approach to the grape. Pink grapefruit, mandarin skin, nectarine to begin. Assertive, crisp and even in the mouth. Flavours move into toasted almonds, baked bread with poached quinces. The cut of crunchy acidity hits the spot. So good. Screwcap. 13.5% alc. **Rating** 95 To 2029 $45 JP
Murrumbateman Pinot Noir 2019 A blend of 5 different pinot noir clones (interestingly, MV6 is not included in the gang) which, on paper, should raise the complexity quotient alone. Youthful in bright red hues and full of brio; the scent of tomato leaf, dried herbs, black tea, wild strawberry and violets engages. Immediately succulent and immersive in red florals and dark spices, wild herbs and rosemary contrasting with supple texture and superfine tannins. Can only go up from here. Screwcap. 13.5% alc. **Rating** 95 To 2030 $50 JP
T&L Vineyard Block One Southern Tablelands Shiraz Viognier 2018 Blend of 94% shiraz, 6% viognier. Whole bunches 35%, natural fermentation,

maturation in French puncheons for 24 months. Fruit from the T&L Vineyard generally makes the final cut for the flagship shiraz, so anticipation is high. Here is a wine of effortless beauty, of the woods and the Aussie bush, wild spice and herbs, black fruits and leathery intrigue, and fine tannic lines. There is an underlying floral intensity that stays with you. Screwcap. 14% alc. **Rating** 95 **To** 2034 $130 JP

Western Vineyard Shiraz Viognier 2018 Blend of 94% shiraz, 6% viognier. Sourced from the Western Vineyard which is also a major contributor to Clonakilla's flagship, Shiraz Viognier. Whole bunches 50%, foot crushed, natural fermentation, 20 months in French oak puncheons. Viognier is subtle but clearly brings the iridescent sheen to the deep purple colour, and accentuates the floral intensity on the bouquet. The effect is riveting. Black peppercorns, black fruits, violet essence offer an inviting introduction. A lightness on the palate belies the depth below of spiced plums, pepper, bay leaf. Elegant oak and firm tannins complete the pretty picture. Screwcap. 14% alc. **Rating** 95 **To** 2029 $130 JP

Ballinderry 2018 Made from 39% cabernet franc, 32% cabernet sauvignon, 29% merlot. Ballinderry is Irish for 'place of the oak', a reference to a giant oak planted on the property when it was founded in 1971. High florals of violets and tea rose across the bouquet; musk and mulberry, bay leaf and clove. The bay leaf carries on the palate, which is dense in flavour. Grainy tannins emphasise a taut, well structured presence. One for the cellar. Screwcap. 14% alc. **Rating** 94 **To** 2033 $50 JP

🍷🍷🍷🍷 **Canberra District Viognier 2019** Rating 93 **To** 2025 $50 JP

Clos Clare ★★★★★

45 Old Road, Watervale, SA 5452 **Region** Clare Valley
T (08) 8843 0161 **www**.closclare.com.au **Open** W'ends 11–5
Winemaker Sam Barry, Tom Barry **Est.** 1993 **Dozens** 1600 **Vyds** 2ha
Clos Clare was acquired by the Barry family in 2007. Riesling continues to be made from the 2ha unirrigated section of the original Florita Vineyard (the major part of that vineyard was already in Barry ownership) and newly introduced red wines are coming from a 49-year-old vineyard beside the Armagh site. Exports to the UK.

🍷🍷🍷🍷 **Watervale Riesling 2019** This is archetypal. Quintessential. Classic. A taut thread of lime juice, grapefruit and candied lemon zest woven by a spindle of pumice, slate and bright acidity. Transparent. A flowing stream of flavour. Inimitably Clare. This will fill out with bottle age. Screwcap. **Rating** 94 **To** 2031 $29 NG ✪

🍷🍷🍷🍷 **The Hayes Boy Grenache 2019** Rating 93 **To** 2025 $26 NG ✪
Cemetery Block Shiraz 2017 Rating 92 **To** 2025 $26 NG

Cloudburst ★★★★★

PO Box 1294, Margaret River, WA 6285 **Region** Margaret River
T (08) 6323 2333 **www**.cloudburstwine.com **Open** Not
Winemaker Will Berliner **Est.** 2005 **Dozens** 450 **Vyds** 0.5ha
An extremely interesting young winery. Will Berliner and wife Alison Jobson spent several years in Australia searching for a place that resonated with them, and on their first visit to Margaret River were immediately smitten, drawn by its biodiversity, beaches, farms, vineyards, community and lifestyle. When they purchased their land in 2004 they hadn't the slightest connection with wine and no intention of ever getting involved. Within 12 months Will's perspective had entirely changed, and in '05 he began planting the vineyard and applying biodynamic preparations, seeking to build microbial life in the soil. They planted the vineyard as if it were a garden, with short rows, and initially planted 0.2ha of each of cabernet sauvignon and chardonnay, and 0.1ha of malbec. By 2020 the vineyard will have doubled in size, but without changing the varieties or their proportions. The packaging is truly striking and imaginative. Exports to the US and the UK.

ŶŶŶŶŶ **Margaret River Cabernet Sauvignon 2017** Precise, alluvial ball-bearing tannins spooling cassis, sage, olive, thyme and brush across a chassis of sexy oak and moreish acidity. A prodigious finish. Expands in the glass. This wine cleans up so much in its path and is destined for greatness. Screwcap. **Rating** 98 **To** 2035 $350 NG

Margaret River Malbec 2017 Among few great malbecs in Australia. Gushing blue fruits, a skein of hedgerow tannin, anise, mocha and soaring violet scents define a wine that alludes to full body by virtue of its reach and extract. Yet feels more mid-weighted. Delicious. Screwcap. **Rating** 97 **To** 2032 $350 NG

ŶŶŶŶŶ **Margaret River Chardonnay 2018** This is more intensely flavoured than I remember vintages past, still with the trademark peachy fruit and riffs of dried mango billowing across seams of salubrious French oak and a creamy nougatine core. Sumptuous. Fealty to place manifests in the vigour of flavour and palate-whetting acidity, steering a long passage. **Rating** 96 **To** 2030 $250 NG

Clover Hill ★★★★★

60 Clover Hill Road, Lebrina, Tas 7254 **Region** Northern Tasmania
T (03) 5459 7900 **www**.cloverhillwines.com.au **Open** 7 days 10–4.30
Winemaker Robert Heywood, Peter Warr **Est.** 1986 **Dozens** 12 000 **Vyds** 23.9ha
Clover Hill was established by Taltarni in 1986 with the sole purpose of making a premium sparkling wine. It has 23.9ha of vineyards (chardonnay, pinot noir and pinot meunier) and its sparkling wine is excellent, combining finesse with power and length. The American owner and founder of Clos du Val (Napa Valley), Taltarni and Clover Hill has brought these businesses and Domaine de Nizas (Languedoc) under the one management roof, the group known as Goelet Wine Estates. Exports to the UK, the US and other major markets.

ŶŶŶŶŶ **Cuvee Exceptionnelle Methode Traditionnelle Blanc de Blancs 2013** Disgorged Nov '19. Bright straw tinged with green. A complex but enticing bouquet with white peach, melon and spice. The palate is bright and lively, still youthful and with further development for those chasing complexity. The residual sugar is 8g/l, and the wine is notable for its freshness and purity. Very elegant, very long. Diam. 12% alc. **Rating** 96 $65 ✪

Cuvee Prestige Late Disgorged Methode Traditionnelle Blanc de Blancs 2008 The fruit was hand-picked from the close-planted A Block, whole-bunch pressed, partial mlf while still in tank, spent over 10 years on tirage, disgorged Dec '19. While still a blanc de blancs, this is much more complex than its siblings, with lemon curd, brioche and white peach flavours. Diam. 12.5% alc. **Rating** 96 $150

Vintage Release Methode Traditionnelle 2014 A mix of 66% chardonnay, 31% pinot noir, 3% pinot meunier; 4 years on tirage, disgorged Sept '18. There is an unusually spicy array of aromas to the bouquet and the depth of fruit must have been significant (the residual sugar is 10g/l). Smart wine at the price. Diam. 12% alc. **Rating** 95 $45

Cuvee Exceptionnelle Methode Traditionnelle Brut Rose 2015 A blend of 61% chardonnay, 33% pinot noir and 6% pinot meunier; it spent 43 months on tirage before disgorgement in Aug '19. The complex bouquet swings along with spice, brioche and wild strawberry. Diam. 12% alc. **Rating** 95 $65

Methode Traditionnelle Tasmanian Cuvee NV The base vintage of '17 was a blend of 59% chardonnay, 37% pinot noir and 4% pinot meunier; traditional method but no info on the date of disgorgement. It has particularly good balance and mouthfeel; creamy/toasty/nutty notes all present. It has the lowest residual sugar of all the Clover Hill wines, the bracing acidity of 9.7g/l more than just a match. It's a stylish, bright and breezy wine and will surely coast along in bottle. Diam. 12.5% alc. **Rating** 94 $34

Methode Traditionnelle Tasmanian Cuvee Rose NV Same '17 base vintage blend as the Cuvee NV. Pale pink without any salmon. It tastes of wild strawberries together with Turkish delight/nougat, and gains freshness from its residual sugar/dosage of 7.5g/l. Diam. 12.5% alc. **Rating** 94 $34

Clyde Park Vineyard

2490 Midland Highway, Bannockburn, Vic 3331 **Region** Geelong
T (03) 5281 7274 **www.clydepark.com.au Open** 7 days 11–5
Winemaker Terry Jongebloed **Est.** 1979 **Dozens** 6000 **Vyds** 10.1ha
Clyde Park Vineyard, established by Gary Farr but sold by him many years ago, has passed
through several changes of ownership. Now owned by Terry Jongebloed and Sue Jongebloed-
Dixon, it has significant mature plantings of pinot noir (3.4ha), chardonnay (3.1ha), sauvignon
blanc (1.5ha), shiraz (1.2ha) and pinot gris (0.9ha), and the quality of its wines is consistently
exemplary. Exports to the UK and Hong Kong.

ŸŸŸŸŸ **Single Block C Geelong Chardonnay 2019** P58 clone planted by the Farr
and Weir families in '79. Whole-bunch pressed, cold-settled, fermented and
matured for 9 months in French oak (75% new), minimal batonnage and partial
mlf. The most striking of all the Clyde Park chardonnays. The intensity of the
fruit has managed to make light work of the new oak, leaving the purity and
elegance of the white peach fruit to occupy centre stage with only a whisper
of grapefruit in the natural acidity. Made by Matt Holmes. Screwcap. 13% alc.
Rating 98 **To** 2039

Single Block B3 Geelong Chardonnay 2019 P58 clone planted '95, whole-
bunch pressed for full solids – wild ferment in French oak (60% new), matured
for 10 months. A very complex struck-match bouquet, the palate needing
10–15 seconds to throw its irresistible power that has a whole grapefruit crushed
into a health juice. This is highly polarising, more Burgundian that Australian.
Made by Ray Nadeson. Screwcap. 13% alc. **Rating** 97 **To** 2034 $75 ✪

Single Block F College Bannockburn Pinot Noir 2019 MV6 planted '88 on
the north-facing slopes of the property. Made using carbonic infusion techniques
with 25% whole bunches on top of destemmed fruit, matured in French oak
(75% new) for 9 months. The bouquet is so intense there's little need to swirl
the glass as the high-toned fusion of spiced fruits and cedary oak fill the senses.
The palate has a unique taste profile with the flavours meeting the tip of the
tongue then following through to the finish. Made by Robin Brockett. Screwcap.
12.5% alc. **Rating** 97 **To** 2034 $75 ✪

Single Block D Geelong Pinot Noir 2019 MV6 wild-fermented with
20% whole bunches, plunged twice daily, matured for 9 months in French
hogsheads (40% new). Very good colour: deep, clear crimson. A rich and
expressive bouquet. The focused palate lively and intense, with complex cherry/
plum fruits foremost. Finely honed tannins on the finish. Made by Robin Brockett.
Screwcap. 13.5% alc. **Rating** 97 **To** 2034 $75 ✪

ŸŸŸŸŸ **Single Block B2 Geelong Pinot Noir 2019** Hand-picked, wild-fermented
with 25% whole bunches, hand-plunged, matured for 9 months in French oak
(60% new). Clear crimson. An altogether more savoury bouquet and palate, the
oak and whole bunch coming through the red berry/pomegranate fruit; the palate
mouthfilling and complete. Made by Scott Ireland. Screwcap. 13% alc. **Rating** 96
To 2032 $75 ✪

Single Block G Geelong Shiraz 2019 This small block has rows running
east–west on black cracking clay, planted '99. Wild-fermented, plunged daily,
10 months maturation in French oak (40% new). Very deep colour. The bouquet
is a symphony of black fruits, licorice and black pepper. The palate is full-bodied
yet pliable, unfolding its wares in a stately fashion: wild blackberry leading, then
spice, quiet tannins and sweet oak. Made by Robin Brockett. Screwcap. 13.5% alc.
Rating 96 **To** 2044 $75 ✪

Geelong Chardonnay 2019 Hand-picked, whole-bunch pressed to French
puncheons and hogsheads (25% new), a small amount of mlf, remained on lees
for 9 months. There's no question that the depth and richness of the fruit is akin
to that of Beechworth, not Yarra Valley, and even less the Mornington Peninsula.
It's a wine that marches to the tune of its own big bass drum. Made by Robin
Brockett. Screwcap. 13% alc. **Rating** 95 **To** 2030 $45

Geelong Pinot Noir 2019 A blend of all 5 blocks/clones, wild-fermented with 35% whole bunches, matured for 9 months in fruit (30% new). Crystal, clear crimson. The fragrant and expressive bouquet offers red cherry/berry fruits with spice and forest floor aromas. A vibrant palate with red fruits to the fore, spice and superfine tannins. Made by Robin Brockett. Screwcap. 13% alc. **Rating** 95 To 2032 $45

Geelong Shiraz 2019 From 2 blocks of PT23 clone, wild-fermented in small batches, 20% whole bunch, matured for 9 months in French puncheons (25% new). Deep crimson-purple. The bouquet has red and black fruits in abundance; the medium-bodied palate a precise reflection of the bouquet, the fruit allowed free play with little competition from the fine tannins. Made by Robin Brockett. Screwcap. 13.5% alc. **Rating** 95 To 2040 $45

Geelong Sauvignon Blanc 2019 Should melt the heart of the most ardent foe of Marlborough sauvignon blanc, believing sauvignon blanc is 'only fit for women to drink'. This has exceptional texture and mouthfeel; its rich stone fruits rimmed with citrussy acidity, the finish long and balanced. Made by Robin Brockett. Screwcap. 13% alc. **Rating** 94 To 2023 $35

Geelong Pinot Gris 2019 Its pale pink colour heralds a warm suffusion of honeysuckle and poached pear on the bouquet, joined on the palate by multi-spices A striking pinot gris that's a real wine. Made by Robin Brockett. Screwcap. 13% alc. **Rating** 94 To 2023 $40

Locale Geelong Pinot Noir 2019 Plenty of cool-climate pinot noir makers would give their eye teeth to have this as their second tier pinot noir and expect to receive more than $30 for it. It's laden with spicy, savoury satsuma plum fruit and the balance to underwrite 3–4 years in the cellar. Made by Robin Brockett. Screwcap. 12.5% alc. **Rating** 94 To 2029 $30 ✪

♟♟♟♟♟ **Locale Geelong Chardonnay 2019 Rating** 93 To 2029 $30
Geelong Rose 2019 Rating 93 To 2021 $35

Coates Wines   ★★★★★

185 Tynan Road, Kuitpo, SA 5172 **Region** Adelaide Hills
T 0417 882 557 www.coates-wines.com **Open** W'ends & public hols 11–5
Winemaker Duane Coates **Est.** 2003 **Dozens** 2500
Duane Coates has a Bachelor of Science, a Master of Business Administration and a Master of Oenology from the University of Adelaide; for good measure he completed the theory component of the Masters of Wine degree in 2005. Having made wine in various parts of the world, and in SA, he is more than qualified to make and market Coates wines. Nonetheless, his original intention was to simply make a single barrel of wine employing various philosophies and practices outside the mainstream; there was no plan to move to commercial production. The key is organically grown grapes. Exports to the UK and the US.

♟♟♟♟♟ **Adelaide Hills The Riesling 2019** Sourced from Kuitpo, this balletic riesling was fermented wild in neutral French wood, an approach common in Europe but seldom used in this country. The result is delicious. Pristine. A transparent stream of kaffir lime, Granny Smith apple, pear gelato and bath salts guided by the oak, rather than obfuscated by it. Among the most exciting domestic rieslings tasted in recent memory. Screwcap. **Rating** 96 To 2031 $35 NG ✪

Adelaide Hills The Semillon Sauvignon Blanc 2019 This incredibly sophisticated wine pays homage to the great whites of Graves, the blend's spiritual home. The culture at Coates is one of adroit restraint: appropriating international experience to the conditions at hand. Lanolin, curd and guava. Despite the wine's approachability, this will age very well mid-term. Screwcap. **Rating** 95 To 2027 $25 NG ✪

Langhorne Creek The Cabernet Sauvignon 2017 This is stellar warm-climate, maritime cabernet. Bay leaf and bouquet garni reel off the first riff. Mint, cassis and a saline lick of tapenade taper the finish, directed long by impeccably appointed oak and a *je ne sais quoi* freshness. A lovely mellifluous wine. Screwcap. **Rating** 95 To 2032 NG

ŸŸŸŸŸ **Adelaide Hills The Sauvignon Blanc 2019** Rating 93 To 2024 $25 NG ✪
The Shiraz Cabernet 2016 Rating 93 To 2031 $30 NG
Organic Adelaide Hills Pinot Noir 2018 Rating 92 To 2025 $35 NG

Cockfighter's Ghost | Poole's Rock   ★★★★★

576 De Beyers Road, Pokolbin, NSW 2320 **Region** Hunter Valley
T (02) 4993 3688 **www**.cockfightersghost.com.au **Open** 7 days 10–5
Winemaker Xanthe Hatcher **Est.** 1988 **Dozens** NFP **Vyds** 38ha
Cockfighter's Ghost and Poole's Rock were founded in 1988 by the late David Clarke OAM, and acquired by the Agnew family in 2011 (who also own the neighbouring Audrey Wilkinson). The brands have kept separate identities, but are made at the same winery. The Cockfighter's Ghost white wines are sourced from key growers in the Adelaide Hills, the red wines entirely from the Agnew family's Chairman's Vineyard in Blewitt Springs, made by Xanthe Hatcher. Jeff Byrne continues overseeing Poole's Rock, with Chardonnay, Semillon and Shiraz from the Hunter Valley and also some small-batch wines including a Pinot Noir from Tasmania. Exports to the US and Canada.

ŸŸŸŸŸ **Poole's Rock Centenary Block Hunter Valley Shiraz 2018** Destemmed, fermented, plunged once a day, maturation in 1yo French puncheons. Deep purple. Wafts of shiitake mushrooms, hoisin, sage. Definitely savoury feel from 120+yo vines, game terrine, earth, red licorice with a big embrace of ripe tannins. Dense. Longevity ensured. Screwcap. 14% alc. Rating 96 To 2045 $120 JP
Poole's Rock Soldier Settler Semillon 2019 Hand-picked, whole-bunch pressed, fermented cool for 15 days, fined and filtered. Classic Hunter semillon with huge appeal now for those who appreciate acidity and crisp apple, honeysuckle, cardamom, citrus tang and a smooth feel. And just imagine how magically this will age from here on? Accessible either way. Screwcap. 11.5% alc. Rating 95 To 2037 $45 JP
Poole's Rock Premiere Hunter Valley Chardonnay 2018 One of the earliest vintages on record and near-perfect ripening conditions resulted in a luscious, elegant chardonnay from one of the Hunter's better producers of the grape. Lemon zest, finger lime, nectarine, lemon myrtle set the scene. On the main stage an accomplished display of succulent fruits and lingering French oak and grippy acidity. Demands attention. Screwcap. 13% alc. Rating 95 To 2037 $40 JP
Cockfighter's Ghost Single Vineyard McLaren Vale Sangiovese Rose 2019 Sourced from one of the more elevated and cooler sites in the Vale, and it shows in a focused, serious rose of some class. Essence of sangiovese, with dusty red cherry, plum, dried herbs, rosemary, raspberry. Super dry to taste, concentrated with clean, driving acidity. Screwcap. 13% alc. Rating 95 To 2026 $25 JP ✪
Poole's Rock Premiere McLaren Vale Shiraz 2018 Hand-picked, destemmed, 20% whole-bunch fermentation, matured in 1yo French puncheons for 9 months. McLaren Vale fruit is transported at a constant 2°C to the Hunter Valley for processing. The tyranny of distance is not felt in the least. Energised, purple-violet, and fragrant throughout. Finely tuned tannins, generous Vale personality, budding complexity. Screwcap. 14.5% alc. Rating 95 To 2035 $40 JP

ŸŸŸŸŸ **Poole's Rock Premiere Hunter Valley Semillon 2019** Rating 93 To 2035 $40 JP
Cockfighter's Ghost Single Vineyard McLaren Vale Sangiovese 2018 Rating 91 To 2031 $25 JP
Cockfighter's Ghost Single Vineyard McLaren Vale Barbera 2019 Rating 90 To 2032 $25 JP

Cofield Wines   ★★★★

Distillery Road, Wahgunyah, Vic 3687 **Region** Rutherglen
T (02) 6033 3798 **www**.cofieldwines.com.au **Open** Mon–Sat 9–5, Sun 10–5
Winemaker Damien Cofield, Brendan Heath **Est.** 1990 **Dozens** 13 000 **Vyds** 15.4ha

Sons Damien (winery) and Andrew (vineyard) have taken over responsibility for the business from parents Max and Karen Cofield. Collectively, they have developed an impressively broad-based product range with a strong cellar door sales base. The Pickled Sisters Cafe is open for lunch Wed–Mon, (02) 6033 2377. A 20ha property at Rutherglen, purchased in 2007, is planted to shiraz, durif and sangiovese.

ΨΨΨΨΨ Pinot Noir Chardonnay 2015 The pale but distinct salmon hue reflects the pinot noir contribution (60%). Traditional fermentation in bottle, spending 24 months on yeast lees prior to disgorgement; the grapes sourced from the Alpine Valleys. With Cofield's experienced hand on the tiller, it is elegant and very well balanced, the strawberry/pomegranate flavours doing the wine proud. Cork. 11.8% alc. **Rating** 92 $28

Alpine Valleys Prosecco NV This hits the spot with its attractive baked apple and spiced pear flavours from Alpine Valleys fruit. Bright lemony acidity, all fresh and lively, then finishes crisp and dry. Crown seal. 11.3% alc. **Rating** 91 $20 JF ✪

King Valley Riesling 2019 Enjoy this now for its vibrancy: lemon sherbet and lime blossom nuances with refreshing acidity from start to finish. Screwcap. 12% alc. **Rating** 90 To 2026 $20 JF ✪

King Valley Pinot Grigio 2018 Half spent 6 hours on skins seeking mid-palate texture, augmented by 15% fermented in used oak. The complex texture/mouthfeel reflects this approach, some might say too much so, but paired with food all will be well. Screwcap. 12.9% alc. **Rating** 90 To 2022 $20 ✪

Rose 2019 Pastel pink with a copper hue; zesty with a mainstay of tangy red fruit and flicker of spice. It's racy across the palate thanks to lemony acidity hurtling towards the finishing line. Screwcap. 12.7% alc. **Rating** 90 To 2021 $24 JF

Rutherglen Shiraz 2017 It's fresh, it's juicy and it offers plenty of flavour without being weighty. The palate is surprisingly taut. You'll find plums and spiced cherries, some sweet and savoury cedary oak and a freshness to the finish. Screwcap. 14.2% alc. **Rating** 90 To 2027 $27 JF

Rutherglen Shiraz 2016 The deep colour is part of a wine that speaks loudly of its geographic origin in the Quartz Vein Vineyard at Wahgunyah. It is rich, verging on plush, but with no cooked/confit fruit characters whatsoever. The alcohol speaks for itself, if only more makers would realise that 14% is more often than not a sweet spot. Screwcap. 14.1% alc. **Rating** 90 To 2031 $26

Rutherglen Sangiovese 2018 A hint of cherries and pips with tangy acidity give this the varietal stamp. It opens up to reveal some squishy ripe fruit, tannins with some give, and a neat savouriness to the finish. Easy drinking. Screwcap. 13.7% alc. **Rating** 90 To 2025 $25 JF

Rutherglen Durif 2016 Durif is the most honest of all red grapes unless it is grown hydroponically in the Riverland. It is full-bodied, but the tannins are soft and embedded in the fruit, and few winemakers waste money on new oak. This mouthfilling wine is a good example of its genre. Screwcap. 14.2% alc. **Rating** 90 To 2026 $26

Rutherglen Muscat NV Mahogany with a brown-olive rim; luscious with fruitcake and sultanas soaked in brandy, salted caramel and burnt orange toffee. More depth than the Topaque. 375ml. Screwcap. 17.5% alc. **Rating** 90 $25 JF

ΨΨΨΨ Sparkling Shiraz 2016 Rating 89 $28

Coldstream Hills   ★★★★★

29–31 Maddens Lane, Coldstream, Vic 3770 **Region** Yarra Valley
T (03) 5960 7000 **www**.coldstreamhills.com.au **Open** 7 days 10–5
Winemaker Andrew Fleming, Greg Jarratt, James Halliday (Consultant) **Est.** 1985
Dozens 25 000 **Vyds** 100ha
Founded by the author, James Halliday, Coldstream Hills is now a small part of TWE with 100ha of owned estate vineyards as its base, three in the Lower Yarra Valley and two in the Upper Yarra Valley. Chardonnay and pinot noir continue to be the principal focus; merlot

and cabernet sauvignon came on-stream in 1997, sauvignon blanc around the same time, Reserve Shiraz later still. Vintage conditions permitting, chardonnay and pinot noir are made in Reserve, Single Vineyard and varietal forms. In addition, Amphitheatre Pinot Noir was made in tiny quantities in 2006 and '13. In '10 a multimillion-dollar winery was erected around the original winery buildings and facilities; it has a capacity of 1500t. There is a plaque in the fermentation area commemorating the official opening on 12 October '10 and naming the facility the 'James Halliday Cellar'. Exports to Singapore, Japan and China.

ΨΨΨΨΨ **Reserve Yarra Valley Chardonnay 2019** You get presence, power and length. This is a detailed, controlled, electric chardonnay with a whole lot to say. A wonderful release. Nashi pear, stone fruit, meal, grilled nut and cooked apple characters manage to feel at once both generous and precise. It's a taut wine in the best of ways. Everything feels ripe and yet everything feels chalky and dry. Top tier. Screwcap. 13% alc. **Rating** 97 **To** 2032 $60 CM ✪

Reserve Yarra Valley Pinot Noir 2019 The best vintages combine power and structure, and this is one of them. It presents a unified front of complex flavour but saves its best for the finish, which fans out and emphasises its quality in the most convincing of ways. A 'wow' wine. Screwcap. 13.5% alc. **Rating** 97 **To** 2034 $85 CM ✪

ΨΨΨΨΨ **Deer Farm Vineyard Yarra Valley Chardonnay 2019** It's the leanest of the latest releases but in time it could easily be the best. It's a wine of excellent line and length. Pear, citrus, white peach and nectarine flavours are presented with toasty, cedary highlights. The important thing is that the long finish is full of flavour. Screwcap. 13.5% alc. **Rating** 96 **To** 2034 $45 CM ✪

The Esplanade Yarra Valley Pinot Noir 2019 Sinewy and structured but with the fruit to make it work. This is a smoky, twiggy wine with dark cherry, chicory and toast characters driving through, and very good length. It's inherently complex, almost autumnal, with spice and herb notes aplenty. When it reaches full maturity it's going to be quite something. Screwcap. 14% alc. **Rating** 96 **To** 2033 $50 CM ✪

Reserve Yarra Valley Cabernet Sauvignon 2018 Both a textbook and a beautiful example of Yarra Valley cabernet. It's gently briary, but its core is pure mid-weight blackcurrant with forest berry notes and slips of oak. Tannin winds through the back half of the wine and length is exemplary. At all points it feels ripe and well fruited. This will age superbly. Screwcap. 14% alc. **Rating** 96 **To** 2043 $60 CM ✪

Deer Farm Vineyard Yarra Valley Pinot Noir 2019 Meat and leafy spice on bones of cranberry, strawberry and cherry. It's a firm, confident release, briary in part, undergrowthy in others, with sweet acidity and smoky length. Complex it most certainly is. Will mature well. Screwcap. 14% alc. **Rating** 95 **To** 2030 $50 CM

Yarra Valley Pinot Noir 2019 A particularly serious, sinewy, sappy release. It's flushed with cranberry and cherry-plum fruit flavour, but there's a great deal of savoury character – woods, twigs, spices – threaded throughout, and the finish is high on structure. This will drink well now, and will mature well into the medium term, if not longer. Screwcap. 13.5% alc. **Rating** 94 **To** 2027 $35 CM

Pinot Noir Chardonnay 2015 Juicy red apples and ripe stone fruit flavours come complexed with cinnamon and sweet brioche. Balance is exemplary as indeed is the maintenance of flavour all the way through the palate. Diam. 12% alc. **Rating** 94 $35 CM

ΨΨΨΨΨ **Yarra Valley Merlot 2018 Rating** 93 **To** 2028 $35 CM

Collalto   ★★★★

Lot 99, Adelaide-Lobethal Road, Lobethal, SA 5241 **Region** Adelaide Hills
T 0429 611 290 **www**.collalto.com.au **Open** Not
Winemaker Revenir (Peter Leske) **Est.** 2006 **Dozens** 800 **Vyds** 8ha

To say this is a business with a difference is a masterly understatement. It has a real vineyard of 5.5ha of pinot noir and 2.5ha of chardonnay planted in 2001; a real viticulturist (Damon Koerner), and a real winemaker (Peter Leske). Its owner (who grew up in the Adelaide Hills) is London-based QC James Drake. Most of the grapes are sold to Petaluma, but enough to make 800–1200 dozen or so a year is held back. The name Collalto describes the high vineyard, and is also a tribute to their mother Palimira (née Tosolini) whose father came from the village of that name just north of Udine, in north-eastern Italy. Exports to the UK.

🍷🍷🍷🍷🍷 **Adelaide Hills Chardonnay 2018** From a single vineyard at Lenswood. After identifying the best fruit, the yields are reduced, hand-picked at night, whole-bunch pressed, fermented in barrel. The result is good, with tension and focus derived from crisp acidity. Oak has been gently handled. Screwcap. 13.5% alc. Rating 95 To 2030 $35 ✪

🍷🍷🍷🍷🍷 **Adelaide Hills Pinot Noir 2018** Rating 91 To 2028 $35

Collector Wines

7 Murray Street, Collector, NSW 2581 (postal) **Region** Canberra District
T (02) 6116 8722 **www**.collectorwines.com.au **Open** Thurs–Mon 10–4
Winemaker Alex McKay **Est.** 2007 **Dozens** 6000 **Vyds** 6ha

Owner and winemaker Alex McKay makes exquisitely detailed wines, bending to the dictates of inclement weather on his doorstep, heading elsewhere if need be. He was part of a talented team at Hardys' Kamberra Winery and, when it was closed down by Hardys' new owner CHAMP, decided to stay in the district. He is known to not speak much, and when he does, his voice is very quiet. So you have to remain alert to appreciate his unparalleled sense of humour. No such attention is needed for his wines, which are consistently excellent, their elegance appropriate for their maker. Exports to Thailand and Japan.

🍷🍷🍷🍷🍷 **Tiger Tiger Chardonnay 2017** From Tumbarumba. There's a lot of matchsticky flare to the nose, so be warned, but the palate is seriously stylish and powerful. This wine glistens and sparks, almost as if it would glow in the dark. White peach and then some honeysuckle, fennel; a chalkiness, texture like satin. When you drink this wine you know that Australian chardonnay has reached a remarkable place. Screwcap. 12.9% alc. Rating 96 To 2029 $38 CM ✪

Summer Swarm Fiano 2019 Excellent concentration of fruit, more than a little character and all the carry through to the finish you could hope for. It's all brine, florals, nashi pears and apples, and it's very good. Screwcap. 13.1% alc. Rating 94 To 2023 $28 CM ✪

Shoreline Sangiovese Rose 2019 Sangiovese 99%, mammolo 1%. It's the palest of copper-pink, it has texture aplenty, it feels fresh and essentially fruity but it tips its hat at savouriness. It feels dry and elegant all the way through, not to mention meticulous. Screwcap. 12.2% alc. Rating 94 To 2022 $24 CM ✪

🍷🍷🍷🍷🍷 **Landfall Pinot Meunier 2018** Rating 93 To 2027 $34 CM
Ledger Gruner Veltliner 2019 Rating 92 To 2023 $32 CM
Marked Tree Red Shiraz 2018 Rating 92 To 2027 $28 CM
Lantern 2018 Rating 91 To 2024 $28 CM
Rose Red City Sangiovese 2016 Rating 91 To 2026 $32 CM

Colmar Estate

790 Pinnacle Road, Orange, NSW 2800 **Region** Orange
T 0419 977 270 **www**.colmarestate.com.au **Open** W'ends & public hols 10.30–5
Winemaker Chris Derrez, Lucy Maddox **Est.** 2013 **Dozens** 2000 **Vyds** 5.9ha

The inspiration behind the name is clear when you find that owners Bill Shrapnel and his wife Jane have long loved the wines of Alsace: Colmar is the main town in that region. The Shrapnels realised a long-held ambition when they purchased an established, high-altitude (980m) vineyard in May 2013. Everything they have done has turned to gold: notably grafting cabernet sauvignon to pinot noir, merlot to chardonnay, and shiraz to pinot gris. The plantings are now 1.51ha of pinot noir (clones 777, 115 and MV6), 1.25ha of chardonnay (clones 95, 96 and P58), 1.24ha of riesling and lesser quantities of sauvignon blanc, pinot gris and traminer.

ŶŶŶŶŶ Orange Chardonnay Pinot Noir 2015 Chardonnay dominant (68%), with ample time on lees evincing a textural authority and detail, along with a waft of croissant and assorted pastry aromas. This is long, searingly dry and mineralic. Thoroughly impressive. Cork. Rating 95 $60 NG
Methode Traditionelle Brut Rose 2017 A cooler vintage. This is a strident fizz with great energy, palate-staining intensity of popping red berry fruit across the mouth and impressive length. A dollop of pinot plays its role well. Nothing out of place; the time on lees long enough to confer a bready complexity without detracting from the effusive crunch. The dosage too, palpably low, in synchronicity with the racy balletic style intended. Cork. Rating 94 $38 NG

ŶŶŶŶŶ Block 5 Orange Riesling 2019 Rating 93 To 2031 $35 NG
Le Moche Pinot Gris Traminer Riesling 2019 Rating 93 To 2024 NG
La Belle Riesling 2019 Rating 93 To 2027 $20 NG ❍
Block 6 Orange Riesling 2019 Rating 92 To 2031 $35 NG
Block 1 Orange Pinot Noir 2018 Rating 92 To 2026 $45 NG
Orange Chardonnay 2017 Rating 91 To 2024 $35 NG
Orange Pinot Rose 2019 Rating 90 To 2020 $28 NG
Orange Pinot Noir 2018 Rating 90 To 2024 $35 NG
Block 3 Orange Pinot Noir 2018 Rating 90 To 2022 NG

Comyns & Co   ★★★★☆

Shop 6, 1946 Broke Road, Pokolbin, NSW 2320 **Region** Hunter Valley
T 0400 888 966 **www**.comynsandco.com.au **Open** 7 days 10–4.30
Winemaker Scott Comyns **Est.** 2015 **Dozens** 2000
The stars came into alignment for Scott Comyns in 2018. Having left Pepper Tree Wines in a state of glory at the end of '15, he went out on his own, establishing Comyns & Co with nothing other than his experience as a winemaker for 17 vintages in the Hunter Valley to sustain him. Then Andrew Thomas founded Thomas Wines in the region and Scott joined him as a full-time winemaker, leaving Comyns & Co as a side activity. That has now all changed, as Missy and Scott have opened a 7-days-a-week cellar door in the Peppers Creek Village, Scott having quit his winemaking role at Thomas Wines.

ŶŶŶŶŶ Single Vineyard Casuarina Hunter Valley Semillon 2019 From the sandy soils of the Casuarina Vineyard. The lemon/lime flavours take on a sherbet-like drive and energy as it is retasted, freshening – not dulling – the palate each time you return to the glass. Great now, will be greater in 7–10 years time. Screwcap. 10% alc. Rating 96 To 2032 $28 ❍
Hunter Valley Pinot Noir Shiraz 2017 An 80/20% blend. There's enough pinot noir expression to satisfy most purists, but that's not all the wine has to offer. There are gently briary/earthy notes that add up to Hunter Valley and suggest that Maurice O'Shea would have approved of the wine. And there's the '17 factor (top vintage) as well. Screwcap. 13.5% alc. Rating 94 To 2032 $35
Reserve Hunter Valley Shiraz 2018 Single vineyard, cropped at only 1t/acre; maturation in French puncheons (500l) for 12 months. More on show than its sibling blend; entices with positive juicy red berry notes. Screwcap. 13.8% alc. Rating 94 To 2038 $60

ŶŶŶŶŶ Reserve Hunter Valley Shiraz Pinot Noir 2018 Rating 93 To 2030 $55
Single Vineyard Pokolbin Estate Hunter Valley Riesling 2019 Rating 92 To 2025 $28
Reserve Hunter Valley Chardonnay 2019 Rating 92 To 2029 $38
Mrs White Hunter Valley Blend 2018 Rating 90 To 2021 $28
Hunter Valley Merlot Cab Franc Rose 2018 Rating 90 To 2021 $28
Hunter Valley Pinot Noir Shiraz 2018 Rating 90 To 2048 $35

Contentious Character   ★★★★

810 Norton Road, Wamboin, NSW 2620 **Region** Canberra District
T (02) 6238 3830 **www.**contentiouscharacter.com.au **Open** Thurs–Sun 11–8
Winemaker Jeremy Wilson **Est.** 2016 **Dozens** 2200 **Vyds** 10ha

Contentious Character brings together Jeremy Wilson (chief winemaker), Ben Jarrett (sales and viticulture), Ross Appleton (operations, finance and viticulture) and Tony Mansfield (marketing and sales). I'm not entirely clear who is the contentious character, but so be it. There are a number of close friends/relatives who have fringe involvement in the business. It's based on 10ha of chardonnay, riesling, pinot noir, shiraz, pinot gris, merlot and cabernet sauvignon, all planted in 1998, almost a decade before Contentious Character purchased the property (then known as Lambert Vineyards). They have tended the grounds, overhauled the kitchen, given the restaurant a facelift and fired up the pizza oven (lunch and dinner Thurs–Sun 12–3, 5–8). The name may be a bit esoteric, but the quality of the wines is certainly not going to cause any problems: they are all very well made.

♀♀♀♀♀ **Dry as a Dead Dingoes Donga Canberra District Riesling 2018** The label does the wine no justice. The wine is fresh, light and crisp, with a lemon sorbet palate. Screwcap. 11% alc. **Rating** 90 **To** 2023 $29
Fifty Shades of Grape Canberra District Pinot Grigio 2019 Grigio without any blush/pink or whatever – as it should be. The flavours span citrus as much as pear or apple, but varietal character isn't a real issue. The price may be a little ambitious. Screwcap. 13.5% alc. **Rating** 90 **To** 2022 $35
Canberra District Stop and Smell the Rose 2019 Vivid, almost iridescent magenta. A well made merlot rose that doesn't rely on residual sugar. Screwcap. 12.4% alc. **Rating** 90 **To** 2022 $29

Cooke Brothers Wines   ★★★★

Shed 8, 89–91 Hill Street, Port Elliot, SA 5212 **Region** South Australia
T 0409 170 684 **www.**cookebrotherswines.com.au **Open** Fri–Mon 11–3
Winemaker Ben Cooke **Est.** 2016 **Dozens** 800

The three brothers (eldest to youngest) are: Simon, Jason and Ben. Ben is the partner of Charlotte Hardy, winemaker/owner of Charlotte Dalton Wines. Ben has had a long career in wine: seven years' retail for Booze Brothers while at university the first time around; two vintages at Langhorne Creek 2000–01; and full-time cellar hand/assistant winemaker at Shaw + Smith '03–12 while undertaking two degrees externally (wine science and viticulture) at CSU from '04–11. If this were not enough, he had three northern Californian vintages at the iconic Williams Selyem winery in '08, '12 and '13. He is now a full-time viticulturist with a vineyard management contracting company that he founded in '12. The elder brothers are not actively involved in the business. Exports to Canada.

♀♀♀♀♀ **Auchi Vineyard Barossa Valley Shiraz 2018** Aged in French oak (20% new) for 16 months. Packs plenty of varietal and regional character into a smooth and polished package. Within a supple texture, blackberry and plum fruit provides the basis, oak adds a touch of sweet spice and the tannin is ripe and just firm enough. Screwcap. 14.5% alc. **Rating** 93 **To** 2030 $29 SC
Auchi Vineyard Barossa Valley Cabernet Sauvignon 2018 Typically minty Barossa cabernet aromas with the varietal character in the ripe, cassis-like spectrum. Sturdy and quite thick through the palate with plenty of sweetish fruit and soft tannin that carries into a finish of good length. A solid citizen that should continue to develop steadily. Screwcap. 14.5% alc. **Rating** 92 **To** 2026 $29 SC
Smiths Vineyard Wrattonbully Shiraz 2018 Had 16 months in 25% new French barriques. A cool-climate shiraz bouquet with some leafy/green peppercorn notes and fruit characters reminiscent of redcurrant and cranberry. Just medium-bodied, the flavours continue in the red-fruited vein with tangy astringency pulling through the finish. Screwcap. 14% alc. **Rating** 91 **To** 2025 $29 SC

ＴＴＴＴ Fox Valley Vineyard Adelaide Hills Pinot Noir 2018 Rating 89 To 2025
$29 SC
Northcott Vineyard Adelaide Hills Cabernet Sauvignon 2018 Rating 89
To 2025 $29 SC

Cooks Lot ★★★★☆

Ferment, 87 Hill Street, Orange, NSW 2800 **Region** Orange
T (02) 9550 3228 **www.cookslot.com.au Open** Tues–Sat 11–5
Winemaker Duncan Cook **Est.** 2002 **Dozens** 4000
Duncan Cook began making wines for his eponymous brand in 2002, while undertaking his
oenology degree at CSU. He completed his degree in '10 and now works with a number of
small growers. Orange is unique in the sense that it has regions at various altitudes; fruit is
sourced from vineyards at altitudes that are best suited for the varietal and wine style. Exports
to China.

ＴＴＴＴＴ Iconique Barrique Pinot Noir 2016 The high, cool climate of Orange is a rich
proving ground for the pinot grape, delivering earnest, complex wines such as
this. Clear, bright blood red. Unleashes red cherry, cranberry, root vegetables and
an arresting riff of sage and dried flowers across the bouquet and palate. It's got a
lot to offer, oh yes, with succulence, creamy oak and char. Impressive. Screwcap.
13.5% alc. Rating 95 To 2028 $50 JP

ＴＴＴＴＴ Iconique Barrique Chardonnay 2016 Rating 92 To 2028 $50 JP
Orange Shiraz 2018 Rating 90 To 2027 $23 JP

Coolangatta Estate ★★★★★

1335 Bolong Road, Shoalhaven Heads, NSW 2535 **Region** Shoalhaven Coast
T (02) 4448 7131 **www.coolangattaestate.com.au Open** 7 days 10–5
Winemaker Tyrrell's **Est.** 1988 **Dozens** 5000 **Vyds** 10.5ha
Coolangatta Estate is part of a 150ha resort with accommodation, restaurants, golf course,
etc. Some of the oldest buildings were convict-built in 1822. The standard of viticulture is
exceptionally high (immaculate Scott Henry trellising) and the contract winemaking is wholly
professional. Coolangatta has a habit of bobbing up with medals at Sydney and Canberra wine
shows, including gold medals for its mature semillons. In its own backyard, Coolangatta won
the trophy for Best Wine of Show at the South Coast Wine Show for 17 out of the show's
18 years.

ＴＴＴＴＴ Aged Release Individual Vineyard Wollstonecraft Semillon 2016 Barely
aged, with a pale quartz-hue; the acidity feels soft and the palate gently sweet.
Hints of citrus still at play. Lovely drink. Screwcap. 12% alc. Rating 95 To 2026
$35 JP
Aged Release Individual Vineyard Wollstonecraft Semillon 2011 This
seems parked in the fresh zone. It's still tight and light. Sure there are toasty, lemon
butter flavours, yet still with a neat line of acidity. It's pitch-perfect now and any
longer ageing is a bonus. Screwcap. 11% alc. Rating 95 To 2025 $55 JF

ＴＴＴＴＴ Estate Grown Semillon 2019 Rating 92 To 2026 $30 JF
Individual Vineyard Wollstonecraft Semillon 2019 Rating 90 To 2026
$30 JF

Coombe Yarra Valley ★★★★

673–675 Maroondah Highway, Coldstream, Vic 3770 **Region** Yarra Valley
T (03) 9739 0173 **www.coombeyarravalley.com.au Open** Tues–Sun 10–5
Winemaker Mark O'Callaghan **Est.** 1998 **Dozens** 7000 **Vyds** 60ha
Coombe Yarra Valley is one of the largest and oldest family estates in the Yarra Valley. Once
home to world famous opera singer Dame Nellie Melba, it continues to be owned and
operated by her descendants, the Vestey family. Coombe's wines come from 60ha of vineyards

planted in 1998 on the site of some of the original vineyards planted in the 1850s. The renovated motor house and stable block now contain the cellar door, providore, gallery and restaurant which overlook the gardens. Exports to the UK and Japan.

ΨΨΨΨΨ **Shiraz 2018** A multi-regional blend from western and north-eastern Victoria and the Barossa. The oak, large-format French and Hungarian, 20% new. The result is: delicious. Boysenberry, lilac, anise, salumi and iodine notes combine for a massage by pulpy grape tannins; the oak a mere adjunct in the background. The fruit streams from fore to aft. Long and easygoing, but with a whiff of sophistication. Screwcap. **Rating** 93 **To** 2024 $37 NG

Tribute Series Yarra Valley Chardonnay 2018 A fine, mid-weighted chardonnay using extended lees time to confer a rich kernel of oatmeal, tatami mat and nougatine riffs at its core. The oak, of a high quality cooperage (all French, 20% new for 10 months), is nestled in well. Stone fruit scents and truffle notes too, but texture is the MO. Mineral-punching length. Yet the mouthfeel is soft and billowing. This will grow into something really nutty and detailed in the mid-term. Screwcap. **Rating** 92 **To** 2024 $60 NG

Pinot Gris 2018 Hand-picked from a northern exposed vineyard, the batches each exhibiting varying shades of ripeness and with that, texture. Partially fermented in wood, with regular stirring. That is a lot of love for a gris. And it shows. Baked apple, pear, blossom and a whiff of marzipan meander along detailed leesy seams, riffing oatmeal and toasted nuts. Broad and textural, but vital and fresh all at once. A fine gris. Screwcap. **Rating** 92 **To** 2023 $30 NG

Rose 2019 Straight pinot, all from the lower lying 777 clonal block. The colour is gorgeous. A pale coral. Sapid scents of loganberry, cumquat, tangerine and orange rind are delivered by a skein of chalky, crunchy freshness. A fine rose attesting to the qualitative trajectory that this category has taken. Screwcap. 13.1% alc. **Rating** 92 **To** 2020 $30 NG

Chardonnay 2018 Mid-weighted and brimming with stone fruit, tangerine and honeydew melon scents. Generous. A style that successfully combines ample flavour and a creamy nutty core, with tension and high quality oak. A style for those who seek flavour as much as for those who like mineral. Screwcap. **Rating** 91 **To** 2024 $37 NG

Tribute Series Pinot Noir 2018 A sappy pinot of good intensity and herbal crusted length. A pallid ruby. Mid-weighted. Fermented in open-top vessels resplendent with a good whack of whole-bunch for structural timbre, complexity and a means to tone the fruit. Of a red berry persuasion, with turmeric, mescal and tomatillo scents – a legacy of the stems. A whiff of forest floor to punctuate the tangy finish. Screwcap. **Rating** 91 **To** 2023 $55 NG

Pinot Noir 2018 A good estate expression. Sassafras. Bing cherry, clove and fecund strawberry scents. Ripe but crunchy. Fresh and far from cloying. The incense-infused tannins – a legacy of the whole-bunch element – tuck in the seams nicely. Screwcap. 13% alc. **Rating** 91 **To** 2023 $37 NG

Tribute Series Shiraz 2018 Blue to blackberry scents mingling with anise, five-spice, clove and lacquer. Iodine-sappy tannins tow it long. A gentle clang of peppery acidity to finish. A solid, appetising, medium-bodied shiraz with a burly intensity. Screwcap. **Rating** 91 **To** 2024 $55 NG

Tribute Series Nellie Melba Blanc de Blancs 2015 Straight chardonnay crafted in the traditional method: second fermentation in bottle, 4 years on lees and a dosage (6.5g/l) that is just above the legal parameter for extra brut; should one make the inevitable comparison to Champagne. Extremely toasty, shimmering with brioche, walnut and tangerine to nectarine scents. Just a bit cloying, but artisanal and aspirational. Cork. **Rating** 91 $55 NG

Estate Sparkling NV A blend of chardonnay (80%) and pinot. A portion was fermented in 1yo French wood before blending and a Charmat secondary fermentation in tank. The oak works exceptionally well, building in structure to balance the gushing stone fruit scents. The core of the wine is dutifully nutty and crème brûlée creamy. A round, rich fizz. Cork. **Rating** 90 $35 NG

Cooter & Cooter

82 Almond Grove Road, Whites Valley, SA 5172 **Region** McLaren Vale
T 0438 766 178 **www**.cooter.com.au **Open** Not
Winemaker James Cooter, Kimberly Cooter **Est.** 2012 **Dozens** 800 **Vyds** 23ha
The cursive script on the Cooter & Cooter wine labels was that of various Cooter family
businesses operating in SA since 1847. James comes from a family with more than 20 years
in the wine industry. Kimberley is also a hands-on winemaker; her father is Walter Clappis, a
veteran McLaren Vale winemaker. Their vineyard, on the southern slopes of Whites Valley, has
18ha of shiraz and 3ha of cabernet sauvignon planted in 1996, and 2ha of old vine grenache
planted in the '50s. They also buy Clare Valley grapes to make riesling.

ΥΥΥΥΥ **Shiraz 2018** Immediately appealing with its juicy fruit, licorice, mocha and
eucalyptus flavours. Pure essence of the Vale, with vitality and freshness; it spent
8 months in seasoned French barrels; no need of new oak as the fruit tannins add
structure. It has its own groove. Screwcap. 14% alc. **Rating** 95 To 2026 $23 JF ✪
Grenache 2018 Since the fruit comes off 73yo vines, it is simply allowed to
shine, unfettered by heavy-handed winemaking. Heady with musk and red berries,
there's a delicacy across the palate with lovely grainy tannins and lively acidity. A
satisfying, gorgeous drink. Screwcap. 14% alc. **Rating** 95 To 2028 $32 JF ✪

ΥΥΥΥΥ **Watervale Riesling 2019 Rating** 92 To 2028 $23 JF ✪

Coppabella of Tumbarumba   ★★★★★

424 Tumbarumba Road, Tumbarumba, NSW 2653 (postal) **Region** Tumbarumba
T (02) 6382 7997 **www**.coppabella.com.au **Open** Not
Winemaker Jason Brown **Est.** 2011 **Dozens** 4000 **Vyds** 71.9ha
Coppabella is owned by Jason and Alecia Brown, owners of the highly successful Moppity
Vineyards in Hilltops. They became aware of the quality of Tumbarumba chardonnay
and pinot noir, in particular the quality of the grapes from the 71ha Coppabella vineyard,
when purchasing grapes for Moppity Vineyards. This was the second vineyard established
(in 1993) by the region's founder, Ian Cowell, but frost and other problems led him
to lease the vineyard to Southcorp, this continued until 2007. The reversion of the
management of the vineyard coincided with several failed vintages, and the owner decided
to close the vineyard and remove the vines. In October '11, at the last moment, the Browns
purchased the vineyard and have since invested heavily in it, rehabilitating the vines and
grafting a number of blocks to the earlier ripening Dijon clones of pinot noir and chardonnay.
Coppabella is run as an entirely separate venture from Moppity.

ΥΥΥΥΥ **Sirius Single Vineyard Chardonnay 2018** Serious chardonnay. Long, smoky
and sophisticated. White peach and grapefruit, cedar wood and flint. A suggestion
of fig. It feels vigorous and energetic from start to finish; indeed it's just a little
mesmerising. Screwcap. 12.5% alc. **Rating** 96 To 2027 $60 CM ✪
Procella Chardonnay 2018 Class act. Powerful, yet long and elegant. Pure white
peach, custard apple, honeysuckle and chalk flavours combine seamlessly with spicy
oak. A beautiful wine. Screwcap. 12.5% alc. **Rating** 95 To 2026 $45 CM
Procella I Hilltops Shiraz 2017 Cold-soaked 5 days, open-fermented, 12 days
on skins, matured in French puncheons and hogsheads (25% new) for 12 months.
This is a luscious, layered wine with an abundance of blackberry, black cherry
and plum wrapped in a custom-designed suit, oak providing the lining. That '17
vintage again. Screwcap. 14% alc. **Rating** 95 To 2037 $45
Procella II Chardonnay 2018 Hand-picked, cold-pressed to tank, partial
ferment in French barriques, partial stirring. Lets the variety and the terroir do
the work, with minimal winemaking inputs. White peach, pink grapefruit are
the cool-climate markers. Has room to develop depth and complexity. Screwcap.
12.5% alc. **Rating** 94 To 2028 $45

ΥΥΥΥΥ **Procella IV Pinot Noir 2018 Rating** 93 To 2030 $45
Sirius Pinot Noir 2018 Rating 91 To 2024 $60 CM

Single Vineyard Sauvignon Blanc 2019 Rating 90 To 2021 $26 CM
Single Vineyard Prosecco 2019 Rating 90 $26 CM

Corang Estate ★★★★

533 Oallen Road, Nerriga, NSW 2622 **Region** Southern New South Wales zone
T 0419 738 548 **www**.corangestate.com.au **Open** By appt
Winemaker Michael Bynon **Est.** 2018 **Dozens** 1000 **Vyds** 1ha
This is the nascent business of Michael and Jill Bynon. Michael has been in the wine industry
in one role or another for 30 years, attending Roseworthy Agricultural College and moving
from a marketing career to join the senior corporate ranks. Most impressive of all is that he has
passed the Master of Wine tasting examination. Jill was a linguist and marketing professional,
speaking Italian, French and Spanish fluently, spending much time in France before moving
to Australia from her native Scotland in 2003. It was here that she met Michael, and having
bought a bush block and erected a small house, they planted 0.5ha each of shiraz and
tempranillo in '18. They also purchase grapes from high altitude vineyards comparable to that
of their own, which is at 600m.

🍷🍷🍷🍷🍷 Hilltops Shiraz 2018 The grapes were supplied from Moppity Vineyard's oldest
blocks, the wine matured in French barriques (33% new). The colour is excellent,
and stands for everything that follows. The medium-bodied palate is supple and
smooth, the fruit (cherry and plum) beautifully balanced. Screwcap. 14% alc.
Rating 95 To 2038 $25 ✪

🍷🍷🍷🍷🍷 Tumbarumba Sauvignon Blanc 2019 Rating 90 To 2021 $25

Corduroy ★★★★

15 Bridge Terrace, Victor Harbour, SA 5211 (postal) **Region** Adelaide Hills
T 0405 123 272 **www**.corduroywines.com.au **Open** Not
Winemaker Phillip LeMessurier **Est.** 2009 **Dozens** 320
Phillip and Eliza LeMessurier have moved to the Adelaide Hills, but are continuing the model
they originally created in the Hunter under the tutelage of Andrew Thomas at Thomas
Wines. In the new environment, they are matching place and variety to good effect.

🍷🍷🍷🍷🍷 Aged Release Blenheim Vineyard Watervale Riesling 2016 Free-run juice,
wild-fermented. You wonder whether there is some residual sugar left in the wine,
but either way, it has helped the development and length of the juicy citrus-driven
fruit. Screwcap. 11.4% alc. Rating 94 To 2029 $28 ✪

🍷🍷🍷🍷🍷 Bowe-Lees Vineyard Adelaide Hills Semillon 2019 Rating 92 To 2027
$24 ✪
Blenheim Vineyard Watervale Riesling 2019 Rating 91 To 2026 $24
Mansfield Adelaide Hills Chardonnay 2018 Rating 90 To 2022 $48

Coriole ★★★★★

Chaffeys Road, McLaren Vale, SA 5171 **Region** McLaren Vale
T (08) 8323 8305 **www**.coriole.com **Open** Mon–Fri 10–5, w'ends & public hols 11–5
Winemaker Duncan Lloyd **Est.** 1967 **Dozens** 30 000 **Vyds** 48.5ha
While Coriole was not established until 1967, the cellar door and gardens date back to 1860,
when the original farm houses that now constitute the cellar door were built. The oldest
shiraz forming part of the estate plantings dates back to 1917, and since '85, Coriole has
been an Australian pioneer of sangiovese and the Italian white variety fiano. More recently, it
has planted picpoul, adding to grenache blanc, negro amaro, sagrantino, montepulciano and
prosecco. Coriole celebrated its 50th anniversary in 2019, presumably counting from the year
of its first commercial wine release. Exports to all major markets.

🍷🍷🍷🍷🍷 Mary Kathleen Reserve Cabernet Sauvignon 2017 A shimmering ruby,
this is exceptional warm–climate cabernet. The usual varietal pointers of
blackcurrant, bouquet garni, graphite and the motley crew of herbs aside, the

tannin management here is skilled, linked with an after-carriage of coffee grind bite. Real detail to these tannins. Compact. A noble sheen married to compelling length. Screwcap. **Rating** 96 **To** 2034 $65 NG ✪

Rubato Reserve Fiano 2019 Confidence with a newly introduced variety manifests in the use of oak, to flex authority and impart textural intrigue. And deservedly so. Coriole, a pioneer with the great Italian varieties, comes up trumps with this call. Apricot pith, white flower, anise and some smokey leesy notes. Detailed, dutifully viscous, long and well placed. Screwcap. **Rating** 95 **To** 2025 $50 NG

Willunga 1920 Single Vineyard McLaren Vale Shiraz 2018 This is a smooth ride. Dense. Mocha, black olive, mulberry, blueberry and spice, with a spool of pepper-doused acidity towing the rear long and effortless. The cedary oak glosses the fabric, rather than ripping it apart. Exceptional warm-climate shiraz. Screwcap. **Rating** 95 **To** 2033 $100 NG

Estate Grown McLaren Vale Grenache 2018 Oooh! Quintessentially McLaren Vale, with those redcurrant jubes, molten kirsch, rosewater, cranberry and pomegranate notes. Sweet-sour, crunchy. Most impressive is the broad brushstroke of tannin, partly due to an intelligent extraction regime and the choice of puncheons (18 months). Drink on the cooler side. In large draughts. Screwcap. **Rating** 95 **To** 2024 $40 NG

McLaren Vale Dancing Fig 2018 Coriole has a number of different species of fig trees that are carefully tended, the figs sold. The autosuggestion is too strong to ignore, and the bouquet of this mourvedre/grenache/shiraz blend has a ripe fig overtone. The palate keeps its focus where it should, with a suite of sultry earthy notes ex the mourvedre, lightened and brightened by the other varieties. Screwcap. 14.5% alc. **Rating** 94 **To** 2030 $28 ✪

Estate McLaren Vale Cabernet Sauvignon 2018 I like cabernet from the Vale. I really do. Despite the inherent generosity and warmth, there remains a transparent connection to varietal personality that too often warmer regions and their morass of flavour tend to obfuscate. This exudes cassis, dried sage, spearmint and bitter chocolate notes, rounded up by a plume of savoury tannins, pliant and moreish. Screwcap. **Rating** 94 **To** 2032 $32 NG

McLaren Vale Montepulciano 2018 Among the finest renditions of this ferruginous variety seen on these shores. I suppose that is not saying much. But this is impressive and, frankly, among the grape varieties laying out the future of viticulture across this parched land. Far from thirsty, monte boasts a floral to meaty whirr across dark succulent cherry notes, nicely plied by frisky medicinal tannins and bright acidity, flecked with olive and strewn herb. I really like this. Very Italianate. Screwcap. **Rating** 94 **To** 2024 $32 NG

🍷🍷🍷🍷🍷 **The Riesling Block Single Vineyard Shiraz 2018** Rating 93 To 2028 NG
The Soloist Single Vineyard McLaren Vale Shiraz 2018 Rating 93 To 2033 $50 NG
Estate McLaren Vale Shiraz 2018 Rating 93 To 2030 $32 NG
Vita Reserve McLaren Vale Sangiovese 2018 Rating 93 To 2030 NG
McLaren Vale Fiano 2019 Rating 92 To 2024 $28 NG
Sparta McLaren Vale Shiraz 2018 Rating 92 To 2030 $26 NG
McLaren Vale Sangiovese 2018 Rating 91 To 2023 $28 NG
McLaren Vale Nero 2019 Rating 91 To 2023 $28 NG
Redstone McLaren Vale Shiraz 2018 Rating 90 To 2024 $20 NG ✪

Corymbia ★★★★★

30 Nolan Avenue, Upper Swan, WA 6069 **Region** Swan Valley
T 0439 973 195 **www**.corymbiawine.com.au **Open** By appt
Winemaker Genevieve Mann, Robert Mann **Est.** 2013 **Dozens** 900 **Vyds** 2.5ha
This is a Flying Winemaker exercise in reverse. Rob Mann was chief winemaker at Cape Mentelle in the Margaret River, where he and wife Genevieve lived. But Rob's father had established a family vineyard in the Swan Valley more than 25 years ago, where Rob and his

father worked together in Rob's early years as a winemaker. The Mann team settled on 0.4ha of tempranillo, 0.2ha of malbec, 0.1ha of cabernet sauvignon and 1.8ha of chenin blanc for the Corymbia wine production. They now live in the Napa Valley in California, where Rob is chief winemaker for the illustrious Newton Winery, coming back for what is obviously a pretty short vintage.

🍷🍷🍷🍷🍷 **Margaret River Cabernet Sauvignon Cabernet Sauvignon 2018** The inaugural release with fruit off the Mann family's organically farmed Calgardup vineyard. The result is a beautifully composed wine. This is all about detail. Heady aromas of mulberries, florals, soy sauce and saltbush with a wisp of menthol. Lots going on, yet medium-bodied with superfine tannins that glide across the palate. A wine of great finesse. 13.5% alc. **Rating** 96 **To** 2033 $64 JF ✪
Rocket's Vineyard Swan Valley Chenin Blanc 2019 Gently spiced with pepper and cinnamon quills. It's floral with some fresh herbs, poached apple, beeswax and refreshing lemon barley water flavours. The palate is altogether racier, almost riesling-like acidity keeping this long and pure, with the right amount of phenolics adding an extra layer. Screwcap. 12.6% alc. **Rating** 95 **To** 2028 $32 JF ✪
Tempranillo Malbec Cabernet Sauvignon 2018 A tight and tidy blend that sticks to a savoury theme with jamon, woodsy spices and fennel, yet all bound to a core of tangy fruit. Lithe, juicy, vibrant, with raw silk tannins and a neat acid line. Totally delicious. Screwcap. 13.5% alc. **Rating** 95 **To** 2026 $42 JF

Cosmo Wines   ★★★★

187 Victoria Road, Chirnside Park, Vic 3116 **Region** Yarra Valley
T 0408 519 461 **www.**cosmowines.com.au **Open** W'ends 11–5, Mon–Fri by appt
Winemaker Lindsay Corby **Est.** 2008 **Dozens** 3000 **Vyds** 2.25ha
Bianchet was established many years ago, but Lou Bianchet passed away without leaving sufficient records, meaning that the planning and liquor licensing approval were required to re-establish the property detail. Three years' work resulted in the creation of a new business structure with all the necessary approvals in place. Lindsay Corby brings an impressive CV, including cellar door sales, laboratory work and vineyard management, leading to teaching 'The art and science of the vine and wine' at La Trobe University and managing the small campus vineyard. An arrangement with the new owners of Bianchet has been finalised, with Lindsay leasing the winery and vineyard, and opening the Cosmo Wines cellar door. Bianchet Bistro is a separate business that sells some of the Cosmo wines as part of their wine list. Exports to China.

🍷🍷🍷🍷🍷 **Reserve Yarra Valley Cabernet Sauvignon 2015** An elegant wine that deserved its silver medal at the Victorian Wines Show '16. Matured with light and medium toast French staves, crossflow filtration cleaned it up very well. Screwcap. 13.7% alc. **Rating** 92 **To** 2030 $50
Sparkling Shiraz NV The base wines are 85% '18 Heathcote shiraz and 15% '11 Yarra Valley cabernet sauvignon, disgorged Oct '19. Another surprise – has length and is not too sweet. Cosmo is a skilled maker of sparkling wines. Screwcap. 13.8% alc. **Rating** 92 $40
Heathcote Shiraz 2015 Crushed, destemmed, open-fermented, oak blocks, plus multiple additions, crossflow-filtered. The cheapest of the 3 Cosmo shirazs, but the best. Screwcap. 14% alc. **Rating** 90 **To** 2021 $40
Sparkling Chardonnay NV The base wines are from '09, '11 and '16. A surprise. The age of the base wines is evident and the 9g/l dosage is balanced. Ready to roll. Crown seal. 12.6% alc. **Rating** 90 $35

🍷🍷🍷🍷 **Estate Verduzzo 2017 Rating** 89 **To** 2022 $30

Costanzo & Sons   ★★★★

602 Tames Road, Strathbogie, Vic 3666 **Region** Strathbogie Ranges
T 0447 740 055 **www.**costanzo.com.au **Open** By appt
Winemaker Ray Nadeson (Contract) **Est.** 2011 **Dozens** 500 **Vyds** 6ha

This is the venture of Joe Costanzo and Cindy Heath; Joe has grapegrowing in his DNA. He was raised on his parents' 20ha vineyard on the Murray River in NSW, the family business selling grapes to Brown Brothers, Seppelt, Bullers and Miranda Wines. By the age of 17 he had decided to follow in their footsteps, working full-time in vineyards and studying viticulture for five years. He and Cindy searched for the perfect vineyard, and in 2011 finally acquired one that had been planted between 1993 and '94 to 1.5ha each of sauvignon blanc and chardonnay and 3ha of pinot noir.

ŶŶŶŶŶ **Single Vineyard Reserve Strathbogie Ranges Pinot Noir 2017** Estate-grown, hand-picked, destemmed, 10 months in French barriques (33% new). Winemaker Ray Nadeson has pulled all the right levers for a generous, supple pinot. Screwcap. 13.5% alc. **Rating** 92 **To** 2027 $35

Methode Traditionelle Single Estate Blanc de Noir 2017 It's 100% pinot noir; traditional method, disgorged Feb '19, 8g/l dosage. Plenty of strawberry fruit; good length and balance. Diam. 12.5% alc. **Rating** 90 $35

ŶŶŶŶ **Single Vineyard Reserve Strathbogie Ranges Sauvignon Blanc 2017** **Rating** 89 **To** 2021 $25

Coulter Wines

6 Third Avenue, Tanunda, SA 5352 (postal) **Region** Adelaide Hills
T 0448 741 773 **www.**coulterwines.com **Open** Not
Winemaker Chris Coulter **Est.** 2015 **Dozens** 720

Chris Coulter had a 22-year previous life as a chef, but fell in love with wine in the early 1990s and managed to fit in a vintage at Coldstream Hills as a cellar rat. In 2007 he undertook a winemaking degree and secured work with Australian Vintage Limited, gaining large volume winemaking experience first in Mildura and then at (the then) Chateau Yaldara in the Barossa Valley, remaining there through '14 under Australian Vintage Limited, and thereafter as part of the 1847 winemaking team after its acquisition of the Yaldara site. Coulter Wines was born in the '15 vintage as a side project, making wines from another universe – nothing other than SO_2 is added, movements are by gravity and the wine is unfiltered where practicable. He purchases and hand-picks grapes from vineyards mainly in the Adelaide Hills. Exports to Singapore.

ŶŶŶŶŶ **C1 Adelaide Hills Chardonnay 2019** A warm, compressed growing season reduced volume, and the fruit yielded was incredibly concentrated. A lick of pungent flintiness segues to a melody of stone fruit flavours, and a creamy core of praline to vanillan oak scents. Mid-weighted with palate-staining intensity, yet there is nothing blowsy about it. With zero pH adjustments, it is dutifully fresh, long and finely poised between imminent pleasure and the potential for greater complexity across a short-term cellaring window. A striking wine. Screwcap. **Rating** 95 **To** 2024 $30 NG ✪

Adelaide Hills Syrah 2019 Hurray for syrah. Doesn't this wine put on a show? It's alive with licoricey, floral, dark cherried flavour; it leaps from the glass, eager to please. Lots of aroma too. Nutty, malty oak also plays a key role without overstepping the mark. It will no doubt age but it's beautiful to drink as a young wine. Screwcap. 14.5% alc. **Rating** 95 **To** 2030 $30 CM ✪

C2 Adelaide Hills Sangiovese 2019 On the one hand it's bright and juicy, on the other it's dry and complex. This is a seriously good sangiovese. Cherried, earthen, woodsy and drifted with smoke, in a positive way. A touch floral too, with cedar wood and briary herb notes over the top. An assertive-but-appropriate frame of tannin on the finish seals the deal and then some. Screwcap. 13.5% alc. **Rating** 95 **To** 2028 $28 CM ✪

C5 Adelaide Hills Barbera 2019 This country makes poor barbera. Sodden! Yet in Chris Coulter's worldly grasp, it comes alive! Peter Frampton in a bottle! Far from prosaic, but that is not – and never is – the point of barbera. The modus is the refreshment factor: the giddy aromas of violet, tar and crushed black fruits, pulpy and joyous, melded with thirst-slaking acidity. A smidgeon of barrel work has imparted textural breadth without getting in the way of the hedonic flow. Kapow! Screwcap. **Rating** 94 **To** 2022 $28 NG ✪

🍷🍷🍷🍷 C3 Adelaide Hills Pinot Noir 2019 **Rating** 93 **To** 2024 $30 NG
Experimental Eden Valley Syrah 2019 **Rating** 92 **To** 2025 $28 NG

Cowaramup Wines ★★★★☆

19 Tassel Road, Cowaramup, WA 6284 **Region** Margaret River
T (08) 9755 5195 **www**.cowaramupwines.com.au **Open** By appt
Winemaker Naturaliste Vintners (Bruce Dukes) **Est.** 1996 **Dozens** 3000 **Vyds** 11ha
Russell and Marilyn Reynolds run a biodynamic vineyard with the aid of sons Cameron (viticulturist) and Anthony (assistant winemaker). Plantings began in 1996 and include merlot, cabernet sauvignon, shiraz, semillon, chardonnay and sauvignon blanc. Notwithstanding low yields and the discipline that biodynamic grapegrowing entails, wine prices are modest. Wines are released under the Cowaramup, Clown Fish and New School labels.

🍷🍷🍷🍷🍷 Clown Fish Ellensbrook Margaret River Cabernet Sauvignon 2016 This has to be among the very best cabernets priced at $20. Sure, it's at the lighter end of the cabernet scale, but that serves to highlight the purity of the fruit. Elegance personified. Screwcap. 14% alc. **Rating** 95 **To** 2031 $20 ✪

🍷🍷🍷🍷 Clown Fish Chardonnay 2019 **Rating** 92 **To** 2022 $20 ✪
Clown Fish Cabernet Merlot 2018 **Rating** 92 **To** 2027 $20 ✪

Coward & Black Vineyards ★★★★

448 Tom Cullity Drive, Wilyabrup, WA 6280 **Region** Margaret River
T (08) 9755 6355 **www**.cowardandblack.com.au **Open** 7 days 9–5
Winemaker Clive Otto (Contract) **Est.** 1998 **Dozens** 1100 **Vyds** 9.5ha
Patrick Coward and Martin Black have been friends since they were five years old. They acquired a property directly opposite Ashbrook and on the same road as Vasse Felix, and began the slow establishment of a dry-grown vineyard; a second block followed five years later. In all there are 2.5ha each of cabernet sauvignon and shiraz, and 1.5ha each of chardonnay, semillon and sauvignon blanc. The cellar door is integrated with another of their businesses, The Margaret River Providore, which sells produce from their organic garden and olive grove.

🍷🍷🍷🍷🍷 The Black Prince Margaret River Cabernet Sauvignon 2018 Hand-picked, crushed and whole-berry ferment, 20 months in oak. The bouquet is crystal clear in its varietal expression with cassis, black olive and bay leaf; the medium-bodied palate in lockstep behind it. Screwcap. 14.8% alc. **Rating** 94 **To** 2029 $35

🍷🍷🍷🍷 Lady Margo Margaret River Rose 2019 **Rating** 91 **To** 2021 $30

cradle of hills ★★★★★

76 Rogers Road, Sellicks Hill, SA 5174 **Region** McLaren Vale
T 0418 826 206 **www**.cradle-of-hills.com.au **Open** By appt
Winemaker Paul Smith **Est.** 2009 **Dozens** 800 **Vyds** 6.51ha
Paul Smith's introduction to wine was an unlikely one: the Royal Australian Navy and, in particular, the wardroom cellar at the tender age of 19. A career change took Paul to the world of high-performance sports, and he met his horticulturist wife Tracy. From 2005 they travelled the world with their two children, spending a couple of years in Europe, working in and learning about the great wine regions and about how fine wine is made. Paul secured a winemaking diploma and they now have 3.46ha of shiraz, 2.67ha of cabernet sauvignon and 0.38ha of mourvedre, supplementing this with purchased grenache and mourvedre.

🍷🍷🍷🍷🍷 Row 23 McLaren Vale Shiraz 2016 From a western facing block in Sellicks, this was hand-picked and, rare for Australia, hand-sorted before a wild fermentation. Resplendent with 15% whole bunch in the mix to confer a spicy savouriness; this rich red is turning out very well. A dollop of cabernet (5%) rears its head over the fray, communicating bouquet garni scents to a melee of saturated dark fruits, anise, iodine and mocha tannins; fine-grained and nicely tuned to a bright future. Screwcap. **Rating** 94 **To** 2029 $45 NG

ŸŸŸŸŸ **Darkside Shiraz Mourvedre 2016** Rating 93 To 2026 $29 NG
Maritime Cabernet Sauvignon 2016 Rating 92 To 2026 $29 NG

Craiglee ★★★★★
785 Sunbury Road, Sunbury, Vic 3429 **Region** Sunbury
T (03) 9744 4489 **www**.craigleevineyard.com **Open** Feb–Dec 1st Sun each month
Winemaker Patrick Carmody **Est.** 1976 **Dozens** 2000 **Vyds** 9.5ha
A winery with a proud 19th-century record, Craiglee recommenced winemaking in 1976 after a prolonged hiatus. Produces one of the finest cool-climate shirazs in Australia, redolent of cherry, licorice and spice in the better (warmer) vintages; lighter bodied in the cooler ones. Mature vines and improved viticulture have made the wines more consistent over the past 10 years or so (except 2011).

ŸŸŸŸŸ **Sunbury Shiraz 2016** Owner/winemaker Pat Carmody in fine touch here with the grape that made his and Craiglee's reputation. Signature black pepper with wild thyme, sage, acacia and ripe, sweet blackberries. Launches into a savoury world of game and earth, and background notes of hoisin and undergrowth. Quite the dark and brooding kind of cool-climate shiraz. A stunner. Screwcap. 14% alc. **Rating** 95 **To** 2040 $60 JP
JADV Shiraz 2016 JADV? It means Just A Dash of Viognier. Just how much of a dash is not clear but the white grape certainly makes its presence felt on the nose with real charm and a persistent presence of high tone florals, musk and orange blossom. They combine well with subtle red fruits and spice. Cuts a dash on the palate with sweet pastille notes to the fore and support from a range of savoury, earthy characters. Screwcap. 13.5% alc. **Rating** 95 **To** 2042 $40 JP
Sunbury Chardonnay 2018 Pat Carmody keeps matters close to his chest, so there are few details about how he approaches this wine. It is resplendent in ripe fruit, with citrus, stone fruit peel and quince paste. In good Craiglee form. Screwcap. 13.5% alc. **Rating** 94 **To** 2032 $40 JP

Craigmoor | Montrose ★★★★★
Craigmoor Road, Mudgee, NSW 2850 **Region** Mudgee
T (02) 6372 2208 **www**.craigmoor.com.au **Open** 7 days 10–4
Winemaker Debbie Lauritz **Est.** 1858 **Dozens** NFP **Vyds** 25ha
Established in 1858, Craigmoor is Mudgee's oldest vineyard and winery. The Oatley family has long owned vineyards in Mudgee and in 2006 they acquired the Montrose winery and the Craigmoor cellar door and restaurant. Montrose was established in 1974 by Carlo Salteri and Franco Belgiorno-Nettis, Italian engineers with a love of fine wine. Coincidentally they were friends of the Oatleys – the two families developing their Montrose and Rosemount wineries almost simultaneously. The cellar door is five minutes' drive from the centre of Mudgee, surrounded by picturesque vines and gum trees on the banks of Eurunderee Creek.

ŸŸŸŸŸ **Craigmoor Artist Series Mudgee Chardonnay 2018** The 50yo vines are vinous treasures, always hand-picked and whole-bunch pressed into new French barriques for wild fermentation. The organoleptic quality of the fruit is thrown into stark relief by the way it has eaten the new oak. The impossible question is the retail price. Screwcap. 12.5% alc. **Rating** 95 **To** 2023 $32 ❂
Montrose Mudgee Black Shiraz 2018 Hand-picked, 20% whole bunches, the balance crushed to small fermenters for a 7-day cold soak, a further week on skins after fermentation, 12–15 months in new and used French barriques. An ornate wine, still youthful, of course, but very, very interesting. Screwcap. 14% alc. **Rating** 95 **To** 2038 $32 ❂

ŸŸŸŸŸ **Craigmoor Artist Series Mudgee Shiraz 2018** Rating 92 To 2038 $32

Craigow ★★★★

528 Richmond Road, Cambridge, Tas 7170 **Region** Southern Tasmania
T 0418 126 027 **www**.craigow.com.au **Open** W'ends 11–4 or by appt
Winemaker Frogmore Creek (Alain Rousseau), Tasmanian Vintners **Est.** 1989
Dozens 800 **Vyds** 8.75ha
Hobart surgeon Barry Edwards and wife Cathy have moved from being grapegrowers with only one wine to a portfolio of impressive wines – with long-lived Riesling of particular quality, closely attended by Pinot Noir – while continuing to sell most of their grapes.

♥♥♥♥♥ Riesling 2019 Craigow was established in '89. I first met with it in the early '90s. Its rieslings always offer a bit more fruit on the sometimes lean Tasmanian wines. This turns back the hands of time, with Rose's lime juice; a benediction of some stature. Screwcap. 12.5% alc. **Rating** 95 **To** 2034 $32 **✪**

Crawford River Wines ★★★★★

741 Hotspur Upper Road, Condah, Vic 3303 **Region** Henty
T (03) 5578 2267 **www**.crawfordriverwines.com **Open** By appt
Winemaker John Thomson, Belinda Thomson **Est.** 1975 **Dozens** 3500 **Vyds** 10.5ha
Time flies, and it seems incredible that Crawford River celebrated its 40th birthday in 2015. Once a tiny outpost in a little-known wine region, Crawford River is now a foremost producer of riesling (and other excellent wines), originally thanks to the unremitting attention to detail and skill of its founder and winemaker, John Thomson. His elder daughter Belinda has worked alongside her father part-time from '04–11 (full-time between June '05–08) and has been chief winemaker since '12. She obtained her viticulture and oenology degree in '02 and has experience in Marlborough (NZ), Bordeaux (France), Tuscany (Italy) and the Nahe (Germany). In '08 she became senior winemaker/technical director of a winery in Spain, travelling back and forth three or four times a year for over eight years. Younger daughter Fiona is in charge of sales and marketing. Exports to the UK.

♥♥♥♥♥ Museum Release Riesling 2013 Even at this age, riesling is only in its young adult phase. This is pristine. Gleaming straw with a green shimmer. Heady aromas and flavours of baked ricotta topped with lemon and lime zest. Steely, and still an intensity to this with its very tight acid line. Fabulous now but no signs of slowing down either. Wow. Screwcap. 13% alc. **Rating** 96 **To** 2033 $82 JF
Young Vines Riesling 2019 Surprisingly reticent yet still a delicious rendition this vintage. If anything, it's more subtle, savoury even. Sure it has the hint of lemon blossom but also wet slate and texture; more phenolic grip. It's riper and all done well. Screwcap. 13.5% alc. **Rating** 95 **To** 2030 $34 JF **✪**
Riesling 2019 The 'old' vines, planted in '75 and '77, hit their straps years ago. Today, this is a wine of provenance. A cool region is not immune to hot/drier weather and this already has some forward toasty, lime marmalade flavours that could advance the ageing process. Drinking beautifully now; there's certainly the acid backbone to keep this afloat. Screwcap. 13% alc. **Rating** 95 **To** 2029 $48 JF
Cabernet Franc 2018 When the stars are aligned, this shines brightly as a pure expression of the variety and place, the vines planted in '77. Imbued with a coolness – ripe certainly, but refined and polished. The palate is seamless, elegant with finely chiselled tannins and lovely acidity driving this to a long finish. Screwcap. 14% alc. **Rating** 95 **To** 2030 $46 JF

♥♥♥♥♡ Rose 2019 **Rating** 92 **To** 2020 $26 JF

Credaro Family Estate ★★★★★

2175 Caves Road, Yallingup, WA 6282 **Region** Margaret River
T (08) 9756 6520 **www**.credarowines.com.au **Open** 7 days 10–5
Winemaker Trent Kelly, Paul Callaghan **Est.** 1993 **Dozens** 10 000 **Vyds** 110ha
The Credaro family first settled in Margaret River in 1922, migrating from northern Italy. Initially a few small plots of vines were planted to provide the family with wine in the

European tradition. However, things began to change significantly in the '80s and '90s, and changes have continued through to 2015. The most recent has been the acquisition of a 40ha property, with 18ha of vineyard, in Wilyabrup (now called the Summus Vineyard) and the expansion of winery capacity to 1200t with 300 000l of additional tank space. Credaro now has seven separate vineyards (150ha in production), spread throughout the Margaret River; Credaro either owns or leases each property and grows/manages the vines with its own viticulture team. Exports to Thailand, Singapore and China.

🍷🍷🍷🍷🍷 **1000 Crowns Margaret River Chardonnay 2018** Hand-picked, whole-bunch pressed, wild-fermented, SO_2 added immediately fermentation completed thus blocking mlf. The Regional Winner in the James Halliday Chardonnay Challenge '19. It was doubtless the extreme precision, length and tension that led the judges to choose this wine. Screwcap. 13% alc. **Rating** 97 **To** 2030 $65 ✪

🍷🍷🍷🍷🍷 **1000 Crowns Margaret River Cabernet Sauvignon 2017** Two estate parcels: the larger from Yallingup, the much smaller from Wilyabrup. Machine-harvested, small static fermenters, both taken to barrel for mlf, and once completed the wine returned to barrel and periodically racked during the 16-month maturation period. Perfectly ripened and balanced. Screwcap. 14.5% alc. **Rating** 96 **To** 2040 $85

Kinship Margaret River Chardonnay 2019 Hand-picked from 2 vineyards, whole-bunch pressed, wild-fermented in 2–3t batches, no mlf, matured in French barriques and puncheons (30% new). Racy style, with 8.3g/l of titratable acidity. Grapefruit leads with white flowers, white peach and good oak handling. Screwcap. 12.5% alc. **Rating** 95 **To** 2027 $35 ✪

Kinship Margaret River Sauvignon Blanc 2019 Wild-fermented with minimal additions other than disciplined use of SO_2 used to block mlf and oxidation. Some of the higher estery tropical fruit characters (as in Five Tales) have been sacrificed, but in their place fermentation and maturation in used French barrels has produced a wine of startling intensity and length. Screwcap. 13% alc. **Rating** 94 **To** 2025 $32

Five Tales Margaret River Sauvignon Blanc 2019 A small parcel from the estate was cold-settled and cool-fermented with what is commonly called 'the sauvignon blanc yeast'. It has the intensity of good Margaret River sauvignon blanc, with a full hand of tropical fruits finishing with a slash of grapefruit. Screwcap. 12% alc. **Rating** 94 **To** 2023 $24 ✪

Kinship Margaret River Cabernet Merlot 2018 Blend of 54% cabernet sauvignon, 35% merlot, 11% petit verdot; estate-grown in Carbunup River, Wilyabrup and Yallingup; vinified separately and matured for 14 months in French barriques. The colour is very good, as are the elegant footsteps of the winemaking team led by Trent Kelly. Screwcap. 14.5% alc. **Rating** 94 **To** 2030 $35

Kinship Margaret River Cabernet Sauvignon 2018 From the 5 estate vineyards, machine-harvested, destemmed, pumped over, some batches cold-soaked matured for 14–16 months in French barriques (30% new). Old-fashioned (but good) bay leaf/green olive notes on the finish. Screwcap. 14.5% alc. **Rating** 94 **To** 2038 $35

🍷🍷🍷🍷 **Kinship Margaret River Shiraz 2018** **Rating** 92 **To** 2038 $35
Kinship Margaret River Fragola 2018 **Rating** 91 **To** 2025 $35
Five Tales Margaret River Shiraz 2018 **Rating** 90 **To** 2033 $24

Crittenden Estate ★★★★★

25 Harrisons Road, Dromana, Vic 3936 **Region** Mornington Peninsula
T (03) 5981 8322 **www**.crittendenwines.com.au **Open** 7 days 10.30–4.30
Winemaker Rollo Crittenden, Matt Campbell **Est.** 1984 **Dozens** 10 000 **Vyds** 4.8ha

Garry Crittenden was a pioneer on the Mornington Peninsula, establishing the family vineyard over 30 years ago and introducing a number of avant-garde pruning and canopy management techniques. Much has changed – and continues to change – in cool-climate vineyard management. Pinot noir and chardonnay remain the principal focus, and in 2015 winemaking returned to the family vineyard on the Mornington Peninsula in a newly built facility, with son Rollo very much in charge. Exports to the UK.

♥♥♥♥♥ Cri de Coeur Mornington Peninsula Savagnin 2015 An impeccable vintage defined by an attenuated cool growing season, this compelling wine is inspired by the great whites of the Jura region, inflected with the nutty influence of *voile* – or the surface yeast known as flor. Whole-bunch pressed to old French wood, the barrels were left on ullage and moved to a well ventilated area to encourage the yeast's growth. They remained there for a whopping 3 years, sans any additions. The result is quite possibly the most exciting white wine in the country: reeling off top notes of dried hay, camomile and cheese cloth; bottom notes of quince and dried fruits. A long weave of viscosity, unctuousness and freshness all at once. Riveting! Cork. **Rating** 97 **To** 2027 $80 NG ✪

♥♥♥♥♥ Cri de Coeur Mornington Peninsula Chardonnay 2018 This is a tour de force. A sensational chardonnay. Rich, pliant and yet so, so fresh. Reminiscent of a top Meursault, this would be hard to discern blind. Or at least I think so, in this moment of immense pleasure. Nougat, roasted hazelnuts, cashew cream, vanillan oak and the most sublime length towed by a skein of pitch-perfect acidity. This goes on and on, buffered by the 11 months spent in 2 classy French barriques. Cork. **Rating** 96 **To** 2032 $80 NG

The Zumma Mornington Peninsula Chardonnay 2018 This cuvee has an effortless conflation of mineral tension, poise and richness. White fig, toasted hazelnut, nougat, a touch of lanolin, nectarine and white peach all teem along juicy acid rails. A wisp of maritime sea spray marks the finish, just in case you didn't know that this is from Mornington. Screwcap. **Rating** 95 **To** 2024 $57 NG

Cri de Coeur Mornington Peninsula Pinot Noir 2018 A complex equation of Pommard, Dijon 114, 115, a sparkling clone and the Aussie battle axe MV6; fermented wild in open-top fermenters with a whack of 50% whole-cluster, prior to 11 months in assorted French oak formats (25% new). The result? The intensity of fruit and herbal dill spike from the whole-bunch quotient is still unresolved. Yet the sappy length, curl of structural authority and carnal desire in the berry scents and forest floor whiff strongly suggest that this wine will age beautifully with a strident confidence. Cork. **Rating** 95 **To** 2028 $80 NG

The Zumma Mornington Peninsula Pinot Noir 2018 A smidgeon of whole-bunches (15%) in the ferment confers a gentle rasp to the tannin profile, melding effortlessly with the classy French oak (30%) to evince a slick authority. Already delicious, moderate cellaring will flesh out the sous-bois, truffled kirsch and root spice scents further. Screwcap. **Rating** 95 **To** 2025 $57 NG

Macvin Fortified Savagnin NV A traditional style of fortified wine inspired by the uber hip Jura region. A blend of flor-inflected dry savagnin from '15, together with '19 savagnin juice, fortified to 17%. Camomile, cheesecloth and a deeper, more resinous mix of chestnut, blossom and Indian spice lead the charge. Take a deep breath because this bedazzles, alone or with foods savoury and a little sweet. Cork. 17% alc. **Rating** 95 NG

Peninsula Chardonnay 2018 Has more weight and texture than most Mornington Peninsula chardonnays, but kept trim and balanced by its bright acidity and creamy cashew notes. Screwcap. 13.4% alc. **Rating** 94 **To** 2027 $34

♥♥♥♥♡ Kangerong Mornington Peninsula Chardonnay 2018 **Rating** 93 **To** 2023 $45 NG
Oggi 2017 **Rating** 93 **To** 2022 $35 NG
Kangerong Mornington Peninsula Pinot Noir 2018 **Rating** 93 **To** 2023 $45 NG
Peninsula Pinot Noir 2018 **Rating** 92 **To** 2024 $34 NG
Los Hermanos Tempranillo 2018 **Rating** 92 **To** 2024 $29
Geppetto Shiraz 2018 **Rating** 90 **To** 2025 $26

Cullarin Block 71 ★★★★☆

125 Vineyards Road, Lake George, NSW 2581 **Region** Canberra District
T (02) 6226 8800 **www**.cullarin.com.au **Open** Not
Winemaker Andrew Thomas, Celine Rousseau **Est.** 1971 **Dozens** 700 **Vyds** 6ha
Dr Edgar Riek was a Canberra-based academic with a brilliant mind and insatiable
curiosity, putting him far ahead of contemporary thought. He was largely responsible for
the establishment of the National Wine Show, and he and Dr John Kirk of Clonakilla
were the first to plant vines in the Canberra District in 1971. Much later Edgar wrote,
'Driving past Lake George, I noticed one spot on the escarpment that was always green, it
had its own spring and was warmer in winter than anywhere else in the region. I thought it
was the perfect place for my vineyard.' He planted 3.9ha (1ha chardonnay, 1ha pinot noir, 1ha
cabernet sauvignon, cabernet franc and merlot (collectively), 0.4ha sauvignon blanc, 0.3ha
riesling and 0.2ha semillon), initially naming the vineyard Cullarin (hence Cullarin Block 71),
later Lake George Winery, in recognition of the shed he had built to process 10t of fruit. After
he sold the property, another 1.4ha were planted in 1998. Owner Peter Wiggs is dedicated
to high quality NSW vineyards. In addition to Cullarin, he owns the Cote d'Or vineyard in
Pokolbin (supplying Andrew Thomas' the Cote Shiraz) and is the majority owner of Eden
Road Wines.

🍷🍷🍷🍷🍷 **Canberra District Syrah 2018** From 48yo vines; hand-picked, part destemmed,
15% whole bunches, fermented with cultured yeasts, pressed to 1–3yo French
barriques once dry and matured for 12 months. The absence of new oak hasn't
distressed the wine in any way; there's an energetic display of vibrant red and
black fruits, finely grained tannins and a long, fresh finish. Screwcap. 13.5% alc.
Rating 95 To 2030 $35 ❂
Canberra District Pinot Noir 2018 Planted by Dr Edgar Riek in '73; hand-
picked, destemmed, 25% whole bunches, wild yeast–open fermented, mlf, thence
to 1–3yo French barriques for 14 months' maturation. Impeccably made, plum
fruit leading red and blue berry fruits, supple finish. Screwcap. 13% alc. **Rating** 94
To 2028 $35

Cullen Wines ★★★★★

4323 Caves Road, Wilyabrup, WA 6280 **Region** Margaret River
T (08) 9755 5277 **www**.cullenwines.com.au **Open** 7 days 10–4.30
Winemaker Vanya Cullen, Andy Barrett-Lennard **Est.** 1971 **Dozens** 20 000 **Vyds** 49ha
A pioneer of Margaret River, Cullen Wines has always produced long-lived wines of highly
individual style from the mature estate vineyard. The vineyard has progressed beyond organic
to biodynamic certification and, subsequently, has become the first vineyard and winery in
Australia to be certified carbon neutral. Winemaking is in the hands of Vanya Cullen, daughter
of the founders; she is possessed of an extraordinarily good palate and generosity to the
cause of fine wine. Exports to all major markets.

🍷🍷🍷🍷🍷 **Vanya Flower Day Margaret River Cabernet Sauvignon 2017** Hand-
picked, wild-fermented in terracotta amphorae, then pressed to French barriques
(66% new) for a further 6 months. The only addition was minimal SO_2,
biodynamic principles followed throughout. The light crimson colour is deceptive,
as is the light to medium-bodied palate. The bouquet is ultra-fragrant, the aromas
and flavours locked into red fruits, cassis and gentle but persistent tannins. Utterly
delicious. Screwcap. 13.5% alc. **Rating** 98 **To** 2040 $500
Vanya Wilyabrup Margaret River Cabernet Sauvignon 2016 From old
estate vines yielding 1.5t/ha picked on a new moon day with a solar eclipse, wild-
fermented in terracotta eggs, 86 days on skins, pressed to 4 French barrels (3 new),
matured for 6 months. A totally harmonious medium to full-bodied cabernet, all
the components precisely (naturally) calibrated; supple cassis, olive and bay leaf
keep watch. 1080 bottles made. Screwcap. 12.5% alc. **Rating** 98 **To** 2046 $500
**Kevin John Legacy Series Fruit Day Margaret River Chardonnay
2016** Wild-fermented in a ceramic egg, then transferred to French puncheons

(50% new) for 10 months maturation. Full but bright colour. No additives makes the natural acidity particularly impressive (and important). Natural winemaking at its very best. Screwcap. 13% alc. **Rating** 97 **To** 2030 $250

ŸŸŸŸŸ **Wilyabrup Cabernet Sauvignon Merlot 2018** Blend of 62% cabernet sauvignon, 37% merlot, 1% cabernet franc. Matured in French oak (25% new) for an average of 6 months. A lifted, quite fragrant bouquet with aromas of bay leaf, fresh green herbs, red berry fruits and cedar. A finely balanced medium–bodied palate, silky and supple with ripe but restrained flavours interwoven with very fine tannin. Poised and precise. Screwcap. 13.5% alc. **Rating** 95 **To** 2030 $39 SC
Vanya Full Moon Wilyabrup Margaret River Cabernet Sauvignon 2017 Hand–picked on a flower day at 2.08pm, the exact cycle of the full moon, from old estate vines; wild–fermented in a terracotta amphora with 90 days on skins, then pressed to a single new barrel for 6 months maturation with no additions. It is still at the dawn of its life, the tannins ripe but needing 3+ years to fully resolve. 261 bottles made. Screwcap. 13.5% alc. **Rating** 95 **To** 2041 $500
Mangan Vineyard Wilyabrup Red Moon 2018 Mix of 61% malbec, 39% petit verdot. An arresting colour in the glass, bright deep crimson right to the edge. The bouquet is like a melange of wild vine and forest berries with raspberry, mulberry and redcurrant among them; a trace of perfume drifting in the background. Juicy and exuberant in the mouth, the red fruit flavours and youthfully grippy tannin vying for attention. Screwcap. 13% alc. **Rating** 94 **To** 2030 $30 SC ✪

Cumulus Vineyards   ★★★★

1705 Euchareena Road, Molong, NSW 2866 **Region** Orange
T 1300 449 860 **www**.cumulusvineyards.com.au **Open** Not
Winemaker Debbie Lauritz **Est.** 1995 **Dozens** 193 000 **Vyds** 508ha
The 508ha Cumulus vineyard (at 600m above sea level) is one of the largest single estates in NSW. The wines are made at the Robert Oatley winery in Mudgee and are released under the Cumulus, Soaring, Climbing, Rolling, Luna Rosa, Block 50, Head in the Clouds, Alte and inkberry labels. Exports to most major markets.

Cupitt's Winery   ★★★★☆

58 Washburton Road, Ulladulla, NSW 2539 **Region** Shoalhaven Coast
T (02) 4455 7888 **www**.cupitt.com.au **Open** 7 days 10–5
Winemaker Rosie Cupitt, Wally Cupitt, Tom Cupitt **Est.** 2007 **Dozens** 7000 **Vyds** 3ha
Griff and Rosie Cupitt run a combined winery and restaurant complex, taking full advantage of their location on the south coast of NSW. Rosie studied oenology at CSU and has more than a decade of vintage experience, taking in France and Italy; she also happens to be the Shoalhaven representative for Slow Food International. The Cupitts have 3ha of vines centred on sauvignon blanc and semillon, and also source fruit from Hilltops, Canberra District, Tumbarumba and Orange. Sons Wally and Tom have now joined the winery.

ŸŸŸŸŸ **Hilltops Fiano 2019** A southern Italian variety going great guns on these shores, with the best results to date largely from warmer climes, somewhat akin to the Campanian countryside outside of Naples. This challenges those precepts. Intelligently picked fully ripe, rather than on acidity. Poached apricot and vanilla pod notes are bound by a twine of herb from thyme to fennel, with a quilt of gentle phenolics folded across a skein of maritime acidity. Rich, texturally compelling and very fresh. An excellent fiano. Screwcap. **Rating** 95 **To** 2024 $34 NG ✪
Provenance Canberra District Chardonnay 2018 A refined chardonnay, boasting fidelity to the estate's culture of flavour while melding it to finer boned acidity and mineral crunch; generous stone fruit scents, creamed cashew, nougat and toasted hazelnut. Powerful, yet fresh enough and effortless. The acidity dutiful. Screwcap. **Rating** 94 **To** 2026 NG

ŢŢŢŢŢ The Pointer Tumbarumba Chardonnay 2018 Rating 93 To 2025 $38 NG
Carolyn's Hilltops Cabernet 2017 Rating 92 To 2025 $40 NG
Hilltops Tempranillo 2019 Rating 92 To 2023 $38 NG
Alphonse Sauvignon 2019 Rating 91 To 2023 $34 NG
Orange Pinot Gris 2019 Rating 91 To 2024 $34 NG
The Pointer Tumbarumba Pinot Noir 2018 Rating 91 To 2023 $40 NG
Hilltops Nebbiolo 2018 Rating 91 To 2024 $46 NG

Curator Wine Company ★★★★☆

28 Jenke Road, Marananga, SA 5355 **Region** Barossa Valley
T 0411 861 604 **www**.curatorwineco.com.au **Open** By appt
Winemaker Tom White **Est.** 2015 **Dozens** 5000 **Vyds** 8ha
This business is owned by Tom and Bridget White, who have made a number of changes in direction over previous years and have now decided to focus on shiraz and cabernet sauvignon from the Barossa Valley, a decision that has been rewarded. The vineyard at Marananga is planted on ancient red soils rich in ironstone and quartzite, and the wines are naturally fermented. Exports to China.

ŢŢŢŢŢ White Label Marananga Vineyard Barossa Valley Shiraz 2017 From the winery block at the estate Marananga Vineyard after rain 'really dialled back on these wines this year'. 40% new French oak, 60% second fill, 5% of the '18 added to 'boost the juiciness'. Although unusual, and regardless of the alcohol, still an attractive wine. Diam. 15% alc. **Rating** 92 To 2027 $85
White Label Stone Well Vineyard Barossa Valley Shiraz 2017 Same vinification as for the White Label Marananga Vineyard Shiraz, and the same addition of 5% from '18. And just as lovely. Diam. 15% alc. **Rating** 92 To 2037 $85
White Label Marananga Vineyard Barossa Valley Cabernet Sauvignon 2017 Wine of the vintage for Curator, which wrote, 'More of a cabernet year than shiraz'. New oak was reduced to 55% French, the rest of the oak was used French and American ex the '15 vintage. It's clear the house style is focused on maximum extraction of body from fully ripe fruit, and isn't departing from it, no matter what. Diam. 15% alc. **Rating** 91 To 2029 $85
Parishes Barossa Valley Shiraz 2018 A complicated mix from younger blocks on the home Marananga Vineyard, a 45yo vineyard at Vine Vale, plus leftovers from other vineyards. Most given 14 months in barrel, 10% from the '19 vintage. Diam. 15% alc. **Rating** 90 To 2028 $25
Greenock Vineyard Shiraz 2018 A new vineyard and wine for Curator. Total new oak 30%, split equally between French and American. Relentlessly full-bodied, the alcohol seeming higher. Diam. 15% alc. **Rating** 90 To 2038 $85
Stonehouse Quartz Block Icon Barossa Valley Shiraz 2016 30–70yo vines in Kalimna, Ebenezer and Moppa, matured in 30% new French oak, the remainder used French and American barrels. Raw power is the house style, modified by the French oak, otherwise old style. Polarising. Diam. 14.9% alc. **Rating** 90 To 2036
Museum Release Barossa Valley Shiraz 2013 A massive wine in every way. Not bottled until Jul '15. Fruit, oak, tannin in scary balance. This isn't wine in the ordinary sense. Diam. 15.5% alc. **Rating** 90 To 2040 $85
Barossa Valley Cabernet Sauvignon 2018 From the home Marananga Vineyard. The heatwave of '18 caused problems, here the yield reduced to 1.5t/acre. Co-fermented with 5% merlot, pressed to French oak (15% new), the balance used American and French oak. The alcohol didn't help its cause, but was inevitable. Diam. 15% alc. **Rating** 90 To 2038 $35
Museum Release Barossa Valley Cabernet Sauvignon 2013 The first vintage; 100% new French oak, a long slow open ferment, racked and bottled Jul '15. The thick, viscous Curator style is still taking shape; the alcohol part of the parcel since day one. Diam. 15.5% alc. **Rating** 90 To 2029 $85

Curly Flat ★★★★★

263 Collivers Road, Lancefield, Vic 3435 **Region** Macedon Ranges
T (03) 5429 1956 **www**.curlyflat.com **Open** Fri–Mon 12–5
Winemaker Matt Harrop, Ben Kimmorley **Est.** 1991 **Dozens** 6000 **Vyds** 13ha
Founded by Phillip Moraghan and Jenifer Kolkka in 1991; Jenifer has been the sole owner of
Curly Flat since 2017. The focus has always been on the vineyard, a dedicated team ensuring
quality is never compromised. Matt Harrop is now overseeing production. Exports to the UK,
Japan and Hong Kong.

🍷🍷🍷🍷 **Western Macedon Ranges Pinot Noir 2018** A small bottling from the
east-facing, coolest blocks; 11% whole bunch, no new oak, but 82% 1yo. Clones
115 and 114 contribute fragrance and supple mouthfeel. The most elegant and
delicate, although persistent, bouquet and palate of the Curly Flat pinots. Screwcap.
13.3% alc. **Rating** 96 **To** 2039 $53 ✪

Macedon Ranges Pinot Noir 2018 This is the main release from all parts
of the vineyard; MV6, 115 and 114 clones, 20% whole bunch, 28 days on skins,
matured for 16 months in oak (20% new). Fine, elegant and fragrant cherry and
pomegranate fruit. Overall balance and length are very good. QED. Available
in half-bottles and magnums as well as 750ml. Screwcap. 13.5% alc. **Rating** 96
To 2040 $53 ✪

Chardonnay 2018 Estate-grown, hand-picked, whole-bunch pressed, wild-
fermented, 35% mlf, matured in French oak (20% new) for 14 months on lees.
Elegant and perfectly balanced, it is maturing at a reassuringly slow pace, promising
more still when fully mature. The flavours are poised between stone fruit and
citrus. Screwcap. 13.3% alc. **Rating** 95 **To** 2025 $46

Central Macedon Ranges Pinot Noir 2018 Wild-fermented MV6 from the
oldest ('92) plantings contributes aromatics and tannins to the blend, 20% whole
bunch, 23 days on skins, 25% new oak. Dark fruits/plums and superfine tannins.
Available from the mailing list only. Screwcap. 13.7% alc. **Rating** 95 **To** 2028 $53

Macedon Ranges Pinot Gris 2019 Hand-picked and whole-bunch pressed.
Three weeks undisturbed under CO_2 before being pressed to barrel is presumably
the source of the salmon-pink hue. Matured for 7 months on lees. The vinification
has resulted in full-on flavour, the residual sugar of 3.4g/l not high enough to
contribute to flavour, just texture. Screwcap. 13.8% alc. **Rating** 94 **To** 2022 $26 ✪

🍷🍷🍷🍷 **Macedon Ranges White Pinot 2019 Rating** 91 **To** 2021 $26
Williams Crossing Pinot Noir 2017 Rating 90 **To** 2025 $29

Curtis Family Vineyards ★★★★

514 Victor Harbor Road, McLaren Vale, SA 5171 **Region** McLaren Vale
T 0439 800 484 **www**.curtisfamilyvineyards.com **Open** Not
Winemaker Mark Curtis **Est.** 1973 **Dozens** 10 000
The Curtis family traces its history back to 1499 when Paolo Curtis was appointed by
Cardinal de Medici to administer Papal lands in the area around Cervaro. (The name Curtis is
believed to derive from Curtius, a noble and wealthy Roman Empire family.) The family has
been growing grapes and making wine in McLaren Vale since 1973, having come to Australia
some years previously. Exports to the US, Canada, Thailand and China.

🍷🍷🍷🍷 **Limited Series McLaren Vale Shiraz 2018** Less winemaking artefact,
especially the oak regime – French barrels (33% new), aged for 18 months –
would allow more freshness and life in. Instead, this dense wine is infused with
sweet smoky flavours, a backdrop against the very ripe fruit with masses of tannin.
It's sturdy and needs lots of air to show signs of life. Diam. 14% alc. **Rating** 89
To 2027 $100 JF

d'Arenberg

Osborn Road, McLaren Vale, SA 5171 **Region** McLaren Vale
T (08) 8329 4888 **www.**darenberg.com.au **Open** 7 days 10–5
Winemaker Chester Osborn, Jack Walton **Est.** 1912 **Dozens** 220000 **Vyds** 197.2ha
Nothing, they say, succeeds like success. Few operations in Australia fit this dictum better than d'Arenberg, which has kept its 100+-year-old heritage while moving into the 21st century with flair and élan. At last count the d'Arenberg vineyards, at various locations, have 37 varieties planted, as well as more than 50 growers in McLaren Vale. There is no question that its past, present and future revolve around its considerable portfolio of richly robed red wines, shiraz, cabernet sauvignon and grenache being the cornerstones. The quality of the wines is unimpeachable, the prices logical and fair. It has a profile in both the UK and the US that far larger companies would love to have. d'Arenberg celebrated 100 years of family grapegrowing in '12 on the property that houses the winery, and the iconic cube cellar door and restaurant. A founding member of Australia's First Families of Wine. Unfortunately the wines submitted for this edition disappeared; Campbell Mattinson's tasting notes for the resubmission of the wines appear on www.winecompanion.com.au. Exports to all major markets.

Dabblebrook Wines

69 Dabblebrook Road, Sellicks Hill, SA 5174 **Region** McLaren Vale
T 0488 158 727 **www.**dabblebrookwines.com **Open** By appt
Winemaker Ian Adam **Est.** 2007 **Dozens** 1000 **Vyds** 10ha
Dabblebrook is the seachange occupation of Ian Adam and Libbi Langford. They left Port Douglas after running a waste management business for 20 years, moving south to find what the larger world offered. They had no plans to establish a wine business, but found a property with 5ha of shiraz and 2ha of grenache, planted in 1990. In the early years they grew grapes for d'Arenberg (shiraz and grenache), an arrangement which ran for five years. Over the same period Ian worked on the Battle of Bosworth vineyards, gaining experience from Joch Bosworth. In 2011 he decided to make the wine for Dabblebrook; a vintage in the Loire Valley has further cemented his role as a winemaker. The red wines are made with little or no machinery, typically hand-plunged and basket-pressed, with minimal additions. Ian's current CV reads: 'Vigneron, part-time flagpole painter, chandelier cleaner (seasonal) and Doer of Lunch'. Exports to Singapore.

ΨΨΨΨΨ **Single Vineyard McLaren Vale Shiraz 2016** Has that fresh, vibrant mouthfeel and flavour perspective ex 35 days on skins, 10% whole bunches, hand-plunged, matured for 13 months in 2yo low toast French oak. A triumph for '16. Screwcap. 13.5% alc. **Rating** 95 **To** 2029 $30 ✪

Row 8 Single Row Single Barrel McLaren Vale Shiraz 2015 Hand-picked, foot-trodden, hand-destemmed, hand-plunged, 25 days on skins, waterbag press, 1 new French hogshead, 26 months, hand-bottled and wax-dipped. There's almost too much extract, certainly enough to warrant cellaring for 5+ years – it does have balance and harmony. Cork. 13% alc. **Rating** 95 **To** 2039 $60

Single Vineyard McLaren Vale Grenache 2017 Hand-picked, fermented with 30% whole bunches, foot-stomped after 10 days, then 20 days on skins, hand-plunged, gently pressed to retain brightness – and succeeded. Brightness is very different from sweet fruit, sweetness ex alcohol and skin fragmentation. Screwcap. 13.5% alc. **Rating** 95 **To** 2027 $30 ✪

Single Vineyard McLaren Vale Grenache Shiraz 2017 No oak exposure for the grenache, the shiraz spending 8 months in aged French oak. The impact of the oak is measured in flavour rather than texture and, in this as well as its sibling, shows the great '17 vintage. Screwcap. 13.5% alc. **Rating** 94 **To** 2029 $30 ✪

Dal Zotto Wines

Main Road, Whitfield, Vic 3733 **Region** King Valley
T (03) 5729 8321 **www.**dalzotto.com.au **Open** 7 days 10–5
Winemaker Michael Dal Zotto, Daniel Bettio **Est.** 1987 **Dozens** 60000 **Vyds** 46ha

The Dal Zotto family is a King Valley institution; ex-tobacco growers, then contract grapegrowers, they are now 100% focused on their Dal Zotto wine range. Founded by Otto and Elena, ownership has now passed to sons Michael and Christian (and their partners Lynne and Simone), who handle winemaking and sales/marketing respectively. Dal Zotto is producing increasing amounts of Italian varieties of consistent quality from its substantial estate vineyard; they were the pioneers of prosecco in Australia with the first planting in 1999. The cellar door is in the centre of Whitfield, and is also home to their Trattoria (open weekends). Exports to the UK, the UAE, the Philippines, Singapore and China appear to be flying.

King Valley Fiano 2019 Crackerjack release. Intensity and character in spades. It's a textured wine with honeysuckle and fleshy stone fruit characters soaring throughout. The price makes it a steal. Screwcap. 13.4% alc. **Rating** 95 **To** 2023 $27 CM ✪

Col Fondo King Valley Prosecco 2019 A beautiful prosecco, crisp, clean and complex at once; refreshing, interesting. Cloudy and perfumed, dry as all hell, pushed with textural fruit, pear through the aftertaste. Style, sophistication, value and more. Crown seal. 11.3% alc. **Rating** 95 $29 CM ✪

King Valley Pinot Bianco 2019 Not quite unctuous but almost there. This is rich and heady with rose petal and ripe citrus flavours, not to mention red apple and spice. It's not inappropriate to call it captivating. Screwcap. 13.2% alc. **Rating** 94 **To** 2022 $27 CM ✪

Tabelo Col Fondo King Valley Prosecco 2018 Cloudy, dry, serious, powerful. In many respects it's the opposite of what you normally get with prosecco and yet it's an uber-traditional expression of the variety. This turns your head and twists your mind. It's slatey, salty, pear-like, barleyed and zesty. There's a kick of smoked fennel to the aftertaste. It's quite something. Crown seal. **Rating** 94 $48 CM

King Valley Pinot Grigio 2019 Rating 93 **To** 2022 $21 CM ✪
King Valley Sangiovese 2018 Rating 93 **To** 2026 $27 CM ✪
King Valley Arneis 2019 Rating 91 **To** 2022 $27 CM
Pucino King Valley Prosecco 2019 Rating 91 $26 CM

Dalfarras ★★★★

PO Box 123, Nagambie, Vic 3608 **Region** Nagambie Lakes
T (03) 5794 2637 **www**.tahbilk.com.au **Open** At Tahbilk
Winemaker Alister Purbrick, Alan George **Est.** 1991 **Dozens** 8750 **Vyds** 20.97ha
The project of Alister Purbrick and artist wife Rosa (née Dalfarra), whose paintings adorn the labels of the wines. Alister is best known as winemaker at Tahbilk (see separate entry), the family winery and home, but this range of wines is intended to (in Alister's words), 'Allow me to expand my winemaking horizons and mould wines in styles different from Tahbilk'.

Prosecco 2019 By prosecco standards this is pretty good. It has some fruit flavour and isn't sweet. Cork. 11% alc. **Rating** 89 $19 ✪

Dalrymple Vineyards ★★★★★

1337 Pipers Brook Road, Pipers Brook, Tas 7254 **Region** Northern Tasmania
T (03) 6382 7229 **www**.dalrymplevineyards.com.au **Open** By appt
Winemaker Peter Caldwell **Est.** 1987 **Dozens** 4000 **Vyds** 17ha
Dalrymple was established many years ago by the Mitchell and Sundstrup families; the vineyard and brand were acquired by Hill-Smith Family Vineyards in late 2007. Plantings are split between pinot noir and sauvignon blanc, and the wines are made at Jansz Tasmania. In '10 Peter Caldwell was appointed, responsible for the vineyard, viticulture and winemaking. He brought with him 10 years' experience at Te Kairanga Wines (NZ) and two years with Josef Chromy Wines. His knowledge of pinot noir and chardonnay is comprehensive. In Dec '12 Hill-Smith Family Vineyards acquired the 120ha property on which the original Frogmore Creek Vineyard was established; 10ha of that property is pinot noir specifically for Dalrymple.

ΨΨΨΨΨ **Cave Block Pipers River Chardonnay 2017** Predictably intense and varietal, a cool site and a cool vintage. The colour is still bright, the bouquet has a complex touch of funk and the palate enjoys wonderful drive. Very Burgundian (minus premox). No surprise that the grapes for this wine were declared by Dalrymple to be of the highest quality. Screwcap. 13% alc. **Rating** 96 **To** 2027 $38 **◐**

Cottage Block Pipers River Pinot Noir 2017 Dense, deep colour. The Cottage Block fruit from this vintage of excellent quality. It's full-bodied, but not muscular; the colour and flavour simply part of the fruit characteristics in a cool vintage with a long, slow ripening pattern. Black and red cherry mingle with plum on the palate. Screwcap. 13% alc. **Rating** 96 **To** 2030 $64 **◐**

Single Site Ouse Pinot Noir 2018 The colour is light, but the bouquet and palate have much more to say than its siblings. The explanation lies in its alcohol, not of itself a good thing, but here signalling ripe fruit, coupled with a touch of new oak. Screwcap. 14.5% alc. **Rating** 95 **To** 2030 $64

Single Site Coal River Valley Pinot Noir 2017 Presumably from the same vineyard as its '16 sibling, the superior texture and depth reflecting the excellent vintage. It's perfumed and spicy, the mouthfeel supple, the flavours a mirror image of the bouquet. Screwcap. 13% alc. **Rating** 95 **To** 2030 $64

Cave Block Pipers River Chardonnay 2018 The wine speaks clearly with its grapefruit edge to the drive and intensity to the fruit, oak thereabouts, the length admirable. Screwcap. 13.5% alc. **Rating** 94 **To** 2028 $38

Pipers River Pinot Noir 2018 The colour is lighter in hue and depth, but there's more fragrance and fruit expression. Just a tad adrift of complete ripeness — so near, yet so far. Screwcap. 13.5% alc. **Rating** 94 **To** 2028 $38

ΨΨΨΨ♀ **Pipers River Sauvignon Blanc 2018** **Rating** 93 **To** 2021 $30 CM
Cottage Block Pipers River Pinot Noir 2018 **Rating** 93 **To** 2028 $64
Single Site Coal River Valley Pinot Noir 2016 **Rating** 92 **To** 2026 $64
Single Site Swansea Pinot Noir 2016 **Rating** 92 **To** 2023 $64

Dalwhinnie ★★★★★

448 Taltarni Road, Moonambel, Vic 3478 **Region** Pyrenees
T (03) 5467 2388 **www**.dalwhinnie.com.au **Open** 7 days 10–5
Winemaker David Jones **Est.** 1976 **Dozens** 3500 **Vyds** 25ha
David and Jenny Jones make wines with tremendous depth of flavour, reflecting the relatively low-yielding but well maintained vineyards. The vineyards are dry-grown and managed organically, hence the low yield, but the quality more than compensates. A 50t high-tech winery allows the wines to be made onsite. It's good to see that Dalwhinnie has been acquired by the Fogarty Wine Group. Exports to the UK, the US and China.

ΨΨΨΨΨ **Moonambel Shiraz 2016** Crushed and destemmed, 8-day ferment, 14 days post-ferment maceration, 17–18 months in French oak (33% new). Full-bodied blackberry/black cherry fruits and substantial tannins need some years yet to resolve and let the fruit shine. Screwcap. 13.5% alc. **Rating** 95 **To** 2041 $62

Moonambel Shiraz 2017 This is only medium-bodied and is red-fruited (the vintage speaking presumably). It was made prior to Dalwhinnie's acquisition by the Fogarty Group, so its future is yet to be charted. Screwcap. **Rating** 94 **To** 2027 $62

ΨΨΨΨ♀ **Moonambel Cabernet 2016** **Rating** 90 **To** 2026 $58

Dalwood ★★★★

700 Dalwood Road, Dalwood, NSW 2335 **Region** Hunter Valley
T (02) 4998 7666 **www**.dalwoodestate.com.au **Open** Long weekends
Winemaker Bryan Currie **Est.** 1828 **Dozens** NFP **Vyds** 23ha
The chain of events making the oldest winery the youngest isn't far removed from the white rabbit appearing out of the magician's hat. George Wyndham was an important figure in the middle of the 19th century, born in 1801 to a wealthy family, he arrived in Australia in 1823

and promptly set about assembling vast agricultural holdings stretching from Inverell to the Liverpool Plains, the Hunter Valley the centrepiece. He berated the Sydney Agricultural Show for holding the Wine Show in February, and for awarding gold medals that weren't in fact 24-carat gold. In 1904 Penfolds purchased Wyndham Estate and renamed it Dalwood. Declining yields attracted the attention of the bean counters, and in 1967 Penfolds sold the winery and vineyard to Perc McGuigan, but retained the Dalwood brand, leaving McGuigan free to rename it Wyndham Estate. In December 2017 TWE (aka Penfolds) sold the Dalwood brand to Sam and Christie Arnaout (who also own Hungerford Hill and its subsidiaries) and Sweetwater Wines. The synergy of this assemblage is obvious.

ŸŸŸŸŸ **Estate Hunter Valley Shiraz 2018** Had 14 months in 25% new oak. The oak is obvious on the medium-bodied palate. Screwcap. 14% alc. **Rating** 90 **To** 2038 $45

ŸŸŸŸ **Estate Hunter Valley Semillon 2019 Rating** 89 **To** 2026 $27

Dandelion Vineyards   ★★★★★

PO Box 138, McLaren Vale, SA 5171 **Region** South Australia
T (08) 8323 8979 **www.dandelionvineyards.com.au Open** Not
Winemaker Elena Brooks **Est.** 2007 **Dozens** NFP **Vyds** 124.2ha
Dandelion Vineyards brings together vineyards spread across the Adelaide Hills, Eden Valley, Langhorne Creek, McLaren Vale, Barossa Valley and Fleurieu Peninsula. Elena Brooks is not only the wife of industry dilettante Zar, but also a gifted winemaker. Exports to all major markets.

ŸŸŸŸŸ **Red Queen of the Eden Valley Shiraz 2017** Made from Colin Krohen's Eden Valley vineyard planted over 100 years ago (1912). Hand-picked with one-third whole bunches, two-thirds crushed on top; open-fermented, 11 days on skins, matured for 30 months in French oak (50% new). The density of the colour is striking, as is the depth and power of the fruit. This is an extraordinary wine, the intensity of its black fruits awe-inspiring; oak and tannins insisting on adding their say. Screwcap. 14.5% alc. **Rating** 98 **To** 2057 $200 ✪

Wonderland of the Eden Valley Riesling 2019 The price of this wine reflects the piercing brilliance of the bouquet and, in particular, the palate. There is some residual sugar, but the acidity totally obscures it. If you buy it, keep some bottles for a minimum of 10 years, allowing the treasure trove of secondary flavours to be liberated. Screwcap. 11.5% alc. **Rating** 97 **To** 2040 $60 ✪

ŸŸŸŸŸ **Lioness of McLaren Vale Shiraz 2018** Matured in French and American oak (mainly used) for 18 months. Deeply coloured crimson-purple. It is redolent of McLaren Vale with layers of black fruits, choc-mint and ripe tannins, the oak important for texture, not flavour. All up, a thoroughly impressive wine at this price. Screwcap. 14.5% alc. **Rating** 95 **To** 2033 $27.50 ✪

Lion's Tooth of McLaren Vale Shiraz Riesling 2018 Clearly eager to showcase the riesling component (as at 5% of the blend it is not necessary to note it on the label), this is quirky but wholly delicious. Makes sense: riesling's zingy acidity imparting life to the swirl of purple to blue fruit references inherent to Vale shiraz. Whole bunches of the latter were fermented with stems, atop riesling skins. Beautifully floral. Think lilac and rosewater. Charming. Crunchy and long. The tannins are like chewing grape skins and the most delicious pulp. Real verve here. **Rating** 95 **To** 2026 $30 NG ✪

Lion's Roar of the Barossa Cabernet Sauvignon 2018 While we seldom associate Barossa with that most stiff upper lipped grape, cabernet, there are many good examples. This is among them. Embellished with the varietal tattoo of dried sage, clove and a whiff of leaf, there is something more nourishing, denser and altogether richer from these parts: black olive, bitter chocolate and cherry bonbon. But what I really love are the tannins: moreish, cocoa-laced and fine-grained. **Rating** 95 **To** 2033 $40 NG

Wishing Clock of the Adelaide Hills Sauvignon Blanc 2019 This is sophisticated sauvignon blanc, defying what is largely an oxymoronic concept in this country. More akin to a textural, herbal light to mid-weighted expression from Graves. Thankfully, too, eschewing the usual bane of sweet/sour tropical fruit references in the name of an effortless flow of greengage, nettle, evergreen and strewn herb. Screwcap. **Rating** 94 **To** 2021 $27 NG ✪

ΨΨΨΨΨ **Enchanted Garden of the Eden Valley Riesling 2019 Rating** 93 **To** 2031 $27 NG ✪

Honeypot of the Barossa Roussanne 2018 Rating 93 **To** 2022 $27 NG ✪

Menagerie of the Barossa Grenache Shiraz Mataro 2018 Rating 93 **To** 2026 $30 NG

Lionheart of the Barossa Shiraz 2018 Rating 92 **To** 2032 $28

Firehawk of McLaren Vale Shiraz 2017 Rating 92 **To** 2032 $60 NG

Pride of the Fleurieu Cabernet Sauvignon 2018 Rating 92 **To** 2033 $28

Damsel of the Barossa Merlot 2018 Rating 91 **To** 2025 $30 NG

Dappled Wine ★★★★★

1 Sewell Road, Steels Creek, Vic 3775 **Region** Yarra Valley
T 0407 675 994 **www**.dappledwines.com.au **Open** By appt
Winemaker Shaun Crinion **Est.** 2009 **Dozens** 800
Owner and winemaker Shaun Crinion was introduced to wine in 1999, working for his winemaker uncle at Laetitia Winery & Vineyards on the central coast of California. His career since then has been so impressive I can't cut it short: 2000 Devil's Lair, Margaret River and Corbett Canyon Vineyard, California; '02 Houghton, Middle Swan; '03 De Bortoli, Hunter Valley; '04–06 Pipers Brook, Tasmania; '06 Bay of Fires, Tasmania; '06–07 Williams Selyem, California; '08 Domaine Chandon, Yarra Valley; '10 Domaine de Montille, Burgundy; '09–present Dappled Wines (plus part-time for Rob Dolan). His longer term ambition is to buy or establish his own vineyard.

ΨΨΨΨΨ **Les Verges Single Vineyard Yarra Valley Chardonnay 2018** From Seville. Hand-picked, cooled overnight, foot-stomped, then a long press straight to oak, wild ferment, no batonnage, 10 months on lees plus 5 months in tank, bottled by gravity. Lovely chardonnay. Screwcap. 13% alc. **Rating** 97 **To** 2028 $40 ✪

ΨΨΨΨΨ **Appellation Yarra Valley Chardonnay 2018** Upper and Lower Yarra fruit; hand-picked, cooled, whole bunch lightly crushed before long pressing unsulphured to French oak (20% new), wild-fermented with no temperature control, no batonnage, on lees for 10 months. Takes shape like a complex knitting pattern. Screwcap. 13% alc. **Rating** 95 **To** 2028 $30 ✪

Appellation Yarra Valley Pinot Noir 2018 From the Upper (mainly) and Lower Yarra. Winemaking involves minimal intervention, cold soak, wild yeast–open fermented with 30% whole bunches, 15% new oak, 10 months on lees, no additions other than SO_2. A pretty pinot still evolving to take texture and structure on board. Screwcap. 13% alc. **Rating** 95 **To** 2028 $30 ✪

Les Bois Single Vineyard Yarra Valley Pinot Noir 2018 From an incredibly steep vineyard. MV6, hand-picked, sorted and chilled, 5 days cold soak, 30% whole bunch, matured in very old large-format oak. Takes a moment to engage gears, then powers along the palate, flashes of spicy/savoury red fruits flying in every direction when it does. Diam. 13% alc. **Rating** 95 **To** 2030 $40

Fin de la Terre Single Vineyard Yarra Valley Syrah 2018 Hand-picked and sorted, cooled, 100% whole bunches in an airtight vessel for 2 weeks then foot-stomped once a week for 5 weeks, pressed to a very old puncheon with full lees and not touched until the following May. It's pretty extreme and it is remarkably good, especially with its retention of dark cherry/spicy fruit flavours. Diam. 13.5% alc. **Rating** 94 **To** 2030 $40

ΨΨΨΨΨ **Limited Release Yarra Valley Pinot Syrah 2018 Rating** 93 **To** 2023 $35

David Franz

94 Stelzer Road, Stone Well, SA 5352 **Region** Barossa Valley
T 0417 454 556 **www.**david-franz.com **Open** 7 days 11–5
Winemaker David Franz Lehmann **Est.** 1998 **Dozens** 6600 **Vyds** 33.92ha

David Franz (Lehmann) is one of Margaret and Peter Lehmann's sons. He took a very circuitous path around the world before establishing his eponymous winery. Wife Nicki accompanied him on his odyssey and, together with their three children, two dogs, a mess of chickens and a surly shed cat, all live happily together in their house and winery. The utterly unique labels stem from (incomplete) university studies in graphic design. Exports to the UK, the US, Japan, Hong Kong and China.

ΨΨΨΨΨ Georgie's Walk Cellar Release Cabernet Sauvignon 2010 A regional collaboration of 60% Barossa, the remainder from the more elevated Eden. A great vintage. Dense. This is exhibiting a progression of fruit scents into the tertiary nether: five-spice, beef bouillon, wet clay, pencil shavings, strewn herb with an accent on bouquet garni and seams of spearmint. Smells like a pot roast; brimming with umami. Screwcap. **Rating** 96 **To** 2028 $100 NG

Cellar Release Eden Valley Riesling 2010 As is the wont here, the free-run and pressings are separated, kicked off ambiently before chilling and fermented cool to palpable dryness. Just prior, the 2 parts are blended. This has aged beautifully. Dry, but billowing with an aged complexity that endows a sense of richness and with that poise, mitigating the razor of acidity scratching beneath. Lemon drop candy, quince, Pez, citrus marmalade and kerosene, yet nothing overt. Just a long linger of flavour and aura of place. Screwcap. **Rating** 95 **To** 2026 $50 NG

Long Gully Road Ancient Vine Semillon 2018 The source was 133 years of age at the time of harvest, sandy loam over marble; madeira clonal material that defines Barossa's unique expression of semillon. Hand-picked and fermented wild and long. Pressings in neutral wood; free-run in tank. Partial malolactic had its way, with the wine remaining unstirred while enriched by extended lees handling, imparting a weave of textural intrigue. This is exceptional. Youthfully nascent, yet a breeze of fennel, thyme and soapy citrus scents ride long over a beam of juicy natural acidity and gentle pucker. I would wager a good 10+ years in the cellar. Screwcap. **Rating** 95 **To** 2030 $27 NG ✪

Marg's Blood Semillon 2010 Borne of the old Madeira clone that furtively roams these parts. Sourced from an ancient plot, 120yo when this elixir was crafted. A long ambient ferment complemented by judicious oak handling has imparted detail while evincing structural authority; this style is seldom seen and scantly appreciated. Lemon drop, curd, quince, lanolin, verdant herb and a billowing vinosity and breadth that stain the cheeks while expanding across the palate. An effortless weave of complexity and verve. The pH metre set to a welcome diplomacy: dutifully fresh, without being severe. Long and mellifluous. Screwcap. **Rating:** 95 **To** 2028 $50 NG

Alexander's Reward Cabernet Sauvignon Shiraz 2015 This sets the bar for a different shade to the Barossan archetype. Not because it is picked green for acid retention, nor stuffed full of herbal stems to mitigate low acidity. This is simply picked at the right moment, exhibiting a poise and grace seldom experienced in this neck of the woods. Plunged thrice daily, before 24 months in a combination of new and used French and American wood; nothing out of place. Bitter chocolate, herb and dark to red fruit allusions. But this is second tier to the lacy tannins and juicy acidity, melding into a compelling textural whole. A lovely wine of a beguiling elegance. Screwcap. **Rating** 95 **To** 2030 $50 NG

Benjamin's Promise Cellar Release Shiraz 2010 A superlative vintage. Reason to salivate as you unscrew the cap; the aromas are a doozy of carnal, smoky, loamy, nourishing warm-climate shiraz. Five-spice, mocha, black plum, anise, tar, lapsang and lilac. Initially, the alcohol is buried, nary a burn. The finish is long and scintillating, carrying the weight of the wine into a zone of relative effortlessness. Screwcap. **Rating** 94 **To** 2026 $100 NG

Plane Turning Right Merlot Petit Verdot Cabernet Sauvignon 2016
Seeing the price brought a grin. This is a real wine: hand-picked and extracted
with integrity, while playing the game of approachability in beautifully massaged
tannins, polished enough to reward those with patience without punishing those
not wanting to cellar this mid to full-weighted, savoury, merlot-dominant red.
Black and redcurrant scents are brushed with sage, soused with tapenade and
infused with bay leaf muddled with damson plum. Real thrust and parry of fruit
to structure. I love this! Screwcap. Rating 94 To 2026 $27 NG ✪

Alexander's Reward Cellar Release Cabernet Sauvignon Shiraz 2010
With 75% cabernet, the remainder shiraz, this wine has become lighter over the
years, without sacrificing any intensity of flavour, nor pedigree of tannin. This
boasts the same tannic detail, length and sheen as the recent expression. Aged
complexity too, of course. Think a bay leaf–infused potpourri of earthy loams,
coffee bean, verdant hedgerow, dark fruit allusions and spearmint lifting the fray.
And yet, there is more power over refinement. A fine wine, nevertheless. Screwcap.
Rating 94 To 2028 $100 NG

ᵱᵱᵱᵱᵱ **Eden Valley Riesling 2019** Rating 93 To 2028 $27 NG ✪
108 Varieties Red Rose 2018 Rating 93 To 2022 $25 NG ✪
1923 Survivor Vines Barossa Grenache Noir 2017 Rating 93 To 2026
$27 NG ✪
Georgie's Walk Cabernet Sauvignon 2015 Rating 93 To 2030 $50 NG
225 Cabernet Sauvignon 2009 Rating 93 To 2032 $200 NG
Nicole Sparkling Cabernet Shiraz NV Rating 93 $75 NG
Eden Edge 2019 Rating 92 To 2025 $25 NG ✪
Alternative View Shiraz 2012 Rating 92 To 2028 $150 NG
Larrikin NV Rating 92 To 2025 $50 NG
Dam Block Barossa Shiraz Grenache 2017 Rating 92 To 2023 $27 NG
H.P. Hydraulic Press Shiraz 2017 Rating 91 To 2023 $25 NG
Nicki's Symphony No. 1 Barossa Cabernet Sauvignon NV Rating 91
To 2024 $25 NG

David Hook Wines ★★★★

Cnr Broke Road/Ekerts Road, Pokolbin, NSW 2320 **Region** Hunter Valley
T (02) 4998 7121 **www**.davidhookwines.com.au **Open** 7 days 10–4.30
Winemaker David Hook **Est.** 1984 **Dozens** 10 000 **Vyds** 8ha
David Hook has over 25 years' experience as a winemaker for Tyrrell's and Lake's Folly, also
doing the full Flying Winemaker bit with jobs in Bordeaux, the Rhône Valley, Spain, the US
and Georgia. The Pothana Vineyard has been in production for almost 40 years and the wines
made from it are given the 'Old Vines' banner. This vineyard is planted on the Belford Dome,
an ancient geological formation that provides red clay soils over limestone on the slopes, and
sandy loams along the creek flats; the former for red wines, the latter for white.

ᵱᵱᵱᵱᵱ **Old Vines Pothana Vineyard Belford Semillon 2019** It's tempting to
describe this as lean and direct, but then it has quite a lot of grapeskin-like texture
and there's an array of flavours to be appreciated. It tastes of green apple and lime
with nashi pear, slate, grapefruit rind and grass characters whispered through.
Nothing sticks out; everything is tucked in close. Screwcap. 10.5% alc. Rating 93
To 2028 $28 CM
Central Ranges Pinot Gris 2019 Fermented in old French oak. It offers a
weight of fruit and wood smoke flavour without getting too heady or indeed
heavy. Nashi pear and apple are the main drivers but oak lends the wine a
presence. Screwcap. 13% alc. Rating 93 To 2022 $35 CM
Orange Sangiovese 2018 Beautiful even flow of flavour. Cherry-plum and
earth, sweet and sour, with woodsy spice notes in the background. It's not a big
wine, but it lingers appreciably. Great for drinking, most especially with food but
for any occasion really. Screwcap. 13% alc. Rating 93 To 2026 $35 CM

Old Vines Pothana Vineyard Belford Chardonnay 2019 Excellent fruit intensity. Pear, peach and citrus flavours burst into cedar wood, toast and nougat. It seems oak-heavy at first, but as it breathes the fruit sears through. It's generally well balanced and will continue to drink well over the next handful of years. Screwcap. 13.5% alc. **Rating** 92 **To** 2026 $32 CM

Orange Barbera 2018 Juicy red-berried fruit, inflections of woodsy spice, a soft musk-like note to the texture/flavour and trademark (for the variety) refreshing acidity. There's a mint/menthol note here too which works well in context; it contributes to the freshness of the theme. Screwcap. 13.5% alc. **Rating** 91 **To** 2024 $35 CM

Dawson & James   ★★★★★

1240B Brookman Road, Dingabledinga, SA 5172 **Region** Southern Tasmania
T 0419 816 335 **www.**dawsonjames.com.au **Open** Not
Winemaker Peter Dawson, Tim James **Est.** 2010 **Dozens** 1200 **Vyds** 3.3ha
Peter Dawson and Tim James had long and highly successful careers as senior winemakers for Hardys/Accolade Wines. Tim jumped ship first, becoming managing director of Wirra Wirra for seven years until 2007. Now both have multiple consulting roles. They have long had a desire to grow and make wine in Tasmania, a desire that came to fruition in '10. Exports to the UK and Singapore.

Pinot Noir 2016 A Tasmanian pinot that has been supremely stylish since first tasted in Jan '18 and is now even better. The richness of the fruit of youth remains in the background; there's a spicy complexity of the mouthfilling flavours. Oak and tannins play their part on the long palate, adding to its longevity. Screwcap. 13.3% alc. **Rating** 98 **To** 2030 $72 ✪

DCB Wine   ★★★★★

505 Gembrook Road, Hoddles Creek, Vic 3139 **Region** Yarra Valley
T 0419 545 544 **www.**dcbwine.com.au **Open** Not
Winemaker Chris Bendle **Est.** 2013 **Dozens** 1300
DCB is a busman's holiday for Chris Bendle, currently a winemaker at Hoddles Creek Estate, where he has been since 2010. He previously made wine in Tasmania, NZ and Oregon, so he is the right person to provide wines that are elegant, affordable and reward the pleasure of drinking (Chris's aim); the wines also offer excellent value. Exports to the UK and Japan.

Whole Bunch Single Vineyard Pinot Noir 2018 Whole bunches from the Lone Star Creek Vineyard tipped directly into 0.8t fermenters and closed with CO_2 in head space, 3 days later foot-stomped and juice commenced fermentation naturally, stomped every 2 days until the ferment reduced to 1°baume, the must pressed to used barriques to complete primary fermentation and mlf. A wine I like a great deal. Screwcap. 13.2% alc. **Rating** 96 **To** 2030 $35 ✪

Single Vineyard Mornington Peninsula Pinot Noir 2018 Clones 114, 115 and MV6 from the Bittern Vineyard transported to the Yarra Valley in the early morning, destemmed, cultured yeast added the next day, 62 dozen made so manipulation of must not difficult, pressed to used barriques. It's a wine that creeps up on you; its bright/clear crimson hue retrospectively waving a flag; its gently spiced red berry fruits and ultrafine tannins making a coherent statement. Fruit-sweet flavours are supple and fine. Screwcap. 13.5% alc. **Rating** 95 **To** 2028 $35 ✪

Yarra Valley Pinot Noir 2018 From vineyards on the northern and southernmost extremities of the Yarra Valley, with very different soils but a similar ripening period; made with the usual vinification process: destemmed after chilling, cultured yeast 48 hours later, no additions made until SO_2 at the end of Apr. Screwcap. 13.5% alc. **Rating** 94 **To** 2025 $23 ✪

Single Vineyard Woori Yallock Pinot Noir 2018 MV6 from the Lone Star Creek Vineyard; chilled, whole berries, 2 days cold soak, cultured yeast, 3 weeks on skins, pressed to barrel (15% new); 159 dozen made. Fragrant red/purple fruit aromas; very good length and balance. Full-bodied in the context of DCB pinot style. Screwcap. 13.5% alc. **Rating** 94 **To** 2027 $35

🍷🍷🍷🍷♀ Single Vineyard Woori Yallock Chardonnay 2018 **Rating** 92 **To** 2026 $35

De Beaurepaire Wines ★★★★☆

182 Cudgegong Road, Rylstone, NSW 2849 **Region** Mudgee
T 0429 787 705 **www**.debeaurepairewines.com **Open** Thurs–Mon 11–4
Winemaker Jacob Stein, John Cassegrain, Lisa Barry (Contract) **Est.** 1998 **Dozens** 7000
Vyds 53ha
The large De Beaurepaire vineyard was planted by Janet and Richard de Beaurepaire in 1998 and is situated on one of the oldest properties west of the Blue Mountains, at an altitude of 570–600m. The altitude, coupled with limestone soils and frontage to the Cudgegong River, provides grapes (and hence wines) very different from the Mudgee norm. The vineyard is planted to merlot, shiraz, cabernet sauvignon, pinot noir, petit verdot, viognier, chardonnay, semillon, verdelho and pinot gris; most of the grapes are sold. Exports to France and Hong Kong.

🍷🍷🍷🍷♀ Victor Rylstone Cabernet Sauvignon 2016 Individual selections from Block A hand-picked, destemmed, 3 days cold soak, 15 days in closed (Potter) fermenter. Medium to full-bodied with fully ripe, but not over the top, blackcurrant fruit flavour. The tannins are also ripe, the oak not a penalty. Screwcap. 15% alc. **Rating** 93 **To** 2036 $60
Jeannette Reserve Rylstone Chardonnay 2017 Hand-picked from particular patches within Block C, destemmed and whole-berry pressed, wild-fermented, 15% mlf, matured for 9 months in French hogsheads (50% new). Stone fruit, melon and citrus; tightly wound and needs time to open up to show its best. Screwcap. 12.5% alc. **Rating** 92 **To** 2035 $60
La Comtesse Rylstone Chardonnay 2017 Machine-harvested, relatively low yield per tonne ex slow press cycles, 85% fermented in stainless steel, 15% in French barrels. Very much fruit-driven; even if not particularly complex, very fresh and crisp. Screwcap. 12% alc. **Rating** 90 **To** 2030 $30
Coeur d'Or Rylstone Botrytis Semillon 2018 A pretty snappy botrytis semillon: complex candied fruits and nuts, good acidity. Screwcap. 14% alc. **Rating** 90 **To** 2021 $45
Bluebird Rylstone Botrytis Viognier 2017 Far from a lost cause; marzipan, apricot and spice working well. Screwcap. 10.8% alc. **Rating** 90 **To** 2023 $50

🍷🍷🍷🍷 Le Marquis Rylstone Cabernet Sauvignon 2017 **Rating** 89 **To** 2027 $30

De Bortoli ★★★★★

De Bortoli Road, Bilbul, NSW 2680 **Region** Riverina
T (02) 6966 0100 **www**.debortoli.com.au **Open** Mon–Sat 9–5, Sun 9–4
Winemaker Darren De Bortoli, Julie Mortlock, John Coughlan **Est.** 1928 **Dozens** NFP
Vyds 367ha
Famous among the cognoscenti for its superb Noble One, which in fact accounts for only a tiny part of its total production, this winery turns out low-priced varietal wines that are invariably competently made. They come from estate vineyards, but also from contract-grown grapes. In June 2012 De Bortoli received a $4.8 million grant from the Federal Government's Clean Technology Food and Foundries Investment Program. This grant supported an additional investment of $11 million by the De Bortoli family in their 'Re-engineering Our Future for a Carbon Economy' project. De Bortoli is a founding member of Australia's First Families of Wine. Exports to all major markets.

🍷🍷🍷🍷🍷 Noble One Botrytis Semillon 2017 Golden yellow-orange. De Bortoli has been out on its own with this wine since '82. It's complex, with glace fruits and spices, yet doesn't cloy. Serve fully chilled and wait for the fireworks. Screwcap. 12.5% alc. **Rating** 95 **To** 2022 $36

Regional Classic Tumbarumba Chardonnay 2018 From the Minutello Vineyard, planted '81. The sheer quality of the fruit — and its clearly articulated varietal character — leaves no room for argument; this is priced well below its value. The flavours are ripe even though framed by pink grapefruit, green apple and white peach. Oak? Don't know/don't care. Screwcap. 13% alc. **Rating** 94 **To** 2025 $22 ✪

ⓎⓎⓎⓎⓎ **Regional Classic Gundagai Shiraz 2017 Rating** 93 **To** 2029 $22 ✪
Deen De Bortoli Vat 8 Heathcote Shiraz 2017 Rating 90 **To** 2027 $15 ✪

De Bortoli (Victoria)   ★★★★★

Pinnacle Lane, Dixons Creek, Vic 3775 **Region** Yarra Valley
T (03) 5965 2271 **www.debortoli.com.au Open** 7 days 10–5
Winemaker Stephen Webber, Sarah Fagan, Andrew Bretherton **Est.** 1987
Dozens 350 000 **Vyds** 520ha

Arguably the most successful of all Yarra Valley wineries, not only in terms of the sheer volume of production but also the quality of its wines. It is run by the husband and wife team of Leanne De Bortoli and Steve Webber, but owned by the De Bortoli family. The wines are released in three quality (and price) groups: at the top Single Vineyard, then Estate Grown and in third place Villages. Small volume labels increase the offer with Riorret Single Vineyard Pinot Noir, Melba, La Bohème, an aromatic range of Yarra Valley wines and Vinoque, enabling trials (at the commercial level) of new varieties and interesting blends in the Yarra. The BellaRiva Italian varietal wines are sourced from the King Valley, and Windy Peak from Victorian regions including the Yarra, King Valley and Heathcote. The PHI wines are made from the 7.5ha Lusatia Park Vineyard established by the Shelmerdine family in the Yarra Valley, purchased in November '15, and from Heathcote. Exports to all major markets.

ⓎⓎⓎⓎⓎ **Section A8 Yarra Valley Syrah 2018** This vineyard was planted in '71 in the earliest days of the revival of the Yarra Valley. The bouquet has some fine French oak on parade but the fruit easily accommodates it. A stylish wine of high quality, with a long future for those with patience. Screwcap. 14.2% alc. **Rating** 97 **To** 2031 $55 ✪

ⓎⓎⓎⓎⓎ **Section A7 Yarra Valley Chardonnay 2018** Hand-picked, whole-bunch crushed, natural ferment in older French oak. From a highly rated vintage. Mid-straw. Finely sculpted chardonnay that looks to its site for inspiration, one known for producing wines of a more delicate disposition. Brings together nectarine, quince, lemon, mandarin skin. Serious stuff. A full complement of chardonnay fineness on the palate of almond meal, stone fruits; bitey quince on the finish and acidity everywhere, and nowhere, such is the balance. Screwcap. 12.5% alc. **Rating** 96 **To** 2032 $55 JP ✪

PHI Single Vineyard Yarra Valley Chardonnay 2018 Whole-bunch pressed, wild ferment in used French oak casks. Vegan/vegetarian friendly. An effortless wine of great poise. Fruit, oak and everything else irresistibly entwined. Citrus, yes! It's there in spades. Lemon, grapefruit pith, apple, nectarine and easy on the spice. Filigree acidity. Screwcap. 12.7% alc. **Rating** 96 **To** 2033 $55 JP ✪

PHI Single Vineyard Yarra Valley Pinot Noir 2018 Hand-picked, combination whole berries and whole bunches, 15–20 days maceration, 10 months in new and used barriques. Vegan/vegetarian friendly. A good year, a great vineyard, what's not to like? Lusatia Park fruit in top form here producing a finely structured, supple wine of some distinction. Seamless, too. Plums, red cherry, lavender, cinnamon, hummus earthiness. Goes and goes. Screwcap. 13.5% alc. **Rating** 96 **To** 2032 $55 JP ✪

The Estate Vineyard Dixons Creek Yarra Valley Shiraz 2018 Open-fermented, wild yeast, the fermentation finished and then matured in French oak. An elegant wine in every respect — fruit, oak use, tannin extraction. It caresses the mouth; the finish long. Screwcap. 14% alc. **Rating** 96 **To** 2033 $30 ✪

The Estate Vineyard Dixons Creek Yarra Valley Chardonnay 2018
Hand-picked, whole-bunch pressed, racked to older French oak casks, wild ferment, lees stirred in late autumn and left to rest until late Nov. Mature vines (the oldest were planted in '76) bring an effortless cool to chardonnay's personality. Everything in its place, no angles or points, just beautifully expressive fruit – grapefruit pith, lemon delicious, quince tartness, almond meal texture, baked bread. Seamless. Screwcap. 12.5% alc. **Rating** 95 **To** 2028 $30 JP ✪

Lusatia Chardonnay 2017 Whole-bunch pressed, racked to older French oak casks, wild ferment, lees stirred at end of fermentation and left to rest. Gravity racked to vat for 6 months on fine lees before bottling. From a prized vineyard in the Upper Yarra Valley, Lusatia is a stellar chardonnay beginning to slowly unwind and reveal. The excellent '17 vintage is allowed to shine. Stone fruits, baked apple, grilled grapefruit, mealy. Walks long and fine, freewheeling citrus and orchard fruit. Screwcap. 12.7% alc. **Rating** 95 **To** 2034 $100 JP

Vinoque Yarra Valley Nebbiolo Rose 2019 Hand-picked, whole-bunch pressed, racked to old barriques, wild ferment, 6 weeks lees contact. A step up from La Boheme in price and quality with greater concentration and serious intent. Made using the nebbiolo grape, the flavours move into dusty raspberries, watermelon and earth. Firm to start, it fills out nicely with a textural quality and will meet all challenges food-wise. Screwcap. 12.8% alc. **Rating** 95 **To** 2025 $25 JP ✪

Riorret Lusatia Park Pinot Noir 2018 The De Bortoli winemaking mantra is precise: 'It's harder to do nothing'. The intensity and complexity of the flavours is striking, as is the length. The finer mouthfeel of Upper Yarra fruit is obvious. Diam. 13.5% alc. **Rating** 95 **To** 2030 $45

Riorret The Abbey Pinot Noir 2018 Open ferment, 18 days maceration, matured on fine lees in new and used casks for 10 months. Gravity at all stages. Vegan/vegetarian friendly. Moves in a different circle to its Lusatia Park sibling. The Abbey Vineyard roams the dark side where there is undergrowth and mushrooms on the forest floor. Shades of cranberry, dried flowers, musk, rhubarb to start. Slides into dark and savoury territory from then on. Tight as. Diam. 13.5% alc. **Rating** 95 **To** 2030 $45 JP

Lusatia Yarra Valley Pinot Noir 2017 Hand-picked, fermented in wooden 5t cuves, 15–20% whole bunch, the balance destemmed. Matured in new and used 228l casks for 11 months and a further 6 months on fine lees in vat before bottling. From one of the best Yarra Valley vintages in years, and one of the region's better sites, comes an exceptional pinot noir of concentration and sheer, unabated enjoyment. Black cherry compote, dried flowers, violets, undergrowth. As it opens it becomes more complex and edgy, wild, smoky, tobacco leaf and forest floor. Hedonistic pleasure. Screwcap. 13.5% alc. **Rating** 95 **To** 2034 $120 JP

Section A5 Yarra Valley Chardonnay 2018 Hand-picked, whole-bunch crushed, wild ferment in used French oak casks. Snow peas, grass, dried herbs, preserved lemon. Assertive, almost brash; definitely on the herbal, grapefruit side. Plenty of moving parts yet to come together, but when they do it will be a lovely, streamlined wine. Screwcap. 12.5% alc. **Rating** 94 **To** 2027 $55 JP

The Estate Vineyard Dixons Creek Yarra Valley Pinot Blanc 2019 Hand-picked, fermentation and maturation in used French oak casks for 5 months. Often compared to chardonnay, but this variety has more in common with fiano with its warm textural support. No matter the similarities, the grape is here to stay and definitely of the moment with its approachable citrus, cut pear, spice and pretty florals. Screwcap. 12.7% alc. **Rating** 94 **To** 2026 $30 JP ✪

♟♟♟♟♟ **La Boheme The Missing Act Yarra Valley Cabernet Sauvignon Sangiovese 2017** Rating 93 To 2025 $22 ✪
Villages Heathcote Tempranillo Touriga 2019 Rating 93 To 2029 $22 JP ✪
Rutherglen Estate Fiano 2019 Rating 92 To 2021 $19 ✪
BellaRiva King Valley Fiano 2019 Rating 92 To 2026 $18 JP ✪
BellaRiva King Valley Sangiovese 2015 Rating 92 To 2025 $18 JP ✪

Rutherglen Estate Tempranillo 2018 Rating 92 To 2030 $24 ☻
Vinoque Willoughby Bridge Vineyard Heathcote Fiano e Greco 2019
Rating 91 To 2021
Vinoque Same Same Yarra Valley Pinot Meunier Pinot Noir 2019
Rating 91 To 2026 $25 JP
Villages Yarra Valley Chardonnay 2018 Rating 90 To 2025 $22 JP
La Boheme Act Three Yarra Valley Pinot Gris 2019 Rating 90 To 2020 $22
Rutherglen Estate Arneis 2019 Rating 90 To 2020 $19 ☻
Vinoque Willoughby Bridge Vineyard Heathcote Fiano e Greco 2018
Rating 90 To 2024 $25 JP
La Boheme Act Two Yarra Valley Dry Pinot Noir Rose 2019 Rating 90
To 2025 $22 JP
Rutherglen Estate Shiraz 2018 Rating 90 To 2038 $24

de Capel Wines

101 Majors Lane, Lovedale, NSW 2320 **Region** Hunter Valley
T 0419 994 299 **www.decapelwines.com.au Open** W'ends by appt
Winemaker Daniel Binet **Est.** 2008 **Dozens** 400 **Vyds** 2.2ha
Owners David and Elisabeth Capel's love of wine and a rural life led them to the purchase of
their 11ha property in 2001 at which time the land (previously used for livestock) was mainly
cleared, with small patches of remnant vegetation. It wasn't until '08 that they undertook
major soil improvements, installed all of the vineyard infrastructure and personally planted
2.2ha of semillon and shiraz under the direction of viticulturist Jenny Bright. They say, 'We
are very fortunate to have the support (and muscle) of our close friends and family who put
in an amazing effort every vintage and help us to hand-pick every single shiraz and semillon
grape that we grow'. It precisely follows the early years (1971–77) of Brokenwood.

🍷🍷🍷🍷🍷 **Gabriela Hunter Valley Shiraz 2018** Hand-picked, matured in American
barrels (30% new). Fresh thanks to 3.5pH and 7.2g/l acidity (and 14% alcohol).
Superfine tannins provide texture. Good wine, but what a jewel it could have been
if French oak had been used. Screwcap. **Rating** 92 To 2038 $39

🍷🍷🍷🍷 **Henry Hunter Valley Chardonnay 2019 Rating** 89 To 2022 $25

De Iuliis

1616 Broke Road, Pokolbin, NSW 2320 **Region** Hunter Valley
T (02) 4993 8000 **www.dewine.com.au Open** 7 days 10–5
Winemaker Michael De Iuliis, Shannon Burgess-Moore **Est.** 1990 **Dozens** 15 000
Vyds 30ha
Three generations of the De Iuliis family have been involved in the establishment of the
vineyard. The family acquired a property at Lovedale in 1986 and planted 18ha of vines in
'90, selling the grapes from the first few vintages to Tyrrell's but retaining increasing amounts
for release under the De Iuliis label. In '99 the land on Broke Road was purchased and a
winery and cellar door were built prior to the 2000 vintage. In '11 De Iuliis purchased 12ha
of the long-established Steven Vineyard in Pokolbin. Winemaker Michael De Iuliis completed
postgraduate studies in oenology at the Roseworthy campus of the University of Adelaide
and was a Len Evans Tutorial scholar. He has lifted the quality of the wines into the highest
echelon. Exports to the US, Belgium, Italy, Singapore and China.

🍷🍷🍷🍷🍷 **Hunter Valley Semillon 2019** Perfectly poised and focused; a wine that's in no
hurry, sure of its 20+ year future, offering different focus as it ages. Its constant
characteristic will be its length, built on citrus/herb and crisp, unwavering tannins.
As the years pass, buttered toast, honey and nuts will build. Screwcap. 10.5% alc.
Rating 96 To 2039 $25 ☻
Single Vineyard Hunter Valley Semillon 2019 The lines are taut, the
flavour is pristine. This bristles through the palate in excellent style, its lemon and
lemongrass flavours strung in precise place. It goes without saying that an excellent
future is in store. Screwcap. 10.8% alc. **Rating** 96 To 2040 $30 CM ☻

Hunter Valley Shiraz 2018 From the celebrated '18 vintage, one of the great years in the Hunter Valley over the past 50. Brilliant crimson. The bouquet and palate present endless portraits of shiraz, but in a calm, measured way. Red, blue, purple and black fruits. Screwcap. 14.5% alc. **Rating** 96 **To** 2040 $25 ✪

Steven Vineyard Hunter Valley Shiraz 2018 The Steven Vineyard was planted on red volcanic soil in '68 and rapidly gained a reputation it will never lose. Michael De Iuliis is a talented winemaker with a very good palate and hasn't missed the opportunity with this wine, its slippery, medium-bodied palate full of bright blackberry and dark cherry fruit and a faint touch of fresh Hunter Valley dirt. Screwcap. 14.5% alc. **Rating** 96 **To** 2043 $40 ✪

LDR Vineyard Hunter Valley Shiraz Touriga 2018 An 80/20% blend with exceptional texture to what I term 'squeaky' tannins. The flow of the fruit is complex. The flavours run to the beat of a different drum, earthy and dark and with more conventional structure. Screwcap. 14% alc. **Rating** 96 **To** 2043 $40 ✪

Aged Release Hunter Valley Semillon 2013 Fresher than a daisy in flavour terms but texturally it has softened into satin. It's just at the start of its prime drinking run now, and will hold and develop for a long while yet. It's citrussy, waxy, musky and driven. It's a classic example of 'line and length'. Screwcap. 10.7% alc. **Rating** 95 **To** 2030 $45 CM

Talga Road Vineyard Hunter Valley Shiraz 2018 The fragrant bouquet is very different from that of Steven Vineyard, its structure more full-bodied with the march and retreat of firm tannins, the fruit never defeated. The freshness of the finish and aftertaste is a feature. Screwcap. 14% alc. **Rating** 95 **To** 2038 $40

Limited Release Hunter Valley Shiraz 2018 Smoked tobacco and general wood smoke characters flash through cherry plum and redcurrant-like fruit. Sweet spice and earth notes play roles too, as does fine-grained, toasty tannin. Not a big wine but intricately well crafted and finished. Screwcap. 14.5% alc. **Rating** 95 **To** 2033 $80 CM

LDR Vineyard Hunter Valley Shiraz 2018 LDR stands for Lovedale Road. This is a medium-weighted red with plenty of character. In fact, it's a neat version of character; everything remains nicely folded and tucked. Earth, meat, wood smoke. Jellied citrus and ripe cherry-plum flavours. All the steps are confident. Screwcap. 13.8% alc. **Rating** 94 **To** 2034 $40 CM

ΨΨΨΨΩ **Limited Release Hunter Valley Chardonnay 2018** Rating 93 To 2025 $45 CM
Special Release Sangiovese 2018 Rating 92 To 2025 $25 CM ✪
Hilltops Tempranillo 2018 Rating 90 To 2024 $25 CM

Deakin Estate | Azahara | La La Land   ★★★

Kulkyne Way, via Red Cliffs, Vic 3496 **Region** Murray Darling
T (03) 5018 5555 **www**.deakinestate.com.au **Open** Sunraysia Cellar Door, Mildura
Winemaker Frank Newman, Aidan Menzies **Est.** 1967 **Dozens** 205 000 **Vyds** 350ha
Deakin Estate is owned by the Wingara Wine Group, in turn owned by Freixenet of Spain. Frank Newman has had a long and varied career, starting at Penfolds working alongside Max Schubert, then Angove (for more than a decade) and BRL Hardy at Renmano. The very large production, with an enlarged range of brands, is only part of the story: with other labels produced at the estate, the annual crush of 2500t for Deakin is doubled, as is the production of bottled wines under those other labels. Deakin Estate's extensive range of varietal wines at $10 all offer excellent value for money. Exports to all major markets.

Deep Woods Estate   ★★★★★

889 Commonage Road, Yallingup, WA 6282 **Region** Margaret River
T (08) 9756 6066 **www**.deepwoods.com.au **Open** Wed–Sun 11–5, 7 days during hols
Winemaker Julian Langworthy, Emma Gillespie **Est.** 1987 **Dozens** 30 000 **Vyds** 14ha
Deep Woods Estate is a key part of the dynamic wine business of Peter Fogarty that includes Millbrook in the Perth Hills, Evans & Tate (70% owned), Margaret River Vintners

and extensive vineyard holdings in Wilyabrup and elsewhere in Margaret River, plus in Smithbrook in Pemberton. The business is the largest producer in WA with 600 000 dozen. There is a similar multifaceted stream in Tasmania, with Tasmanian Vintners (a 50/50% deal between Peter and Tasmanian businessman Rod Roberts), the acquisition of the outstanding Lowestoft Vineyard planted in the 1980s with pinot noir in high-density configuration and a 120ha vineyard site at Forcett. Lake's Folly in the Hunter Valley was the first move, Dalwhinnie in the Pyrenees the most recent acquisition. Exports to Germany, Malaysia, Singapore, Japan and China.

Reserve Margaret River Chardonnay 2018 Hand-picked parcels of the best blocks were whole-bunch pressed and fermented in new and used French oak, then a best barrels selection was made. A super elegant wine, fresh and lively; its white peach/grapefruit held in a gentle embrace of oak. Screwcap. 13% alc. Rating 97 To 2030 $50 ✪

Reserve Margaret River Cabernet Sauvignon 2017 Sourced entirely from the original estate vines planted in '87, matured for 18 months in new and used French oak. A wine of immediate power, coupled with the balance to guide it through the decades ahead. The flavours are grounded on blackcurrant and bay leaf, the tannins ripe. Screwcap. 14.5% alc. Rating 97 To 2042 $70 ✪

Yallingup Grand Selection Single Vineyard Margaret River Cabernet Sauvignon 2017 Had 14 days on skins, then straight to barrel (60% new) for 19 months maturation, then a selection of the best barrels. A very expressive and fragrant bouquet sets the hares running for this intense wine sourced from the self-described jewel in Deep Woods' crown. This is a super elegant and pure expression of cabernet with a virtually indefinite future. Screwcap. 14% alc. Rating 97 To 2057 $135 ✪

Margaret River Shiraz et al 2018 'Et al' adds malbec and grenache to the mix. Deep crimson-purple. The most striking feature of the wine is the management of the tannins, which adds to the texture and structure without diminishing the unusual (for Margaret River) array of fruits. Trophy Adelaide Wine Show '19. Screwcap. 14.5% alc. Rating 96 To 2038 $20 ✪

Hillside Margaret River Cabernet Sauvignon 2018 A complex blend, mainly from Yallingup Hills plus a small percentage from Wilyabrup; 92% cabernet sauvignon, 5% merlot and 3% malbec; vinified separately, matured in French oak (20% new) for 16 months. An amazing expression of modern style, in particular, Yallingup. Densely coloured, it explores sombre black fruits, then breaks free and is fresh on the finish. An exceptional bargain. Trophy Best Cabernet Perth Wine Show '19. Screwcap. 14.5% alc. Rating 96 To 2038 $28 ✪

Margaret River Sauvignon Blanc 2019 Some barrel ferment with lees stirring employed, enhancing the texture being the main aim. Abundant varietal expression from go to whoa, with all manner of fruit to be found, ranging from passionfruit and citrus to more tropical aspects like mango and guava. It's ripe and flavoursome on the palate, but there's the crispness of acidity; and yes, it does have texture. Screwcap. 13% alc. Rating 95 To 2022 $20 SC ✪

Hillside Margaret River Chardonnay 2019 Primarily from the southern Margaret River Rowe Road Vineyard; whole-bunch pressed and fermented and aged in French barriques, 20% new. Dials things up a notch from the Estate chardonnay, with an extra degree of richness in the fruit and slightly more oak impact. Outstanding depth and length of flavour with a lingering aftertaste. Screwcap. 12.5% alc. Rating 95 To 2026 $28 SC ✪

Harmony Margaret River Rose 2019 No indication as to the variety or varieties involved here, but no matter, let's just taste the wine. Strawberry, as is often the case with rose, supplies the most obvious fruit character on the bouquet, and you can find watermelon in there as well. It's dry and quite savoury, but juicy as well, and beautifully textured. Good stuff. Screwcap. 13% alc. Rating 95 To 2020 $15 SC ✪

Single Vineyard Margaret River Cabernets 2018 A blend of the Bordeaux varieties (74% cabernet sauvignon, 12% merlot and 7% each of cabernet franc and malbec). In best Deep Woods fashion, makes you wonder what are the most attractive characters/flavours of this fruit-filled luscious wine? The answer is all. Screwcap. Rating 95 To 2038

Margaret River Chardonnay 2019 Shows a level of complexity beyond its dollar value. Citrus and stone fruit lead the way on the bouquet, with some minerality and high quality oak input, nutty and toasty, very neatly integrated. Excellent mouthfeel; flavours also in the grapefruit/white peach/nectarine spectrum; a good measure of acidity providing freshness and length on the palate. Screwcap. 13% alc. Rating 94 To 2026 $20 SC ○

Margaret River Chardonnay 2018 Complex wine, celebrating Margaret River as its birthplace. Fruit (white peach, nectarine and grapefruit), oak (barrel ferment, with toasted cashews and soft toast) and acidity (providing overall balance and length) all joining the party. Yet more celebrations anon. Bargain. Screwcap. 13% alc. Rating 94 To 2025 $20 ○

Margaret River Rose 2019 A blend of tempranillo and shiraz that was largely pressed to tank for fermentation, but a small portion barrel-fermented. Ultra pale salmon-pink; An authoritative wine from start to finish, with a sour cherry and herbal flavour spectrum for a wine that has a very good track record. Screwcap. 13% alc. Rating 94 To 2021 $30 ○

Margaret River Cabernet Sauvignon Merlot 2018 Mostly from the Yallingup Hills, a lesser amount from Wilyabrup and small parcels of malbec and cabernet franc included; 18 months maturation in tight-grained French oak. Red fruit, cedary oak and hints of bay leaf and mint are the main players on the bouquet; the palate quite densely packed with flavour, the tannin firmly in control as it moves towards the finish. Screwcap. 14% alc. Rating 94 To 2030 $35 SC

Single Vineyard Margaret River Cabernet Franc 2019 The first time this wine has appeared in the treasure trove of Deep Woods' portfolio. Time will tell whether it continues but on the evidence of this wine it should do so. The opening stanza is of ripe/rich raspberries, then foresty tannins on the finish. Still getting all of its affairs in order. Screwcap. 14.5% alc. Rating 94 To 2035 $35

ΨΨΨΨΨ **Ivory Semillon Sauvignon Blanc 2019** Rating 91 To 2022 $15 SC ○

del Rios of Mt Anakie   ★★★★☆

2320 Ballan Road, Anakie, Vic 3221 **Region** Geelong
T (03) 5284 1227 **www.**delrios.com.au **Open** W'ends 11–5
Winemaker Gus del Rio **Est.** 1996 **Dozens** 5000 **Vyds** 17ha
Gus del Rio, of Spanish heritage, established a vineyard in 1996 on the slopes of Mt Anakie, northwest of Geelong (chardonnay, pinot noir, cabernet sauvignon, sauvignon blanc, shiraz, merlot and marsanne). The wines are made onsite in the fully equipped winery, which includes a bottling and labelling line able to process over 150t. The Hildegard Aura wines are a joint venture of Gus del Rio, John Durham and Doug Neal. Exports to Hong Kong and China.

ΨΨΨΨΨ **Geelong Marsanne 2012** No information provided but I'd guess the wine was fermented and matured in used French oak. Honeysuckle and crushed citrus leaves and/or pith; it's pure and fresh, with exceptionally good mouthfeel. Screwcap. 13.6% alc. Rating 95 To 2025 $22 ○

Geelong Chardonnay 2017 Hand-picked, whole-bunch pressed, fermented and matured for 10 months in oak. Has good definition, with stone fruit and citrus contributing to the long palate. Very different, and better than, its Reserve sibling. Screwcap. 13.5% alc. Rating 94 To 2029 $28 ○

ΨΨΨΨΨ **Geelong Rose 2019** Rating 93 To 2021
Geelong Cabernet Sauvignon 2015 Rating 92 To 2035
Carmen King Valley Tempranillo 2016 Rating 90 To 2024 $25

Delamere Vineyards ★★★★★

Bridport Road, Pipers Brook, Tas 7254 **Region** Northern Tasmania
T (03) 6382 7190 **www**.delamerevineyards.com.au **Open** 7 days 10–5
Winemaker Shane Holloway, Fran Austin **Est.** 1982 **Dozens** 5000 **Vyds** 13.5ha
Delamere was one of the first vineyards planted in the Pipers Brook area. It was purchased by
Shane Holloway and wife Fran Austin and their families in 2007. Shane and Fran are in charge
of viticulture and winemaking. The vineyard has been expanded with 4ha of pinot noir and
chardonnay. Exports to China.

♟♟♟♟♟ **Block 3 Chardonnay 2016** Wow – what a harmonious wine. Superfine and
long with layers of flavour comprising white stone fruit, lemon rind, ginger spice
and beautifully handled oak that adds just the right amount of seasoning. Although
it has a savoury drive to it with a hint of leesy complexity, it remains ultra-fresh
and satisfying. This is something very special. Alas, a mere 510 bottles produced.
Diam. 13.1% alc. **Rating** 97 **To** 2026 $110 JF ✪

♟♟♟♟♟ **Pinot Noir 2017** This offers glorious aromas of raspberries, florals, damp forest
floor and charcuterie all pointing to a complex wine. And it delivers on the palate
with cherries and pips, lacy fine tannins and cleansing, tangy acidity. Finesse in a
glass. Screwcap. 13.6% alc. **Rating** 96 **To** 2026 $50 JF ✪
Blanc de Blancs 2013 Whole-bunch pressed grapes, wild-fermented and full
mlf, tiraged Oct '13, 5 years on lees before disgorgement. It is riveting and racy,
with spice and brioche notes balanced – and lengthened – by lemony acidity.
It has the capacity to age for another 5 years for those seeking complexity, not
freshness. Diam. 13% alc. **Rating** 96 $60 ✪
Cuvee NV A pinot noir chardonnay blend plus a generous proportion of reserve
wine. Traditional method provides excellent mouthfeel, yet leaves the fruit flavours
untouched and the length intact. Diam. 13.4% alc. **Rating** 96 $35 ✪
Chardonnay 2018 Hand-picked, whole-bunch pressed, fermented in
Burgundian-coopered oak. Harmony and balance are the keywords for this lovely
Tasmanian chardonnay. White stone fruit, apple and grapefruit are gently kissed
by French oak, leaving the finish fresh and clear. Screwcap. 13.3% alc. **Rating** 95
To 2026 $50
Chardonnay 2017 A wine of substance; it comes together seamlessly. Stone fruit,
lemon peel, leesy and nutty nuances, the oak neatly integrated and adding more
complex spice notes. Fuller-bodied, and some funky sulphides add to the overall
pleasure of drinking this. Screwcap. 13.5% alc. **Rating** 95 **To** 2027 $50 JF
Rose 2019 Very pale pastel pink. It's a lovely rose, vibrant and lively with red
berries. Tangy lemon acidity is the driver yet it is textural and detailed. Screwcap.
12.5% alc. **Rating** 95 **To** 2022 $30 JF ✪
Hurlo's Rose 2017 This is a rose with serious intent – made from pinot noir, it
spent 10 months in French oak with a whopping 50% new, not that you would
know it. It is in the savoury spectrum yet still has hints of red berries, lemon
zest and ginger spice. Textural, tangy, complex, detailed and satisfying. Screwcap.
13.5% alc. **Rating** 95 **To** 2025 $80 JF
Pinot Noir 2018 Typical pale red, equally typically misleads with its implication
of light varietal expression. This is an intense wine, with rose petals and wild
strawberries amid wafts of forest floor. Screwcap. 13.4% alc. **Rating** 95 **To** 2029
$50
Rose NV Pale salmon-pink. It is 100% pinot noir, traditional method, no details
of tirage/dosage. It manages to have both worlds at its feet: finesse and red fruits
on the one hand, creamy texture on the other. Diam. 13.2% alc. **Rating** 95 $35 ✪

♟♟♟♟♟ **Naissante Pinot Noir 2018 Rating** 91 **To** 2028 $30

Delatite

390 Pollards Road, Mansfield, Vic 3722 **Region** Upper Goulburn
T (03) 5775 2922 **www.**delatitewinery.com.au **Open** 7 days 10–5
Winemaker Andy Browning **Est.** 1982 **Dozens** 16 000 **Vyds** 27.25ha

With its sweeping views across to the snow-clad alps, this is uncompromising cool-climate viticulture. Increasing vine age (the earlier plantings were between 1968–82, others between '84–2011) and the adoption of organic (and partial biodynamic) viticulture, have also played a role in providing the red wines with more depth and texture. The white wines are as good as ever. All are wild-yeast fermented. In '11 Vestey Holdings Limited, the international pastoral giant, acquired a majority holding in Delatite and has said it represents one of 'what we hope will be a number of agricultural businesses here'. Exports to Japan and China.

ŸŸŸŸŸ **Catherine's Block Reserve Gewurztraminer 2019** This is a truly exceptional wine. Lacy acidity curtails the variety's inherent tendency towards excess. The usual cavalcade of exotica is present: tropical fruits, orange blossom and honeysuckle. Yet the overall impression is of great finesse and uncanny refinement. This is already a delicious wine, with moderate ageing to deliver even greater complexity. Among the finest dessert wines from this country. Screwcap. **Rating** 97 **To** 2027 $30 NG ✪

ŸŸŸŸŸ **Late Harvest Riesling 2019** Riesling is truly this estate's tour de force. Lime cordial, tonic, grapefruit and other citrus fruit allusions stream across pumice and wet rocky mineral tension, sublimating sweetness to the point of palpable dryness. This is very fine. Balletic, even. Vibrant but juicy. Nothing brittle. Streamlined and long. Delicious. Screwcap. **Rating** 96 **To** 2034 $28 NG ✪

Deadman's Hill Gewurztraminer 2018 A pioneer with this variety, the estate has really lifted its game. Once, aromatics were too often sacrificed to retain freshness. The result may have been higher acidity, but the phenolics were ropy and the exuberance was lost. Not any more. A resinous yellow segues to punchy notes of rosewater, lychee and orange blossom. Ginger, even. Dutifully fresh but, more importantly, texturally detailed with sound use of oak. Long and eminently satisfying. Among the national benchmarks. Screwcap. **Rating** 95 **To** 2024 $28 NG ✪

Pinot Gris 2019 This is an exceptional gris, a harbinger of a style that is increasingly versatile at the table and reflective of this country's more sophisticated dining culture. These mid-weighted highly textural wines are founded, too, in greater winemaking expertise: ambient yeast and neutral wood. After all, gris does not need too much embellishment, but the confidence to allow baked autumnal fruit notes to ease across gentle phenolics. This does so in style. Screwcap. **Rating** 95 **To** 2025 $28 NG ✪

Vivienne's Block Reserve Riesling 2019 Hand-picked across an esteemed 49yo block, this cuvee is only made in exceptional years. Delicate of weight and sublimely finessed, belying an intensity of flavour that grows in the glass: grapefruit, quince, apricot and lemon zest. The acidity is relaxed and gently talcy. This will develop with patience, despite its understated nature at present. Screwcap. **Rating** 94 **To** 2039 $49 NG

ŸŸŸŸŸ **Riesling 2019 Rating** 93 **To** 2029 $28 NG
Sauvignon Blanc 2019 Rating 93 **To** 2023 $28 NG
Polly's Block Reserve Chardonnay 2017 Rating 93 **To** 2032 $49 NG
Dungeon Gully Malbec Merlot 2017 Rating 93 **To** 2023 $35 NG
Tempranillo 2018 Rating 92 **To** 2024 $35 NG
Mansfield Blend 2017 Rating 91 **To** 2022 $28 NG
Tempranillo Rose 2019 Rating 91 **To** 2020 $28 NG
Pinot Noir 2018 Rating 91 **To** 2026 $35 NG
Yarra Chardonnay 2017 Rating 90 **To** 2026 NG
High Ground Shiraz 2018 Rating 90 **To** 2024 NG

Delinquente Wine Co

31 Drayton Street, Bowden, SA 5007 **Region** Riverland
T 0437 876 407 **www**.delinquentewineco.com **Open** By appt
Winemaker Con-Greg Grigoriou **Est.** 2013 **Dozens** 7000
A Hollywood actress once said, 'I don't care what they say about me as long as they spell my name right'. Con-Greg Grigoriou might say, 'I don't care how bad people think my wine labels are as long as they remember them'. Con-Greg grew up on a vineyard in the Riverland and spent a lot of time in wineries with his father and grandfather. He has decided to concentrate on southern Italian grape varieties. It's a virtual winery operation, buying fruit from growers who share his vision and having the wine made wherever he is able to find a facility prepared to assist in the making of micro-quantities. Delinquente is getting a lot of airplay from the smart set, and it's no surprise to see production jump from 600 to 7000 dozen. Exports to the UK, the US, Canada, South Korea, Singapore, Japan, Taiwan, Hong Kong and NZ.

Roxanne the Razor Riverland Negroamaro Nero d'Avola 2019 A blend of negroamaro and nero d'Avola that's as bright and breezy as a summer's day. A focus on juicy and tangy red fruits infused with Mediterranean herbs; easy tannins add some grip on the finish alongside vibrant acidity. Could be chilled in warm weather. Screwcap. 13% alc. **Rating** 91 **To** 2023 $25 JF
The Bullet Dodger Riverland Montepulciano 2019 Works off a dark cherry theme with kirsch and fruit compote spiced with cinnamon and fresh herbs. Some meaty reduction adds to the appeal. Lively and juicy with enough tannin to keep one's interest beyond a glass. Screwcap. 13.2% alc. **Rating** 90 **To** 2024 $25 JF

Dell'uva Wines

15 Murray Street, Greenock, SA 5360 **Region** Barossa Valley
T (08) 8562 8297 **www**.delluvawines.com.au **Open** Sun–Thurs 10–5.30, Sat 10–7
Winemaker Wayne Farquhar **Est.** 2014 **Dozens** 500 **Vyds** 20ha
Owner and winemaker Wayne Farquhar moved from horticulture to viticulture, acquiring his first vineyard in 1979. His viticultural career was low-key for a number of years, but having tasted wines from all over the world during a decade of business travel, he decided to establish Dell'uva Wines off the back of his existing (conventional) vineyard on the western ridge of the Barossa Valley. In short order he established small plots of an A–Z of varieties: aglianico, albarino, ansonica, arinto, barbera, cabernet sauvignon, canaiolo nero, carmenere, carnelian, chardonnay, dolcetto, durif, fiano, freisca, garnacha, graciano, grillo, lagrein, merlot, marsanne, mencia, montepulciano, moscato bianco, mourvedre, negroamaro, nero d'Avola, pinot blanc, pinot grigio, pinot noir, primitivo, roussanne, sagrantino, sangiovese, saperavi, shiraz, tannat, tempranillo, touriga nacional, verdelho, vermentino, verdicchio and viognier. With only 20ha available, the production of each wine is limited, the vinification as unconventional as the vineyard mix, utilising barrels, ceramic eggs, demijohns and tanks. The winemaking techniques throw maximum attention onto the inherent quality of the varieties, and this story has a long way to run. Exports to China.

Eliza Shiraz 2015 High octane, melding a razor's edge of volatility with sapid cherry-chocolate fruit scents. Bristling with tang, this cuvee somehow works if given the right map at the table: rich meats, blue cheeses or dark bitter chocolate. Screwcap. **Rating** 89 **To** 2022 $40 NG

Denton Viewhill Vineyard

Viewhill Vineyard, 160 Old Healesville Road, Yarra Glen, Vic 3775 **Region** Yarra Valley
T 0402 346 686 **www**.dentonwine.com **Open** By appt
Winemaker Luke Lambert **Est.** 1997 **Dozens** 2500 **Vyds** 31.3ha
Leading Melbourne architect John Denton and son Simon began the establishment of the vineyard with a first stage planting in 1997, completing the plantings in 2004. The name Viewhill derives from the fact that a granite plug 'was created 370 million years ago, sitting above the surrounding softer sandstones and silt of the valley'. This granite base is most unusual in the Yarra Valley and, together with the natural amphitheatre that the plug created,

has consistently produced exceptional grapes. The principal varieties planted are pinot noir, chardonnay and shiraz, with lesser quantities of nebbiolo, cabernet sauvignon, merlot, cabernet franc and petit verdot. Exports to Japan and Hong Kong.

ΨΨΨΨΨ **Denton Shed Chardonnay 2019** The bouquet is unremarkable; the palate the opposite, instantly filling the mouth with ripe white peach, nectarine and a hint of custard apple. Citrussy acidity rounds off the long palate. Screwcap. 13% alc. **Rating** 95 **To** 2029 $30 ✪

Yarra Valley Pinot Noir 2017 A wine that has all the complexity provided by the cool vintage. Buzzing with complex aromas of forest floor and its inhabitants, of rose petals, spices, wild raspberries – almost but not quite ripe – and fine tannins. Diam. 13% alc. **Rating** 95 **To** 2027 $45

Nebbiolo 2016 This is a very good nebbiolo with good colour, bright red and blue fruits and no aggressive tannins. It also has a savoury/silky subtext to its long palate. Diam. 14% alc. **Rating** 95 **To** 2038 $48

Denton Shed Nebbiolo Rose 2019 From the most recent plantings of new clones; whole-bunch pressed, wild-fermented in old oak. Salmon-pink. Very complex juicy red fruits on a carpet of savoury spices. Screwcap. 12.5% alc. **Rating** 94 **To** 2021 $30 ✪

ΨΨΨΨΨ **Denton Shed Pinot Noir 2019** **Rating** 93 **To** 2030 $30

Deviation Road

207 Scott Creek Road, Longwood, SA 5153 **Region** Adelaide Hills
T (08) 8339 2633 **www**.deviationroad.com **Open** 7 days 10–5
Winemaker Kate Laurie **Est.** 1999 **Dozens** 10 000 **Vyds** 11.05ha
Continuing a five-generation family winemaking tradition, Hamish and Kate Laurie created their first wine (Pinot Noir) from the 30-year-old Laurie family-owned vineyard on Deviation Road in 2002. In '04 Hamish and Kate purchased their property at Longwood, which is the current home to 4ha of shiraz and pinot noir, the winery and tasting room. Disgorging equipment from Kate's family's Manjimup winery, originally imported from Champagne, was shipped to the Adelaide Hills in '08 enabling the first Deviation Road traditional method sparkling wine release. Hamish and Kate consistently produce wines that represent the cool-climate terroir of the Adelaide Hills. Exports to the UK, the US and Hong Kong.

ΨΨΨΨΨ **Mary's Reserve Adelaide Hills Shiraz 2017** Mostly whole berry–open fermented, 12% coming from a 100% whole-bunch ferment; 16 months in French oak (30% new). Light to medium-bodied but buzzing with red berry flavour and texture highlights. Some may question the wine's insouciant mouthfeel, but I enjoy it. Screwcap. 13.5% alc. **Rating** 95 **To** 2027 $45

Southcote Adelaide Hills Blanc de Noirs 2017 From 100% pinot noir clone D2V5; hand-picked, whole-bunch pressed, disgorged Oct '19, 8g/l dosage. The Deviation Road sparkling wines are, of course, traditional method. The palest salmon. It has very good texture and grip, the dosage nigh on perfect for a blanc de noirs with its dry characters. Diam. 12.5% alc. **Rating** 95 $55

Beltana Adelaide Hills Blanc de Blancs 2013 Given another 12 months on lees since tasted by Ned Goodwin and seems every bit as fresh as it was when he wrote: 'This expansive, rich wine has spent an extended 5 years on lees, which for me, considering the acid levels, pH and fruit ripeness even in cooler Australian zones, seems just about the maximum level of ambition. A fully loaded nose oozes toasted nuts, marzipan, spiced quince and tarte tatin flavours across a creamy, broad-shouldered core of nourishment. This stains the cheeks and swoons the nose.' Diam. 12.5% alc. **Rating** 95 $100

Altair Adelaide Hills Brut Rose NV A blend of pinot noir and chardonnay grown at Lenswood and Piccadilly Valley, 80% from '17. Hand-picked, whole-bunch pressed, largely fermented in tank, a small percentage of pinot made as a red wine. Delicious rose, with small red fruits/berries, and a supple mouthfeel. Bargain. Cork. 12.5% alc. **Rating** 95 $35 ✪

Adelaide Hills Chardonnay 2018 A well made chardonnay, all the inputs skilfully handled. Fermentation and 6 months maturation in used French barrels works well with the medium-weight fruit; natural citrussy acidity a feature. Screwcap. 12.5% alc. **Rating** 94 **To** 2026 $45

Adelaide Hills Pinot Gris 2019 Hand-picked fruit fermented with wild and cultured yeast, 30% in aged French oak. Unmistakable varietal aromas of ripe pear and red apple, like the scents in an autumn orchard. A beautifully textured wine, the oaked component playing its part no doubt, enhancing the natural gris mouthfeel. Freshness, length of flavour and fine acidity all positives as well. Screwcap. 12.5% alc. **Rating** 94 **To** 2022 $30 SC ✪

Adelaide Hills Pinot Noir 2018 The accent is on plums and ripe notes of spice and tannin moving through on the finish and aftertaste. Screwcap. 13% alc. **Rating** 94 **To** 2028 $45

Loftia Adelaide Hills Vintage Brut 2017 A 60/40% pinot noir/chardonnay base; hand-picked, whole-bunch pressed, 24 months on tirage, 8g/l dosage, disgorged Oct '19. The pinot shows in the palate. Kate Laurie hasn't forgotten her studies in Champagne. This is elegant, but not at the cost of character. Diam. 12.5% alc. **Rating** 94 $48

♥♥♥♥♀ **Adelaide Hills Pinot Noir 2019 Rating** 91 **To** 2027 $45

Devil's Cave Vineyard   ★★★★☆

250 Forest Drive, Heathcote, Vic 3523 **Region** Heathcote
T 0438 110 183 **www**.devilscavevineyard.com **Open** By appt
Winemaker Luke Lomax, Steve Johnson **Est.** 2012 **Dozens** 1200 **Vyds** 0.4ha
This is an acorn and oak story. After retiring from 40+ years of business in Heathcote, Steve and Gay Johnson purchased a property to enjoy their retirement. In 2010 they planted 0.4ha of shiraz, and in '12 Steve asked Luke Lomax (his niece's husband and a winemaker at Yabby Lake and Heathcote Estate) to help with the first vintage of 33 dozen bottles. The camaraderie was such that the Johnsons formed a partnership with Luke and Jade Lomax, and it's been onwards and upwards since, with an impressive collection of gold and silver medals for the Shiraz. The winery's name comes from an adjacent cave known locally as the Devil's Cave. Exports to Thailand.

♥♥♥♥♀ **Devil's Baie Pinot Gris 2019** An inviting and refreshing wine with spiced poached pears and red apple. Quite tight and racy although there's some texture woven through. Simple yet pleasant. Screwcap. 13% alc. **Rating** 90 **To** 2022 $25 JF

♥♥♥♥ **Heathcote Shiraz 2018 Rating** 89 **To** 2027 $36 JF

Devil's Corner   ★★★★☆

The Hazards Vineyard, Sherbourne Road, Apslawn, Tas 7190 **Region** East Coast Tasmania
T (03) 6257 8881 **www**.devilscorner.com.au **Open** 7 days 10–5
Winemaker Tom Wallace, Anthony De Amicas **Est.** 1999 **Dozens** 70 000 **Vyds** 190ha
This is one of the separately managed operations of Brown Brothers' Tasmanian interests, taking The Hazards Vineyard on the east coast as its chief source – it is planted to pinot noir, chardonnay, sauvignon blanc, pinot gris, riesling, gewurztraminer and savagnin. The avant-garde labels mark a decided change from the past and also distinguish Devil's Corner from the other Tasmanian activities of Brown Brothers. Exports to all major markets.

♥♥♥♥♥ **Mt Amos Pinot Noir 2017** A wine of exceptional length and intensity, its varietal character ablaze with finely articulated fruit spices and lingering tannins. Has blossomed since first tasted in Jan '19, but has an even brighter future for patient pinot lovers. Screwcap. 13% alc. **Rating** 95 **To** 2027 $65

Resolution Pinot Gris 2019 Intensity and personality, a great deal of both. Here's a gris to crow about. It has a sweet edge and plenty of acid drive. Apple, nectarine, lychee, musk and lime. Brings the room to life. Lovely wine. Screwcap. 14% alc. **Rating** 94 **To** 2023 $34 CM

ŢŢŢŢŢ Sauvignon Blanc 2019 Rating 93 To 2022 $20 CM ✪
Resolution Pinot Noir 2018 Rating 93 To 2029 $34 CM
Chardonnay 2018 Rating 92 To 2024 $22 CM ✪
Riesling 2019 Rating 91 To 2025 $20 CM ✪
Resolution Riesling 2019 Rating 91 To 2026 $34 CM

Devil's Lair ★★★★★

Rocky Road, Forest Grove via Margaret River, WA 6286 **Region** Margaret River
T (08) 9759 2000 **www**.devils-lair.com **Open** Not
Winemaker Ben Miller, Matt Godfrey **Est.** 1990 **Dozens** NFP
Having rapidly carved out a high reputation for itself through a combination of clever
packaging and impressive wine quality, Devil's Lair was acquired by Southcorp in 1996. The
estate vineyards have been substantially increased since, now with sauvignon blanc, semillon,
chardonnay, cabernet sauvignon, merlot, shiraz, cabernet franc and petit verdot, supplemented
by grapes purchased from contract growers. Production has increased from 40000 dozen
to many times greater, largely due to its Fifth Leg and Dance with the Devil wines. Exports to
the UK, the US and other major markets.

ŢŢŢŢŢ Margaret River Cabernet Sauvignon 2018 Top class, young cabernet
sauvignon can have a hauteur, a reserve, an arrogance driven by its self-
acknowledged excellent and layered power. You don't have to like it, but you do
need to respect it – and be confident that in 15–20 years' time it will sweep all
before it. This is such a wine. Screwcap. 14% alc. **Rating** 97 To 2038 $50 ✪

ŢŢŢŢŢ Margaret River Chardonnay 2019 Fermented and matured in French
barriques (40% new) for 9 months. Precise and focused on high quality fruit
picked early to preserve natural acidity. Stone fruit and pink grapefruit easily deal
with the oak. It's a style that is well established, less baroque than many, working
on the less-is-more principle. Screwcap. 13% alc. **Rating** 95 To 2032
Dance with the Devil Margaret River Chardonnay 2018 No question, this
is a very smart chardonnay. Partial wild ferment and the use of large-format oak
have held a light up to the quality of the wine. Its length and balance are spot on;
the pink grapefruit and white peach add another layer to dance with. Exceptional.
Screwcap. 13.5% alc. **Rating** 95 To 2028 $25 ✪
Margaret River Chardonnay 2018 High quality estate-grown fruit is the
foundation of the wine; mature vines a part of the story. The flavours encompass
white peach, nectarine and cashew in a stream of citrussy acidity. Screwcap.
13% alc. **Rating** 94 To 2026 $50

ŢŢŢŢŢ The Hidden Cave Margaret River Cabernet Shiraz 2017 Rating 93
To 2029 $24 ✪
Dance with the Devil Margaret River Cabernet Sauvignon 2018
Rating 92 To 2030 $25 ✪
The Hidden Cave Margaret River Chardonnay 2018 Rating 91 To 2023 $24

Dewey Station Wines ★★★☆

14 Jane Street, Smithfield, SA 5114 **Region** Barossa Valley
T 0476 100 245 **www**.deweystationwines.com.au **Open** Not
Winemaker Stefan Dewey **Est.** 2017 **Dozens** 620
This micro-business will grow, but by exactly how much and when depends on your vision
of the glass – I say it's half full. Winemaker Stefan Dewey has covered a lot of ground since
2007, all within the Barossa Valley. He worked in retail, distribution and marketing (enrolling
in the wine marketing course at the University of Adelaide) before taking the ultimate step of
beginning to make wine. He and wife Eleanor share a conviction that wine should be shared
with friends and lots of laughter. Boring, it should not be. But there has to be a limit, and I'll
declare my hand by saying the label designs and production names will only ever gain niche
market shares. But, of course, if you establish that niche, demand drawing supply, the game
changes. A small quantity is exported to the UK and Japan.

ΨΨΨΨ **Moonglow Barossa Valley Grenache Rose 2019** From 70yo vines; some skin contact giving the pale pink hue; 50/50% fermentation in used oak and stainless steel. Sweetness ex the deliberate stop to fermentation was overdone. Screwcap. 12.5% alc. **Rating** 89 **To** 2021 $20

The Mars Express Barossa Shiraz 2019 50% from the Scholz Estate in Ebenezer, 50% from Leon Koch in Altona, 28% whole bunch, matured for 8 months in French oak (10% new). Has balance and, of course, complexity. There is increasing interest in the softening impact of whole-bunch fermentation; plenty to dwell on over a glass or two. Screwcap. 14.5% alc. **Rating** 89 **To** 2029 $25

Venus Express Barossa GSM Grenache Shiraz Mataro 2019 A complex blend even when simplified thus: 77% grenache, 21% shiraz, 2% mataro; 27% whole bunch, 3.5% new oak, 8 months maturation. There's an abundance of red, blue, purple and black fruits, and no tannins or oak to fight with. Sheer simple drinking, no need for patience. Screwcap. 14.5% alc. **Rating** 89 **To** 2025 $25

Off The Beaten Track Barossa Graciano 2019 Hmmm. Destemmed, not crushed, 30% in new oak for 6 weeks, pressed at 3° baume, a mix of new and used oak. Savoury/sweet or vice versa. Screwcap. 14% alc. **Rating** 89 **To** 2024 $25

Dexter Wines

210 Foxeys Road, Tuerong, Vic 3915 (postal) **Region** Mornington Peninsula
T (03) 5989 7007 **www**.dexterwines.com.au **Open** Not
Winemaker Tod Dexter **Est.** 2006 **Dozens** 1200 **Vyds** 7.1ha
Tod Dexter travelled to the US with the intention of enjoying some skiing; having done that, he became an apprentice winemaker at Cakebread Cellars, a well known Napa Valley establishment. After seven years he returned to Australia and the Mornington Peninsula, and began the establishment of his vineyard in 1987; planted to pinot noir (4ha) and chardonnay (3.1ha). To keep the wolves from the door he became winemaker at Stonier and leased his vineyard to them. Having left Stonier to become the Yabby Lake winemaker, and spurred on by turning 50 in 2006 (and at the urging of friends), he and wife Debbie established the Dexter label. The quality of his wines has been impeccable, the Pinot Noir especially so. Exports to the UAE and Japan.

ΨΨΨΨΨ Mornington Peninsula Pinot Noir 2018 The perfumed blossom scents of the bouquet are signals not to be missed because of the light, clear colour. The wine builds progressively as it journeys through the mouth to the lifted finish. Screwcap. 14% alc. **Rating** 95 **To** 2029 $60

Mornington Peninsula Chardonnay 2018 Advanced colour for its age, albeit with no visible hint of brown, just luscious, mouthfilling chardonnay flavours; white peach, rockmelon and zesty acidity are mouth-watering. Screwcap. 13.5% alc. **Rating** 94 **To** 2027 $40

Di Sciascio Family Wines

2 Pincott Street, Newtown, Vic 3220 **Region** Victoria
T 0417 384 272 **www**.dsaswines.com.au **Open** Not
Winemaker Matthew Di Sciascio, Andrew Santarossa **Est.** 2012 **Dozens** 3000
Matthew Di Sciascio's journey through wine has been an odyssey of Homeric proportions. His working life began as an apprentice boilermaker in his father's business. In 1991 he accompanied his father on a trip to Italy, where a shared bottle of wine in the kitchen of his uncle's house sowed the seed that flowered back in Australia. After helping his father and friends with garage winemaking, the vinous pace increased in '97 with vineyard work in the Yarra Valley and enrolment in Dookie Agricultural College's viticultural course. It accelerated further with the establishment of Bellbrae Estate in Geelong and enrolling (in 2002) in the new Deakin University wine and science degree, graduating in '05 as co-dux. In Dec '10 the responsibility for seriously ill parents and a young daughter led to the decision to sell his share of Bellbrae to his financial partners, and (in '12) to start this venture.

♟♟♟♟♟ D'Sas Heathcote Sangiovese 2018 A blend of Brunello and Chianti clones, this is among the finest renditions of this fecund and capricious variety I have yet tasted on domestic shores. A dark mottled ruby; it looks the part. The nose is restrained with but a hint of dark cherry, tar and anise. The tannins are firm and frisky, boasting strong fidelity to the archetype. The grip is the schtick. This is what sangiovese does. Put it with food, sit back and let this take you on a textural journey. Screwcap. **Rating** 95 **To** 2023 $40 NG

♟♟♟♟♟ D'Sas Pinot Gris 2019 **Rating** 92 **To** 2024 $32 NG
D'Sas Heathcote Shiraz 2018 **Rating** 91 **To** 2026 $40 NG
D'Sas King Valley Prosecco 2019 **Rating** 90 $32 NG

Dickinson Estate ★★★★★

2414 Cranbrook Road, Boyup Brook, WA 6244 **Region** Blackwood Valley
T (08) 9769 1080 **www.dickinsonestate.com.au Open** Not
Winemaker Coby Ladwig, Luke Eckersley **Est.** 1994 **Dozens** 6000 **Vyds** 8.52ha
Trevor and Mary Dickinson went from a 20-year life at sea with the Australian Navy to becoming farmers at Boyup Brook in 1987. They learned on the job, initially cropping and breeding sheep for wool, then cattle and fat lambs. In '94 they diversified further, planting shiraz, chardonnay, sauvignon blanc and cabernet sauvignon, and appointing the highly experienced team of Coby Ladwig and Luke Eckersley to make the wines. Exports to the UK and China.

♟♟♟♟♟ Limited Release Blackwood Valley Cabernet Sauvignon 2018 As with the Single Vineyard wine, the varietal character is on show, but here the new oak seems a little more prominent – this is an observation, not a criticism. It's a smooth and polished expression of youthful cabernet with good depth of fruit in the soft and sweetish vein of the winery style. Well integrated tannin provides structure without being too obvious. Screwcap. 14.6% alc. **Rating** 93 **To** 2028 $40 SC
Limited Release Blackwood Valley Shiraz 2018 Almost identical winemaking to the Single Vineyard wine, but with a slightly longer fermentation and a higher percentage (35%) of new oak. Unsurprisingly it shares similar qualities to its sibling, but there's just a bit more of everything: the colour is deeper; there's an extra degree of richness to the fruit; and the oak contribution is dialled up a notch. Screwcap. 14.5% alc. **Rating** 92 **To** 2028 $40 SC
Single Vineyard Blackwood Valley Sauvignon Blanc 2019 Had 6 hours skin contact in the press, and 4 months on fine lees with weekly stirring. Shows light but authentic varietal aromas on the bouquet with some green herb and mineral (or maybe lees) characters most prominent. It's a similar theme on the palate with mouthfeel rather than volume of flavour carrying it through, and freshness on the finish a positive. Screwcap. 12.9% alc. **Rating** 90 **To** 2022 $18 SC ✪
Single Vineyard Blackwood Valley Cabernet Sauvignon 2018 No mistaking the variety as you smell this wine. Aromas of blackcurrant, mint, cedar and some green leafy character (not Margaret River bay leaf) on display. Smoothly textured through the palate with an even spread of flavours that reflect the bouquet, and soft tannin to finish. Screwcap. 14.4% alc. **Rating** 90 **To** 2025 $25 SC

♟♟♟♟ Single Vineyard Blackwood Valley Shiraz 2018 **Rating** 89 **To** 2025 $25 SC

DiGiorgio Family Wines ★★★★☆

14918 Riddoch Highway, Coonawarra, SA 5263 **Region** Coonawarra
T (08) 8736 3222 **www.digiorgio.com.au Open** 7 days 10–5
Winemaker Peter Douglas, Bryan Tonkin **Est.** 1998 **Dozens** 25 000 **Vyds** 353.53ha
Stefano DiGiorgio emigrated from Abruzzo, Italy in 1952. Over the years, he and his family gradually expanded their holdings at Lucindale to 126ha. In '89 he began planting cabernet

sauvignon, chardonnay, merlot, shiraz and pinot noir. In 2002 the family purchased the historic Rouge Homme winery and its surrounding 13.5ha of vines from Southcorp. The plantings have since been increased to almost 230ha, the lion's share to cabernet sauvignon. The enterprise offers full winemaking services to vignerons in the Limestone Coast zone. Exports to all major markets.

ΨΨΨΨΨ **Kongorong Riesling 2019** The freshness here is to be devoured, it is so zesty and clean. Is this going to be the white grape variety for the emerging Mount Gambier wine region? This little beauty is a good indication. Pale straw hue. Lemon sherbet brightness on the bouquet with lime zest, spring blossom and apple spice, nougat. Shades of honeysuckle, Pink Lady apple and that arresting zestiness on the palate that endures. Enhanced by precision acidity and hints of Germanic-style spice. Screwcap. 11.5% alc. **Rating** 95 **To** 2031 $20 JP ✪

ΨΨΨΨΨ **Coonawarra Chardonnay 2017 Rating** 93 **To** 2029 $29 JP
Dolcetto Rose 2019 Rating 93 **To** 2024 $20 JP ✪
Kongorong Pinot Noir 2016 Rating 93 **To** 2026 $29 JP
Coonawarra Shiraz 2016 Rating 93 **To** 2031 $29 JP
Lucindale Limestone Coast Botrytis Semillon 2018 Rating 93 **To** 2026 JP
Kongorong Riesling 2018 Rating 92 **To** 2035 $20 JP ✪
Coonawarra Chardonnay 2018 Rating 92 **To** 2029 $29 JP
Coonawarra Cabernet Sauvignon 2016 Rating 92 **To** 2032 $29 JP
Traditional Method Blanc de Blanc 2017 Rating 92 $35 JP
Coonawarra Sparkling Merlot 2016 Rating 92 $29 JP
Montepulciano 2016 Rating 91 **To** 2026 $25 JP
Lucindale Pinot Noir Chardonnay NV Rating 91 $20 JP ✪

Dinny Goonan   ★★★★★

880 Winchelsea-Deans Marsh Road, Bambra, Vic 3241 **Region** Geelong
T 0438 408 420 **www.**dinnygoonan.com.au **Open** Jan 7 days, Nov–Jun w'ends
Winemaker Dinny Goonan, Angus Goonan **Est.** 1990 **Dozens** 1500 **Vyds** 5.5ha
The genesis of Dinny Goonan dates back to 1988, when Dinny bought a 20ha property near Bambra, in the hinterland of the Otway Coast. Dinny had recently completed a viticulture diploma at CSU and initially a wide range of varieties was planted in what is now known as the Nursery Block, to establish those best suited to the area. As these came into production Dinny headed back to CSU, where he completed a wine science degree. Production is focused on shiraz and riesling, with more extensive plantings of these varieties.

ΨΨΨΨΨ **Single Vineyard Geelong Riesling 2019** So, this is what the Otway Coast can do with riesling. More, please! It's complex and delicious with real presence in the glass. Opens with nashi pear, preserved lemon, orange rind and a granitic mineral character. Moves into well defined riesling territory of lemon, grapefruit with a smidge of lime cordial lifted on tangy acidity. A mover and shaker. Screwcap. 12% alc. **Rating** 95 **To** 2031 $27 JP ✪
Chardonnay 2019 A firm-footed chardonnay. Light tropical scents, quince, baked apple, almond meal riff. It's early days. The acidity is keen and juicy, fruit is keeping a lemony-grapefruit buzz and oak, well, it's on the q.t. at the moment. Light on its feet and super elegant – vegan friendly, to boot. There is a lot to like and enjoy here. Screwcap. 13% alc. **Rating** 94 **To** 2027 JP
Single Vineyard Geelong Shiraz 2018 The addition of a small amount of viognier is obvious from the beautiful, translucent purple hue and vibrant aromas. The white grape contributes so much energy and lift. A classy shiraz all round. Spice-laced blackberry, black cherry, violet fineness on the palate. The role of French oak (25% new) cannot be underestimated in presenting a wine of such poise. Screwcap. 14% alc. **Rating** 94 **To** 2029 $32 JP

ΨΨΨΨΨ **Outlier Riesling 2018 Rating** 91 **To** 2025 $49 JP
Geelong Pinot Noir 2019 Rating 91 **To** 2027 $35 JP

Dionysus Winery

1 Patemans Lane, Murrumbateman, NSW 2582 **Region** Canberra District
T 0411 730 724 **www**.dionysus-winery.com.au **Open** W'ends & public hols 10–5
Winemaker Michael O'Dea **Est.** 1998 **Dozens** 1000 **Vyds** 4ha

Michael and Wendy O'Dea founded the winery while they had parallel lives as public servants in Canberra. They have now retired, and devote themselves full-time to Dionysus. They purchased their property in 1996 and planted chardonnay, sauvignon blanc, riesling, viognier, merlot, pinot noir, cabernet sauvignon and shiraz between '98 and 2001. Michael has completed an associate degree in winemaking at CSU and is responsible for viticulture and winemaking; Wendy has completed various courses at the Canberra TAFE and is responsible for wine marketing and (in their words) 'nagging Michael and being a general slushie'.

🍷🍷🍷🍷🍷 **Canberra District Riesling 2019** Excellent intensity and focus. Citrus, slate, chalk and brine flavours burst energetically through the palate. It's a dry, direct style with very good length and, indeed, cellaring potential. Screwcap. 12.5% alc. **Rating** 94 **To** 2030 CM

🍷🍷🍷🍷🍷 **C.B. Young Canberra District Shiraz 2018 Rating** 93 **To** 2034 $60 CM
Canberra District Shiraz Viognier 2018 Rating 93 **To** 2030 $30 CM
Canberra District Chardonnay 2019 Rating 90 **To** 2025 CM
Canberra District Cabernet Sauvignon 2018 Rating 90 **To** 2027 $30 CM

Dirt Candy

39 Hobart Road, New Lambton, NSW 2305 **Region** Hunter Valley
T 0412 510 594 **www**.dirtcandy.com.au **Open** Not
Winemaker Daniel Payne **Est.** 2017 **Dozens** 400

Winemaker Daniel Payne and design and marketer wife Jenni are the owners of this at times decidedly natural business. They purchase varieties of various grapes from various places to make the wines; some of which are artisanal, some good, and all worthy of discussion. The wines from Hunter Valley grapes are the core of the business.

🍷🍷🍷🍷🍷 **The Natural Orange Riesling 2019** 'Natural' in this case refers to the organic viticulture employed. Winemaking is quite conventional, including a minimal sulphur addition. Attractive varietal aromas with scents of lemon and lime and sweet citrus blossom. Fresh and light on its feet through the palate with some tanginess to the flavours tapering into a soft acid finish. Screwcap. 12.5% alc. **Rating** 90 **To** 2026 $24 SC
The Little Circus Red Blend 2019 Half a dozen eclectic varieties in this blend, sourced from as many Hunter vineyards. Fermented together (including a portion of whole bunch) with some traminer skins included, matured in French puncheons. It's light and fresh, perfumed and spicy; various red berry aromas and flavours mingling with more savoury notes. Perfect to accompany a gourmet pizza. Screwcap. 13.5% alc. **Rating** 90 **To** 2024 $24 SC

🍷🍷🍷🍷 **The One Hunter Valley Chardonnay 2019 Rating** 89 **To** 2024 $27 SC
The Gamechanger Hunter Valley Rose 2019 Rating 89 **To** 2021 $24 SC
The Ruby Rabbit Hunter Valley Rose Pet Nat 2019 Rating 89 $27 SC

Dr Edge

5 Cato Avenue, West Hobart, Tas 7000 (postal) **Region** Southern Tasmania
T 0439 448 151 **www**.dr-edge.com **Open** Not
Winemaker Peter Dredge **Est.** 2015 **Dozens** 700 **Vyds** 1.5ha

After working as a winemaker for Petaluma, Peter Dredge moved to Tasmania in 2009, spending 7 years within the Accolade group, becoming chief winemaker at Bay of Fires. He moved proactively to become a consultant and self-employed winemaker, to shortcircuit the uncertainty then existing around Accolade and its future. In '15 he sourced a small amount of pinot noir from Joe Holyman of Stoney Rise and Gerald Ellis of Meadowbank to start his own label. He made the wine at Moorilla as a contract client with sole control of the winemaking process. In '15, during vintage, the Ellis family, owners of Meadowbank, approached Pete to form a partnership to relaunch Meadowbank. As part of the deal, Meadowbank gave Pete a sole lease arrangement to 1.5ha of pinot noir from the '16 vintage and onwards. Exports to the UK, the US and South-East Asia.

ŸŸŸŸŸ **North Tasmania Chardonnay 2019** Fruit off Peter Dredge's vineyard in the Tamar Valley and made in line with the other single site chardonnays; it's the most complete of the 3. Subtle aromas with a mix of florals, oyster shell and citrus, with some sulphide flint. It has laser definition, tight and linear – but not mean or too lean – with lemon saline and mouth-watering freshness. Screwcap. 12.5% alc. **Rating** 95 **To** 2030 $50 JF

East Tasmania Chardonnay 2019 Made identically to the other single site offerings, fruit from Hazards Vineyard owned by Brown Brothers. Good tension to this; steely, brisk acidity; and linear in shape. It's infused with lemon barley water, a squirt of lemon juice, aniseed and pure flavours. Incredibly tight and refreshing. Screwcap. 12.5% alc. **Rating** 95 **To** 2030 $50 JF

Tasmania Chardonnay 2019 A blend of all 3 single vineyards comprising 60% Derwent Valley, 30% Tamar Valley and 10% East Coast. A good combo with the same intense precision and length as the other chardonnays but the flavours seem somewhat bolstered, a sum of its parts perhaps. Lemon drops and zest, lemon saline, aniseed and lovely creamy, ginger fluff flavours across the palate from the lees. The acidity is electric, it lights this up. Screwcap. 12.5% alc. **Rating** 95 **To** 2030 $50 JF

Tasmania Pinot Noir 2019 Just the one pinot this vintage but a very good offering. A whorl of dark fruit infused with cloves, smoky and reductive with salami and prosciutto flavours. Savoury in attitude yet whole-bunch appeal comes through – ripe rhubarb–like stems. Buoyant, textural raw silk–like tannins and neat acidity to close. It renders this mouth–watering as well as satisfying. Screwcap. 12.5% alc. **Rating** 95 **To** 2030 $50 JF

Tasmania Riesling 2019 Some whole-bunches in the ferment, aged 9 months in oak; an off-dry style and a smorgasbord of flavour with precision. This is Tasmanian riesling after all. A depth of flavour with a raft of citrus, freshly cut green apple, pickled ginger and a splash of lemon barley cordial. It has texture aplenty with some clotted cream across the palate, an assured footing to the very end. Lovely acid line and a delicious drink. Screwcap. 12.5% alc. **Rating** 95 $35 JF ✪

Dodgy Brothers   ★★★★★

PO Box 655, McLaren Vale, SA 5171 **Region** McLaren Vale
T 0450 000 373 **www.**dodgybrotherswines.com **Open** Not
Winemaker Wes Pearson **Est.** 2010 **Dozens** 2000

This is a partnership between Canadian-born Flying Winemaker Wes Pearson, viticulturist Peter Bolte and grapegrower Peter Sommerville. Wes graduated from the University of British Columbia's biochemistry program in 2008, along the way working at wineries including Chateau Leoville Las Cases in Bordeaux. Also in '08 he and his family moved to McLaren Vale, and after working at several wineries, he joined the Australian Wine Research Institute as a sensory analyst. Peter Bolte has over 35 vintages in McLaren Vale under his belt and was the original Dodgy Brother. Peter Sommerville's vineyard provides cabernet sauvignon, cabernet franc and petit verdot for the Dodgy Brothers Bordeaux blend. Exports to Canada.

ŸŸŸŸŸ **Juxtaposed Old Vine Grenache 2018** Aromatically satisfying and awash with bright, red fruit laced with savoury flavours, fresh herbs and red licorice. It's medium-bodied, juicy and mouth-watering with tangy raspberry sorbet–like acidity. Screwcap. 14.5% alc. **Rating** 95 **To** 2026 $29 JF ✪

ŸŸŸŸŸ **Juxtaposed Bigger Boat Fiano 2018 Rating** 93 **To** 2022 $26 JF ✪
Sellicks Foothills McLaren Vale Shiraz 2018 Rating 92 **To** 2025 $25 JF ✪

Juxtaposed Cabernet Franc 2017 Rating 92 To 2024 $29 JF
Juxtaposed Sangiovese Rose 2019 Rating 90 To 2021 $25 JF
Juxtaposed Old Vine Shiraz 2017 Rating 90 To 2027 $29 JF
Juxtaposed Old Vine Grenache 2017 Rating 90 To 2023 $29 JF

DogRidge Wine Company ★★★★

129 Bagshaws Road, McLaren Flat, SA 5171 **Region** McLaren Vale
T (08) 8383 0140 **www**.dogridge.com.au **Open** 7 days 11–5
Winemaker Fred Howard **Est.** 1991 **Dozens** 16 000 **Vyds** 56ha
Dave and Jen Wright (co-owners with Fred and Sarah Howard) had a combined background of dentistry, art and a CSU viticultural degree when they moved from Adelaide to McLaren Flat to become vignerons. They inherited shiraz and grenache vines planted in the early 1940s as a source for Chateau Reynella fortified wines, and their vineyards now range from 2001 plantings to some of the oldest vines in the immediate district. Quality at one end, value-packed at the other end. Exports to Canada, Singapore and Japan.

TTTTT **Shirtfront McLaren Vale Shiraz 2016** Shirtfront is said to encapsulate the DogRidge 'front on and fearless' approach to life. It does that. Nuance is not something you tend to appreciate in DogRidge reds. However, Shirtfront carries its 15% alcohol well and it's good to see balance across all of the essential ingredients from fruit (tossed earth, leather, chocolate, high spice), oak (vanilla pod, bbq sauce) and tannins (savoury, rounded). Big and beautiful is the way. Screwcap. **Rating** 94 **To** 2030 $28 JP ○

TTTTT **The Pup McLaren Vale Shiraz 2017 Rating** 93 **To** 2029 $20 JP ○
Noble Rot McLaren Vale Sticky White Frontignac 2019 Rating 93 **To** 2025 $25 JP ○
Square Cut McLaren Vale Cabernet 2016 Rating 92 **To** 2027 $28 JP
The Pup McLaren Vale Sauvignon Blanc 2019 Rating 91 **To** 2024 $20 JP ○

DogRock Winery ★★★★★

114 Degraves Road, Crowlands, Vic 3377 **Region** Pyrenees
T 0409 280 317 **www**.dogrock.com.au **Open** By appt
Winemaker Allen Hart **Est.** 1998 **Dozens** 1000 **Vyds** 6.2ha
This is the venture of Allen (now full-time winemaker) and Andrea (viticulturist) Hart. Having purchased the property in 1998, the planting of shiraz, riesling, tempranillo, grenache, chardonnay and marsanne began in 2000 (0.2ha of touriga nacional added in '16 and arinto and azal in '20). Given Allen's former post as research scientist/winemaker with Foster's, the attitude taken to winemaking is unexpected. The estate-grown wines are made in a low-tech fashion, without gas cover or filtration; the Harts say, 'All wine will be sealed with a screwcap and no DogRock wine will ever be released under natural cork bark'. DogRock installed the first solar-powered irrigation system in Australia, capable of supplying water 365 days a year, even at night or in cloudy conditions.

TTTTT **Degraves Road Single Vineyard Pyrenees Shiraz 2018** Hand-picked, wild-fermented, matured in French oak (50% new) for 14 months. Deep crimson-purple; laden with luscious black fruits and blood plum flavours, complexed by tar, spice and anise; the tannins ripe and balanced. Terrific full-bodied wine reflecting the great vintage. Screwcap. 14% alc. **Rating** 97 **To** 2043 $38 ○

TTTTT **Grampians Touriga Nacional 2019** Made with 90% touriga nacional, 10% shiraz; only 15 dozen bottles. Crushed, open-fermented, 8 days on skins, hand-plunged, matured for 10 months in a 4yo French (Troncais) barrel. Vivid hue. Perfumed, akin to a Dutch miniature painting, finely detailed and silky in the mouth. If I had made the wine I might not have been able to sell it. Screwcap. 13% alc. **Rating** 96 **To** 2029 $30 ○
Pyrenees Shiraz 2018 Matured for 12 months in French oak (40% new). A medium to full-bodied shiraz in company with its sibling, a similar mix of black

fruits and plums, tannin and a positive touch of oak. Impressive wine reflecting the vintage. Screwcap. 13.5% alc. **Rating** 95 To 2038 $30 ✪

Grampians Tempranillo 2019 Made with 95% tempranillo, 5% shiraz; crushed, wild yeast–open fermented over 7 days, matured for 12 months, 30% new French oak, 10% American. Vivid colour. A lively, medium-bodied tempranillo with classic cherry/berry fruits dressed in a fine gauze of tannins and a kiss of oak. Screwcap. 13.5% alc. **Rating** 94 To 2029 $30 ✪

TTTTT **Degraves Road Riesling 2019 Rating** 93 To 2034 $28
Degraves Road Reserve Chardonnay 2019 Rating 93 To 2029

Domaine A   ★★★★★

105 Tea Tree Road, Campania, Tas 7026 **Region** Southern Tasmania
T (03) 6260 4174 **www**.domaine-a.com.au **Open** Fri–Mon 10–5
Winemaker Conor van de Reest **Est.** 1973 **Dozens** 5000 **Vyds** 11ha
Effective from 1 March 2020 ownership of Domaine A passed from Peter Althaus, its long-term custodian, to Moorilla Estate. There were no changes to existing employees, with Conor van de Reest continuing the position he has held since 2007. The inclusion of Domaine A's stock in the sale will be of particular relevance with the opening of Mona's 172-room hotel on the Moorilla property in '22. Mona is Australia's largest private museum showing ancient, modern and contemporary art. It is founded by philanthropist and collector David Walsh. Mona opened in January '11. Exports to Singapore, Japan, Hong Kong and China.

TTTTT **Stoney Vineyard Pinot Noir 2018** Hand-picked and bunch-sorted, crushed, open-fermented, 11 days on skins, matured in used French oak for 8 months. An unexpectedly expressive bouquet of red flowers and warm baker's spices; the long, juicy palate with layers of fruits ranging from pomegranate to plum. Screwcap. 13.8% alc. **Rating** 95 To 2030 $38

Cabernet Sauvignon 2010 Includes 4% each of cabernet franc and merlot, and 2% petit verdot; matured in French barriques for 30 months, not fined or filtered. This has, by far, the best balanced cabernet fruit expression and fine tannins. Above all else, it is ripe. Cork. 14% alc. **Rating** 95 To 2035 $120

Stoney Vineyard Cabernet Sauvignon 2016 Includes 4% each of merlot and cabernet franc; matured in 2yo French oak. In true Domaine A style, reluctant to allow the fruit to escape the bonds of tannin and acidity, yet its balance can't be denied. Diam. 14.4% alc. **Rating** 94 To 2041 $38

TTTTT **Pinot Noir 2013 Rating** 93 To 2033 $90
Stoney Vineyard Sauvignon Blanc 2018 Rating 91 To 2022 $36

Domaine Asmara   ★★★★★

Gibb Road, Toolleen, Vic 3551 **Region** Heathcote
T (03) 5433 6133 **www**.domaineasmara.com **Open** 7 days 9–6.30
Winemaker Sanguine Estate **Est.** 2008 **Dozens** 3000 **Vyds** 12ha
Chemical engineer Andreas Greiving had a lifelong dream to own and operate a vineyard, and the opportunity came along with the global financial crisis. He was able to purchase a vineyard planted to shiraz, cabernet sauvignon, cabernet franc, durif and viognier, and have the wines contract-made. The venture is co-managed by dentist wife Hennijati. The red wines are made from controlled yields of 1–1.5t/acre, hence their concentration. Exports to the UK, Vietnam, Malaysia, Hong Kong and China.

TTTTT **Reserve Heathcote Cabernet Sauvignon 2018** 25% fermented in barrel, 75% wild-fermented in stainless steel open fermenters, matured for 10 months in French barriques (10% new). This is rich and ripe with cassis gliding over the tannin structure that's meant to be a calling card of the variety. But it doesn't take your breath away. Cork. 14.5% alc. **Rating** 95 To 2029 $45

Reserve Heathcote Shiraz 2018 75% open-fermented, 25% wild yeast–barrel fermented, then taken to French barriques (30% new) for 10 months. Has much to say, but the heat generated by the alcohol cannot be disguised, although it still leaves ultra-ripe fruit in place. Cork. 15.5% alc. **Rating** 94 **To** 2025 $49

Infinity Heathcote Shiraz 2018 50% barrel-fermented, 50% in open stainless steel vats, matured for 15 months in French barriques (75% new). Dense crimson-purple. As you get towards the mid-palate, there is an illusion that you are chewing the wine as the oak and tannins join the alcohol. Very difficult to score. Cork. 16% alc. **Rating** 94 **To** 2025 $88

♀♀♀♀♀ **Private Reserve Heathcote Durif 2018** Rating 91 **To** 2028 $59

Domaine Naturaliste ★★★★★

160 Johnson Road, Wilyabrup, WA 6280 **Region** Margaret River
T (08) 9755 6776 **www.**domainenaturaliste.com.au **Open** Not
Winemaker Bruce Dukes **Est.** 2012 **Dozens** 12000 **Vyds** 21ha

Bruce Dukes' career dates back over 30 years, its foundations built around a degree in agronomy from the University of WA, followed by a masters degree in viticulture and agronomy from the University of California (Davis). A four-year stint at Francis Ford Coppola's iconic Niebaum–Coppola winery in the Napa Valley followed. Back in WA Bruce worked with a consultancy and contract winemaking business in Margaret River in 2000. His winery was set up to handle small and large amounts of fruit, but it was not until '12 that he made his own wine under the Domaine Naturaliste label. The quality of all the wines is excellent. Exports to the UK, the US, Canada and China.

♀♀♀♀♀ **Artus Margaret River Chardonnay 2018** The grapes come from Karridale in the distinctly cool, Southern Ocean–influenced, far south of Margaret River. Whole-bunch pressed, cloudy juice and wild ferment in 40% new French barriques, cultured mlf. White stone fruit flavours build richness and structure. Screwcap. 13% alc. **Rating** 97 **To** 2030 $49 ✪

♀♀♀♀♀ **Sauvage Margaret River Sauvignon Blanc 2017** The naked power of the sauvignon blanc that fuels this wine is exceptional. Its fiercely unsweetened lemon fruit and zest ensure it will outlive the patience of many who buy it expecting a developed wine. The fact it has swept past 3 vintages will only serve to increase their surprise. Screwcap. 13% alc. **Rating** 96 **To** 2037 $30 ✪

Floris Margaret River Chardonnay 2018 All about complexity and texture. The richer fruit from the Wallcliffe district absorbing 10 months in French barriques (30% new, but low-medium toast). Fresh grapefruit takes care of the oak of a carefully built wine. Screwcap. 13% alc. **Rating** 96 **To** 2026 $30 ✪

Discovery Margaret River Chardonnay 2018 Sourced from Wilyabrup and Carbunup. It is built on a deep-set core of natural acidity and deliberate fermentation and maturation in used French barriques. An elegant wine with perfect balance and length, the jasmine scents of the bouquet deliciously seductive. Screwcap. 13% alc. **Rating** 95 **To** 2027 $24 ✪

Rachis Margaret River Syrah 2018 The sheer power and intensity of this wine are utterly exceptional – it's as if two 750ml bottles had been compressed by some arcane process into a single bottle. Neither the modest alcohol nor the Margaret River provenance give a clue about the clash of cymbals on the palate; black fruits shutting all else back into the cellar for a minimum of 5 years maturation. Screwcap. 14% alc. **Rating** 95 **To** 2041 $30 ✪

Rebus Margaret River Cabernet Sauvignon 2017 Engages you in a split second with its pirouette of juicy redcurrant, blackcurrant, spice and bay leaf. No need for introspection, just sheer hedonistic enjoyment. Screwcap. 14% alc. **Rating** 94 **To** 2032 $36

Domenica Wines ★★★★★

651 Wangaratta-Beechworth Road, Beechworth, Vic 3747 **Region** Beechworth
T (03) 5728 1612 **www.**domenicawines.com.au **Open** By appt
Winemaker Peter Graham **Est.** 2012 **Dozens** 1500 **Vyds** 5ha

Domenica Wines is the reincarnation of the previous Ergo Sum joint venture between Rick Kinzbrunner, Michel Chapoutier and Peter Graham. Domenica was established in 2012 when Peter Graham purchased the shares of Kinzbrunner and Chapoutier, and he is now the sole owner and winemaker of the business. He has had 15 years winemaking in Beechworth, and in particular worked both growing and making the wines from the (now) Domenica vineyard since it first produced fruit. Shiraz, roussanne and marsanne are considered by Peter Graham to have a natural affinity with the warm, dry summers, granitic soils, slopes and altitude provided by Beechworth. Beechworth's two major varieties are shiraz and chardonnay, and these are cornerstones for Domenica Wines.

ŸŸŸŸŸ **Meeting of Minds Beechworth Chardonnay 2017** Fine wine. Unforced. Flush with grapefruit, almond, cream and toast flavours though the truth is that it presents as one. Harmony is its middle name. Length is its surname. It's just now entering a prime drinking zone. Screwcap. 13.2% alc. **Rating** 95 To 2026 $45 CM
Beechworth Nebbiolo 2017 Light in colour and – indeed – on its feet, but seriously stern and dry through the finish, as is nebbiolo's wont. Rusty tannin aplenty, orange oil notes, flashes of licorice, tea and black cherry. Very good length. It takes a long time to come up in the glass but it's worth the wait. Authentic nebbiolo. Screwcap. 14% alc. **Rating** 95 To 2032 $48 CM

ŸŸŸŸŸ **Beechworth Pinot Noir 2017 Rating** 93 To 2027 CM

Dominique Portet ★★★★★

870–872 Maroondah Highway, Coldstream, Vic 3770 **Region** Yarra Valley
T (03) 5962 5760 **www**.dominiqueportet.com **Open** 7 days 10–5
Winemaker Ben Portet **Est.** 2000 **Dozens** 15 000 **Vyds** 6.3ha
Dominique Portet was bred in the purple. He spent his early years at Chateau Lafite (where his father was régisseur), and was one of the first Flying Winemakers, commuting to Clos du Val in the Napa Valley where his brother was also a winemaker. He then spent over 20 years as managing director of Taltarni and Clover Hill. After retiring from Taltarni, he moved to the Yarra Valley, a region he had been closely observing since the mid-1980s. In 2000 he found the site he had long looked for and built his winery and cellar door, planting a quixotic mix of viognier, sauvignon blanc and merlot. Son Ben is now executive winemaker, leaving Dominique with a roving role as de facto consultant and brand marketer. Ben himself has a winemaking CV of awesome scope, covering all parts of France, South Africa, California and four vintages at Petaluma. Exports to Canada, India, Dubai, Hong Kong, Singapore, Malaysia and Japan.

ŸŸŸŸŸ **Yarra Valley Cabernet Sauvignon 2018** Includes 3% cabernet franc and 1% petit verdot; matured in French oak (35% new) for 14 months. Marries intensity, purity and silky mouthfeel. It has length and balance to the medium-bodied cassis-dominant flavours. Cork. 13.5% alc. **Rating** 96 To 2038 $60 ✪
Origine Yarra Valley Chardonnay 2019 Hand-picked, chilled, whole-bunch pressed, fermented in French puncheons (40% new), matured for 9 months. Gleaming straw-green. A perfectly pitched chardonnay: the fruit midway between stone fruit and citrus; the oak largely absorbed by the fruit, providing texture as much as flavour. Screwcap. 13% alc. **Rating** 95 To 2029 $48
Fontaine Yarra Valley Cabernet Sauvignon 2018 Includes 86% cabernet sauvignon, 6% merlot, 5% cabernet franc, 2% petit verdot and 1% malbec; matured for 10 months in French oak (30% new). It's bred in the purple but needs 5–10 years to fully reveal the inherent balance and finesse of the blackcurrant fruit and green olive flavours. Value++. Screwcap. 13.5% alc. **Rating** 94 To 2038 $22 ✪
Yarra Valley Blanc de Blancs 2015 Hand-picked chardonnay from a very steep Upper Yarra vineyard on red volcanic soil. Whole-bunch pressed, the first fermentation in tank with 6 months on lees, the second ferment on tirage for 3 years on lees before disgorgement and a further 12 months on cork prior to release. Attractive wine, well made. Diam. 12.5% alc. **Rating** 94 $45

ŸŸŸŸŸ **Fontaine Rose 2019 Rating** 92 To 2020 $22 ✪

Dorrien Estate ★★★★★

Cnr Barossa Valley Way/Siegersdorf Road, Tanunda, SA 5352 **Region** Barossa Valley
T (08) 8561 2235 **www**.cellarmasters.com.au **Open** Not
Winemaker Nick Badrice **Est.** 1988 **Dozens** 1 million **Vyds** 109.6ha
Dorrien Estate is the physical base of the vast Cellarmasters network – the largest direct
sales outlet in Australia. It also makes wine for many producers across Australia at its modern
winery, which has a capacity of 14.5 million litres in tank and barrel; however, a typical make
of each wine will be little more than 1000 dozen. Most of the wines made for others are
exclusively distributed by Cellarmasters. Acquired by Woolworths in May 2011.

ŸŸŸŸŸ **Krondorf Bowen & Schiller The Growers Grenache Shiraz Mourvedre**
2017 Immediately and immensely appealing, for it is light on its feet for a
Krondorf. It has plenty of substance with a more savoury take to the blend. Fresh
red berries, cinnamon and pepper, jamon and Vegemite with plush tannin and
toasty-charry oak on the finish. Screwcap. 14.5% alc. **Rating** 93 **To** 2027 $27 JF ✪
Krondorf The Growers Miles & Koch Barossa Cabernet Sauvignon 2017
The richness, the blackberry essence and scorched earth aromas plant this firmly
in the Barossa. It's lively and fresh with shapely tannins and a smoothness across the
fuller-bodied palate. Screwcap. 14.5% alc. **Rating** 93 **To** 2028 $27 JF ✪
Stonyfell Bin 62 Langhorne Creek Cabernet Sauvignon Shiraz Malbec
2018 Definitely the sum of its parts. A neat mix of ripe blackberries, plums,
choc-mint, soy sauce and wafts of warm earth. Oak shows itself on the full-bodied
palate but the fleshy, plump tannins and acidity, keeps this on track. Screwcap.
14.5% alc. **Rating** 92 **To** 2030 $37 JF
Krondorf Old Salem Barossa Shiraz 2018 Flavour in abundance, that's for
sure. Lurking underneath the lashings of American and French oak is a mix of
plums and blackberry essence, mocha, mint and aniseed. Densely weighted across
the palate, yet the tannins are plush, almost velvety, and there's a succulence that
entices. Screwcap. 14.5% alc. **Rating** 91 **To** 2033 $35 JF
Black Wattle Vineyards The Icon Mount Benson Chardonnay 2018
Really tightly wound with some whiffy sulphides and oak spices. Definitely in the
citrus spectrum with the acidity skating past the creamy-leesy flavours. Screwcap.
13.5% alc. **Rating** 90 **To** 2026 $43 JF
Avon Brae Moculta Eden Valley Shiraz 2018 Amazing purple-black hue,
the same shade of the sweet plum-cherry-accented fruit within. Added extras of
mocha molten chocolate, cinnamon plus cedary-vanillan oak imparting loads of
sweetness. It's full-bodied, dense with ripe tannins, yet everything comes together.
Screwcap. 14.4% alc. **Rating** 90 **To** 2030 $30 JF
William Light Clare Valley Shiraz 2018 Inky purple hue. Violets with a fair
amount of mint/eucalyptus infusing the black plums spiced with cinnamon. Lots
of sweet cedary-clove oak lingering across the full-bodied palate, yet buoyant with
the exuberance of youth. Screwcap. 14.5% alc. **Rating** 90 **To** 2027 $40 JF

DOWIE DOOLE ★★★★★

695 California Road, McLaren Vale, SA 5171 **Region** McLaren Vale
T 0459 101 372 **www**.dowiedoole.com **Open** 7 days 10–5
Winemaker Chris Thomas **Est.** 1995 **Dozens** 25000 **Vyds** 90ha
DOWIE DOOLE was founded in 1995 by Drew Dowie and Norm Doole. They had been
connected to the McLaren Vale community for many years as grapegrowers in the region.
Vineyard management is now led by champions of sustainable viticulture practices Dave
Gartelmann and Drew Dowie. In May '16, with winemaker and managing director Chris
Thomas leading a group of like-minded investors, DOWIE DOOLE acquired 35ha of vines
of the 53ha Conte Tatachilla Vineyard, book-ended by 50-year-old bushvine grenache
and grafted (in '12) vermentino, aglianico and lagrein. In October '18, DOWIE DOOLE
purchased Possum Vineyard, including its vineyards in Blewitt Springs and 500t winery.
Exports to all major markets.

ΨΨΨΨΨ **Reserve McLaren Vale Shiraz 2017** Remarkable balance given the concentration of flavour. It's big and a little old school in its styling but it makes it all work and then some. It tastes of coffee grounds and blackberry, sweet plum and tar; the tannin coming with infusions of saltbush, toast and malt. Volume and momentum are both excellent, as is the fine-grained spread of tannin. A-class quality. Diam. 14.5% alc. **Rating** 96 **To** 2038 $95 CM

The Banker McLaren Vale Shiraz 2017 Concentrated, syrupy shiraz with malt and clove flavours flooding through roasted plum, salted licorice and asphalt. There's an assertiveness to the tannin but it's hand-in-glove with the fruit. It's both substantial and svelte. Diam. 14.5% alc. **Rating** 95 **To** 2035 CM

The Architect Blewitt Springs McLaren Vale Shiraz 2017 1500 bottles made. A robust delicacy. Dark choc-mint and sweet plum flavours offer both intensity of flavour and a degree of elegance; no mean feat. Indeed the way fresh-but-full-bodied fruit tucks into appropriately applied cedar wood oak is quite something here. It's a class act from start to finish. Diam. 14.5% alc. **Rating** 95 **To** 2035 CM

Estate McLaren Vale Shiraz 2018 Matured in 60% French oak, 40% American; 15% new oak. Creamy vanilla characters glide over smooth plum-shot fruit. A tried and true formula, done well here. Gum leaf and caramel notes add more to the show, but firm tannin keeps it all nicely in control. Not a foot wrong. Screwcap. 14.5% alc. **Rating** 94 **To** 2032 $25 CM ❂

Cali Road McLaren Vale Shiraz 2017 Resiny oak exerts a clear influence, and the integration of fruit and tannin isn't as seamless as it is with some of its siblings, but this is still pretty impressive. Ample plum/toast/clove/musk flavours with creamy mouthfeel and good length. Screwcap. 14.5% alc. **Rating** 94 **To** 2033 $60 CM

Estate McLaren Vale Cabernet Sauvignon 2018 Matured in 90% French oak, 10% American. It's worth decanting this, it really builds as it breathes. It's curranty, kirsch-like and solid with bay leaf, cedar-cream and choc-mint flavours impressing on the palate. Tannin is firm, dusty and confidence-building. You take a sip and feel as though you can rely on this wine. Screwcap. 14.4% alc. **Rating** 94 **To** 2033 $25 CM ❂

Mr G's C.S.M. 2016 The mix is 48% cabernet sauvignon, 45% shiraz and 7% merlot; matured for 24 months in 50/50% American and French oak. Coffee-cream and blackcurrant/redcurrant flavours turn on the charm. It's a well balanced and integrated red with plenty of stuffing and no signs of untidiness. It spreads out impressively on the finish too. Diam. 14.5% alc. **Rating** 94 **To** 2032 $35 CM

ΨΨΨΨΦ **McLaren Vale Rose 2019 Rating** 93 **To** 2021 $25 CM ❂
G&T Grenache & Tempranillo 2018 Rating 93 **To** 2027 $25 CM ❂
Estate McLaren Vale Chenin Blanc 2019 Rating 92 **To** 2024 $25 CM ❂
B.F.G. McLaren Vale Grenache 2019 Rating 92 **To** 2028 $30 CM
Estate Adelaide Hills Sauvignon Blanc 2019 Rating 91 **To** 2022 $30 CM
C.T. McLaren Vale Shiraz 2017 Rating 91 **To** 2027 $35 CM

Drayton's Family Wines   ★★★★☆

555 Oakey Creek Road, Pokolbin, NSW 2321 **Region** Hunter Valley
T (02) 4998 7513 **www**.draytonswines.com.au **Open** Mon–Fri 8–5, w'ends 10–5
Winemaker Edgar Vales, John Drayton **Est.** 1853 **Dozens** 40 000 **Vyds** 72ha
Six generations of the Drayton family have successively run the family business. It is now in the hands of Max Drayton, and sons John and Greg. The family has suffered more than its fair share of misfortune over the years, but has risen to the challenge. Edgar Vales is the chief winemaker after previous experience as assistant winemaker with David Hook and First Creek Wines. His arrival coincided with the release of a range of high quality wines. The wines come in part from blocks on the estate vineyards that are over 120 years old and in prime Hunter Valley locations. Exports to Ireland, Bulgaria, Turkey, Vietnam, Malaysia, Indonesia, Singapore, Taiwan and China.

ŸŸŸŸŸ Susanne Semillon 2013 From the estate Old Flat Vineyard planted in the 1890s. Still incredibly light green-quartz, the palate underlining its ancestry. In world-class form for a wine from vines over 100yo, having the best of both worlds, perfect balance and length, protected by the screwcap and immaculate winemaking. 11.5% alc. Rating 98 To 2038 $60 ✪

ŸŸŸŸŸ Vineyard Reserve Pokolbin Semillon 2018 From the family Oakey Vineyard, fermented with cultured yeast. Slightly less power and depth than its '19 sibling, but has more elegance and finesse. Screwcap. 11.5% alc. Rating 94 To 2038 $35
Vineyard Reserve Pokolbin Chardonnay 2019 From the oldest planting of PF clone chardonnay planted in the mid-'60s. Hand-picked, free-run juice fermented in French oak (20% new), stirred for 3 months, lesser stirring for a further 4 months. The expected overworked characters didn't appear. Instead bright and fresh grapefruit, apple and melon flavours; the oak not excessive. Screwcap. 13% alc. Rating 94 To 2023 $35
Vineyard Reserve Pokolbin Shiraz 2018 Includes 60% from the estate Old Flat Vineyard planted in the 1890s, 40% from the Bull Paddock Vineyard planted in the '60s and '70s. Hand-picked, destemmed and crushed, open-fermented with cultured yeast, matured in 3yo French oak. Good colour; blackberry, oak and a splash of Hunter Valley earth. Made sensibly to let the vintage, place and variety all have their say. Great value given its provenance. Screwcap. 14% alc. Rating 94 To 2048 $35 ✪
Joseph Hunter Valley Shiraz 2013 From the Old Flat Vineyard planted in the 1890s, matured for 11 months in used French oak. Rich and ripe black fruits, a flicker of dark chocolate borrowed from McLaren Vale. The juicy finish puts the icing on the cake. Screwcap. 13.5% alc. Rating 94 To 2028 $90

ŸŸŸŸŸ Vineyard Reserve Pokolbin Semillon 2019 Rating 92 To 2034 $35
Vineyard Reserve Reserve Pokolbin Touriga Nacional 2019 Rating 92 To 2025 $35
Vineyard Reserve Pokolbin Tempranillo 2019 Rating 91 To 2029 $35

Driftwood Estate ★★★★★

3314 Caves Road, Wilyabrup, WA 6282 **Region** Margaret River
T (08) 9755 6323 **www.**driftwoodwines.com.au **Open** 7 days 10.30–5
Winemaker Kane Grove **Est.** 1989 **Dozens** 15 000 **Vyds** 22ha
Driftwood Estate is a well established landmark on the Margaret River scene. Quite apart from offering a casual dining restaurant capable of seating 200 people (open 7 days for lunch and dinner) and a mock Greek open-air theatre, its wines feature striking and stylish packaging and opulent flavours. Its wines are released in three ranges: The Collection, Artifacts and Oceania. Exports to the UK, Canada, Singapore and China.

ŸŸŸŸŸ Single Site Margaret River Cabernet Sauvignon 2017 Includes 95% cabernet sauvignon, 5% petit verdot. Such a well rounded wine. It feels complete. Blackcurrant, plum, peppercorn and dark chocolate flavours roll persuasively through the palate. Tannin is fine-grained and length is impressive. It's not overly big or muscular because it doesn't have to be; everything is in its rightful place. Screwcap. 14.3% alc. Rating 95 To 2036 $70 CM
Artifacts Margaret River Cabernet Sauvignon 2017 It's not a lively red but it's certainly a substantial one. It's a roasted, meaty, blackberry-soaked wine with dry woodsy spice notes aplenty and a kick of red licorice on the finish. Tannin has been well played, dusty/bay leaf notes are present but not dangerous, and everything feels as though it's been deliberately placed. Screwcap. 14.5% alc. Rating 94 To 2031 $35 CM
Artifacts Margaret River Malbec 2017 Mostly malbec, smaller amounts of petit verdot, cabernet sauvignon and cabernet franc. Matured in both tank and French oak (33% new) for 18 months. It's a powerful rendition of the variety. A core of blackberry, leather and earth meets toast, licorice and menthol. It

remains silken even as it pours it on. The finish still feels slightly awkward but time
will take care of it. 14% alc. **Rating** 94 To 2030 $33 CM

☥☥☥☥☥ Artifacts Semillon Sauvignon Blanc 2019 Rating 93 To 2024 $30 CM
Artifacts Chardonnay 2019 Rating 93 To 2025 $35 CM
Artifacts Shiraz 2017 Rating 92 To 2028 $32 CM
The Collection Cabernet Merlot 2017 Rating 92 To 2028 $25 CM ✪
The Collection Chardonnay 2019 Rating 91 To 2024 $25 CM
The Collection Sauvignon Blanc 2019 Rating 90 To 2022 $25 CM
The Collection Shiraz Cabernet Sauvignon 2017 Rating 90 To 2026
$25 CM

Duke's Vineyard   ★★★★★

Porongurup Road, Porongurup, WA 6324 **Region** Porongurup
T (08) 9853 1107 **www**.dukesvineyard.com **Open** 7 days 10–4.30
Winemaker Castle Rock (Robert Diletti) **Est.** 1998 **Dozens** 3500 **Vyds** 10ha
When Hilde and Ian (Duke) Ranson sold their clothing manufacturing business in 1998, they
were able to fulfil a long-held dream of establishing a vineyard in the Porongurup subregion
of Great Southern with the acquisition of a 65ha farm at the foot of the Porongurup Range.
They planted shiraz and cabernet sauvignon (3ha each) and riesling (4ha). Hilde, a successful
artist, designed the beautiful, scalloped, glass-walled cellar door sales area, with its mountain
blue cladding. Great wines at great prices.

☥☥☥☥☥ Magpie Hill Reserve Riesling 2019 Hand-picked, whole-bunch pressed,
minimal SO$_2$. One-year-old riesling doesn't come more powerful or intense than
this brilliant Porongurup example, with glorious lime/lemon fruit and a whipcord
of acidity giving the backbone for a long, oh so long, life. Screwcap. 12.5% alc.
Rating 98 To 2053 $42 ✪
Magpie Hill Reserve Cabernet Sauvignon 2018 A superb cabernet that
will be calling the shots for decades to come. Its richness is spectacular because
it parallels the wine's power. Endless peaks of supple blackcurrant and cassis
make light of the varietal tannins that can dog cabernet. The price rendered me
speechless. Screwcap. 13.5% alc. **Rating** 98 To 2048 $35 ✪
Magpie Hill Reserve Shiraz 2018 Estate-grown, small parcels. The colour
is deep, the palate exceptionally focused and full-bodied, yet it has the Duke's
lightness of touch courtesy of contract winemaking by Rob Diletti of Castle
Rock. This is a great wine with a very long future. Screwcap. 14.5% alc.
Rating 97 To 2048 $35 ✪
The Morrissey 2018 An estate blend of cabernet and shiraz. There's nothing
that the human combination of Duke Ranson, in and around the vineyard, and
the skills of winemaker Robert Diletti can't achieve. The breathless flavours,
structure and texture of this striking blend are, quite simply, superb. Glistening
black cherries, satsuma plum and finely wrought tannins are all on parade.
Screwcap. 13.8% alc. **Rating** 97 To 2043 $90 ✪

☥☥☥☥☥ Single Vineyard Riesling 2019 Those who regularly buy and drink Duke's
Riesling should need no persuasion. You can already see the magic of the
indissoluble marriage of lime, Granny Smith apple and a whisper of stone fruit
flavours that gently capture the bouquet and palate; 'gently' simply because the
balance is so perfect. Screwcap. 12.5% alc. **Rating** 96 To 2034 $26 ✪
The Whole Bunch Shiraz 2018 Hand-picked, open-fermented with
100% whole bunches, 5–6 days on skins. Superb violet-crimson colour; there is
no mention of oak, but the vibrant, highly spiced red fruits are the epitome of
successful whole-bunch fermentation. There is every reason to drink it now, but
keep it longer if you can. Screwcap. 13% alc. **Rating** 96 To 2028 $60 ✪
Single Vineyard Shiraz 2018 Typical Duke's Shiraz, with the elegance of a
ballet dancer floating across the stage lifted by unseen strands of tannins. Screwcap.
14% alc. **Rating** 95 To 2030

Single Vineyard Cabernet Sauvignon 2018 Duke's Vineyard and winemaker Robert Diletti are a match made in vinous heaven, whether it be riesling, shiraz or cabernet. The special quality stems from purity and (for the reds), silky tannins. Screwcap. 13.2% alc. Rating 95 To 2038

ɪɪɪɪ **Single Vineyard Rose 2019** Rating 89 To 2021 $20

Dune Wine ★★★★★

PO Box 9, McLaren Vale, SA 5171 **Region** McLaren Vale
T 0403 584 845 **www**.dunewine.com **Open** Not
Winemaker Duncan Lloyd, Peter Lloyd **Est.** 2017 **Dozens** 1700 **Vyds** 8ha
This is the project of Duncan and Peter Lloyd (of Coriole fame) using fruit sourced from a single vineyard in Blewitt Springs. The brothers grew up immersed in a world of wine, olive oil, illegal goat's cheese and great food. Both worked in kitchens from the age of 13 and continued to develop a love of good food and wine. Duncan studied winemaking before leaving McLaren Vale to work in Tasmania and Margaret River, and then in Chianti and the Rhône Valley. He returned to McLaren Vale as he couldn't understand why you would want to live anywhere else. Peter also left the area after university, with eclectic occupations in France and England. He shares Duncan's views on McLaren Vale, though for now he lives in Melbourne. Exports to Sweden and Taiwan.

ɪɪɪɪɪ **Desert Sands McLaren Vale Shiraz 2018** The yield was less than 1t/acre, open-fermented, matured for 12 months in 10% new oak. It's hard to separate the intensity, acidity, fruit and tannins – don't waste valuable drinking time. Screwcap. 14.1% alc. **Rating** 97 To 2038 $60 ✪

ɪɪɪɪɪ **Blewitt Springs McLaren Vale Shiraz 2018** Fermented with a combination of whole berry and some whole bunch. It's only medium-bodied, but packs a punch from its cleverly pitched black fruits, spice, licorice and cherry. Value+ is a Dune consistency. Screwcap. 14% alc. **Rating** 95 To 2040 $26 ✪
Bonaire McLaren Vale Rose 2019 Carignan, shiraz and sangiovese; the juice fully oxidised to reduce phenolics pre-fermentation in used oak. Bone dry, savoury and complex spicy/rose powder palate. The usual high quality from Dune. Screwcap. 12.5% alc. **Rating** 94 To 2023 $26 ✪
The Empty Quarter 2018 Grenache, mourvedre, shiraz and touriga; co-fermented, matured for 12 months in used French oak. Very good colour and a freshness to the flavour, at once savoury and bursting with red and purple fruits. This is a very rare (and interesting) co-ferment, all 4 varieties needing to ripen at the same time. Screwcap. 14.3% alc. **Rating** 94 To 2035 $28 ✪
Pyla 2018 The vineyard is planted to negroamaro, nero d'Avola, grenache, mourvedre, montepulciano and carignan. Somehow this band of varieties is persuaded to ripen at the same time, and hence are co-fermented in a wax-lined concrete fermenter. It's as complex as its blend suggests, with red, blue and purple flavours, and persistent tannins. Screwcap. 13.5% alc. **Rating** 94 To 2030 $32

ɪɪɪɪɪ **Tirari 2018** Rating 93 To 2022 $26 ✪
El Beyda 2019 Rating 90 To 2023 $26

Dutschke Wines ★★★★★

Lot 1 Gods Hill Road, Lyndoch, SA 5351 **Region** Barossa Valley
T (08) 8524 5485 **www**.dutschkewines.com **Open** By appt
Winemaker Wayne Dutschke **Est.** 1998 **Dozens** 5000 **Vyds** 15ha
Winemaker and owner Wayne Dutschke set up business with uncle (and grapegrower) Ken Semmler in 1990 to produce their first wine. Since then, Dutschke Wines has built its own small winery around the corner from Ken's vineyard and the portfolio has increased. While Wayne has now been making small-batch wines for over 20 years; his use of whole-berry ferments, open fermenters, basket presses and a quality oak regime have all remained the same. He was crowned Barossa Winemaker of the Year in 2010, inducted into the Barons

of Barossa in '13 and is the author of a children's book about growing up in a winery called *My Dad has Purple Hands*. Exports to the US, Canada, Denmark, Germany, the Netherlands, Taiwan and China.

🍷🍷🍷🍷 **Oscar Semmler Lyndoch Barossa Valley Shiraz 2017** This is benchmark shiraz for those who like something quintessentially Barossa, albeit, with freshness, flow and a *je ne sais quoi* elegance. The oak transcends the other cuvees in terms of impact, melding with the inevitable dark fruit references to impart a malty, toasty warmth. Long. A bit tangy, but this will age very well as each component comes into step. Screwcap. **Rating** 94 To 2032 $80 NG

🍷🍷🍷🍷 **St Jakobi Single Vineyard Lyndoch Barossa Valley Shiraz 2018** Rating 93 To 2030 $45 NG
SAMI St Jakobi Vineyard Lyndoch Barossa Valley Cabernet Sauvignon 2018 Rating 93 To 2028 $38 NG
GHR Neighbours Barossa Valley Shiraz 2018 Rating 92 To 2028 $35 NG
Jackson St Jakobi Vineyard Barossa Valley Cabernet Shiraz 2018 Rating 91 To 2026 $38 NG

Eagles Rest Wines

65 Maxwells Road, Pokolbin, NSW 2320 **Region** Hunter Valley
T 0428 199 888 **www**.eaglesrestwines.com.au **Open** By appt
Winemaker Xanthe Hatcher **Est.** 2007 **Dozens** 1000 **Vyds** 20ha
Eagles Rest has flown under the radar since its establishment in 2007, and still does. The estate is planted to 8ha of chardonnay, 7ha shiraz, 3ha semillon and 2ha verdelho.

🍷🍷🍷🍷 **Gully Block Hunter Valley Semillon 2016** Hand-picked, whole-bunch pressed, controlled temperature fermentation (14°–18°C) for 14 days. The colour is still to develop but the semillon flavours take centre stage; the acidity is likely high, the pH low. Great bargain. Screwcap. 11.5% alc. **Rating** 95 To 2026 $35 **✪**
Maluna Block Hunter Valley Shiraz 2018 Hand-picked, 50yo vines, destemmed, open-fermented, 6 days cold soak, hand-plunged, 18 days on skins, 10 months maturation in used French oak. Deep colour; multiple layers of blackberry/black cherry. A curiously low level of tannin extract. Screwcap. 13.7% alc. **Rating** 94 To 2038 $50

🍷🍷🍷🍷 **Maluna Block Hunter Valley Shiraz 2011** Rating 92 To 2031 $60

Earthworks

PO Box 551, Tanunda, SA 5352 **Region** Barossa Valley
T (08) 8561 3200 **www**.earthworkswines.com **Open** Not
Winemaker Sam Wigan, Marc van Halderen **Est.** 2003 **Dozens** 10 000 **Vyds** 15ha
Earthworks was founded by the Lindner and Bitter families in 2003. Both have been centrally involved in the Barossa wine industry for many years and were able to persuade the marketing arm of the Hill-Smith Family/Yalumba/Negociants Australia, to handle the domestic distribution of the wine. When the arrangement was extended internationally via Negociants International, part of the business was purchased by the Hill-Smith Family, reinforcing their sales, winemaking and marketing efforts with an equity position in Earthworks. Exports to the UK, the US, Canada and NZ.

Eddie McDougall Wines

PO Box 2012, Hawthorn, Vic 3122 **Region** King Valley/Margaret River
T 0413 960 102 **www**.eddiemcdougallwines.com.au **Open** Not
Winemaker Eddie McDougall **Est.** 2007 **Dozens** 6000
Eddie McDougall is an award-winning winemaker, wine judge, columnist and host of the 13-episode TV series *The Flying Winemaker* on Discovery network's TLC. In 2012 Eddie was named one of the 'Top 20 People Changing the Way We Eat and Drink' by *Time Out Hong*

Kong. Eddie's winemaking credentials extend over a decade of experience with some of the world's most influential wineries. He has made wines with the likes of Vietti (Barolo), Mas de Daumas Gassac (Languedoc), Deep Woods Estate (Margaret River), Giant Steps (Yarra Valley) and O'Leary Walker (Clare Valley). Eddie holds a Bachelor of International Business from Griffith University and a post-graduate Diploma of Wine Technology and Viticulture from the University of Melbourne. In '13 he was one of 12 elite wine professionals selected for the annual Len Evans Tutorial, regarded as the world's most esteemed wine education program. Exports to Singapore, the Philippines, Hong Kong, Macau, Taiwan and China.

♟♟♟♟♟ **Margaret River Cabernets 2017** A deep ruby, this is a youthful wine. Full-bodied, but showing little but a nascent shade of what it will become. Pulpy. Puppy fat cherry, cassis and vanillan scents. Ball bearing tannins, nicely lubricated, serve as the undercarriage. The oak, yet to be fully absorbed, is classy and cedar-edged. This will be a fine, savoury expression in time. Screwcap. 14.5% alc. **Rating** 93 **To** 2029 $45 NG
King Valley Pinot Grigio 2019 Has all the indicia for pinot gris: dry, crisp pear and apple fruit creating length rather than depth. Screwcap. 13.5% alc. **Rating** 90 **To** 2022 $22
Little Pig Margaret River Rose 2019 A more recent vintage gives this gently coral hued rose more crunch. More energy. Greater length and refreshment factor. Tangerine, rosewater, musk and strawberry careen along some talcy acid lines. Easy enough to plunder a bottle. Screwcap. 12.8% alc. **Rating** 90 **To** 2020 $18 NG ☺
King Valley Prosecco NV A palpably dry prosecco, tucking in gushing scents of baked apple, Asian pear and alpine herbs with a chewy froth and gentle acid seams. A joyous drink. Crown seal. 12% alc. **Rating** 90 $22 NG

Eden Hall   ★★★★☆

6 Washington Street, Angaston, SA 5353 **Region** Eden Valley
T 0400 991 968 **www.**edenhall.com.au **Open** At Taste Eden Valley
Winemaker Phil Lehmann **Est.** 2002 **Dozens** 6000 **Vyds** 34ha
David and Mardi Hall purchased the historic Avon Brae Estate in 1996. The 120ha property has been planted to cabernet sauvignon (the lion's share, with 13ha), riesling (9.25ha), shiraz (6ha) and smaller amounts of merlot, cabernet franc and viognier. The majority of the production is contracted to Yalumba, St Hallett and McGuigan Simeon, with 10% of the best grapes held back for the Eden Hall label. Exports to Canada, NZ and China.

♟♟♟♟♟ **Block 4 Eden Valley Shiraz 2018** This is a delicious, full-bodied, silken red. Sourced from a single block of the Avon Brae vineyard. Fealty to place evident across a soaring violet, crushed rock, clove, boysenberry, kirsch and anise-scented nose. The palate billows nicely, the aromas reverberating across it. The French oak (40% new), well nestled. The finish juicy, plush and nicely sappy; a riff of coffee bean tannin as a final accent. Screwcap. 14.5% alc. **Rating** 93 **To** 2033 $40 NG
Springton Eden Valley Cabernet Sauvignon 2018 A deep crimson, with bright vermilion edges. Great colour! Mint, thyme, dried sage, Christmas cake spice and cassis billow across beautifully appointed oak pillars. For this style of warm-climate, rich cabernet, the tannins are impeccably massaged into the fray. A lovely drink. Well measured. Screwcap. 14% alc. **Rating** 93 **To** 2032 $25 NG ☺
Reserve Eden Valley Riesling 2019 Hewn from grapes of several select rows across a prized block. A medium yellow, smelling considerably riper than the modest alcohol suggests. Candied Meyer lemon. Spa salts, pink grapefruit, quince and lime juice as backups. A ripe, warm year to be sure, but the structural gears are well set. Dutiful acidity, a gentle chew and a strident forceful flourish across the finish. Screwcap. 11.5% alc. **Rating** 92 **To** 2029 $35 NG
Springton Eden Valley Riesling 2019 This has less intensity and mettle than the Reserve cuvee, but the drinkability factor is high. In light of the warm conditions, this has an effortless flow. Gentle. Balletic. Orange blossom, honeysuckle and citrus marmalade notes coat the cheeks and linger long. Screwcap. 11% alc. **Rating** 91 **To** 2027 $22 NG ☺

Block 3 Eden Valley Cabernet Sauvignon 2018 A great colour, as is the estate's wont. French oak introduces the nose, with scents of cedar and spice, then blackcurrant, bouquet garni, tapenade and extremely ripe black cherry beckon one in to play. This is a dense, take-no-prisoners sort of wine. The finish warm and porty, with a clang of tannins to conclude. Time will tell, but I much prefer the Springton cuvee. Screwcap. 14.8% alc. **Rating** 91 **To** 2033 $40 NG
Springton Eden Valley Shiraz 2018 A meld of fruit from 2 blocks across the Avon Brae site. Ample blue fruit references, black cherry, lilac and licorice blackstrap. Rich and warming. Yet despite the modest use of French oak (15% new), this finishes with edgy tannins and acidity. A little time may settle them. Screwcap. 14.5% alc. **Rating** 90 **To** 2028 $25 NG

Eden Road Wines   ★★★★★

3182 Barton Highway, Murrumbateman, NSW 2582 **Region** Canberra District
T (02) 6226 8800 **www**.edenroadwines.com.au **Open** Wed–Sun 11–4.30
Winemaker Celine Rousseau **Est.** 2006 **Dozens** 12000 **Vyds** 5ha
The name of this business, now entirely based in the Canberra District, reflects an earlier time when it also had a property in the Eden Valley. That has now been separated and since 2008 operations have focused on Hilltops, Canberra District and Tumbarumba wines. Eden Road purchased the former Doonkuna winery and mature vineyard, and its marketing was greatly assisted by winning the Jimmy Watson Trophy in '09. Exports to the UK and the US.

ⵟⵟⵟⵟⵟ **The Long Road Syrah 2018** From the estate Murrumbateman vineyard and Chalker's Crossing (Hilltops); fully destemmed and fermented with batches of whole and lightly crushed berries, matured in 3yo French puncheons. Every aspect parked so neatly. Great future. Screwcap. 13% alc. **Rating** 95 **To** 2040 $25 ✪
Canberra Syrah 2018 A 50/50% mix from Eden Road's vineyards at Murrumbateman and Lake George. Destemmed, fermented with batches of whole or partly crushed berries, matured for 18 months in French puncheons (20% new). It is only medium-bodied but has unlimited drive and power from its 13.5% alcohol that translates into a raft of black fruits/spice and licorice notes. Screwcap. **Rating** 95 **To** 2035 $35 ✪
Tumbarumba Chardonnay 2018 From the Maragle and Courabyra vineyards; destemmed and lightly crushed, 30% of the free-run juice direct to French puncheons, settled juice from tanks to 30% new French oak. A complex, full-bodied wine with white peach, nectarine and fig flavours. Screwcap. 13.5% alc. **Rating** 94 **To** 2030 $35
Tumbarumba Pinot Noir 2018 From the Courabyra Vineyard and includes 8% pinot meunier; the pinot noir was open-fermented with 30% whole bunches, the pinot meunier destemmed and open-fermented, matured in French puncheons (no age specified). A powerful statement about place. Screwcap. 14% alc. **Rating** 94 **To** 2028 $25 ✪
Canberra Malbec 2019 From the Lake George vineyard; fully destemmed, 25% whole berries, 75% lightly crushed, pressed into used barriques for mlf and 6 months development; 10% shiraz from Lake George also included. Exceptional power and intensity for a wine with such low alcohol. Screwcap. 12.5% alc. **Rating** 94 **To** 2040 $30 ✪

ⵟⵟⵟⵟⵡ **The Long Road Tumbarumba Chardonnay 2018** **Rating** 93 **To** 2028 $25 ✪
The Long Road Hilltops Pinot Gris 2019 **Rating** 92 **To** 2021 $25 ✪
The Long Road Tumbarumba Pinot Noir 2018 **Rating** 90 **To** 2023 $25

Edenmae Estate Wines   ★★★★

7 Miller Street, Springton, SA 5235 **Region** Eden Valley
T 0409 493 407 **www**.edenmae.com.au **Open** Fri–Sun 10–6
Winemaker Michelle Barr **Est.** 2007 **Dozens** 1800 **Vyds** 12ha

Owner/winemaker Michelle Barr runs Edenmae on a minimal intervention/organic viticulture basis. The vineyard is planted to riesling and shiraz (4ha each), pinot noir and cabernet sauvignon (2ha each); most around 40yo, some younger. Its cellar door offers their full portfolio for tasting and local platters.

1847 | Chateau Yaldara ★★★★★

Chateau Yaldara, Hermann Thumm Drive, Lyndoch, SA 5351 **Region** Barossa Valley
T (08) 8524 0200 **www**.1847wines.com **Open** 7 days 10–5
Winemaker Chris Coulter, Gabriel Morgan **Est.** 1947 **Dozens** 50000 **Vyds** 100ha
1847 Wines is wholly owned by Chinese group Treasure Valley Wines. The year 1847 is when Barossa pioneer Johann Gramp planted his first vines in the region; there is in fact no other connection between Gramp and the business he established and that of 1847 Wines, other than the fact that the 80ha estate is in the general vicinity of Gramp's original plantings. A 1000t winery was built in 2014, handling the core production together with new varieties and blends. This was underpinned by the acquisition of Chateau Yaldara in '14, providing a major retail outlet and massively enhanced production facilities. Exports to the US, Canada, Germany, Morocco, Sri Lanka, Vietnam, Singapore, Taiwan, Hong Kong and China.

🍷🍷🍷🍷🍷 **1847 Special Aged 20 Years Old Tawny NV** More muted on the nose than you might expect, but the palate rams home its message. Rancio, fruitcake, brandy and sweet raisin flavours pour it on. Cork. 19.5% alc. **Rating** 91 $100 CM
Yaldara Rose 2019 Single vineyard rose made with grenache and sangiovese. Pale crimson in colour and showing plenty of verve on the palate. Apple and strawberry flavours team with cream and dry herbs. Good lift and life. Good drink. Screwcap. 12.5% alc. **Rating** 90 **To** 2022 $20 CM ❂

Eisenstone ★★★★★

56 Murray Street, Tanunda, SA 5352 **Region** Barossa Valley
T 0417 827 851 **www**.eisenstone.com.au **Open** By appt 10–5
Winemaker Stephen Cook **Est.** 2014 **Dozens** 500
Stephen Cook took a circuitous route to winemaking: his first occupation on leaving school in NZ was a nine-year stint with a local bank. The decision to up stakes and travel in SA brought him into contact with wine and he returned to NZ and completed a bachelor of science degree and a master's in biochemisty. Even then, he says, not with the intention of becoming a winemaker. On a whim he called into a small local winery to 'buy a few grapes' and a deal was struck that he would exchange his time in lieu of payment. 'From the first moment I was was hooked'. He returned to SA and secured the Roseworthy Graduate Diploma in Oenology. A vintage in California filled his wanderlust; a varied career in the Barossa Valley followed, working for large wineries, rising steadily up the ranks in a 20-year career. In 2014 he decided to take a small plunge and embark on Eisenstone, its translation meaning the ironstone soil on which the early settlers planted their vineyards. He only makes single vineyard or single district shiraz, eschewing all other varieties. He is only interested in high quality grapes, the use of top quality oak the tool to capture the message of the interaction between shiraz and its particular place. Exports to China.

🍷🍷🍷🍷🍷 **Dimchurch vd. Ebenezer Barossa Valley Shiraz 2018** The vineyard, with its 70+yo vines, is that of 6th generation grower Adrian Hoffman; matured in French oak (50% new) for 20 months. This is a very elegant medium–bodied wine that has soaked up the new oak without hesitation, leaving the fresh fruit flavours free to depart from the normal Barossa Valley black spectrum and explore red berry flavours. The tannins are fine, the wine showing no sign of bottling 1 month before tasting. Screwcap. 14.5% alc. **Rating** 97 **To** 2040 $100 ❂
Greenock Barossa Valley Shiraz 2017 The grapes were grown by Kym Teusner on his personal vineyard on Roennfeldt Road along the western ridge of the Barossa Valley. Matured in French oak (50% new) for 20 months. Has the qualities that I see (and enjoy) as the mark of a special vintage: lighter

footfall, more spice and savoury nuances, and a long finish that expands like the peacock's tail. The special bonus is a final surge of fresh red fruits. Cork. 14.5% alc. **Rating** 97 **To** 2037 $75 ✪

▼▼▼▼▼ **Greenock Barossa Valley Shiraz 2018** Matured in French oak (30% new) for 20 months, 133 dozen made. It's full-bodied, flush with black fruits and in normal Barossa Valley style. Screwcap. 14.5% alc. **Rating** 96 **To** 2043 $75 ✪

Stockwell Barossa Valley Shiraz 2018 The red ironstone soils sweep across the northeast of the Barossa Valley including the Stockwell district. Matured in French oak (50% new) for 20 months. This is a very attractive medium-bodied wine with notes of spice and licorice studded in the blackberry and plum fruit; the tannins playing a gentle hand. Screwcap. 14.5% alc. **Rating** 96 **To** 2038 $75 ✪

Nitschke Road vd. Greenock Barossa Valley Shiraz 2018 The grapes were grown by Angelo de Fazio at his Nitschke Road Vineyard; the wine matured in French oak (50% new) for 22 months. Deep and such an intense crimson-purple, it stains the glass as it's swirled. It is voluptuous and very full-bodied; the tannins submerged, as is the oak. 66 dozen. Screwcap. 14.5% alc. **Rating** 95 **To** 2048 $100

Marananga Barossa Valley Shiraz 2017 Matured in French oak (30% new) for 20 months, 66 dozen made. Here the impact of the richness associated with Marananga cuts across the '17 vintage mark. Thus it conforms to the longer term expectations of style, which is no bad thing. Screwcap. 14.5% alc. **Rating** 95 **To** 2035 $75

Elderslie

PO Box 93, Charleston, SA 5244 **Region** Adelaide Hills
T 0404 943 743 **www**.eldersliewines.com.au **Open** Not
Winemaker Adam Wadewitz **Est.** 2015 **Dozens** 600 **Vyds** 8ha
Elderslie brings together two families with wine in their veins. In their respective roles as winemaker (Adam Wadewitz) and wine marketer (Nicole Roberts), they bring a wealth of experience gained in many parts of the wine world. They each have their partners (Nikki Wadewitz and Mark Roberts) onboard and also have real-life jobs. In 2016 Nicole accepted the position of executive officer of the Adelaide Hills Wine Region, having had brand development roles with three of the Hills' leading winemakers: Shaw + Smith, Grosset and The Lane Vineyard. Adam carved out a career at the highest imaginable level, aided by becoming joint dux of the Len Evans Tutorial in 2009. He was senior winemaker at Best's, where he made the '12 Jimmy Watson winner; became the youngest judge to serve as a panel chair at the National Wine Show; and is now senior winemaker for Shaw + Smith and their associated Tolpuddle Vineyard in Tasmania.

▼▼▼▼▼ **Hills Blend #2 Adelaide Hills Pinot Meunier Pinot Noir Gamay 2018** Excellent colour and clarity, deep but bright (in pinot terms). It's not particularly rich, but is very intense, focused, spicy and long. Screwcap. 13.5% alc. **Rating** 95 **To** 2027 $42

Hills Blend #1 Adelaide Hills Pinot Blanc 2018 Combines power and finesse; citrus, grass and cashew all in play. The result is a wine of exceptional mouthfeel and length, unlike the usual rather drab pinot blancs. So, don't tie it down. Screwcap. 12.5% alc. **Rating** 94 **To** 2025 $42

Elderton

3–5 Tanunda Road, Nuriootpa, SA 5355 **Region** Barossa Valley
T (08) 8568 7878 **www**.eldertonwines.com.au **Open** Mon–Fri 10–5, w'ends & hols 11–4
Winemaker Julie Ashmead, Brock Harrison **Est.** 1982 **Dozens** 45 000 **Vyds** 65ha
The founding Ashmead family, with mother Lorraine supported by sons Allister and Cameron, continues to impress with their wines. Julie Ashmead (married to Cameron), fifth-generation winemaker at Campbells in Rutherglen, is head of production, overseeing viticulture and winemaking. Elderton has two vineyards: one in the Barossa Valley at Greenock (originally planted by the Helbig family in 1915, purchased in 2010, consisting

of shiraz, grenache, carignan, mourvedre, cabernet sauvignon, chardonnay and semillon); the other one is the Craneford Vineyard in the Eden Valley (planted to shiraz, cabernet sauvignon, riesling and chardonnay). Energetic promotion and marketing in Australia and overseas are paying dividends. Elegance and balance are the keys to these wines. Exports to all major markets.

ΥΥΥΥΥ **Western Ridge Barossa Valley Shiraz 2017** Only the second release – the first in '14 and a mere 1147 bottles made – sold via cellar door. Make the trip because this is very good. Be greeted by a dark garnet hue; a mass of ripe fruit infused with mint, baking spices, black chocolate and roasted coffee bean, but the drive is altogether savoury and meaty. Quite decadent. The palate voluminous, shiny and impressive. Ripe tannins and terrific length seal the deal. Screwcap. 14.5% alc. **Rating** 96 **To** 2037 $80 JF

Command Barossa Shiraz 2017 This commands respect thanks to the fruit coming off 123yo vines and the care taken from that moment right through to the winemaking. It is powerful and divine. Lush with the dark fruit coated with chocolate, pepper and coffee. The palate feels all velvety with the tannins neatly placed, the oak integrated. With a glass in hand enjoy a sense that all's well with the world. Screwcap. 14.9% alc. **Rating** 96 **To** 2037 $145 JF

Fifteen Single Vineyard Shiraz 2016 Single vineyard block planted in 1915, hence the name, and described as a 'massive blockbuster'. Mmm, it comes in an absurdly heavy bottle. That aside, it's one for the cellar. A flood of soused dark plums, tobacco, molasses, licorice and soy sauce; firm tooth-coating tannins and volume across the palate. There is a green walnut character wafting in and out, it's distracting. Still, fans of massive blockbusters, rejoice. Cork. 15% alc. **Rating** 96 **To** 2036 $350 JF

Ode to Lorraine Barossa Valley Cabernet Shiraz Merlot 2017 A glorious, superb blend of 58% cabernet sauvignon, 37% shiraz and 5% merlot. It is heady with violets, cassis and woodsy spices. The full-bodied palate impresses with its gloss, its detail; neat acidity and firm tannins inform its ageing potential. Harmony in a glass. Screwcap. 14.5% alc. **Rating** 96 **To** 2037 $60 JF ✪

Western Ridge Barossa Valley Grenache Carignan 2019 There is something about this blend. It makes you sit up, take notice and relish the flavours and lightness of touch. And yet, there's laser precision to the acidity, the grainy tannins in tow, the gorgeous red fruit and spice flavours. It's the Barossa without the boom. Lovely wine. Screwcap. 13.9% alc. **Rating** 95 **To** 2029 $60 JF

Barossa GSM 2018 This blend of 44% grenache, 31% shiraz, 25% mourvedre has come together fabulously and is immediately pleasurable. Tangy, ripe, juicy fruit spiced with musk, juniper and woodsy spices. Fuller-bodied but not a blockbuster; compact tannins and freshness throughout. Great stuff. Screwcap. 14.7% alc. **Rating** 95 **To** 2028 $35 JF ✪

ΥΥΥΥΦ **Neil Ashmead Grand Tourer Shiraz 2018** **Rating** 93 **To** 2033 $60 JF
Barossa Valley Golden Semillon 2019 **Rating** 93 **To** 2026 $30 JF
Barossa Shiraz 2017 **Rating** 92 **To** 2030 $35 JF
Barossa Merlot 2018 **Rating** 90 **To** 2026 $35 JF
Barossa Cabernet Sauvignon 2017 **Rating** 90 **To** 2028 $35 JF

Eldorado Road ★★★★★

46–48 Ford Street, Beechworth, Vic 3747 **Region** North East Victoria zone
T (03) 5725 1698 **www**.eldoradoroad.com.au **Open** Fri–Sun 11–5
Winemaker Paul Dahlenburg, Ben Dahlenburg, Laurie Schulz **Est.** 2010 **Dozens** 1500
Vyds 4ha

Paul Dahlenburg (nicknamed Bear), Lauretta Schulz (Laurie) and their children have leased a 2ha block of shiraz planted in the 1890s with rootlings supplied from France (doubtless grafted) in the wake of phylloxera's devastation of the Glenrowan and Rutherglen plantings. Bear and Laurie knew about the origins of the vineyard, which was in a state of serious decline after years of neglect. The owners of the vineyard were aware of its historic importance and were more than happy to lease it. Four years of tireless work reconstructing the old vines has resulted in tiny amounts of exceptionally good shiraz; they have also planted a small area of nero d'Avola and durif.

⚑⚑⚑⚑⚑ **Perseverance Old Vine Shiraz 2017** This deserves some respect, so don't rush it. Let it breathe and come to life, for the fruit comes off vines planted in the 1890s and there's a dash of ugni blanc in the mix given it's dotted throughout the vineyard. This unfurls to reveal a delicacy and yet it's full of the flavour of zesty red fruits, a hint of licorice and more besides. It's the contentment across the palate and the astonishingly fine and pure tannins that really set this apart. Screwcap. 14.3% alc. **Rating** 96 **To** 2035 $65 JF ○

Onyx Durif 2018 A durif that's approachable and immensely pleasurable to drink is generally rare, but this is one. It is not extracted or killed with oak. Instead, the quality fruit shines through. It's remarkably juicy with pliant yet decisive tannins and a freshness throughout. Screwcap. 14.5% alc. **Rating** 96 **To** 2030 $37 JF ○

Beechworth Chardonnay 2018 Layers of flavour from stone fruit and figs to creamed honey, grilled almonds and toasty brioche. Thankfully it doesn't fall into the too big or blowsy territory as there's a citrus bent to the acidity. Screwcap. 13.6% alc. **Rating** 95 **To** 2027 $37 JF

Quasimodo Nero d'Avola Durif Shiraz 2017 A 50/33/17% split, fermented separately then blended, each variety adding their strengths to the final wine. Juiciness and brightness of the nero d'Avola fruit really shines through, along with some meaty reductive characters adding a more savoury overlay. Tannins are ripe and neatly pitched, as is the medium-bodied palate and its overall immediate appeal. Screwcap. 13.4% alc. **Rating** 95 **To** 2025 $29 JF ○

Comrade Nero d'Avola 2018 Eldorado Road has found its groove with this southern Italian variety – its '16 Riserva arguably the finest made in Australia – and this is no wallflower either. It's beautifully fragrant, super bright with juicy red fruits and more complexing notes of squid ink. Medium-bodied yet tightly framed with fine grainy tannins, and acidity that is so lively it pops. Screwcap. 13.3% alc. **Rating** 95 **To** 2026 $37 JF

Beechworth Syrah 2018 This inaugural release kickstarts with an excellent purple-crimson hue; reductive at first with meaty nuances but that soon gives way to a flush of dark sweet red fruits, oak spice, licorice and warm earth. It's still tight – almost linear – thanks to its fresh and lively acidity, with the grippy tannins and charry oak needing time to settle. Screwcap. 13% alc. **Rating** 94 **To** 2030 $37 JF

⚑⚑⚑⚑⚑ **Luminoso Rose 2019 Rating** 92 **To** 2022 $25 JF ○

Eldridge Estate of Red Hill   ★★★★★

120 Arthurs Seat Road, Red Hill, Vic 3937 **Region** Mornington Peninsula
T 0414 758 960 **www**.eldridge-estate.com.au **Open** Mon–Fri 12–4, w'ends & hols 11–5
Winemaker David Lloyd **Est.** 1985 **Dozens** 1000 **Vyds** 3ha
The Eldridge Estate vineyard was purchased by David and (the late) Wendy Lloyd in 1995. Major retrellising work has been undertaken, changing to Scott Henry, and all the wines are estate-grown and made. David also planted several Dijon-selected pinot noir clones (114, 115 and 777), which have been contributing since 2004; likewise the Dijon chardonnay clone 96. Attention to detail permeates all he does in vineyard and winery. Exports to the US.

⚑⚑⚑⚑⚑ **Wendy Chardonnay 2018** The second single vineyard chardonnay off the rank, crafted with Burgundian clones 95 and 96. More resinous. Umami creaminess. Toasted nuts, praline and vanillan-cedar oak tones. A weightier palate that is still, in the scheme of things, medium-bodied and restrained, belying the wine's thrumming intensity. The integration of each component is impeccable. Again, an air of generosity despite the underlying tension and precision. These are not wines reliant on sulphuric matchstick aromas, but on high quality fruit, sensitive handling and propitious sites. Screwcap. **Rating** 97 **To** 2028 NG

ŢŢŢŢŢ **Clonal Blend Pinot Noir 2018** Destemmed, cold soaked and fermented wild, as is the wont at this address. The point of difference, aside from the blend of 7 clones, is the Darwinian selection of the 4 best barrels, 1 being new. For me, this is the more structured brethren of the estate Single Vineyard. A return to the thirst-slaking tannins, expansive and rolling across the mouth. Sapid cherry, a sluice of orange zesty acidity and some fecund strawberry to spindly sandalwood notes, bound to a seam of classy oak. This is distinctive, delicious and for those who like great pinot. Screwcap. **Rating** 96 **To** 2030 NG

PTG 2019 A blend of 60% pinot noir, 40% gamay. It's the vinification that is intriguing and very successful. Called Carbo-Crush, the whole bunches are placed in a tank with no additions of any kind, the tank sealed and after a week a handful of bunches are removed and tasted – if there is an explosion of CO_2, the bunches are destemmed and fermented dry (if no explosion the tank is resealed for a few more days). The bouquet is rich and complex, the palate likewise. Screwcap. 13.5% alc. **Rating** 95 **To** 2039 $35

Single Vineyard Pinot Noir 2018 A mesh of 6 clones, dry-grown and planted in front of the property. Fully destemmed, soaked and fermented under the aegis of natural yeasts, before ageing for 16 months in French oak (20% new). The result is a pallid ruby, bristling with intent while belying the intensity of flavour that is to come: sour cherry, loganberry and other alpine red fruits. The tannins are attenuated, slaty and thirst-quenching, melding with maritime acidity to pull the melee long. This stands defiant and righteous in the face of so much pinot in this country made with excessive whole-bunches. Screwcap. **Rating** 95 **To** 2026 $65 NG

Chardonnay 2018 A fine vintage for the variety. A barrel-fermented blend of 2 clones. Beautifully proportioned. Mid-weighted. The nose an effortless meld of white fig, stone fruits and hazelnut, with a whiff of flint conferring gentle tension, rather than shrillness. Generous of flavour and yet far from a lair. The oak, well massaged into the fray. Maker David Lloyd is well versed in Burgundy and it shows. A mellifluous wine of precision and juicy length. Screwcap. **Rating** 94 **To** 2026 $50 NG

ŢŢŢŢ♀ **Single Clone Pinot Noir 2018** Rating 93 **To** 2028 NG

Elgee Park   ★★★★★

24 Junction Road, Merricks North, Vic 3926 **Region** Mornington Peninsula
T (03) 5989 7338 **www**.elgeeparkwines.com.au **Open** At Merricks General Wine Store
Winemaker Geraldine McFaul (Contract) **Est.** 1972 **Dozens** 1600 **Vyds** 4.4ha
The pioneer of the Mornington Peninsula in its 20th-century rebirth, owned by Baillieu Myer and family. The vineyard is planted to riesling, chardonnay, viognier (some of the oldest vines in Australia), pinot gris, pinot noir, merlot and cabernet sauvignon. The vineyard is set in a picturesque natural amphitheatre with a northerly aspect, looking out across Port Phillip Bay towards the Melbourne skyline.

ŢŢŢŢŢ **Mornington Peninsula Chardonnay 2018** Hand-picked, wild-fermented, matured for 11 months in French barriques. Gleaming quartz-green hue; lemongrass, citrus and Meyer lemon juice flavours have an umbrella protecting them. A complex wine with strands pulling in numerous directions. Screwcap. 13.2% alc. **Rating** 95 **To** 2028 $50

ŢŢŢŢ♀ **Mornington Peninsula Pinot Noir 2018** Rating 93 **To** 2028 $50
Mornington Peninsula Riesling 2018 Rating 91 **To** 2025 $30
Mornington Peninsula Cuvee Brut 2015 Rating 91 $50
Mornington Peninsula Pinot Gris 2018 Rating 90 **To** 2023 $35

Elgo Estate

2020 Upton Road, Upton Hill, Vic 3664 **Region** Strathbogie Ranges
T (03) 5798 5563 **www**.elgoestate.com.au **Open** Not
Winemaker Grant Taresch **Est.** 1999 **Dozens** 5000 **Vyds** 100ha
Elgo Estate, owned by the Taresch family, is located high in the hills of the Strathbogie Ranges, 125km northeast of Melbourne, a stone's throw from the southern end of the Heathcote region. Elgo Estate is committed to sustainable viticulture reflecting and expressing the characteristics of this cool-climate region. Two distinct wine portfolios via the Allira and Elgo Estate labels are produced. All of the wines are 100% estate-grown from their three vineyards in the region, with plantings dating back to the early 1970s. Elgo Estate was the first winery in Australia to be fully powered by self-generated renewable wind energy. The installation of a 30m tall 150kW wind turbine in 2007 enables Elgo to save around 400t of greenhouse gas emissions per year, while generating enough electricity to power the winery twice over; the excess green electricity is fed back into the main power grid. In '12 Elgo purchased the Mount Helen Vineyard from Robert Kirby. Exports to China.

Strathbogie Ranges Cabernet Sauvignon 2013 This is a nicely aged, mature bottle of dry red, in need of little patience. Produced to the limited tune of 100 dozen. Cassis, vanillan oak scents and bay leaf to black olive–soused tannins define the aroma to mid-palate. A stream of juicy acidity tows it all long and effortless. Nothing is out of place. Screwcap. **Rating** 92 **To** 2022 $26 NG

Allira Strathbogie Ranges Chardonnay 2019 Rating 89 **To** 2023 $16 NG ✪

Ellis Wines

3025 Heathcote-Rochester Road, Colbinabbin, Vic 3559 (postal) **Region** Heathcote
T 0401 290 315 **www**.elliswines.com.au **Open** Not
Winemaker Guy Rathjen **Est.** 1998 **Dozens** 3000 **Vyds** 54.18ha
Bryan and Joy Ellis own this family business, daughter Raylene Flanagan is the sales manager, and seven of the vineyard blocks are named after family members. For the first 10 years the Ellises were content to sell the grapes to a range of distinguished producers. However, since then a growing portion of the crop has been vinified. Exports to Hong Kong.

Premium Heathcote Shiraz 2016 This is 100% estate-grown. Small open fermenters, plunged 4–6 times daily, matured in French oak (50% new) for 14 months. High quality Heathcote shiraz; intense, long and intricately detailed black fruits, spice, pepper and licorice. Screwcap. 14.8% alc. **Rating** 97 **To** 2036 $70 ✪

Signature Label Heathcote Shiraz 2017 Estate-grown, open-fermented, 14 days on skins, pressed to French and American oak (30% new) for 12 months maturation. The colour is good, the bouquet and palate better still. Plum and blackberry fruit provide the lattice work of the texture. Gold medal Melbourne Wine Awards '17. Screwcap. 14.8% alc. **Rating** 95 **To** 2037 $35 ✪

Signature Label Heathcote Rose 2019 Rating 92 **To** 2021 $25 ✪

Eloper Wines

27 Arthur Street, Unley, SA 5061 (postal) **Region** Adelaide Hills
T 0437 199 728 **www**.eloperwines.com.au **Open** Not
Winemaker Revenir, Peter Dawson (Consultant) **Est.** 2018 **Dozens** 1300 **Vyds** 2.12ha
'Eloper' was born of the notion to 'escape without permission'. After a busy corporate life in the resources sector, Mick and Melissa Anstey yearned to return home to the Adelaide Hills for a life on the land and some fine wine. Their purchase of a historic 31.5ha Kuitpo property in 2014 was serendipitous: it was a piece of farming land once owned by Sir Douglas Mawson, complete with an abandoned gold mine and 5 acres of mature sauvignon blanc. The Pottery Road Vineyard, planted in 1996, had previously been a source of fruit for Starvedog Lane and

Shaw + Smith. The Ansteys have restructured the vineyard from spur pruning to cane pruning in an effort improve uniformity and fruit quality, and have also planted shiraz. It is one of the latest ripening sites in the Adelaide Hills. A collaboration with David Blows and the Springhill Vineyard at Macclesfield provides tempranillo and shiraz – this vineyard was planted in '98 at the behest of Hardys and is well known to Peter Dawson.

🍷🍷🍷🍷🍷 **Adelaide Hills Sauvignon Blanc 2019** Night-harvested, only the free-run used. Tropical fruits, a squeeze of Meyer lemon juice and crisp acidity make a sauvignon blanc with above average character. Screwcap. 12.2% alc. **Rating** 91 **To** 2021 $25

Adelaide Hills Syrah 2018 Hand-picked, wild-fermented with 40% whole bunches, matured in large-format Taransaud French oak (40% new) for 10 months. The colour and the body of the wine are in the clasp of the oak, but will likely break free during the next 3–5 years. Screwcap. 14% alc. **Rating** 90 **To** 2032 $40

🍷🍷🍷🍷 **Adelaide Hills Tempranillo 2018** **Rating** 89 **To** 2022 $25

Emilian ★★★★

1295 Mt Dandenong Tourist Road, Kalorama, Vic 3766 (postal) **Region** Yarra Valley
T 0421 100 648 **www**.emilian.com.au **Open** Not
Winemaker Robin Querre **Est.** 2015 **Dozens** 300

Robin Querre is the fourth generation of a family involved in winemaking since 1897, variously in Saint Emilion and Pomerol, France. Robin commenced studies in medicine at the University of Bordeaux, but changed to oenology in 1990. He studied under some of the Bordeaux greats (such as Yves Glories, Denis Dubourdieu and Aline Lonvaud), and worked vintages at Chateau Canon and Moueix (under Jean-Claude Berrouet, who was supervising Chateau Petrus), as well as at Rudd Estate in the Napa Valley. This led Robin to work in research, travelling to Australia, Germany, Austria, Switzerland, England, Japan and Israel. He currently works for Laffort Oenology, a private research company based in Bordeaux, developing, producing and selling oenological products to winemakers. He and wife Prue also make small quantities of very good wine at Allinda in the Yarra Valley.

🍷🍷🍷🍷🍷 **Single Vineyard Yarra Valley Syrah Cabernet Sauvignon en Rose 2019** Two-thirds shiraz, one-third cabernet sauvignon. Hand-picked direct to press, 7 days on lees skins, racked for clear juice to ferment, aged on lees for 6 months. Excellent texture, unusual but highly enjoyable and every bit as important as the spicy red fruit flavours. Screwcap. 12.5% alc. **Rating** 94 **To** 2021 $25 ✪

🍷🍷🍷🍷🍷 **Single Parcel Chardonnay 2019** **Rating** 92 **To** 2029 $37
Yarra Valley L'assemblage Rouge 2019 **Rating** 92 **To** 2030 $35

Eperosa ★★★★★

Lot 552 Krondorf Road, Tanunda, SA 5352 **Region** Barossa Valley
T 0428 111 121 **www**.eperosa.com.au **Open** Fri 11–2.30, Sat 11–5 & by appt
Winemaker Brett Grocke **Est.** 2005 **Dozens** 1000 **Vyds** 8.75ha

Eperosa owner and *Wine Companion 2021* Winemaker of the Year Brett Grocke qualified as a viticulturist in 2001 and, through Grocke Viticulture, consults and provides technical services to over 200ha of vineyards spread across the Barossa Valley, Eden Valley, Adelaide Hills, Riverland, Langhorne Creek and Hindmarsh Valley. He is ideally placed to secure small parcels of organically managed grapes, hand-picked, whole-bunch fermented and foot-stomped, and neither filtered nor fined. The wines are of impeccable quality – the use of high quality, perfectly inserted, corks will allow the wines to reach their full maturity decades hence. Exports to the UK, the US, Canada and China.

🍷🍷🍷🍷🍷 **Magnolia 1896 Shiraz 2017** The vines are pruned by hand; shoot and bunch thinning also by hand. The grapes are hand-picked and sorted; 1265 bottles made. Terrific colour clarity. The wine is full-bodied yet balanced to the point of elegance, with blackberry fruit trellised on ripe tannins. Why so cheap? Cork. 14.9% alc. **Rating** 98 **To** 2040 $80 ✪

L.R.C. Shiraz 2017 '144 shiraz, a few riesling, one mataro and a lone stranger make up a stand of vines that once formed the boundary row of an old vineyard.' The boundary row has survived the vineyard's loss to housing developments, saved by a partnership between the Light Regional Council and Grocke Viticulture. What a beautiful wine, taken to a vinous heaven by the vintage and modest alcohol. It's visibly full of red and black fruits, and will live as long as the (high quality) cork holds. 13.8% alc. **Rating** 98 **To** 2037 $45 ✪

Krondorf Grenache 2017 From a single block planted in 1903; 1584 bottles made. One of the best Barossa Valley grenaches I've tasted. It has a magical mix of finesse, power and length; the finish and aftertaste a circus ring of sparkling red fruits. A glorious wine at a giveaway price. Cork. 14.6% alc. **Rating** 97 **To** 2032 $30 ✪

Stonegarden 1858 Grenache 2017 This is from the oldest vineyard in the Eperosa band – indeed it is the oldest I know of that has remained in constant production; it is now heritage-listed. The wine fills the mouth with sweet dark fruit (not sugar-sweet) and a cage of fine, earthy tannins. It's a wine that I retasted numerous times, always finding new and delicious flavours and textures to enjoy. Includes 3% mataro and 2% shiraz. Cork. 14.5% alc. **Rating** 97 **To** 2047 $60 ✪

♟♟♟♟♟ **Magnolia 1965 Shiraz 2017** The 4 best barrels from the vines planted in '65 on the Magnolia Vineyard. In typical Brett Grocke style, every aspect of viticulture is done by hand and the vineyard is run organically. Matured in French hogsheads for 15 month. It is supple, but sits within a frame of perfect fruit – the blessing of the vintage and the vigneron who is constantly vigilant. Grossly underpriced. Cork. 14.9% alc. **Rating** 96 **To** 2040 $35 ✪

Barossa Valley Mataro Shiraz 2017 I nearly blindsided myself with this wine thanks to my general disappointment with Barossa Valley mataro. This is another thing altogether. It's a blend of 75% mataro from the Hoffman Sand Block at Ebenezer and 25% shiraz from the Magnolia Road Vineyard at Vine Vale. The mataro was green bunch-thinned post veraison and matured in a 1650l foudre; the organically farmed shiraz also bunch-thinned and aged in French hogsheads. It's supple and silky, the mouthfeel superb Cork. 13.7% alc. **Rating** 96 **To** 2042 $25 ✪

Ernest Schuetz Estate Wines   ★★★★

778 Castlereagh Highway, Mudgee, NSW 2850 **Region** Mudgee
T 0402 326 612 **www.ernestschuetzestate.com.au Open** W'ends 10.30–4.30
Winemaker Liam Heslop **Est.** 2003 **Dozens** 4500 **Vyds** 4.1ha

Ernest Schuetz's involvement in the wine industry started in 1988 at the age of 21. Working in various liquor outlets and as a sales representative for Miranda Wines, McGuigan Simeon and, later, Watershed Wines gave him an in-depth understanding of all aspects of the wine market. In 2003 he and wife Joanna purchased the Arronvale Vineyard (first planted in '91), at an altitude of 530m. When the Schuetzs acquired the vineyard it was planted to merlot, shiraz and cabernet sauvignon, and they have since grafted 1ha to riesling, pinot blanc, pinot gris, zinfandel and nebbiolo. The cellar door overlooks the vineyard. Exports to Vietnam, Hong Kong and China.

♟♟♟♟♟ **Epica XVI Amarone Method Mudgee Shiraz Cabernet 2016** Painstaking attention to detail and bunch-by-bunch handling as each is laid on drying racks with no bunches touching. They are left for 28 days before crushed and destemmed and fermented, matured for 30 months in French hogsheads (50% new). The wine is an unqualified success. Unctuous flavours of crystallised fruits and bitter chocolate, raisin fruitcake and endless spices all in true Amarone style. Screwcap. 16% alc. **Rating** 96 **To** 2050 $70 ✪

♟♟♟♟ **Terra X Mudgee Dry Rose 2019 Rating** 89 **To** 2021 $18 ✪
Terra X Mudgee Dry Rose 2018 Rating 89 **To** 2020 $18 ✪
Family Reserve Single Vineyard Mudgee Black Cabernet Sauvignon 2017 Rating 89 **To** 2024 $30

Espier Estate

Room 1208, 401 Docklands Drive, Docklands, Vic 3008 **Region** South Eastern Australia
T (03) 9670 4317 **www**.jnrwine.com **Open** Mon–Fri 9–5
Winemaker Sam Brewer **Est.** 2007 **Dozens** 25 000
This is the venture of Robert Luo and Jacky Lin. Winemaker Sam Brewer has been closely
linked with the business since its establishment. The principal focus is affordable, good value
wines. The Espier Estate wines are made at the family-owned boutique winery of Yarran
Wines, which is also partly owned by Robert and Jacky. Exports to Asia.

Estate 807

807 Scotsdale Road, Denmark, WA 6333 **Region** Denmark
T (08) 9840 9027 **www**.estate807.com.au **Open** Thurs–Sun 11–4
Winemaker Mike Garland **Est.** 1998 **Dozens** 1500 **Vyds** 4.2ha
Dr Stephen Junk and Ola Tylestam purchased Estate 807 in 2009. Stephen was a respected
embryologist working in IVF, while Ola came from a financial background. They chose the
property due to its range of pinot noir and chardonnay clones (there are also plantings of
cabernet and sauvignon blanc). Farm animals are used in the vineyard: chickens and ducks eat
the pests, and sheep and alpacas provide manure and keep the vineyard neat and tidy.

Evans & Tate

Cnr Metricup Road/Caves Road, Wilyabrup, WA 6280 **Region** Margaret River
T (08) 9755 6244 **www**.evansandtate.com.au **Open** 7 days 10.30–5
Winemaker Matthew Byrne, Lachlan McDonald **Est.** 1970 **Dozens** NFP **Vyds** 12.3ha
The history of Evans & Tate has a distinct wild west feel to its ownership changes since
1970, when it started life as a small two-family-owned business centred on the Swan
District. Suffice it to say, it was part of a corporate chess game between McWilliam's Wines
and the Fogarty Wine Group. Vineyards, brands, a viticultural services business and existing
operations encompassing Deep Woods, Smithbrook, Millbrook and Pemberton Estate, plus
Selwyn Viticultural Services, will become part of the production facility and other assets of
Margaret River Vintners. It is now 100% owned by Fogarty, who previously held 70%. This
doubles Fogarty's production to 600 000 dozen, cementing its place as the largest producer of
WA wine. Exports to all major markets.

ΨΨΨΨΨ **Redbrook Reserve Margaret River Chardonnay 2014** The utterly fantastic
quartz-green hue sets the antennae waving furiously. The bouquet is first out of
the blocks but it's the drive, the freshness, the pink grapefruit and Granny Smith
apple flavours that are the mark of a Margaret River chardonnay of the highest
rank. Its show record is partly summarised on the bottle. Screwcap. 12.5% alc.
Rating 97 **To** 2024 $65 ✪

ΨΨΨΨΨ **Redbrook Reserve Margaret River Chardonnay 2017** Fermented wild, no
mlf, 11 months in oak (only 13% new) before spending a further 12 months in
tank on lees prior to bottling. It puts on a clean pure display but then it also has
excellent intensity and length. Apple, white peach, pear and cedar wood flavours
are presented crisp-but-creamy, the result as delicious as it is impressive. Screwcap.
13.1% alc. **Rating** 95 **To** 2027 $65 CM
Redbrook Estate Margaret River Shiraz 2018 Vines planted in '75;
80% whole-bunch ferment, all pressings included, 13 months in French oak
(13% new). Licorice, violets, stems, nuts and black cherries. It puts on a complex
display, seamless too; its soft fruit and texture pulling a wide gamut of flavours
along for the ride. Tannin is incredibly fine-grained and its nutty length has plenty
going for it. This is a mid-weight shiraz with a whole lot to offer. Screwcap.
14.5% alc. **Rating** 95 **To** 2032 $40 CM
Redbrook Estate Margaret River Cabernet Merlot 2017 An even but
satisfying flow of elegant flavour. It's ripe and sweet but it's also dusty and well
shaped; it combines plushness with persistence. Fine-grained tannin, licorice notes,

florals and sweet herbs; everything here is in excellent order. Screwcap. 14.5% alc.
Rating 95 To 2034 $40 CM
Redbrook Reserve Margaret River Cabernet Sauvignon 2016 Cabernet
with a sweet-fruited smile on its face. It's ripe and polished with smoked cedar
wood slipped hand-in-glove into pure, ripe cassis, chocolate and peppermint. It's
pretty much impossible to review or drink this wine without uttering the word
'seductive'. Screwcap. **Rating** 95 To 2035 CM

ҶҶҶҶҶ **Broadway Chardonnay 2018 Rating** 93 To 2024 $29 CM
Broadway Cabernet Sauvignon 2018 Rating 92 To 2027 $29 CM
Breathing Space Cabernet Sauvignon 2018 Rating 92 To 2027 $19 CM ⊙
Breathing Space Rose 2019 Rating 90 To 2021 $19 CM ⊙

Evoi Wines

529 Osmington Road, Bramley, WA 6285 **Region** Margaret River
T 0437 905 100 **www**.evoiwines.com **Open** 7 days 10–5
Winemaker Nigel Ludlow **Est.** 2006 **Dozens** 10 000
NZ-born Nigel Ludlow has a Bachelor of Science in Human Nutrition but, after a short
career as a professional triathlete, he turned his attention to grapegrowing and winemaking,
with a Graduate Diploma in Oenology and Viticulture from Lincoln University, NZ. Time at
Selaks was a stepping stone to Flying Winemaking stints in Hungary, Spain and South Africa,
before a return as senior winemaker at Nobilo. He thereafter moved to Victoria, and finally
to Margaret River. It took time for Evoi to take shape, the first vintage of chardonnay being
made in the lounge room of Nigel's house. By 2010 the barrels had been evicted to more
conventional storage and since '14 the wines have been made in leased space at a commercial
winery. Quality has been exceptional. Exports to the UK, the Caribbean, Norway and
Hong Kong.

ҶҶҶҶҶ **Reserve Margaret River Chardonnay 2018** Hand-picked, vacuum-pressed,
full solids–barrel fermentation, 20% mlf, batonnage for 12 months. Wonderful
mouthfeel and varietal expression; the oak and mlf adding complexity to the core
of grapefruit and white peach; the length quite special. Curiously not bottled until
Oct '19. Screwcap. 13.5% alc. **Rating** 97 To 2033 $69 ⊙
Margaret River Chardonnay 2018 Selectiv'-harvested for whole berries, wild-
fermented – part in barrel, part in tank – 20% mlf and persistent reduction. Classic
grapefruit and white peach aromas and flavours. Screwcap. 13.5% alc. **Rating** 97
To 2030 $32 ⊙
Reserve Margaret River Cabernet Sauvignon 2018 Hand-picked,
fermented in small parcels, pressed to French barriques to finish primary and mlf.
This is a blend of the top barrels, and what a wine it is! I've never been able to
understand why finishing the ferment in oak should be used for shiraz but not
cabernet. I put my money where my mouth is on that 35 years ago. Screwcap.
14.5% alc. **Rating** 97 To 2038 $120 ⊙

ҶҶҶҶҶ **Margaret River Cabernet Sauvignon 2016** That this comes from a very
good Margaret River cabernet vintage is self-evident; yes, they are all good, but
this is even better. It is firm where it should be, with fine blackcurrant fruit right
through the palate, especially the mid-palate. Screwcap. 14.5% alc. **Rating** 95
To 2036 $35 ⊙
Margaret River Sauvignon Blanc Semillon 2018 An 80/20% blend harvested
at night, fermented in tank, a small part on solids. In its own way, as predictable
as Marlborough; and also at unbeatable prices. Passionfruit to capsicum, terrific
length. Screwcap. 13% alc. **Rating** 94 To 2026 $24 ⊙
Margaret River Malbec 2018 Hand-picked, open-fermented, hand-plunged,
12 months in French oak. Bright colour. A scented bouquet and a juicy rainbow
of flavours of red and black cherry, spice and licorice. Screwcap. 14.5% alc.
Rating 94 To 2033 $35

ŶŶŶŶŶ art by Evoi Reserve Margaret River Chardonnay 2018 Rating 93
To 2029 $30
art by Evoi Blackwood Valley Cabernet Sauvignon 2018 Rating 93
To 2028 $27 ✪

Faber Vineyard ★★★★★

233 Haddrill Road, Baskerville, WA 6056 **Region** Swan Valley
T (08) 9296 0209 **www**.fabervineyard.com.au **Open** Fri–Sun 11–4
Winemaker John Griffiths **Est.** 1997 **Dozens** 4000 **Vyds** 4.5ha
John Griffiths, former Houghton winemaker, teamed with wife Jane Micallef to found Faber
Vineyard. They have established shiraz, verdelho (1.5ha each), brown muscat, chardonnay
and petit verdot (0.5ha each). John says, 'It may be somewhat quixotic, but I'm a great fan of
traditional warm-area Australian wine styles, wines made in a relatively simple manner that
reflect the concentrated ripe flavours one expects in these regions. And when one searches,
some of these gems can be found from the Swan Valley.' Exports to Hong Kong and China.

ŶŶŶŶŶ **Ferguson Valley Semillon 2019** Sourced from the Rascals Corner Vineyard.
Hand-picked, chilled overnight, crushed, pressed and barrel fermented in seasoned
oak and bottled early. This youngster is still feeling its way, but barrel fermentation
has certainly aided its early attraction and drinkability, not to mention the drinker's
interest. Apple peel, quince, white peach, lemon zest. It will age with grace.
Screwcap. 12% alc. **Rating** 93 **To** 2027 $34 JP
Grand Liqueur Muscat NV Pours like molasses, has the visual appeal of treacle,
so you know you are moving up age-wise on the fortified classification system.
Grand is the second top tier with an average age of 11–20 years, definitely serious
territory; and here we have a weighty example, literally. It moves like syrup. It's
dark and concentrated with malty-raisin, fruitcake, walnut paste nuttiness. Dense
to taste, a bit heavy too, with golden syrup, nougat and honey. 375ml. Screwcap.
18% alc. **Rating** 93 JP
Swan Valley Verdelho 2019 Explores the rich tropical fruit vein running
through the grape: guava, melon, passionfruit, pineapple. It's a pretty, sweet-
tinged little number that builds and builds on the palate, with a honeysuckle
aromatic quality that is highly appealing. Texture is the key to not only immediate
enjoyment but ongoing drinkability into the future, together with some
understated, nutty acidity. Screwcap. 13.5% alc. **Rating** 90 **To** 2025 $24 JP
Swan Valley Petit Verdot 2018 Petit verdot is no shrinking violet. Often,
as a stand alone, it can be a thumping presence in the glass. Here, it is certainly
generous in nature, but it also exudes a certain grace and charm. Dark fruits
abound on the aroma with hoisin and tobacco savoury notes. The palate is sweet-
fruited and sure-footed with grainy tannins and noticeable oak. Give it time.
Screwcap. 14.5% alc. **Rating** 90 **To** 2035 $34 JP

ŶŶŶŶ **Chardonnay 2018** Rating 89 To 2026 JP
Swan Valley Chenin Blanc 2019 Rating 89 To 2027 $24 JP
Riche Swan Valley Shiraz 2018 Rating 89 To 2032 $27 JP
Donnybrook Durif 2018 Rating 89 To 2028 $43 JP
Frankland River Malbec 2018 Rating 89 To 2028 $35 JP

Fallen Giants ★★★★★

4113 Ararat-Halls Gap Road, Halls Gap, Vic 3381 **Region** Grampians
T (03) 5356 4252 **www**.fallengiants.com.au **Open** Wed–Mon 10–5
Winemaker Justin Purser **Est.** 1969 **Dozens** 2750 **Vyds** 10.5ha
I first visited this vineyard when it was known as Boroka Vineyard and marvelled at the
location in the wild country of Halls Gap. It wasn't very successful: Mount Langi Ghiran
acquired it in 1998 but by 2013 it had outlived its purpose. It was then that the opportunity
arose for the Drummond family, led by Aaron, to purchase the somewhat rundown vineyard.
They moved quickly; while the '13 vintage was made at Mount Langi Ghiran, thereafter it

was managed under contract by Circe Wines (Aaron Drummond's partnership business with Dan Buckle).

ΨΨΨΨΨ Grampians Riesling 2019 Aromas of apple and pear, citrus blossom and minerals all swirling around in the bouquet. A burst of lime juice as soon as it hits the mouth, then fanning out into riper citrus flavours as it moves along the palate. That slatey minerality detected in the bouquet seems to be integral to the acidity which drives through the finish, and lingers on and on in the aftertaste. Screwcap. 12% alc. **Rating** 95 **To** 2034 $30 SC ✪

Block 3 Grampians Shiraz 2018 From a higher point on the same vineyard as the Grampians Shiraz; 14 months in French oak (25% new). A darker, richer wine than its sibling, with more depth to the black fruit characters on the bouquet and palate, and more of a cedary oak influence. It's ripe as cool-climate shiraz goes, but complex and lingering flavours and fine tannin are the defining elements. Screwcap. 14.5% alc. **Rating** 95 **To** 2038 $60 SC

Grampians Shiraz 2018 Fruit from a 50yo vineyard at Halls Gap, grey loam with ironstone. Aged 12 months in French oak (10% new). The bouquet is archetypal cool-climate shiraz with gamey, leathery, herbal and peppery characters very much to the fore. Fruit is more apparent on the palate, ripe but restrained, red and black berries with tangy tannin astringency and very good length of flavour. Screwcap. 14.5% alc. **Rating** 94 **To** 2035 $35 SC

ΨΨΨΨ Grampians Cabernet Sauvignon 2018 **Rating** 93 **To** 2033 $35 SC

Farmer's Leap Wines   ★★★★

41 Hodgson Road, Padthaway, SA 5271 **Region** Padthaway
T (08) 8765 5155 **www**.farmersleap.com **Open** 7 days 10–4
Winemaker Renae Hirsch **Est.** 2004 **Dozens** 12000 **Vyds** 357ha
Scott Longbottom and Cheryl Merrett are third-generation farmers in Padthaway. They commenced planting the vineyard in 1995 on the family property and now there are shiraz, cabernet sauvignon, chardonnay and merlot. Initially the majority of the grapes were sold, but increasing quantities held for the Farmer's Leap label have seen production rise. Exports to Canada, Singapore, South Korea, Japan, Taiwan, Hong Kong and China.

ΨΨΨΨ Padthaway Shiraz 2015 It's in good shape. Rich and ripe with black plums doused in spices, licorice and soy sauce. A touch syrupy with firm tannins working across the full-bodied palate. Not complex, but you'd take it to a bbq. Screwcap. 14.5% alc. **Rating** 91 **To** 2024 $25 JF

Padthaway Shiraz 2016 Packed with the flavours of stewed plums, currants, licorice, wood smoke and a hint of regional mint. Fuller-bodied but not too big, tannins are plush and there's great appeal at this price point. Screwcap. 14.5% alc. **Rating** 90 **To** 2025 $25 JF

Random Shot Padthaway Shiraz 2016 A region that punches above its weight. This is still youthful yet takes in savoury flavours of licorice, boot polish and varnishy oak. Tannins are stern but less obvious with hearty dishes. Screwcap. 14.5% alc. **Rating** 90 **To** 2025 $18 JF ✪

Farr | Farr Rising   ★★★★★

27 Maddens Road, Bannockburn, Vic 3331 **Region** Geelong
T (03) 5281 1733 **www**.byfarr.com.au **Open** Not
Winemaker Nick Farr **Est.** 1994 **Dozens** 5500 **Vyds** 13.8ha
By Farr and Farr Rising continue to be separate brands from separate vineyards, the one major change being that Nick Farr has assumed total responsibility for both labels, leaving father Gary free to pursue the finer things in life without interruption. This has in no way resulted in any diminution in the quality of the Pinot Noir, Chardonnay, Shiraz and Viognier made. The vineyards are based on ancient river deposits in the Moorabool Valley. There are six different soils spread across the Farr property, with the two main types are: rich, friable red and black volcanic loam; and limestone, which dominates the loam in some areas. The other soils are

quartz gravel through a red volcanic soil, ironstone (called buckshot) in grey sandy loam with a heavy clay base, sandstone base and volcanic lava. The soil's good drainage and low fertility are crucial in ensuring small yields of intensely flavoured fruit. Exports to the UK, Canada, Denmark, Sweden, Hong Kong, Singapore, Taiwan, the Maldives, China and Japan.

ΨΨΨΨΨ **By Farr Chardonnay 2019** Stunning chardonnay. Flinty, peach-driven, toasty; sweet with spice and cedar wood, but smoky and minerally in spades. Powerful up front and all the way through before fully setting sail on the finish. A complete wine if ever there was one. Diam. 13.5% alc. **Rating** 97 **To** 2028 CM

GC Chardonnay by Farr 2018 Those long trails of flavour. That texture of satin. The way depth meets breadth without breaking stride. Classic chardonnay with white peach, grapefruit, grilled nut and flint notes lighting up the glass. It has a powerful body in elegant robes; it will mature gloriously. Diam. 13% alc. **Rating** 97 **To** 2030 CM

Farrside by Farr Geelong Pinot Noir 2018 It takes time in the glass for assertive cedar wood oak to settle into the fruit, but at all steps along the way this wine oozes quality and class. You're in the most skilled of hands here. Wood smoke, assorted cherries, twiggy spice notes, flavour-infused acidity and fine-grained tannin. It's a truly beautiful wine. Cork. 13.5% alc. **Rating** 97 **To** 2030 CM

By Farr Shiraz 2018 A special wine. It's all tang and undergrowth, cherries and peppery spices; but putting names to the individual flavours doesn't do the overall effect justice. This is a wine of fresh-faced beauty; it's a glance and a wink and a nod, all rolled into one. It tastes like a kind of magic. Cork. 13.5% alc. **Rating** 97 **To** 2032 CM

ΨΨΨΨΨ **Farr Rising Chardonnay 2019** The sheer crackle of quality. There's a flintiness to the nose, but the palate is pure, powerful and long. It's seamless in its own, formidable way. Ripe stone fruit, crushed fennel seeds, citrus rind and smoked oatmeal characters purr throughout. A beauty. Diam. 13.5% alc. **Rating** 96 **To** 2028 CM

RP Pinot Noir by Farr 2017 There's a bit of extra brood and scaffold here. It's a stern, spicy, tannic pinot with beetroot and earthy flavours folded into black cherry and red plum. Its acidity comes laden with spice, its tannin flecked with dry leaves, its fruit notes rise as if from the ground. It's not overdone but oak has added cushions to the texture. Its quality is right up there. Cork. 13.5% alc. **Rating** 96 **To** 2030 CM

Sangreal by Farr Geelong Pinot Noir 2018 Liquid roses, strawberry compote, fragrant garden herbs; the sweet joy of spring. It's structural and sturdy and yet it's ever so pretty. There's a tanginess to the acidity and a smokiness to the oak, both of which work in context. Every step is confident. Now or later, it will seduce. Cork. 13.5% alc. **Rating** 96 **To** 2030 CM

Tout Pres by Farr Pinot Noir 2017 The Tout Pres world is always a complex one. This is where sap is zapped by wood smoke, undergrowth is fired by autumn leaves. There's fruit, there's forest, there are roots dug into earth. The nuances come like dimples on a gold ball; such is their number, such is their integration. Don't drink now, drink later. Cork. 13.5% alc. **Rating** 96 **To** 2030 CM

Feathertop Wines   ★★★★☆

Great Alpine Road, Porepunkah, Vic 3741 **Region** Alpine Valleys
T (03) 5756 2356 **www.**feathertopwinery.com.au **Open** Fri–Sun 10–5
Winemaker Kel Boynton, Nick Toy **Est.** 1987 **Dozens** 9000 **Vyds** 16ha

Kel Boynton has a beautiful vineyard, framed by Mt Feathertop rising above it. The initial American oak input has been softened in more recent vintages to give a better fruit–oak balance. Kel has planted a spectacular array of 22 varieties, headed by savagnin, pinot gris, vermentino, sauvignon blanc, fiano, verdelho, riesling, friulano, pinot noir, tempranillo, sangiovese, merlot, shiraz, montepulciano and nebbiolo; with smaller plantings of prosecco, pinot meunier, dornfelder, durif, malbec, cabernet sauvignon and petit verdot. Exports to Austria.

♀♀♀♀♀ **Vintage Prosecco 2018** Bottle-fermented, 12 months on lees, traditional method. A grape at home in the King and Alpine valleys, prosecco invariably shines. It helps that the '18 vintage was considered a 'winemaker's dream' by founder/winemaker Kel Boynton. Neutral in colour; wisteria, jasmine florals, lemon sherbet tang. Turns serious on the palate with real depth and complexity: almond meal, apple compote and that prosecco vivaciousness and zest for life. Crown seal. 11.5% alc. **Rating** 95 $40 JP

♀♀♀♀♀ **Alpine Valleys Savagnin 2018 Rating** 93 To 2026 $30 JP
Limited Release Fiano 2019 Rating 91 To 2026 $30 JP
Limited Release Friulano 2018 Rating 91 To 2028 $30 JP
Blanc de Blanc Methode Traditionnelle 2012 Rating 91 $50 JP
Alpine Valleys Pinot Gris 2019 Rating 90 To 2026 $30 JP
Alpine Valleys Rose 2019 Rating 90 To 2024 $30 JP
Alpine Valleys Shiraz 2016 Rating 90 To 2026 $30 JP
Limited Release Nebbiolo 2017 Rating 90 To 2035 $30 JP

Fermoy Estate   ★★★★★

838 Metricup Road, Wilyabrup, WA 6280 **Region** Margaret River
T (08) 9755 6285 **www.fermoy.com.au Open** 7 days 10–5
Winemaker Jeremy Hodgson **Est.** 1985 **Dozens** 25 000 **Vyds** 27.28ha
A long-established winery with plantings of semillon, sauvignon blanc, chardonnay, cabernet sauvignon and merlot. The Young family acquired Fermoy Estate in 2010 and built a larger cellar door which opened in '13, signalling the drive to increase domestic sales. It is happy to keep a relatively low profile, however difficult that may be given the quality of the wines. Jeremy Hodgson brings with him a first class honours degree in oenology and viticulture, and a CV encompassing winemaking roles with Wise Wines, Cherubino Consultancy and, earlier, Plantagenet, Houghton and Goundrey Wines. Exports to Thailand, Fiji, Singapore, Japan and China.

♀♀♀♀♀ **Reserve Margaret River Shiraz 2018** 30% whole bunches, 40% new French oak. It's a filigreed wine, inherently spicy, detailed and fine but with a good push of cherry-plum fruit, the latter aided by swish, smoky oak. This has been very nicely put together. It gives nods to both savouriness and fruitiness but finesse is its main quality marker. Screwcap. 14% alc. **Rating** 95 To 2028 CM
Margaret River Merlot 2018 It impresses from the outset. It offers a serious amount of flavour and while it feels soft through the mid-palate it's firm through the finish. It's a merlot with presence. Blackcurrant and redcurrant, tobacco and wild fragrant herbs, bay. It fires along in fine style and finishes with a resounding kick. Screwcap. 14.5% alc. **Rating** 95 To 2035 $30 CM ✪
Margaret River Cabernet Sauvignon 2017 19 months in French oak, 33% new. It's fluid, well fruited and well structured. It offers blackcurrant, tobacco, cedar wood and bay leaf flavours, all of which ripple beautifully out through the finish. Gold medal Margaret River Wine Show '19. Screwcap. 14% alc. **Rating** 95 To 2034 CM
Reserve Margaret River Cabernet Sauvignon 2017 A substantial red wine but a svelte one. Creamy oak on curranty fruit with mulberry, tobacco and bay leaf as highlights. There's quite a lot of oak here but the balance hasn't been thrown. Fruit quality is exemplary. Screwcap. 14% alc. **Rating** 95 To 2037 CM
Reserve Margaret River Semillon 2018 Semillon 95%, chardonnay 5%. Fermented in 100% new French oak before, after 2 months, being transferred to 100% seasoned oak. Pungent thistle and tropical fruit aromatics lead to a well powered, well balanced palate of precision and poise. It's good drinking now, but its future is bright. Screwcap. 12.8% alc. **Rating** 94 To 2028 CM

♀♀♀♀♀ **Reserve Margaret River Chardonnay 2018 Rating** 93 To 2027 CM
Margaret River Cabernet Merlot 2017 Rating 93 To 2030 CM
Margaret River Chardonnay 2018 Rating 92 To 2026 CM

Margaret River Semillon Sauvignon Blanc 2019 Rating 90 **To** 2023 CM
Margaret River Rose 2019 Rating 90 **To** 2021 $25 CM
Sparkling Chardonnay Pinot Noir 2016 Rating 90 $40 CM

Fernfield Wines ★★★

112 Rushlea Road, Eden Valley, SA 5235 **Region** Eden Valley
T 0402 788 526 **www**.fernfieldwines.com.au **Open** Fri–Mon 11–4
Winemaker Rebecca Barr, Scott Barr **Est.** 2002 **Dozens** 1500 **Vyds** 0.7ha

The establishment date of 2002 might, with a little poetic licence, be shown as 1864. Bryce Lillecrapp is the fifth generation of the Lillecrapp family; his great-great-great-grandfather bought land in the Eden Valley in 1864, subdividing it in 1866, establishing the township of Eden Valley and building the first house, Rushlea Homestead. Bryce restored this building and opened it in 1998 as a bicentennial project; it now serves as Fernfield Wines' cellar door. Ownership has now passed to daughter Rebecca Barr and husband Scott.

🍷🍷🍷🍷 **Barossa Late Harvest Semillon 2016** Only 100 dozen made, the possibility of problems from micro-vinification neatly avoided. The wine is well off-dry, and would have been better had the acidity of 6.5g/l been 8g/l and if the residual sugar (which is in fact 8g/l) was 6.5g/l. Screwcap. 13.5% alc. **Rating** 89 $22

Ferngrove ★★★★★

276 Ferngrove Road, Frankland River, WA 6396 **Region** Frankland River
T (08) 9363 1300 **www**.ferngrove.com.au **Open** By appt
Winemaker Craig Grafton, Adrian Foot **Est.** 1998 **Dozens** NFP **Vyds** 220ha

Known for producing consistent examples of cool-climate wines across multiple price brackets. The Ferngrove stable includes the Stirlings, Orchid, Frankland River and Symbols ranges. Ferngrove Vineyards Pty Ltd enjoys the benefits of majority international ownership, but remains Australian-run. Exports to all major markets.

🍷🍷🍷🍷🍷 **Black Label Frankland River Malbec 2018** A wine that has won a couple of worthwhile gold medals and a trophy. It looks like malbec with its deep, inky colour; and it smells like malbec with those distinctive mulberry/raspberry aromas. There's plenty of flavour, soft, supple and fresh-fruited; the tannin kicking in on the finish to firm things up. Easy to see why the judges liked it. Screwcap. 14% alc. **Rating** 95 **To** 2025 $22 SC ✪

King Frankland River Malbec 2018 Consummate malbec! Made me happy. Damson plum, tobacco leaf and gently chewy and pliant tannins, all creating the new world order. A delicious wine. Screwcap. **Rating** 95 **To** 2023 $38 NG

Black Label Frankland River Sauvignon Blanc 2019 Will have easy appeal for sauvignon blanc fans, brimming with varietal aromas that run the gamut from tropical fruit to just-mown green grass, and replete with fresh, juicy flavour. There's just enough acidity to keep things on track without being obvious. It pretty much ticks all the boxes for this style and price range. Screwcap. 12% alc. **Rating** 94 **To** 2021 $22 SC ✪

Estate Frankland River Shiraz 2018 A fine shiraz that pushes the envelope across a firm carriage of tannin, very ripe fruit and salubrious oak handling. As a package, it works well: blueberry, violet, tar, iodine, smoked meat and cushy vanillan pod oak. Cork. **Rating** 94 **To** 2026 $40 NG

🍷🍷🍷🍷🍷 **Cossack Frankland River Riesling 2019 Rating** 93 **To** 2027 $30 NG
Diamond Frankland River Chardonnay 2018 Rating 93 **To** 2026 $32 NG
Dragon Frankland River Shiraz 2018 Rating 93 **To** 2026 $38 NG
Majestic Frankland River Cabernet Sauvignon 2018 Rating 93 **To** 2028 $38 NG
Reserve Dragon Cabernet Shiraz 2017 Rating 93 **To** 2028 $110 NG
Independence Great Southern Cabernet Sauvignon 2018 Rating 92 **To** 2025 $26 NG

Black Label Aromatic Frankland River Off-Dry Riesling 2019 Rating 92
$22 SC ✪
Independence Tempranillo 2018 Rating 91 To 2023 $23 ✪
Independence Great Southern Riesling 2019 Rating 90 To 2022 $26 NG
Frankland River Chardonnay 2018 Rating 90 To 2023 $222 NG
Frankland River Cabernet Sauvignon 2018 Rating 90 To 2024 $22 NG

Fetherston Vintners   ★★★★★

1/99A Maroondah Highway, Healesville, Vic 3777 **Region** Yarra Valley
T 0417 431 700 **www.**fetherstonwine.com.au **Open** Not
Winemaker Chris Lawrence **Est.** 2015 **Dozens** 1500
The establishment of Fetherston Vintners in 2015 by Chris Lawrence and Camille Koll was,
in hindsight, the logical consequence of their respective careers in wine, food and hospitality.
Chris began his career in the kitchen in establishments all over Australia. In '09 he enrolled in
the science (oenology) degree with the University of Southern Queensland, graduating in '14
as valedictorian, receiving the Faculty Medal for Science. During his time at Yering Station
('10–14) he worked his way up from junior cellar hand to assistant winemaker. A vintage at
Domaine Serene in Oregon's Willamette Valley in '12 gave him further insight into the study
of great chardonnay and pinot noir. In '14 he took on the role of winemaker at Sunshine
Creek in the Yarra Valley. Camille is Yarra born and bred, growing up in Hoddles Creek. After
finishing school, she began a 7-year stint at Domaine Chandon, giving her invaluable insight
into professional branding, marketing and customer service. She is now working in hospitality
management as her day job. Chris's late grandfather was Tony Fetherston.

🍷🍷🍷🍷🍷 Yarra Valley Chardonnay 2018 Fruit sourced from Gembrook, Dixons
          Creek and Coldstream; each with different clones. Fermented wild on full solids,
          aged for 8 months in French puncheons (28% new). There's an easy, unforced
          complexity to this wine and a sense of balance. Stone fruit, nutty oak, minerality
          and creaminess of texture all play their part. Fine acidity too. Screwcap. 13.5% alc.
          Rating 95 To 2028 $35 SC ✪
          Single Vineyard Yarra Valley Pinot Noir 2018 MV6 clone from the
          Tibooburra Vineyard; 40% whole bunch, 8 months in French puncheons
          (35% new). A fine and almost ethereal bouquet, unmistakably pinot but you
          feel the site is expressing itself as well. Elegant in structure, with subtle red berry
          flavours and a whisper of oak; the tannin seems light, but it carries the wine
          convincingly through the finish. Screwcap. 13% alc. Rating 95 To 2030 $35 SC ✪
          Single Vineyard Pyrenees Nebbiolo 2017 From the Malakoff Vineyard;
          150 days on skins, aged in 100% French oak (17% new). Noticeably pale in colour
          which is no surprise. A fragrant, aromatic bouquet showing floral perfume, anise-
          like herbs and red-berried fruit. It's quite light-bodied but the delicacy and gentle
          persistence win you over. Drink now or cellar? Screwcap. 13.5% alc. **Rating** 94
          To 2024 $35 SC

🍷🍷🍷🍷🍷 Iris Yarra Valley Chardonnay 2018 Rating 93 To 2025 $28 SC
          Peony Yarra Valley Rose 2019 Rating 93 To 2023 $28 SC
          Fungi Yarra Valley Pinot Noir 2019 Rating 93 To 2026 $28 SC
          Sakura Single Vineyard Yarra Valley Pinot Noir Syrah 2018 Rating 92
          To 2025 $28 SC

Fighting Gully Road   ★★★★★

Kurrajong Way, Mayday Hill, Beechworth, Vic 3747 **Region** Beechworth
T 0407 261 373 **www.**fightinggully.com.au **Open** By appt
Winemaker Mark Walpole, Adrian Rodda **Est.** 1997 **Dozens** 3500 **Vyds** 8.3ha
Mark Walpole (who began his viticultural career with Brown Brothers in the late 1980s) and
partner Carolyn De Poi found their elevated north-facing site south of Beechworth in 1995.
They commenced planting the Aquila Audax Vineyard in '97 with cabernet sauvignon and
pinot noir, subsequently expanding with significant areas of sangiovese, tempranillo, shiraz,

petit manseng and chardonnay. In 2009 they were fortunate to lease the oldest vineyard in the region, planted by the Smith family in 1978 to chardonnay and cabernet sauvignon – in fact, Mark shares the lease with long-time friend Adrian Rodda (see A. Rodda Wines). Mark says, 'We are now making wine in a building in the old and historic Mayday Hills Lunatic Asylum – a place that should be full of winemakers!' Exports to Hong Kong.

ŸŸŸŸŸ **Beechworth Chardonnay 2018** A humdinger of a chardonnay with no shortage of flavour, from sweet stone fruit and grapefruit to powdered ginger and oak spices. There's an opulence. It's fuller-bodied and laced with leesy, creamy flavours; then the citrus tones and funky flint kick in; the finish tight and linear. Super cool. Umpteen awards at the North East Wine Challenge '19, including trophy for Best Wine of Show. Screwcap. 13% alc. **Rating** 97 **To** 2028 $40 JF ❂
Black Label La Longa Sangiovese 2017 The second release in the reserve Black Label range. What sets it apart is the overall restraint, especially in ripeness and the wine's underlying tension. Excellent fruit, but more a savoury wine: earthy, new leather, oak spice, black cherries and pips, Italian bitter herbs, steely and energetic with precision tannins. This is outstanding Australian sangiovese. Screwcap. 14% alc. **Rating** 97 **To** 2030 $85 JF ❂

ŸŸŸŸŸ **Beechworth Sangiovese 2018** Cherries and amaro. Mediterranean herbs and red flowers. Wood spices and warm earth. This is topnotch, with its lighter-framed palate yet bright acid line and slinky tannins. Most important, drinkability writ large. Screwcap. 14% alc. **Rating** 96 **To** 2027 $32 JF ❂
Beechworth Pinot Noir 2018 At first, this is tight, restrained and seemingly lightweight. Starts with florals, cherry pips and scorched earth fragrance. More cherry compote on the sinewy palate with a ferrous overlay. Grainy tannins neatly hewn and the fresh acidity is key. It takes time to reveal and appeal. Better still, let it be for another year or so. Screwcap. 13.5% alc. **Rating** 95 **To** 2028 $35 JF ❂
Beechworth Sangiovese 2017 The colour is distinctly developed (although bright), the palate in a very different world of cherries of all types from savoury through to red and dark aromas and flavours. The sangiovese tannins are there, of course, duty-bound to provide the structure the variety has as its birthright. Screwcap. 14% alc. **Rating** 94 **To** 2027 $30 ❂
Moelleux Beechworth Petit Manseng 2018 An exotic and complex wine of real interest to nerds. Honeycomb, nuts and a flourish of sweetness. 375ml. Screwcap. 12% alc. **Rating** 94 **To** 2027 $32

ŸŸŸŸŸ **Beechworth Rose 2019 Rating** 93 **To** 2022 $26 JF ❂

Finestra   ★★★★

PO Box 120, Coldstream, Vic 3770 **Region** Yarra Valley
T (03) 9739 1690 **Open** Not
Winemaker Alan Johns, Bruce Lang **Est.** 1989 **Dozens** 500 **Vyds** 2.9ha
Owners Bruce and Jo-Anne Lang have combined professional careers and small-scale winemaking for over 30 years. In the early 1970s they gained vacation employment with Yarra Valley wineries and at the end of that decade they joined with friends in acquiring the old Brown Brothers' Everton Hills vineyard near Beechworth. In 1987 they acquired their property adjacent to Yeringberg, overlooking Domaine Chandon, beginning the establishment of the vineyard in '89 and extending it in '96. With a total of 2.9ha of pinot noir, chardonnay, shiraz and cabernet sauvignon, it is small and, until 2002, all of the grapes were sold to two major Yarra Valley wineries. Since then 50% of the grapes have been used for the Finestra label.

ŸŸŸŸŸ **Dalla Mia Yarra Valley Shiraz 2018** A well judged, light to mid-weighted shiraz, with an emphasis on savouriness over sweet fruit. For the better. A skein of peat to pepper-grind acidity conferring an elegance and crunch to floral scents and a blue-fruited palate. Screwcap. **Rating** 92 **To** 2023 $27 NG
Dalla Mia Yarra Valley Cabernet 2017 Mid-weighted and savoury, although a little hotter this year. Akin to a Petit Châteaux style: currant, herb and sage to

bouquet garni scents, skirting along a bow of gently rustic astringency. Nothing polished necessarily, but nourishing, brimming with personality and good drinking. Screwcap. **Rating** 92 **To** 2025 $30 NG

Dalla Mia Yarra Valley Pinot Noir 2018 A twiggy, savoury pinot, of a charming, old school predilection. From 100% MV6, 30% whole bunch. Woodsy truffled scents and sarsaparilla melded to sour cherry. Firmly boned following 18 months in a combination of French oak of various moulds. Screwcap. **Rating** 91 **To** 2023 $27 NG

Finniss River Vineyard   ★★★★☆

2/13 Cadell Street, Goolwa, SA 5214 **Region** Currency Creek
T 0432 546 065 **www**.finnissvineyard.com.au **Open** 7 days 10–4
Winemaker Andrew Hercock **Est.** 1999 **Dozens** 3200 **Vyds** 65.3ha
The Hickinbotham family established several great vineyards, the last of these being that of Finniss River in 1999. The planting mix was good, dominated by 31.3ha of shiraz and 20.9ha of cabernet sauvignon. Between then and February 2015, when Adam and Lauren Parkinson purchased the vineyard, all the grapes were sold, which brought Adam – during his time as general manager of a winery in McLaren Vale, as well as general manager of one of Australia's largest vineyard management companies – into contact with the family and its grapes. Grape sales will remain for the foreseeable future, but the cellar door is the outlet for local sales. Exports to the US, Singapore and China.

♆♆♆♆♆ **Reserve Series Block 5 Shiraz 2016** Crushed and destemmed, open-·fermented, 12 days on skins, matured for 30 months in oak (20% new French). Opulence with a big O. You have to respect it, for it's been well done and has time to go. Cork. 15.5% alc. **Rating** 95 **To** 2033 $65

♆♆♆♆♀ **Reserve Series Block 1 Cabernet Sauvignon 2016 Rating** 92 **To** 2036 $65

Fire Gully   ★★★★☆

Metricup Road, Wilyabrup, WA 6280 **Region** Margaret River
T (08) 9755 6220 **www**.firegully.com.au **Open** By appt
Winemaker Dr Michael Peterkin **Est.** 1988 **Dozens** 5000 **Vyds** 13.4ha
A 6ha lake created in a gully ravaged by bushfires gave the name. In 1998 Mike Peterkin of Pierro purchased it. He manages the vineyard in conjunction with former owners Ellis and Margaret Butcher. He regards the Fire Gully wines as entirely separate from those of Pierro. The vineyard is planted to cabernet sauvignon, merlot, shiraz, semillon, sauvignon blanc, chardonnay, viognier and chenin blanc. Exports to all major markets.

♆♆♆♆♆ **Margaret River Shiraz 2015** Attention to detail has provided further proof of the compatibility of Margaret River and shiraz. It's alive with purple fruits, silky tannins and quality oak. It's more difficult than it looks to create wine such as this. Includes 9.5% viognier. Screwcap. 14.5% alc. **Rating** 95 **To** 2035 $33

♆♆♆♆♀ **Margaret River Cabernet Sauvignon Merlot 2017 Rating** 90 **To** 2027 $26

Firetail   ★★★★★

21 Bessell Road, Rosa Glen, WA 6285 **Region** Margaret River
T (08) 9757 5156 **www**.firetail.com.au **Open** 7 days 11–5
Winemaker Bruce Dukes, Peter Stanlake **Est.** 2002 **Dozens** 1200 **Vyds** 3.8ha
Jessica Worrall and Rob Glass are fugitives from the oil and gas industry. In 2002 they purchased a vineyard in Margaret River that had been planted between 1979 and '81 to sauvignon blanc, semillon and cabernet sauvignon; and have also planted chardonnay and malbec. The wines are made by Bruce Dukes and Peter Stanlake (Jessica has a Masters of Wine Technology and Viticulure from the University of Melbourne). The wine quality is exemplary.

♆♆♆♆♆ **Margaret River Semillon 2013** Amazing wine. Toasty developments add intrigue to flavour, texture and balance. Gentle Meyer lemon and lemon tart

flavours are seductive, but not the least brash. First tasted over 5 years ago and has
prospered since then. Screwcap. 12.1% alc. **Rating** 95 **To** 2028 $23 ✪

Margaret River Cabernet Sauvignon 2017 Had 8 months' maturation in
barrel, no fining. While the the '17 vintage was described as 'challenging' by
the winemaker, the wine drinker will fall for this wine's subtle, reserved charms.
Margaret River's luscious volume is turned down a notch, including the eucalyptus
signature. Violet, florals combine with sweet blackberry, background spice, coffee
grounds. Sweeps easily across the palate with integrated tannins. A firm elegance
on display. Diam. 13.5% alc. **Rating** 95 **To** 2034 $33 JP ✪

Margaret River Cabernet Sauvignon 2018 The purity of varietal expression
has been enhanced by a hands-off approach in the winery, resulting in a young
cabernet of rare beauty. Diam. 13.4% alc. **Rating** 94 **To** 2033 $33

🍷🍷🍷🍷 **Margaret River Rose 2019 Rating** 89 **To** 2026 $19 JP ✪

First Creek Wines

600 McDonalds Road, Pokolbin, NSW 2320 **Region** Hunter Valley
T (02) 4998 7293 **www.**firstcreekwines.com.au **Open** Mon–Wed 9–6, Thurs–Sat 9–7,
Sun 9–5
Winemaker Liz Silkman, Shaun Silkman, Greg Silkman **Est.** 1984 **Dozens** 60 000
First Creek Wines is the family business of Greg Silkman (managing director and winemaker),
son Shaun Silkman (chief operating officer and winemaker) and Shaun's wife Liz (née Jackson,
chief winemaker). The quality of the wines has been consistently exemplary and there is every
reason to believe this will continue in the years to come. Associated business First Creek
Winemaking Services is the main contract winemaker operating in the Hunter Valley. Exports
to Singapore, Japan and China.

🍷🍷🍷🍷🍷 **Hunter Valley Shiraz 2017** A medium-bodied wine that captures the great
vintage and frames it with delicate French oak. There are red and black fruit notes
and fine, faintly earthy tannins adding to the texture of what will be a near-endless
future. Screwcap. 13.5% alc. **Rating** 97 **To** 2047 $30 ✪

🍷🍷🍷🍷🍷 **Oakey Creek Single Vineyard Semillon 2019** Pickled fennel, grapefruit pulp,
lemon drop and bitter almond. Delicious, melding well with the gently phenolic
scrape across the palate that defines the '19 vintage. I'm very fond of '19. There
is an intense thrust of extract as this opens, juxtaposed beautifully against a parry
of structure, allowing the flavours to twist and turn long. Exceptional wine in the
making. Screwcap. **Rating** 96 **To** 2034 $60 NG ✪

Single Vineyard Murphys Semillon 2017 Elegance, purity, balance, length –
each ticks the box, enlivening the mouth and making it difficult to resist the
temptation to swallow it during tasting. The flavour and mouthfeel take shape
from the first sip and don't back off. Screwcap. **Rating** 96 **To** 2032 $80

Winemaker's Reserve Hunter Valley Semillon 2017 Has abundant high
quality flavour for a 2yo semillon, and has a gold-plated guarantee it won't
disappoint those who leave it for the next 3 years. There's even stone fruit lurking
in the shadows. Screwcap. **Rating** 95 **To** 2030 $60

Hunter Valley Semillon 2017 Bright straw-green, less developed than its '18
sibling. The bouquet and palate are another thing, with very impressive length
and focus, the mouth asking for more please. Meyer lemon and lime coalesce.
Screwcap. **Rating** 95 **To** 2030 $30 ✪

Merton Chardonnay 2019 Hunter chardonnay is an interesting beast, tucking
a contemporary thread of mineral pungency beneath an altogether more generous
weave of stone fruit, tropical inflections and pumice. This is such a chardonnay.
Admirable tension marking a delicious wine. Best enjoyed across the mid-term.
Screwcap. **Rating** 95 **To** 2026 $60 NG

Winemaker's Reserve Hunter Valley Chardonnay 2019 Restrained and
taut, despite the Hunter predilection to gush stone fruit scents across the seams.
The vanillan pod oak, beautifully appointed as the seatbelt. With a workout in

the glass, this can't be restrained and yet, it is bloody delicious. Long, detailed, streamlined and yet, oh so generous. Screwcap. **Rating** 95 **To** 2027 $65 NG

Balmoral Single Vineyard Chardonnay 2017 An immaculately structured and textured palate that opens up further with each taste. There are some florals, but the main drive comes from the blend of white peach, rockmelon and grapefruit. Subtle use of French oak ex barrel fermentation another plus. Screwcap. **Rating** 95 **To** 2023 $80

Winemaker's Reserve Hunter Valley Chardonnay 2017 Whether there is or isn't a hint of reduction on the bouquet, it's blown away by the satin-smooth palate, its white peach and creamy cashew flavours sweeping all before it. Theoretically, the Hunter Valley was never an obvious place to grow and make chardonnay, and climate change should have made it impossible. Screwcap. 12.5% alc. **Rating** 95 **To** 2027 $60

Hunter Valley Chardonnay 2018 Early picking to retain natural acidity and freshness has worked. Special attention to the use of new French oak has also been impeccably handled, the theme continued with white-fleshed stone fruit and rockmelon, balanced by notes of citrus on the finish. Screwcap. 12.5% alc. **Rating** 94 **To** 2028 $30 ○

Hunter Valley Chardonnay 2017 Unusual scented floral notes to the bouquet are made irrelevant by the power and concentration of the palate with its ripe stone fruit and rockmelon flavours. The freshness of the wine is heightened by its balance. Screwcap. 12.5% alc. **Rating** 94 **To** 2023 $30 ○

♟♟♟♟♟ **Single Vineyard Murphys Semillon 2019 Rating** 93 **To** 2034 $60 NG
Hunter Valley Semillon 2018 Rating 93 **To** 2028 $30
Balmoral Single Vineyard Chardonnay 2019 Rating 93 **To** 2025 $60 NG
Hunter Valley Shiraz 2018 Rating 92 **To** 2025 $30 NG
Winemaker's Reserve Hunter Valley Semillon 2019 Rating 91 **To** 2029 $65 NG
Marrowbone Road Hunter Valley Shiraz 2018 Rating 90 **To** 2024 $65 NG

First Drop Wines ★★★★★

Beckwith Park, Barossa Valley Way, Nuriootpa, SA 5355 **Region** Barossa Valley
T (08) 8562 3324 **www.firstdropwines.com Open** Mon–Sat 10–4, Sun 11–4
Winemaker Matt Gant, Anna Higgins **Est.** 2005 **Dozens** 20 000
The First Drop Wines of today has been transformed since its establishment in 2005. It now has its own winery, part of the old Penfolds winery at Nuriootpa, shared with Tim Smith Wines. The group of buildings is called Beckwith Park in honour of the man who did so much groundbreaking work for Penfolds: Ray Beckwith OAM, recipient of the Maurice O'Shea Award, who died in '12, but not before his 100th birthday. The quality of the First Drop wines would have made Ray Beckwith smile in appreciation. Exports to the UK, the US, Canada, Denmark, Japan, Hong Kong and China.

♟♟♟♟♟ **Cold Sweat Craneford Syrah 2016** Very fine with detailed tannins that coat the mouth, corral the fruit and coax the saliva, serving as the wine's opus. Otherwise, black and blue fruits, five-spice, mocha and intensely lifted florals that serve as the regional postcode. A polished sheath. Thoroughly delicious. Screwcap. 14% alc. **Rating** 96 **To** 2028 $75 NG ○

Cold Sweat Wilton Syrah 2016 Clearly the priorities at this address lie with the more expensive, less interventionist wines. A more artisanal approach: hand-picking, open ferments and indigenous yeasts, with a spicing from 20% whole bunch in the mix. Full-bodied. Glossy on approach. Violet, smoked meats, blueberry, iodine, clove and a souk of exotic spice. Attractive aromas. The finish is defined by a twine of oak (16 months French oak, 50% new) melded to whole-cluster fibre, needing time to harmonise. It will. Screwcap. 14% alc. **Rating** 94 **To** 2026 $75 NG

♟♟♟♟♟ **Two Percent Barossa Shiraz 2018 Rating** 93 **To** 2025 $38 NG
Cold Sweat Moculta Syrah 2016 Rating 93 **To** 2028 $75 NG

Mother's Milk Barossa Shiraz 2018 Rating 92 To 2024 $25 NG ✪
Liebfraumilk Barossa Valley Shiraz 2017 Rating 92 To 2025 $50 NG
Mere et Fils Adelaide Hills Chardonnay 2018 Rating 91 To 2023 $25 NG
The Matador Barossa Garnacha 2018 Rating 91 To 2022 $25 NG
Minchia Adelaide Hills Montepulciano 2016 Rating 90 To 2023 $38 NG

First Foot Forward   ★★★★★

6 Maddens Lane, Coldstream, Vic 3770 **Region** Yarra Valley
T 0402 575 818 **www**.firstfootforward.com.au **Open** By appt
Winemaker Martin Siebert **Est.** 2013 **Dozens** 500
Owner and winemaker Martin Siebert's daytime job is at Tokar Estate, where he has been
chief winemaker for a number of years. In 2013 he had the opportunity to purchase pinot noir
and chardonnay from a mature vineyard in The Patch – high in the Dandenong Ranges on
the southern edge of the Yarra Valley. It is cooler and wetter than the floor of the Yarra Valley,
so much so that the fruit is consistently picked after Tokar's cabernet sauvignon, reducing the
stress that might otherwise have occurred. He says that so long as the fruit is available, he will
be purchasing it, adding other wines from the Yarra Valley broaden the offer to quality-focused
restaurants and specialty wine stores around Melbourne.

🍷🍷🍷🍷♀ **Upper Yarra Valley Chardonnay 2018** Has the distinctive edge of finesse that
so often is part and parcel of the Upper Yarra – it's not as dependant on vintage
as is the Lower Yarra. Subtle oak is the finishing touch, wild ferment another step.
Screwcap. 13% alc. **Rating** 93 **To** 2027 $28
Yarra Valley Pinot Noir 2018 MV6 from a block at Coldstream, hand-
picked, destemmed, no whole bunches, 3 weeks on skins, held on lees in French
hogsheads (30% new) until Nov '18. Light red. Slippery mouthfeel is unusual,
but pleasantly so. The colour suggests early consumption. Screwcap. 13.5% alc.
Rating 92 **To** 2024 $28

First Ridge   ★★★★

Cnr Castlereagh Highway/Burrundulla Road, Mudgee, NSW **Region** Mudgee
T 0407 701 014 **www**.firstridge.com.au **Open** 7 days 10–4
Winemaker James Manners **Est.** 1998 **Dozens** 5000 **Vyds** 20ha
Sydney architect John Nicholas and wife Helen have established a 20ha vineyard on
undulating hillsides above the open valley below. The soils vary from shallow topsoils of
basalt and quartz on the highest ridges to deeper loams over neutral clays. Barbera and
sangiovese and vermentino are planted on the ridges; fiano, pinot grigio, tempranillo, shiraz
and merlot on the deeper soils. The vineyard manager, Colin Millot, began work in McLaren
Vale over 30 years ago, moving to Mudgee in 1995 to manage the Rosemount Hill of Gold
and Mountain Blue vineyards. James Manners (son of famed chef Ned Manners) plays his part
in realising the desire of the Nicholases to 'enjoy tables of abundant food, friends and fiery
conversation, not unlike a vibrant Italian table'.

🍷🍷🍷🍷♀ **Mudgee Vermentino 2019** This is good. The best white of the pack. Saline
and chalky, the texture riding *uber alles*. Quince, ripe stone fruits and a saline-
grippy nourishment. Broad and layered, yet fresh and long. Bravo! Screwcap.
Rating 93 **To** 2023 $24 NG ✪
Mudgee Barbera 2017 This does a good enough job as an homage to
Piemonte's everyday fountain of youthful vibrancy; pulpy red to black fruits, violet
and tar. Barbera. Among the most versatile varieties in the world when done well.
Drink young and on the cooler side. Screwcap. **Rating** 91 **To** 2023 $30 NG
Mudgee Barbera 2016 While I firmly believe that barbera is best maximised
in its youth to take advantage of meagre tannins and bright, blueberry-clad acidity,
juicy and energetic; this proves that there is a brief holding pattern. Yet the fruit
has segued from its primary pulpy freshness into something a little stern. Still alive,
sure; the oak handling imparting a shimmy of mocha and caraway. A good wine,
implicating this site and address for even better wines in the future. Screwcap.
Rating 91 **To** 2022 $30 NG

Mudgee Fiano 2019 This is good. Some neutral oak handling and lees work has deemed it a bit of a chardonnay look-alike, but the fruit is clearly of very high quality, auguring for a bright future should a little more courage come into the equation. Quince, fennel and apricot make it broader. Screwcap. **Rating** 90 **To** 2022 $28 NG

Fishbone Wines

422 Harmans Mill Road, Wilyabrup, WA 6285 **Region** Margaret River
T (08) 9755 6726 **www**.fishbonewines.com.au **Open** 7 days 10–4.30
Winemaker Stuart Pierce **Est.** 2009 **Dozens** 15 000 **Vyds** 9.1ha
Fishbone Wines' 9.1ha vineyard includes chardonnay, tempranillo and cabernet sauvignon; and 1ha of newer plantings of malbec, vermentino and pinot noir. The Fishbone wines are created with minimal intervention. The range includes the 'accessible' Blue Label range, single vineyard Black Label Margaret range and the 'icon' Joseph River wines. The restaurant features a Japanese-inspired menu with a terrace overlooking the property. Exports to the US, Canada, Dubai, Singapore, Taiwan and China.

🍷🍷🍷🍷🍷 **Black Label Margaret River Cabernet Sauvignon Merlot 2018** A 77/33% blend: the cabernet from the Fishbone Vineyard, the merlot ex Rosa Glen. An elegant wine, totally under the driving instructions of the cabernet with black olive tapenade and dusty tannins. Screwcap. 14.2% alc. **Rating** 94 **To** 2033 $40

🍷🍷🍷🍷🍷 **Black Label Margaret River Tempranillo 2018** Rating 92 To 2032 $40
Black Label Margaret River Chardonnay 2018 Rating 91 To 2030 $35

Flametree

Cnr Caves Road/Chain Avenue, Dunsborough, WA 6281 **Region** Margaret River
T (08) 9756 8577 **www**.flametreewines.com **Open** 7 days 10–5
Winemaker Cliff Royle, Julian Scott **Est.** 2007 **Dozens** 20 000
Flametree, owned by the Towner family (John, Liz, Rob and Annie), has had extraordinary success since its first vintage in 2007. The usual practice of planting a vineyard and then finding someone to make the wine was turned on its head: a state-of-the-art winery was built, and grape purchase agreements signed with growers in the region. Show success was topped by the winning of the Jimmy Watson Trophy with its '07 Cabernet Merlot. If all this were not enough, Flametree has secured the services of winemaker Cliff Royle. Exports to the UK, Canada, Indonesia, Malaysia, Singapore, Papua New Guinea, Fiji and Hong Kong.

🍷🍷🍷🍷🍷 **S.R.S. Wallcliffe Margaret River Syrah 2018** An exhaustive and exhausting vinification program – including conveyance of whole bins and refrigeration, drying of stalks after destemming – was rewarded by a wine with a fascinating progression of flavours, some remaining, others leaving/changing their profile. The activity on the back-palate and finish is a significant attribute. Screwcap. 14% alc. Rating 96 To 2043 $45 ✪
S.R.S. Wilyabrup Margaret River Cabernet Sauvignon 2017 Selectiv'-harvested, wild yeast–open fermented, 30 days skin contact, 17 months in French oak (50% new). Full-bodied, but no over-extraction. A long life ahead. Screwcap. 14% alc. Rating 96 To 2037 $85
Margaret River Chardonnay 2018 From 4 districts along Margaret River; 30% fermented in new oak, 8% mlf, matured for 9 months in oak. A lot of effort and high quality inputs have gone into making a classy chardonnay, with ever-changing facets as the wine travels along the palate and lingering finish; nothing dominant. Drink and be happy – it's a steal. Screwcap. 13% alc. Rating 95 To 2028 $29 ✪
Margaret River Cabernet Sauvignon 2017 Hand-picked and Selectiv'-harvested, matured for 14 months in French oak (35% new). A classy wine, all the inputs precisely balanced. Screwcap. 14% alc. Rating 95 To 2032 $45
S.R.S. Wallcliffe Margaret River Chardonnay 2018 Elegant and very fresh coming up to its third year. Sophisticated winemaking, reacting to the grapes in

the press with options still open; not formulaic. Citrus, pear and white peach, all very subtle. Screwcap. 13% alc. **Rating** 94 **To** 2023 $65

Margaret River Pinot Rose 2019 Intelligent winemaking. Chilled overnight, wild-fermented in old puncheons on pinot gris lees, a small amount of pinot gris juice included. A concerted (and successful) mission to introduce flavour and structure complexity. Screwcap. 13% alc. **Rating** 94 **To** 2021 $25 ✪

ꕥꕥꕥꕥꕥ **Embers Cabernet Sauvignon 2017 Rating** 91 **To** 2027 $20 ✪
Embers Chardonnay 2018 Rating 90 **To** 2022 $20 ✪

Flaxman Wines   ★★★★★

662 Flaxmans Valley Road, Flaxmans Valley, SA 5253 **Region** Eden Valley
T 0411 668 949 **www.**flaxmanwines.com.au **Open** Thurs 11–4, Fri–Sat 11–5, Sun 11–4
Winemaker Colin Sheppard **Est.** 2005 **Dozens** 1500 **Vyds** 2ha
After visiting the Barossa Valley for over a decade, Melbourne residents Colin Sheppard and wife Fi decided on a tree-change and in 2004 found a small, old vineyard overlooking Flaxmans Valley. It consists of 90-year-old riesling, 90-year-old shiraz and 70 year-old semillon. The vines are dry-grown, hand-pruned and hand-picked and treated – say the Sheppards – as their garden. Yields are restricted to under 4t/ha and exceptional parcels of locally grown grapes are also purchased. Colin has worked at various Barossa wineries and his attention to detail (and understanding of the process) is reflected in the consistent high quality of the wines. Exports to China.

ꕥꕥꕥꕥꕥ **Estate Eden Valley Shiraz 2017** The grapes come from 80yo dry-grown vines on the small estate vineyard; 120 dozen made. Well, well, what a wine! The bouquet is exceptionally fragrant, the palate a glorious combination of elegance and intensity. The finish is long, the aftertaste of the forest fruits and a box full of spices. Screwcap. 14% alc. **Rating** 97 **To** 2047 $120 ✪

ꕥꕥꕥꕥꕥ **Double Up Barossa & Eden Valleys Shiraz 2017** A 50/50% Barossa Valley/ Eden Valley blend. The bouquet sends the antennae into overdrive, and indeed this is a brilliant wine that has gloried in the '17 weather. Black and red fruits are part of the great quality of the wine, tannins and oak along for the ride. The sour note is only 50 dozen bottles made. Screwcap. 14% alc. **Rating** 96 **To** 2047 $50 ✪

Paladin Barossa Valley Shiraz 2017 As with its siblings, the colour is bright and youthful. The history of Flaxman Wines in the *Wine Companion* leaves no room for discussion – Colin Sheppard is a very, very talented winemaker who grows or sources great grapes. If only he could persuade the weather gods to replicate the '17 vintage conditions so he could make the Barossa Valley produce grapes that mimic those of the Eden Valley as they do here. 120 dozen made, fine-boned and oh so long. Screwcap. 13.5% alc. **Rating** 96 **To** 2052 $30 ✪

Shhh Eden Valley Cabernet Sauvignon 2017 Deep colour. A penetrating, intense wine with laser-cut cabernet varietal flavours; cassis/blackcurrant to the fore, firm but precise tannins bringing up the rear. Some '17 cabernets (from noted producers) failed the ripeness test, but this doesn't even blink. Screwcap. 14% alc. **Rating** 96 **To** 2047 $50 ✪

Eden Valley Riesling 2019 From 90yo estate vines yielding 0.65t/acre. Has soared over any issues from the very warm vintage, with a fragrant citrus blossom bouquet and a palate that has layers of lime/lemon flavours and ample acidity. Screwcap. 12% alc. **Rating** 95 **To** 2032 $30 ✪

The Stranger 2017 A blend of 55% Barossa shiraz, 45% Eden Valley cabernet sauvignon; fermented separately, matured for 22 months in barrel, the shiraz in American, the cabernet in French oak. Complex, spicy savoury black fruits are in command; texture/structure its strength. Screwcap. 14% alc. **Rating** 94 **To** 2032 $40

Flowstone Wines

★★★★★

11298 Bussell Highway, Forest Grove, WA 6286 **Region** Margaret River
T 0487 010 275 **www**.flowstonewines.com **Open** By appt
Winemaker Stuart Pym **Est.** 2013 **Dozens** 1500 **Vyds** 2.25ha

Veteran Margaret River winemaker Stuart Pym's career constituted long-term successive roles: beginning with Voyager Estate in 1991, thereafter with Devil's Lair, and finishing with Stella Bella in '13, the year he and Perth-based wine tragic Phil Giglia established Flowstone Wines. In '03 Stuart had purchased a small property on the edge of the Margaret River Plateau in the beautiful Forest Grove area, progressively planting chardonnay, cabernet sauvignon, gewurztraminer and more recently touriga. From '17, Flowstone leased a vineyard at Karridale, planted to long-established sauvignon blanc and chardonnay, having previously purchased part of the crop for its regional wines. The lease puts the vineyard on par with the estate plantings; the best fruit is retained, the balance sold. Thus Queen of the Earth Sauvignon Blanc appeared for the first time in '17, joining the estate chardonnay and cabernet Queens. Exports to the UK.

🍷🍷🍷🍷🍷 **Queen of the Earth Margaret River Sauvignon Blanc 2018** Fermented and matured in a single 600l demi-muid. This is very different from its Margaret River sibling, exceptionally complex and powerful, yet with extraordinary purity to its citrus-dominant varietal expression. Screwcap. 12.3% alc. **Rating** 97 **To** 2027 $55 ✪

Margaret River Chardonnay 2017 From the Karridale Vineyard. The vinification doesn't change from one year to the next, except for the gestation period from grape to glass, here over 41 months. The flow of fruit flavours is mesmerising, moving through peach and co. to grapefruit and co. 450 dozen made. Screwcap. 13.5% alc. **Rating** 97 **To** 2042 $36 ✪

Queen of the Earth Margaret River Chardonnay 2017 Hand-picked, whole-bunch pressed, fermented and matured in French barriques (50% new). Exceptional depth to its structure and texture; luxuriantly ripe and supple. Clotted cream is swept away by acidity on the aftertaste. Screwcap. 12.7% alc. **Rating** 97 **To** 2045 $55 ✪

Queen of the Earth Margaret River Cabernet Sauvignon 2016 The first Queen of the Earth Cabernet Sauvignon from the Home Block in Forest Grove. Open-fermented, 2.5 weeks on skins post-fermentation pressed to thin-staved French barriques for 3 years, gravity bottled, 15 months in bottle before release, 110 dozen made. A great Margaret River vintage and (as always) a great wine; flows along and across the mouth without a ripple. Screwcap. 14% alc. **Rating** 97 **To** 2047 $74 ✪

🍷🍷🍷🍷🍷 **Moonmilk Margaret River Shiraz Grenache 2018** Made with 60% shiraz crushed and destemmed to open fermenters and amphorae; 37% whole-bunch grenache open-fermented; and 3% viognier, matured in barrique (5+yo) and three 20yo cognac puncheons. Every bit as exotically (yet harmoniously) rich as expected. Screwcap. 14% alc. **Rating** 96 **To** 2030 $21 ✪

Margaret River Gewurztraminer 2018 Hand-picked, whole-bunch pressed, fermented in aged barrels for 15 months. Highly perfumed talc, spice and rosewater scents. The palate more than just lives up to the promise of the bouquet. It's a ripper. Stuart Pym has pulled this rabbit out of the hat before and knows how it's done. Screwcap. 14% alc. **Rating** 95 **To** 2025 $32 ✪

Margaret River Sauvignon Blanc 2018 Made with as much care as a red wine, using many of the same steps. It presents its varietal fruit and structure as a wine with a full-scale cellaring future, unique in Australia. 410 dozen made. Screwcap. 13.5% alc. **Rating** 95 **To** 2023 $32 ✪

Moonmilk Margaret River Shiraz Grenache 2017 The wine has great integrity but would cause no end of trouble in an options game as you endeavour to reconcile intense red fruits with precise, disciplined mouthfeel and length. It is this cool-climate cut that takes you away from the softer cadence of most of the cool-grown examples of this blend. Screwcap. 14% alc. **Rating** 95 **To** 2032 $22 ✪

Moonmilk White 2019 A blend of 68% savagnin, 24% viognier, 5% gewurztraminer, 3% sauvignon blanc. Made from fully ripe grapes, each variety whole-bunch pressed to old barrels and amphorae, held on lees for 6 months. Apricot and citrus flavours are light on their feet. Screwcap. 13% alc. **Rating** 94 To 2029 $21 ✪

Margaret River Cabernet Sauvignon Touriga 2016 A 68/32% blend matured separately for 24 months in French barriques (20% new), then blended and given a further 24 months maturation. Complex wine, hints of coffee grounds and preserved lemon before the fruits break free; supported by tannins. Screwcap. 14% alc. **Rating** 94 To 2029 $36

Flying Fish Cove ★★★★★

Caves Road, Wilyabrup, WA 6280 **Region** Margaret River
T (08) 9755 6600 **www.**flyingfishcove.com **Open** By appt
Winemaker Simon Ding, Damon Easthaugh **Est.** 2000 **Dozens** NFP **Vyds** 25ha
Flying Fish Cove has two strings to its bow: contract winemaking for others and the development of its own brand. Long-serving winemaker Simon Ding had a circuitous journey before falling prey to the lure of wine. He finished an apprenticeship in metalwork in 1993. In '96 he obtained a Bachelor of Science, then joined the Flying Fish Cove team in 2000. Exports to the UK, the US, Canada and Malaysia.

🍷🍷🍷🍷🍷 **Margaret River Chardonnay 2018** Elegance (with a capital E) was written before another word for this tasting note. This stands apart from all the other districts, reflecting its position in the far southeast corner of Margaret River and the accumulated experience that brings the softest of winemaker thumbprints into play. Screwcap. 12.6% alc. **Rating** 96 To 2028 $22 ✪

🍷🍷🍷🍷🍷 **Margaret River Shiraz 2018 Rating** 93 To 2028 $22 ✪
Margaret River Cabernet Merlot 2016 Rating 90 To 2026 $22

Forbes & Forbes ★★★★★

20 Hooper Road, Strathalbyn, SA 5255 **Region** Eden Valley
T 0478 391 304 **www.**forbeswine.com.au **Open** At Taste Eden Valley, Angaston
Winemaker Colin Forbes **Est.** 2008 **Dozens** 1200 **Vyds** 3.2ha
This venture is owned by Colin and Robert Forbes, and their respective partners. Colin says, 'I have been in the industry for a "frightening" length of time', beginning with Thomas Hardy & Sons in 1974. Colin is particularly attached to riesling and the property owned by the partners in Eden Valley has 2ha of the variety (plus 0.5ha each of merlot and cabernet sauvignon and 0.2ha of cabernet franc). Exports to Japan and China.

🍷🍷🍷🍷🍷 **Single Vineyard Eden Valley Riesling 2018** The rieslings at this address demonstrate a mastery of the Eden Valley idiom: picked on ripeness, little grating or too hard; the vinosity of gnarled old vines ... the telltale kaffir lime scents. This, too, will make beautiful old bones due to the thrust of fruit and parry of freshness. **Rating** 95 To 2033 $20 NG ✪

Cellar Matured Eden Valley Riesling 2010 An impressive riesling, all the more so because of the prodigious complexity imparted by bottle age: quinine, cumquat and a sash of candied citrus rind, all melded to a whiff of kerosene. The acidity, a driver, but far from hard. All well appointed. Vinous old vine (90yo) oomph to boot. Screwcap. **Rating** 95 To 2023 $32 NG ✪

Fraternal Blend 2011 From among the coolest years on record, this is a wine of which all of those involved should be immensely proud! Restrained, elegant, precise and impeccably long, sans the green unresolved tannins that mar so many SA reds. Propitiously situated? Prodigious handling? Surely both! Bitter chocolate, ample dark fruit, dank foresty notes and a lovely pin bone flourish to the granular tannins. Screwcap. **Rating** 95 To 2023 $28 NG ✪

Alexander Murray 2014 Merlot, cabernet sauvignon, cabernet franc. This is a fine, pointed, mid-weighted and highly savoury Right Bank Bordeaux blend with ample time left in the tank, despite it being a (slightly) aged release. Currant allsorts, graphite, mulch and pencil shavings, with a refreshing smear of mint and dried herb across the finish. This will make fine old bones even if the acidity, at present, is a bit aggressive. Screwcap. **Rating** 94 **To** 2029 $32 NG

Forest Hill Vineyard   ★★★★★

Cnr South Coast Highway/Myers Road, Denmark, WA 6333 **Region** Great Southern
T (08) 9848 2399 **www**.foresthillwines.com.au **Open** Thurs–Sun 10.30–4.30
Winemaker Liam Carmody, Guy Lyons **Est.** 1965 **Dozens** 12000 **Vyds** 65ha
This family-owned business is one of the oldest 'new' winemaking operations in WA and was the site of the first grape plantings in Great Southern in 1965. The Forest Hill brand became well known, aided by the fact that a '75 Riesling made by Sandalford from Forest Hill grapes won nine trophies. The quality of the wines made from the oldest vines (dry-grown) on the property is awesome (released under the numbered vineyard block labels). Exports to Taiwan, Hong Kong, Singapore and China.

ＹＹＹＹＹ **Block 1 Mount Barker Riesling 2019** Vines planted '65; hand-picked and sorted, chilled, whole-bunch pressed, free-run juice cool-fermented, on lees until Oct '19. A wonderful riesling with mouth-watering intensity and purity to the lime/lemon/mineral drive of the palate and aftertaste. Only 60 dozen made. Screwcap. 12.5% alc. **Rating** 98 **To** 2039 $45 ✪
Block 2 Mount Barker Riesling 2018 Block 2 was planted in '75, a foundation block for viticulture in southwest Australia. Hand-picked and sorted, pressed and chilled for fermentation. The wine has 9.2g/l of acidity and attacks the mouth like a whirling dervish but doesn't compromise the fruit. Screwcap. 12.5% alc. **Rating** 97 **To** 2033 $35 ✪
Block 9 Mount Barker Shiraz 2018 Relentless attention to detail to capture the richness of the fruit with several hand-picks, small batch–open fermentation variously with whole berries and whole bunches, 12 months maturation in French oak (15% new). Gold medals Perth and Melbourne. Deep colour. Velvet-lined black fruits, licorice, pepper and rounded tannins. Screwcap. 14% alc. **Rating** 97 **To** 2047 $60 ✪

ＹＹＹＹＹ **Block 2 Mount Barker Riesling 2019** Vines planted '75; several pickings, whole-bunch pressed, chilled, fermented with some solids, part wild, part cultured yeast, when fermentation finished blended with the ferment lees. Has as much impact as Block 1, but not the same intensity and purity. Screwcap. 12.5% alc. **Rating** 96 **To** 2034 $35 ✪
Highbury Fields Cabernet Sauvignon 2018 From Blocks 5, 6 and 7; Selectiv'-harvested, 12 months in French barriques, the wine including 14% malbec. Gold medal WA Wine Show '19 and gold (best in region) Halliday Cabernet Challenge '19. Luscious blackcurrant fruit, bay leaf and fine tannins. Screwcap. 14% alc. **Rating** 96 **To** 2038 $24 ✪
Block 5 Mount Barker Cabernet Sauvignon 2018 Vines planted '75. Hand-sorted, chilled, cold soak, post-ferment maceration, matured for 15 months in French barriques (30% new). A full-bodied towering wine oozing black fruits, yet retaining balance for a future as long as your patience lasts. Screwcap. 13.5% alc. **Rating** 96 **To** 2048 $65 ✪
Mount Barker Riesling 2019 Hand-picked with multiple passes, largely whole-bunch pressed, a small part crushed and pressed, the juice cold-settled and cool-fermented. For riesling nerds, the titratable acidity is a towering 9g/l, residual sugar 2.2g/l. Rain fell through the growing season exactly when it was needed, the season basically dry. The Meyer lemon, lime and apple zest provide all the fruit background expected. Screwcap. 13% alc. **Rating** 95 **To** 2034 $26 ✪
Mount Barker Chardonnay 2019 Hand-picked Gingin and Dijon clones, chilled, matured in French barriques and puncheons (20% new). All worth it because there is great drive and intensity to the fruit, oak simply putting a bow on the parcel. Screwcap. 13% alc. **Rating** 95 **To** 2027 $30 ✪

Block 8 Mount Barker Chardonnay 2018 Hand-picked and sorted, chilled, whole-bunch pressed, wild-fermented in French oak (25% new), matured for 6 months. While the oak is obvious on the bouquet, the sheer power and intensity of the palate sweeps the floor clean for the fruit to take control and keep it active in the mouth long after the wine has been swallowed. Screwcap. 13% alc. Rating 95 To 2030 $45

Mount Barker Shiraz 2018 Made in the same way as its Highberry Fields sibling, with a whole-berry fermentation in open fermenters, then matured in French oak (15% new). It is exceptionally intense and will richly repay cellaring, but needs time. Screwcap. 14% alc. Rating 94 To 2043 $30 ✪

Mount Barker Cabernet Sauvignon 2018 Hand-picked, open-fermented, matured for 15 months in French barriques (25% new). Part of a close-knit family of wines from Blocks 5, 6 and 7; the vinification very similar. Here the tannins are still a little restive. Screwcap. 13.8% alc. Rating 94 To 2038 $32

♈♈♈♈♈ Highbury Fields Great Southern Shiraz 2018 Rating 92 To 2033 $22 ✪
Highbury Fields Chardonnay 2019 Rating 91 To 2025 $24

Forester Estate   ★★★★★

1064 Wildwood Road, Yallingup, WA 6282 Region Margaret River
T (08) 9755 2788 www.foresterestate.com.au Open At Rivendell Estate
Winemaker Kevin McKay, Todd Payne Est. 2001 Dozens 52000 Vyds 33.5ha
Forester Estate is owned by Kevin and Jenny McKay. Winemaker Todd Payne has had a distinguished career, starting in the Great Southern, thereafter the Napa Valley, back to Plantagenet, then Esk Valley in Hawke's Bay, plus two vintages in the Northern Rhône Valley, one with esteemed producer Yves Cuilleron in 2008. His move back to WA completed the circle. The estate vineyards are planted to sauvignon blanc, semillon, chardonnay, cabernet sauvignon, shiraz, merlot, petit verdot, malbec and fer. Exports to Switzerland and Japan.

♈♈♈♈♈ Margaret River Chardonnay 2018 Wild-fermented and matured for 8 months in French oak (40% new). One of those wines that make you relax and enjoy it. Supple, long and smooth stone fruits hand in hand with grapefruit. Screwcap. 13.5% alc. Rating 95 To 2030 $40

Yelverton Reserve Margaret River Chardonnay 2017 Block selection, hand-picked, whole-bunch pressed, only the first 500l used, wild-fermented, 54% mlf to reduce malic acid, matured for 10 months in barriques and puncheons (45% new). Supple and smooth stone fruit and hints of cream and toast. Ready when you are. Screwcap. 11.5% alc. Rating 95 To 2027 $70

Home Block Margaret River Shiraz 2016 The Home Block is always shoot and bunch-thinned to reduce the crop. Hand-picked, 5% whole bunches in the bottom of the fermenter, the remainder destemmed on top, 9 days on skins, pressed to French oak (40% new) for 14 months maturation, 75% with full solids. It is a wine of power, precision and length. Screwcap. 14% alc. Rating 95 To 2040 $40

Margaret River Sauvignon Blanc 2019 Partial barrel ferment gives the best of both worlds, leaving the wine crisp and bright while adding textural complexity. It also extends the window of opportunity to enjoy an extra year or two. Screwcap. 12.5% alc. Rating 94 To 2022 $30 ✪

♈♈♈♈♈ Margaret River Cabernet Sauvignon 2017 Rating 91 To 2032 $40
Margaret River Rose 2019 Rating 90 To 2021 $27

Four Sisters   ★★★

199 O'Dwyers Road, Tabilk, Vic 3608 Region Central Victoria
T (03) 5736 2400 www.foursisters.com.au Open Not
Winemaker Alan George, Jo Nash, Alister Purbrick Est. 1995 Dozens 40000
The four sisters who inspired this venture were the daughters of the late Trevor Mast, a great winemaker who died before his time. The business is owned by the Purbrick family (the

owner of Tahbilk). It orchestrates the purchase of the grapes for the brand and also facilitates the winemaking. The production is wholly export-focused, with limited sales in Australia. It exports to 15 countries including China, and that number may well diminish if Chinese distribution fulfils all its potential.

Four Winds Vineyard ★★★★☆

9 Patemans Lane, Murrumbateman, NSW 2582 **Region** Canberra District
T (02) 6227 0189 **www**.fourwindsvineyard.com.au **Open** Thurs–Mon 10–4
Winemaker Highside Winemaking **Est.** 1998 **Dozens** 4000 **Vyds** 11.9ha
Graeme and Suzanne Lunney planted the first vines in '98, moving to the Four Winds property full-time in '99 and making the first vintage in 2000. Daughter Sarah and her husband John now oversee the vineyard and cellar door operations. A distinguished vineyard, selling part of the crop to highly regarded producers, part reserved for its own brand.

🍷🍷🍷🍷🍷 Chapel Block Canberra District Riesling 2019 This is a lovely, racy riesling; citrus fruits and vibrant, but balanced, acidity chasing each other around the mouth, continuing onto the aftertaste. Screwcap. 11.2% alc. **Rating** 95 **To** 2029 $28 ✪

Gundagai Sangiovese Rose 2019 Very pale salmon-pink suggests brief skin contact, but the spicy/savoury bouquet lays the scene for a complex, dry wine. The palate continues the theme, dry yet pomegranate-fruity. Very smart wine. Screwcap. 11.3% alc. **Rating** 94 **To** 2021 $27 ✪

Kyeema Canberra District Shiraz 2018 This is the first vintage of Kyeema Vineyard grapes following the acquisition of the long-established Kyeema property. Blackberry and plum fruits are shot through with spice, pepper and firm (not dry) tannins. Oak plays a minimal role on the medium-bodied palate. Screwcap. 13.7% alc. **Rating** 94 **To** 2039 $37

🍷🍷🍷🍷♀ Kyeema Canberra District Shiraz Viognier 2018 **Rating** 93 **To** 2033 $42
Canberra District Sparkling Riesling 2019 **Rating** 93 $27 ✪

Fowles Wine ★★★★★

Cnr Hume Freeway/Lambing Gully Road, Avenel, Vic 3664 **Region** Strathbogie Ranges
T (03) 5796 2150 **www**.fowleswine.com **Open** 7 days 9–5
Winemaker Victor Nash, Lindsay Brown **Est.** 1968 **Dozens** 80 000 **Vyds** 120ha
This family-owned winery is led by Matt Fowles, with chief winemaker Victor Nash heading the winemaking team. The large vineyard is primarily focused on riesling, chardonnay, shiraz and cabernet sauvignon, but also includes arneis, vermentino, pinot gris, sauvignon blanc, pinot noir, mourvedre, sangiovese and merlot. Marketing is energetic, with the well known Ladies who Shoot their Lunch label available as large posters, the wines also available presented in a 6-bottle gun case. Exports to the UK, the US, Canada and China.

🍷🍷🍷🍷♀ Stone Dweller Single Vineyard Strathbogie Ranges Mourvedre 2018 A new addition. The fruit coming off vines planted in '10, wild fermentation and aged in used French puncheons. An appealing outcome with its savoury outlook all pepper and salami with a hint of black fruits. Medium-bodied with parching tannins thankfully tamed by a succulence and refreshing finish. Screwcap. 14% alc. **Rating** 92 **To** 2025 $25 JF ✪

Ladies who Shoot their Lunch Riesling 2019 It's so racy with its dousing of lemon and lime juice, zest and pith. It's really dry, yet has an appealing shape to the palate, as in not all lean and mean. Blossoms on the finish. Screwcap. 12% alc. **Rating** 91 **To** 2026 $35 JF

The Exception King Valley Saperavi 2018 I actually take exception to the bottle weighing nearly 2kg. Enticing aromas of warm earth, juniper, cardamom and black plums. The palate is fuller-bodied but not heavy despite the extraction and thumping of oak. Diam. 14.5% alc. **Rating** 91 **To** 2027 $50 JF

Ladies who Shoot their Lunch Wild Ferment Chardonnay 2018 It's not a shy wine with its stone fruit, honeydew and creamy, leesy flavours coated in sweet, vanillan oak. A style that you can recommend to fans of big chardonnay. Screwcap. 13.2% alc. **Rating** 90 **To** 2025 $35 JF

The Rule Strathbogie Ranges Shiraz 2018 It's dense and ripe, yet prominent acidity holds everything in place. Expect a wave of dark plums, baking spices and cedary-coconutty oak. Full-bodied but not too heavy as there is a brightness followed by firm tannins, somewhat drying on the finish. A well formed bicep is needed to lift the heavy bottle. Sigh. Diam. 14.5% alc. **Rating** 90 **To** 2028 $50 JF

Stone Dwellers Single Vineyard Strathbogie Ranges Cabernet Sauvignon 2018 A dusting of spices, cassis, licorice and warm terracotta work their way through to the palate. It's well composed with firm tannins, and tempting at this price point. Screwcap. 14.5% alc. **Rating** 90 **To** 2026 $25 JF

Fox Creek Wines ★★★★★

140 Malpas Road, McLaren Vale, SA 5171 **Region** McLaren Vale
T (08) 8557 0000 **www.**foxcreekwines.com **Open** 7 days 10–5
Winemaker Ben Tanzer, Steven Soper **Est.** 1995 **Dozens** 35 000 **Vyds** 21ha
Fox Creek has a winemaking history that dates back to 1984 when Helen and Dr Jim Watts purchased a 32ha property in McLaren Vale. The winery has been upgraded to handle the expanded production of Fox Creek, the increase a function of demand for the full-flavoured, robust red wines that make up the portfolio. Part of the estate vineyard dates back to the early 1900s, providing the Old Vine Shiraz that carries the Fox Creek banner. Exports to all major markets.

ŸŸŸŸŸ **Old Vine McLaren Vale Shiraz 2018** Open-fermented, 10 days on skins, plunged twice daily. In line with Fox Creek's approach across its red wines, fermentation finished in barrel (100% new), matured for 20 months. Deep, intense colour. The wine isn't full-bodied in the ordinary sense thanks to the balance of black fruits, oak and tannins; the mouthfeel supple and fresh. Screwcap. 14.5% alc. **Rating** 97 **To** 2043 $68 ✪

ŸŸŸŸŸ **Short Row McLaren Vale Shiraz 2017** Fermented on skins for 8–11 days, 90% completing fermentation in new and used barrels coopered in France, Australia and/or the US (predominantly dried for 3 years) matured for 20 months. The savoury, spicy palate has the indelible stamp of the '17 vintage from the opening sniff to the last taste. Screwcap. 14.5% alc. **Rating** 95 **To** 2037 $38

Postmaster McLaren Vale GSM 2018 A blend of 53% shiraz from 70yo vines, matured in used oak; 35% 60yo and 80yo grenache in used puncheons; 12% mourvedre in new and used puncheons. A barrel selection was detailed and complex, but has repaid the time taken. It's a really attractive GSM, the price a mystery given the cost and quality of the wine – a great bargain. Screwcap. 14.5% alc. **Rating** 95 **To** 2030 $29 ✪

Three Blocks McLaren Vale Cabernet Sauvignon 2017 Made with Rubik's Cube complexity using some high class fruit amid very elaborate use of oak, the only constants 8–19 days on skins and completion of fermentation in barrel. It's almost by-the-by to mention the quality of the wine, another example of Fox Creek's generosity (bordering on profligate) in selling what is a beautifully structured and weighted cabernet. Screwcap. 14.5% alc. **Rating** 95 **To** 2032 $38

Limited Release McLaren Vale Grenache 2018 Hand-plunged twice daily during fermentation, pressed to used puncheons to complete fermentation and maturation. I'm right on board with this technique, one I stumbled on with the Brokenwood Shiraz '73 and used until I stopped hands-on winemaking. It works as well with this grenache as with shiraz et al, giving a lightness of touch to the red spicy fruit and the lingering finish. Screwcap. 14.5% alc. **Rating** 94 **To** 2028 $38

Limited Release McLaren Vale Nero d'Avola 2019 Standard ultra small-batch Fox Creek vinification, open-fermented, 8 days on skins, matured in used

French puncheons. Vivid colour; flavour-sweet red fruits. Lovely wine for food. Screwcap. 13.5% alc. **Rating** 94 **To** 2026 $38

🍷🍷🍷🍷🍷 **Reserve McLaren Vale Shiraz 2016 Rating** 90 **To** 2031 $90
Limited Release McLaren Vale Tempranillo 2019 Rating 90 **To** 2025 $38

Foxeys Hangout
★★★★★

795 White Hill Road, Red Hill, Vic 3937 **Region** Mornington Peninsula
T (03) 5989 2022 **www.**foxeys-hangout.com.au **Open** W'ends & public hols 11–5
Winemaker Tony Lee, Michael Lee **Est.** 1997 **Dozens** 14000 **Vyds** 3.4ha
After 20 successful years in hospitality operating several cafes and restaurants (including one of Melbourne's first 'gastro-pubs' in the early 1990s), brothers Michael and Tony Lee planted their first vineyard in '97 at Merricks North. The venture takes its name from the tale of two fox hunters in the '30s hanging the results of their day's shooting in opposite branches of an ancient eucalypt, using the tree as their scorecard. Michael and Tony also manage the former Massoni Vineyard at Red Hill established by Ian Home, planting more chardonnay and pinot noir and opening their cellar door. Michael makes the sparkling wines, Tony (a qualified chef) makes the table wines and also cooks for the cellar door kitchen.

🍷🍷🍷🍷🍷 **White Gates Mornington Peninsula Chardonnay 2018** Powerful chardonnay boasting serious length. This is top tier. It tastes of stone fruit, toffee apples, bran, cream and wood smoke, and while the palate gives you plenty, the real drama is on the finish. Quite wonderful. Screwcap. 13.5% alc. **Rating** 96 **To** 2028 $45 CM ✪

Mornington Peninsula Chardonnay 2017 Fortune favours the bold. Seeking phenolics, 15% was whole bunch–wild fermented in tank, then pressed to barrel to complete fermentation, the balance pressed to barrel at inception with retention of full solids, 50% undergoing mlf, matured in French hogsheads (25% new). It has intensity, length, a great balance and mouthfeel. A tribute to the year and to the winemaking. Screwcap. 13% alc. **Rating** 96 **To** 2027 $38 ✪

Mornington Peninsula Pinot Noir 2018 In terrific form. Powerfully fruited, alive with spice and confidently structured. It doesn't just woo you, it reassures you. Dark macerated cherries, wood smoke, flings of herbs and assorted woodsy spices. There's a garden herb element here that is most attractive, matched as it is to nutty oak. From ear to ear the quality is excellent. Screwcap. 13.5% alc. **Rating** 96 **To** 2030 $38 CM ✪

Shiraz 2018 Unusual scents of wildflowers à la garrigue. The vintage was tailor-made for Mornington Peninsula shiraz, and the Lee brothers took full advantage. It has layers of black fruits, spices and light colour; the tannins positive. Screwcap. 13.5% alc. **Rating** 96 **To** 2038 $45 ✪

Red Lilac Single Vineyard Chardonnay 2018 Bright straw-green. Crisp, lively and pure fruits open the door wide from the first sip. Grapefruit is the centrepiece, with room all around waiting to be occupied with associated fruit flavours. The wine has, of course, been barrel-fermented, which has imparted some flavour, but more importantly, texture. Screwcap. 13.5% alc. **Rating** 95 **To** 2026 $45

Mornington Peninsula Chardonnay 2018 It's well filled out with varietal flavour, but it finishes with a cool, dry reserve. Stone fruit, meal, toast, tropical fruit and flint characters put on a classy display before the finish really seals the deal. Screwcap. 13% alc. **Rating** 95 **To** 2030 $38 CM

White Gates Mornington Peninsula Pinot Gris 2019 Textural, composed, complete gris. Seamless is the word. Shells, pears, honeysuckle and apples. It has depth but it also has carry. Indeed, it lingers beautifully through the finish. Screwcap. 14% alc. **Rating** 95 **To** 2025 $45 CM

Red Fox Mornington Peninsula Pinot Noir 2018 Entry level for Foxeys restaurant clients and cellar door, designed (by barrel selection) to be fruit forward. This isn't a giveaway price and is thoroughly deserved; it has vibrant red fruits with touches of oak and tannins. Attractive, indeed seductive. Screwcap. 13.5% alc. **Rating** 94 **To** 2023 $28 ✪

Kentucky Road 777 Single Vineyard Pinot Noir 2018 Clone 777 was grafted onto older vines in '10. The hue of this full purple-crimson is very striking. It has a depth and concentration not often found in other pinots in '18. It's an open question where this wine will head, and when it will reach its peak. Screwcap. 13.5% alc. **Rating** 94 **To** 2028 $65

Scotsworth Farm Mornington Peninsula Pinot Noir 2018 Such a powerful pinot. This is where delicacy exits and significant spice-shot varietal flavour marches in. It's stern, tannic, slightly stewy, undergrowthy and solid. Where it goes from here will be interesting. **Rating** 94 **To** 2028 $65 CM

ᵀᵀᵀᵀᵀ **Pinot Gris 2019 Rating** 93 **To** 2022 $30 CM
Pinot Gris 2018 Rating 93 **To** 2021 $28
Rose 2019 Rating 93 **To** 2022 $28 CM
Rose 2018 Rating 93 **To** 2021 $28
Late Harvest Pinot Gris 2018 Rating 92 **To** 2022 $28

Frankland Estate ★★★★★

Frankland Road, Frankland, WA 6396 **Region** Frankland River
T (08) 9855 1544 **www**.franklandestate.com.au **Open** Mon–Fri 10–4, w'ends by appt
Winemaker Hunter Smith, Brian Kent **Est.** 1988 **Dozens** 20 000 **Vyds** 34.5ha
A significant operation, situated on a large sheep property owned by Barrie Smith and Judi Cullam. The vineyard has been established progressively since 1988. The introduction of an array of single vineyard rieslings has been a highlight, driven by Judi's conviction that terroir is of utmost importance, and the soils are indeed different; the Isolation Ridge Vineyard is organically grown. Frankland Estate has held important International Riesling tastings and seminars for more than a decade. Exports to all major markets.

ᵀᵀᵀᵀᵀ **Poison Hill Riesling 2019** Organically certified, this address has loosened up a conventional strut of austerity to a swagger of confidence, textural detail and poise. This new stance is embellished with optimally ripe fruit evincing care, love for the land and authority. This is a rich and spicy riesling, reminiscent of great Germanic expressions over the sour Aussie norm. A forcefield of palate-staining intensity. This is juicy, powerful and complex. Compelling length. Quince, lemon oil, apricot and tonic. Screwcap. **Rating** 97 **To** 2029 $45 NG ✪

ᵀᵀᵀᵀᵀ **Mourvedre 2018** An expression of this marvellous variety far from the hot SA norm where, too often, sheer extract and ripeness obfuscates a ferruginous personality. Conversely, this speaks with a ferrous growl. Dried tobacco, salami, tapenade, dark cherry, satsuma plum and Asian spice meet their maker, as a clang of iron-clad tannins let us all know who is in charge. I would like to simply drink the bottle. Screwcap. **Rating** 96 **To** 2025 $32 NG ✪

Alter Weg Riesling 2019 Another riesling breaking the reductive mould and seeking texture through skin-inflection, barrel fermentation and maturation (11 months). The result is outstanding. Quince, grapefruit pulp, apricot and lemon squash scents rally along a pungent mineral beam, accented with a gentle pucker. Scintillating length. Great purity. A celebration of organic fruit and handling. The way forward! Screwcap. **Rating** 95 **To** 2031 $35 NG ✪

Smith Cullam Syrah 2018 An idyllic selection across the Isolation Ridge zone. And it shows. Clearly. Strongly. Distinctively. The tannins more polished; the peppery blueberry to dark cherry scents, vibrant and transparent. This is delicious, with a fidelity to the Frankland briar and olive scents palpable, pure and uncluttered. Screwcap. **Rating** 95 **To** 2035 $120 NG

Shiraz 2017 A superb estate release, drinking like a savoury highly aromatic paean to a luncheon quaffer from the Northern Rhône. Olive, charcuterie, iodine, blueberry and a long peppery skein of jitterbug freshness. A great drink now and across the mid-term. Screwcap. **Rating** 95 **To** 2025 $30 NG ✪

Organic Touriga Nacional 2018 More of this, please! Hard to spit. Far from prosaic and yet a conflation of regional scrub and menthol scents, gorgeous florals and a jubey, bouncy palate exuding dark cherry, tobacco leaf, anise and bitter chocolate notes. Lip-smacking and dangerous. Juicy acidity driving it all long. Scored on sumptuousness. Screwcap. **Rating** 95 **To** 2024 $32 NG ✪

Isolation Ridge Riesling 2019 Hewn of fruit from a marginal ironstone-lain site, this is a different kettle of fish to the pungent power of Poison Hill. More linear. Greater tension, perhaps, while exhibiting a flavour spectrum of grapefruit pulp, lemon zest, fennel and lemongrass. More citric, herbal and wet stone slaty. No less intense, but less generous in the here and now. Bodes well for a bright, long future. Screwcap. **Rating** 94 **To** 2031 $45 NG

Riesling 2019 This is an excellent estate riesling, boasting ripeness and the sort of succulent fruit that the Australian obsession with pH/acidity seldom facilitates. Talc, bath salts and grapefruit pulp. Tingly. Jittering with energy. Yet the streamlined juiciness, pulling the saliva across the mouth while instigating thirst and hunger, is the sign of a versatile, food-friendly wine. Excellent. Screwcap. **Rating** 94 **To** 2028 $30 NG ✪

Smith Cullam Riesling 2019 Named after the founders, Barrie Smith and Judi Cullam. Off-dry and crafted from a plot-by-plot-by-row selection across the most propitious sites. Lemon squash, candied citrus zest, mountain herb and tonic. A transparent stream of uncluttered riesling scents, neither too dry and sour, nor excessively fruity and dainty. Make no mistake, despite its ethereal flow, this mid-weighted riesling packs a punch across a long finish of sap and crunch, the dollop of sugar mitigating the grape's soprano acidity. Screwcap. **Rating** 94 $65 NG

♏♏♏♏♀ **Alter Weg Riesling 2018** Rating 93 **To** 2028 $30
Museum Release Isolation Ridge Vineyard Riesling 2010 Rating 93 **To** 2024 $65 NG
Isolation Ridge Shiraz 2018 Rating 93 **To** 2026 $45 NG
Cabernet Sauvignon 2018 Rating 93 **To** 2027 $30 NG
Rocky Gully Riesling 2019 Rating 92 **To** 2025 $20 NG ✪
Chardonnay 2018 Rating 92 **To** 2024 $30 NG
Rocky Gully Shiraz 2017 Rating 92 **To** 2021 $18 NG ✪
Rocky Gully Cabernets 2017 Rating 92 **To** 2023 $18 NG ✪

Fraser Gallop Estate   ★★★★★

493 Metricup Road, Wilyabrup, WA 6280 **Region** Margaret River
T (08) 9755 7553 **www**.frasergallopestate.com.au **Open** 7 days 11–4
Winemaker Clive Otto, Ellin Tritt **Est.** 1999 **Dozens** 10 000 **Vyds** 20ha

Nigel Gallop began the development of the vineyard in 1999, planting cabernet sauvignon, semillon, petit verdot, cabernet franc, malbec, merlot, sauvignon blanc and multi-clone chardonnay. The dry-grown vines have modest yields, followed by kid-glove treatment in the winery. With Clive Otto (formerly of Vasse Felix) onboard, a 300t winery was built. The wines have had richly deserved success in wine shows and journalists' reviews. Exports to the UK, Sweden, Thailand, Indonesia and Singapore.

♏♏♏♏♏ **Parterre Margaret River Cabernet Sauvignon 2016** Includes 7% petit verdot, 5% cabernet franc and 4% malbec. Tasted at the end of a group of cabernets, it had the essence of cabernet missing from the other wines. After 18 months in new and used French oak, it presents all the tension between cassis/blackcurrant on the one hand and finely etched cabernet tannins on the other. The balance and mouthfeel are exceptional. Screwcap. 14% alc. **Rating** 97 **To** 2041 $50 ✪

♏♏♏♏♏ **Palladian Margaret River Chardonnay 2018** Pale straw-green; in the subtle, tightly woven style of Fraser Gallop's chardonnays. The subtlety of the label designs and the 3 different chardonnays can be confusing. This beautifully balanced and very long wine has Granny Smith apple, white peach and nectarine all contributing. The role of each is small, the finish clear. Screwcap. 13.5% alc. **Rating** 96 **To** 2032 $110

Palladian Margaret River Cabernet Sauvignon 2016 A case of achieving more by doing less, if ever there was one. The bouquet is fragrant, full of blackcurrant and bramble spice. Oak and tannins are both there, but neither able to be separately analysed. Only medium-bodied. A rare example of top class cabernet. Screwcap. 14% alc. **Rating** 96 **To** 2036 $110

Margaret River Cabernet Merlot 2018 Oh so easy – simply grow the grapes, pick when ripe, crush and ferment, mature in French oak, wait for the synergy, bottle when ready. Here the magic starts: cassis/blackcurrant, a touch of tapenade, ripe but deferent tannins and a waft of sweet cigar box. Screwcap. 14% alc. **Rating** 95 **To** 2028 $26 ✪

Parterre Margaret River Cabernet Sauvignon 2017 Includes 86.2% cabernet sauvignon and small amounts of petit verdot, merlot, cabernet franc and malbec; matured in used French oak for 18 months. A fresh, lively medium-bodied Bordeaux blend, tannins and oak unimportant. Elegance and purity are its watchwords. Screwcap. 13.5% alc. **Rating** 95 **To** 2037 $50

Margaret River Malbec 2018 The Clare Valley, Langhorne Creek and Margaret River share what is often regarded as a second-rate variety, its best use is as a blend component. Well, there are enough very good, fleshy dark fruits to prove it's capable of making really pleasing wines. This, with its plush fruits and ripe tannins, proves the point. Screwcap. 14% alc. **Rating** 95 **To** 2038 $33 ✪

Margaret River Chardonnay 2019 Whole-bunch pressed, wild-fermented in barrel. Crystal clear; does raise the question of confusion between sauvignon blanc and early picked chardonnay. I am perfectly happy with the energy and freshness of this wine, and equally relaxed about any trade-off. Grapefruit and white peach push my buttons, the oak influence very subtle; as much to do with texture as flavour. Screwcap. 12.5% alc. **Rating** 94 **To** 2026 $26 ✪

🍷🍷🍷🍷🍷 **Margaret River Ice Pressed Chardonnay 2019** **Rating** 92 **To** 2021 $35
Margaret River Rose 2019 **Rating** 90 **To** 2021 $24

Freeman Vineyards ★★★★★

101 Prunevale Road, Prunevale, NSW 2587 **Region** Hilltops
T 0429 310 309 **www.**freemanvineyards.com.au **Open** By appt
Winemaker Dr Brian Freeman, Xanthe Freeman **Est.** 2000 **Dozens** 5000 **Vyds** 173ha
Dr Brian Freeman spent much of his life in research and education, in the latter with a role as head of CSU's viticulture and oenology campus. In 2004 he purchased the 30-year-old Demondrille Vineyard. He has also established a vineyard next door. In all has 22 varieties that range from staples such as shiraz, cabernet sauvignon, semillon and riesling through to more exotic, trendy varieties such as tempranillo, corvina, rondinella and harslevelu.

🍷🍷🍷🍷🍷 **Aged Release Rondinella Corvina Secco 2007** Still has its particular savoury/spicy/plum/dried fruit blend. The tannins play a positive part. Screwcap. 15% alc. **Rating** 93 **To** 2023 $70

Altura Vineyard Nebbiolo 2016 An ominous blackish edge to the hue (from the pH or the variety?). Rose petal/spice/violets. The tannins are under control, although dryish à la nebbiolo. Screwcap. 14% alc. **Rating** 92 **To** 2026 $40

Rondo Rondinella Rose 2019 Part of the wine was (for the first time) fermented in used oak, which has resulted in the salmon colour. The bouquet is part floral, part spicy for a high-yielding variety. The palate packs a punch with its slippery acidity on high volume. Screwcap. 12.8% alc. **Rating** 90 **To** 2022 $20 ✪

Freycinet ★★★★★

15919 Tasman Highway via Bicheno, Tas 7215 **Region** East Coast Tasmania
T (03) 6257 8574 **www.**freycinetvineyard.com.au **Open** Oct–Apr 7 days 10–5,
May–Sept 7 days 10–4
Winemaker Claudio Radenti, Lindy Bull **Est.** 1979 **Dozens** 9000 **Vyds** 15.9ha
The Freycinet vineyards are situated on the sloping hillsides of a small valley. The soils are brown dermosol on top of Jurassic dolerite; and the combination of aspect, slope, soil and heat

summation produces red grapes with unusual depth of colour and ripe flavours. One of the foremost producers of pinot noir, with an enviable track record of consistency – rare in such a temperamental variety. The Radenti (sparkling), Riesling and Chardonnay are also wines of the highest quality. In 2012 Freycinet acquired part of the neighbouring Coombend property from Brown Brothers. The 42ha property extends to the Tasman Highway and includes a 5.75ha mature vineyard and a 4.2ha olive grove. Exports to the UK and Singapore.

ŸŸŸŸŸ **Riesling 2019** Ever reliable, and one of my favourite Tasmanian rieslings. It has laser-like precision, its lime-infused fruit simply nodding to the 8.5g/l of titratable acidity. No frills winemaking other than (perhaps) the selection of a Mosel Valley isolate yeast. Screwcap. 13.5% alc. **Rating** 96 **To** 2034 $32 ✪

R3 Radenti Chardonnay Pinot Noir NV Radenti is doing a Krug, moving from single vintage (the last '11) to a multi-vintage blend. R3 is a blend of 3 vintages: '12 (40%), '13 (44%), '14 (16%); the overall blend 70% chardonnay and 30% pinot noir. It is vibrant, with fresh fruit flavours in a complex, textured frame. Cork. 12.5% alc. **Rating** 96 $65 ✪

Wineglass Bay Sauvignon Blanc 2018 Hand-picked when very ripe, 70% fermented in tank, 30% in used barriques with specialist yeasts, matured for 8 months. Gold medal from the Six Nations Challenge held in Australia. A just reward for a wine that pays no attention to Tasmania's reluctance to produce good sauvignon blanc. Screwcap. 13.8% alc. **Rating** 95 **To** 2023 $28 ✪

Pinot Noir 2018 Hand-picked, 95% whole berry, 5% whole bunch, 28 and 48 days on skins (for 80% and 20% of the wine respectively), matured for 16 months in French oak (36% new). Radically different from Louis. Medium-bodied with spicy/savoury notes from start to finish. Both this and Louis need time for the tannins to soften. Screwcap. 14% alc. **Rating** 95 **To** 2030 $75

Botrytis NV Only the third botrytic wine in the estate's history, this is straight sauvignon blanc, blended across 3 recent benevolent years: '16 (50%), '17 (25%) and '18 (the remainder). The residual sugar is Germanic of proportion, yet the whiplash of acidity that unfurls across the tail wrestles it into a sense of poise, grace and flow, as it drives across the mouth delivering notes of candied quince, persimmon and pineapple, accented with a gentle verdant waft. Screwcap. 10% alc. **Rating** 95 **To** 2028 $35 NG ✪

Chardonnay 2018 40yo vines, hand-picked, crushed, fermented in French barriques (26% new), matured for 10 months, stirred every 3 weeks. Relies on purity and focus, rather than complexity, and will age with grace. Screwcap. 13.5% alc. **Rating** 94 **To** 2030 $45

Louis Pinot Noir 2018 Mainly G5V12 clone; 95% whole berry, 5% whole-bunch rotary fermented, 42–48 days on skins, matured for 14 months in French oak (18% new). Deep colour. A perfumed/oriental spice bouquet. A rich full-bodied (for pinot) palate with depth of fruit and tannins – the latter more obvious than expected. Screwcap. 14% alc. **Rating** 94 **To** 2033 $45

Cabernet Merlot 2016 Includes 70% cabernet sauvignon, 22% merlot, 8% cabernet franc; matured for 30 months in French (31% new). It is medium to full-bodied with power to burn. Blackcurrant, black olive, bay leaf and firm but not abrasive tannins all add up coherently. Screwcap. 14% alc. **Rating** 94 **To** 2038 $45

ŸŸŸŸŸ **Louis Chardonnay 2018 Rating** 92 **To** 2026 $28
Shiraz 2016 Rating 90 **To** 2028 $60

Frog Choir Wines   ★★★★

PO Box 635, Margaret River, WA 6285 **Region** Margaret River
T 0427 777 787 **www.**frogchoir.com **Open** At Redgate Wines cellar door
Winemaker Naturaliste Vintners (Bruce Dukes) **Est.** 1997 **Dozens** 250 **Vyds** 1.2ha
Kate and Nigel Hunt have a micro-vineyard equally split between shiraz and cabernet sauvignon. It has immaculate address credentials: adjacent to Leeuwin Estate and Voyager Estate; 6km from the Margaret River township. The hand-tended vines are grown without the use of insecticides.

♥♥♥♥♥ **Margaret River Shiraz Cabernet Sauvignon 2012** Mix of 63.3% shiraz, 36.7% cabernet. Full-bodied. It is still a young, powerful wine; its best years in front of it. Screwcap. 14.9% alc. **Rating** 94 **To** 2032 $28 ✪

♥♥♥♥♀ **Margaret River Shiraz Cabernet Sauvignon 2015 Rating** 92 **To** 2030 $28

Gala Estate   ★★★★★

14891 Tasman Highway, Cranbrook, Tas 7190 **Region** East Coast Tasmania
T 0408 681 014 **www.**galaestate.com.au **Open** 7 days 10–4
Winemaker Pat Colombo, Keira O'Brien **Est.** 2009 **Dozens** 5000 **Vyds** 11ha
This vineyard is situated on a 4000ha sheep station, with the sixth, seventh and eighth generations – headed by Robert and Patricia (nee Amos) Greenhill – custodians of the land granted to James Amos in 1821. It is recognised as the second oldest family business in Tasmania. The 11ha vineyard is heavily skewed to pinot noir (7ha), the remainder planted (in descending order of area) to chardonnay, pinot gris, riesling, shiraz and sauvignon blanc. The main risk is spring frost, and overhead spray irrigation serves two purposes: it provides adequate moisture for early season growth and frost protection at the end of the growing season.

♥♥♥♥♥ **Black Label Chardonnay 2018** Hand-picked, chilled, whole-bunch pressed, wild-fermented, matured for 10 months on lees in new and used French oak. This is up with Gala's best, vibrantly fresh yet generous and complex. Pink grapefruit/white peach may be clichés, but they're here in spades. Screwcap. 13% alc. **Rating** 97 **To** 2030 $65 ✪

♥♥♥♥♥ **Black Label Chardonnay 2017** Very well made. The bouquet and palate share the complexity bonus. There's an almost savoury edge to the grapefruit and stone fruit du. This, plus natural acidity, confers length well above normal. Screwcap. 13.8% alc. **Rating** 96 **To** 2030 $65 ✪
White Label Pinot Noir 2017 Wonderfully spicy and entrancing, the fresh, vibrant, red-berried palate picking up where the bouquet left off. Length and balance are its calling cards, the value for money needing no comment. Screwcap. 13.4% alc. **Rating** 96 **To** 2032 $32 ✪
Black Label Pinot Gris 2018 Identical vinification to the '19. Nougat varietal character comes through strongly. A wonderfully complex pinot gris, a genuine food style. Retasted after 3 hours in the glass, and the nougat (and pear) were undiminished. Screwcap. 13.5% alc. **Rating** 95 **To** 2023 $65
White Label Pinot Rose 2018 Pale salmon-pink hue. Strawberries and cream. It's a really attractive wine that should be served in a black glass to overcome the instinctive negative reaction to the colour. Screwcap. 12.5% alc. **Rating** 95 **To** 2022 $32 ✪
Black Label Sparkling Vintage Rose 2016 No disgorgement details, but it is traditional method pinot chardonnay, suggesting circa 3 years on lees. Pale salmon-pink. Classy wine. The low dosage works well, brightening the fruit component. Diam. 13.5% alc. **Rating** 95 $65
White Label Riesling 2019 No frills winemaking, none needed. An apple and citrus blossom bouquet, then a supple, balanced palate offering plenty now, and more still in the years to come. The acidity is ample, not fearsome. Screwcap. 12.5% alc. **Rating** 94 **To** 2029 $32
White Label Pinot Gris 2019 Destemmed, 12-hours cold soak, special yeasts used (including the 'sauvignon blanc' yeast). Full pink ex skin contact; 5 months on lees has added to the mid-palate; a crisp finish. Fresh, vibrant phenolics are a plus, nashi pear the driver. Screwcap. 13.5% alc. **Rating** 94 **To** 2023 $32
White Label Syrah 2018 Light, bright colour. Light-bodied, fresh lively red cherry fruit. Quite likely to show its best over the next 2–3 years. Screwcap. 13.5% alc. **Rating** 94 **To** 2025 $32

♥♥♥♥♀ **White Label Sauvignon Blanc 2019 Rating** 93 **To** 2024 $32
White Label Pinot Gris 2018 Rating 93 **To** 2022 $32
White Label Pinot Noir 2018 Rating 93 **To** 2028 $32
White Label Chardonnay 2019 Rating 91 **To** 2023 $32

Galafrey

Quangellup Road, Mount Barker, WA 6324 **Region** Mount Barker
T (08) 9851 2022 www.galafreywines.com.au **Open** 7 days 10–5
Winemaker Kim Tyrer **Est.** 1977 **Dozens** 3500 **Vyds** 13.1ha
The Galafrey story began when Ian and Linda Tyrer gave up high-profile jobs in the emerging computer industry and arrived in Mount Barker to start growing grapes and making wine, the vine-change partially prompted by their desire to bring up their children-to-be in a country environment. The dry-grown vineyard they planted continues to be the turning point, the first winery established in an ex-whaling building (long since replaced by a purpose-built winery). The premature death of Ian at a time when the industry was buckling at the knees increased the already considerable difficulties the family had to deal with, but deal with it they did. Daughter Kim Tyrer is now CEO of the business, with Linda still very much involved in the day-to-day management of Galafrey. Exports to Canada and Singapore.

ΨΨΨΨΨ **Dry Grown Vineyard Mount Barker Riesling 2019** 100% free-run juice. Straw coloured with green highlights. Mount Barker florals, in particular a distinct lavender note mixed with lemon sherbet and lime zest. So fine, restrained. Green apple and kaffir lime leaf mingle on a palate of true finesse. A youngster with an eye on the future. Gold medal Perth Wine Awards '19. Screwcap. 12.5% alc. Rating 96 To 2035 $25 JP ✪

Galli Estate

1507 Melton Highway, Plumpton, Vic 3335 **Region** Sunbury
T (03) 9747 1444 www.galliestate.com.au **Open** 7 days 11–5
Winemaker Alasdair Park **Est.** 1997 **Dozens** 10 000 **Vyds** 160ha
Galli Estate has two vineyards: Heathcote, which produces the red wines (shiraz, sangiovese, nebbiolo, tempranillo, grenache and montepulciano) and the cooler climate vineyard at Plumpton in Sunbury, producing the whites (chardonnay, pinot grigio, sauvignon blanc and fiano). All wines are biodynamically estate-grown and made, with wine movements on the new moon. Exports to Canada, Singapore, China and Hong Kong.

ΨΨΨΨΨ **Adele Nebbiolo 2017** More Barbaresco in style than Barolo, Adele resides in the prettier, finer interpretation of the Piedmontese grape. Nevertheless, it shares the beguiling, lifted floral aromas common to both Italian styles. The palate is irresistibly savoury and inviting with cherry, fig, orange peel, dried fruit and rose petal. The grape's notorious tannins are tamed and in balance. Screwcap. 14.5% alc. Rating 95 To 2032 $38 JP

ΨΨΨΨ♀ **Camelback Grenache 2018** Rating 91 To 2026 $20 JP ✪
Camelback Man Is Not A Camel Montepulciano 2018 Rating 91 To 2027 $20 JP ✪
Camelback Man Is Not A Camel Rose 2019 Rating 90 To 2025 $20 JP ✪

Gapsted Wines

3897 Great Alpine Road, Gapsted, Vic 3737 **Region** Alpine Valleys
T (03) 5751 9100 www.gapstedwines.com.au **Open** 7 days 10–5
Winemaker Michael Cope-Williams, Toni Pla Bou, Matt Fawcett **Est.** 1997
Dozens 250 000 **Vyds** 256.1ha
Gapsted is the major brand of the Victorian Alps Winery, which started life (and continues) as a large-scale contract winemaking facility. The quality of the wines made for its own brand has led to the expansion of production not only under that label, but also under a raft of subsidiary labels. As well as the substantial estate plantings, Gapsted sources traditional and alternative grape varieties from the King and Alpine valleys. Exports to Canada, Germany, Norway, Sweden, Russia, the UAE, India, Thailand, South Korea, Malaysia, Singapore, Vietnam, Cambodia, Hong Kong, China and Japan.

ΨΨΨΨΨ **Ballerina Canopy Heathcote Shiraz 2018** Packed tight and ready for an extended time in the bottle, the Ballerina Canopy is always a good bet for the cellar. Deep, dense purple hues typical of Heathcote. Plush, aromatic scent with a good dose of Aussie bush amid the blackberry, cassis and cedar. The big takeaway with this wine is the structural integrity and powdery tannins. It's well built. Screwcap. 14% alc. **Rating** 94 **To** 2030 $31 JP

Ballerina Canopy Alpine Valleys Durif 2018 Under the flagship label, and up to the task, comes a durif that delivers ripe fruit and sturdy tannins in a mid-weighted style that reveals a more stylish side of the grape. Deepest purple in hue. Savoury introduction with black cherries, cassis and plum fruits and striking star anise. Ripe, supple and well composed with discreet, coffee-mocha oak playing a feature role. There's a lot to like here. Screwcap. 14.5% alc. **Rating** 94 **To** 2031 $31 JP

ΨΨΨΨ **Limited Release Single Vineyard King Valley Pinot Blanc 2019 Rating** 93 **To** 2023 $25 JF ✪

Limited Release King Valley Fiano 2019 Rating 92 **To** 2026 $25 JP ✪

Garagiste ★★★★★

4 Lawrey Street, Frankston, Vic 3199 (postal) **Region** Mornington Peninsula
T 0439 370 530 **www.**garagiste.com.au **Open** Not
Winemaker Barnaby Flanders **Est.** 2006 **Dozens** 2200 **Vyds** 3ha
Barnaby Flanders was a co-founder of Allies Wines (see separate entry) in 2003, with some of the wines made under the Garagiste label. Allies has now gone its own way and Barnaby has a controlling interest in the Garagiste brand. The focus is on the Mornington Peninsula. The grapes are hand-sorted in the vineyard and again in the winery. Chardonnay is whole-bunch pressed, barrel-fermented with wild yeast in new and used French oak, mlf variably used, 8–9 months on lees. Seldom fined or filtered. Exports to the UK, Canada, Norway, Singapore, Japan, Hong Kong and China.

ΨΨΨΨΨ **Merricks Mornington Peninsula Pinot Noir 2018** A light ruby hue segues to an inviting nose, boasting sap and a density far from the candied red-fruited regional norm. Sapid cherry scents, damson plum, Asian five-spice, wood smoke and sandalwood. Nebbioloesque. The compact tannins curl across the mouth, long-chained, pliant and just firm enough. Each component integrates beautifully to draw the flavours long while evincing an authority and welcome savouriness, without any obvious greenness. Very fine. Screwcap. **Rating** 95 **To** 2026 NG

Terre de Feu Mornington Peninsula Pinot Noir 2017 A mid-weighted pinot of scintillating vibrancy, embedded with the mescal and turmeric scents that serve as whole-cluster's legacy. Yet the juiciness of the mid-palate, the intensity of red berry flavours and a medicinal whiff behind the bunchy cladding, are all impressive. Framed by a carapace of nicely wrought tannins melded with saliva-sucking acidity, these are factors that augur well for a bright future across the mid-term. Screwcap. **Rating** 95 **To** 2026 $75 NG

Terre Maritime Mornington Peninsula Chardonnay 2018 A limey green glint segues to a flinty vibrancy of curd, lanolin and lemon drop. This is racy, yet generous and juicy all at once; the phalanx of maritime salinity and acidity far from forced, but merely seducing the flavours to a long energetic finish across a vanillan praline core. Screwcap. **Rating** 94 **To** 2025 $75 NG

ΨΨΨΨ **Merricks Chardonnay 2018 Rating** 93 **To** 2025 $45 NG

Le Stagiaire Pinot Gris 2019 Rating 93 **To** 2022 $30 NG

Merricks Pinot Noir Cuve Beton 2018 Rating 93 **To** 2024 NG

Le Stagiaire Chardonnay 2019 Rating 92 **To** 2023 $30 NG

Cotier Wines Pinot Gris 2018 Rating 92 **To** 2021 NG

Cotier Wines Gewurztraminer 2018 Rating 91 **To** 2021 $30 NG

Le Stagiaire Pinot Noir 2018 Rating 91 **To** 2021 NG

Cotier Wines Riesling 2018 Rating 90 **To** 2023 NG

Garden & Field   ★★★★☆

PO Box 52, Angaston, SA 5353 **Region** Eden Valley/Barossa Valley
T (08) 8564 2435 **www**.tasteedenvalley.com.au **Open** At Taste Eden Valley
Winemaker Peter Raymond **Est.** 2009 **Dozens** 100 **Vyds** 5.6ha
One of those stories that seem to be too good to be true. It is over 100 years since the Schilling
family cleared the land of its granite boulders, built cottages from the rocks and planted
a vineyard. In the late 1970s the property was sold and when the Vine Pull Scheme was
legislated, the new owners were quick to remove the vines. Another decade passed and the
property was again on the market. Eventually viticulturist Peter Raymond and wife Melissa
purchased it and set about preparing 3.6ha for planting. As they arrived one Saturday morning
to begin the long task, they found a group of octogenarian men armed with picks and shovels,
there to help plant 3500 vines on what they regarded as holy viticultural land, desecrated by
the Vine Pull Scheme. Penfolds now buys most of the grapes for its RWT Shiraz at tip-top
prices, but the Raymonds keep enough to make a small amount of wine each year.

🍷🍷🍷🍷🍷 **Gnadenberg Road Barossa Shiraz 2017** The '17 vintage allowed wicket
keeper Peter Raymond to have his cake and eat it. This wine is generous and
stacked with blackberry and blueberry fruit flavours, yet shows no heat or over-
extraction. Cork. 14.4% alc. **Rating** 94 **To** 2027 $95

Garners Heritage Wines   ★★★★

32–34 Conran Drive, Ocean Grove, Vic 3226 (postal) **Region** Strathbogie Ranges
T 0410 649 030 **www**.garnerswine.com.au **Open** Not
Winemaker Lindsay Brown **Est.** 2005 **Dozens** 600 **Vyds** 1.8ha
Leon and Rosie Garner established Garners Heritage Wines in 2005, celebrating their
10th anniversary in '15. A multi-vintage future for Leon and Rosie Garner stretched out
with the completion of their vineyard and early wine show successes but it was cut short by
Leon's death in '16 after a long battle with cancer. The 1.8ha vineyard that produced high
class award-winning shiraz has now been sold, Rosie retaining the label and wine stock. The
wines are sold via the website, email or phone orders; '18 was the last vintage. Exports to
Hong Kong.

🍷🍷🍷🍷🍷 **The Whanau Reserve Strathbogie Ranges Shiraz 2018** Follows in the
footsteps of the '17 and marks the last vintage to be made. 'Whanau' is a Maori
word used to describe extended family and friends. The wine is destined to be
sold to loyal clients and the Melbourne Sandbelt golf clubs. It is full-bodied but
balanced; the palate rich, its future secure. Screwcap. 15.2% alc. **Rating** 94 **To** 2038
$30 ♻

🍷🍷🍷🍷♀ **Bookend Strathbogie Ranges Vintage Port 2017** Rating 90 $18 ♻

Gartelmann Wines   ★★★★★

701 Lovedale Road, Lovedale, NSW 2321 **Region** Hunter Valley
T (02) 4930 7113 **www**.gartelmann.com.au **Open** Mon–Sat 10–5, Sun 10–4
Winemaker Jorg Gartelmann, Liz Silkman, Rauri Donkin **Est.** 1996 **Dozens** 6500
In 1996 Jan and Jorg Gartelmann purchased what was previously the George Hunter Estate –
16ha of mature vineyards, most established by Oliver Shaul in '70. In a change of emphasis, the
vineyard was sold and Gartelmann now sources its grapes from the Hunter Valley and other
NSW regions, including the cool Rylstone area in Mudgee.

🍷🍷🍷🍷🍷 **Shiraz 2017** A warm drought year, but for sheer intensity and tenacity of fruit,
an impressive vintage. This is a rich loamy wine, framed by a swathe of firm earthy
tannins. These corral a wave of blue fruits, red plum, Asian spice and anise. I like
this. A lot. Strong fealty to place. Traditional school. Quintessentially Hunter.
Screwcap. **Rating** 96 **To** 2037 NG
Museum Release Benjamin Hunter Valley Semillon 2014 This hails from
very old vines on deep sandy loams. A testimonial to how well these sprightly

wines cellar. And yet this is barely middle-aged, at least in the regional context. A medium yellow with a glint of green. Telltale aromas of citrus marmalade, buttered toast, quince and lemon drop. Long and vibrant. From a textbook year, I would hedge my bets on an even finer future. Screwcap. **Rating** 95 To 2029 NG

ŢŢŢŢ͡Ţ **Benjamin Hunter Valley Semillon 2019** Rating 93 To 2031 $27 NG ✪
Phillip Alexander Mudgee Cabernet Merlot 2016 Rating 93 To 2028 $30 NG
Stephanie Orange Pinot Gris 2019 Rating 90 To 2021 $27 NG
Joey Mudgee Merlot 2017 Rating 90 To 2023 $30 NG

Gatt Wines

417 Boehms Springs Road, Flaxman Valley, SA 5235 **Region** Eden Valley
T (08) 8564 1166 **www**.gattwines.com **Open** At Taste Eden Valley
Winemaker David Norman **Est.** 1972 **Dozens** 8000 **Vyds** 56.24ha
When you read the hyperbole that sometimes accompanies the acquisition of an existing wine business, about transforming it into a world class operation, it is easy to sigh and move on. When Ray Gatt acquired Eden Springs, he proceeded to translate words into deeds. As well as the 19.15ha Eden Springs Vineyard, he also acquired the historic Siegersdorf Vineyard (now 21.79ha) on the Barossa floor and the neighbouring Graue Vineyard (15.3ha). The change of name from Eden Springs to Gatt Wines in 2011 was sensible. Exports to the UK, Canada, France, Sweden, Denmark, Germany, Finland, Italy, South Korea, Japan, Macau, Hong Kong and China.

ŢŢŢŢŢ **High Eden Riesling 2017** From the estate vineyard at 460m altitude. Has greater depth and richness than its Eden Springs sibling, but not the same focus. Both are high quality wines, but the balance of this wine effortlessly brings the flavours through to the long palate and lingering aftertaste. High alcohol doesn't spoil the wine. Screwcap. 13% alc. **Rating** 96 To 2032 $30 ✪
Eden Springs High Eden Riesling 2017 Highly focused, crisp and intense, reflecting the vintage and good vineyard. Citrus blossom tells of the bracing fruit and minerally/crunchy acidity. Finesse and precision. Screwcap. 11% alc. **Rating** 95 To 2030 $30 ✪
High Eden Riesling 2010 Glorious straw-green hue. It's behaving like a 2–3yo riesling, not a 9yo. Crisp and dry, citrus blossom aromas and flavours are joined by green apple on the long and taut palate. Screwcap. 12% alc. **Rating** 95 To 2023 $35 ✪
Old Vine Barossa Valley Shiraz 2014 From a single vineyard planted in '72, matured for 15 months in new French oak. Excellent colour, the fruit having easily accounted for the time in oak. The flavours are ripe and full, the alcohol simply part of the wine. Screwcap. 14.5% alc. **Rating** 95 To 2034 $100
High Eden Shiraz 2010 Has retained exceptional colour and overall freshness; red and black cherry fruit, silky tannins and positive oak in balanced abundance. Age has also given the wine a savoury element that adds to the quality. Screwcap. 14.5% alc. **Rating** 95 To 2028 $60
High Eden Shiraz 2014 A generously fruited 5yo wine with discussion between the red (raspberry, cherry) fruits backing up purple (plum) and black (blackberry) flavours; oak and tannins relegated to the back benches. Screwcap. 13% alc. **Rating** 94 To 2029 $60

ŢŢŢŢŢ **Barossa Valley Cabernet Sauvignon 2014** Rating 93 To 2029 $60
Old Vine Barossa Valley Shiraz 2010 Rating 92 To 2030 $100
Barossa Valley Shiraz 2010 Rating 92 To 2025 $60
Eden Springs High Eden Cabernet Sauvignon 2015 Rating 92 To 2025 $40
Eden Springs High Eden Shiraz 2014 Rating 91 To 2025 $40
Eden Springs Barossa Cabernet Sauvignon 2015 Rating 91 To 2025 $40
Eden Springs High Eden Pinot Gris 2016 Rating 90 To 2021 $30
Barossa Valley Shiraz 2014 Rating 90 To 2029 $60

Gembrook Hill ★★★★★

Launching Place Road, Gembrook, Vic 3783 **Region** Yarra Valley
T (03) 5968 1622 **www**.gembrookhill.com.au **Open** By appt
Winemaker Andrew Marks **Est.** 1983 **Dozens** 1500 **Vyds** 5ha

Ian and June Marks established Gembrook Hill, one of the oldest vineyards in the southernmost part of the Upper Yarra Valley. The northeast-facing vineyard is in a natural amphitheatre; the low-yielding sauvignon blanc, chardonnay and pinot noir are not irrigated. The minimal approach to winemaking produces wines of a consistent style with finesse and elegance. The unexpected death of Ian in March 2017, and the decision of former winemaker Timo Mayer to concentrate on his own label, left son Andrew Marks in charge of winemaking at Gembrook Hill (and his own label, The Wanderer). Exports to the UK, the US, Denmark, Japan and Malaysia.

♥♥♥♥♥ **Yarra Valley Sauvignon Blanc 2018** Always among the finest renditions in the country, eschewing the sweet/sour tropical projectile of flavours in the name of something ethereal but punchy, slaty and mineral-pungent. Herbal and palate-staining. Intensity! A brethren to the great expressions of the Loire, à la Sancerre. Nothing obviously fruity about this. Some nettle and greengage. Yet it is the drive, the palate whetting thirst for more, the texture; these factors are the mettle of this wine. **Rating** 95 **To** 2023 $33 NG ✪
Blanc de Blancs 2013 Six years on lees and 5g/l of dosage to placate a straight chardonnay from, arguably, the coolest site in the Yarra. It works a treat. Doughy. Brioche. Slaty to chalky mineral seams of thrumming intensity. And yet, just generous enough. Impeccably tuned. Cork. **Rating** 95 $57 NG
Yarra Valley Pinot Noir 2018 The first time I visited this site at the upper crest of the Yarra, hedging Gippsland, it was snowing. This is truly a cool-climate wine in the Australian context. Transparent. Vivid. Crunchy, driven by rails of juicy natural acidity. Sour cherry and strawberry scents. Elemental, perhaps. But vivacious, eminently drinkable and absolutely delicious. Among my favourite domestic expressions of this grape. Cork. **Rating** 94 **To** 2024 $55 NG

♥♥♥♥♡ **Yarra Valley Chardonnay 2018 Rating** 93 $45 NG

Gemtree Wines ★★★★★

167 Elliot Road, McLaren Flat, SA 5171 **Region** McLaren Vale
T (08) 8323 8199 **www**.gemtreewines.com **Open** 7 days 10–5
Winemaker Mike Brown, Joshua Waechter **Est.** 1998 **Dozens** 90 000 **Vyds** 123ha

Gemtree Wines is owned and operated by husband and wife team Melissa and Mike Brown. Mike (winemaker) and Melissa (viticulturist) firmly believe it is their responsibility to improve the land for future generations, and the vineyards are farmed organically and biodynamically. Exports to the US, Canada, Sweden, Denmark, Norway, Finland, Japan, China and NZ.

♥♥♥♥♥ **Obsidian McLaren Vale Shiraz 2018** From 20–80yo vines; whole-berry fermentation, no crushing, no whole bunches, every last vinification detail carefully considered and implemented precisely. It's remarkable how much power can be harnessed without a hint of strain. Elegance and harmony are 2 of the keys. Cork. 14.5% alc. **Rating** 97 **To** 2043 $90 ✪

♥♥♥♥♥ **Uncut McLaren Vale Shiraz 2018** The colour is deep, holding its hue to the rim. It's rich, full-bodied in the winery style, the palate a well of black fruit flavours, spices, dark chocolate and tannins; the latter the life support system. Screwcap. 14.5% alc. **Rating** 95 **To** 2043 $30 ✪
Ernest Allan McLaren Vale Shiraz 2018 From 20–60yo vines; destemmed, open-fermented, 7 days on skins, fermentation and 18 months' maturation completed in French oak (50% new). Supple, smooth, dark purple/black fruits; tannins and oak are simply there to observe. Cork. 14.5% alc. **Rating** 95 **To** 2038 $60

Small Batch McLaren Vale Grenache 2019 From a single vineyard planted '37; hand-picked, destemmed whole berries, 5% whole bunches, open-fermented, 7 days on skins, only free-run juice, matured for 6 months in used French barriques. Red berries, red flowers, red spices, all in a delicious floating web. Cork. 14% alc. **Rating** 95 **To** 2032 $50

Small Batch McLaren Vale Mataro 2019 From 30yo vines; hand-picked, destemmed, whole berries, open-fermented, 8 days on skins, only free-run juice, 3 months in old puncheons, 3 months in a concrete egg. A rare thing: a mataro that is full of juicy fruit and soft tannins. Cork. 14% alc. **Rating** 95 **To** 2034 $50

Luna Temprana McLaren Vale Tempranillo 2019 A fresh, juicy array of plush red cherry/berry fruit has unexpectedly positive, fine tannins bringing texture and structure into play with the varietal fruit. Bargain. Screwcap. 13% alc. **Rating** 94 **To** 2024 $25 **○**

ΨΨΨΨΨ **Bloodstone Shiraz 2019** Rating 93 To 2034 $20 **○**
Cinnabar Grenache Shiraz Mataro 2019 Rating 93 To 2027 $30
Moonstone Savagnin 2019 Rating 92 To 2022 $25 **○**
Cinnabar Grenache Shiraz Mataro 2018 Rating 92 To 2030 $30
Small Batch Cabernet Sauvignon 2019 Rating 92 To 2032 $50
The Phantom Red 2019 Rating 92 To 2030 $50
Bloodstone Shiraz 2018 Rating 91 To 2033 $20 **○**

Geoff Merrill Wines ★★★★★

291 Pimpala Road, Woodcroft, SA 5162 **Region** McLaren Vale
T (08) 8381 6877 **www**.geoffmerrillwines.com.au **Open** Mon–Fri 10–4.30, Sat 12–4.30
Winemaker Geoff Merrill, Scott Heidrich **Est.** 1980 **Dozens** 55 000 **Vyds** 45ha
If Geoff Merrill ever loses his impish sense of humour or his zest for life, high and not-so-high, we shall all be the poorer. The product range consists of three tiers: premium (varietal); Reserve, being the older wines, reflecting the desire for elegance and subtlety of this otherwise exuberant winemaker; and, at the top, Henley Shiraz. Exports to all major markets.

ΨΨΨΨΨ **Henley McLaren Vale Shiraz 2012** An exceptional, high quality, perfectly inserted cork guarantees a long life ahead – after all, it's already 8yo, having spent the first 3 years of its life in oak. A very good vintage, cork and oak all add up to a special version of Henley. 14.5% alc. **Rating** 97 **To** 2052 $185

ΨΨΨΨΨ **Parham Cabernet Sauvignon 2016** McLaren Vale 85%, Coonawarra 15%; 27 months in new American hogsheads. The fruit has done a pretty good job of absorbing that oak, blackcurrant and blackberry just shading mocha and cedar. At present it's a densely packed wine, yet to really spread its wings, but there's impressive depth of flavour, no doubt, with very high quality tannin as well. Patience required. Cork. 14.5% alc. **Rating** 95 **To** 2036 $95 SC

Bush Vine McLaren Vale Grenache Rose 2019 Geoff Merrill has been making bright pink rose just like this for 40 years; grenache the vehicle, with 6 hours on skins the start; a juicy but dry finish. Screwcap. 13.5% alc. **Rating** 94 **To** 2022 $24 **○**

Jacko's McLaren Vale Shiraz 2014 Matured in new and used American and French hogsheads for 29 months. The oak plays a major role in shaping the aromas and flavours of this old style, full-bodied shiraz. What is certain is its staying power. Screwcap. 14.5% alc. **Rating** 94 **To** 2034 $31

Reserve McLaren Vale Shiraz 2014 Matured for 30 months in new and used American and French hogsheads and puncheons. Retains excellent, bright-rimmed crimson-purple colour. The fate of the wine will be determined by one's like or dislike of oak. Otherwise, the mouthfeel is surprisingly elegant, the palate long. Screwcap. 14.5% alc. **Rating** 94 **To** 2039 $65

ΨΨΨΨΨ **Reserve Cabernet Sauvignon 2014** Rating 93 To 2029 $51 SC
Reserve Chardonnay 2018 Rating 90 To 2023 $39

Geoff Weaver

2 Gilpin Lane, Mitcham, SA 5062 (postal) **Region** Adelaide Hills
T (08) 8272 2105 **www**.geoffweaver.com.au **Open** Not
Winemaker Geoff Weaver **Est.** 1982 **Dozens** 3000 **Vyds** 12.3ha
This is the business of one-time Hardys chief winemaker Geoff Weaver. The Lenswood
vineyard was established between 1982 and '88, and invariably produces immaculate riesling
and sauvignon blanc and long-lived chardonnays. The beauty of the labels ranks supreme.
Exports to the UK, Hong Kong and Singapore.

Lenswood Riesling 2019 Fermented in old barriques, 7 months on lees, a small
amount of residual. Terrific intensity of both fruit flavour and acidity, softened
only slightly by time in oak and that glimpse of sweetness. It tastes of green apples
and lime, mineral and florals; the momentum carried through to a sustained finish.
Screwcap. 11.5% alc. **Rating** 96 **To** 2030 $25 CM ◐
Single Vineyard Adelaide Hills Chardonnay 2016 Deep gold. A wine that
is now all about complexity, which will continue to build, but at a slower pace
than hitherto. Different, and all the better for it. Screwcap. 13.5% alc. **Rating** 95
To 2026 $45
Single Vineyard Adelaide Hills Sauvignon Blanc 2018 Geoff Weaver's
sauvignon blancs have always had a flavour wheel and mouthfeel of their own.
A plaited rope of gooseberry, exotic tree fruits and white peaches and cream make
this a compelling wine. The Adelaide Hills and sauvignon have always given each
other a hug. Screwcap. 13.5% alc. **Rating** 94 **To** 2023 $25 ◐

George Wyndham

167 Fullarton Road, Dulwich, SA 5065 (postal) **Region** South Eastern Australia
T (08) 8131 2400 **www**.georgewyndham.com **Open** Not
Winemaker Steve Meyer **Est.** 1828 **Dozens** 450 000 **Vyds** 75ha
Named in honour of George Wyndham, who planted Australia's first commercial shiraz
vineyard in 1830 at Dalwood in the Hunter Valley. Originally Dalwood Wines until 1970,
then Wyndham Estate ('70–2015), the wines were renamed George Wyndham in '15. The
Bin range, led by Bin 555 Shiraz, often represents good value for money, as do the 'George'
wines (I am George, George the Fixer). At the top is Black Cluster (shiraz) from the Hunter
Valley. The wines are made and bottled in the Barossa Valley. Exports to Canada, Europe
and Asia.

I Am George Limestone Coast Chardonnay 2018 100% fermented in
French oak (20% in new hogsheads). Yes, the Limestone Coast can produce
elegant wine with clear-cut varietal character, here with a mix of white peach
and citrus. Screwcap. 13.4% alc. **Rating** 90 **To** 2023 $20 ◐

Georges Wines

32 Halifax Street, Adelaide, SA 5000 (postal) **Region** Clare Valley
T (08) 8366 2266 **www**.georgeswines.com **Open** Not
Winemaker O'Leary Walker **Est.** 2004 **Dozens** 5000 **Vyds** 36ha
This venture began with Nick George's acquisition of the Springwood Vineyard in the
Armagh Valley district of the Clare Valley. The 10ha vineyard was planted between 1996
and 2000, shiraz by some distance the most important of the varieties. Nick understood the
proud history of the vineyard, which for a number of years supplied Leasingham with all of its
grapes. He appointed O'Leary Walker as contract winemaker, an astute move. In '17 Georges
Wines acquired Olssen's 26ha vineyard at Auburn, lifting its vineyards to 36ha and allowing
an expansion in the production of new and existing wines.

Exile Watervale Riesling 2019 The flavours get up and running fast, but it
saves its biggest push for the finish. It's driven by dry lemon and lime flavours and
it shoots straight into quality territory. Screwcap. 12.5% alc. **Rating** 92 **To** 2027
$20 CM ◐

The Dam Break Clare Valley Shiraz 2017 Single vineyard shiraz, dry-grown. It puts on a hearty show. Blackcurrant, mint and assorted red berry flavours combine to pleasing effect, toasty oak and clove notes rounding it out. Essentially fresh but it's just starting to mellow; it will drink well any time over the next 5–10 years. Screwcap. 14.5% alc. **Rating** 92 **To** 2030 $35 CM

Ghost Rock Vineyard ★★★★★

1055 Port Sorrell Road, Northdown, Tas 7307 **Region** Northern Tasmania
T (03) 6428 4005 **www**.ghostrock.com.au **Open** 7 days 11–5
Winemaker Justin Arnold **Est.** 2001 **Dozens** 12000 **Vyds** 30ha
Cate and Colin Arnold purchased the former Patrick Creek Vineyard (planted exclusively to pinot noir in 1989) in 2001. The vineyards, situated among the patchwork fields of Sassafras to the south and the white sands of the Port Sorell Peninsula to the north, now total 30ha: pinot noir (14 clones) remains the bedrock of the plantings, with other varieties including chardonnay, pinot gris, riesling and sauvignon blanc. Ownership has passed to son Justin and his wife Alicia (who runs the cooking school and cellar door). Justin's experience in the Yarra Valley (Coldstream Hills), Margaret River (Devil's Lair) and Napa Valley (Etude) has paid dividends – the business is going from strength to strength, and the capacity of the relatively new 100t winery may need to be expanded. Exports to Japan.

🍷🍷🍷🍷🍷 **Riesling 2019** An exceptional riesling that is neither afraid of acidity – almost pixelated in its transparency – nor optimal physiological ripeness, promoting fruit and flavour. Lemon oil, quince, nashi pear and pink grapefruit, beamed long and mellifluous. Screwcap. **Rating** 95 **To** 2027 $32 NG ✪
Pinot Gris 2019 This is as good as gris gets. Defined by a sluice of nashi pear gelato welded to a gentle breeze of detailed phenolics, what's not to like? The lick of sugar works beautifully and yet the end result is palpably dry. Screwcap. **Rating** 95 **To** 2023 $30 NG ✪
Zoe Brut Rose 2016 Has 60% pinot, the rest chardonnay. This is delicious fizz, carved with an indelibly creamy froth that can only come from a traditional second fermentation in bottle and ample time on lees, conferring a toasty richness and considerable detail: pinot noir–centric strawberry cheesecake, vanilla and brioche. A sluice of oak imbuing textural intrigue while evincing structural authority. Cork. **Rating** 95 $38 NG

🍷🍷🍷🍷🍷 **P3 Rose 2019 Rating** 93 **To** 2020 $30 NG
Oulton XP Pinot Noir 2018 Rating 93 **To** 2023 $50 NG
Pinot Noir 2018 Rating 93 **To** 2025 $38 NG
Catherine Cuvee Exceptionelle 2015 Rating 93 $50 NG
Chardonnay 2018 Rating 91 **To** 2022 $34 NG
Bonadale 2CL Pinot Noir 2018 Rating 91 **To** 2023 $50 NG
Supernatural Pinot Noir 2018 Rating 90 **To** 2022 $29 NG

Giaconda ★★★★★

30 McClay Road, Beechworth, Vic 3747 **Region** Beechworth
T (03) 5727 0246 **www**.giaconda.com.au **Open** By appt
Winemaker Rick Kinzbrunner **Est.** 1982 **Dozens** 3000 **Vyds** 4.5ha
These wines have a super cult status and, given the small production, are extremely difficult to find; they are sold chiefly through restaurants and via their website. All have a cosmopolitan edge befitting Rick Kinzbrunner's international winemaking experience. The Chardonnay is one of Australia's greatest and is made and matured in the underground wine cellar hewn out of granite. This permits gravity flow and a year-round temperature range of 14–15°C, promising even more for the future. Exports to the UK, the UAE and China.

🍷🍷🍷🍷🍷 **Estate Vineyard Chardonnay 2016** Still basking in the sunlight of its vibrant freshness and, at the same time, its complexity. The Giaconda '16, '17 and '18 chardonnays are magnificent. It is frowned upon these days to mention Burgundy, but on the scale of weight and complexity, these are the Montrachets, the Grand

Crus of the Australian chardonnay landscape. The freshness and clarity of this wine keeps it right at the top. Screwcap. 13.5% alc. **Rating** 98 **To** 2036

Estate Vineyard Chardonnay 2017 The sheer power and depth of this wine is unique, no other Australian chardonnay can rival it. Its balance of stone fruit, grilled nuts and citrussy acidity is impeccable, transforming into the extreme length of the palate. Will live forever. Screwcap. 13.5% alc. **Rating** 98 **To** 2032 $115 ✪

Warner Vineyard Shiraz 2016 Excellent colour, still holding its primary crimson-purple hue. This is exceptionally intense and complex, deep robes of velvet wrapping the palate in an embrace that is sheer perfection. Tannins are part of the picture but are completely resolved. Screwcap. 14% alc. **Rating** 98 **To** 2046

Estate Vineyard Pinot Noir 2017 In the tradition of Giaconda Estate pinots, generosity is a subtext to red and black cherry fruit; the tannins underpin the length of a wine of great quality. The vintage was perfect for pinot, giving the certainty of at least 10 years development of spice and violets among other secondary characters. Screwcap. 14% alc. **Rating** 97 **To** 2032 $84 ✪

Estate Vineyard Shiraz 2016 Deeper in colour than the '17, the starting point of consistent aromas and flavours. Blackberry, licorice and pepper tumble merrily across the palate, framed by fine-grained tannins and oak that provide the structure to support the fruit extravaganza. Cork. 14% alc. **Rating** 97 **To** 2041

🍷🍷🍷🍷🍷 **Nantua Les Deux Chardonnay 2018** Rich, creamy/toasty chardonnay with layered complexity from start to finish. It is on the finish that the very high quality of the wine becomes obvious, for it is fresh and vibrant. The aftertaste brings another range of flavours drawing saliva from the mouth. Screwcap. 13.5% alc. **Rating** 96 **To** 2031

Nantua Les Deux Chardonnay 2017 Sits comfortably alongside its '18 sibling, reducing the expected gap, which is no criticism of either wine. There is elegance built into the heart of this wine. It flows along the palate with white peach leading the way followed by grapefruit and a wisp of cream. Screwcap. 13.5% alc. **Rating** 96 **To** 2032

Estate Vineyard Shiraz 2017 A super elegant shiraz. It is medium-bodied but has great length, and a very expressive bouquet with spice and cedary nuances to the black cherry fruit. Savoury complexity will slowly grow as the wine strolls through the next 20 or 30 years. Cork. 13.5% alc. **Rating** 96 **To** 2037 $84

Nantua Les Deux Nebbiolo 2015 This is a nebbiolo that doesn't need a lion/tannin tamer to allow the fruits freedom to express themselves. Bramble, forest and raspberry flavours sweep along the palate in fine style. Screwcap. 14% alc. **Rating** 95 **To** 2031

Nantua Les Deux Nebbiolo 2016 Very good colour for nebbiolo, no browning evident. You need to keep a tight grip on the tannins and focus on the glistening red fruits on the fore-palate. Time in bottle will be repaid. Screwcap. 14% alc. **Rating** 94 **To** 2029

Giant Steps   ★★★★★

314 Maroondah Highway, Healesville, Vic 3777 **Region** Yarra Valley
T (03) 5962 6111 **www**.giantstepswine.com.au **Open** 7 days 11–4
Winemaker Phil Sexton, Steve Flamsteed, Jess Clark **Est.** 1997 **Dozens** 30 000 **Vyds** 60ha
In May 2016 the sale by Giant Steps of the Innocent Bystander brand and stock was completed. The former Innocent Bystander restaurant and shop has been substantially remodelled to put the focus on the high quality, single vineyard, single varietal wines in what is demonstrably a very distinguished portfolio. Its vineyard resources comprise the Sexton Vineyard (32ha) in the Lower Yarra and Applejack Vineyard (13ha) in the Upper Yarra; there is also the Primavera Vineyard in the Upper Yarra under long-term supervised contract and Tarraford Vineyard in the Lower Yarra under long-term lease. Exports to the UK, the US and other major markets.

🍷🍷🍷🍷🍷 **Yarra Valley Chardonnay 2019** Hand-picked, chilled, whole-bunch pressed, wild fermentation on full solids, no stirring, no mlf, matured in French oak (10% new) for 8 months. The bouquet is slightly funky/reduced, but it's elegance and purity that are the essence of this wine, made by a master of the art. Screwcap. 13% alc. **Rating** 98 **To** 2032 $37 ✪

Nocton Vineyard Tasmania Pinot Noir 2018 Clones MV6 and D2V5 were wild-fermented separately in open fermenters with 100% whole bunches. The innate power is awesome, but it seduces thanks to a silky texture and vibrant red fruits. Screwcap. 14% alc. **Rating** 98 **To** 2030 $75 ✪

♟♟♟♟♟ **Clay Ferment Ocarina Yarra Valley Chardonnay 2019** A parcel of fruit from each of Giant Steps' single vineyard sites, whole-bunch pressed to 675l clay eggs for wild yeast–open fermentation, the lids sealed with clay for maturation. It's harder to do nothing they say. There's a beautiful pattern in the mouth, reflecting no pumping (just gravity), no fining, no filtration. Screwcap. 13% alc. **Rating** 96 **To** 2030 $60 ✪

Applejack Vineyard Yarra Valley Chardonnay 2018 Hand-picked, whole-bunch pressed, no additions, wild-fermented in French puncheons (20% new), matured for 8 months with stirring for the first month. A spotless bouquet and an elegant palate of great length. Stone fruits and melon are threaded through a faint gauze of acidity, oak barely seen. This is an exercise in balance and the certainty of future greatness. Screwcap. 13% alc. **Rating** 96 **To** 2028 $50 ✪

Wombat Creek Vineyard Yarra Valley Chardonnay 2018 At 420m, Wombat Creek is the highest vineyard site in the Yarra Valley, with a gentle northeast-facing slope of volcanic red soil. The vinification sees the wine bottled by gravity, not fined, and only coarse-filtered, as is the case with its siblings. Although the acidity is not adjusted (like its siblings), it feels softer and fruitier, pink grapefruit at work. Screwcap. 13.5% alc. **Rating** 96 **To** 2030 $50 ✪

Applejack Vineyard Yarra Valley Pinot Noir 2018 A great vineyard producing great wines. The perfumed, flowery (violets) bouquet and a highly focused palate bring whole-bunch tannins into play, with a gently savoury finish. Seductive. Screwcap. 13.5% alc. **Rating** 96 **To** 2029 $60 ✪

Wombat Creek Vineyard Yarra Valley Pinot Noir 2018 At the opposite end of the spectrum to its Sexton Vineyard sibling. Elegant, light-bodied and wonderfully fragrant; faintly savoury ex whole bunches but overall its strawberry, red cherry and pomegranate flavours carry the day on the very long palate. Screwcap. 13.5% alc. **Rating** 96 **To** 2030 $60 ✪

Harry's Monster 2018 A blend of cabernet, merlot and petit verdot from the single vineyard planted by Phil Sexton in '97. It is of a style seldom encountered in the Yarra Valley. Rich cassis fruit cut by finely ground tannins on a long palate. Quite something. Screwcap. 14% alc. **Rating** 96 **To** 2043 $55 ✪

Sexton Vineyard Yarra Valley Chardonnay 2018 Identical vinification to its siblings, the intention to place all the emphasis on the site. A wine with substance and depth, and a (non-residual sugar) touch of fruit sweetness. I am confident that the individual personality of each sibling will express itself more over the next 2 years. Screwcap. 13% alc. **Rating** 95 **To** 2028 $50

Tarraford Vineyard Yarra Valley Chardonnay 2018 Tarraford Vineyard is located in a small valley that provides protection and a cooler site climate than adjacent parts of the Yarra Valley floor, with consequently higher natural acidity (7.6g/l) than any of its siblings. The vinification remains identical, deliberately leaving the minerally shell intact. Screwcap. 13% alc. **Rating** 95 **To** 2028 $50

LDR Yarra Valley Pinot Noir Syrah 2019 Hand-picked, wild yeast, co-fermented in small open fermenters with 50% whole bunches, matured for 5 months in large French oak vats. A very cleverly made wine (in terms of pre-planning) that is yet another example of the intrinsic worth of this blend. Red and black cherry, spice and pepper all held in a fine net of tannins. Screwcap. 13.5% alc. **Rating** 95 **To** 2034 $37

Primavera Vineyard Yarra Valley Pinot Noir 2018 Deceptively light colour and body, but you have to wait until the wine opens its peacock's tail on the finish. As it does so, a wave of red fruits, violets, spices and forest notes flood the senses. Whole-bunch vinification is the key. Screwcap. 13.5% alc. **Rating** 95 **To** 2030 $60

Yarra Valley Syrah 2018 A particularly expressive shiraz with interleaving, luscious purple/dark red fruits with classy ripe tannins. Drink now or in 20 years, or any time in between. Screwcap. 14% alc. **Rating** 95 **To** 2040 $37

Tarraford Vineyard Yarra Valley Syrah 2018 Includes 50/50% Blocks 4 and 5, vinified separately. Block 4 was created from the original planting of Block 5 that included the Red Dog clone. The Block 5 ferment was 100% whole bunches, the bunches removed, destemmed and returned; Block 4 was 100% destemmed and given 7 days post-ferment maceration. It's a wine with intensity and extreme complexity, a long future ahead. Screwcap. 14% alc. **Rating** 95 **To** 2038 $50

Yarra Valley Rose 2019 Hand-picked pinot noir from the Sexton Vineyard, whole-bunch pressed with only free-run juice used, the pressings used in the LDR (light dry red). Ultra pale pink. The haunting bouquet suggests walking through a strawberry field, the mouthfeel dry yet long and juicy, the flavours spanning wild strawberries and pomegranate. Screwcap. 12.5% alc. **Rating** 94 **To** 2022 $25 ✪

Sexton Vineyard Yarra Valley Pinot Noir 2018 Full crimson-purple. A powerful wine with red and purple fruits, bramble and whole-bunch tannins all tumbling along the palate, but doing so in synergy with each other. Needs a few years in the cellar. Screwcap. 13.5% alc. **Rating** 94 **To** 2032 $60

Gibson ★★★★★

190 Willows Road, Light Pass, SA 5355 **Region** Barossa Valley
T (08) 8562 3193 **www**.gibsonwines.com.au **Open** 7 days 11–5
Winemaker Rob Gibson **Est.** 1996 **Dozens** 11 000 **Vyds** 12.4ha
Rob Gibson spent much of his working life as a senior viticulturist for Penfolds, involved in research tracing the characters that particular parcels of grapes give to a wine, which left him with a passion for identifying and protecting what is left of the original vineyard plantings in Australia. He has a vineyard (merlot) in the Barossa Valley at Light Pass, and one in the Eden Valley (shiraz and riesling) and also purchases grapes from McLaren Vale and the Adelaide Hills. Exports to Germany, Taiwan and China.

♛♛♛♛♛ **Australian Old Vine Collection Eden Valley Shiraz 2017** A complete wine with the composure of Eden Valley fruit from old vines. It comes at you with an amalgam of red and black fruits, florals, the right amount of spice and oak (no details supplied) and beautiful tannins. A glorious, heady drink. Cork. 14.5% alc. Rating 96 To 2040 $115 JF

♛♛♛♛♛ **The Dirtman Barossa Shiraz 2018** Rating 93 To 2033 $35 JF
The Smithy Barossa Shiraz Cabernet 2017 Rating 93 To 2028 $32 JF
Duke Barossa Grenache Shiraz 2018 Rating 93 To 2028 $32 JF

Gilbert Family Wines ★★★★★

137 Ulan Road, Mudgee, NSW 2850 **Region** Orange/Mudgee
T (02) 6373 1371 **www**.gilbertfamilywines.com.au **Open** Sun–Thurs 10–4, Fri–Sat 10–5
Winemaker Simon Gilbert, Will Gilbert **Est.** 2004 **Dozens** 15 000 **Vyds** 25.81ha
The Gilbert Family Wine Company was established in 2004 by fifth-generation winemaker Simon Gilbert; sixth-generation Will Gilbert took over the reins in '14. Will draws on extensive Old and New World winemaking experience to push boundaries with different techniques and ideas to make the Gilbert Family wines from Orange and Mudgee. Gilbert + Gilbert wines from the Eden Valley draw from the family history – Joseph Gilbert of Pewsey Vale was the first to plant grapes in the Eden Valley in 1847. Exports to the UK, the US, Canada, Norway, Denmark, Japan, Taiwan, Hong Kong and China.

♛♛♛♛♛ **Gilbert + Gilbert Single Vineyard Eden Valley Riesling 2017** It's still early days for this 3yo wine born of an idyllic vintage for Eden Valley riesling. Natural acidity and low pH provide the launching pad for the classic lime and lemon flavours. It's still building its fruit signature, notes of toasty maturity still far off. Screwcap. 12.4% alc. **Rating** 95 **To** 2029 $28 ✪

Gilbert Barrel Select Orange Pinot Noir 2018 Similar vinification to its 777 sibling except for sorting at harvest, 25% whole bunch, the wine drained off at 3.5° baume to finish fermentation in new French barrels, plus a 990l specialised roll barrel filled with destemmed fruit and rolled daily during wild fermentation, then pressed to a new French puncheon. It is a resounding success with intense, complex, savoury forest floor and bramble fruits. Screwcap. 13.3% alc. **Rating** 95 To 2029 $48

🍷🍷🍷🍷🍷 **Gilbert Mudgee Rose 2019** Rating 92 To 2021 $24
Gilbert 777 Orange Pinot Noir 2018 Rating 92 To 2026 $42
Gilbert Orange Shiraz 2018 Rating 92 To 2038 $36
Gilbert Orange Riesling 2018 Rating 91 To 2027 $26
Gilbert L.C.R. Orange Chardonnay 2017 Rating 91 To 2025 $42
Gilbert Orange Pinot Noir 2018 Rating 90 To 2025 $28

Gilberts   ★★★★★
30138 Albany Highway, Kendenup via Mount Barker, WA 6323 **Region** Mount Barker
T (08) 9851 4028 **www**.gilbertwines.com.au **Open** Fri–Mon 10–5
Winemaker West Cape Howe **Est.** 1985 **Dozens** 3000 **Vyds** 9ha
Once a part-time occupation for third generation sheep and beef farmers Jim and Beverly Gilbert, but now a full-time job and a very successful one. In 2014 the fourth generation, sons Clinton and Matthew, joined the management of the business. The mature vineyard (shiraz, chardonnay, riesling and cabernet sauvignon) coupled with contract winemaking at West Cape Howe, has long produced high class wines. Exports to Canada.

🍷🍷🍷🍷🍷 **Mount Barker Riesling 2019** The best part of this attractive riesling is the juicy, zesty 'snap' of crunchy acidity and lime cordial flavour combining on the tongue. It brightens the palate as the best rieslings do, and broadens out across the palate like a search party looking for taste buds to tingle. A wine that shows why Mount Barker is a premier riesling producer in this country. First rate drinking and cellaring potential. Screwcap. 12% alc. **Rating** 96 To 2032 $24 JP ⊘
Estate Hand Picked Mount Barker Chardonnay 2018 Pressed, whole cluster, barrel ferment, aged in French oak (30% new), 10–12 months on lees. Still working things out; the chardonnay notes are slowly revealing more of their personality. Wait a little while and this will be a blooming good drink. Undertones of melon, peach and pink grapefruit with a light nuttiness. Leesy, lanolin creaminess across the palate with fruit unfurling in the background. Screwcap. 13.5% alc. **Rating** 94 To 2030 $35 JP

🍷🍷🍷🍷🍷 **Dry Mount Barker Rose 2019** Rating 93 To 2025 $20 JP ⊘

Gioiello Estate   ★★★★☆
350 Molesworth-Dropmore Road, Molesworth, Vic 3718 **Region** Upper Goulburn
T 0437 240 502 **www**.gioiello.com.au **Open** Not
Winemaker Scott McCarthy (Contract) **Est.** 1987 **Dozens** 3000 **Vyds** 8.97ha
The Gioiello Estate vineyard was established by a Japanese company and originally known as Daiwa Nar Darak. Planted between 1987 and '96, it accounts for just under 9ha of a 400ha property of rolling hills, pastures, bushland, river flats, natural water springs and billabongs. Now owned by the Schiavello family, the vineyard continues to produce high quality wines.

🍷🍷🍷🍷🍷 **Upper Goulburn Merlot 2017** Hand-picked, destemmed and crushed into small open fermenters, matured for 18 months in French oak. No frills other than the benefit of the '17 vintage that invests the wine with very good length and a pleasing finish. Screwcap. 14% alc. **Rating** 95 To 2040 $27 ⊘
Old Hill Upper Goulburn Chardonnay 2018 Hand-picked, fermented in French barriques, matured on lees for 8 months. Good fruit expression and intensity; grapefruit and white peach lead the way, oak impact minimal. Screwcap. 12.6% alc. **Rating** 94 To 2027 $35

🍷🍷🍷🍷🍷 **Upper Goulburn Syrah 2017** Rating 92 To 2027 $27
Upper Goulburn Chardonnay 2019 Rating 91 To 2024 $20 ⊘

Gisborne Peak

69 Short Road, Gisborne South, Vic 3437 **Region** Macedon Ranges
T (03) 5428 2228 **www.gisbornepeakwines.com.au Open** 7 days 11–4
Winemaker Rob Ellis **Est.** 1978 **Dozens** 1800 **Vyds** 5.5ha
Bob Nixon began the development of Gisborne Peak way back in 1978, planting his dream vineyard row by row. The tasting room has wide shaded verandahs, plenty of windows and sweeping views. The vineyard is planted to pinot noir, chardonnay, semillon, riesling and lagrein.

🍷🍷🍷🍷🍷 **Macedon Ranges Riesling 2019** Hand-picked, whole-bunch pressed, cultured yeast. Starts demurely before progressively building intensity to the lime and green apple and its foundation of lemony acidity. As the '16 vintage will attest – Trophy (white varieties other than chardonnay) Macedon Ranges Wine Show '19 – will benefit greatly from 5+ years in bottle. Screwcap. **Rating** 94 **To** 2029 $39
Macedon Ranges Chardonnay 2018 Hand-picked, whole-bunch pressed, fermented in 3+yo French oak, matured for 12 months. Surprising depth and complexity; not easy to see where it's coming from. Screwcap. 13.1% alc.
Rating 94 **To** 2026 $38

🍷🍷🍷🍷🍷 **Semillon 2019 Rating** 92 **To** 2029 $29
Two Blocks Blend Pinot Noir 2017 Rating 92 **To** 2025 $39
Semillon 2016 Rating 91 **To** 2031 $29
Pinot Rose 2018 Rating 91 **To** 2021 $32
Riesling 2018 Rating 90 **To** 2025 $39
Two Blocks Blend Pinot Noir 2016 Rating 90 **To** 2026 $39

Glaetzer-Dixon Family Winemakers

93 Brooker Avenue, Hobart, Tas 7000 **Region** Southern Tasmania
T 0417 852 287 **www.gdfwinemakers.com Open** By appt
Winemaker Nick Glaetzer **Est.** 2008 **Dozens** 2500
History does not relate what Nick Glaetzer's high-profile Barossa Valley winemaker relatives thought of his decision to move to Tasmania in 2005, to make cutting-edge cool-climate styles. Obviously wife Sally approves. While his winemaking career began in the Barossa Valley, he reached into scattered parts of the New World and Old World alike, working successively in Languedoc, the Pfaltz, Margaret River, Riverland, Sunraysia, the Hunter Valley and Burgundy. Exports to the US, Canada, the Netherlands and Singapore.

🍷🍷🍷🍷🍷 **Mon Pere Shiraz 2017** Cool-grown, but not to the point of exaggeration. The 10th consecutive release of this wine grown in the Coal River district, and one of the best thanks to its balance and ripe plum/blackberry fruit. Savoury tannins complete the picture. Screwcap. 13.8% alc. **Rating** 95 **To** 2032 $65
Uberblanc Riesling 2018 Texture and structure are the key elements of this wine, part from acidity, part from fermentation with the inclusion of some solids. Citrus, apple and pear are all contributors to a wine that speaks of its Tasmanian origins. Screwcap. 12.5% alc. **Rating** 94 **To** 2030 $26 ✪

Glaetzer Wines ★★★★★

PO Box 824 Tanunda, SA 5352 **Region** Barossa Valley
T (08) 8563 0947 **www.glaetzer.com Open** Not
Winemaker Ben Glaetzer **Est.** 1996 **Dozens** 15 000 **Vyds** 20ha
With a family history in the Barossa Valley dating back to 1888, Glaetzer Wines was established by Colin Glaetzer after 30 years of winemaking experience. Son Ben worked in the Hunter Valley and as a Flying Winemaker in many of the world's wine regions before returning to Glaetzer Wines and assuming the winemaking role. The wines are made with great skill and abundant personality. Exports to all major markets.

🍷🍷🍷🍷🍷 **Anaperenna 2018** A blend of 82% shiraz (30–100yo vines), 18% cabernet sauvignon (80–130yo vines) yielding 2.5t/ha; open-fermented, hand-plunged, matured for 16 months in new hogsheads (92% French, 8% American). Full-bodied, plum blackberry, supple tannin, good oak. Easy to argue this is too cheap. Cork. 14.5% alc. **Rating** 96 **To** 2038 $52 ✪

Amon-Ra Barossa Valley Shiraz 2018 From vines 50–130yo in Ebenezer yielding 2t/ha; open-fermented, hand-plunged 3 times daily, matured for 16 months in new hogsheads (5% American). Full-bodied to the point where it's difficult to give any guidance for cellaring time. Similarly, what will be the quality of the wine as it steadily develops – the points somewhere in the middle of the range of possibilities. Cork. 15% alc. **Rating** 95 **To** 2030 $100

♥♥♥♥♀ **Bishop Barossa Valley Shiraz 2018 Rating** 93 **To** 2035 $33
Wallace Barossa Valley Shiraz Grenache 2018 Rating 93 **To** 2024 $23 ✪

Glen Eldon Wines   ★★★★★

143 Nitschke Road, Krondorf, SA 5352 **Region** Barossa Valley
T (08) 8568 2644 **www**.gleneldonwines.com.au **Open** By appt
Winemaker Richard Sheedy **Est.** 1997 **Dozens** 6000 **Vyds** 50ha
Owners Richard and Mary Sheedy (and their four children) have established the Glen Eldon property in the Eden Valley. The shiraz and cabernet sauvignon come from their vineyards in the Barossa Valley; viognier and merlot are contract-grown; the riesling is from the Eden Valley. Exports to the US, Canada and China.

♥♥♥♥♀ **Barossa Cabernet Sauvignon 2015** Matured in French oak and American hogsheads for 18–24 months. A full-bodied cabernet with ripe blackcurrant fruit and substantial tannins. Needs more time. The question is whether the tannins will outlive the fruit or vice versa. Screwcap. 14% alc. **Rating** 93 **To** 2025 $35

♥♥♥♥ **Old Vine Series Barossa Shiraz 2014 Rating** 89 **To** 2025 $300

Glenguin Estate   ★★★★★

Milbrodale Road, Broke, NSW 2330 **Region** Hunter Valley
T (02) 6579 1009 **www**.glenguinestate.com.au **Open** Thurs–Mon10–5
Winemaker Robin Tedder MW, Rhys Eather **Est.** 1993 **Dozens** 2000 **Vyds** 6ha
Glenguin Estate was established by the Tedder family, headed by Robin Tedder MW. It is close to Broke and adjacent to Wollombi Brook. The backbone of the production comes from almost 30-year-old plantings of Busby clone semillon and shiraz. Tannat (1ha) and a new planting of grafted semillon, with cuttings from Braemore/HVD complete the picture. Vineyard manager Andrew Tedder, who has considerable experience with organics and biodynamics, is overseeing the ongoing development of Glenguin's organic program.

♥♥♥♥♥ **Glenguin Vineyard Semillon 2019** A single plot of sandy loam over red basalt is responsible for this lightweight semillon, weighing in at a more traditional 11% alc. Fermented wild too. Unusual still in these parts. This is very good. Scintillating intensity of flavour with palpably natural acidity and a waft of phenolic pucker making all the difference to the wine's digestibility. Nothing too tangy. Nothing out of place. Lemon oil, grapefruit pulp and dried tatami. Lovely stuff. On the softer side, but all the better for it. Screwcap. **Rating** 95 **To** 2029 $27 NG ✪

Aristea Shiraz 2018 A site of gravelly clay; 25% whole bunch and a more ambitious sleight of hand across 16 months in French oak (50% new) confer authority. This is needed given the density and compelling vinosity of the wine. Texturally compelling. Red and black plum, a waft of Asian exotica, a gentle twist of the pepper grinder and welcome oak pillars for direction. This will age sumptuously. Screwcap. **Rating** 95 **To** 2040 $60 NG

Cellar Aged Schoolhouse Block Shiraz 2014 Things are a changin' in the Hunter, at least at this prescient estate: 40% whole bunch and 12 months in French oak puncheons (30% new) before a further 4 years of bottle age. This is good, while only reaching middle age rather than optimal maturity. Plenty of life

left. Boysenberry, five-spice, satsuma plum and a swathe of leather-clad tannins.
Screwcap. **Rating** 94 To 2033 $70 NG

ΤΤΤΤΩ **Schoolhouse Shiraz 2018 Rating** 93 To 2030 $45 NG
Stonybroke Shiraz 2018 Rating 92 To 2026 $30 NG
The Sticky Botrytised Semillon 2018 Rating 92 To 2025 NG

Glenlofty Wines

123 Glenlofty-Warrenmang Road, Glenlofty, Vic 3469 (postal) **Region** Pyrenees
T (03) 5354 8228 **www**.glenloftywines.com.au **Open** Not
Winemaker Andrew Koerner, Chris Smales **Est.** 1995 **Dozens** 15 000 **Vyds** 132ha
The vineyard was established by Southcorp after exhaustive soil and climate research to
supply grapes for Seppelt and Penfolds wines. In August 2010 Treasury Wine Estates sold
the vineyard to Canadian-based Roger Richmond-Smith and winemaking moved to Blue
Pyrenees Estate. Glenlofty Wines subsequently purchased the nearby 30ha Decameron
Station, bringing the total vineyard holdings to over 130ha. In April '19 Glenlofty Wines also
purchased Blue Pyrenees Estate, making it the largest producer in the Pyrenees. Exports to
Canada, Singapore, NZ and China.

ΤΤΤΤΤ **The Ridge Block Pyrenees Shiraz 2017** The Ridge Block is one of the top
blocks each year, this parcel standing out and vinified separately, matured in French
oak (60% new). Intense blackberry, spice, licorice and pepper join hands with the
tannins to balance the impact of the French oak. All good. Screwcap. 14% alc.
Rating 95 To 2037 $60
The Decameron Block Pyrenees Cabernet Sauvignon 2017 This block
is typically one of Glenlofty's best cabernet locations; it clearly was in '17. The
18 months in used French and American oak has helped provide texture without
aggression. Screwcap. 14% alc. **Rating** 94 To 2032 $60

ΤΤΤΤΩ **Estate Pyrenees Marsanne Roussanne 2017 Rating** 90 To 2023 $34

Glenwillow Wines

Bendigo Pottery, 146 Midland Highway, Epsom, Vic 3551 **Region** Bendigo
T 0428 461 076 **www**.glenwillow.com.au **Open** Fri–Sun & public hols 10.30–5
Winemaker Adam Marks **Est.** 1999 **Dozens** 500 **Vyds** 2.8ha
Peter and Cherryl Fyffe began their vineyard at Yandoit Creek, 10km south of Newstead, in
1999. They planted 1.8ha of shiraz and 0.3ha of cabernet sauvignon, later branching out with
0.6ha of nebbiolo and 0.1ha of barbera. Planted on a mixture of rich volcanic and clay loam
interspersed with quartz and buckshot gravel, the vineyard has an elevated north-facing aspect,
which minimises the risk of frost.

ΤΤΤΤΤ **Bendigo Cabernet Sauvignon 2016** Destemmed and crushed, plus
10% whole bunches, matured in French oak (20% new). An attractively juicy
cabernet, medium-bodied but long and bordering on succulent. The second glass
will quickly follow the first. Screwcap. 14% alc. **Rating** 94 To 2026 $30 ✪

ΤΤΤΤΩ **Bendigo Nebbiolo d'Yandoit 2016 Rating** 90 To 2026 $32

Golden Ball

1175 Beechworth-Wangaratta Road, Beechworth, Vic 3747 **Region** Beechworth
T 0406 018 280 **www**.goldenball.com.au **Open** By appt
Winemaker James McLaurin **Est.** 1996 **Dozens** 1100 **Vyds** 3.2ha
The Original Vineyard is on one of the original land grants in the Beechworth region, planted
by James McLaurin in 1996, mainly to chardonnay, shiraz (in 2013 grafted to chardonnay),
cabernet sauvignon, merlot and malbec; with lesser plantings of petit verdot, sagrantino and
savagnin. The Lineage Vineyard was planted in '08 to shiraz, followed by lesser plantings of
petit verdot, sagrantino and savagnin. No insecticides are used, only copper, sulphur, milk and

oil as foilage sprays. The wines are aged in 33% new French oak, the remainder 2–4 years old. The low yields result in intensely flavoured wines, which are found in Melbourne's best restaurants and a handful of local and Melbourne retailers. Exports to Singapore and China.

🍷🍷🍷🍷🍷 **Saxon Beechworth Shiraz 2016** Hand-picked, 48 hours' cold soak, wild-fermented, matured for 18 months in French oak (33% new). Stops short of being overripe and has a richness to the black fruit and licorice flavours. Diam. 14.6% alc. **Rating** 95 **To** 2030 $55

🍷🍷🍷🍷 **Gallice Cabernet Merlot Malbec 2016 Rating** 89 **To** 2027 $55

Golden Grove Estate ★★★★☆

Sundown Road, Ballandean, Qld 4382 **Region** Granite Belt
T (07) 4684 1291 **www.**goldengroveestate.com.au **Open** 7 days 9–4
Winemaker Raymond Costanzo **Est.** 1993 **Dozens** 4000 **Vyds** 12.4ha
Golden Grove Estate was established by Mario and Sebastian Costanzo in 1946, producing stone fruits and table grapes. The first wine grapes (shiraz) were planted in '72 but it was not until '85, when ownership passed to (CSU graduate) son Sam and his wife Grace, that the use of the property began to change. In '93 chardonnay and merlot joined the shiraz, followed by cabernet sauvignon, sauvignon blanc and semillon. The baton has been passed down another generation to CSU graduate Ray Costanzo, who has lifted the quality of the wines remarkably and has also planted tempranillo, durif, barbera, malbec, mourvedre, vermentino and nero d'Avola. Its consistent wine show success over recent years with alternative varieties is impressive.

🍷🍷🍷🍷🍷 **Granite Belt Rose Brose 2019** A blend of shiraz, sangiovese and grenache, augmented by notes of barrel ferment. The result is a wine bursting with red fruits at its heart; darker notes adding yet more flavour, texture and structure. Seriously good. Screwcap. 12.2% alc. **Rating** 94 **To** 2021 $20 ○

🍷🍷🍷🍷🍷 **Joven Granite Belt Tempranillo 2018 Rating** 92 **To** 2023 $30
Granite Belt Durif 2018 Rating 92 **To** 2038 $30
Granite Belt Vermentino 2019 Rating 91 **To** 2021 $30

Golding Wines ★★★★★

52 Western Branch Road, Lobethal, SA 5241 **Region** Adelaide Hills
T (08) 8189 4500 **www.**goldingwines.com.au **Open** 7 days 11–5
Winemaker Darren Golding, Natasha Mooney **Est.** 2002 **Dozens** 5000 **Vyds** 26.12ha
The Golding family story began in the Adelaide Hills three generations ago through market gardening and horticulture. Viticulture became part of the picture in 1995 when their Western Branch Road Vineyard was planted. Darren and Lucy Golding took the helm in 2002, launching the Golding Wines brand. Viticultural holdings have increased recently with the purchase of more vineyard and new plantings of gamay and dornfelder added to the existing pinot noir, shiraz, chardonnay, savagnin, pinot gris and sauvignon blanc. The cellar door within their rustic sandstone barn has recently been refurbished. Exports to the UK, the US, Canada, Hong Kong, the Philippines, Malaysia, Singapore and China.

🍷🍷🍷🍷🍷 **Ombre Gamay 2019** This is very good. Beaujolais-inspired notes of muddled cherry and damson plum with a lash of gently verdant tannins, pliant and expansive across the palate. These are the opus of this light to barely mid-weighted wine. They scratch the cheeks, pull out the saliva and prepare one for the next glass. And the next. Juicy, savoury and damn delicious! Hand-picked and wild-fermented, with a dash of whole bunch and a smidgen of oak. Screwcap. **Rating** 94 **To** 2023 $35 NG

🍷🍷🍷🍷🍷 **The Purveyor Adelaide Hills Pinot Noir 2019 Rating** 90 **To** 2025 $25 NG

Goldman Wines

11 Ercildoune Street, Cessnock, NSW 2325 (postal) **Region** Hunter Valley
T 0467 808 316 **www**.goldmanwines.com.au **Open** Not
Winemaker Various contract **Est.** 2014 **Dozens** 1500
Owner Callan Goldman grew up in the Hunter Valley, coming into contact with many of
the people involved in growing grapes or making wine (or both) in the region. But his real
job then and now is working as a civil engineer in northwest WA to fund his various wine
production plans. Jo Marsh of Billy Button Wines makes the majority of the impressive
portfolio at her new winery in the Ovens Valley.

Margaret River Chardonnay 2018 'We spent 10 years working in WA, so
it was inevitable Goldman Wines would have wine made in Margaret River.' It
was contract made at Flametree, wild-fermented in French barriques (60% new),
spending 8 months in barrel. This is by some distance the best of the Goldman
portfolio. Screwcap. 14% alc. **Rating** 93 **To** 2028 $35
Alpine Valleys Shiraz 2018 Made by Jo Marsh at Billy Button Wines. Bright
crimson-purple. It is medium-bodied with red and black cherry fruit supported by
a veneer of French oak and fine tannins. Attractive, well balanced and structured.
Screwcap. 14.5% alc. **Rating** 93 **To** 2033 $35
JohannesBurg Hunter Valley Semillon 2018 Radically different label designs
and complex family ownership don't help to clarify the family story. However, this
is a well made wine with good varietal expression. Screwcap. 12.1% alc. **Rating** 92
To 2025 $27
Alpine Valleys Chardonnay 2017 As for all the Alpine Valleys wines in the
portfolio, contract-made by Jo Marsh. This was wild-fermented in French oak
(30% new) and matured for 10 months. An attractive wine, every step taken in the
vinification just what was needed to frame the grapefruit and white peach flavours.
Screwcap. 13.5% alc. **Rating** 91 **To** 2027 $40
Alpine Valleys Shiraz 2017 Light to medium-bodied. Well made. The
30% new oak pushing the envelope to some degree but not tearing it. Sweet
black and red fruits join fine tannins, making the wine an each way bet. Screwcap.
14.5% alc. **Rating** 90 **To** 2025 $35

Alpine Valleys Chardonnay 2018 **Rating** 89 **To** 2022 $35

Gomersal Wines

203 Lyndoch Road, Gomersal, SA 5352 **Region** Barossa Valley
T (08) 8563 3611 **www**.gomersalwines.com.au **Open** Wed–Mon 10–5
Winemaker Barry White, Peter Pollard **Est.** 1887 **Dozens** 10 200 **Vyds** 20.2ha
The 1887 establishment date has a degree of poetic licence. In 1887 Friedrich W Fromm
planted the Wonganella Vineyards, following that with a winery on the edge of the Gomersal
Creek in '91; it remained in operation for 90 years, finally closing in 1983. In 2000 a group
of friends 'with strong credentials in both the making and consumption ends of the wine
industry' bought the winery and re-established the vineyard, planting 17ha of shiraz, 2.2ha
of mourvedre and 1ha of grenache. Exports to Switzerland, Iceland, South Korea, Singapore,
China and NZ.

Estate Grown Barossa Valley Shiraz 2016 I am trying to work out why
this costs so much given that the vines are young, the fruit machine-picked and
the elevage stock standard. The oak? 60% new French, for 22 months. The wine
is surprisingly vibrant with purple fruits, floral scents and finely wrought grape
tannins conflated with a phalanx of oak. Liquorice blackstrap and smoked meats
too. An impressive wine for the idiom. Screwcap. **Rating** 91 **To** 2028 $60 NG
Lyndoch Road Barossa Valley Shiraz Mataro 2017 This has but 8% of
mataro in the blend. This wine will please many, the bitter choc-mocha-bourbon
oak defining the fray of oozing black fruits, hints of violet and licorice. Round,
generous and powerful, if not oaky. Screwcap. **Rating** 90 **To** 2024 $25 NG

Gotham Wines

8 The Parade West, Kent Town, SA 5067 **Region** South Australia
T (08) 7324 3031 **www**.gothamwines.com.au **Open** Not
Winemaker Peter Pollard **Est.** 2004 **Dozens** 84000
In 2014 a group of wine enthusiasts, including former BRL Hardy CEO Stephen Millar, came together to purchase the Gotham Wines brands. The intention was (and is) to build on the existing domestic and export distribution of the wines, which include Wine Men of Gotham, Gotham, Stalking Horse and Step X Step brands from Langhorne Creek, Clare Valley, Barossa Valley and McLaren Vale. Exports to most major markets.

ΨΨΨΨΨ **Langhorne Creek Cabernet Sauvignon 2018** Decent flow of berried fruit flavour, an appropriate churn of tannin and satisfying length. You can drink this now or any time over the next handful of years and it will provide pleasure. Screwcap. 14% alc. **Rating** 90 **To** 2027 $20 CM ✪

ΨΨΨΨ **Langhorne Creek Shiraz 2018 Rating** 89 **To** 2026 $20 CM

Grace Farm

741 Cowaramup Bay Road, Gracetown, WA 6285 **Region** Margaret River
T (08) 9384 4995 **www**.gracefarm.com.au **Open** By appt
Winemaker Jonathan Mettam **Est.** 2006 **Dozens** 3000 **Vyds** 8.19ha
Situated in the Wilyabrup district, Grace Farm is the small, family-owned vineyard of Elizabeth and John Mair. It takes its name from the nearby coastal hamlet of Gracetown. Situated beside picturesque natural forest, the vineyard is planted to cabernet sauvignon, chardonnay, sauvignon blanc and semillon with smaller amounts of cabernet franc, petit verdot and malbec. Viticulturist Tim Quinlan conducts tastings (by appointment), explaining Grace Farm's sustainable viticultural practices.

ΨΨΨΨΨ **Reserve Margaret River Cabernet Sauvignon 2015** Closed and brooding, but with ample fruit, tannin, texture and length. Archetype of the cellaring red. Balance is one of its main virtues but so too is a weight of pure, ripe flavour. Time will be rewarded. Screwcap. 14% alc. **Rating** 95 **To** 2040 $60 CM

Grampians Estate ★★★★★

1477 Western Highway, Great Western, Vic 3377 **Region** Grampians
T (03) 5354 6245 **www**.grampiansestate.com.au **Open** 7 days 10–5
Winemaker Andrew Davey, Tom Guthrie **Est.** 1989 **Dozens** 2000 **Vyds** 8ha
Graziers Sarah and Tom Guthrie began their diversification into wine in 1989, but their core business continues to be fat lamb and wool production. They have acquired the Garden Gully winery at Great Western, giving them a cellar door and a vineyard with 140+-year-old shiraz and 100+-year-old riesling. Grampians Estate followed its success of being Champion Small Winery of Show at the Australian Small Winemakers Show for the second year running in '18 by winning the Premier's Trophy for Champion Wine of Victoria in '19. These successes have led to a major expansion of the cellar door. Exports to China.

ΨΨΨΨΨ **Streeton Reserve Shiraz 2017** By far the most elegant wine in the stable. This is a taut mainline of pepper grind acidity towing scents of iodine, blueberry and mace long and far down the throat. The oak is impeccably nestled into the fold. Again, indelibly marked with the potpourri of spice and eucalyptus of the Grampians. Screwcap. 14% alc. **Rating** 96 **To** 2037 $75 NG ✪

St Ethel's Shiraz 2016 A single vineyard, the vines dating back to the 1880. This delivers in terms of a sudden leap from the lower tier wines into a scope of not just power, but riper and well toned tannins. These service the avalanche of fruit cascading from fore to aft. An impressively vinous wine of compelling length, showcasing the Grampians tapestry of scents and flavours: anise, mint, bitter chocolate and unctuous dark fruit. 14.5% alc. **Rating** 95 **To** 2036 $50 NG

Rutherford Sparkling Shiraz 2017 Sparkling shiraz is one of the very few truly unique Australian contributions to the wine world. It sits well at the table, be it with richer, spicy meat dishes or blue cheese. This is a very good example: mottled dark fruits spurt across the mouth, all underlain by a carriage of Grampians peppercorn acidity and a sumptuous creamy texture following its second fermentation in bottle. Long and joyous. Cork. **Rating** 95 $35 NG ✪

🍷🍷🍷🍷♀ **St Ethel's 1878 Vines Shiraz 2017 Rating** 93 To 2035 $150 NG
Arawatta Shiraz 2018 Rating 92 To 2030 $30 NG
Rhymney Shiraz 2018 Rating 90 To 2030 $30 NG

Grandeur Wellington ★★★★

201 Blewitt Springs Road, McLaren Flat, SA 5171 **Region** McLaren Vale
T 0414 188 588 **www**.grandeurwellington.com.au **Open** By appt
Winemaker Tony De Lisio, Anthony De Lisio **Est. Dozens** 12 000
After sifting through the scant evidence on the website, the name of the owner 'Fountain of Fortune Five Pty Ltd', its quaint language and the amount of oak used in fashioning the wines, this has all the appearance of a business created for the China market and is quite possibly Chinese-owned. Whether or not that is the case, the quality of the wines from the '17 vintage is consistently good. Exports to Hong Kong and China.

🍷🍷🍷🍷🍷 **Gen62 McLaren Vale Cabernet Sauvignon 2017** Open-fermented, hand-plunged, 9–14 days on skins, matured for 18 months in 80% French and 20% American barriques (50% new). This is a serious wine, the fruit able to do battle with the oak. Cork. 14.7% alc. **Rating** 94 To 2037 $35

🍷🍷🍷🍷♀ **Cellar Reserve Shiraz 2017 Rating** 90 To 2030 $90
Gen69 Shiraz 2017 Rating 90 To 2037 $35
Cellar Reserve Cabernet Sauvignon 2017 Rating 90 To 2027 $90

Granite Hills ★★★★★

1481 Burke and Wills Track, Baynton, Vic 3444 **Region** Macedon Ranges
T (03) 5423 7273 **www**.granitehills.com.au **Open** 7 days 11–5
Winemaker Llew Knight, Christian James **Est.** 1970 **Dozens** 5000 **Vyds** 11.5ha
Granite Hills is one of the enduring classics, having pioneered the successful growing of riesling and shiraz in an uncompromisingly cool climate. The vineyard includes riesling, chardonnay, shiraz, cabernet sauvignon, cabernet franc, merlot and pinot noir (the last also used in its sparkling wine). The Rieslings age superbly, and the Shiraz was the forerunner of the cool-climate school in Australia. Exports to Japan and China.

🍷🍷🍷🍷🍷 **Knight Macedon Ranges Riesling 2018** This wine is often closed and shy when first released, taking several years to get into its stride. There are always exceptions and this is one. There is a richness to the fruit flavours, all in the citrus spectrum, also with unexpected complexity. Screwcap. 13% alc. **Rating** 95 To 2033 $25 ✪
Knight Macedon Ranges Gruner Veltliner 2018 The spicy, peppery varietal character of gruner veltliner is in full stride from the word go, reinforcing its presence each time it is retasted. The very cool Macedon climate works synergistically with the varietal fruit through to the long finish and aftertaste. Gruner veltliner is a kissing cousin of riesling as it expands with time in bottle. Screwcap. 13% alc. **Rating** 95 To 2025 $25 ✪
Knight Macedon Ranges 1971 Block Riesling 2018 From the original riesling vines planted in '71. Delicate lemony scents lead to a textural, well weighted riesling with an above-average sense of presence. Its quality is built on mouthfeel, weight of fruit and flow. Screwcap. 13% alc. **Rating** 94 To 2029 $30 CM ✪
The Gordon 2013 Includes 56% cabernet sauvignon, 26% cabernet franc and 18% merlot. Brings back memories of Tom Lazar in his prime. This is juicy,

vibrantly fresh; the fruits primarily ranging through the red spectrum (cherry/berry) but also offering notes of spice. Excellent balance and length. Screwcap. 14.5% alc. **Rating** 94 **To** 2028 $30 ✪

ŸŸŸŸŸ Knight Macedon Ranges Chardonnay 2016 **Rating** 92 **To** 2025 $30 CM
Knight Macedon Ranges Gamay Noir 2018 **Rating** 92 **To** 2025 $30 CM
Knight Macedon Ranges Chardonnay 2015 **Rating** 91 **To** 2030 $30
Knight Macedon Ranges Gamay Noir 2017 **Rating** 91 **To** 2023 $30
Knight Macedon Ranges Pinot Noir 2015 **Rating** 91 **To** 2027 $30 CM
Knight Macedon Ranges Pinot Blanc 2018 **Rating** 90 **To** 2024 $25
Knight Macedon Ranges Shiraz 2014 **Rating** 90 **To** 2026 $30 CM

Grant Burge   ★★★★★

279 Krondorf Road, Barossa Valley, SA 5352 **Region** Barossa Valley
T (08) 8563 7675 **www**.grantburgewines.com.au **Open** 7 days 10–5
Winemaker Craig Stansborough **Est.** 1988 **Dozens** 400 000
Grant and Helen Burge established the eponymous Grant Burge business in 1988. It grew into one of the largest family-owned wine businesses in the valley. In February 2015, Accolade Wines announced it had acquired the Grant Burge brand and the historic Krondorf Winery. The 356ha of vineyards remain in family ownership and will continue to supply premium grapes to the Accolade-owned business. Exports to all major markets.

ŸŸŸŸŸ **40 Year Old Super Rare Fortified Tawny NV** The colour is deep. Grenache (35%), shiraz and mourvedre (31% each) are to all intents and purposes the blend, now so wound up in the coils of its flavours like a large python it's hard to identify any single flavour source. Christmas pudding, burnt toffee, Oriental spices and fruit are just the start of the flavour catalogue. The rancio isn't particularly strong. The colour is yet to go brown and there's no olive on the rim. But – and it's a big but – it finishes fresh. Vino-Lok. 19.5% alc. **Rating** 98 $450

ŸŸŸŸŸ **Corryton Park Barossa Cabernet Sauvignon 2017** Machine-harvested, crushed and destemmed, open-fermented, 6–8 days on skins, wild and cultured yeast, matured in French hogsheads (65% new) for 18 months, 5% merlot blended in. All handed on a plate ex the vintage, the vineyard and the courage to use this amount of new French oak, and no attempt to over-extract. Screwcap. 14% alc. **Rating** 96 **To** 2032 $44 ✪

The Vigneron Centenarian Barossa Semillon 2016 From the Zerk family's 102yo block of semillon. Treated with the respect it deserved: picked early to maintain acidity and avoid higher baume/alcohol, whole-bunch pressed, cool-fermented with cultured yeast. Meyer lemon and green apple flavours are the drivers of the pure and youthful palate. Screwcap. 11.5% alc. **Rating** 95 **To** 2045 $30 ✪

Meshach 2016 From 60+yo vines with around 18 months in a combination of new and older French and American oak. A wine with undoubted richness and power, but there's a controlled, almost taut feel about it as well. There's plenty of ripe fruit and oak, but there's also a minerally quality running through it with firm, but not overwhelming tannin keeping a tight rein. Screwcap. 14.4% alc. **Rating** 95 **To** 2036 $200 SC

The Holy Trinity 2017 A 47.9/36.5/15.6% GSM blend; separately vinified, crushed and destemmed, open-fermented, 6–8 days on skins, matured for 16 months in used French puncheons and hogsheads. Holy trinity or holy vintage? I'll take both, for they have both made the wine so enjoyable – a tumble of red and purple fruits in a skein of silk. Screwcap. 14% alc. **Rating** 95 **To** 2032 $44

Cameron Vale Barossa Cabernet Sauvignon 2017 With 94.2% cabernet sauvignon, the balance petit verdot, merlot and shiraz. Destemmed whole berry, open ferments, matured in a mix of oaks and ages, the most significant 15% new French hogsheads for 15 months. Yet another wine that shines thanks to the vintage. Elegant, medium-bodied, blackberry/cassis, fine tannins and good oak management. Screwcap. 14.5% alc. **Rating** 95 **To** 2037 $27 ✪

Shadrach 2016 Has 91.6% cabernet sauvignon, the balance merlot and petit verdot. Matured for 15 months in a mix of new and older French hogsheads. A dense sort of bouquet at this stage, comprised of black fruits with a cedary oak presence and some earthy/gamey characters. Deep, dark flavours saturate the palate and linger on the finish but are yet to fully reveal themselves. Screwcap. 14.3% alc. Rating 95 To 2036 $105 SC

The Vigneron Co-Ferment Barossa Cabernet Sauvignon Petit Verdot Merlot 2015 A 42/40/18% blend; matured in French oak (40% new) for 26 months. A difficult feat, but has worked well. Blackcurrant, bay leaf and black olive are fused by the time in barrel. Screwcap. 14.5% alc. Rating 95 To 2040 $50

Reserve Eden Valley Riesling 2015 Details are a bit sketchy but this wine is a trophy and multiple gold medal winner at capital city wine shows. The 11.9% alcohol is a good figure for Eden Valley riesling. No pronounced colour development, and while it's showing some aged honey and hay characters on the bouquet and palate, it still has verve and freshness. Just a whisker short of gold for me. Screwcap. Rating 94 To 2027 $30 SC ❂

Balthasar Eden Valley Shiraz 2017 Matured in French oak for 18 months with a barrel selection for the final blend. Spicy red fruit with a hint of chocolate and an earthy/leathery character on the bouquet, moving into a palate generous in flavour but with a restrained and quite softly textured feel. An interesting wine. Eden Valley elegance presented in an open and approachable style. Ready now. Screwcap. 14.5% alc. Rating 94 To 2025 $44 SC

🍷🍷🍷🍷🍷 **The Vigneron Centenarian Barossa Semillon 2015** Rating 93 To 2025 $30 SC

East Argyle Vigneron Collection Adelaide Hills Pinot Gris 2019 Rating 93 To 2022 $27 SC ❂

The Vigneron The Natural Barossa Valley Shiraz 2015 Rating 93 To 2035 $50

Abednego 2017 Rating 93 To 2027 $90 SC

Nebu Barossa Cabernet Shiraz 2017 Rating 92 To 2030 $90

Thorn Eden Valley Riesling 2019 Rating 91 To 2029 $27 SC

Grape Farm Winery   ★★★☆

107 McAdams Lane, Moonambel, Vid 3478 **Region** Pyrenees
T (03) 5467 2145 **www**.grapefarmwinery.com.au **Open** Fri–Sun 11–5
Winemaker Heath Stevenson **Est.** 1976 **Dozens** 1000 **Vyds** 3.6ha
Grape Farm Winery was established back in 1976 when the vineyard was acquired by chef Heath and mental health professional Karina Stevenson. They have learnt on the job, carrying all of the vineyard work, Heath the self-taught winemaker. The wines are estate-grown; the low-yielding vineyard managed organically.

# Graphite Road   ★★★★

1163 Graphite Road, Manjimup, WA 6258 **Region** Manjimup
T 0408 914 836 **www**.graphiteroad.com.au **Open** By appt
Winemaker Kim Horton **Est.** 2017 **Dozens** 4250 **Vyds** 9ha
The business was founded by Bente and Vic Peos, with their three daughters being the fourth generation of the family involved in the wine industry. From a young age they worked in the vineyard with their parents and share a combined love for wine and food. Graphite Road is the name of the thoroughfare in South Western Australia leading to the township of Manjimup. The road winds through state forests filled with towering Karri trees, crossing the Gairdner River and passing the historic 'One Tree Bridge' on the journey through the scenic natural landscape. Exports to China.

🍷🍷🍷🍷🍷 **Walker & Wilde Manjimup Shiraz 2017** It's medium-bodied; full of rich, dark cherry/berry fruits with a velvety mouthfeel, dark chocolate also in play. Soft tannins, integrated oak. Screwcap. 14% alc. Rating 94 To 2027 $32

ŶŶŶŶŶ Walker & Wilde Chardonnay 2019 Rating 92 To 2029 $32
Walker & Wilde Cabernet Sauvignon 2017 Rating 92 To 2032 $32

Green Door Wines   ★★★★

1112 Henty Road, Henty, WA 6236 **Region** Geographe
T 0439 511 652 **www**.greendoorwines.com.au **Open** Thurs–Sun 11–4.30
Winemaker Ashley Keeffe, Vanessa Carson **Est.** 2007 **Dozens** 1200 **Vyds** 4ha
Ashley and Kathryn Keeffe purchased what was then a rundown vineyard in '06. With
a combination of new and pre-existing vines, the vineyard includes fiano, mourvedre,
grenache, verdelho, tempranillo and shiraz. The wines are made in a small onsite winery using
a range of winemaking methods, including the use of amphora pots.

ŶŶŶŶŶ El Toro Geographe Tempranillo 2018 This bursts onto the palate with
vibrant, tangy, juicy red-berried fruit. In the mix: dabs of red licorice, charcuterie
and woodsy spices. The acidity keeps everything humming along and the fine-
sandpaper tannins in check. Screwcap. 14% alc. **Rating** 95 To 2026 $25 JF

ŶŶŶŶŶ Amphora Geographe Monastrell 2018 Rating 93 To 2024 $35 JF

Greenock Estate   ★★★★

12A Basedow Road, Tanunda, SA 5352 **Region** Barossa Valley
T (08) 8563 2898 **www**.greenockestate.com **Open** Fri–Tues
Winemaker Jo Irvine **Est.** 1948 **Dozens** NFP
The establishment date is that of the Kurtz Family vineyards, which supply Greenock Estate
with its grapes. The first Greenock Estate wine was made in 2002 and the first wines reached
Asia in '09. Exports to Hong Kong, Macau and China.

ŶŶŶŶŶ Premium Selection Barossa Shiraz Cabernet 2016 A big, cuddly, generous
wine with nuance is hard to find, but here it is. The classic Aussie blend is done
proud. Abundant blackberry, cinnamon, nutmeg, Aussie bush and licorice. Sweet
spice is queen. As a colleague would say, there's a lot of everything but not too
much of anything. Fine-edged coffee, mocha oak and smooth tannins bring both
richness and definition. Cork. 14.5% alc. **Rating** 94 To 2031 JP

ŶŶŶŶŶ Angas King A3 Barossa Valley Shiraz 2016 Rating 91 To 2042 $45 JP
Angas King Old Barossa Reserve Shiraz 2016 Rating 91 To 2045 JP
Angas King A7 McLaren Vale Shiraz 2016 Rating 90 To 2040 $45 JP

Greenstone Vineyards   ★★★★★

179 Glenview Road, Yarra Glen, Vic 3775 **Region** Yarra Valley/Heathcote
T (03) 9730 1022 **www**.greenstonevineyards.com.au **Open** Thurs–Mon 10–5
Winemaker Han Tao Lau, Sam Atherton, David Li **Est.** 2003 **Dozens** 20 000
Vyds 39.2ha
In January 2015 the former Sticks Winery (originally Yarra Ridge, established in 1982)
was purchased by a group of investors, along with the Greenstone brand and vineyard in
Heathcote. The Greenstone vineyard, just north of the Heathcote township at Colbinabbin
at the base of the Camel Range, derives its names from the soils on which the 20ha of vines
are planted (the lion's share to 17ha of shiraz). The Yarra Valley vineyard is planted mainly to
chardonnay (11.7ha) and also includes 4.1ha of pinot noir and smaller plantings of sauvignon
blanc, viognier, cabernet sauvignon and petit verdot. Exports to China.

ŶŶŶŶŶ Estate Series Yarra Valley Chardonnay 2018 From the oldest block of
clone P58, fermentation in French hogsheads (35% new), matured on lees for
10 months. Bright, youthful hue. Elegant from start to finish, the fruit driving the
show without even pausing for breath. Will become more ballsy with a few more
years in bottle. Screwcap. 12.6% alc. **Rating** 95 To 2033 $30
Estate Series Heathcote Shiraz 2017 The estate vineyard has 7 clones,
all included in this wine, which was matured in French oak (29% new) for

20 months. The mouthfeel, balance and length are all first class, as are the tannins, which entice a second sip. All up, quite a lovely medium-bodied wine. Screwcap. 14.7% alc. Rating 95 To 2037 $30 ☉
MMM Mataro 2018 Crushed, wild-fermented, 3 weeks on skins, matured for 16 months in used French oak. Relatively light colour. This doesn't have an axe of tannins suspended above your neck, rather a fruit core wrapped with a filmy satin swathe à la Wendouree. Screwcap. 13.9% alc. **Rating 94 To 2028 $30** ☉

♍♍♍♍♀ **Estate Series Heathcote Sangiovese 2016** Rating 93 To 2029 $30
Estate Series Yarra Valley Pinot Noir 2018 Rating 92 To 2028 $32
Estate Series Yarra Valley Sauvignon Blanc 2018 Rating 90 To 2025 $30

GREENWAY Wines   ★★★★☆

350 Wollombi Road, Broke, NSW 2330 **Region** Hunter Valley
T 0418 164 382 **www.**greenwaywines.com.au **Open** W'ends 10–4.30 (closed Jan)
Winemaker Michael McManus, Daniel Binet **Est.** 2009 **Dozens** 450 **Vyds** 6.5ha
GREENWAY Wines is a small family-owned and operated business. The sustainably managed vineyard is nestled against Wollombi Brook near Broke. The single vineyard estate wines, only produced in the best vintages, are available from the cellar door and online.

♍♍♍♍♍ **The Architect Hunter Valley Shiraz 2018** Balance is key. Sweet cherry-plum flavours combine with earth and oak-spice characters to put on a silken, beautifully integrated show. Not a single foot has been put wrong. Fine-grained tannin and sustained length seals the quality experience. Screwcap. 13.5% alc. Rating 95 To 2035 $40 CM

♍♍♍♍♀ **Favoloso Fiano 2019** Rating 92 To 2022 $26 CM
Hunter Valley Pinot Grigio 2018 Rating 91 To 2020 $26 CM

Griffin Wines   ★★★★

231 Brockhurst Road, Kuitpo, SA 5172 **Region** Adelaide Hills
T 0408 815 623 **www.**griffinwinesdirect.com **Open** By appt
Winemaker Darryl Catlin **Est.** 1997 **Dozens** 300 **Vyds** 26ha
The Griffin family planted pinot noir, merlot, chardonnay, sauvignon blanc and shiraz in 1997, having owned the property for over 30 years; the vines are cane-pruned and the grapes hand-picked. Situated 3km from Kuitpo Hall, its 350m elevation gives sweeping views over the valley below.

♍♍♍♍♀ **Adelaide Hills Shiraz 2018** Fuller than the '17 version but with a similar profile; redcurrant and cherry, anise and flowery herb notes. It draws you in and keeps you there. Screwcap. 14.5% alc. Rating 93 To 2028 $28 CM
Adelaide Hills Shiraz 2017 200 dozen made. Perfumed and peppery with sweet raspberry, cherry, anise and floral elements putting on an attractive show. It's neat and contained, and medium-weight at most, but there's a lot to like about this wine. Screwcap. 14.5% alc. Rating 93 To 2027 $28 CM

Groom   ★★★★☆

28 Langmeil Road, Tanunda, SA 5352 (postal) **Region** Barossa Valley
T (08) 8563 1101 **www.**groomwines.com **Open** Not
Winemaker Daryl Groom **Est.** 1997 **Dozens** 1500 **Vyds** 27.8ha
The full name of the business is Marschall Groom Cellars, a venture owned by David and Jeanette Marschall and their six children, and Daryl and Lisa Groom and their four children. Daryl was a highly regarded winemaker at Penfolds before he moved to Geyser Peak in California. Years of discussion between the families resulted in the purchase of a 35ha block of bare land adjacent to Penfolds' 130-year-old Kalimna Vineyard. Shiraz was planted in 1997, giving its first vintage in '99. The next acquisition was an 8ha vineyard at Lenswood in the Adelaide Hills, planted to sauvignon blanc. In 2000, 3.2ha of zinfandel was planted on the Kalimna Bush Block. Exports to the US and China.

▼▼▼▼▼ **Barossa Valley Shiraz 2018** From 20yo vines; crushed and destemmed, cultured yeast, 6–9 days on skins, 18 months in 55% American and 45% French oak (30% new). A textured, medium-bodied shiraz; oak surprisingly assertive, but Daryl Groom's long experience will reassure confidence that fruit, tannin and oak will coalesce and flow in a single stream. Cork. 14.5% alc. **Rating** 95 **To** 2038 $50
Bush Block Barossa Valley Zinfandel 2018 Estate-grown bushvine zinfandel with a little shiraz; matured for 12 months in French and American oak (25% new). It is full to the brim with spicy red fruits, the tannins soft, the oak balanced. A loaves and fishes exercise with only 200 dozen made. Cork. 14.5% alc. **Rating** 94 **To** 2028 $30 ✪

▼▼▼▼▽ **Adelaide Hills Sauvignon Blanc 2019 Rating** 90 **To** 2021 $24

Grosset   ★★★★★

King Street, Auburn, SA 5451 **Region** Clare Valley
T 1800 088 223 **www**.grosset.com.au **Open** 10–5 Wed–Sun (Spring)
Winemaker Jeffrey Grosset, Brent Treloar **Est.** 1981 **Dozens** 11 000 **Vyds** 21ha
Jeffrey Grosset wears the unchallenged mantle of Australia's foremost riesling maker. Grosset's pre-eminence is recognised both domestically and internationally; however, he merits equal recognition for the other wines in his portfolio: Semillon Sauvignon Blanc from Clare Valley/ Adelaide Hills, Chardonnay and Pinot Noir from the Adelaide Hills and Gaia, a Bordeaux blend from the Clare Valley. These are all benchmarks. His quietly spoken manner conceals a steely will. Trial plantings (2ha) of fiano, aglianico, nero d'Avola and petit verdot suggest some new wines may be gestating. Exports to all major markets. Best value winery in the *Wine Companion 2018*. Exports to all major markets.

▼▼▼▼▼ **Polish Hill Clare Valley Riesling 2019** The sails of the ship are still tightly furled but the length and balance will stand the wine well as it ages (for decades), elaborating on the flavours of the Polish Hill River district as it always does. Screwcap. 12.5% alc. **Rating** 96 **To** 2035 $63 ✪
Gaia 2017 Gaia demands attention and respect in equal measure. Do take time to admire its balance of savouriness to fruit, it's calmness and class. Expect pomegranate and boysenberries with dabs of licorice, rolled tobacco and cedary oak with a touch of green walnut. Medium-bodied and the plush yet textured tannins render the wine ready for immediate drinking but will reward those who wait. Screwcap. 13.7% alc. **Rating** 96 **To** 2030 $89 JF
Springvale Clare Valley Riesling 2019 Slightly deeper colour than the Polish Hill, although why it should be thus I don't know. The bouquet and palate march in tune, bringing Meyer lemon, lime and green apple into play from the outset. It's dangerously easy to drink. Screwcap. 12.8% alc. **Rating** 95 **To** 2034 $45
Apiana Clare Valley Fiano 2019 Full of poached quinces and pears drizzled with honey, cream and a sprinkling of ginger powder. Lots of texture and phenolics at play with almost a beeswax feel across the palate. Fresh acidity to keep everything buoyant. Screwcap. 12.5% alc. **Rating** 95 **To** 2026 $45 JF
Piccadilly Valley Pinot Noir 2018 Ah, the perfume. Heady with florals, wild strawberries, morello cherries and aromas of humus/forest floor, it is possible to spend more time inhaling than tasting. The palate doesn't disappoint even if the bouquet is far more appealing. More time needed for the pronounced acidity and raspy tannins to settle around the core of tangy-juicy fruit. Screwcap. 14% alc. **Rating** 95 **To** 2030 $78 JF

▼▼▼▼▽ **Piccadilly Chardonnay 2018 Rating** 93 **To** 2030 $66 JF
Nereus 2017 Rating 92 **To** 2027 $50 JF

Grove Estate Wines   ★★★★☆

4100 Murringo Road, Young, NSW 2594 **Region** Hilltops
T (02) 6382 6999 **www**.groveestate.com.au **Open** 7 days 9.30–4.30
Winemaker Brian Mullany, Tim Kirk, Bryan Martin **Est.** 1989 **Dozens** 4000 **Vyds** 100ha

Grove Estate Vineyard was re-established in 1989 by Brian and Suellen Mullany on the site where grapes were first planted in Lambing Flat (Young) in 1861 by Croation settlers who brought vine cuttings with them from Dalmatia. One of the original pickers' huts has been refurbished as the cellar door. Further plantings in '98 were made on their Bit O' Heaven Vineyard, the two sites with vastly different soils. The wines are made at Clonakilla by Tim Kirk and Bryan Martin. Exports to China.

🍷🍷🍷🍷🍷 **Sommita Hilltops Nebbiolo 2018** Fantastic release. All wild ferment, no new oak. It's a wine of substance and firmness but it remains delicate. Ground coffee, cherry, woodsy spices and roses. It feels hand-sewn. Lovely lingering length. Screwcap. 13.5% alc. **Rating** 95 **To** 2030 $60 CM

Hilltops Rose 2019 Rose made with nebbiolo, sangiovese, barbera and muscadelle. Lifted red-berried aromas lead to a dry-but-fruity palate with wood-spice and dry-spice characters woven through. Frisky, textural and satisfying. Screwcap. 13% alc. **Rating** 94 **To** 2023 $25 CM ✪

Hilltops Shiraz 2018 It's well fruited. It uses reduction to positive effect; it's woodsy and clovey but at heart it's black-cherried and ripe. Fine tannins, impeccable balance and a satisfying finish complete a quality picture. Screwcap. 14% alc. **Rating** 94 **To** 2028 $30 CM ✪

The Cellar Block Shiraz 2018 It's not an obvious shiraz, it seems quite reserved, which just goes to show that viognier (3%) doesn't always do what you think it will. The quality of the black-cherried fruit, though, is clear, as are notes of meaty/woodsy spices, smoke and cedar. Floral characters emerge gradually with air, as do fine-grained tannins. You can cellar this wine with confidence over the medium term. Screwcap. 14% alc. **Rating** 94 **To** 2032 $38 CM

🍷🍷🍷🍷🍷 **Think Outside The Circle Fiano 2019** **Rating** 92 **To** 2023 $20 CM ✪

The Italian Hilltops Sangiovese Barbera Fiano 2018 **Rating** 92 **To** 2024 $28 CM

Murringo Way Hilltops Chardonnay 2018 **Rating** 91 **To** 2025 $20 CM ✪

Hilltops Primitivo 2018 **Rating** 91 **To** 2024 $30 CM

Grove Hill ★★★

120 Old Norton Summit Road, Norton Summit, SA 5136 **Region** Adelaide Hills
T 0402 838 932 **www.**grovehill.com.au **Open** By appt
Winemaker Margeurite Giles, Sam Giles **Est.** 1978 **Dozens** NFP

Horticulturist Charles Giles established the Grove Hill property in 1846 as an orchard and exotic plant nursery in a secluded valley near Norton Summit. The property has remained in the Giles family, Margeurite Giles and son Sam the current owners. Two sites were chosen for vines, the initial plantings made in the late 1970s and early '80s replaced by close-planted, dry-grown vines in '88. Chardonnay and pinot noir make up the main section on the valley floor, with a small section of pinot noir on a steep hillside block. Several historic buildings remain; the wines are matured in a large stone cellar.

🍷🍷🍷🍷 **Adelaide Hills Chardonnay 2016** Hand-picked, whole-bunch pressed, wild-fermented, matured in French oak. It is extraordinarily youthful, beyond any 3.5yo barrel-fermented chardonnay. By definition, it hasn't yet developed the complexity one would expect. Screwcap. 13.5% alc. **Rating** 89 **To** 2025 $80

Adelaide Hills Chardonnay 2015 Hand-picked, whole-bunch pressed, matured in French oak. Does show some development and also the impact of oak. Screwcap. 13.9% alc. **Rating** 89 **To** 2024 $80

Rubra Adelaide Hills Pinot Noir 2016 Hand-picked, wild-fermented using whole bunches. Very light, developed colour. The palate is initially savoury, then sweet fruits become more apparent. Screwcap. 13% alc. **Rating** 89 **To** 2021 $80

Growers Gate

8 The Parade West, Kent Town, SA 5067 **Region** South Australia
T 0432 74 107 **www**.growersgate.com.au **Open** Not
Winemaker Peter Pollard **Est.** 2010 **Dozens** 32 000

Growers Gate was established in 2010 by a collection of like-minded grapegrowers in SA. The range has gradually expanded to include Brut Cuvee, Sauvignon Blanc, Pinot Grigio, Chardonnay, Moscato, Rose, Shiraz and Cabernet Sauvignon. Exports to the UK, Canada, Germany, the UAE, Oman, Vietnam, Malaysia and Japan.

Gumpara Wines

410 Stockwell Road, Light Pass, SA 5355 **Region** Barossa Valley
T 0419 624 559 **www**.gumparawines.net.au **Open** By appt
Winemaker Mark Mader **Est.** 1999 **Dozens** 1000 **Vyds** 21.53ha

In 1856 the Mader family left Silesia to settle in SA, acquiring a 25ha property at Light Pass. Over the generations, farming and fruit growing gave way to 100% grapegrowing; six generations later, in 2000, Mark Mader produced the first wine under the Gumpara label. After success with shiraz, Mark branched out into semillon made from a small parcel of almost 90-year-old estate vines. The portfolio may be small but it's certainly diverse, also with Vermentino, Grenache and a range of fortified wines. The name Gumpara comes from the words 'gum' reflecting the large red gumtrees on the property and 'para', the local Aboriginal word for river. Exports to the US and China.

🍷🍷🍷🍷 **Mader Reserve Barossa Shiraz 2015** Molten cherry-choc, mint and bourbon-scented oak drive across the palate. This is an immense wine that coats the palate while overwhelming it, all at once. Will surely have many fans. Cork. **Rating** 89 **To** 2030 NG

Gundog Estate

101 McDonalds Road, Pokolbin, NSW 2320 **Region** Hunter Valley/Canberra District
T (02) 4998 6873 **www**.gundogestate.com.au **Open** 7 days 10–5
Winemaker Matthew Burton **Est.** 2006 **Dozens** 7000 **Vyds** 5ha

Matt Burton makes four different Hunter semillons, and shiraz from the Hunter Valley, Murrumbateman and Hilltops. The cellar door is located in the historic Pokolbin schoolhouse, next to the old Rosemount/Hungerford Hill building on McDonalds Road. The Burton McMahon wines are a collaboration between Matt Burton and Dylan McMahon of Seville Estate, and focus on the Yarra Valley. In 2016 Gundog opened a second cellar door at 42 Cork Street, Gundaroo (Thurs–Sun 10–5). Exports to the UK.

🍷🍷🍷🍷🍷 **Marksman's Canberra District Shiraz 2018** One of the best wines in the Gundog portfolio. Each aspect of the wine is more exactly expressed, reflecting the fact that only the best barrels are selected from the Canberra District wine in the current year. It is lighter-bodied than its siblings, yet more persuasive. Very high quality wine. Screwcap. 13.5% alc. **Rating** 96 **To** 2038 $60 ☺
Smoking Barrel Red 2018 It's 100% shiraz; 57% Hunter Valley, 43% Canberra District; the Canberra component fermented with 25% whole bunches. There's no question about the synergy the wine creates; it's particularly complex and lively, with red and black fruits both seeking to occupy centre stage, the finish very long yet fruit – not tannin – engendered. First made in '14, this is only the third release. Screwcap. 13.5% alc. **Rating** 96 **To** 2040 $35 ☺
Canberra District Riesling 2019 From the highly regarded Four Winds Vineyard. The opening stanza of the palate is of purity and balance, then the fun starts as the flavours build intensity in a classic, dry mould. Minerally acidity, crushed citrus leaves and Granny Smith apple rush through to a mouth-watering finish and aftertaste. Screwcap. 12% alc. **Rating** 95 **To** 2034 $40
The Chase Hunter Valley Semillon 2019 While the chemistry (and the vinification) of the 2 Gundog semillons from '19 is similar, this wine has more

fruit intensity and complexity; its balance very good. Screwcap. 11% alc. **Rating** 95 To 2030 $35 ✪

Canberra District Shiraz 2018 Each parcel of fruit is a combination of whole bunch and whole berries, initially cold-soaked, then fermented with cultured yeast, matured for 12 months in French puncheons. Vibrantly fresh, the fruit flavours cover the full span of red to black, the tannins firm. Screwcap. 13.5% alc. **Rating** 95 **To** 2038 $40

Rare Game Hunter Valley Shiraz 2018 A highly rated wine from the patch of the Somerset Vineyard planted in the '70s and Tinklers Vineyard 49 Block, both low-yielding, crumbly red soils. The wine immediately proclaims its quality with its freshness of flavours and innate balance that the vineyard achieves with apparent ease. Screwcap. 13% alc. **Rating** 95 **To** 2038 $60

Wild Hunter Valley Semillon 2019 Has had the works thrown at it: part clear-fermented in stainless steel to dryness, some with a little residual sugar, some cloudy-juice barrel ferment, some 100% whole-bunch fermented, part with 30% on skins and extended maceration. It's not surprising that the wine will evolve well. Screwcap. 10.5% alc. **Rating** 94 **To** 2029 $35

Hilltops Shiraz No. 1 2018 Adjacent to the Freeman Vineyard, the 2 blocks made in the same way unless unexpected weather intervenes. Machine-harvested, short soak, 5–7 days ferment, thence to French puncheons (25% new) for 14 months. The maturation period was judged to perfection. Very powerful, but well balanced. Screwcap. 13.5% alc. **Rating** 94 **To** 2038 $35

Squire's Shiraz 2018 Whether intentionally or otherwise is a moot point, but this blend (75% Hilltops from the Freeman and Moppity vineyards and 25% Canberra District from Wallaroo and Four Winds) is particularly noted as an early drinking style. It's very fresh, the slender tannins rustling in the wind, the aftertaste sultry. Screwcap. 13.5% alc. **Rating** 94 **To** 2035 $35

Hunter Valley Off-Dry Semillon 2019 If you don't have a guide dog, you might well miss the residual sugar. Either way, it's a pretty delicious wine and that residual sugar will prolong the development of the wine over time. Screwcap. 8.5% alc. **Rating** 94 $30 ✪

🍷🍷🍷🍷 **Hilltops Shiraz No. 2 2018 Rating** 93 **To** 2035 $35
Hunter's Semillon 2019 Rating 92 **To** 2027 $30

Guthrie Wines ★★★★★

661 Torrens Valley Road, Gumeracha, SA 5253 **Region** Adelaide Hills
T 0413 332 083 **www**.guthriewines.com.au **Open** By appt
Winemaker Hugh Guthrie **Est.** 2012 **Dozens** 1500

Growing up on his family's farm in the Adelaide Hills, Hugh Guthrie developed an early interest in the wines and vineyards of the region, completing a Masters of Oenology at the University of Adelaide before working in wineries around Australia and abroad. Most recently he was a winemaker at The Lane Vineyard, winner of many awards for its wines. Wife Sarah's interest has always been more in drinking than in making wine, and her work as an anaesthetist and mother is already a more than full-time job. Looking after the business side of Guthrie Wines mops up any of her spare time. In 2014 Hugh held his breath, jumped, quit his day job, and became full-time winemaker at Guthrie Wines.

🍷🍷🍷🍷 **Wild Gruner 2019** Hand-picked, whole-bunch pressed, wild-fermented in French oak (50% new), matured for 3 months on lees. A strong varietal affirmation on the bouquet, then a juicy, lingering palate. Screwcap. 13% alc. **Rating** 94 To 2027 $25 ✪

🍷🍷🍷🍷 **The Mondo Sauvignon Blanc 2019 Rating** 91 **To** 2023 $22 ✪
Ashton Pinot Noir 2019 Rating 90 **To** 2024 $30

Haan Estate

148 Siegersdorf Road, Tanunda, SA 5352 **Region** Barossa Valley
T (08) 8562 4590 **www**.haanestate.com.au **Open** Not
Winemaker Daniel Graham (Contract) **Est.** 1993 **Dozens** 5000 **Vyds** 16.3ha
Established in 1993 by the Haan Family, Haan Estate is enjoying a revival under the direction
of George Zaal and associate Mingrong Meng of Shanghai. The estate vineyard is planted to
shiraz (5.3ha), merlot (3.4ha), cabernet sauvignon (3ha), viognier (2.4ha), cabernet franc (1ha)
and malbec, petit verdot and semillon (0.4ha each). Oak use is determined by the vintage and
the wines are matured for up to 24 months in new and used barrels and puncheons. The
oak undoubtedly plays a role in the shaping of the style of the Haan wines, but it is perfectly
integrated and the wines have the fruit weight to carry the oak. Exports to Switzerland, the
Czech Republic, China and other markets.

ŸŸŸŸŸ **Wilhelmus 2017** A blend of cabernet sauvignon, merlot, cabernet franc, malbec
and petit verdot. Machine-picked, crushed, destemmed, cultured yeast, 6 days
on skins, mlf, matured in French oak for 24 months. Attractive display of florals,
black fruits, nutmeg, cinnamon and chocolate buds. The generosity imbued in this
cabernet is well managed and it retains a strong cabernet fruit focus rather than
leaning towards oak or alcohol. Leafy and sweet-fruited, it sings. Cork. 15% alc.
Rating 95 **To** 2032 $65 JP

ŸŸŸŸŸ **Barossa Valley Merlot Prestige 2017 Rating** 92 **To** 2031 $65 JP
Barossa Valley Shiraz Prestige 2017 Rating 91 **To** 2037 $65 JP

Haddow + Dineen

c/- Bruny Island Cheese Co, 1807 Bruny Island Main Road, Great Bay, Tas 7150 **Region**
Tasmania
T 0412 478 841 **www**.haddowanddineen.com.au **Open** 7 days 9–5
Winemaker Jeremy Dineen, Nick Haddow **Est.** 2017 **Dozens** 800 **Vyds** 2.6ha
This is a collaborative winemaking project involving winemaker Jeremy Dineen and
cheesemaker Nick Haddow. Jeremy has been the Chief Winemaker for Josef Chromy
since 2005, his knowledge and skill self-evident. Nick Haddow is a unique phenomenon. Since
1995 he has received 10 grants, many substantial, and (by coincidence) 10 significant awards.
He travels the world amassing exceptional knowledge about cheese, gaining unsurpassed
international recognition. Haddow + Dineen has a single vineyard at the mouth of the
Tamar River with 1.6ha of pinot noir and 1ha of pinot gris. Their wines have no additions
other than a small amount of SO_2, and are not fined or filtered. Moreover, each barrel is
bottled as is, with no blending. They say, 'We value maximum consideration over minimum
intervention … for every wine there are a thousand choices [that could be made] or simply
employ vigilant inaction.'

ŸŸŸŸŸ **Grain of Truth Pinot Gris 2018** Hand-picked, whole-bunch pressed, wild-
fermented in barrel. There's no question, the wine oozes wild honey from its
bouquet and palate, yet doesn't cloy. Very skilled winemaking for a thoroughly
left field, out there wine. You only have to glimpse the bottle to know there's
something new here. Screwcap. 13.5% alc. **Rating** 95 **To** 2021 $48

Hahndorf Hill Winery

38 Pain Road, Hahndorf, SA 5245 **Region** Adelaide Hills
T (08) 8388 7512 **www**.hahndorfhillwinery.com.au **Open** 7 days 10–5
Winemaker Larry Jacobs **Est.** 2002 **Dozens** 6000 **Vyds** 6.5ha
Larry Jacobs and Marc Dobson, both originally from South Africa, purchased Hahndorf Hill
Winery in 2002. Before migrating, Larry had given up a career in intensive care medicine in
1988 when he bought an abandoned property in Stellenbosch and established the near-iconic
Mulderbosch Wines. It was purchased at the end of '96 and the pair eventually found their
way to Australia and Hahndorf Hill. In 2006, their investment in the winery and cellar door
was rewarded by induction into the South Australian Tourism Hall of Fame. In '07 they began

converting the vineyard to biodynamic status and they were among the first to implement a carbon offset program. They imported three clones of gruner veltliner from Austria and another variety, St Laurent. In '16 the winery was awarded Best Producer of Show <100t at the Adelaide Hills Wine Show, and their wines too have had trophy and medal success. Exports to the UK, Singapore, Japan and China.

ŸŸŸŸŸ **Adelaide Hills Pinot Grigio 2019** I took this wine up to the house after my daily tasting to make sure I hadn't lost my senses. (I hadn't.) A storm-induced crop loss of 60% saw the grapes hand-picked from 2 Adelaide Hills sites, chilled overnight, whole-bunch pressed and flash-oxygenated to eliminate anthocyanin colour contribution, then cool-fermented in stainless steel. An ever so fine distillation of nashi pear, a prodigiously long palate and crunchy acidity. Three gold medals and a trophy in '19. Screwcap. 12.5% alc. **Rating** 96 **To** 2025 $25 ✪

GRU Adelaide Hills Gruner Veltliner 2018 Very complex vinification with 3 different approaches to batches picked at varying stages of ripeness. Gruner stands tall over all other alternative white varieties, with a range of fruit and mineral flavours, a brush of white pepper, but above all else, texture and length. Screwcap. 12.5% alc. **Rating** 96 **To** 2028 $29 ✪

Reserve Adelaide Hills Gruner Veltliner 2017 Showing signs of development as expected – colour (although bright), depth, richness and complexity. It would have been easy to overplay any of the steps of vinification, counterintuitively, it is closest to the gruner veltliners of Austria, particularly. Screwcap. 13% alc. **Rating** 96 **To** 2027 $45 ✪

White Mischief Adelaide Hills Gruner Veltliner 2019 Made in a New World fruit-driven style emphasising a broad range of varietal primary fruits. Hand-picked, chilled for 24 hours in small slotted bins, pressed, free-run fermented separately from the pressings then blended back to provide textural play, left on gross lees for a time. Screwcap. 13% alc. **Rating** 95 **To** 2026 $24 ✪

GRU Adelaide Hills Gruner Veltliner 2019 Brutal crop loss, 6 clones hand-picked over 3 specific days, each parcel vinified very differently, including a yeast to reduce primary fruit and 30% wild-fermented in used barriques before blending. Has that precision that is the hallmark of Hahndorf Hill, leaving a mouth-watering intensity and texture. Gold medal Hobart Wine Show '19. Screwcap. 13% alc. **Rating** 95 **To** 2024 $29 ✪

White Mischief Adelaide Hills Gruner Veltliner 2018 The accent is on fruit rather than texture or structure. Its intensity is remarkable, the length a reflection of that intensity. Gruner veltliner's white pepper on the bouquet stands out long and clear, and the fruits range through stone fruit to citrus, none dominant. Gold medal National Wine Show '18. Screwcap. 13% alc. **Rating** 95 **To** 2030 $24 ✪

Adelaide Hills Rose 2019 A blend of 37% pinot noir, 28% merlot, 27% trollinger and 8% tannat (a first-time inclusion); each hand-picked specifically for this wine, each crushed for free-run juice to prevent colour pick-up. Delicately framed and poised, it is a special rose, given as much care as any dry red or white wine. Gold medal Melbourne International Wine Competition '19. Screwcap. 12.5% alc. **Rating** 95 **To** 2021 $24 ✪

ŸŸŸŸŸ **Adelaide Hills Shiraz 2017** **Rating** 92 **To** 2029 $40
Zsa Zsa Adelaide Hills Zweigelt 2018 **Rating** 90 **To** 2023 $35

Hamelin Bay   ★★★★☆

McDonald Road, Karridale, WA 6288 **Region** Margaret River
T (08) 9758 6779 **www.hbwines.com.au** **Open** 7 days 10–5
Winemaker Richard Drake-Brockman **Est.** 1992 **Dozens** 5000 **Vyds** 23.5ha

The Hamelin Bay vineyard was established by the Drake-Brockman family, pioneers of the region. Richard Drake-Brockman's great-grandmother, Grace Bussell, was famous for her courage when, in 1876, aged 16, she rescued survivors of a shipwreck not far from the mouth of the Margaret River. Richard's great-grandfather Frederick, known for his exploration of the Kimberley, read about the feat in Perth's press and rode 300km on horseback to meet her — they married in 1882. Hamelin Bay's vineyard and winery is located within a few kilometres of Karridale, at the intersection of the Brockman and Bussell highways, which were named in honour of these pioneering families. Exports to the UK, Canada, Malaysia, Singapore and China.

🍷🍷🍷🍷🍷 **Five Ashes Reserve Margaret River Shiraz 2018** An impressive swathe of blue to dark fruit allusions, iodine, a smear of black olive and peppery accents across the mouth. Fully flared oak, however, makes this a proposition for the future, rather than approachable right now. That said, the juicy acidity, smothered in clove and pepper, augurs well. Screwcap. **Rating** 95 **To** 2030 $55 NG
Five Ashes Vineyard Margaret River Shiraz 2018 Molten ruby. This is promising aromatically: blueberry, olive pith, iodine, salumi. The tannins are well nestled, the acidity a zip-code thread of pepper grind to clove, tying up the seams. Very well handled. Screwcap. **Rating** 94 **To** 2028 $33 NG

🍷🍷🍷🍷🍷 **Five Ashes Vineyard Chardonnay 2017 Rating** 91 **To** 2023 $33 NG
Rampant Red 2018 Rating 91 **To** 2024 $22 NG ✪
Sauvignon Blanc 2019 Rating 90 **To** 2020 $26 NG
Semillon Sauvignon Blanc 2019 Rating 90 **To** 2020 $26 NG
Five Ashes Vineyard Cabernet Sauvignon 2017 Rating 90 **To** 2025 $33 NG

Handpicked Wines   ★★★★★

50 Kensington Street, Chippendale, NSW 2008 **Region** Various
T (02) 9475 7888 **www**.handpickedwines.com.au **Open** Mon–Fri 11–10, w'ends 10–10
Winemaker Peter Dillon, Jonathon Mattick **Est.** 2001 **Dozens** 100 000 **Vyds** 83ha
Handpicked Wines is a multi-regional business with a flagship vineyard and winery on the Mornington Peninsula and vineyards in the Yarra Valley, Tasmania and Barossa Valley. They also make wines from many of Australia's leading fine wine regions. Five of Handpicked's vineyards focus on high quality pinot noir and chardonnay – two in Tasmania's Tamar Valley, Capella Vineyard in the Mornington Peninsula and two in the Yarra Valley, including Wombat Creek in the Upper Yarra, the highest elevation vineyard in the valley. Director of winemaking Peter Dillon travels extensively to oversee quality throughout the regions, he and assistant winemaker Jonathon Mattick work closely with a team of viticulturists who manage the vineyards. The cellar door in Sydney's CBD brings the wines together in a stylish retail and hospitality venue. Exports to the US, Canada, the Philippines, South Korea, Cambodia, Malaysia, Singapore, Japan, Taiwan and China.

🍷🍷🍷🍷🍷 **Capella Vineyard Mornington Peninsula Pinot Noir 2018** A red wine sibling to the majestic Capella Chardonnay, this is a thickly curbed pinot, with a strong band of structural integrity: impeccable oak handling, bunch, cool-climate acidity and fibrous tannins. The red fruit allusions are tucked in, restrained, discreet. They will come to the fore. This is highly impressive, shying away from the medicinal sweetness of so many Aussie pinots thanks to the tannic bind. **Rating** 97 **To** 2027 $80 NG ✪

🍷🍷🍷🍷🍷 **Capella Vineyard Mornington Peninsula Chardonnay 2018** This is an impressive contemporary expression of domestic chardonnay: a conflation of chablis-like flint and toasted hazelnut, curd and stone fruits flowing effortlessly and long across a thread of juicy acidity and mineral tension. Burgundian. All augurs for a long future. A stamp of authority for this producer. Screwcap. **Rating** 96 **To** 2030 $60 NG ✪
Highbow Hill Vineyard Yarra Valley Chardonnay 2017 This is mid-weighted and tightly furled, with flinty mineral crunch welded to classy oak, proving the structural enforcement. A work out in the glass reveals some stone fruit and leesy accents, but it is the kinetic energy and palate-staining length that suggest a very bright further for this cuvee. Screwcap. **Rating** 96 **To** 2029 $60 NG ✪

Collection Mornington Peninsula Pinot Noir 2018 Fecund strawberry notes careen along gently fibrous tannins, expansive and spindly. Acidity, palpably natural. Lovely structure and density to this. Light years ahead of the Yarra Collection. A richly tapestried pinot. **Rating** 95 **To** 2025 $60 NG

Highbow Hill Vineyard Yarra Valley Pinot Noir 2017 A light ruby, beaming vivid aromas of strawberry, mulch, Asian spice, red and black cherry and sarsaparilla. Loads of flavour. Rich even, but far from a loosely knit wine. There is an undercarriage of well massaged tannins across grape, stem and oak, corralling it all into a sheath of sapid intensity and full barrelled length. Very good. Screwcap. **Rating** 95 **To** 2026 $80 NG

Collection Mornington Peninsula Chardonnay 2019 A seamless chardonnay exuding scents of white peach, cream of cashew to nougatine, fig and truffled curd. The seams of oak guide the billow of flavour, while a thread of juicy maritime acidity tows it all long. Loosely knit, but still focused. Screwcap. **Rating** 94 **To** 2026 $45 NG

Wombat Creek Vineyard Yarra Valley Chardonnay 2018 This is a discreet chardonnay revealing white fig, melon and gentle vanillan oak tones melded to leesy nougatine and oatmeal scents, unfolding with a brisk workout in the glass. Classy cool-climate chardonnay, boding well for a bright future. Screwcap. **Rating** 94 **To** 2030 $60 NG

ΨΨΨΨΨ **Collection Yarra Valley Chardonnay 2018** **Rating** 93 **To** 2026 $45 NG
Wombat Creek Vineyard Yarra Valley Pinot Noir 2018 **Rating** 93 $80 NG
Collection Tasmania Pinot Noir 2018 **Rating** 93 **To** 2025 $60 NG
Trial Batch Pyrenees Nebbiolo Rose 2019 **Rating** 92 **To** 2020 $29 NG
Collection Yarra Valley Pinot Noir 2016 **Rating** 92 **To** 2025 $60
Collection Barossa Valley Grenache 2018 **Rating** 92 **To** 2024 $70 NG
Collection Yarra Valley Cabernet Sauvignon 2014 **Rating** 92 **To** 2023 $80 NG
Collection Yarra Valley Pinot Noir 2018 **Rating** 91 **To** 2024 $60 NG
Regional Selections Margaret River Cabernet Sauvignon 2017 **Rating** 91 **To** 2026 $25 NG
Regional Selections Yarra Valley Chardonnay 2018 **Rating** 90 **To** 2024 $25
Regional Selections Yarra Valley Cabernet Sauvignon 2017 **Rating** 90 **To** 2025 $25 NG

Hanging Rock Winery   ★★★★★

88 Jim Road, Newham, Vic 3442 **Region** Macedon Ranges
T (03) 5427 0542 **www.**hangingrock.com.au **Open** 7 days 10–5
Winemaker Robert Ellis **Est.** 1983 **Dozens** 20 000 **Vyds** 14.5ha
The Macedon area has proved marginal in spots and the Hanging Rock vineyards, with their lovely vista towards the Rock, are no exception. John Ellis thus elected to source additional grapes from various parts of Victoria to produce an interesting and diverse range of varietals at different price points. In 2011 John's children Ruth and Robert returned to the fold: Robert has an oenology degree from the University of Adelaide, after that working as a Flying Winemaker in Champagne, Burgundy, Oregon and Stellenbosch. Ruth has a degree in wine marketing from the University of Adelaide. Exports to the UK, the US and other major markets.

ΨΨΨΨΨ **The Jim Jim Three 2019** Gewurztraminer, riesling, pinot gris. This is a delicious wine, lightweight but intensely aromatic and flavourful across a long, talcy finish. The intensity of lychee, orange blossom, Granny Smith apple and lime notes are belied by a relaxed, confident gait across the palate. Effortless. Poised. Compact. Fine. Screwcap. **Rating** 94 **To** 2024 $30 NG ○

ΨΨΨΨΨ **Jim Jim Macedon Ranges Sauvignon Blanc 2019** **Rating** 93 **To** 2023 $30 NG
Tarzali Riesling 2019 **Rating** 92 **To** 2029 $25 NG ○

Bendigo Cabernet Sauvignon 2018 Rating 92 To 2026 $25 NG ✪
Jim Jim Macedon Ranges Pinot Noir 2018 Rating 91 To 2025 $50 NG
Cambrian Rise Heathcote Shiraz 2018 Rating 91 To 2028 $35 NG
Heathcote Shiraz 2017 Rating 91 To 2027 $75 NG
Macedon Cuvee NV Rating 91 $50 NG
Jim Jim Macedon Ranges Pinot Noir 2017 Rating 90 To 2024 $50 NG
Rich Reef Shiraz 2018 Rating 90 To 2026 $25 NG

Happs ★★★★★

575 Commonage Road, Dunsborough, WA 6281 **Region** Margaret River
T (08) 9755 3300 **www**.happs.com.au **Open** 7 days 10–5
Winemaker Erl Happ, Mark Warren **Est.** 1978 **Dozens** 15 000 **Vyds** 35.2ha
One-time schoolteacher, potter and winemaker Erl Happ is the patriarch of a three-generation family. More than anything, Erl has been a creator and experimenter: building the self-designed winery from mudbrick, concrete form and timber; and making the first crusher. In 1994 he planted a new 30ha vineyard at Karridale to no less than 28 varieties, including some of the earliest plantings of tempranillo in Australia. The Three Hills label is made from varieties grown at this vineyard. Erl passed on his love of pottery to his son Myles, and Happs Pottery now has four potters, including Myles. Exports to the US, Denmark, the Netherlands, Malaysia, the Philippines, Vietnam, Hong Kong, China and Japan.

🍷🍷🍷🍷♀ **Three Hills Shiraz 2018** This is a very good medium to full-bodied shiraz with good varietal expression and attendant oak. The tannins are ripe and fine. Screwcap. 14% alc. **Rating** 93 To 2033 $60
Margaret River Sauvignon Blanc Semillon 2018 A 64/36% blend, wild-fermented in used French oak. The shoe fits perfectly, ready to wear with no adjustment. Screwcap. 12.8% alc. **Rating** 92 To 2023 $24 ✪
Fields of Gold Margaret River Chardonnay 2018 The vineyard is the first in Margaret River to see the sun in the morning, reflecting the gold of the rays. Poetry to one side, this is a chardonnay you could enjoy at any hour of the day. Screwcap. 13.6% alc. **Rating** 92 To 2025 $30
Three Hills Cabernet Merlot 2018 A very different wine to its sibling, despite the similarity of the blend, with red fruits swinging along a light to medium-bodied oak; tannins present but not dangerous. The cool climate of Karridale was Erl Happ's happy hunting ground for varietal expression across traditional and new varieties. Screwcap. 14.2% alc. **Rating** 91 To 2029 $30
iSeries Margaret River Pinot Noir 2019 Happs says this variety is an anomaly for Margaret River, but that he's found a clone and a cooler vineyard that produce good pinot noir. One swallow (horrible pun) doesn't make a summer, but this wine does indeed have good varietal character and has been allowed to do its thing without embellishment in the winery. A light-bodied red-berry line of fruit has a spicy/savoury offset. Screwcap. 13.6% alc. **Rating** 90 To 2023 $17 ✪
Three Hills Cabernet Franc 2018 Here's a red flower peeping out through its bramble surroundings, secure that no-one is going to take it away for purpose pure or foul. Screwcap. 13.4% alc. **Rating** 90 To 2029 $38

🍷🍷🍷 **Margaret River Verdelho 2019** Rating 89 To 2022 $20
Three Hills Grenache 2018 Rating 89 To 2022 $38
Margaret River Cabernet Merlot 2018 Rating 89 To 2028 $24

Hardys ★★★★★

202 Main Road, McLaren Vale, SA 5171 **Region** McLaren Vale
T (08) 8329 4124 **www**.hardyswines.com.au **Open** Sun–Fri 11–4, Sat 10–4
Winemaker Nic Bowen **Est.** 1853 **Dozens** NFP
The 1992 merger of Thomas Hardy and the Berri Renmano group may have had some elements of a forced marriage, but the merged group prospered over the next 10 years. It was so successful that a further marriage followed in early 2003, with Constellation Wines of the

US the groom and BRL Hardy the bride, creating the largest wine group in the world (the Australian arm was known as Constellation Wines Australia or CWA); but it is now part of the Accolade Wines group. The Hardys wine brands are headed by Thomas Hardy Cabernet Sauvignon, Eileen Hardy Chardonnay, Pinot Noir and Shiraz; then the Sir James range of sparkling wines; next the HRB wines, the William Hardy quartet; then the expanded Oomoo range and the Nottage Hill wines. The 'Big Company' slur is ill deserved – these are some of Australia's greatest wines. Exports to all major markets.

ŶŶŶŶŶ Eileen Hardy Chardonnay 2017 While this has been tightened up in fealty to more contemporary trends – mineral crunch and linearity – it is still a richer expression of this great grape than many. Ample stone fruit references strut along a stage of flint and oak. Plenty of moxie. Long and energetic. And in an age of regional singularity, this applies the classic Australian approach of inter-regional blending across the Yarra and Tasmania, all to maximise potential, complexity and poise. For your benefit. Screwcap. **Rating** 96 **To** 2029 $118 NG
Tintara Sub Regional Blewitt Springs McLaren Vale Shiraz 2018 This is sumptuous warm-climate shiraz, managing to effortlessly bridle cool-climate florals, tapenade and iodine scents, with black cherry and blue fruit persuasions, more suggestive of home turf. Quintessentially Blewitt Springs. The oak (25% new French), svelte tannins and crackling thread of peppery acidity provide ample seams to rein in the explosion of flavour, while towing the carnival long. Screwcap. **Rating** 95 **To** 2033 $80 NG
Barrel Selected Rare Liqueur Sauvignon Blanc NV Made akin to a tawny port, with controlled oxidative handling across a blend of youthful and very old wines, this fortified is delicious. Resinous, layered and very long. Lemon curd wafts beneath toasted nuts, gingerbread, date and molasses to dried walnut rancio notes. Given the uncanny varietal choice, there must be plenty of sauvignon in need of a spruce up. Far from the typical fortified base. Cork. **Rating** 95 $100 NG
Brave New World McLaren Vale Grenache Shiraz Mourvedre 2017 An 86/10/4% blend; part hand, part machine-picked, 10% whole-bunch fermentation, 10 days on skins, 6 months in used oak, but French and American staves. Bursts with the fresh fruit serenade ex the '17 vintage, and is great now. Cellar if you will, but why do so? Value+. Screwcap. 14.5% alc. **Rating** 94 **To** 2027 $25 ✪

ŶŶŶŶŶ HRB Shiraz 2018 **Rating** 93 **To** 2030 $35 NG
Eileen Hardy Shiraz 2016 **Rating** 93 **To** 2036 $154 NG
Insignia Limestone Coast Chardonnay 2019 **Rating** 92 **To** 2023 NG
HRB Chardonnay 2018 **Rating** 92 **To** 2025 $35 NG
Char No. 3 McLaren Vale Shiraz 2018 **Rating** 92 **To** 2026 $26 NG
Tintara Reserve McLaren Vale Grenache 2018 **Rating** 92 **To** 2026 $70 NG
The Chronicles 7th Green McLaren Vale Cabernet Sauvignon 2017 **Rating** 91 **To** 2024 $16 NG ✪
The Chronicles Butcher's Gold Shiraz 2017 **Rating** 90 **To** 2025 NG
Char No. 3 Cabernet Sauvignon NV **Rating** 90 **To** 2028 $26 NG

Hare's Chase ★★★★★

PO Box 46, Melrose Park, SA 5039 **Region** Barossa Valley
T (08) 8277 3506 **www**.hareschase.com **Open** Not
Winemaker Peter Taylor **Est.** 1998 **Dozens** 5000 **Vyds** 16.8ha
Hare's Chase is the creation of two families, headed respectively by Peter Taylor as winemaker, with over 30 vintages' experience and Mike de la Haye as general manager; they own a 100+-year-old vineyard in the Marananga Valley area of the Barossa Valley. The simple, functional winery sits at the top of a rocky hill in the centre of the vineyard, which has some of the best red soil available for dry-grown viticulture. In 2016 Peter and Mike said, 'After 15 years of developing Hare's Chase, we are starting to believe we may one day give up our day job'. Exports to the US, Canada, Switzerland, Singapore, Hong Kong, Malaysia and China.

ŶŶŶŶŶ Marananga Barossa Valley Cabernet Shiraz 2017 The ancient soils of the Marananga subregion, close to the Barossa Valley floor, are renowned for producing red wines rich in blue fruits and juniper with intense colour. The area offers a singularly individual Barossa flavour profile and almost effortless structure as evidenced in this wine with its blue and red fruits, mulberry, bouquet garni, celery salt. Tannins are powdery, oak stays on the low down. Screwcap. 14.5% alc. Rating 95 To 2031 $38 JP

Cellar Reserve 100 Year Old Barossa Valley Grenache 2018 Vines planted in 1912. Gently destemmed retaining whole berries, cool ferment in open fermenters, aged for 15 months in new and seasoned French puncheons. An intelligent winemaking approach, capturing the more elegant qualities of the variety and its provenance. Perfumed and gently sweet-fruited, harmonious throughout. Screwcap. 14.5% alc. **Rating** 94 **To** 2030 $38 SC

ŶŶŶŶŶ **Ironscraper Barossa Valley Shiraz 2018** Rating 93 To 2032 $35 SC
Cellar Reserve Barossa Valley Grenache Shiraz Mataro 2018 Rating 93 To 2028 $38 SC
Cellar Reserve Cabernet Sauvignon 2018 Rating 93 To 2030 $38 SC
Cellar Reserve Cabernet Franc 2018 Rating 93 To 2028 $38 SC
Tempranillo 2018 Rating 91 To 2025 $25 SC

Harewood Estate ★★★★★

1570 Scotsdale Road, Denmark, WA 6333 **Region** Denmark
T (08) 9840 9078 **www**.harewood.com.au **Open** Fri–Mon 11–5 (school hols 7 days)
Winemaker James Kellie **Est.** 1988 **Dozens** 15 000 **Vyds** 19.2ha
In 2003 James Kellie, responsible for the contract making of Harewood's wines since 1998, purchased the estate with his father and sister as partners. A 300t winery was constructed, offering both contract winemaking services for the Great Southern region and the ability to expand the Harewood range to include subregional wines. In January 2010 James, together with wife Careena, purchased his father's and sister's shares to become 100% owners. Exports to the UK, the US, Denmark, Sweden, Switzerland, Indonesia, Hong Kong, Malaysia, Macau, Singapore, China and Japan.

ŶŶŶŶŶ **Porongurup Riesling 2019** Perhaps the most delicate of the single vineyard Harewood rieslings from this release, but it comes at no expense to intensity. Sweet citrus, apple and lemon barley water are the themes on the bouquet; and the palate is an exercise in perfect balance, the fruit flavours finding their way all around the mouth but held in a web of taut acidity. Screwcap. 12.5% alc. **Rating** 96 **To** 2034 $30 SC ✪

Mount Barker Riesling 2019 Intense varietal aroma on the bouquet with various citrus and floral characters involved and a touch of spiced apple. Sweet-fruited, the flavours build towards the back of the palate. It's really on the finish and in the aftertaste that it displays its quality. Screwcap. 12.5% alc. **Rating** 95 **To** 2034 $30 SC ✪

Frankland River Riesling 2019 Lime juice and talc aromas lead the way to a palate which seems a little fuller than its stable mates, but at no sacrifice to elegance and poise. This is a beautifully textured wine; the lemony acidity is gently persistent throughout, finishing with a flourish on the farewell. This is the one to drink first. Screwcap. 13% alc. **Rating** 95 **To** 2034 $30 SC ✪

Denmark Riesling 2019 Quite a different style from the Mount Barker. Less fruit and florals in the bouquet but more minerality. Juicy acidity dominates the palate, wrapping up the lemon and grapefruit flavours tightly – to be released with more time in the bottle. Of the group, this is the one asking most to be cellared. Screwcap. 12% alc. **Rating** 95 **To** 2034 $30 SC ✪

Denmark Pinot Noir 2018 Had 15 months new French oak. Dried flowers, cranberry, red plum, sea spray, a whiff of the Aussie bush. There's a whole lot of sweet, lifted aromatics erupting in the glass, establishing a real sense of place. Gives every appearance of being lighter and breezier than it actually is. The white pepper provides a lasting memory. Screwcap. 14% alc. **Rating** 94 **To** 2024 $21 JP ✪

Great Southern Shiraz 2017 Had 18 months in 20% new French oak. Frankland River fruit forms the basis of very approachable shiraz which has been afforded some impressive oak handling given its price point. Such a pretty, inviting nose with florals to the forefront with red berry spice and sage. It glides across the palate, carrying a host of black and red fruits, vanilla and spicy sundries. Screwcap. 14.5% alc. **Rating** 94 **To** 2025 $21 JP ❂

❦❦❦❦❦ **Great Southern Sauvignon Blanc Semillon 2019 Rating** 93 **To** 2024 $21 JF ❂
Great Southern Cabernet Merlot 2017 Rating 92 **To** 2027 $21 JF ❂
Reserve Great Southern Cabernet Sauvignon 2018 Rating 92 **To** 2030 $34 JF
Reserve Denmark Semillon Sauvignon Blanc 2018 Rating 90 **To** 2026 $27 JP
Reserve Great Southern Chardonnay 2018 Rating 90 **To** 2025 $34 JF
Flux-III Denmark Chardonnay 2017 Rating 90 **To** 2027 $29 JP
Denmark Pinot Noir 2019 Rating 90 **To** 2024 $20 SC ❂
Flux-V Great Southern Pinot Noir 2018 Rating 90 **To** 2023 $29 JP
Great Southern Shiraz 2018 Rating 90 **To** 2025 $20 SC ❂

Hart & Hunter ★★★★★

Gabriel's Paddock, 463 Deasys Road, Pokolbin, NSW 2325 **Region** Hunter Valley
T (02) 4998 7645 **www.hartandhunter.com.au Open** Thurs–Mon 10–4
Winemaker Damien Stevens, Jodie Belleville **Est.** 2009 **Dozens** 2500
This is the venture of winemaking couple Damien Stevens and Jodie Belleville. The grapes are purchased from highly regarded growers within the Hunter. The emphasis on single vineyard wines and small-batch processing. Continuing success for the venture led to the opening of a cellar door in late 2014, offering not only the three best known Hunter varieties but also experimental wines and alternative varieties.

❦❦❦❦❦ **Museum Release Single Vineyard Series Oakey Creek Semillon 2015**
Subdued and far more reserved than the Remparts but with a crackling energy that is effusive. Lemon oil, curd, quince and grapefruit pulp. A gentle chew, with the acidity buried in the fray. Long. Structurally refined; acidity and phenolics of equal importance. Fine. Very. **Rating** 95 **To** 2029 NG
Museum Release Single Vineyard Series Oakey Creek Semillon 2013
Blissfully mature Hunter semillon when, somehow, all the shins of acidity and jangle of elbows come into play. Lanolin, buttered toast, lime tonic and lemon curd. This is mellifluous with the undeniable chassis of early picked acidity towing the rear and pulling the meld long. Screwcap. **Rating** 95 **To** 2028 NG
Single Vineyard Series The Hill Shiraz 2017 Sturdier. Real tannic amplitude. Structurally forceful; almost ferrous. This is light years from the Ablington, validating the producer's decision to separate these expressions. Darker fruit; finer boned. Resinous, dense and complex. Very. This will reward patience. Screwcap. **Rating** 95 **To** 2032 NG

❦❦❦❦❦ **Hunter River Riesling 2018 Rating** 93 **To** 2033 $35 NG
Single Vineyard Series Hart Vineyard Semillon 2019 Rating 93 **To** 2031 $30 NG
Museum Release Single Vineyard Series The Remparts Semillon 2015 Rating 93 **To** 2027 NG
Single Vineyard Series Ablington Shiraz 2017 Rating 93 **To** 2029 $47 NG
75 Days Chardonnay 2018 Rating 92 **To** 2024 $42 NG
Single Vineyard Series Twenty Six Rows Chardonnay 2018 Rating 92 **To** 2025 $40 NG
Single Vineyard Series Oakey Creek Semillon 2019 Rating 91 **To** 2029 $30 NG
Single Vineyard Series Old Vine Shiraz 2016 Rating 90 **To** 2026 $50 JP

Hart of the Barossa ★★★★★

Cnr Vine Vale Road/Light Pass Road, Tanunda, SA 5352 **Region** Barossa Valley
T 0412 586 006 **www.**hartofthebarossa.com.au **Open** Fri–Sat 11–4 or by appt
Winemaker Michael Hart, Alisa Hart, Rebekah Richardson **Est.** 2007 **Dozens** 2000
Vyds 6.5ha

The ancestors of Michael and Alisa Hart arrived in SA in 1845, their first address (with seven children) a hollow tree on the banks of the North Para River. Michael and Alisa personally tend the vineyard, which is the oldest certified organic vineyard in the Barossa Valley and includes a patch of 110-year-old shiraz. The quality of the wines coming from these vines is exceptional; unfortunately, there is only enough to fill two hogsheads a year (66 dozen bottles). The other wines made are also impressive, particularly given their prices. Exports to Germany, Hong Kong and China.

♥♥♥♥♥ **Ye Faithful Limited Release Old Vine Shiraz 2015** Hand-picked, crushed and destemmed, 10 days on skins, twice-daily pumpovers, matured for 24 months in new French oak. Against all expectations, the fruit has made light work of the oak and does so in medium-bodied style. The mouthfeel is very good, supple and smooth, the wine just cruising along. Screwcap. 14.5% alc. **Rating** 95 To 2030 $115
The Blesing Cabernet Sauvignon 2017 Hand-picked, crushed and destemmed, 10 days on skins, twice-daily pumpovers, 18 months in 75% American and 25% French oak (25% new). The '17 vintage has bequeathed the wine good varietal expression courtesy of low(ish) alcohol and a savoury/slightly herbal black olive wedding party. Screwcap. 13.7% alc. **Rating** 95 To 2032 $50

♥♥♥♥♡ **Vine Vale Mataro 2019 Rating** 92 To 2029 $25 ✪
Ye Brave Limited Release Shiraz 2016 Rating 91 To 2036 $30

Harvey River Estate ★★★★

Third Street, Harvey, WA 6220 **Region** Geographe
T (08) 9729 2085 **www.**harveyriverestate.com.au **Open** 7 days 10–4
Winemaker Stuart Pierce **Est.** 1999 **Dozens** 20000 **Vyds** 18.5ha

Harvey River Estate has a long and significant tradition of winemaking in WA's southwest. The Sorgiovanni family have been farming and making wine on the original property since Guiseppe (Joe) arrived from Italy in 1928. Orchards evolved into a standalone business and Harvey Fresh went on to become one of WA's largest milk and juice processors. The Harvey River Estate label was established in 1999, the range of popular varietals designed to be enjoyed in the short to medium term including Sauvignon Blanc, Chardonnay, Sauvignon Blanc Semillon, Rose, Merlot, Shiraz, Cabernet Sauvignon. The fruit for these wines is predominantly from the family-owned vineyards in Geographe. Exports to the US, Canada, Singapore and China.

♥♥♥♥ **Merlot 2018** The front and main back labels claim WA as its place of origin, Geographe in small print. Clear mulberry; olive/savoury less insistent. Very good value, the varietal character is well established by the wine. Screwcap. 14% alc. **Rating** 89 To 2028 $18 ✪

Haselgrove Wines ★★★★★

187 Sand Road, McLaren Vale, SA 5171 **Region** McLaren Vale
T (08) 8323 8706 **www.**haselgrove.com.au **Open** By appt
Winemaker Alex Sherrah **Est.** 1981 **Dozens** 45000 **Vyds** 9.7ha

Italian-Australian industry veterans Don Totino, Don Luca, Tony Carrocci and Steve Maglieri decided to purchase Haselgrove 'over a game of cards and couple of hearty reds' in 2008. They have completely changed the product range, the modern small-batch winery producing the Legend Series ($85–$150), the Origin Series ($30–$40), the Alternative Series ($24), First Cut ($22) and the 'H' by Haselgrove Series ($15). Exports to Canada, Germany, Malaysia, South Korea, Hong Kong, China and NZ.

ŸŸŸŸŸ **The Cruth McLaren Vale Shiraz 2018** Destemmed to open fermenters, 14 days on skins, pressed to new and 1yo French hogsheads for 18 months maturation, every barrel tasted for selection. The most complete tannin profile from oak and vineyard with blueberries dipped in dark chocolate flavours. Totally compelling in the context of McLaren Vale style. Diam. 14.5% alc. **Rating** 96 **To** 2043 $150

The Ambassador Single Vineyard McLaren Vale Shiraz 2018 From estate vineyards planted in '72 on sand over clay soils in an east–west row orientation the batches matured separately in new and used French oak for 18 months, every barrel tasted for selection. This borders on outright elegance; balance and length also gaining points; the fruits a blackberry/blueberry mix. A very good regional wine. Diam. 14.5% alc. **Rating** 96 **To** 2041 $85

Col Cross Single Vineyard McLaren Vale Shiraz 2018 Crushed but not destemmed, a cool open fermentation, 12 days on skins, matured in new and used French hogsheads for 18 months, each barrel tasted for suitability for the blend. If full-bodied is what you are after, this is a good place to start. Ponderous for sure, but it is balanced. Diam. 14.5% alc. **Rating** 95 **To** 2038 $90

The Lear McLaren Vale Shiraz 2018 Follows in the fermentation footsteps of its siblings, maturation in new and 1yo French hogsheads for 18 months before a barrel selection. Savoury black fruits and a surge of heat on the finish keep this wine out of the very best. Screwcap. 14.5% alc. **Rating** 94 **To** 2038 $90

Protector McLaren Vale Cabernet Sauvignon 2018 Destemmed, open-fermented, 12 days on skins, pressed to new and used French oak for completion of fermentation and maturation, blended after 16 months. There's so much to enjoy here, except for a fox terrier nip on the finish ex tannins. Screwcap. 14% alc. **Rating** 94 **To** 2038 $40

ŸŸŸŸŸ **Catkin McLaren Vale Shiraz 2018 Rating** 92 **To** 2038 $40
Switch GSM McLaren Vale Grenache Shiraz Mourvedre 2018 Rating 92 **To** 2028 $40
Vine Sean McLaren Vale Grenache 2018 Rating 91 **To** 2024 $30
First Cut McLaren Vale Shiraz 2018 Rating 90 **To** 2029 $23

Hay Shed Hill Wines   ★★★★★

511 Harmans Mill Road, Wilyabrup, WA 6280 **Region** Margaret River
T (08) 9755 6046 **www.**hayshedhill.com.au **Open** 7 days 10–5
Winemaker Michael Kerrigan **Est.** 1987 **Dozens** 24 000 **Vyds** 18.55ha
Mike Kerrigan, former winemaker at Howard Park, acquired Hay Shed Hill in late 2006 (with co-ownership by the West Cape Howe syndicate) and is now the full-time winemaker. He had every confidence that he could dramatically lift the quality of the wines and has done precisely that. The estate-grown wines are made under the Vineyard, White Label and Block series. The Block series showcases the ultimate site-specific wines, made from separate blocks within the vineyard. The Pitchfork wines are made from contract-grown grapes in the region. Exports to the UK, the US, Denmark, Singapore, Japan, Hong Kong and China.

ŸŸŸŸŸ **Block 2 Margaret River Cabernet Sauvignon 2017** Block 2 has the oldest vines on the vineyard, reflected in the depth of varietal fruit aroma and the palate. It has been singularly well made, drawing out the full array of blackcurrant, bay leaf and black olive fruits. The texture, structure and balance rest on ripe tannins, making a complete wine. Screwcap. 14% alc. **Rating** 97 **To** 2042 $60 ❂

ŸŸŸŸŸ **Block 1 Margaret River Semillon Sauvignon Blanc 2018** Block 1 has some of the oldest semillon and sauvignon blanc vines on the property. It's rare to find such a combination of finesse, elegance, intensity and length. The barrel ferment element is of minor importance but does contribute to this special wine. Screwcap. 11.5% alc. **Rating** 96 **To** 2023 $30 ❂

Block 6 Margaret River Chardonnay 2018 From the coolest block on the vineyard, free-run juice direct to French barrels (35% new), no mlf, no stirring,

11 months on lees. More restrained than most quality chardonnays from the Margaret River, Yarra Valley, etc. Screwcap. 13% alc. **Rating** 96 **To** 2030 $40 ❂

Margaret River Chardonnay 2018 Estate-grown. The bouquet is very pure, pointing to the restraint of the palate where white stone fruit, apple and grapefruit do the talking. It was barrel-fermented, which has left its imprint on both the bouquet and palate. The way the wine has developed to date makes me certain it will grow old with grace, a long way down the track. Great value. Screwcap. 13% alc. **Rating** 95 **To** 2029 $28 ❂

Margaret River Cabernet Sauvignon 2018 Dry-grown estate vineyard, 10 days' open fermentation, pressed to French barriques, some new, for 18 months. Powerful, balanced wine, cabernet tannins a feature, adding to the present and future length. Bargain price. Screwcap. 14.5% alc. **Rating** 95 **To** 2033 $28 ❂

Morrison's Gift 2018 A Bordeaux blend of cabernet sauvignon, cabernet franc, merlot, malbec and petit verdot; the name reflecting the '70s Sussex Vale name change to Hay Shed Hill in '89 when Barry and Liz Morrison purchased, expanded and rehabilitated the vineyard. Matured for 18 months in French barriques, it has excellent balance and length to its blackcurrant fruit flavours. Screwcap. 14% alc. **Rating** 95 **To** 2030 $25 ❂

Margaret River Sauvignon Blanc Semillon 2019 Far more depth than many unoaked SBS blends. The fruit is rich and complex, lychee and guava held in control by grassy/citrus notes ex the semillon and good acidity. Has cellaring capacity if you want. Screwcap. 12.5% alc. **Rating** 94 **To** 2024 $21 ❂

Margaret River Cabernet Merlot 2017 This is a good Margaret River Bordeaux blend. It marries supple, rich blackcurrant fruit with tannins that are manifestly ripe. The overall balance and length are in good company with each other, the price excellent value. Screwcap. 14.5% alc. **Rating** 94 **To** 2030 $22 ❂

Margaret River Malbec 2017 From the Happs Vineyard at Karridale with a seldom used (in Australia) overhead trellis system. Hand-picked, small open fermenters, matured for 12 months in French barriques (20% new). The colour is deep, and the wine full-bodied; a strong savoury shaft penetrating plummy fruit. One to cellar and spring a surprise 20 years down the track. Screwcap. 14.5% alc. **Rating** 94 **To** 2037 $30 ❂

♟♟♟♟♟ Rose 2019 **Rating** 93 **To** 2022 $22 ❂
Pitchfork Pink 2019 **Rating** 91 **To** 2022 $17 ❂
Pitchfork Semillon Sauvignon Blanc 2019 **Rating** 90 **To** 2022 $16 ❂
Pitchfork Shiraz 2018 **Rating** 90 **To** 2021 $17 ❂
Cabernet Merlot 2018 **Rating** 90 **To** 2022 $22

Hayes Family Wines   ★★★★★

102 Mattiske Road, Stone Well, SA 5352 **Region** Barossa Valley
T 0499 096 812 **www**.hayesfamilywines.com **Open** Fri–Sun & public hols 11–5
Winemaker Andrew Seppelt **Est.** 2014 **Dozens** 1000 **Vyds** 5ha
Hayes Family Wines is a small family-owned wine producer nestled among organically farmed vineyards in Stone Well on the western ridge of the Barossa Valley. The Hayes family has 25+ years of agriculture and business experience. Shiraz, Grenache, Mataro and Semillon are produced from the old vineyard in Stone Well, and also from Ebenezer and Koonunga in the northern Barossa.

♟♟♟♟♟ Vineyard Series Primrose Vineyard Barossa Valley Mataro 2019 Sourced from a tiny patch of bushvines dry-grown on the Schulz Vineyard in Ebenezer. An extremely powerful, full-bodied wine that manages to also have a juicy lift and a mix of spicy/earthy tannins. Mataro seldom scales the heights exemplified by this wine in '19. Screwcap. 14% alc. **Rating** 97 **To** 2049 $40 ❂

♟♟♟♟♟ Vineyard Series Primrose Vineyard Barossa Valley Shiraz 2018 The grapes come from a tiny patch high in the hills of the famed Schulz Vineyard in Ebenezer. Full-bodied but with all its components in total harmony, letting

the light shine in on its inherent dark-fruited complexity. Screwcap. 14% alc.
Rating 96 To 2038 $60 ✪

Estate Block 2 Barossa Valley Grenache 2019 Bright colour. A fragrant
wine with lifted fruits and rose petal aromas, then an elegant, light-bodied palate of
red fruits and a waft of spice. The balance is exact, the tannins fine, the finish long.
Only 50 dozen made. Screwcap. 14% alc. Rating 96 To 2027 $40 ✪

**Vineyard Series Glengrae Old Bush Block Barossa Valley Grenache
2019** This is all about contained power reflecting a 'lost' 0.8ha dry-grown block
on an exposed ridge that yielded 750kg of fruit. Its perfumed bouquet foretells a
wine that, while delicate, has a long, lingering palate destined to live for decades.
A gift horse of rare magnitude. Screwcap. 14.4% alc. Rating 96 To 2034 $40 ✪

Winemaker's Selection Barossa Valley Grenache 2018 Made from very old
bushvines in Ebenezer; the wine aged in a ceramic egg for 4 months, thereafter
in old used barrels. It has the immediate savoury freshness of old vines picked at
optimum ripeness; the length too, is excellent. The price seems ridiculously low.
Screwcap. 13.5% alc. Rating 96 To 2030 $40 ✪

Estate Field Blend Barossa Valley Grenache Shiraz Mataro 2019 A true
field blend, grown on the family's organic estate vineyard on the Western ridge.
Vivid, deep crimson-purple. This is a luscious wine of great quality; black and
red fruits swapping places with purple; ripe tannins adding a dimension. Only
75 dozen made. Screwcap. 13.8% alc. Rating 96 To 2035 $40 ✪

Estate Block 3 Barossa Valley Mataro 2019 From the estate vineyard at
Stone Well, sharing the disparate low yields of the vintage, also the power and
concentration. The colour is deep purple-crimson with a bright rim, the bouquet
floral, the palate full-bodied yet with great balance between dark berry fruit, earthy
notes and ripe tannins. Will live for decades. Only 50 dozen made. Screwcap.
14.5% alc. Rating 96 To 2049 $40 ✪

**Vineyard Series Koonunga Creek Block South Barossa Valley Grenache
2019** From an old hand-tended bush block yielding less than 1t/a. Hand-picked,
20 days on skins, 9 months in used French oak. This doesn't attempt to conceal its
power, the deep colour a giveaway. It carries its weight without complaint. Only
50 dozen made. Screwcap. 15% alc. Rating 95 To 2034 $40

Bon Ami Cabernet & Shiraz 2018 A regional and varietal blend of
60% Coonawarra cabernet and 40% Barossa Valley shiraz. Excellent colour; the
Barossa shiraz is from Ebenezer, which explains the power of this component.
Screwcap. 14.4% alc. Rating 95 To 2038 $80

Show Reserve Rare Batch No. 1 Very Old Tawny NV Includes 35% 40yo
tawny, 35% 35yo touriga and 30% 20yo tawny; less than 400 bottles released each
year. The colour change from red to purple is almost complete, the age confirmed
by the bouquet and the palate. It is intense and shows the contribution made by
the oldest components and the youngest. The latter gives the wine its freshness,
the former a sheen of rancio. The wine shouldn't be cellared, for there is no
more complexity to be had. Keep it cool once opened. 500ml. Diam. 20% alc.
Rating 95 $120

Regional Series Barossa Valley Shiraz 2018 The deep crimson-purple
colour waves the flag of a full-bodied shiraz, abounding with black fruits of every
kind. The well of fruit will outdistance the generous tannin and oak contributions.
Screwcap. 13.8% alc. Rating 94 To 2038 $35

Estate Stone Well Block 1 Barossa Valley Shiraz 2018 Bright, full purple-
crimson hue. The wine is nakedly full-bodied, earthy blackberry fruit locked in
combat with ripe but uncompromising tannins. There's oak somewhere in the fray,
but it's hard to detect. The one thing the wine needs is time – lots of it. Screwcap.
14% alc. Rating 94 To 2043 $60

Sam's Barossa Valley Grenache 2019 Positively ripples with muscular power
that is inherent in the wine, not the result of extraction, and has nothing to do

with fruit left on the vine too long. Choose the moment or leave it in the cellar. 165 dozen made. Screwcap. 14.5% alc. **Rating** 94 **To** 2030 $28 ⊙

ŶŶŶŶŶ Barossa Valley Blanc 2019 **Rating** 92 **To** 2025 $35

Head in the Clouds ★★★★

36 Neate Avenue, Belair, SA 5052 **Region** Adelaide Hills
T 0404 440 298 **www.**headinthecloudswines.com **Open** Not
Winemaker Ashley Coats **Est.** 2008 **Dozens** 260
Head in the Clouds is a family-run microbusiness that, by virtue of its size, is able to lavish attention to detail on sourcing its intake of contract-grown grapes and on the vinification of its wines. The wines are distributed statewide by Glenn Beale.

ŶŶŶŶŶ Clare Valley Riesling 2019 The sheer vibrancy and quality make comparisons invidious. The acidity is pure and fine, in no way threatening the lime juice fruit. From a single vineyard in Watervale. 119 dozen made. Screwcap. 12.5% alc. **Rating** 94 **To** 2031 $19 ⊙

ŶŶŶŶŶ GSM 2016 **Rating** 91 **To** 2027 $26
Paeroa Vineyard Mataro 2017 **Rating** 91 **To** 2029 $26
Inkwell Vineyard McLaren Vale Zinfandel 2018 **Rating** 91 **To** 2030 $26

Head Wines ★★★★★

PO Box 58, Tanunda, SA 5352 **Region** Barossa Valley
T 0413 114 233 **www.**headwines.com.au **Open** Feb–Apr by appt
Winemaker Alex Head **Est.** 2006 **Dozens** 10000
Head Wines is the venture of Alex Head. In 1997, he finished a degree in biochemistry from Sydney University. Experience in fine wine stores, importers and an auction house was followed by vintage work at wineries he admired: Tyrrell's, Torbreck, Laughing Jack and Cirillo Estate. The names of the wines reflect his fascination with Côte-Rôtie in the Northern Rhône Valley. The two facing slopes in Côte-Rôtie are known as Côte Blonde and Côte Brune. Head's Blonde comes from an east-facing slope in the Stone Well area, while The Brunette comes from a very low-yielding vineyard in the Moppa area. In each case, open fermentation (with whole bunches) and basket pressing precedes maturation in French oak. Exports to the UK, the US, Denmark, the Netherlands, Singapore and China.

ŶŶŶŶŶ The Redhead Menglers Hill Barossa Shiraz 2018 From 70yo vines, open-fermented with 30% whole bunches, matured in French oak (40% new). The wine has wonderful drive, taking focus and balance on board for the voyage, sailing through fields of purple and black fruits. Screwcap. 14% alc. **Rating** 97 **To** 2040 $100 ⊙
The Brunette Moppa Barossa Shiraz 2017 The soils are red clays with mixed ironstone and quartz; the vineyard has a perfect easterly slope. Open-fermented with 20% skin retention, 2 weeks on skins, matured in French barriques (33% new), 200 dozen made. Deep crimson. Superb mouthfeel and varietal expression are anchored by red and black cherry fruit. Medium to full-bodied, but not heavy. Screwcap. 14.5% alc. **Rating** 97 **To** 2042 $60 ⊙

ŶŶŶŶŶ Head Red Barossa Shiraz 2018 There's a lot happening here, all of it good. Includes 80% sourced from the Eden Valley, 20% from the Barossa Valley; co-fermented on skins for 14 days, matured in French oak (10% new), the barrel size ranging from 225l to 2250l. There's a poultice of red and black fruits and ribbons of fine, ripe tannins. You can't deny a wine like this. Screwcap. 14.5% alc. **Rating** 96 **To** 2038 $25 ⊙
Old Vine Barossa Shiraz 2018 Includes 10% grenache. The old vines range between 35 and 160yo, all situated in the Eden Valley; open-fermented, 14 days on skins, matured in French oak (20% new), 250 dozen made. It is a highly fragrant

wine, the grenache contributing to the fresh red and black cherry fruits. Screwcap. 14.5% alc. **Rating** 96 **To** 2040 $35 ✪

The Blonde Stone Well Barossa Shiraz 2017 The vineyard soil is red clay sand with a deep limestone base, blonde in colour. Open-fermented with 10% stems retained, matured in French oak (30% new), 300 dozen made. Vibrant wine, light to medium-bodied with fresh and vibrant red fruits and silky tannins. Screwcap. 14.5% alc. **Rating** 96 **To** 2037 $50 ✪

Head Red Barossa GSM 2019 A blend of 50% grenache, 30% mataro and 20% shiraz from 25–76yo vines; wild yeast-open fermented with 10% whole bunches, 14 days on skins, daily plunging and pumpovers, 500 dozen made. Beautifully and harmoniously structured and textured; clarity and purity its watchwords. Screwcap. 14.2% alc. **Rating** 96 **To** 2030 $26 ✪

The Blonde Stone Well Barossa Shiraz 2018 The vineyard in Stone Well at 280m practises sustainable farming techniques, including straw mulches. Open-fermented, 100% whole bunch, matured in French oak, 300 dozen made. Delicious surge/uplift on the finish. Screwcap. 14% alc. **Rating** 95 **To** 2033 $50

The Brunette Moppa Barossa Shiraz 2018 Hand-picked, wild-fermented with 20% whole bunches, matured in French barriques (40% new), 200 dozen made. Deep colour. A profound and rich wine – a marriage of elegance and opulence. Screwcap. 13.5% alc. **Rating** 95 **To** 2038 $65

Head Red Barossa Montepulciano 2018 Hand-picked, fermented with some whole bunches, matured in a 23yo 2250l foudre for 12 months. Manages to provide all the fruit one could wish for without any hint of over-extraction. Balance and length are both impeccable in a vintage that wasn't always easy. Screwcap. 13.5% alc. **Rating** 95 **To** 2028 $25 ✪

The Contrarian Barossa Shiraz 2018 From the Eden Valley; hand-picked, open-fermented with 50% whole bunches, matured for 12 months on fine lees in a 2250l 4yo French foudre. Gloriously rich and supple, the medium-bodied palate gives a velvety mouthfeel and some chocolate. Screwcap. 14% alc. **Rating** 94 **To** 2038 $40

🍷🍷🍷🍷🍷 **Cellar Reserve Barossa Shiraz 2018** Rating 93 To 2028 $22 ✪
Head Red Barossa GSM 2018 Rating 93 To 2028 $25 ✪

Heartland Wines   ★★★★

The Winehouse, Wellington Road, Langhorne Creek, SA 5255 **Region** Langhorne Creek
T (08) 8333 1363 **www**.heartlandwines.com.au **Open** 7 days 10–5
Winemaker Ben Glaetzer **Est.** 2001 **Dozens** 50000 **Vyds** 200ha
Heartland is a joint venture of veteran winemakers Ben Glaetzer and Scott Collett. It focuses on cabernet sauvignon and shiraz from Langhorne Creek, with John Glaetzer (Ben's uncle and head winemaker at Wolf Blass for over 30 years) liaising with his network of growers and vineyards. Ben makes the wines at Barossa Vintners. Exports to all major markets.

🍷🍷🍷🍷🍷 **Sposa e Sposa 2016** A blend of 55% lagrein, 45% dolcetto from Langhorne Creek; the lagrein matured in new French hogsheads, the dolcetto in stainless steel. Typical Ben Glaetzer, weaving seductive mouthfeel and flavours for the price of a tram ticket. Screwcap. 14.5% alc. **Rating** 91 **To** 2023 $19 ✪

Langhorne Creek Shiraz 2016 Terrific value for a generous wine with dark berry fruits, a lick of dark chocolate and soft tannins. Drink anywhere, any time. Screwcap. 14.5% alc. **Rating** 90 **To** 2025 $19 ✪

Spice Trader Langhorne Creek Shiraz Cabernet Sauvignon 2016 A 50/50% blend fermented and matured separately in used French and American oak for 12 months. Remarkably fresh and equally good at the price. Screwcap. 14.5% alc. **Rating** 90 **To** 2029 $17 ✪

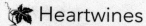

Heartwines ★★★★★

7–9 Keele Street, Collingwood, Vic 3066 **Region** McLaren Vale/Beechworth
T 0408 432 456 **www.**heartandsoil.com.au **Open** Not
Winemaker Peter Fraser, Tessa Brown, Mark Kelly **Est.** 2015 **Dozens** 800
Melbourne wine importer, distributor and retailer Randall Pollard (and partner Paula
Munroe) has friends in many places in the world of wine. Obtaining grapes from the altar of
grenache grown on the high sands of Blewitt Springs and having the high priest Peter Fraser
make the wine is a feat of no mean dimension. And he's got a few more tricks up his sleeve.
Exports to the UK.

ŸŸŸŸŸ **Danger Organic Vines Blewitt Springs Shiraz 2018** The vibrancy and
quality of Blewitt Springs seldom fails to make an above-average wine, this shiraz
among them. Its low alcohol allows the wine extra room for expressing its place
and variety; dark cherry and plum to the fore. The oak (all used except for one
barrel) is yet more of the same. Screwcap. 13.5% alc. **Rating** 95 **To** 2038 $29 ✪
Archie Old Bush Vines Blewitt Springs Grenache 2018 From 70yo
bushvines, wild-fermented as whole berries, matured in used French oak. There is
an exciting freshness to the varietal expression, taking in all things red, making this
a special wine. Screwcap. 13.5% alc. **Rating** 95 **To** 2030 $38
Archie Old Bush Vines Blewitt Springs Grenache 2017 Bright, vibrant and
fresh in every respect: colour, aromas, flavours and tannins; oak out of the action in
flavour terms. This is a wine for drinking, not sipping, nor careful deconstruction/
analysis. Lovely stuff. Screwcap. 14.5% alc. **Rating** 95 **To** 2025 $38

ŸŸŸŸŸ **Victor Central Beechworth Chardonnay 2017 Rating** 93 **To** 2026 $29
Ruby McLaren Vale Rose 2018 Rating 92 **To** 2021 $27
La Biche King Valley Fiano 2018 Rating 91 **To** 2022 $29

Heathcote Estate ★★★★★

Drummonds Lane, Heathcote, Vic 3523 (postal) **Region** Heathcote
T (03) 5974 3729 **www.**yabbylake.com **Open** Not
Winemaker Tom Carson, Chris Forge, Luke Lomax **Est.** 1999 **Dozens** 5000 **Vyds** 34ha
Heathcote Estate and Yabby Lake Vineyard are owned by the Kirby family of Village
Roadshow Ltd. They purchased a prime piece of Heathcote red Cambrian soil in 1999,
planting shiraz (30ha) and grenache (4ha). The wines are matured exclusively in French oak.
The arrival of the hugely talented Tom Carson as group winemaker has added lustre to the
winery and its wines. Exports to the US, the UK, Canada, Sweden, Singapore, Hong Kong
and China.

ŸŸŸŸŸ **Single Vineyard Shiraz 2018** Full crimson-purple; a medium to full-bodied
palate, remarkable given its modest alcohol; flavours of cherry and plum within
a palisade of neatly controlled tannin and French oak. Screwcap. 13.5% alc.
Rating 95 **To** 2033 $50

Heathcote II ★★★

290 Cornella-Toolleen Road, Toolleen, Vic 3551 **Region** Heathcote
T (03) 5433 6292 **www.**heathcote2.com **Open** W'ends 11–5 or by appt
Winemaker Peder Rosdal **Est.** 1995 **Dozens** 500 **Vyds** 6.5ha
This is the venture of Danish-born, French-trained Flying Winemaker (California, Spain and
Chablis) Peder Rosdal and viticulturist Lionel Flutto. The establishment of the vineyard dates
back to 1995, with further plantings since of shiraz (with the lion's share of 2.7ha), cabernet
sauvignon, cabernet franc, merlot, tempranillo and grenache. The vines are dry-grown on the
famed red Cambrian soil. The wines are made onsite using hand-plunging, basket pressing and
(since 2004) French oak maturation. Exports to Denmark, Japan and Singapore.

ŸŸŸŸ **Tempranillo 2016** Wow! What a difference a degree or so of alcohol makes.
Still firmly of the smudgy dark fruit, mocha and bitter chocolate mould, this
is altogether lighter, more fragrant and far, far easier to drink. Cork. 14% alc.
Rating 89 **To** 2023 $39 NG

Heathcote Winery ★★★★☆

185 High Street, Heathcote, Vic 3523 **Region** Heathcote
T (03) 5433 2595 **www**.heathcotewinery.com.au **Open** 7 days 10–5
Winemaker Rachel Gore **Est.** 1978 **Dozens** 8000 **Vyds** 11ha

The cellar door of Heathcote Winery is situated in the main street of Heathcote, housed in a restored miner's cottage built by Thomas Craven in 1854 to cater for the huge influx of gold miners. The winery is immediately behind the cellar door. The first vintage was processed in 1983, following the planting of the vineyards in '78. Shiraz and Shiraz Viognier account for 90% of the production.

ⵝⵝⵝⵝⵝ **Slaughterhouse Paddock Single Vineyard Shiraz 2018** This struts its stuff with ease, from the bold, ripe flavours with a hint of regional bay leaf to the full-bodied palate doused in charry/sweet oak. Plump ripe tannins soften the edges. Screwcap. 14.5% alc. **Rating** 93 **To** 2030 $55 JF

Mail Coach Shiraz 2018 Dark fruits, spicy with a flash of Heathcote bracken and herbs. It's not too big, the tannins firm yet ripe with a fresh acid line keeping it lively. Well played. Screwcap. 14.5% alc. **Rating** 91 **To** 2028 $35 JF

Heathvale ★★★★★

300 Saw Pit Gully Road, via Keyneton, SA 5353 **Region** Eden Valley
T 0407 600 487 **www**.heathvale.com **Open** By appt
Winemaker Trevor March, Tony Carapetis (Consultant) **Est.** 1987 **Dozens** 1200
Vyds 7.8ha

The origins of Heathvale go back to 1865, when William Heath purchased the property, building the homestead and establishing the vineyard. The wine was initially made in the cellar of the house, which still stands on the property (now occupied by owners Trevor and Faye March). The vineyards were re-established in 1987 and consisted of shiraz, cabernet sauvignon, riesling, sagrantino and tempranillo. Between 2011 and '12 fundamental changes for the better took place – stylish new labels are but an outward sign of the far more important changes to wine style, with the winemaking now under the control of consultant Tony Carapetis (Quattro Mano) and the introduction of French oak. There are now 4.5ha of chardonnay, 4ha shiraz, 2ha cabernet sauvignon, 1.3ha riesling and 0.5ha sangiovese (1ha of tempranillo is planned to be replaced with shiraz in '20). Exports to China.

ⵝⵝⵝⵝⵝ **The Reward Eden Valley Barossa Shiraz 2018** The reward for the rejuvenation of the entire vineyard. Deeply robed in colour, it is full-bodied but keeps a sense of place (and balance). The fine-grained tannins and quality French oak (30% new) add to the lustre of a fine return to the *Wine Companion*. Screwcap. 15% alc. **Rating** 95 **To** 2038 $50

The Encounter Eden Valley Barossa Cabernet Sauvignon 2018 Cold-soaked, wild yeast with co-inoculation of mlf yeast, basket-pressed to French oak (30% new), no fining. There are whispers of McLaren Vale and Langhorne Creek to accompany the main tune of dark blackcurrant and tapenade fruit. Screwcap. 14.5% alc. **Rating** 95 **To** 2038 $50

The Encounter Eden Valley Barossa Cabernet Sauvignon 2016 The packaging of this range of Heathvale wines is very stylish, even if not informative. The fruit was perfectly ripe, the tannins likewise, blackcurrant and olive tapenade mouthfilling. The length and overall balance and mouthfeel can't be faulted. Screwcap. 13.5% alc. **Rating** 95 **To** 2033 $50

The Belief Eden Valley Sagrantino 2018 Sagrantino was grafted onto 34yo chardonnay, the vines netted to prevent bird damage. Heathvale reds are always picked by hand in 1–2t lots for quality control. Matured in French oak. This is the only sagrantino that I've tasted that has good mouthfeel, structure and ripe red and purple fruits. Screwcap. 14.5% alc. **Rating** 94 **To** 2029 $45

ⵝⵝⵝⵝⵝ **Estate Barossa Cabernet Sauvignon 2018** Rating 93 **To** 2030 $27
The Belief Eden Valley Sagrantino 2017 Rating 93 **To** 2030 $45

Hedonist Wines

Rifle Range Road, McLaren Vale, SA 5171 **Region** McLaren Vale
T (08) 8323 8818 **www.**hedonistwines.com.au **Open** Not
Winemaker Walter Clappis, Kimberly Cooter, James Cooter **Est.** 1982 **Dozens** 18 000
Vyds 35ha

Walter Clappis has been making wine in McLaren Vale for 40 years, and over that time
has won innumerable trophies and gold medals, including the prestigious George Mackey
Memorial Trophy with his 2009 The Hedonist Shiraz, chosen as the best wine exported from
Australia that year. He now has daughter Kimberly and son-in-law James Cooter (both with
impressive CVs) supporting him on the winery floor. The estate plantings of shiraz, cabernet
sauvignon, tempranillo and grenache are the cornerstones of the business. Exports include the
UK, the US, Canada, Singapore, Thailand and China.

ŶŶŶŶŶ **The Hedonist McLaren Vale Sangiovese 2018** Ooh la la! The wrong
vernacular, perhaps, but this is joyous! A celebration of all that is – and can be –
with this cantankerous, voluminous variety. And when it is good, it is lip-smacking
and delicious. Few other red grape varieties facilltate so many dining options.
A curb of frisky tannin and curl of herb offset sour cherry and bergamot notes.
Crunchy. Long. Really delicious, based on saliva-sucking succulence alone. Ready
for the next glass? I am! Screwcap. **Rating** 94 **To** 2023 $25 NG ✪

ŶŶŶŶ♀ **The Hedonist Shiraz 2018 Rating** 93 **To** 2024 $25 NG ✪
Ecology Shiraz 2018 Rating 92 **To** 2023 $35 NG
The Hedonist Cabernet Sauvignon 2018 Rating 92 **To** 2026 $25 NG ✪
The Hedonist Tempranillo 2019 Rating 92 **To** 2024 $25 NG ✪
Grenache 2018 Rating 91 **To** 2023 $35 NG

Heggies Vineyard

Heggies Range Road, Eden Valley, SA 5235 **Region** Eden Valley
T (08) 8561 3200 **www.**heggiesvineyard.com **Open** By appt
Winemaker Teresa Heuzenroeder **Est.** 1971 **Dozens** 15 000 **Vyds** 62ha

Heggies was the second of the high-altitude (570m) vineyards established by the Hill-
Smith family. Plantings on the 120ha former grazing property began in 1973; the principal
varieties are riesling, chardonnay, viognier and merlot. There are also two special plantings: a
1.1ha reserve chardonnay block and 27ha of various clonal trials. Exports to all major markets.

ŶŶŶŶŶ **Estate Eden Valley Riesling 2019** It's rather shy. Delicate aromas and flavours:
a hint of citrus, spice and florals with the finest acid line. This will unfurl in time,
and it will be worth the wait (although it's perfectly understandable to want a glass
now). Screwcap. 11.5% alc. **Rating** 95 **To** 2029 $26 JF ✪
Single Block Estate Vineyard Reserve Eden Valley Chardonnay 2017
It's pleasing to have some shape here. It's still tight, but there's fruit flavour. Splashes
of lemon, mandarin peel and a dash of ginger spice. It's delicately floral too. Oak
is seamlessly integrated, with enough funky sulphides to warrant a disco move.
Screwcap. 13.5% alc. **Rating** 95 **To** 2028 $50 JF
Eden Valley Botrytis Riesling 2019 Offers delight with every sip. It balances
gorgeous flavours of lemon drops, lemon barley cordial and ginger spice with
wafts of honeysuckle. The botrytis flavours are subtle, acidity the key to balancing
sweetness. 375ml. Screwcap. 10.5% alc. **Rating** 95 **To** 2025 $28 JF ✪

ŶŶŶŶ♀ **Estate Eden Valley Riesling 2018 Rating** 92 **To** 2028 $26 JF
Estate Eden Valley Chardonnay 2018 Rating 90 **To** 2027 $31 JF
Single Block Estate Vineyard Reserve Eden Valley Chardonnay 2016
Rating 90 **To** 2028 $50 JF

Heifer Station

PO Box 5082, Orange, NSW 2800 **Region** Orange
T 0407 621 150 **www**.heiferstation.com **Open** 7 days 11–5
Winemaker Daniel Shaw, Nadja Wallington **Est.** 1999 **Dozens** 450 **Vyds** 24.3ha
Founders Phillip and Michelle Stivens both grew up on the land but spent over 25 years in
the corporate world: Phillip as owner-operator of real estate offices in Parkes and Orange,
Michelle working in the Attorney-General's Department. When their five adult children left
the nest, they decided to retire to the land and grow fat cattle. When Heifer Station, a property
Phillip had admired for years, came onto the market they did not hesitate to purchase it. There
was an existing 25ha vineyard, planted in 1998, barely visible through the blackberries, and
their intention was to remove the vines. But locals argued they should not do so, pointing to
the ideal soils: red loam over limestone. After much contemplation, they agreed to give the
vineyard a go and it has indeed proved its worth. In January 2016 they opened a cellar door,
housed in a 100-year-old woolshed on the property.

ŸŸŸŸŸ **Single Vineyard Orange Shiraz 2018** Whole berries wild-fermented, matured
for 12 months in French oak (30% new). A lively medium-bodied palate with
a sprinkle of pepper and spices. Well made, high quality outcome. Screwcap.
14.5% alc. **Rating** 90 **To** 2028 $45

Heirloom Vineyards

PO Box 39, McLaren Vale, SA 5171 **Region** Adelaide zone
T (08) 8323 8979 **www**.heirloomvineyards.com.au **Open** Not
Winemaker Elena Brooks **Est.** 2004 **Dozens** NFP
This is (yet another) venture for Zar Brooks and his wife Elena. They met during the
2000 vintage and one thing led to another, as they say. Dandelion Vineyards and Zonte's
Footstep came along first, and continue, but other partners are involved in those ventures. The
lofty aims of Heirloom are 'to preserve the best of tradition, the unique old vineyards of SA,
and to champion the best clones of each variety, embracing organic and biodynamic farming'.
The quality of the wines has been consistently very good. Exports to all major markets.

ŸŸŸŸŸ **A'Lambra Eden Valley Shiraz 2017** Exceptionally powerful, rich and full-
bodied shiraz with multiple layers of black fruits, tar, licorice and full-on, but
ripe, tannins. Striking, potentially long-lived style. Screwcap. 14.5% alc. **Rating** 96
To 2047 $80
Alcazar Castle Adelaide Hills Pinot Noir 2019 This producer's highest
quality Adelaide Hills fruit; bunch-sorted, naturally open-fermented, matured in
seasoned first use French barriques and finally a barrel selection of the best. It's
an impressive wine. Powerful varietal aromas and intensely cedary oak on the
bouquet; and a silky, supple palate with depth and length of flavour. Should age
very well too. Screwcap. 13.5% alc. **Rating** 95 **To** 2031 $80 SC
Eden Valley Riesling 2018 Attractive wine, citrus surrounding a core of
tropical/passionfruit at its heart. The acidity is on the money, freshening the finish
without smothering the fruit. Screwcap. 11.5% alc. **Rating** 94 **To** 2030 $30 ✪

ŸŸŸŸŸ **Eden Valley Riesling 2019 Rating** 93 **To** 2034 $30 SC
Alcala McLaren Vale Grenache 2018 Rating 93 **To** 2023 $80
Coonawarra Cabernet Sauvignon 2017 Rating 93 **To** 2030 $40 SC
Adelaide Hills Sauvignon Blanc 2019 Rating 92 **To** 2022 $30 SC
Adelaide Hills Pinot Grigio 2019 Rating 92 **To** 2022 $30 SC
The Velvet Fog Adelaide Hills Pinot Noir 2018 Rating 91 **To** 2023 $40 SC
Anevo Fortress McLaren Vale Grenache Touriga Tempranillo 2018
Rating 91 **To** 2026 $80

Helen & Joey Estate   ★★★★☆

12–14 Spring Lane, Gruyere, Vic 3770 **Region** Yarra Valley
T 1800 989 463 **www.**helenandjoeyestate.com.au **Open** 7 days 10–5
Winemaker Meg Brodtmann MW **Est.** 2011 **Dozens** 20 000 **Vyds** 23.81ha
This is the venture of Helen Xu, who purchased the large Fernando Vineyard on Spring Lane in 2010. It is planted to pinot noir, cabernet sauvignon, merlot, chardonnay, pinot gris, shiraz and sauvignon blanc. Helen's background is quite varied. She has a Masters degree in analytical chemistry and was a QA manager for Nestlé for several years. She now owns a business in Shanghai, working with textile ink development together with husband Joey. They currently split their time between China and Australia. Exports to the US, Singapore, Japan and China.

♟♟♟♟♟ **Alena Single Vineyard Yarra Valley Chardonnay 2018** Hand-picked, whole-bunch pressed, a slow wild ferment in French puncheons, full lees retained. The wine has excellent texture and structure; mouth-watering pink grapefruit and white peach providing emphatic fruit through to the finish. Screwcap. 12.5% alc. Rating 96 To 2030 $50 ✪

♟♟♟♟♡ **Wayward Child Ilion 2018** Rating 92 To 2023 $35
Layla Single Vineyard Yarra Valley Chardonnay 2018 Rating 92 To 2025 $35
Alena Single Vineyard Yarra Valley Pinot Noir 2018 Rating 92 To 2027 $50
Inara Yarra Valley Pinot Noir 2019 Rating 90 To 2025 $25
Wayward Child Serendip 2018 Rating 90 To 2030 $50

Helen's Hill Estate   ★★★★★

16 Ingram Road, Lilydale, Vic 3140 **Region** Yarra Valley
T (03) 9739 1573 **www.**helenshill.com.au **Open** 7 days 10–5
Winemaker Scott McCarthy **Est** 1984 **Dozens** 15 000 **Vyds** 53ha
Helen's Hill Estate is named after the previous owner of the property, Helen Fraser. Venture partners Andrew and Robyn McIntosh and Roma and Allan Nalder combined childhood farming experience with more recent careers in medicine and finance to establish and manage the day-to-day operations of the estate. It produces two labels: Helen's Hill Estate and Ingram Rd, both made onsite. Scott McCarthy started his career early by working vintages during school holidays before gaining diverse and extensive experience in the Barossa and Yarra valleys, Napa Valley, Languedoc, the Loire Valley and Marlborough. The winery, cellar door complex and elegant 140-seat restaurant command some of the best views in the valley. Exports to the Maldives, Hong Kong and China.

♟♟♟♟♟ **The Smuggler Single Clone Yarra Valley Pinot Noir 2017** The magic of the cool '17 vintage suggests some whole bunch when in fact none was used. Savoury complexity creates drive and intensity, spicy/foresty notes to the fore, and linger long on the finish and aftertaste. I love this style of pinot. Screwcap. 12.8% alc. Rating 97 To 2033 $60 ✪

♟♟♟♟♟ **Breachley Block Single Vineyard Yarra Valley Chardonnay 2018** Intense and powerful. Layers of white peach, cashew and pink grapefruit fill the mouth. Has immaculate balance and all the length expected of a high class Yarra Valley chardonnay. Development is assured. Screwcap. 12.8% alc. Rating 95 To 2029 $35 ✪
Long Walk Single Vineyard Yarra Valley Pinot Noir 2019 A rich and deep pinot with satsuma plum the dominant player, promising much for the future as spicy notes build. The tannin and oak management (9 months in French puncheons, 30% new) is spot on. Screwcap. 13.1% alc. Rating 95 To 2032 $35 ✪

Helm ★★★★★

19 Butt's Road, Murrumbateman, NSW 2582 **Region** Canberra District
T (02) 6227 5953 **www.**helmwines.com.au **Open** Thurs–Mon 10–5
Winemaker Ken Helm, Stephanie Helm **Est.** 1973 **Dozens** 6000 **Vyds** 12ha
Ken Helm celebrated his 44th vintage in 2020. Over the years he has achieved many things,
through dogged persistence on the one hand, vision on the other. Riesling has been an all-
consuming interest, ultimately rewarded with rieslings of consistently high quality. He has also
given much to the broader wine community, extending from the narrow focus of the Canberra
District to the broad canvas of the international world of riesling: in '00 he established the
Canberra International Riesling Challenge. He retired as Chairman in '16, but keeps an active
eye on the Challenge. In '14 his youngest child Stephanie (and husband Ben Osborne, Helm's
vineyard manager) purchased Yass Valley Wines, rebranding it as The Vintner's Daughter (see
separate entry). He also persuaded Stephanie to join him as winemaker at Helm. In '17 Helm
completed construction of a separate 40000l insulated winery with a double-refrigeration
system dedicated to the production of riesling, the old winery now producing cabernet
sauvignon. Exports to the UK.

ỹỹỹỹỹ **Premium Canberra District Riesling 2019** Slightly deeper colour than its
siblings and the flavour dial is set, waiting to lift off once all the jigsaw pieces have
been put in their due place. Then there's a magic carpet ride as all the citrus fruits
run their course through to the finish and aftertaste. Screwcap. 11% alc. **Rating** 96
To 2034 $58 ✪
Classic Dry Canberra District Riesling 2019 In one sense 'classic dry' says it
all. Freshness and a hint of Granny Smith apple texture built around firm, crunchy
acidity that exponentially increases the length of the back-palate and finish.
Screwcap. 11% alc. **Rating** 95 To 2029 $38
Premium Canberra District Cabernet Sauvignon 2017 From the
Lustenberger Vineyard, matured for 2 years in oak, this a selection of the best
barrels. It has ripe cassis/blackcurrant fruit with no hint of mint or green notes.
It is medium-bodied and has effortless length, the tannins adding to the quality.
Screwcap. 13.5% alc. **Rating** 95 To 2037 $70
Tumbarumba Riesling 2019 There's a blend of Meyer lemon and a
counterbalance of passionfruit flower, the acidity moulded into the fruit flavours.
It's very different but has been part of the Helm range since '12. Screwcap.
11% alc. **Rating** 94 To 2030 $30 ✪
Canberra District Cabernet Sauvignon 2017 This vintage saw some of the
best cabernets made to date by Helm, this not far behind the Premium. It is (only)
medium-bodied with ripe blackcurrant fruit, a nice touch of ripe tannins and a
twitch of oak. Screwcap. 13.5% alc. **Rating** 94 To 2030 $40

ỹỹỹỹỹ **Central Ranges Orange Riesling 2019** **Rating** 93 To 2027 $30

Hemera Estate ★★★★★

1516 Barossa Valley Way, Lyndoch, SA 5351 **Region** Barossa Valley
T (08) 8524 4033 **www.**hemeraestate.com.au **Open** 7 days 10–5
Winemaker Jason Barrette **Est.** 1999 **Dozens** 20000 **Vyds** 44ha
Hemera Estate was originally founded by Darius and Pauline Ross in 1999 as Ross Estate
Wines. The name change came about in 2012 after the business was sold to Winston Wine.
This purchase also saw renewed investment in the winery, vineyard and tasting room, and a
focus on consistently producing high quality wines. Running very much on an estate basis, the
winery and tasting room are located on the 44ha vineyard in the southern Barossa Valley; it's
planted to 11 varieties, with blocks of old vine grenache (105yo) and riesling (48yo). Exports
to China.

ỹỹỹỹỹ **JDR Barossa Valley Shiraz 2017** From the estate and trusted growers, this
flagship wine is only made in exceptional years such as '17. Destemmed and
crushed, open-fermented with manual pumpovers, towards the end of maturation
the wine drained and pressed to new French and American barrels for 17 months

maturation, then the best barrels selected. This is a stealth bomber, its rainbow of black fruits and seasonings from all sides refusing to be ejected once the tasting process was complete. Screwcap. 14.3% alc. **Rating** 98 **To** 2057 $120 **○**

Limited Release Home Block Barossa Valley Shiraz 2017 Exclusively sourced from the estate Block 3A, vinification identical to its siblings with one exception: it is matured in predominantly new French oak, and I find the result perfect. Glossy black cherry and blackberry fruit take centre stage, oak left to the sides in a very good support role. Screwcap. 14.5% alc. **Rating** 97 **To** 2037 $60 **○**

ΨΨΨΨΨ **Limited Release Aurora Barossa Valley Shiraz 2017** From selected vineyards in the northern Barossa Valley, the vinification identical to its more expensive siblings. The bouquet is a tribute to the oak. As with all these top Hemera wines, not fined or filtered. It has an edge to its power, adding to the mouthfeel. Screwcap. 14.5% alc. **Rating** 96 **To** 2046 $80

Barossa Valley Shiraz 2017 Destemmed and crushed into open fermenters, manual pumpovers twice-daily, 20 months in 56% new French and American oak. A wine of energy, focus and length, with lovely spicy/savoury notes from the fruit and oak. Great balance from a respectful winemaking approach. Screwcap. 14.5% alc. **Rating** 95 **To** 2043 $40

Limited Release Coonawarra Cabernet Sauvignon 2017 Fruit from Katnook Estate; destemmed/crushed and open-fermented, matured for 17 months in 77% new French oak; the final wine a barrel selection. The first sniff takes you to Coonawarra straight away with it's distinctive choc-mint character, cedary oak providing a backdrop. It's quite plush, but structured and long. Will age well. Screwcap. 13.5% alc. **Rating** 95 **To** 2032 $80 SC

Limited Release Coonawarra Barossa Valley Cabernet Shiraz 2017 Pays homage to Australia's greatest red wine – 1962 Penfolds Bin A. This is a 57.5/42.5% blend, with 77% new French and American oak. While there's a lot of oak, it has the drive, energy and length of the '17 vintage that will carry it forward for years, while the oak settles down. Screwcap. 13.7% alc. **Rating** 95 **To** 2037 $80

ΨΨΨΨΩ **Barossa Valley Cabernet Sauvignon 2017** **Rating** 93 **To** 2032 $40

Henschke ★★★★★

1428 Keyneton Road, Keyneton, SA 5353 **Region** Eden Valley
T (08) 8564 8223 **www**.henschke.com.au **Open** Mon–Sat 9–4.30
Winemaker Stephen Henschke **Est.** 1868 **Dozens** 30 000 **Vyds** 109ha
Henschke is the foremost medium-sized wine producer in Australia. Stephen and Prue Henschke have taken a crown jewel and polished it to an even greater brilliance. In this 2021 edition of the *Wine Companion*, it has a staggering six wines with 97–99 points, and a further 13 with 95–96 points. Year on year they have quietly added labels for single vineyards, single varieties or blends. The wines hail from the Eden Valley (the majority), the Barossa Valley or the Adelaide Hills. There's a compelling logic and focus – no excursions to McLaren Vale, Coonawarra, etc. There are now four wines from the Hill of Grace Vineyard: the icon itself, Hill of Roses (also shiraz), Hill of Peace (semillon) and Hill of Faith (mataro); the last two are only made in exceptional years. Recognition as Winery of the Year is arguably long overdue. Exports to all major markets.

ΨΨΨΨΨ **Hill of Grace 2015** Henschke says the '15 vintage provided stunning and elegant Eden Valley shiraz with extraordinary flavours, purity of fruit and acid balance. And indeed that's a fair description of this medium-bodied Hill of Grace. The colour is still bright, clear crimson-purple, and the beautifully balanced fruit flavours are vibrantly fresh. It would be easy to underestimate the likely longevity of this wine. One of the all-time greats. Vino-Lok. 14.5% alc. **Rating** 99 **To** 2045 $865

Hill of Roses 2016 The vines were 26yo in '16, too young for inclusion in Hill of Grace, notwithstanding its undoubted quality; matured for 14 months in French hogsheads (30% new). There's not a single hair out of place in a perfectly framed,

medium-bodied shiraz. Bred in the purple. Vino–Lok. 14.5% alc. **Rating** 98
To 2046 $390

Tappa Pass Vineyard Selection Barossa Shiraz 2017 Very good colour; the
cool vintage has produced a finely wrought, intense and powerful wine with a
special array of forest berry/dark spices and hints of sweet earth. The palate is very
long and persistent, and has perfect balance of fruit, oak and tannins. Vino–Lok.
14.5% alc. **Rating** 97 **To** 2042 $115 ✪

Mount Edelstone 2016 The vineyard was planted in 1912; hand-picked,
matured in 80% French and 20% American hogsheads (19% new). The vintage
was challenging but this shiraz shows no sign of that. The wine is full-bodied,
very complex and very long; the tannins expertly massaged and drawn under the
fruit. Blackberry, tar and bitter dark chocolate all contribute to what will be a very
long-lived wine. Screwcap. 14.5% alc. **Rating** 97 **To** 2051 $225

The Wheelwright Vineyard 2016 From the estate Eden Valley vineyard. It is
medium to full-bodied and fast out of the box in revealing wild blackberry fruits
with a savoury/bramble backdrop. Oak has been a means to an end, the taste
minimal, leaving room for ripe tannins to complete the picture of yet another high
quality shiraz. Vino–Lok. 14.5% alc. **Rating** 97 **To** 2046 $130 ✪

Cyril Henschke 2016 Some of the vines were planted by Cyril Henschke in the
'60s. Matured in French hogsheads (35% new) for 18 months. Deep but brightly
coloured. This is a no holds barred, full-bodied Eden Valley cabernet sauvignon
that will live for decades, blessed by a screwcap. Blackcurrant fruit, touches of
cedary oak, black olive, bay leaf and earthy tannins are all on parade. 14.5% alc.
Rating 97 **To** 2046 $165

ꙮꙮꙮꙮꙮ **Julius Eden Valley Riesling 2019** The perfumed citrus and apple blossom
bouquet wastes no time in catching attention with its promise of juicy, citrus-
accented fruit on the long, even palate – which it duly delivers. No surprise it
won gold medals at the Adelaide and Barossa wine shows in '19. Great now,
it will be better still 5+ years down the track. Screwcap. 11.5% alc. **Rating** 96
To 2034 $45 ✪

Apple Tree Bench 2016 A blend of 52% Eden Valley shiraz, 48% Barossa Valley
cabernet; matured in 71% French and 29% American hogsheads (16% new) for
18 months. This over-delivers in terms of its satin and velvet mouthfeel and the
celebration of the blackberry, blackcurrant and cherry fruits. The balance and
length will repay cellaring if you are looking for a wine with a long life that will
please whenever you choose to drink it. Screwcap. 14.5% alc. **Rating** 96 **To** 2046
$70 ✪

Abbotts Prayer Vineyard 2018 A blend of 57% merlot, 43% cabernet
sauvignon; matured in French hogsheads (10% new) for 18 months. This is a
particularly enjoyable Abbotts Prayer. The seamless union of merlot and cabernet
translating as a perfectly balanced juicy stream of red and blackcurrant fruit; oak
and tannins there or thereabouts, but no more. Screwcap. 14.5% alc. **Rating** 96
To 2038 $105

Cyril Henschke 2015 To be precise, includes 1% cabernet franc; matured
in French hogsheads (20% new) for 18 months. An almost monastic portrait
of cabernet, the power of the fruit making the oak and tannin contributions
(relatively) unimportant. Blackcurrant, bramble, blackberry and black olive are the
lead players. Screwcap. 14.5% alc. **Rating** 96 **To** 2045 $165

Green's Hill Adelaide Hills Riesling 2018 Intense high quality riesling with
no winemaking tricks (simply cold-fermented in stainless steel), but given a
saloon car ride by its low pH (3.07) and titratable acidity (6.84g/l), balanced with
12.5% alcohol. It has length and balance, but it's the combination of lime juice,
green apple and slate that makes the wine. Screwcap. **Rating** 95 **To** 2038 $35 ✪

Hill of Peace 2015 Planted by fourth-generation Louis Henschke in '52 on the
Hill of Grace Vineyard; matured for 9 months in used barriques. There is no use
comparing it to other Australian semillons; this is out on its own and is incredibly
good. The real question is how many years/decades will pass before it reaches
optimum maturity. Screwcap. 12% alc. **Rating** 95 **To** 2045 $60

Percival's Mill Adelaide Hills Gruner Veltliner 2019 A cut above most Australian gruner veltliners, and many from overseas. It has totally delicious, sea breeze-fresh flavours that dance along the palate with tinker bells of acidity keeping the party going. I'm going to taste some more tonight to reassure myself it's as good as I think it is right now. Screwcap. 12% alc. **Rating** 95 **To** 2023 $38

Hill of Roses 2015 From the Hill of Grace Vineyard; matured in French hogsheads (55% new) for 18 months. It oozes high quality shiraz fruit from every pore, but this is for the long run. The oak is presently a little too much of a good thing and goes close to smothering the fruit – give it 5–10 years and it will be a stunning wine. Vino-Lok. 14.5% alc. **Rating** 95 **To** 2048 $390

Keyneton Euphonium 2016 Matured in French and American hogsheads (18% new) for 18 months. The bouquet does indeed bellow from the glass like that euphonium. It has a swag of red, black and purple fruits all in tune. Something very different for drinking now. Screwcap. 14.5% alc. **Rating** 95 **To** 2026 $60

Keyneton Euphonium 2015 A blend of 66% shiraz, 19% cabernet sauvignon, 10% merlot and 5% cabernet franc; matured in French hogsheads (20% new) for 18 months, the grapes picked over 2 months. It's a fragrant, elegant wine; the fruit flavours akin to piano keys; a fine web of tannins and oak completing the picture. Screwcap. 14.5% alc. **Rating** 95 **To** 2035 $60

Abbotts Prayer Vineyard 2016 A 76/24% blend of cabernet sauvignon and merlot from the Adelaide Hills estate vineyard; matured in French hogsheads (20% new) for 18 months. The vines flourished in the warmer vintage, as might be expected, providing a wine of excellent depth and structure; the flavours of blackcurrant/cassis intermingling with savoury herbal notes. Vino-Lok. 14.5% alc. **Rating** 95 **To** 2041 $105

Marble Angel Vineyard Cabernet Sauvignon 2014 Matured in French hogsheads (28% new) for 18 months. While the wine still has a long way to go, some of the tannins have softened and hints of violets and gentle spices add to the bouquet. It should really open up as it nears its 10th birthday. Vino-Lok. 14% alc. **Rating** 95 **To** 2034 $75

The Rose Grower Eden Valley Nebbiolo 2015 Classic rose petal, powder puff and spice aromas swirl around on the bouquet, the palate providing more of the same until the finish and aftertaste when tannins appear. They provide an essential framework for the wine, giving it the ability to stand up to virtually any dish, especially Italian. Vino-Lok. 13.5% alc. **Rating** 95 **To** 2031 $50

Five Shillings 2018 A 70/30% blend of shiraz and mataro; matured in used French (78%) and American (22%) hogsheads for 8 months. This a delicious medium-bodied wine with fresh, supple fruit flavours of spice, licorice and juicy red and blue jujube. Screwcap. 14.5% alc. **Rating** 94 **To** 2028 $33

Henry's Seven 2018 Includes 67% shiraz, 17% grenache, 10% mataro and 6% viognier from the Eden and Barossa valleys. Shiraz/viognier dominates the blend, but does so without bluster – indeed this is a wine with javelin-like linearity that is from fruit and acid, not tannins or oak. This could be a sleeper, stealing the show in 10+ years. Screwcap. 14.5% alc. **Rating** 94 **To** 2038 $37

Henry's Seven 2017 Includes 73% shiraz, 17% grenache and 5% each of mataro and viognier. The wine has a zesty freshness that is normally associated with white wines, but without any suggestion of green fruit, just the vintage. There's every reason to drink this now while its bigger brothers go through their limbering up exercises. Screwcap. 14.5% alc. **Rating** 94 **To** 2027 $37

ȲȲȲȲȲ **Giles Adelaide Hills Pinot Noir 2017** **Rating** 93 **To** 2022 $55
Croft Adelaide Hills Chardonnay 2017 **Rating** 92 **To** 2027 $50
Innes Vineyard Littlehampton Adelaide Hills Pinot Gris 2018 **Rating** 92 **To** 2021 $37
Peggy's Hill Eden Valley Riesling 2019 **Rating** 91 **To** 2026 $25 CM
Croft Adelaide Hills Chardonnay 2018 **Rating** 90 **To** 2027 $50
Archer's Vineyard Adelaide Hills Chardonnay 2017 **Rating** 90 **To** 2022 $35
The Alan Lenswood Pinot Noir 2015 **Rating** 90 **To** 2025 $93

Henskens Rankin of Tasmania ★★★★

PO Box 67, Sandy Bay, Tas 7005 **Region** Southern Tasmania
T (03) 6288 8508 **www**.henskensrankin.com **Open** Tues–Sat 10–2 by appt
Winemaker Frieda Henskens, Keira O'Brien **Est.** 2010 **Dozens** 275

Sparkling specialist Henskens Rankin of Tasmania was founded in 2010 while working for a local contract winemaker (now Tasmanian Vintners) with the aim of exploring distinctive Tasmanian styles of sparkling wine. That working relationship has continued for the Vintage Brut (limited releases of 2500 bottles), which spends a minimum of 6 years on yeast lees. Frieda makes the other wines elsewhere in tiny batches, typically fermented with wild yeast in barrels, they may also undergo wild tirage and wild malolactic fermentation in bottle and/or tirage with residual grape sugar. These wines also find their way into the Vintage Brut blend.

🍷🍷🍷🍷🍷 Brut Rose 2013 Bottle no. 193/830. A 50/50% blend of chardonnay and pinot noir, disgorged Jun '19. Pale salmon-pink; the white peach of the chardonnay and the wild strawberry of the pinot are joined in vinous holy matrimony. Such dosage as there was is hidden in the satin of the fruit. Lovely wine. Diam. 13.4% alc. **Rating** 96 $95

Hentley Farm Wines

Cnr Jenke Road/Gerald Roberts Road, Seppeltsfield, SA 5355 **Region** Barossa Valley
T (08) 8562 8427 **www**.hentleyfarm.com.au **Open** 7 days 11–5
Winemaker Andrew Quin **Est.** 1999 **Dozens** 20 000 **Vyds** 44.7ha

Keith and Alison Hentschke purchased Hentley Farm in 1997, as a mixed farming property with an old vineyard. Keith has thoroughly impressive credentials, having studied agricultural science at Roseworthy, graduating with distinction, later adding an MBA. During the 1990s he had a senior production role with Orlando, before moving on to manage Fabal, one of Australia's largest vineyard management companies. Establishing Hentley Farm might seem all too easy but it required all of his knowledge to create such a great vineyard. A total of 38.2ha were planted between '99 and 2005. In '04 an adjoining 6.5ha vineyard, christened Clos Otto, was acquired. Shiraz dominates the plantings, with 32.5ha. Situated on the banks of Greenock Creek, the vineyard has red clay loam soils overlaying shattered limestone, lightly rocked slopes and little topsoil. *Wine Companion 2015* Winery of the Year. Exports to the US and other major markets.

🍷🍷🍷🍷🍷 Clos Otto Barossa Valley Shiraz 2017 Typically destemmed, open-fermented, 22 months in French oak (66% new). The vintage was always likely to produce the mix of intensity and generosity, and it is indeed that. The luscious blackberry and satsuma plum fruit of the medium to full-bodied palate has a faintly savoury trimming that adds to the overall appeal. Lovely wine. Cork. 14.8% alc. **Rating** 97 To 2047 $209

Museum Release The Beauty Barossa Valley Shiraz 2015 First tasted Jan '17, no change in price. 'Includes 3% viognier, destemmed only, co-fermented, 9 days on skins, matured in French oak (35% new) for 16 months. Vivid crimson-purple. Fruit, oak and tannins are in perfect alignment, all expressive; the juicy blackberry and satsuma plum fruit has clearly gained freshness from the viognier, and allows textural complexity free play. A lovely Barossa Valley shiraz.' This elegant and fragrant wine is even more enjoyable now. Screwcap. 15% alc. **Rating** 97 To 2035 $85 **O**

H Block Shiraz Cabernet 2017 A 67/33% blend flooded with complex flavours ex 66% new French oak for 22 months. Counterintuitively, but pleasingly, it is lighter on its feet than its siblings. A tapestry of red, blue and black fruits, the tannins fine and integrated. If you like, it has more '17 vintage character. Cork. 14.8% alc. **Rating** 97 To 2045 $187

🍷🍷🍷🍷🍷 The Creation Barossa Valley Shiraz 2017 As deep and vibrant colour as its siblings. The decision to delay picking until such a high baume is interesting – it has resulted in a broader canvas of fruit and of texture/structure, and there's no trade off of heat or imbalance. The lingering aftertaste is of savoury spices, licorice, blackberry confit, cedary oak and ancient balsamic vinegar. Cannot be gainsaid. Cork. 15.5% alc. **Rating** 96 **To** 2047 $187

Museum Release The Beast Barossa Valley Shiraz 2015 First tasted Mar '17 – no change in price or points. 'Well I don't know about The Beast, but this is power in liquid form, taking no prisoners. It is unequivocally full-bodied and should ideally be allowed to mature for a minimum of 5 years, preferably 10. Its black fruits are shot through with spice, licorice and savoury tannins that would do cabernet proud.' Cork. 15.5% alc. **Rating** 96 **To** 2045 $120

Museum Release Clos Otto Barossa Valley Shiraz 2014 First tasted by Campbell Mattinson in Feb '16, the price now increased from $190. I haven't changed his tasting note, but have lifted the points from 95. 'Full-bodied in every sense. Rich, thick, powerful: its muscles bulging with sweet, blackberried, jam-stuffed fruit; its limbs of licorice and coffeed oak rippling with chunky ropes of tannin. You could moor ships to this. Its flavours reach into deep, inky pools; the finish pulls it all safely into harbour.' Cork. 14.8% alc. **Rating** 96 **To** 2040 $305

Barossa Valley Shiraz 2018 The usual mix of polished elegance and discreet power. The accent is on the fruit, not oak, and the balance ensures a long future. Plum and blackberry fruit, a dash of spice and licorice are on the money. Screwcap. 14.5% alc. **Rating** 95 **To** 2033 $32 ✪

The Beauty Barossa Valley Shiraz 2018 Wet skins of viognier (3%) co-fermented, destemmed, closed fermentation for 6 days, matured in French oak (35% new) for 20 months. In archetypal Hentley Farm mode. Deeply layered and polished black fruits and tannins, and just the right amount of new oak. Screwcap. 14.5% alc. **Rating** 95 **To** 2033 $69

The Beast Barossa Valley Shiraz 2017 Follows the vinification pattern of Clos Otto but there the similarity ends. A texture and structure of licorice, graphite, black cherry and a powerful thrust of tannins are in sufficient balance to warrant the time (a minimum of 5 years, better still 25) the wine needs to calm down. Cork. 15% alc. **Rating** 95 **To** 2042 $99

E Block Shiraz 2017 Grown on this producer's highest altitude block on Mt Rufus in Seppeltsfield. A wine of real fruit intensity first and foremost, like an essence of blackberry and plum. The flavour quickly saturates the palate in a linear sort of way and then fans out in a combination with the ripe tannin and some warmth on the finish. Needs time to fully unfold. Cork. 15.2% alc. **Rating** 95 **To** 2037 $500 SC

Eden Valley Riesling 2019 Good wine, its varietal and regional expressions spot on. The lemon citrus accent of the Eden Valley comes through without any equivocation; signed off with minerally/slatey acidity on the long finish. Screwcap. 11.8% alc. **Rating** 94 **To** 2029 $24.50 ✪

🍷🍷🍷🍷🍷 **Villain & Vixen Barossa Shiraz 2019** Rating 93 To 2026 $28 SC
Black Beauty Sparkling Shiraz NV Rating 93 $69 SC
Villain & Vixen Barossa Shiraz 2018 Rating 92 To 2035 $28
The Stray Mongrel 2019 Rating 92 To 2026 $32 SC
Barossa Valley Rose 2019 Rating 91 To 2021 $24
Barossa Valley Viognier 2019 Rating 90 To 2021 $47

Hentyfarm Wines ★★★★☆

250 Wattletree Road, Holgate, NSW 2250 **Region** Henty
T 0423 029 200 **www.**hentyfarm.com.au **Open** By appt
Winemaker Ray Nadeson, Jono Mogg **Est.** 2009 **Dozens** 800
Dr John Gladstones names the Henty GI the coolest climate in Australia, cooler than Tasmania and the Macedon Ranges. This is both bane and blessing, for when it's cold, it's bitterly so. The other fact of life it has to contend with is its remoteness, lurking just inside the SA/Victorian border. The rest is all good news, for this region is capable of producing riesling, chardonnay and pinot noir of the highest quality. Seppelt's Drumborg Vineyard focuses on riesling, pinot noir and chardonnay; Crawford River on riesling; both adding lustre to the region. In 2009 Jonathan (Jono) Mogg and partner Belinda Low made several weekend trips in the company

of (then) Best's winemaker Adam Wadewitz and his partner Nikki. They were able to buy grapes from renowned Henty grower Alastair Taylor and the first vintage of Chardonnay was made in '09. The portfolio now also includes Riesling, Gewurztrainer, Pinot Gris, Pinot Noir, Pinot Meunier and The Farm Barossa Shiraz. The wines are made by Ray Nadeson at Lethbridge Wines. Exports to China.

▼▼▼▼▼ **Riesling 2019** Typical Henty riesling: charged with Tahitian lime, crushed citrus leaves, Meyer lemon and acidity that is the servant of the fruit. Screwcap. 12% alc. Rating 96 To 2034 $25 ✪

▼▼▼▼▽ **Pinot Noir 2018** Rating 93 To 2024 $35
Pinot Noir 2017 Rating 90 To 2028 $35

Herbert Vineyard   ★★★★☆
Bishop Road, Mount Gambier, SA 5290 **Region** Mount Gambier
T 0408 849 080 **www**.herbertvineyard.com.au **Open** By appt
Winemaker David Herbert **Est.** 1996 **Dozens** 550 **Vyds** 1.77ha
David and Trudy Herbert have 1.77ha planted to pinot noir (1.32ha), with smaller amounts of cabernet sauvignon, cabernet franc, shiraz, pinot gris and merlot. They have built a two-level (mini) winery overlooking a 1300-square metre maze, which is reflected in the label logo.

Heritage Estate   ★★★★★
Granite Belt Drive, Cottonvale, Qld 4375 **Region** Granite Belt
T (07) 4685 2197 **www**.heritagewines.com.au **Open** 7 days 9–5
Winemaker John Handy **Est.** 1992 **Dozens** 5000 **Vyds** 10ha
Heritage Estate (owned by Robert and Therese Fenwick) has two estate vineyards in the Granite Belt: one at Cottonvale (north) at an altitude of 960m, where it grows white varieties; and the other at Ballandean (south), a slightly warmer site, where red varieties and marsanne are planted. Heritage Estate has been a prolific award-winner in various Qld wine shows. The weather gyrations since 2012 are reminiscent of the run of Burgundy, France with its up and down frost, hail and rain issues. Nice to have some comparison, I suppose ('13, '14 and '17 also suffered, '18 and '19 bouncing back).

▼▼▼▼▼ **Old Vine Reserve Granite Belt Shiraz 2018** 60yo vines; 2 weeks pre and post-ferment maceration with 3–4 punchdowns daily, matured in French oak (20% new). Deep colour. A luscious and rich shiraz, blackberry and plum both having much to say in agreement with each other. Soft tannins and oak provide a high quality each-way wine. Screwcap. 14.5% alc. Rating 95 To 2038 $35 ✪
Granite Belt Tempranillo 2019 2 days' cold soak, cool-fermented at 18°C for 5 days, pressed to second-use French oak for completion of ferment, matured for 5 months. Sensitive winemaking. Screwcap. 13% alc. Rating 95 To 2025 $30 ✪
Old Vine Reserve Shiraz Viognier 2019 Shiraz from 60+yo vines co-fermented with 6% viognier. Viognier (as usual with Heritage) is crushed with high SO_2 in cold storage and, when warmed, is highly aromatic in the shiraz ferment. Post-ferment maceration of 3 weeks was needed. Screwcap. 13.8% alc. Rating 94 To 2029 $40

▼▼▼▼▽ **Granite Belt Fiano 2019** Rating 92 To 2025 $30
Granite Belt Pinot Gris 2019 Rating 90 To 2021 $28

Heritage Wines   ★★★☆
399 Seppeltsfield Road, Marananga, SA 5355 **Region** Barossa Valley
T (08) 8562 2880 **www**.heritagewinery.com.au **Open** Mon–Fri 10–5, w'ends 11–5
Winemaker Stephen Hoff **Est.** 1984 **Dozens** 3000 **Vyds** 8.3ha
A little-known winery that deserves a wider audience, for veteran owner/winemaker Stephen Hoff is apt to produce some startlingly good wines. At various times the Riesling (from old Clare Valley vines), Cabernet Sauvignon and Shiraz (now the flagbearer) have all excelled. The

vineyard is planted to shiraz (5.5ha), cabernet sauvignon (2.5ha) and malbec (0.3ha). Exports to the UK, Thailand, Hong Kong, Malaysia and Singapore.

⚆⚆⚆⚆⚆ **Barossa Semillon 2019** Already showing signs of development, but all are good. Bright green hue. The palate full of citrus, honey and a hint of toast. Drink now if you want the best of all worlds, later if you enjoy the depth and complexity of aged semillon. Screwcap. 12% alc. **Rating** 92 **To** 2029 $15 ✪

"Heroes" Vineyard ★★★

495 Murroon Road, Murroon, Vic 3243 **Region** Geelong
T 0490 345 149 **www.**heroesvineyard.com **Open** By appt
Winemaker James Thomas **Est.** 2016 **Dozens** 1500 **Vyds** 3.9ha
James Thomas was 16 when his parents planted a vineyard in the UK in 1996. He came to Australia in 2004. After achieving a postgraduate degree in oenology from La Trobe, he spent four years as assistant winemaker at Bannockburn Vineyards, followed by three years of making sparkling wine in England. Returning to Australia in '14, his homing pigeon instinct led him to become head winemaker at Clyde Park for the '14–16 vintages (inclusive). Wanting to establish his own winery, he looked at many possible sites in Geelong but didn't imagine he would be able to find a 3.4ha vineyard planted to pinot noir, shiraz, riesling and sauvignon blanc. He is deeply wedded to organic vineyard practices and is moving towards certification. He has also increased the plantings with 0.5ha chardonnay. I was much taken by the sophistication of the labels, even more by the quality of his wines.

⚆⚆⚆⚆ **Das Helden Otway Hinterland Geelong Riesling 2018** The fermentation was arrested by cooling and filtering the wine to prevent any unwanted recurrence of fermentation. It's distinctly, but not heroically, sweet, and doesn't cloy. Screwcap. 7.6% alc. **Rating** 89 $32

Hesketh Wine Company ★★★★☆

28 The Parade, Norwood, SA 5067 **Region** South Australia
T (08) 8362 8622 **www.**heskethwinecompany.com.au **Open** Not
Winemaker James Lienert, Keeda Zilm, Andrew Hardy **Est.** 2006 **Dozens** 40 000
Headed by Jonathon Hesketh, this is part of WD Wines Pty Ltd, which also owns Parker Coonawarra Estate and St John's Road in the Barossa Valley. Jonathon spent seven years as the global sales and marketing manager of Wirra Wirra, and two and a half years as general manager of Distinguished Vineyards in NZ. He is also the son of Robert Hesketh, one of the key players in the development of many facets of the SA wine industry. Jonathon says, 'After realising long ago that working for the man (Greg Trott) was never going to feed two dogs, four children, two cats, four chickens and an ever-so-patient wife, the family returned to Adelaide in early 2006 to establish Hesketh Wine Company'. Exports to all major markets.

⚆⚆⚆⚆⚆ **Regional Selections Eden Valley Riesling 2018** This is good. Kaffir lime scents segue to a juicy line of crunchy, green apple acidity. Tightly furled now but with enough weight on the bones. Plows long. Screwcap. **Rating** 92 **To** 2026 $20 NG ✪

Midday Somewhere Shiraz 2018 Miracle of miracles! A wine at this price that is not reductive. Raspberry to black cherry fruits waft effortlessly, lifted by gentle lilac florals, soft tannins and a breeze of acidity. **Rating** 92 **To** 2022 $15 NG ✪

Subregional Treasures Penola Coonawarra Cabernet Sauvignon 2018 A mid-weighted, savoury cabernet with a strong emphasis on a flow of crème de la cassis fruit and some verdant herb and mulch. Some twiggy tannins bind and shape the wine; saline acidity giving it sap and modest length. A solid drink. **Rating** 92 **To** 2026 $30 NG

Regional Selections Barossa Valley Shiraz 2018 An easier going expression than many. Full-weighted but plump, gentle and more medium-bodied. Redcurrant, blueberry, bergamot, lilac and anise. The tannins melt, juxtaposed against an acid line punching a bit shrill. This is already breachable. Screwcap. 14.5% alc. **Rating** 91 **To** 2024 NG

Subregional Treasures Ebenezer Barossa Valley Grenache 2018 Grenache of a lighter shade, crafted with plenty of whole berry by the smell of it. Cranberry, bergamot and strawberry, with a spicy herbal undercurrent. Ripe and crunchy. Australian fruit sweet but nothing excessive. Drink on the cooler side. Screwcap. **Rating** 91 **To** 2023 $22 NG ✪

Twist of Fate Cabernet Sauvignon 2018 This is a strong wine with cassis, dried herb, black olive and a bulwark of sage-doused tannins curbing the exuberance. A strong fealty to place too, with a lick of briny energy across the finish. **Rating** 91 **To** 2025 $15 NG ✪

Regional Selections Coonawarra Cabernet Sauvignon 2018 More fruit than many a neighbour; gushing blackcurrant, plum and blueberry corralled by seams of nicely managed sage and tapenade-doused tannins. The acidity, bright. The oak well handled. Otherwise, eminently drinkable and good across the mid-term. Screwcap. 14.5% alc. **Rating** 91 **To** 2026 NG

Bright Young Things Limestone Coast Sauvignon Blanc 2019 This is rather good. Capsicum, greengage and guava. Neither slipping too far into the vegetal stream of things, nor into to the talcy sweet/sour tropical spectrum. Hits the right stride. Screwcap. **Rating** 90 **To** 2020 $15 NG ✪

Regional Selections Adelaide Hills Sauvignon Blanc 2019 Typically regional. Geeengage, nettle, lemongrass and assorted green herb jitterbug along beams of acidity doused with guava. There is a beginning, middle and end to this. Nothing out of whack. Screwcap. **Rating** 90 **To** 2020 $20 NG ✪

Hewitson ★★★★★

66 Seppeltsfield Road, Nuriootpa, SA 5355 **Region** Adelaide zone
T (08) 8212 6233 **www**.hewitson.com.au **Open** 7 days 9–5
Winemaker Dean Hewitson **Est.** 1996 **Dozens** 35 000 **Vyds** 4.5ha

Dean Hewitson was a winemaker at Petaluma for 10 years, during which time he managed to do three vintages in France and one in Oregon, as well as undertaking his Masters at the University of California, Davis. It is hardly surprising that the wines are immaculately made from a technical viewpoint. Dean sources 30+-year-old riesling from the Eden Valley and 70+-year-old shiraz from McLaren Vale; he also makes a Barossa Valley Mourvedre from vines planted in 1853 at Rowland Flat, and Barossa Valley Shiraz and Grenache from 60-year-old vines at Tanunda. Exports to the UK, the US and other major markets.

🍷🍷🍷🍷🍷 **Gun Metal Eden Valley Riesling 2019** Low yields across the Clare and Eden valleys occasioned by the relentlessly dry growing season have come good with very concentrated flavours. Give it 5 years and we will know whether the cost of low yields has been offset by the complexity and quality. Screwcap. 12.5% alc. **Rating** 94 **To** 2030 $28 ✪

Miss Harry Barossa Valley Grenache Shiraz Mourvedre 2017 Vinified with 45% whole bunches and minimal SO_2, using solar energy and water recycling. A very attractive light to medium-bodied palate with spices coming from all directions; the fruit flavours red, purple and black; the tannin load minimal. It's soft but not weak or thin, just ready to drink without further ageing. Screwcap. 14% alc. **Rating** 94 **To** 2022 $26 ✪

🍷🍷🍷🍷 **Old Garden Vineyard Mourvedre 2015** **Rating** 91 **To** 2029 $88

Heydon Estate ★★★★★

325 Tom Cullity Drive, Wilyabrup, WA 6280 **Region** Margaret River
T (08) 9755 6995 **www**.heydonestate.com.au **Open** 7 days 10–5
Winemaker Mark Messenger **Est.** 1988 **Dozens** 1800 **Vyds** 10ha

Margaret River dentist and cricket tragic George Heydon and wife Mary have been involved in the region's wine industry since 1995. They became 50% partners in Arlewood and when that partnership was dissolved in 2004, they retained the property and the precious 2ha of cabernet sauvignon and 2.5ha of Gingin clone chardonnay planted in 1988. Additional plantings from '95 include Dijon chardonnay clones, sauvignon blanc, semillon, shiraz and petit verdot. The estate is now biodynamic; near neighbour Vanya Cullen inspired the decision. Exports to the UK, Singapore and Hong Kong.

ŦŦŦŦŦ **The Streaker Single Vineyard Margaret River Chardonnay 2018**
George Heydon (and family) are dedicated to the artistry of wine (their words). Winemaker Mark Messenger is the 12th man, giving this chardonnay free rein with its extreme – and convincing – length. Screwcap. 13.5% alc. **Rating** 95 **To** 2027 $60

The Hallowed Turf Single Vineyard Margaret River Chardonnay 2017 Light straw-green. Exemplifies the depth and richness of Margaret River chardonnay with white stone fruit striking the first runs. Positive oak adds to a long innings. Screwcap. 13.5% alc. **Rating** 95 **To** 2030 $30 ✪

The Willow Single Vineyard Margaret River Chardonnay 2017 Hand-picked Gingin clone, wild-fermented in French oak (50% new), matured for 12 months. A mix of white peach, grapefruit and nectarine. Bright and fresh. Screwcap. 14% alc. **Rating** 95 **To** 2027 $60

The Willow Single Vineyard Margaret River Chardonnay 2016 Has developed with grace, oak a backstop for the full-bodied, rich fruit. It will outrun many of its contemporaries, caring not that it is countercultural to the quest for finesse of modern winemakers. Screwcap. 13.5% alc. **Rating** 95 **To** 2026 $60

The Willow Single Vineyard Margaret River Chardonnay 2015 The spine of acidity that runs through the Heydon Estate chardonnays is the key to their freshness and their length. It also allows the fruit flavours to expand without going over the top. A blind tasting with some of the more generous Yarra Valley chardonnays would prove interesting. Screwcap. 13.5% alc. **Rating** 95 **To** 2025 $60

The Sledge Single Vineyard Margaret River Shiraz 2015 Includes 96% shiraz and 4% viognier; co-fermented to produce a juicy array of supple red fruit flavours, finished with soft tannins and a whisper of cedary oak. Screwcap. 15% alc. **Rating** 95 **To** 2030 $40

W.G. Grace Single Vineyard Margaret River Cabernet Sauvignon 2015 Bright crimson-purple. An elegant medium-bodied cabernet with all its elements in balance: fruit, oak tannins and acidity. Cassis/blackcurrant flavours set the course, followed by the other components, even if their manifestations change their intensity as they age. Screwcap. 14% alc. **Rating** 95 **To** 2030 $75

The Sledge Single Vineyard Margaret River Shiraz 2016 Machine-harvested, matured in a mix of French and American oak (30% new). A wine that is content with its place in vinous life; all in balance, all appealing. Screwcap. 15% alc. **Rating** 94 **To** 2036 $40

W.G. Grace Single Vineyard Margaret River Cabernet Sauvignon 2014 A more substantial wine than its '15 sibling, with warmer/richer aromas and flavours yet still (just) within the parameters of medium-bodied. If there is a significant difference, it's style, because both wines have great balance. Screwcap. 14.5% alc. **Rating** 94 **To** 2029 $75

The Declaration Single Vineyard Margaret River Blanc de Blancs 2016 Hand-picked Gingin clone chardonnay, fermented in second-use French oak, 6 months on lees, second ferment in bottle, 3 years on yeast lees, disgorged with 2.75g/l dosage. Generous. Low dosage (seldom so precise) was exactly the right choice. Very good decisions throughout, including early picking. Cork. 12.6% alc. **Rating** 94 $35

ŦŦŦŦŦ **The Hallowed Turf Single Vineyard Margaret River Chardonnay 2018**
Rating 91 **To** 2024 $30

The Doc Single Vineyard Margaret River Cabernet Petit Verdot 2017
Rating 91 **To** 2027 $45

Chin Music Single Vineyard Margaret River Fume Blanc 2019 **Rating** 90 **To** 2023 $25

Chin Music Single Vineyard Margaret River Sauvignon Blanc 2018
Rating 90 **To** 2021 $25

Hickinbotham Clarendon Vineyard ★★★★★

92 Brooks Road, Clarendon, SA 5157 **Region** McLaren Vale
T (08) 8383 7504 **www.**hickinbothamwines.com.au **Open** By appt
Winemaker Chris Carpenter **Est.** 2012 **Dozens** 4800 **Vyds** 87ha
Alan Hickinbotham established the vineyard bearing his name in 1971 when he planted dry-grown cabernet sauvignon and shiraz in contoured rows on the sloping site. He was a very successful builder; this is his first venture into wine but his father, Alan Robb Hickinbotham, had a long and distinguished career, co-founding the oenology diploma at Roseworthy in '36. In 2012 Clarendon, and the stately sandstone house on the property, was purchased by Jackson Family Wines; it is run as a separate business from Yangarra Estate Vineyard, with different winemaking teams and wines. Exports to all major markets.

ΤΤΤΤΤ **The Peake McLaren Vale Cabernet Shiraz 2018** From vines planted in '71. Hand-picked, destemmed, fermented separately on skins for 18 days, matured for 15 months in high quality French barrels. The best shiraz and cabernet are selected to showcase this long-time Australian blend. If there's a better one, I haven't seen it. This is a beautiful wine, red and black fruits holding hands as they so brilliantly throw off the shackles of the hot vintage. Screwcap. 14% alc. **Rating** 99 **To** 2048 $175 **○**

Brooks Road McLaren Vale Shiraz 2018 From the '71 contour plantings; hand-picked, 50% crushed, 40% destemmed, 10% whole bunch, gentle extraction during 18 days on skins, no pressings used, 6 months on lees, then racked to foudre and puncheons (30% new) for 9 months. This oak use will continue in all releases post '18. Extremely complex and intense, but perfectly balanced red and black fruits, tannins a feature. Screwcap. 14.5% alc. **Rating** 98 **To** 2048 $150 **○**

The Revivalist McLaren Vale Merlot 2018 The perfume, the nuance, the power. This takes the merlot grape and knocks it out of the park. It's ripped with both fruit flavour and tannin, it's smoked with an appropriate level of oak and it feels authoritative through the finish. In short, it's a pearler. Screwcap. 14.5% alc. **Rating** 97 **To** 2033 $75 CM **○**

Trueman McLaren Vale Cabernet Sauvignon 2018 This is a superb cabernet. Dusty, dry and herbal but awash with sweet, boysenberried, blackcurrant-drenched fruit. It lays down oodles of flavour, not to mention tannin, but it's fragrant and frisky at the same time. One sip and you can't let go; it has you in its thrall. Screwcap. 14.5% alc. **Rating** 97 **To** 2043 $75 CM **○**

ΤΤΤΤΤ **The Nest McLaren Vale Cabernet Franc 2018** Excellent flow of ripe, berried, fruit-driven flavour with grass, dust and herb notes as complexing inflections. Perfectly integrated and yet assertive; dusty tannin through the back half of the wine. There are lots of highlights. Velvety mouthfeel and the perfect application of cedar wood oak add finishing touches to a dramatically high quality red wine. Screwcap. 14.5% alc. **Rating** 96 **To** 2036 $75 CM **○**

Hidden Creek ★★★★☆

Eukey Road, Ballandean, Qld 4382 **Region** Granite Belt
T (07) 4684 1383 **www.**hiddencreek.com.au **Open** Mon & Fri 11–3, w'ends 10–4
Winemaker Andy Williams **Est.** 1997 **Dozens** 1000 **Vyds** 2ha
A beautifully located vineyard and winery at 1000m on a ridge overlooking the Ballandean township and the Severn River Valley. The granite boulder–strewn hills mean that the 70ha property only provides 2ha of vineyard, in turn divided into three different blocks planted to shiraz and merlot. Other varieties are sourced from local growers. The business is owned by a group of Brisbane wine enthusiasts. Queensland Winery of the Year, Queensland Wine Awards '18.

ΤΤΤΤΤ **Granite Belt Tempranillo 2018** The consistency in the quality of Hidden Creek's winemaking has to be unreservedly congratulated. This wine is yet another example: 5% viognier was co-fermented, maturation in used French hogsheads for 12 months. Lacy tannins provide texture and structure to red and

black cherry fruit; the length equally impressive. Screwcap. 13.5% alc. **Rating** 95
To 2030 $40

♟♟♟♟♟ **Granite Belt Syrah 2018** Rating 91 To 2030 $35
Granite Belt Viognier 2019 Rating 90 To 2021 $35

Highbank ★★★★★

Riddoch Highway, Coonawarra, SA 5263 **Region** Coonawarra
T 1800 653 311 **www**.highbank.com.au **Open** By appt
Winemaker Dennis Vice **Est.** 1986 **Dozens** 2000 **Vyds** 4ha
Mount Gambier lecturer in viticulture Dennis Vice makes small quantities of single vineyard
chardonnay, merlot, sauvignon and Coonawarra cabernet. The wines are sold through local
restaurants and the cellar door, with limited Melbourne distribution. The major part of the
grape production is sold. Exports to the US, Thailand, Singapore, Japan and China.

♟♟♟♟♟ **Family Reserve Single Vineyard Coonawarra Cabernet Sauvignon
2015** This is a lovely wine – a Coonawarra cabernet masterclass. Elegant aromas
of blackcurrant and redcurrant mesh seamlessly with notes of cedar and dark
chocolate, while subtle herbal characters add a cool-climate varietal counterpoint.
It's medium-bodied, almost svelte in structure, but seamless in texture with
red fruit and savoury flavours framed by fine tannin. Cork. 14% alc. **Rating** 95
To 2030 $89 SC

♟♟♟♟♟ **Single Vineyard Coonawarra Merlot 2015** Rating 93 To 2025 $59 SC

Higher Plane ★★★★★

98 Tom Cullity Drive, Cowaramup, WA 6284 **Region** Margaret River
T (08) 9755 9000 **www**.higherplanewines.com.au **Open** At Juniper Estate
Winemaker Mark Messenger **Est.** 1996 **Dozens** 3000 **Vyds** 18.38ha
Higher Plane was purchased by Roger Hill and Gillian Anderson, owners of Juniper Estate, in
2006. The brand was retained with the intention of maintaining the unique and special aspects
of the site in the south of Margaret River distinct from those of Wilyabrup in the north.
The close-planted vineyard is sustainably farmed using organic principles. Sons Nick and
Tom (formerly a winemaker in the Yarra Valley) are now running the business. Chardonnay,
sauvignon blanc and cabernet sauvignon are the major plantings with smaller amounts of
fiano, syrah and malbec.

♟♟♟♟♟ **Reserve Margaret River Chardonnay 2018** Single vineyard, whole-bunch
pressed to barrel, wild ferment or as Mark Messenger calls it 'free range'. No malo
and stays in French barriques, 40% new, for 10 months with some lees stirring
early in its life. This is all about restrained power. It's a fabulous outcome of intense
grapefruit and lemon sprinkled with powdered ginger and creamy curd flavours.
It's the pure acidity that drives this and contains it all. Brilliant. Screwcap. 13% alc.
Rating 96 To 2029 $40 JF ✪
Margaret River Fume Blanc 2019 A stylish, complex yet thoroughly delicious
wine. It has the right amount of texture, creamy nuances and smokiness of oak to
balance the refreshing citrussy, feijoa, pine needles and basil flavours of sauvignon
blanc. Moreish and more please. Screwcap. 13% alc. Rating 95 To 2025 $25 JF ✪
Margaret River Cabernet Malbec 2017 This super blend consistently
punches above its medium-bodied weight. All balance here with its cassis, juniper,
cinnamon and Margaret River scrub aromas. The palate cruises to the finishing
line with oak in place and fine-sandy tannins going along for the ride. Lovely
wine. Screwcap. 13.9% alc. Rating 95 To 2030 $25 JF ✪
Margaret River Syrah 2018 Red and black cherries establish the rhythm of the
wine, spices filling any gaps in the fruit – though it's hard to see any. Sprightly oak
and fruit tannins add to the complexity. Astute winemaking. Screwcap. 13.5% alc.
Rating 94 To 2033 $24.99 ✪

Reserve Margaret River Cabernet Sauvignon 2015 Always lovely to taste this. It offers up restraint, elegance and fruit purity in equal measure. Its medium-bodied palate has a dusting of spice to the cassis and mulberry fruit as fine-grained tannins edge out to the long finish. Screwcap. 13.8% alc. **Rating** 94 **To** 2028 $40 JF

Forest Grove Chardonnay 2018 Rating 92 **To** 2026 $25 JF ✪
Fiano 2019 Rating 92 **To** 2024 $25 JF ✪

Highland Heritage Estate ★★★★

4698 Mitchell Highway, Orange, NSW 2800 **Region** Orange
T (02) 6363 5602 **www.**highlandheritageestate.com.au **Open** 7 days 10–5
Winemaker John Hordern, Rex D'Aquino **Est.** 1985 **Dozens** 5000 **Vyds** 15ha
Owned and operated by the D'Aquino family, the vineyard, restaurant and cellar door are on 125ha located 3km east of Orange, with a heliport offering scenic flights and tours. The vineyard is planted to 15ha of chardonnay, sauvignon blanc, riesling, pinot noir, merlot and shiraz. At an elevation of 900m, on deep alluvial and rich basalt soils, the cool to cold climate and long growing season produce elegant reds and crisp, clean whites. Exports to all major markets.

Orange Dry Riesling 2019 Abundant lime and Meyer lemon fruit, the crisp acidity in no need of residual sugar to provide balance – it's already there. Some question about the gold medal it won at the Canberra International Riesling Challenge '19. The overall impact is of a delicate riesling. I'll engage in a spot of fence sitting. Screwcap. 12.1% alc. **Rating** 93 **To** 2025 $25 ✪
Nikki D Orange Riesling 2019 The 60g/l of residual sugar is balanced by 9.3g/l of titratable acidity. It is definitely sweet, but more in a kabinett style than spatlese. Nice wine. Screwcap. 8.5% alc. **Rating** 93 **To** 2025 $25 ✪
Orange Syrah 2017 The impact of partial barrel ferment and 18 months' maturation in new and 1yo American oak is substantial, but doesn't obliterate the fruit. The flavours are in the dark cherry/satsuma plum spectrum, the tannins soft. Screwcap. 13% alc. **Rating** 92 **To** 2029 $32
Methode Traditionelle Cuvee Brut 2017 A mix of 70% pinot noir, 30% chardonnay from Orange, 24 months on lees in bottle with low dosage. Attractive bouquet with toasty, nutty aromas to the fore, more subdued fruit and floral notes in the background. A positive attack on the palate, quite dry through the middle, then finishing with crispness and flavour in the aftertaste. A good aperitif style. Cork. 12% alc. **Rating** 92 $55 SC
Orange Sauvignon Blanc 2019 Lives up to the region's reputation for sauvignon blanc. It's fresh, crisp and has a range of flavours from citrus through to savoury. Screwcap. 13.5% alc. **Rating** 90 **To** 2021 $25

Hill-Smith Estate ★★★★☆

Flaxmans Valley Road, Eden Valley, SA 5235 **Region** Eden Valley
T (08) 8561 3200 **www.**hillsmithestate.com **Open** Not
Winemaker Teresa Heuzenroeder **Est.** 1979 **Dozens** 5000 **Vyds** 12ha
The Eden Valley vineyard sits at an altitude of 510m, providing a cool climate that extends the growing season; rocky, acidic soil coupled with winter rainfall and dry summers, results in modest crops. The Parish Vineyard in the Coal River Valley of Tasmania was purchased from Frogmore Creek in 2012.

Eden Valley Chardonnay 2018 There's a flintiness to the nose and a mealy character to the palate, but this is sweet with peach and cooked apple flavour yet, despite its best efforts, the wine just seems a little simple. It doesn't lack flavour though. Indeed it's highly varietal and it presents in neat/tidy fashion; good things both. Screwcap. 13.5% alc. **Rating** 90 **To** 2023 CM

Hillcrest Vineyard ★★★★★

31 Phillip Road, Woori Yallock, Vic 3139 **Region** Yarra Valley
T (03) 5964 6689 **www**.hillcrestvineyard.com.au **Open** By appt
Winemaker Dylan McMahon **Est.** 1970 **Dozens** 600 **Vyds** 5.25ha
The small, effectively dry-grown vineyard was established by Graeme and Joy Sweet, and is now owned by Shirley Zhang and family. The high quality pinot noir, chardonnay, merlot and cabernet sauvignon grown on the property were particularly important resources when Coldstream Hills was in its infancy. Exports to China.

🍷🍷🍷🍷🍷 **Premium Yarra Valley Chardonnay 2019** Has greater weight than the Village, but the overall mouthfeel and flavour bundle is very similar. Not a skerrick of info for any of the Hillcrest wines is frustrating. Cork. 13% alc. **Rating** 94 **To** 2029
Premium Yarra Valley Pinot Noir 2019 The vineyard was planted 48 years ago. The wine shares the power of its Village sibling but also has more texture and a longer finish. Cork. 13.5% alc. **Rating** 94 **To** 2030

🍷🍷🍷🍷♀ **Village Yarra Valley Chardonnay 2019 Rating** 93 **To** 2028
Village Yarra Valley Pinot Noir 2019 Rating 92 **To** 2030
Estate Yarra Valley Cabernet Sauvignon 2019 Rating 91 **To** 2029

Hither & Yon ★★★★★

17 High Street, Willunga, SA 5172 **Region** McLaren Vale
T (08) 8556 2082 **www**.hitherandyon.com.au **Open** 7 days 11–4
Winemaker Richard Leask **Est.** 2012 **Dozens** 15000 **Vyds** 88ha
Brothers Richard and Malcolm Leask started Hither & Yon in 2012, the Old Jarvie label added in '16. The grapes are sourced from 88ha of family vineyards at seven sites scattered around McLaren Vale. Currently there are 14 varieties, with more to come. Richard manages the vineyards and makes the wine, while Malcolm runs the historic cellar door in Willunga, along with production, sales and marketing. The Hither & Yon labels feature the brands' ampersand, created by a different artist for each wine, and having won many domestic and international design awards. Old Jarvie (www.oldjarvie.com.au) focuses on varietal blends. Exports to Canada, Germany, Denmark, Sweden, Singapore, Hong Kong and China.

🍷🍷🍷🍷🍷 **McLaren Vale Shiraz 2018** Oh come all ye faithful lovers of McLaren Vale shiraz. It's hard to say whether the variety or the region is the most important – and true – contributor to the depth and outright richness of this shiraz. The tannins also ring true to the theme, leaving no doubt about its longevity. Screwcap. 14.5% alc. **Rating** 95 **To** 2038 $29 ✪
Leask McLaren Vale Grenache 2018 Vines planted in the '40s; whole-berry ferment with 10% whole bunches, cultured yeast and aged in French puncheons for 17 months. There's a lightness across the palate from fine sandpaper tannins and cherry and raspberry fruit. It's a lovely wine with savoury inputs and not at all confected. A whiff of pine needle/Mediterranean herbs comes and goes. Cork. 14.5% alc. **Rating** 95 **To** 2030 $100 JF
McLaren Vale Grenache Touriga 2019 What appeals is how the fruit does the talking, winemaking merely the guide. Made in a fresh, drink-now style yet with some depth and shape thanks to its grainy tannins and savoury overlay. Delicious. Screwcap. 14.5% alc. **Rating** 95 **To** 2026 $33 JF ✪
McLaren Vale Grenache Mataro 2018 Classic southern Rhône Valley style, with the wild herbs and spices of the garrigue giving pleasure in the aromas and flavours alike. It will be hard to keep your hands off it, but it could be a knockout with more time in bottle. Screwcap. 14.5% alc. **Rating** 95 **To** 2030 $29 ✪
McLaren Vale Nero d'Avola 2018 At the upper end of the scale for nero d'Avola. It is varietal, and certain to burst into song with appropriate Italian cuisine. Screwcap. 14.5% alc. **Rating** 95 **To** 2028 $29 ✪

🍷🍷🍷🍷♀ **McLaren Vale Tempranillo 2019 Rating** 92 **To** 2026 $29 JF

Hobbs Barossa Ranges

550 Flaxman's Valley Road, Angaston, SA 5353 **Region** Barossa
T 0427 177 740 **www**.hobbsvintners.com.au **Open** At Vino Lokal, Tanunda
Winemaker Pete Schell, Chris Ringland (Consultant), Allison Hobbs, Greg Hobbs
Est. 1998 **Dozens** 1700 **Vyds** 6.2ha

Hobbs of Barossa Ranges is the high profile, if somewhat challenging, venture of Greg and Allison Hobbs. The estate vineyards revolve around 1ha of shiraz planted in 1905, 1ha planted in '88, 1ha planted in '97 and 1.82ha planted in 2004; 0.4ha of old white frontignac was removed in '09, giving space for another small planting of shiraz. The viticultural portfolio is completed with 0.6ha of semillon planted in the 1960s and an inspired 0.4ha of viognier ('88). All the wines, made by Peter Schell (at Spinifex), push the envelope. The only conventionally made wine is the Shiraz Viognier, with a production of 130 dozen. Gregor Shiraz, in Amarone-style shiraz in full-blooded table-wine mode, and a quartet of dessert wines are produced by cane cutting, followed by further desiccation on racks. The Grenache comes from a Barossa floor vineyard; the Semillon, Viognier and White Frontignac from estate-grown grapes. The Tin Lids wines are made with 'the kids', Sean, Bridget and Jessica. Exports to the UK, the US, Singapore, Taiwan and China.

🍷🍷🍷🍷🍷 **1905 Shiraz 2017** Hand-picked, destemmed and crushed, wild-yeast fermented, pressed to new French hogsheads for 2 years. While there's a density to the flavours from soused plums to baking spices, there's also a brightness. The palate is silky and glossy, the tannins plush. All in all, a super fine drink. Diam. 14.5% alc. Rating 96 To 2037 $170 JF

🍷🍷🍷🍷🍷 **Gregor Shiraz 2017** Rating 93 To 2030 $150 JF
Tin Lids Aria Secca Shiraz 2018 Rating 92 To 2028 $50 JF
Tin Lids Shiraz Cabernet Sauvignon 2018 Rating 90 To 2030 $50 JF
Tin Lids Fortified Grenache 2004 Rating 90 $65 JF

Hoddles Creek Estate

505 Gembrook Road, Hoddles Creek, Vic 3139 **Region** Yarra Valley
T (03) 5967 4692 **www**.hoddlescreekestate.com.au **Open** By appt
Winemaker Franco D'Anna, Chris Bendle **Est.** 1997 **Dozens** 30000 **Vyds** 33.3ha

The D'Anna family established their vineyard on a property that had been in the family since 1960. The vines (chardonnay, pinot noir, sauvignon blanc, cabernet sauvignon, pinot gris, merlot and pinot blanc) are hand-pruned and hand-harvested. A 300t, split-level winery was built in 2003. Son Franco is the viticulturist and inspired winemaker; he started work in the family liquor store at age 13, graduating to chief wine buyer by the time he was 21. He completed a Bachelor of Commerce at the University of Melbourne before studying viticulture at CSU. A vintage at Coldstream Hills, then two years' vintage experience with Peter Dredge at Witchmount and, with Mario Marson (ex Mount Mary) as mentor in '03, has put an old head on young shoulders. The Wickhams Road label uses grapes from an estate vineyard in Gippsland as well as purchased grapes from the Yarra Valley and Mornington Peninsula. Exports to the UK, Denmark, Brazil, Dubai, Japan and China.

🍷🍷🍷🍷🍷 **Road Block Chardonnay 2017** Planted on an east-facing terraced hill slope. It's quite certain the wine was barrel-fermented with a percentage of new French oak, but it's been soaked up by the fruit. It's an intricately polished wine, the fruit/ oak/acid balance sheer perfection, its longevity impossible to guess. Screwcap. 12.5% alc. Rating 98 To 2032 $60 ✪
DML Mornington Peninsula Pinot Noir 2018 Perfect colour. The complexity of the bouquet is immediate with a cupboard full of spices; the impact of the palate even greater than that of the bouquet with layered dark cherry fruit with a fine-spun latticework of fruit and oak. Diam. 13.5% alc. Rating 98 To 2032 $60 ✪

🍷🍷🍷🍷🍷 **1er Yarra Valley Chardonnay 2018** The bouquet is very complex ex well controlled barrel fermentation. The palate has focus and balance: the grapes picked at precisely the right moment; the fruit flavours of white peach, grapefruit and Granny Smith apple in perfect balance and harmony; the length that of top Yarra Valley chardonnay. Yarra Valley chardonnay responds like a violin in the hands of an 18th century musician. Screwcap. 13.2% alc. **Rating** 96 **To** 2028 $50 ✪

Yarra Valley Pinot Noir 2019 Hand-picked and sorted, wild-fermented, 21 days on skins, 10 months in French oak (25% new). Deep colour. The bouquet and palate flow with black cherry/berry fruits, violets and spices lurking in its depths. The palate has abundant power that will sustain the wine for years to come. The richness of the plush fruit got better and better on retasting. Screwcap. 13.2% alc. **Rating** 96 **To** 2030 $25 ✪

DML Yarra Valley Pinot Noir 2019 MV6; hand-picked and sorted, whole berry–open fermented, matured for 10 months in French oak (25% new). The colour isn't as bright as its Mornington Peninsula sibling, but the bouquet is carried on an exotic array of spices and forest berries. The palate is typical Yarra Valley with drive coming from red fruits and superfine, savoury tannins. Diam. 13.5% alc. **Rating** 96 **To** 2031 $60 ✪

1er Yarra Valley Pinot Noir 2018 Bright, clear colour. A highly perfumed/scented, spicy bouquet leads into a beautifully structured and weighted palate. Hints of forest add to the complexity and simultaneously the length of the red-berried palate. Screwcap. 13.2% alc. **Rating** 96 **To** 2028 $50 ✪

Yarra Valley Chardonnay 2018 This has the typical energy, finesse and drive that makes Hoddles Creek wines a 'must buy' year in, year out. It has all the power needed to cruise through the next 10 years. Grapefruit, Granny Smith apple and stone fruit decorated with a necklace of bracing acidity. Screwcap. 13.2% alc. **Rating** 95 **To** 2028 $22 ✪

DML Mornington Peninsula Pinot Noir 2019 Clones 114, 115; hand-picked and sorted, cold soak, 14 days on skins. Has more altitude and precision than many from the Mornington Peninsula in this difficult vintage. Fragrant red cherry and blood plum, superfine tannins. Complex and balanced. Diam. 13.5% alc. **Rating** 95 **To** 2030 $60

Yarra Valley Pinot Noir 2018 When you have a vineyard site as good as Hoddles Creek Estate and lavish it with consitent care, the result is preordained. This is an elegant, spice-infused wine with tannins providing the boundary fence, fruit filling the centre. The length and balance can't be faulted. Screwcap. 13.2% alc. **Rating** 95 **To** 2030 $25 ✪

PSB Pinot Noir 2018 From a close-planted single block of MV6 and Pommard clones. A fragrant, fresh armful of red berries. It's the length of the wine that arrests most attention, although it is accompanied by depth to its blood plum fruit. As usual, Hoddles Creek Estate rises above the dictates of a difficult vintage. Screwcap. 13.2% alc. **Rating** 95 **To** 2028 $60

Yarra Valley Chardonnay 2019 High quality clones; hand-picked, crushed and destemmed, fermented in tank with wild and cultured yeast, matured in French oak (25% new) for 10 months. Small wonder that my head snapped back when I tasted the wine before reading the vinification notes – it's fresh and juicy right through to the mid-palate, before some of the complexity makes its appearance. A vintage response. Screwcap. 13.2% alc. **Rating** 94 **To** 2026 $22 ✪

Wickhams Road Gippsland Pinot Noir 2019 It knocks the price out of the park. There's a generosity to the fruit in varietal terms, complemented perfectly by firm, stringy tannin. It tastes of herbs, sap and spices with cherry-rhubarb pushing through. There's a tangy cranberried aspect too. No hesitation. Screwcap. 13.5% alc. **Rating** 94 **To** 2025 $19 CM ✪

🍷🍷🍷🍷 **Yarra Valley Pinot Gris 2019 Rating** 93 **To** 2024 $22 ✪
Wickhams Road Yarra Valley Pinot Noir 2019 Rating 93 **To** 2025 $19 CM ✪

Hofer Family Wines

7 Cambridge Street, Reynella, SA 5161 (postal) **Region** Fleurieu Peninsula
T 0410 521 592 **www**.facebook.com/southernfleurieuwine **Open** Not
Winemaker Marcus Hofer, Dave Sinclair **Est.** 2017 **Dozens** 400
A winery that is in its infancy, intending to grow production over the years to the point where
it will be a legacy for Marcus Hofer's children. It is an adjunct to his job as an employed
winemaker, buying the grapes on a yearly basis keeps costs down.

ΨΨΨΨΨ **Southern Fleurieu Montepulciano 2018** Brightly coloured. The wine is juicy,
bordering on plush; the fruit not threatened by tannins. A mix of sour and morello
cherries does well on the palate. A useful wine at this price. Screwcap. 13.5% alc.
Rating 90 **To** 2023 $25
Southern Fleurieu Montepulciano 2017 Sits alongside its Lagrein sibling,
with fresh, although gentle, red fruits and good balance. This is all about delicacy,
not raw power. Screwcap. 13.5% alc. **Rating** 90 **To** 2023 $25

ΨΨΨΨ **Langhorne Creek Barbera 2018** **Rating** 89 **To** 2028 $25
Langhorne Creek Lagrein 2017 **Rating** 89 **To** 2027 $25

Hollydene Estate

3483 Golden Highway, Jerrys Plains, NSW 2330 **Region** Hunter Valley
T (02) 6576 4021 **www**.hollydeneestate.com **Open** Mon–Thurs 10–4, Fri 10–9, Sat 9–9,
Sun 9–4
Winemaker Matt Burton **Est.** 1965 **Dozens** 7000 **Vyds** 80ha
Karen Williams has three vineyards and associated properties, all established in the 1960s. They
are Hollydene Estate, Wybong Estate and Arrowfield; the latter one of the original vinous
landmarks in the Upper Hunter. The three vineyards produce grapes for the Hollydene
Estate and Juul labels. Hollydene also makes sparkling wines from the Mornington Peninsula.
Exports to Germany, Indonesia and China.

ΨΨΨΨΨ **Show Reserve Upper Hunter Valley Chardonnay 2018** It's not showy but
it is soft and easy to like. Light layers of flavour from stone fruit and citrus to some
leesy, nutty nuances. Screwcap. 13% alc. **Rating** 90 **To** 2022 JF

Holm Oak

11 West Bay Road, Rowella, Tas 7270 **Region** Northern Tasmania
T (03) 6394 7577 **www**.holmoakvineyards.com.au **Open** 7 days 11–5
Winemaker Rebecca Duffy **Est.** 1983 **Dozens** 15 000 **Vyds** 15ha
Holm Oak takes its name from its grove of oak trees, planted around the beginning of the
20th century and originally intended for the making of tennis racquets. Winemaker Rebecca
Duffy, daughter of founders Ian and Robyn Wilson, has extensive winemaking experience in
Australia and California; and husband Tim, a viticultural agronomist, manages the vineyard
(pinot noir, cabernet sauvignon, chardonnay, riesling, sauvignon blanc and pinot gris with
small amounts of merlot, cabernet franc and arneis). Exports to the UK, the US and Japan.

ΨΨΨΨΨ **Riesling 2019** The perfumed, flowery bouquet leads into a mouth-watering blast
of citrus sorbet and flinty acidity. A wine that underlines the belief that Tasmanian
riesling and pinot noir are the 2 best varietal wines of the island. Screwcap.
12.5% alc. **Rating** 96 **To** 2039 $28 ✪
Arneis 2019 Well, well, this is a revelation; 25% of the juice was fermented in
a Nomblot egg, 75% in old oak barrels. Grapefruit/honeysuckle/lychee aromas
are precisely replicated on the delicious palate. Just when you wonder whether
it's a bit too much, Tasmanian acidity puts you back on track. Screwcap. 13% alc.
Rating 96 **To** 2023 $28 ✪
The Protege Pinot Noir 2019 Made to be enjoyed now. Early picking and no
oak are the cornerstones of a pinot full of joy. Destemmed and fermented on skins
for 10 days, using yeasts known to enhance fruit aromatics. Strawberry, red cherry

and spice fill the senses. Outstanding example of the style. Screwcap. 13% alc.
Rating 95 To 2023 $25 ○

Pinot Noir 2018 Wild-yeast fermented in small open fermenters, 10 months'
ageing in French oak (25% new). Shows typically cool-climate pinot characters
of sappy spice and twiggy undergrowth but it has a sense of ripeness as well.
The cherry flavours are towards being sweet-fruited and there's a suggestion of
strawberry. A touch of cedary oak fits in nicely. A lovely wine. Screwcap. 13% alc.
Rating 95 To 2028 $35 SC ○

Sparkling Rose 2017 Includes 60% pinot noir, 40% chardonnay. Pale blush
pink. Strawberry fruit comes through with absolute clarity, so the description
of strawberries and cream is as unavoidable as it is correct. Diam. 12% alc.
Rating 95 $50

Chardonnay 2018 Harvested at 12° baume to retain acidity, pressed and racked
to barrel for natural ferment, 20% mlf, 10 months' maturation in new and older
French oak. The early picking has accentuated the citrus aromas and flavours with
white-fleshed stone fruit and some spicy oak in the background. It's textured
and long on the palate with a lingering, lemony aftertaste. Screwcap. 12.5% alc.
Rating 94 To 2025 $35 SC

The Wizard Pinot Noir 2018 Hand-picked, wild yeast–open fermented
with 30% whole bunches, frequent plunging, pressed to barrel (60% new). The
vinification started with pruning, continuing with first-stage barrel selection
reduced to 30 barrels and, finally, 24. Clear purple-crimson hue. Smoky oak is
coupled with a palate of sheer power, red cherries the fuel. Screwcap. 13.5% alc.
Rating 94 To 2033 $65

♈♈♈♈♈ **Pinot Gris 2019** Rating 93 To 2022 $28
Pinot Noir Chardonnay NV Rating 92 $40

Home Hill   ★★★★★

38 Nairn Street, Ranelagh, Tas 7109 **Region** Southern Tasmania
T (03) 6264 1200 **www.**homehillwines.com.au **Open** 7 days 10–5
Winemaker Gilli Lipscombe, Paul Lipscombe **Est.** 1994 **Dozens** 3300 **Vyds** 9ha
Terry and Rosemary Bennett planted their first 0.5ha of vines in 1994 on gentle slopes in the
beautiful Huon Valley. The plantings have gradually been increased to 9ha, including pinot
noir, chardonnay and sylvaner. Home Hill has had great success with its exemplary pinot noirs,
consistent multi-trophy and gold medal winners in the ultra-competitive Tasmanian Wine
Show. Impressive enough but pales into insignificance in the wake of winning the Jimmy
Watson Trophy at the Melbourne Wine Awards '15. Exports to Singapore.

♈♈♈♈♈ **Estate Pinot Noir 2018** Southern Tasmania's Home Hill is one of the leaders in
redefining the boundaries of world class pinot in Australia. The depth and richness
of its spiced cherries, blood plums and finely ground tannins drive a finish that
seems to have no end. Screwcap. 13.9% alc. Rating 98 To 2033 $45 ○
Kelly's Reserve Pinot Noir 2018 Wild-fermented with 10% whole bunches, a
barrel selection with 50% new French oak. Super colour. This is at the tip of the
pyramid of the remarkable Home Hill pinots; the silky mouthfeel unique unto
itself yet from a family bound by their common ancestry. Here the perfume of
the bouquet soars from the glass the moment it is swirled. Screwcap. 13.9% alc.
Rating 98 To 2035 $75 ○

♈♈♈♈♈ **Kelly's Reserve Chardonnay 2017** From the oldest vines on the property. The
very cool climate invests the wine with a freshness and delicacy that is remarkable,
especially the way it has absorbed its new oak contribution. Great value. Screwcap.
13.5% alc. Rating 96 To 2030 $35 ○
Landslide Pinot Noir 2018 Tasmania's Huon Valley is at the southernmost and
nigh on coolest part of Australia. And this is a glorious wine at any price, let alone
$28. It is supple and feline, dripping plum, strawberry and blueberry fruits, cosseted
by finely presented, sweet tannins. Screwcap. 13.7% alc. Rating 96 To 2030 ○

♈♈♈♈♈ **Sauvignon Blanc 2018** Rating 90 To 2021 $25

Horner Wines

188 Palmers Lane, Pokolbin, NSW 2325 **Region** Hunter Valley
T 0477 222 121 **www**.hornerwines.com.au **Open** Not
Winemaker Ashley Horner **Est.** 2013 **Dozens** 14500

Ashley and Lauren Horner have a certified organic vineyard planted to chardonnay, viognier and shiraz. Grapes are also sourced from organic vineyards in Orange and Cowra. Ashley had a 14-year career working at Rosemount Estate, Penfolds, Kamberra Estate, Saint Clair (NZ) and Mount Pleasant, ultimately becoming winemaker at Tamburlaine and completing a Diploma in Wine Technology at Dookie College. Lauren has a degree in hospitality/tourism and is now involved in the running of Horner Wines. The move from grapegrowing to winemaking was precipitated by the fall in demand for grape. They sell the wines through www.nakedwines.com.au.

Family Reserve Chardonnay 2019 This cuts straight to the chase with its citrus profile. A lean style with some toasty nuances, lemon curd with the oak in check. Refreshing. Screwcap. 13.2% alc. **Rating** 90 **To** 2026 $26 JF
Organic Orange Rose 2019 An orange hue to the candy red. Tangy cranberries and their ensuing tartness, spicy with crunchy acidity. All in all, refreshing and dry. Screwcap. 12.5% alc. **Rating** 90 **To** 2021 $25 JF

Houghton

★★★★★

4070 Caves Road, Wilyabrup, WA 6280 **Region** Swan Valley
T (08) 9755 6042 **www**.houghton-wines.com.au **Open** 7 days 10–5
Winemaker Ross Pamment **Est.** 1836 **Dozens** NFP

Houghton's reputation was once largely dependent on its (then) White Burgundy, equally good when young or 5 years old. In the last 20 years its portfolio changed out of all recognition, with a kaleidoscopic range of high quality wines from the Margaret River, Frankland River, Great Southern and Pemberton regions to the fore. The Jack Mann and Gladstones red wines stand at the forefront, but to borrow a saying of the late Jack Mann, 'There are no bad wines here'. In November 2019 the Houghton property was sold to the Yukich family, who had acquired part of the property in 1990 and established Oakover Wines. The reunited vineyard will be relaunched as Nikola Estate, in honour of Nikola Yukich, who emigrated from Croatia and planted vines in the Swan Valley over 90 years ago. The Houghton brand is retained by Accolade, with the winemaking moved to its Nannup winery in the Blackwood Valley, adjacent to the Frankland River and Margaret River, the sources of most of its grape production. Exports to the UK and Asia.

Gladstones Margaret River Cabernet Sauvignon 2017 From a dry-grown single vineyard in Wilyabrup. Selectiv'-harvested or hand-picked and sorted, open-fermented 10 days, basket-pressed, matured for 15 months in French barriques. A long-established classic Margaret River cabernet, every step along the way precisely measured. Screwcap. 13.5% alc. **Rating** 98 **To** 2042 $100 ✪
Jack Mann Single Vineyard Frankland River Cabernet Sauvignon 2017 Hand-picked and sorted, destemmed, whole-berry wild ferments, 10 days on skins, 16 months in Bordeaux-coopered barriques (50% new). This is a full-bodied cabernet, but is so well structured you barely notice. It will only take the first 5 years of a 25+-year life for it to seem medium-bodied. Screwcap. 14% alc. **Rating** 98 **To** 2045 $175 ✪
Wisdom Margaret River Cabernet Sauvignon 2017 Houghton clone; Selectiv'-harvested or hand-picked and sorted, destemmed whole berries, wild yeast–open fermented, 10 days on skins, matured for 13 months in French oak (33% new). Fragrant bouquet, fruit, oak and tannins all building a very, very impressive picture. Margaret River's climate is second to none. Screwcap. 14% alc. **Rating** 97 **To** 2037 $40 ✪

C.W. Ferguson Frankland River Cabernet Malbec 2017 A rich 68/32% blend; wild yeast–open fermented, matured in Bordeaux-coopered barriques (33% new) for 16 months. Frankland River offers the ability to make cabernet of intensity and length, yet makes no demands on the taster for the calibrated flow along the palate. Screwcap. 14% alc. **Rating** 96 To 2037 $78

ŸŸŸŸ♀ **Wisdom Pemberton Chardonnay 2018** Rating 93 To 2030 $40
Crofters Pemberton Margaret River Chardonnay 2018 Rating 92 To 2023 $20 ✪
White Classic Dry White 2018 Rating 90 To 2026 $13 JP ✪
Crofters Frankland River Shiraz 2017 Rating 90 To 2027 $19 JP ✪
Crofters Frankland River Cabernet Sauvignon 2017 Rating 90 To 2027 $19 JP ✪

House of Arras   ★★★★★

Bay of Fires, 40 Baxters Road, Pipers River, Tas 7252 **Region** Northern Tasmania
T (03) 6362 7622 **www.**houseofarras.com.au **Open** Mon–Fri 11–4, w'ends 10–4
Winemaker Ed Carr **Est.** 1995 **Dozens** NFP
The rise and rise of the fortunes of the House of Arras has been due to two things: the exceptional skills of winemaker Ed Carr, and its access to high quality Tasmanian chardonnay and pinot noir. While there have been distinguished sparkling wines made in Tasmania for many years, none has so consistently scaled the heights of Arras. The complexity, texture and structure of the wines are akin to that of Bollinger RD and Krug; the connection stems from the 7–15+ years the wines spend on lees prior to disgorgement.

ŸŸŸŸŸ **EJ Carr Late Disgorged 2005** A mix of 69% chardonnay and 31% pinot noir spent 13 years on tirage, and a low dosage of 3.1g/l. It takes Australian sparkling onto a level of texture and complexity that no other producer can even seek to achieve. Comparisons with Krug or Bollinger are valid, regardless of preferences. Cork. 12.5% alc. **Rating** 99 $230 ✪
Rose 2009 A blend of 69.6% pinot noir and 30.4% chardonnay with some reserve wines. A spectacular 9 years on tirage/lees. Salmon-pink. How can a wine of this age be as delicate, fresh and red-fruited as this? A knockout in every respect. Cork. 12.5% alc. **Rating** 98 $105 ✪

ŸŸŸŸŸ **Brut Elite NV Cuvee No. 1501** Includes 49.4% pinot noir, 41.6% chardonnay, 9% pinot meunier; 32 months on lees, 9.2g/l dosage. Fresh, vibrant multitude of flavours from white peach and citrus to nougat and brioche, then a burst of cleansing acidity on the finish. Cork. 12.5% alc. **Rating** 95 $53

House of Cards   ★★★★★

3220 Caves Road, Yallingup, WA 6282 **Region** Margaret River
T (08) 9755 2583 **www.**houseofcardswine.com.au **Open** 7 days 10–5
Winemaker Travis Wray **Est.** 2011 **Dozens** 5000 **Vyds** 12ha
House of Cards is owned and operated by Elizabeth and Travis Wray; Travis managing the vineyard and making the wines, Elizabeth managing sales and marketing. The name of the winery is a reflection of the gamble that all viticulturists and winemakers face every vintage: 'You have to play the hand you are dealt by Mother Nature'. They only use estate-grown grapes, open-top fermentation, hand-plunging and manual basket pressing. It's certainly doing it the hard way, but it must seem all worthwhile when they produce wines of such quality.

ŸŸŸŸŸ **Three Card Monte Single Vineyard Margaret River Sauvignon Blanc 2019** Hand-picked, destemmed, crushed to fermentation bins and sealed for 8 days, pressed to barrel (French oak, 25% new) and wild-fermented, matured for 11 months. Wow. Has layered, complex fruit that is deliciously fresh with tropical notes running alongside intense Meyer lemon acidity. Screwcap. 11.9% alc. **Rating** 95 To 2023 $28 ✪
The Royals Single Vineyard Margaret River Chardonnay 2019 Hand-picked, chilled overnight, whole-bunch pressed, only free-run juice used, wild fermented, 30% mlf, matured in French oak (53% new) for 12 months.

A high quality wine with remarkable drive and intensity. Grapefruit leads the flavour. Screwcap. 13.2% alc. **Rating** 95 **To** 2029 $54

Ace of Spades 2018 For the first time, 100% cabernet sauvignon with 2 new clones: one ex Houghton, the other ex Chateau Margaux. Hand-picked and sorted, open-fermented, 30 days on skins, repeated plunging, matured for 18 months in French oak (50% new). It's medium-bodied but feline in the way it creeps up on you – initially simply pretty, but its structure and texture become apparent on retasting, the fruit keeping pace. All up, a cabernet of distinction. Screwcap. 14.2% alc. **Rating** 95 **To** 2033 $65

Black Jack Single Vineyard Margaret River Malbec 2018 Hand-picked, 10% of the juice drained off, wild yeast–open fermented, matured for 18 months in French oak (25% new). Powerful satsuma plum with exotic spice notes. Lots of character. Screwcap. 14.2% alc. **Rating** 95 **To** 2033 $48

Dead Man's Hand Margaret River Shiraz 2018 60% whole bunch fermentation, matured in French oak for 14 months. It ticks all the boxes bar one: the jigsaw of the components is yet to mesh. Screwcap. 14.5% alc. **Rating** 94 **To** 2038 $26 ○

🍷🍷🍷🍷♀ **Lady Luck Petit Verdot 2017** **Rating** 93 **To** 2037 $58
Kings in the Corner Cabernet Merlot 2017 **Rating** 92 **To** 2026 $26 NG
The Royals Cabernet Sauvignon 2017 **Rating** 92 **To** 2029 $40 NG
The Joker Sauvignon Blanc 2019 **Rating** 90 **To** 2022 $21 ○

Howard Park   ★★★★★

Miamup Road, Cowaramup, WA 6284 **Region** Margaret River
T (08) 9756 5200 **www.**burchfamilywines.com.au **Open** 7 days 10–5
Winemaker Janice McDonald, Mark Bailey **Est.** 1986 **Dozens** NFP **Vyds** 183ha
Over the last 30 or so years the Burch family has slowly acquired vineyards in Margaret River and Great Southern. The Margaret River vineyards range from Leston in Wilyabrup to Allingham in southern Karridale; Great Southern includes Mount Barrow and Abercrombie (the latter acquired in 2014), with Houghton cabernet clones, planted in 1975, all in Mount Barker. At the top of the portfolio are the Howard Park Abercrombie Cabernet Sauvignon and the Allingham Chardonnay, followed by the rieslings, chardonnay and sauvignon blanc; next come pairs of shiraz and cabernet sauvignon under the Leston and Scotsdale labels. The Miamup and the Flint Rock regional ranges were established in 2012. MadFish produces the full range of varietal wines, Gold Turtle the second tier of MadFish. The feng shui–designed cellar door is a must-see. A founding member of Australian First Families of Wines. Exports to all major markets.

🍷🍷🍷🍷🍷 **Howard Park Margaret River Chardonnay 2018** Wild yeast–barrel fermented. Immaculate vinification of the best fruit has produced maximum results for a great wine at a fair price. White peach, melon and pink grapefruit are joined at the hip. Screwcap. 13% alc. **Rating** 97 **To** 2033 $58 ○

Howard Park Abercrombie Margaret River Mount Barker Cabernet Sauvignon 2017 Hand-picked and sorted, destemmed, fermented in header-board vats or small open stainless steel vats, part pressed at dryness (fruit vibrancy), part given extended maceration (structure). High quality Margaret River cabernet made for a long life with decades of change to texture and structure. Screwcap. 14% alc. **Rating** 97 **To** 2042 $150 ○

Howard Park ASW Margaret River Cabernet Sauvignon Shiraz 2017 The result of decades of investment in the Leston Vineyard; the cabernet from Block 29, the shiraz from Block 17; vinified separately, the wine is taken to American barriques for maturation. This wine must please Janice McDonald mightily, for it is seriously elegant and complex with a full array of fruit and secondary flavours. Screwcap. 14% alc. **Rating** 97 **To** 2047 $100 ○

🍷🍷🍷🍷🍷 **Howard Park Museum Release Mount Barker Riesling 2013** A riesling that retains a youthful glow and carries its age well. Mineral, lightly toasted, spring blossom, lantana, lime pith and more. The palate goes on and on, and with it a rising intensity in developed riesling characters with acidity keeping things tight. This is why people get excited by aged riesling. Screwcap. 12% alc. **Rating** 96 **To** 2025 $41 JP ✪

Howard Park Porongurup Riesling 2019 Made in identical fashion to the Mount Barker. Has that edge of elegance that is particular to Porongurup, and will retain that through its journey to full maturity 10 years hence. Screwcap. 12% alc. **Rating** 95 **To** 2030 $35 ✪

Howard Park Flint Rock Great Southern Riesling 2018 The wine builds layers of intensity each time it is retasted. A classic Great Southern mix of lime, lemon, apple and pear aromas and flavours. Length is a given, as is a long future. Screwcap. 12% alc. **Rating** 95 **To** 2031 $28 ✪

Howard Park Margaret River Sauvignon Blanc 2019 Predominantly cool-fermented sauvignon blanc in tank, with a smaller amount fermented in oak; Howard Park making the process seem easy, which it's not. Aromas and flavours play snakes and ladders with the interplay of fruit, oak and acidity. Screwcap. 13% alc. **Rating** 95 **To** 2023 $31 ✪

Howard Park Allingham Margaret River Chardonnay 2018 Hand-picked, chilled, hand-sorted, wild-fermented in French oak (40% new), 9 months in barrel, some mlf. Elegant and detailed, the finish ramping up the complexity and length. Screwcap. 13% alc. **Rating** 95 **To** 2027 $89

Howard Park Mount Barker Riesling 2019 Settled bright, free-run juice given a long, cold ferment. First class wine. Layers of flavour before a long, fresh finish. Screwcap. 12% alc. **Rating** 94 **To** 2027 $34

Howard Park Flint Rock Mount Barker Chardonnay 2018 Key descriptors from the '18 vintage in Mount Barker are 'ripeness' and 'power'. They apply equally here. A fresh, juicy chardonnay with fruit dominant and subtle backup oak. Generous stone fruit, melon, ruby grapefruit. Expansive palate. Peachy, nutty, creamy and mouthfilling. Screwcap. 13% alc. **Rating** 94 **To** 2028 $29 JP ✪

Howard Park Porongurup Riesling 2018 **Rating** 93 **To** 2032 $35 JP
MadFish Gold Turtle Great Southern Riesling 2018 **Rating** 93 **To** 2025 $25 ✪
Howard Park Miamup Margaret River Cabernet Sauvignon 2017 **Rating** 93 **To** 2030 $32
Howard Park Miamup Margaret River Chardonnay 2018 **Rating** 91 **To** 2027 $28
Howard Park Miamup Margaret River Rose 2018 **Rating** 91 **To** 2024 $28 JP
MadFish Gold Turtle Margaret River Cabernet Sauvignon Merlot 2017 **Rating** 91 **To** 2029 $25
Puppet Master Chardonnay 2018 **Rating** 90 **To** 2026 $26
MadFish Chardonnay 2018 **Rating** 90 **To** 2023 $20 ✪
Howard Park Flint Rock Great Southern Pinot Noir 2018 **Rating** 90 **To** 2028 $32
MadFish Vera's Cuvee Methode Traditionnelle NV **Rating** 90 $26
Howard Park Methode Traditionnelle Blanc de Blancs NV **Rating** 90 $89

Howard Vineyard ★★★★★

53 Bald Hills Road, Nairne, SA 5252 **Region** Adelaide Hills
T (08) 8188 0203 **www**.howardvineyard.com **Open** Tues–Sun 10–5
Winemaker Tom Northcott **Est.** 2005 **Dozens** 6000 **Vyds** 60ha

Howard Vineyard is a family-owned Adelaide Hills winery set among towering gum trees, and terraced lawns. Pinot noir, chardonnay, pinot gris and sauvignon blanc are sourced from the 470m altitude Schoenthal 'Beautiful Valley' Vineyard near Lobethal, while Howard's Nairne Vineyard, in the warmer Mt Barker district, is home to shiraz, cabernet sauvignon and cabernet franc. All the wines are estate-grown. Winemaker Tom Northcott has a Bachelor Degree in Viticulture and Oenology from the University of Adelaide, and has worked vintages in the South of France, Barossa Valley, Western Australia and Tasmania. Exports to Hong Kong and China.

ΨΨΨΨΨ **Amos Adelaide Hills Shiraz 2017** Fruit from low yielding 15yo vines was amplified by a long pre-ferment cold soak. To excellent effect. Fermented with 25% whole-bunches. Semi-carbonic aromas of lilac, blue and black fruits, iodine, tapenade and salumi are bright and highly attractive. Best, though, is the impressively long finish. The pixelated peppery tannic detail, compelling. Cork. 13.7% alc. **Rating** 96 **To** 2026 $55 NG ✪
Amos Adelaide Hills Cabernet Sauvignon 2017 A gentle, medium-bodied and highly savoury cabernet, drinking more like a warmer year from the Loire than a wine of Bordeaux, simply by virtue of the delicate leafy structural attributes. Make no mistake, this is delicious! Blackcurrant, mint, graphite and a whiff of bitter chocolate meander along a balletic beam of finely wrought tannins. Lovely tannins! So different from the norm and all the better for it. Cork. 13.8% alc. **Rating** 95 **To** 2029 $55 NG
Adelaide Hills Shiraz 2018 Partly hand-picked and fermented carbonic, presumably with stems intact. The result, though, sumptuous, combining a quintessentially coolish expression of Australian fruit, ramrod and pure. Think black cherry and boysenberry. Soaring florals lifting. To follow, a finely tuned cadence of salami, pepper, Asian spice, Pastis and mocha oak. Good now and across a shortish mid-term in the cellar. Screwcap. **Rating** 94 **To** 2024 $35 NG

ΨΨΨΨ♀ **Adelaide Hills Cabernet Franc Rose 2019 Rating** 93 **To** 2022 $35 NG
Adelaide Hills Pinot Gris 2019 Rating 92 **To** 2024 $25 NG ✪
Block Q Adelaide Hills Sauvignon Blanc 2019 Rating 91 **To** 2024 $25 NG
Amos Adelaide Hills Chardonnay 2018 Rating 91 **To** 2025 $50 NG
Adelaide Hills Gruner Veltliner 2019 Rating 91 **To** 2023 $30 NG
Adelaide Hills Cabernet Sauvignon 2017 Rating 91 **To** 2023 $30 NG
Adelaide Hills Sauvignon Blanc 2019 Rating 90 **To** 2021 $20 NG ✪
Adelaide Hills Rose 2019 Rating 90 **To** 2020 $20 NG ✪
Adelaide Hills Pinot Noir Chardonnay 2019 Rating 90 $30 NG

Hugh Hamilton Wines ★★★★★

94 McMurtrie Road, McLaren Vale, SA 5171 **Region** McLaren Vale
T (08) 8323 8689 **www.**hughhamiltonwines.com.au **Open** 7 days 11–5
Winemaker Nic Bourke **Est.** 1991 **Dozens** 18 500 **Vyds** 21.4ha
In 2014, fifth-generation family member Hugh Hamilton handed over the reins to daughter Mary. She developed the irreverent black sheep packaging. But it's more than simply marketing: the business will continue to embrace both mainstream and alternative varieties, its 85-year-old shiraz and 65-year-old cabernet sauvignon at its Blewitt Springs vineyard providing the ability to develop the Black label. There have been changes: in the way the vines are trellised, picking and fermenting in small open fermenters, using gravity for wine movements and maturation in high quality French oak. The cellar door is lined with the original jarrah from Vat 15 of the historic Hamilton's Ewell winery, the largest wooden vat ever built in the Southern Hemisphere. Exports to the UK, the US, Canada, Denmark, Germany, Switzerland, Finland, South Korea, Singapore, Japan and China.

ΨΨΨΨΨ **Black Blood II McLaren Vale Shiraz 2018** Of the 3 single site Black Blood wines, this, from the Church Vineyard in McMurtrie Road, shines the most brightly. It's complete. It's balanced. A waft of wet iron filings and violets, then a whorl of black plums and cherry pips spiced with cinnamon flow across the full-bodied palate abetted by ripe yet silky tannins. Screwcap. 14.9% alc. **Rating** 96 **To** 2035 $79 JF
The Oddball McLaren Vale Saperavi 2017 Trademark saperavi colour – an inky purple with a flash of red. Fragrant with red roses and spices, enticing. It is full-bodied, rich and ripe, packing a lot of flavour yet persimmon-like tannins and a vivacity to the acidity manage to keep this in tip-top shape. Cork. 15.2% alc. **Rating** 96 **To** 2027 $70 JF ✪

Aroma Pagoda 2019 A multi-regional blend and different make-up to the previous vintage, this comprising mostly riesling and pinot gris with decent glugs of gewurztraminer and sauvignon blanc. It's a ripper. Refreshing from the word go with its lemon accents and crunchy pear with a hint of rose. It's a neat blend with texture, drive and a kiss of sweetness on the finish. Screwcap. 12.8% alc. **Rating** 95 To 2021 $25 JF ✪

Black Blood I McLaren Vale Shiraz 2018 From the Cellar Vineyard in McMurtrie Road. The richest, densest of the 3 Black Blood wines, yet it doesn't get bogged down in winemaking artefact. Layers of black cherries, plums and licorice infused with iodine and nori. Full-bodied for sure, but the palate is bright and juicy with some gentle grip to the tannins. Neatly played. Screwcap. 14.9% alc. **Rating** 95 To 2032 $79 JF

Tonnellerie Damy McLaren Vale Shiraz 2017 The idea behind the trio of Tonnellerie shirazs is to take fruit from the same vineyard make them identically, the only difference is the choice of cooperage. At a pinch, this leads for its balance and complexity. The core of dark, sweet plums/cherries is perfectly embedded in the smoky-savoury oak flavours with the fruit and wood tannins neatly meshed. Screwcap. 14.8% alc. **Rating** 95 To 2032 $50 JF

Tonnellerie Francois Freres McLaren Vale Shiraz 2017 Burgundian cooper Francois Freres barrels are distinctive for their cherry sweet–savoury profile and extra tannin layer across the wine; and perfectly suited to this full-bodied shiraz. Appealing toasty, cedar flavours with a dusting of baking spices and firm tannins to close. As with the other Tonnellerie wines, just 25 dozen made. Screwcap. 14.8% alc. **Rating** 95 To 2032 $50 JF

Black Ops McLaren Vale Shiraz Saperavi 2018 Black Ops is now part of the Exotica range focussing on saperavi – this at 40% with 60% shiraz. While the Vale is famous for the latter, Hugh Hamilton is renowned for his Georgian addiction. This is a wonderful combo: a whorl of the darkest fruits, licorice and Middle Eastern spices with determined tannins across a structured palate. It all works. Everything in sync. Screwcap. 14.9% alc. **Rating** 95 To 2028 $33 JF ✪

Three Bags Full 2018 You have to be a member of Hugh Hamilton's Black Sheep Club to buy this – worth joining to get it. It's a GSM split 51/42/7%, and it flies the flag for bright, ripe fruit with a savoury thread ensuring the fruit sweetness is kept in check. Full-bodied with supple satisfying tannins; while it has the brightness and boldness of youth, it'll temper down in time. Screwcap. 14.8% alc. **Rating** 95 To 2030 $33 JF ✪

The Nimble King McLaren Vale Cabernet Sauvignon 2018 A glorious purple-black. Heady aromas of violets, cassis and blackberries with tannins smooth as silk as they sashay across the full-bodied palate. An impressive cabernet. Membership of the Black Sheep Club is essential to buy this. Screwcap. 14.6% alc. **Rating** 95 To 2030 $50 JF

♥♥♥♥♡ **Shearer's Cut McLaren Vale Shiraz 2018 Rating** 93 To 2026 $25 JF ✪
Tonnellerie Vicard McLaren Vale Shiraz 2017 Rating 93 To 2030 $50 JF
The Trickster Adelaide Hills Pinot Grigio 2019 Rating 92 To 2021 $20 JF ✪
Black Blood III McLaren Vale Shiraz 2018 Rating 92 To 2030 $79 JF
Cornucopiacation Shiraz 2018 Rating 92 To 2028 $30 JF
Ancient Earth McLaren Vale Shiraz 2017 Rating 92 To 2030 $50 JF
The Mongrel McLaren Vale Sangiovese 2018 Rating 92 To 2024 $25 JF ✪
The Villain McLaren Vale Cabernet Sauvignon 2018 Rating 91 To 2026 $30 JF
The Ratbag McLaren Vale Merlot 2018 Rating 90 To 2022 $25 JF

Hugo   ★★★★☆

246 Elliott Road, McLaren Flat, SA 5171 **Region** McLaren Vale
T (08) 8383 0098 **www**.hugowines.com.au **Open** Mon–Fri 10–5, Sat–Sun 10.30–5
Winemaker Renae Hirsch, Brian Light **Est.** 1982 **Dozens** 8000 **Vyds** 20ha

Came from relative obscurity to prominence in the late 1980s with some lovely ripe, sweet reds, which, while strongly American oak–influenced, were outstanding. It picked up the pace again after a dull period in the mid-'90s and has made the most of the recent run of good vintages. The estate plantings include shiraz, cabernet sauvignon, chardonnay, grenache and sauvignon blanc with part of the grape production sold. Exports to Canada.

𝕐𝕐𝕐𝕐𝕐 **McLaren Vale Shiraz 2016** As usual, great value on offer. Dark plums and licorice with lots of woodsy spices. It's fuller bodied and starts out fleshy, almost glossy. It is still quite oaky, adding sweetness across the palate, but nothing jarring. Screwcap. 14.5% alc. **Rating** 92 **To** 2028 $25 JF ✪
McLaren Vale Shiraz Cabernet 2018 A 52/48% split that has gelled, offering lots of spice, dark berries with a whisper of cassis, licorice and aniseed. Fuller bodied with tannins firmly in place yet, in-between a succulence to the fruit, just a nagging green bitter walnut pinch to the finish. Screwcap. 14.5% alc. **Rating** 91 **To** 2028 $28 JF
McLaren Vale Grenache 2019 The price seems to have dropped significantly compared with previous years. Fruit still comes off bushvines planted in '51; whole-bunch fermentation and aged in used French hogsheads for 7 months. Red fruit mingles with more savoury elements of pepper and earth, while the tannins have a decent grip on the finish. Screwcap. 13.5% alc. **Rating** 91 **To** 2028 $28 JF

Humis Vineyard   ★★★★

3730 Heathcote-Rochester Road, Corop, Vic 3559 **Region** Heathcote
T 0419 588 044 www.humisvineyard.com **Open** By appt
Winemaker Cathy Branson **Est.** 2011 **Dozens** 800 **Vyds** 13.5ha
Both the wine labels and the letter from Hugh Jones to me giving the background to his and wife Michelle's venture share a battered, old-fashioned typeface. The letter was as interesting for what it didn't say as for what it did, although there was a connection in an improbable way because my mother Muriel's house name was Missy, also Michelle's nickname. The snapshot approach of the website's 'About Us' explains that in 2010, with the wine industry on its knees and a drought in full swing in Heathcote, Hugh saw a dusty paddock running down to a dry Lake Cooper with a 'for sale' sign. The decision was obvious: buy and promise that then very young twins, son Tex and daughter Mallee, wouldn't be too neglected. The ace in the hole was the irrigation water available to the property.

𝕐𝕐𝕐𝕐 **Heathcote Grenache 2018** Estate-grown, the vineyard planted '12; matured in used French oak. Very light colour. Gentle fruit. Drink now. Screwcap. 13.5% alc. **Rating** 89 **To** 2020 $20
Heathcote Grenache Shiraz 2017 An 80/20% single vineyard blend. Very light colour and flavour. No mention of oak. Screwcap. 12.3% alc. **Rating** 89 **To** 2020 $20

Hundred of Comaum   ★★★★

242 Comaum School Road, Coonawarra, SA 5263 **Region** Coonawarra
T 0438 005 051 www.hundredofcomaum.com.au **Open** 7 days 10–6
Winemaker Gavin Hogg **Est.** 1999 **Dozens** 4000 **Vyds** 9.6ha
Stephen Moignard sits defiantly on an ancient backhoe with the registration plate DAVNET, even though the backhoe is not registered and the plate came from a Ferrari he once owned. He was briefly CEO of the publicly listed DAVNET, rising from 4c a share in 1999 to $5 just before the tech wreck of 2002 took it back to 10c. He made the BRW Rich List for one year, which excited the interest of various regulators. He says, 'You would be right to ask whether eight years of fighting de factos, ASIC and the ATO has sent [me] around the twist. Who cares? I'll die here, and I can even dig the hole.' These days he has cabernet sauvignon, shiraz and riesling planted on Lot 1, Comaum School Road, Coonawarra, hence the brand name Hundred of Comaum. Steve offers vineyard accommodation with cabins, glamping tents and even air-filled bubble apartments. Exports to China.

♀♀♀♀♀ **Reserve Coonawarra Cabernet Sauvignon 2012** The screwcap has been invaluable in allowing this medium-bodied cabernet to handle the first 8 years of its life with ease. Cassis fruit, quality oak and fine-grained tannins are all on the same page. 14% alc. **Rating** 93 **To** 2027

Flagship Coonawarra Cabernet Sauvignon 2018 An attractive, very well balanced wine, its best years to come. It has not been hit with oak staves et al, and easily handles its alcohol with redcurrant and blackcurrant fruit, the tannins fine. Diam. 15% alc. **Rating** 91 **To** 2030

Hungerford Hill   ★★★★☆

2450 Broke Road, Pokolbin, NSW 2320 **Region** Hunter Valley
T (02) 4998 7666 **www**.hungerfordhill.com.au **Open** Sun–Thurs 10–5, Fri–Sat 10–6
Winemaker Bryan Currie **Est.** 1967 **Dozens** 22000 **Vyds** 5ha
Sam and Christie Arnaout purchased Hungerford Hill in December 2016, planning to refocus the 50-year-old label on its Hunter Valley origin, also adding significant new Lower Hunter vineyards at Sweetwater and Dalwood – the oldest continuously operating vineyard in Australia (see separate entries). Hungerford Hill will use these vineyards to bolster its Hunter Valley wines while continuing its 20+-year association with the cool-climate Tumbarumba and Hilltops regions. Exports to all major markets.

♀♀♀♀♀ **Revee Vineyard Tumbarumba Chardonnay 2017** Tumbarumba stars again in a high altitude, cool-climate chardonnay that combines delicacy and power in the best way possible. Old vines (Revee was planted in '81) and a cooler year than some have helped. To drink it is to wander through an orchard of citrus, nectarines and quince, and further into a wild place. Brisk acidity heightens the senses. Screwcap. 13.5% alc. **Rating** 95 **To** 2032 $55 JP

Revee Vineyard Tumbarumba Pinot Noir 2018 The MV6 workhorse clone does another mighty fine job here in tandem with the always reliable, cool-climate Tumbarumba region. Solid red colour and big presence in the glass with aromas of wild strawberry and cherry, leafy, dusty beets and cinnamon. Then it gets serious with good depth of complexity and length. Cherry jelly shots bring a lighter moment. Screwcap. 13.5% alc. **Rating** 94 **To** 2030 $65 JP

Hilltops Tempranillo Graciano 2019 Clearly made to enjoy in its youth, it boasts an exuberant personality with a softness and the kind of versatility that will put it in the good books with many a sommelier. Mouth-watering dark cherries, stewed plums, summer pudding and spice. A balanced, tightly knit palate brimming with primary fruit goodness. Drink sooner rather than later. Screwcap. 13.5% alc. **Rating** 94 **To** 2026 $45 JP

Dalliance Methode Champenoise 2017 A blend of pinot meunier, pinot noir and chardonnay from the high and mighty Tumbarumba wine region. It's a fleshy, succulent sparkling with aromas of white peach, melon, white flowers, confection and biscuit. The thread of preserved lemon provides a point of difference, a touch of savouriness, with mouthfilling chalk texture. Cork. 12.5% alc. **Rating** 94 $45 JP

♀♀♀♀♀ **Tumbarumba Pinot Gris 2019** **Rating** 93 **To** 2026 $27 JP ✪
Tumbarumba Chardonnay 2017 **Rating** 92 **To** 2030 $40 JP
Hunter Valley Fiano 2019 **Rating** 92 **To** 2027 $27 JP
H.H. Classic Hunter Valley Shiraz NV **Rating** 92 **To** 2032 $45 JP
Heavy Metal 2018 **Rating** 92 **To** 2030 $55 JP
Hilltops Pinot Grigio 2019 **Rating** 91 **To** 2025 $27 JP
Hilltops Shiraz 2018 **Rating** 91 **To** 2030 $45 JP
Tumbarumba Fume Blanc 2018 **Rating** 90 **To** 2026 $27 JP
Hunter Valley Vermentino 2019 **Rating** 90 **To** 2026 $27 JP
Tumbarumba Pinot Noir 2018 **Rating** 90 **To** 2026 $45 JP
Liqueur Muscat NV **Rating** 90 $50 JP

Huntington Estate ★★★★★

Ulan Road, Mudgee, NSW 2850 **Region** Mudgee
T 1800 995 931 **www**.huntingtonestate.com.au **Open** Mon–Sat 10–5, Sun 10–4
Winemaker Tim Stevens **Est.** 1969 **Dozens** 13 000 **Vyds** 43.8ha

Since taking ownership of Huntington Estate from the founding Roberts family, Tim Stevens has sensibly refrained from making major changes. The policy of having older vintage wines available is continuing, making the cellar door a first port of call for visitors to Mudgee. Exports to China.

ɯɯɯɯɯ Block 3 Mudgee Cabernet Sauvignon 2015 Destemmed and crushed into small wooded fermenters, half pressed after 2 weeks, the other half after 4 weeks, matured for 18 months in French oak (33% new). It fully meets Huntington's description of elegance and, I would add, purity with a very strong sense of place. The varietal expression is exact. Screwcap. 13.1% alc. **Rating** 96 **To** 2035 $75 ✪
Mudgee Shiraz 2017 A blend of the best 4 estate blocks; crushed, fermented for 10 days, matured for 16 months in used American oak. Bright, full colour. Oak, fruit and fine tannins are sewn together by the balance and elegance of this medium–bodied shiraz. Screwcap. 14.1% alc. **Rating** 95 **To** 2030 $32 ✪
Special Reserve Mudgee Cabernet Sauvignon 2016 From 48yo vines; vinified in large open–top wooden fermenters, sealed after conclusion of fermentation for a month on skins, 18 months maturation in French barriques (40% new). With a long list of forebears that were honoured in the Mudgee Wine Show, it speaks with utmost clarity of its sense of place with a swell of earthy tannins backing up blackcurrant fruit. Screwcap. 14.5% alc. **Rating** 95 **To** 2036 $45
Special Reserve Mudgee Semillon 2019 Processed swiftly, cool–fermented and early bottled. Lemongrass, lemony acidity et al is in place for a gradual move to the complexity and richness 10+ years hence. Screwcap. 11.7% alc. **Rating** 94 **To** 2032 $35
Special Reserve Mudgee Shiraz 2017 Deep, bright colour. Full–bodied, overflowing with luscious purple and black fruits and lashings of oak. Finesse is not part of the landscape, this doesn't need it. What it does need is time. Screwcap. 14.4% alc. **Rating** 94 **To** 2040 $45
Basket Dried Mudgee Shiraz 2016 An experiment to ascertain what happens to the tannins if the grapes are harvested early, here at 10.5°baume. They were placed in drying trays and stored for 3 weeks with fans blowing continuously, then fermented normally and matured in barrel for 18 months. Its intensity of dark fruit flavours, supported by firm tannins, was recognised by the Mudgee Wine Show '19 with the trophy for Best Museum Red Wine. Screwcap. 15.5% alc. **Rating** 94 **To** 2031 $75

ɯɯɯɯ Special Reserve Mudgee Merlot 2018 Rating 90 **To** 2028 $45

Hurley Vineyard ★★★★★

101 Balnarring Road, Balnarring, Vic 3926 **Region** Mornington Peninsula
T (03) 5931 3000 **www**.hurleyvineyard.com.au **Open** 1st Fri & w'end each month 11–5
Winemaker Kevin Bell **Est.** 1998 **Dozens** 1100 **Vyds** 3.5ha

It's never as easy as it seems. Despite leading busy city lives, Kevin Bell and wife Tricia Byrnes have done most of the hard work in establishing Hurley Vineyard themselves, with some help from family and friends. Kevin completed the applied science (wine science) degree at CSU, drawing on a wide circle of fellow pinot noir makers in Australia and Burgundy. He has not allowed a significant heart issue to prevent him continuing with his first love.

ɯɯɯɯɯ Garamond Balnarring Mornington Peninsula Pinot Noir 2018 Garamond has well and truly inveigled its way onto our pinot noir landscape as one of the finest. It has presence. It reflects the 1.2ha easterly site of MV6 with such detail, the vines planted 20 years ago. Everything is perfectly placed here: the aromatics are heady and enticing, the palate serene with raw silk tannins and a gentle persuasion throughout. Bravo. Diam. 13.4% alc. **Rating** 97 **To** 2030 $85 JF ✪

🍷🍷🍷🍷🍷 **Hommage Balnarring Mornington Peninsula Pinot Noir 2018** The darkest hue of the trio of single-site offerings, and what a wine! Harmony in a glass, with red cherries and raspberries, star anise, woodsy spices and more besides. Medium-bodied with the oak seamlessly integrated and exceptional tannins, all velvety and smooth. Fabulous. Diam. 13.5% alc. **Rating** 96 **To** 2030 $70 JF ✪

Estate Balnarring Mornington Peninsula Pinot Noir 2018 One of the best value pinots from the Peninsula. It has quality stamped across it – the estate is a blend of the 3 single sites, the sum of its parts. Heady aromatics, a delicacy throughout, but still detailed tannins and refreshing acidity gliding across the smooth palate. Diam. 13.4% alc. **Rating** 95 **To** 2028 $45 JF

Lodestone Balnarring Mornington Peninsula Pinot Noir 2018 Welcome back Lodestone – none made in '17. From the warmest of the 3 single sites, so more dark cherries and juniper, earth and hummus with orange zest. Just shy of fuller bodied; plush tannins ensue as does a refreshing line of acidity making this satisfying to the very last drop. Diam. 13.4% alc. **Rating** 95 **To** 2028 $70 JF

Hutton Vale Farm

Stone Jar Road, Angaston, SA 5353 **Region** Eden Valley
T (08) 8564 8270 **www.**huttonvale.com **Open** By appt
Winemaker Kym Teusner **Est.** 1960 **Dozens** 1500 **Vyds** 27ha

John Howard Angas arrived in SA in 1843 and inter alia gave his name to Angaston, purchasing and developing significant farming property close to the still embryonic town. He named part of this Hutton Vale and it is this property that is now owned and occupied by his great-great-grandson John and wife Jan Angas. In 2012, the Angas family and Teusner Wines shook hands on a new partnership arrangement, under which the Angases grow the grapes and Kym Teusner is responsible for the winemaking, sales and marketing of Hutton Vale wines. The vineyards in question first caught Kym's attention when he was at Torbreck and he fulfilled a long-term ambition with the new agreement. Just when the future seemed assured, the vineyards were badly affected by a grass fire in August '14. While much of the vineyard has regenerated, some of the oldest grenache vines were completely destroyed, as were 55 of the magnificent 500-year-old gum trees that are part of the striking landscape of Hutton Vale. Small quantities of its wines are exported to China.

🍷🍷🍷🍷🍷 **Eden Valley Shiraz 2016** The names of the Angas family and of the Hutton Vale Farm have been part of the fabric of the Eden Valley, with continued ownership during 6 generations, the 7th (brother and sister Stuart and Caitlin) now also actively involved. This is a beautiful wine; its aroma, its palate, its weight, its varietal and regional expression giving rise to a continuous stream of velvety pleasure. Flawless. Screwcap. 15% alc. **Rating** 97 **To** 2036 $75 ✪

🍷🍷🍷🍷🍷 **Eden Valley Grenache Mataro 2016** A blend accidentally created when the vineyard was planted to grenache and around 10% of the vineyard block failed due to drought, mataro unknowingly supplied for the replanting. Hand-picked, open-fermented, matured in French puncheons for 24 months. Fair and square – wonderfully elegant red fruits and spicy, savoury notes. Screwcap. 15% alc. **Rating** 96 **To** 2031 $75 ✪

Eden Valley Cabernet Sauvignon 2016 Open-fermented, 8 days on skins, 26 months in French barriques (35% new), plus 20 months in bottle before release. Cassis/blackcurrant notes plus mint and briar. The tannins are still on the lookout for a fight, so proceed with caution. Screwcap. 15% alc. **Rating** 94 **To** 2041 $75

Eden Valley Riesling 2019 As anticipated, barely off-dry – the touch of sweetness appears briefly on the tip of the tongue to be promptly displaced by a touch of acidity almost on the same spot. Screwcap. 10% alc. **Rating** 94 $35

Hutton Wines

PO Box 1214, Dunsborough, WA 6281 **Region** Margaret River
T 0417 923 126 **www**.huttonwines.com **Open** Not
Winemaker Michael Hutton **Est.** 2006 **Dozens** 300
This is another venture of the Hutton family of Gralyn fame, with Michael Hutton, who returned to the Margaret River region in 2005, establishing this micro-business the following year, while continuing his architectural practice. Tiny quantities of semillon sauvignon, chardonnay and cabernet sauvignon are produced; hardly enough to threaten Gralyn.

🍷🍷🍷🍷🍷 Triptych Margaret River Chardonnay 2019 It's unclear the difference between this and the reserve, which is nearly double the price. If the accompanying note is correct, this relies on more new French oak at 54%, and adds plenty of flavour and layers, yet the fruit is taking it in its stride. Creamed honey, grapefruit, lovely acid line and all in all, impressive. Screwcap. 12.7% alc. Rating 95 To 2028 $40 JF

🍷🍷🍷🍷🍷 Graffiti Chardy 2019 Rating 90 To 2024 $25 JF
Triptych Reserve Chardonnay 2019 Rating 90 To 2027 $75 JF

Idavue Estate

470 Northern Highway, Heathcote, Vic 3523 **Region** Heathcote
T 0429 617 287 **www**.idavueestate.com **Open** W'ends 10.30–5
Winemaker Andrew Whytcross, Sandra Whytcross **Est.** 2000 **Dozens** 600 **Vyds** 5.7ha
Owners and winemakers Andrew and Sandra Whytcross produce award-winning wines; the vineyard managed by Andy, the winery run using normal small-batch winemaking techniques. Shiraz is the flagship wine, with cabernet sauvignon, chardonnay and semillon also grown and made on the estate. The Barrelhouse cellar door is adorned with music paraphenalia and guitars, and regularly holds blues music events.

🍷🍷🍷🍷🍷 Heathcote Cabernet Sauvignon 2016 As is the case with its Shiraz sibling, this is impressive value. Indeed, it is more than that. The varietal expression is clear, and the mouthfeel balanced. Screwcap. 14% alc. Rating 94 To 2030 $20 ✪

🍷🍷🍷🍷🍷 Heathcote Shiraz 2017 Rating 90 To 2037 $25 ✪

Idyll Wine Co.

265 Ballan Road, Moorabool, Vic 3221 **Region** Geelong
T (03) 5228 4888 **www**.idyllwineco.com.au **Open** Mon–Fri 10–5
Winemaker Toby Wanklyn, Vassily Pestretsov **Est.** 2015 **Dozens** 1.2 million **Vyds** 6ha
By 1861 Geelong was Victoria's largest wine region with 225ha under vine, rising to 400ha in '69 with 50 individual vineyards. By '75 it reached the peak of its success, its dream then soured by the arrival of phylloxera and the decision by the government to order the removal of all vines just as the cure (grafting onto American rootstocks) was proved. It took nigh-on 100 years for (grafted) vines to be planted again in the region by vet Daryl Sefton and relentless promoter wife Nini. By 1966 Idyll Vineyard was established with 20ha of shiraz, cabernet sauvignon and gewurztraminer. The Seftons were making and selling wines until their retirement in the '80s. This is the site of the vast winery owned by private investment group Costa Asset Management. The winery can process 15 000t of grapes each vintage and store 18 million litres of wine in refrigerated stainless steel tanks. Idyll has 3 branches: first, wines based on grapes purchased from regions spread across southeastern Australia; second, branded wines at low prices; and third, bulk wine or cleanskin wines. A large part of all these wines are sold to Chinese-based customers. Exports to most major markets.

In Dreams

3/436 Johnston Street, Abbotsford, Vic 3067 **Region** Yarra Valley
T (03) 8413 8379 **www**.indreams.com.au **Open** Not
Winemaker Nina Stocker **Est.** 2013 **Dozens** 1200

'Hand-crafted wines begin with a dream, the dream of what might be as the first vine is planted.' Nina Stocker sources pinot noir and chardonnay from three low yielding vineyards in the cool Upper Yarra Valley. The cooler microclimate of the area lends itself to traditional winemaking techniques, such as small-batch fermentation and delicate use of French oak, which allow the fruit to express itself.

🍷🍷🍷🍷🍷 **Yarra Valley Chardonnay 2019** From 5 vineyards, each parcel kept separate, all fermented in French oak (10% new), 40% underwent mlf, each batch sat on full lees for 9 months before blending. On the leaner side of chardonnay with pronounced lemony acidity; taut and tastes of cold steel. Concentrated and yet to do a full reveal. Screwcap. 13% alc. **Rating** 94 **To** 2035 JP

Indigo Vineyard ★★★★★

1221 Beechworth–Wangaratta Road, Everton Upper, Vic 3678 **Region** Beechworth
T (03) 5727 0233 **www**.indigovineyard.com.au **Open** 7 days 11–4
Winemaker Stuart Hordern, Marc Scalzo **Est.** 1999 **Dozens** 6000 **Vyds** 46.15ha
Indigo Vineyard has a little over 46ha of vineyards planted to 11 varieties, including the top French and Italian grapes. The business was and is primarily directed to growing grapes for sale to Brokenwood, but since 2004 increasing amounts have been vinified for the Indigo label. The somewhat incestuous nature of the whole business sees the Indigo wines being made at Brokenwood (Marc Scalzo makes the Pinot Grigio). Exports to France.

🍷🍷🍷🍷🍷 **Beechworth Pinot Grigio 2019** Sourced from Everton Upper. Think grigio is the simple sister to gris? Here is a wine to change your mind with deep, concentrated aromas of delicious apple, hay, jasmine, nashi pear. Reaches for new ground with the variety; a full exposition of flavour possibilities from pear tatin and citrus to biscuit. A distinct savoury texture and zesty acidity noted. Screwcap. 13.5% alc. **Rating** 95 **To** 2026 $25 JP ❂
Beechworth Pinot Noir 2018 Hand-picked, wild ferment with 25% whole bunches, matured in French oak for 11 months (30% new). Another pinot noir name to remember from the Beechworth region showing how it's done. Walks a brisk and savoury line with wood smoke, fungal undergrowth nuances amid the cherry and spice. On the darker side mood-wise. An autumnal kind of wine, brooding with forest floor, tomato leaf. Should travel well over time. Screwcap. 12.7% alc. **Rating** 95 **To** 2028 $25 JP ❂
Beechworth Rose of Pinot Noir 2019 Under the ownership of Brokenwood, Indigo Vineyard is kicking goals whether it is with pinot noir or a pinot noir rose. Tantalising watermelon pink hues. Complex aromatics with dusty wild raspberries, cranberry, black tea, herbs. Clean, bright on the taste buds: pomegranate, raspberry bonbon, black tea, dried herbs. Doesn't mind a bit of hard chilling. Screwcap. 13.5% alc. **Rating** 94 **To** 2024 $25 JP ❂

Inner City Winemakers ★★★★

28 Church Street, Wickham, NSW 2293 **Region** Hunter Valley
T (02) 4962 3545 **www**.innercitywinemakers.com.au **Open** Tues–Sun 10–5
Winemaker Rob Wilce **Est.** 2010 **Dozens** 900
Owner/winemaker Rob Wilce has over 20 years' experience in the business, mainly spent with wine companies in the Hunter Valley. While his job was in marketing and sales, he has worked many vintages with different winemakers in the valley, learning the basic winemaking skills. He realised he simply didn't have the capital to establish a vineyard and winery, and so came up with the idea of a virtual winery, purchasing a small warehouse at Wickham, on the edge of Newcastle's CBD and harbour. The small warehouse was too small right from the word go, and is now 'ridiculously small', but he spreads vintage intake by buying grapes from the Hunter Valley, Orange, Hilltops and New England, thus starting in January and finishing at the end of April. He says his winemaking can best be described as rustic, with Heath Robinson winemaking equipment, but it gets the job done. He has a wine club with just under 200 members, they do the wine marketing for him; and two part-time employees who join him during vintage.

ŦŦŦŦ♀ **Indenture Cabernet Sauvignon 2017** From Moppity, machine-harvested at
night, crushed and destemmed, fermented in a 1000l Flexcube with French staves.
Medium-bodied, very good varietal character, cassis, fine tannins. Good wine, no
issues of any description. Screwcap. 13.5% alc. **Rating** 91 **To** 2029 $40
Vintage Chardonnay 2018 Sourced from Tumbarumba, matured for 6 months.
A well made chardonnay from one of the best regions for cool-grown fruit
(altitude dependent) in NSW. One of the better wines in the Inner City portfolio.
Screwcap. 13% alc. **Rating** 90 **To** 2024 $28

ŦŦŦŦ **Hunter Valley Verdelho 2019** **Rating** 89 **To** 2020 $25

Innocent Bystander   ★★★★☆

316 Maroondah Highway, Healesville, Vic 3777 **Region** Yarra Valley
T (03) 5999 9222 www.innocentbystander.com.au **Open** 7 days 11–9
Winemaker Joel Tilbrook, Cate Looney, Geoff Alexander, Katherine Brown, Tom Canning
Est. 1997 **Dozens** 49000 **Vyds** 45ha
On 5 April 2016 Brown Brothers and Giant Steps announced that the Innocent Bystander
brand (including Mea Culpa) and stock had been sold to Brown Brothers. As part of the
acquisition, Brown Brothers purchased the White Rabbit Brewery site adjacent to Giant
Steps and this has become the cellar door home of Innocent Bystander. Its business is in two
completely different wine categories, both fitting neatly together. On the one hand is the
big volume (confidential) of vintage moscato, the grapes coming from the King Valley; and
non vintage prosecco, similarly sourced. The other side of the business is the premium, high
quality Yarra Valley single varietal wines with substantial brand value. Exports to the UK, the
US and other major markets.

ŦŦŦŦŦ **Mea Culpa Yarra Valley Syrah 2017** Savoury to the nth degree, but well
balanced and nicely fleshed with fruit. It tastes of licorice and black cherry, plum,
peppercorn and choc-mint. And while it's moreish it's also stitched with fine-
grained tannin. Walk around this wine and view it from every side and you'll
become more and more impressed. Screwcap. 14% alc. **Rating** 95 **To** 2030
$49 CM

ŦŦŦŦ♀ **Yarra Valley Pinot Noir Rose 2019** **Rating** 91 **To** 2022 $20 CM ✪
Yarra Valley Chardonnay 2018 **Rating** 90 **To** 2024 $25 CM

Iron Cloud Wines   ★★★★★

Suite 16, 18 Stirling Highway, Nedlands, WA 6009 (postal) **Region** Geographe
T 0401 860 891 www.ironcloudwines.com.au **Open** Not
Winemaker Michael Ng **Est.** 1999 **Dozens** 2500 **Vyds** 11ha
In 2003 owners Warwick Lavis and Geoff and Karyn Cross purchased the then-named
Pepperilly Estate, which had been planted in 1999 on red gravelly loam soils. Peppermint
trees line the Henty Brook, the natural water source for the vineyard. In 2017 Michael Ng,
chief winemaker for Rockcliffe, succeeded Coby Ladwig (who made the '15 and '16 vintage
wines). Exports to China.

ŦŦŦŦŦ **Rock of Solitude Single Vineyard Ferguson Valley Shiraz 2018** Machine-
harvested, crushed and destemmed, wild yeast–open fermented, 2–3 weeks on
skins, matured for 12 months in French oak (30% new). Intense black fruits
harbour a stream of licorice and multi-spices. There's great length and balance, and
you keep returning to the very high quality fruit the vineyard provides. Will live
for decades. Screwcap. 14.5% alc. **Rating** 96 **To** 2040 $32 ✪
The Alliance Ferguson Valley Cabernet Sauvignon Malbec 2018 With
57% cabernet sauvignon, 29% malbec and 14% petit verdot. Machine-harvested,
crushed and destemmed, a mix of wild and cultured yeast, 2–3 weeks on skins, a
soft press to barrel (30% new) for 18 months maturation. A full-bodied, complex
wine: the fruit singing soprano, tannins the base. An imposing wine by any
standards. It does need time. Screwcap. 14.5% alc. **Rating** 96 **To** 2043 $45 ✪

Rock of Solitude Single Vineyard Ferguson Valley Chardonnay 2019
Hand-picked, whole-bunch pressed, wild-fermented in French oak (52% new),
matured for 9 months. A very interesting wine. The flavour and texture of the
fruit tightly coupled, aided by acidity; the aftertaste with a European feel. Screwcap.
13.5% alc. **Rating** 95 **To** 2030 $32 **☉**

Pepperilly Single Vineyard Ferguson Valley Shiraz 2018 Machine-
harvested, crushed and destemmed, open-fermented, 2–3 weeks on skins, matured
for 10 months in French oak. There's a lot on offer here for a wine at this price.
While only medium-bodied, there's depth and complexity to the waves of red
and black fruits interwoven with tannins and a burst of spices and black pepper.
Screwcap. 13.5% alc. **Rating** 95 **To** 2038 $25 **☉**

**Rock of Solitude Single Vineyard Ferguson Valley Purple Patch GSM
2018** A blend of 85% grenache, 10% mourvedre, 5% shiraz; open-fermented,
10 days on skins, matured for 10 months in French oak (20% new). It's more
precise in terms of its flavour than McLaren Vale, the grenache less warm – you
might assume from the taste that shiraz is the dominant part. It carries its alcohol
extraordinarily well. Screwcap. 15% alc. **Rating** 94 **To** 2033 $32

⓯⓯⓯⓯ⓥ **Pepperilly Single Vineyard Ferguson Valley Sauvignon Blanc Semillon
2019** Rating 93 **To** 2023 $25 **☉**

Pepperilly Single Vineyard Ferguson Valley Rose 2019 Rating 90
To 2021 $25

Iron Gate Estate ★★★★

Cnr Oakey Creek Road/Ingles Lane, Pokolbin, NSW 2320 **Region** Hunter Valley
T (02) 4998 6570 **www.**irongateestate.com **Open** 7 days 10–4
Winemaker Geoff Broadfield, Jade Hafey **Est.** 1996 **Dozens** 4500 **Vyds** 8.7ha
Iron Gate Estate would not be out of place in the Napa Valley, which favours bold architectural
statements made without regard to cost; no expense was spared in equipping the winery or on
the lavish cellar door facilities. The winery and its equipment have been upgraded since the
arrival in 2018 of veteran winemaker Geoff Broadfield, who has reshaped the business plan.
The Classic range comes exclusively from estate fruit, while the Primera range includes wines
that are the best expression of a given variety from the estate and NSW regions. Fenix is a
60/40% blend of Mudgee cabernet sauvignon and shiraz made in limited quantities.

⓯⓯⓯⓯ⓥ **Primera Shiraz 2018** Made with 65% from Mudgee, 35% from the Hunter
Valley; vinified separately, the wine matured in Hungarian and American
hogsheads. The vintage was of high quality in both regions. The wine is full-
bodied, needing time to lose some of its puppy fat. Screwcap. 14.5% alc. **Rating** 90
To 2038 $40

Fenix Cabernet Shiraz 2018 A 60/40% blend; matured in second-use French
oak, production limited to 2000 bottles per year. It is a fleshy, medium-bodied
wine with soft tannins and good balance. Drink now or later. Cork. 14.5% alc.
Rating 90 **To** 2028 $75

Primera Tempranillo 2018 From the Hunter Valley; crushed and destemmed,
static fermenter for 7 days with pumpovers, matured in second-use American
hogsheads for 5 months. Well made with bright cherry varietal fruit and a long,
balanced finish. Screwcap. 14.6% alc. **Rating** 90 **To** 2027 $50

⓯⓯⓯⓯ **Primera Chardonnay 2019** Rating 89 **To** 2023 $30

Hunter Valley Verdelho 2019 Rating 89 **To** 2021 $25

Primera Rose 2019 Rating 89 **To** 2020 $30

Ironwood Estate ★★★

2191 Porongurup Road, Porongurup, WA 6234 **Region** Porongurup
T (08) 9853 1126 **www.**ironwoodestatewines.com.au **Open** Wed–Mon 11–5
Winemaker Wignalls Wines (Michael Perkins) **Est.** 1996 **Dozens** 2500 **Vyds** 5ha

Ironwood Estate was established in 1996 under the ownership of Mary and Eugene Harma. An estate vineyard of riesling, sauvignon blanc, chardonnay, shiraz, merlot and cabernet sauvignon (in more or less equal amounts) was planted on a northern slope of the Porongurup Range. Exports to Japan and Singapore.

ŸŸŸŸ **Reserve Porongurup Chardonnay 2018** Mid-straw gold. Ripe peaches and nectarines, oak imparting spices and a sweetness. A hint of flint adding another layer of flavour but overall, a simple, easy drink. Screwcap. 14.1% alc. **Rating** 89 **To** 2024 $26 JF

Irrewarra   ★★★★

101 Kellys Lane, Bannockburn, Vic 3331 **Region** Western Victoria zone
T (03) 5281 1733 **www**.irrewarravineyard.com.au **Open** Not
Winemaker Nick Farr **Est.** 2015 **Dozens** 900 **Vyds** 3.2ha
Freehold owners of the Irrewarra Vineyard, John and Bronwyn Calvert, had had little success in persuading the vines to yield adequately, and Nick Farr jumped at the chance of securing a long-term lease of the 2.4ha of pinot noir and 0.8ha of chardonnay. The Irrewarra brand is completely separate from By Farr and Farr Rising.

ŸŸŸŸŸ **Pinot Noir 2017** Predominantly red berry fruits, medium-bodied, balanced oak/tannins. Diam. 13% alc. **Rating** 93 **To** 2029 $60
Chardonnay 2018 The bouquet is odd/flat – not reduced, but it stops there. The palate is complex, much more in the Farr style. Diam. 12.5% alc. **Rating** 92 **To** 2028 $60

Irvine   ★★★★★

PO Box 308, Angaston, SA 5353 **Region** Eden Valley
T (08) 8564 1110 **www**.irvinewines.com.au **Open** Not
Winemaker Rebekah Richardson **Est.** 1983 **Dozens** 15 000 **Vyds** 111ha
When James (Jim) Irvine established his eponymous winery, he chose a singularly difficult focus for the business: the production of great merlot from the Eden Valley. Throughout the years of establishment, and indeed thereafter, he was a much-in-demand consultant, bobbing up in all sorts of places. Yet when he decided to sell the business in 2014, its potential was greatly increased with the dowry provided by the purchasing Wade and Miles families. In 1867 Henry Winter Miles planted 0.8ha of shiraz. Successive generations of the Miles family had added to the vineyard portfolio from 1967, both acquiring existing vineyards and planting others (Ben's Block vineyard at Penrice is home to 120-year-old vines). Henry's great-grandson Peter Miles and partner John Wade collectively own 160ha spread through the Barossa and Eden valleys, although only 80ha fall within the new Irvine partnership. Exports to the UK, Switzerland, the UAE, Singapore, Malaysia, Japan, Taiwan, Hong Kong and China.

ŸŸŸŸŸ **James Irvine Eden Valley Grand Merlot 2016** Cold-soaked to maximise colour and glean aromatic intensity; maturation in quality French oak (2 years) has conferred bitter chocolate-espresso doused tannins. The wine is rich, plush and salubrious, beaming dark fruit references with an attractive bitterness evincing a welcome savouriness. It reminds me of something from California, just one-third of the price. Cork. **Rating** 93 **To** 2029 $130 NG
The Earl Eden Valley Cabernet Franc 2017 Surprisingly mature vines (30yo+) yielding intense fruit of great purity. A gentle extraction was followed by 12 months in French wood. The result is sappy dense ruby; mid to fullish; and pulpy-generous-savoury all at once. This is delicious, and on the cooler side. Chilli, spearmint, bitter chocolate, violet and dark cherry scents. The acidity well tuned. The finish is fresh, crunchy and long. Drink for its youthful vibrancy. Screwcap. **Rating** 93 **To** 2024 $35 NG
The Estate Eden Valley Merlot 2018 Fermented cool with no extended maceration. A wise approach in the age of pulpy, bouncy, fruit-forward mid-weighted expressions. Imminently swiggable. A smidgeon of oak (10%) applied for guidance. Black plum, Asian spice, a riff of anise and a chord of mint. Good drinking. Screwcap. **Rating** 91 **To** 2023 $30 NG

Spring Hill Eden Valley Pinot Gris 2019 This is a fine gris, attesting to the excitement around the category on these shores. A lick of skin contact and post-ferment stirring have served to build texture. The acidity, a bit obtuse given varietal tendencies towards moderation. Yet a stream of pear gelato, baked apple, blossom and quince notes rallies around a juicy core. Good drinking. Screwcap. **Rating** 90 **To** 2023 $24 NG

ᵀᵀᵀᵀ **Spring Hill Eden Valley Riesling 2019** **Rating** 89 **To** 2025 $24 NG

J&J Wines

67 Rivers Lane, McLaren Vale, SA 5172 **Region** McLaren Vale
T (08) 8323 9098 **www**.jjwines.com.au **Open** Thurs–Sun 11–4
Winemaker Goe DiFabio **Est.** 1998 **Dozens** 5000 **Vyds** 5.5ha
J&J has been owned and operated by three generations of the Mason family. The estate vineyards are organically managed but are significantly supplemented by contract-grown grapes. It has come a long way since 2004, the first year when some of the estate grapes were vinified to make wine for the private use of the family. Exports to Taiwan and China.

Jack Estate ★★★★

15025 Riddoch Highway, Coonawarra, SA 5263 **Region** Coonawarra
T (08) 8736 3130 **www**.jackestate.com **Open** By appt
Winemaker Conrad Slabber **Est.** 2011 **Dozens** 10 000 **Vyds** 221ha
Jack Estate was founded in 2011 by a group of grapegrowers who acquired the large Mildara Blass winery in Coonawarra. Wines are sourced from the estate vineyards in Coonawarra (1ha of cabernet sauvignon) and the Murray Darling (200ha). Jack Estate also sources grapes from neighbouring grapegrowers in Coonawarra and Wrattonbully to complete their three-tiered range. Exports to Malaysia, Singapore, the Philippines, Thailand and China.

ᵀᵀᵀᵀᵀ **Coonawarra Chardonnay 2018** Machine-harvested, fermented in used French oak with cultured yeast, matured for 5 months. A surprise gold medal at the Limestone Coast Wine Show. All the emphasis is on the fruit and thus obviously appealed to the judges; its mix of stone fruit, grapefruit and honeydew melon all contributing. Screwcap. 13% alc. **Rating** 92 **To** 2025 $22 ☺
Coonawarra Wrattonbully Cabernet Sauvignon 2017 Machine-harvested, crushed and destemmed, roto-fermented with cultured yeast, 10 days on skins, matured for 18 months in 20% new oak (15% French, 5% American). A sturdy, medium to full-bodied wine. Screwcap. 14% alc. **Rating** 90 **To** 2029 $25

Jack Rabbit Vineyard ★★★★

85 McAdams Lane, Bellarine, Vic 3221 **Region** Geelong
T (03) 5251 2223 **www**.jackrabbitvineyard.com.au **Open** 7 days 10–5
Winemaker Nyall Condon **Est.** 2010 **Dozens** 5000 **Vyds** 25ha
Nestled onsite next to the acclaimed Jack Rabbit Restaurant are 25ha of vineyards planted equally to pinot noir and cabernet sauvignon. Wines are also made from 50ha of vines planted across the Bellarine Peninsula.

ᵀᵀᵀᵀᵀ **Bellarine Peninsula Riesling 2019** Expressive, light to mid-weighted riesling careening along talcy acid rails while exuding guava, Granny Smith apple and citrus blossom scents. The energy is palpable; the grip far from brittle. This is smart. Screwcap. **Rating** 91 **To** 2028 $35 NG

ᵀᵀᵀᵀ **The Bellarine Shiraz 2018** **Rating** 89 **To** 2023 $45 NG
Geelong Cabernet Sauvignon Shiraz 2017 **Rating** 89 **To** 2026 $34 NG

Jackson Brooke

126 Beaconsfield Parade, Northcote, Vic 3070 (postal) **Region** Henty
T 0466 652 485 **www**.jacksonbrookewine.com.au **Open** Not
Winemaker Jackson Brooke **Est.** 2013 **Dozens** 120

Jackson Brooke graduated from the University of Melbourne in 2004 with a science degree and, having spent a summer working at Tarrington Vineyards, went on to study oenology at Lincoln University in NZ. A vintage at Wedgetail Estate in the Yarra Valley was followed by stints in Japan, Southern California and then three years as assistant winemaker to Ben Portet. With his accumulated knowledge of boutique winemaking he has abandoned any idea of building a winery for the foreseeable future, renting space in the little winery at Tarrington Vineyards. He has edged up annual production from 1t in '13 to 3t in '15 and 6t in '16 (15–20t is the ultimate goal).

♀♀♀♀♀ **Henty Pinot Meunier 2019** Very light, clear colour, rose depth. Has a perfumed, wildflower bouquet; the palate surprising with its garden of cultivated red fruits, pomegranate and rhubarb. Sweet rather than savoury. Drink sooner than later. Screwcap. 12.5% alc. **Rating** 95 **To** 2026 $28 ⊙
Henty Chardonnay 2018 From Henty's Cobboboonee Vineyard; 66% basket-pressed to tank, the remainder to a new French puncheon. Opens quietly, then quick as a flash the grapefruit acidity (and flavour) takes control. Only 150 dozen made. Screwcap. 12.5% alc. **Rating** 94 **To** 2030 $28 ⊙
Henty Meunier Rose 2019 Whole-bunch pressed to tank for fermentation without settling, one-third transferred to barrel for mlf, the remainder racked to tank, blended and bottled in Sept. Pale pink. Rose petals, summer flowers and talc aromas. A supple palate, doing more by doing less. Screwcap. 12.5% alc. **Rating** 94 **To** 2021 $22 ⊙

♀♀♀♀♀ **Blok 49 Henty Chardonnay 2019 Rating** 92 **To** 2028 $28

Jackson's Hill Vineyard   ★★★★

Mount View Road, Mount View, NSW 2321 **Region** Hunter Valley
T 1300 720 098 www.jacksonshill.com.au **Open** By appt
Winemaker Greg Walls **Est.** 1983 **Dozens** 10000 **Vyds** 10ha
One of the low-profile operations on the spectacularly scenic Mount View Road, making small quantities of estate-grown wine sold through the cellar door and Australian Wine Selectors. Exports to China.

Jacob's Creek   ★★★★☆

2129 Barossa Valley Way, Rowland Flat, SA 5352 **Region** Barossa Valley
T (08) 8521 3000 www.jacobscreek.com **Open** 7 days 10–5
Winemaker Dan Swincer **Est.** 1973 **Dozens** 5700000 **Vyds** 740ha
Jacob's Creek (owned by Pernod Ricard) is one of the largest selling brands in the world and the global success of the base range has had the perverse effect of prejudicing many critics and wine writers who fail (so it seems) to objectively look behind the label and taste what is in fact in the glass. Exports include the UK, the US, Canada, China and other major markets.

♀♀♀♀♀ **1819 The Birth of Johann Barossa Coonawarra Shiraz Cabernet 2015** From 70% Barossa Valley shiraz and 30% Coonawarra cabernet sauvignon; the components vinified and matured separately. The shiraz spent 12 days on skins in a Potter fermenter and matured for 20 months in oak, the cabernet in an open 10t fermenter and matured for 16 months. It's a full-bodied wine with tannins still to fully integrate but lashings of black fruits to handle this need. Cork. 14.1% alc. **Rating** 96 **To** 2035 $120
Expedition Barossa Valley Shiraz 2016 Machine-harvested, fermented as a single parcel in a small open fermenter with as many whole berries as possible, matured in 50% new French oak, 25% new American hogsheads, the balance used-Hungarian oak. Flamboyantly full-bodied; a joust between fruit, tannins and, the winner, oak. Happily high alcohol wasn't in the picture. Cork. 14.3% alc. **Rating** 94 **To** 2046 $80
Johann Barossa Valley Shiraz Cabernet 2013 From 60% Barossa Valley shiraz, 40% Coonawarra cabernet sauvignon. The shiraz comes from the Willandra Vineyard on the banks of Jacob's Creek in the Barossa Valley planted 1921,

the cabernet from vines planted in '93. It's ultra full-bodied and needs a bare minimum of another 10 years before it will be enjoyable. Screwcap. 14.5% alc. **Rating** 94 **To** 2050 $120

🍷🍷🍷🍷♀ **Reserve Adelaide Hills Chardonnay 2019** **Rating** 90 **To** 2021 $18 ✪
Barossa Signature Chardonnay 2018 **Rating** 90 **To** 2023 $20 SC ✪
Reserve Chardonnay Pinot Noir 2018 **Rating** 90 $20 ✪

Jaeschke's Hill River Clare Estate ★★★★★

406 Quarry Road, Clare, SA 5453 **Region** Clare Valley
T (08) 8843 4100 **www.**hillriverclareestate.com.au **Open** 7 days 10–4
Winemaker Steve Baraglia, Angela Meaney **Est.** 1980 **Dozens** 1750 **Vyds** 180ha
The Jaeschke family has been broadacre farming in the Hill River district for over 50 years. In May 2010 they purchased the neighbouring 180ha vineyard established by Penfolds in 1980. It is planted to 16 varieties, including 21.2ha of riesling, the success of which has led to a stream of trophies and gold medals since '13, the first entry in wine shows. The venture began as the idea of daughter Michelle, with the expectation a medal or two. The success led to the use of one of the Atco huts on the property, a card table set up as a tasting bench, bypassed if you arrive with BYO picnic food, use of the onsite bbq facilities encouraged. A cellar door grant from PIRSA has led to a substantial facilities upgrade. In March '20, four vintages of the Riesling ('16 to '19) were available at $18 a bottle, the '15 at $25. If you are a Wine Club member, the price (for a 12-bottle case) is $194, or $16.16 a bottle, freight free.

🍷🍷🍷🍷🍷 **Polish Hill River Valley Riesling 2017** There's a torrent of lime juice here. It's a very distinguished wine that will live long, holding aloft the sceptre of the kingdom. The intensity of the flavours will change over the years, but won't introduce another theme as many do. Screwcap. 12% alc. **Rating** 96 **To** 2032 $18 ✪
Polish Hill River Valley Riesling 2016 A hint of straw has found its way into the still-pale hue. This is a wine of total control and precision. It's quite possible that this and the '17 will end up as the most preferred of all the vintages to date. Screwcap. 11.5% alc. **Rating** 95 **To** 2029 $18 ✪

🍷🍷🍷🍷♀ **Polish Hill River Valley Riesling 2018** **Rating** 93 **To** 2028 $18 ✪
Polish Hill River Valley Sangiovese 2017 **Rating** 93 **To** 2027 $17 ✪
Polish Hill River Valley Riesling 2015 **Rating** 92 **To** 2030 $25 ✪
Polish Hill River Valley Riesling 2019 **Rating** 90 **To** 2029 $18 ✪
Polish Hill River Valley Shiraz 2016 **Rating** 90 **To** 2022 $17 ✪
Polish Hill River Valley Barbera 2015 **Rating** 90 **To** 2022 $17 ✪

James & Co Wines ★★★★

136 Main Street, Rutherglen, Vic 3685 **Region** Beechworth
T 0447 341 373 **www.**jamesandcowines.com.au **Open** Thurs–Mon 11–6
Winemaker Ricky James **Est.** 2011 **Dozens** 750
Ricky and Georgie James intended to buy land in Beechworth and establish a vineyard planted primarily to sangiovese. They say, 'Serendipity led us to Mark Walpole, and we were given the chance to purchase fruit from his Fighting Gully Road Vineyard'. They have set up their home and cellar door in Rutherglen and intend to float between the two regions.

🍷🍷🍷🍷♀ **Beechworth Sangiovese 2018** The fruit quality shines through this vintage and restraint in the winemaking has produced a juicy and vibrant drink. Hints of cherries and raspberries, a dash of spice and herbs with surprisingly reticent tannins. Screwcap. 14% alc. **Rating** 90 **To** 2024 $35 JF

James Estate ★★★★

951 Bylong Valley Way, Baerami, NSW 2333 **Region** Hunter Valley
T (02) 6547 5168 **www.**jamesestatewines.com.au **Open** 7 days 10–4.30
Winemaker Alex Finnie, Giacomo Soldani **Est.** 1997 **Dozens** 10 000 **Vyds** 86ha

James Estate has had an unsettled corporate existence at various times since 1997, but has now straightened the ship under the ownership of Sydney-based businessman Sam Fayad. The vineyard is planted to shiraz, cabernet sauvignon, merlot, petit verdot, cabernet franc, semillon, chardonnay and verdelho. Cellar doors operate at Baerami, in the Upper Hunter, and at 1210 Hermitage Road, Pokolbin, in the Lower Hunter.

♟♟♟♟ **Upper Hunter Valley Semillon 2019** Dry to the point of drying. Lemon, slate and hay flavours sheet through the palate before puckering through the finish. Screwcap. 10% alc. **Rating** 89 **To** 2028 $20 CM
Upper Hunter Valley Chardonnay 2019 Just enough peach, lemon and lime flavour to keep you happy. No oak flavour or texture to be seen. It's a crisp style of chardonnay. Screwcap. 13% alc. **Rating** 89 **To** 2023 $20 CM

Jansz Tasmania

1216B Pipers Brook Road, Pipers Brook, Tas 7254 **Region** Northern Tasmania
T (03) 6382 7066 **www**.jansz.com **Open** 7 days 10–4
Winemaker Teresa Heuzenroeder **Est.** 1985 **Dozens** 38 000 **Vyds** 30ha
Jansz is part of Hill-Smith Family Vineyards and was one of the early sparkling wine labels in Tasmania, stemming from a short-lived relationship between Heemskerk and Louis Roederer. Its 15ha of chardonnay, 12ha of pinot noir and 3ha of pinot meunier correspond almost exactly to the blend composition of the Jansz wines. It is the only Tasmanian winery entirely devoted to the production of sparkling wine (although the small amount of Dalrymple Estate wines is also made here), which is of high quality. Part of the former Frogmore Creek Vineyard purchased by Hill-Smith Family Vineyards in December 2012 is dedicated to the needs of Jansz Tasmania. Exports to all major markets.

♟♟♟♟♟ **Late Disgorged 2011** This prodigious fizz has spent at least 8 years on lees, before recent disgorgement. Billowing pastry notes a go go. More impressive, though, is the layered and finely detailed texture. Then the impressive finish: forceful, long and finessed. Chardonnay at the fore. Laden with iodine, sea spray and oyster shell notes. Very fine. Cork. **Rating** 95 $56 NG
Vintage Rose 2015 A superior wine to the non-rose of the same vintage, the red wine addition evincing generosity and sass, while evocative of strawberry, cream, brioche and a whiff of orange zest. This is round, detailed, rich feeling and utterly delicious. The dosage sits well. Cork. **Rating** 95 $53 NG
Premium Tasmania Cuvee NV Long a staple across the festive season, this is always a quality domestic sparkling. Best is the integration: creamy yet fresh; rich yet ethereal. Neither the yeast-derived toastiness, nor the cool-climate acidity, sticking out over the other. Scents of autumnal fruits, nuts, brûlée and nougat pulled long and gently saline. Cork. **Rating** 94 $30 NG ✪

♟♟♟♟♀ **Single Vineyard Vintage Chardonnay 2014 Rating** 93 $65 NG
Premium Rose NV Rating 93 $30 NG
Vintage Cuvee 2015 Rating 90 $47 NG

Jarressa Estate Wines

114 Blewitt Springs Road, McLaren Flat, SA 5171 **Region** McLaren Vale
T 0478 517 999 **www**.jarressaestate.com **Open** By appt
Winemaker Michael Petrucci (Contract) **Est.** 2007 **Dozens** 10 000 **Vyds** 5ha
Proprietor Jarrad White established Jarressa Estate in 2007, taking its name from his childhood home of broadacre cropping and stud cattle at Kadina, north of Adelaide. He is now a 20-vintage veteran of the wine community, with 10 years working for Penfolds in both Australia and California. Jarressa was initially a hobby venture, making wine to be sold to family and friends, but changed shape after a Chinese-based wine importer shared a bottle of Jarressa. A joint venture was formed, Jarrad making the wine and Li Hui responsible for sales and marketing. It took another significant step with the acquisition of the 5ha Cape Barren Vineyard, prior to this time the wines were made from purchased fruit. Exports to Vanuatu and China.

ŶŶŶŶŶ **Regional Reveal The Hills McLaren Vale Shiraz 2018** Matured for 18 months in 85% French and 15% American hogsheads (20% new). Another Jarressa wine to carry its alcohol lightly, the mouthfeel supple and without heat, red cherry joining the party. Obviously from a cool part of McLaren Vale. Screwcap. 15% alc. **Rating** 95 **To** 2038 $56

Regional Reveal The Flats McLaren Vale Shiraz 2018 Matured for 18 months in 90% French and 10% American hogsheads (20% new). Attractive wine; good control of extract and oak, the fruits spanning plum and cherry with a coat of dark chocolate. Screwcap. 14.5% alc. **Rating** 95 **To** 2038 $56

Whites Road Roundabout McLaren Vale Shiraz 2017 Jarressa certainly keeps attention with dazzlingly different artwork for its labels. This is a very good wine, right at the heart of (good) '17 flavours and style. From 2 vineyards with different crushing and fermentation controls, matured for 16 months in French oak (20% new). Screwcap. 14.5% alc. **Rating** 95 **To** 2042 $42

Regional Reveal The Foothills McLaren Vale Shiraz 2018 Matured for 18 months in 80% French and 20% American hogsheads (25% new). Powerful and intense with blackberry to the fore, backed up by plum, licorice and spice. It's a fresh wine, the tannin neatly controlled by the fruit. Alcohol isn't the problem it can be. Screwcap. 15% alc. **Rating** 94 **To** 2038 $56

Post The Love By Air Mail Barossa Shiraz 2017 A powerful shiraz destemmed and crushed, yeast added to the fermenter forthwith, pumped over twice a day 'for better colour, tannin and flavour extraction', pressed to second-fill oak for 11 months' maturation. The 14.5% alcohol in '17 is what should be the normal result. Screwcap. **Rating** 94 **To** 2037 $28 ✪

ŶŶŶŶŶ **Copper Triangle McLaren Vale Shiraz 2018 Rating** 93 **To** 2038 $38
Methode Traditionnelle Adelaide Hills Vintage Cuvee 2015
Rating 90 $35

Jasper Hill ★★★★★

Drummonds Lane, Heathcote, Vic 3523 **Region** Heathcote
T (03) 5433 2528 **www.**jasperhill.com.au **Open** By appt
Winemaker Ron Laughton, Emily McNally **Est.** 1979 **Dozens** 2000 **Vyds** 26.5ha
The red wines of Jasper Hill are highly regarded and much sought after. As long as vintage conditions allow, these are wonderfully rich and full-flavoured wines. The vineyards are dry-grown and managed organically. Exports to the UK, the US, Canada, France, Denmark, Hong Kong and Singapore.

ŶŶŶŶŶ **Georgia's Paddock Heathcote Shiraz 2018** Deep crimson-purple. A full-bodied version by Jasper Hill with blackberry, plum and spicy notes. While it is large, it is balanced and has ample tannins for the long term. Cork. 15.5% alc. **Rating** 95 **To** 2038 $82

Emily's Paddock Heathcote Shiraz Cabernet Franc 2018 There is only 5% cabernet franc but it is open to Jasper Hill to disclose it on the front label. It is a finely balanced wine with polished tannins and clearly expressed shiraz varietal character. Cork. 14.5% alc. **Rating** 95 **To** 2032 $108

Georgia's Paddock Heathcote Nebbiolo 2018 Described by Langtons as 'an extremely elegant palate that immediately hits you with mouthpuckering tannins, particularly after swallowing. Lovely clean acid finish.' With quivering palate I tasted it, fearing the worst, only to find the best – a nebbiolo that sent all the right messages. For the record, the quality of the cork was perfect. 13.5% alc. **Rating** 95 **To** 2038 $66

jb Wines ★★★☆

PO Box 530, Tanunda, SA 5352 **Region** Barossa Valley
T 0408 794 389 **www.**jbwines.com **Open** By appt
Winemaker Joe Barritt **Est.** 2005 **Dozens** 900 **Vyds** 18ha

The Barritt family has been growing grapes in the Barossa since the 1850s. This particular venture was established in 2005 by Lenore, Joe and Greg Barritt. It is based on shiraz, cabernet sauvignon and chardonnay (with tiny amounts of zinfandel, pinot blanc and clairette) planted between 1972 and 2003. Greg runs the vineyard operations; Joe, with a Bachelor of Agricultural Science from the University of Adelaide, followed by 10 years of winemaking in Australia, France and the US, is now the winemaker.

ΨΨΨΨ **Sobels Barossa Valley Cabernet Sauvignon 2017** Winemaker Joe Barritt makes plush, full-blooded Barossan reds. This is a good example of his work with super ripe cabernet fruit together with suggestions of exotic spices and Barossan earth. French and American oak play a role adding cigar box warmth. Finishes long. Screwcap. 14.7% alc. **Rating** 91 **To** 2032 $25 JP

Jeanneret Wines   ★★★★★

Jeanneret Road, Sevenhill, SA 5453 **Region** Clare Valley
T (08) 8843 4308 www.jeanneretwines.com **Open** Mon–Sat 10–5, Sun 12–5
Winemaker Ben Jeanneret, Harry Dickinson **Est.** 1992 **Dozens** 18000 **Vyds** 36.5ha
Ben Jeanneret has progressively built the range and quantity of wines he makes at the onsite winery. In addition to the estate vineyards, Jeanneret has grape purchase contracts with owners of an additional 20ha of hand-pruned, hand-picked, dry-grown vines spread throughout the Clare Valley. The rieslings are very good indeed. Exports to Canada, Sweden, Japan and China.

ΨΨΨΨΨ **Aged Release Big Fine Girl Clare Valley Riesling 2013** Thank goodness producers like Jeanneret have a museum release programme in place. Mid-gold, bright. Just crossed over from youth to maturity. Lightly toasty, minerally, orange peel, lime cordial. Real depth here, glace fruits, savoury, grilled grapefruit, honeysuckle. So much to enjoy now but that keen acidity indicates a long life ahead. Screwcap. 12.7% alc. **Rating** 95 **To** 2030 $35 JP ✪
Clare Valley Malbec 2018 It's reassuring to find a producer who takes malbec seriously as a stand-alone variety, embracing its full, expressive self. Hedonistic and intense with black cherry, spiced plums, stewed rhubarb, prune and earth. The palate glides effortlessly with layers of fruit and savoury flavours, and well tuned tannins. Screwcap. 14.9% alc. **Rating** 95 **To** 2030 $28 JP ✪

ΨΨΨΨΨ **Big Fine Girl Clare Valley Riesling 2019 Rating** 92 **To** 2035 $25 JP ✪
Single Vineyard Watervale Riesling 2018 Rating 90 **To** 2028 $30
Rose 2019 Rating 90 **To** 2026 $25 JP

Jenke Vineyards   ★★★★

1857 Barossa Valley Way, Rowland Flat, SA 5352 **Region** Barossa Valley
T (08) 8524 4154 www.jenkevineyards.com.au **Open** By appt
Winemaker Rod Chapman **Est.** 1989 **Dozens** 1000 **Vyds** 40ha
The Jenke family have been growing grapes in the southern Barossa continuously since their arrival from Germany in 1854. Jenke is now in the hands of seventh-generation Mark and Rebecca Jenke. The vineyards have an average age of 40 years, with the oldest shiraz dating back to 1926. A rejuvenation of new plantings in the early '90s strengthened the varietal mix of traditional varieties with new ones. The cellar door is located in the original settlers' cottage built in the 1850s.

ΨΨΨΨΨ **7th Generation Single Vineyard Barossa Valley Shiraz 2018** From a single vineyard at Rowland Flat; open-fermented 8 days, pumpovers, free-run and pressings into 50% new French and 50% new American oak from a local cooperage. Rich, ultra-full-bodied in velvety robes of black fruits and oak, the tannins obliterated. Screwcap. 14.5% alc. **Rating** 94 **To** 2038 $35
Family Icon Barossa Valley Shiraz 2016 The wine was chosen from the best barrels of the '16 vintage. It's got excellent fruit flavour and mouthfeel. There's also a generous oak contribution that will settle over time. Cork. 15% alc. **Rating** 94 **To** 2036 $90

????? **7th Generation Semillon 2019** Rating 89 To 2022 $22
7th Generation Merlot 2018 Rating 89 To 2028 $30
7th Generation Cabernet Sauvignon 2018 Rating 89 To 2028 $30

Jericho Wines

13 Moore Street, Willunga, SA 5172 (postal) **Region** Adelaide Hills/McLaren Vale
T 0410 519 945 **www**.jerichowines.com.au **Open** Not
Winemaker Neil Jericho, Andrew Jericho **Est.** 2012 **Dozens** 3000
In this venture the whole family is involved. The winemaking team consists of father and son,
Neil and Andrew Jericho. Neil has over 45 years of winemaking experience in Rutherglen,
King Valley and the Clare Valley; and Andrew over 15 years in McLaren Vale working as
senior winemaker for Maxwell Wines and Mollydooker. Andrew obtained his Bachelor of
Oenology from the University of Adelaide (in 2003) and then moved outside the square for
experience at the highly regarded Grace Vineyard in the Shanxi Province of China. Wife Kaye
is an experienced vintage widow, eldest daughter Sally has marketing and accounting degrees
(she worked for Wine Australia for 10 years). Youngest son Kim was torn between oenology,
hospitality and graphic design; he opted for the latter, hence designing the highly standout
label and Jericho branding. Exports to Singapore and China.

????? **Selected Vineyards Adelaide Hills Fume Blanc 2019** A mid-gold hue.
Enticing aromas of roasted almonds and grilled pineapple topped with lemon curd.
Savoury and complex on the palate with almost mouth-watering acidity to close.
A really good drink. Screwcap. 13.5% alc. **Rating** 93 To 2024 $26 JF ✪
Selected Vineyards Adelaide Hills Fiano 2019 Full of golden fruit from
quince to yellow peaches and more luscious flavours of honeycomb and ginger
cream. There's a ripeness, a fleshiness, yet a decent acid line and phenolic grip
that put this in the more interesting fiano camp. Screwcap. 13.5% alc. **Rating** 92
To 2024 $26 JF
Selected Vineyards Adelaide Hills Rose 2019 A 3-way pinot blend: noir,
meunier and gris. A delightful outcome. Spiced cherries, cranberries, refreshing
poppy acidity and super dry finish. Screwcap. 13% alc. **Rating** 92 To 2022 $26 JF
Single Vineyard McLaren Vale Shiraz 2016 Holding this back for more bottle
age has helped the wine settle, although it is still a little nervy, if astonishingly
youthful. No doubt its acid profile helped. A mix of redcurrants and blackberries,
mocha and red licorice with woodsy spices; the oak imparting more grip to
the tannins. Overall, the palate is rather smooth and savoury. Diam. 14.4% alc.
Rating 92 To 2028 $42 JF
Selected Vineyards McLaren Vale GSM 2018 Grenache at 85% leads the
show with musk, red fruits and its delicious spiciness; its grainy tannins taking
centre stage. The 12% shiraz and 3% mourvedre are decent backup singers adding
some savoury elements and ensuring drinkability writ large. Screwcap. 14.2% alc.
Rating 92 To 2027 $26 JF
Selected Vineyards Adelaide Hills Tempranillo 2018 Mightily floral and
attractive. The flavours are forward and ready to rip, but it's not light on or dainty.
Anise, honey, redcurrant and boysenberry flavours jostle for position. Not hard to
like. Screwcap. 13.5% alc. **Rating** 91 To 2024 $26 CM
Selected Vineyards S3 McLaren Vale Shiraz 2018 Works off a savoury
theme mostly with the fruit surprisingly reticent. Woodsy spices, licorice, charred
meats and salami with slightly drying, grainy tannins. It's a rustic wine in a way,
made to be enjoyed now. Screwcap. 14.2% alc. **Rating** 90 To 2025 $26 JF

🍇 Jilyara of Wilyabrup

2 Heath Road, Wilyabrup, WA 6280 (postal) **Region** Margaret River
T (08) 9755 6575 **www**.jilyara.com.au **Open** Not
Winemaker Kate Morgan, Laura Bowler **Est.** 2017 **Dozens** 4000 **Vyds** 9.7ha
Craig Cotterell and partner Maria Bergstrom planted the 9.7ha Jilyara Vineyard in 1995,
finishing the task the following year. Until 2017 the crop was sold to other producers in the

region, but the game changed that year. They have 6.4ha of cabernet sauvignon, 0.9ha each of malbec and sauvignon blanc, 0.8ha of chardonnay, 0.4ha of merlot and 0.3ha of petit verdot. There are three tiers: at the top The Williams' Block duo of Chardonnay and Cabernet Sauvignon (incorporating small amounts of malbec and petit verdot) at $75; next comes the Heath Road banner ($35) with Chardonnay, Malbec and Cabernet Sauvignon (also including some malbec and petit verdot); the last group is Honeycomb Corner ($22) with a Sauvignon Blanc and Cabernet Sauvignon (with some merlot and malbec), the price particularly appealing for the Cabernet. The packaging is very smart, a design-house dream, visually bringing together the local Noongar language of 'Djilyaro' for bee (there is a beehive at each corner of the block). Professional winemaking, a detailed marketing strategy and an interesting website with the odd fanciful assertion from the PR front. Exports are planned for Sweden, Denmark and China.

ㅜㅜㅜㅜㅜ **The Williams' Block Margaret River Cabernet Sauvignon 2018** From 24yo vines, the blend includes 8.5% malbec and 5.5% petit verdot. A rich and luscious, utterly seductive medium to full-bodied wine. The tannins are somewhere there because the texture and structure give the wine harmony. Screwcap. 14.5% alc. **Rating** 97 **To** 2043 $75 ◐

ㅜㅜㅜㅜㅜ **The William's Block Margaret River Chardonnay 2018** A fulsome back label testimonial to the male members of the family is justified by the complexity of the ripe white peach, nectarine and contrasting citrus/lemon curd flavours. Oak has played a significant role, managing to make its contribution to texture and structure without impinging on the varietal character. Screwcap. 13% alc. **Rating** 95 **To** 2028 $75
Heath Road Margaret River Cabernet Sauvignon 2018 Includes 7.5% each of petit verdot and malbec. Immaculately balanced and presented. It's an example of a very great year in a string of such vintages. Blackcurrant, forest fruits then more savoury notes on the finish – pure cabernet. Screwcap. 14.5% alc. **Rating** 95 **To** 2038 $35 ◐

ㅜㅜㅜㅜ **Honeycomb Corner Margaret River Cabernet Sauvignon 2018** **Rating** 93 **To** 2027 $22 ◐
Heath Road Margaret River Malbec 2018 Rating 92 **To** 2028 $35
Honeycomb Corner Margaret River Sauvignon Blanc 2018 Rating 91 **To** 2021 $22 ◐
Heath Road Margaret River Chardonnay 2018 Rating 91 **To** 2024 $35
Heath Road Margaret River Chardonnay 2019 Rating 90 **To** 2022 $35

Jim Barry Wines   ★★★★★

33 Craig Hill Road, Clare, SA 5453 **Region** Clare Valley
T (08) 8842 2261 **www.**jimbarry.com **Open** Mon–Fri 9–5, w'ends & hols 9–4
Winemaker Peter Barry, Tom Barry, Ben Marx **Est.** 1959 **Dozens** 80 000 **Vyds** 355ha
The patriarch of this highly successful wine business, Jim Barry, died in 2004, but the business continues under the active involvement of the second generation, led by the irrepressible Peter Barry, plus brothers John and Mark; the third generation represented by two of Peter and Sue Barry's children, Tom and Sam. Sam's wife Olivia has set a whirlwind pace, graduating with a Bachelor of Science in Commerce from the University of Adelaide, then a Masters of Wine Business. Peter, John and Mark purchased the famed Florita Vineyard in 1986 (one of the oldest vineyards in the Clare Valley, planted in 1962). Tom and Sam also purchased Clos Clare in 2008 with its high quality vineyards (see separate entry). Jim Barry Wines is able to draw upon 320ha of mature Clare Valley vineyards, plus 35ha in Coonawarra. In November '16, Jim Barry Wines released the first commercial Assyrtiko grown and made in Australia. A founding member of Australia's First Families of Wine. Winery of the Year *Wine Companion 2020*. Exports to all major markets.

ㅜㅜㅜㅜㅜ **The Armagh Clare Valley Shiraz 2017** Largely standard vinification with individual blocks ex the Armagh Vineyard; 10 days on skins, some blocks given 3 weeks' post-ferment maceration. Elegance isn't the aim of The Armagh, but the

'17 vintage has made it easy. Richly flavoured with dark fruits. Savoury tannins balance and lengthen the palate. Screwcap. 13.8% alc. **Rating** 96 **To** 2042 $325

The McRae Wood Clare Valley Shiraz 2017 Standard vinification made irrelevant by the luscious, juicy red and black fruits that continue to seduce the palate right through to the finish and aftertaste. One of the best vintages to date. Screwcap. 14.3% alc. **Rating** 96 **To** 2047 $70 ✪

The Florita Clare Valley Riesling 2019 No frills winemaking simply because none was needed. The great vineyard and significant vine age give the wine an extra volume of citrus and Granny Smith apple flavour. The acidity is especially good for the vintage. A classic. Screwcap. 12.5% alc. **Rating** 95 **To** 2032 $60

The Benbournie Clare Valley Cabernet Sauvignon 2016 From separate blocks on the Armagh Vineyard planted in '64; 10 days on skins, 50% with an additional 2 weeks' post-ferment maceration. Elegant wine with tannins and other extract at a low level. Varietal fruit is clear as a day, 13.5% alcohol the key. Screwcap. **Rating** 95 **To** 2036 $80

The James Clare Valley Cabernet Malbec 2016 Two blocks on the Armagh Vineyard were vinified and matured separately, some parcels on skins for 3 weeks post-ferment, matured in hogsheads. The return of the pressings to the wine has added to the already full-bodied palate. It is a powerhouse with the structure and balance to merit extended cellaring. Screwcap. 14% alc. **Rating** 95 **To** 2046 $350

Clare Valley Assyrtiko 2019 Hand-picked, destemmed, 90% cool-fermented in stainless steel, 10% in barrel. Very intelligent winemaking invests the wine with firm acidity creating texture and structure. Clingstone peach fruit demands to be appreciated as it wraps itself around the lemon curd acidity. Screwcap. 12% alc. **Rating** 94 **To** 2030 $35

Lodge Hill Clare Valley Shiraz 2017 Fruit is its strong point: supple and balanced blackberry and plum are refreshed by moderate alcohol (and the vintage). Excellent value. Screwcap. 13.9% alc. **Rating** 94 **To** 2030 $25 ✪

♟♟♟♟♙ **The Forger Clare Valley Shiraz 2018 Rating** 93 **To** 2035 $35
Single Vineyard Watervale Shiraz 2018 Rating 92 **To** 2038 $35

John Duval Wines ★★★★★

PO Box 622, Tanunda, SA 5352 **Region** Barossa Valley
T (08) 8562 2266 **www.**johnduvalwines.com **Open** At Vino Lokal, Tanunda
Winemaker John Duval, Tim Duval **Est.** 2003 **Dozens** 8000
John Duval is an internationally recognised winemaker, having been the custodian of Penfolds Grange during his role as chief red winemaker from 1986–2002. He established his eponymous brand in 2003 after almost 30 years with Penfolds and provides consultancy services to clients all over the world. While his main focus is on old vine shiraz, he has extended his portfolio with other Rhône varieties. John was joined in the winery by son Tim in '16. Exports to all major markets.

♟♟♟♟♟ **Entity Barossa Shiraz 2018** Entity is always a complete, fabulous wine. Nothing out of place. Cherry-picking fruit from sites off old vines across the Eden and Barossa valleys. It is so polished, there's a sheen. Flavours of black fruits, licorice and woodsy spices all in sync. The key is beautifully shaped and plush tannins. Wonderful wine. Screwcap. 14.5% alc. **Rating** 97 **To** 2038 $55 JF ✪

Eligo The Barossa Shiraz 2017 John Duval is a master blender. This is all about the best of the vintage, fruit from various sites across the Barossa and Eden valleys, to morph into the mighty Eligo. A powerhouse of flavour yet never loses focus. Dark plums infused with star anise, cinnamon, Dutch licorice and soy sauce. Full-bodied with velvety rich tannins. It gets the most oak – French hogsheads (54% new), aged 18 months, and needs time to settle in. It will. Cork. 14.5% alc. **Rating** 97 **To** 2040 $120 JF ✪

Annexus Barossa Valley Mataro 2018 It's all about putting the spotlight on fruit from a dry-grown centenarian vineyard in Light Pass. I love this. It's a commanding wine. It oscillates between deep, dark, spicy fruit to savoury, meaty flavours. It's long and pure, with poised yet determined tannins. I doubt mataro gets any better than this. Screwcap. 14.5% alc. **Rating** 97 **To** 2038 $70 JF ✪

Annexus Barossa Valley Mataro 2017 Matured for 15 months in used French oak. This is a glorious manifestation of the '17 vintage, its cool conditions retaining freshness of fruit at a very modest alcohol level. A sheer pleasure to drink. Screwcap. 13.5% alc. **Rating** 97 **To** 2032 $70 ✪

♟♟♟♟♟ **Annexus Barossa Grenache 2018** When 90% of the fruit comes off an Eden Valley ancestor vineyard (over 150yo) and 10% off old bushvines from northern Barossa, just take time to appreciate what's in the glass. The wine unfurls with a heady elixir of sweet, briary fruit, gently spiced with a savoury overlay. It is lithe, not too big, yet flavoursome. Fine sandpaper tannins are perfectly poised and the acidity shines. Lovely drinking. Screwcap. 14% alc. **Rating** 96 **To** 2033 $70 JF ✪

Annexus Barossa Grenache 2017 John Duval was the maker of Penfolds Grange for 16 short years. The positive outcome was his ability to create his own wines, originally alone, now with son Tim. A feature of this wine is its modest alcohol, which most (myself included) might miss unless it was pointed out. Screwcap. 13.5% alc. **Rating** 96 **To** 2031 $70 ✪

Plexus Barossa Shiraz Grenache Mourvedre 2018 A very satisfying combo with no variety fighting for the lead. Expect a melody of red fruits lightly spiced with a fleck of herbs for good measure, and meaty-stock flavours too. The savoury and shapely tannins in tune with the more medium-weighted palate. Finishes fresh and buoyant. A ripper drink. Screwcap. 14.5% alc. **Rating** 95 **To** 2030 $40 JF

♟♟♟♟♀ **Plexus Marsanne Roussanne Viognier 2019 Rating** 92 **To** 2027 $30 JF
Concilio Grenache Shiraz 2018 Rating 91 **To** 2028 $30 JF

John Kosovich Wines   ★★★★★

Cnr Memorial Ave/Great Northern Hwy, Baskerville, WA 6056 **Region** Swan Valley/Pemberton
T (08) 9296 4356 **www**.johnkosovichwines.com.au **Open** Wed–Mon 10–4.30
Winemaker Anthony Kosovich **Est.** 1922 **Dozens** 2000 **Vyds** 10.9ha

The Kosovich family, headed by Jack Kosovich and his brothers, immigrated from Croatia shortly before the outbreak of World War I. After cutting railway sleepers in the southwest of WA and thereafter in the goldmines of Kalgoorlie, Jack purchased the property in 1922; the first vines planted in that year still grace the entrance to the winery. Cutting railway sleepers by axe made digging the underground cellar seem easy, and a 7m white gum beam cut from a tree felled by Jack in the hills nearby became the supporting structure for the cellar roof; the axe used by Jack to shape the beam hangs from it today. John took over winemaking aged 15 after the death of his father, making fortified wines and rough red wines which remained the staple of the business until the 1960s when John made the then-bold move to change the vineyard to produce white wines. Riesling was the first variety planted, chenin blanc, chardonnay and verdelho followed. In '89 John established a 3.5ha vineyard in Pemberton, changing the face of the business forever, albeit continuing with the magnificent Rare Muscat. The winery was known as Westfield Wines until 2003 when, prompted by John's 50th vintage, the name was changed to John Kosovich Wines. In 1995 John became a member of the Order of Australia for his long contribution to the wine industry and in '04 won the prestigious Jack Mann Medal for services to the WA wine industry; in the same year the winery won the trophy for Best WA Small Producer at the Perth Wine Show. Son Anthony (Arch) took over the winemaking and is looking forward to the 100-year anniversary in 2022.

♟♟♟♟♟ **Bottle Aged Reserve Swan Valley Chenin Blanc 2014** From 40yo estate vines; hand-picked, fermented in tank, bottled Oct '14, aged in bottle for 6 years before release. Bright, full yellow-green. At the peak of its life, providing the opportunity to have your vinous cake and eat it. Toasty flavours give way to citrussy acidity that will continue to give zesty freshness for years to come. A special wine. Screwcap. 13% alc. **Rating** 95 **To** 2029 $40

Rare Muscat NV This has an average age of 20 years. The grapes are usually picked at 28° baume – little more than raisins. Only good vintages are used in the ageing process, the vintages represented here are '84, '96, '02 and '03. It is a fresh solera, keeping the levels of volatile acidity under control. Lusciously rich, Callard & Bowser toffee, part ginger biscuit, part crystallised fruits dipped in chocolate. Diam. 19% alc. **Rating** 95 **$**95

Swan Vineyard Field Blend White 2019 A blend of 39% semillon, 34% verdelho, 18% chardonnay and 9% sauvignon blanc; co-fermented in one batch, cool-fermented for 18 days, then 4 months on light yeast lees. A vivid portrait of the Swan Valley at its best; zesty and tangy, and some synergy going on under the bedclothes. Screwcap. 13% alc. **Rating** 94 **To** 2026 **$**25 ✪

ⵡⵡⵡⵡⵡ **Bottle Aged Reserve Chenin Blanc 2013** Rating 93 To 2028 $36
MPV Malbec Petit Verdot 2018 Rating 92 To 2029 $32
Reserve Cabernet Malbec 2016 Rating 90 To 2027 $45

Jones Road   ★★★★★

2 Godings Road, Moorooduc, Vic 3933 **Region** Mornington Peninsula
T (03) 5978 8080 **www.**jonesroad.com.au **Open** W'ends 11–5
Winemaker Travis Bush **Est.** 1998 **Dozens** 6000 **Vyds** 26.5ha
After establishing a very large and very successful herb-producing business in the UK, Rob Frewer and family migrated to Australia in 1997. By a circuitous route they ended up with a property on the Mornington Peninsula, planting pinot noir and chardonnay, then pinot gris, sauvignon blanc and merlot. They have since leased another vineyard at Mt Eliza and purchased Ermes Estate in 2007.

ⵡⵡⵡⵡⵡ **Nepean Mornington Peninsula Pinot Noir 2018** Good colour, deep but bright. The most powerful of the Jones Road '18 pinots, only 250 dozen made. Every scrap of flavour and tannin has been captured, the road not easy to follow. Comparisons with the lovely '17 aren't fair, but can't be ignored. Screwcap. 14% alc. **Rating** 94 **To** 2028 $60

Mornington Peninsula Syrah 2017 A small patch of estate vines received maximum care, and no less in the winery, exulting the '17 vintage. The wine has a core of dark cherry/forest berry fruit, garnished with spices and polished leather. It's a very good cool-climate shiraz. Screwcap. 13.3% alc. **Rating** 94 **To** 2037 $38

ⵡⵡⵡⵡⵡ **Mornington Peninsula Pinot Noir 2018** Rating 93 To 2028 $38
Mornington Peninsula Chardonnay 2018 Rating 92 To 2021 $38
Mornington Peninsula Pinot Gris 2018 Rating 92 To 2021 $32

Josef Chromy Wines   ★★★★★

370 Relbia Road, Relbia, Tas 7258 **Region** Northern Tasmania
T (03) 6335 8700 **www.**josefchromy.com.au **Open** 7 days 10–5
Winemaker Jeremy Dineen, Ockie Myburgh **Est.** 2004 **Dozens** 40 000 **Vyds** 60.32ha
Joe is at it again. After escaping from Czechoslovakia in 1950, he established Blue Ribbon Meats, used the proceeds of that sale to buy Rochecombe and Heemskerk vineyards, then sold those and established Tamar Ridge before it, too, was sold. This time Joe has invested $40 million in another wine-based business. If this were not remarkable enough, Joe is in his late-80s and has recovered from a major stroke. The foundation of the new business is the Old Stornoway Vineyard with 60ha of mature vines, the lion's share planted to pinot noir and chardonnay. Joe's grandson, Dean Cocker, is business manager of the restaurant, cellar door and function and wine centre within the homestead. They offer WSET (Wine & Spirit Education Trust) courses. Exports to all major markets.

ⵡⵡⵡⵡⵡ **Block 17 Pinot Noir 2014** A single barrel selection from one of the estate's favourite blocks. Open-fermented with 25% whole bunches, matured in French barriques for 11 months. It has retained the energy and layered complexity since first tasted in Mar '18. Luscious and velvety black cherry fruit has exotic spices spun throughout, providing a complex flavour base, expanding into the persistent flavours of the long, lingering finish. Screwcap. 13.8% alc. **Rating** 97 **To** 2024 $150 ✪

ΨΨΨΨΨ   **Chardonnay 2018** Excellent wine. It is complex and vibrant, with barrel ferment characters to the fore on both bouquet and palate, grapefruit the spearhead in both instances. The flavours are notably fresh, the finish long. Screwcap. 13.5% alc. **Rating** 96 **To** 2029 $38 ✪

ΨΨΨΨΨ   **PEPIK Chardonnay 2018 Rating** 91 **To** 2027 $25
Pinot Gris 2018 Rating 91 **To** 2020 $28
Tasmanian Cuvee Methode Traditionelle NV Rating 91 $32
PEPIK Sparkling Rose NV NV Rating 90

Journey Wines ★★★★★

2/26 Hunter Road, Healesville, Vic 3777 (postal) **Region** Yarra Valley
T 0427 298 098 **www.**journeywines.com.au **Open** Not
Winemaker Damian North **Est.** 2011 **Dozens** 3000
The name chosen by Damian North for his brand is particularly appropriate given the winding path he has taken before starting (with his wife and three children) his own label. Originally a sommelier at Tetsuya's, he was inspired to enrol in the oenology course at CSU, gaining his first practical winemaking experience as assistant winemaker at Tarrawarra Estate. Then, with family in tow, he moved to Oregon's Benton-Lane Winery to make pinot noir, before returning to become winemaker at Leeuwin Estate for five years. The wheel has turned full circle as the family has returned to the Yarra Valley, securing 2ha of chardonnay, 2.5ha of pinot noir and 2ha of shiraz under contract arrangements, and making the wines at Medhurst. Exports to the UK, Singapore, Thailand and China.

ΨΨΨΨΨ   **Small Batch Lone Star Creek Pinot Noir 2017** 20% whole bunches, though it feels like more. Electrically spiced with autumn leaf, clove, twig, walnut and mulch characters swinging through vibrant red cherry and strawberry. It's a firm, earnest, smoky pinot – serious is the word – with murky undergrowth characters and plenty of texture. Its flavour profile is no-holds-barred but it's balanced and svelte. It will mature well. Screwcap. 13% alc. **Rating** 96 **To** 2030 $60 CM ✪
Yarra Valley Chardonnay 2018 It's an elegant, fluid, textural chardonnay with white peach, custard apple and vanilla cream characters washing through to a sustained, stony finish. This will mature beautifully over the next handful of years. Screwcap. 13% alc. **Rating** 94 **To** 2027 $40 CM
Heathcote Fiano 2019 The combination of texture, flavour and length here is a winner in anyone's book. It's pulpy and ripe but it plays savoury cards and smoky barrel–induced ones too. It wouldn't be far-fetched to call this compelling. Screwcap. 13.5% alc. **Rating** 94 **To** 2024 $26 CM ✪
Yarra Valley Pinot Noir 2018 It's a wine of inherent complexity. It's fine-boned and slender, but there's enough texture and flavour to satisfy and then you get to the nuances, which are many. It's an undergrowthy pinot, and a spicy one, but macerated fruit carries throughout and cedary oak has been expertly applied. Sure, safe hands here. Screwcap. 14% alc. **Rating** 94 **To** 2029 $40 CM
Heathcote Shiraz 2017 It's an alert shiraz, vibrant with fruit and spice notes, satiny to the touch, tannic in an integrated way, well finished. It's not especially deep in colour or flavour, but then it's certainly not underpowered either. Texture is key, so too balance and length. Screwcap. 14% alc. **Rating** 94 **To** 2030 $40 CM

JS Wines ★★★★☆

42 Lake Canobolas Road, Nashdale, Orange, NSW 2800 **Region** Orange
T 0433 042 576 **www.**jswine.com.au **Open** Not
Winemaker Philip Shaw, Nadja Wallington, Drew Tuckwell **Est.** 2015 **Dozens** NFP
Vyds 16.6ha
I simply can't resist quoting the opening to the background information provided: 'Located on the west side of Australia's agricultural province of New South Wales. JS Wines' estate is about 8km from the centre of Orange, 3 hours' drive from Sydney'. The vineyard and the quality of

the wines brings together three winemakers who have long-term firsthand knowledge of the Orange region. This business expects to sell virtually all of its wines in China.

♥♥♥♥♡ Sea Wave Cabernet Sauvignon 2018 As with all of the JS wines, no regional claim on the front or back label. A well made cabernet with black fruits set in the flesh of a full-bodied style. Screwcap. 14.8% alc. **Rating** 91 **To** 2030 $40
Blue Sea Shiraz 2018 If you aren't sensitive to lots of oak, this wine will appeal; the underlying fruit with attractive dark cherry flavours and overall good balance. Screwcap. 14.5% alc. **Rating** 90 **To** 2028 $40

♥♥♥♥ Black Swan Pinot Gris 2018 Rating 89 **To** 2020 $35
Reserve Blue Sea Shiraz 2018 Rating 89 **To** 2026 $40

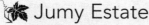

Jumy Estate   ★★★★☆

28 Ellsworth Crescent, Camberwell, Vic 3124 (postal) **Region** Yarra Valley/Grampians
T 0433 591 617 **www.**odevine.com.cn **Open** Not
Winemaker Ben Haines **Est.** 2015 **Dozens** 2000
Jumy Estate was founded in 2015 by leading architect Linda Wang and structural engineer Roy Zhang. Highly regarded winemaker Ben Haines' brief is to produce wines that are engaging and distinct, and capture the sense of place. Exports to China.

♥♥♥♥♥ ODE19 Jumy Signature Series Grampians Cabernet Sauvignon 2018 Machine-harvested with an optical destemmer that allows 15% of berries to pass through for gentle crushing, open-fermented, 27 days on skins, matured in French barriques (10% new) for 18 months, only one rack and return in that time. A delicious, medium-bodied cabernet, the tannins a feature of the long, balanced palate. Diam. 14% alc. **Rating** 96 **To** 2038 $38 **☺**
ODE19 Jumy Signature Series Yarra Valley Pinot Noir 2019 MV6, 100% whole bunches in a sealed vat for 5 days for partial carbonic maceration, destemmed for wild yeast–alcoholic fermentation, 2 weeks on skins, matured in barriques for 10 months. Well made, with a spicy/savoury stream of cherry cola and plum fruit running through from start to finish. Excellent length and aftertaste. Diam. 13% alc. **Rating** 94 **To** 2026 $35

♥♥♥♥♡ ODE19 Jumy Signature Series Grampians Shiraz 2018 Rating 90 **To** 2030 $35

Juniper   ★★★★★

98 Tom Cullity Drive, Cowaramup, WA 6284 **Region** Margaret River
T (08) 9755 9000 **www.**juniperestate.com.au **Open** 7 days 10–5
Winemaker Mark Messenger **Est.** 1973 **Dozens** 12 000 **Vyds** 19.5ha
Roger Hill and Gillian Anderson purchased the Wrights' Wilyabrup property in 1998, driven by the 25-year-old vineyard with dry-grown cabernet as the jewel in the crown. They also purchased complementary vineyards in Forest Grove (Higher Plane) and Wilyabrup; the vineyards are sustainably farmed using organic principles. Sons Nick and Tom (formerly a winemaker in the Yarra Valley) are now running the business. The Juniper Crossing and Small Batch wines are sourced from the three vineyards, while the Single Vineyard releases are made only from the original vineyard on Tom Cullity Drive. Exports to the UK, the US, Singapore, Hong Kong and China.

♥♥♥♥♥ Estate Margaret River Aquitaine Rouge 2017 A 51/22/16/7/4% cabernet sauvignon/malbec/merlot/petit verdot/cabernet franc. Old vine cabernet sauvignon is the foundation stone for this showcase of Bordeaux grape varieties. Deep purple-garnet. A captivating single vineyard wine that melds the different grape personalities beautifully. Margaret River briary regional character on display with well defined cabernet flavours in the cassis/crushed vine-leaf spectrum and kitchen mint and dark chocolate bitters. A fine-featured, elegant red wine. Screwcap. 14% alc. **Rating** 96 **To** 2040 $38 JP **☺**

Estate Margaret River Aquitaine Blanc 2018 A 63/37% sauvignon blanc/semillon. Aquitaine celebrates the similarity of wine styles made in Margaret River and in the region of Aquitaine in France. It's not such a long bow. Pale-light straw. Gooseberry, nettle, bean, straw and celery salt intense aromas. Subtly moves into more concentrated fruit depth with a flinty, citrus, quince fruit expression. Snappy and tart to taste. It's like discovering Margaret River SBS all over again. This is how it's meant to be. Screwcap. 13.5% alc. **Rating** 95 **To** 2026 $33 JP ✪

Crossing Margaret River Semillon Sauvignon Blanc 2019 A 52/48% blend. Fruitful division of labour exhibited with the grassy, hay notes of semillon intertwined with the exuberant passionfruit pulp, tropical fruit bowl of summery sauvignon blanc. The 2 marry beautifully, thoughtfully, throughout. Screwcap. 12.5% alc. **Rating** 95 **To** 2026 $20 JP ✪

Estate Single Vineyard Margaret River Shiraz 2017 A most persuasively elegant argument to buy a lot more Margaret River shiraz! Filled to brimming with cooler climate expressed red fruits of cranberry, plum, dried redcurrant. Utterly seductive in the mouth, silky, velvety. Nothing out of place. Screwcap. 14% alc. **Rating** 95 **To** 2036 $40 JP

Estate Single Vineyard Margaret River Cabernet Sauvignon 2016 A single vineyard cabernet sauvignon with just a little help from its friends: malbec/merlot/cabernet franc (4.5% each). A wine for the ages – it would be a crime to drink it now. This will be a test of will. Leafy blackcurrant, blueberry interplay with toasty, spicy oak in the background. Mid-weighted with a real depth of flavour intensity of coffee grounds, wet earth, petrichor and assured fine tannins. Screwcap. 14% alc. **Rating** 95 **To** 2042 $70 JP

Estate Margaret River Chardonnay 2018 From best blocks on 2 vineyards at Wilyabrup and Forest Grove. A barrel-selected chardonnay with enticing, ripe aromas of stone fruit, melon and inviting butteriness. Ticks all the boxes from textural mouthfeel to supportive oak and appealing buttered toast complexities. Screwcap. 13% alc. **Rating** 94 **To** 2030 $40 JP

Small Batch Margaret River Rose 2019 Bright, full crimson hue touched by salmon. A rich, layered rose with a mix of crunchy/juicy flavours all suggesting extended skin contact or some barrel ferment (or both). Interesting wine with plenty to say for itself. Screwcap. 12.5% alc. **Rating** 94 **To** 2021 $25 ✪

Small Batch Margaret River Cabernet Sauvignon 2016 An 86/5/5/4% blend of cabernet sauvignon, malbec, merlot and petit verdot. There's a lot of high quality Margaret River fruit deftly handled in the winery for the price. The cabernet tannin structure gives the wine its ticket into the future, years down the track. Screwcap. 14% alc. **Rating** 94 **To** 2031 $25 ✪

Estate Margaret River Malbec 2017 A fine follow-up to the excellent '16 vintage; the '17 offers an earthy, gutsy red to get your teeth into. But not just yet. If you can wait, the pleasure will double; it's still in building mode. Deep garnet. Turned earth, prune, blackberry, star anise – bright on the bouquet. Generous in fruit and dressed in smart oak with chewy tannins, the best is yet to come. Screwcap. 14% alc. **Rating** 94 **To** 2034 $40 JP

♟♟♟♟♟ **Crossing Sauvignon Blanc 2018** Rating 93 To 2021 $22 ✪
Crossing Semillon Sauvignon Blanc 2019 Rating 93 To 2025 $22 ✪
Small Batch Fiano 2019 Rating 93 To 2023 $27 ✪
Crossing Shiraz 2017 Rating 93 To 2027 $25 ✪
Small Batch Tempranillo 2018 **Rating** 93 **To** 2030 $27 ✪
Crossing Chardonnay 2018 **Rating** 92 **To** 2026 $20 JP ✪
Small Batch Fiano 2018 Rating 92 To 2023 $25 ✪
Estate Cane Cut Riesling 2018 Rating 92 To 2027 $27 JP

Just Red Wines   ★★★★☆

2370 Eukey Road, Ballandean, Qld 4382 **Region** Granite Belt
T (07) 4684 1322 **www**.justred.com.au **Open** 7 days 10–5
Winemaker Tony Hassall, Michael Hassall **Est.** 1998 **Dozens** 1500 **Vyds** 2.8ha

Tony, Julia and Michael Hassall have planted shiraz and merlot (plus later additions of cabernet sauvignon, tannat and viognier) at an altitude of just under 900m. They minimise the use of chemicals wherever possible, but do not hesitate to protect the grapes if weather conditions threaten an outbreak of mildew or botrytis.

ПППП **CMT Granite Belt Cabernet Sauvignon Merlot Tannat 2018** A 42/38/20% blend, fermented in open and closed pots. A juicy sweet blend, the tannat cleverly handled, as was the whole blend for that matter. Excellent value. Screwcap. 13.7% alc. **Rating** 92 **To** 2028 $19 ✪

ПППП **Daily Red Granite Belt Shiraz 2019 Rating** 89 **To** 2022 $16 ✪

Kaesler Wines   ★★★★★
Barossa Valley Way, Nuriootpa, SA 5355 **Region** Barossa Valley
T (08) 8562 4488 **www**.kaesler.com.au **Open** 7 days 11–5
Winemaker Reid Bosward, Stephen Dew **Est.** 1990 **Dozens** 20 000 **Vyds** 36ha
The first members of the Kaesler family settled in the Barossa Valley in 1845. The vineyards date back to '93, but the Kaesler family ownership ended in 1968. Kaesler Wines was eventually acquired by a small group of investment bankers (who have since purchased Yarra Yering), in conjunction with former Flying Winemaker Reid Bosward and wife Bindy. Reid's experience shows through in the wines, which come from estate vineyards adjacent to the winery and from 10ha in the Marananga area that includes shiraz planted in 1899. The Small Valley Vineyard wines, made by Stephen Dew, are produced from 49ha in the Adelaide Hills. Exports to all major markets.

ПППП **The Bogan 2018** From 2 vineyards – Marananga planted in 1899 and Nuriootpa in 1965. It's a magical combo because this is gorgeous. Really vibrant and fragrant with florals, a whorl of fresh red berries and blackberries across the palate, but not too much and not too sweet, with some choc-mint too. Tannins are neatly poised and the palate surprisingly mid-weighted. Cork. 14.5% alc. **Rating** 96 **To** 2035 $55 JF ✪
Old Bastard Barossa Valley Shiraz 2017 While this toys with the riper spectrum with its soy sauce and licorice blackstrap flavours, it somehow gets pulled back into its shapely groove. The fruit is lovely – off vines planted in 1893 – the tannins silky if powerful, abetted by the 35% new French oak, yet the line of bright acidity keeps this buoyant. Somehow, it just works. Cork. 15% alc. **Rating** 96 **To** 2037 $250 JF
Alte Reben Barossa Valley Shiraz 2017 Big Barossa Red. Expect black fruits, licorice, aged balsamic vinegar and menthol with sweet oak flavours hovering. It's on the cusp of being too ripe but the acidity and fleshy tannins, plus its drive, keep it in check. One for the fans. Cork. 15% alc. **Rating** 95 **To** 2030 $150 JF
Barossa Valley Barbera 2016 This keeps giving with every sip. Starts with black cherries and pips, spice and lots of florals. The medium–bodied palate fills with fleshy ripe sweet fruit, soft easy tannins and a neat acid lift to the finish. Maturation in used French barriques has imparted woodsy flavours and a slight green walnut bitterness on the finish. Screwcap. 14.5% alc. **Rating** 95 **To** 2026 $35 JF ✪
Old Vine Barossa Valley Shiraz 2017 An abundance of flavour with all manner of ripe fruit, compote and baking spices. While the sweet oak needs to settle, everything else is kept in shape by refreshing raspberry sorbet–like acidity. Cork. 15% alc. **Rating** 94 **To** 2030 $90 JF
Barossa Valley Cabernet Sauvignon 2018 Some charm here with bright cassis and boysenberry compote flavours, plus an array of spices. The palate remains just shy of full-bodied, so there's a bit of verve. Oak plays its part, not dominating. And there is a freshness on the finish. Cork. 14% alc. **Rating** 94 **To** 2030 $35 JF

ПППП **Avignon 2017 Rating** 93 **To** 2027 $35 JF
Old Vine Barossa Valley Semillon 2019 Rating 91 **To** 2026 $25 JF
The Bogan 2017 Rating 91 **To** 2030 $55 JF

WOMS Shiraz Cabernet 2018 Rating 90 **To** 2033 $150 JF
The Fave Barossa Valley Grenache 2019 Rating 90 **To** 2022 $35 JF

Kalleske ★★★★★

6 Murray Street, Greenock, SA 5360 **Region** Barossa Valley
T (08) 8563 4000 **www**.kalleske.com **Open** 7 days 10–5
Winemaker Troy Kalleske **Est.** 1999 **Dozens** 20 000 **Vyds** 50ha

The Kalleske family has been growing and selling grapes on a mixed farming property at Greenock for over 140 years. Sixth-generation Troy Kalleske, with brother Tony, established the winery and created the Kalleske label in 1999. The vineyard is planted mainly to shiraz (31ha) and grenache (7ha), with smaller amounts of chenin blanc, semillon, viognier, cabernet sauvignon, mataro, durif, petit verdot, tempranillo and zinfandel. The vines vary in age, with the oldest dating back to 1875; the overall average age is around 50 years. All are grown biodynamically. Exports to all major markets.

🍷🍷🍷🍷🍷 **Johann Georg Old Vine Single Vineyard Barossa Valley Shiraz 2017** This wine sits unchallenged at the head of the Kalleske shiraz tree. The grapes were treated with the care and attention they deserved in a small open fermenter for 12 days using a heading down screen that submerged the cap, pressed to French hogsheads (new and used) for 2 years. It's got a juicy, supple mouthfeel with an unexpected lightness and finesse. Screwcap. 14.5% alc. **Rating** 98 **To** 2052 $175 ✪

Eduard Old Vine Barossa Valley Shiraz 2017 The vines in question were 46–112yo in '17 from 3 vineyards. Like all the Kalleske wines, deep magenta. The flavours hit at high speed; blackberry, plum, licorice and dark chocolate immediately establishing themselves in all corners of the mouth. Despite this naked power, the wine is so well balanced and so long that it's a pleasure to drink. Screwcap. 14.5% alc. **Rating** 97 **To** 2047 $90 ✪

🍷🍷🍷🍷🍷 **Moppa Barossa Valley Shiraz 2018** The wine is medium to full-bodied, complex in a relaxed fashion and very, very drinkable. All the wines from '17 have a special quality thanks to the vintage, described by Kalleske as 'exceptional'. Screwcap. 14.5% alc. **Rating** 95 **To** 2033 $30 ✪

🍷🍷🍷🍷 **Greenock Barossa Valley Shiraz 2018 Rating** 93 **To** 2038 $45
Clarry's Barossa Valley GSM 2019 Rating 92 **To** 2022 $23 ✪

Kangarilla Road Vineyard ★★★★★

Kangarilla Road, McLaren Vale, SA 5171 **Region** McLaren Vale
T (08) 8383 0533 **www**.kangarillaroad.com.au **Open** Mon–Fri 9–5, w'ends 11–4
Winemaker Kevin O'Brien **Est.** 1997 **Dozens** 25 000 **Vyds** 14ha

In January 2013 Kangarilla Road founders Kevin O'Brien and wife Helen succeeded in breaking the mould for a winery sale, crafting a remarkable win-win outcome. They sold their winery and surrounding vineyard to Gemtree Wines, which has had its wine made at Kangarilla Road since '01 under the watchful eye of Kevin. The O'Briens have retained their adjacent JOBS vineyard and the Kangarilla Road wines continue to be made by Kevin at the winery. Luck of the Irish, perhaps. Exports to the UK, the US and other major markets.

🍷🍷🍷🍷 **Black St Peters McLaren Vale Zinfandel 2019** Judging by my tech sheet, this hails from an older vineyard (planted in 1975) than the Primitivo albeit the DNA is the same, the clone the same and yet, the nomenclature different. The intensity, vibrancy and carry across the mouth too is starkly different. This has impressive density to saturated blue to dark fruit scents; the signature twist of Aperol orange bitters and a long, succulent finish. Outstanding value. Screwcap. **Rating** 92 **To** 2023 $25 NG ✪

Q McLaren Vale Shiraz 2017 Unbelievable to me that a wine of this price was machine-harvested. The price presumably a communication of the time in barrel: 24 months in French (100% new). Salubrious, I suppose, for this sort of thing. The oak certainly serves to tame the pH tweaks, resulting in a curvaceous rich red, dense and plush. Black fruits, bitter chocolate to coffee grind, anise and cedar. Screwcap. **Rating** 91 **To** 2029 $70 NG

McLaren Vale Primitivo 2018 There is something unadulterated and primary about this wine. Candied orange zest meshed with a sweet-sour red-berry tang. Really attractive. This is intuitive and easygoing, and very easy to drink, attesting to the bright future of warm climate Italian indigenes on these shores. Screwcap. **Rating** 91 **To** 2023 $25 NG

Blanche Point Formation McLaren Vale Shiraz 2019 A coastal vineyard near Maslins Beach, lending a salinity to the swirl of black and blue fruit references. Gently extracted with a floating cap in open-top fermenters – the estate's signature. Shiraz's lilac florals enticing, as usual. A bitter choc-coffee grind oak element, adding to the complexity. The pH work obtuse. Screwcap. **Rating** 90 **To** 2026 $45 NG

The Devil's Whiskers McLaren Vale Shiraz 2018 A single vineyard sourcing in Seaview. An open-top fermentation before maturation in French hogsheads for 18 months. Blood plum, blueberry, licorice blackstrap and some exotic spice scents careening their way across a tangy finish. Screwcap. **Rating** 90 **To** 2026 $40 NG

ȚȚȚȚ **McLaren Vale Shiraz 2018** Rating 89 To 2028 $25

 # Kanoetree Wines

147 Watson Park Road, Angas Plains, SA 5255 **Region** Langhorne Creek
T 0417 307 208 **www**.kanoetree.com.au **Open** Not
Winemaker David Haeusler **Est.** 2016 **Dozens** 800 **Vyds** 5.88ha

Branches of the Haeusler family have lived in Langhorne Creek for years. When the family agreed that the former dairy farm (with two large red gums bearing the evidence that two aboriginal canoes had been cut from their bark) should be divided between the two brothers, David and Sue Haeusler knew that one use for their property was viticulture. David had worked in the wine industry all his life: first in his uncle's vineyard, thereafter assisting in the set up of a nearby winery. He continued as assistant winemaker and production manager while obtaining a diploma in wine marketing. In 1993 and '94 Sue and David planted shiraz, malbec, cabernet sauvignon, merlot and verdelho, intending to sell the grapes. When demand slowed they set up a small winery using their engineering and electrical skills. A new shiraz block was planted in 2014 and in '16 the first grapes were crushed for their newly-created label. Since '17 all the grapes have been crushed, part sold in bulk, part kept for their own label.

ȚȚȚȚȚ **Langhorne Creek Shiraz 2017** The first estate release from its 26yo vines; open-fermented in small stainless steel pots, matured in American oak. Has the benediction of its Langhorne Creek terroir, which seldom fails to produce red wines with a softly cushioned generosity. The vintage was another plus. Screwcap. 15% alc. **Rating** 90 **To** 2027 $22

Haeusler Crossing Langhorne Creek Shiraz Cabernet 2017 Bright crimson. The region, blend and the vintage join hands to produce a medium-bodied wine with a degree of elegance and good balance. Screwcap. 14.4% alc. **Rating** 90 **To** 2027 $22

Langhorne Creek Malbec 2017 Deep, bright crimson. Langhorne Creek has a high reputation for malbec and this levels up to that reputation with luscious plum fruit/plum cake and soft tannins. Screwcap. 14.6% alc. **Rating** 90 **To** 2027 $22

ȚȚȚȚ **Langhorne Creek Cabernet Sauvignon 2017** Rating 89 To 2021 $22

Karrawatta

164 Greenhills Road, Meadows, SA 5201 **Region** Adelaide Hills
T (08) 8537 0511 **www**.karrawatta.com.au **Open** 7 days 11–4
Winemaker Mark Gilbert **Est.** 1996 **Dozens** 6000 **Vyds** 59.25ha

Mark Gilbert is the great-great-great-grandson of Joseph Gilbert, who established the Pewsey Vale vineyard and winery in 1847. Joseph Gilbert had named the property Karrawatta, but adopted Pewsey Vale after losing the toss of a coin with his neighbour. The Karrawatta of today has 12.43ha of vines in the Adelaide Hills, 38.07ha in Langhorne Creek and 8.75ha in McLaren Vale. The vineyards are all hand-pruned, the small-batch wines fashioned with minimum intervention. Exports to the US, Canada and Hong Kong.

ŢŢŢŢŢ **Dairy Block Adelaide Hills Shiraz 2018** It puts on a rich, seductive, complex display powered by black cherry, ripe plum and black pepper flavours. Briary/clovey/woodsy notes hover throughout, as does a suggestion of smoky reduction. It's juicy, well shaped and enormously enjoyable to drink. Screwcap. 14.8% alc. **Rating** 95 **To** 2030 $38 CM

Joseph Langhorne Creek Shiraz 2017 From the family's vineyard; matured for 18 months in French oak. Interesting wine, with a distinctly savoury edge, dark chocolate à la McLaren Vale, and a long palate. The wine will live as long as your patience. Screwcap. 15% alc. **Rating** 95 **To** 2040 $54

Ace of Trumps Chapel Hill Road McLaren Vale Shiraz 2017 Matured in French oak (30% new) for 10 months. A full-bodied shiraz with layers of purple and black fruits, ripe tannins throughout and lashings of oak. Its components are balanced, and a long future awaits. Screwcap. 15% alc. **Rating** 95 **To** 2037 $54

Ace of Trumps Chapel Hill Road McLaren Vale Shiraz 2018 Sweet-fruited and plush, attractively oaked too, but with a firm, imposing finish. This is a wine to win you over. It tastes of cloves, malt, sweet plum and chocolate, and while it has plenty of heft, it's not syrupy or overdone. Screwcap. 14.7% alc. **Rating** 94 **To** 2032 $54 CM

Joseph Langhorne Creek Shiraz 2018 The accent is on sweet fruit, blackberried and slightly jammy, with toasty/clovey accents adding both grain and breadth. This is a sizeable shiraz: mouthfilling, generous to a fault but shaped well through the finish. Sweet caramel–like oak and saltbush notes only adds to the seduction. Screwcap. 14.9% alc. **Rating** 94 **To** 2034 $54 CM

Christo's Paddock Langhorne Creek Cabernet Sauvignon 2018 The fruit is sweet and flowing, the oak is nicely tucked in, the tannin is dusty and complementary. It floods your mouth with curranty flavours before presenting chocolate, mint, violet and cream-caramel characters as a kind of icing. It's very good. Screwcap. 14.9% alc. **Rating** 94 **To** 2035 $54 CM

Spartacus Langhorne Creek Cabernet Sauvignon Malbec Shiraz 2018 A wealth of fruit, lots of muscle and a warm-but-satisfying finish. This really steps up and gives you everything it's got. Tar, mint, dark chocolate, raisin and sweet tobacco flavours do the grunt work. The finish is spread with firm tannin. There's lots here to chew on. Cork. 14.9% alc. **Rating** 94 **To** 2036 CM

ŢŢŢŢŢ **Anna's Adelaide Hills Sauvignon Blanc 2019** **Rating** 93 **To** 2022 $30 CM
The Meddler Langhorne Creek Malbec 2018 **Rating** 93 **To** 2030 $54 CM
Anth's Garden Adelaide Hills Chardonnay 2018 **Rating** 92 **To** 2025 $46 CM
Sophie's Hill Adelaide Hills Pinot Grigio 2018 **Rating** 92 **To** 2021 $26
Sophie's Hill Adelaide Hills Pinot Grigio 2019 **Rating** 91 **To** 2022 $30 CM

KarriBindi   ★★★★☆

111 Scott Road, Karridale, WA 6288 (postal) **Region** Margaret River
T (08) 9758 5570 **www**.karribindi.com.au **Open** Not
Winemaker Kris Wealand **Est.** 1997 **Dozens** 1500 **Vyds** 32.05ha
KarriBindi is owned by Kevin, Yvonne and Kris Wealand. The name comes from Karridale and the surrounding karri forests, and from Bindi, the home town of one of the members of the Wealand family. In Nyoongar, 'karri' means strong, special, spiritual, tall tree; 'bindi' means butterfly. The Wealands have established sauvignon blanc (15ha), chardonnay (6.25ha), cabernet sauvignon (4ha), plus smaller plantings of semillon, shiraz and merlot. KarriBindi also supplies a number of high-profile Margaret River wineries. Exports to Singapore and China.

ŢŢŢŢŢ **Margaret River Semillon Sauvignon Blanc 2019** A 60/40% blend, 8% of the sauvignon blanc barrel-fermented. A gold medal at the highly competitive Margaret River Wine Show and silver medals from Perth and Hobart reflect the combination of fruit, texture and structure. Will match many cuisines. Screwcap. 12.5% alc. **Rating** 94 **To** 2023 $20 ◐

Margaret River Chardonnay 2018 Hand-picked, whole-bunch pressed, wild-fermented, 20% mlf, matured for 10 months in 30% new oak. Its balance allows the wine to run fluidly across and along the palate, paying no attention to its alcohol. Screwcap. 13.8% alc. **Rating** 94 **To** 2029 $30 ◐

Margaret River Shiraz 2018 Crushed and destemmed, matured for 15 months in French oak (25% new). Medium to full-bodied. The oak handling ticks the box, framing the fresh array of spicy black cherry and satsuma plum fruits; the tannins also in sync. Great value. Screwcap. 13.9% alc. **Rating** 94 **To** 2033 $25 ◐

♈♈♈♈♈ **Margaret River Sauvignon Blanc 2019 Rating** 90 **To** 2022 $20 ◐

Katnook ★★★★★

Riddoch Highway, Coonawarra, SA 5263 **Region** Coonawarra
T (08) 8737 0300 **www.**katnookestate.com.au **Open** Mon–Fri 10–5, w'ends 12–5
Winemaker Tim Heath **Est.** 1979 **Dozens** 90000 **Vyds** 198ha
Second in size in the region to Wynns Coonawarra Estate, Katnook has taken significant strides since acquisition by Freixenet, the Spanish cava producer. Once Katnook sold most of its grapes, but it now sells only 10%. The historic stone woolshed in which the second vintage in Coonawarra (1896) was made, and which has served Katnook since 1980, has been restored. Likewise, the former office of John Riddoch has been restored and is now the cellar door; the former stables serve as a function area. Well over half of the total estate plantings are cabernet sauvignon and shiraz; the Odyssey Cabernet Sauvignon and Prodigy Shiraz are the duo at the top of a multi-tiered production. In March 2018 Freixenet announced that Henkell, the Oetker Group's sparkling wine branch, had acquired 50.67% of Freixenet's shares, creating the world's leading sparkling wine group. In the same month, and by coincidence, Katnook announced that Tim Heath, Cloudy Bay's chief winemaker for the previous 14 years, had taken up the role at Katnook following the death of long-term incumbent Wayne Stehbens. Exports to all major markets.

♈♈♈♈♈ **Estate Sauvignon Blanc 2019** This has always been a complex sauvignon and for me arguably the standout wine across the estate's legacy. Distinctive parcel-to-parcel ferments across a judicious swathe of barrel work and lees handling, produces a wine that is inimitable and uncanny. Who would think that this region is capable of such complexity? Lemon curd, greengage, guava and a curb of beautifully handled oak corralling the party. Screwcap. **Rating** 95 **To** 2023 $25 NG ◐

Prodigy Shiraz 2015 This is a nostalgic sort of wine that packs huge appeal. Oozing with blueberry, black cherry and a hint of kirsch; the nicely wrought tannins imbue a sophistication to the melee while imparting tone. The acidity feels right enough, giving pull to a long, nourishing finish. The sort of wine that allows you to have your cake and eat it too. Cork. **Rating** 95 **To** 2035 $110 NG

Estate Cabernet Sauvignon 2017 This mid to full-weighted wine is initially defined by the carapace of largely French oak in which it was aged for 12 months. Tight. Drawn across cedar and vanilla, this needs time in the cellar to fill out. With air, the growing whisper in the glass of cassis, green olive, strewn herb and sage comes to the fore; the oak tannins soften. This stands to be a very fine Connawarra cabernet as the grape tannins are of pixelated detail, ethereal and finely wrought, pulling it all long. The lingering impression is finesse. Really impressive wine. Screwcap. **Rating** 95 **To** 2032 $40 NG

The Caledonian Cabernet Shiraz 2017 The Katnook wines from this address have become gentler, effortless, more poised. No longer over-extracted and whacked up with a barrage of tannins, oak or otherwise. Rewardingly, there is a strong fealty to the famed terra rossa strip manifest across pliant tannins, bumptious dark to red fruit tones, hints of pencil lead and a ferrous waft across the detailed finish. This savoury red is a real pleasure to drink. Screwcap. 14% alc. **Rating** 94 **To** 2032 $55 NG

ŸŸŸŸŶ Founder's Block Chardonnay Pinot Noir NV Rating 93 $23 NG ✪
Founder's Block Chardonnay 2018 Rating 92 To 2023 $18 NG ✪
Estate Shiraz 2017 Rating 92 To 2030 $40 NG
Amara Vineyard Cabernet Sauvignon 2016 Rating 92 To 2032 $55 NG
Estate Riesling 2019 Rating 91 To 2027 $25 NG
Estate Chardonnay 2018 Rating 91 To 2023 $29 NG
Estate Merlot 2017 Rating 91 To 2028 $40 NG
Founder's Block Cabernet Sauvignon 2017 Rating 91 To 2024 $20 NG ✪
Founder's Block Sparkling Shiraz 2017 Rating 90 $23 NG

Kay Brothers Amery Vineyards ★★★★★

57 Kays Road, McLaren Vale, SA 5171 **Region** McLaren Vale
T (08) 8323 8211 **www**.kaybrothersamerywines.com **Open** Mon–Fri 10–4.30, w'ends &
public hols 12–4.30
Winemaker Duncan Kennedy, Colin Kay (Consultant) **Est.** 1890 **Dozens** 11 000
Vyds 22ha
A traditional winery with a rich history and just over 20ha of priceless old vines. The red
and fortified wines can be very good. Of particular interest is Block 6 Shiraz, made from
120+-year-old vines. Both vines and wines are going from strength to strength. Celebrated its
130th anniversary in 2020. Exports to the US, Canada, Switzerland, Germany, Malaysia, Hong
Kong, Singapore, South Korea, Thailand and China.

ŸŸŸŸŸ Block 6 McLaren Vale Shiraz 2017 Block 6 is a 1.4ha east-facing block of
125yo vines with very complex soils. Hand-picked, crushed and destemmed,
11 days on skins, matured for 20 months in French and American puncheons
(40% new). If ever there was an iron fist in a velvet glove this is it, but with one
qualification: the iron fist was created by a master sculptor; the wine quite special,
and fully deserving its price. Screwcap. 14.5% alc. **Rating** 97 To 2047 $125 ✪

ŸŸŸŸŸ Hillside McLaren Vale Shiraz 2017 Hillside allows Kay to blend Block 11 (on
the exposed tip of the hill with shallow sandy loam over limestone and sandstone,
wind and sun keeping the yield low) with the higher yielding New Block 6 (dark
chocolate loam and clay), matured in American and French oak for 20 months.
An exceptional Kay Brothers wine that has elegance to burn. Screwcap. 14.5% alc.
Rating 95 To 2037 $49
Griffon's Key Reserve Grenache 2018 From the best vines on the Amery
Vineyard; open-fermented, matured for 11 months in used French puncheons.
Generosity is its second name: liqueur-filled dark chocolate, contrast with savoury
nuances and ripe tannins. The 'Reserve' label is deserved. Screwcap. 14.5% alc.
Rating 94 To 2039 $49

ŸŸŸŸŶ Basket Pressed McLaren Vale Shiraz 2018 Rating 93 To 2033 $29
Basket Pressed McLaren Vale Grenache 2018 Rating 92 To 2035 $29
Cuthbert McLaren Vale Cabernet Sauvignon 2017 Rating 90 To 2022 $49
Basket Pressed McLaren Vale Mataro 2018 Rating 90 To 2028 $29
Nero d'Avola 2018 Rating 90 To 2027 $35

Keith Tulloch Wine ★★★★★

Hermitage Road, Pokolbin, NSW 2320 **Region** Hunter Valley
T (02) 4998 7500 **www**.keithtullochwine.com.au **Open** 7 days 10–5
Winemaker Keith Tulloch, Brendan Kaczorowski, Alisdair Tulloch **Est.** 1997
Dozens 10 000 **Vyds** 10.1ha
Keith Tulloch is, of course, a member of the Tulloch family, which has played a leading role
in the Hunter Valley for over a century. Formerly a winemaker at Lindemans and Rothbury
Estate, he developed his own label in 1997. There is the same almost obsessive attention to
detail, the same almost ascetic intellectual approach, the same refusal to accept anything but the
best as that of Jeffrey Grosset. In April 2019 the winery became the first Hunter Valley winery

to become certified carbon neutral under the National Carbon Offset Standard (NCOS). Exports to the UK, Ireland, the UAE, Indonesia and Japan.

ΨΨΨΨΨ **Field of Mars Block 2A Hunter Valley Semillon 2017** Hailing from a vineyard planted in 1968 on old silty riverbed sand, this is a pristine and incredibly transparent expression of featherweight semillon. A beguiling intensity of citrus fruit, apricot and chalky salinity staining the palate. Real extract here. Compact, yet very ripe. Tightly coiled before unleashing a thrust of flavour and parry of juicy acidity, driving it long and into a bright future. Screwcap. **Rating** 96 **To** 2034 $50 NG ✪

The Doctor Hunter Valley Shiraz 2017 A blend of equal parts Field of Mars and Kester barrels: the best from the prodigious '17 vintage. Mid-ruby. An outstanding first impression with a strong whiff of anise, violet, charcuterie, nori and succulent blue to dark fruits. Juicy. Rich, but not overt. Mocha oak well nestled. The tannic carriage is slick and finely tuned, driving the cavalcade of immense extract long. Screwcap. **Rating** 96 **To** 2032 $150 NG

Field of Mars Block 3B Hunter Valley Semillon 2017 Situated on the eastern side of the Block. The soils heavier than the 2A plot; the wine more robust and – in the context of lightweight semillon – more powerful. This is like squeezing the juice from the ripest quince, blending it with candied lemon rind, pink grapefruit and chalk, and serving it up. Delicious. Screwcap. **Rating** 95 **To** 2032 $50 NG

Field of Mars Block 6 Hunter Valley Chardonnay 2017 Hand-picked across the powdery alluvials planted in 1968. Destemmed and crushed. Hallelujah! Makes a change from the whole-bunch pressing norm in this country and the sameness too often produced. Racked to a François Frères oak regime, fermented wild and aged on heavy solids for 10 months, 25% new wood. A light yellow hue segues to a soprano of palate-staining nectarine, white peach and blossom notes. Impressive intensity and compelling length. Oak-scented vanillan core. Beautifully crafted. Screwcap. **Rating** 95 **To** 2025 $60 NG

The Wife Hunter Valley Shiraz 2018 A meld of 90% shiraz, the remainder viognier. Co-fermented as an homage to intelligent winemaking and to Côte-Rôtie, the blend's spiritual home. Mid-weighted. The viognier setting a mid-ruby hue while lifting syrah to a balletic persona: lilac, red cherry, salumi, satsuma plum and rosewater meandering along a skein of peppery acidity and granular tannin. A highly refined expression, best drunk during its youthful exuberance. Screwcap. **Rating** 95 **To** 2027 $65 NG

Bainton Vineyard Hunter Valley Shiraz 2018 This is a delicious, medium-bodied red with a mellifluous flow from fore to aft. Nothing too sweet, over the top or acerbic. It just sits in the mouth with a confident gait and effortless poise. Low yielding dry-grown fruit, a judicious amount of extraction bearing a real tannic gait and classy oak (Francois Frères for 18 months; 25% new). All about texture. Screwcap. **Rating** 95 **To** 2030 $48 NG

Eagles Rest Vineyard Chardonnay 2019 An impressive chardonnay boasting a mineral pungency and seams of high quality oak, melding as a carriage of thirst-slaking vibrancy and impressive length. Nectarine, tangerine and poached apricot with vanillan oak and praline at the core. Lighter of body. Real thrust of fruit and intensity of flavour. Screwcap. **Rating** 94 **To** 2027 $40 NG

The Kester Hunter Valley Shiraz 2018 A rich shiraz of dark fruit persuasions, licorice and violet notes, all strung across a chassis of coffee-grind tannins. Moreish. A conflation of the best shiraz parcels of the estate holdings. Forceful of flavour and tenacious of finish. Screwcap. **Rating** 94 **To** 2032 $75 NG

ΨΨΨΨΨ **Latara Vineyard Hunter Valley Semillon 2019** Rating 93 To 2029 $32 NG
Museum Release Hunter Valley Semillon 2013 Rating 93 To 2025 $60 NG
Field of Mars Block 1 Viognier 2019 Rating 93 To 2024 $55 NG
McKelvey Vineyard Hunter Valley Shiraz 2018 Rating 93 To 2032 $48 NG
Tawarri Vineyard Hunter Valley Shiraz 2018 Rating 93 To 2028 $48 NG
McKelvey Vineyard Chardonnay 2019 Rating 92 To 2025 $40 NG

Hunter Valley Shiraz Viognier 2018 Rating 92 To 2025 $36 NG
Hunter Valley Semillon 2019 Rating 91 To 2029 $30 NG
Hunter Valley Chardonnay 2019 Rating 91 To 2023 $35 NG
Museum Release The Kester Shiraz 2012 Rating 90 To 2025 NG

Kellermeister ★★★★★

Barossa Valley Highway, Lyndoch, SA 5351 **Region** Barossa Valley
T (08) 8524 4303 **www**.kellermeister.com.au **Open** 7 days 9.30–5.30
Winemaker Mark Pearce **Est.** 1976 **Dozens** 30000 **Vyds** 20ha
Since joining Kellermeister from Wirra Wirra in 2009, Mark Pearce has successfully worked
through challenging times to ensure the survival of the winery and its brands; and upon
the retirement of founders Ralph and Val Jones in late '12, the Pearce family acquired the
business. Surrounded by a young, close-knit team, Mark is committed to continuing to build
on the legacy that the founders began more than 40 years ago. His winemaking focus is on
continuing to preserve Kellermeister's best wines, while introducing new wines made with
the intention of expressing the purity of the provenance of the Barossa. Exports to the US,
Canada, Switzerland, Denmark, Israel, Taiwan, China and Japan.

🍷🍷🍷🍷 **The Meister Eden Valley Shiraz 2017** From the best parcels of shiraz on
the Fechner Vineyard planted in 1908. It marries power and concentration with
finesse and impeccable balance. The red and purple/cherry and plum fruits have
the finest threads of tannins invisibly woven into the palate. Mouth-watering and
lipsmacking are words seldom, if ever, used in connection with an Eden Valley
shiraz. Screwcap. 14.5% alc. **Rating** 98 **To** 2047 $250
**Rocamora Ancestor Vine Stonegarden Vineyard Eden Valley Grenache
2018** It is extraordinary how many winemakers line up for their share of the
1858 grenache vines. Terrific colour and depth; this is truly unique and treated
with utmost respect by all who share in its bounty, Kellermeister no exception.
The wine is so densely layered you simply wonder how long it will live. Screwcap.
14% alc. **Rating** 98 **To** 2058 $175 ✪
Black Sash Barossa Valley Shiraz 2017 Made from 100yo vines grown in
Ebenezer; matured in new and used French hogsheads. A wine with a proud record
of success. It has great finesse, elegance and balance; Mark Pearce has used every
advantage the vintage offered. Screwcap. 14.5% alc. **Rating** 97 **To** 2042 $79 ✪

🍷🍷🍷🍷 **The Wombat General Hand Picked Eden Valley Riesling 2019** Sourced
from the best riesling block on the Fechner Vineyard; whole-bunch pressed,
free-run juice of only 450l/t. Takes the mouth captive, intense lime/lemon fruit
building inexorably from the start to the finish, bright acidity adding to the drive
and purity of the finish. Screwcap. 12% alc. **Rating** 96 **To** 2034 $25 ✪
Wild Witch Barossa Shiraz 2016 This demonstrates the skill of Mark Pearce as
he takes parcels from the powerful northern and vibrant eastern Barossa and silky
Eden Valley fruit, employing his typical approach of new and used French oak. It's
intense and deep, but doesn't threaten as its name might suggest. What is beyond
doubt is its longevity. Screwcap. 14.8% alc. **Rating** 96 **To** 2056 $85
**Threefold Farm Single Vineyard The Firstborn Barossa Valley Shiraz
2018** Mark Pearce's intuitive winemaking (and familiarity with his family's
vineyard) seldom misses a trick. It's medium to full-bodied; its rich blackberry
and juicy fruitcake flavours neatly circumscribed by fine, ripe tannins. Screwcap.
14% alc. **Rating** 95 **To** 2038 $45
The Funk Wagon GSM Barossa Grenache Shiraz Mataro 2015 This is
developing very attractive secondary spices and cedary oak nuances, all different
but all in harmony. Old estate vines presumably been the major contributor
to a wine of real character. Screwcap. 14.5% alc. **Rating** 95 **To** 2030 $30 ✪
Barossa Vineyards Shiraz 2015 From a patchwork of vineyards across the
Barossa and Eden valleys; matured in used French hogsheads. Outstanding value
at this price. Medium to full-bodied fruits ranging through blackberry and plum,
the oak integrated, the tannins firm but supple. Screwcap. 14.5% alc. **Rating** 94
To 2030 $20 ✪

Wild Witch Barossa Shiraz 2015 This is so densely coloured it paints the inside of the glass as it is swirled in similar fashion (well, almost) to Seppeltsfield 100 Year Old Para. It's a full-bodied wine but its alcohol will not interrupt your enjoyment. Screwcap. 14.8% alc. **Rating** 94 **To** 2030 $85

Threefold Farm Missy Moo Single Vineyard Barossa Valley Mataro 2018 Kellermeister is one of the relatively few able to deliver a 100% mataro that happily stands on its own, rather than be a jigsaw piece of critical importance. It's savoury but has a heart of glistening black fruits. Screwcap. 14% alc. **Rating** 94 **To** 2038 $45

♟♟♟♟♟ **Topsy Turvy Frozen Pressed Dessert Wine 2018** Rating 92 $32
The Pious Pioneer Barossa Shiraz 2016 Rating 90 **To** 2036 $28
Threefold Farm Missy Moo Single Vineyard Barossa Valley Mataro 2016 Rating 90 **To** 2026 $45

Kellybrook ★★★★★

Fulford Road, Wonga Park, Vic 3115 **Region** Yarra Valley
T (03) 9722 1304 **www**.kellybrookwinery.com.au **Open** Thurs–Mon 10–5
Winemaker Stuart Dudine **Est.** 1962 **Dozens** 3000 **Vyds** 8.4ha
The vineyard is at Wonga Park, one of the gateways to the Yarra Valley. A very competent producer of both cider and apple brandy (in Calvados style) as well as table wine. When it received its winery licence in 1970, it became the first winery in the Yarra Valley to open its doors in the 20th century, a distinction often ignored or forgotten.

♟♟♟♟♟ **Estate Yarra Valley Chardonnay 2018** Light yellow–straw hue, suggesting energy in store. The mid-weighted palate is tautly strung by subtle malty oak as well as by a gentle clench of mineral flintiness. Cashew, stone fruit accents. All meandering along a beam of juicy acidity. This is a delicate chardonnay of precision and effortlessness. Highly Burgundian. Screwcap. **Rating** 95 **To** 2024 $35 NG ✪

Willowlake Vineyard Pinot Noir 2018 A pallid ruby segueing to a soothing wash of wild red berry fruits, tomatillo, turmeric and orange zest. Unadulterated deliciousness from this prized Upper Yarra single site. Without the obtuse clutter of green tannins or excessive oak. Transparent. Ethereal. Already delicious, this will grow in stature with short-term cellaring. Screwcap. **Rating** 95 **To** 2024 $45 NG

Malakoff Vineyard Pyrenees Range Shiraz 2017 A lauded vineyard that, in the wrong hands, produces wines of drying menthol notes. Not the case here. This is pulpy, alive and joyous. Savoury, compact and mid-weighted. Beautifully moulded tannins, gentle but palpable, encasing blue to dark fruit allusions, seaweed, black olive and lilac to anise notes. All beamed long by juicy pepper grind acidity. Rack and returns sensibly casting off reductive pong. Relaxed and beautifully understated. Cork. **Rating** 94 **To** 2027 $45 NG

♟♟♟♟♟ **Yarra Valley Pinot Noir 2018** Rating 93 **To** 2025 $30 NG
Estate Yarra Valley Cabernet Sauvignon 2017 Rating 93 **To** 2027 $35 NG
Estate Yarra Valley Shiraz 2017 Rating 92 **To** 2025 $35 NG
Blanc de Blancs 2018 Rating 92 $40 NG
Yarra Valley Shiraz 2017 Rating 91 **To** 2022 $30 NG
Sparkling Rose 2018 Rating 91 $40 NG

Kelman Vineyard ★★★★☆

2 Oakey Creek Road, Pokolbin, NSW 2320 **Region** Hunter Valley
T (02) 4991 5456 **www**.kelmanvineyard.com.au **Open** Thurs–Mon 10–4
Winemaker Xanthe Hatcher **Est.** 1999 **Dozens** 1300 **Vyds** 9ha
Kelman Vineyard is a community development spread over 40ha, with 9ha under vine. The estate is scattered with traditional country cottages and homesteads; vines, olive and lemon groves meander between the dwellings. Named in honour of William Kelman who travelled

to Australia with John Busby (father of James Busby) in 1824, marrying John's daughter Katherine on the ship to Australia.

🍷🍷🍷🍷🍷 **Barrel Selection Reserve Hunter Valley Shiraz 2018** Hand-picked and sorted, crushed and destemmed, 4 weeks on skins, matured for 10 months in used French oak. The implicit suggestion is the great vintage will do the work, and that's correct. It is a perfectly weighted shiraz, full of soft black/purple fruits and ripe, benign tannins. It will cruise past '38 if reasonably cellared. Screwcap. 13.9% alc. **Rating** 95 **To** 2038 $35 ✪

🍷🍷🍷🍷🍷 **Hunter Valley Semillon 2019 Rating** 93 **To** 2029 $24 ✪
Hunter Valley Tempranillo 2018 Rating 93 **To** 2028 $24 ✪
Late Disgorged Blanc de Blancs 2015 Rating 91 $36
First Block Hunter Valley Chardonnay 2019 Rating 90 **To** 2025 $24

Kennedy   ★★★★★

Maple Park, 224 Wallenjoe Road, Corop, Vic 3559 (postal) **Region** Heathcote
T (03) 5484 8293 www.kennedyvintners.com.au **Open** Not
Winemaker Glen Hayley (Contract) **Est.** 2002 **Dozens** 3000 **Vyds** 29.2ha
Having been farmers in the Colbinabbin area of Heathcote for 27 years, John and Patricia Kennedy were on the spot when a prime piece of red Cambrian soil on the east-facing slope of Mt Camel Range became available for purchase. They planted 20ha of shiraz in 2002. As they gained knowledge of the intricate differences within the site, further plantings of shiraz, tempranillo and mourvedre followed in '07. The Shiraz is made in small open fermenters, using indigenous yeasts and gentle pigeage before being taken to French oak for maturation.

🍷🍷🍷🍷🍷 **Cambria Heathcote Shiraz 2017** Kennedy's flagship shiraz is a barrel selection incorporating the best parcels of fruit and has come together brilliantly. A harmonious blend of red and black fruits, a hint of charry oak, spice and an appealing amaro–walnut-skin edge. It's not a big wine – the antithesis to what one might think of Heathcote shiraz – with velvety tannins and a litheness throughout. Highly drinkable. Highly enjoyable. Screwcap. 13.5% alc. **Rating** 96 **To** 2030 $36 JF ✪
Pink Hills Heathcote Rose 2019 A pale copper hue. It has the tang and acid kick of the variety – mourvedre with texture across the palate thanks to wild fermentation in barrel, and kept neat and tight as there's no mlf. Delicious. Screwcap. 13.5% alc. **Rating** 95 **To** 2022 $24 JF ✪
Heathcote Shiraz 2017 A restrained, savoury style that works off a medium-bodied palate with the right amount of appealing flavours. Expect some just-ripe red plums, a dusting of baking spices, dried herbs and cherry pips. And with its soft and supple tannins and approachability, it's ready now. Screwcap. 13.5% alc. **Rating** 95 **To** 2027 $27 JF ✪

Kensington Wines   ★★★★★

1590 Highlands Road, Whiteheads Creek, Vic 3660 **Region** Upper Goulburn
T (03) 5796 9155 www.kensingtonwines.com.au **Open** Sun 11–5
Winemaker Nina Stocker, Frank Bonic **Est.** 2010 **Dozens** 15 000 **Vyds** 4ha
This is the venture of husband and wife Anddy and Kandy Xu, born and raised in China but now residents in Australia. They have created a broad portfolio of wines by sourcing grapes and wines mostly from regions across Victoria, but also SA. While the primary market is China (and other Asian countries), the wines have not been made with residual sugar sweetness and are also sold in Australia. Kandy and Anddy's purchase of the Rocky Passes Vineyard (and cellar door) in the Upper Goulburn region in 2015 was a significant development in terms of their commitment to quality Australian wine. Kandy has broadened her own experience and wine qualifications by completing the WSET diploma and undertaking a vintage at Brown Brothers. She was co-founder of the Chinese Wine Association of Australia and continues as the chair. She has translated wine books into Mandarin, including my *Top 100 Wineries of Australia*. Exports to China and other Asian countries.

♟♟♟♟♟ **Benalla Shiraz 2017** Hand-picked, crushed and destemmed, open-fermented with wild and cultured yeast, matured in French oak (30% new) for 18 months. This is a high quality shiraz that has made the most of the cool vintage. It has layers of cherry and plum fruit supported by ripe tannins and cedary oak. It is a pleasure to drink now, but will live for decades with the protection of the screwcap. Very elegant packaging. 14.8% alc. **Rating** 95 **To** 2037 $65

Rutherglen Durif 2018 A very well made durif with a typical deep/opaque colour. Satsuma plum and black fruits have an earthy/savoury backdrop/aftertaste; the mouthfeel and balance are good. Easy to drink now or in a decade. Clever label design. Screwcap. 14.5% alc. **Rating** 95 **To** 2033 $40

♟♟♟♟♟ **Old Vine Series Glenrowan Shiraz 2018 Rating** 93 **To** 2030 $150
Rocky Passes Vineyard Shiraz 2017 Rating 91 **To** 2030 $65
Selected Edition Merlot 2018 Rating 90 **To** 2028 $22

Kerrigan + Berry   ★★★★★

PO Box 221, Cowaramup, WA 6284 **Region** South West Australia zone
T (08) 9755 6046 **www**.kerriganandberry.com.au **Open** At Hay Shed Hill
Winemaker Michael Kerrigan, Gavin Berry **Est.** 2007 **Dozens** 1200
Owners Michael Kerrigan and Gavin Berry have been making wine in WA for a combined period of over 40 years and say they have been most closely associated with the two varieties that in their opinion define WA: riesling and cabernet sauvignon. This is strictly a weekend and after-hours venture, separate from their respective roles as chief winemakers at Hay Shed Hill (Michael) and West Cape Howe (Gavin). They have focused on what is important, and explain, 'We have spent a total of zero hours on marketing research, and no consultants have been injured in the making of these wines'. Exports to the UK, Denmark, Singapore and China.

♟♟♟♟♟ **Mt Barker Great Southern Riesling 2019** Low crops/small berries were shared between the Great Southern and Clare/Eden valleys alike, with local conditions making vintage generalisations doubly dangerous – exacerbated by the need to wait 5 years until the situation stabilises. In the meantime the sheer power of the citrus family flavours will need highbrow Chinese/Japanese dishes from the sea or lowbrow fish and chips. Screwcap. 12% alc. **Rating** 93 **To** 2039 $30

Kilgour Wines   ★★★★

25 McAdams Lane, Bellarine, Vic 3223 **Region** Geelong
T 0448 785 744 **www**.kilgourwines.com **Open** Public hols & by appt
Winemaker Alister Timms **Est.** 2017 **Dozens** 700 **Vyds** 8ha
While this business has roots in the Bellarine Peninsula dating back to 1989, its reappearance in 2017 is a different venture altogether. Anne Timms planted the original vineyard in '89, opening Kilgour Estate. In 2010 she sold the 3.2ha title with the Kilgour Estate winery, the winery label and a separate 2ha of vines to David and Lyndsay Sharp who renamed the business Jack Rabbit. Anne Timms retained 8ha of vines surrounding the Jack Rabbit property and for the next five years sold the grapes to other wineries. In '17 she retained part of the crop, with Alister Timms (chief winemaker at Shadowfax) making the Kilgour Wines under contract at Shadowfax.

♟♟♟♟♟ **Bellarine Chardonnay 2019** Hand-picked, whole-bunch pressed, wild-fermented in French hogsheads (33% new), matured for 10 months. Unusual. There is a constant flow of sweet fruit with a suggestion of some unfermented sugar. Screwcap. 13% alc. **Rating** 90 **To** 2025 $50

Bellarine Pinot Gris 2019 No viticultural or winemaking information to hand, but we know this region is suited to pinot gris. This example hits the mark pretty well with aromas of ripe pear and stone fruit varietal character on the bouquet, and a palate with generous flavour and good texture. It's not a wine of nuance or complexity but it rates well for drinkability, which is a considerable virtue. Screwcap. 13% alc. **Rating** 90 **To** 2023 $30 SC

Bellarine Rose 2019 No mention of the variety (or varieties) here, but I note that the '17 vintage was a pinot noir saignee style. It has a slightly orange tinge in the glass and I'm sure I can detect blood orange in the bouquet, along with the more expected strawberry and red berry characters. It has a sweetly-fruited palate with some richness of mouthfeel, and a fairly soft finish. Screwcap. 13% alc. **Rating** 90 **To** 2023 $25 SC

♥♥♥♥ **Bellarine Pinot Noir 2019 Rating** 89 **To** 2029 $40

Kilikanoon Wines ★★★★★

Penna Lane, Penwortham, SA 5453 **Region** Clare Valley
T (08) 8843 4206 **www.**kilikanoon.com.au **Open** 7 days 11–5
Winemaker Kevin Mitchell, Barry Kooij, Jarrad Steele, Peter Warr **Est.** 1997
Dozens 100 000 **Vyds** 120ha
Kilikanoon has travelled in the fast lane since winemaker Kevin Mitchell established it in 1997 on the foundation of 6ha of vines he owned with father Mort. With the aid of investors, its 100 000-dozen production comes from over 100ha of estate-owned vineyards and access to the best grapes from a total of over 2000ha across SA. Between 2013 and early '14 all links between Kilikanoon and Seppeltsfield were ended; the sale of Kilikanoon's share in Seppeltsfield, together with the sale of Kilikanoon's Crowhurst Vineyard in the Barossa Valley, led to the purchase by Kilikanoon of the winery which it had previously leased, and of the Mount Surmon Vineyard. The small-batch Mr Hyde wines are produced from individual vineyards/blocks in the Clare Valley. Exports to most major markets.

♥♥♥♥♥ **Kavel's Flock Barossa Valley Shiraz 2016** Shiraz was the standout variety in the '16 Barossa Valley vintage; the warm, dry conditions providing dense colours and rich flavours. This wine definitely fits the bill with an incredible inky red concentration in the glass that bodes well for what follows. A powerful presence in the glass with the blackest blackcurrant intensity, aniseed and dark chocolate. Screwcap. 14.5% alc. **Rating** 97 **To** 2027 $20 JP ✪

♥♥♥♥♥ **Killerman's Run Clare Valley Riesling 2018** The Clare riesling style is undergoing a slight style adjustment to include a touch of residual sugar, and it's working. Citrus blossom, kaffir lime, cardamom and grapefruit aromas. The palate starts steely with brisk acidity but launches into a mid-palate texture that isn't noticeably sweet but definitely rounds out the acid bite. Don't overchill. Screwcap. 12.5% alc. **Rating** 95 **To** 2028 $25 JP ✪

Covenant Clare Valley Shiraz 2017 A mesh of premium vineyard fruit and an 18 month passage across quality French oak, this is a salubrious, full-bodied and glossy wine. A deep crimson verging on opaque. A firm bulwark of coffee grind–mocha tannins prolongs scents of violet, blue to blackberry persuasions and crushed rock long and far across the palate. The tannins define, etch and shape this, keeping it from an over-the-top persuasion. Just. Very good, if hedonism is your cup of tea. Screwcap. **Rating** 95 **To** 2031 $55 NG

Oracle Clare Valley Shiraz 2016 Long an iconic wine, particularly among American critics, this has revealed a lighter shade of late. The fruit, no longer desiccated. Dense and impressive, if this is your schtick. Powerful, sure. But energetic, long and far from drying. An arsenal of sexy oak meets licorice blackstrap, smoked meats, blue to black fruits and a squeegee of anise-scented acidity. Screwcap. **Rating** 95 **To** 2031 $96 NG

Mort's Block Watervale Riesling 2019 The superior quality of '19 shines through. Light, pushing mid-weighted. This is scintillating with fruit purity, intensity of flavour and unbridled length. The acidity, nicely melded. Citrus allusions shimmer along a juicy spine. This is benchmark Clare. Long, dry and chalky, without excessive rasp. Screwcap. **Rating** 94 **To** 2031 $25 NG ✪

Killerman's Run Clare Valley Grenache Shiraz Mataro 2017 Oh so savoury with a touch of wildness. May not be everyone's cup of GSM but it has its good points such as smoked meaty gameness, prune, red licorice and stewed plums on the nose, followed by super smooth presence in the mouth. Grenache makes the running and provides a distinctive walk on the wild side. Screwcap. 14.5% alc. **Rating** 94 **To** 2025 $20 JP ✪

Tregea Reserve Clare Valley Cabernet Sauvignon 2018 Low yielding fruit, hand-picked. The range of Cabernets at this address is like no other. The saturation of fruit, miraculously fidelitous to variety and place, is impressive. Blackcurrant and mulberry, anise and tapenade, sage and bouquet garni barrage across the mouth, staining every pore. Powerful, but not galumphing. Long and impressive. Like eating wine, rather than drinking it. Screwcap. **Rating** 94 **To** 2035 $96 NG

Blocks Road Clare Valley Cabernet Sauvignon 2016 From 46yo vineyards. This is delicious. Clearly a fine year, the sheer density of the fruit compelling. Given cabernet's stern predilections, nothing jammy. Just a phalanx of cassis, dried sage, green olive and hedgerow billowing across the fully loaded palate, toned by fine grape and oak tannins. A fine wine. Screwcap. **Rating** 94 **To** 2028 $40 NG

♥♥♥♥♀ **Pearce Road Clare Valley Semillon 2019** Rating 93 To 2036 $30 NG
Kelly 1932 Clare Valley Grenache 2015 Rating 93 To 2025 $96 NG
Killerman's Run Clare Valley Cabernet Sauvignon 2017 Rating 93 To 2026 $20 JP ✪
Killerman's Run Clare Valley Riesling 2019 Rating 92 To 2026 $22 NG ✪
Mort's Reserve Watervale Riesling 2018 Rating 92 To 2027 $55 NG
Pearce Road Clare Valley Semillon 2018 Rating 92 To 2032 $30 NG
Prodigal Clare Valley Grenache 2017 Rating 92 To 2025 $33 NG
Baudinet Blend Clare Valley Grenache Shiraz Mataro 2017 Rating 92 To 2024 $55 NG
Killerman's Run Clare Valley Shiraz 2018 Rating 91 To 2023 $22 NG ✪
Killerman's Run Clare Valley Shiraz 2017 Rating 91 To 2025 $20 JP ✪
Attunga 1865 Clare Valley Shiraz 2015 Rating 91 To 2028 $250 NG
Killerman's Run Clare Valley Cabernet Sauvignon 2018 Rating 91 To 2024 $22 NG ✪
Baudinet Clare Valley Mataro 2016 Rating 91 To 2024 $44 NG
Kavel's Flock Barossa Valley Shiraz 2017 Rating 90 To 2024 $20 JP ✪

Killerby   ★★★★

4259 Caves Road, Wilyabrup, WA 6280 **Region** Margaret River
T (08) 9755 5983 **www**.killerby.com.au **Open** Not
Winemaker Craig Grafton **Est.** 1973 **Dozens** NFP **Vyds** 4ha
Owned by Ferngrove since 2008, Killerby has relaunched, opening its architect-designed 'Cellar Store' (with one of the longest tasting benches in Australia) in '13. With a variety of local produce available, it pays homage to the history of the Killerby family (in the late 1930s Benjamin George Lee Killerby established a general store to supply the region, while grandson Benjamin Barry Killerby planted one of the first vineyards in Geographe in '73). Exports to the UK.

♥♥♥♥♀ **Margaret River Great Southern Cabernet Merlot 2017** This offers outstanding value. Mid-weighted, highly savoury, impeccably poised and long. Currant, graphite, pencil lead and a waft of dried sage. Classic aromas in place. A lunchtime claret à l'Australien! Screwcap. **Rating** 92 **To** 2025 $20 NG ✪

Great Southern Margaret River Chardonnay 2018 This is a taut, flavourful chardonnay with a degree of complexity that belies the favourable pricing. Tangy flavours of nectarine and a hint of toasted cashew careen along a spine of crackling acidity. A whiff of oak directs proceedings while imparting a dash of complexity. Screwcap. **Rating** 91 **To** 2023 $20 NG ✪

Kimbarra Wines

422 Barkly Street, Ararat, Vic 3377 **Region** Grampians
T 0428 519 195 **www**.kimbarrawines.com.au **Open** By appt
Winemaker Peter Leeke, Justin Purser, Adam Richardson **Est.** 1990 **Dozens** 180
Vyds 11ha

Peter Leeke has 8.5ha of shiraz, 1.5ha of riesling and 1ha of cabernet sauvignon – varieties that have proven best suited to the Grampians region. The particularly well made, estate-grown wines deserve a wider audience.

Great Western Shiraz 2018 Ripeness has been pushed to the limit but while it's warm it doesn't feel overcooked and there's still a good deal of spice. This is a tasty shiraz if ever there was one. Ripe plums, florals, smoky oak, cloves and peppers. The executive summary is that it's delicious but it's more than just that. Screwcap. 14.9% alc. **Rating** 95 **To** 2032 $30 CM ✪

Great Western Riesling 2019 Intensity of flavour combined with a dry, far-reaching finish. That's a combination not to be sneezed at. Leafy lime, almost an earthiness, the rind of lemons. It's a highly strung riesling, best served with a few years on it. Screwcap. 11% alc. **Rating** 94 **To** 2034 $30 CM ✪

Great Western Cabernet Sauvignon 2018 Rating 92 **To** 2028 $28 CM

Kimbolton Wines

29 Burleigh Street, Langhorne Creek, SA 5255 **Region** Langhorne Creek
T (08) 8537 3002 **www**.kimboltonwines.com.au **Open** 7 days 10–4
Winemaker Contract **Est.** 1998 **Dozens** 2000 **Vyds** 55ha

The Kimbolton property originally formed part of the Potts Bleasdale estate. In 1946 it was acquired by Henry and Thelma Case, grandparents of current owners brother and sister Nicole Clark and Brad Case. The grapes from the vineyard plantings (cabernet sauvignon, shiraz, malbec, fiano, carignan and montepulciano) are sold to leading wineries, with small amounts retained for the Kimbolton label. The name comes from a medieval town in Bedfordshire, UK, from which some of the family's ancestors emigrated. Kimbolton opened its cellar door in December '18, constructed from 'a unique mix of high gloss navy industrial shipping containers' and timber, includes a rooftop viewing platform.

The Rifleman Adelaide Hills Chardonnay 2018 Whole-bunch pressed and barrel-fermented in French oak (10% new). A further 8 months in neutral wood to impart breadth and warmth. This is nicely done, built around a reckoning of poise, drinkability and just the right amount of everything: white fig, melon scents; a nougat to creamed cashew core; and gentle vanillan oak pillars to guide the melee long. Screwcap. **Rating** 92 **To** 2024 $36 NG

Langhorne Creek Carignan 2019 The quintessential Languedocienne variety. The guts of the Mediterranean, planted as far back as 1911 on these shores. Made in a very gentle manner, forsaking structure in the name of partial carbonic scents of rosewater, red berry fruits and baking spice. An easygoing wine made to guzzle at a good chill. Screwcap. **Rating** 91 **To** 2021 $28 NG

Bella Monte Sparkling Montepulciano 2017 Langhorne Creek promises great things with the sort of sturdy vine material found in central to southern Italy. Far from thirsty and capable of obviating the gushing fruit inherent to SA with ferrous tannins and an innate savouriness, montepulciano is one such example. Frothy and joyous, yet amaro-savoury. Blackberry, anise and briar teem along an energetic bead. Plenty to like. Cork. **Rating** 91 $36 NG

Langhorne Creek Montepulciano Rose 2019 A gentle coral. A lash of cumquat, herb and tangerine laced acidity drives notes of musk stick, strawberry and fermentative bath salt scents long. Crunchy and moreish. A good drink. Screwcap. **Rating** 90 **To** 2021 $22 NG

Langhorne Creek Cabernet Sauvignon 2016 Rating 89 **To** 2023 $25 NG

King River Estate

3556 Wangaratta–Whitfield Road, Wangaratta, Vic 3678 **Region** King Valley
T (03) 5729 3689 **www**.kingriverestate.com.au **Open** Fri–Sun & public hols 11–5
Winemaker Dennis Clarke **Est.** 1996 **Dozens** 2000 **Vyds** 13ha
First planted in 1990, King River Estate sits alongside the King River in the heart of the King Valley in Victoria's northeast. The almost 30-year-old vines produce an array of wines which reflect the character and Italian influence of the region. It came under new ownership in 2018; it is still very much a family-run business, new investment has reinvigorated the winery and the cellar door experience. Prosecco made a its debut in '18, while the Flying Duck range adds some zest to the line-up. Exports to China and Singapore.

ꢁꢁꢁꢁꢁ **King Valley Barbera 2015** Machine-harvested, open-fermented, 9 days on skins, matured in barrel for 18 months. Good depth to the colour of this medium-bodied wine with its combination of juicy and savoury flavours. The tannins are soft, the overall balance good. Screwcap. 15% alc. **Rating** 90 **To** 2030 $25

ꢁꢁꢁꢁ **Flying Duck King Valley Rose 2019** **Rating** 89 **To** 2020 $22
King Valley Prosecco 2019 **Rating** 89 $22

Kings Landing

9 Collins Place, Denmark, WA 6333 (postal) **Region** Great Southern
T 0432 312 918 **www**.kingslandingwines.com.au **Open** Not
Winemaker Coby Ladwig, Luke Eckersley **Est.** 2015 **Dozens** 6000 **Vyds** 9ha
Winemakers Coby Ladwig and Luke Eckersley have spent many years making wines for others, so this is in some ways a busman's holiday. But it's also a serious business, with 9ha of vineyard plantings (3ha of chardonnay and 2ha each of shiraz, riesling and cabernet sauvignon) making this much more than a virtual winery. Watch this space!

ꢁꢁꢁꢁꢁ **Mount Barker Cabernet Sauvignon 2018** The scent of gum leaves, the flavours of blackcurrant, the swirls of wood smoke. This is a red wine of power and length which – when combined with strong fruit and appropriate oak – make for an all-round impressive package. Tannin too is firm and ripe. The cellaring potential of this wine is excellent. Screwcap. 14.5% alc. **Rating** 95 **To** 2036 $32 CM ✪
Mount Barker Riesling 2019 Excellent concentration of lime-driven flavour and the length to match. Slate, lemon-sorbet and musk-like notes help to drive it along. You wouldn't call it a textural wine but it has more texture than your average riesling. Has the ring of confidence. Screwcap. 12.8% alc. **Rating** 94 **To** 2028 $32 CM
Mount Barker Shiraz 2018 Medium to full-bodied, neat as a pin, ripe blue and blackberried fruit, a mesh of fine-grained tannin. Everything in good order. Floral notes combine with nutty oak to add a certain prettiness. Nothing but positives. Screwcap. 14.4% alc. **Rating** 94 **To** 2034 $32 CM
The Last Knight Shiraz 2018 Had 25 days on skins, 50% new French oak, all fermented as whole berries with a small inclusion of stalks. It's a complex, reductive wine with good colour and concentration and an excellent spread of tannin. Some folks will find this a little too reductive; it has a rubber-smoke aspect to it. But its bold heart is well balanced and framed, and its length is impressive. Screwcap. 14.6% alc. **Rating** 94 **To** 2036 $80 CM

ꢁꢁꢁꢁꢁ **Frankland River Malbec 2019** **Rating** 91 **To** 2031 $32 CM

Kingsley Grove

49 Stuart Valley Drive, Kingaroy, Qld 4610 **Region** South Burnett
T (07) 4162 2229 **www**.kingsleygrove.com **Open** 7 days 10–5
Winemaker Michael Berry, Patricia Berry, Simon Berry **Est.** 1998 **Dozens** 850
Vyds 10ha

Michael and Patricia Berry and Edward Devereux have a substantial vineyard near Kingaroy, an area better known for growing peanuts. The VSP-trellised vines are grown in a north–south orientation that best accommodates the hot Queensland summer sun with a computer-controlled irrigation system. The wines are made onsite, Michael and Patricia having undertaken viticulture studies at the University of Melbourne.

Kingston Estate Wines   ★★★★

Sturt Highway, Kingston-on-Murray, SA 5331 **Region** South Australia
T (08) 8243 3700 **www.**kingstonestatewines.com **Open** Not
Winemaker Bill Moularadellis, Brett Duffin, Steve Warne **Est.** 1979 **Dozens** 100 000
Vyds 3100ha
Kingston Estate, under the direction of Bill Moularadellis, has its production roots in the Riverland region, but also has long-term purchase contracts with growers in the Clare Valley, Adelaide Hills, Coonawarra, Langhorne Creek and Mount Benson. It has also spread its net to take in a wide range of varietals, mainstream and exotic, under a number of brands at various price points. Kingston Estate has been very active in purchasing vineyards, trebling the holdings from 1000ha to 3100ha. Exports to all major markets.

ŸŸŸŸŸ **Clare Valley Cabernet Sauvignon 2018** Machine-harvested, fermentation
        on skins for 5 days, pressed, mlf, maturation in French and American oak. Yes, it's
        super generous, ripe and plummy but with real dash. For the price, this is fab value.
        There is a wealth of fruit power – wild blackberry, bramble – with stewed rhubarb,
        earth, dark spices and chocolate. Smooth, supple with chewy tannins, smart oak.
        Plenty to enjoy here. Screwcap. 14.5% alc. **Rating** 93 **To** 2036 $19 JP ✪
        Clare Valley Shiraz 2018 Machine-picked, 5–7 days on skins during ferment,
        maturation in French and American oak barrels. Winemaker Bill Moularadellis
        looks to the Clare Valley for definition and complexity in shiraz. We might
        include power too. This is a wine of tremendous ease, it just unfurls in rich,
        velvety folds across the tongue with blackcurrant, stewed plums, blue fruits, licorice
        blackstrap and chocolate. Almost all the major food groups are here with the
        arrival of smoked, cured charcuterie on the palate amid ripe, earthy tannins. It's a
        busy wine. 14% alc. **Rating** 90 **To** 2030 $19 JP ✪

ŸŸŸŸ **Semillon 2019 Rating** 89 **To** 2025 $19 JP ✪

Kirrihill Wines   ★★★★

12 Main North Road, Clare, SA 5453 **Region** Clare Valley
T (08) 8842 4087 **www.**kirrihillwines.com.au **Open** 7 days 11–4
Winemaker Susan Mickan **Est.** 1998 **Dozens** 35 000 **Vyds** 600ha
The Kirrihill story started in the late 1990s. The aim was to build a business producing premium wines from temperate vineyards that represent the unique characters of the Clare Valley. Grapes are sourced from specially selected parcels of Kirrihill's 600ha of vineyards. Susan (Susie) Mickan, with vintage experience in Australia, Spain, China and the US, joined Kirrihill as chief winemaker in December 2018. Exports to all major markets.

ŸŸŸŸŸ **Gleeson & Co Clare Valley Riesling 2019** This is delicate, balletic across
        the mouth, intensely flavoured and long. Kaffir lime, grapefruit pulp, bath salts
        and lemon zest. Dry, but not harsh. A riesling with a bright future. Screwcap.
        Rating 93 **To** 2030 $25 NG ✪
        Piccoli Lotti Mount Lofty Ranges Montepulciano 2018 This is delicious.
        A variety of the future. When the last shiraz vine has withered, the sturdy
        montepulciano will be going strong as it has in the Marche and Abruzzo regions
        of Italy for so long. Ferrous, pulpy and plenty rich without being hard, especially
        when made as sensitively as this: gently extracted across plenty of whole berries.
        Violet, black fruit allusions and a thread of anise, olive, briar and charcuterie. The
        tannins are pliant, iron-rich and handled with aplomb, drawing one in for another
        sip. Screwcap. **Rating** 93 **To** 2025 $27 NG ✪

Regional Selection Clare Valley Cabernet Sauvignon 2018 A fine regional cabernet. While known for shiraz, perhaps it is cabernet from the Clare that is more expressive and synergistic with quality expressions from elsewhere. Inimitable currant, leaf, graphite and a motley sash of herbal aromas. This couldn't be anything else. The tannins too are firm but nicely melded into the fray. The oak, an adjunct. Screwcap. **Rating** 92 **To** 2028 $19 NG ✪

E.B.'s The Settler Watervale Riesling 2019 Long, succulent and full of vigour. Finger lime juicy. A saline line of acidity, not too brittle. Chalky and spa-salt scented. A good drink with a bright future. Screwcap. **Rating** 91 **To** 2029 $35 NG

Gleeson & Co Clare Valley Shiraz 2018 This capacious red was fermented in large-format wood, imparting a textural breadth conducive to the uber style: quintessentially full-bodied Clare. Mint, blueberries, licorice allsorts and creamy seams given tension by a reductive bow of iodine mineral. Screwcap. **Rating** 91 **To** 2024 $25 NG

Regional Selection Clare Valley Shiraz 2018 A rich, highly regional wine that is firmly of place and type: dark fruit references, violet scents and a whiff of fennel are slung across nicely wrought bitter chocolate—coffee grind tannins. The envelope is pushed, but not too far. Screwcap. **Rating** 91 **To** 2025 $19 NG ✪

Gleeson & Co Clare Valley Riesling 2018 Already developing a whiff of petroleum, this is a lightweight, delicate riesling best drunk in the mid-term. Quince, pear and lime curd. A little short, but plenty fresh enough. Screwcap. **Rating** 90 **To** 2024 $25 NG

Piccoli Lotti Adelaide Hills Pinot Grigio 2019 Solid grigio, splaying varietal scents of nashi pear, green apple and orange blossom along tangy acid rails. An attractive expansion of sweet fruit across the midriff gives this wine the juice it needs to push to a satisfying crunchy finish. Screwcap. **Rating** 90 **To** 2021 $27 NG

ՈՈՈՈ **Piccoli Lotti Clare Valley Sangiovese Rose 2019** **Rating** 89 **To** 2020 $27 NG

KJB Wine Group

2 Acri Street, Prestons, NSW (postal) **Region** McLaren Vale
T 0409 570 694 **Open** Not
Winemaker Kurt Brill **Est.** 2008 **Dozens** 750
KJB Wine Group Pty Ltd is the venture of Kurt Brill, who began his involvement in the wine industry in 2003, largely through the encouragement of his wife Gillian. He commenced a marketing degree through the University of Adelaide but switched to the winemaking degree at CSU in '08, finally graduating in '19. Fruit is sourced from growers in different parts of McLaren Vale, made in small volumes with sales along the eastern seaboard of Australia. Kurt also has international winemaking experience gained in Bordeaux and Fleurie, France. Exports to the UK and the Netherlands.

ՈՈՈՈՈ **Land of the Vines Bush Vine McLaren Vale Grenache 2018** Appealing flavours of raspberries, boiled lollies and musk sticks tempered by savoury notes and the texture of grainy tannins. Lighter bodied, soft and supple. Screwcap. 14.5% alc. **Rating** 91 **To** 2025 $30 JF

🍇 Klahn Estate ★★★★

960 Light Pass Road, Vine Vale, SA 5352 **Region** Barossa Valley
T 0411 495 565 **www**.klahnestate.com.au **Open** 7 days 10–5
Winemaker Julian Midwinter, Tim Smith **Est.** 2016 **Dozens** 15 000 **Vyds** 22ha
This family-owned business acquired its first vineyard – John's Block – four years ago. The winery/cellar door was built on this property and further acquisitions have resulted in the present portfolio of 11ha shiraz, 9ha cabernet sauvignon and 2ha merlot. The wines submitted for this edition of the *Wine Companion* were variously sourced from McLaren Vale, Barossa Valley, Clare Valley and Langhorne Creek; shiraz the focus. They were all from '16 and '17, nothing more recent. A curious Clare Valley Merlot is branded Squid Ink. Exports to Vietnam and China.

🍷🍷🍷🍷 **MuSeUM McLaren Vale Shiraz 2017** The back label suggests vibrant plum-red colour and hints of mint, earth, mocha, blackberry, blackcurrant and dark plum fruits. It didn't miss anything (other than, perhaps chocolate). All up, it is a breezy, fresh wine that has all the hallmarks of the great vintage. Screwcap. 14.5% alc. **Rating** 90 **To** 2023 $20 ◯

Vera Klahn Premium Reserve Barossa Valley Shiraz 2016 Significantly deeper colour and richer in body than its sibling. Its black fruits are pure shiraz; blackberry, blackcurrant, licorice and gently savoury tannins all contributing. Diam. 14.5% alc. **Rating** 90 **To** 2030 $35

Knappstein   ★★★★★

2 Pioneer Avenue, Clare, SA 5453 **Region** Clare Valley
T (08) 8841 2100 **www**.knappstein.com.au **Open** 7 days 10–4
Winemaker Michael Kane, Mike Farmilo (Consultant) **Est.** 1969 **Dozens** 75 000
Vyds 114ha
Knappstein's full name is Knappstein Enterprise Winery, reflecting its history before being acquired by Petaluma, then part of Lion Nathan, followed by Accolade. It is now in private ownership. Despite these corporate chessboard moves, wine quality has remained excellent. The wines are produced from substantial mature estate Enterprise, Ackland, Yertabulti and The Mayor's vineyards. Exports to all major markets.

🍷🍷🍷🍷 **Bryksy's Hill Vineyard Watervale Riesling 2015** Gentle development but it still basically presents as fresh and young. Excellent intensity of lime and orange-driven flavour with blossomy highlights. Well textured and finished as well. It's sitting pretty for drinking now-ish, though it responds well to air/decanting (yes, for a riesling). Screwcap. 13% alc. **Rating** 94 **To** 2029 $30 CM ◯

🍷🍷🍷🍷 **Clare Valley Riesling 2019 Rating** 93 **To** 2027 $22 CM ◯
Wickham Estate Reserve McLaren Vale Shiraz 2016 Rating 92 **To** 2029 $38 CM
Wickham Estate Estate McLaren Vale Shiraz 2015 Rating 92 **To** 2032 $75 CM
Wickham Estate Reserve McLaren Vale Cabernet Sauvignon 2016 Rating 91 **To** 2028 $38 CM
Clare Valley Malbec 2018 Rating 91 **To** 2027 $22 CM ◯
Clare Valley Rose 2019 Rating 90 **To** 2021 $22 CM

Koerner Wine   ★★★★☆

935 Mintaro Road, Leasingham, SA 5452 **Region** Clare Valley
T 0408 895 341 **www**.koernerwine.com.au **Open** By appt
Winemaker Damon Koerner **Est.** 2014 **Dozens** 2000 **Vyds** 60ha
Brothers Damon and Jonathan (Jono) Koerner grew up in the Clare Valley but flew the coop to work and study in other parts of Australia and abroad. The substantial vineyards had been owned and managed by their parents, Anthony and Christine Koerner, for 35 years, but they have passed ownership and management of the vineyards on to their sons. While the major part of the crop is sold to other wineries, in 2016 Damon made 11 wines. A major point of difference from other Clare Valley wineries is the use of synonyms for well known varieties, as well as adopting Australian name usage, turning the world upside down with left-field winemaking practices. Exports to the UK, the US, Canada, Belgium, the Netherlands, Korea, Singapore and Japan.

🍷🍷🍷🍷 **Pigato Vermentino 2019** Most Australian winemakers treat the alternative Italian grape, vermentino, as they would chardonnay. Here, it is treated like semillon with early picking and low alcohol. The results are mesmerising. The grape loves it. Pretty aromatics and citrus blossom lead the wine, while the palate is all about spice, nougat and orange peel savouriness and texture. Skin contact adds the right amount of phenolic grip. Diam. 11.3% alc. **Rating** 93 **To** 2025 $30 JP

Vivian Cabernet Sangiovese 2018 The 2 fit nicely into each other's groove, much like a traditional Aussie cabernet shiraz. The nose is cabernet cool and sangiovese bounce: all blackberries, plum, violets and a peppermint/pepper intrigue. Fine with powdery tannins, it's a delicate and pretty mix of varietal expressions. More please. Screwcap. 13.2% alc. **Rating** 93 **To** 2030 $50 JP

Cot 18 Bass Hill Vineyard Malbec 2018 A total violet love fest in the glass with the rising and dominant scent of crushed violets with mulberry and macerated plums and cherries. It is one of the most distinctive and idiosyncratic wines around. And it gets better with fruit that is lush, tannins that are soft and oak at its supportive best. Diam. 12.5% alc. **Rating** 93 **To** 2026 $35 JP

La Korse 2019 A mix of 35/34/17/9/5% sangiovese/grenache/malbec/sciacarello/carignan. An ode to Corsican-style light and easy dry reds, and it works a treat. The light savouriness is a fine adjunct to the blackberry, red cherry, blood plum, cherry cola notes and lifted florals in the wine. It's light on its feet, the powdery tannins help, together with an acid crunch. Diam. 12.2% alc. **Rating** 92 **To** 2026 $30 JP

Mammalo 2018 One of the traditional inclusions in Chianti, it is great to see the mammolo grape out on its own. It translates as 'bashful', but not here with its pretty florals, aromatics and redcurrant, cherry, red fruits and spice. Drink early and often. Diam. 13.2% alc. **Rating** 92 **To** 2026 $40 JP

Classico Cabernet Malbec 2018 With 81/19% cabernet sauvignon/malbec. Koerner dances to the beat of a different drum, which in this case brings out a highly fragrant, juicy cabernet blend that behaves like a plummy soft red for early consumption. It also boasts a savoury sour cherry, fruit peel, rose edge that you would just love to see again with some bottle age under its belt. Diam. 12.9% alc. **Rating** 90 **To** 2025 $50 JP

ŸŸŸŸ **The Clare 2018 Rating** 89 **To** 2024 $30 JP

Koonara ★★★★☆

44 Church Street, Penola, SA 5277 **Region** Coonawarra
T (08) 8737 3222 **www.**koonara.com **Open** Mon–Thurs 10–5, Fri–Sat 10–6, Sun 10–4
Winemaker Peter Douglas (Consultant) **Est.** 1988 **Dozens** 10000 **Vyds** 9ha
Trevor Reschke planted the first vines on the Koonara property in 1988. Peter Douglas, formerly Wynns' chief winemaker before moving overseas for some years, has returned to the district and is consultant winemaker. After 10 years of organic viticulture practises, Koonara's vineyards in Coonawarrra were certified organic in 2017. Since '13 Koonara have leased and managed the Kongorong Partnership Vineyard in Mount Gambier, which had previously sold its grapes to Koonara. Exports to Russia, Malaysia and China.

ŸŸŸŸŸ **Lucy and Alice Limestone Coast Pinot Gris 2019** Includes 50% from Mount Gambier providing the structure and 50% from Mount Benson giving the mid-palate flesh. The highly aromatic bouquet of nashi pear and nougat is matched by the citrus-riddled acidity of the finish. Over-delivers. Screwcap. 11.5% alc. **Rating** 92 **To** 2022 $20 ✪

Ambriel's Gift Family Reserve Coonawarra Cabernet Sauvignon 2016 Machine-harvested, whole-berry fermented, 10 days on skins, matured for 26 months in French hogsheads (30% new). A medium to full-bodied cabernet with mocha/cocoa overtones to the plush fruit before tannins come to life with a kick. Screwcap. 14% alc. **Rating** 92 **To** 2036 $40

Emily May Limestone Coast Rose 2019 Pale lipstick pink. Rose is a cruel fate for sangiovese but this is neatly made, residual sugar kept at bay. Screwcap. 12% alc. **Rating** 90 **To** 2020 $20 ✪

1,000 Sundowns Coonawarra Cabernet Sauvignon 2017 Not much depth to the colour but whole-berry fermentation has produced a clear, ripe palate, and 12 months in French oak (10% new) has worked well. Screwcap. 14% alc. **Rating** 90 **To** 2027 $30

Koonowla Wines

18 Koonowla Road, Auburn, SA 5451 **Region** Clare Valley
T (08) 8849 2270 **www**.koonowla.com **Open** W'ends & public hols 10–5
Winemaker O'Leary Walker Wines **Est.** 1997 **Dozens** 6000 **Vyds** 48.77ha
Koonowla is an historic Clare Valley property situated just east of Auburn. It was first planted with vines in the 1890s and by the early 1900s was producing around a quarter of a million litres of wine annually. A disastrous fire in '26 destroyed the winery and wine stocks, and the property converted to grain and wool production. Replanting of vines began in '85 and accelerated in the early '90s. Owned and operated by Andrew Michael there are currently around 50ha of shiraz, cabernet sauvignon, riesling, merlot and semillon. Exports to the UK, Scandinavia, Vietnam, Malaysia, China and NZ.

Clare Valley Riesling 2019 Easy drinking style; soft citrus fruit and good balance. Screwcap. 12.5% alc. **Rating** 90 **To** 2022 $25

The Ringmaster Clare Valley Riesling 2019 Rating 89 **To** 2021 $20

Kooyong ★★★★★

PO Box 153, Red Hill South, Vic 3937 **Region** Mornington Peninsula
T (03) 5989 4444 **www**.kooyongwines.com.au **Open** At Port Phillip Estate
Winemaker Glen Hayley **Est.** 1996 **Dozens** 13 000 **Vyds** 33.4ha
Kooyong, owned by Giorgio and Dianne Gjergja, released its first wines in 2001. The vineyard is planted to pinot noir (20ha), chardonnay (10.4ha) and, more recently, pinot gris (3ha). In July '15, following the departure of Sandro Mosele, his assistant of six years, Glen Hayley, was appointed to take his place. The Kooyong wines are made at the state-of-the-art winery of Port Phillip Estate, also owned by the Gjergjas. Exports to the UK, Canada, Belgium, the Netherlands, Singapore, Hong Kong, Japan and China.

Estate Mornington Peninsula Pinot Noir 2018 An altogether stylish pinot noir, supple and long with spicy fine tannins providing the structure for dark fruit to drape itself on. There's a freshness to the wine that is the key to its success. Screwcap. 13.5% alc. **Rating** 96 **To** 2030 $54 ✪

Estate Mornington Peninsula Chardonnay 2018 Builds slowly. The bouquet remains defiant in refusing to spark; the palate initially shy, then progressively gaining territory as the mid and back-palate bring a carefully composed fruit salad onto the table. Screwcap. 13% alc. **Rating** 94 **To** 2026 $44

Farrago Single Block Mornington Peninsula Chardonnay 2018 Whole-bunch pressed, wild-fermented in French barriques (15% new), matured for 11 months. Has the energy and drive often lacking from Mornington Peninsula chardonnay (no mlf?). A fresh, citrussy finish. Screwcap. 13.5% alc. **Rating** 94 **To** 2028 $61

Faultline Single Block Mornington Peninsula Chardonnay 2018 Somewhat fuller, although the freshness is similar. No batonnage may be the key, as well as minimal new oak (15%). Screwcap. 13% alc. **Rating** 94 **To** 2030 $61

Beurrot Mornington Peninsula Pinot Gris 2019 Beurrot is a very old Burgundian name for pinot gris, a variety that can be grown there. Here the grapes were whole-bunch pressed to old oak, wild-fermented and bottled without fining. The cool climate and vinification have produced a wine of considerable flavour and character. Screwcap. 14% alc. **Rating** 94 **To** 2022 $32

Clonale Chardonnay 2019 Rating 92 **To** 2027 $34
Meres Single Block Pinot Noir 2018 Rating 92 **To** 2027 $76
Haven Single Block Pinot Noir 2018 Rating 91 **To** 2027 $76
Ferrous Single Block Pinot Noir 2018 Rating 90 **To** 2022 $76

Kooyonga Creek

2369 Samaria Road, Moorngag, Vic 3673 **Region** North East Victoria zone
T (03) 9629 5853 **www**.kooyongacreek.com.au **Open** Fri–Sun & public hols 11–5
Winemaker Barry Saunders, Luis Simian **Est.** 2011 **Dozens** 5000 **Vyds** 8ha
When you read the name of this winery, you expect to find it somewhere on or near the
Mornington Peninsula. In fact it's a very long way to the North East Victoria zone, where
Barry and Pam Saunders planted 8ha of vineyards on their farm and released the first wines
under the name Kooyonga Chapel in 2003. They planted a sensibly focused range of 1.6ha
each of shiraz, cabernet sauvignon, merlot, chardonnay and sauvignon blanc, and what started
as a hobby has now become a business. Family and friends help with the peak seasons (picking
and pruning). Having initially been sold locally under the Kooyonga Chapel brand, the name
has been changed and distribution into the Melbourne market has begun.

ŸŸŸŸŸ **Sauvignon Blanc 2018** Traditional machine-harvested. Two cultured yeasts were
used to good effect giving the wine an extra level of tropical fruit and citrussy
acidity. Screwcap. 12.5% alc. **Rating** 90 **To** 2020 $20 ✪
Shiraz 2017 Machine-harvested, crushed and destemmed, 8-day ferment, 22 days'
post-ferment maceration, matured in hogsheads (5% new) for 14 months. A
surprise packet thanks to '17. Fresh, with complexity to go with the freshness.
Screwcap. 14% alc. **Rating** 90 **To** 2027 $20 ✪

ŸŸŸŸ **Fume Blanc 2016 Rating** 89 **To** 2021 $20

Kosciuszko Wines

PO Box 57, Campbell, ACT 2612 **Region** Tumbarumba
T 0417 036 436 **www**.kosciuszkowines.com.au **Open** Not
Winemaker Robert Bruno **Est.** 2007 **Dozens** 1000
Kosciuszko Wines is the latest wine business venture of the energetic Bill Mason and wife
Maria. Bill has been distributing wine in Canberra since 2004, with a small but distinguished
list of wineries, which he represents with considerable marketing flair. In '18 Bill purchased
Kosciuszko Wines from founding winemaker Chris Thomas after working with Chris and
Kosciuszko Wines for a number of years. Bill sources his fruit from pioneering grapegrower
Julie Cullen, from her vineyard in Jingellic Road, Tumbarumba.

ŸŸŸŸŸ **Tumbarumba Pinot Noir 2015** From 10yo MV6 clone; hand-picked, open-
fermented with 20% whole bunches, the remainder destemmed and crushed,
3 days cold soak, matured for 10 months, 33% new oak. There are a couple of off
notes, but the glass is near full. Screwcap. 13.4% alc. **Rating** 92 **To** 2025 $25 ✪
Tumbarumba Pinot Noir 2018 The lengthy back label says nothing of
relevance about the vinification of the wine, but there's no doubting its
Tumbarumba provenance, nor, of course, its varietal makeup. The flavours are
at the dark fruit end of the pinot spectrum; plum and black cherry aromas and
flavours with the first signs of spice emerging, and more to come. Screwcap.
13.5% alc. **Rating** 91 **To** 2026 $25
Tumbarumba Pinot Noir 2017 80% crushed and destemmed, 20% whole
bunches, 6 days on skins, matured for 8 months in French oak (20% new). A well
handled wine with plum and cherry fruit to the fore, backed by light tannins.
Screwcap. 13.5% alc. **Rating** 91 **To** 2027 $25

Krinklewood Biodynamic Vineyard

712 Wollombi Road, Broke, NSW 2330 **Region** Hunter Valley
T (02) 6579 1322 **www**.krinklewood.com **Open** Fri–Sun & long w'ends 10–5
Winemaker Rod Windrim, PJ Charteris (Consultant) **Est.** 1981 **Dozens** 10000
Vyds 19.9ha
Krinklewood is a family-owned, certified biodynamic, organic winery. Every aspect of the
property is managed in a holistic and sustainable way; Rod Windrim's extensive herb crops,
native grasses and farm animals all contribute to biodynamic preparations to maintain healthy

soil biology. The small winery is home to a Vaslin Bucher basket press and two Nomblot French fermentation eggs, a natural approach to winemaking. Exports to Hong Kong.

TTTTY **Basket Press Shiraz 2018** Part from the best estate block and part from a friend's biodynamic vineyard in McLaren Vale. Foot-plunged, then transferred to Italian and French oak open fermenters, matured in new and used French oak for 10 months. Impressive wine with a very good future. Screwcap. 13.8% alc. **Rating** 93 **To** 2038 $50

Chardonnay 2018 Apart from 1 month less in oak, the details of alcohol, pH and titratable acidity (in each case 6.8g/l) are the same for all the '18 chardonnays. The overall result for this version is a fresher wine. It is also less expensive. Screwcap. 13% alc. **Rating** 90 **To** 2025 $32

TTTT **Semillon 2019 Rating** 89 **To** 2027 $24
Basket Press Chardonnay 2018 Rating 89 **To** 2022 $40

Kurtz Family Vineyards ★★★☆

731 Light Pass Road, Angaston, SA, 5353 **Region** Barossa Valley
T 0418 810 982 **www**.kurtzfamilyvineyards.com.au **Open** By appt
Winemaker Steve Kurtz **Est.** 1996 **Dozens** 2500 **Vyds** 15.04ha
The Kurtz family vineyard is at Light Pass. It has 9ha of shiraz, the remainder planted to chardonnay, cabernet sauvignon, semillon, sauvignon blanc, petit verdot, grenache, mataro and malbec. Steve Kurtz has followed in the footsteps of his great-grandfather Ben Kurtz, who first grew grapes at Light Pass in the 1930s. During a career working first at Saltram and then at Foster's until 2006, Steve gained invaluable experience from Nigel Dolan, Caroline Dunn and John Glaetzer, among others. Exports to the US and China.

TTTTY **Schmick Barossa Shiraz 2015** While no details forthcoming, tasting this next to the '14 revealed some backing off here with the extraction and overripe flavours generally. The oak not so all-consuming. By no means a wall flower but this has ripe fresh fruit, roasted coffee beans and licorice. Full-bodied, the tannins plump and giving. There's energy across the palate. Faith restored. Screwcap. 15% alc. **Rating** 93 **To** 2030 $85 JF

Kyberd Hills ★★★★☆

PO Box 208, Red Hill, Vic 3937 **Region** Mornington Peninsula
T 0417 556 836 **www**.kyberdhillswines.com.au **Open** Not
Winemaker Michael Kyberd **Est.** 2017 **Dozens** 400 **Vyds** 2ha
After making wine on the Mornington Peninsula for other people for 20 years, Michael Kyberd finally got around to starting a brand, with his wife Nicolette and friends Kim and David Wilson as partners. Starting with a combination of leased vineyard and purchased grapes, and focussing on pinot noir and chardonnay, the plan is to plant a vineyard on their property in Red Hill. The winemaking style is gentle with minimal extraction and intervention, purity is the desired outcome. Hopefully such words as folly and regret will disappear from their conversation in less than a decade.

TTTTT **Main Creek Road Vineyard Mornington Peninsula Chardonnay 2018** This and its sibling were made in identical fashion, but this is fresher and has better colour. Both were barrel-fermented (no details of age or origin of oak provided) and allowed to undergo limited mlf, matured for 8 months. This is bright and fresh with good acidity. Screwcap. 13.2% alc. **Rating** 94 **To** 2028 $50

L.A.S. Vino ★★★★

PO Box 361, Cowaramup, WA 6284 **Region** Margaret River
T **www**.lasvino.com **Open** Not
Winemaker Nic Peterkin **Est.** 2013 **Dozens** 800

Owner Nic Peterkin is the grandson of the late Diana Cullen (Cullen Wines) and the son of Mike Peterkin (Pierro). After graduating from the University of Adelaide with a Masters Degree in Oenology and travelling the world as a Flying Winemaker, he came back to roost in Margaret River with the ambition of making wines that are a little bit different, but also within the bounds of conventional oenological science. The intention is to keep the project small. Exports to the UK, Singapore and Japan.

ΨΨΨΨΨ **CBDB Margaret River Chenin Blanc Dynamic Blend 2018** The first vintage from a certified biodynamic unkempt, sprawling (no trellising), unpruned vineyard in Yallingup where pigs, geese, guinea fowl and cows roam free. Unsurprisingly, the bunches were picked at various degrees of ripeness, chilled overnight, whole-bunch pressed, 70% fermented in French barriques, 305 in clay amphorae, no mlf, no fining or filtration. How it didn't go through mlf is anyone's guess. It's a big wine that is worth the story. Diam. 14% alc. **Rating** 92 **To** 2024 $50
Whole Bunch Ferguson Valley Grenache 2018 A 100% whole-bunch fermentation has led to a light colour, but hasn't compromised the light-bodied aromas and flavours of a red-fruited wine with clear varietal character. Diam. 13.5% alc. **Rating** 90 **To** 2025 $50

ΨΨΨΨ **Albino Margaret River PNO 2018 Rating** 89 **To** 2021 $45

La Bise
★★★★☆

38A Murray Street, Tanunda, SA 5352 **Region** Adelaide Hills
T 0439 823 251 **www**.labisewines.com.au **Open** By appt
Winemaker Natasha Mooney **Est.** 2006 **Dozens** 3000
This is a reasonably significant busman's holiday for Natasha Mooney, a well known and highly regarded winemaker whose 'day job' (her term) is to provide winemaking consultancy services for some of SA's larger wineries. This allows her to find small, unique parcels of grapes that might otherwise be blended into large-volume brands. She manages the arrangements so that there is no conflict of interest, making wines that are about fruit and vineyard expression. She aims for mouthfeel and drinkability without high alcohol, and for that she should be loudly applauded.

ΨΨΨΨΨ **The Thief? Barossa Valley Grenache Shiraz Mataro 2017** Bright colour; this is the modern face of GSM. Good natural acidity gives the flavours a brightness and freshness that is often compromised at higher levels. There are red fruits (pomegranate), purple and blue all to be found. Good to go tonight, or in 5 years' time. Screwcap. 14% alc. **Rating** 95 **To** 2025 $33 ✪

ΨΨΨΨΨ **Whole Bunch Pressed Pinot Gris 2018 Rating** 93 **To** 2022 $22 ✪
Le Petite Frais Rose 2018 Rating 93 **To** 2021 $22 ✪
Limited Release Chardonnay 2017 Rating 92 **To** 2030 $45 JP
Sangiovese 2018 Rating 91 **To** 2026 $25 JP
Sangiovese 2017 Rating 91 **To** 2022 $22 ✪
Chardonnay 2018 Rating 90 **To** 2030 $33 JP
The Kiss Field Blend White 2019 Rating 90 **To** 2025 $25 JP
Nero d'Avola 2018 Rating 90 **To** 2023 $33 JP

La Kooki Wines
★★★★★

12 Settlers Retreat, Margaret River, WA 6285 **Region** Margaret River
T 0447 587 151 **www**.lakookiwines.com.au **Open** Not
Winemaker Eloise Jarvis, Glenn Goodall **Est.** 2017 **Dozens** 335
Except for the fact that the proprietors of La Kooki have accumulated 42 years of winemaking between them, there would be little or nothing to say about a winery that has a small wine portfolio. Two detailed A4 sheets cover the conception and birth of La Kooki's Rose, one stating the quantity made as 114 dozen, the other 250 dozen. Either way, you'd better be quick, because it's an unusual wine.

ŸŸŸŸŸ **Margaret River Rose Blonde 2019** Hand-picked pinot noir, whole-bunch pressed to 6 barriques, wild-fermented, SO_2 added to prevent mlf. Jumping out of its skin – quite exceptional. On a warm summer day at a Chinese restaurant I'd drink this in preference to a bottle of Domaine de la Romanée-Conti (well, almost). It's so mouth-watering, it leaves you wondering whether it was too good to be true. A further mouthful tells you, no, it's that good. Screwcap. 12.5% alc. **Rating** 95 **To** 2021 $25 ✪
Ten Foot Ferguson Valley Tempranillo 2018 Hand-picked, single vineyard, destemmed to single berries, from which point on the whole fermentation process was managed by foot, actually 10 because it's a family of 5. After gentle pressing, the wine was poured into 5 used barriques for 9 months' maturation. It's a lovely tempranillo (that includes 3% cabernet) of great purity being sold for a song. Screwcap. 14% alc. **Rating** 95 **To** 2025 $25 ✪

ŸŸŸŸŸ **Carbonic Blanc Margaret River Verdelho 2019 Rating** 90 **To** 2020 $25

La Linea   ★★★★★

36 Shipsters Road, Kensington Park, SA 5068 (postal) **Region** Adelaide Hills
T (08) 8431 3556 www.lalinea.com.au **Open** Not
Winemaker Peter Leske **Est.** 2007 **Dozens** 3500 **Vyds** 6.64ha
La Linea is a partnership of several experienced wine industry professionals, including Peter Leske and David LeMire MW. Peter was among the first to recognise the potential of tempranillo in Australia and his knowledge of it is reflected in the three wine styles made from the variety: Tempranillo Rose, Tempranillo blended from several Adelaide Hills vineyards and Norteno, from a single vineyard at the northern end of the Hills. Two rieslings are produced under the Vertigo label: TRKN (short for trocken) and the off-dry 25GR (25g/l residual sugar). Exports to the UK.

ŸŸŸŸŸ **Sureno Adelaide Hills Tempranillo 2017** A selection of the 4 best barrels from the many available from this great vintage. The 'numbers' (alcohol/residual sugar/pH/titratable acidity) are identical to the standard '17. All you need to know is that the flavour set is oh so close, and what is different is a subtle shift upwards in the weight of this wine. Screwcap. 13.7% alc. **Rating** 96 **To** 2030 $35 ✪
Adelaide Hills Tempranillo 2017 It's hard to recall 2 vintages more different than the cool, drawn out, fragrant '17 and the hectic, hot '18; yet wine delights in upsetting generalities. Thus the chemical composition of the '17 and '18 La Linea tempranillos are nigh-on identical. This is far more savoury, spicy and elegant. A lovely wine bringing the year, the variety and the place to a perfect finish. Screwcap. 13.7% alc. **Rating** 95 **To** 2030 $27 ✪

ŸŸŸŸŸ **Adelaide Hills Tempranillo 2018 Rating** 92 **To** 2025 $27
Adelaide Hills Tempranillo Rose 2019 Rating 91 **To** 2021 $24
Vertigo 25GR Adelaide Hills Riesling 2019 Rating 91 $24

La Pleiade   ★★★★

c/- Jasper Hill, Drummonds Lane, Heathcote, Vic 3523 **Region** Heathcote
T (03) 9602 1570 www.mchapoutier.com.au **Open** By appt
Winemaker Ron Laughton, Michel Chapoutier **Est.** 1998 **Dozens** 500 **Vyds** 9ha
A joint venture of Michel and Corinne Chapoutier and Ron and Elva Laughton. In spring 1998 a vineyard of Australian and imported French shiraz clones was planted. The vineyard is run biodynamically and the winemaking is deliberately designed to place maximum emphasis on the fruit quality. Exports to the UK, the US, France, Singapore and Hong Kong.

ŸŸŸŸŸ **Heathcote Shiraz 2016** Long a collaborative effort between the Laughton family and Michel Chapoutier, this is a brooding wine that exudes a floral joyousness meshed with deftly tuned tannins and compelling intensity of flavour. Sure, there is an undeniable gravitas and power to the underbelly of dark fruit, licorice blackstrap, mocha and tapenade allusions, yet there is also an uncanny effortlessness defined by an MO of poise. Cork. **Rating** 94 **To** 2031 $68 NG

La Prova ★★★★★

102 Main Street, Hahndorf, SA 5245 **Region** Adelaide Hills
T (08) 8388 7330 **www**.laprova.com.au **Open** 1st w'end of the month 11–5 or by appt
Winemaker Sam Scott **Est.** 2009 **Dozens** 5000
Sam Scott's great-grandfather worked in the cellar for Max Schubert and passed his knowledge down to Sam's grandfather. It was he who gave Sam his early education. Sam enrolled in business at university, continuing the casual retailing with Booze Brothers – which he'd started while at school – picking up the trail with Baily & Baily. Next came wine wholesale experience with David Ridge, selling iconic Australian and Italian wines to the trade. This led to a job with Michael Fragos at Tatachilla in 2000 and since then he has been the 'I've been everywhere man', working all over Australia and in California. He moved to Bird in Hand winery at the end of '06, where Andrew Nugent indicated that it was about time he took the plunge on his own account and this he has done. Exports to the UK and Singapore.

ΨΨΨΨΨ **Adelaide Hills Fiano 2019** To be contentious and prefer the less expensive, minimally oaked and less winemaking-infused cuvee feels contrarian. But it feels good! Both fianos at this address are stellar! Yet this has more of the resinous Mediterranean feel: fennel, white flower, apricot and lemon oil. The cadence of freshness just right; gently oily, mid to full-weighted and rapier-long. Screwcap. **Rating** 95 **To** 2024 $26 NG ✪
Monaciello Adelaide Hills Aglianico 2015 Earthy, loamy and dank. In a good way. Ferrous. Tobacco and black fruits with a pickled cherry riff. The tannins, however, are what define this wine. What make it so darn delicious. They slake the thirst while coaxing every bit of saliva from the mouth. They billow against the cheeks and stain every crevice. A fidelitous representation of any aglianico tasted outside of the grape's spiritual home of Campania or Basilicata. Cracking wine! Screwcap. **Rating** 95 **To** 2028 $35 NG ✪
Pilota Adelaide Hills Fiano 2018 Hewn of fruit from the first plantings in the Hills, hailing from '05, this is a broad, textural expression derived from a wild barrel ferment and extended lees time. Oatmeal, apricot, ripe quince and nectarine. The intensity and length of this, prodigious. Complex and powerful. Highly textural. Yet while this reminds me of contemporary expressions in Campania, I find that winemaking obfuscates varietal personality. A very impressive wine, nevertheless. Screwcap. **Rating** 94 **To** 2024 $35 NG
Adelaide Hills Aglianico Rosato 2019 Among the country's better roses, a category that has become crowded with quality. Tangerine, orange blossom and cumquat scents careen across a vibrant dry finish; of an admirable pulpy intensity. A wild ferment and a little oak and voila! Screwcap. **Rating** 94 **To** 2021 $25 NG ✪

ΨΨΨΨΦ **McLaren Vale Nero d'Avola 2018 Rating** 93 **To** 2023 $26 NG ✪
Adelaide Hills Barossa Valley Sangiovese 2018 Rating 92 **To** 2023 $26 NG
Rusco Adelaide Hills Barbera 2018 Rating 92 **To** 2022 $35 NG
Brusco Adelaide Hills Nebbiolo 2016 Rating 92 **To** 2036 $45 NG
King Valley Prosecco 2019 Rating 91 $25 NG
Adelaide Hills Pinot Grigio 2019 Rating 90 **To** 2021 $25 NG

Lake Breeze Wines ★★★★★

Step Road, Langhorne Creek, SA 5255 **Region** Langhorne Creek
T (08) 8537 3017 **www**.lakebreeze.com.au **Open** 7 days 10–5
Winemaker Greg Follett **Est.** 1987 **Dozens** 20 000 **Vyds** 90ha
The Folletts have been farmers at Langhorne Creek since 1880, and grapegrowers since the 1930s. Part of the grape production is sold, but the quality of the Lake Breeze wines is

exemplary, with the red wines particularly appealing. Exports to the UK, the US, Canada, Switzerland, Denmark, Germany, Peru, Singapore, Hong Kong, Japan and China.

🍷🍷🍷🍷🍷 **Section 54 Langhorne Creek Shiraz 2018** Select parcels were fermented in small open-top fermenters before ageing in high quality French oak for 15 months. This is delicious. Pulpy. Floral. An easy flow of rich dark-berry fruit references splayed across detailed tannins and ample spice. The oak is there. But it serves a purpose: to corral the wine's inherent generosity. Screwcap. **Rating** 94 **To** 2026 $25 NG ✪
The Drake 2014 A blend of cabernet (70%) and shiraz, this is a fully loaded homage to a quintessential Australian blend. The cabernet, the dough; the shiraz, the warmth in the centre. Fermented in French wood (90% new) for a whopping 20 months, this is aspirational. The old vine material provides ample stuffing, with the result a seamless, highly savoury mould of floral scents, berry fruits, finely tuned sage-brushed tannins and ambitious oak tones that, nevertheless, fit the billing. This will age very well. Screwcap. **Rating** 94 **To** 2035 $80 NG

🍷🍷🍷🍷🍷 **Winemaker's Selection Shiraz 2018 Rating** 93 **To** 2033 $45 NG
Cabernet Sauvignon 2018 Rating 91 **To** 2026 $25 NG
Bullant Chardonnay 2019 Rating 90 **To** 2023 $17 NG ✪
Bullant Cabernet Merlot 2018 Rating 90 **To** 2028 $17 NG ✪

Lake Cooper Estate   ★★★★☆

1608 Midland Highway, Corop, Vic 3559 **Region** Heathcote
T (03) 9387 7657 **www**.lakecooper.com.au **Open** W'ends & public hols 11–5
Winemaker Paul Boulden, Richard Taylor **Est.** 1998 **Dozens** 12 000 **Vyds** 29.8ha
Lake Cooper Estate is a substantial venture in the Heathcote region, set on the side of Mt Camel Range with panoramic views of Lake Cooper, Greens Lake and the Corop township. In 2019 plans for the construction of a 300t winery, cellar door, restaurant and accommodation were announced, with a complete overhaul of winemaking practices by the highly experienced Paul Boulden and Richard Taylor. Viticulturist Shane Bartel will oversee new plantings of shiraz and grenache and a move towards sustainable practices in the vineyard. Exports to China.

🍷🍷🍷🍷🍷 **Marsanne 2018** This is very good, coming from an understanding that Marsanne demands optimal ripeness as much as it is reliant on a waft of phenolics for its structural reins. Dried tatami mat, apricot pith, blossom. But nothing exuberant. A wine that boasts great versatility at the table. Highly Rhône-like and far better than the skinny wines that are too often lauded on these shores. Mistaken identity? This is the real deal. Screwcap. **Rating** 95 **To** 2024 $40 NG

🍷🍷🍷🍷🍷 **Chardonnay 2018 Rating** 93 **To** 2024 $40 NG
Well Rhapsody Reserve Shiraz 2018 Rating 93 **To** 2028 $149 NG
Reserve Shiraz 2017 Rating 92 **To** 2029 $80 NG
Well Bin 1989 Cabernet Sauvignon 2017 Rating 92 **To** 2032 $90 NG

Lake George Winery   ★★★★★

173 The Vineyards Road, Lake George, NSW 2581 **Region** Canberra District
T (02) 9948 4676 **www**.lakegeorgewinery.com.au **Open** Thurs–Sun 10–5
Winemaker Nick O'Leary, Anthony McDougall **Est.** 1971 **Dozens** 3000 **Vyds** 8ha
Lake George Winery was established by legend-in-his-own-lifetime Dr Edgar Riek, who contributed so much to the Canberra District and the Australian wine industry. It has now passed into the hands of Sarah and Anthony McDougall, and the 47-year-old dry-grown chardonnay, pinot noir, cabernet sauvignon, semillon and merlot plantings have been joined by shiraz, tempranillo, pinot gris, viognier and riesling. The winemaking techniques include basket-pressing and small-batch barrel maturation.

🍷🍷🍷🍷♀ Riesling 2019 Quintessential riesling aromas of lemon zest, pink grapefruit, bath salts and green apple. Rewardingly, the acidity is not hard, but a long slaty flow. Screwcap. **Rating** 92 **To** 2031 $27 NG
Chardonnay 2019 Barrel fermented (25% new French oak) before settling in tank to tighten things up while emphasising the fruit. A pleasant, mid-weighted chardonnay, pillowed with vanillan oak to cashew and nougat notes, creamy at the core. Tangy acidity tows the rear. Screwcap. **Rating** 90 **To** 2024 $25 NG

Lake's Folly ★★★★★

2416 Broke Road, Pokolbin, NSW 2320 **Region** Hunter Valley
T (02) 4998 7507 **www**.lakesfolly.wine **Open** 7 days 10–4 while wine available
Winemaker Rodney Kempe **Est.** 1963 **Dozens** 4500 **Vyds** 13ha
The first of the weekend wineries to produce wines for commercial sale, long revered for its Cabernet Sauvignon and nowadays its Chardonnay. Just as they should, terroir and climate produce a distinct wine style. Lake's Folly no longer has any connection with the Lake family, having been acquired some years ago by Perth businessman Peter Fogarty. Peter's family company previously established the Millbrook Winery in the Perth Hills and has since acquired Deep Woods Estate in Margaret River and Smithbrook Wines in Pemberton, so is no stranger to the joys and agonies of running a small winery. Peter has been an exemplary owner of all the brands, providing support where needed but otherwise not interfering.

🍷🍷🍷🍷🍷 Hunter Valley Cabernets 2018 Blend of cabernet sauvignon, merlot, petit verdot and shiraz. The classic Folly Hunter red blend rarely ceases to amaze with its great subtlety and finesse, even in a challenging year such as '18 which was hot, drought-affected and short. The wine is in great form with a mellifluous aroma of fine-edged fruit, leaf, dark chocolate and the prettiest violets. The wine fairly glides with poise, balance and some of the smartest, seamless oak. Everything is in its place. Screwcap. 13.5% alc. **Rating** 96 **To** 2042 $70 JP ✪
Hill Block Shiraz 2018 Only the second release of a Hill Block 100% shiraz under the Lake's Folly label, makes you wish we had seen these beauties earlier. Startling bright purple colour. Rises like an expensive perfume from the glass; ripe cassis, blackberry, vanilla bean and rich spices giving the impression of a quiet power. The palate is summer berry, plum, a bit of tang here, smooth tannins there. The power of the wine is deceptive; rest assured it's there. Screwcap. 14% alc. **Rating** 95 **To** 2037 $100 JP

🍷🍷🍷🍷♀ Hill Block Chardonnay 2019 **Rating** 93 **To** 2032 $70 JP
Hunter Valley Chardonnay 2019 **Rating** 91 **To** 2027 $70 JP

Lambert Estate ★★★

55 Long Gully Way, Angaston, SA 5353 **Region** Barossa Valley
T (08) 8564 2222 **www**.lambertestate.com.au **Open** 7 days 11–5
Winemaker Kirk Lambert, Vanessa Lambert **Est.** 1986 **Dozens** 10 000 **Vyds** 40ha
James (Jim) and Pamela Lambert are the owners of the recently renamed Lambert Estate (previously Stanley Lambert Wines), with son Kirk and wife Vanessa now winemakers. Like his parents, Kirk was born in Wisconsin and followed his parents' footsteps to the University of Wisconsin. Graduating as a mechanical engineer, he worked for several years for General Electric but decided to move to Australia and, after working in the vineyard and winery for some years, obtained his Masters degree in Oenology from the University of Adelaide. In 2003 Jim and Pamela purchased a 24ha vineyard planted in 1986 and subsequently expanded to 40ha with shiraz, riesling, chardonnay, cabernet sauvignon, zinfandel, tempranillo, grenache, mourvedre, merlot and viognier. A futuristic winery and cellar door was opened in May 2015. Exports to the US, Canada, Germany, China and other major markets.

Landaire   ★★★★☆

PO Box 14, Padthaway, SA 5271 **Region** Padthaway
T 0417 408 147 **www**.landaire.com.au **Open** Not
Winemaker Pete Bissell **Est.** 2012 **Dozens** 2000 **Vyds** 200ha

David and Carolyn Brown have been major grapegrowers in Padthaway over the past
18 years, David having had a vineyard and farming background, Carolyn with a background
in science. Landaire has evolved from a desire, after many years of growing grapes at their
Glendon Vineyard, to select small quantities of the best grapes and have them vinified by Pete
Bissell, chief winemaker at Balnaves. It has proved a sure-fire recipe for success. A cellar door
and accommodation is planned. Exports to the UK, Hong Kong and China.

ŸŸŸŸŸ **Padthaway Chardonnay 2017** Estate-grown Dijon clones 95 and 77, hand-
         picked, whole-bunch pressed direct to barrel (25% new), matured for 11 months.
         A stylish wine with a gently creamy edge to the palate, although in no way
         muffling the varietal fruit expression carried by the cool vintage. Screwcap.
         13% alc. **Rating** 95 **To** 2030 $37
         Padthaway Tempranillo 2019 Estate, hand-picked, small open fermenters,
         50% whole bunches, 50% crushed on top, hand-plunged, matured in used French
         oak. Bright colour; lively, juicy rush of red berry fruits. Simply delicious. Screwcap.
         14.3% alc. **Rating** 94 **To** 2027 $35

ŸŸŸŸ **Padthaway Vermentino 2018** **Rating** 89 **To** 2023 $30
         Padthaway Estate Eliza Brut Rose 2018 **Rating** 89 $35

Landhaus Estate   ★★★★★

102 Main Street, Hahndorf, SA 5245 **Region** Barossa Valley/Adelaide Hills
T 0418 836 305 **www**.landhauswines.com.au **Open** Thus–Mon 11–5
Winemaker Kane Jaunutis **Est.** 2002 **Dozens** 18 000 **Vyds** 1ha

John, Barbara and son Kane Jaunutis purchased Landhaus Estate in 2002, followed by 'The
Landhaus' cottage and 1ha vineyard at Bethany. Bethany is the oldest German-established
town in the Barossa (1842) and the cottage was one of the first to be built. Kane has worked
vintages for Mitolo and Kellermeister, as well as managing East End Cellars, one of Australia's
leading fine wine retailers. John brings decades of owner/management experience and
Barbara 20 years in sales and marketing. Rehabilitation of the estate plantings and establishing
a grower network have paid handsome dividends. Exports to Canada, Singapore and China.

ŸŸŸŸŸ **Rare Barossa Valley Shiraz 2015** A one-barrel wine made from old, low-
         yielding vines in the Barossa's famous Ebenezer district. The word 'rare' is
         probably well deserved in this case. Garnet in colour, dense in aroma, but it is the
         ultra-expressive palate that you come to concentrate on. Blue fruits, sage, licorice
         blackstrap, Barossa game meshes seamlessly with fine tannins. A keeper. Screwcap.
         14.3% alc. **Rating** 96 **To** 2030 $140 JP
         Classics Barossa Valley Shiraz Cabernet Sauvignon 2017 A classic Aussie
         red. Sweet-centered, archetypal, unconstrained; blackcurrant, cherry ripe, chocolate,
         clove, toasty, vanillan oak. Supple and slippery with just a lick of savouriness. Fulfils
         most, if not all, of the requirements of Australia's national red, and a little more.
         Screwcap. 14% alc. **Rating** 94 **To** 2030 $40 JP
         Mourvedre Grenache 2017 A 50/50% blend sourced from low-yielding
         70–100yo vineyards in Ebenezer, Kalimna and Moppa. Starts with a bang, all
         energy and vibrancy. Mourvedre (aka mataro) reveals its pretty side – leafy, rose,
         florals, red cherry – and takes the lead on the bouquet. Licorice, stewed plums
         and telltale grenache confectionery are a presence on the palate. The fruit sings.
         Screwcap. 14% alc. **Rating** 94 **To** 2025 $20 JP ✪

ŸŸŸŸŸ **Classics Barossa Valley Shiraz 2017** **Rating** 92 **To** 2028 $50 JP
         Classics Barossa Valley Mourvedre Grenache Shiraz 2017 **Rating** 90
         To 2026 $30 JP
         Classics Barossa Valley Grenache 2017 **Rating** 90 **To** 2025 $27 JP

Lane's End Vineyard ★★★★★

885 Mount William Road, Lancefield, Vic 3435 **Region** Macedon Ranges
T (03) 5429 1760 **www**.lanesend.com.au **Open** By appt
Winemaker Howard Matthews, Kilchurn Wines **Est.** 1985 **Dozens** 400 **Vyds** 2ha
Pharmacist Howard Matthews and family purchased the former Woodend Winery in 2000,
with 1.8ha of chardonnay and pinot noir (and a small amount of cabernet franc) dating back
to the mid-1980s. The cabernet franc has been grafted over to pinot noir and the vineyard
is now made up of 1ha each of chardonnay and pinot noir (five clones). Howard has been
making the wines for over a decade.

🍷🍷🍷🍷🍷 **Macedon Ranges Chardonnay 2017** Single block, whole-bunch pressed,
wild-fermented and matured for 11 months in French oak (33% new). Has the
drive and zest expected of '17, handsomely delivered. An intense amalgam of
grapefruit juice and pith, Granny Smith apple flesh and core; the oak perfectly
integrated. Screwcap. 13.2% alc. **Rating** 96 **To** 2029 $35
Macedon Ranges Pinot Noir 2018 MV6 and Dijon clones, wild-fermented
with 15% whole bunches, the remainder destemmed, 21 days on skins, matured
for 18 months in extra fine-grained Tonnellerie Mercurey oak (50% new). Superb
deep purple-crimson through to the rim; a voluptuous plum compote style.
Good now, but once its puppy fat is polished off it will be very good. Screwcap.
13.5% alc. **Rating** 96 **To** 2038 $50 ✪
L'autre Macedon Ranges Pinot Noir 2018 From 40yo MV6, wild-fermented
with 5% whole bunches, the remainder destemmed, 18 days on skins, 8 months in
second and third-use French oak. Good hue; red and purple flowers, part field/part
forest, are very attractive. Screwcap. 13.5% alc. **Rating** 95 **To** 2028 $29 ✪

🍷🍷🍷🍷🍷 **Cottage Macedon Ranges Chardonnay 2018 Rating** 91 **To** 2027 $25

Lange Estate ★★★★

633 Frankland-Cranbrook Road, Frankland River, WA 6396 **Region** Frankland River
T 0438 511 828 **www**.langestate.com.au **Open** Not
Winemaker Liam Carmody **Est.** 1997 **Dozens** 4000 **Vyds** 20ha
The eponymous Lange Estate is owned and run by the family: Kim and Chelsea, their children
Jack, Ella and Dylan, together with parents Don and Maxine. The vineyard is situated in
the picturesque Frankland River, tucked away in the far northwestern corner of the Great
Southern. The vineyard, with an elevation of almost 300m and red jarrah gravel loam soils,
produces wines of great intensity. Exports to China.

🍷🍷🍷🍷🍷 **Providence Road Frankland River Shiraz 2018** The most balanced of the '18
shirazs. A core of spicy very ripe red fruit and pleasing earthy aromas and florals.
Medium-bodied with fine tannins and charry oak easing out onto a savoury finish.
Screwcap. 14.5% alc. **Rating** 90 **To** 2027 $32 JF

Langmeil Winery ★★★★★

Langmeil Road, Tanunda, SA 5352 **Region** Barossa Valley
T (08) 8563 2595 **www**.langmeilwinery.com.au **Open** 7 days 10.30–4.30
Winemaker Paul Lindner **Est.** 1996 **Dozens** NFP **Vyds** 33.12ha
Langmeil Winery, owned and operated by the Lindner family, is home to what may be the
world's oldest surviving shiraz vineyard, The Freedom 1843. It was planted by Christian
Auricht, a blacksmith who fled religious persecution in his native Prussia and sought a new
life for his family in Australia. The historic, now renovated, site was once an important trading
post and is also the location of the Orphan Bank Vineyard. This plot of shiraz vines, originally
planted in the '60s, was transplanted from the centre of Tanunda to the banks of the North
Para River in 2006. Exports to all major markets.

🍷🍷🍷🍷🍷 **Wattle Brae Eden Valley Riesling 2019** The smallest vintage since '00. The
analysis is striking: a pH of 2.85, 8.1g/l titratable acidity and the clever retention

of 4.7g/l of residual sugar. The very low yield has been a major help to an elegant, intense riesling. Screwcap. 11% alc. **Rating** 95 To 2034 $30 ✪

The Freedom 1843 Barossa Shiraz 2017 Langmeil has always believed the vines were planted in 1843, the first in the Barossa Valley, but there is some dispute about this. The wine was matured in French hogsheads and barriques (44% new) for 24 months. It's an important wine, and a good one, but I wish the alcohol and oak had been lower. Screwcap. 15% alc. **Rating** 95 To 2037 $145

Jackaman's Barossa Cabernet Sauvignon 2017 From low-yielding vines planted '59, '64 and '71 at Lyndoch and Light Pass; matured in French hogsheads (57% new, 43% second use). It all comes together very well, cassis-accented cabernet fruit clear and bright through the oak. Attractive cabernet. Screwcap. 15% alc. **Rating** 95 To 2032 $70

Pure Eden Barossa Shiraz 2017 From vines planted in the 1890s in Flaxman Valley; matured for 23 months in French oak (34% new). You can see the quality and nature of the fruit, but have to struggle with the oak which puts a curtain around the fruit. Screwcap. 14% alc. **Rating** 94 To 2032 $145

🍷🍷🍷🍷♀ **Orphan Bank Barossa Shiraz 2017** Rating 93 To 2030 $70
Blacksmith Barossa Cabernet Sauvignon 2017 Rating 93 To 2032 $30
Kernel Barossa Cabernet Sauvignon 2017 Rating 92 $50
Valley Floor Barossa Shiraz 2017 Rating 90 To 2029 $30
Hallowed Ground Barossa Shiraz 2017 Rating 90 To 2037 $50

Lansdowne Vineyard

180 Forreston Road, Forreston, SA 5233 **Region** Adelaide Hills
T 0402 505 763 www.lansdownevineyard.com **Open** Not
Winemaker Tim Smith, Simon Greenleaf **Est.** 2003 **Dozens** 500 **Vyds** 18.6ha
Lansdowne's vineyard was planted between 1996 and 2004. It takes its name from the late Victorian house built at Forreston in 1896. Since the 1940s a 3m cedar hedge has been trimmed with 'Lansdowne', creating a local landmark. Janet and Brendan Cameron purchased the house and existing vineyard in 2002, and have since retrained and replanted the vineyard to its current mix of viognier, chardonnay, semillon, pinot gris, pinot noir and sauvignon blanc. Most of the grapes are sold, but since 2005 small quantities have been held for the Lansdowne Vineyard label. The Camerons are moving to an organic regime for the vineyard.

Lark Hill   ★★★★★

31 Joe Rocks Road, Bungendore, NSW 2621 **Region** Canberra District
T (02) 6238 1393 www.larkhill.wine **Open** Wed–Mon 11–4
Winemaker Dr David Carpenter, Sue Carpenter, Chris Carpenter **Est.** 1978 **Dozens** 6000 **Vyds** 10.5ha
The Lark Hill vineyard is situated at an altitude of 860m, offering splendid views of the Lake George escarpment. The Carpenters have made wines of real quality, style and elegance from the start, but have defied all the odds (and conventional thinking) with the quality of their pinot noirs in favourable vintages. Significant changes have come in the wake of son Christopher gaining three degrees – including a double in wine science and viticulture through CSU – and the biodynamic certification of the vineyard. In 2011 Lark Hill purchased one of the two Ravensworth vineyards from Michael Kirk, with plantings of sangiovese, shiraz, viognier, roussanne and marsanne; they have renamed it Dark Horse and manage it biodynamically, having achieved NASAA cetification in '14.

🍷🍷🍷🍷🍷 **Lark Hill Vineyard Canberra District Riesling 2019** Planted in '78 with the Pewsey Vale clone; hand-picked, whole-bunch pressed, fermented with cultured yeast. Another synergistic example of the union between place and variety – bright and crisp, lime and minerality. Screwcap. 12% alc. **Rating** 94 To 2029 $45

🍷🍷🍷🍷♀ **Dark Horse Vineyard Syrah 2017** Rating 93 To 2030 $55
Lark Hill Vineyard Pinot Noir 2018 Rating 92 To 2028 $55
Lark Hill Vineyard Chardonnay 2018 Rating 90 To 2027 $55

Larry Cherubino Wines

3462 Caves Road, Wilyabrup, WA 6280 **Region** Western Australia
T (08) 9382 2379 **www**.larrycherubino.com **Open** 7 days 10–5
Winemaker Larry Cherubino, Andrew Siddell, Matt Buchan **Est.** 2005 **Dozens** 8000
Vyds 120ha

Larry Cherubino has had a particularly distinguished winemaking career, first at Hardys Tintara, then Houghton and thereafter as consultant/Flying Winemaker in Australia, NZ, South Africa, the US and Italy. He has developed three ranges: at the top is Cherubino (Riesling, Sauvignon Blanc, Shiraz and Cabernet Sauvignon); next The Yard, single vineyard wines from WA; and last the Ad Hoc label, all single region wines. The range and quality of his wines is extraordinary, the prices irresistible. The runaway success of the business has seen the accumulation of 120ha of vineyards, the appointment of additional winemakers and Larry's own appointment as director of winemaking for Robert Oatley Vineyards. Exports to the UK, the US, Canada, Ireland, Switzerland, Hong Kong, South Korea, Singapore, China and NZ.

Cherubino Great Southern Riesling 2019 All the tightness, precision and intensity of the palate have been prophesied by the bouquet and reinforced by the aftertaste. Meyer lemon, lime and Granny Smith apple are welded together by the core of acidity that will underwrite the longevity of the wine. Screwcap. 12.5% alc. **Rating** 97 **To** 2029 $35 ✪

Cherubino Porongurup Riesling 2019 There's a laser precision to riesling from Porongurup as this attests. A touch of lavender to the citrus blossom, grapefruit alongside Meyer lemon and mouth-watering chalky acidity. Long, pure and classy. Screwcap. 12.2% alc. **Rating** 96 **To** 2030 $40 JF ✪

Cherubino Margaret River Chardonnay 2018 Impressive from the start, offering the best regional flavours. Stone fruit, grapefruit, creamy honeycomb, ginger spice and flint; oak neatly in place yet playing a part. Complex, powerful and utterly delicious. Screwcap. 13.5% alc. **Rating** 96 **To** 2028 $50 JF ✪

Cherubino Gingin Wilyabrup Chardonnay 2018 A real energy and drive here with a more linear, taut structure compared with its Dijon/Karridale sibling. Mouth-watering flavours of pink grapefruit, lemon with struck-match, flinty sulphides. Laser precision across the palate but there's give, it's not lean and mean. It has power and drive with refreshing acidity to the very end. Screwcap. 13.5% alc. **Rating** 96 **To** 2028 $39 JF ✪

Cherubino Frankland River Cabernet Sauvignon 2017 It starts out all serious and broody offering a hint of the savouriness with licorice, meat stock and wormwood. It's full-bodied with densely packed tannins and yet, it doesn't feel weighty. It unfurls with aplomb and while it's a pleasure to drink now, time will be its benefactor. Screwcap. 14% alc. **Rating** 96 **To** 2035 $110 JF

Cherubino Laissez Faire Riesling 2019 A real thirst quencher thanks to its lemon sorbet acidity, saline crunch and zippy palate. It's all about citrus flavours and is lip-smackingly good. Screwcap. 12.4% alc. **Rating** 95 **To** 2029 $29 JF ✪

Uovo Frankland River Riesling 2017 The Uovo range has been a revelation despite the absence of any detail about it. Still, no better example than this riesling that has a beautiful acid line with layers of flavour and texture. Lemon and ginger curd, fresh citrus and plenty of juiciness across the palate with a dash of sweetness softening the finish. Screwcap. 11% alc. **Rating** 95 **To** 2030 $30 JF ✪

Cherubino Beautiful South White Wine 2018 From the best blocks of sauvignon blanc from a selection of Great Southern vineyards. It was wild-fermented and matured in French oak for 6 months. It can be cellared for at least a decade. It's a powerful wine, acidity providing all the structure required for this to prove true. Screwcap. 13.2% alc. **Rating** 95 **To** 2038 $35 ✪

Ad Hoc Hen & Chicken Pemberton Chardonnay 2018 The name refers to the Gingin clone that produces radically different sized berries on each bunch. The result is a wine with great concentration and depth that will leave all other chardonnays at this price gasping for breath – there is a full panoply of chardonnay

fruit flavours from melon to vanilla and white peach. Screwcap. 13% alc.
Rating 95 To 2025 $21 ✪

Cherubino Dijon Karridale Chardonnay 2018 Dijon, as in clones 95 and
96 grown in Karridale. A mighty fine result. Moreish, savoury with grapefruit,
pomelo, ginger spice and sweet oak influence. Fuller bodied, creamy across the
palate and yet reined in by refreshing, lithe acidity. Screwcap. 13.5% alc. **Rating** 95
To 2028 $39 JF

Cherubino Laissez Faire Porongurup Chardonnay 2018 No shortage of
flavour with grapefruit, stone fruit and oak spices. A juiciness across the palate
with fresh acidity plus creamy leesy influence, but not too much. This only spent
6 months in new and used French oak but it feels more substantial. Very good
drinking now. Screwcap. 13% alc. **Rating** 95 **To** 2028 $39 JF

Uovo Great Southern Chardonnay 2017 Frustrating not having more
information. Regardless, this is a gem. Tight, linear with a fine acid line yet layers
of flavour and a real depth. Stone fruit, lemon with ginger cream, fabulous texture,
almost chalky. Screwcap. 12% alc. **Rating** 95 **To** 2027 $60 JF

Cherubino Laissez Faire Frankland River Fiano 2019 Fiano can handle oak,
but not too much. The back label states whole-bunch pressed and partial-barrel
fermentation. It has more phenolic grip as a result. It's textural and honeyed on
the palate. Lemon blossom, fresh herbs with lots of ginger and spices on the nose.
Really good. Screwcap. 13.6% alc. **Rating** 95 **To** 2024 $29 JF ✪

Cherubino Laissez Faire Great Southern Vermentino 2018 It has a depth
of flavour often missing with Australian renditions. Sure it has the lemon saline
allure, the camomile and blossom, but it's the palate that stands out – textural, some
phenolics adding a comment. Screwcap. 12% alc. **Rating** 95 **To** 2024 $29 JF ✪

Cherubino Laissez Faire Field Blend 2018 Gewürztraminer, pinot grigio,
riesling and pinot blanc form the quartet. No information other than the back
label claiming hand-harvested and natural fermentation. It tastes as if there's been
some skin contact, heady aromatics spicy and citrussy with the palate in tow. Well
handled phenolics and a savoury, moreish finish. Love it. Screwcap. 12.8% alc.
Rating 95 To 2025 $29 JF ✪

Cherubino Laissez Faire Syrah 2018 Estate-grown (Riversdale Vineyard);
hand-picked and sorted, matured for 10 months in French oak. This is high
quality shiraz fruit handled with attention to detail. It is fragrant and juicy, long
and very well balanced. Texture and structure in a medium-bodied guise, and a
cornucopia of black fruits. Screwcap. 14% alc. **Rating** 95 **To** 2033 $39

Cherubino Frankland River Shiraz 2018 It has regional appeal aplenty –
black–blue fruits, squid ink and black pepper; on first pour, somewhat hammered
by lots of varnishy-sweet-charry oak. Yet all that fades with air, to reveal a vibrancy
and plushness. Ripe, dense tannins and appealing in the end. Screwcap. 14% alc.
Rating 95 To 2030 $55 JF

Uovo Frankland River Grenache 2018 This is the essence of grenache. Heady
aromatics of florals, red fruits, musk and a touch of cherry cola, but it's the palate
that makes this special. Medium-bodied with fine-grained tannins and, while the
fruit is delicious, the enjoyment is in its savouriness. Grenache in Frankland River
is proving to be something special. Screwcap. 14% alc. **Rating** 95 **To** 2030 $60 JF

The Yard Riversdale Frankland River Cabernet Sauvignon 2017 The
substantial Riversdale Vineyard was originally planted in the mid-'90s, so
the vines are relatively young. One can only imagine how good it will be in
another 10 years. Not that this wine needs any excuses, it's classic cabernet with
blackcurrant, black olive and bay leaf aromas/flavours supported by firm tannins
that are the markers of prime quality cabernet sauvignon. Screwcap. 13.7% alc.
Rating 95 To 2040 $35 ✪

Cherubino Rivers End Cabernet Sauvignon 2017 Percentage unknown but
a blend of fruit is from Frankland River and Margaret River, the latter taking the
lead: mulberry, earth, lead pencil and warm spices. Lots to take away and enjoy
with its soft, shapely tannins and freshness throughout. It's in the zone. Screwcap.
13.8% alc. **Rating** 95 **To** 2032 $40 JF

Cherubino Margaret River Cabernet Sauvignon 2017 Fruit sourced from Wilyabrup sites so it is full of cassis, mulberries, licorice and violets. A lovely start. A vibrancy throughout with finely chiselled tannins and bright acidity working across the medium-bodied palate. Approachable now and will reward the patient. Screwcap. 14.5% alc. **Rating 95 To** 2033 **$75** JF

Cherubino Beautiful South Red Wine 2017 A blend of cabernet sauvignon and malbec from the Riversdale Vineyard in Frankland River. Shot with savoury flavours of licorice, warm earth and wood spices. There's a flutter of leafy freshness, cassis with captivating tannins. Screwcap. 13.8% alc. **Rating 95 To** 2030 **$40** JF

Ad Hoc Wallflower Great Southern Riesling 2019 Rating 94 To 2027 **$21** ✪

Apostrophe Stone's Throw Great Southern Riesling Gewurztraminer Pinot Blanc 2019 Rating 94 To 2023 **$16** ✪

LC Great Southern Malbec 2018 Rating 94 To 2030 **$25** ✪

Latitude 34 Wine Co

St Johns Brook, 283 Yelverton North Road, Yelverton, WA 6281 **Region** Margaret River
T (08) 9417 5633 **www.**latitude34wineco.com **Open** By appt
Winemaker Robert Olde, Andrew Dawson **Est.** 1997 **Dozens** 70 000 **Vyds** 120ha
Family-owned and operated, Latitude 34 Wine Co was established in 1997 with their first vineyards in the Blackwood Valley (83ha), followed in '98 by the St Johns Brook Vineyard in Yallingup (37ha). A 1200t winery with temperature-controlled wine storage was built in 2004. The wines are released under the St Johns Brook, Optimus, The Blackwood and Crush labels. Exports to the UK, the US and other major markets including China.

🍷🍷🍷🍷🍷 **Raison d'Etre Chatenait 2018** Hand-picked Gingin chardonnay clone from the best block, free-run juice wild-fermented in barrel with some solids and stirring, 20% new oak. Brisk and fresh; grapefruit and Granny Smith apple. Screwcap. 12.5% alc. **Rating 95 To** 2038 **$36**

Raison d'Etre Riserva BDX 2017 Blend of 92% cabernet sauvignon, 8% malbec; crushed and destemmed, matured for 18 months in French barriques. A full-bodied and tightly structured tower of black fruits, yet has minimal tannins, hence texture. Will definitely change (for the better) with age. Screwcap. 13.7% alc. **Rating 94 To** 2037 **$55**

🍷🍷🍷🍷🍷 **St Johns Brook Single Vineyard Margaret River Chardonnay 2018 Rating 92 To** 2027 **$34**

St Johns Brook Reserve Margaret River Chardonnay 2018 Rating 91 To 2025 **$50**

St Johns Brook Single Vineyard Margaret River Shiraz 2017 Rating 91 To 2027 **$34**

Raison d'Etre Tinta De Toro 2018 Rating 91 To 2030 **$36**

St Johns Brook Single Vineyard Margaret River Cabernet Sauvignon 2017 Rating 90 To 2027 **$34**

Laurel Bank

130 Black Snake Lane, Granton, Tas 7030 **Region** Southern Tasmania
T (03) 6263 5977 **www.**laurelbankwines.com.au **Open** By appt
Winemaker Greer Carland **Est.** 1986 **Dozens** 1700 **Vyds** 3.5ha
Laurel Bank was established by Kerry Carland in 1986 but deliberately kept a low profile by withholding release of most of its early wines. When the time came, Kerry entered the Hobart Wine Show in '95 and won the trophy for Most Successful Tasmanian Exhibitor. The moderate slope of the north-facing vineyard overlooking the Derwent River has two radically different soil types: one high vigour, the other low. Intelligent matching of variety and soil has led to a natural balance and (relative) ease of canopy management – and balanced wines.

🍷🍷🍷🍷🍷 **Cabernet Merlot 2018** A solid Bordeaux blend, fully suggestive of how pockets of the Island State can now ripen these varieties with alacrity. Blackberry, cassis and verdant herb scents are strung across a chassis of cedar-vanillan oak. This needs

a little time but will shape up well across the mid-term. Screwcap. **Rating** 92
To 2030 $33 NG

Riesling 2018 This intensely flavoured riesling can, and will, be so much more
in the future. The ripeness, à point; the acidity, juicy rather than grating. More
risk-taking will pay dividends. Quince, grapefruit pulp, candied citrus zest and bath
salts. Long and refreshing enough. Screwcap. **Rating** 91 **To** 2026 $25 NG

Pinot Noir 2018 Lots of whole-berry semi-carbonic lift going on here: violet,
Turkish delight and pulpy, grapey blue fruits. Fermented wild. Almost Beaujolais-
like in its effusive drinkability. Far from prosaic but an easy drink. Screwcap.
Rating 90 **To** 2023 $39 NG

♛♛♛♛ **Sauvignon Blanc 2019 Rating** 89 **To** 2023 $25 NG

Leasingham ★★★★★

PO Box 57, Clare, SA 5453 **Region** Clare Valley
T 1800 088 711 **www**.leasingham-wines.com.au **Open** Not
Winemaker Matt Caldersmith **Est.** 1893 **Dozens** NFP

Leasingham has experienced death by a thousand cuts. First, its then owner, CWA, sold its
Rogers Vineyard to Tim Adams in 2009. CWA then unsuccessfully endeavoured to separately
sell the winemaking equipment and cellar door, while retaining the winery. In January '11
Tim Adams purchased the winery, cellar door and winemaking equipment, making the once-
proud Leasingham a virtual winery (or brand). The quality of the wines has not suffered.
Exports to the UK and Canada.

♛♛♛♛♛ **Cellar Release Classic Clare Riesling 2015** Always an interesting wine to
taste as it typically combines classic Clare (no pun) Valley riesling characters with a
more individual, herbal quality; that holds true here. At 5yo it's just getting into its
stride with toasty aromas mingling with the scents of lime juice and garrigue, and
the richness of maturity developing in the flavours. Drink now or later. Screwcap.
12.8% alc. **Rating** 95 **To** 2030 $56 SC

Classic Clare Shiraz 2017 Hand-picked from 40yo vines. Winemaking
apparently identical to its Cabernet Sauvignon sibling. A little more peppery spice
and a little less ripe fruit on the bouquet of this release than usual, with some
minerally character in there as well. Blackberry provides the main flavour thrust on
a medium-bodied palate, the sweet-edged tannin providing the length. Screwcap.
14.5% alc. **Rating** 94 **To** 2030 $76 SC

Classic Clare Cabernet Sauvignon 2017 Open-fermented with wild yeast,
aged for 16 months in French oak. Unusually approachable for a young Classic
Clare, presenting as a wine that doesn't even seem to require cellaring. It's rich
and actually quite soft, although there's no questioning the depth here with layers
of flavours offering blackcurrant, mint chocolate and toasty oak framed by ripe,
gentle tannin. Screwcap. 14% alc. **Rating** 94 **To** 2030 $79 SC

Leconfield ★★★★★

Riddoch Highway, Coonawarra, SA 5263 **Region** Coonawarra
T (08) 8737 2326 **www**.leconfieldwines.com **Open** Mon–Fri 11–4.30, w'ends 11–4
Winemaker Paul Gordon, Tim Bailey **Est.** 1974 **Dozens** 25 000 **Vyds** 43.7ha

Sydney Hamilton purchased the unplanted property that was to become Leconfield in 1974,
having worked in the family wine business for over 30 years until his retirement in the mid-
'50s. When he acquired the property and set about planting it he was 76 and reluctantly bowed
to family pressure to sell Leconfield to nephew Richard in '81. Richard has progressively
increased the vineyards to their present level, over 75% dedicated to cabernet sauvignon – for
long the winery's specialty. Exports to most major markets.

♛♛♛♛♛ **Coonawarra Cabernet Franc 2018** From a single estate block; 9 days on skins,
10% matured in French oak, the balance in used French and American oak. This
succeeds in some vintages, not others. This is a resounding success: generously
flavoured, seductively textured and exceptional structure. It's all juicy black

fruits with a border of tapenade. And the price! Screwcap. 14.5% alc. **Rating** 96
To 2033 $29 ○

The Sydney Reserve Coonawarra Cabernet Sauvignon 2016 This is a
stellar red. Cassis melds with an exploration of the more intriguing side of this
stiff-upper-lipped variety: graphite, lead and a sense of mineral. A feeling of ball
bearings popping across the mouth, lubricating the saliva and preparing one for
the next sip. Long and impressive. Screwcap. 14% alc. **Rating** 95 To 2031 $80 NG

La Sevillana Coonawarra Rose 2019 Estate-grown merlot; 75% free-run cool-
fermented in stainless steel as if it was an aromatic white, 25% wild-fermented
at ambient temperatures and partial mlf. This complex approach has paid big
dividends. It fills the mouth with red berry fruits; the mouthfeel excellent, residual
sugar playing no part. Screwcap. 13% alc. **Rating** 94 To 2020 $26 ○

ㅇㅇㅇㅇㅇ **Hamilton Block Coonawarra Cabernet Sauvignon 2018 Rating** 93
To 2025 $25 NG ○
Coonawarra Cabernet Sauvignon 2018 Rating 93 To 2028 $35 NG
McLaren Vale Shiraz 2018 Rating 92 To 2028 $26
Coonawarra Petit Verdot 2018 Rating 92 To 2025 $29 NG
Old Vines Coonawarra Riesling 2019 Rating 91 To 2026 $26 NG
Coonawarra Chardonnay 2018 Rating 91 To 2024 $26 NG
Coonawarra Merlot 2018 Rating 91 To 2026 $26 NG
Syn Rouge Sparkling Shiraz NV Rating 91 $18 NG ○

Leeuwin Estate ★★★★★

Stevens Road, Margaret River, WA 6285 **Region** Margaret River
T (08) 9759 0000 **www**.leeuwinestate.com.au **Open** 7 days 10–5
Winemaker Tim Lovett, Phil Hutchison **Est.** 1973 **Dozens** 50 000 **Vyds** 121ha
This outstanding winery and vineyard is owned by the Horgan family, founded by Denis
and Tricia, who continue their involvement, with son Justin Horgan and daughter Simone
Furlong joint chief executives. The Art Series Chardonnay is, in my opinion, Australia's finest
example based on the wines of the last 30 vintages. The move to screwcap brought a large
smile to the faces of those who understand just how superbly the wine ages. The large estate
plantings, coupled with strategic purchases of grapes from other growers, provide the base for
high quality Art Series Cabernet Sauvignon and Shiraz; the hugely successful, quick-selling
Art Series Riesling and Sauvignon Blanc; and lower priced Prelude and Siblings wines.
Exports to all major markets.

ㅇㅇㅇㅇㅇ **Art Series Margaret River Chardonnay 2017** This achieves another step
up the quality ladder for Leeuwin Estate, seemingly impossible. There's been no
change in the vinification, nor in the vineyard. The change is an increase in the
intensity of the flavours and hence their length and aftertaste. It's an extraordinary
wine, among the greatest of Burgundy (and elsewhere in the world). Whatever
you expect from its future development will be delivered. Screwcap. 13.5% alc.
Rating 99 To 2032 $109 ○
Art Series Margaret River Chardonnay 2016 The perfumed perfection of
the bouquet and the wonders of the palate – an ever-shifting mosaic of white
stone fruit, rock melon, grapefruit, Granny Smith apple and custard apple – reign
supreme. Oak? Yes, it's there, although subtle. Acidity? Yes, the giver of life now
and into the future. Screwcap. 13.5% alc. **Rating** 99 To 2046 $104 ○
Art Series Margaret River Cabernet Sauvignon 2016 After berry sorting,
cold soak and maceration, pumping over 3 times daily, the wine pumped to
French barriques for mlf and 9 months maturation. The Art Series range has a
clear family approach to each wine, a focus and sophistication that brings certainty
to its long-term maturity. Screwcap. 13.5% alc. **Rating** 97 To 2036 $71 ○

ㅇㅇㅇㅇㅇ **Prelude Vineyards Margaret River Chardonnay 2018** Leeuwin Estate has
the game sewn up with this entry point wine. It's so precise, so balanced, so pure.
The distinction between fruit and oak is impossible to gauge, the length magical.
Screwcap. 13.5% alc. **Rating** 96 To 2030 $35 ○

Art Series Margaret River Shiraz 2017 Open and closed fermenters with 20% whole bunches, plunged/pumped over daily, pressed to new and used barrels for a total of 18 months in oak. Deep, bright purple-crimson; after early (10 years±) hesitation about the synergy that might be gained from this marriage of wine and place, all doubts were comprehensively answered. Lovely medium to full-bodied blackberry and co flavours. Screwcap. 13.5% alc. **Rating** 95 To 2037 $39

ΨΨΨΨΨ Prelude Vineyards Cabernet Sauvignon 2017 **Rating** 93 To 2037 $30
Art Series Sauvignon Blanc 2019 **Rating** 92 To 2023 $30
Art Series Riesling 2019 **Rating** 90 To 2023 $22
Pinot Noir Chardonnay Brut 2017 **Rating** 90 $35

Lenton Brae Wines

3887 Caves Road, Margaret River, WA 6285 **Region** Margaret River
T (08) 9755 6255 **www.**lentonbrae.com **Open** 7 days 10–5
Winemaker Edward Tomlinson **Est.** 1982 **Dozens** NFP **Vyds** 7.3ha
The late architect Bruce Tomlinson built a strikingly beautiful winery (heritage-listed by the Shire of Busselton) that is now in the hands of winemaker son Edward (Ed), who consistently makes elegant wines in classic Margaret River style. A midwinter (French time) trip to Pomerol in Bordeaux to research merlot is an indication of his commitment. Exports to the UK.

ΨΨΨΨΨ Margaret River Semillon Sauvignon Blanc 2019 Stainless-steel fermented with aromatic yeasts, semillon from Wilyabrup, sauvignon blanc from Karridale. Highly expressive bouquet with an abundance of the herbaceous and tropical/citrus/stone fruit aromas these varieties can produce in this region. It's lively and juicy in the mouth, with attractive semillon flavours providing the main thrust on the palate. Screwcap. 12.5% alc. **Rating** 93 To 2023 $24 SC ✪
Lady Douglas Margaret River Cabernet Sauvignon 2018 With 5% merlot included, 14 months in French barriques. Shows some very distinctively Margaret River cabernet traits on the bouquet with bay leaf, black olive and cedary wood polish wound around the currant fruit. Generous ripe red and blackberry flavours on the palate, with fine but persistent tannin carrying it through the finish. Screwcap. 13.5% alc. **Rating** 93 To 2033 $38 SC
Margaret River Merlot 2018 The inaugural release. An interesting bouquet, a bit gamey and earthy with the oak having an influence. Fruit comes through more clearly on the palate, the red-berried flavours quite soft and rich, fitting the usual expectation of merlot. Ripe, almost sweet tannin rounds it out. Screwcap. 14% alc. **Rating** 92 To 2028 $38 SC
Margaret River Cabernet Merlot 2018 Smaller portions of petit verdot and malbec also included in this blend. Cassis, mulberry, cedar and a touch of green leaf are all apparent in the bouquet and you can see (or smell) the different varieties playing a part. It's smoothly textured along the palate, the flavours mostly a mirror image of the aromas, the tannin well woven into the fabric. Good drinking. Screwcap. 14.5% alc. **Rating** 92 To 2030 $28 SC
Southside Margaret River Chardonnay 2018 Wild ferment in new and used French hogsheads, some fining, unfiltered. An interesting style, seemingly not made to be a crowd pleaser. Not a lot of primary fruit on the bouquet, the effect of the oak handling apparent, although it's not an 'oaky' wine. Textured on the palate with some sweetness of fruit. It isn't totally convincing for me but may be for others. Screwcap. 13.5% alc. **Rating** 90 To 2023 $30 SC
Margaret River Pinot Blanc 2019 Subtle aromas of autumnal fruit with what appears to be some skins or lees character, or perhaps it's a varietal thing. Lightly weighted on the palate but fresh and somewhat savoury, the flavour pulling up a little short but the acidity lingering well into the finish. Screwcap. 13.5% alc. **Rating** 90 To 2022 $30 SC

Margaret River Pinot Blanc 2018 Wild-fermented in used French hogsheads, no mlf. This is the third commercial release. Is it simply to provide more choice (which I'll buy) or some extra quality over chardonnay et al (which I won't)? Screwcap. 12.5% alc. **Rating** 90 **To** 2032 $30

Leo Buring ★★★★★

Sturt Highway, Nuriootpa, SA 5355 **Region** Eden Valley/Clare Valley
T 1300 651 650 **Open** Not
Winemaker Tom Shanahan **Est.** 1934 **Dozens** NFP
Between 1965 and 2000 Leo Buring was Australia's foremost producer of rieslings, with a rich legacy left by former winemaker John Vickery. After veering away from its core business into other varietal wines, it has now refocused on riesling. Top of the range are the Leopold Derwent Valley and the Leonay Eden Valley rieslings, supported by Clare Valley and Eden Valley rieslings at significantly lower prices, and expanding its wings to Tasmania and WA.

🍷🍷🍷🍷🍷 **Leonay Riesling 2019** An Aussie icon with a track record to prove it. Plenty of juice on the skeletal bones of shock wave acidity and mineral pungency: lemon, green apple, Rose's lime, talc, pumice, quince and apricot. Long, juicy and boasting real flow. This bodes very well for a long life. Screwcap. **Rating** 95 **To** 2034 $40 NG

🍷🍷🍷🍷🍷 **Clare Valley Riesling Dry 2019 Rating** 92 **To** 2031 $20 NG ⊙

Leogate Estate Wines ★★★★★

1693 Broke Road, Pokolbin, NSW 2320 **Region** Hunter Valley
T (02) 4998 7499 **www**.leogate.com.au **Open** 7 days 10–5
Winemaker Mark Woods **Est.** 2009 **Dozens** 30 000 **Vyds** 127.5ha
Since purchasing the substantial Brokenback Vineyard in 2009 (a key part of the original Rothbury Estate, with the majority of vines over 50 years old), Bill and Vicki Widin have wasted no time. Initially the Widins leased the Tempus Two winery but prior to the '13 vintage they completed the construction of their own winery and cellar door. They have also expanded the range of varieties, supplementing the long-established 30ha of shiraz, 25ha of chardonnay and 3ha of semillon with between 0.5 and 2ha of each of verdelho, viognier, gewurztraminer, pinot gris and tempranillo. They have had a string of wine show successes for their very impressive portfolio. In '16 Leogate purchased a 61ha certified organic vineyard at Gulgong (Mudgee) planted to shiraz, cabernet sauvignon and merlot. Leogate has an impressive collection of back-vintage releases available on request. Exports to the UK, the US, Malaysia, Hong Kong and China.

🍷🍷🍷🍷🍷 **The Basin Reserve Hunter Valley Shiraz 2018** The grapes come from a small patch of east-facing vines. Youthful, bright colour; medium to full-bodied. The tannin texture and structure are the architects of the wine and its long future, the fruits in a blackberry/plum spectrum. The 14 months in French hogsheads (15% new) has also built the context of the wine; the remaining oak, second and third use, another building block. Screwcap. 14% alc. **Rating** 96 **To** 2048 $115
Western Slopes Reserve Hunter Valley Shiraz 2018 The name speaks for itself, but one of the strengths of this winery's releases is the modest alcohol at which full ripeness has been achieved. The innate balance virtually guarantees a very long life, demonstrating this (for me at least) in the context of tastings of Hunter shiraz over many decades. Screwcap. 14% alc. **Rating** 96 **To** 2048 $115
Aged Release Malabar Reserve Hunter Valley Shiraz 2014 Vinification near-identical to the '18, the wine benefiting from the extra years in bottle. That said, it deserves another 6 years minimum to reach its peak, one that it will hold indefinitely. Screwcap. 14% alc. **Rating** 96 **To** 2048 $100
Creek Bed Reserve Hunter Valley Semillon 2019 At once more intense and more elegant than its Brokenback Vineyard sibling, and will provide great pleasure once it moves through the 5–10-year period of gaining maturity.

The lime/lemon/lemongrass flavours of today will become adjuncts to lightly browned and buttered toast. Screwcap. 11% alc. **Rating** 95 **To** 2039 $30 ✪
Malabar Reserve Hunter Valley Shiraz 2018 Hand-picked, crushed and destemmed, 10 days on skins, matured in 90% French and 10% American hogsheads of various ages for 14 months. Most attractive varietal fruit flavours spanning cherry, plum and blackberry fruit supported by ripe, round tannins. Screwcap. 14.5% alc. **Rating** 95 **To** 2038 $70
Aged Release Brokenback Vineyard Hunter Valley Shiraz 2014 Identical vinification (or near enough) to the '18. Moving along the maturity scale at a leisurely pace with decades still to go. Screwcap. 14% alc. **Rating** 95 **To** 2038 $70

🍷🍷🍷🍷🍷 **Brokenback Vineyard Semillon 2019 Rating** 93 **To** 2034 $22 ✪
H10 Block Reserve Chardonnay 2018 Rating 92 **To** 2021 $52
Vicki's Choice Reserve Chardonnay 2017 Rating 92 **To** 2023 $70
Brokenback Vineyard Chardonnay 2016 Rating 90 **To** 2021 $26

Lerida Estate   ★★★★☆

The Vineyards, Old Federal Highway, Lake George, NSW 2581 **Region** Canberra District
T (02) 4848 0231 **www.**leridaestate.com.au **Open** 7 days 10–5
Winemaker Campbell Meelis **Est.** 1997 **Dozens** 10 000 **Vyds** 11.69ha
Lerida Estate owes a great deal to the inspiration of Dr Edgar Riek; it is planted immediately to the south of Edgar's former Lake George vineyard. Lerida is planted mainly to pinot noir, with pinot gris, chardonnay, shiraz, merlot and cabernet franc and viognier also on site. Michael and Tracey McRoberts purchased Lerida in 2017 and significant expansion is underway. They have leased a 20-year-old shiraz vineyard (4ha) in the heart of Murrumbateman and shiraz has overtaken pinot noir as the predominant variety produced. The Glen Murcutt–designed winery, barrel room, cellar door and restaurant have spectacular views over Lake George. Exports to China.

🍷🍷🍷🍷🍷 **Cullerin Canberra District Riesling 2019** This is one of those wines with all the bits in place: citrussy aromatics, spice, fresh acidity, the touch of phenolics on the finish adding a layer of complexity. And yet, it's enjoyable too, without having to overthink things. Screwcap. 12.5% alc. **Rating** 93 **To** 2028 $38 JF
Canberra District Shiraz 2018 Falls into medium-bodied territory with its flush of red fruits, a sprinkling of black pepper and baking spices. Gritty tannins and a savouriness throughout. Ironically, the least expensive shiraz is the pick of the '18s. Screwcap. 13.9% alc. **Rating** 92 **To** 2027 $27 JF
Cullerin Saignee Canberra District Rose 2019 Bright cherry hue. Soft, plush with hints of strawberries, star anise and rose petals. Finishes somewhat sweet yet still refreshing and enjoyable Screwcap. 13.5% alc. **Rating** 90 **To** 2020 $38 JF

Lethbridge Wines   ★★★★★

74 Burrows Road, Lethbridge, Vic 3222 **Region** Geelong
T (03) 5281 7279 **www.**lethbridgewines.com **Open** Mon–Fri 11–3, w'ends 11–5
Winemaker Ray Nadeson, Maree Collis **Est.** 1996 **Dozens** 6000 **Vyds** 10ha
Lethbridge was founded by scientists Ray Nadeson, Maree Collis and Adrian Thomas. In Ray's words, 'Our belief is that the best wines express the unique character of special places'. As well as understanding the importance of terroir, the partners have built a unique straw-bale winery, designed to recreate the controlled environment of cellars and caves in Europe. Winemaking is no less ecological: hand-picking, indigenous-yeast fermentation, small open fermenters, pigeage (foot-stomping) and minimal handling of the wines throughout the maturation process are all part and parcel of the highly successful Lethbridge approach. Ray also has a distinctive approach to full-blown chardonnay and pinot noir. There is also a contract winemaking limb to the business. Exports to the UK, Denmark, Singapore, Thailand and China.

🍷🍷🍷🍷🍷 **Botrytis Riesling TBA 2018** Trockenbeerenauslese – indeed, one of the best examples of this style I have tasted. Extraordinarily rich and intense; the acidity not searing as so often is the case, just balancing the sublime concentration of dried and sugar-coated fruit. Screwcap. 11.5% alc. **Rating** 99 **To** 2048 $90 ○

Allegra 2017 50/50% mix of P58/Dijon chardonnay clones, the vines planted in '81; hand-picked, whole-bunch pressed, wild-fermented, matured in new French oak. Exceedingly powerful and complex. Needs to be chilled on a warm/hot day, but is quite something. Screwcap. 14% alc. **Rating** 97 **To** 2032 $90 ○

🍷🍷🍷🍷🍷 **Shiraz 2018** From the home block; hand-picked and sorted, fermented with 50% whole bunches, matured in new French barriques, 106 dozen made. The finish makes it a special wine. Screwcap. 13.5% alc. **Rating** 96 **To** 2040 $48 ○

Allegra 2016 The same Mt Duneed source and vinification as its sibling. Impressive chardonnay, just '16 versus '17 vintage. Screwcap. 14.5% alc. **Rating** 95 **To** 2026 $90

Mietta Pinot Noir 2017 A very good pinot noir that has taken full advantage of the '17 vintage. The 80% whole-bunch vinification may not appeal to all, but I am more than happy with the forest floor and soaring spices. The use of 100% new French oak was justified and has been almost entirely absorbed by the fruit. Screwcap. 13% alc. **Rating** 95 **To** 2027 $90

Rebenberg Geelong Shiraz 2018 The vineyard at Mt Duneed was planted in '69. Hand-picked, wild-fermented with 50% whole bunches, matured for 11 months in French oak (50% new), 109 dozen made. Generous, but not excessive – a full and round compote of black fruit and fine-grained tannins. Screwcap. 14.5% alc. **Rating** 95 **To** 2038 $55

Indra 2017 Hand-picked, wild-fermented with 30% whole bunches, matured for 11 months in new French barriques, 151 dozen made. In the full-bodied, heroic Lethbridge style, impressive and enjoyable. A long future. Screwcap. 13.5% alc. **Rating** 95 **To** 2030 $90

Dr Nadeson Riesling 2019 Fermented in stainless steel and a 1300l foudre, 16.45g/l residual sugar. Sourced from Henty, the coolest region of the Australia mainland; its acidity masking the sugar well. Will develop superbly for 20+ years. Screwcap. 11% alc. **Rating** 95 $35 ○

Chardonnay 2018 Hand-picked, whole-bunch pressed, wild-fermented in French oak (30% new), matured for 11 months. Nice work – it all comes together very well. Screwcap. 13.5% alc. **Rating** 94 **To** 2028 $48

Que Syrah Syrah 2018 Fermented in a 3000l wooden cuve, 20 days on skins, pressed and returned to the same cuve for 10 months maturation. Very rich, concentrated and complex. Too much of everything? Some would say so today, but not in 10 years. Screwcap. 14.5% alc. **Rating** 94 **To** 2038 $35

🍷🍷🍷🍷🍷 **Il regalo di compleanno Nebbiolo 2017** **Rating** 90 **To** 2037 $55

Leura Park Estate   ★★★★☆

1400 Portarlington Road, Curlewis, Vic 3222 **Region** Geelong
T (03) 5253 3180 **www.**leuraparkestate.com.au **Open** Thurs–Sun 10–5, 7 days Jan
Winemaker Darren Burke **Est.** 1995 **Dozens** 3000 **Vyds** 17ha
Leura Park Estate's vineyard is planted to riesling, shiraz, sauvignon blanc, pinot gris, pinot noir, chardonnay and cabernet sauvignon. Owners David and Lyndsay Sharp are committed to minimal interference in the vineyard and have expanded the estate-grown wine range (Sauvignon Blanc, Pinot Gris, Chardonnay, Pinot Noir and Shiraz) to include Vintage Grande Cuvee. The next step was the erection of a winery for the 2010 vintage, leading to increased production and ongoing wine show success.

🍷🍷🍷🍷🍷 **Yublong Limited Release Geelong Cabernet Sauvignon 2018** Micro-fermented in small batches prior to 10 months in high quality French oak – the estate's wont. This is a delicate cabernet, yet fully flavoured in the respect that the wine is beautifully detailed with fine-boned tannins guiding every riff of flavour long: red and blackcurrant, bouquet garni and a breeze of pyrazine herb. Fine, pointed and highly savoury, boasting an uncanny elegance and drinkability. Screwcap. Rating 95 To 2029 $42 NG

Limited Release Block 1 Reserve Chardonnay 2018 Hand-picked, sourced from a propitiously sited block and aged for 10 months in smart French oak. This is a rewarding richer expression, particularly in the current clime of thinner, more linear styles. Toasted hazelnut, creamed cashew, oatmeal and ample nougat creaminess meander with plush stone fruit aspersions. Very well put together and frankly, delicious, billowing and long. Screwcap. **Rating** 94 **To** 2025 $45 NG

Bellarine Peninsula Chardonnay 2018 I like this. A whiff of gunflint mineral reduction soon disperses to reveal ripe apricot, nectarine and white peach notes. The thrust of fruit and parry of nicely layered oak is impressive. Nothing is exaggerated: neither on the heavy side, nor on the side of abstemiousness. This plays the contemporary card of mineral energy, while appeasing the crowd in need of flavour and nourishment. Very well done. Screwcap. **Rating** 94 **To** 2026 $35 NG

♟♟♟♟♟ **Bellarine Peninsula Pinot Noir 2018** Rating 93 To 2024 $45 NG
Geelong Sauvignon Blanc 2018 Rating 92 To 2023 $24 NG ✪
Bellarine Peninsula Shiraz 2017 Rating 91 To 2023 $45 NG
Pinot Gris 2018 Rating 90 To 2023 $30 NG

Levrier by Jo Irvine   ★★★★☆

PO Box 70, Nuriootpa, SA 5355 **Region** South Australia
T (08) 8562 3888 **www**.levrierwines.com.au **Open** By appt
Winemaker Joanne Irvine **Est.** 2017 **Dozens** 3000

What do I and Jo Irvine have in common? The only person in the world able to answer that question is myself, not – as you might guess – Jo. Because I'm sure that she doesn't know that in my younger days I was a part-owner of two greyhounds, neither of which were as fast as those they raced against. 'Levrier' is French for greyhound, and Jo has looked after retired racing greyhounds for 20 years, currently Georgie and Daphne, who hang out at her winery. The wines she now makes on her own account are given the names of famous racing greyhounds. Jo's second career is as a skilled contract winemaker. At age 35 she gave up her occupation as a theatre nurse and joined her father Jim Irvine, having enjoyed gap years travelling internationally and doing vintages in the US. In a reversal of roles, she made wines for her father, notably his Grand Merlot, the last vintage in 2014, after which he sold his business. Jo was in no hurry to hang her shingle up until all the pieces were in place: grape supply, winemaking, maturation and packaging. The old saying 'Slow boat to China' fits well with Jo's wines.

♟♟♟♟ **Barossa Chardonnay 2017** Unoaked Eden Valley chardonnay given a (small) lease on life by the vintage. Screwcap. 13% alc. **Rating** 89 **To** 2021 $25

Lienert Vineyards   ★★★★☆

Box 5, Lienert Road, She Oak Log, SA 5371 **Region** Barossa Valley
T (08) 8524 9062 **www**.lienert.wine **Open** By appt
Winemaker James Lienert **Est.** 2001 **Dozens** 2000 **Vyds** 70ha

Lienert Vineyards is a partnership between brothers John and James Lienert, who have converted the family's farmland on the Barossa Valley's western ridge from cropping to vineyards, planting the first vines in the distinctive terra rossa soils in 2001. John manages the vineyard, which also supplies fruit to a number of Barossa wineries. James makes wines under the Lienert Vineyards and Jack West labels from selected blocks.

♟♟♟♟♟ **Barossa Valley Shiraz 2016** For all practical reasons, identical vinification to its '17 sibling. The wine itself is very different, more savoury than sweet, and with clear-cut Barossa flavours, the tannins ripe and balanced. Screwcap. 14.3% alc. **Rating** 95 **To** 2036 $45

Barossa Valley Shiraz 2017 Wild-fermented in small (2t) fermenters, 10–12 days on skins, matured in hogsheads (12% new) for 18 months. The flavours are intense and rich, the fruit sweet (not residual sugar-sweet), the line long. Screwcap. 14.3% alc. **Rating** 94 **To** 2032 $45

🍷🍷🍷🍷♀ **Barossa Valley Mataro 2018 Rating** 92 **To** 2028 $45

Lightfoot & Sons ★★★★★

Myrtle Point Vineyard, 717 Calulu Road, Bairnsdale, Vic 3875 **Region** Gippsland
T (03) 5156 9205 **www.**lightfootwines.com **Open** Fri–Sun 11–5
Winemaker Alastair Butt, Tom Lightfoot **Est.** 1995 **Dozens** 10000 **Vyds** 29.3ha
Brian and Helen Lightfoot have established pinot noir, shiraz, chardonnay, cabernet sauvignon and merlot; the lion's share to pinot noir and shiraz. The soil is very similar to that of Coonawarra with terra rossa over limestone. Most of the grapes are sold (as originally planned) to other Victorian winemakers. With the arrival of Alastair Butt (formerly of Brokenwood and Seville Estate) and supported by son Tom, production has increased and may well rise further. Second son Rob has also come onboard, bringing 10 years' experience in sales and marketing.

🍷🍷🍷🍷🍷 **River Block Gippsland Shiraz 2018** We get a meat-strewn, pepper-tossed, twiggy shiraz served with plenty of fruit and silky-smooth texture. In other words we get a fantastic wine with plenty of interest. Tannin has largely melted in, though there's enough – especially when combined with exquisite balance and impeccable length – to make you think that this will mature swimmingly. Screwcap. 13.9% alc. **Rating** 96 **To** 2032 $55 CM ✪

Myrtle Point Vineyard Gippsland Chardonnay 2018 Pressed direct to a mix of hogsheads and puncheons (15% new) from 3 forests/3 coopers, 10% undergoing mlf. The Lightfoot chardonnays are very similar, the differences lying as much in the vineyard as the winery. The overall light touch in vinification also brings the wines closer together. Screwcap. 12.6% alc. **Rating** 95 **To** 2026 $30 ✪

Home Block Gippsland Chardonnay 2017 Only 222 dozen bottles made despite the perfect growing season, the limitation being the small parcel from within the Home Block. Had 11 months' maturation in oak. The fruit aromas and flavours span white peach, grapefruit and melon; the oak no more than a textural play. Screwcap. 13.2% alc. **Rating** 95 **To** 2030 $50

Gippsland Pinot Noir Shiraz 2018 A 50/50% blend, all destemmed and all into French oak. This blend always sounds like a good idea but it rarely works as well as it has here. This is both well fleshed and fine-grained, its dark berry notes teaming beautifully with nut, herb, cedar wood and sweet spice notes; the finish full of get-up-and-go. It's a mid-weight red with quality nailed to the mast. Screwcap. 13.7% alc. **Rating** 95 **To** 2029 $40 CM

Myrtle Point Vineyard Gippsland Pinot Noir 2018 Sturdy, almost beefy, with macerated cherry and woodsy spice characters pushing through. It's a somewhat backward, earthen, more-bass-than-treble wine with sweet, toasty, malty characters as highlights and good momentum through the finish. Again you'd bet that it will age well. Screwcap. 13.8% alc. **Rating** 94 **To** 2027 $30 CM ✪

🍷🍷🍷🍷♀ **Myrtle Point Vineyard Gippsland Shiraz 2018 Rating** 93 **To** 2027 $30 CM
Cliff Block Gippsland Pinot Noir 2017 Rating 92 **To** 2026 $55 CM
Myrtle Point Vineyard Gippsland Rose 2019 Rating 90 **To** 2022 $25 CM

Lillydale Estate ★★★★

Davross Court, Seville, VIC 3139 **Region** Yarra Valley
T 0422 962 888 **www.**lillydaleestate.com **Open** Not
Winemaker Franco D'Anna **Est.** 1975 **Dozens** 3000 **Vyds** 5ha
Lillydale Estate was established in 1975 by Alex White and Martin Grinbergs, fugitives from Carlton & United Breweries, where they were scientists. They were at the forefront of the

development of Yarra Valley chardonnay style in the early '80s, but in '94 the winery, brand and vineyards were acquired by McWilliam's. In August 2012, ownership changed once again when a subsidiary of the very large Wuxi Electronics and Instruments Industry Co. Ltd (of China) acquired the property. The intention is to slowly build the brand, protecting the reputation it has gained over the years. Exports to China.

ͰͰͰͰͰ **Yarra Valley Pinot Noir 2019** Deep colour. The fragrant bouquet sets the scene for a complex earthy/savoury palate, plum driving the engine room with spice trimmings. Screwcap. 14.3% alc. **Rating** 93 **To** 2029 $37

Yarra Valley Gewurztraminer 2019 Gewurztraminer's varietal expression is often a no-show but it's on parade here. It's true the wine doesn't have Alsace power but lychee, passionfruit and guava are all delicately painted on the senses; the aftertaste fresh and clean. Screwcap. 12.5% alc. **Rating** 91 **To** 2023 $30

Yarra Valley Chardonnay 2019 Barrel ferment/oak influence is light but the quality of the fruit is good with typical Yarra Valley length. Screwcap. 13.5% alc. **Rating** 90 **To** 2024 $37

Lillypilly Estate ★★★★★

47 Lillypilly Road, Leeton, NSW 2705 **Region** Riverina
T (02) 6953 4069 **www**.lillypilly.com **Open** Mon–Sat 10–5.30, Sun by appt
Winemaker Robert Fiumara **Est.** 1982 **Dozens** 11 000 **Vyds** 27.9ha
Botrytised white wines are by far the best offering from Lillypilly, with the Noble Muscat of Alexandria unique to the winery. These wines have both style and intensity of flavour and can age well. Their table wine quality is always steady – a prime example of not fixing what is not broken. Exports to the UK, the US, Canada and China.

ͰͰͰͰͰ **Noble Blend 2018** Sauvignon blanc and muscat of Alexandria morph into a mid-gold-amber. Beautifully fresh with apricot studded with preserved ginger, glace lemon, saffron cream and truffled honey. Fresh acidity ensuring this soars. 375ml. Screwcap. 12% alc. **Rating** 95 **To** 2025 $32 JF ✪

Museum Release Noble Harvest 2012 Don't keep this golden-orange sweetie any longer. It's gorgeous now with its heady aromas of lemon/lime marmalade on toast, but mostly poached pears drizzled with a saffron-honey glaze. While there's acidity cutting a clean line through the richness and sweetness across the palate, there's a tipping point and soon this will start to dip. Screwcap. 11% alc. **Rating** 95 **To** 2021 $42 JF

Angelo Blend Fiumara 7 NV Tawny with a red sheen. Very fresh and heady with gingerbread and panettone, hazelnut toffee, soused raisins and baking spices. A brandy flavour to the spirit, the palate is smooth, warming and this is a delight to drink. 375ml. Screwcap. 18% alc. **Rating** 95 **To** $27 JF ✪

Lindenderry at Red Hill ★★★★☆

142 Arthurs Seat Road, Red Hill, Vic 3937 **Region** Mornington Peninsula
T (03) 5989 2933 **www**.lindenderry.com.au **Open** W'ends 11–5
Winemaker Barnaby Flanders **Est.** 1999 **Dozens** 1000 **Vyds** 3.35ha
Lindenderry at Red Hill is a sister operation to Lancemore Hill in the Macedon Ranges and Lindenwarrah at Milawa. It has a 5-star country house hotel, conference facilities, a function area, day spa and restaurant on 16ha of gardens. It also has a little over 3ha of vineyards, planted equally to pinot noir and chardonnay 20 years ago. Notwithstanding the reputation of the previous winemakers for Lindenderry, the wines now being made by Barney Flanders are the best yet. He has made the most of the estate-grown grapes, adding cream to the cake by sourcing some excellent Grampians shiraz.

ͰͰͰͰͰ **Mornington Peninsula Chardonnay 2018** Peninsula chardonnay at its cool, crisp best courtesy of flinty sulphides and citrussy acidity. Stone fruits and savoury grilled almonds with fig build and build in the mouth. It's deceptively on the leaner side with good length and persistence. Screwcap. 13% alc. **Rating** 92 **To** 2027 $35 JP

Macedon Ranges Pinot Noir 2018 A profoundly different expression of pinot noir a thousand miles away from the sweet fruit and spice style. Think rosemary, thyme, hummus, tobacco leaf and dried earth. It's savoury and sinewy in tannins. Grows on you with each sip. Screwcap. 13% alc. **Rating** 92 **To** 2025 $40 JP
Mornington Peninsula Pinot Noir 2018 Polar-opposite to its Macedon Ranges sibling with a lighter, brighter red hue and sweeter, finer fruit expression. Wild strawberries, raspberries, red plums engage. Pulses with life and freshness on the palate, all juicy fruits with dried herb and spice support but there is depth here too. This is no simple pushover. Screwcap. 13% alc. **Rating** 92 **To** 2026 $40 JP
Grampians Shiraz 2018 A soft and elegant shiraz that is easy to make friends with. Fresh blackberries, blood plums and loaded with spice. The palate is a repeat with the red fruits emerging later on the palate together with attractive regional menthol characters. Tannins are densely packed and the result is one supple wine. Screwcap. 13.5% alc. **Rating** 90 **To** 2031 $40 JP

Lindsay Wine Estate | DB Wines

15 Vine Vale Road, Tanunda, SA 5352 **Region** Barossa Valley
T (08) 8563 3858 **www.**lindsaywineestate.com.au **Open** 7 days 11–5
Winemaker Matt Dunning **Est.** 2012 **Dozens** 25 000 **Vyds** 10.4ha
There's not much that can be said about this venture other than the founders', Matt Dunning and Will Bolton, love of music, art and wine – music in the form of 4000 vinyl records on tap. The website speaks for itself, as do the wines. Exports to Denmark, Russia, Brazil, Singapore, NZ, Taiwan, Hong Kong and China.

Lindsay Wine Estate Barossa Valley Semillon 2017 This wine has only 550l extraction/t (700l usually achieved); 50% matured for 9 months on lees, stirred monthly. If it had a screwcap rather than a one-piece cork, it would be looking at a 10-year development pattern (à la Hunter Valley) but experience demonstrates it's not possible to predict when and how it will develop, no 2 bottles the same. The irony is the quality of the cork, and the way it has been inserted. My points are for the wine as it is today. 13.5% alc. **Rating** 90 **To** 2020 $50

The Lindsay Collection The Selector Barossa Valley Shiraz 2017 **Rating** 89 **To** 2032 $20
The Lindsay Collection The Sumit Barossa Valley Shiraz 2016 **Rating** 89 **To** 2032 $40

Lino Ramble

11 Gawler Street, Port Noarlunga, SA 5167 **Region** McLaren Vale
T 0409 553 448 **www.**linoramble.com.au **Open** W'ends 12–5
Winemaker Andy Coppard **Est.** 2012 **Dozens** 3500
After 20 years of working for other wine companies, big and small, interstate and international, Andy Coppard and Angela Townsend say, 'We've climbed on top of the dog kennel, tied a cape around our necks, held our breaths, and jumped'. And if you are curious about the name (as I was), the story has overtones of James Joyce's stream of consciousness mental rambles. Exports to Canada and Japan.

Simon Says McLaren Vale Saperavi 2018 This treads a richer ground, mottled with darker fruit, herb, root spice and chewy, granular anise-clad tannins. That said, it remains in the mould of this address' pulpy, fleshy and joyously drinkable style despite a firmer, more tremulous ground across Saperavi's tannic carapace. All for the best. Screwcap. **Rating** 93 **To** 2023 $40 NG
Treadlie Shiraz 2019 A delicious Vale shiraz exuding a whiff of neoprene tension before spiralling into blue to dark fruit allusions, dried seaweed, charcuterie and a smudge of black olive, lacing a gentle waft of tannin. The freshness is apt. The wine, on the richer side of mid-weight. **Rating** 92 **To** 2025 $20 NG ✪
Blind Man's Bluff McLaren Vale Bastardo 2019 This is a wonderful and immensely enjoyable lightish sassy red, seared with a core of McLaren Vale

warmth. Known as trousseau in the uber-fashionable Jura, this goes under the Portuguese moniker. Think a swirl of ripe red berries soused with root spice, a dash of pepper, orange rind, strewn herb, tamarind and anise. This coaxes one in for another glass, then another. Dangerous stuff in the most beautiful sense. This country should make more wines like this. Screwcap. **Rating** 92 **To** 2022 $30 NG
Tom Bowler McLaren Vale Nero d'Avola 2018 This is a slurpy nero that manages to curb the grape's jammy and dusty tendencies in the name of blueberry, pine, kirsch and a whiff of lilac, lifted by a bright tang inherent to the gently extractive nature of the whole-berry regime. Delicious! Screwcap. **Rating** 91 **To** 2021 $30 NG
Pee Wee McLaren Vale Nero d'Avola Novello 2019 This is a lightly quashed red of bright bing cherry, cumquat, candied orange rind and inherent freshness, so intrinsic to its lightweighted 'smashability'. Thrills with chill! Screwcap. **Rating** 90 **To** 2020 $25 NG

♟♟♟♟ **Yoyo Pinot Gris 2019 Rating** 89 **To** 2022 $20 NG

Lisa McGuigan Wines

2198 Broke Road, Pokolbin, NSW 2320 **Region** Various
T 0418 424 382 **www.**lisamcguiganwines.com **Open** Thurs–Mon 11–5
Winemaker Liz Silkman, Lisa McGuigan **Est.** 2010 **Dozens** 10 000
Lisa McGuigan is a fourth-generation member of a famous Hunter Valley winemaking dynasty, started many decades ago by Perc McGuigan and more recently (and perhaps more famously) led by Brian McGuigan. In 1999 Lisa started Tempus Two from her garage, and under the McGuigan-Simeon (now Australian Vintage) umbrella, the volume rose to 250 000 dozen before she left in 2007 to start a retail wine business. In '10 she turned full circle, starting her own business in the Hunter Valley and using the winemaking skills of Liz Silkman, whom she had headhunted for Tempus Two, and who is now also chief winemaker at First Creek Wines. Lisa opened her cellar door in December '19. Located within the Blaxland's complex on Broke Road, the VAMP venue and wine room brings together wine, oysters, art and fashion.

Liz Heidenreich Wines ★★★★★

PO Box 783, Clare, SA 5453 **Region** Clare Valley
T 0407 710 244 **www.**lizheidenreichwines.com **Open** Thurs–Mon 11–5
Winemaker Liz Heidenreich **Est.** 2018 **Dozens** 1300 **Vyds** 6ha
In 1866 Liz Heidenreich's great-great-grandfather Georg Adam Heidenreich, a Lutheran minister, was sent from Hamburg to the Barossa Valley to provide religious care and instruction for those living in the parish of Bethany. In 1936 Liz Heidenreich's grandfather planted vines at Vine Vale; those vines still in production, still owned and managed by the Heidenreich family. After 15 years as an intensive care nurse, Liz decided to follow her family heritage and enrolled in a post-graduate winemaking degree course at the University of Adelaide. After working in many different winemaking regions in Australia and abroad, she says her spiritual wine homes are the Barossa and Clare valleys. The red wines she makes are from the family-owned old vines in the Barossa Valley, while her other focus of riesling comes from the Clare Valley, more particularly O'Leary Walker, where she makes small parcels of fruit and also undertakes the contract winemaking of Peter Teakle wines. Exports to China.

♟♟♟♟♟ **Watervale Riesling 2019** The yields were very low across the Clare Valley in '19 but the quality was very high. This wine achieves the difficulty of dealing with flavours going over-the-top without losing the brightness and freshness the palate displays. It's lemon/lime/green apple sorbet all in one mouthful. Acidity of 7.5g/l and a pH of 2.88 are the indicia of a high quality riesling wherever it may be grown. Screwcap. 11.5% alc. **Rating** 96 **To** 2030 $24 ✪
Barossa Valley Shiraz 2017 Hand-picked early in the morning, 20–day ferment, matured for 18 months in French oak (25% new). Lovely wine, the

built-in superfine tannins a feature giving light and shade to a wine that took full advantage of the year. Screwcap. 14.7% alc. **Rating** 95 **To** 2037 $30 ✪

Lobethal Road Wines ★★★★★

2254 Onkaparinga Valley Road, Mount Torrens, SA 5244 **Region** Adelaide Hills
T (08) 8389 4595 **www**.lobethalroad.com **Open** W'ends & public hols 11–5
Winemaker David Neyle, Michael Sykes **Est.** 1998 **Dozens** 6500 **Vyds** 10.5ha
Dave Neyle and Inga Lidums bring diverse, but very relevant, experience to the Lobethal Road vineyard; the lion's share planted to shiraz, with smaller amounts of chardonnay, tempranillo, sauvignon blanc and graciano. Dave has been in vineyard development and management in SA and Tasmania since 1990. Inga has 25+ years' experience in marketing and graphic design in Australia and overseas, with a focus on the wine and food industries. The property is managed with minimal chemical input. Exports to the UK and Switzerland.

♟♟♟♟♟ **Adelaide Hills Pinot Gris 2019** Hand-picked, whole-bunch pressed into stainless steel and 2–3yo French barriques, 20% barrel-fermented, partial mlf. A very good example of why pinot gris is suited to the Adelaide Hills; the high, cool region zeroing in on the grape's spiced-up personality. So delicious. Spiced apple, nougat, nashi pear. Screwcap. 13% alc. **Rating** 95 **To** 2025 $25 JP ✪
Carey Gully Adelaide Hills Pinot Noir 2017 Carey Gully is high (550m) in the Adelaide Hills and eminently suited to streamlined, herbal-edged pinot noir. Stays true to the cool-climate model of cranberry, red cherry, white pepper and tomato leaf aromas. Goes on to explore similar ground with the addition of a light gaminess. Sustained finish. Screwcap. 11.8% alc. **Rating** 94 **To** 2028 $25 JP ✪
Maja Late Disgorged 2012 Chardonnay-based sparklings are riding a popularity wave at the moment, but late-disgorged examples are a rare treat. It takes great personal and financial patience to mature a wine on lees for 7 years. This is a powerful sparkling that works plush flavours of gingerbread, grilled grapefruit and nuts into a taut frame. Diam. 12% alc. **Rating** 94 $45 JP

♟♟♟♟♛ **Adelaide Hills Rose 2019** Rating 93 To 2025 $25 JP ✪
Adelaide Hills Sauvignon Blanc 2019 Rating 92 To 2026 $22 JP ✪
Adelaide Hills Shiraz 2017 Rating 91 To 2026 $25 JP
Adelaide Hills Chardonnay 2018 Rating 90 To 2025 $25 JP
Adelaide Hills Tempranillo 2018 Rating 90 To 2026 $25 JP

Lofty Valley Wines ★★★★☆

110 Collins Road, Summertown, SA 5141 **Region** Adelaide Hills
T 0400 930 818 **www**.loftyvalleywines.com.au **Open** W'ends by appt
Winemaker Peter Leske **Est.** 2004 **Dozens** 400 **Vyds** 3ha
Medical practitioner Dr Brian Gilbert began collecting wine when he was 19, flirting with the idea of becoming a winemaker before being pointed firmly in the direction of medicine by his parents. Thirty or so years later he purchased a blackberry and gorse-infested 12ha property in the Adelaide Hills, eventually obtaining permission to establish a vineyard. Chardonnay (2ha) was planted in 2004 and 1ha of pinot noir in '07, both on steep slopes.

♟♟♟♟♟ **Ascent Single Vineyard Adelaide Hills Chardonnay 2018** White peach, white flowers, cream and cedar wood flavours charge through the palate in impressive fashion. This is a powerful chardonnay, its quality clear. It finishes taut and tense but give it another year or 2 in the bottle and it will really sing. Screwcap. 13.4% alc. **Rating** 95 **To** 2028 $35 CM ✪

♟♟♟♟♛ **Pinot Noir Rose 2019** Rating 93 To 2023 $30 CM
Steeped Single Vineyard Pinot Noir 2018 Rating 93 To 2030 $40 CM

Logan Wines   ★★★★☆

Castlereagh Highway, Apple Tree Flat, Mudgee, NSW 2850 **Region** Mudgee/Orange
T (02) 6373 1333 **www**.loganwines.com.au **Open** 7 days 10–5
Winemaker Peter Logan, Jake Sheedy **Est.** 1997 **Dozens** 50 000
Logan is a family-owned and operated business with its emphasis on cool-climate wines
from Orange and Mudgee. The business is run by husband and wife team Peter (winemaker)
and Hannah (sales and marketing). Peter majored in biology and chemistry at Macquarie
University, moving into the pharmaceutical world working as a process chemist. In a reversal
of the usual roles, his father encouraged him to change careers and Peter obtained a Graduate
Diploma in Oenology from the University of Adelaide in 1996. The winery and tasting room
are situated on the Mudgee vineyard but the best wines are all made from grapes grown in
the Orange region. Exports to the EU, Japan and other major markets.

ꝐꝐꝐꝐꝐ Vintage M Orange Cuvee 2016 Traditionally crafted across the 3 principal
Champagne varieties (chardonnay dominant at 63%) with extended time on lees
(33 months). The dosage is a meagre 2g/l. The first whiff reminds me of walking
past bakeries in the early hours in Paris: brioche and glaze. The palate, creamy but
impressively fresh. Nothing austere but a stream of palpably natural acidity driving
length of finish and desire for another glass. An apero-style extraordinaire. Cork.
Rating 95 $40 NG

ꝐꝐꝐꝐꝐ Weemala Orange Sauvignon Blanc 2018 Rating 93 To 2022 $20 NG ✪
Weemala Orange Gewurztraminer 2019 Rating 92 To 2022 $20 NG ✪
Orange Sauvignon Blanc 2019 Rating 92 To 2023 $25 NG ✪
Orange Chardonnay 2019 Rating 92 To 2024 $27 NG
Clementine de la mer 2019 Rating 92 To 2022 $25 NG ✪
Ridge of Tears Mudgee Shiraz 2017 Rating 92 To 2024 $50 NG
Orange Shiraz 2017 Rating 92 To 2022 $28 NG
Weemala Orange Riesling 2019 Rating 91 To 2025 $20 NG ✪
Ridge of Tears Orange Shiraz 2017 Rating 91 To 2023 $50 NG
Weemala Central Ranges Merlot 2017 Rating 91 To 2022 $20 NG ✪
Orange Cabernet Merlot 2016 Rating 91 To 2022 $28 NG
Weemala Mudgee Tempranillo 2018 Rating 91 To 2022 $20 NG ✪
Weemala Orange Pinot Gris 2019 Rating 90 To 2022 $20 NG ✪
Hannah Orange Rose 2019 Rating 90 To 2020 $23 NG

 # Lone Palm Vineyard   ★★★☆

PO Box 288, Tanunda, SA 5352 **Region** Barossa Valley
T 0411 861 604 **www**.lonepalmvineyard.com.au **Open** Not
Winemaker Thomas White **Est.** 2019 **Dozens** 1500 **Vyds** 7ha
Lone Palm has 7ha of shiraz, planted in 1992, at Marananga on the western ridge of the
Barossa Valley. The vineyard gets its name from a single old palm tree next to the original
cottage, built in the late 1800s. The wines are made in a generous style, open-fermented slowly
and gently basket-pressed. The wines are available from the website and www.winesdirect.
com.au. Exports to China.

ꝐꝐꝐꝐ Crossings Barossa Valley Shiraz 2017 Two clones, vinified separately, blended
post-mlf, 14 months in barrel. Light to medium-bodied, easy drinking. Diam.
15% alc. Rating 89 To 2027 $60
Hillside Barossa Valley Shiraz 2017 Westerly facing block, mulched with straw
and bird netting. Medium-bodied. Has depth, but little or no personality. Diam.
15% alc. Rating 89 To 2023 $120
Selection Barossa Valley Shiraz 2017 Counterintuitively, the 16% alcohol
isn't as obvious as the 15% in the Hillside Shiraz. It's really hard to understand the
rationale for the pricing. What other virtues the wines have, they are all much
the same. Diam. Rating 89 To 2025 $250

Longline Wines

PO Box 131, McLaren Vale, SA 5171 **Region** McLaren Vale/Adelaide Hills
T 0415 244 124 **www**.longlinewines.com.au **Open** Not
Winemaker Paul Carpenter **Est.** 2013 **Dozens** 800
The name reflects the changing nature of the Carpenter family's activities. Over 40 years ago
Bob Carpenter gave up his job as a bank manager to become a longline fisherman at Goolwa;
this was in turn replaced by a move to McLaren Vale for farming activities. Son Paul graduated
from the University of Adelaide and began his professional life as a cereal researcher for the
university, but a vintage job at Geoff Merrill Wines at the end of his university studies led him
to switch to winemaking. Over the next 20 years he worked both locally and internationally,
in the Rhône Valley and Beaujolais and at Archery Summit in Oregon. Back in Australia he
worked for Hardys and Wirra Wirra, and is currently senior winemaker at Hardys Tintara.
Together with partner Martine, he secures small parcels of outstanding grapes from four
grower vineyards of grenache and shiraz (three vineyards in McLaren Vale, the fourth in the
Adelaide Hills).

♟♟♟♟♟ Albright McLaren Vale Grenache 2018 A dry-grown single vineyard planted
in '47 on the edge of Onkaparinga Gorge in Blewitt Springs. About 25% whole
bunches and wild ferment, 22 days on skins then pressed to a concrete egg and left
on lees for 9 months, bottled unfined and unfiltered. Given all that and the price,
what a bargain. It segues from the juicy red fruits and musk lollies into savoury
territory quickly. Lighter framed with neat sandy tannins and refreshing acidity.
Delicious drinking. Screwcap. 14.5% alc. **Rating** 95 **To** 2028 $26 JF ✪
GSM McLaren Vale Grenache Shiraz Mourvedre 2018 As with the other
Longline wines, this is stamped with drinkability thanks to the 55/25/20% split
perfectly proportioning the outcome. Heady aromas and vibrant flavours of red
berries, cinnamon and a hint of mint, yet quite savoury. Everything just sits right.
It's medium-weighted, buoyant as the supple tannins with some raw silk texture
glide across the palate Screwcap. 14.5% alc. **Rating** 95 **To** 2028 $22 JF ✪

♟♟♟♟♟ Bimini Twist McLaren Vale Rose 2019 **Rating** 93 **To** 2022 $20 JF ✪

Longview Vineyard

Pound Road, Macclesfield, SA 5153 **Region** Adelaide Hills
T (08) 8388 9694 **www**.longviewvineyard.com.au **Open** 7 days 11–5
Winemaker Ben Glaetzer, Michael Sykes **Est.** 1995 **Dozens** 30 000 **Vyds** 58.7ha
With a lifelong involvement in wine and hospitality, the Saturno family have been at the
helm of Longview since 2007. Further plantings of barbera, gruner veltliner, new clones of
chardonnay and pinot grigio have been added to the existing 20-year-old shiraz, cabernet
sauvignon, nebbiolo and sauvignon blanc. Winemaking is overseen by Ben Glaetzer, in close
consultation with Peter and Mark Saturno. A new cellar door and kitchen was unveiled in
'17, adding to 12 accommodation suites, a popular function room and unique food and wine
events in the vineyard. This family-owned, estate-grown producer exports to 14 countries,
including the UK, Ireland, the US, Canada, Denmark, the Netherlands, Hungary, Germany,
Singapore, Thailand, Hong Kong and China.

♟♟♟♟♟ Adelaide Hills Nebbiolo Riserva 2018 The real deal. Alluring nebbiolo scent,
floral intensity underwritten by a dried herbal intrigue and a quiet power. Rose
petal, plum, orange rind, grilled almond with a whiff of licorice. The grape's
notorious tannins are tamed, just enough, allowing a glimpse into the beauty
beneath. An absorbing wine. Diam. 14% alc. **Rating** 96 **To** 2033 $50 JP ✪
Yakka Adelaide Hills Shiraz 2017 Matured for 15 months in new and used
French hogsheads. A most attractive wine that has taken full advantage of the
'17 vintage: finesse, length and elegance. The red and black cherry/berry fruits
intermingle with notes of spice and oak. The balance and length of this medium-
bodied wine can't be faulted. Screwcap. 14% alc. **Rating** 95 **To** 2037 $30 ✪
Devil's Elbow Adelaide Hills Cabernet Sauvignon 2017 Always a star
performer, Devil's Elbow is consistently blessed each vintage with energy and life

that you can taste. Black and red soused berries, baked earth, leather, warm spice. Reveals some savoury influences, grainy tannins and a touch of rusticity that all adds up. Keeps you coming back for more. Screwcap. 14% alc. **Rating** 95 **To** 2032 $30 JP ✪

Fresco Red 2019 Fresco is in the vino novello style, intended for early drinking. A blend of nebbiolo, pinot nero, sangiovese and barbera. It bursts with sunny, fruit intensity of cranberry, red cherry, pomegranate bite and rosehip. No oak, just the sheer joy of drinking this jubey, tasty youngster, maybe even chilling it down when the temperature rises. It's that kind of wine. Screwcap. 13% alc. **Rating** 95 **To** 2030 $26 JP ✪

Nebbiolo Rosato 2019 Bright salmon-pink. Talk about relaxed, this is one laidback, subtle rose with a broad-ranging application at the table. It's super versatile due in large part to its fine textured dusty, white pepper, sour cherry properties delivered via bright acidity. Lick of confection on the finish is a lasting gift. Screwcap. 12.5% alc. **Rating** 94 **To** 2027 $26 JP ✪

ΨΨΨΨ℘ Iron Knob Riesling 2019 **Rating** 93 **To** 2029 $21 ✪
Whippet Sauvignon Blanc 2019 **Rating** 92 **To** 2024 $21 JP ✪
Vista Shiraz Barbera 2018 **Rating** 92 **To** 2025 $24 ✪
Barbera 2018 **Rating** 91 **To** 2026 $40 JP

Loonie Wine Co   ★★★★★

RSD1436 Meadows Road, Willunga, SA 5172 **Region** McLaren Vale
T 0428 581 177 **www**.monterrawines.com.au **Open** Not
Winemaker Mike Farmilo, Daniel Zuzolo **Est.** 2014 **Dozens** 20000 **Vyds** 15ha
Yet another venture by Canadian-born and raised (but long-term McLaren Vale resident) Norm Doole (in partnership with Mike Farmilo and Nick Whiteway). A grapegrower for decades, Norm founded DOWIE DOOLE with Drew Dowie in 1995. Loonie Wine Co (formerly Monterra) has been a centre of activity in McLaren Vale in recent years. It flew under the radar when established in 2014, busy with barrel finance and logistics and Norm Doole's mind-spinning roles with the Willunga Basin Water Company, Southern Adelaide Economic Development Board and Boar's Rock. Wines are made from the Adelaide Hills, McLaren Vale, Barossa Valley and Fleurieu Peninsula. Exports to the US, Canada, Sri Lanka, Malaysia, Thailand, Singapore, Hong Kong and China.

ΨΨΨΨΨ Monterra Reserve McLaren Vale Shiraz 2017 From 4 vineyards, separately vinified and matured for 18 months before blending. A Star Wars hero, its intensity and length brooking no argument. Blackberry, dark chocolate and French oak follow the style of previous vintages, '17 giving added presence. Screwcap. 14.5% alc. **Rating** 96 **To** 2037 $40 ✪
Colab and Bloom McLaren Vale Grenache 2018 Light, clear colour. A bright and fresh grenache; red berries, red fruits and spice all speak out from a very well made wine, in particular its low (for grenache) alcohol. A long, ultra-juicy and fresh finish. Screwcap. 14% alc. **Rating** 95 **To** 2028 $25 ✪
Monterra Reserve Fleurieu Cabernet Sauvignon 2017 Another great Monterra red, but then '17 was a tailor-made vintage for cabernet in the Fleurieu. Has length thanks to dill pickle tannins (which I mean as a compliment). Screwcap. 14.5% alc. **Rating** 95 **To** 2032 $22 ✪

ΨΨΨΨ℘ Colab and Bloom McLaren Vale Montepulciano 2018 **Rating** 91 **To** 2026 $25
Monterra Mt Pleasant Adelaide Hills Pinot Noir 2018 **Rating** 90 **To** 2025 $28
Monterra Fleurieu Shiraz 2018 **Rating** 90 **To** 2025 $22
Colab and Bloom Fleurieu Tempranillo 2018 **Rating** 90 **To** 2024 $25

Lost Buoy Wines

c/- Evans & Ayers, PO Box 460, Adelaide, SA 5001 **Region** McLaren Vale
T 0400 505 043 **www**.lostbuoywines.com.au **Open** Not
Winemaker Phil Christiansen **Est.** 2010 **Dozens** 8000 **Vyds** 18.5ha
The Lost Buoy vineyard and estate is perched high on the cliffs at Port Willunga in McLaren Vale, overlooking the Gulf of St Vincent. The 6ha 'home block' is planted to grenache and shiraz, the region's foundation varieties. The red wines are made by experienced local contract winemaker Phil Christiansen. Rose is made from estate-grown grenache, while a series of white wines, sourced from McLaren Vale and Adelaide Hills, are made by experienced local winemakers. Exports to Canada, Singapore and Hong Kong.

McLaren Vale Shiraz 2017 Has that '17 red vintage stamped all over it: vibrant varietal fruit expression, an overarching elegance, spicy tannins underpinning the length of the palate, and a finish that simply says 'more please'. Screwcap. 14.5% alc. **Rating** 94 **To** 2032 $25 ○

McLaren Vale Grenache 2018 A most attractive grenache with striking purity of varietal flavour, picked at the right moment. Clear crimson-purple, the red fruits bounce off savoury nuances (a percentage of whole bunch used?) on the long finish. Screwcap. 14% alc. **Rating** 94 **To** 2033 $25 ○

Lou Miranda Estate

1876 Barossa Valley Way, Rowland Flat, SA 5352 **Region** Barossa Valley
T (08) 8524 4537 **www**.loumirandaestate.com.au **Open** Mon–Fri 10–4, w'ends 11–4
Winemaker Lou Miranda, Angela Miranda **Est.** 2005 **Dozens** 20 000 **Vyds** 23.29ha
Lou Miranda's daughters Lisa and Victoria are the driving force behind the estate, albeit with continuing hands-on involvement from Lou. The jewels in the crown of the estate plantings are 0.5ha of mourvedre planted in 1897 and 1.5ha of shiraz planted in 1907. The remaining vines have been planted gradually since '95, the varietal choice widened by cabernet sauvignon, merlot, chardonnay and pinot grigio. Exports to all major markets.

Master Piero Barossa Valley Shiraz 2016 A wine dedicated to future generations. Deep lush garnet throughout. Scents of the Aussie saltbush, sage and thyme enhance a wine with a big Barossa stamp of ripe black fruit and panforte spice. Glossy, a touch flamboyant to taste but never alcoholic or extracted, it is dense and powerful on the palate. A wine to put down for those future generations. Diam. 14.5% alc. **Rating** 96 **To** 2050 $167 JP

Old Vine Barossa Valley Shiraz Mataro 2016 Christmas comes early in a shiraz/mataro chock-full of sweet, plump raisiny fruitcake and plum pudding characters. Built large and complex, less for speedy drinking and more for the cellar, which will give the wine time to resolve the high tone American oak influence. From the old school of Barossa red winemaking, it is also a celebration of old vines with the mataro planted in 1898. Screwcap. 14.5% alc. **Rating** 94 **To** 2029 $90 JP

Super Luigi 2018 An unusual blend, but then a winemaker only turns 70 once. Lou Miranda put sagrantino and shiraz together and aged it in medium-toast American oak barrels for 12 months. Sagrantino is the dominant partner, bringing a bouquet of pretty flowers to the party: violet, acacia, peony. On the palate, cabernet raises its head, twisting back and forth from a foundation of solid tannin to a pantry of cooking spices; five-spice and wild berries add an exotic touch. Cork. 14.5% alc. **Rating** 94 **To** 2045 $53 JP

Leone Barossa Valley Pinot Grigio 2019 Rating 90 **To** 2027 $26 JP
Single Vineyard Barossa Valley Shiraz 2015 Rating 90 **To** 2030 $90 JP

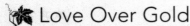 # Love Over Gold

PO Box 117, Nuriootpa, SA 5355 **Region** Barossa Valley
T 0437 091 277 **www**.loveovergold.com.au **Open** Not
Winemaker Contract **Est.** 2014 **Dozens** 400 **Vyds** 6.25ha
Loved by all who knew him, Bob McLean stood large (one nickname was The Jolly Green Giant) over many parts of the SA wine industry and in 1997 he purchased a block of shiraz in the Eden Valley planted by the Pollner family in 1858, tended by the family for almost 150 years. Bob became very ill, ultimately passing away in April 2015. He was a friend of one of the Barossa's most esteemed grapegrowers, Joel Matschoss, who effectively looked after the vineyard in the last years of Bob's life. In '14 Joel showed the fruit to Pierre-Henri Morel, newly arrived from the Northern Rhône Valley, where he had been Michel Chapoutier's right-hand man. Pierre-Henri was so impressed, he and Joel purchased the fruit, vinified it and Love Over Gold was born. In '16 they created Avenue to Gold from a younger block on the same property. A joint venture followed between Joel, Pierre-Henri, Michael Twelftree and Tim Hower to acquire the property. The plan is to expand the vineyard size and to buy parcels of high quality Eden Valley fruit, including grenache. Exports to the UK, the US, Canada, France, Korea, Singapore and China.

ÿÿÿÿÿ Eden Valley Shiraz 2014 Exceptionally clever packaging with a double-sheet label. The infinitely painstaking vinification might be seen to justify the price, particularly in export markets. The colour is still bright, the blackberry and satsuma plum fruit well balanced, the structure good. Diam. **Rating** 96 To 2029 $300

Avenue to Gold Mengler's Hill Eden Valley Shiraz 2016 Hand-picked and sorted with infinite care and patience berry by berry, and where whole bunches used, damaged berries removed. Full-bodied, but not to excess. The flavours range from plum through to blackberry, but with a juicy generosity. Fruit, oak and tannins are exactly proportioned. Diam. 14.5% alc. **Rating** 95 To 2031 $70

Eden Valley Shiraz 2015 Bottle no. 451. Four signatures on the label, one a highly regarded Eden Valley grower, one a winemaker, one a marketing consultant, the last not known to me. This is a good wine, the oak a little pushy but it can easily be ignored. Cork. 14.1% alc. **Rating** 94 To 2029 $300

ÿÿÿÿÿ Avenue to Gold Mengler's Hill Shiraz 2017 Rating 91 To 2027 $70

Lowe Wines

Tinja Lane, Mudgee, NSW 2850 **Region** Mudgee
T (02) 6372 0800 **www**.lowewine.com.au **Open** 7 days 10–5
Winemaker David Lowe, Paul Martung **Est.** 1987 **Dozens** 15 000 **Vyds** 41.3ha
Lowe Wines has undergone a number of changes in recent years, the most recent being the acquisition of Louee and its two vineyards. The first is at Rylstone, led by shiraz, cabernet sauvignon, petit verdot and merlot, with chardonnay, cabernet franc, verdelho and viognier making up the balance. The second is on Nullo Mountain, bordered by Wollemi National Park, at an altitude of 1100m (high by any standards) and often the coolest location in Australia. Lowe Wines continues with its organic profile. The Tinja property has been in the Lowe family ownership for five generations.

ÿÿÿÿÿ Block 8 Organic Mudgee Shiraz 2017 Matured in new and 1yo French puncheons for 12 months, then in used 4500l American oak casks. No niggles here – it is a very good medium-bodied, supple shiraz with abundant red cherry and berry fruit; the tannins resolved. The balance impeccable. Screwcap. 14.6% alc. Rating 95 To 2037 $35 ✪

Organic Mudgee Zinfandel 2017 Open-fermented in wax-lined fermenters, part matured in French and American puncheons, part in a 4500l foudre for 2 years. It exceeds expectations with a spicy tapestry of red and purple fruits, ripe spicy tannins and a long finish. Cork. 14.8% alc. **Rating** 94 **To** 2030 $75

ÿÿÿÿ Block 5 Organic Mudgee Shiraz 2017 Rating 89 $50

Lyons Will Estate ★★★★☆

60 Whalans Track, Lancefield, Vic 3435 **Region** Macedon Ranges
T 0412 681 940 **www**.lyonswillestate.com.au **Open** 4th w'end of each month 11–5
Winemaker Oliver Rapson, Renata Morello **Est.** 1996 **Dozens** 1100 **Vyds** 4.2ha
Oliver Rapson (with a background in digital advertising) and Renata Morello (a physiotherapist with a PhD in public health) believe the Macedon Ranges has the best of both worlds: less than an hour's drive to Melbourne, ideal for pinot and chardonnay and still sparsely settled. The property had 2ha of vines planted in 1996: pinot noir clones D5V12, D4V2 and 115 and chardonnay. They have extended the pinot noir to 1.2ha, increasing the 115 and introducing MV6, and planted 1ha each of riesling and gamay. Oliver makes the Pinot Noir and Chardonnay, Renata the Riesling and Gamay.

🍷🍷🍷🍷🍷 Macedon Ranges Pinot Noir 2017 Clones D5V12, 115, D4V2 and MV6, vinified separately; hand-picked, bunch-sorted, 85% destemmed, 15% whole bunches, open-fermented, 12 months in French barriques (20% new), not fined or filtered. Clarity of colour, of varietal red cherry, of mouthfeel, of length, of ripeness. Diam. 12.5% alc. **Rating** 96 **To** 2030 $37 ❂

Macedon Ranges Riesling 2019 Hand-picked, destemmed, 6–8 hours skin contact, fermented in used oak, matured for 3 months. Bright straw-green. The vinification may have helped with the acidity (which is quite soft) but hasn't impacted on the juicy citrus and lemon curd flavours. The indicative response is simple – just drink it. Diam. 12% alc. **Rating** 94 **To** 2030 $36

Macedon Ranges Chardonnay 2018 Hand-picked, fermented in barrel (20% new), matured for 11 months on lees. Has that edgy acidity ex no mlf that underwrites its longevity. Diam. 13% alc. **Rating** 94 **To** 2030 $39

🍷🍷🍷🍷🍷 Macedon Ranges Gamay 2018 **Rating** 91 **To** 2028 $39

M. Chapoutier Australia ★★★★☆

141–143 High Street, Heathcote, Vic 3523 **Region** Pyrenees/Heathcote
T (03) 5433 2411 **www**.mchapoutieraustralia.com **Open** W'ends 10–5 or by appt
Winemaker Michel Chapoutier **Est.** 1998 **Dozens** 8000 **Vyds** 48ha
M. Chapoutier Australia is the eponymous offshoot of the famous Rhône Valley producer. The business focuses on vineyards in the Pyrenees, Heathcote and Beechworth with collaboration from Ron Laughton of Jasper Hill and Rick Kinzbrunner of Giaconda. After first establishing a vineyard in Heathcote adjacent to Jasper Hill (see La Pleiade), Chapoutier purchased the Malakoff Vineyard in the Pyrenees to create Domaine Terlato & Chapoutier (the Terlato & Chapoutier joint venture was established in 2000; Terlato still owns 50% of the Malakoff Vineyard). In '09 Michel Chapoutier purchased two neighbouring vineyards, Landsborough Valley and Shays Flat; all these are now fully owned by Tournon. (Tournon consists of Landsborough Valley and Shays Flat estates in the Pyrenees and Lady's Lane Estate in Heathcote.) Exports to all major markets.

🍷🍷🍷🍷🍷 Domaine Terlato and Chapoutier L-Block Pyrenees Shiraz 2015 Hand-picked from the 0.9ha block, crushed and destemmed, wild-fermented, 35 days on skins, 15 months' maturation in French oak (20% new). Very bright colour for its age. Medium-bodied, juicy red cherry/plum fruit, lively spice and fine tannins on the long, well balanced finish. Cork. 15% alc. **Rating** 95 **To** 2030 $80

Tournon Lady's Lane Vineyard Heathcote Shiraz 2016 Hand-picked and bunch-sorted, wild-fermented in a concrete tank, 35 days on skins, matured for 15 months in French oak (20% new). Good colour. A fresh, medium-bodied palate with finely polished tannins woven through red and purple fruits. Cork. 14% alc. **Rating** 94 **To** 2036 $50

🍷🍷🍷🍷🍷 Tournon Mathilda Shiraz 2017 **Rating** 90 **To** 2027 $18 ❂
Domaine Terlato and Chapoutier Lieu-Dit Malakoff Pyrenees Shiraz 2016 **Rating** 90 **To** 2031 $40
Tournon Landsborough Vineyard Pyrenees Grenache 2016 **Rating** 90 **To** 2026 $30

Mac Forbes

Graceburn Wine Room, 11A Green Street, Healesville, Vic 3777 **Region** Yarra Valley/
Strathbogie Ranges
T (03) 9005 5822 **www**.macforbes.com **Open** Sun–Mon 12–7, Thurs–Sat 12–11
Winemaker Mac Forbes, Hannah Hodges **Est.** 2004 **Dozens** 6000

Mac Forbes cut his vinous teeth at Mount Mary, where he was winemaker for several years before heading overseas in 2002. He spent two years in London working for Southcorp in a marketing liaison role, then travelled to Portugal and Austria to gain further winemaking experience. He returned to the Yarra Valley prior to the '05 vintage, purchasing grapes to make his own wines. He has a two-tier portfolio: first, the Victorian range, employing unusual varieties or unusual winemaking techniques; and second, the Yarra Valley range of multiple terroir-based offerings of chardonnay and pinot noir. Exports to the UK, the US, Canada, Norway, Thailand, Singapore, Hong Kong and China.

Villages Woori Yallock Pinot Noir 2019 MV6, hand-picked and sorted, 20% crushed and destemmed, fermented with 60% whole berry, 20% whole bunch, 13 days on skins, matured in old oak and a large concrete vat. Much deeper in colour than prior vintages. Red berries and plum, superfine tannins. Diam. **Rating** 96 **To** 2032 $55 ○

Hugh 2017 Made from 50% cabernet sauvignon, 25% cabernet franc, 23% petit verdot and 2% merlot; 90% whole berry, 10% whole bunch, wild yeast–open fermented, 12 days on skins, matured in small old oak for 13 months. Bright, moderately deep hue. Medium-bodied but has the drive and impact one might expect from a fuller-bodied wine thanks to the synergy of the blend in the hands of Mac Forbes and the quality of the vintage. Cork. 12.5% alc. **Rating** 96 **To** 2042 $75 ○

EB47 Concrete Kingdom Riesling 2019 Hand-picked from a vineyard at 800m in the Strathbogie Ranges, crushed and destemmed, wild-fermented, normally with some residual sugar but this vintage fermented dry. A very expressive palate, lime/lemon and crisp acidity dispute primacy but, because the balance is so good, neither prevails. Screwcap. 11% alc. **Rating** 95 **To** 2030 $50

Villages Gladysdale Chardonnay 2019 Made with 60% Mendoza, 40% P58 clones; hand-picked, crushed and destemmed, fermented and matured in old small-format barrels for 10 months. A chardonnay of class and substance, white peach and nectarine girdled by citrussy acidity. Has the length for which Yarra Valley chardonnay is known. Diam. **Rating** 95 **To** 2030 $55

Villages Yarra Junction Pinot Noir 2019 Hand-picked and sorted, open-fermented, 20% crushed and destemmed, 45% whole berry, 35% whole bunch, matured in old oak and a large concrete vat. Lighter in hue than its sibling, but bright and clear. Excellent bouquet, fragrant rose petal and cherry blossom aromas. The palate is spicy, the red fruits with complex texture and structure underpinning the fruit. Diam. **Rating** 95 **To** 2029 $55

Yarra Valley Syrah 2018 Hand-picked, the bunches hand-sorted, 20% crushed and destemmed, 50% whole berry, 30% whole bunch, wild-fermented, 14 days on skins, matured for 10 months in small old oak. A delicious medium-bodied shiraz, supple and smooth, red fruits in the lead, fine-spun tannins extending the long finish. Screwcap. 12.5% alc. **Rating** 95 **To** 2038 $30 ○

EB40 Flaming Nebbiolo 2017 Hand-picked and sorted, wild-fermented with 100% whole berries, 25 days on skins, matured in large and small old oak for 12 months. Bright, light garnet-red. A mix of every known cherry from fresh to maraschino on the bouquet. Nebbiolo is a wolf in sheep's clothing with its tannins, super length is the SWALK. Cork. 13.5% alc. **Rating** 95 **To** 2032 $45

Villages Woori Yallock Chardonnay 2019 Clone I10V1, identical vinification to Gladysdale. There is a trace of reduction on the bouquet, the palate with savoury grapefruit and white peach flavours. Diam. **Rating** 94 **To** 2029 $55

Yarra Valley Pinot Noir 2018 Hand-picked, bunch-sorted, 40% crushed and destemmed, 30% whole berry, 30% whole bunch, wild-fermented, 18 days on skins, matured in small and large French oak (5% new) for 11 months. Highly fragrant and pure in Mac Forbes style. Spicy elements emerging. Still youthful. Screwcap. 11% alc. **Rating** 94 **To** 2028 $30

🍷🍷🍷🍷 **Spring Riesling 2019 Rating** 93 **To** 2030 $30
Yarra Valley Chardonnay 2018 Rating 93 **To** 2028 $30
RS3 Strathbogie Ranges Riesling 2019 Rating 92 **To** 2029 $42

Macaw Creek Wines ★★★★

Macaw Creek Road, Riverton, SA 5412 **Region** Mount Lofty Ranges zone
T (08) 8847 2657 **www**.macawcreekwines.com.au **Open** By appt
Winemaker Rodney Hooper **Est.** 1992 **Dozens** 8000 **Vyds** 10ha
The property on which Macaw Creek Wines is established has been owned by the Hooper family since the 1850s but development of the estate vineyards did not begin until 1995. The Macaw Creek brand was established in '92 with wines made from grapes from other regions. Rodney Hooper is a highly qualified and skilled winemaker with experience in many parts of Australia and in Germany, France and the US. Exports to Canada, Sweden, Norway, the Netherlands, Finland and China.

🍷🍷🍷🍷 **Reserve Basket Pressed Mount Lofty Ranges Malbec 2018** No indication why this is a reserve or what that means. Still, the colour is deep, vibrant, inky purple. Appealing aromas from violets, black plums to sweet tobacco. The medium-bodied palate is surprisingly tight; sinewy grainy tannins and piercing acidity keeps this lively. Screwcap. 13.5% alc. **Rating** 90 **To** 2026 $35 JF

McGlashan's Wallington Estate ★★★★★

225 Swan Bay Road, Wallington, Vic 3221 **Region** Geelong
T (03) 5250 5760 **www**.mcglashans.com.au **Open** Thurs–Sun 11–5, Jan 7 days
Winemaker Robin Brockett (Contract) **Est.** 1996 **Dozens** 2500 **Vyds** 12ha
Russell and Jan McGlashan began the establishment of their vineyard in 1996. Chardonnay (6ha) and pinot noir (4ha) make up the bulk of the plantings, the remainder shiraz and pinot gris (1ha each). The wines are made by Robin Brockett, with his usual skill and attention to detail. The cellar door offers food and music, with four cottages offering vineyard accommodation.

🍷🍷🍷🍷 **Bellarine Peninsula Pinot Grigio 2019** Pours pale pastel pink. Bruised pear and baked apples spiced with cinnamon. Some phenolics add to the texture yet a reserved style. Screwcap. 13% alc. **Rating** 90 **To** 2021 $30 JF
Bellarine Peninsula Pinot Noir 2018 Soft and gentle with its light cherry flavour, spiced with cinnamon. Some grip to the tannins, but it's a drink-now style. No need to overthink it. Screwcap. 13.5% alc. **Rating** 90 **To** 2025 $34 JF

McGuigan Wines ★★★★☆

447 McDonalds Road, Pokolbin, NSW 2320 **Region** Hunter Valley
T (02) 4998 4111 **www**.mcguiganwines.com.au **Open** 7 days 9.30–5
Winemaker Thomas Jung **Est.** 1992 **Dozens** 4.3 million **Vyds** 2000ha
McGuigan Wines is an Australian wine brand operating under parent company Australian Vintage Ltd. McGuigan represents four generations of Australian winemaking and, while its roots are firmly planted in the Hunter Valley, its vine holdings extend across SA, from the Barossa Valley to the Adelaide Hills and the Eden and Clare valleys, into Victoria and NSW. McGuigan Wines' processing facilities operate out of three core regions: the Hunter Valley, Sunraysia and the Barossa Valley. Exports to all major markets.

🍷🍷🍷🍷🍷 **The Shortlist Eden Valley Riesling 2019** Harvested and pressed off skins immediately, cultured yeast ferment, clarified, bottled. Sourced from low yielding, old vines and made to perfectly protect and amplify the purity and beauty of Eden Valley riesling. Concentration of fruit flavour is the key with layer upon layer of deep lemon and lime flavours with lifted florals. Utterly beguiling. Screwcap. 12% alc. **Rating** 96 **To** 2031 $29 JP ✪

The Shortlist Hunter Valley Semillon 2019 A classic Hunter Valley semillon right here with early picked fruit, lowish alcohol, fermentation in stainless steel tanks with aromatic yeast and little else. Sings from the hymn book. Straw-green in hue. Beautiful aromatics of spring blossom and jasmine, lemon curd, nashi pear. Fruit purity is maintained throughout. Zesty, lemony acidity refreshes. Screwcap. 11.3% alc. **Rating** 94 **To** 2030 $30 JP **☉**

The Shortlist Adelaide Hills Chardonnay 2018 Wild ferment in oak, aged in new French hogsheads and lees stirred for 8 months. Another Adelaide Hills chardonnay showcasing the region's innate ability to produce stunning, varietally intense examples of the grape. It captures nectarine, white peach, mandarin, almond meal, struck-match on the nose. Palate is warm and generous and a touch savoury. Hits all the high notes. Screwcap. 13% alc. **Rating** 94 **To** 2031 $29 JP **☉**

The Shortlist Barossa Valley Shiraz 2017 Here McGuigan looks to the Barossa for a different style of shiraz for its The Shortlist portfolio. Barossa power and oomph is present from the word go. Toast, roasted nuts, vanilla pod, intense blackberry pastille, clove, licorice and more on the nose. This is a big wine, a tad extractive, that wears its 16 months in new French and American oak with pride. McGuigan came to the Barossa, it saw, it conquered. Screwcap. 14.5% alc. **Rating** 94 **To** 2034 $29 JP **☉**

🍷🍷🍷🍷⟨ **The Shortlist Cabernet Sauvignon 2017** **Rating** 92 **To** 2031 $29 JP
Personal Valley Chardonnay 2018 **Rating** 91 **To** 2027 $50 JP
Bin 9000 Semillon 2019 **Rating** 90 **To** 2028 $25 JP
The Shortlist Chardonnay 2017 **Rating** 90 **To** 2027 $30
Personal Reserve Shiraz 2018 **Rating** 90 **To** 2030 $75 JP
The Shortlist Shiraz 2016 **Rating** 90 **To** 2036 $30
The Shortlist Montepulciano 2018 **Rating** 90 **To** 2025 $29 JP
The Shortlist Montepulciano 2017 **Rating** 90 **To** 2027 $30

McHenry Hohnen Vintners ★★★★★

5962 Caves Road, Margaret River, WA 6285 **Region** Margaret River
T (08) 9757 7600 **www**.mchenryhohnen.com.au **Open** 7 days 10.30–4.30
Winemaker Jacopo Dalli Cani **Est.** 2004 **Dozens** 7500 **Vyds** 50ha
The McHenry and Hohnen families have a long history of grapegrowing and winemaking in Margaret River. They joined forces in 2004 to create McHenry Hohnen with the aim of producing wines honest to region, site and variety. Vines have been established on the McHenry, Calgardup Brook and Rocky Road properties, all farmed biodynamically. Exports to the UK, Singapore, Japan and China.

🍷🍷🍷🍷🍷 **Rolling Stone 2016** Cabernet sauvignon 36%, malbec 27%, merlot 27%, petit verdot 10%. It sits on the bolder side of medium weight but it's elegant and superbly persistent. It presents a velvety flow of blackcurrant, dark chocolate, gravel, peppercorn and wood smoke–like flavours and, while the pull of tannin is strong, the flow of fruit will not be halted. Sensational example of a Margaret River cabernet blend. Screwcap. 14.8% alc. **Rating** 97 **To** 2045 $125 CM **☉**

🍷🍷🍷🍷🍷 **Burnside Vineyard Margaret River Chardonnay 2018** It's a flinty, funky chardonnay on the one hand, and powerful and long on the other. This really does establish its quality in emphatic terms. Nectarine, fig, grapefruit, grilled nut and spice characters drive through the wine's more matchsticky notes. There's a pure, strong drive of acidity running from start to finish too. It's a top drawer release. Screwcap. 13.2% alc. **Rating** 96 **To** 2029 $65 CM **☉**

Hazel's Vineyard Margaret River Chardonnay 2018 This single vineyard series is full of stars but this is arguably the brightest of them in the intensity of fruit and the corresponding length of flavour. It attacks straight up and simply doesn't let go. It's polished and tidy but boy, does its motor hum. Screwcap. 13.3% alc. **Rating** 96 **To** 2031 $65 CM **☉**

Hazel's Vineyard Margaret River Cabernet Sauvignon 2017 Firm, perfumed, well fruited and impressive. A beautiful example of the glory of cabernet. Minted blackcurrant, chicory and dark chocolate flavours cruise authoritatively through the palate. Everything here is in high class order. Screwcap. 13.8% alc. **Rating** 96 **To** 2039 $70 CM ○

Calgardup Brook Vineyard Margaret River Chardonnay 2018 Fine-boned and lengthy, but it doesn't leave flavour behind. Elegant power is a good way to describe it. It's flinty but not too much so, fleshed with stone fruit, touched up with meal and green apple, and intricately complex to close. All the while sweet fruit flows. It's an easy wine to get excited about. Screwcap. 13.3% alc. **Rating** 95 **To** 2029 $65 CM

Hazel's Vineyard Margaret River Syrah 2018 It was 100% whole bunch, matured in a single 2800l cask. Inherently savoury as you'd expect with roasted nut, twig and peppery spice notes running wild. There's a good push of cherry-plum fruit, graphite and gum leaf notes. It has a perfumed sweetness despite the charge of peppers. It's a beauty. Screwcap. 13.5% alc. **Rating** 95 **To** 2033 $40 CM

Hazel's Vineyard Margaret River Zinfandel 2017 100% destemmed, short cold soak, matured in used American hogsheads. Excellent colour; shows the 50+ years of experience by David Hohnen dating back to his days in California. Its polished display of cherries leaves no room for doubt – this is a lovely wine at a lipsmacking price. Screwcap. 14.2% alc. **Rating** 95 **To** 2027 $38

Laterite Hills Margaret River Chardonnay 2018 From 3 estate vineyards, made in the same way as the 3 single vineyard wines: whole-bunch pressed, oxidative handling, wild yeast and retention of full solids, matured in tank for 3 months on lees. It has built great depth, but less length. Screwcap. 13.3% alc. **Rating** 94 **To** 2025 $38

Hazel's Vineyard Grenache Shiraz Mourvedre 2018 Savoury to its back teeth, but well fruited and textured, not to mention lengthy. It's a nutty, buoyant, boysenberried shiraz with personality galore but with succulence and softness. Screwcap. 14.2% alc. **Rating** 94 **To** 2029 $40 CM

Margaret River BDX 2018 Mostly malbec and cabernet sauvignon with a dash of petit verdot. It's sweet-fruited and svelte with plenty of juicy, berried fruit and the perfume to match. Redcurrant and blackcurrant with peppercorn and cedar wood. Hums along before keen tannin drags it all into line. Screwcap. 14% alc. **Rating** 94 **To** 2033 $40 CM

ŸŸŸŸŸ **Burnside Vineyard Sauvignon Blanc 2018 Rating** 93 **To** 2021 $28
Rocky Road Shiraz 2016 Rating 92 **To** 2030 $25 ○
Rocky Road Semillon Sauvignon Blanc 2018 Rating 90 **To** 2022 $20 ○

McKellar Ridge Wines   ★★★★★

2 Euroka Avenue, Murrumbateman, NSW 2582 **Region** Canberra District
T 0407 482 707 **www.**mckellarridgewines.com.au **Open** W'ends 10–4
Winemaker John Sekoranja, Marina Sekoranja **Est.** 2005 **Dozens** 800 **Vyds** 5.5ha
Dr Brian Johnston established McKellar Ridge in 2005 and after 10 years decided it was time to retire. John and Marina Sekoranja worked with Brian for 12 months before purchasing the winery in July '17. Brian continued to provide support as winemaking consultant during vintage while John and Marina completed Bachelor of Wine Science degrees at CSU. The change has seen an increase in the number of wines available, including from Tumbarumba.

ŸŸŸŸŸ **Canberra District Shiraz 2018** Hand-picked and sorted, 85% crushed and destemmed, 15% whole bunches, 5 days' cold soak, open-fermented, matured in French oak (30% new) for 10 months. A fine cool-climate shiraz with many years, indeed decades, in front of it. Screwcap. 13.9% alc. **Rating** 95 **To** 2043 $45
Canberra District Shiraz Viognier 2018 Co-fermented, 4% viognier, matured in French oak (33% new) for 10 months. The impact of the French oak outweighs that of the fruit early in its life, but in a few years the lovely red and purple fruits will emerge on top. All up, a very good wine. Screwcap. 13.6% alc. **Rating** 95 **To** 2033 $38

ŸŸŸŸ **Canberra District Riesling 2019 Rating** 89 **To** 2022 $28

McLaren Vale III Associates   ★★★★☆

309 Foggo Road, McLaren Vale, SA 5171 **Region** McLaren Vale
T 1800 501 513 **www**.mclarenvaleiiiassociates.com.au **Open** Mon–Fri 9–5, w'ends &
public hols 11–5
Winemaker Campbell Greer **Est.** 1999 **Dozens** 12000 **Vyds** 34ha
McLaren Vale III Associates is a very successful boutique winery owned by Mary and John
Greer and Reg Wymond. An impressive portfolio of estate-grown wines allows them control
over quality and consistency, and thus success in Australian and international wine shows.
The signature wine is Giant Squid Ink Reserve Shiraz. Exports to the US, Canada, Indonesia,
Hong Kong, Singapore, South Korea, Japan and China.

♥♥♥♥♥ The Album Reserve Shiraz 2018 A best barrel selection of what would
appear to be highly extracted and tannic wines that need a minimum of 5 years,
preferably more. Some of the language used on the label is, well, eclectic. It
is a massive, full-bodied shiraz, the hope being that it will retain the balance
it presently has for 10 years. It is that hope that drives the points. Screwcap.
14.5% alc. **Rating** 95 **To** 2038 $80
Squid Ink Reserve Shiraz 2018 'Reserve' doesn't appear on the front label and
the back label is often impossible to understand – a better translation is needed,
filling in the gaps as it were. The grapes are cold-soaked for 2 days, the wine
pressed to American hogsheads (75% new) at 3.5° baume, remaining in oak for
18 months. Full-bodied, dripping with black fruits. Screwcap. 14.5% alc. **Rating** 94
To 2038 $65

♥♥♥♥♡ Abyssal Shiraz 2018 Rating 93 To 2038 $150

McLeish Estate   ★★★★★

462 De Beyers Road, Pokolbin, NSW 2320 **Region** Hunter Valley
T (02) 4998 7754 **www**.mcleishestatewines.com.au **Open** 7 days 10–5
Winemaker Andrew Thomas (Contract) **Est.** 1985 **Dozens** 8000 **Vyds** 17.3ha
Bob and Maryanne McLeish have established a particularly successful business based on estate
plantings. The wines are of consistently high quality, and more than a few have accumulated
show records leading to gold medal–encrusted labels. The quality of the grapes is part of the
equation; the other, the skills of winemaker Andrew Thomas. Over the years, there have been
many trophies and medals, the majority won in the Hunter Valley and Sydney Wine shows.
Exports to the UK, the US and Asia.

♥♥♥♥♥ Cellar Reserve Hunter Valley Semillon 2014 Always a joy to see a cellar
reserve Hunter semillon, and to experience the world-beating charm of aged
semillon from that part of the world. The green apple and citrus characters
of youth are now evolving into so much more: spring blossom, honeysuckle
aromatics with apple tarte tatin and wow, the poached quince is so zingy. Acidity
keeps everything looking fresh. Screwcap. 11% alc. **Rating** 95 **To** 2028 $80 JP
Reserve Hunter Valley Shiraz 2018 Black fruits, pepper, clove and toasted,
nutty oak present a persuasive reserve argument. Taut in structure, savoury notes
are introduced: Hunter dusty back roads with vanilla and lively pepperiness.
Oak casts its shadow, tannins are tight and chalky. You would be doing yourself a
huge disfavour to open now. Screwcap. 13.45% alc. **Rating** 95 **To** 2031 $65 JP
Reserve Hunter Valley Merlot 2017 From the famed '17 Hunter Valley
vintage, comes a stand-alone merlot that rocks. Swish it around a few times and
the perfume grows with redcurrant, stewed plums, cinnamon, panforte. Walks the
line between edgy savouriness and juicy, fruit power. Its 10 months in French oak
has brought some svelte moves. Screwcap. 13% alc. **Rating** 95 **To** 2031 $65 JP
Hunter Valley Semillon 2019 A bright young thing that explores both sides
of the semillon grape with warmer light tropicals and classic cooler lemon butter
citrus notes throughout. And there's a textural component too. Love the mix; the
crunchy acidity is the icing on the cake. Doubt this will ever see the inside of

a cellar, such is its instant, drink-me-now appeal. Screwcap. 11% alc. **Rating** 94
To 2027 $30 JP ○

♀♀♀♀♀ Hunter Valley Chardonnay 2018 Rating 93 To 2028 $30 JP
Hunter Valley Cabernet Sauvignon Shiraz 2018 Rating 93 To 2029 $35 JP
Hunter Valley Merlot 2018 Rating 91 To 2028 $30 JP
Dwyer Hunter Valley Rose 2019 Rating 90 To 2025 $23 JP

McPherson Wines

6 Expo Court, Mount Waverley, Vic 3149 **Region** Nagambie Lakes
T (03) 9263 0200 **www**.mcphersonwines.com.au **Open** Not
Winemaker Jo Nash **Est.** 1968 **Dozens** 500w 000 **Vyds** 262ha

McPherson Wines is, by any standards, a substantial business. Its wines are largely produced for
the export market, with enough sales in Australia to gain some measure of recognition here.
Made at various locations from the estate vineyards and contract-grown grapes, they represent
very good value. McPherson Wines is a joint venture between Andrew McPherson and
Alister Purbrick (Tahbilk), both of whom have had a lifetime of experience in the industry.
Quality is unfailingly good. Exports to all major markets.

♀♀♀♀♀ Don't tell Gary. 2018 From a single vineyard in the Grampians, matured in
French puncheons, 80% new. Shows all the hallmarks of shiraz from this region
with black fruit, licorice and spice, but differs from most in that it's completely
approachable so young. It has structure and tannin but feels like it's ready and
raring to be drunk now, which seems to be the house style. Screwcap. 14.5% alc.
Rating 93 To 2025 $24 SC ○
Jo Nash Single Vineyard Shiraz 2018 From a vineyard in the Strathbogie
Ranges; fermented naturally in small open-pot fermenters, aged for 12 months
in French puncheons. A cool-climate expression of the variety, this seems a little
closed at present although you can see that there are black fruits, licorice and
spice characters within the wine that will emerge more fully with time. Screwcap.
14.5% alc. **Rating** 90 To 2028 $38 SC
Jo Nash Single Vineyard Cabernet Sauvignon 2018 Fruit sourced from a
vineyard on the banks of the Goulburn River. Fermented with wild yeast, separate
parcels spending between 6 and 12 months in French barriques. Red berries are
the main theme on the bouquet with a touch of chocolate (perhaps oak) in the
background. Medium-bodied and quite soft and sweet-fruited on the palate, it's
ready to go now. Screwcap. 14.5% alc. **Rating** 90 To 2028 $38 SC

♀♀♀♀ Jo Nash Single Vineyard Pinot Noir 2018 Rating 89 To 2025 $38 SC
Bella Luna Nero d'Avola 2018 Rating 89 To 2023 $19 SC ○

McWilliam's

Jack McWilliam Road, Hanwood, NSW 2680 **Region** Riverina
T (02) 6963 3400 **www**.mcwilliams.com.au **Open** Wed–Sat 10–4
Winemaker Andrew Higgins, Russell Cody, Harry Kinsman **Est.** 1916 **Dozens** NFP
Vyds 455.7ha

The best wines of this Riverina winery are from other regions (either in whole or in part),
notably Hilltops, Yarra Valley, Tumbarumba and Margaret River. As McWilliam's viticultural
resources have expanded, it has been able to produce regional blends, of startlingly good value,
from across Australia. The winery rating is strongly reliant on the exceptional value for money
of the Hanwood Estate and Inheritance labels. McWilliam's is the owner of Mount Pleasant
(Hunter Valley) and Barwang (Hilltops), the value of which will become ever more apparent
as the ability of these brands to deliver world class wines at appropriate prices is leveraged by
group chief winemaker Jim Chatto (see separate entries for each winery). McWilliam's is a
founding member of Australia's First Families of Wine and is 100% owned by the McWilliam
family. Exports to all major markets.

Magpie Estate ★★★★★

PO Box 126, Tanunda, SA 5352 **Region** Barossa Valley
T (08) 8562 3300 **www**.magpieestate.com **Open** At Rolf Binder
Winemaker Rolf Binder, Noel Young **Est.** 1993 **Dozens** 10 000 **Vyds** 16ha
A partnership between two Rhône-philes: Barossa winemaker, Rolf Binder and UK wine impresario, Noel Young. Fruit is sourced from a group of select growers, with the acquisition of the Smalltown Vineyard in Ebenezer providing estate-grown fruit from the 2017 vintage. Each fruit batch is kept separate, giving the winemakers more blending options. The intent is to make wines that have a sense of place and show true Barossa characters, wines that are complex with a degree of elegance. The winemaking style is focused on minimal intervention, with an aversion to massive extract and over-oaked wines. Rolf and Noel say they have a lot of fun making these wines but they are also very serious about quality. Exports to the UK, Canada, Denmark, Poland, Finland and Singapore.

🍷🍷🍷🍷 **The Election Barossa Valley Shiraz 2016** Part hand-picked, part machine-harvested, 7 days on skins, all new oak, 75% French and 25% American, for 22 months. Supple medium-bodied black fruits, soft tannins, plum fruit; the length and balance spot on. Screwcap. 14% alc. **Rating** 95 **To** 2036 $60

🍷🍷🍷🍷 **The Sack Barossa Valley Shiraz 2017 Rating** 93 **To** 2030 $30
Wit & Shanker Cabernet Sauvignon 2017 Rating 93 **To** 2035 $30
The Black Craft Barossa Valley Shiraz 2018 Rating 92 **To** 2028 $30
The Schnell Barossa Valley Shiraz Grenache 2018 Rating 90 **To** 2025 $25
The Good Luck Club Barossa Valley Cabernet Sauvignon 2017
Rating 90 **To** 2030 $25

Main & Cherry ★★★★★

Main Road, Cherry Gardens, SA 5157 **Region** Adelaide Hills
T 0431 692 791 **www**.mainandcherry.com.au **Open** By appt
Winemaker Michael Sexton **Est.** 2010 **Dozens** 2500 **Vyds** 4.5ha
Michael Sexton grew up on the property and graduated in oenology from the University of Adelaide in 2003. Grapes from the existing shiraz plantings were sold to other wineries but in '10 the first single vineyard Shiraz was made and the Main & Cherry brand name chosen. Since then plantings of bushvine grenache and mataro have been made. The business continues to grow with the purchase of an established vineyard in Clarendon planted to 2.4ha of shiraz and 0.9ha of grenache (the plantings at the Cherry Gardens Vineyard consist of 0.8ha shiraz and 0.2ha each of mataro and grenache). Exports to Vietnam and China.

🍷🍷🍷🍷 **Clarendon McLaren Vale Shiraz 2018** A single vineyard, hand-picked fruit, 15% whole bunches into small open fermenters, wild yeast, 16 days on skins then basket-pressed to old French oak, aged 1 year. Unfined and unfiltered. Seamless. Winemaker Michael Sexton has a knack for teasing out something special. Fuller-bodied with a core of excellent fruit, layered with spice and a depth of flavour. The tannins are sublime – ripe, smooth and silky – the finish seemingly endless. Diam. 14.3% alc. **Rating** 96 **To** 2033 $50 JF ✪
On Skins Adelaide Hills Pinot Gris 2019 An attractive copper-pink. The free-run juice and pressings were fermented on viognier skins for 8 days in 200l beeswax-lined terracotta pots, wild fermentation then basket-pressed to old French oak, 4 months. Reticent aromas, a touch of pepper, florals and baked quince but it's a rage party on the palate. Textural with no shortage of refreshing Campari-tangy acidity and neat phenolics. A real thirst-quencher. Diam. 12.6% alc. **Rating** 95 **To** 2025 $35 JF ✪
Adelaide Hills Pinot Meunier 2019 It's rare to find pinot meunier as a straight varietal, and as lovely as this. Unencumbered by heavy-handed winemaking – wild fermentation, 12 days on skins, basket-pressed to older French oak for 8 months. A delicacy here with its florals, tangy raspberries and fresh herbs. It's lighter framed and so enjoyable thanks to its soft acidity and fine tannins. Diam. 13.2% alc. **Rating** 95 **To** 2028 $40 JF

Adelaide Hills Pinot Noir 2019 At first, deceptively light and delicate. It builds gently. Fragrant with spiced cherries, forest floor and truffle notes. Tangy and juicy, cleansing acidity a driver taking the supple, shapely tannins along for the smooth ride. Some might argue this lacks puissance; I think it's ethereal and beautiful. Diam. 12.8% alc. **Rating** 95 **To** 2028 $35 JF ✪

McLaren Vale Grenache 2019 Fruit hand-picked off a single vineyard in Blewitt Springs, fermented in beeswax lined 200l terracotta pots, 25% whole bunches then basket-pressed to older French oak for 6 months. The result, a very fine, elegant style. Expect spicy, juicy fruit (not too much), raw silk-like tannins and drinkability stamped all over. Diam. 13.8% alc. **Rating** 95 **To** 2027 $30 JF ✪

McLaren Vale Sangiovese 2019 You'd be hard pressed to find a better value drink-now Aussie sangiovese than this beauty, and that should be celebrated. Full of juicy, vibrant cherry fruit, a flutter of dried herbs and earthy spices yet it remains in a savoury spectrum. It's lighter framed with pleasantly grippy, textural tannins. Gorgeous wine. Love it. Screwcap. 13.6% alc. **Rating** 95 **To** 2024 $26 JF ✪

♆♆♆♆♆ **Adelaide Hills Pinot Grigio 2019 Rating** 93 **To** 2024 $25 JF ✪

Main Ridge Estate ★★★★★

80 William Road, Red Hill, Vic 3937 **Region** Mornington Peninsula
T (03) 5989 2686 www.mre.com.au **Open** Mon–Fri 12–4, w'ends 12–5
Winemaker James Sexton, Linda Hodges, Nat White (Consultant) **Est.** 1975
Dozens 1200 **Vyds** 2.8ha
Quietly spoken and charming Nat and Rosalie White founded the first commercial winery on the Mornington Peninsula. It has an immaculately maintained vineyard and equally meticulously run winery. In December 2015, ownership of Main Ridge Estate passed to the Sexton family, following the retirement of Nat and Rosalie after 40 years. Tim and Libby Sexton have an extensive background in large-scale hospitality, first in the UK, then with Zinc at Federation Square, Melbourne and at the MCG. Son James Sexton is completing the Bachelor of Wine Science at CSU. Nat continues as a consultant to Main Ridge.

♆♆♆♆♆ **Mornington Peninsula Chardonnay 2018** Follows in the footsteps of prior vintages, always generous and satisfying – and quite different from most Mornington Peninsula chardonnays. This is layered and rich, citrus on buttered toast to arrive later in the development cycle. Screwcap. 13.8% alc. **Rating** 95 **To** 2028 $65

Half Acre Mornington Peninsula Pinot Noir 2018 An attenuated vintage with a spread of physiological ripeness manifest in impeccably tuned – if very ripe – grapes. A darker tone of fruit, rather than red. Blue scents, too. Succulent with the sheer fruit extract spread across the mouth. Yet what makes this full-weighted pinot delicious is the saline, thirst-slaking briary tannins. Real, moreish grippiness here, mitigating the fruit sweetness while corralling the whole into a savoury meld of nourishment and sappy, spicy length. **Rating** 95 **To** 2026 $90 NG

The Acre Mornington Peninsula Pinot Noir 2018 Made to the same fully destemmed timbre; across the same oak regime. Less propitiously rewarded components based on site-fruit-barrel selection. I am beginning to think that as the joint gets warmer, this notion of hierarchy is likely to be scuttled. Effete. Last year I preferred the freshness and lighter gauze of this cuvee. This year, it is head-to-head. **Rating** 95 **To** 2026 $75 NG

Majella ★★★★★

Lynn Road, Coonawarra, SA 5263 **Region** Coonawarra
T (08) 8736 3055 www.majellawines.com.au **Open** 7 days 10–4.30
Winemaker Bruce Gregory, Michael Marcus **Est.** 1969 **Dozens** 30 000 **Vyds** 60ha
The Lynn family has been in residence in Coonawarra for over four generations, starting as storekeepers, later graduating into grazing. The Majella property was originally owned by Frank Lynn, then purchased in 1960 by nephew George, who ran merinos for wool

production and prime lambs. In '68 Anthony and Brian (the Prof) Lynn established the vineyards, since joined by Peter, Stephen, Nerys and Gerard. Bruce Gregory has been at the helm for every wine made at Majella. The Malleea is one of Coonawarra's classics, The Musician one of Australia's most outstanding red wines selling for less than $20 (having won many trophies and medals). The largely fully mature vineyards are principally shiraz and cabernet sauvignon, with a little riesling and merlot. Exports to the UK, Canada and Asia.

ΨΨΨΨΨ **GPL68 Coonawarra Cabernet Sauvignon 2015** Made from the original cabernet sauvignon vines planted in '68. There's a sturdiness to the tannin but this is essentially an even-tempered cabernet with cassis and bay leaf flavours pushing persuasively towards a dusty, ripe, convincing finish. There are no dips, no hiccups and no heavy-handedness apparent; it's balanced just-so in the best of ways. Screwcap. 14.5% alc. **Rating** 96 **To** 2040 $130 CM
Coonawarra Cabernet Sauvignon 2017 Pristine blackcurrant and bay leaf flavours come whispered with toasty, cedar wood oak. Truth is though, that it tastes of Coonawarra and of cabernet sauvignon and of not much else, in the best of ways. Essence of the variety and of the region. It draws confidently through the palate and is satisfying, and then some, through the finish. Screwcap. 14.5% alc. **Rating** 95 **To** 2036 $35 CM ◐
The Malleea 2015 Prime quality. Smooth as silk. Pure, rich blackcurrant, plum and boysenberry with cedar highlights. Acidity is slightly nervy but the quality of fruit more than compensates. Indeed sweet fruit flavour extends beautifully out through the finish. Screwcap. 14.5% alc. **Rating** 95 **To** 2040 $80 CM

ΨΨΨΨΨ **Shiraz 2017 Rating** 93 **To** 2032 $30 CM
Merlot 2018 Rating 93 **To** 2032 $30 CM
The Musician Cabernet Shiraz 2018 Rating 93 **To** 2026 $18 CM ◐

Mallee Estate Wines

20055 Renmark Avenue, Renmark, SA 5341 **Region** Riverland
T (08) 8595 1088 **www**.malleeestatewines.com.au **Open** 7 days 10.30–5
Winemaker Jim Markeas **Est.** 1998 **Dozens** 70000 **Vyds** 53ha
Peter and Eleni Markeas migrated to Australia in the early 1960s. In '68 they purchased their first mixed fruit block in Renmark and were looking at retirement in '94, a time when many family blocks were for sale. Their son Arthur, who was living in Adelaide at the time, encouraged Peter to take the opposite course and purchase the neighbour's 8ha block giving room for expansion and specialisation. The crux of the deal was that youngest son Jim, then in year 11 at high school, should abandon his career aspirations as a cabinetmaker and instead enrol into the wine science degree at CSU. The plan was realised and production grew, but then drought and oversupply issues led them to investigate the US market. In the wake of the GFC, they abandoned the US and went instead to China, where their wines proved popular at their price. Today Mallee Estate is successful in the US market and has also seen the Chinese market grow substantially; the sales in Australia of negligible importance.

Mandala   ★★★★★

1568 Melba Highway, Dixons Creek, Vic 3775 **Region** Yarra Valley
T (03) 5965 2016 **www**.mandalawines.com.au **Open** Mon–Fri 10–4, w'ends 10–5
Winemaker Charles Smedley, Don Pope **Est.** 2007 **Dozens** 10500 **Vyds** 29ha
Mandala is owned by Charles Smedley, who acquired the established vineyard in 2007. The vineyard has vines up to 25 years old, but the spectacular restaurant and cellar door complex is a more recent addition. The vineyards are primarily at the home base in Dixons Creek, with chardonnay (9.1ha), pinot noir (6.1ha), cabernet sauvignon (4.4ha), sauvignon blanc (2.9ha), shiraz (1.7ha) and merlot (0.4ha). There is a separate 4.4ha vineyard at Yarra Junction planted entirely to pinot noir with an impressive clonal mix. Exports to China.

ΨΨΨΨΨ **Yarra Valley Chardonnay 2018** This is a fine mid-weighted chardonnay. Transparent, precise. Hewn across a beam of reductive tension and judicious oak handling, this crunchy wine corrals apricot, cantaloupe and white fig into a tightly woven kernel of energy. Juicy. Nothing sour, nor brittle. A benchmark at this price, surely. Screwcap. **Rating** 95 **To** 2025 $30 NG ✪

The Mandala Compass Yarra Valley Chardonnay 2018 A selection of the strongest performing plots. Hand harvested, whole-bunch pressed and fermented on full solids. 10 months in French wood, 30% new. Tight. Defined by oak at this nascent stage. Truffle, curd, nougat and cashew. This requires confidence in the fruit to transcend its oaky carriage. With a work-out in the glass and the billow of stone fruit that emerges, I have that confidence. Screwcap. **Rating** 95 **To** 2029 $60 NG

Yarra Valley Pinot Noir 2018 A 100% whole-berry fermentation, 9 months' barrel maturation in 28% new French oak. Engaging pinot noir. Whole-berry fermentation brings a hedonistic perfume that carries with it lifted fresh berries, dried flowers, violets. There's elegance in the glass and an honest accounting of the grape with little oak interference. Supple tannins provide the backdrop to a real little head-turner. Screwcap. 13.2% alc. **Rating** 95 **To** 2030 $30 JP ✪

Yarra Valley Shiraz 2018 Yarra meets a peripheral Northern Rhône pocket. Think Crozes. Perhaps Saint Joseph. Far from prosaic, this is a delicious rendition of pulp, perfume and all that syrah/shiraz can deliver when in the right hands and in the right possie. Think violet, blueberry, nori, tapenade, a whiff of meat and a skein of peppery acidity for length, freshness and a big grin. Drink in large draughts. No point in ageing. Reduction massaged into pleasure. Screwcap. **Rating** 95 **To** 2023 $30 NG ✪

The Mandala Butterfly Yarra Valley Cabernet Sauvignon 2017 Hand-picked in one batch from a Darwinian 20 rows in Dixon's Creek. A 12-day ferment, followed by an additional 30 days in vat with lid closed. Then, French wood for 22 months. An ambitious approach. And judging by the quality of currany fruit and tannic astringency – typically Yarra green bean – a good one. Poised. Plenty in store. Mid-weighted and beautifully savoury, if not angular now. I would hold this with great optimism. Screwcap. **Rating** 95 **To** 2032 $60 NG

Yarra Valley Cabernet Sauvignon 2018 This has been extracted with precision and early to mid-term drinking in mind, without sacrificing flavour or the integrity of cabernet's inherent graphite tannic strictures. There is a dollop of merlot (11%) and franc (4%) for fill and lift respectively. Delicious. Currant and berry fruit. Hedgerow tannins, gently guiding. This is gorgeous Yarra cabernet Screwcap. **Rating** 94 **To** 2028 $30 NG ✪

Yarra Valley Blanc de Blancs 2016 The first fermentation took place in tank and a skerrick (10%) of oak. Thereafter, a second fermentation and 24 months on lees. Well judged, although could be a bit fresher. Like drinking a savoury doughnut, billowing with yeasty inflections. A whiff of stone fruit and mandarin acidity across the finish. Cork. **Rating** 94 $35 NG

🍷🍷🍷🍷🍷 Yarra Valley Pinot Noir 2019 **Rating** 93 **To** 2024 $30 NG
Yarra Valley Chardonnay 2019 **Rating** 92 **To** 2025 $30 NG
Yarra Valley Rose 2019 **Rating** 92 **To** 2020 $20 NG ✪
Yarra Valley Shiraz 2017 **Rating** 92 **To** 2027 $30 JP

Mandoon Estate   ★★★★★

10 Harris Road, Caversham, WA 6055 **Region** Swan District
T (08) 6279 0500 **www**.mandoonestate.com.au **Open** 7 days 10–5
Winemaker Ryan Sudano, Lauren Pileggi **Est.** 2009 **Dozens** 10 000 **Vyds** 40ha
Mandoon Estate, headed by Allan Erceg, made a considerable impression with its wines in a very short time. In 2008 the family purchased a site in Caversham in the Swan Valley. Construction of the winery was completed in time for the first vintage in '10. They have also purchased 20ha in Margaret River. Winemaker Ryan Sudano has metaphorically laid waste to Australian wine shows with the quality of the wines he has made from the Swan Valley, Frankland River and Margaret River.

ΨΨΨΨΨ Reserve Research Station Margaret River Cabernet Sauvignon 2015
From the iconic Bramley Research Station Vineyard originally planted by the
WA Dept of Agriculture in '76 and rehabilitated by Mandoon Estate. Its show
awards include 6 gold medals (including Margaret River Wine Show '16 and '18)
and 11 silver medals. It has a veritable flood of cassis fruit, the tannins typical of
good cabernet and only sufficient to keep hold of the fruit. Screwcap. 14% alc.
Rating 96 **To** 2035 $84

Reserve Frankland River Shiraz 2016 Vivid crimson-purple. Classic cool-
grown shiraz with black cherry/blackberry, licorice and black pepper all within a
medium-bodied frame. Screwcap. 14.5% alc. **Rating** 95 **To** 2036 $49

Margaret River Cabernet Merlot 2016 This 80/20% blend isn't ablaze with
power and richness, if anything it's the reverse. What it does have is excellent
balance, texture and structure. It is a neatly developing gold medal wine with
years left in front of it. Three trophies, 5 gold medals, 11 silver and bronze awards.
Screwcap. 14% alc. **Rating** 95 **To** 2031 $29 ✪

ΨΨΨΨ Margaret River Sauvignon Blanc 2019 Rating 89 **To** 2021 $23

Manly Produce   ★★★

PO Box 1, Watervale, SA 5452 **Region** Clare Valley
T 0439 317 331 **www**.manlyproduce.com.au **Open** Not
Winemaker Contract **Est.** 2018 **Dozens** 130 **Vyds** 28.5ha
This is the venture of sisters Jessica and Abbey Smythe who grew up in country Victoria,
moved to the fashion industry in Melbourne and are in the process of consolidating the
28.5ha family vineyard and farm in Watervale. Jessica's partner and in-laws have assisted the
process, with the grape production from plantings of riesling, grenache, shiraz and cabernet
sauvignon sold to local wineries. The object is to develop experience in all facets of wine
production from grape to bottle to sales and marketing.

Manser Wines   ★★★★

c/- 3 Riviera Court, Pasadena, SA 5042 (postal) **Region** Adelaide Hills
T 0400 251 168 **www**.manserwines.com.au **Open** Not
Winemaker Phil Christiansen **Est.** 2015 **Dozens** 1000 **Vyds** 6ha
Phil Manser has a long history of involvement in the wine industry in various parts of the
world and has now teamed up with brother Kevin and father Bernie to run the family
vineyard. The vineyard was established by Tim James, a skilled winemaker with senior
winemaking and management roles at Hardys and Wirra Wirra. He planted the vineyard to
four clones of shiraz, planted randomly throughout the vineyard in 1997, a common practice
in France. The Mansers acquired the property in 2015, Tim remaining an enthusiastic
spectator during vintage. They also source fruit from a 65-year-old vineyard in Blewitt Springs
and a third vineyard on the McMurtrie Mile which feeds their One Mad Moment range.
Contract winemaker Phil Christiansen looks after the destinies of a considerable number of
vineyards throughout McLaren Vale.

ΨΨΨΨΨ Block 4 Adelaide Hills Shiraz 2017 Hand-picked, crushed and destemmed,
matured in 100% new French oak. Less new oak and/or a shorter time in
barrel would have made an even better wine. Screwcap. 13.7% alc. **Rating** 93
To 2037 $55

Dad's Block Adelaide Hills Shiraz 2018 Matured in 4yo barrels for
18 months. Full-bodied black fruits, tar, licorice and some savoury characters of
uncertain origin. Screwcap. 14.3% alc. **Rating** 92 **To** 2030 $30

One Mad Moment McLaren Vale Shiraz Grenache 2018 Deep crimson-
purple. This full-bodied wine has all the black fruits and tannins of shiraz and
none of the juicy red fruits of grenache. Good balance and structure. Screwcap.
14.3% alc. **Rating** 92 **To** 2038 $30

One Mad Moment McLaren Vale Shiraz Grenache 2017 A 56/44% blend
from Blewitt Springs, 65yo and 85yo vines respectively, picked on the same day

but not co-fermented, the shiraz vinified for extraction, the grenache gently handled, both matured in 4yo American oak. All good except for the 15.7% alcohol. Screwcap. **Rating** 92 **To** 2029 $30

Many Hands Winery ★★★★★

2 Maxwells Road, Coldstream, Vic 3770 **Region** Yarra Valley
T 0400 035 105 **www.**manyhandswinery.com.au **Open** Fri–Mon 10–5
Winemaker Tony Indomenico **Est.** 2010 **Dozens** 1000 **Vyds** 2.6ha
Owners Jennifer Walsh and Tony Indomenico were looking for a tree change when in 2010 they came across a 2.6ha vineyard that had been planted in 1982 to six mainstream varieties, but not always looked after. The first task was to rehabilitate the vineyard and thereafter build a restaurant offering Italian food reflecting Tony's Sicilian heritage. The restaurant opened in '17 and has been well received.

♟♟♟♟♟ Yarra Valley Pinot Noir 2017 Hand-picked clone MV6, bunch-sorted by hand, 14 days on skins with cultured yeast, matured for 12 months in French oak (35% new). The vintage drives the intense, full flavours. Good length and balance, likewise varietal expression. Very good value, better still with further time in bottle. Diam. 13.5% alc. **Rating** 95 **To** 2032 $35 ✪
Yarra Valley Cabernet Sauvignon Cabernet Franc 2018 Cabernet sauvignon 35%, cabernet franc 25%, merlot and malbec 15% each and petit verdot 10%. Hand-picked and sorted, crushed and destemmed, 80% fermented in tank, 20% in barrel, 15–25 days' maceration, matured for 12 months in French oak (35% new). Deep colour. Ultra-concentrated, especially the cabernet, cassis flowing all over the place, the tannins inconsequential. This is the full glass. Diam. 13.5% alc. **Rating** 95 **To** 2040 $42

♟♟♟♟♀ Yarra Valley Rose 2018 **Rating** 90 **To** 2021 $36

Marchand & Burch ★★★★★

PO Box 180, North Fremantle, WA 5159 **Region** Great Southern
T (08) 9336 9600 **www.**burchfamilywines.com.au **Open** Not
Winemaker Janice McDonald, Pascal Marchand **Est.** 2007 **Dozens** 2000 **Vyds** 8.46ha
A joint venture between Canadian-born and Burgundian-trained Pascal Marchand and Burch Family Wines. Grapes are sourced from single vineyards and, in most cases, from single blocks within those vineyards (4.51ha of chardonnay and 3.95ha of pinot noir, in each case variously situated in Mount Barker and Porongurup). Biodynamic practices underpin the viticulture in the Australian and French vineyards, and Burgundian viticultural techniques have been adopted in the Australian vineyards (e.g. narrow rows and high-density plantings, Guyot pruning, vertical shoot positioning and leaf and lateral shoot removal). Exports to the UK, the US and other major markets.

♟♟♟♟♟ Mount Barker Chardonnay 2018 Each hand-picked parcel is hand-sorted, cooled, whole-bunch pressed, only the free-run juice used, wild fermented in French oak (40% new), matured for 9 months, some mlf encouraged in each batch. Its quality cannot be gainsaid, all the flavours in balance, the length good. Screwcap. 13% alc. **Rating** 96 **To** 2032 $78
Margaret River Shiraz 2018 Small-batch winemaking, some whole-bunch addition, matured for 18 months in new and used French barriques. Medium-bodied with an aromatic red fruit bouquet, moving to purple and black on the palate. Screwcap. 14.5% alc. **Rating** 95 **To** 2033 $60
Villages Shiraz 2018 Destemmed to open fermenters with 15–20% whole bunches, pneumatic plunging throughout fermentation, one puncheon (500l) run off at 4° baume, the remainder to used oak. Highly fragrant, medium-bodied, supple and juicy. The oak handling has created a cedary/spicy note and the tannins are 100% integrated. Screwcap. 14.5% alc. **Rating** 95 **To** 2030 $39
Villages Pinot Noir 2018 From the Mount Barrow Vineyard. Fermented with 5–10% whole bunches, one puncheon run off from each fermenter while still

actively fermenting, once dry, pressed to puncheons (20% new) for 6–9 months' maturation. You have to hope that increasing maturity of vines will see greater varietal expression. Screwcap. 13.5% alc. **Rating** 94 **To** 2028 $39

ȶȶȶȶȶ **Villages Chardonnay 2018 Rating** 93 **To** 2030 $39
Villages Rose 2019 Rating 93 **To** 2021 $26 ✪
Mount Barrow Mount Barker Pinot Noir 2018 Rating 92 **To** 2036 $60

Margan Family   ★★★★★

1238 Milbrodale Road, Broke, NSW 2330 **Region** Hunter Valley
T (02) 6579 1317 **www.**margan.com.au **Open** 7 days 10–5
Winemaker Andrew Margan **Est.** 1997 **Dozens** 25 000 **Vyds** 98ha
Andrew Margan, following in his late father's footsteps, entered the wine industry over 20 years ago working as a Flying Winemaker in Europe, then for Tyrrell's. The growth of the Margan Family business over the following years has been the result of unremitting hard work and a keen understanding of the opportunities Australia's most visited wine region provides. They have won innumerable awards in the tourism sector, against competition in the Hunter Valley, across NSW and Australia. The next generation looks similarly set to cover all bases when their parents retire: eldest son Ollie is finishing a double degree in winemaking and viticultural science at the University of Adelaide; daughter Alessa is studying communications at UTS while working in wine and food PR; and younger son James is enrolled in economics at the University of Sydney. Andrew has continued to push the envelope in the range of wines made, without losing focus on the varieties that have made the Hunter famous. He planted barbera in 1998 and since then has progressively added mourvedre, albarino, tempranillo and graciano. Exports to the UK, the US, Sweden and Hong Kong.

ȶȶȶȶȶ **Aged Release Hunter Valley Shiraz 2014** Released when 5yo; '14 following in the footsteps of '07 and '11. From 40+yo estate vines, a mid-press fraction from each batch taken to new French oak to finish fermentation. The great colour signals a vibrant palate of pulsating red fruits, the length utterly exceptional. The balance gives the wine a life span Maurice O'Shea would have admired and he only had corks. Screwcap. 13.5% alc. **Rating** 97 **To** 2054 $100 ✪

ȶȶȶȶȶ **Aged Release Hunter Valley Semillon 2014** Released in May '19 having moved along the development curve, bringing intense fruit in a green spectrum onto a bracing background of crunchy acidity. Screwcap. 12.5% alc. **Rating** 96 **To** 2030 $50 ✪
White Label Fordwich Hill Hunter Valley Shiraz 2018 Estate-grown on red volcanic soils with very low yield, matured for 10 months in 1yo French barriques. A great Hunter Valley vintage faithfully reflected in the bottle. Its elegance and texture are first class, the fine tannins asking how long into the future will they be married to the plum and cherry fruit. Screwcap. 13.5% alc. **Rating** 96 **To** 2043 $50 ✪
White Label Ceres Hill Hunter Valley Semillon 2019 From 30yo vines on grey alluvial clay, the fruit naturally fermented on solids and held on yeast lees for an extended time. The winemaking approach has clearly provided some extra texture and fullness to the palate, retaining the expected freshness and acidity. The citrus, green herb and mineral characters are classic Hunter semillon. To drink now or cellar is win-win. Screwcap. 11.5% alc. **Rating** 95 **To** 2034 $35 SC ✪
Aged Release Hunter Valley Semillon 2015 Hand-picked, crushed and destemmed, cultured yeast, 5 years bottle age before release. Is 5 the magic number for Hunter semillon? No longer a pup, it starts to reveal a little more personality of buttered toast, spiced apple, lantana and fig. Soft and spicy, we start to see the integration of fruit and acidity with just a hint of sweet pear. Bright and juicy acidity sweeps the mouth clean. Screwcap. 11.5% alc. **Rating** 95 **To** 2031 $50 JP
Breaking Ground Hunter Valley Albarino 2019 Hand-picked, crushed and destemmed, wild ferment on full solids, extended contact on lees. A Spanish grape making itself at home in this country, fitting in largely because it enjoys warm,

maritime regions and keeps its acidity. This is another great release from Margan who is helping lead the way with the variety. Honeysuckle, grapefruit pith, lemon-lime zest and striking lemony acidity are hallmarks but it is the oyster shell, saline zip throughout that really makes you sit up and take notice. Screwcap. 12% alc. Rating 95 To 2027 $30 JP ✪

White Label BC4 Hunter Valley Shiraz 2018 From a block of 50yo shiraz vines grafted to 6 clones sourced from heritage vineyards in Pokolbin. This is from a single clone chosen to highlight the fresh fruit flavours achieved with limited oak influence and early bottling. The '18 vintage also helped. Screwcap. 13.5% alc. Rating 95 To 2033 $45

Hunter Valley Shiraz 2017 From 40yo estate vines on a patch of red volcanic soil in Fordwich. The wine is still very fresh, black and red cherry leading the way, the more usual black fruits in a support role. The price is very appealing indeed. Screwcap. 13.5% alc. Rating 95 To 2032 $25 ✪

Breaking Ground Saxonvale Hunter Valley Shiraz Mourvedre 2018 From low-yielding 60yo estate vines, the 80/20% blend co-fermented and matured for 18 months in French barriques (10% new). An expressive fruit-driven bouquet is parlayed into a medium-bodied, elegant palate of red and black fruits. Impressive wine; freshness and balance. Screwcap. 14% alc. Rating 95 To 2038 $40

White Label Fordwich Hill Hunter Valley Semillon 2018 The Fordwich Hill Vineyard is planted on red volcanic soil more usual for red wines, but there's no downside to what is a classic Hunter semillon from a hot but dry vintage. Lemongrass, lemon, citrus and Granny Smith apple flavours are neatly framed by crisp acidity. Screwcap. 11.5% alc. Rating 94 To 2033 $30 ✪

White Label Ceres Hill Hunter Valley Semillon 2018 The vines were planted in '89 on a grey clay east-facing hillside. Its flavour profile is anchored by crisp acidity that will serve the wine well as it ages and the fruit swells. Screwcap. 11% alc. Rating 94 To 2033 $35

Rose & Bramble Hunter Valley Rose 2019 An esoteric blend, primarily of merlot and barbera, with a portion barrel-fermented. The rose of the name is a reflection of the bouquet, not the style, and there is much to be enjoyed with this blend in both terms of sour cherry flavours and mouthfeel. Screwcap. 12.5% alc. Rating 94 To 2022 $25 ✪

Breaking Ground Saxonvale Hunter Valley Mourvedre 2018 Usually part of the field blend, and is in fact the first 100% mourvedre made in the Hunter Valley so far. Several rows of the varietal were identified and picked, then vinified as a single parcel. It's a very persuasive example of mourvedre grown a hemisphere away from its European home. Screwcap. 14% alc. Rating 94 To 2033 $40

🍷🍷🍷🍷 **White Label Fordwich Hill Hunter Valley Semillon 2019** Rating 93 To 2032 $30 SC

White Label BC4 Hunter Valley Shiraz 2019 Rating 93 To 2030 $45 JP

Breaking Ground Ripasso 2014 Rating 93 To 2026 $75 SC

Breaking Ground Ceres Hill Hunter Valley Barbera 2018 Rating 92 To 2027 $40

White Label Timbervines Chardonnay 2019 Rating 91 To 2036 $50 JP

White Label Hunter Valley Chardonnay 2018 Rating 91 To 2022 $40

Breaking Ground Timbervines Hunter Valley Tempranillo Graciano Shiraz 2018 Rating 91 To 2028 $40

Hunter Valley Botrytis Semillon 2016 Rating 90 To 2026 $25 SC

Margaret Hill Vineyard ★★★★

18 Northcote Avenue, Balwyn, Vic 3103 (postal) **Region** Heathcote
T (03) 9836 2168 **www**.guangtiangroup.com.au **Open** Not
Winemaker Ben Portet **Est.** 1996 **Dozens** 1100 **Vyds** 12.5ha

Formerly known as Toolleen Vineyard, the name Margaret Hill Vineyard was chosen by owner Linchun Bao (and wife Chunye Qiu) after they acquired the business from the Huang family in 2010. They have upgraded the vineyard equipment and irrigation system and are restoring full health and vigour to the vineyard, which is equally split between cabernet sauvignon and shiraz. Wines are released under the Margaret Hill and Kudo labels. The quality of the vineyard and the skill of contract winemaker Ben Portet have together been responsible for the high quality of the wines. Exports to China.

🍷🍷🍷🍷🍷 **Kudo Heathcote Shiraz 2018** Hand-picked, matured in French oak for 14 months. A high quality Heathcote shiraz, threading the needle through the eye of the drought, both flavour and its supple texture giving no sign of stress. Perfect cork, perfectly inserted. 14% alc. **Rating** 95 **To** 2038

🍷🍷🍷🍷♀ **Kudo Heathcote Cabernet Sauvignon 2018 Rating** 92 **To** 2028

🌿 Marion's Vineyard  ★★★★★

361 Deviot Road, Deviot, Tas, 7275 **Region** Northern Tasmania
T (03) 6394 7434 **www**.marionsvineyard.com.au **Open** 7 days 11–5
Winemaker Cynthea Semmens **Est.** 1979 **Dozens** 3500 **Vyds** 8ha

Marion's Vineyard was established by young Californian couple Marion and Mark Semmens, backyard winemakers in their home state, who purchased a 14ha rundown apple orchard on the Tamar River in 1980. They had seen the property on a holiday trip to Tasmania the year before, knew instantly that it would make a great vineyard site and returned home to sell their house and possessions that wouldn't come with them. With blood, sweat and tears they planted 4ha of chardonnay, pinot noir, cabernet and Muller Thurgau, subsequently doubling the size. Daughter Cynthea left Tasmania to ultimately obtain a wine marketing degree from Roseworthy and an oenology degree from CSU. She travelled the world undertaking vintages, gaining invaluable experience. Back in Australia she worked for Tatachilla and Hardys Tintara when she met husband-to-be winemaker David Feldheim. They returned to Tasmania in 2010, Cynthea contract-making Marion's Vineyard wines and establishing their own small business Beautiful Isle Wines in '13. In '19, Marion, Cynthea, David and Nick (Cynthea's brother) jointly bought Mark's share of Marion's Vineyard, fulfilling a long-desired succession plan.

🍷🍷🍷🍷🍷 **Chardonnay 2018** Hand-picked in the early morning, the press (and the winery) 30m away, whole-bunch pressed to French puncheons (20% new) for wild ferment, some mlf and 10 months' maturation, then crossflow-filtered to bottle. This has been superbly handled, the wine faultless in its varietal expression, mouthfeel, length and balance. Screwcap. 12.4% alc. **Rating** 97 **To** 2030 $40 ✪

🍷🍷🍷🍷🍷 **Syrah 2016** Hand-picked, open-fermented with 15% whole bunches, 10 days on skins, matured in French puncheons (18% new) for 15 months, the bottles gravity-filled. It's medium-bodied with red cherry and plum plus a garnish of spice and black pepper, the tannins supple, the balance good. Screwcap. 13% alc. **Rating** 95 **To** 2040 $55

Chardonnay 2017 From 40yo vines. Natural acidity is important but sometimes mlf occurs unbidden. This is as fresh as a daisy with grapefruit, white peach and green apple. Screwcap. 12.5% alc. **Rating** 94 **To** 2019 $40

Pinot Gris 2018 Hand-picked, whole-bunch pressed with some lees to used French barriques for wild ferment and natural mlf, lees stirred for 10 months. Has all the mouthfeel sought, in particular the texture of nashi pear/apple fruit. A very good pinot gris. Screwcap. 12.5% alc. **Rating** 94 **To** 2023 $32

Pinot Noir 2018 Hand-picked MV6, whole-berry wild yeast–open fermented, hand-plunged for 8 days, pressed to French barriques (15% new), racked after 12 months, the wine bottled by gravity, not fined or filtered. Its fresh fruits are in the red berry/pomegranate spectrum. Another 3–4 days on the vine might have made an even better wine. Screwcap. 13% alc. **Rating** 94 **To** 2028 $45

🍷🍷🍷🍷♀ **Tempranillo 2018 Rating** 93 **To** 2029 $50
Pinot Noir 2017 Rating 90 **To** 2027 $45
Syrah 2015 Rating 90 **To** 2025 $50

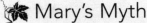 Mary's Myth

144 Johnsons Road, Balhannah, SA 5242 **Region** South Australia
T 0447 608 479 **www.**marysmyth.com.au **Open** Not
Winemaker Alister McMichael **Est.** 2018 **Dozens** 550
This is the as-yet small venture of three childhood friends: Alister McMichael, Evan Starkey and Millie Haigh. Alister grew up in the Adelaide Hills in the late 1990s and after finishing his studies headed to the Mosel Valley to absorb Old World treatment of riesling. His return was not to Australia, but the northern Canterbury district of NZ where for six months he was exposed to minimalistic vinification approaches plus biodynamic/organic inputs. Then he was off again, this time to the very cool Finger Lakes of Upstate New York. While the primary purpose was, of course, to continue the pursuits of riesling, he also observed the making of pinot noir and cabernet franc in such an unlikely environment. Finally back in the Adelaide Hills, Mary's Myth was conceived; the name inspired by the discovery that each of their grandmother's names was Mary.

ΨΨΨΨΨ **Clare Valley Riesling 2019** Radically different from its '18 sibling. A much more relaxed palate feel and texture and ripe citrus and Granny Smith apple flavours – but not entirely at the expense of the '18 structure. Screwcap. 12% alc. **Rating** 94 **To** 2032 $22 ✪

ΨΨΨΨΨ **Clare Valley Riesling 2018 Rating** 93 **To** 2030 $22 ✪

Massena Vineyards

92 Moppa Springs Road, Greenock, SA 5360 **Region** Barossa Valley
T 0408 821 737 **www.**massena.com.au **Open** By appt
Winemaker Jaysen Collins **Est.** 2000 **Dozens** 5000 **Vyds** 4ha
Massena Vineyards draws upon 1ha each of mataro, saperavi, petite syrah and tannat at Nuriootpa, also purchasing grapes from other growers. It is an export-oriented business, although the wines can also be purchased by mail order, which, given both the quality and innovative nature of the wines, seems more than ordinarily worthwhile. Exports to the US, Canada, France, Switzerland, Denmark, South Korea, NZ, Hong Kong and China.

ΨΨΨΨΨ **Stonegarden Single Vineyard Eden Valley Grenache 2018** Old bushvines planted in 1857 prove they still have the X-factor. One batch of fruit destemmed and popped into a ceramic egg on skins for several months (not specified) then into used puncheons; the second batch, whole-bunch fermented in used puncheons. Happy to report this is a sterling drink. It has poise, incredibly velvety tannins, a suppleness and beautiful fruit – which is the very heart of this wine. Cork. 14.5% alc. **Rating** 96 **To** 2028 $70 JF ✪

Stonegarden Single Vineyard Eden Valley Riesling 2019 What makes this stand out is its texture. It has body not just racy acidity. Sure it has heady citrus blossom and ginger spice aromas but the palate cruises along with flavours of lime-curd and lemon tart. Fabulous. Screwcap. 12.5% alc. **Rating** 95 **To** 2029 $32 JF ✪

The Eleventh Hour Barossa Valley Shiraz 2018 A paucity of information but here fruit sourced from vineyards in Greenock, Stone Well and Vine Vale; some whole bunches, some extended skin contact and basket-pressed to used French oak barriques and puncheons for 18 months. Unfined and unfiltered. It's come together brilliantly. It has richness and a depth of flavour matched to a brightness and vivacity across its fuller-bodied palate. Supple, savoury tannins and just lovely fruit shining through. Screwcap. 14.5% alc. **Rating** 95 **To** 2033 $43 JF

The Moonlight Run 2018 Mataro, grenache, shiraz. Teetering on the edge of being too ripe and yet the rich flavours and voluminous palate somehow suck you right in. Blackberry pastilles, all manner of baking spices with pliant and plump tannins yet there is a freshness throughout. Screwcap. 14.5% alc. **Rating** 95 **To** 2028 $32 JF ✪

Massoni

30 Brasser Avenue, Dromana, Vic 3936 **Region** Pyrenees/Mornington Peninsula
T (03) 5981 0711 **www**.massoniwines.com **Open** By appt 10–4.30
Winemaker Adam Dickson **Est.** 1984 **Dozens** 30000 **Vyds** 277.5ha
Massoni is a substantial business owned by the Pellegrino and Ursini families, and is a venture
with two completely distinct arms. In terms of vineyard and land size, by far the larger is the
GlenKara Vineyard in the Pyrenees (269ha). It also has 8.5ha on the Mornington Peninsula
where Massoni started and where it gained its reputation. In 2012 Massoni purchased the
former Tucks Ridge/Red Hill winemaking facility at Dromana. Exports to China.

Pyrenees Cabernet Sauvignon 2013 From the Glenkara Vineyard, matured
for 18 months in French oak. In exceptional condition, the cassis/blackcurrant
fruit in a framework of quality French oak and ripe tannins. Almost too good to
be true. Screwcap. 15% alc. **Rating** 94 To 2038 $25 ✪

El Nino Pyrenees Cabernet Sauvignon 2013 Rating 93 To 2028 $15 ✪
Mornington Peninsula Chardonnay 2016 Rating 91 To 2026 $30
Pyrenees Shiraz 2013 Rating 90 To 2025 $25

Maverick Wines

981 Light Pass Road, Vine Vale, Moorooroo, SA 5352 **Region** Barossa Valley
T 0402 186 416 **www**.maverickwines.com.au **Open** Mon–Tues 1.30–4.30 or by appt
Winemaker Ronald Brown, Leon Deans **Est.** 2004 **Dozens** 10000 **Vyds** 61.7ha
This is the business established by highly experienced vigneron Ronald Brown. It has
evolved, now with seven vineyards across the Barossa and Eden valleys, all transitioned into
biodynamic grape production. The vines range from 40 to almost 150 years old, underpinning
the consistency and quality of the wines. Exports to the UK, France, Russian, Thailand, Japan
and China.

Ahrens' Creek Barossa Valley Shiraz 2017 The 18ha vineyard (with 3ha of
ancestor vine shiraz) was planted in the 1870s by the Lehmann family. Hand-
picked, open-fermented, matured for 22 months in French oak. The quality of
the wine is awesome, its intensity, its focus and its length all of the highest quality.
Diam. 14% alc. **Rating** 98 To 2047 $120 ✪
Trial Hill Eden Valley Shiraz 2017 From an 8ha organic vineyard (with 1.6ha
of old vine shiraz), everything done by hand that could possibly be managed this
way. The freshness of the wine is such that it might coast through 40–50 years
if well stored, the Diam cork perfectly inserted. There is a shimmering red fruit
heart to the wine, small black fruits and fine tannins never likely to break that line
of this awesome wine. 13% alc. **Rating** 97 To 2050 $120 ✪
Ahrens' Creek Barossa Valley Cabernet Sauvignon 2017 Hand-picked,
24 hours' cold soak, small open fermenters, pressed to new French oak for
22 months, only 4 barriques made. A very high quality wine, beautiful line, length
and balance. Diam. 14% alc. **Rating** 97 To 2047 $120 ✪

The Maverick Barossa Shiraz Cabernet Sauvignon 2017 A blend of
2 barriques of shiraz and 1 barrique of cabernet sauvignon. Small open fermenter,
matured for 22 months. Delicious wine, harmonious cassis fruit, superfine tannins;
balanced and long. Diam. 14% alc. **Rating** 96 To 2047 $300
Trial Hill Eden Valley Grenache 2018 Eden Valley's climate is cooler
compared to the Barossa Valley, delivering wines that move more fluidly and with
more grace. Screwcap. 14.5% alc. **Rating** 95 To 2028 $140
Ahrens' Creek Old Vine Barossa Valley Grenache 2018 The weight and
flavour is very different from the '17. It is more traditional Barossa Valley and
not to be denigrated for that. Mouthfilling plum and Turkish delight flavours.
Screwcap. 14.5% alc. **Rating** 94 To 2030 $140

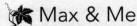 # Max & Me

Eden Valley Hotel, 11 Murray Street, Eden Valley, SA 5235 **Region** Eden Valley
T 0403 250 331 **www.**maxandme.com.au **Open** 7 days 12–5
Winemaker Philip Lehmann **Est.** 2011 **Dozens** 900 **Vyds** 10.22ha
Max is the name of a German shepherd x whippet cross purchased by Phil Lehmann from the RSPCA pound and who introduced Phil to his wife-to-be Sarah during a visit to the Barossa. A dog lover from way back, she fell in love with Max and Phil made it clear she wouldn't get Max unless she married him (Phil). Phil had previously purchased the Boongarrie Estate (on Keyneton Road, at an elevation of 430–460m) with 5.25ha of shiraz and 4.97ha of cabernet sauvignon. They converted the vineyard to (non-certified) organic management, with no herbicides and only copper/sulphur sprays. The benefits are self-evident, reflected in the high quality of the wines made since '11. Sarah raises their two small children and manages direct wine sales. The future is for modest growth, planting riesling and grenache.

Boongarrie Vineyard Eden Valley Shiraz 2017 Selectiv'-harvested at night, open-fermented, maceration pigeage, 9 days on skins, maturation in French hogsheads and puncheons (30% new) for 18 months. A shiraz of great quality and style with the dark berry fruits, the tannins and the oak in perfect harmony. Only 220 dozen made. Screwcap. 14.6% alc. **Rating** 97 **To** 2037 $60 ✪

Boongarrie Vineyard Whole Bunch Eden Valley Syrah 2017 Hand-picked in the first flush of berry ripeness, allowing 30% whole-bunch inclusion in small open fermenters and pigeage for maceration, 10 days on skins, pressed to old French puncheons for 12 months, 140 dozen made. The Max & Me wines all have a touch of magic, this has a bit extra as the fruit flavours float above the tannin and oak components. Screwcap. 14.3% alc. **Rating** 97 **To** 2042 $50 ✪

Boongarrie Vineyard Eden Valley Shiraz 2015 Excellent growing season, yet microscopic yield (0.3t/acre), a hangover from '14. The first vintage with the Pellenc Selectiv' harvester, matured for 18 months in French oak (30% new). Slightly different flavour set, in part due to extra years in bottle, promising great things for the younger wines. Supple balance and harmony are the watchwords. Screwcap. 14.4% alc. **Rating** 96 **To** 2035 $65 ✪

Boongarrie Vineyard Eden Valley Cabernet Sauvignon 2018 The strength and cooler climate of Eden Valley comes in handy in vintages such as '18. Selectiv'-harvested, primary fermentation in open grape receival bins, maturation in French hogsheads (33% new) for 17 months. Bright crimson; fresh, juicy cassis flavours all point to careful control of pH. All things considered, this is a top-flight wine; 190 dozen made. Screwcap. 14.3% alc. **Rating** 96 **To** 2040 $50 ✪

Boongarrie Vineyard Eden Valley Shiraz 2018 This is the House Block, established '98 with cuttings from the Poonawatta Vineyard. Selectiv'-harvested, matured in French hogsheads (50% new) for 19 months, 170 dozen made. Deep crimson-purple, unexpected given the limited maceration. The bouquet and palate are quick to join in, with fresh dark fruits, fine tannins and oak carried with ease by the fruit. Screwcap. 14.8% alc. **Rating** 95 **To** 2038 $60

Boongarrie Vineyard Eden Valley Cabernet Sauvignon 2017 From the east-facing bottom block, Selectiv'-harvested, primary fermentation in grape bins, 65% of the must (cuvee) 35 days' maceration, the other portion on skins for 16 days, the combined parcels matured in French hogsheads (30% new) for 17 months, 190 dozen made. It flaunts its sexy oak in a devil-may-care reprise. Screwcap. 14.6% alc. **Rating** 95 **To** 2037 $50

The House Blend Boongarrie Vineyard Eden Valley Cabernet Sauvignon Shiraz 2018 Both components from the estate, fermentation and maturation as usual, 200 dozen made. Also as usual, the richness and generosity of the wine is exceptional. It is hard to tear yourself away from simply smelling as well as tasting. Screwcap. 14.5% alc. **Rating** 95 **To** 2038 $40

The House Blend Boongarrie Vineyard Eden Valley Cabernet Sauvignon Shiraz 2017 The year was unusual with cabernet and shiraz ripening at the same time (shiraz is usually first); 50% of this wine was co-fermented and left on skins for a month, the other parcels separately vinified, all parcels matured in French hogsheads. A very complex wine of high quality. Whether it captured '17 is another question. Screwcap. 14.7% alc. **Rating** 95 **To** 2036 $40

Woodcarvers Vineyard Mirooloo Road Eden Valley Riesling 2019 Juicy lemon citrus and Granny Smith apple flavours are neatly tied down by minerally acidity that refreshes the mouth on the aftertaste; 270 dozen made. Screwcap. 11.7% alc. **Rating** 94 **To** 2029 $30 ○

Woodcarvers Vineyard Mirooloo Road Eden Valley Riesling 2018 The second Eden Valley release; pressed, cold-settled prior to racking to ferment. It is already rich and open for business however many years await its optimum maturity. Screwcap. 12.7% alc. **Rating** 94 **To** 2025 $30 ○

Boongarrie Vineyard Eden Valley Cabernet Sauvignon 2015 Selectiv'-harvested at night, open-fermented in a grape bin with pigeage for maceration, 10 days on skins, matured in French oak (20% new) for 18 months, 60 dozen made. It's early days but the style foreshadows that which emerged so well so soon thereafter. Screwcap. 14.6% alc. **Rating** 94 **To** 2023 $55

ΨΨΨΨΨ **Boongarrie Vineyard Whole Bunch Eden Valley Syrah 2018 Rating** 93 **To** 2025 $50

Maxwell Wines   ★★★★☆

Olivers Road, McLaren Vale, SA 5171 **Region** McLaren Vale
T (08) 8323 8200 **www**.maxwellwines.com.au **Open** 7 days 10–5
Winemaker Kate Petering, Mark Maxwell **Est.** 1979 **Dozens** 30 000 **Vyds** 40ha

Maxwell Wines has carved out a reputation as a premium producer in McLaren Vale, making some excellent red wines in recent years. The majority of the vines on the estate were planted in 1972, including 19 rows of the highly regarded Reynella clone of cabernet sauvignon. The Ellen Street shiraz block in front of the winery was planted in '53. In a region abounding with first class restaurants (and chefs), Maxwell has responded to the challenge with extensive renovations to the restaurant and cellar door. Kate Petering, formerly chief winemaker at Mount Langi Ghiran, was appointed head winemaker in March '19. Exports to all major markets.

ΨΨΨΨΨ **Four Roads McLaren Vale Grenache 2018** This is firmly of place. Pumice to chalky tannins corral molten kirsch, cranberry, pomegranate, anise and vanilla pod scents; salty acidity propelling it all long. A fine grenache reflective of an exciting time in the Vale. Screwcap. **Rating** 95 **To** 2024 $28 NG ○

Minotaur Reserve McLaren Vale Shiraz 2016 A big step up in price from the rest of the range and rightly so. Intense. Pulverising. Opaque. Saturated mulberry and blueberry notes billow to smoked meat and bbq scents. Not for the faint of heart. Iodine and anise serve as varietal zip codes. When all is a said and done, the sheen of fruit, piney oak and smooth piste of tannins can't be denied. Cork. **Rating** 94 **To** 2028 $95 NG

ΨΨΨΨΨ **Kangaroo Island Shiraz 2018 Rating** 92 **To** 2030 $25 NG ○
Fresca McLaren Vale Grenache 2019 Rating 92 **To** 2022 $25 NG ○
Lime Cave McLaren Vale Cabernet Sauvignon 2018 Rating 92 **To** 2030 $40 NG
Lime Cave McLaren Vale Cabernet Sauvignon 2016 Rating 92 **To** 2036 $40
Small Batch Clan Wine Club McLaren Vale Petit Verdot 2018 Rating 92 **To** 2026 $30 NG
Little Demon McLaren Vale Grenache Rose 2019 Rating 91 **To** 2021 $20 ○
Clan Wine Club Nero d'Avola 2019 Rating 91 **To** 2023 $36 NG
Ellen Street McLaren Vale Shiraz 2017 Rating 90 **To** 2024 $40 NG

Mayer

★★★★★

66 Miller Road, Healesville, Vic 3777 **Region** Yarra Valley
T (03) 5967 3779 **www**.timomayer.com.au **Open** By appt
Winemaker Timo Mayer **Est.** 1999 **Dozens** 2000 **Vyds** 3ha

Timo Mayer, also winemaker at Gembrook Hill Vineyard, teamed with partner Rhonda Ferguson to establish Mayer on the slopes of Mt Toolebewong, 8km south of Healesville. The steepness of those slopes is presumably 'celebrated' in the name given to the vineyard (Bloody Hill). Pinot noir has the lion's share of the high-density vineyard, with smaller amounts of shiraz and chardonnay. Mayer's winemaking credo is minimal interference and handling, and no filtration. The Empire of Dirt wines are a collaboration between son Rivar Ferguson-Mayer and UK importer Ben Henshaw. Exports to the UK, France, Germany, Denmark, Sweden, Singapore and Japan.

♥♥♥♥♥ **Yarra Valley Nebbiolo 2019** Here the oft talked about but seldom seen similarity between pinot noir and nebbiolo is striking. Timo Mayer has made a beautiful wine; its clarity of crimson colour, its violet and rose petal aromas and delicate red cherry/pomegranate palate utterly bewitching. There's not a trace of green/mint/underripe flavours. By far the highest points I've given for an Australia nebbiolo. Diam. 13% alc. **Rating** 98 **To** 2033 $58 ✪

♥♥♥♥♥ **Empire of Dirt Yarra Valley Sauvignon Blanc 2019** This is a ripper. Flush with citrussy goodness with lemon bath salts, zest, orange curd and Fever Tree Mediterranean tonic. There's depth yet a neat acid line keeping it tight, tangy and super delicious. Bravo. Diam. 12.5% alc. **Rating** 95 **To** 2024 $25 JF ✪
Yarra Valley Pinot Noir 2019 Hand-picked, 25% of the grapes from the Bloody Hill Vineyard, whole bunch, semi-carbonic, semi-macerated, 3 weeks on skins, 25% new oak. This is the most powerful of the Mayer pinots. Spiced satsuma plum. Good depth, good future. Diam. 13% alc. **Rating** 95 **To** 2032 $58
Empire of Dirt Yarra Valley Cabernet Sauvignon 2019 Fruit comes off fellow winemaker Behn Payten's vineyard in Healesville. Glorious dark red-purple. Wildly heady with hints of cassis, florals and pencil shavings. The palate is lighter framed but not simple. It has a juiciness and very fine tannins making it delicious and ready to pour. Love it. Diam. 13% alc. **Rating** 95 **To** 2025 $25 JF ✪
Yarra Valley Syrah 2019 Very fresh and bright fruits in a cherry/plum/spice spectrum. Medium-bodied, supple, smooth and very long. Diam. 13% alc. **Rating** 94 **To** 2029 $58
Yarra Valley Merlot 2019 A merlot that's a pleasure to taste and drink. The purity of the flavours are halfway between red cherry and plum. Supple, silky mouthfeel and good length. Diam. 13% alc. **Rating** 94 **To** 2029 $58

♥♥♥♥♀ **Empire of Dirt Yarra Valley Pinot Gris 2019** **Rating** 93 **To** 2022 $25 JF ✪
Dr Mayer Yarra Valley Pinot Noir 2019 **Rating** 93 **To** 2030 $58
Yarra Valley Cabernet 2019 **Rating** 91 **To** 2026 $58

Mayford Wines

★★★★★

6815 Great Alpine Road, Porepunkah, Vic 3740 **Region** Alpine Valleys
T (03) 5756 2528 **www**.mayfordwines.com **Open** By appt
Winemaker Eleana Anderson **Est.** 1995 **Dozens** 800 **Vyds** 3.9ha

The roots of Mayford go back to 1995, when Brian Nicholson planted a small amount of shiraz, chardonnay and tempranillo. Further plantings of shiraz, tempranillo, cabernet sauvignon and malbec have increased the vineyard to 3.9ha; more plantings are planned. In their words, 'In-house winemaking commenced shortly after Brian selected his seasoned winemaker bride in 2002'. Wife and co-owner Eleana Anderson was a Flying Winemaker, working four vintages in Germany while completing her wine science degree at CSU (having much earlier obtained an arts degree). Vintages in Australia included one at Feathertop (also at Porepunkah), where she met her husband-to-be. Initially, she was unenthusiastic about tempranillo, which Brian had planted after consultation with Mark Walpole, Brown Brothers' viticulturist. But since making the first vintage in '06, she has been thoroughly enamoured of the variety. Eleana practises minimalist winemaking, declining to use enzymes, cultured yeasts, tannins and/or copper. Exports to Singapore.

🍷🍷🍷🍷🍷 **Porepunkah Tempranillo 2018** Mayford's hidden valley just keeps turning out top-flight tempranillo. This is as good as any release so far. It's savoury as much as sweet, juicy with flavour as much as it is structured and controlled. Ample flavour without going overboard and a sustained finish. Give it a couple of years in bottle and then start tucking in. Screwcap. 13.9% alc. **Rating** 96 **To** 2029 $40 CM ❂
Porepunkah Shiraz 2017 Excellent spread of flavour and the balance to match. This is another tip-top release. Trademark black cherry flavours almost move into plum; toast and chicory characters come thanks to oak; peppercorn is part of the wine's story. Ultrafine but assertive tannin exerts a certain confidence. All the right moves. Screwcap. 13.9% alc. **Rating** 95 **To** 2035 $42 CM

🍷🍷🍷🍷🍷 **Porepunkah Chardonnay 2018 Rating** 93 **To** 2025 $40 CM

Maygars Hill Winery   ★★★★☆

53 Longwood–Mansfield Road, Longwood, Vic 3665 **Region** Strathbogie Ranges
T 0402 136 448 **www.**maygarshill.com.au **Open** By appt
Winemaker Contract **Est.** 1997 **Dozens** 900 **Vyds** 3.2ha
Jenny Houghton purchased this 8ha property in 1994, planting shiraz (1.9ha) and cabernet sauvignon (1.3ha). The name comes from Lieutenant Colonel Maygar, who fought with outstanding bravery in the Boer War in South Africa in 1901 and was awarded the Victoria Cross. In World War I he rose to command the 8th Light Horse Regiment, winning yet further medals for bravery. The 100th anniversary of Lieutenant Colonel Maygar's death was in 2017. The Shiraz and Cabernet Sauvignon, both in Reserve and standard guise, have been consistently excellent for a number of years. Exports to China.

🍷🍷🍷🍷🍷 **Reserve Shiraz 2017** Maygars Hill vineyard celebrated 20 years in '17; it also marked 100 years since Lt Colonel Maygar's death. It was also a brilliant vintage, producing a medium-bodied wine with intensity and length to its black and red cherry fruit. The balance is exemplary. Screwcap. 14% alc. **Rating** 96 **To** 2037 $42 ❂
Shiraz 2018 In classic Maygars Hill style: the fruit rich and textured, not the least extractive and the oak balanced. Screwcap. **Rating** 94 **To** 2028 $30 ❂
Cabernet Sauvignon 2017 The cool, sometimes wet, growing season was ideal for cabernet sauvignon, enhancing varietal cassis fruit, backed by bay leaf and the occasional hint of Central Victorian mint. This is a lovely wine. Screwcap. 14.1% alc. **Rating** 94 **To** 2032 $28 ❂

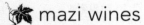 mazi wines   ★★★★

5 Wilbala Road, Longwood, SA 5153 **Region** McLaren Vale
T 0406 615 553 **www.**maziwines.com.au **Open** Not
Winemaker Alex Katsaros, Toby Porter **Est.** 2016 **Dozens** 1500
Lifelong friends Toby Porter and Alex Katsaros always talked about making wine together as an adjunct to their day jobs in wine. Toby has been a winemaker at d'Arenberg for 15+ years and Alex had 10 years' experience working with alternative varieties here and abroad. They decided to only make roses, and more power to them in doing so. Moreover, McLaren Vale is the sole source for their grapes, focusing on grenache, but happy to work with bushvine mataro. The aim is to produce fresh wines with vibrant fruit, normally by crushing and pressing the grapes for a cool ferment in stainless steel, but maturation in old French oak can (and has) been used to build palate complexity without sacrificing fruit. The derivation of the name is as simple as that of their raison d'être – it is Greek for together. Exports to the US, Singapore and Hong Kong.

🍷🍷🍷🍷🍷 **Limited Release McLaren Vale Rose 2019** Made predominantly from mourvedre with a splash of grenache, matured for 5 months in used French oak.

It's a very delicate (very good) style with a juicy texture/flavour. Odd decision to use a cork – drink soon. 13% alc. **Rating** 94 **To** 2020 $44

🍷🍷🍷🍷🍷 **McLaren Vale Grenache Rose 2019 Rating** 90 **To** 2020 $25

Mazza Wines   ★★★★

PO Box 480, Donnybrook, WA 6239 **Region** Geographe
T (08) 9201 1114 **www**.mazza.com.au **Open** Not
Winemaker Contract **Est.** 2002 **Dozens** 1000 **Vyds** 4ha
David and Anne Mazza were inspired by the great wines of Rioja and the Douro Valley, and continue a long-standing family tradition of making wine. They have planted the key varieties of those two regions: tempranillo, graciano, bastardo, souzao, tinta cao and touriga nacional. They believe they were the first Australian vineyard to present this collection of varieties on a single site and I am reasonably certain they are correct. Exports to the UK.

🍷🍷🍷🍷🍷 **Geographe Tinta Cao 2015** Uses the standard Mazza vinification map of hand-picking, 10% whole bunches, 10% crushed, 10 days on skins, 9 months in used French oak. The most successful of the '15 releases with good balance, texture and structure. There are spice and pepper nuances to the bright red cherry fruits, leaving the mouth refreshed (and looking for a second glass). Screwcap. 12.5% alc. **Rating** 94 **To** 2030 $30 ○

🍷🍷🍷🍷🍷 **Geographe Touriga Nacional 2017 Rating** 90 **To** 2025 $32
Geographe Graciano 2016 Rating 90 **To** 2026 $30

Meadowbank Wines   ★★★★★

652 Meadowbank Road, Meadowbank, Tas 7140 **Region** Southern Tasmania
T 0439 448 151 **www**.meadowbank.com.au **Open** Not
Winemaker Peter Dredge **Est.** 1976 **Dozens** 1000 **Vyds** 52ha
In 1976 Gerald and Sue Ellis picked the first grapes from their large Glenora property at the top end of the Derwent River, having planted the vines in '74. There have been four major expansions since, most recently a 10ha planting of pinot noir, chardonnay, syrah and gamay in 2016, lifting the total to 52ha, the major part as fully mature vines. Meadowbank Wines opened its cellar door and restaurant in July '00 at Cambridge in the Coal River Valley. The wines were made next door at what is now Frogmore Creek. Eventually Frogmore Creek purchased Meadowbank's cellar door and restaurant (since they didn't previously have either), leaving Meadowbank to concentrate on further developing its vineyards. Meadowbank supplies grapes to six or so small wineries and also leases 32ha to Accolade. Peter Dredge, having been intimately associated with the vineyard for six years, formed a partnership with the Ellis family (Gerald, Sue, daughter Mardi and her husband, Alex Dean) to relaunch Meadowbank. The wines are made by Peter at Moorilla Estate from the portion of vineyard set aside for the Meadowbank wines. Exports to South-East Asia.

🍷🍷🍷🍷🍷 **Riesling 2019** Hand-picked, whole-bunch pressed, wild-fermented, 4 months on lees, 50% in stainless steel, 50% in used French barriques. One of those wines that captures you just as you are about to move on, for it has a veritable peacock's tail finish, expanding dramatically with the intensity of its lime juice fruit. Screwcap. 12% alc. **Rating** 95 **To** 2034 $35 ○
Chardonnay 2019 Hand-picked, whole-bunch pressed, wild-fermented in French puncheons and barriques (10% new), matured for 9 months. A high quality chardonnay with an intense varietal mix of grapefruit and white peach, oak in the back pocket. Screwcap. 12.5% alc. **Rating** 95 **To** 2029 $50
Gamay 2019 Utterly exceptional. Crimson lit from within. The palate too is a breath of spring air in an orchard in full bloom. Mandatory immediate drinking. Screwcap. 12% alc. **Rating** 95 **To** 2023 $45

Medhurst   ★★★★★

24–26 Medhurst Road, Gruyere, Vic 3770 **Region** Yarra Valley
T (03) 5964 9022 **www**.medhurstwines.com.au **Open** Thurs–Mon & public hols 11–5
Winemaker Simon Steele **Est.** 2000 **Dozens** 6000 **Vyds** 12ha

The wheel has come full circle for Ross and Robyn Wilson. In the course of a very distinguished corporate career, Ross was CEO of Southcorp when it brought the Penfolds, Lindemans and Wynns businesses under its banner. Robyn spent her childhood in the Yarra Valley, her parents living less than a kilometre away from Medhurst. The vineyard is planted to low-yielding sauvignon blanc, chardonnay, pinot noir, cabernet sauvignon and shiraz vines. The winery focuses on small-batch production and also provides contract winemaking services. The visual impact of the winery has been minimised by recessing the building into the slope of land and locating the barrel room underground. The building was recognised for its architectural excellence at the Victorian Architecture Awards. The arrival of Simon Steele (his loss much mourned by Brokenwood) has enhanced the already considerable reputation of Medhurst.

ΨΨΨΨΨ **Reserve Yarra Valley Chardonnay 2018** From 6 rows of a block planted east–west, protected from northerly winds. Top class vinification: 65% new French oak folded within intense, layered white flower/white peach/grapefruit flavours; exceptional length for this single batch; 50 dozen made. Screwcap. 12.5% alc. **Rating** 97 **To** 2028 $70 ✪

ΨΨΨΨΨ **Estate Vineyard Chardonnay 2019** Hand-picked, whole-bunch pressed, wild-fermented and matured in French oak (30% new) for 10 months. An elegant chardonnay, well balanced and long in true Yarra Valley style. While there is an element of restraint, white peach, nectarine and grapefruit are seamlessly united and incorporate cashew/toasted almond complexity. Screwcap. 12.5% alc. **Rating** 96 **To** 2030 $44 ✪

YRB 2019 With 50% pinot noir, 50% shiraz. A great example of a blend that was not even thought of not so long ago, now a permanent feature of the landscape. Medium-bodied. One of its great strengths is the supple mouthfeel, tannins and oak relegated to the back row as luscious cherry fruit takes control. A great success for the vintage. Screwcap. 13% alc. **Rating** 96 **To** 2039 $44 ✪

Reserve Yarra Valley Pinot Noir 2018 Picked from the middle of a block on the middle of the north-by-northwest slope; destemmed, 17 days on skins, 50% new Dargaud & Jaegle oak, 50 dozen made. The perfumed cherry and plum fruit already sings like a bird as the perfume builds. Screwcap. 13% alc. **Rating** 96 **To** 2023 $70 ✪

Reserve Yarra Valley Cabernet 2017 From 20 rows, hand-picked and sorted in the vineyard, destemmed, 30 days on skins, maximum fermentation temperature 25°C, 110 dozen made. Superb vibrant crimson-purple. Silky mouthfeel after 18 months in tightly wrought oak (70% new) and cabernet tannins soar on the finish. Screwcap. 13% alc. **Rating** 96 **To** 2042 $70 ✪

Estate Vineyard Rose 2019 A blend of whole-bunch pressed cabernet sauvignon and shiraz that has succulent mouthfeel and balance. It's one of those wines that won't take no for an answer, demanding the second sip, indeed mouthful, as you find more to enjoy each time you return. Screwcap. 13% alc. **Rating** 95 **To** 2021 $25 ✪

Estate Vineyard Pinot Noir 2019 Hand-picked and sorted, 90% whole berry, 10% whole bunch, 10–15 days on skins, matured in French oak (29% new) for 10 months. Light, clear purple-crimson. Purity is the watchword for both the bouquet and palate, with just a shimmer of tannins, the oak influence not obvious. Silky red fruits are particularly appealing. Screwcap. 13% alc. **Rating** 95 **To** 2030 $50

ΨΨΨΨΨ **Estate Vineyard Sauvignon Blanc 2019** **Rating** 93 **To** 2022 $27 ✪

Meerea Park ★★★★★

Pavilion B, 2144 Broke Road, Pokolbin, NSW 2320 **Region** Hunter Valley
T (02) 4998 7474 **www**.meereapark.com.au **Open** 7 days 10–5
Winemaker Rhys Eather **Est.** 1991 **Dozens** 10 000
This is the project of Rhys and Garth Eather, whose great-great-grandfather, Alexander
Munro, established a famous vineyard in the 19th century, known as Bebeah. While the
range of wines chiefly focuses on semillon and shiraz, it extends to other varieties (including
chardonnay) and also into other regions. Meerea Park's cellar door is located at the striking
Tempus Two winery, owned by the Roche family, situated on the corner of Broke Road and
McDonald Road. It hardly need be said that the quality of the wines, especially with 5 years'
cellaring, is outstanding. Exports to the UK, the US, Canada, Singapore and China.

ΨΨΨΨΨ **Terracotta Individual Vineyard Hunter Valley Semillon 2013** Brilliantly
coloured, it has a delicious collage of lime, honey and mineral flavours. Its purity
and mouthfeel are striking. Drinking the wine now is not a sin if you have
some more in the further recesses of your cellar. Screwcap. 11.5% alc. **Rating** 96
To 2033 $35 ✪
Hell Hole Individual Vineyard Hunter Valley Shiraz 2018 Opaque colour;
this is Hunter shiraz from a great, dry vintage. Juicy plum and blackberry fruit,
then the light to medium-bodied palate holds fast to the finish and aftertaste.
Delicious now with fruit ascendant – drink tonight or in 20+ years' time.
Screwcap. 14% alc. **Rating** 95 **To** 2038 $60
**Cellar Release Alexander Munro Individual Vineyard Hunter Valley
Shiraz 2014** This is a perfect example of a medium-bodied Hunter Valley shiraz.
It has now opened its wings to expose all of its intricate complexities, yet is only
6yo. The almost freakish thing is its indefinite future – think O'Shea. Screwcap.
14% alc. **Rating** 95 **To** 2034 $150
Terracotta Individual Vineyard Hunter Valley Semillon 2015 The coming
of age has just arrived – honey glistens in the backdrop, the foreground still held
firm by acidity, just as it should be. Screwcap. 11% alc. **Rating** 94 **To** 2024 $35

ΨΨΨΨΨ **XYZ Hunter Valley Shiraz 2018** **Rating** 93 **To** 2038 $25 ✪
Indie Individual Vineyard Hunter Valley Cabernet Sauvignon 2018
Rating 93 **To** 2038 $30
Alexander Munro Individual Vineyard Hunter Valley Chardonnay 2019
Rating 91 **To** 2026 $45
Indie Individual Vineyard Hunter Valley Marsanne Roussanne 2018
Rating 91 **To** 2025 $30
Indie Individual Vineyard Hunter Valley Pinot Shiraz 2018 **Rating** 91
To 2038 $30
Hell Hole Individual Vineyard Hunter Valley Semillon 2019 **Rating** 90
To 2024 $30
Alexander Munro Individual Vineyard Hunter Valley Chardonnay 2018
Rating 90 **To** 2022 $45
XYZ Hunter Valley Rose 2019 **Rating** 90 **To** 2022 $25

Mercuri Estate ★★★

9484 Horrocks Highway, Clare, SA 5453 **Region** Clare Valley
www.mercuriestate.com **Open** Not
Winemaker Justin Ardill **Est.** 2015 **Dozens** 5000
This is the venture of Ennio Mercuri, whose family has had a 50-year history in
the manufacturing industry. It's been a staged development, which gained massively with the
acquisition of the 52.6ha Cardinham Estate vineyard, with a history of wines made from
St Clare Vineyard at Leasingham and pinot grigio sourced from the Adelaide Hills. This will
give rise to a number of ranges of wines in the future, along with purchased fruit from selected
sites in other SA regions. Exports to Canada and China.

Mérite Wines ★★★★

PO Box 167, Penola, SA 5277 **Region** Wrattonbully
T 0437 190 244 **www**.meritewines.com **Open** Not
Winemaker Mike Kloak **Est.** 2000 **Dozens** 2000 **Vyds** 40ha

Mérite Wines was established in 2000. It was the end of Mike Kloak and Colleen Miller's protracted search for high quality viticultural land, with a particular focus on the production of merlot utilising recently released clones that hold the promise of producing wine of a quality not previously seen. However, it's not a case of all eggs in the same basket; malbec, cabernet sauvignon and shiraz have also been planted. It was not until '13 that the first small amount of wine was made (most of the grapes were, and will continue to be, sold to other winemakers).

🍷🍷🍷🍷🍷 **Single Vineyard Wrattonbully Merlot 2016** Excellent dark purple hue.
Bright, ripe blackberries, currants and plums mingle with menthol and savoury notes of coffee grounds and woodsy spices. While there's a succulence across the palate, this carries some heft partly from oak, which also imparts bitter green walnut–like tannins that clip the finish. Screwcap. 14.2% alc. **Rating** 93 **To** 2030 $60 JF

Wrattonbully Merlot Rose 2019 A pale pink-copper hue. A frisky rose with pomegranate tang and fresh lemon-orange juice. There's just enough seasoning of ginger spice and fresh herbs with its citrus-sorbet acidity ensuring this is a lively, refreshing drink. Screwcap. 13% alc. **Rating** 92 **To** 2022 $24 JF ○

Merricks Estate ★★★★★

Thompsons Lane, Merricks, Vic 3916 **Region** Mornington Peninsula
T (03) 5989 8416 **www**.merricksestate.com.au **Open** 1st w'end of month, Jan every w'end
Winemaker Simon Black (Contract) **Est.** 1977 **Dozens** 2500 **Vyds** 4ha

Melbourne solicitor George Kefford, with wife Jacky, runs Merricks Estate as a weekend and holiday enterprise. It produces distinctive, spicy, cool-climate shiraz, which has accumulated an impressive array of show trophies and gold medals. As the current tasting notes demonstrate, the fully mature vineyard and skilled contract winemaking by Simon Black are producing top class wines. Exports to Hong Kong.

🍷🍷🍷🍷🍷 **Mornington Peninsula Chardonnay 2018** Hand-picked and sorted, fermented and matured for 12 months in French oak (25% new), partial mlf. A major success for Merricks Estate, with succulent stone fruit flavours, oak merely a support. Screwcap. 13.4% alc. **Rating** 95 **To** 2028 $35 ○

Mornington Peninsula Shiraz 2015 Quite apart from the extra year's age of the Thompson's Lane, this estate wine is substantially fuller bodied with blackberry, licorice and pepper. Mornington Peninsula shiraz was once dogged by issues of (not) ripening, there's no such problem today. Screwcap. 13.8% alc. **Rating** 95 **To** 2035 $35 ○

🍷🍷🍷🍷🍷 **Thompson's Lane Chardonnay 2019** Rating 92 To 2023 $25 ○
Thompson's Lane Shiraz 2016 Rating 92 To 2021 $25 ○
Mornington Peninsula Cabernet Sauvignon 2015 Rating 92 To 2030 $30
Thompson's Lane Pinot Noir 2019 Rating 91 To 2029 $25

Merum Estate ★★★

PO Box 840, Denmark, WA 6333 **Region** Great Southern
T (08) 9848 3443 **www**.merumestate.com.au **Open** Not
Winemaker Harewood Estate (James Kellie) **Est.** 1996 **Dozens** 4000

Merum Estate stirred from slumber after morphing from grower and winemaker to pure grapegrowing after the 2006 vintage in '10. Another change in direction has since seen the sale of the Pemberton vineyard established by Mike Melsom, Mike's retirement and a restructure in partnership with the Capelli family (of The Lake House Denmark).

Mewstone Wines   ★★★★★

11 Flowerpot Jetty Road, Flowerpot, Tas 7163 **Region** Southern Tasmania
T 0439 367 653 **www**.mewstonewines.com.au **Open** 7 days 10–4
Winemaker Jonathan Hughes **Est.** 2011 **Dozens** 4000 **Vyds** 3.65ha

Brothers Matthew and Jonathan (Jonny) Hughes established Mewstone Vineyard on the banks of the D'Entrecasteaux Channel in the tiny hamlet of Flowerpot in 2011. The vineyard is planted on a former cherry orchard, the original 2ha since expanded to 3.65ha consisting mainly of pinot noir (2.1ha) with smaller plantings of riesling, shiraz and chardonnay. Jonny is the winemaker in this family venture; he studied winemaking in NZ before working in Langhorne Creek, Central Otago, Mornington Peninsula, Barolo, Hunter Valley and Okanagan Valley in British Columbia. Heading home to Tasmania, Jonny worked in various roles within the local wine industry before settling in as the assistant winemaker at Moorilla Estate for seven years. With the vineyard established to produce the single site Mewstone wines, the brothers have embarked on a second label, Hughes & Hughes, which focuses on Tasmania as a whole. Purchasing quality grapes from other local vineyards, this label uses slightly unconventional winemaking techniques that Jonny encountered on his world travels. Small-batch production means he can put maximum effort in. Best New Winery in the *Wine Companion 2019*. Exports to Singapore and Hong Kong.

🍷🍷🍷🍷🍷 **D'Entrecasteaux Channel Chardonnay 2018** Estate-grown, pressed straight to barrel, wild-fermented, not fined. Has excellent length, line and focus. Grapefruit and white peach are conventional flavours, the X-factors here are the mouthfeel and lifted aftertaste. Screwcap. 13.2% alc. **Rating** 97 **To** 2029 $60 ☉
Hughes & Hughes Pinot Noir 2018 With 10% whole bunch, 5 months' maturation in oak. Unfined, unfiltered. It's the quiet ones you have to watch, the ones that sneak under your guard and infiltrate your senses. A slow, subtle approach, hints of a quiet presence that grows. Pomegranate here, raspberry clafoutis there, wild rosemary. They gather on the palate and intensify. Herbals add charm. Tannins offer a savoury polish. Screwcap. 13.2% alc. **Rating** 97 **To** 2030 $34 JP ☉

🍷🍷🍷🍷🍷 **D'Entrecasteaux Channel Riesling 2018** Hand-picked, destemmed, soaked, pressed to used French oak for wild fermentation, then kept on lees for 2 months. An extremely interesting – and enjoyable – wine that has harnessed Tasmanian acidity, the flavour blends citrus with custard apple before a bright finish. Screwcap. 12.9% alc. **Rating** 96 **To** 2028 $50 ☉
Hughes & Hughes Chardonnay 2018 Powerfully expressive chardonnay sourced from Tasmania's Derwent Valley that continues to cement the producer's growing reputation for quality. Grapefruit, citrus, mandarin zest, white peach and struck-match aromas. Beautifully integrated oak is a feature and that typical Tassie acid raciness brings with it a long, lingering aftertaste. Screwcap. 13.2% alc. **Rating** 96 **To** 2032 $34 JP ☉
D'Entrecasteaux Channel Pinot Noir 2018 Excellent hue and clarity. High class canopy management and clear vision about style, hence vinification, has resulted in the full canvas of red and black cherry, spice and a perfectly judged winemaker thumbprint. Screwcap. 13.2% alc. **Rating** 96 **To** 2038 $65 ☉
Hughes & Hughes Chardonnay 2019 70% whole-bunch pressed, 30% cold-soaked on skins, wild-fermented in French oak (15% new), partial mlf, not fined or filtered. It all comes together perfectly with a mouthfeel that is harmonious not challenging, the flavours midway between stone fruit and citrus. Screwcap. 13.2% alc. **Rating** 95 **To** 2029 $35 ☉
Hughes & Hughes Pinot Noir 2019 Hand-picked, wild-fermented with 15% whole bunch, 85% whole berry, not fined or filtered. No shrinking violet. Spiced plum, fine-grained tannins. No mention of oak at any stage, although it has to have been used. Screwcap. 13.8% alc. **Rating** 95 **To** 2030 $35 ☉
Hughes & Hughes Riesling 2019 From the vineyards in the north, east and south of Tasmania (the west never to be planted). The bouquet is attractive, with some floral notes. The palate springs up with explosive power, passionfruit, crushed

lime leaves and minerally acidity; it has particularly good balance and length. Screwcap. 12.9% alc. **Rating** 94 **To** 2029 $30 ❂

Hughes & Hughes Sauvignon Blanc 2019 From a single vineyard in the Coal River Valley, fermented in stainless steel with a portion on skins. Sauvignon blanc is typically sulky in Tasmania, but Mewstone has caused it to be happy, with juicy fruit and citrussy acidity. Screwcap. 13.2% alc. **Rating** 94 **To** 2022 $30 ❂

Hughes & Hughes Pinot Gris 2019 Wild-fermented in barrel and stainless steel. Aromas of musk, talc, powder puff and rose petals. The result? Bloody marvellous. Screwcap. 12.7% alc. **Rating** 94 **To** 2021 $30 ❂

🍷🍷🍷🍷 **Hughes & Hughes Rose 2019 Rating** 90 **To** 2021 $30
D'Entrecasteaux Channel Syrah 2018 Rating 90 **To** 2026 $75

Mia Valley Estate ★★★★

203 Daniels Lane, Mia Mia, Vic 3444 **Region** Heathcote
T (03) 5425 5515 **www**.miavalleyestate.com.au **Open** 7 days 10–5
Winemaker Norbert Baumgartner, Pamela Baumgartner, Nick Baumgartner **Est.** 1999
Dozens 1000 **Vyds** 3.2ha

Norbert and Pamela Baumgartner both had indirect connections with wine, and a direct interest in drinking it. In the early 1980s, based in Melbourne, they began a search for suitable vineyard land. However, it proved too difficult to find what they wanted and the plans were put on hold. It took until '98 for them to discover their property: 40ha with softly undulating land and the Mia Mia (pronounced mya-mya) Creek running through it. They planted 1.6ha of shiraz and in 2002 produced their first vintage. It encouraged them to plant another 1.6ha. Along the way Norbert completed winemaking and viticulture courses and worked with David Anderson of Wild Duck Creek, and Peter Beckingham. They made their wines for the '02 to '05 vintages in their air-conditioned garage in Melbourne. In '05 they converted the vineyard shed into a mini-winery, expanding it in '06 to a winery and temporary accommodation, commuting on weekends from Melbourne until '09. They then contended with the '09 bushfires, the '11 rains, floods and disease, a '12 vintage more than they could handle, '14 decimated by frosts and late '15 and '16 severe drought. Are they giving up? No sign of it so far. They have been joined in the winery by son Nick. Exports to the UK, the US, Japan and China.

🍷🍷🍷🍷 **Reserve Heathcote Shiraz 2016** It finishes warm but in general this hefty red carries its alcohol well, not the least because it's packed with sweet, jammy, choc-coated flavour. Licorice allsorts and Jaffa orange flavours do all they can to seduce you. Diam. 16% alc. **Rating** 92 **To** 2028 $35 CM

Heathcote Cabernet Malbec 2017 Mint and chocolate flavours flow into plum, earth and leather. It's an amiable red with decent shape. While it will hold, it's best consumed soonish. Screwcap. 13.4% alc. **Rating** 90 **To** 2025 $30 CM

🍷🍷🍷🍷 **Heathcote Cabernet Sauvignon 2017 Rating** 89 **To** 2026 $30 CM

Michael Hall Wines ★★★★★

103 Langmeil Road, Tanunda, SA 5352 **Region** Mount Lofty Ranges zone
T 0419 126 290 **www**.michaelhallwines.com **Open** Fri–Sat 11–5 or by appt
Winemaker Michael Hall **Est.** 2008 **Dozens** 2500

For reasons no longer relevant (however interesting) Michael Hall was once a jewellery valuer for Sotheby's in Switzerland. He came to Australia in 2001 to pursue winemaking – a lifelong interest – and undertook the wine science degree at CSU, graduating as dux in '05. His vintage work in Australia and France is a veritable who's who of producers: in Australia with Cullen, Giaconda, Henschke, Shaw + Smith, Coldstream Hills and Veritas; in France with Domaine Leflaive, Meo-Camuzet, Vieux Telegraphe and Trevallon. He is now involved full-time with his eponymous brand and the wines are as impressive as his experience suggests they should be. Exports to the UK and the US.

ŶŶŶŶŶ **Piccadilly and Lenswood Adelaide Hills Sauvignon Blanc 2019** From 2 vineyards: Ben's Block part-fermented on skins, the remainder pressed and fermented in barrel; and the Hill Block tank-fermented, matured for 9 months in barrel. Suffice it to say this is a delicious, mouthfilling sauvignon blanc of rare quality. Screwcap. 13.3% alc. **Rating** 96 **To** 2024 $38 **☉**

Flaxman's Valley Eden Valley Syrah 2018 Hand-picked, 95% whole berries, 5% whole bunches, 18 months in French oak (20% new). Michael Hall nailed this one. Lively medium-bodied black cherry/berry fruits, spice, pepper, fine-grained tannins, the oak not obtrusive. Screwcap. 13.6% alc. **Rating** 96 **To** 2038 $50 **☉**

Stone Well Barossa Valley Shiraz 2018 Hand-picked, destemmed, wild yeast–open fermented, matured in French oak (10% new) for 18 months. Plucks the bass strings here in a full-bodied, black-fruited wine with ripe tannins. Thoroughly enjoyable. Screwcap. 14.5% alc. **Rating** 96 **To** 2038 $50 **☉**

Piccadilly Adelaide Hills Chardonnay 2018 Hand-picked, whole-bunch pressed, wild-fermented in French puncheons (20% new), 34% mlf, 9 months on lees. The mlf was perfectly judged, leaving the mouthfeel fresh and grapefruit in the driver's seat. Has length and class to burn. Screwcap. 13.5% alc. **Rating** 95 **To** 2028 $50

Lenswood Adelaide Hills Pinot Noir 2018 Hand-picked, wild yeast–open fermented with 61% whole bunches, matured for 11 months in French oak (35% new). The whole bunch works very well, exotic spiced perfume extended by savoury nuances to the clearly articulated varietal fruit. Screwcap. 13.6% alc. **Rating** 95 **To** 2029 $50

Sang de Pigeon Barossa Valley Shiraz 2018 Hand-picked, destemmed, wild yeast–open fermented, 18 months in French oak (20% new). The complex bouquet gives the illusion of whole bunch (zero used). There's a lightness of touch that was difficult to achieve in '18. Interesting wine. Screwcap. 14.5% alc. **Rating** 94 **To** 2028 $30 **☉**

ŶŶŶŶŶ **Greenock Barossa Valley Roussanne 2019 Rating** 92 **To** 2028 $38

Michel Marie   ★★★★★

PO Box 204, Yenda, NSW 2681 **Region** Riverina
T 0411 718 221 **www**.michelmarie.co **Open** Not
Winemaker Sam Brewer **Est.** 2013 **Dozens** 250 **Vyds** 21ha

Michel and Marie Nehme married in 1969 and migrated to Australia, ultimately moving to the Riverina to bring up their children, including daughter Julie. In the 1980s, after the De Bortoli success of Noble One in 1982, the family decided to only grow botrytis semillon from the 21ha vineyard, selling the grapes until 2013. Michel took great delight in being named the King of Rot but tragedy loomed when he developed pancreatic cancer. With bittersweet timing, the '15 and '16 vintages of the Botrytis Semillon made for them by friend and neighbour Sam Brewer (of Yarran Wines) both won gold medals at the Royal Melbourne Wine Awards '18, the '16 emerging with the trophy. One week after Julie Nehme came back home with the trophy, her father succumbed to cancer. De Bortoli won a silver medal at the same show. Both the '15 and '16 are for sale online, with the '13 museum stock in small quantity and not for sale. Exports to China.

ŶŶŶŶŶ **Nehme Vineyard Botrytis Semillon 2013** This is the freshest of the 3 Michel Marie botrytis semillons, picked at a lower baume and ultimately made at a better baume/sugar level. Screwcap. 11.5% alc. **Rating** 96 **To** 2022

Nehme Vineyard Botrytis Semillon 2016 From 33yo vines, hand-picked, direct to press (as whole bunches). Deep gold; luscious and rich; cumquat, crystallised fruits, nougat. Screwcap. 12.4% alc. **Rating** 95 **To** 2024 $55

Nehme Vineyard Botrytis Semillon 2015 Less luscious than the '16, the acidity marginally out of whack but still a very good example of the class, that acidity making winners as well as losers. Screwcap. 11.6% alc. **Rating** 95 **To** 2025 $55

Michelini Wines ★★★★

Great Alpine Road, Myrtleford, Vic 3737 **Region** Alpine Valleys
T (03) 5751 1990 **www**.micheliniwines.com.au **Open** 7 days 10–5
Winemaker Matt Kilby **Est.** 1982 **Dozens** 18000 **Vyds** 60ha
The Michelini family are among the best known grapegrowers of the Buckland Valley in northeast Victoria. Having migrated from Italy in 1949, they originally grew tobacco, diversifying into vineyards in '82. The main vineyard, on terra rossa soil, is at an altitude of 300m, mostly with frontage to the Buckland River. The Devils Creek Vineyard was planted in '91 on grafted rootstocks with merlot and chardonnay taking the lion's share. A vineyard expansion program has seen the plantings reach 60ha. Exports to China.

ΨΨΨΨΨ Emo Selection Sangiovese 2017 Machine-harvested, whole-berry fermentation, 48 hours' cold soak, 3 weeks on skins, pressed to 1yo French oak, matured for 12 months. Has good varietal expression. Screwcap. 14% alc. **Rating** 93 **To** 2027 $65
Italian Selection Sangiovese 2018 Machine-harvested, 20% whole-bunch fermentation in open fermenters, 14 days on skins, pressed straight to French oak (20% new), matured for 12 months. Pretty red fruits but the oak needs to settle. Screwcap. 13.5% alc. **Rating** 91 **To** 2030 $25

ΨΨΨΨ Italian Selection Pinot Grigio 2019 Rating 89 **To** 2021 $25
Merlot 2018 Rating 89 **To** 2023 $20

Mike Press Wines ★★★★★

PO Box 224, Lobethal, SA 5241 **Region** Adelaide Hills
T (08) 8389 5546 **www**.mikepresswines.com.au **Open** Not
Winemaker Mike Press **Est.** 1998 **Dozens** 12000 **Vyds** 22.7ha
Mike and Judy Press established their Kenton Valley Vineyards in 1998, when they purchased 34ha of land in the Adelaide Hills at an elevation of 500m. They planted mainstream cool-climate varieties (merlot, shiraz, cabernet sauvignon, sauvignon blanc, chardonnay and pinot noir) intending to sell the grapes to other wine producers. Even an illustrious 43-year career in the wine industry did not prepare Mike for the downturn in grape prices that followed and that led to the development of the Mike Press wine label. They produce high quality sauvignon blanc, chardonnay, rose, pinot noir, merlot, shiraz, cabernet merlot and cabernet sauvignon, which are sold at mouth-wateringly low prices. I've decided to give this winery/maker proprietary five stars because there is no other producer offering estate-grown and made wines at prices to compete with these.

ΨΨΨΨΨ Single Vineyard Adelaide Hills Merlot 2017 Very good colour. There is an abundance of red and blackberry fruits, and more texture and structure to go with that fruit; maturation in French and American oak for 12 months the key. As always, great value for money. Screwcap. 14.6% alc. **Rating** 92 **To** 2025 $15 ✪
Adelaide Hills Sauvignon Blanc 2018 Fresh, bright, breezy and crisp; the flavour spectrum in green pea, grass and apple flavours. Screwcap. 13.5% alc. **Rating** 90 **To** 2022 $15 ✪

Miles from Nowhere ★★★★☆

PO Box 128, Burswood, WA 6100 **Region** Margaret River
T (08) 9264 7800 **www**.milesfromnowhere.com.au **Open** Not
Winemaker Rory Clifton-Parks, Gary Stokes **Est.** 2007 **Dozens** 20000 **Vyds** 46.9ha
Miles from Nowhere is one of the two wineries owned by Franklin and Heather Tate. Franklin returned to Margaret River in 2007 after working with his parents establishing Evans & Tate from 1987 to 2005. The Miles from Nowhere name comes from the journey Franklin's ancestors made over 100 years ago from Eastern Europe to Australia: upon their arrival, they felt they had travelled 'miles from nowhere'. The plantings include petit verdot, chardonnay, shiraz, sauvignon blanc, semillon, viognier, cabernet sauvignon and merlot, spread over two vineyards planted over 20 years ago. Exports to the UK, the US, Canada, Asia and NZ.

🍷🍷🍷🍷♀ **Best Blocks Margaret River Chardonnay 2018** Flavour by the bucket load starting with ripe nectarines and peaches, layers of cream and lemon curd flecked with ginger spice. Some funky sulphides and tangy acidity do their bit to rein things in. Screwcap. 13.5% alc. **Rating** 90 **To** 2026 $32 JF

Best Blocks Margaret River Cabernet Sauvignon 2018 No mistaking its regional thumbprint with boysenberry, blackberry and black olive to the fore. It's fuller bodied, ripe with tart acidity and gritty tannins to close. Screwcap. 14.5% alc. **Rating** 90 **To** 2028 $32 JF

Milhinch Wines   ★★★★☆

27 Gerald Roberts Road Seppeltsfield, SA 5355 **Region** Barossa Valley
T 0412 455 553 www.seizetheday.net.au **Open** By appt
Winemaker Contract **Est.** 2003 **Dozens** 1200 **Vyds** 4ha
In 1999 Peter Milhinch and Sharyn Rogers established 2ha each of shiraz and cabernet sauvignon near Greenock Creek, which flows through their property. At the foot of their vineyard is the award-winning Seppeltsfield Vineyard Cottage, a restored 1860s German settlers cottage offering luxury accommodation for one couple. The cottage restoration and Peter and Sharyn's wine production began in 2003, when Peter was recovering from a serious illness. The Seize the Day phrase on their wine labels acknowledges their journey through adversity, as Peter notes, 'Carpe Diem – we never know what tomorrow may bring!'

🍷🍷🍷🍷🍷 **Seize The Day Barossa Valley Shiraz 2016** A standout vintage offers a different perspective to the '15 vintage release. The '16 is more fruit-obvious and seems finer despite the same alcohol level. Less bolshie all round: cassis, cinnamon, pepper, clove, coffee, chocolate and leather. The volume is turned down compared to '15 and as a result it's better balanced. Screwcap. 14.5% alc. **Rating** 95 **To** 2035 $120 JP

Seize The Day Barossa Valley Shiraz 2015 A good year in the Barossa has produced a solid wine that doesn't pretend to be anything other than what it is. Garnet. Shiitake mushroom, meaty, game, blackcurrant, chocolate – there's certainly a lot happening before the wine hits the lips. Acacia, thyme, sage, blackcurrant pastille sweetness, dark chocolate, Cherry Ripe-cum-panforte. Thick, chunky, meaty and heavy. Tannins are up to the challenge. Screwcap. 14.7% alc. **Rating** 94 **To** 2033 $120 JP

Millbrook Winery   ★★★★★

Old Chestnut Lane, Jarrahdale, WA 6124 **Region** Perth Hills
T (08) 9525 5796 www.millbrookwinery.com.au **Open** Wed–Mon 10–5
Winemaker Damian Hutton, Adair Davies **Est.** 1996 **Dozens** 10 000 **Vyds** 8ha
Millbrook is situated in the historic town of Jarrahdale, southeast of Perth. Located at the picturesque Chestnut Farm, the property backs on to the Serpentine River and is nestled among jarrah forests. Chestnut Farm dates back to the 19th century, when the original owner planted an orchard and grapevines in 1865, providing fruit to the local timber-millers in Jarrahdale. In 1996 Chestnut Farm and Millbrook Winery were bought by Peter and Lee Fogarty, marking the family's first entry into the wine business. Together with their children John, Mark and Anna they planted the vineyard. In 2001 a state-of-the-art winery was completed, including a restaurant. In addition to the 8ha estate, Millbrook draws on vineyards in prime locations across WA for sauvignon blanc, vermentino, fiano, chardonnay, tempranillo, grenache, mourvedre and pedro ximenez. Exports to Germany, Malaysia, Hong Kong, Singapore, China and Japan.

🍷🍷🍷🍷🍷 **Limited Release Pedro Ximenez NV** Among the very noble varieties of Spain, pedro ximenez's home is in the semi-arid turf of Andalusia, near Cordoba. Toffee, walnut and varnish here. Treacly acidity serves as a righteous pillar of sense and restraint, miraculously transforming the immense sweetness into a sense of savouriness. Made across a solera, fractionally blended to deliver one of Australia's finest interpretations. Screwcap. 18.5% alc. **Rating** 97 $60 NG ✪

ŸŸŸŸŸ Single Vineyard Geographe Chardonnay 2019 Hand-picked, chilled to 5°C, whole-bunch pressed to barriques (40% new) with full solids. A lovely wine, immaculate balance and length, grapefruit/nectarine fruit, freshness the order of the day. Screwcap. 13.5% alc. Rating 95 To 2029 $35 ☉
Limited Release Chardonnay 2018 Hand-picked from the 52 Stones Vineyard in the Ferguson Valley; chilled, whole-bunch pressed, wild-fermented, 100% mlf, matured in French oak (70% new). Very intense and long, the mlf certainly needed to soften the acidity. A very classy wine with a lengthy future. Screwcap. 14% alc. Rating 95 To 2028 $50

ŸŸŸŸŸ Estate Viognier 2019 Rating 93 To 2022 $40
Regional Range Geographe Grenache Shiraz Mourvedre 2019 Rating 93 To 2030 $25 ☉
Estate Shiraz Viognier 2018 Rating 92 To 2029 $40
Regional Range Margaret River Sauvignon Blanc 2019 Rating 91 To 2022 $25 SC
Regional Range Perth Hills Viognier 2019 Rating 91 To 2022 $25
Single Vineyard Frankland River Shiraz 2018 Rating 91 To 2038 $35
Regional Range Margaret River Fiano 2019 Rating 90 To 2022 $25 SC

Millon Wines   ★★★★☆

48 George Street, Williamstown, SA 5351 **Region** Eden Valley
T (08) 8524 6691 **www**.millonwines.com.au **Open** Not
Winemaker Angus Wardlaw **Est.** 2013 **Dozens** 20 000
Millon Wines has three vineyards: one in the Eden Valley, the second in the Barossa Valley and the third in the Clare Valley. Winemaker Angus Wardlaw, with a degree in wine science from CSU and experience in the Clare Valley as winemaker at Kirrihill Wines, 'believes the Eden Valley is the future of the Barossa' (see separate entry for his family business, Brothers at War). He makes the Millon wines with a minimalist approach.

ŸŸŸŸŸ Clare's Secret Shiraz 2017 The value for money of this deeply coloured wine verges on absurdity. If twice the price, it would still star. Single vineyard, destemmed whole berries are open-fermented, 15 days on skins, pressed to French hogsheads (20% new) for 15 months' maturation. It wasn't fined (vegan) and is perfectly balanced. I'm not deducting points but the packaging isn't appropriate. Screwcap. 13.5% alc. Rating 95 To 2037 $18 ☉

ŸŸŸŸŸ Clare's Secret Cabernet Sauvignon 2017 Rating 91 To 2032 $18 ☉

Milton Vineyard   ★★★★★

14635 Tasman Highway, Swansea, Tas 7190 **Region** East Coast Tasmania
T (03) 6257 8298 **www**.miltonvineyard.com.au **Open** 7 days 10–5
Winemaker John Schutz, Anna Pooley, Justin Bubb **Est.** 1992 **Dozens** 11 000
Vyds 19.8ha
Michael and Kerry Dunbabin have one of the most historic properties in Tasmania, dating back to 1826. The property is 1800ha, meaning the vineyard (9ha of pinot noir, 6ha pinot gris, 1.5ha chardonnay, 1ha each of gewurztraminer and riesling, plus 10 rows of shiraz) has plenty of room for expansion.

ŸŸŸŸŸ Pinot Noir 2018 From a very good vintage for Tasmania's east coast wineries. The colour is excellent, the bouquet blooming with scents of cherry blossom, the palate providing a platform with sustained fine tannins. Screwcap. 13.8% alc. Rating 95 To 2028 $38
Dunbabin Family Reserve Shiraz 2016 Shiraz from Tasmania is definitely a thing, as the growing number of producers can attest. White pepper is a signature with both this wine and previous vintages. Dried herbs and leafy characters. Bright red and blue fruits take a back step to all that herbal/spice/pepper action. A cool

expression all round but note the mellow tannins. Screwcap. 14% alc. **Rating** 95
To 2026 $58 JP

🍷🍷🍷🍷🍷 **Pinot Gris 2019** Rating 92 To 2021 $28
Gewurztraminer 2018 Rating 91 To 2024 $28
Freycinet Coast Pinot Noir Rose 2019 Rating 91 To 2021 $28

Ministry of Clouds ★★★★★

39A Wakefield Street, Kent Town, SA 5067 **Region** Various
T 0417 864 615 **www**.ministryofclouds.com.au **Open** By appt
Winemaker Julian Forwood, Bernice Ong, Tim Geddes **Est.** 2012 **Dozens** 3500 **Vyds** 9ha
Bernice Ong and Julian Forwood say, 'The name Ministry of Clouds symbolises the
relinquishing of our past security and structure (ministry) for the beguiling freedom,
independence and adventure (clouds) inherent in our own venture'. I doubt whether there are
two partners in a relatively young wine business with such extraordinary experience in sales
and marketing of wine, stretching back well over 20 years. They bypassed owning vineyards
or building wineries, instead headhunting key winemakers in the Clare Valley and Tasmania
for riesling and chardonnay respectively, and the assistance of Tim Geddes at his winery in
McLaren Vale, where they make the red wines. In 2016 they took the plunge and purchased
part of the elevated Seaview block adjacent to Chapel Hill, Samuels Gorge, Coriole and
Hardys' Yeenunga Vineyard, with 7ha of shiraz and 2ha of cabernet sauvignon. They have
enlisted the very experienced Richard Leaske to help manage the vineyard. Exports to the
UK, Sweden, Malaysia, Singapore and Hong Kong.

🍷🍷🍷🍷🍷 **Onkaparinga Rocks Single Vineyard McLaren Vale Shiraz 2018** Whole-
berry, open-fermented, matured for 12 months in old and new French puncheons.
This is the ringmaster of the Ministry of Clouds shirazs, cracking the tannin whip
over the juicy black fruits. Striking wine. The cool site with its thin veneer of soil
over rocky subsoil is at work here. Screwcap. 14.5% alc. **Rating** 96 To 2048 $65 ✪
McLaren Vale Shiraz 2018 From an estate block in Onkaparinga and a Blewitt
Springs parcel. Hand-picked, 12% whole bunches, the remainder whole berries,
matured for 12 months in large-format used French oak. This has a bright and
lively bouquet and an equally expressive palate of red cherry peppered with spice
and splashes of licorice. Screwcap. 14.1% alc. **Rating** 96 To 2038 $32 ✪
Single Vineyard Blewitt Springs Shiraz 2018 Hand-picked, destemmed,
open-fermented, matured in used French hogsheads for 12 months. This is a
magisterial wine, totally centred on black fruits: blackberry to the fore, dark cherry
and licorice in support. It is one of those wines that you absolutely know will be
very long lived. Screwcap. 14.5% alc. **Rating** 96 To 2048 $65 ✪
Tasmania Chardonnay 2018 From the Coal River and Derwent valleys,
whole-bunch pressed direct to used French oak for wild ferment and 10 months'
maturation. Surprisingly attractively rich in the mouth, balance achieved through
natural acidity and (possibly) mlf. Screwcap. 12.9% alc. **Rating** 95 To 2026 $48
McLaren Vale Grenache 2018 Hand-picked from a 98yo bushvine vineyard;
saw a little time in old French oak, the intention to focus on the fruit and its low
alcohol (for grenache). It is a grenache with the potential longevity of a top class
Rhône producer. Given its provenance, it's absurdly cheap. Screwcap. 13.9% alc.
Rating 95 To 2040 $38

🍷🍷🍷🍷🍷 **McLaren Vale Tempranillo Grenache 2018** Rating 92 To 2029 $32

Minnow Creek ★★★★☆

42 Frontenac Avenue, Panorama, SA 5041 (postal) **Region** McLaren Vale
T 0404 288 108 **www**.minnowcreekwines.com.au **Open** Not
Winemaker Tony Walker **Est.** 2005 **Dozens** 1600
Tony Walker spent 6 years as winemaker at Fox Creek, after two previous vintages in Beaujolais
and Languedoc. He founded Minnow Creek in 2005, not with any fanfare of (marketing)

trumpets but simply to make very good wines that reflected their place and their variety, the Lopresti family providing many of the grapes for the best red wines of Minnow Creek.

ɤɤɤɤɤ The Black Minnow McLaren Vale Sangiovese Cabernet Sauvignon 2018 An 80/20% blend, vinified separately, blended after 18 months in French oak. Full-flavoured. It will age well. Screwcap. 13.5% alc. **Rating** 90 **To** 2026 $21 ◎

ɤɤɤɤ McLaren Vale Shiraz 2017 Rating 89 $29

Mino & Co Wines

113 Hanwood Avenue, Hanwood, NSW 2680 **Region** Riverina
T (02) 6963 0200 **www**.minoandco.com.au **Open** Mon–Fri 8–5, Sat by appt
Winemaker Sam Trimboli **Est.** 1997 **Dozens** 20 000
The Guglielmino family, specifically father Domenic and sons Nick and Alain, founded Mino & Co in 1997. From the outset they realised that their surname could cause problems of pronunciation, so they simply took the last four letters for the name of their business. Mino & Co has created two brands: Signor Vino and A Growers Touch. Signor Vino covers wines made from Italian varieties sourced from the Adelaide Hills, Riverina and Riverland. The A Growers Touch brand covers traditional varieties, often with local growers who have been working with the family for over two decades. The wines are made at Hanwood Winery (established on what was once a drive-in cinema). Exports to the UK, China and NZ.

ɤɤɤɤɤ Signor Vino Pinot Grigio 2019 This is a fine expression of unadulterated, sassy grigio. The core of fruit is nashi gelato to baked apple spice. The phenolic rails are gentle. The acidity fresh but not obtrusive. A good call. Screwcap. **Rating** 91 **To** 2021 $21 NG ◎
A Growers Touch Shiraz 2018 A whiff of reductive tension soon eases the clutch, jettisoning this rich red into a world of purple fruit scents, licorice, root spice and lilac aromas. Well crafted, tasting as if from a far cooler place than the Riverina. The tannins and acidity, a little grating. Screwcap. **Rating** 91 **To** 2024 $20 NG ◎
A Growers Touch Durif 2018 A series featuring the farmer of each block/ variety on the label. A really nice touch. Opaque. Liquid density coats the mouth, with a bridle of herbal to vanillan oak tannins staining the cheeks. A force. Yet the aromas are floral. The fruit, pulpy and blue. Nothing desiccated or dried out. **Rating** 91 **To** 2026 $20 NG ◎

ɤɤɤɤ Signor Vino Fiano 2019 Rating 89 **To** 2021 $21 NG

Mr Barval Fine Wines

7087 Caves Road, Margaret River, WA 6285 **Region** Margaret River
T 0481 453 038 **www**.mrbarval.com **Open** 7 days 11–5
Winemaker Robert Gherardi **Est.** 2015 **Dozens** 1300
Robert Gherardi was born with wine in his blood. As a small boy he'd go to Margaret River to pick grapes with three generations of his extended Italian family. The grapes were taken to his grandmother's suburban backyard to begin the fermentation, followed by a big lunch or dinner to celebrate the arrival of the new vintage-to-be. Nonetheless, his first degree was in marine science and biotechnology; while completing the course he worked in an independent wine store in Perth. Having tasted his way around the world in the bottle, at age 25 he enrolled in the full oenology and viticulture degree. This led to employment at Moss Wood for four years, then Brown Hill Estate as assistant winemaker and finally to Cullen for three years. Vanya Cullen encouraged him to travel to Barolo and work with Elio Altare for three harvests over a five-year period. This included moving to Barolo with his wife and children to experience the full four seasons of viticulture and winemaking. He returns to Italy each year for his boutique travel business, with customised tours of Barolo, Valtellina and further north. And so he arrived at the name for his winery: Margaret River, Barolo and Valtellina. Exports to Singapore and Hong Kong.

ΨΨΨΨΨ **Margaret River Chardonnay 2019** Hand-picked from 3 vineyards in Wilyabrup and Karridale, whole-bunch pressed direct to French barriques for wild fermentation and maturation. A beautiful chardonnay in every respect – line, length and balance. A pure varietal rendition. Screwcap. 13.3% alc. **Rating** 96 **To** 2030 $40 ❂

ΨΨΨΨ♀ **Vino Rosso 2018 Rating** 93 **To** 2030 $29
Mistral 2019 Rating 92 **To** 2025 $29
Nebbia 2019 Rating 90 **To** 2025 $35

Mr Mick   ★★★★

7 Dominic Street, Clare, SA 5453 **Region** Clare Valley
T (08) 8842 2555 **www**.mrmick.com.au **Open** 7 days 10–5
Winemaker Tim Adams, Brett Schutz **Est.** 2011 **Dozens** 30 000 **Vyds** 145ha
This is the venture of Tim Adams and wife Pam Goldsack. The name was chosen to honour KH (Mick) Knappstein, a legend in the Clare Valley and the broader Australian wine community. Tim worked at Leasingham Wines with Mick between 1975 and '86, and knew him well. When Tim and Pam acquired the Leasingham winery in January 2011, together with its historic buildings, it brought the wheel full circle. Various commentators (including myself) have used Mick's great one-liner: 'There are only two types of people in the world: those who were born in Clare, and those who wish they had been'. Exports to China and NZ.

ΨΨΨΨ♀ **Clare Valley Riesling 2019** From 4 named Clare vineyards. It overflows with Meyer lemon, lime and Granny Smith apple inputs on the bouquet and palate alike. If there's any residual sugar it's far from obvious. This is as honest as the day is long, and terrific value. Screwcap. 11.5% alc. **Rating** 90 **To** 2026 $17 ❂
Clare Valley Tempranillo 2017 Matured for 18 months in French oak. An elegant, light to medium-bodied wine. It's hard to see its long time in oak; what is there, needed polishing. No matter, at $17 it's a gift horse. Screwcap. 13.5% alc. **Rating** 90 **To** 2024 $17 ❂

Mr Riggs Wine Company   ★★★★★

169 Douglas Gully Road, McLaren Flat, SA 5171 **Region** McLaren Vale
T 1300 946 326 **www**.mrriggs.com.au **Open** Mon–Fri 9–5
Winemaker Ben Riggs **Est.** 2001 **Dozens** 20 000 **Vyds** 7.5ha
With over a quarter of a century of winemaking experience, Ben Riggs is well established under his own banner. Ben sources the best fruit from individual vineyards in McLaren Vale, Clare Valley, Adelaide Hills, Langhorne Creek, Coonawarra and from his own Piebald Gully Vineyard (shiraz and viognier). Each wine expresses the essence of not only the vineyard but also the region's terroir. The vision of the Mr Riggs brand is unpretentious and personal: 'To make the wines I love to drink'. He drinks very well. Exports to the US, Canada, Denmark, Sweden, Germany, the Netherlands, Switzerland, Singapore, NZ, Hong Kong and China.

ΨΨΨΨΨ **McLaren Vale Shiraz 2017** This is the distilled essence of McLaren Vale: full-bodied black fruits, dark chocolate, licorice and tar – and then a superb juicy finish that demands the next mouthful be tasted forthwith. Tannins and oak lend appropriate support. Diam. 14.5% alc. **Rating** 97 **To** 2047 $50 ❂

ΨΨΨΨΨ **The Chap 2012** This, says Ben Riggs, is 'my icon wine'. A blend of 55% McLaren Vale shiraz and 45% Coonawarra cabernet sauvignon, the parcels open-fermented and kept separate for 2 years in oak (80% French, 20% American, 35% new), a barrel selection made 3 months before bottling. This is unashamedly full-bodied and needs another 10 years for the rich black fruits and ripe tannins to soften and fully mesh. As a matter of interest, 2.7g/l of residual sugar is part of the picture. Diam. 14.5% alc. **Rating** 95 **To** 2042 $100

ΨΨΨΨ♀ **Mr Brightside McLaren Vale Grenache Rose 2019 Rating** 93 **To** 2022 $22 SC ❂
Outpost Coonawarra Cabernet 2018 Rating 93 **To** 2030 $25 SC ❂

Piebald Adelaide Hills Syrah 2018 Rating 92 To 2038 $30
Yacca Paddock Adelaide Hills Tempranillo 2018 Rating 91 To 2026 $30
Watervale Riesling 2019 Rating 90 To 2029 $25 SC
Mr Brightside Adelaide Hills Pinot Gris 2019 Rating 90 To 2021 $20 ✪
Mr Brightside Preservative Free McLaren Vale Shiraz 2019 Rating 90
To 2022 $22 SC
Mr Brightside Eurotrash 2017 Rating 90 To 2024 $22 SC

Mitchell   ★★★★☆

Hughes Park Road, Sevenhill via Clare, SA 5453 **Region** Clare Valley
T (08) 8843 4258 **www**.mitchellwines.com **Open** 7 days 10–4
Winemaker Andrew Mitchell, Simon Pringle **Est.** 1975 **Dozens** 15000 **Vyds** 75ha
One of the stalwarts of the Clare Valley, established by Jane and Andrew Mitchell, producing
long-lived rieslings and cabernet sauvignons in classic regional style. The range now includes
very creditable semillon, grenache and shiraz. A lovely old stone apple shed is the cellar door
and upper section of the upgraded winery. Children Angus and Edwina are now working
in the business, heralding generational changes. Over the years the Mitchells have established
or acquired 75ha of vineyards on four excellent sites, some vines over 60 years old; all are
managed organically, with biodynamic composts used for over a decade. Exports to the UK,
the US, Canada, Denmark, Singapore, Taiwan, Hong Kong, China and NZ.

🍷🍷🍷🍷🍷 **McNicol Clare Valley Shiraz 2008** Oak has been absorbed by the fruit, the
tannins ditto and balanced. An attractive mature 12yo wine. Screwcap. 14.5% alc.
Rating 94 **To** 2026 $60

🍷🍷🍷🍷♀ **Sparkling Peppertree NV** Rating 93 $45 SC
Kinsfolk Grenache 2017 Rating 92 To 2027 $40
Sevenhill Vineyard Clare Valley Cabernet Sauvignon 2015 Rating 92
To 2030 $28 JF
Kinsfolk Shiraz 2015 Rating 90 To 2027 $40

Mitchell Harris Wines   ★★★★★

38 Doveton Street North, Ballarat, Vic 3350 **Region** Ballarat
T (03) 5331 8931 **www**.mitchellharris.com.au **Open** Sun–Tues 11–6, Wed 11–9,
Thurs–Sat 11–11
Winemaker John Harris **Est.** 2008 **Dozens** 2300
Mitchell Harris Wines is a partnership between Alicia and Craig Mitchell and Shannyn and
John Harris. John, the winemaker, began his career at Brown Brothers, then spent eight years
as winemaker at Domaine Chandon in the Yarra Valley, cramming in Northern Hemisphere
vintages in California and Oregon. The Mitchell and Harris families grew up in the Ballarat
area and have an affinity for the Macedon and Pyrenees regions. While the total make is not
large, a lot of thought has gone into the creation of each of the wines, which are sourced
from the Pyrenees, Ballarat and Macedon regions. In 2012 a multipurpose space was created
in an 1880s brick workshop and warehouse providing a cellar door, bar and education facility.
Exports to China.

🍷🍷🍷🍷🍷 **Sabre 2016** A 55/45% chardonnay/pinot noir blend, tiraged Oct '16, disgorged
Dec '19, 4g/l dosage. Winemaker John Harris learnt much from the late Dr Tony
Jordan when he was a winemaker at Domaine Chandon, skills such as tightness of
style and refinement of flavour. Sabre is greater than the sum of its parts – a blend
of Henty, Pyrenees, Macedon Ranges – and exudes a coolness and fine line, and
length of taut acidity. Smoky, toasty complexity. Oyster shell, nougat mingling with
almond amaretti. Diam. 11.2% alc. **Rating** 95 $50 JP
Sabre Rose 2015 Chardonnay/pinot noir. Tiraged Nov '15, disgorged Jun '19,
3g/l dosage. A master sparkling maker at the top of his game, John Harris shows
his Domaine Chandon training off with each release. Pale salmon-blush. Tight
bead, pinot-led smoky and strawberry scent. Extended yeast age produces inviting

flavours of cherry kernel, pomegranate, roast nuts. Seamlessly balanced, crunchy acidity. Diam. 11.5% alc. **Rating** 95 $60 JP

Rose 2019 A 70/30% pinot noir/sangiovese blend. Orange-damask rose. The nose is all summery and inviting with sliced watermelon, cut strawberries and raspberries, floral/spice confection. Boasts a dusty, breezy palate with sangiovese's fingerprints all over it, especially the sour cherry intensity. So refreshing, it can take some serious chilling. Screwcap. 11.7% alc. **Rating** 94 **To** 2025 $28 JP ✪

Peerick Vineyard Pyrenees Shiraz 2018 Includes 3% viognier; co-fermented, matured in 1–5yo French hogsheads for 15 months, no fining. Campari, warm spices, plum, red berries. There is a noticeable savouriness, hard to pinpoint but prune and wild thyme comes close. Soft and fine with sinewy tannins. Rouses the appetite. Screwcap. 13.5% alc. **Rating** 94 **To** 2030 $35 JP

♟♟♟♟♟ **Pyrenees Sauvignon Blanc Fume 2019** Rating 93 To 2026 $28 JP
Wightwick Vineyard Ballarat Chardonnay 2018 Rating 93 To 2030 $32 JP
Wightwick Vineyard Ballarat Pinot Noir 2018 Rating 93 To 2028 $38 JP
Pyrenees Shiraz 2019 Rating 93 To 2027 $40 JP
Curious Winemaker Pyrenees Shiraz 2019 Rating 92 To 2026 $30 JP
Pyrenees Sangiovese 2019 Rating 92 To 2027 $28 JP
Peerick Vineyard Pyrenees Cabernet Sauvignon 2018 Rating 90 To 2030 $32 JP

Mitchelton   ★★★★★

Mitchellstown via Nagambie, Vic 3608 **Region** Nagambie Lakes/Heathcote
T (03) 5736 2222 **www**.mitchelton.com.au **Open** 7 days 10–5
Winemaker Andrew Santarossa **Est.** 1969 **Dozens** 35 000 **Vyds** 118ha
Mitchelton was founded by Ross Shelmerdine. He had a splendid vision for the striking winery, restaurant, observation tower and surrounding vineyards. The expected volume of tourism did not eventuate and the business became embroiled in a long-running dispute. In 1994 it was acquired by Petaluma but, once again, did not deliver the expected financial return, notwithstanding the long and faithful service of chief winemaker Don Lewis or the quality of its best wines. In August 2012 a new chapter opened for Mitchelton, with the completion of an acquisition agreement by Gerry Ryan OAM and son Andrew. Gerry founded caravan company Jayco in 1975 and, as a consequence of the success of that company, has a virtually unlimited budget to take Mitchelton to the next level. Exports to China.

♟♟♟♟♟ **Spring Single Block Heathcote Shiraz 2017** If you wanted to be picky you might say that the oak runs slightly ahead of the fruit, but this is a very fine shiraz: powerful but detailed, intricately tannic, long-flavoured and impressive. The berried fruit is beautifully ripened, it gives clear nods to savouriness and the lingering smoky aftertaste is seriously delicious. Screwcap. 14.4% alc. **Rating** 96 **To** 2038 $60 CM ✪

Estate Grown Heathcote Shiraz 2017 Such a finely crafted red wine. Most of the best wines are medium–bodied and this shows why. It doesn't push too hard, it allows time for more complex notes to show through, it feels layered and it feels hand-stitched. Its fruits are mostly in the red/black cherry sphere and they come laced with woodsy spice and a superfine layer of creamy oak. It will develop beautifully. Screwcap. 14.3% alc. **Rating** 96 **To** 2032 $40 CM ✪

Single Vineyard Toolleen Heathcote Shiraz 2017 There's real power to this wine but it's not at the expense of elegance. It's a satiny shiraz with black cherry-plum and clove flavours and a light coating of chocolate and coffee cream. Tannin is fine and silty. Everything feels harmonious and the length is sound. Screwcap. 14.4% alc. **Rating** 95 **To** 2032 $50 CM

Roussanne 2019 Smoky, toasty, flinty and complex. A serious white, made to impress. Sweet stone fruit and melon flavour through its core, vanilla bean characters coming through with air. It's a textural white wine made for richer fare, and it's a steal at the price. Screwcap. 13.5% alc. **Rating** 94 **To** 2025 $25 CM ✪

♟♟♟♟♀ **Marsanne 2019** Rating 93 To 2027 $25 CM ✪
Chardonnay 2019 Rating 92 To 2024 $25 CM ✪
Preece Bendigo Cabernet Sauvignon 2018 Rating 92 To 2027 $20 CM ✪
Preece Nagambie Chardonnay 2018 Rating 91 To 2023 $20 CM ✪
Estate Grown Shiraz 2018 Rating 91 To 2026 $25 CM
Blackwood Park Riesling 2019 Rating 90 To 2025 $20 CM ✪
Preece Grenache Rose 2019 Rating 90 To 2021 $20 CM ✪
Preece Heathcote Shiraz 2018 Rating 90 To 2024 $20 CM ✪

Mitolo Wines ★★★★★

141 McMurtrie Road, McLaren Vale, SA 5171 **Region** McLaren Vale
T 1300 571 233 **www**.mitolowines.com.au **Open** 7 days 10–5
Winemaker Ben Glaetzer **Est.** 1999 **Dozens** 40 000
Mitolo had a meteoric rise once Frank Mitolo decided to turn a winemaking hobby into a business. In 2000 he took the plunge into the commercial end of the business, inviting Ben Glaetzer to make the wines. Split between the Jester range and single vineyard wines, Mitolo began life as a red wine–dominant brand but now produces a range of varietals. In November '17 Mitolo opened their $3 million tasting room, restaurant and event space with a flourish. Exports to all major markets.

♟♟♟♟♟ **Savitar McLaren Vale Shiraz 2016** From a single block, crushed and destemmed, matured in 100% new French oak for 18 months. It is a tribute to the power of the fruit that it has been able to stand alongside the oak, the combination absorbing the tannins. Will be very long lived. Screwcap. 14.5% alc. **Rating** 95 To 2051 $85
Ourea McLaren Vale Sagrantino 2018 This is very good sagrantino. Physiologically, arguably the most phenolic grape variety known to man, sagrantino's wines are inevitably full-bodied and equipped for richer foods. This is no exception. The accents on darker fruit tones. Saturated with extract and a thrumming chord of tannin from fore to aft, this is savoury and delicious. Appetising. More, please. Screwcap. 14.5% alc. **Rating** 95 To 2028 $39 NG
Of the Wind Adelaide Hills Chardonnay 2019 Delicious, with effortless poise between fruit weight and acidity. Nicely restrained and far from fruity. It billows rather than sears. Gentle stone fruit accents, notes of oatmeal, toasted nuts and nougat. The oak is nicely nestled; the finish long and expansive. A delicious wine. Screwcap. 12.5% alc. **Rating** 94 To 2027 $49 NG

♟♟♟♟♀ **Savitar McLaren Vale Shiraz 2017** Rating 93 To 2029 $89 NG
G.A.M. McLaren Vale Shiraz 2016 Rating 93 To 2031 $60
Marsican McLaren Vale Shiraz 2016 Rating 93 To 2029 $235 NG
7th Son 2017 Rating 93 To 2026 $39 NG
Jester Cabernet Sauvignon 2017 Rating 93 To 2029 $25 NG ✪
Of the Earth Adelaide Hills Pinot Noir 2019 Rating 92 To 2026 $49 NG
Angela McLaren Vale Shiraz 2017 Rating 92 To 2025 $39 NG
Marsican McLaren Vale Shiraz 2015 Rating 92 To 2027 $235 NG
Jester McLaren Vale Malbec 2018 Rating 92 To 2023 $25 NG ✪
Jester McLaren Vale Vermentino 2019 Rating 91 To 2022 $25 NG
Serpico Cabernet Sauvignon 2018 Rating 91 To 2031 $89 NG
Cinquecento McLaren Vale Sangiovese 2019 Rating 91 To 2025 $39 NG
Jester McLaren Vale Shiraz 2017 Rating 90 To 2030 $25

MOJO Winemakers ★★★★

99 Maud Street, Unley, SA 5061 **Region** South Australia
T (08) 8124 9020 **www**.mojowine.com.au **Open** Not
Winemaker Matt Talbot **Est.** 2000 **Dozens** 9000
MOJO Winemakers source grapes from across SA, collaborating with vineyard owners to create expressions of some of Australia's most highly regarded wine styles from the most suitable regions in SA; Coonawarra Cabernet Sauvignon, Barossa Shiraz, white wines from

the Adelaide Hills and a Moscato. The labels of each wine are a collaboration that showcases different contemporary Australian artists. Exports to the US, Canada, NZ and china.

🍷🍷🍷🍷🍷 **Bruno Barossa Valley Shiraz 2018** Aged in new and older French and American hogsheads for 10 months. Barossa shiraz with plenty of oomph, but in a contemporary, approachable style. Aromas of ripe blackberry and plum with tar/graphite notes and a generous, juicy palate with grippy but balanced tannin. Screwcap. 14.5% alc. **Rating** 92 **To** 2028 $30 SC
04 Limestone Coast Sauvignon Blanc 2019 The Limestone Coast does quite well with sauvignon blanc. Plenty of varietal character here across the usual spectrum, with a more satisfying mouthfeel and length than many examples at this price. It's fairly simple, but effective, and very easy to drink. Screwcap. 13.5% alc. **Rating** 90 **To** 2022 $20 SC ☺
01 Fleurieu Peninsula Pinot Grigio 2019 Gently whole-bunch pressed to avoid colour or phenolic pick-up, no oak. It's not pink but light bronze. The variety won't be denied. Nashi pear and ripe apple provide the theme on the bouquet and palate, and the winemaking approach has successfully achieved the desired freshness. Screwcap. 13% alc. **Rating** 90 **To** 2022 $20 SC ☺

🍷🍷🍷🍷 **02 Barossa Valley Shiraz 2018 Rating** 89 **To** 2023 $20 SC
03 McLaren Vale Cabernet Sauvignon 2018 Rating 89 **To** 2023 $20 SC

Molly's Cradle   ★★★★

17/1 Jubilee Avenue, Warriewood, NSW 2102 **Region** Hunter Valley
T (02) 9979 1212 **www**.mollyscradle.com.au **Open** By appt
Winemaker Liz Silkman **Est.** 2002 **Dozens** 20000 **Vyds** 15ha
Steve Skidmore and Deidre Broad created the Molly's Cradle brand concept in 1997, moving to reality with the first planting of estate vines in 2000, the first vintage following in '02. They have verdelho, chardonnay, merlot, shiraz and petit verdot, but also look to other regions to supplement the estate-grown grapes. Exports to India, Indonesia and China

Momentum Wines   ★★★★

55 King William Street, Kent Town, SA 5067 **Region** South Australia
T 0438 314 040 **www**.momentumfoodandwine.com.au **Open** Not
Winemaker Nick Walker, David O'Leary **Est.** 2006 **Dozens** 30000
Momentum Wines is owned by John Hood and Sandra North. John has had a distinguished career as an accountant and business advisor to organisations ranging from privately owned to multinationals. Sandra North also has had an impressive career spanning 25 years in export, seven of those years for Yalumba between the late 1990s and early 2000s. It is a virtual winery, owning neither vineyards nor winery. They source grapes from Kangaroo Island, Clare Valley and McLaren Vale. O'Leary Walker makes the wines, with Nick Walker handling the white wines and David O'Leary the reds. Exports to the UK, the US, Canada, South Korea, Japan and China.

🍷🍷🍷🍷🍷 **Henri's Book Limited Release Clare Valley Shiraz 2015** A no-holds-barred, full-bodied shiraz small batch–fermented in 2t and 4t fermenters, matured in French oak (25% new) for 2 years. Over-delivers in usual fashion for Momentum. Take into account the cork and you have the thumbprint of exports to ponder. 15% alc. **Rating** 94 **To** 2035 $25 ☺

🍷🍷🍷🍷🍷 **Chapter Two McLaren Vale Cabernet Sauvignon 2017 Rating** 93 **To** 2032 $25 ☺

Mon Tout   ★★★☆

PO Box 283, Cowaramup, WA 6284 **Region** Margaret River
T (08) 9336 9600 **www**.montout.com.au **Open** Not
Winemaker Janice McDonald, Mark Bailey **Est.** 2014 **Dozens** NFP **Vyds** 28ha

Mon Tout ('my everything' in French) is the venture of second-generation vigneron Richard Burch, son of Jeff and Amy Burch of Howard Park. The wines are crafted from small parcels of hand-picked fruit from sustainably farmed vineyards and are made with natural ferments and minimal-intervention winemaking. The wines are bottled without filtration or fining and minimal to no sulphur (100% vegan friendly).

🍷🍷🍷 **Kind Animals Red 2019** Includes 50% shiraz, 40% pinot noir, 10% grenache from Great Southern and the Swan Valley. A slight acidic nip on the finish. Screwcap. 13.5% alc. **Rating** 89 **To** 2029 $30

Montalto   ★★★★★

33 Shoreham Road, Red Hill South, Vic 3937 **Region** Mornington Peninsula
T (03) 5989 8412 **www.**montalto.com.au **Open** 7 days 11–5
Winemaker Simon Black **Est.** 1998 **Dozens** 12 000 **Vyds** 47ha
John Mitchell and family established Montalto in 1998, but the core of the vineyard goes back to '86. It is planted to pinot noir, chardonnay, pinot gris, riesling, shiraz, tempranillo and sauvignon blanc. Intensive vineyard work opens up the canopy, with yields of 3.7–6.1t/ha. Wines are released in three ranges: the flagship Single Vineyard, Montalto and Pennon Hill. Montalto leases several external vineyards that span the peninsula, giving vastly greater diversity of pinot noir sources and greater insurance against weather extremes. There is also a broad range of clones adding to that diversity. Montalto has hit new heights with its wines from these blocks. Exports to the Philippines and China

🍷🍷🍷🍷🍷 **Single Vineyard Tuerong Block Mornington Peninsula Chardonnay 2018**
A very different style to The Eleven, with more emphasis on varietal fruit on both the bouquet and palate. The mouthfeel is juicy to the point of being slippery, leaving a trail of multi stone and citrus fruits in its wake. Gold medal Victorian Wine Show '19. Screwcap. 12.8% alc. **Rating** 96 **To** 2027 $60 ✪
Single Vineyard Merricks Block Mornington Peninsula Pinot Noir 2018
A highly expressive bouquet, suggesting a period of carbonic maceration pre destemming and/or crushing. The colour is the brightest of the Montalto pinots, with more purple-crimson. The palate lives up to, if not exceeds, the promise of the bouquet with whole-bunch flavours doing the heavy lifting. Screwcap. 13.7% alc. **Rating** 96 **To** 2029 $70 ✪
Single Vineyard Tuerong Block Mornington Peninsula Pinot Noir 2018
Good depth and hue. The complex flavours and texture are the product of the warmest Montalto site. Cherry and plum each claim to be the leader and they aren't easy to split. This has more body than its siblings. Screwcap. 13.6% alc. **Rating** 96 **To** 2030 $70 ✪
Estate Mornington Peninsula Shiraz 2018 From a vineyard in the warm Tuerong district. Good colour. An aromatic bouquet points to the inclusion of some whole-bunch fruit, reinforced by the complex palate with spiced black cherry, wild blackberry, licorice and bitter chocolate all in a wreath of finely tuned tannins. Screwcap. 14.2% alc. **Rating** 96 **To** 2038 $50 ✪
Single Vineyard The Eleven Mornington Peninsula Chardonnay 2018
Exclusively from the Eleven Estate rows planted in '86, matured for 11 months in French oak (40% new). The bouquet immediately proclaims its complexity with a savoury/funky mix, the palate more restrained and long. Gold medal Victorian Wine Show '19. Screwcap. 12.8% alc. **Rating** 95 **To** 2026 $60
Estate Mornington Peninsula Pinot Noir 2018 A bright, light crimson hue is a propitious start but it's the finish of the palate that is the best starting point, for it's here the full complexity of the wine is revealed. Fresh and blanched cherries and strawberries carry the conversation for a considerable time. All happy. Screwcap. 13.7% alc. **Rating** 95 **To** 2033 $50
Pennon Hill Mornington Peninsula Shiraz 2018 Light but bright crimson-purple. It is elegant and lively, in best cool-climate style; savoury/spicy notes are in balance with black cherry fruit. Drink it soon while it has the brightness of fruit. Screwcap. 14.2% alc. **Rating** 95 **To** 2025 $34 ✪

Single Vineyard Red Hill Block Mornington Peninsula Pinot Noir 2018
From the north face of the estate Red Hill South vineyard at 110m, the plantings
going back to '86. Light, clear colour. It's a pretty wine with purity a feature
and no obvious manifestations of winemaker Simon Black's adventuresome
vinification. Screwcap. 13.7% alc. **Rating** 94 **To** 2027 $70

ŢŢŢŢŢ **Pennon Hill Chardonnay 2019** Rating 92 To 2023 $30
Estate Chardonnay 2018 Rating 91 To 2022 $45
Pennon Hill Pinot Gris 2019 Rating 90 To 2021 $27

Montara ★★★★★

76 Chalambar Road, Ararat, Vic 3377 **Region** Grampians
T (03) 5352 3868 **www**.montarawines.com.au **Open** 1st Fri each month 11–late
Winemaker Simon Fennell **Est.** 1970 **Dozens** 3000 **Vyds** 19.2ha
Montara gained considerable attention for its pinot noirs during the 1980s and continues
to produce wines of distinctive style under the ownership of no less than six siblings of the
Stapleton family. As I can attest from several visits over the years, the view from the cellar door
is one of the best in the Grampians region. Simon Fennell, with an extensive winemaking
history, including assistant winemaker at Best's Wines, and with direct knowledge of the
Grampians region, has replaced long-serving winemaker Leigh Clarnette. Exports to the US,
Canada, Indonesia, Taiwan, Hong Kong and China.

ŢŢŢŢŢ **Chalambar Road Reserve Grampians Shiraz 2017** From 48yo vines; hand-
picked, open-fermented with 20% whole bunch and 1% viognier, 10 days on
skins, 16 months in French oak (30% new). Medium-bodied, fully ripened fruit
with plum and blackberry fruits, fine tannins and neatly integrated oak, the finish
long and convincing. Screwcap. 14.5% alc. **Rating** 95 **To** 2037 $70
Grampians Riesling 2019 From 2 estate blocks; night-harvested, skin contact
in the press, part of the free-run fermented in French barrels, the remainder cool-
fermented in stainless steel, stopped with 9g/l residual sugar. Made to be enjoyed
tonight. Screwcap. 12% alc. **Rating** 94 **To** 2025 $27 ✪
Grampians Sauvignon Blanc 2019 Night-harvested, part cool-fermented in
stainless steel, part wild-fermented at a higher temperature in French barriques,
fermentation stopped with 5g/l of residual sugar. A seriously good outcome.
Screwcap. 12.5% alc. **Rating** 94 **To** 2025 $27 ✪
Grampians Shiraz 2018 From 2 estate vineyards 30–48yo; open-fermented with
10% whole bunches, pressed to French oak (15% new) for 16 months. Very spicy
throughout the bouquet and palate, berries of all shapes and sizes with a coating of
savoury tannins. Screwcap. 14.5% alc. **Rating** 94 **To** 2030 $30 ✪

ŢŢŢŢŢ **Grampians Cabernet Sauvignon 2017** Rating 93 To 2032 $30
Grampians Pinot Noir 2018 Rating 90 To 2024 $30

Monty's Leap ★★★★

45821 South Coast Highway, Kalgan, WA 6330 **Region** Albany
T (08) 9845 7880 **www**.montysleap.com.au **Open** Tues–Sun 11–5
Winemaker Castle Rock (Robert Diletti) **Est.** 1996 **Dozens** 6000
Hospitality and IT professionals Phil Shilcock and Michelle Gray purchased the former
Montgomery's Hill in October 2017 and have launched the Monty's Leap brand. They had
long shared the dream of owning a vineyard and restaurant, and jumped at the opportunity
when Montgomery's came up for sale. The mature vineyard (planted in 1996–97 by
founders Pamela and Murray Montgomery) is planted on the banks of the Kalgan River,
16km northeast of Albany.

ŢŢŢŢŢ **The Mulberry Block Great Southern Chardonnay 2018** This will please
those who want more flavour and oomph to their chardonnay. It's not over the top
but it has ripe stone fruit, melon and ginger spice infused with sweet oak. Slippery
texture thanks to the creamy, buttery lees influence. Screwcap. 13% alc. **Rating** 91
To 2025 $40 JF

Single Vineyard Great Southern Cabernet Sauvignon 2018 Excellent crimson hue. Singing with regional charm all blackberries, currants, bitumen and leafy freshness, plus cedary oak to the fore. The tannins are well placed. A slight green edge to the finish, but certainly a vitality to this. It's appealing now but a reasonable cellaring proposition. Screwcap. 14% alc. **Rating** 90 **To** 2028 $35 JF

Moores Hill Estate ★★★★★

3343 West Tamar Highway, Sidmouth, Tas 7270 **Region** Northern Tasmania
T (03) 6394 7649 **www**.mooreshill.com.au **Open** 7 days 10–5
Winemaker Julian Allport **Est.** 1997 **Dozens** 5000 **Vyds** 7ha
The Moores Hill Estate vineyard (owned by winemaker Julian Allport and Fiona Weller plus Tim and Sheena High) consists of pinot noir, riesling, pinot gris and chardonnay, with a very small amount of cabernet sauvignon and merlot. The vines are located on a northeast-facing hillside, 5km from the Tamar River and 30km from Bass Strait. Moores Hill became Tasmania's first 100% solar-powered winery in 2017, the wines all made onsite.

⦿⦿⦿⦿⦿ **Pinot Gris 2019** I still remember the pinot gris we were called upon to judge at the Tasmanian Wine Show decades ago, and our incomprehension of the style. In a sense, this takes another giant step forward – Julian Allport has found his own way to a glorious gris, running counter to some mainstream abhorrence of any colour. Subtle pink, yet bronze. Pear, toffee apple, spice and Tahitian lime. Screwcap. 13.5% alc. **Rating** 97 **To** 2023 $30 ✪

⦿⦿⦿⦿⦿ **Riesling 2019** Delicious. Lime/lemon rippling along the palate, the acidity of prime importance but not the least fierce or aggressive. Ten years won't tire the wine, so long is its palate. Screwcap. 11.5% alc. **Rating** 95 **To** 2029 $30 ✪
Chardonnay 2018 Very much in the Moores Hill credo: small batch, whole-bunch pressed, wild fermentation in 30% new French oak, lees stirring, 50% mlf (Tasmanian acidity in the gun), 10 months' maturation in oak. A wine to please everyone with white peach, nectarine and grapefruit gently framed by an airbrush of oak. Screwcap. 13.2% alc. **Rating** 95 **To** 2021 $35 ✪
Pinot Noir 2018 After meticulous management of the vine canopy, made with whole-bunch fermentation, matured for 12 months in French oak (30% new). It all works. This is an attractive Tasmanian pinot noir with an abundance of plummy fruit, fine tannins and a kiss of quality oak. Screwcap. 13.5% alc. **Rating** 95 **To** 2033 $40
Methode Traditionelle Blanc de Noir NV The entire process from growing the pinot noir through to disgorgement and everything inbetween is carried out by hand onsite, with a minimum of 36 months on tirage. Pink-salmon. A super generous, full-bodied sparkling wine with some Bollinger-like richness and complexity. Diam. 12.5% alc. **Rating** 95 $55

Moorilla Estate ★★★★★

655 Main Road, Berriedale, Tas 7011 **Region** Southern Tasmania
T (03) 6277 9900 **www**.moorilla.com.au **Open** Wed–Mon 9.30–5
Winemaker Conor van der Reest **Est.** 1958 **Dozens** 11 000 **Vyds** 15.36ha
Moorilla Estate was the second winery to be established in Tasmania in the 20th century, Jean Miguet's La Provence beating it to the punch by two years. However, through much of the history of Moorilla Estate, it was the most important winery in the state, if not in size then as the icon. Magnificently situated on a mini-isthmus reaching into the Derwent River, it has always been a must-visit for wine lovers and tourists. Production is around 90t/year, sourced entirely from the vineyards around Moorilla and its St Matthias Vineyard (Tamar Valley). The winery is part of an overall development said by observers (not Moorilla) to have cost upwards of $150 million. Its raison d'être is the establishment of an art gallery (MONA) that has the highest atmospheric environment accreditation of any gallery in the Southern Hemisphere, housing both the extraordinary ancient and contemporary art collection assembled by Moorilla's owner, David Walsh, and visiting exhibitions from major art museums around the world. Exports to South Korea, Hong Kong and China.

ΨΨΨΨΨ **Muse Extra Brut Methode Traditionelle 2014** Terrific intensity, complexity and length. Red apple, sweet pastry, citrus and creamed honey flavours power deliciously through the mouth. One sniff/sip and you're both impressed and hooked. A great advertisement for Australian/Tasmanian sparkling wine. Diam. 12.5% alc. **Rating** 96 $54 CM ✪

Cloth Label Late Disgorged 2008 Both powerful and complex but what length, what elegance. This biscuity, citrussy, yeasty release boasts both character and dare. The line of acidity through the finish is challenging but ultimately (and then some) successful. It's a statement wine in the best of ways. Diam. 11.4% alc. **Rating** 96 $145 CM

Muse Moorilla Vineyard Pinot Noir 2015 Has more drive and complexity than the very developed colour would suggest; the bouquet fragrant and spicy; the palate following suit. Screwcap. 13.9% alc. **Rating** 94 **To** 2025 $65

ΨΨΨΨΨ **Muse Riesling 2017** **Rating** 93 **To** 2029 $42 CM
Muse St Matthias Vineyard Chardonnay 2017 **Rating** 93 **To** 2028 $45 CM

Moorooduc Estate ★★★★★

501 Derril Road, Moorooduc, Vic 3936 **Region** Mornington Peninsula
T (03) 5971 8506 **www**.moorooducestate.com.au **Open** 7 days 11–5
Winemaker Dr Richard McIntyre, Jeremy Magyar **Est.** 1983 **Dozens** 4000 **Vyds** 10.4ha
Richard McIntyre has taken Moorooduc Estate to new heights, having completely mastered the difficult art of gaining maximum results from wild-yeast fermentation. Starting with the 2010 vintage, there was a complete revamp of grape sources and hence changes to the tiered structure of the releases. These changes were driven by the simple fact that the estate vineyards had no possibility of providing the 4000–6000 dozen bottles of wine sold each year. The entry-point wines under the Devil Bend Creek label remain principally sourced from the Osborn Vineyard. The mid-priced Chardonnay and Pinot Noir are no longer single-estate vineyard wines and are now simply labelled by vintage and variety. Next come the Robinson Vineyard Pinot Noir and Chardonnay, elevated to reserve wine status, priced a little below the ultimate 'Ducs' (The Moorooduc McIntyre). Exports to the UK, the US, Hong Kong and China.

ΨΨΨΨΨ **Robinson Vineyard Chardonnay 2018** This vineyard gives fruit of a cooler aura with greater tension than others. Subdued. Subtle stone fruit and nougatine allusions. But it is the stony mesh of juicy acidity and pungent mineral that service tenacious persistence and length. The flavours be damned! This wine is all about texture, a coiled restraint and a cool confidence. The oak a mere adjunct. Delicious. Screwcap. **Rating** 96 **To** 2028 $60 NG ✪

Pinot Gris On Skins 2018 A versatile wine that can be treated either as a light red or richer rose. A gorgeous tangerine hue. Limpid. Scents of orange zest, quinine, tomatillo, mandarin and crushed strawberry. Moreish, crunchy and devilishly long with a fibrous skein of spicy tannins. Neither prosaic, nor simple. Just dangerously easy to drink. Scored as a benchmark for the idiom. Screwcap. **Rating** 95 **To** 2022 $40 NG

Robinson Vineyard Pinot Noir 2018 A lighter shade of Mornington, singing a soprano of bright red berry fruits and autumnal forest scents. Lifted and highly aromatic. Almost ethereal. Crunchy and saliva-sucking. Defined by an immaculate patina of tannin that is herb-inflected, yet ripe; detailed, yet svelte. A fine pinot of textural intrigue and freshness. Screwcap. **Rating** 95 **To** 2026 $60 NG

The Moorooduc McIntyre Pinot Noir 2018 A pinot of compelling flavour intensity and refined, granular tannins. These are a product of site, judicious extraction and well appropriated oak regime (15 months; 20% new French). Ferrous. Black cherry, satsuma plum and Asian spice. Forceful. Long and plush without being fat or sweet. The tannins – grape and oak – operate as ample reins to the wine's exuberance. Screwcap. **Rating** 95 **To** 2026 $80 NG

The Moorooduc McIntyre Chardonnay 2018 Mealy. Oatmeal. Apricot pith, white peach and a core of truffled praline and toasted nuts. More Meursault than anything else. The oak impeccably nestled. Intense, prickly mineral and expanding nicely with time in the glass. Fine length. A warmer sandy site with a clay substrata. Screwcap. **Rating** 94 **To** 2024 **$**80 NG

🍷🍷🍷🍷 **Chardonnay 2018 Rating** 93 **To** 2023 **$**40 NG
Pinot Gris 2018 Rating 93 **To** 2024 NG
Pinot Noir 2018 Rating 93 **To** 2023 **$**40 NG
NV Rating 93 **$**60 NG

Moortangi Estate ★★★☆

120 Wills Road, Dixons Creek, Vic 3775 **Region** Yarra Valley
T (03) 9600 4001 **www**.moortangiestate.com.au **Open** Not
Winemaker Sergio Carlei **Est.** 2002 **Dozens** 300 **Vyds** 5.75ha

Paul and Pamela Hyland purchased a beautiful grazing property at Dixons Creek already christened 'Moortangi'. They planted the north-facing paddocks with shiraz (4ha), cabernet sauvignon (0.9ha), merlot (0.5ha) and viognier (0.35ha), and while waiting for the vines to mature purchased shiraz from Heathcote for their first vintage. They have continued to make the Old Vine Heathcote Shiraz from vines planted in the 1950s in grey loam soils, the Cambrian Shiraz from red soils. By 2009 the vines were flourishing and they anticipated their first vintage but the Black Saturday bushfires devastated the property, destroying the majority of their vines. In '10 they saw shoots on their main planting of shiraz and they have since laboriously resurrected the vineyard on a vine-by-vine basis and now oversee what they regard as an exceptional vineyard. They say their love of wine brought them to this place; it has been sorely tested, but ultimately fulfilled.

🍷🍷🍷🍷 **Yarra Valley Dry Red 2012** Why label a Yarra Valley shiraz Dry Red? It's showing some age but the glass is more than half full and the price is right. Don't delay consuming it. Diam. 13.5% alc. **Rating** 90 **To** 2022 **$**25

Moppity Vineyards ★★★★★

Moppity Road, Young, NSW 2594 (postal) **Region** Hilltops
T (02) 6382 6222 **www**.moppity.com.au **Open** Not
Winemaker Jason Brown **Est.** 1973 **Dozens** 30 000 **Vyds** 66.54ha

Jason Brown and wife Alecia, with backgrounds in fine wine retail and accounting, purchased Moppity Vineyards in 2004 when it was already 31 years old. Initially they were content to sell the grapes to other makers, but that changed with the release of the '06 Shiraz, which won top gold in its class at the London International Wine & Spirit Competition. In Nov '09 the '08 Eden Road Long Road Hilltops Shiraz, made from Moppity Vineyards grapes, won the Jimmy Watson Trophy. These awards are among a cascade of golds for its shirazs, Riesling, Tumbarumba Chardonnay and Cabernet Sauvignon. Production (and sales) have soared and all the grapes from the estate are now used for the Moppity Vineyards brand. The Lock & Key range provides exceptional value for money. Moppity has also established Coppabella, a separate venture, in Tumbarumba. Exports to the UK and China.

🍷🍷🍷🍷🍷 **Escalier Hilltops Shiraz 2016** Shiraz from a '73-planted block, co-fermented with viognier. Medium in weight but threaded with beautiful, fine-grained tannin and boasting significant elegance. It tastes of red berries, bay leaves, smoky oak and sweet spice but it's the carry through the finish that really marks its quality. Not a big wine by any stretch but exquisitely well crafted. Screwcap. 14% alc. **Rating** 96 **To** 2035 **$**130 CM

Lock & Key Hilltops Cabernet Sauvignon 2017 Over 23 days on skins, matured in new and used French oak. Bell-clear varietal character; juicy cassis fruit fills the bouquet and palate alike, oak and tannins where you need/expect them to be. Length and balance tick their boxes. Exceptional value. Screwcap. 13.9% alc. **Rating** 95 **To** 2030 **$**25 ✪

Cato La Lucha Hilltops Tempranillo 2017 Two clones grafted onto 43yo rootstocks, the fruit cold-soaked pre-fermentation, matured in new French oak for 12 months. This is the second vintage after the first won gold medals at Sydney and Canberra. It is labrador-friendly and you'd have to have a hard heart (or tongue) not to love it. Screwcap. 13.5% alc. **Rating** 95 **To** 2029 $35 **◐**

Lock & Key Hilltops Merlot 2018 Briary, juicy, characterful and persistent. It's distinctive in a good way; highly fragrant (tobacco), supple-textured, traced with sweet coffee notes and run with mulberried fruit. If you're looking for a good merlot, buy this. Screwcap. 14% alc. **Rating** 94 **To** 2027 $25 CM **◐**

Cato La Pendenza Hilltops Sangiovese 2017 Matured in used French barriques for 12 months. Proves that sangiovese can be fun to drink any time, anywhere. Bright red fruits have just the right amount of fine tannins. Screwcap. 14% alc. **Rating** 94 **To** 2023 $35

♟♟♟♟♟ **Crafted Hilltops Syrah Nouveau 2018** **Rating** 93 **To** 2024 $30 CM
Reserve Hilltops Shiraz 2017 **Rating** 93 **To** 2027 $80 CM
Crafted Hilltops Grenache Shiraz 2018 **Rating** 93 **To** 2025 $30 CM
Lock & Key Tumbarumba Sauvignon Blanc 2019 **Rating** 92 **To** 2021 $25 CM **◐**
Lock & Key Tumbarumba Chardonnay 2018 **Rating** 92 **To** 2024 $25 JP **◐**
Tumbarumba Chardonnay 2018 **Rating** 92 **To** 2026 $35 CM
Lock & Key Hilltops Rose 2019 **Rating** 92 **To** 2021 $25 CM **◐**
Lock & Key Hilltops Shiraz 2018 **Rating** 92 **To** 2026 $25 CM **◐**
Crafted Hilltops Shiraz 2018 **Rating** 92 **To** 2026 $30 CM
Crafted Hilltops Shiraz 2017 **Rating** 92 **To** 2026 $30 CM
Crafted Hilltops Cabernet Sauvignon 2018 **Rating** 92 **To** 2027 $30 CM
Lock & Key Tumbarumba Sauvignon Blanc 2018 **Rating** 91 **To** 2025 $25 JP
Lock & Key Tumbarumba Rose 2018 **Rating** 91 **To** 2026 $25 JP
Lock & Key Single Vineyard Tumbarumba Pinot Noir 2019 **Rating** 91 **To** 2024 $25 CM
Crafted Hilltops Cabernet Sauvignon 2017 **Rating** 91 **To** 2027 $30 CM
Lock & Key Tumbarumba Chardonnay Pinot Noir 2018 **Rating** 90 $25 JP

🍇 Mordrelle Wines   NR

411 River Road, Hahndorf, SA 5243 **Region** Adelaide Hills
T 0448 859 454 www.mordrellewines.com.au **Open** By appt
Winemaker Martin Moran **Est.** 2010 **Dozens** 2000
Martin Moran says he is the only Argentinian in Australia to have studied viticulture and winemaking in Mendoza, who makes very good malbec, plays a classical guitar built by his father's uncle in 1933 and has created enormous Argentinian bbqs to feed big crowds. Unfortunately the wines submitted did not arrive.

Morris   ★★★★★

Mia Mia Road, Rutherglen, Vic 3685 **Region** Rutherglen
T (02) 6026 7303 www.morriswines.com **Open** Mon–Sat 9–5, Sun 10–5
Winemaker David Morris **Est.** 1859 **Dozens** 100 000 **Vyds** 96ha
One of the greatest of the fortified winemakers, ranking an eyelash behind Chambers Rosewood. Morris has changed the labelling system for its sublime fortified wines with a higher-than-average entry point for the (Classic) Liqueur Muscat; Topaque and the ultra-premium wines are being released under the Old Premium Liqueur (Rare) label. The art of these wines lies in the blending of very old and much younger material. These Rutherglen fortified wines have no equivalent in any other part of the world (with the honourable exception of Seppeltsfield in the Barossa Valley). In July 2016 Casella Family Brands acquired Morris after decades of uninterested ownership by Pernod Ricard.

♟♟♟♟♟ **Old Premium Rare Topaque NV** Rare is in a class of its own. Extraordinary. Taking on umami complexity, dark chocolate studded with salt flakes, raisins soaked in molasses and more. Rich and sweet but definitely not burdened by all that because it has life, a lemony acidity and a freshness throughout. Screwcap. 17.5% alc. **Rating** 99 $90 JF **◐**

Old Premium Rare Liqueur Rutherglen Muscat NV A lot of emotion can be found in a glass of rare, as only time can produce this. Extraordinarily complex with its umami flavours, brittle burnt toffee, Eccles cakes and an array of Middle Eastern baking spices. Beautifully composed, fresh and a joy to behold. And drink. Screwcap. 17% alc. **Rating** 98 $90 JF ✪

Cellar Reserve Grand Liqueur Rutherglen Topaque NV Deep chocolate brown-olive; toffee and coffee, lemon drops and salted caramels. It's luscious, the palate silky smooth, the balance perfect. 500ml. Screwcap. 17.3% alc. **Rating** 97 $50 JF ✪

ΨΨΨΨΨ **Cellar Reserve Grand Liqueur Rutherglen Muscat NV** A deep walnut hue. Imagine chocolate licorice bullets, lemon drops, aged balsamic vinegar, pepper and baking spices – they are all in this glorious elixir. The palate as rich as molasses yet incredibly fresh with the spirit perfectly matched. Screwcap. 17.3% alc. **Rating** 96 $50 JF ✪

CHM Rutherglen Shiraz 2013 Fabulous dark garnet. It's so rich, deep and flavoursome, where to start? No shortage of oak, no shortage of tannins and yet, this doesn't drag anything down. Wafts of leather, spiced plums with an Aussie bush fragrance. It smells of Rutherglen. Screwcap. 15% alc. **Rating** 95 To 2033 $50 JF

CHM Rutherglen Durif 2013 A wonderful deep dark red hue. Like its Shiraz sibling, it's made with serious intention and cellaring. An abundance of ripe flavours from poached fruit to tar and warm bitumen. Lashings of oak that somehow just work. The tannins are bolshie and firm yet there's a line of acidity keeping this ever-so above board. Archetypal Rutherglen durif at its best. Screwcap. 15% alc. **Rating** 95 To 2033 $60 JF

Cellar Reserve Grand Rutherglen Tawny NV Tawny with a shimmer of ruby. There's a brandy-esque aroma with licorice and raisins, toffee apples and aged balsamic vinegar. Very fresh yet has a richness and depth from age. Screwcap. 19% alc. **Rating** 95 $50 JF

Old Premium Rare Rutherglen Tawny NV Ruby-tawny hue. A strong whiff of volatility and spirit, but the palate compensates admirably. Aged balsamic vinegar, brittle toffee, coffee and chocolate licorice and aniseed balls. Lemony acidity cuts through the richness, the palate tight and bright. 500ml. Screwcap. 20% alc. **Rating** 94 $90 JF

Classic Rutherglen Muscat NV Mahogany with a ruby glint; a lovely entree to the muscat style with this first tier. Lemon cake studded with raisins, caramel and toffee. Luscious and sweet, the acidity keeping it in check. 500ml. Screwcap. 17.5% alc. **Rating** 94 $25 JF ✪

ΨΨΨΨΩ **Bin 186 Rutherglen Shiraz 2016** Rating 93 To 2030 $25 JF ✪
Black Label Rutherglen Muscat NV Rating 93 $20 JF ✪
Sparkling Shiraz Durif NV Rating 92 $25 JF ✪
Classic Rutherglen Topaque NV Rating 91 $25 JF
Mia Aged Amber Apera NV Rating 91 $50 JF

🍇 Moss Brothers   ★★★★

8 Wattle Place, Margaret River, WA 6285 **Region** Margaret River
T 0402 010 352 **www**.mossbrotherswines.com.au **Open** Not
Winemaker Laura Bowler **Est.** 1984 **Dozens** 5600 **Vyds** 16.03ha
This is the reincarnation of the Moss Brothers brand, though not its vineyards, which were acquired by Amelia Park in 2015. It is a parallel business to Trove Estate. Paul Byron and Ralph Dunning are the major forces in both ventures, both with extensive whole-of-business expertise across Australia. (Paul Byron's has focused on Margaret River.) Exports to the US and China.

ΨΨΨΨΩ **Moses Rock Margaret River Cabernet Sauvignon 2018** Matured for 10 months in French oak (10% new). Medium-bodied cassis fruit, the tannins in need of more grooming. Screwcap. 14.5% alc. **Rating** 92 To 2028 $32

Fidium Margaret River Shiraz 2018 Destemmed, matured in French oak (25% new) for 18 months. A complex wine. Medium-bodied aromas and flavours from red to earthy black olive. Screwcap. 14.5% alc. **Rating** 90 **To** 2028 $50

ŶŶŶŶ **Moses Rock Sauvignon Blanc 2019** Rating 89 To 2021 $32
Moses Rock Chardonnay 2019 Rating 89 To 2023 $32

Moss Wood ★★★★★

926 Metricup Road, Wilyabrup, WA 6284 **Region** Margaret River
T (08) 9755 6266 **www**.mosswood.com.au **Open** By appt
Winemaker Clare Mugford, Keith Mugford **Est.** 1969 **Dozens** 11 000 **Vyds** 18.14ha
Widely regarded as one of the best wineries in the region, producing glorious chardonnay, power-laden semillon and elegant cabernet sauvignon that lives for decades. Moss Wood also owns the RibbonVale Estate, the wines treated as vineyard-designated within the Moss Wood umbrella. Exports to all major markets.

ŶŶŶŶŶ **Wilyabrup Margaret River Cabernet Sauvignon 2016** Includes 5% petit verdot and 4% cabernet franc; hand-picked, destemmed, open-fermented, matured in French barriques (18% new). A luscious, plush cabernet; its voluptuous palate trimmed by dry herbs and foresty notes. A great vintage maximised by the thoughtful vinification. Screwcap. 14% alc. **Rating** 99 **To** 2051 $128 ○
Wilyabrup Margaret River Chardonnay 2018 Bright, light straw-green. Rich and layered stone fruit (white and yellow peach) and fig balanced by citrussy acidity. Oak handling is of a higher order – as befits the wine. Screwcap. 14% alc. **Rating** 97 **To** 2028 $85 ○

ŶŶŶŶŶ **Amy's 2018** Moss Wood's Bordeaux blend of cabernet sauvignon, merlot, malbec and petit verdot. Deep but bright crimson-purple foretells what is to come: a rich yet refined medium-bodied wine, oak and tannins present but not the least obvious. Screwcap. 14% alc. **Rating** 96 **To** 2038 $43 ○
Wilyabrup Margaret River Semillon 2019 Pressed, the juice transferred to stainless steel tanks and settled for 48 hours, seeded with multiple yeast cultures and fermented at 18°C, bottled as soon as possible in Jul. Smooth as silk with a velvet trim. It has multiple layers of fruit and can silence any food match. Screwcap. 14% alc. **Rating** 95 **To** 2030 $44
Ribbon Vale Margaret River Merlot 2017 Full of nervous energy. Its plummy fruit on one side and earthy, herbal acidity and freshness on the other. This will be ready when you are. Screwcap. 14% alc. **Rating** 94 **To** 2032 $77
Ribbon Vale Margaret River Cabernet Sauvignon 2017 Has the nervous energy of its '18 sibling but the herbal, forest floor characters show the door to the fruit. Bordeaux lovers may enjoy this wine. Screwcap. 13.5% alc. **Rating** 94 **To** 2032 $77

ŶŶŶŶ **Wilyabrup Margaret River Pinot Noir 2017** Rating 89 To 2027 $77

Mount Avoca ★★★★★

Moates Lane, Avoca, Vic 3467 **Region** Pyrenees
T (03) 5465 3282 **www**.mountavoca.com **Open** 7 days 11–4
Winemaker David Darlow **Est.** 1970 **Dozens** 15 000 **Vyds** 23.46ha
A winery that has long been one of the stalwarts of the Pyrenees region, owned by third-generation Matthew Barry. The estate vineyards (shiraz, sauvignon blanc, cabernet sauvignon, chardonnay, merlot, cabernet franc, tempranillo, lagrein, viognier, sangiovese, nebbiolo and semillon) are organically managed. The Moates Lane wines are partly or wholly made from contract-grown grapes, but other releases are estate-grown. Mount Avoca has continued to implement organic practises and has obtained full organic certification for some of the estate-grown wines. The winery was certified organic in 2016. Exports to China.

ŶŶŶŶŶ **Estate Old Vine Pyrenees Shiraz 2018** Sumptuous shiraz. What is rewarding while tasting across the shiraz hierarchy at this address, is the ascension of complexity, detail and density. Most of all, however, is the synergistic thread of drinkability across all cuvees. This, rightly, is the finest. The tannins are beautifully wrought, defining a gush of blue and boysenberry fruit, a swab of black olive and iodine. Effortless. Screwcap. **Rating** 95 **To** 2030 $38 NG

🍷🍷🍷🍷🍷 **Estate Pyrenees Shiraz 2018** Rating 93 $28 NG
Estate Pyrenees Merlot 2018 Rating 92 To 2023 $38 NG
Moates Lane Shiraz 2018 Rating 91 To 2023 $21 NG ✪
Moates Lane Sauvignon Blanc 2019 Rating 90 To 2020 $21 NG ✪

Mount Benson Estate ★★★★★

329 Wrights Bay Road, Mount Benson, SA 5275 **Region** Mount Benson
T 0417 996 796 **www**.mountbensonestate.com.au **Open** Sept–Jun 7 days 10–5
Winemaker Contract **Est.** 1988 **Dozens** 800 **Vyds** 24.2ha
The future of Mount Benson isn't easy to foresee. Both climate and soil offer rich rewards for those who understand the extreme differences between the four seasons (for humans as well as vines). The newly installed owners of Mount Benson Estate have one obvious advantage: husband Brian Nitschinsk served for 39 years in the Australian Navy, retiring as a commander engineer. Figuratively, Mount Benson (a puny rise measured in only tens of metres) has one foot in the Southern Ocean and one foot on the ground, so Brian should feel right at home. Wife Carolyn was a secondary school teacher specialising in art and visual communication. Thus, the cold windswept landscape of winter is something they will be able to cope with. The legacy of two generations of the founding Wehl family has already demonstrated the ability of the vineyard to produce shiraz of exceptional quality, cabernet sauvignon not far behind.

🍷🍷🍷🍷🍷 **Syrah 2016** Whole-berry fermented, extended skin contact, matured in French oak (15% new) for 12 months. Light to medium-bodied, it has a spicy shaft of flavour, partly cool-grown shiraz and partly oak. Screwcap. 14.3% alc. **Rating** 90 **To** 2023 $40

🍷🍷🍷🍷 **Rose of Syrah 2017** Rating 89 To 2019 $25
Cabernet Sauvignon 2016 Rating 89 To 2026 $25

Mount Eyre Vineyards ★★★★

173 Gillards Road, Pokolbin, NSW 2320 **Region** Hunter Valley
T 0438 683 973 **www**.mounteyre.com **Open** At The Garden Cellars
Winemaker Andrew Spinaze, Mark Richardson, Michael McManus **Est.** 1970
Dozens 3000 **Vyds** 45.5ha
This is the venture of two families whose involvement in wine extends back several centuries in an unbroken line: the Tsironis family in the Peleponnese, Greece; and the Iannuzzi family in Vallo della Lucania, Italy. Their largest vineyard is at Broke, with a smaller vineyard at Pokolbin. The three principal varieties planted are chardonnay, shiraz and semillon, with small amounts of merlot, viognier, chambourcin, verdelho, negro amaro, fiano and nero d'Avola.

🍷🍷🍷🍷🍷 **Three Ponds Grosser Hunter Valley Chardonnay 2019** A barrel selection of the best of the vintage. A rich wine. Toasty, nutty French oak mingling with stone fruit on the bouquet and showing a similar theme on the palate; a textural mouthfeel and ripe fruit balanced by light but persistent acidity. A good wine that is still getting into its stride. Screwcap. 13.2% alc. **Rating** 93 **To** 2026 $48 SC
Three Ponds Holman Hunter Valley Nero d'Avola 2017 From the estate Holman Vineyard in Pokolbin; open-fermented, matured in French oak for 12 months, made by Michael McManus. The region imparts as much as the variety – all of which goes to make a very pleasing medium-bodied red wine. Screwcap. 14.5% alc. **Rating** 93 **To** 2023 $45
Three Ponds Hunter Valley Shiraz 2018 From the estate Holman Vineyard in Pokolbin; open-fermented, matured in French oak for 15 months, made by Mark Richardson. Fully reflects the excellent vintage. Soft tannins, good mouthfeel; rich blood plum and dark cherry fruit. Screwcap. 13% alc. **Rating** 92 **To** 2030 $30

Three Ponds Hunter Valley Chardonnay 2019 Fermented and aged in tight grain French oak. Melony fruit greets you on the bouquet but it's fighting for attention with the oak, which is perhaps a little too obvious at this stage. There's ample sweet-fruited flavour on the palate and, while softness is the overall impression, there's enough acidity to provide a clean finish of good length. Screwcap. 13.5% alc. **Rating** 90 **To** 2024 $28 SC

Three Ponds Hunter Valley Fiano 2019 Does show some of the textural qualities fiano is noted for; both the bouquet and palate have a range of tree fruit flavours. Fermented largely dry. Screwcap. 13.3% alc. **Rating** 90 **To** 2024 $30

Three Ponds Holman Hunter Valley Nero d'Avola 2018 Nero d'Avola is seldom put off, its soft red cherry/berry flavours and wine structure always come good (or at least try to). The question of price is another issue. Screwcap. 14.5% alc. **Rating** 90 **To** 2023 $45

♟♟♟♟ **Three Ponds Hunter Valley Semillon 2019 Rating** 89 **To** 2030 $20
Monkey Place Creek Hunter Valley Rose 2019 Rating 89 **To** 2020 $23
Monkey Place Creek Hunter Valley Shiraz 2018 Rating 89 **To** 2025 $25

Mount Horrocks

The Old Railway Station, Curling Street, Auburn, SA 5451 **Region** Clare Valley
T (08) 8849 2243 **www.**mounthorrocks.com **Open** W'ends & public hols 10–5
Winemaker Stephanie Toole **Est.** 1982 **Dozens** 3500 **Vyds** 9.4ha
Owner/winemaker Stephanie Toole has never deviated from the pursuit of excellence in the vineyard and winery. She has three vineyard sites in the Clare Valley, each managed using natural farming and organic practices. The attention to detail and refusal to cut corners is obvious in all her wines. The cellar door is in the renovated old Auburn railway station. Exports to the UK, China and other major markets.

♟♟♟♟♟ **Watervale Riesling 2019** This offers the commodity in short supply in '19: finesse. It has all the varietal flavours that make riesling what it is – mouth-watering, vibrant, crisp and long – riding high on a magic carpet. Screwcap. 12.5% alc. **Rating** 95 **To** 2034 $40

Clare Valley Cabernet Sauvignon 2018 A mid to full-weighted cabernet with mint, sap, blackcurrant and bouquet garni. Pliant tannins doused with sage galvanise the flavours. Highly savoury. Very versatile. The oak and unobtrusive acidity are beautifully positioned to let this run for a decade or more. Screwcap. **Rating** 95 **To** 2033 $46 NG

Clare Valley Semillon 2019 A warmer vintage. What this lacks in the way of linearity and precision, it gains in terms of amplitude and aromatic complexity: lemon oil and hedgerow segue to ripe quince, all offset by an intoxicating skein of fennel. Almost pastis-like. Nestled seams of oak service the textural opus. Delicious and light years from the tensile Hunter expression. Best not drunk too cold. Screwcap. **Rating** 94 **To** 2026 NG

♟♟♟♟♟ **Clare Valley Nero d'Avola 2018 Rating** 92 **To** 2022 $40 NG

Mount Langi Ghiran Vineyards

80 Vine Road, Bayindeen, Vic 3375 **Region** Grampians
T (03) 5354 3207 **www.**langi.com.au **Open** 7 days 10–5
Winemaker Adam Louder, Jess Robertson, Darren Rathbone **Est.** 1969 **Dozens** 60 000 **Vyds** 65ha
A maker of outstanding cool-climate peppery shiraz, crammed with flavour and vinosity, and very good cabernet sauvignon. The shiraz has long pointed the way for cool-climate examples of the variety. The business was acquired by the Rathbone family group in 2002. The marketing is integrated with the Yering Station and Xanadu Estate wines, a synergistic mix with no overlap. Wine quality is exemplary. Exports to all major markets.

♥♥♥♥♥ **Langi Grampians Shiraz 2018** Hand-picked, wild-fermented with 80% whole bunches and 20% whole berries, 2–3 weeks on skins, matured for 18 months in French barriques (18% new), 280 dozen made. Wonderfully, tumultuously intense yet balanced; black licorice and herbal/foresty nuances all in play. Screwcap. 14.8% alc. **Rating** 99 **To** 2053 $200 ❂

♥♥♥♥♥ **Mast Shiraz 2018** The late Trevor Mast was the founder of Mount Langi Ghiran and for so long its sole winemaker. Many things have changed since then, all good. Open-fermented with 65% whole bunches, 35% whole berries, pressed to French barriques (none new). The absence of new oak has not diminished it in any way, a simple recognition that Trevor Mast's financial constraints meant little money for oak. Screwcap. 14.8% alc. **Rating** 96 **To** 2038 $90
Cliff Edge Grampians Shiraz 2018 Was 50% hand-picked, 50% machine-harvested (traditional), part whole berry, part crushed, 2 weeks on skins with cultured yeast, 14 months in French barriques (30% new). The Grampians at its most seductive. Medium-bodied with supple dark fruits, licorice, spice and soft tannins. Screwcap. 14.5% alc. **Rating** 96 **To** 2032 $35 ❂
Talus Grampians Shiraz 2018 A blend of some of the best parcels from the Mount Langi Ghiran property; 80% hand-picked, open-fermented with 75% whole berries/25% whole bunches, matured for 18 months in French barriques (25% new), 600 dozen made. If you didn't know otherwise, you might think red fruits have joined the black, or viognier or raspberries (wild or cultivated). Screwcap. 14.8% alc. **Rating** 96 **To** 2038 $60 ❂
Cliff Edge Cabernet Sauvignon Merlot 2018 A 79/21% blend, both varieties hand-picked, whole berries in small open fermenters, 3 weeks on skins, matured for 18 months in French barriques (30% new). High quality fruit and attention to detail. Screwcap. 14.8% alc. **Rating** 95 **To** 2033 $35 ❂

♥♥♥♥♡ **Billi Billi Shiraz 2017 Rating** 93 **To** 2024 $18 ❂
Talus Grampians Riesling 2019 Rating 92 **To** 2029 $35
Cliff Edge Grampians Riesling 2019 Rating 92 **To** 2026 $25 ❂
Billi Billi Pinot Gris 2019 Rating 91 **To** 2022 $18 ❂
Cliff Edge Grampians Pinot Gris 2019 Rating 91 **To** 2023 $25

Mt Lofty Ranges Vineyard   ★★★★★

Harris Road, Lenswood, SA 5240 **Region** Adelaide Hills
T (08) 8389 8339 **www**.mtloftyrangesvineyard.com.au **Open** Fri–Sun 11–5
Winemaker Peter Leske, Taras Ochota **Est.** 1992 **Dozens** 3000 **Vyds** 4.6ha
Mt Lofty Ranges is owned and operated by Sharon Pearson and Garry Sweeney. Nestled high in the Lenswood subregion of the Adelaide Hills at an altitude of 500m, the very steep north facing vineyard (pinot noir, sauvignon blanc, chardonnay and riesling) is hand-pruned and hand-picked. The soil is sandy clay loam with a rock base of white quartz and ironstone, and irrigation is kept to a minimum to allow the wines to display vintage characteristics.

♥♥♥♥♥ **Adelaide Hills Shiraz 2018** From 20+yo vines, multiple clones; hand-picked, matured for 10 months in French oak (25% new). There's a multi-spice backbone to a wine of deceptive power. Tannins present but acting in concert. Screwcap. 14% alc. **Rating** 96 **To** 2048 $35 ❂
S&G Adelaide Hills Shiraz 2018 From 20+yo vines, multiple clones; hand-picked, 100% whole bunch, matured in 1yo French barrels for 10 months. Strange (though very good) that the whole-bunch vinification intensifies the length and depth of the black cherry fruits while also adding texture. Screwcap. 13.3% alc. **Rating** 96 **To** 2038 $85
S&G Lenswood Chardonnay 2018 Three clones, 1yo barrels, 10 months. The accent is firmly on the fruit, which delivers and then some. Screwcap. 13.2% alc. **Rating** 95 **To** 2027 $85

Aspire Adelaide Hills Shiraz 2018 Identical vinification to its varietal sibling, less than 100 dozen made. Classic cool-grown shiraz with a perfumed bouquet; spice, pepper and cedar oak all singing from the same page. Screwcap. 14% alc. Rating 95 To 2033 $55

Old Apple Block Lenswood Chardonnay 2018 Identical vinification to Aspire but different clones. Curiously, the 25% new French oak is more obvious and complex here, the wine likewise. Screwcap. 13% alc. **Rating** 94 **To** 2026 $32

S&G Lenswood Pinot Noir 2018 From 25yo vines, multiple clones; hand-picked, 100% whole bunch, matured for 10 months in second-use French oak, less than 50 dozen made. Superior colour to its '18 siblings. The varietal bouquet and palate are also distinctly better with juicy cherry-accented fruit to the fore, whole-bunch notes no more than an echo. Screwcap. 12.8% alc. **Rating** 94 **To** 2026 $85

ŢŢŢŢŢ **Aspire Lenswood Chardonnay 2018** Rating 93 To 2027 $55
Home Block Lenswood Riesling 2019 Rating 90 To 2026 $30
Aspire Lenswood Pinot Noir 2018 Rating 90 To 2025 $55

Mount Majura Vineyard ★★★★★

88 Lime Kiln Road, Majura, ACT 2609 **Region** Canberra District
T (02) 6262 3070 **www**.mountmajura.com.au **Open** 7 days 10–5
Winemaker Dr Frank van de Loo **Est.** 1988 **Dozens** 4000 **Vyds** 9.3ha
Vines were first planted in 1988 by Dinny Killen on a site on her family property that had been especially recommended by Dr Edgar Riek; its attractions were red soil of volcanic origin over limestone with reasonably steep east and northeast slopes providing an element of frost protection. The tiny vineyard has been significantly expanded since it was purchased in '99. Blocks of pinot noir and chardonnay have been joined by pinot gris, shiraz, tempranillo, riesling, graciano, mondeuse and touriga nacional. Much attention has been focused on tempranillo with six clones planted: D8V12, D8V13, CL770, T306, requena and tinta roriz. Three single site tempranillos (Road Block, Dry Spur and Little Dam) are more recent arrivals. The Mount Majura flagship remains the Canberra District Tempranillo with volume and quality cementing its place. All the grapes used come from these estate plantings. One of the star performers in the Canberra District.

ŢŢŢŢŢ **Canberra District Shiraz 2018** Hand-picked, 25% whole bunches, matured in French barriques for 16 months. Gold medals Small Winewise Vignerons Wine Show and Canberra Regional Wine Show '19. Elegance personified with flavour and texture a continuum joined at the hip. Screwcap. 14% alc. **Rating** 96 **To** 2030 $38 ✪

Rock Block 2018 The 0.363ha block was planted with 4 clones of tempranillo in '00; Frank van der Loo using the standard pre-fermentation cold soak, wild yeast and hand-plunging; 49 dozen made. There is a large bowl of flowers and a distinctive array of soft spices. This is my choice of this group of tempranillos, but I do wonder why a mixed dozen (with the main release leading the way) wasn't part of the release. Screwcap. 14% alc. **Rating** 96 **To** 2039 $65 ✪

Canberra District Riesling 2019 Early summer heat and drought reduced yields before mild conditions in Mar; hand-picked, free-run juice, the cool ferment stopped with 6g/l residual sugar manifested as lime and candied lemon, the flavours building with each additional sip. Lovely wine. Gold medal Winewise Small Vigneron Awards '19. Screwcap. 12% alc. **Rating** 95 **To** 2031 $29 ✪

Canberra District Tempranillo 2018 This is Mount Majura's 16th release of tempranillo, making it an early player. Pre and post-fermentation maceration have built the power and savoury notes to the many faces of the wine and ensured its long future. Firm, dry finish. Screwcap. 14% alc. **Rating** 95 **To** 2038 $48

Little Dam 2018 Originally planted to pinot noir in '00, grafted to tempranillo in '04. A distinctly floral bouquet with an unexpected lead of violets, the medium-bodied palate offers a finely balanced play between small-berry fruits and firm but fine tannins. Screwcap. 14.5% alc. **Rating** 95 **To** 2038 $65

Dry Spur 2018 Originally planted to merlot in '96 but progressively replanted/grafted to tempranillo through to '06. Only 50 dozen made, attention to detail inevitable. This is as juicy as you could expect from any tempranillo. Red and blue fruits caress the mouth through to the aftertaste. Screwcap. 14% alc. **Rating** 94 **To** 2038 $65

Canberra District Mondeuse 2019 Described by the winemaker as 'filling the space left by pinot noir' as climate change inexorably alters our viticultural landscape. There's little similarity of aroma or flavour, but the parallel is in the just medium weight and fruit-driven structure. Red and black berries, peppery spice and piquant astringency it's defining characters. I want to drink it with a gourmet pizza. Screwcap. 13% alc. **Rating** 94 **To** 2025 $32 SC

ΨΨΨΨΥ **Chardonnay 2018** Rating 93 To 2028 $29 SC
Graciano 2019 Rating 93 To 2025 $32 SC
Lime Kiln Red 2018 Rating 92 To 2023 $26 SC
TSG Tempranillo Shiraz Graciano 2017 Rating 92 To 2023 $34 SC
The Silurian Pinot Noir Chardonnay 2018 Rating 92 $32 SC

Mount Mary ★★★★★

Coldstream West Road, Lilydale, Vic 3140 **Region** Yarra Valley
T (03) 9739 1761 **www.**mountmary.com.au **Open** Not
Winemaker Sam Middleton **Est.** 1971 **Dozens** 4500 **Vyds** 18ha

Mount Mary was one of the foremost pioneers of the rebirth of the Yarra Valley after 50 years without viticultural activity. From the outset they produced wines of rare finesse and purity. Today its star shines brighter than that of any of the 169 producers in the Yarra Valley. The late founder, Dr John Middleton, practised near-obsessive attention to detail long before that phrase slid into oenological vernacular. He relentlessly strove for perfection and all four of the wines in the original Mount Mary portfolio achieved just that (within the context of each vintage). Charming grandson Sam Middleton is equally dedicated. An all-encompassing recent tasting of every vintage of these four wines left me in no doubt he is making even better wines since assuming the winemaker mantle in June 2011. In '08 Mount Mary commenced a detailed program of vine improvement, in particular assessing the implications of progressively moving towards a 100% grafted vineyard to provide immunity from phylloxera. Part involved a move to sustainable organic viticulture and ongoing use of straw mulch to retain as much moisture as possible in the vineyard. Winery of the Year in the *Wine Companion 2018*. Exports to the UK, the US, Denmark, Hong Kong, Singapore, South Korea and China.

ΨΨΨΨΨ **Yarra Valley Quintet 2018** Stands proudly at the head of the Mount Mary portfolio. A blend of 44% cabernet sauvignon, 30% merlot, 16% cabernet franc and 5% each of malbec and petit verdot; each variety handled according to its structure. Open/static fermenters, wood/stainless steel, 10–14 days on skins, 35% new oak from a range of coopers and forests, 16–20 months in barrel. Mesmerisingly silky with a kaleidoscope of fruit and secondary flavours. Cork. 13% alc. **Rating** 99 **To** 2048 $155 ✪

Yarra Valley Chardonnay 2018 Multiple clones, hand-picked, crushed and destemmed, fermented French oak (30% new), matured for 11 months. Pale straw-green. Extremely focused and wrapped in a skein of citrussy acidity, the palate of extreme length, its future guaranteed by its screwcap. Just when you think the Mount Mary wines can't get any better (at the point of release), they do. 13% alc. **Rating** 98 **To** 2038 $110 ✪

Yarra Valley Pinot Noir 2018 Bunch-sorted on vibrating tables, Oscillys-destemmed whole berries, 10–14 days on skins, matured 14–18 months in oak (25% new). Not a hair out of place, all the boxes with big ticks. A perfumed bouquet with rose petals and tantalising hints of forest, the vibrantly fresh palate with a diamond-clear stream of red fruits and spices. The length is awesome. Cork. 13.3% alc. **Rating** 98 **To** 2038 $140 ✪

Marli Russell by Mount Mary RP2 2018 With 50% grenache, 20% each of shiraz and mourvedre, 10% cinsaut; each variety vinified separately. Bunch-sorted on vibrating tables, then berry-sorted by Oscillys machine, 10–14 days on skins, matured for 14–18 months in French oak (10% new). Pure class, pure Mount Mary; long and silky. Screwcap. 13% alc. **Rating** 97 **To** 2038 $75 ○

ŸŸŸŸŸ **Yarra Valley Triolet 2018** An estate-grown blend of 68% sauvignon blanc, 24% semillon and 8% muscadelle; matured for 11 months in barrel. Has exceptional drive, complexity and balance; its longevity proved by multi-vintage vertical tastings. Its backbone of acidity has ample lime/lemon curd/fresh-cut grass to encourage a second glass. Diam. 13% alc. **Rating** 95 **To** 2028 $95

Marli Russell by Mount Mary RP1 2018 With 40% each of marsanne and roussanne, 20% clairette; fermented and matured in used French oak. The discipline of thought and deed is the anchor of the Mount Mary approach to every wine in its portfolio, this crisply savoury wine a prime example. It's harder to do less, but if the situation requires it, so be it. Screwcap. 13% alc. **Rating** 94 **To** 2038 $55

Mount Pleasant ★★★★★

401 Marrowbone Road, Pokolbin, NSW 2320 **Region** Hunter Valley
T (02) 4998 7505 **www.**mountpleasantwines.com.au **Open** 7 days 10–4
Winemaker Adrian Sparks **Est.** 1921 **Dozens** NFP **Vyds** 88.2ha
The glorious Elizabeth and Lovedale semillons are generally commercially available with four to five years of bottle age; they are treasures with a consistently superb show record. Mount Pleasant's individual vineyard wines, together with the Maurice O'Shea memorial wines, add to the lustre of this proud name. The appointment of Jim Chatto as group chief winemaker in 2013 and the '14 vintage – the best since 1965 – has lifted the range and quality of the red wines back to the glory days of Maurice O'Shea, who founded Mount Pleasant and proved himself one of Australia's great winemakers. Winery of the Year in the *Wine Companion 2017*. Exports to all major markets.

ŸŸŸŸŸ **1946 Vines Rosehill Vineyard Hunter Valley Shiraz 2018** A quite extraordinary release. It's dense with red-berried fruit but also with earth and spice. There are minor signs of oak but this wine is all about fruit and place. It's the Hunter Valley distilled into a red wine. It's floral, its flavours are spread wide and long, it feels captivating from start to finish. Get a T-shirt made: Rosehill We Love You. Screwcap. 13.5% alc. **Rating** 98 **To** 2050 $135 CM ○

1965 Vines Rosehill Vineyard Hunter Valley Shiraz 2018 It's hard to think of superlatives when your breath has been taken away. This reaches into full-bodied territory and makes it its own. It's floral, earthen, boysenberried, rushed with cherries and plush with plum. Drinking it is like diving into a remote country creek; one sip and you're in another world. Tannin. We have to talk about tannin. It's not just an aspect, it's a hill on which the wine is built. Think of a date between now and 2100 and, if well stored, this wine will likely still have wonders to impart. Screwcap. 14% alc. **Rating** 98 **To** 2050 $135 CM ○

Mountain C Light Bodied Dry Red 2018 From '46-planted vines, Rosehill Vineyard. More medium-bodied than light but no-one's complaining. This is so sure-footed it could walk a tightrope in the dark. It's red-fruited, spice-laced, impeccably well structured and sensationally long through the finish. The word seductive is apt, but so too is the word elegant. It's a beautiful wine in anyone's language. Screwcap. 13% alc. **Rating** 97 **To** 2040 CM

Mountain D Full Bodied Dry Red 2018 Living treasure of a wine. Incredibly well structured and incredibly regional in its flavour profile. Earth, violets, red and black cherry, graphite and wood smoke characters. It sits on the fuller side of medium-bodied and reaches to the long side of persistent. It will mature wonderfully. Screwcap. 14% alc. **Rating** 97 **To** 2045 $75 CM ○

🍷🍷🍷🍷🍷 **1921 Vines Old Paddock Vineyard Hunter Valley Shiraz 2018** High on structure and on fruit. Excellent concentration though it remains medium in weight. Plum and red cherry with hints of deeper blackberry. Earth and spice. A clove-like character. Really fresh, really firm, really good. Screwcap. 13.5% alc. **Rating** 96 **To** 2038 $135 CM

Mountain A Medium Bodied Dry Red 2018 It couldn't be any more Hunter if it tried. It sits just on the bolder side of medium weight, it's underpinned by earth and dry spice, it's essentially red-berried but there are suede, saltbush and roasted nuts characters rippling through. There's a dusting of musk stick too. You'd bet on this having a long, beautiful future. Screwcap. 14% alc. **Rating** 96 **To** 2042 CM

Old Paddock & Old Hill Hunter Valley Shiraz 2018 All things considered this is a bit of a steal. The history, the class in the bottle, the potential longevity, the importance. It's a beautiful medium-weight red wine. It tastes of musk, earth, peppercorn and ripe red/black cherries. It has vigour and momentum, yet it feels settled and controlled. It sings through the finish. It doesn't put a foot wrong. Screwcap. 14% alc. **Rating** 96 **To** 2038 $55 CM ✪

Rosehill Vineyard Hunter Valley Shiraz 2018 It's not a 'look at me' wine, but it's so beautifully well fruited, balanced and flavoured. This is a seriously good option for the cellar. The tannin is ripped with earth and coffee notes, the fruit is black-cherried and bountiful, it's svelte of texture and sustained through the finish. It's both faultless and characterful and, all things considered, extremely well priced. Screwcap. 14% alc. **Rating** 96 **To** 2040 $50 CM ✪

Mothervine Hunter Valley Pinot Noir 2017 Roars back into form. One word: character. Clean character. It's firm, red-fruited, sure-footed, a little spicy and low in oak. It's light but it feels confident. You just feel as though you're in good hands. Lengthy finish. A good strike of earthen tannin. Wood smoke as afters. Screwcap. 13% alc. **Rating** 95 **To** 2032 $40 CM

Mount Henry Hunter Valley Shiraz Pinot Noir 2018 The tension between tannin, acidity, savoury nuances and fruit is high. It feels as though all the components here are sitting straight and alert. Earth, rust, iodine, black cherry and plum notes all make contributions, as does malty oak. It's not dense but it feels robust; it's a wine of presence. It's easy to see this wine maturing fantastically. Screwcap. 14% alc. **Rating** 95 **To** 2038 CM

🍷🍷🍷🍷🍷 **1946 Vines Lovedale Vineyard Hunter Valley Semillon 2019** **Rating** 93 **To** 2029 $75 CM

Eight Acres Hunter Valley Semillon 2019 **Rating** 93 **To** 2032 $35 CM

Marrowbone Road Hunter Valley Fiano 2018 **Rating** 93 **To** 2023 $30 CM

High Paddock Hunter Valley Shiraz 2018 **Rating** 93 **To** 2032 $35 CM

Creek Block Hunter Valley Tempranillo Touriga 2018 **Rating** 93 **To** 2026 $30 CM

Isabelle Hunter Valley Rose 2019 **Rating** 91 **To** 2021 $20 CM ✪

Mount Stapylton Wines   ★★★★

1212 Northern Grampians Road, Laharum, Vic 3401 **Region** Grampians
T 0429 838 233 **www**.mts-wines.com **Open** Not
Winemaker Don McRae **Est.** 2002 **Dozens** 300 **Vyds** 1ha

Mount Stapylton's vineyard is planted on the historic Goonwinnow Homestead farming property at Laharum, on the northwest side of the Grampians, in front of Mt Stapylton. In 2017 the vineyard lease was purchased from founder Howard Staehr by the Staehr family and is now being run as an addition to their mixed farming enterprise.

🍷🍷🍷🍷🍷 **Grampians Shiraz 2018** An elegant mid-weighted shiraz, displaying all the benign regional influences and none of the negative ones. Aromas of plum, redcurrant and blackberry sashay effortlessly along a skein of peppery acidity. Finely tuned, fresh and graceful. Thankfully. The finish is long with a velour of gentle, sappy tannins. These could have been more amply extracted rather than relying on oak to provide the grip. Just a bit easy and sweet at the back end, but a delicious fluid wine nevertheless. Screwcap. **Rating** 93 **To** 2028 $45 NG

Mount Terrible ★★★★★

289 Licola Road, Jamieson, Vic 3723 **Region** Central Victoria zone
T (03) 5777 0703 **www**.mountterriblewines.com.au **Open** By appt
Winemaker John Eason **Est.** 2001 **Dozens** 350 **Vyds** 2ha
John Eason and wife Janene Ridley began the long, slow (and at times very painful) business of establishing their vineyard just north of Mt Terrible in 1992 – hence the choice of name. In 2001 they planted 2ha of pinot noir (MV6, 115, 114 and 777 clones) on a gently sloping, north-facing river terrace adjacent to the Jamieson River. DIY trials persuaded John to have the first commercial vintage in '06 contract-made. He has since made the wines himself in a fireproof winery built on top of an underground wine cellar. John has a sense of humour second to none, but must wonder what he has done to provoke the weather gods, alternating in their provision of fire, storm and tempest. Subsequent vintages have provided some well earned relief. Exports to the UK.

🍷🍷🍷🍷🍷 Jamieson Pinot Noir 2017 Hand-picked, chilled before crushing, 20% whole bunches, matured in French oak (33% new). A most attractive wine that has flourished in the cool vintage. Screwcap. 13.5% alc. **Rating** 95 **To** 2030 $45

Mount Trio Vineyard ★★★★☆

2534 Porongurup Road, Mount Barker WA 6324 **Region** Porongurup
T (08) 9853 1136 **www**.mounttriowines.com.au **Open** By appt
Winemaker Gavin Berry, Andrew Vesey, Caitlin Gazey **Est.** 1989 **Dozens** 3500
Vyds 8.5ha
Mount Trio was established by Gavin Berry and wife Gill Graham (plus business partners) shortly after they moved to the Mount Barker area in late 1988, Gavin to take up the position of chief winemaker at Plantagenet, which he held until 2004, when he and partners acquired the now very successful and much larger West Cape Howe. They have increased the estate plantings to 8.5ha with pinot noir (3.4ha), riesling (3.3ha), shiraz (1ha) and chardonnay (0.8ha). Exports to the UK, Denmark and China.

🍷🍷🍷🍷🍷 Home Block Porongurup Pinot Noir 2018 A barrel selection, the grapes coming from the oldest vines. A big hit of pinot character on the bouquet with gamey sour cherry characters overlaid by toasty oak. The cherry theme flows onto the palate, delivering it with a sweet-fruited, ripe feel and ample generosity of flavour. Has plenty to offer now but complexity will develop in time. Screwcap. 14% alc. **Rating** 95 **To** 2028 $35 SC ✪

🍷🍷🍷🍷🍷 Porongurup Riesling 2019 **Rating** 93 **To** 2024 $22 SC ✪

Porongurup Syrah 2018 **Rating** 93 **To** 2028 $22 SC ✪
Porongurup Pinot Noir 2018 **Rating** 92 **To** 2025 $22 SC ✪

Mount View Estate ★★★★★

Mount View Road, Mount View, NSW 2325 **Region** Hunter Valley
T (02) 4990 3307 **www**.mtviewestate.com.au **Open** Mon–Sat 10–5, Sun 10–4
Winemaker Scott Stephens **Est.** 1971 **Dozens** 5000 **Vyds** 16ha
Mount View Estate's vineyard was planted by the very knowledgeable Harry Tulloch almost 50 years ago; he recognised the quality of the red basalt volcanic soils of the very attractive hillside site. Prior owners John and Polly Burgess also purchased the adjoining Limestone Creek Vineyard in 2004 (planted in 1982), fitting it seamlessly into Mount View Estate's production. The quality of the wines is outstanding. The business changed hands in '16, now owned by a Chinese national with no further details available. Exports to China.

🍷🍷🍷🍷🍷 Museum Release Reserve Hunter Valley Semillon 2014 The nose on this wine is beguiling. It's all hay and honey, lemon pie and lanolin; the palate then following faithfully and impressively on. A burst of life and we're done. There's a great deal on offer here. Screwcap. 11.5% alc. **Rating** 95 **To** 2026 CM

Reserve Hunter Valley Shiraz 2018 It's about as full-bodied as Hunter Valley shiraz gets and neat as a pin to boot. It's fleshed with roasted plum and red cherry flavours, it's laced with dark soil and it carries high notes of sweet spice. Tannin pulls far back through the wine without ever altering its momentum. It has cellar worthiness written all over it. Screwcap. 14% alc. **Rating** 95 **To** 2036 $45 CM

Flagship Hunter Valley Shiraz 2018 Toast, redcurrant and smoked spice characters come edged with Vegemite and brandied raisin. It's a deep-set wine and a full-bodied one; its sweep of dry tannin carried along by the crush of fruit. Its robust persona is bound to serve it well over time. Screwcap. 14% alc. **Rating** 94 **To** 2040 $85 CM

Reserve Hunter Valley Petite Syrah 2018 First release from a block grafted from cabernet to durif/petite syrah in '17. Matured in French oak (33% new). There's grunt to the fruit and there's grunt to the tannin. No holds have been barred. It tastes of plum, toast, Bonox and florals, the latter rich and heady. Entirely convincing. Screwcap. 14.5% alc. **Rating** 94 **To** 2030 $45 CM

ŢŢŢŢ♀ **Reserve Hunter Valley Semillon 2019 Rating** 93 **To** 2030 CM
Reserve Hunter Valley Chardonnay 2018 Rating 93 **To** 2026 $45 CM

Mountadam ★★★★★

High Eden Road, Eden Valley, SA 5235 **Region** Eden Valley
T 0427 089 836 **www**.mountadam.com.au **Open** By appt
Winemaker Phil Lehmann **Est.** 1972 **Dozens** 30000 **Vyds** 148ha

Founded by the late David Wynn for the benefit of winemaker son Adam, Mountadam was (somewhat surprisingly) purchased by Möet Hennessy Wine Estates in 2000. In 2005, Mountadam returned to family ownership when it was purchased by David and Jenni Brown from Adelaide. David and Jenni have worked to bring the original Mountadam property back together with the purchase of Mountadam Farm in 2007 and the High Eden Vineyard from TWE in '15, thus reassembling all of the land originally purchased by David Wynn in the late 1960s. Phil Lehmann stepped into the role of chief winemaker in 2019, with extensive experience in the Barossa and Eden valleys at Peter Lehmann, Yalumba, Teusner, WD Wines and his own label Max & Me. Exports to the UK, Canada, France, Switzerland, Poland, Hong Kong and China.

ŢŢŢŢŢ **Eden Valley Chardonnay 2018** Has unexpected vigour and life with grapefruit leading white peach by the hand. The palate is long, well balanced, and such oak as is there, is well integrated. Screwcap. 12.5% alc. **Rating** 94 **To** 2023 $28 ✪

ŢŢŢŢ♀ **Eden Valley Riesling 2019 Rating** 92 **To** 2028 $28

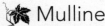 # Mulline ★★★★★

19/33 Fisher Parade, Ascot Vale, Vic 3032 (postal) **Region** Geelong
T 0402 409 292 **www**.mulline.com **Open** Not
Winemaker Ben Mullen **Est.** 2019 **Dozens** 700

This is the venture of Ben Mullen and business partner Ben Hine, the derivation of the winery name self-evident. Ben Mullen grew up in the Barossa Valley and studied oenology at the University of Adelaide, graduating in 2012. His journey thereafter was in the purple, working at Yarra Yering, Oakridge, Torbreck and Leeuwin Estate, Domaine Dujac in Burgundy in '13 (lighting a fire for pinot noir and chardonnay), Craggy Range in NZ ('15), coming back to Geelong as winemaker for Clyde Park in '17–18. Here he made the wine that won the Shiraz Trophy at the National Wine Show (for the '17 vintage) and the Geelong Trophy at the Australian Pinot Noir Challenge. Ben Hine also came from SA, and worked in hospitality for many years before obtaining his law degree; he is working full-time as a lawyer. When they met, it was he who took the running in creating the brand and the business structure behind it. In wine terms, this means a range of single vineyard wines at the top, backed by the Geelong region range (and no wines from elsewhere).

ŦŦŦŦŦ **Single Vineyard Portarlington Chardonnay 2019** Selectiv'-harvested,
pressed direct to oak (30% new Austrian) with full solids at 10°C for wild-yeast
fermentation. This is a wine initially all about mouthfeel/texture/structure until
the back-palate and finish, when pithy grapefruit notes break free to populate the
aftertaste with all manner of primary fruit, juice and zest contesting first place.
Screwcap. 13% alc. **Rating** 97 **To** 2029 $50 ✪
Single Vineyard Bannockburn Syrah 2019 Hand-picked, wild yeast–open
fermented with 25% whole bunches, twice-daily pumpovers, 10 days on skins,
pressed to oak (20% new) for mlf, no further movement pre-blending/bottling.
Good colour. Spicy black pepper and licorice. Great line and length to its ocean
of sweet black fruits. Screwcap. 13% alc. **Rating** 97 **To** 2039 $50 ✪

ŦŦŦŦŦ **Single Vineyard Bannockburn Fume Blanc 2019** Hand-picked, stomped
on and held on skins for 24 hours in a cool room, then pressed directly to barrel
with full solids, wild-fermented, 30% transferred to one new hogshead of Austrian
oak, the balance to used French barriques; blended and bottled Nov '19. The
retention of some tropical nuances is remarkable, the length and complexity less so.
Screwcap. 13.5% alc. **Rating** 96 **To** 2027 $50 ✪
Single Vineyard Sutherlands Creek Pinot Noir 2019 From 100% MV6
planted '98 on the Strathmore Vineyard; wild yeast–open fermented with
30% whole bunches, pressed to oak, no movement for 9 months before blending
and bottling. Light, bright crystal-clear crimson. The bouquet is complexed by a
mix of berry, earth and spice. A light-bodied palate follows, albeit with red fruits
and pomegranate joining the party. Screwcap. 13% alc. **Rating** 95 **To** 2029 $50
Geelong Pinot Gris 2019 From the Austin's Vineyard at Sutherlands Creek.
The fruit was machine-harvested, 30% fermented on skins for 7 days with twice-
daily punch downs, 70% pressed to tank and cold-fermented until dry, 120 dozen
made. Full-on salmon-pink. There is a fusion of red, citrus and pear aromas and
flavours. Screwcap. 12.5% alc. **Rating** 94 **To** 2023 $30 ✪

ŦŦŦŦ♀ **Geelong Rose 2019** **Rating** 93 **To** 2022 $30

Munari Wines ★★★★★

Ladys Creek Vineyard, 1129 Northern Highway, Heathcote, Vic 3523 **Region** Heathcote
T (03) 5433 3366 **www**.munariwines.com **Open** Tues–Sun 11–5
Winemaker Adrian Munari **Est.** 1993 **Dozens** 3000 **Vyds** 6.9ha
Established on one of the original Heathcote farming properties, Ladys Creek Vineyard is
situated on the narrow Cambrian soil strip 11km north of the town. Adrian Munari has
harnessed traditional winemaking practices to New World innovation to produce complex,
fruit-driven wines that marry concentration and elegance. They are produced from estate
plantings of shiraz, cabernet sauvignon, merlot, cabernet franc and malbec. Exports to France,
Denmark, Taiwan and China.

ŦŦŦŦŦ **Ladys Pass Heathcote Shiraz 2017** Move up the shiraz ladder at Munari and
the fruit concentration and complexity level goes up a notch. Colour, too. Dark
purple hues are in keeping with a region with some of the deepest red wine
colours in the country. Spice-accentuated black fruits, black olive savouriness and a
glimmer of toasted char. Supple with real poise on the palate. Screwcap. **Rating** 95
To 2034 $40 JP
The Gun Picker Shiraz Cabernet 2017 A more concentrated version of
the '16, powerfully so, mining deeper and more expressive flavour components.
Game and leather mix with concentrated black fruits and spice. Red berries
show up on the palate bringing a brightness. Texture is creamy, oak and tannin
integrated. Everything is in its place. Screwcap. **Rating** 95 **To** 2032 $30 JP ✪
Heathcote Rose 2019 The grape responsible for the picture-perfect rose-
salmon blush and discreet, red cherry–infused perfume is grenache. Its delightfully
dusty, gentle confection and raspberry and watermelon individual flavour
components all add up to a winning rose. Mouth-watering acidity finishes the job.
Screwcap. 12.8% alc. **Rating** 94 **To** 2025 $25 JP ✪

The Gun Picker Shiraz Cabernet 2016 A 60/40% shiraz/cabernet sauvignon blend. This is the scent of the Australian bush: turned red earth, briar, wild thyme and dusty roads. Intoxicating stuff. It's joined by blackberry, wild berries and bitter dark chocolate. Taut and deserving of a decant, it goes long and smooth. Screwcap. 13.8% alc. **Rating** 94 **To** 2032 **$30** JP ✪

India Red Heathcote Cabernet Sauvignon 2017 The '17 vintage in the Heathcote region has been described as 'perfect', which fits with the spring and lift in this 3yo and is why it works so well. Dense black fruits, licorice block, pastille confection and entwined throughout; dried herbs suggestive of garden mint and sage. Medium in weight, it's bolstered by a mineral intensity and fine tannins. Bright as a button. Screwcap. **Rating** 94 **To** 2032 **$30** JP ✪

🍷🍷🍷🍷🍸 **Late Harvest Viognier 2019 Rating** 93 **To** 2028 **$30** JP
The Beauregard Heathcote Shiraz 2017 Rating 90 **To** 2028 **$25** JP

Murdoch Hill   ★★★★★

260 Mappinga Road, Woodside, SA 5244 **Region** Adelaide Hills
T (08) 8389 7081 **www**.murdochhill.com.au **Open** By appt
Winemaker Michael Downer **Est.** 1998 **Dozens** 4000 **Vyds** 20.48ha
A little over 20ha of vines have been established on the undulating, gum tree–studded countryside of Charlie and Julie Downer's 60-year-old Erika property, 4km east of Oakbank. In descending order of importance, the varieties planted are sauvignon blanc, shiraz, cabernet sauvignon and chardonnay. Son Michael, with a Bachelor of Oenology degree from the University of Adelaide, is winemaker. Exports to the UK and China.

🍷🍷🍷🍷🍷 **The Rocket Limited Release Adelaide Hills Chardonnay 2019** A cull of the best barrels, the fruit hailing from 2 propitious sites in the Piccadilly Valley and lower, at Lobethal. Fermented wild in tight-grained French barriques and puncheons for 10 months (50% new). Malolactic (75%) serviced a softening while imbuing poise. Judging by this, all chardonnay makers should use this ilk of wood from whatever coopers it came from. This is sexy wine. Impeccable. Subdued yet searing of the sort of intensity of flavour that augurs for the brightest of futures. Writing of fruit references here is pointless. This wine is about texture, indelibly imprinted with a sense of place and the finest craftsmanship. Deservedly at the top of the tier. Screwcap. **Rating** 97 **To** 2029 **$80** NG ✪

🍷🍷🍷🍷🍷 **The Tilbury Adelaide Hills Chardonnay 2019** More tightly woven, restrained and nascent than the estate chardonnay, although jittering with an energy that only patience, time or an aggressive decant will unspool. Confident, unfettered and finely tuned. Nothing astride or unnecessary. Curd, apricot, grapefruit pulp and nectarine lurk beneath a veneer of classy oak (9 months, 30% new barriques). The intensity written. The finish long. Screwcap. **Rating** 95 **To** 2027 **$48** NG

The Surrey Single Vineyard Piccadilly Valley Pinot Meunier 2018 A western aspect, very low yielding, planting on shallow gravelly soil, wild-fermented with 50% whole bunches, matured for 6 months in used barriques. The colour is good, the bouquet an expressive mix of red cherry and strawberry fruit. Has good mouthfeel and length. Screwcap. 13% alc. **Rating** 95 **To** 2026 **$40**

The Phaeton Piccadilly Valley Adelaide Hills Pinot Noir 2019 Sourced from 3 separate Piccadilly Valley sites across Dijon clones 114 and 115, together with the Pommard/Aussie stalwart, MV6. And delicious it is too. A dash of whole bunch evinces some herbal cladding, 35% new oak serving as a directive pillar buried beneath the sapid cherry, wood smoke, root spice and autumnal leafy scents. Long and nourishing. Highly satisfying pinot. Screwcap. **Rating** 94 **To** 2025 **$48** NG

Cronberry Block Oakbank Adelaide Hills Syrah 2017 Estate-grown, 5 picking days from the cool vintage, fermented with 15% whole bunches, matured for 12 months in French barriques and puncheons (20% new). Elegant wine. Red berries with spices and black pepper run through the light to medium-bodied, well balanced palate. Screwcap. **Rating** 94 **To** 2030 **$30** ✪

🍷🍷🍷🍷🍷 Adelaide Hills Syrah 2018 Rating 93 To 2024 $30 NG
Limited Release Falcon Adelaide Hills Syrah Pinot Noir 2018 Rating 93
To 2026 $50 NG
Adelaide Hills Sauvignon Blanc 2019 Rating 92 To 2022 $25 NG ✪
Adelaide Hills Chardonnay 2019 Rating 92 To 2026 $25 NG ✪
Adelaide Hills Pinot Noir 2019 Rating 92 To 2024 $30 NG
The Surrey Single Vineyard Piccadilly Valley Pinot Meunier 2019
Rating 92 To 2023 $40 NG
Limited Release Vis-a-Vis Adelaide Hills Cabernet Franc 2019 Rating 92
To 2023 $35 NG
Limited Release Vis-a-Vis Adelaide Hills Cabernet Franc 2018 Rating 91
To 2030 $36
The Sulky Adelaide Hills Riesling 2019 Rating 90 To 2025 $36 NG
Limited Release Ridley Adelaide Hills Pinot x Three 2018 Rating 90
To 2025 $36

Murrumbateman Winery

13 McIntosh Circuit, Murrumbateman, NSW 2582 **Region** Canberra District
T 0432 826 454 **www.**murrumbatemanwinery.com.au **Open** Wed–Thurs 12–4,
Fri–Sat 10–5
Winemaker Bobbie Makin **Est.** 1972 **Dozens** 3500 **Vyds** 4ha
Draws upon 4ha of estate-grown sauvignon blanc and shiraz. It also incorporates an à la carte
restaurant and function room, together with picnic and bbq areas.

🍷🍷🍷🍷🍷 Riesling 2019 Hand-picked, no frills winemaking. There's no question that the
Canberra District produces first class riesling if the vintage conditions are normal
(or better). The beautiful lime, Meyer lemon and passionfruit flavour reservoir calls
you back again and again. Screwcap. 11.5% alc. Rating 96 To 2034 $30 ✪

🍷🍷🍷🍷🍷 Wine Dogs Pinot Grrris 2018 Rating 93 To 2020 $25 ✪
Shiraz 2017 Rating 90 To 2025 $50
Merlot 2018 Rating 90 To 2027 $25
Sangiovese 2018 Rating 90 To 2025 $25
Kay's Off Dry Riesling 2019 Rating 90 $30

MyattsField Vineyards

Union Road, Carmel Valley, WA 6076 **Region** Perth Hills
T (08) 9293 5567 **www.**myattsfield.com.au **Open** Fri–Sun & public hols 11–5
Winemaker Josh Davenport, Rachael Davenport, Josh Uren **Est.** 1997 **Dozens** 4000
Vyds 4.5ha
MyattsField Vineyards is owned by Josh and Rachael Davenport. Both have oenology
degrees and domestic and Flying Winemaker experience, especially Rachael. In 2006 they
decided they would prefer to work for themselves. They left their employment, building a
winery in time for the '07 vintage. Their vineyards include cabernet sauvignon, merlot, petit
verdot, shiraz and chardonnay. They also purchase small parcels of grapes from as far away as
Manjimup. Exports to Singapore and Taiwan.

🍷🍷🍷🍷🍷 Chardonnay 2016 Hand-picked, a long, cool fermentation in French hogsheads
(50% new), no mlf. Travelling slowly and smoothly along the development
tracks. An impressive stone fruit/melon/citrus trio. Screwcap. 14% alc. Rating 94
To 2025 $24 ✪

🍷🍷🍷🍷🍷 Mourvedre 2017 Rating 93 To 2027 $26 ✪
Riesling 2018 Rating 91 To 2028 $20 ✪
Vermentino 2019 Rating 90 To 2022 $20 ✪
Shiraz Mourvedre Viognier 2017 Rating 90 To 2026 $26
Methode Traditionelle Chardonnay Pinot Noir 2016 Rating 90

Naked Run Wines

36 Parawae Road, Salisbury Plain, SA 5109 (postal) **Region** Clare Valley/Barossa Valley
T 0408 807 655 **www**.nakedrunwines.com.au **Open** Not
Winemaker Steven Baraglia **Est.** 2005 **Dozens** 1200
Naked Run is the virtual winery of Jayme Wood, Bradley Currie and Steven Baraglia; their skills ranging from viticulture through to production, and also to the all-important sales and marketing (and not to be confused with Naked Wines). Riesling, shiraz and cabernet are sourced from Clare Valley, grenache from the Williamstown area of the Barossa Valley and shiraz from Greenock.

🍷🍷🍷🍷🍷 Place in Time Sevenhill Clare Valley Riesling 2015 Feel the Clare Valley riesling purity and power in this aged beauty. The vibrancy and youthfulness, still going strong in its fifth year, can only ensure a continued long future. Explosive lime and lemon sherbet liveliness countered with developing toastiness. The palate is fine and chalky with no sharp edges. What a wine! Screwcap. 12% alc. Rating 96 To 2032 $40 JP ✪

🍷🍷🍷🍷🍷 BWC Barossa Valley Shiraz 2017 Rating 92 To 2028 $28 JP
The Aldo Barossa Valley Grenache 2018 Rating 91 To 2026 $24 JP
Der Zweite Clare Valley Riesling 2019 Rating 90 To 2026 $28 JP
Hill 5 Clare Valley Shiraz Cabernet 2018 Rating 90 To 2031 $24 JP

Nannup Estate ★★★★☆

Lot 25 Perks Road, Nannup, WA 6275 **Region** Blackwood Valley
T (08) 9756 2005 **www**.nannupestate.com.au **Open** Not
Winemaker Michael Ng, Ryan Aggiss **Est.** 2017 **Dozens** 5000 **Vyds** 14.43ha
Nannup Estate (with the vineyard held under this title) is owned by Mark Blizzard and family, and the adjacent Nannup Ridge Estate under another title owned by Ray Fitzgerald and family. Until recently, these two properties were both farmed together as a single property, although the grapes went to the respective families once harvested. The vineyard sits high on the granite ridges of the Blackwood River escarpment. During the growing season the vines enjoy long hours of sunshine followed by moderate coastal breezes in the afternoons and cool evenings – idyllic growing conditions. Abundant water, granite loam soils and low frost and disease pressure all contribute to reliable quality and consistent vintages. The first 6ha of vines were planted in 1998, with subsequent plantings in 2000 and '06. The vineyard now comprises almost 14.5ha of cabernet sauvignon, merlot, chardonnay, tempranillo and malbec. Exports to China.

🍷🍷🍷🍷🍷 Rolling Hills Chardonnay 2019 Dijon clones 76, 95 and 96; fermented and matured in French oak (35% new). Has surprising depth to the fruit given the lowish alcohol. Impressive wine with more to come. Screwcap. 12.5% alc. Rating 94 To 2029 $35
Phillip Stanley Cabernet Sauvignon 2017 Crushed and destemmed, tank-fermented, pressed to French oak (45% new) for 14 months' maturation. Oak and fruit tannins go hand in glove to defeat the fruit – let's hope it fights back (there is every chance it will). Screwcap. 13.5% alc. Rating 94 To 2037 $45

🍷🍷🍷🍷🍷 Rolling Hills Malbec 2018 Rating 93 To 2033 $35
Rolling Hills Merlot 2018 Rating 91 To 2029 $35
Rolling Hills Cabernet Sauvignon 2018 Rating 90 To 2028 $35

Nannup Ridge Estate

PO Box 2, Nannup, WA 6275 **Region** Blackwood Valley
T (08) 9286 2202 **www**.nannupridge.com.au **Open** Not
Winemaker Bruce Dukes **Est.** 1998 **Dozens** 4000 **Vyds** 16ha
The business is owned by the Fitzgerald brothers, who purchased the then unplanted property from the family that had farmed it since the early 1900s. They established 16ha of mainstream varieties backed by a (then) grape sale agreement with Houghton and Constellation.

They still regard themselves as grapegrowers but have successful wines skilfully contract-made by celebrated winemaker Bruce Dukes. Terrific value is par for the course. Exports to China.

ŶŶŶŶŶ **Epic Shiraz 2018** Whole-berry fermented in tank, 12 days on skins, matured for 16 months in French oak (35% new). Striking texture and structure of the full-bodied palate, fine-ground tannins woven through the blackberry and plum fruit. A long life ahead. Screwcap. 14.3% alc. **Rating** 95 **To** 2038 $28 **◎**

Epic Cabernet Sauvignon 2018 Machine-harvested, crushed, tank-fermented, 18 days on skins, fermentation finished in barrel, matured for 16 months in French oak (40% new). A pure rendition of cabernet, medium to full-bodied, the tannins plaited around the resilient palate. A long future. Screwcap. 14.1% alc. **Rating** 95 **To** 2043 $28 **◎**

Cabernet Sauvignon 2017 Crushed and destemmed, fermented in tank, 18 days on skins, fermentation finished in barrel, 16 months in French oak (40% new). A very precise wine, the fruit having made light work on their way to the finish where tannins patiently wait for their moment, but there's no argument. Screwcap. 14.8% alc. **Rating** 95 **To** 2042 $25 **◎**

Perks Road Cabernet Merlot 2018 A 52/48% blend; crushed, 10–12 days on skins, tank fermented, matured in French oak (30% new) for 10 months. A juicy medium-bodied wine with good varietal expression. As with all the Nannup Ridge Estate wines, the applause should be directed to the vineyard. Screwcap. 14.1% alc. **Rating** 94 **To** 2033 $23 **◎**

ŶŶŶŶŶ **Perks Road Merlot 2018 Rating** 93 **To** 2035 $23 **◎**
Voller Rose 2019 Rating 90 **To** 2022 $16 **◎**

Narkoojee ★★★★★

170 Francis Road, Glengarry, Vic 3854 **Region** Gippsland
T (03) 5192 4257 **www**.narkoojee.com **Open** 7 days 10.30–4.30
Winemaker Axel Friend **Est.** 1981 **Dozens** 5000 **Vyds** 13.8ha
Narkoojee, originally a dairy farm owned by the Friend family, is near the old gold-mining town of Walhalla and looks out over the Strzelecki Ranges. The wines are produced from the estate vineyards, with chardonnay accounting for half the total. Former lecturer in civil engineering and extremely successful amateur winemaker, Harry Friend, changed horses in 1994 to take joint control of the vineyard and winery with son Axel, and they haven't missed a beat since; their skills show through in all the wines. Exports to China.

Nashdale Lane Wines ★★★★★

125 Nashdale Lane, Nashdale, NSW 2800 **Region** Orange
T 0458 127 333 **www**.nashdalelane.com **Open** 7 days 11–5
Winemaker Chris Derrez, Lucy Maddox **Est.** 2016 **Dozens** 5000 **Vyds** 15.31ha
Nashdale Lane began as a dream following Nick and Tanya Segger's brief working holiday on a tiny vineyard in Tuscany in 2001, becoming reality in '17 with the purchase of an 18-year-old vineyard. Nick grew up on the family farm in the UK, which became one of the largest suppliers of organic produce in the UK. He majored in French and business at Brunel University. Tanya has a career in journalism, PR and advertising. They have appointed Chris Derrez and Lucy Maddox as contract winemakers, setting up their cellar door in a refurbished apple packing shed on the property. The vineyard is planted mainly to chardonnay, shiraz, pinot gris and sauvignon blanc, with smaller amounts of riesling, pinot noir, tempranillo and arneis. Visitors to Nashdale Lane can stay in luxury cabins set among the vines. Exports to the UK.

ŶŶŶŶŶ **Orange Shiraz 2018** Crushed to small open fermenters, cold soak, pressed to French oak (30% new), matured for 14 months. This is a truly delicious cool-climate style, full to overflowing with every type of cherry imaginable. The oak and fine-grained tannins are vehicles to add spicy notes to the palate. Screwcap. 13.5% alc. **Rating** 96 **To** 2038 $35 **◎**

Legacy Orange Pinot Noir 2018 A wine that has spicy/savoury red and purple fruits from the outset. But it's not until the finish and aftertaste that its intensity and power ex barrel ferment take hold, sweeping all other flavours to one side. The wine is made using barrels that have been modified with the creation of a large (150mm) bung hole in the head of the barrel that stands vertically (the original small bung hole in the side of the barrel tightly sealed). Screwcap. 13.5% alc. **Rating** 95 **To** 2026 $55

Orange Riesling 2019 The vinification directed to the preservation of the perfume and flavours of the wine has worked very well indeed. Lime, lemon and apple blossom aromas surge from the glass when swirled, and need no prodding to fill the mouth with the same suite of flavours and their crisp finish. Screwcap. 12% alc. **Rating** 94 **To** 2029 $30 ✪

🍷🍷🍷🍷🍷 **Orange Chardonnay 2018** **Rating** 93 **To** 2027 $35
Legacy Orange Tempranillo 2018 **Rating** 92 **To** 2033 $55
Orange Pinot Gris 2019 **Rating** 90 **To** 2021 $28

Nazaaray ★★★★

266 Meakins Road, Flinders, Vic 3929 **Region** Mornington Peninsula
T 0407 391 991 **www**.nazaaray.com.au **Open** Sat–Mon 11–4
Winemaker Paramdeep Ghumman **Est.** 1996 **Dozens** 800 **Vyds** 2.4ha

Paramdeep Ghumman is, as far as I am aware, the only Indian-born winery proprietor in Australia. He and his wife purchased the Nazaaray vineyard property in 1991. An initial trial planting of 400 vines in '96 was gradually expanded to the present level of 2.4ha of pinot noir, pinot gris, sauvignon blanc and shiraz. Notwithstanding the micro size of the estate, all the wines are made and bottled onsite. Exports to Hong Kong.

🍷🍷🍷🍷🍷 **Single Vineyard Mornington Peninsula Chardonnay 2018** Hand-picked, whole-bunch pressed, fermented in French oak (20% new). In the slender mouthfeel/style typical of the Mornington Peninsula. Has its appeal. Screwcap. 13.6% alc. **Rating** 91 **To** 2029 $45

🍷🍷🍷🍷 **Single Vineyard Mornington Peninsula Pinot Gris 2019** **Rating** 89 **To** 2020 $33
Barrabool Hills Single Vineyard Mornington Peninsula Shiraz 2018 **Rating** 89 **To** 2022 $45

Nepenthe ★★★★

93 Jones Road, Balhannah, SA 5242 **Region** Adelaide Hills
T (08) 8398 8899 **www**.nepenthe.com.au **Open** 7 days 10–5
Winemaker James Evers **Est.** 1994 **Dozens** 40 000 **Vyds** 93ha

Nepenthe quickly established its reputation as a producer of high quality wines, but founder Ed Tweddell died unexpectedly in 2006 and the business was purchased by Australian Vintage Limited the following year. The winery was closed in '09 and winemaking operations transferred to McGuigan Wines (Barossa Valley). The Nepenthe winery has since been purchased by Peter Leske and Mark Kozned, and provides contract winemaking services via their Revenir venture. Nepenthe has 93ha of close-planted vines in the Adelaide Hills, with an exotic array of varieties. Exports to all major markets.

🍷🍷🍷🍷🍷 **Pinnacle Ithaca Adelaide Hills Chardonnay 2018** Chardonnay in full flight. Ripe peach and tropical fruit meets citrus, flint and wood smoke. It convinces on power alone but there's nuance, length and no shortage of X-factor. Screwcap. 13.5% alc. **Rating** 94 **To** 2025 $35 CM

Adelaide Hills Cabernet Sauvignon 2017 Open-fermented, matured in French oak (some new) for 10 months. An elegant, supple, medium-bodied cabernet, replete with cassis and bay leaf. The tannin and oak contributions are as they should be. Excellent value. Screwcap. 13% alc. **Rating** 94 **To** 2027 $22 ✪

♟♟♟♟♀ Altitude Pinot Noir 2017 Rating 93 To 2025 $22 ✪
Altitude Sauvignon Blanc 2019 Rating 92 To 2021 $22 CM ✪
Altitude Pinot Gris 2019 Rating 92 To 2021 $20 CM ✪
Pinot Noir Rose 2019 Rating 92 To 2021 $22 CM ✪
Altitude Pinot Noir 2018 Rating 92 To 2024 $22 CM ✪
Altitude Shiraz 2016 Rating 92 To 2031 $22 ✪
Tempranillo 2017 Rating 92 To 2025 $22 ✪
Altitude Sauvignon Blanc 2018 Rating 91 To 2020 $22 ✪
Pinot Noir Rose 2018 Rating 91 To 2020 $22 ✪
Winemaker's Selection Lenswood Vineyard Zinfandel 2018 Rating 91
To 2024 $35 CM
Pinnacle Gate Block Shiraz 2017 Rating 90 To 2025 $35 CM
Altitude Shiraz 2017 Rating 90 To 2024 $20 CM ✪

New Era Vineyards   ★★★★★

PO Box 391, Woodside, SA 5244 **Region** Adelaide Hills
T 0413 544 246 www.neweravineyards.com.au **Open** Not
Winemaker Robert Baxter, Iain Baxter **Est.** 1988 **Dozens** 1500 **Vyds** 13ha
The New Era vineyard is situated over a gold reef that was mined for 60 years until 1940,
when all recoverable gold had been extracted. The vineyard was mostly contracted to Foster's
and now includes shiraz, pinot noir, cabernet sauvignon, tempranillo, sangiovese, touriga
nacional, sauvignon blanc and montepulciano. Much of the production is sold to other
winemakers in the region. The small amount of wine made has been the subject of favourable
reviews. Exports to Taiwan.

♟♟♟♟♟ Barrel Select Adelaide Hills Shiraz 2018 In '12 and '16 Bob and Iain Baxter
selected a small number of barrels of exceptional quality and called the wine
Barrel Select. They say this wine is better than any previous vintage, matured in
new French oak from various coopers. It has more of everything, oak and tannins
dominant, and needs 5–7 years to calm down – it has unlimited quality if given
this time. Screwcap. 14.5% alc. **Rating** 96 To 2048 $50 ✪
Basket Pressed Adelaide Hills Cabernet Sauvignon 2016 Small
open fermenters, extended maceration on skins, basket pressed into French
oak, 15 months ageing. Immediately, resolutely cabernet sauvignon! Great to see
the grape variety so enhanced and celebrated without too much winemaking
noise in the background. Textbook descriptors all round: blackcurrant, cinnamon,
clove and violets with just a light leafy theme throughout. Gently grippy palate to
close. Screwcap. 14.1% alc. **Rating** 96 To 2034 $27 JP ✪
Barrel Select Adelaide Hills Pinot Noir 2017 Clones 114, 115, D4V2,
MV6 and 777 were mostly destemmed and chilled prior to a 5-day cold
soak, wild fermentation in parallel with a Brunello cultured yeast, matured for
12 months in used French hogsheads. A complex pinot with the suggestion of
whole bunch when there was none – a win-win scenario. Red fruits grow as
the wine is retasted. Screwcap. 14% alc. **Rating** 95 To 2032 $35 ✪
Adelaide Hills Syrah 2018 Ideal conditions meant a generous crop was fully
ripened. Vinified in 2 batches with different clones, one parcel given extended
post-ferment maceration, then a 2-stage blending process followed by 12 months'
maturation in new and used French hogsheads. This is a high quality wine, full of
delicious black fruits on the long, supple palate; the oak balanced and integrated.
Screwcap. 14% alc. **Rating** 95 To 2038 $33 ✪
Basket Pressed Adelaide Hills Merlot 2016 Adelaide Hills merlot is a
rare bird but it certainly sings a pretty tune. Winemaking is spot on, delivering
complexity of flavour within a relatively modest, medium-bodied framework.
Aromatics shine – dark rose, violets, florals – mixing with blackberry, pomegranate
and a subtle herbaceousness. Lingers long. Screwcap. 14% alc. **Rating** 95 To 2030
$27 JP ✪
Langhorne Creek Touriga Nacional 2018 Destemmed, cultured yeast, 12 days
on skins, 12 months in American and French hogsheads, not fined or filtered.

Impressive wine. A deep well of dark fruits on the bouquet foreshadows the medium-bodied palate with its ultra-supple and round cascade of spiced fruits. Total seduction. Screwcap. 14% alc. **Rating** 95 **To** 2030 $33 **○**

🍷🍷🍷🍷🍷 **Adelaide Hills Sangiovese 2018 Rating** 93 **To** 2030 $33
Adelaide Hills Tempranillo 2018 Rating 92 **To** 2030 $33
Adelaide Hills Pinot Rose 2018 Rating 91 **To** 2024 $22 JP **○**

Newbridge Wines   ★★★☆

18 Chelsea Street, Brighton, Vic 3186 (postal) **Region** Bendigo
T 0417 996 840 **www**.newbridgewines.com.au **Open** At Newbridge Hotel
Winemaker Mark Matthews, Andrew Simpson **Est.** 1996 **Dozens** 300 **Vyds** 1ha
The Newbridge property was purchased by Ian Simpson in 1979, partly for sentimental family history reasons and partly because of the beauty of the property situated on the banks of the Loddon River. It was not until '96 that Ian decided to plant shiraz. Up to and including the 2002 vintage the grapes were sold to several local wineries. Ian retained the grapes and made wine in '03, and lived to see that and the following two vintages take shape before his death. The property is now run by his son Andrew, the wines contract-made by Mark Matthews with enthusiastic support from Andrew.

🍷🍷🍷🍷🍷 **Bendigo Shiraz 2017** An unusual lavender-pine-needle herbal note and seemingly more than a regional character. Lots of oak infusing the spiced dark plums and juniper berries with a dusting of cocoa and savoury, meaty flavours. The surprise is the fine, smooth tannins and its medium-bodied structure. Screwcap. 14% alc. **Rating** 90 **To** 2027 $25 JF

Ngeringa   ★★★★★

119 Williams Road, Mount Barker, SA 5251 **Region** Adelaide Hills
T (08) 8398 2867 **www**.ngeringa.com **Open** By appt
Winemaker Erinn Klein **Est.** 2001 **Dozens** 2500 **Vyds** 5.5ha
Erinn and Janet Klein say, 'As fervent practitioners of biodynamic wine growing, we respect biodynamics as a sensitivity to the rhythms of nature, the health of the soil and the connection between plant, animal and cosmos. It is a pragmatic solution to farming without the use of chemicals and a necessary acknowledgement that the farm unit is part of a great whole.' It is not an easy solution and the Kleins have increased the immensity of the challenge by using ultra-close vine spacing of 1.5m × 1m, necessitating a large amount of hand-training of the vines plus the use of a tiny crawler tractor. Lest it be thought they have stumbled onto biodynamic growing without understanding wine science, they teamed up while studying at the University of Adelaide in 2000 (Erinn – oenology, Janet – viticulture/wine marketing) and then spent time looking at the great viticultural regions of the Old World, with a particular emphasis on biodynamics. The JE label is used for the basic wines, Ngeringa only for the very best (NASAA Certified Biodynamic). Exports to Belgium, Norway, Japan, Hong Kong and China.

🍷🍷🍷🍷🍷 **Iluma Vineyard Adelaide Hills Syrah 2017** It's inherently savoury but there's excellent fruit power and the structure to match. This is a prime example of just how good Adelaide Hills shiraz/syrah can be. Cherry-plum flavours with licorice, graphite, twig and herb notes. There's a dry, velvety aspect to the texture and very good length. Picture perfect. Cork. 13.8% alc. **Rating** 96 **To** 2035 $55 CM **○**
Adelaide Hills Rose 2018 Raspberry and cranberry flavours come infused with anise. It's juicy and vibrant, but there's a substance to it, particularly through the finish. Screwcap. **Rating** 94 **To** 2022 $30 CM **○**

🍷🍷🍷🍷🍷 **Summit Vineyard Chardonnay 2017 Rating** 93 **To** 2027 CM
Single Vineyard Pinot Noir 2017 Rating 93 **To** 2026 $45 CM

Nick Haselgrove Wines ★★★★★

281 Tatachilla Road, McLaren Vale, SA 5171 **Region** Adelaide zone
T (08) 8383 0886 **www.**nhwines.com.au **Open** By appt
Winemaker Nick Haselgrove, Marcus Hofer **Est.** 1981 **Dozens** 10 000

After various sales, amalgamations and disposals of particular brands, Nick Haselgrove now owns The Old Faithful (the flagship brand, see separate entry), Blackbilly, Clarence Hill, James Haselgrove and The Wishing Tree brands. Exports to the US and other major markets including Canada, Hong Kong and China.

ΤΤΤΤΤ **James Haselgrove Futures McLaren Vale Shiraz 2017** Single vineyard planted in 1910; hand-picked, open ferment, 15 months' maturation. Old vines play a prominent role here from the deep concentration of fruit, so intense, which allows for – and encourages – a fuller expression of oak to a natural-born structure. The '17 vintage was on the cooler side with extended ripening time. It has brought a touch of class and a peppery, fine-edged finish. Diam. 14% alc. **Rating** 95 **To** 2042 $50 JP
Blackbilly Single Vineyard Old Vine McLaren Vale Grenache 2016 What joy to celebrate old bushvine grenache from a single vineyard that is 100+yo. And such sensitive low-key winemaking that allows the fruit to shine from an open ferment with the inclusion of a small amount of whole bunches – which lifts the aroma beautifully – and maturation in old, large-format French oak puncheons. A classy display of grenache with black cherries, generous florals, stewed plums with a hint of musk confection all dressed in a medium-bodied beauty of a wine. Diam. 14% alc. **Rating** 95 **To** 2043 $25 JP ✪

ΤΤΤΤΥ **Reserve McLaren Vale Cabernet Sauvignon 2017 Rating** 92 **To** 2035 $45 JP
Clarence Hill Adelaide Cabernet Sauvignon 2017 Rating 92 **To** 2025 $18 JP ✪
Clarence Hill Red Label McLaren Vale Shiraz 2017 Rating 90 **To** 2027 $35
Reserve McLaren Vale Shiraz 2016 Rating 90 **To** 2034 $45 JP

Nick O'Leary Wines ★★★★★

149 Brooklands Road, Wallaroo, NSW 2618 **Region** Canberra District
T (02) 6230 2745 **www.**nickolearywines.com.au **Open** By appt
Winemaker Nick O'Leary **Est.** 2007 **Dozens** 12 000 **Vyds** 11ha

At the ripe old age of 28, Nick O'Leary had been involved in the wine industry for over a decade, working variously in retail, wholesale, viticulture and winemaking. Two years earlier he had laid the foundation for Nick O'Leary Wines, purchasing shiraz from local vignerons (commencing in 2006); riesling following in '08. His wines have had extraordinarily consistent success in local wine shows and competitions since the first vintages, and are building on that early success in spectacular fashion. At the NSW Wine Awards '15, the '14 Shiraz was awarded the NSW Wine of the Year trophy, exactly as the '13 Shiraz was in the prior year – the first time any winery had won the award in consecutive years.

ΤΤΤΤΤ **White Rocks Riesling 2019** It seems all the Nick O'Leary rieslings are made identically and therefore, what a difference a place makes. Fruit comes off the 45yo Westering Vineyard, one of the oldest in the Canberra District. The wine is explosive. Lemon juice and zest are in the mix, but key is the laser precision line of acidity across the palate. A mineral sensation with just a hint of creamy texture. Screwcap. 12% alc. **Rating** 96 **To** 2034 $38 JF ✪
Bolaro Shiraz 2018 The key to enjoying Nick O'Leary's reds is time – to allow the wines (and enjoyment) to unfurl. This beautiful wine has fantastic fruit at its heart. It pulses with energy, lively acidity and superfine yet decisive tannins and length like no tomorrow. A very classy, cool shiraz. Screwcap. 13.5% alc. **Rating** 96 **To** 2030 $55 JF ✪
Heywood Shiraz 2018 Everything about this refined red delights: its purple-ruby hue; it's heady aromatics a mix of florals, spice and fruit. Plus seamlessly

integrated oak, and fine tannins and detail across the medium–bodied palate.
Screwcap. 13.5% alc. **Rating** 95 **To** 2028 $35 JF ☻

ŢŢŢŢŢ **Riesling 2019 Rating** 93 **To** 2028 $25 JF☻
Shiraz 2018 Rating 93 **To** 2028 $30 JF
Heywood Riesling 2019 Rating 92 **To** 2027 $32 JF
Heywood Red Blend 2019 Rating 92 **To** 2024 $32 JF
Canberra District Sangiovese 2019 Rating 92 **To** 2025 $32 JF
Seven Gates Tempranillo 2018 Rating 90 **To** 2024 $32 JF

Nick Spencer Wines ★★★★★

11 Loch Street, Yarralumla, ACT 2600 (postal) **Region** Gundagai
T 0419 810 274 **www.**nickspencerwines.com.au **Open** Not
Winemaker Nick Spencer **Est.** 2017 **Dozens** 2500
No winemaker's career starts newborn with receiving a degree in oenology at the University
of Adelaide. The desire to make wine comes well before the inception to the studies.
Some string the process out, others don't even undertake the process. Nick Spencer didn't
procrastinate. In the early years he worked for Rosemount Estate, Coldstream Hills, Madew
Wines and Tertini. He won the biggest wine show trophy in 2009: the Jimmy Watson; in '11
he was a Len Evans Tutorial scholar and in '14 was a finalist in the Young Gun of Wine and
a finalist in the *Gourmet Traveller* Winemaker of the Year. He has travelled extensively through
France, NZ and California, and in '14 made wine in Khakheti in Georgia. Having lead the
team at Eden Road for seven years, he finally moved to establish his own business in '17. His
two regions of interest are Tumbarumba and Gundagai – adjoining but very different. The
quality of his wines from Gundagai make him the captain of that ship.

ŢŢŢŢŢ **Tumbarumba Gruner Veltliner 2018** While made simply – 12 hours' skin
contact, lightly pressed and fermented in stainless steel then bottled in May – it
packs a lot of flavour and texture effortlessly, so it glides across the palate. In the
complex mix, a whisper of white florals, nashi pear, daikon and green apple with
some wild nettles and fennel. It's also flinty with a smidge of white pepper to seal
the varietal deal. Screwcap. 12.5% alc. **Rating** 95 **To** 2022 $30 JF ☻

916 ★★★★☆

916 Steels Creek Road, Steels Creek, Vic 3775 (postal) **Region** Yarra Valley
T (03) 5965 2124 **www.**916.com.au **Open** Not
Winemaker Ben Haines **Est.** 2008 **Dozens** 200 **Vyds** 2ha
Established by John Brand and Erin-Marie O'Neill, 916 is one of two wineries in the *Wine
Companion* using three digits as their name, the other 919. A year after they acquired their 8ha
property, bushfires destroyed their home and all their possessions but they rebuilt their lives
and home, reinvesting in wine and vineyard alike. The focus is on pinot noir alone and in
understanding the impact of subtle differences in the soil and subsoil on the wines they
produce. 'Each bottle is protected by various mechanisms to ensure product integrity, and
serial number validation entitles collectors to future pre-release allocations.' Exports to the
US, China and Singapore.

ŢŢŢŢŢ **South Yarra Valley Pinot Noir 2018** This is the better wine, at least in this
vintage. More interesting. More flavour intensity, length and layered complexity
across the Indian spice–infused bunch element; a whiff of volatility, sapid cherry
notes and fecund strawberry. Cork. **Rating** 93 **To** 2025 $90 NG
West Yarra Valley Pinot Noir 2018 Turf of gravel and yellow clay. Lots of
whole berry and bunch in the mould. A pallid ruby, light weight and mescal-
herbal at the first whiff: a legacy of the stems. Strawberry and mulch. Ethereal, but
needs more. Cork. **Rating** 92 **To** 2024 $90 NG

919 Wines
★★★★☆

39 Hodges Road, Berri, SA 5343 **Region** Riverland
T 0408 855 272 **www.**919wines.com.au **Open** Wed–Sun & public hols 10–5
Winemaker Eric Semmler, Jenny Semmler **Est.** 2002 **Dozens** 2000 **Vyds** 17ha
Eric and Jenny Semmler have been involved in the wine industry since 1986 and have a special interest in fortified wines. Eric made fortified wines for Hardys and worked at Brown Brothers. Jenny has worked for Strathbogie Vineyards, Pennyweight Wines and St Huberts. They have planted micro-quantities of varieties for fortified wines: palomino, durif, tempranillo, muscat à petits grains, tinta cao, shiraz, tokay and touriga nacional. They use minimal water application, deliberately reducing the crop levels, practising organic and biodynamic techniques. In 2011 they purchased the 12.3ha property at Loxton they now call Ella Semmler's Vineyard.

♟♟♟♟♟ **Classic Topaque NV** Winemaker Eric Semmler has a fine reputation with fortifieds. The Riverland and his skills mesh nicely. With topaque (aka muscadelle) the sweetness appears to be toned down a fraction and there is greater liveliness and freshness compared to the muscat. Wields typical topaque lush characters throughout: golden syrup, malt, prune, barley sugar, butterscotch. Mouthfilling and so, so drink-me. Spot on clean, bright, neutral spirit and balance. Screwcap. 19% alc. **Rating** 95 $42 JP

♟♟♟♟♀ **Vermentino 2019 Rating** 93 **To** 2026 $28 JP
Sparkling Durif NV Rating 93 $45 JP
Classic Tawny NV Rating 93 $40 JP
Durif 2017 Rating 92 **To** 2038 $48 JP
Pale Dry Apera NV Rating 92 $40 JP
Touriga Nacional 2015 Rating 91 **To** 2027 $42 JP
Ella Semmler's Orchard Shiraz 2019 Rating 90 **To** 2028 $22 JP
Shiraz 2019 Rating 90 **To** 2026 $45 JP
Classic Muscat NV Rating 90 $42 JP

Nintingbool
★★★★

56 Wongerer Lane, Smythes Creek, Vic 3351 (postal) **Region** Ballarat
T 0429 424 399 **www.**nintingbool.com.au **Open** Not
Winemaker Peter Bothe **Est.** 1998 **Dozens** 600 **Vyds** 2ha
Peter and Jill Bothe purchased the Nintingbool property in 1982 and built their home in '84, using bluestone dating back to the goldrush period. They established an extensive Australian native garden and home orchard but in '98 diversified by planting pinot noir, plus a further planting the following year lifting the total to 2ha. Ballarat is one of the coolest mainland regions and demands absolute attention to detail (and a warm growing season) for success.

♟♟♟♟♀ **Pinot Noir 2017** The vineyard at Smythes Creek, west of Ballarat, is on 'harsh' goldfields soil and at a decent elevation of 425m. It delivers a sinewy, mineral-edged pinot noir, a style increasingly associated with the Ballarat region. Red fruits inhabit the wine: redcurrant, sour cherry, cranberry with nettle, weed, forest floor. The fine herbal line is maintained on the palate. It's a cold climate, firm expression – unlike most pinots you taste. Screwcap. 14% alc. **Rating** 93 **To** 2026 $35 JP
Smythes Creek Rose 2019 A 80/20% pinot noir/shiraz blend. Fermented in a combination of barrels and stainless steel tanks. Medium salmon in colour and bursting with summer pudding, raspberry, red cherry aromas and flavours. On the fuller, generous side. A-meal-in-a-glass kind of rose in no need of any food accompaniment. Screwcap. 12.9% alc. **Rating** 90 **To** 2025 $23 JP

♟♟♟♟ **Smythes Creek Chardonnay 2019 Rating** 89 **To** 2028 $29 JP
Blanc de Noir 2017 Rating 89 $35 JP

Noble Red

13 Eastrow Avenue, Donnybrook, Vic 3064 (postal) **Region** Heathcote
T 0400 594 440 **www**.nobleredwines.com **Open** Not
Winemaker Roman Sobiesiak **Est.** 2002 **Dozens** 1200 **Vyds** 6ha
Roman and Margaret Sobiesiak acquired their property in 2002. It had 0.25ha of shiraz planted in the 1970s. A progressive planting program has seen the area increase to 6ha: shiraz (3.6ha) accounting for the lion's share, the remainder equally split to tempranillo, mourvedre, merlot and cabernet sauvignon. They adopted a dry-grown approach, which meant slow development during the prolonged drought, but their commitment remains undimmed. Indeed, visiting many wine regions around the world and working within the industry locally has increased their determination. Exports to Europe and China.

🍷🍷🍷 **Heathcote Carmenere 2017** Screwcap. 14.5% alc. **Rating** 89 **To** 2027 $28

Noble Road Wines | Genders Vintners ★★★☆

33–37 Wright Street, Adelaide, SA 5000 **Region** South Australia
T (08) 8212 6959 **www**.nobleroadwine.com **Open** 7 days 11–4
Winemaker Scott Curtis, Diana Genders **Est.** 1922 **Dozens** 100000 **Vyds** 118.5ha
In 1922, after serving in WWI, Reginald Curtis migrated to Australia from Cornwall in England. In the same year Reginald planted the Curtis family vineyard on 32 acres of land in Waikerie, SA. His son Gordon Curtis was one of the first students to graduate from Roseworthy, specialising in viticulture. The Curtis vineyard supplied grapes to G. Gramp & Sons (later Orlando). In 2007 third generation Scott Curtis, with extended wine industry experience, became chief winemaker of Noble Road Wines. The venture has 100ha of vines in the Clare Valley, 10ha in the Barossa and 8.5ha in McLaren Vale. Exports to the US, Singapore, Japan, Hong Kong, Taiwan and China.

Nocton Vineyard

373 Colebrook Road, Richmond, Tas 7025 **Region** Southern Tasmania
T (03) 6260 2688 **www**.noctonwine.com.au **Open** Thurs–Mon 10–4, Tues–Wed by appt
Winemaker Frogmore Creek (Alain Rousseau) **Est.** 1998 **Dozens** 8000 **Vyds** 33.16ha
Nocton Vineyard is the reincarnation of Nocton Park. After years of inactivity (other than the ongoing sale of the grapes from what is a first class vineyard) it largely disappeared. Wines are released under the Nocton Vineyard and Willow (Reserve) labels. The quality across the two labels is very good. Exports to China.

🍷🍷🍷🍷 **Sauvignon Blanc 2018** Far from the madding crowd as far as domestic sauvignon goes, Coal River offers a point of real difference. While this is punchy, febrile and highly aromatic, it is juicier and attractively citric, fully green-apple-to-guava ripe and more thirst-slaking-herbal and pungent than those from better known regions. This has enough intensity and weight to handle oak. Screwcap. **Rating** 93 **To** 2022 $29 NG

Merlot 2018 This is impressive. Plum, dried tobacco, spearmint, bitter chocolate and a firm enough skein of tannin meld nicely. The oak, both well selected and appointed, serves the fray. The finish is long with the tannic rub boding well for a mid-term future in the cellar. Screwcap. **Rating** 93 **To** 2025 $29 NG

Tasmania Sparkling NV Includes 60% pinot and 40% chardonnay, made in the traditional method with 2 years of lees ageing and the addition of older wines at disgorgement, aged in older oak. Good gear. More of an apero style than a rich, creamy one. That said, the leesy detail imbues complexity to notes of baked apple, nashi pear and oyster shell. The dosage appears minimal, promoting a saline freshness and a refreshing plume of a finish. Cork. **Rating** 93 $35 NG

Sparkling Rose NV Made in the traditional fashion, this straight pinot is equipped with 18 months on lees and a bolstering of older reserve material at disgorgement, aged in neutral wood. The result is pointed, palpably dry and creamy across the midriff, staining the cheeks with notes of sour cherry, raspberry and ume. The finish, of good length and poise. Cork. **Rating** 92 $38 NG

ΨΨΨΨ   Coal River Valley Chardonnay 2018 Rating 89 To 2023 $29 NG
        Coal River Valley Pinot Noir 2018 Rating 89 To 2023 $32 NG

Nocturne Wines ★★★★★

PO Box 111, Yallingup, WA 6282 **Region** Margaret River
T 0477 829 844 **www**.nocturnewines.com.au **Open** Not
Winemaker Alana Langworthy, Julian Langworthy **Est.** 2007 **Dozens** 1300 **Vyds** 8ha
Alana and Julian Langworthy were newly minted winemakers when they met in SA over
15 years ago and set up a small winery project called Nocturne Wines. The intention
was to make small quantities of project wines as an adjunct to their day jobs as employed
winemakers. The enlightened Peter Fogarty, owner of WA's fastest growing wine business
(Fogarty Family Wines), raised no objection to Nocturne Wines when he appointed Julian
chief winemaker in 2011. Nocturne has been able to buy the Sheoak Vineyard (former
Jimmy Watson–producing vineyard – Harvey River Bridge 2010), with its 4ha of mature
cabernet sauvignon vines, but Nocturne wines are still produced in modest quantities. The
flood of show awards will, indeed, be enhanced by the arrival of Nocturne alongside Deep
Woods Estate. Exports to the UK.

ΨΨΨΨΨ   **Tassell Park Vineyard Margaret River Chardonnay 2018** From a 0.37ha site
         on the Tassell Park Vineyard; whole-bunch pressed to new and used puncheons,
         wild-fermented, no intervention until SO_2 in Sept '18. A wine with the precision
         of a rapier as you taste it. It's slightly reductive, which I see as a positive. It certainly
         leaves the mouth fresh. Screwcap. 13% alc. **Rating** 97 To 2033 $53 ✪
         Sheoak Vineyard Margaret River Cabernet Sauvignon 2018 Destemmed,
         matured in French oak (25% new) for 15 months. Nothing to it really, once
         you've done this as often as Julian Langworthy. Has all the quality of the luscious
         cassis fruit and ripe tannins. Screwcap. 14% alc. **Rating** 97 To 2042 $53 ✪

ΨΨΨΨΨ   **Carbunup SR Sangiovese Nebbiolo Rose 2019** Very complex vinification
         with different pathways for 60% sangiovese and 40% nebbiolo. It's worked
         brilliantly, the blend a perfumed garden of red flowers led by roses. The wine is
         equally expressive in the mouth, yet treads lightly thanks to the absence of heavy
         phenolics et al. A wine to be revered yet quickly consumed – have your wine and
         drink it too. Screwcap. 13% alc. **Rating** 96 To 2023 $31 ✪
         Treeton SR Chardonnay 2018 A complex wine sourced from 2 vineyards;
         hand-picked, whole-bunch pressed direct to new and used puncheons, wild-
         fermented, no intervention until Aug when SO_2 added. Freshness is the golden
         key that comes with the first taste. Screwcap. 13% alc. **Rating** 95 To 2028 $35 ✪
         Yallingup SR Cabernets 2018 Includes 87% cabernet from the Langworthy's
         Sheoak Vineyard and 13% merlot from a neighbouring vineyard. It's very,
         very fresh. Red berries need to pay respect to their betters. Screwcap. 14% alc.
         Rating 95 To 2038 $35 ✪

Norfolk Rise Vineyard ★★★★

Limestone Coast Road, Mount Benson, SA 5265 **Region** Mount Benson
T (08) 8768 5080 **www**.norfolkrise.com.au **Open** Not
Winemaker Alice Baker **Est.** 2000 **Dozens** 20 000 **Vyds** 130ha
Norfolk Rise Vineyard is by far the largest and most important development in the Mount
Benson region. It is owned by privately held Belgian company G and C Kreglinger, which
was established in 1797. In early 2002 Kreglinger acquired Pipers Brook Vineyard and has
since maintained the separate brands of Pipers Brook and Norfolk Rise. There are 46 blocks of
sauvignon blanc, pinot gris, pinot noir, shiraz, merlot and cabernet sauvignon, allowing a range
of options in making the six single-variety wines in the portfolio. The business has moved
from the export of bulk wine to bottled wine, which gives significantly better returns to the
winery. Exports to the US, Canada, Europe and Asia.

ΨΨΨΨ   **Limestone Coast Pinot Noir 2019** Fruit sourced from estate and local growers
        in Robe and Mount Benson. Aged for 6 months in used French barriques. Light

and bright varietal cherry fruit from go to whoa; a hint of toasty oak adding some interest. It's soft and smoothly textured through the palate with gentle astringency completing the finish. Screwcap. 12% alc. **Rating** 89 **To** 2024 $18 SC ✪

Norton Estate

758 Plush Hannans Road, Lower Norton, Vic 3401 **Region** Western Victoria zone
T (03) 5384 8235 **www**.nortonestate.com.au **Open** Fri–Sun & public hols 11–4
Winemaker Best's Wines **Est.** 1997 **Dozens** 1200 **Vyds** 5.66ha
In 1996 the Spence family purchased a rundown farm at Lower Norton and, rather than looking to the traditional wool, meat and wheat markets, trusted their instincts and planted vines on the elevated, frost-free, buckshot rises. The surprising vigour of the initial planting of shiraz prompted further plantings of shiraz, cabernet sauvignon and sauvignon blanc, plus a small planting of the American variety 'Norton'. The vineyard is halfway between the Grampians and Mt Arapiles, 6km northwest of the Grampians region, and has to be content with the Western Victoria zone, but the wines show regional Grampians character and style.

🍷🍷🍷🍷🍷 **Arapiles Run Shiraz 2018** The most Rhône-like of the bunch with a higher proportion of whole bunch (20%) to tannin ratio, helping to tone the wine into a more savoury mould. Turmeric and exotic Indian spice on the nose. Blue fruit allusions too. Clove and pepper-clad tannins, juicy and moreish peppery acidity. This is very good. Screwcap. **Rating** 94 **To** 2030 $38 NG

🍷🍷🍷🍷🍷 **Wendy's Block Shiraz 2018** Rating 92 To 2030 $65 NG
Cabernet Sauvignon 2018 Rating 92 To 2026 $25 NG ✪
Sauvignon Blanc 2019 Rating 90 To 2023 $25 NG
Rockface Shiraz 2018 Rating 90 To 2026 $25 NG

Nova Vita Wines

11 Woodlands Road, Kenton Valley, SA 5235 **Region** Adelaide Hills
T (08) 8356 0454 **www**.novavitawines.com.au **Open** Wed–Sun 11–5
Winemaker Mark Kozned **Est.** 2005 **Dozens** 20000 **Vyds** 49ha
Mark and Jo Kozned's 30ha Woodlands Ridge Vineyard is planted to chardonnay, sauvignon blanc, pinot gris and shiraz. They subsequently established the Tunnel Hill Vineyard, with 19ha planted to pinot noir, shiraz, cabernet sauvignon, sauvignon blanc, semillon, verdelho, merlot and sangiovese. The name Nova Vita reflects the beginning of the Kozned's new life, the firebird on the label coming from their Russian ancestry – it is a Russian myth that only a happy or lucky person may see the bird or hear its song. They are building a new winery and cellar door at the Woodlands Ridge Vineyard and they expect the first small-batch varietal wines to be made in 2020. The majority of the wines are made at Revenir. Exports to the US, Finland, Thailand, Singapore and China.

🍷🍷🍷🍷🍷 **Project K The GTR Adelaide Hills 2019** Project K is a new range of low-intervention wines and the style will vary each year. In this instance, a co-ferment of pinot gris, traminer and riesling results in a pale orange-pink. It's really fragrant with blood orange juice and zest, pickled ginger and lots of florals. The palate is quite textural, phenolic, yet fresh as a daisy. Screwcap. 12.5% alc. **Rating** 95 **To** 2023 $40 JF

🍷🍷🍷🍷🍷 **Firebird Adelaide Hills Pinot Grigio 2019** Rating 93 To 2022 $20 JF ✪
Firebird Adelaide Hills Pinot Noir 2018 Rating 92 To 2024 $35 JF
Firebird Adelaide Hills Saignee Rose 2019 Rating 90 To 2021 $20 JF ✪

Nugan Estate

580 Kidman Way, Wilbriggie, NSW 2680 **Region** Riverina
T (02) 9362 9993 **www**.nuganestate.com.au **Open** Mon–Fri 9–5
Winemaker Daren Owers **Est.** 1999 **Dozens** 500000 **Vyds** 606ha

Nugan Estate arrived on the scene like a whirlwind. It is an offshoot of the Nugan Group headed by Michelle Nugan (until her retirement in Feb 2013), inter alia the recipient of an Export Hero Award in '00. The wine business is now in the energetic hands of Matthew Nugan. Exports to the UK, the US, Canada, the EU and Asia.

ΤΤΤΤΩ **McLaren Parish Vineyard McLaren Vale Shiraz 2018** A delicious wine tattooed with the fealty of place: blue fruits and Christmas cake spice. Aged in a combination of French and American oak, pillars that guide the fray long. Sumptuous and creamy. A skein of peppery acidity towing it all long. An accent of clove and smoked meat to finish. Screwcap. 14.5% alc. **Rating** 93 To 2026 $26 NG ✪

Alfredo Second Pass Shiraz 2017 An Italian-inspired approach of passing the newly fermented wine across the pomace of a denser dried grape iteration fermented prior. This is very good. Highly successful. Bravo! The lilac, blue fruit references, spice and smoked meat references, as to be expected. However, this approach provides detailed, fibrous tannins, gritty and grapey. These are the wine's totem and a very welcome one for the sake of drinkability and salvation. Screwcap. 14% alc. **Rating** 93 To 2025 $20 NG ✪

Manuka Grove Vineyard Riverina Durif 2016 This sturdy phenolically endowed grape variety thrives in warm, dry conditions such as the Riverina. Saturated scents of black plum, cherry, five-spice and crushed black rock; ferrous and mineral. The palate, unashamedly rich but smooth from fore to aft, is punctuated by impeccably massaged tannins going the melee long. As far as drinkable durif goes, this is a benchmark. Screwcap. 14.5% alc. **Rating** 93 To 2028 $26 NG ✪

Frasca's Lane Vineyard King Valley Chardonnay 2018 Cooler climate sourcing, this mid-weighted, juicy and highly appealing chardonnay reaps the dividends. Honeydew melon, apricot, white peach and nectarine scents teem along well appointed nougatine oak and a long trail of subalpine acidity. Plenty of wine for the price. Screwcap. 13.5% alc. **Rating** 91 To 2023 $22 NG ✪

Cookoothama Darlington Point Shiraz 2017 Polished rich red. Dark fruit flavours meld sumptuously with coffee-vanilla-bean oak, beautifully integrated. A flourish of anise and floral notes across the long finish. Exemplary winemaking. Screwcap. 14% alc. **Rating** 91 To 2025 $17 NG ✪

Matriarch McLaren Vale Shiraz 2012 A whole-berry ferment confers pulp and a floral, grapey juiciness. A cavalcade of French and American oak (24 months), structural mettle and a pipeline along which the fruit flavours are funnelled. Long. The pH adjustments clang a little but for a buxom fully loaded style, this is well put together. Screwcap. 15% alc. **Rating** 91 To 2024 $79 NG

La Brutta Zinfandel Petite Sirah 2017 This is an uncanny blend of 2 physiologically sturdy and highly charged varieties, seldom seen outside of California's Amador County. The result is powerful. But plenty fresh and pulpy. Not too worked. Saturated dark fruit persuasions, bitter chocolate, violet, smouldering herb and barbecued meat scents corral across a beam of well applied tannins and oak. Screwcap. 14.5% alc. **Rating** 91 To 2023 $28 NG

Frasca's Lane Vineyard Pinot Grigio 2019 A definitive grigio and a solid one; the green apple crunch and curb of herbal chew and acidity is brighter than that of a more viscous gris. Even if, of course, gris and grigio are DNA replicates. Nashi pear and fennel too. A good drink. Screwcap. 13% alc. **Rating** 90 To 2022 $22 NG

Scruffy's Single Vineyard Riverina Shiraz 2017 An abstemious parcel-by-parcel selection, micro-vinifications and a combination of French and American oak (25% new). The result is rich and soft, the only real tannins being a gentle etching of piney oak. Boysenberry, licorice and cherry bonbon. A sumptuous wine for the here and now. Screwcap. 14% alc. **Rating** 90 To 2024 $17 NG ✪

Cookoothama Darlington Point Cabernet Merlot 2016 The wines under this label are highly reliable. Close to the hearth, heart and operational facilities, presumably. Blackcurrant, clove, tapenade, hedgerow and mocha-oak-sage-clad tannins, gently pliant, to direct the billowing warmth of fruit. A satisfying drink. Screwcap. 14% alc. **Rating** 90 **To** 2023 $17 NG ○

ŸŸŸŸ **Talinga Park Rose 2019 Rating** 89 **To** 2020 $14 NG ○

Nuova Scuola Wines   ★★★☆

167 Tipperary Road, Redgate, Qld 4605 **Region** South Burnett
T 0408 850 595 **www**.nuovascuola.com.au **Open** Thurs–Sun 10.30–4.30
Winemaker Sarah Boyce, Stefano Radici **Est.** 2017 **Dozens** 350
Winemakers Sarah Boyce and Stefano Radici met in NZ in 2009, fell in love and haven't looked back since. They have been working side by side in many different wineries in many parts of the world including Italy, France, Canada, the US, NZ, Mexico and – of course – Australia. Queensland's South Burnett has its limitations but they believe the climate is ideal for Iberian and Italian varieties such as barbera, nebbiolo, tempranillo, sangiovese and viognier. The demand for these varieties is increasing rapidly and while currently purchasing grapes, they plan to establish their own vineyard.

ŸŸŸŸŸ **Nebbiolo 2018** By far the most difficult of all wines to make – colour, bitter tannin, diminished fruit. This is the best of the Nuova Scuola wines, its 14 months in barrel safely navigated, the red cherry fruits and savoury tannins all in balance. Screwcap. 12.8% alc. **Rating** 90 **To** 2028 $25

O'Leary Walker Wines   ★★★★★

7093 Horrocks Highway, Leasingham, SA 5452 **Region** Clare Valley/Adelaide Hills
T 1300 342 569 **www**.olearywalkerwines.com **Open** Mon–Sat 10–4, Sun 11–4
Winemaker David O'Leary, Nick Walker, Jack Walker, Luke Broadbent **Est.** 2001
Dozens 20 000 **Vyds** 45ha
David O'Leary and Nick Walker together had more than 30 years' experience as winemakers working for some of the biggest Australian wine groups when they took the plunge in 2001 and backed themselves to establish their own winery and brand. Initially the principal focus was on the Clare Valley with 10ha of riesling, shiraz and cabernet sauvignon the main plantings; thereafter attention swung to the Adelaide Hills where they now have 35ha of chardonnay, cabernet sauvignon, pinot noir, shiraz, sauvignon blanc and merlot. The vineyards were certified organic in 2013. O'Leary Walker also has a cellar door in the Adelaide Hills at 18 Oakwood Road, Oakbank at the heritage-listed former Johnson Brewery established in 1843 (7 days 11–4). Exports to the UK, Ireland, Canada, the UAE, Asia and Japan.

ŸŸŸŸŸ **Polish Hill River Riesling 2019** Machine-harvested at night, destemmed and crushed, gently pressed for free-run. There's a sorbet-like energy and bounce to the wine. The crunchy electricity of the fruit on the palate is exhilarating, driving the long finish. Screwcap. 11.5% alc. **Rating** 96 **To** 2034 $28 ○
Polish Hill River Armagh Shiraz 2017 From the 2 estate vineyards: one in the warmer Armagh district, the other in the cooler Polish Hill River. Fermented with some whole bunches, 27 days on skins, matured for 2 years in French oak (25% new). Good colour opens the batting; length and oak aplenty, all in balance. Screwcap. 14.5% alc. **Rating** 95 **To** 2042 $30 ○
Oakbank Adelaide Hills Shiraz 2018 Full of vibrant fruit flavours ranging from red to purple to black, garnished by spice, pepper and licorice. Balanced and coherent. Screwcap. 14% alc. **Rating** 94 **To** 2043 $40

ŸŸŸŸŸ **Watervale Riesling 2019 Rating** 93 **To** 2024 $25 ○
Oakbank Adelaide Hills Sauvignon Blanc 2019 Rating 93 **To** 2023 $25 ○
Oakbank Adelaide Hills Pinot Noir 2019 Rating 90 **To** 2029 $35
Blue Cutting Rd Polish Hill River Cabernet Sauvignon Merlot 2017 Rating 90 **To** 2027 $22

Oakdene

255 Grubb Road, Wallington, Vic 3221 **Region** Geelong
T (03) 5256 3886 **www.**oakdene.com.au **Open** 7 days 10–4
Winemaker Robin Brockett, Marcus Holt **Est.** 2001 **Dozens** 8000 **Vyds** 32ha

Bernard and Elizabeth Hooley purchased Oakdene in 2001. Bernard focused on planting the vineyard (shiraz, pinot gris, sauvignon blanc, pinot noir, chardonnay, merlot, cabernet franc and cabernet sauvignon) while Elizabeth worked to restore the 1920s homestead. Much of the wine is sold through the award-winning Oakdene Restaurant and cellar door. The quality is exemplary, as is the consistency of that quality; Robin Brockett's skills are on full display. A new vineyard (11km from Oakdene) planted in '17 (to shiraz, pinot noir, pinot gris, chardonnay, sauvignon blanc, merlot, riesling, cabernet franc and cabernet sauvignon) has increased the plantings from 12ha to 32ha.

♥♥♥♥♥ **Liz's Single Vineyard Bellarine Peninsula Chardonnay 2018** Stunning chardonnay! Unabashedly rich but tensile, energetic and incredibly long. The stone fruit references and notes of dried mango are almost sublimated by a saline maritime freshness, beautifully appointed oak and Meursault-like suggestions of toasted hazelnut and curd. Oakdene's tattoo of intensity of flavour melded by quality fruit, a fine site and a deft winemaking hand. Screwcap. **Rating** 96 To 2026 $35 NG ✪

Bellarine Peninsula Shiraz 2018 Open-fermented in small pots, then matured in French oak for 11 months. A most attractive assemblage of bright, supple red and purple fruits, the oak hovering but not threatening the fruit, the tannins exemplary, the pinch of spice well selected. Screwcap. 14.1% alc. **Rating** 95 To 2033 $24 ✪

Bellarine Peninsula Late Harvest Riesling 2019 A stellar wine, loading extract and an uncanny intensity of flavour into an ethereal, featherweight package. Sublime! Nashi pear, talc and Granny Smith apple with merely a semblance of sweetness sublimated by a whiplash of acidity. And yet 135g/l of sugar. Very fine. Screwcap. **Rating** 95 To 2024 $23 NG ✪

Ly Ly Single Vineyard Bellarine Peninsula Pinot Gris 2019 This mid-weighted gris has been treated with as much love and care as any in the land. Oak, nicely worked into the fray, imparts textural detail while conferring a structural authority to riffs of bitter almond, marzipan, baking spice and ripe apple. Long, pointed and intense of flavour. Screwcap. **Rating** 94 To 2024 $24 NG ✪

Peta's Single Vineyard Bellarine Peninsula Pinot Noir 2018 An ambient ferment in open-top pots, smattered with 20% whole-bunch, before completion in French barriques (30% new). The result is a rich pinot with a spicy brood and pallid hue. Cherry cola, root spice and satsuma plum notes billow across a hinge of woodsy tannins, earthen scents and cardamom to turmeric-soused acidity. Screwcap. **Rating** 94 To 2026 $43 NG

♥♥♥♥♡ **Jessica Single Vineyard Bellarine Peninsula Sauvignon 2019** Rating 93 To 2022 $28 NG

Bellarine Peninsula Chardonnay 2018 Rating 93 To 2024 $24 NG ✪

William Single Vineyard Bellarine Peninsula Shiraz 2018 Rating 93 To 2026 $43 NG

Bellarine Peninsula Sauvignon Blanc 2019 Rating 92 To 2021 $24 NG ✪

Bellarine Peninsula Rose 2019 Rating 92 To 2020 $24 NG ✪

Bellarine Peninsula Pinot Noir 2018 Rating 92 To 2023 $24 NG ✪

Bellarine Peninsula Pinot Grigio 2019 Rating 91 To 2022 $24 NG

Bernard's Single Vineyard Bellarine Peninsula Cabernets 2018 Rating 91 To 2026 NG

Oakridge Wines

★★★★★

864 Maroondah Highway, Coldstream, Vic 3770 **Region** Yarra Valley
T (03) 9738 9900 **www**.oakridgewines.com.au **Open** 7 days 10–5
Winemaker David Bicknell, Tim Perrin **Est.** 1978 **Dozens** 35 000 **Vyds** 61ha
Winemaker and CEO David Bicknell has proved his worth time and again as an extremely
talented winemaker. At the top of the Oakridge brand tier is 864, all Yarra Valley vineyard
selections, only released in the best years (Chardonnay, Pinot Noir, Shiraz, Cabernet
Sauvignon, Riesling); next is the Oakridge Local Vineyard Series (the Chardonnay, Pinot
Noir and Sauvignon Blanc come from the cooler Upper Yarra Valley; the Shiraz, Cabernet
Sauvignon and Viognier from the Lower Yarra); and the Over the Shoulder range, drawn from
all of the sources available to Oakridge (Sauvignon Blanc, Pinot Grigio, Pinot Noir, Shiraz
Viognier, Cabernet Sauvignon). The estate vineyards are Oakridge Vineyard, Hazeldene
Vineyard and Henk Vineyard. Exports to the UK, the US, Canada, Sweden, the Netherlands,
Norway, Fiji, Papua New Guinea, Singapore, Hong Kong and China.

🍷🍷🍷🍷🍷 **864 Single Block Release Aqueduct Block Henk Vineyard Yarra Valley
Chardonnay 2018** A very small make. Hand-picked, chilled overnight, whole-
bunch pressed to puncheons for wild ferment, aged on lees for 10 months before
transfer to stainless steel and a further 6 months' maturation. Joyously concentrated,
but self-contained. Screwcap. 13.5% alc. **Rating** 97 **To** 2028 $90 ✪
**864 Single Block Release Close Planted Block Oakridge Vineyard Yarra
Valley Syrah 2018** 5300 vines/ha, hand-picked, destemmed, wild-fermented
with maximum pigeage to extract maximum tannins, matured in French
puncheons (10% new) for 19 months. An extremely attractive, velvety wine, the
relatively low alcohol allowing the fruit to have all the say. Screwcap. 13% alc.
Rating 97 **To** 2038 $90 ✪

🍷🍷🍷🍷🍷 **Vineyard Series Henk Yarra Valley Chardonnay 2018** It's no coincidence
that all 4 of the Oakridge Vineyard Series chardonnays come from the Upper
Yarra – it is higher and cooler, and was the perfect place for the very warm
vintage. The bouquet is slightly richer than Barkala and Hazeldene, and the palate
follows suit. Drink this first (although there's no hurry). Screwcap. 13.7% alc.
Rating 96 **To** 2029 $42 ✪
Vineyard Series Willowlake Yarra Valley Chardonnay 2018 This is the
oldest Upper Yarra vineyard and one of the largest in either the Upper or
Lower Yarra. The mouthfeel and thus the fruit/oak acid balance are all singing
the same note. It has great length and aftertaste. Ironically the only one of these
4 chardonnays not entered in the Yarra Valley Wine Show. Screwcap. 13.4% alc.
Rating 96 **To** 2030 $42 ✪
Vineyard Series Barkala Yarra Valley Chardonnay 2018 The Barkala
Vineyard has east–west facing slopes on red volcanic soil in the Upper Yarra.
David Bicknell has a winemaking approach of letting terroir and site climate
determine quality/style. This is beautifully restrained. Bright fruit in a classic
grapefruit/white peach spectrum. Screwcap. 13.5% alc. **Rating** 96 **To** 2029 $42 ✪
Vineyard Series Henk Yarra Valley Pinot Noir 2018 Clones 777 and MV6,
the standard Oakridge vinification ever seeking maximum expression of the
variety and sense of place. Good colour. The penetration of the wine is a feature
deriving from the inherent purity and natural balance of red and black cherry
fruit. Wonderful wine. Screwcap. 13.1% alc. **Rating** 96 **To** 2033 $45 ✪
**864 Single Block Release Aqueduct Block Henk Vineyard Yarra Valley
Pinot Noir 2018** The vinification of 10% whole bunches in the bottom of the
fermenter, whole berries on top, matured for 10 months in French oak (10% new)
is the cornerstone for all the Oakridge pinots. Brilliantly clear colour. A superbly
handled, supple, very long palate. Life and brightness features. Screwcap. 13.1% alc.
Rating 96 **To** 2033 $90
Vineyard Series Oakridge Yarra Valley Shiraz 2018 Destemmed over
30% whole bunches in the bottom of the fermenter. Part velvety rich, part

savoury spicy. From the warm, high yielding and at times chaotic vintage, this is remarkable. Screwcap. 13.2% alc. **Rating** 96 **To** 2038 $45 **O**

864 Single Block Release Winery Block Oakridge Vineyard Yarra Valley Cabernet Sauvignon 2018 Hand-picked and sorted to static fermenters, 4 days' cold soak, daily delestage, wild-fermented, 14 days' post-ferment maceration, matured in French barriques (40% new) for 15 months. Immaculate balance of blackcurrant fruit, oak and tannins. The fresh fruit flavours are protected by the low alcohol. 13% alc. **Rating** 96 **To** 2048 $90

Vineyard Series Hazeldene Yarra Valley Chardonnay 2018 There's never any mention of the age or source (other than French) of the oak because oak is merely a means of fermentation. The bouquet has a slight, hard-to-pin-down character but the palate is of dazzling purity and finesse, fruit posing no questions. Screwcap. 13.2% alc. **Rating** 95 **To** 2029 $42

Vineyard Series Willowlake Yarra Valley Pinot Noir 2018 From 3 blocks planted '80–82. The colour is deceptively light, as is the weight of the palate. Like all top class pinots, its class comes through on the finish and aftertaste. Screwcap. 13.6% alc. **Rating** 95 **To** 2030 $45

Vineyard Series Hazeldene Yarra Valley Pinot Noir 2018 Has well above average complexity and drive, the style in the mainstream of Oakridge pinot noir. Screwcap. 13.3% alc. **Rating** 95 **To** 2030 $45

Vineyard Series Barkala Yarra Valley Cabernet Sauvignon 2018 Held on skins for 4 weeks after fermentation before 18 months' maturation in French oak. Bright crimson-purple. It is an elegant cabernet that has flourished in the warm vintage – the Upper Yarra sometimes poses challenges but not here. The tannins are savoury and fine, adding to the quality of the wine. Screwcap. 13% alc. **Rating** 95 **To** 2038 $42

Original Vineyard Cabernet Sauvignon 2018 Picked 15 days after the 864 from a single block in the Upper Yarra, 6 weeks on skins, matured in French barriques (35% new) for 16 months with regular racking. Has a particular flavour and feel accurately described by Oakridge as 'fine-grained old school claret' without any green notes. Screwcap. 13.3% alc. **Rating** 95 **To** 2038 $65

Yarra Valley Chardonnay 2018 David Bicknell's masterly handling of Yarra Valley chardonnay has long been proven in wine shows around the country. He's never been afraid to push the envelope (the acidity in this wine, for example), nor test the benefits/downsides of controlled reduction (barely here). Screwcap. 12.9% alc. **Rating** 94 **To** 2032 $30 **O**

Vineyard Series Oakridge Yarra Valley Cabernet Sauvignon 2018 From the west side of the vineyard around the winery. A lengthy and complex vinification over 2 months sends a strong, savoury message courtesy of its austere feel and flavour; 40% new oak has been totally integrated. Screwcap. 13% alc. **Rating** 94 **To** 2048 $45

ỸỸỸỸỌ **Yarra Valley Pinot Noir 2018 Rating** 93 **To** 2025 $30
Vineyard Series Willowlake Yarra Valley Sauvignon 2018 Rating 92 **To** 2021 $28
Meunier 2019 Rating 90 **To** 2023 $28
Sparkling Meunier Rose 2017 Rating 90 $40

Oates Ends   ★★★★★

22 Carpenter Road, Wilyabrup, WA 6280 **Region** Margaret River
T 0401 303 144 **www**.oatesends.com.au **Open** By appt
Winemaker Cath Oates **Est.** 1998 **Dozens** 1000 **Vyds** 11ha

Oates Ends are the new wines from Cath Oates, who returned home to Margaret River after an international winemaking career spanning 15 years. Made from the family Wilagri Vineyard, planted in 1999 and now owned and managed by viticulturist brother Russ Oates, Oates Ends is the culmination of both of their respective experience and wine philosophies. The vineyard is run on sustainable farming principles. Sheep are a big part of the vineyard program with winter mowing a given and they are ever increasingly being relied upon for leaf plucking during the growing season. The name comes from the shed wine made for family and friends in the early 2000s from the ends of the rows the harvesters missed and acknowledges the importance of family farming traditions. Exports to Canada and Singapore.

ҮҮҮҮҮ **Margaret River Sauvignon Blanc Semillon 2019** Four small parcels of 57% sauvignon blanc and 43% semillon; hand-picked over 10 days, crushed, pressed to used French barriques for co-fermentation followed by 4 months' maturation on lees in barrel for mlf that was fully justified analytically and organoleptically due to very high acidity given the very cool vintage. Responsive winemaking. Screwcap. 12.5% alc. **Rating** 95 **To** 2024 $24 **☉**
Margaret River Tempranillo 2018 The bright crimson hue signals a bright, juicy red cherry and pomegranate-filled bouquet and palate. Just when you think there's nothing more to say, an extra plume lifts the finish with a flourish not to be missed. Screwcap. 13.5% alc. **Rating** 95 **To** 2028 $28 **☉**

ҮҮҮҮҶ **Margaret River Cabernet Sauvignon 2016 Rating** 93 **To** 2029 $48
Margaret River Tempranillo Rose 2019 Rating 90 **To** 2020 $24

Occam's Razor | Lo Stesso ★★★★★

c/- Jasper Hill, Drummonds Lane, Heathcote, Vic 3523 **Region** Heathcote
T (03) 5433 2528 **www.**jasperhill.com.au **Open** By appt
Winemaker Emily McNally, Georgia Roberts **Est.** 2001 **Dozens** 370 **Vyds** 2.5ha
Emily McNally (nee Laughton) decided to follow in her parents' footsteps after first seeing the world and having a range of jobs. Having grown up at Jasper Hill, winemaking was far from strange, but she decided to find her own way, buying grapes from a small vineyard owned by Jasper Hill employee Andrew Conforti and his wife Melissa. She made the wine 'with guidance and inspiration from my father'. The name comes from William of Ockham (1285–1349), also spelt Occam, a theologian and philosopher responsible for many sayings, including that appearing on the back label of the wine, 'what can be done with fewer is done in vain with more'. Lo Stesso is made by Emily and friend Georgia Roberts, who purchase 2.5t of fiano from a vineyard in Heathcote, making the wine at Jasper Hill. Exports to the UK, the US, Canada and Singapore.

ҮҮҮҮҮ **Lo Stesso Heathcote Fiano 2019** Lo Stesso is nailing this variety, aiming stylistically for a flavoursome, riper and textural style. Expect chargrilled peaches topped with lemon curd and creamed honey, but this is not sweet. With a true Italian leaning, it is savoury, moreish with neatly handled phenolics. Super drink. Screwcap. 14% alc. **Rating** 95 **To** 2027 $32 JF **☉**

ҮҮҮҮҶ **Occam's Razor Heathcote Shiraz 2018 Rating** 93 **To** 2030 $46 NG

Ochota Barrels ★★★★★

Merchants Road, Basket Range, SA 5138 **Region** Adelaide Hills
T 0400 798 818 **www.**ochotabarrels.com **Open** Not
Winemaker Taras Ochota **Est.** 2008 **Dozens** 900 **Vyds** 0.5ha
Taras Ochota has had an incredibly varied career as a winemaker after completing his oenology degree at the University of Adelaide. He has not only made wine for top Australian producers, but has had a Flying Winemaker role in many parts of the world, most recently as consultant winemaker for one of Sweden's largest wine-importing companies, working on Italian wines from Puglia and Sicily made specifically for Oenoforos. Wife Amber has accompanied him to many places, working in a multiplicity of technical and marketing roles. Exports to the UK, the US, Canada, Denmark, Norway and Japan.

ҮҮҮҮҮ **Control Voltage +5VOV Chardonnay 2019** This tensile chardonnay is imbued with real authority following varying degrees of skin maceration across batches, together with lees stirring. Tightly coiled, it is a take-no-prisoners sort of wine, reliant on a pungent whiplash of mineral as much as a vibrato of acidity for pulse and flow. Texture over fruit. Palate-staining intensity. This leaves a strong impression of place and a cool gaze of confidence. Cork. **Rating** 95 **To** 2025 $60 NG

Impeccable Disorder Pinot Noir 2019 This pinot is a leap forward structurally, embellished with a bunchy rasp, detailed astringency and well appointed oak pillars guiding red berry allusions, wood smoke and scents of sandalwood. Tightly furled upon opening, this demands patience and/or an aggressive decant. A lovely wine of sapid flavour and precision. Cork. **Rating** 95 **To** 2025 $80 NG

I am the Owl Syrah 2019 This has been among the standouts of the range for some time, setting a vibrant aromatic cadence at a modest alcohol level without any hint of greenness. Lifted notes of nori, violet, camphor, clove, black olive and smoked meats; the breadth of wood toning the melee nicely. Pulpy across the midriff with a skein of peppery acidity towing it long and vibrant. Cork. **Rating** 94 **To** 2025 $40 NG

ＹＹＹＹＹ **Weird Berries in the Woods Gewurztraminer 2019 Rating** 93
To 2022 $35 NG
Slint Chardonnay 2019 Rating 93 **To** 2024 $40 NG
The Mark of Cain Pinot Meunier 2019 Rating 93 **To** 2022 $40 NG
A Forest Pinot Noir 2019 Rating 93 **To** 2025 $40 NG
Fugazi Grenache 2019 Rating 92 **To** 2023 $40 NG
From the North Mourvedre 2019 Rating 91 **To** 2024 $40 NG
The Price of Silence Gamay 2019 Rating 90 **To** 2022 $40 NG
The Green Room McLaren Vale Grenache 2019 Rating 90 **To** 2021 $35 NG

Oliver's Taranga Vineyards ★★★★★

246 Seaview Road, McLaren Vale, SA 5171 **Region** McLaren Vale
T (08) 8323 8498 **www**.oliverstaranga.com **Open** 7 days 10–4
Winemaker Corrina Wright **Est.** 1841 **Dozens** 10 000 **Vyds** 85.42ha
William and Elizabeth Oliver arrived from Scotland in 1839 to settle in McLaren Vale. Six generations later, members of the family are still living on the Whitehill and Taranga farms. The Taranga property has 15 varieties planted (the lion's share to shiraz and cabernet sauvignon with lesser quantities of chardonnay, chenin blanc, durif, fiano, grenache, mataro, merlot, petit verdot, sagrantino, semillon, tempranillo, viognier and white frontignac). Corrina Wright (the Oliver family's first winemaker) makes the wines. In 2021 the family celebrates 180 years of grapegrowing. Exports to the UK, Denmark, Finland and Singapore.

ＹＹＹＹＹ **HJ McLaren Vale Shiraz 2017** Part from the oldest estate block (planted '48), and Rayments clone 1654 (planted '96); destemmed, berry-sorted, lightly crushed, 3 days' cold soak, wild yeast–open fermented, pressed at 1°baume for primary and mlf in French oak (35% new). Great fruit, great vintage, great winemaking. Screwcap. 14.5% alc. **Rating** 98 **To** 2047 $75 ✪

ＹＹＹＹＹ **Small Batch McLaren Vale Grenache 2019** Hand-picked from the Old Block planted in '65; destemmed, berry-sorted, lightly crushed, wild yeast–open fermented, bottled Dec '19. It's on the full-bodied side but the texture and structure promote the luscious (not jammy) fruit. A lovely traditional wine. Screwcap. 14% alc. **Rating** 96 **To** 2030 $30 ✪

DJ McLaren Vale Cabernet Sauvignon 2017 From 45yo Reynell clone; destemmed and berry-sorted, lightly crushed, 3 days' cold soak, wild yeast–open fermented, completion of ferment and mlf in French hogsheads (35% new), extended barrel ageing, bottled Sept '19. In McLaren Vale '17 was a great vintage and cabernet benefited more than any other variety. The wine is finely structured, it's blackcurrant fruit with a purebred savoury backdrop. Screwcap. 14% alc. **Rating** 95 **To** 2037 $65

Corrina's Small Batch McLaren Vale Cabernet Shiraz 2018 Made only in the years when both varieties ripen at the same time, thus permitting – indeed encouraging – co-fermentation. It's unashamedly full-bodied but also has the balance to underwrite a lengthy maturation process. Screwcap. 13.5% alc. **Rating** 95 **To** 2038 $32 ✪

Small Batch McLaren Vale Mencia 2019 Progressively planted '16–19, this is the second vintage, Oliver's the leader of the pack of the handful of mencia producers. Hand-picked, open-fermented, no additions other than SO_2 post mlf (as are all the Oliver's red wines), pressed at dryness to used French hogsheads. Supple, smooth, spiced black fruits; great balance and length. A surprise packet. Screwcap. 13% alc. **Rating** 95 To 2029 $32 ✪

Small Batch McLaren Vale Brioni's Blend 2018 A blend of touriga, mataro and shiraz. A very interesting bouquet of dark chocolate, spice, fresh earth and blackberry; all translated to the palate, that is full of juicy flavours and buttressed by tannins. Screwcap. 13.5% alc. **Rating** 94 To 2030 $32

Small Batch McLaren Vale Tempranillo 2018 This is a matador looking for a bull to accompany it to a bbq that would make Spain proud, and a feast for the neighbouring farm. Screwcap. 13% alc. **Rating** 94 To 2025 $32

Small Batch McLaren Vale Sagrantino 2017 One fermenter pressed at 1°baume to barrel for mlf, the other left in the vat for 4 months post-ferment with richer tannin, the former with florals on the bouquet. It is surprising that the tannins needed assistance but the result speaks for itself with very spicy/bramble flavours and good structure. Screwcap. 13.5% alc. **Rating** 94 To 2030 $42

🍷🍷🍷🍷🍷 **McLaren Vale Shiraz 2018** Rating 93 To 2033 $30
Chica Small Batch Mencia Rose 2019 Rating 92 To 2021 $25 ✪

One Block   ★★★★★

Nyora Road, Mt Toolebewong, Vic 3777 **Region** Yarra Valley
T 0419 186 888 **www.**jaydenong.com **Open** By appt
Winemaker Jayden Ong **Est.** 2010 **Dozens** 1500 **Vyds** 5ha

Jayden Ong, a first-generation Eurasian-Australian, was infected by the wine bug working at the Melbourne Wine Room from 2000–06. He has moved with bewildering speed across many facets of the industry since then: wedging in vintages at Curly Flat ('06), Moorooduc Estate ('07) and Allies/Garagiste ('08–09) while completing the CSU oenology course; he also opened Cumulus Inc., a restaurant and bar in Melbourne, with superstar chef Andrew McConnell and business partners; he continues to mentor the Cumulus wine team. Apart from an annual pilgrimage to France to further his grapegrowing and winemaking experience, he went to Italy in '06 and '12, Germany in '10, Spain in '11 and '13, and California in '14. He founded One Block in '10 with the philosophy of making single vineyard wines 'from quality individual vineyard sites where the variety grown suits the site', making 100 dozen of his first love – chardonnay – in '10. In '15 he and partner Morgan Ong purchased a small property and home at Mt Toolebewong, 700m above sea level, in the Yarra Valley. They immediately began biological site preparation for a close-planted vineyard with three new clones of chardonnay. He also leases the dry-grown Chestnut Hill vineyard and winery at Mount Burnett, and has begun conversion of the vineyard to organic and biological farming methods. He doesn't intend to slow down, with all sorts of projects in mind for the coming years. A star in the making. Exports to the UK, Singapore and China.

🍷🍷🍷🍷🍷 **Moonlit Forest Light Chilled Red 'Carter' Yarra Valley Rose 2018** Blend of white and red grapes; hand-picked, aged in seasoned barrels and puncheons for 12 months. Looks a treat, with an aroma to match of just-picked red cherries, wild raspberry, peonies and iris florals. Notes of confection are counterpoised brilliantly by sour cherry and cranberry. Lively with bouncy acidity. Definitely no lightweight. Diam. 13% alc. **Rating** 95 To 2029 $25 JP ✪

La Maison de Ong The Hermit Yarra Valley Syrah 2018 A proponent of minimal intervention, Jayden Ong has fashioned a voluptuous, no-frills winemaking syrah that shines with near-perfect fruit intensity. Laden with ripe tannins and fine-trimmed oak, the dense, black, high-spiced fruit is allowed the freedom to express itself beautifully. Diam. 13.5% alc. **Rating** 95 To 2031 $48 JP

Moonlit Forest Pinot Noir Syrah PS I Love You 2018 What a stunner! Fragrant and fruit-driven, seamless and so seductive. A heady scent of dried flowers, cranberry, black cherry and chocolate. The 2 grapes glide across the palate as one, with just a touch of licorice for added excitement. A most persuasive argument for more of this kind of blend, originally made famous by Maurice

O'Shea in the 1930–50s in the Hunter Valley. Diam. 13% alc. **Rating** 95 **To** 2026 $28 JP ✪

Red Hill Mornington Peninsula Pinot Gris 2018 Gingerbread, Pink Lady apple, hay, crystallised pear. A complex gris that works the spiced, lightly savoury aspect of the grape; akin to an Alsatian interpretation, where it's all about depth and texture and the role of phenolics, less about upfront fruitiness. A different experience to many a gris available in the marketplace. Diam. 13% alc. **Rating** 94 **To** 2027 $30 JP ✪

🍷🍷🍷🍷🍷 **Chestnut Hill Mount Burnett Chardonnay 2017 Rating** 92 **To** 2028 $42 JP
Mt Burnett Sauvignon Blanc 2017 Rating 90 **To** 2026 $32 JP

Oparina Wines   ★★★★☆

126 Cameron Road, Padthaway, SA 5271 **Region** Padthaway
T 0448 966 553 **www**.oparina.com.au **Open** Not
Winemaker Phil Brown, Sue Bell **Est.** 1997 **Dozens** 500 **Vyds** 44ha
Oparina is the venture of Phil and Debbie Brown (along with father Terry and the three third-generation Brown children). Phil grew up in the Padthaway region on the family farm, moving to the Barossa Valley to study and then teach agriculture. He returned to the family farm (with newly planted vineyards) in 1998, simultaneously enrolling in (and completing) an oenology degree. The majority of the grapes are sold, shiraz and cabernet sauvignon finding their way into top tier wines such as Penfolds Bin 389, Bin 707 and St Henri. Family and community commitments limited the amount of time he could devote to winemaking and in '14 Sue Bell of Bellwether Wines was contracted to make the wines, with input from Phil. Further vineyard plantings were made in '16 with small blocks of less traditional varieties.

🍷🍷🍷🍷🍷 **Campion's Run Limited Release Padthaway Shiraz 2017** Hand-picked
from the extensive estate plantings. Deep crimson-purple. Aromas of black fruits, polished leather and spice translate directly to the well balanced, full-bodied palate. Everything available has been used in framing this luscious wine. Screwcap. 14.8% alc. **Rating** 94 **To** 2037 $50

🍷🍷🍷🍷🍷 **Campion's Run Limited Release Padthaway Cabernet Sauvignon 2017**
Rating 92 **To** 2027 $50

Orange Mountain Wines   ★★★★

10 Radnedge Lane, Orange, NSW 2800 **Region** Orange
T (02) 6365 2626 **www**.orangemountain.com.au **Open** Wed–Fri 9–3, w'ends 9–5
Winemaker Terry Dolle **Est.** 1997 **Dozens** 3000 **Vyds** 1ha
Having established the business back in 1997, Terry Dolle made the decision to sell the Manildra Vineyard in 2009. He now makes wine from small parcels of hand-picked fruit, using an old basket press and barrel maturation. These are in principle all single vineyard wines reflecting the terroir of Orange.

🍷🍷🍷🍷🍷 **1397 Shiraz Viognier 2018** A 93/7% co-fermented blend, matured for
18 months in new and 1yo oak. Deep, bright crimson-purple. It's savoury and spicy, but also juicy and very long. A success. Screwcap. 14% alc. **Rating** 94 **To** 2029 $50

🍷🍷🍷🍷🍷 **Limited Release Riesling 2018 Rating** 93 **To** 2026 $25 ✪
Master Joshua Shiraz Viognier 2018 Rating 91 **To** 2030 $35

Orbach Family Wines   ★★★★

57 Rokeby Street, Collingwood, Vic 3066 **Region** South Australia
T (03) 9417 5757 **www**.sidegate.com.au **Open** Mon–Fri 8–5
Winemaker Josef Orbach **Est.** 2001 **Dozens** 50 000
Orbach Family Wines is a Melbourne-based multi-regional producer, specialising in cool-climate reds and whites. Founder Josef Orbach lived and worked in the Clare Valley from 1994 to '98 at Leasingham, and completed a winemaking degree at the University of Melbourne

in 2010. It is a classic negociant business, buying grapes and/or wines from various regions. The wines are released under the Side Gate and Georgie Orbach labels. Exports to the US and China.

ΨΨΨΨΩ **Side Gate Art Series Adelaide Hills Tempranillo Pinot Noir 2018**
Tempranillo is the mainstay of the blend at 70%, servicing a plump medium-bodied red. Highly versatile at the table, with a juiciness that belies most domestic expressions of this Iberian variety. I can only think that pinot's svelte nature underpins it all. Dark cherry, satsuma plum and five-spice notes are bound by a weave of savoury tannins, dusty and pliant. This is a good drink. Screwcap. **Rating** 91 **To** 2024 $25 NG
Side Gate Art Series Adelaide Hills Tempranillo 2018 A large-framed wine that is as pulpy, grapey and joyous as it is astringent and twiggy across the finish. This said, it is among the better renditions of this grape in Australia and I have faith that the components will meld in time. Dark fruit allusions, anise and violet. Screwcap. **Rating** 91 **To** 2024 $25 NG

ΨΨΨΨ **Georgie Orbach Riverina Rose 2019 Rating** 89 **To** 2020 $10 NG ✪

Orlando ★★★★

Barossa Valley Way, Rowland Flat, SA 5352 **Region** Barossa Valley
T (08) 8521 3111 www.pernod-ricard-winemakers.com **Open** Not
Winemaker Dan Swincer **Est.** 1847 **Dozens** 8000 **Vyds** 14ha
Orlando is the parent who has been separated from its child, Jacob's Creek (see separate entry). While Orlando is over 170 years old, Jacob's Creek is little more than 45 years old. For what are doubtless sound marketing reasons, Orlando aided and abetted the separation, but the average consumer is unlikely to understand the logic and, if truth be known, is unlikely to care.

Ottelia ★★★★☆

2280 V&A Lane, Coonawarra, SA 5263 **Region** Coonawarra
T 0409 836 298 www.ottelia.com.au **Open** Thurs–Mon 10–4
Winemaker John Innes **Est.** 2001 **Dozens** 8000 **Vyds** 9ha
John and Melissa Innes moved to Coonawarra intending, in John's words, to 'stay a little while'. The first sign of a change of heart was the purchase of a property ringed by red gums and with a natural wetland dotted with *Ottelia ovalifolia*, a native water lily. They still live in the house they built there. John worked as winemaker at Rymill Coonawarra while Melissa established a restaurant. After 20 years, John left Rymill to focus on consultancy work throughout the Limestone Coast and to establish and run Ottelia. Exports to Malaysia, Thailand, Singapore, Japan and China.

ΨΨΨΨΨ **Mount Gambier Riesling 2019** One of the coolest maritime sites on the mainland and doesn't the riesling grape enjoy it! Mineral, sea breeze, saline with underlying spice and super attractive florals, welcome the drinker. Then it's on to an energised palate with grapefruit pith, lemon and musk finishing with a cold, slatey acidity. A name to remember for riesling lovers. Screwcap. 11% alc. **Rating** 95 **To** 2034 $25 JP ✪

ΨΨΨΨΩ **Mount Gambier Chardonnay 2019 Rating** 91 **To** 2030 $28 JP
Coonawarra Shiraz 2017 Rating 90 **To** 2031 $28 JP

Ouse River Wines ★★★★

PO Box 40, Ouse, Tas 7140 **Region** Southern Tasmania
T (03) 6287 1309 www.ouseriverwines.com.au **Open** Not
Winemaker Anna Pooley (Contract) **Est.** 2002 **Dozens** 240 **Vyds** 17.8ha
Ouse River Wines is one of the most interesting developments in Tasmania. Bernard and Margaret Brain own a 1000ha property north of Ouse at the top end of the Derwent Valley, on the edge of the central highlands. They run nine enterprises on the property, including the vineyard that is the furthest inland in Tasmania. It has a continental climate and a diurnal

temperature range during ripening of 7°C more than the areas surrounding Hobart. In the early 1990s Bernard and Margaret attended wine-tasting classes run by Phil Laing, which prompted the planting of a trial area of six varieties to see whether they would ripen. In 2002 they approached Ray Guerin to see what he thought: the answer was a contract with Hardys for 10 years. The first planting of 1ha in late '02 was followed by 1ha planted each year until '06; further plantings over the years resulted in a total of 6.55ha of pinot noir, 10.25ha of chardonnay and 1ha of riesling. The pinot has been used by House of Arras from the second vintage and in every vintage since. Ouse River's grapes continue to be sought after, which has driven substantial new plantings on their ample land.

ΨΨΨΨΨ **Chardonnay 2018** Dijon clones 76 and 95; whole-bunch pressed, wild-fermented in French barriques (25% new), matured for 10 months. A powerful, savoury style; grapefruit zest and pith; pleasingly long, dry finish. Screwcap. 13.2% alc. **Rating** 95 **To** 2028 $45

ΨΨΨΨΨ **Pinot Noir 2018 Rating** 90 **To** 2026 $45

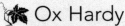 Ox Hardy ★★★★★

28 The Parade, Norwood, SA 5067 (postal) **Region** McLaren Vale
T (08) 8362 8622 **www.**oxhardywines.com.au **Open** Not
Winemaker Andrew Hardy **Est.** 2018 **Dozens** NFP **Vyds** 45ha

It's difficult to overstate the importance of this winery. Its unbroken family line goes back to 1850 and Andrew's great-great-grandfather Thomas Hardy, oft described as the father of the SA wine industry. The interwoven links between the family and the eponymous Hardys Wines have seen an unbroken history of supply of grapes to and from the epicentre of wine production under the Thomas Hardy name for 167 years. How much by design or chance is immaterial, but some of the best vineyards in McLaren Vale and its surrounds have remained in the hands of members of the family outside the corporate structure. One such is the Upper Tintara Vineyard, established by Dr AC Kelly in 1861, purchased by Thomas Hardy in '71. In '91 he expanded the plantings with shiraz, now called Ancestor Vines, and the vineyard has been the prime source of Hardy's Eileen Hardy for 48 years. Small amounts of shiraz were made by Andrew and his late father Bob as a hobby. Since 2008 each vintage has been 70 dozen (other than '09 and '11 declassified); the '08 released in June '19, with subsequent vintages to be an ongoing annual release.

ΨΨΨΨΨ **1891 Ancestor Vines Upper Tintara Vineyard McLaren Vale Shiraz 2008**
Oh my. What a beautiful wine to launch this label. And what a compliment to one of the greatest vineyards in McLaren Vale. It caresses the palate with its purple and black fruits, supple tannins and freshness on the finish. It is medium-bodied yet has the insistent power of a full-bodied wine. Screwcap. 14.5% alc. **Rating** 99 **To** 2038 $225 ✪

Slate Fermented Shiraz 2018 Deep crimson-purple. A full-bodied shiraz that shows no inclination to pull its considerable punches. It goes without saying tannins are in the mix but it's the black fruits, licorice, spice, bitter chocolate flavours framed by quality oak that do the heavy lifting. The most remarkable quality is the way it leaves the mouth fresh. Screwcap. 14.5% alc. **Rating** 98 **To** 2050 $80 ✪

1891 Ancestor Vines Upper Tintara Vineyard McLaren Vale Shiraz 2010 There's magic in this wine, starting with its brilliant crimson-purple colour through to the rim, the bouquet telling you this is no false dawn. Its purity, balance and attention to detail are akin to a miniature painting from the 16th century. Red fruits skip around the perimeter of the gloriously long finish. Screwcap. 14.5% alc. **Rating** 97 **To** 2030 $225

ΨΨΨΨΨ **1891 Ancestor Vines Upper Tintara Vineyard McLaren Vale Shiraz 2012** There's a distinct change of mood here: the fruits are black, the tannins are firm, the dark chocolate and fresh earth aromas are all those of a young, powerful wine refusing to take no for an answer. Its hewn from the bowels of the earth but has exceptional balance that will ease its way through the 3 or so years down the track prior to its release. Screwcap. **Rating** 95 **To** 2040 $225

Blewitt Springs McLaren Vale Grenache 2019 From old bushvines in Blewitt Springs; hand-picked by grower Robert Natale, two 2t fermenters, 500kg of whole bunches on the bottom, the balance destemmed and crushed on top, hand-plunged 3 times daily for 15 days, 6 months in used French barriques and hogsheads before blending. Spicy scented aromas; a classic blend of red fruits and berries led by cherries and raspberries, finished with powdery tannins. Screwcap. 14.5% alc. **Rating** 95 **To** 2030 $38

Upper Tintara Vineyard McLaren Vale Shiraz 2016 This is from the right side of the family blanket. Its blackberry, plum and dark chocolate flavours are accompanied by masculine tannins, made for a winter's day and roasted ox. Screwcap. 14.5% alc. **Rating** 94 **To** 2036 $38

Oxford Landing Estates   ★★★☆

PMB 31, Waikerie, SA 5330 **Region** Riverland
T (08) 8561 3200 **www.**oxfordlanding.com.au **Open** Not
Winemaker Andrew La Nauze **Est.** 1958 **Dozens** NFP **Vyds** 260ha
Oxford Landing Estate is, so the website tells us, 'A real place, a real vineyard. A place distinguished by clear blue skies, rich red soil and an abundance of golden sunshine'. In the 60+ years since the vineyard was planted, the brand has grown to reach all corners of the world. Success has been due to over-delivery against expectations at its price points and it has largely escaped the scorn of the UK wine press. In 2008 a five-year experiment began to determine whether a block of vines could survive and produce an annual crop with only 10% of the normal irrigation. The result showed that the vines could survive but with a crop production of between 40% and 65%. There is also 1ha of native vegetation for every 1ha of vineyard. Exports to the UK, the US and NZ.

Paisley Wines   ★★★★☆

158 Horns Road, Angaston, SA 5353 **Region** Barossa Valley
T 0491 377 737 **www.**paisleywines.com.au **Open** Not
Winemaker Derek Fitzgerald **Est.** 2017 **Dozens** 1800 **Vyds** 5ha
Derek Fitzgerald made wines for nearly 20 years in WA, Langhorne Creek and the Barossa Valley before gentle persuasion by wife Kirsten led to the decision to make wine on their own account. The three varieties produced are classic Barossa: grenache, mataro and shiraz. They are made in three ranges: Mixed by DJ Deadly Turntable, Paisley Fabric Range and top-of-the-ticket Paisely Celtic Range. Derek has winkled out some small parcels of grapes from long-proven vineyards up to 70 years old. Adelaide Hills Fiano completes the range.

 Silk Barossa Valley Shiraz 2018 From 30+yo vines, 85% from Ebenezer, 15% Eden Valley. Identical vinification to Boombox but this has greater intensity to its jet black fruits, and more texture. Screwcap. 14.5% alc. **Rating** 94 **To** 2033 $30 ○

Mixed by DJ Deadly Boombox Shiraz 2018 Rating 92 To 2023 $25 ○

Palmer Wines   ★★★★★

1271 Caves Road, Dunsborough, WA 6281 **Region** Margaret River
T (08) 9756 7024 **www.**palmerwines.com.au **Open** 7 days 10–5
Winemaker Mark Warren, Bruce Dukes, Clive Otto **Est.** 1977 **Dozens** 6000 **Vyds** 51.39ha
Steve and Helen Palmer have mature plantings of cabernet sauvignon, sauvignon blanc, shiraz, merlot, chardonnay and semillon, with smaller amounts of malbec and cabernet franc. Recent vintages have had major success in WA and national wine shows.

 Reserve Margaret River Chardonnay 2018 Hand-picked, wild yeast, barrel-fermented (30% new French oak), no mlf, 10 months on lees with stirring. Hits the bullseye with its cascade of stone fruit that flood the mouth, pulled back into shape by crisp, intense acidity. Screwcap. 13.5% alc. **Rating** 95 **To** 2030 $35 ○

Margaret River Cabernet Sauvignon 2018 Includes 10% malbec and 5% merlot, separately vinified, 13–16 days on skins, 18 months in French oak. Upfront blackcurrant fruit, black olive/bay leaf nuances, firm tannins. Screwcap. 15% alc. Rating 95 To 2033 $30 ✪

Margaret River Shiraz 2018 Matured for 12 months in French oak. A powerful wine with strong texture/structure. Black fruits dominate. Long palate and finish. Needs at least 5 years to show its best. Screwcap. 14.3% alc. Rating 94 To 2035 $30 ✪

🍷🍷🍷🍷🍷 Margaret River Malbec 2018 Rating 93 To 2028 $30
Krackerjack Bin 717 Margaret River Shiraz 2017 Rating 92 To 2032 $25 ✪
The Grandee Reserve Margaret River Cabernets 2018 Rating 92
To 2038 $37
Margaret River Cabernet Franc 2018 Rating 91 To 2026 $30
Margaret River Sauvignon Blanc 2019 Rating 90 To 2022 $22
Krackerjack Bin 917 Margaret River Cabernet Shiraz 2017 Rating 90
To 2032 $25

Paracombe Wines

294B Paracombe Road, Paracombe, SA 5132 **Region** Adelaide Hills
T (08) 8380 5058 **www.**paracombewines.com **Open** By appt
Winemaker Paul Drogemuller **Est.** 1983 **Dozens** 15 000 **Vyds** 22.1ha
Paul and Kathy Drogemuller established Paracombe Wines in 1983 in the wake of the devastating Ash Wednesday bushfires. The winery is located high on a plateau at Paracombe, looking out over the Mount Lofty Ranges, and the vineyard is run with minimal irrigation and hand-pruning to keep yields low. The wines are made onsite, with every part of the production process through to distribution handled from there. Exports to the UK, Canada, Denmark, Sweden, Luxembourg, Singapore and China.

🍷🍷🍷🍷🍷 The Reuben 2015 Includes 37% cabernet sauvignon, 32% merlot, 23% cabernet franc, 6% malbec and 2% shiraz; matured in French oak for 18 months. As Paracombe is apt to do, this is a fresh, youthful and delicious Bordeaux blend. The price is as seductive as the wine. Screwcap. 14.4% alc. Rating 93 To 2035 $25 ✪
Adelaide Hills Shiraz 2015 Crushed and destemmed, 10–14 days on skins in open fermenters and tank, matured in French oak (30% new) for 18 months. Medium-bodied. Complex with a flavour set unique to Paracombe. It's very youthful, again surprising given the absence of tannins. Screwcap. 14.5% alc. Rating 92 To 2030 $25 ✪
Somerville Adelaide Hills Shiraz 2013 Part crushed and destemmed, part whole-berry ferments, 21 days on skins, 36 months in new French oak. This is the whole box and dice. What you see is what you get – it's BIG. Cork. 15.5% alc. Rating 92 To 2030 $70
Adelaide Hills Cabernet Sauvignon 2015 Crushed and destemmed, open-fermented and roto-fermented, 10–14 days on skins, matured in French oak (20% new) for 18 months. Very youthful colour. Medium-bodied with a hint of leaf. Developing well. Screwcap. 14.5% alc. Rating 92 To 2030 $25 ✪
Adelaide Hills Pinot Noir Chardonnay NV A 50/50% base wine blend with up to 26 years of reserve wines available for the dosage. Pale bronze colour. Strong in flavour but less finesse. Crown seal. 12% alc. Rating 92 $35
Adelaide Hills Shiraz Viognier 2014 Has 3% viognier blended in after fermentation in open and roto fermenters, 10–14 days on skins, 18 months in French oak (30% new). The trademark Paracombe bouquet of ripe fruit announces a soft, full-flavoured wine. Screwcap. 14.8% alc. Rating 90 To 2029 $23
Adelaide Hills A Trio of Pinot Sparkling Rose NV A fresh blend of pinot gris, pinot noir and pinot blanc. Vivid light pink. Lovely fresh red fruits and a crisp, dry finish. Cork. 12.1% alc. Rating 90 $27

🍷🍷🍷🍷 Adelaide Hills Cabernet Franc 2016 Rating 89 To 2026 $30

Paradigm Hill

26 Merricks Road, Merricks, Vic 3916 **Region** Mornington Peninsula
T 0408 039 050 **www.**paradigmhill.com.au **Open** W'ends 12–5
Winemaker Dr George Mihaly **Est.** 1999 **Dozens** 1500 **Vyds** 4.2ha
Dr George Mihaly (with a background in medical research, biotechnology and pharmaceutical industries) and wife Ruth (a former chef and caterer) realised a 30-year dream of establishing their own vineyard and winery, abandoning their previous careers to do so. George had all the necessary scientific qualifications and built on those by making the 2001 Merricks Creek wines, moving to home base at Paradigm Hill in '02, all along receiving guidance and advice from Nat White of Main Ridge Estate. The vineyard, under Ruth's control with advice from Shane Strange, is planted to 2.1ha of pinot noir, 0.9ha of shiraz, 0.82ha of riesling and 0.38ha of pinot gris. Exports to the US, Germany, Denmark, Sweden, Singapore and China.

ŸŸŸŸŸ **Les Cinq Mornington Peninsula Pinot Noir 2018** Matured for 14 months.
As sophisticated and charming as previous vintages, Les Cinq oozes class. Perfumed with a mix of fresh raspberry, red cherry, dried flowers. A quiet starter – reserved even – but builds in the mouth, gaining intensity with blackforest undergrowth, dark chocolate, supple tannins. **Rating** 96 **To** 2032 $89 JP
Mornington Peninsula Pinot Gris 2019 Beautifully captures the gris reputation as a meal in a glass. Nectarines, honey, hazelnuts, sour dough messages to start. Warm, rich and adventurous on the palate, wandering into exotic spice and honeysuckle. Fills every part of the mouth, building and building with a pop of acidity and freshness to close. Shows what's possible from one of the better regions in the country for pinot gris, and that's a lot. **Rating** 95 **To** 2030 $55 JP
Adesso Mornington Peninsula Pinot Noir 2018 MV6; 18 months in second-use French oak. Sinewy, herb-infused and controlled, this is a persuasive reason why the MV6 clone shines across southern Victoria. It's generous and plush, but not overly so. Exudes pure varietal expression with a fine tannin overlay. Built to last, just give it time. **Rating** 95 **To** 2030 $79 JP
Transition Mornington Peninsula Rose 2019 This is one sophisticated, exceptional rose. Who knew rose could be so serious? A barely-there red berry vibe – cherries, raspberries, strawberries – moves straight into overdrive on the palate with crushed vine leaves, juicy raspberry and slushy pomegranate pearls. Screwcap. 11.6% alc. **Rating** 94 **To** 2026 $37 JP
L'ami Sage Mornington Peninsula Pinot Noir 2018 Clones MV6 and 115; matured for 14 months in 37% new oak. On the leafier, taut side of the pinot equation with cranberry, barely ripe red fruits, dusty beets. Not generous on the palate, at least not yet. Highly structured with drying tannins and a smack of tart acidity to close. **Rating** 94 **To** 2032 $69 JP

ŸŸŸŸŸ **Col's Block Mornington Peninsula Shiraz 2018 Rating** 92 **To** 2032 $48 JP

Paradise IV

45 Dog Rocks Road, Batesford, Vic 3213 (postal) **Region** Geelong
T (03) 5276 1536 **www.**paradiseivwines.com.au **Open** Not
Winemaker Douglas Neal **Est.** 1988 **Dozens** 800 **Vyds** 3.1ha
The former Moorabool Estate was renamed Paradise IV for the very good reason that it is the site of the original Paradise IV Vineyard, planted in 1848 by Swiss vigneron Jean-Henri Dardel. It is owned by Ruth and Graham Bonney. The winery has an underground barrel room and the winemaking turns around wild-yeast fermentation, natural mlf, gravity movement of the wine and so forth. Exports to China.

ŸŸŸŸŸ **J.H. Dardel 2018** Most of the harvest was whole-berry fermented, a lesser amount with whole-bunch carbonic maceration in a sealed vat, all parcels wild-fermented. The result is a highly spiced medium-bodied wine with a lattice work of tannins after 18 months' maturation in French oak (20% new). Screwcap. 13.8% alc. **Rating** 95 **To** 2038 $77

J.H. Dardel 2017 Bright, deep crimson-purple. A lovely shiraz reflecting the cool, slow ripening vintage. The medium-bodied, spicy palate is replete with red fruits and fine tannins. Screwcap. 13.8% alc. **Rating** 95 **To** 2032 $77

Geelong Chardonnay 2018 Doug Neal dealt with the warm weather of the vintage by cutting back on new oak to 20% and holding mlf down to 20%. It has resulted in a crisp style that will flourish with a few more years in bottle, however well it is drinking at the moment. Screwcap. 13% alc. **Rating** 94 **To** 2028 $62

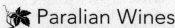 **Chaumont 2018 Rating** 93 **To** 2030 $62
Blanche 2018 Rating 92 **To** 2028 $37

Paralian Wines ★★★★★

21 Eden Terrace, Port Willunga, SA 5171 **Region** McLaren Vale/Adelaide Hills
T 0413 308 730 **www**.paralian.com.au **Open** By appt
Winemaker Skye Salter, Charlie Seppelt **Est.** 2018 **Dozens** 450

Charlie Seppelt and Skye Salter have covered many miles and worked in many places since they met in 2008 working the vintage at Hardys Tintara in McLaren Vale. By the time they took the plunge and established Paralian Wines in '18 they had accumulated 46 vintages between them, working for others. The name is a noun for someone who lives by the sea. Charlie's first exposure to McLaren Vale was as a vintage casual at d'Arenberg and it was vinous love at first sight. He and Skye headed off overseas, a high point undertaking vintage in Burgundy. He headed back to Australia, she went on to the Languedoc, seemingly ideal, but found it as depressing as Burgundy had been inspirational. They agreed McLaren Vale, and in particular Blewitt Springs, was the place they wanted to make grenache and shiraz with high fragrance and brightness, grenache joining pinot noir as a high class wine to be enjoyed young or much later. No fining or additions are used other than SO$_2$ and little requirement for new oak. Watch this space.

Springs Hill Vineyard McLaren Vale Shiraz 2019 Given 25% whole bunch, foot-trodden in a 131yo open concrete vat, cold soak, 23 days on skins, matured for 9 months in hogsheads (10% new), no additions, not fined or filtered. An exceptional wine with the vibrancy of dark berry fruits, vigorous spices and fine but persistent tannins all suggesting a cool-climate origin (but not so). Screwcap. 14% alc. **Rating** 97 **To** 2039 $42 ✪

Springs Hill Vineyard McLaren Vale Shiraz 2018 12% whole bunches are crushed by feet, the remainder of the grapes crushed and destemmed on top, the wine spending 25 days on skins including cold soak and post fermentation. It is medium to full-bodied but steps lightly, easily absorbing the 9% new French oak and tannins that run through the perfectly balanced and very long palate. Fresh fruit purity is common to all Paralian wines. Screwcap. 14% alc. **Rating** 96 **To** 2038 $42 ✪

Marmont Vineyard McLaren Vale Grenache 2018 Wild-fermented with 17% whole bunches in wax-lined concrete vats, 24 days on skins, 9 months' maturation in used oak. Bright, clear colour. It has a medium-bodied silky array of red and purple fruits with a fine-spun tannin backdrop to provide longevity. Delicious stuff. Screwcap. 14% alc. **Rating** 96 **To** 2028 $42 ✪

Grenache Shiraz 2017 A 52/48% blend. The colour is deeper than the Grenache, the bouquet and palate both making an immediate impact with juicy layers of plum and blackberry fruit and a soft cushion of tannins to close. Balance and structure are the DNA of the best McLaren Vale red wine. Screwcap. 14% alc. **Rating** 96 **To** 2033 $36 ✪

Bowyer Ridge Vineyard Adelaide Hills Chardonnay 2019 Clones 76 and 96; free-run juice wild-fermented in a new puncheon and used barriques. It offers remarkable texture, complexity also part of the deal. Fresh Granny Smith apple, grapefruit and toasted almond/cashew. A farewell of grapefruit to freshen the mouth. Screwcap. 13.5% alc. **Rating** 95 **To** 2030 $49

Marmont Vineyard McLaren Vale Grenache 2019 Given 20% whole bunch ex small berries and thick skins, matured for 9 months in old puncheons.

Lipsmacking pomegranate/acidity mark the sidelines for the red fruits that scramble for attention on the long palate. Definitely a thinking person's grenache. Screwcap. 14% alc. **Rating** 95 **To** 2029 $42

Paringa Estate   ★★★★★

44 Paringa Road, Red Hill South, Vic 3937 **Region** Mornington Peninsula
T (03) 5989 2669 **www**.paringaestate.com.au **Open** 7 days 11–5
Winemaker Lindsay McCall, Jamie McCall **Est.** 1985 **Dozens** 15 000 **Vyds** 30.5ha
Schoolteacher-turned-winemaker Lindsay McCall became known for an absolutely exceptional gift for winemaking across a range of styles but with immensely complex pinot noir and shiraz leading the way. The wines have an unmatched level of success in the wine shows and competitions that Paringa Estate is able to enter; the limitation being the relatively small production of the top wines in the portfolio. His skills are no less evident in contract winemaking for others. But time has passed and son Jamie joined the winemaking team in 2012, after completing winemaking and viticulture at the University of Adelaide, Waite Campus. He was put in charge of winemaking at Paringa Estate in '17 following five home vintages and one in Oregon, focusing on pinot noir. Exports to the UK, Denmark, Ukraine, Singapore, Japan, Hong Kong and China.

🍷🍷🍷🍷🍷 **The Paringa Single Vineyard Pinot Noir 2018** Structured, powerful and long. All you really need to know is that this bristles with quality. It's tangy and it's not sweet but it's powered by concentrated strawberry notes. It also floats herb notes throughout and races with dry roasted spice characters. Orange oil, or something like it, adds a lifted, flowery note. It's pure quality and class. Screwcap. 13.5% alc. **Rating** 97 **To** 2029 CM

🍷🍷🍷🍷🍷 **The Paringa Single Vineyard Chardonnay 2018** A powerful wine but, most importantly, it's also a balanced one. It doesn't lean heavily on any one area despite the amount of juicy stone fruit flavour and attachment of smoky, cedary oak. There are whispers of flint, fennel and fig but for the most part it operates on sure, firm rails from start to finish. Its best days are a couple of years away. Screwcap. 13.5% alc. **Rating** 95 **To** 2027 $80 CM

The Paringa Single Vineyard Shiraz 2018 Leans towards black pepper rather than white. It has elements of reduction but its tones remain woody, walnutty and smoky. Its core is run with black cherry, its acidity is nestled, its tannin firm without causing any bumps. Balance is its middle name, persistence its surname. Cellar this with confidence. Screwcap. 14% alc. **Rating** 95 **To** 2035 $80 CM

Robinson Vineyard Pinot Noir 2018 A succulent, sweet, smoky display of boysenberry, garden herbs, blood orange and woodsy spice. Medium weight in a varietal context; subtle of tannin; a twigginess to the aftertaste. It's neither a profound nor a forced wine but we get an array, a display, a touch of intrigue. It satisfies. Screwcap. 13.5% alc. **Rating** 94 **To** 2026 CM

Estate Pinot Noir 2018 I love the concentration of this; the focus. It has purity in its sights and it never wavers. It has cedary oak but the fresh intensity of the fruit and the near-casual inflections of spice keep everything directed towards the fan of the finish. Screwcap. 13.5% alc. **Rating** 94 **To** 2027 $65 CM

Estate Shiraz 2018 There's a splash of white pepper but essentially it's a fruit-driven, attractively textured, mid-weight red with cherry-plum flavours in the driving seat. Peppercorn notes and spice-shot tannin finish things off nicely. Not a foot wrong. Screwcap. 14% alc. **Rating** 94 **To** 2028 CM

🍷🍷🍷🍷🍷 **Peninsula Chardonnay 2019** Rating 93 To 2026 $29 CM
Estate Chardonnay 2018 Rating 93 To 2026 $45 CM
Estate Pinot Gris 2019 Rating 93 To 2021 $25 CM ✪
Peninsula Pinot Noir 2019 Rating 93 To 2025 $29 CM
Peninsula Shiraz 2018 Rating 93 To 2027 CM
Estate Riesling 2019 Rating 92 To 2026 CM

Parish Lane Wines

4 Moirs Road, Upper Kalgan, WA 6328 **Region** Great Southern
T (08) 9846 1220 **www**.parishlanewines.com.au **Open** By appt
Winemaker Mike Garland, Andrew Milbourne **Est.** 1997 **Dozens** 550 **Vyds** 2ha
Richard and Julie Parish moved from Perth to Albany in 1995 seeking a lifestyle change
and planning to grow lavender. This they did for a couple of years until friends, who had a
vineyard, suggested the small property would be ideal for growing grapes. They planted the
first vines in '97, entering a steep learning curve. The vineyard has 1ha of merlot and 0.5ha
each of chardonnay and pinot noir (the last as the result of a grafting program); cabernet
sauvignon is purchased from a local grower.

Small Batch Great Southern Cabernet Merlot 2012 A lovely nose of
currant, anise, sage and strewn herb serves up reason to be confident. Medium to
full-bodied. Resolved, nicely tuned tannins inferring that this will be best soonest.
That said, bags of life left. A lovely drink at its apogee of maturity. Screwcap.
Rating 92 **To** 2021 $25 NG ❂

Small Batch Great Southern Merlot 2011 Rating 89 **To** 2021 $25 NG

Parker Coonawarra Estate

15688 Riddoch Highway, Penola, SA 5263 **Region** Coonawarra
T (08) 8737 3525 **www**.parkercoonawarraestate.com.au **Open** 7 days 10–4
Winemaker James Lienert, Andrew Hardy, Keeda Zilm **Est.** 1985 **Dozens** 30 000
Vyds 20ha
Parker Coonawarra Estate is at the southern end of Coonawarra, on rich terra rossa soil
over limestone. Cabernet sauvignon is the dominant variety (17.45ha), with minor plantings
of merlot and petit verdot. It is now part of WD Wines, which also owns Hesketh Wine
Company, St John's Road, Vickery Wines and Ox Hardy. Production has risen substantially
since the change of ownership. Exports to all major markets.

First Growth 2016 A cabernet with a lengthy history of excellence. It is from
a single vineyard planted in '85. The vines are fully mature and the blackcurrant
fruit revels in the generous proportion of new French oak allocated to it every
year. Screwcap. 14.5% alc. **Rating** 96 **To** 2046 $110
S.B.W. Hungry Lou Shiraz Tokay 2018 Includes 91% shiraz (65% from the
Schutz Vineyard in the Barossa Valley, 26% from Kidman in Coonawarra) and
9% old bushvine muscadelle (also from Schutz). It's a full-bodied number with
some very good fruit. Screwcap. 14% alc. **Rating** 95 **To** 2040 $50

Terra Rossa Cabernet Sauvignon 2018 Rating 93 **To** 2038 $34
S.B.W. Napoleon Cabernet Montepulciano 2018 Rating 93 **To** 2029 $30
Terra Rossa Shiraz 2018 Rating 92 **To** 2030 $34
Shiraz 2018 Rating 90 **To** 2030 $24

Passel Estate

655 Ellen Brook Road, Cowaramup, WA 6284 **Region** Margaret River
T (08) 9717 6241 **www**.passelestate.com **Open** 7 days 10.30–5
Winemaker Bruce Dukes **Est.** 1994 **Dozens** 1500 **Vyds** 6.7ha
Wendy and Barry Stimpson were born in England and South Africa respectively and, during
numerous visits to Margaret River over the years, fell in love with the region's environment.
They made Margaret River home in 2005 and in '11 purchased the vineyard, which is
planted to shiraz, cabernet sauvignon and chardonnay. Viticulturist Andy Ferreira manages the
vineyard with sustainable practices, keeping yields restricted to 6.5–7t/ha. The very talented
and highly experienced contract winemaker Bruce Dukes is responsible for the wines. Exports
to Singapore and Hong Kong.

Lot 71 Reserve Margaret River Syrah 2016 30% whole bunches were tipped
into an empty open fermenter, 70% destemmed berries poured on top, minimal

plunging during the carbonic maceration phase followed by pigeage, matured for 10 months in French puncheons with batonnage. With a degree of hesitation, I have assumed the rich fruit will lighten the oak burden, there is so much fruit here. Screwcap. 14% alc. **Rating** 95 **To** 2035 $65

Margaret River Chardonnay 2017 Chilled, pressed to French barriques (35% new), 33% mlf, matured on lees for 10 months. White peach and melon fruit are cradled by well balanced and integrated oak and creamy cashew notes ex mlf. Screwcap. 13% alc. **Rating** 94 **To** 2027 $38

🍷🍷🍷🍷♀ **Margaret River Cabernet Sauvignon 2017** Rating 93 To 2025 NG
Margaret River Sauvignon Blanc 2018 Rating 92 To 2020 $30
Margaret River Shiraz 2017 Rating 91 To 2023 NG

Passing Clouds   ★★★★★

30 Roddas Lane, Musk, Vic 3461 **Region** Macedon Ranges
T (03) 5348 5550 **www.passingclouds.com.au** **Open** 7 days 10–5
Winemaker Cameron Leith **Est.** 1974 **Dozens** 5500 **Vyds** 5ha
Graeme Leith and son Cameron undertook a monumental change when they moved the entire operation that started way back in 1974 in Bendigo to its new location at Musk, near Daylesford. The vines at Bendigo had been disabled by ongoing drought and all manner of pestilence, and it was no longer feasible to continue the business there. However, they still have a foot in Bendigo courtesy of their friends, the Adams at Rheola. Graeme has now left the winemaking in the hands of Cameron, instead using his formidable skills as a writer. Cameron and wife Marion have made a coup with the establishment of a new train stop (and dedicated platform) at the Passing Clouds cellar door and winery at Musk. The venture is the result of a collaboration between Passing Clouds, Spa Country Railway and the Victorian Regional Development Wine Growth Fund. The development has led to the incorporation of a restaurant (open Mon–Fri) and structured tastings built around the food. Exports to all major markets.

🍷🍷🍷🍷🍷 **Estate Macedon Ranges Chardonnay 2018** From 21yo vines, 14% skin contact, matured for 10 months (22% new oak). Very attractive chardonnay, thanks to the vineyard and some very slick winemaking. Screwcap. 13.6% alc. **Rating** 95 **To** 2027 $47

The Angel 2018 There's a large amount of blackcurrant populating this cabernet sauvignon. It's rich, layered and has a tempering finish of black olive. Issues with its screwcap may possibly have impacted the palate, but I don't think so. 13.4% alc. **Rating** 94 **To** 2033 $53

🍷🍷🍷🍷♀ **Graeme's Shiraz Cabernet 2018** Rating 92 To 2025 $34
Estate Macedon Ranges Pinot Noir 2019 Rating 91 To 2023 $26
Estate Macedon Ranges Pinot Noir 2018 Rating 91 To 2026 $47
Bendigo Shiraz 2018 Rating 91 To 2035 $34
Kilmore Pinot Noir 2019 Rating 90 To 2029 $29

Patina   ★★★★★

109 Summerhill Lane, Orange, NSW 2800 **Region** Orange
T (02) 6362 8336 **www.patinawines.com.au** **Open** W'ends 11–5
Winemaker Gerald Naef **Est.** 1999 **Dozens** 2500 **Vyds** 3ha
Gerald Naef's home in Woodbridge in California was surrounded by the vast vineyard and winery operations of Gallo and Robert Mondavi. It would be hard to imagine a more different environment than that provided by Orange. Gerald and wife Angie left California in 1981, initially establishing an irrigation farm in northwest NSW; 20 years later they moved to Orange and by 2006 Gerald was a final-year student of wine science at CSU. He set up a micro-winery at the Orange Cool Stores, his first wine the trophy-winning '03 Chardonnay.

🍷🍷🍷🍷🍷 **Museum Release Reserve Orange Chardonnay 2004** Fermented and matured on lees for 12 months in new and used French oak. There is so much texture to the palate it might be seen as sweet, but it's not. What it does have is a classic mix of grapefruit, white peach and apple. Screwcap. 12.3% alc. **Rating** 95 **To** 2025 $50

Scandalous Riesling 2017 This is a really attractive wine. Scents of lime and apple blossom lead to a perfectly balanced, intensely flavoured palate; the 26g/l of residual sugar leading to thoughts of a Mosel Valley kabinett. Screwcap. 10.3% alc. **Rating** 95 $25 ✪

Jezza 2016 Merlot, cabernet franc and cabernet sauvignon. It's a solid, well structured red with beef stock, blackcurrant, briary herb and fresh spearmint characters laid on. It's a polished wine but it feels sturdy. Choc-orange characters play a modest but positive role. If well stored, it will carry the next 10 years with ease. Screwcap. 14% alc. **Rating** 94 **To** 2031 $65 CM

Museum Release Orange Cabernet Merlot 2006 Includes 44% cabernet sauvignon, 40% merlot, 12% shiraz, 4% cabernet franc; separately fermented, matured in French and American barrels. It's at the peak of its life but it won't fade away any time soon. Screwcap. 13.5% alc. **Rating** 94 **To** 2026 $55

Museum Release Orange Cabernet Sauvignon 2006 Fully mature. Choc-mint flavours start the ball rolling for what is an attractive wine. It is ready now, with little to gain from cellaring past '26 at the latest. Cork. 13.2% alc. **Rating** 94 **To** 2026 $55

♟♟♟♟♟ **Museum Release Orange Merlot 2009 Rating** 92 **To** 2029 $30
Reserve Orange Chardonnay 2016 Rating 91 **To** 2023 $45
Orange Pinot Noir 2017 Rating 90 **To** 2024 $45

Patrick of Coonawarra   ★★★★★

Cnr Ravenswood Lane/Riddoch Highway, Coonawarra, SA 5263 **Region** Coonawarra
T (08) 8737 3687 **www.**patrickofcoonawarra.com.au **Open** 7 days 10–5
Winemaker Luke Tocaciu **Est.** 2004 **Dozens** 5000 **Vyds** 93.5ha
Patrick Tocaciu (who died in 2013) was a district veteran, with prior careers at Heathfield Ridge Winery and Hollick Wines. Wrattonbully plantings (almost 55ha) cover all the major varieties, while in Coonawarra the low-yielding Home Block (cabernet sauvignon) is supplemented by a second vineyard of 17.5ha of cabernet and smaller amounts of reisling and sauvignon blanc. Patrick of Coonawarra also carries out contract winemaking for others. Son Luke, with a degree in oenology from the University of Adelaide and vintage experience in Australia and the US, has taken over in the winery.

♟♟♟♟♟ **Grande Reserve Cabernet Sauvignon 2012** A barrel selection from the best vintages from Home Block Vineyard; 30 months in French oak, then 4 years cellaring at the winery. It is opulent yet well balanced. Repeated tastings reveal a wine of great class with a long future. Cork. 14% alc. **Rating** 97 **To** 2042 $125 ✪

♟♟♟♟♟ **Estate Grown Riesling 2019** From the estate's 2 vineyards in Coonawarra and Wrattonbully that combine synergistically to dance around maypoles of grainy acidity and slinky lime juice, 6g/l of residual sugar judged to perfection. Screwcap. 11.5% alc. **Rating** 95 **To** 2027 $25 ✪

Joanna Wrattonbully Shiraz 2014 From the premium south-facing estate block, 20 days on skins, matured in French and American oak for 28 months. It has a pleasantly savoury make-up throughout the palate and aftertaste, and is developing slowly yet with certainty. Screwcap. 14% alc. **Rating** 94 **To** 2039 $45

Home Block Cabernet Sauvignon 2014 Fermented in a 10t open vat with extended maceration for up to 30 days, matured for 2 years in French and American oak, predominantly 50% new French medium toast barriques. That the fruit stands up to this is remarkable, and the cost in time and oak means the wine is underpriced. Screwcap. 13.8% alc. **Rating** 94 **To** 2034 $45

♟♟♟♟♟ **P Series by Patrick Limestone Coast Rose 2019 Rating** 90 **To** 2021 $19 ✪
Estate Grown Wrattonbully Shiraz 2014 Rating 90 **To** 2029 $29

Patrick Sullivan Wines

146 Peterson Road, Ellinbank, Vic 3821 **Region** Gippsland
T 0439 729 780 **www.**patricksullivan.com.au **Open** Not
Winemaker Patrick Sullivan **Est.** 2011 **Dozens** 2000 **Vyds** 10ha

Patrick Sullivan is the 'been everywhere, done everything' man, planting vines at age 15 and
heading to London three years later. Viticulture studies followed, coupled with working at
Vina di Anna, a winery in Sicily, thereafter appointed international wine buyer for Vina
di Anna's owner, a London-based wine distribution business. Back in Australia, he became
increasingly interested in Gippsland and the Baw Baw district in particular; winemaker
Bill Downie was his guide both there and thereafter in the Yarra Valley. His beliefs and
practices took shape over this time, notably sustainability/biodynamics and ultra-close spacing
of 7000 vines/ha. In 2014 he and wife Megan purchased the 69ha property now called
Tumblestone Farm, sitting on red volcanic soil over sandstone at the base of the Strzelecki
Ranges. The couple live on the farm with their two young children and have planted pinot
noir and chardonnay that are still coming into full bearing. In the meantime he works with
chardonnay vineyards in the Baw Baw Shire: Millstream, Bullswamp and Ada River. The '19
vintage wines are released in September '20. Exports to the UK, the US, Canada, Sweden,
Norway, South Korea, Japan and China.

Ada River Chardonnay 2018 Uses 50% P58 clone, 50% I10V1; hand-picked,
whole-bunch pressed, wild-fermented in French oak (30% new), matured for
12 months. White peach/nectarine, soft acidity. Cork. 12.8% alc. **Rating** 91
To 2020 $65

Millstream Chardonnay 2018 Has developed more quickly than Ada River
(probably due to the cork), but vinified identically. If this development is typical,
drink (and enjoy) immediately, for it's an attractive wine. Cork. 12.8% alc.
Rating 90 To 2020 $65

Patritti Wines

13–23 Clacton Road, Dover Gardens, SA 5048 **Region** Adelaide zone
T (08) 8296 8261 **www.**patritti.com.au **Open** Mon–Sat 9–5, Dec 7 days
Winemaker James Mungall, Ben Heide **Est.** 1926 **Dozens** 190 000 **Vyds** 16ha

A family-owned business with impressive vineyard holdings of 10ha of shiraz in Blewitt
Springs and 6ha of grenache at Aldinga North. The surging production points to success in
export and also to the utilisation of contract-grown as well as estate-grown grapes. Patritti is
currently releasing wines of very high quality at enticing prices and a range of lesser quality
wines at unfathomably low prices. The JPB Single Vineyard celebrates Giovanni Patritti, who
arrived in Australia in 1925; he sold his wines under the 'John Patritti Brighton' label. Exports
to the UK, Sweden, Germany, Poland, India, Vietnam and China.

McLaren Vale Rare Old Fortified Chardonnay NV The ambient
fermentation was muted at the very beginning with the addition of the spirit.
Following 3 years in wooden vats, this fortified wine was then aged further in old
and very old puncheons for 15 years. Stunning! The spirit is beautifully integrated,
composing an elixir of compelling mahogany, creme caramel, cheesecloth, varnish,
rosewater, grape spice, date and a carnival of Moroccan souk scents. The finish
is infinitesimal. Among the finest fortifieds of my tasting experience this year.
Rating 98 NG

Adelaide Hills Sauvignon Blanc 2019 Rating 93 To 2022 $24 ❂
Adelaide Hills Pinot Grigio 2019 Rating 93 To 2023 $24 ❂
JPB Single Vineyard Shiraz 2018 Rating 92 To 2030 $65 NG
Lot Three Single Vineyard McLaren Vale Shiraz 2018 Rating 91 To 2028
$40 NG
Merchant McLaren Vale Cabernet Sauvignon 2018 Rating 91 To 2028
$25 NG
Merchant McLaren Vale Shiraz 2018 Rating 90 To 2026 $25 NG

Merchant McLaren Vale Grenache Shiraz Mourvedre 2018 Rating 90
To 2026 $25 NG
Barossa Valley Saperavi 2017 Rating 90 To 2027 $30

Paul Conti Wines

529 Wanneroo Road, Woodvale, WA 6026 **Region** Greater Perth zone
T (08) 9409 9160 **www**.paulcontiwines.com.au **Open** Tues–Sun 11–4
Winemaker Paul Conti, Jason Conti **Est.** 1948 **Dozens** 4000 **Vyds** 11ha
Third-generation winemaker Jason Conti has assumed control of winemaking, although
father Paul (who succeeded his own father in 1968) remains involved in the business. Over
the years Paul challenged and redefined industry perceptions and standards. The challenge for
Jason is to achieve the same degree of success in a relentlessly and increasingly competitive
market environment, and he is doing just that. Plantings at the Carabooda Vineyard have
been expanded with tempranillo, petit verdot and viognier, and pinot noir and chardonnay
are purchased from Pemberton. In a further extension, a property at Cowaramup in Margaret
River with sauvignon blanc, shiraz, cabernet sauvignon, semillon, muscat and malbec has been
acquired. The original 2ha of shiraz at the Mariginiup Vineyard remains the cornerstone.
Exports to Japan.

🍷🍷🍷🍷 Margaret River Cabernet Sauvignon 2018 A smidgeon of malbec in
the blend promotes some floral lift and a glossy sheen of blue fruits nestled
amid cabernet's currant, sage and green olive. This is straight shooting regional
cabernet, highly reflective of place and with that, rewarding. Screwcap. **Rating** 91
To 2024 NG

🍷🍷🍷🍷 Mariginiup Shiraz 2018 Rating 89 To 2024 $28 NG

Paul Osicka

Majors Creek Vineyard at Graytown, Vic 3608 **Region** Heathcote
T (03) 5794 9235 **www**.paulosickawines.com.au **Open** By appt
Winemaker Simon Osicka **Est.** 1955 **Dozens** NFP **Vyds** 13ha
The Osicka family arrived from Czechoslovakia in the early 1950s. Vignerons in their own
country, their vineyard in Australia was the first new venture in central and southern Victoria
for over half a century. With the return of Simon Osicka to the family business, there have
been substantial changes. Simon held senior winemaking positions at Houghton, Leasingham,
and as group red winemaker for Constellation Wines Australia, interleaved with vintages in
Italy, Canada, Germany and France, working at the prestigious Domaine Jean-Louis Chave
for the '10 vintage. The fermentation of the red wines has been changed from static to open
fermenters and French oak has replaced American. Extensive retrellising of the 65-year-old
estate plantings is now complete. Installation of a conveyor belt enables 100% berry sorting
and eliminates pumping; installation of new vats is another improvement. Paul Osicka, Simon's
father, passed away in 2019 after 50 vintages and over 60 years of involvement in the vineyards.
Exports to Denmark.

🍷🍷🍷🍷🍷 Moormbool Heathcote Shiraz 2018 Made only if the vintage reveals
something uniquely interesting. Sourced from a particular spot within the
vineyard – '50s plantings on deeper loam soils. It's a commanding wine. Perfectly
structured and poised. The '18 wines are special, they are the last vintage that Paul
Osicka worked; he died in June '19. This is a fitting tribute. Screwcap. 14.5% alc.
Rating 96 To 2033 $50 JF ❂
Heathcote Majors Creek Vineyard Shiraz 2018 I've always had a soft spot
for Paul Osicka's wines. A producer whose attention to detail flows from the
vineyard to the winery, not so much marketing. Respect. This has all the regional
hallmarks – the blue fruits, bay leaf and warm earth – but also its own unique
DNA. A depth of flavour without being too much. It's glossy with smooth, supple
tannins and finishes long. Screwcap. 14.5% alc. Rating 95 To 2030 $35 JF ❂
Majors Creek Vineyard Heathcote Cabernet Sauvignon 2018 Not sure
how this gets to be so polished and refined. It's more in the savoury spectrum

with decisive tannins moving across the full-bodied palate, although the ride is smooth. It does have a touch of cassis, licorice and bitumen. Screwcap. 14.5% alc. Rating 95 To 2030 $35 JF ❂

🍷🍷🍷🍷🍷 Heathcote Riesling 2019 Rating 93 To 2027 $25 JF ❂

Paulett Wines ★★★★★

752 Jolly Way, Polish Hill River, SA 5453 **Region** Clare Valley
T (08) 8843 4328 **www.**paulettwines.com.au **Open** 7 days 10–5
Winemaker Neil Paulett, Jarrad Steele **Est.** 1983 **Dozens** 35 000 **Vyds** 79.5ha
The Paulett story is a saga of Australian perseverance, commencing with the 1982 purchase of a property with 1ha of vines and a house, promptly destroyed by the terrible Ash Wednesday bushfires the following year. Son Matthew joined Neil and Alison Paulett as a partner in the business some years ago; he is responsible for viticulture on the property holding, much expanded following the purchase of a large vineyard at Watervale. The winery and cellar door have wonderful views over the Polish Hill River region, the memories of the bushfires long gone. Exports to the UK, Denmark, Germany, Singapore, Malaysia, China and NZ.

🍷🍷🍷🍷🍷 Polish Hill River Riesling 2019 This is a delicious riesling, a true rendition of the variety, courtesy of a blend of Rose's lime juice, Meyer lemon, passionfruit and Granny Smith apple held in a fine web of acidity. Time will bring change, but it's a purely personal decision to drink it now or later. Best have a bob each way. Screwcap. 12% alc. **Rating** 95 To 2035 $30 ❂
Polish Hill River Aged Release Riesling 2015 Attesting to the ageing capacity of Clare riesling, particularly that from the limestone substrata of Polish Hill, this is very fine. Lemon buttered toastiness. Citrus marmalade. Yet dry, grapefruit pulpy and dense; the aromas reverberating across the long, balletic palate. The hard acidity, the caveat. Screwcap. **Rating** 95 To 2027 NG
Watervale Semillon 2019 This is a delicious mid-weighted and vibrant wine. Gently soapy of texture with riffs of lemon oil, quince and lemongrass splayed across a lattice of thirst-slaking acidity, saline and slaty. Like biting into a melody of ripe citrus. Long and crunchy. Screwcap. **Rating** 94 To 2027 NG
Clare Valley Shiraz 2017 Fresh, vibrant shiraz, the vintage written all over it. Medium-bodied at best, but has all the length one could wish for. Why the cheap twin top cork? 13.5% alc. **Rating** 94 To 2029 $40
Polish Hill River Late Harvest Riesling 2018 This wine doesn't really need to be labelled 'late harvest'. While it was clearly picked later than usual, inflecting the aroma with high tones of tangerine, cumquat, lime cordial and dried mango, the juicy acid line effectively negates any palpable sweetness. The end effect, particularly if paired with gentle spice, is dry. The miracle of riesling! Screwcap. Rating 94 To 2026 $24 NG ❂

🍷🍷🍷🍷🍷 Clare Valley Riesling 2018 Rating 93 To 2030 $35
Polish Hill River Chardonnay 2018 Rating 91 To 2023 $25 NG
Polish Hill River Shiraz 2017 Rating 91 To 2025 $30 NG
Brielle Watervale Grenache 2019 Rating 91 To 2025 $42 NG
Polish Hill River Cabernet Merlot 2017 Rating 91 To 2025 NG
Polish Hill River Cabernet Merlot 2016 Rating 91 To 2034 $30 JP
Andreas Polish Hill River Shiraz 2017 Rating 90 To 2028 NG
Trillians Polish Hill River Brut NV Rating 90 $30 NG
Trillians Sparkling Red NV Rating 90 $30 NG

Paulmara Estates ★★★★★

144 Seppeltsfield Road, Nuriootpa, SA 5355 **Region** Barossa Valley
T 0417 895 138 **www.**paulmara.com.au **Open** By appt
Winemaker Paul Georgiadis **Est.** 1999 **Dozens** 350 **Vyds** 12.8ha
Born to an immigrant Greek family, Paul Georgiadis grew up in Waikerie, where his family had vineyards and orchards. His parents worked sufficiently hard to send him first to St Peters

College in Adelaide and then to the University of Adelaide to do a marketing degree. He became the whirlwind grower-relations manager for Southcorp and one of the best known faces in the Barossa Valley. Paul and wife Mara established a vineyard in 1995, planted to semillon, shiraz, sangiovese, merlot and cabernet sauvignon. Part of the production is sold and the best shiraz makes the Syna Shiraz ('syna' being Greek for together).

ŸŸŸŸŸ Limited Release Syna Barossa Valley Shiraz 2018 Hand-picked, destemmed, matured for 20 months in French oak (70% new), held in bottle for a further 6 months before release. The wine is an exercise in harmony, the black cherry fruit/black cherry compote exercising relaxed control over the oak and tannins. Cork. 14% alc. Rating 96 To 2048 $60 ✪
APOTIGI Barossa Valley Cabernet Sauvignon 2018 Estate-grown 30+yo vines, destemmed to static fermenters, matured for 20 months in French hogsheads (70% new). Full-bodied and intense, yet supple and elegant. The tannins are polished and the oak swims in the wake of blackberry, dark cherry and dark plum. The magic is the way the wine manages to convey its message with such ease. Cork. 14% alc. Rating 96 To 2043 $100

ŸŸŸŸŸ The Marriage Barrel Selection Barossa Valley Cabernet Shiraz 2018 Rating 93 To 2033 $60
Brasco's Montepulciano Graciano 2018 Rating 90 To 2022 $21 ✪

Paxton '
★★★★★

68 Wheaton Road, McLaren Vale, SA 5171 **Region** McLaren Vale
T (08) 8323 9131 **www**.paxtonwines.com **Open** 7 days 10–5
Winemaker Dwayne Cunningham, Kate Goodman (Consultant) **Est.** 1979
Dozens 25 000 **Vyds** 82.5ha
David Paxton is of one Australia's most successful and respected viticulturists, with a career spanning over 40 years. He started his successful premium grower business in 1979 and has been involved with planting and managing some of the most prestigious vineyards in McLaren Vale, Barossa Valley, Yarra Valley, Margaret River and Adelaide Hills for top global wineries. There are six vineyards in the family holdings in McLaren Vale: Thomas Block (25ha), Jones Block (22ha), Quandong Farm (18ha), Landcross Farm (2ha), Maslin (3ha) and 19th (12.5ha). All are certified organic and biodynamic, making Paxton one of the largest biodynamic producers in Australia. The vineyards have some of the region's oldest vines, including the 125-year-old EJ shiraz. His principal focus is on his own operations in McLaren Vale with Paxton Wines, established in '98 as a premium shiraz, grenache and cabernet producer. The cellar door sits on Landcross Farm, a historic 1860s sheep farm in the original village consisting of limestone houses and shearing shed. Exports to the UK, the US, Canada, Denmark, France, Germany, Sweden, the Netherlands, Russia, Finland, Japan, Malaysia, Singapore, Hong Kong, Taiwan and China.

ŸŸŸŸŸ Thomas Block McLaren Vale Grenache 2018 An elegant grenache that speaks loudly about place and variety. The balance, texture, structure and flavour of red fruits run the length of the palate. It was the first vineyard David Paxton acquired (in '79), in a unique side valley with very cool mornings and with some vines dating back to 1887. Screwcap. 14% alc. Rating 96 To 2033 $35 ✪

ŸŸŸŸŸ MV McLaren Vale Shiraz 2018 Rating 93 To 2026 $22 JF ✪
AAA McLaren Vale Shiraz Grenache 2018 Rating 92 To 2024 $22 JF ✪
McLaren Vale Cabernet Sauvignon 2018 Rating 92 To 2028 $25 ✪
NOW McLaren Vale Shiraz 2019 Rating 91 To 2021 $25 JF
McLaren Vale Grenache 2019 Rating 91 To 2025 $35 JF
Quandong Farm Single Vineyard McLaren Vale Shiraz 2018 Rating 90 To 2029 $30 JF
Jones Block Single Vineyard McLaren Vale Shiraz 2017 Rating 90 To 2030 $45 JF

Payne's Rise

10 Paynes Road, Seville, Vic 3139 **Region** Yarra Valley
T (03) 5964 2504 www.paynesrise.com.au **Open** Thurs–Sun 11–5
Winemaker Franco D'Anna (Contract) **Est.** 1998 **Dozens** 2000 **Vyds** 5ha
Tim and Narelle Cullen have progressively established 5ha of cabernet sauvignon, shiraz, pinot noir, chardonnay and sauvignon blanc since 1998. They carry out all the vineyard work. Tim is also a viticulturist for a local agribusiness. Narelle is responsible for sales and marketing. The contract-made wines have won both gold medals and trophies at the Yarra Valley Wine Show since '10, echoed by success at the Victorian Wine Show. Exports to China.

ΨΨΨΨΨ **Yarra Valley Chardonnay 2019** From the much in-demand Upper Yarra, a chardonnay with class and richness in fruit: ripe nectarine, white peach, grilled pineapple, fig. Expansive on the palate, building flavour and mouthfeel through the means of smart oak and brought into line with a nice ping of acidity. Screwcap. 13% alc. **Rating** 95 **To** 2030 $30 JP **✿**
Mr Jed Yarra Valley Pinot Noir 2018 Hand-picked, destemmed, straight to fermenter, cold soak for 3 days, aged in new (20%), 1yo (20%) and 2–3yo oak for 10 months, no fining or filtration. The cloudy, cherry-red appearance is nothing to be concerned about, indeed it's an indication that all the pinot goodies have not been fined or filtered away. A vibrant, youthful look and scent of fresh cherries, raspberries, cranberries with floral musk, dried flowers. Juicy-fruited, the palate works the mouth with energy. Screwcap. 13.6% alc. **Rating** 95 **To** 2028 $35 JP **✿**
Yarra Valley Cabernet Sauvignon 2018 Hand-picked, destemmed, cold soak, wild ferment, post-ferment maceration for 2 weeks, pressed, transferred to new, first and second fill barriques for 14 months, no fining or filtration. Planted in '99, the Seville Vineyard is hitting its straps and producing some super elegant wines. Deep, purple-garnet. Dusty, toasty, black fruits to burn, and spice. Kicks off on the palate with sweet fruit, fine-edged tannin and smart, tobacco leaf, cedar oak. So hard to resist right now. Screwcap. 13.6% alc. **Rating** 94 **To** 2029 $35 JP

ΨΨΨΨΩ **Redlands Yarra Valley Shiraz 2018 Rating** 91 **To** 2030 $35 JP

Peccavi Wines

1121 Wildwood Road, Yallingup Siding, WA 6282 **Region** Margaret River
T 0409 544 630 www.peccavi-wines.com **Open** By appt
Winemaker Brian Fletcher, Jeremy Muller **Est.** 1996 **Dozens** 6000 **Vyds** 16.5ha
Jeremy Muller was introduced to the great wines of the world by his father when he was young and says he spent years searching New and Old World wine regions (even looking at the sites of ancient Roman vineyards in England), but did not find what he was looking for until one holiday in Margaret River. There he found a vineyard in Yallingup that was available for sale and he did not hesitate. He quickly put together an impressive contract winemaking team and appointed Colin Bell as viticulturist. The wines are released under two labels: Peccavi for 100% estate-grown fruit (all hand-picked) and No Regrets for wines with contract-grown grapes and estate material. The quality of the wines is very good, reflecting the skills and experience of Brian Fletcher. Exports to the UK, Canada, Sweden, Malaysia, Singapore, Japan, Hong Kong and China.

ΨΨΨΨΨ **Margaret River Sauvignon Blanc 2017** A blend of citrus and herbal aromas and flavours; considerable length and intensity. Screwcap. 13% alc. **Rating** 94 **To** 2022 $42

ΨΨΨΨ **Margaret River Syrah 2015 Rating** 89 **To** 2024 $52

Peel Estate

290 Fletcher Road, Karnup, WA 6176 **Region** Peel
T (08) 9524 1221 www.peelwine.com.au **Open** 7 days 10–5
Winemaker Will Nairn, Mark Morton **Est.** 1973 **Dozens** 4000 **Vyds** 4ha

Peel's icon wine is the Shiraz, a wine of considerable finesse and with a remarkably consistent track record. Every year Will Nairn holds a Great Shiraz Tasting for six-year-old Australian shirazs and pits Peel Estate (in a blind tasting attended by 100 or so people) against Australia's best; it is never disgraced. The wood-matured Chenin Blanc is another winery specialty. Exports to the UK and China.

🍷🍷🍷🍷🍷 **Wood Matured Chenin Blanc 2017** Preserved lemon and tropical fruit characters, an itch of oak, an impeccable line and length. It's rich in a good way; it still manages to crackle its way along the palate. Screwcap. 12.5% alc. **Rating** 93 **To** 2023 $30 CM

Old Vine Shiraz 2013 Mellow flavours of leather, chocolate, toast and blackberry jam lead to a warm-but-satisfying finish. It's expressive, laced with tannin, warm-to-hot and characterful. Importantly, at no point along the length of the palate does it lose control. Screwcap. 15% alc. **Rating** 92 **To** 2025 $60 CM

Penfolds ★★★★★

30 Tanunda Road, Nuriootpa, SA 5355 P16 **Region** Barossa Valley
T (08) 8568 8408 **www.**penfolds.com **Open** 7 days 9–5
Winemaker Peter Gago **Est.** 1844 **Dozens** NFP

Penfolds is the star in the crown of Treasury Wine Estates (TWE) but its history predates the formation of TWE by close on 170 years. Its shape has changed in terms of its vineyards, its management, its passing parade of great winemakers and its wines. There is no other single winery brand in the New or the Old World with the depth and breadth of Penfolds. Retail prices range from less than $20 to $900 for Grange, which is the cornerstone, produced every year, albeit with the volume determined by the quality of the vintage, not by cash flow. There is now a range of regional wines of single varieties and the Bin Range of wines that includes both regional blends and (in some instances) varietal blends. Despite the very successful Yattarna and Reserve Bin A chardonnays, and some impressive rieslings, this remains a red wine producer at heart. Exports to all major markets.

🍷🍷🍷🍷🍷 **Bin 144 Yattarna Chardonnay 2017** Sourced from Tasmania, Tumbarumba and Adelaide Hills; 8 months in French oak (50% new). The blending must have taken weeks to finalise. Opens with a fanfare of aromas and flavours and increases its impact through to the incredibly long finish and aftertaste. Best Yattarna yet. Screwcap. 13% alc. **Rating** 99 **To** 2037 $175 ○

Bin 95 Grange 2015 Includes 2% cabernet sauvignon, matured for 20 months in new American hogsheads. Bang. The first whiff cries Grange. A lifted, fragrant, harmonious blend of fruit, oak (American, of course) and finely pitched tannins. Faultless. It's all relative but this is starting to relax its grip. And the length is very, very special. Cork. 14.5% alc. **Rating** 99 **To** 2055 $900

Bin 798 RWT Barossa Valley Shiraz 2017 Matured for 15 months in French hogsheads (70% new). Deep, vibrant colour. The bouquet is very expressive, speaking of a legion of black fruits, licorice, plum and spice, none of which prepare you for the sheer power of this amazing wine and its untold depths. Cork. 14.5% alc. **Rating** 98 **To** 2042 $200 ○

Bin 389 Cabernet Shiraz 2017 A 54/46% blend from McLaren Vale, Barossa Valley, Padthaway and Wrattonbully; matured for 12 months in American hogsheads (29% new). Complex and compelling, the bouquet setting the scene and the palate filling it. Black fruits, gently vanillan oak, superfine but persistent tannins are but the start. Cork. 14.5% alc. **Rating** 97 **To** 2037 $100 ○

🍷🍷🍷🍷🍷 **Reserve Bin A Adelaide Hills Chardonnay 2018** Matured for 8 months in French barriques (40% new). Bright straw-green. As ever, Penfolds has this label nailed. It is a magical combination of power and finesse, thanks in part to low pH and high acidity. It is just starting to stretch its legs. Screwcap. 13% alc. **Rating** 96 **To** 2030 $125

Bin 28 Kalimna Shiraz 2017 From the Barossa Valley, McLaren Vale and Padthaway; matured for 12 months in used American hogsheads. Deep, bright crimson. The battle lines are there before you smell or taste the wine: Penfolds' black-fruited depth and power on the one hand, the elegant vintage stamp on the other. Its balance and structure are the guarantee of a very long life. Cork. 14.5% alc. **Rating** 96 **To** 2037 $50 ❂

Bin 128 Coonawarra Shiraz 2017 Matured for 12 months in French hogsheads (25% new). Good depth to the colour (as expected) and brightness of hue. Black cherry, blackberry, plum, all within a carefully tailored embrace of French oak. Fine tannins add more to the impact and length. Cork. 14.5% alc. **Rating** 96 **To** 2032 $60 ❂

Bin 407 Cabernet Sauvignon 2017 From Padthaway, McLaren Vale, Barossa Valley, Coonawarra and Wrattonbully; matured in French (18% new) and American (14% new) hogsheads. Great colour. Blackcurrant, licorice, dark chocolate and spices run through the bouquet and palate alike, splitting and reforming in a dance of cassis and spices of all kinds. There is life and energy to spare here. Another major success. Cork. 14.5% alc. **Rating** 96 **To** 2032 $100

Bin 23 Adelaide Hills Pinot Noir 2018 From Henty, Tasmania and the Adelaide Hills; matured for 8 months in French barriques (17% new). Bright, clear crimson. In the same class as its compelling '17 sibling. Red cherry, pomegranate, fine tannins, deft oak handling. Cork. 14.5% alc. **Rating** 95 **To** 2029 $50

St Henri Shiraz 2016 Includes 5% cabernet sauvignon, matured for 12 months in 50+yo large oak vats. The dark, deep colour alerts you to the vintage. This is a wine for future generations to enjoy. It is stacked with extract of black fruits and tannins, its elevage at work. Cork. 14.5% alc. **Rating** 94 **To** 2055 $135

🍷🍷🍷🍷🍷 **Bin 150 Marananga Shiraz 2017 Rating** 93 **To** 2037 $100
Bin 138 2017 Rating 92 **To** 2028 $60
Bin 51 Eden Valley Riesling 2019 Rating 91 $40

Penfolds Magill Estate   ★★★★★

78 Penfold Road, Magill, SA 5072 **Region** Adelaide zone
T (08) 8301 5569 **www**.penfolds.com **Open** 7 days 9–6
Winemaker Peter Gago **Est.** 1844 **Dozens** NFP **Vyds** 5.2ha
This is the birthplace of Penfolds, established by Dr Christopher Rawson Penfold in 1844. His house is still part of the immaculately maintained property that includes 5.2ha of precious shiraz vines used to make Magill Estate Shiraz and the original and subsequent winery buildings, most still in operation or in museum condition. In May 2015 Penfolds unveiled the redevelopment of Magill Estate with the opening of a new cellar door (where visitors can taste Grange by the glass) and Magill Estate Kitchen, a casual dining environment with a grazing menu built on local and fresh ingredients and meant for sharing. The much-awarded Magill Estate Restaurant, with its panoramic views of the city, remains a temple for sublime food and wine matching. Exports to al major markets.

🍷🍷🍷🍷🍷 **Magill Estate Shiraz 2017** Matured for 17 months in French (30% new) and American (20% new) oak. This gives the elegance lurking in many of the Penfolds wines free play. It's colour is lighter, the fruit restrained, and it is only on the finish that its pedigree asserts itself. Cork. 14% alc. **Rating** 94 **To** 2034 $150

Penley Estate   ★★★★★

McLeans Road, Coonawarra, SA 5263 **Region** Coonawarra
T (08) 8736 3211 **www**.penley.com.au **Open** 7 days 10–4
Winemaker Kate Goodman, Lauren Hansen **Est.** 1988 **Dozens** 48 000 **Vyds** 111ha
In 1988 Kym, Ang and Bec Tolley joined forces to buy a block of land in Coonawarra – Penley Estate was underway, the amalgamation of a 5th generation wine family Penfold and Tolley. In 2015 Ang and Bec took full ownership of the company. They have made a number of changes, welcoming general manager Michael Armstrong and, even more importantly, appointing Kate Goodman as winemaker. Behind the scenes Ang's husband David Paxton, one of Australia's foremost viticulturists, has been working as a consultant, with improvements

in vineyard performance already evident. In December '17, Penley also opened a cellar door in the main street of McLaren Vale. Exports to all major markets.

ＹＹＹＹＹ **Eos Coonawarra Shiraz Cabernet Sauvignon 2017** A 24-hour cold soak, small 2t fermenters, matured in French oak (45% new). A very elegant and balanced medium-bodied blend, which has profited greatly from its alcohol of 14%. The fruit has given the oak a cuff across the ears because it is not the least assertive, the tannins also exact. Cork. **Rating** 96 **To** 2040 $100

Helios Coonawarra Cabernet Sauvignon 2018 Wild yeast–open fermented, one batch kept on skins for extended maceration, matured for 18 months in French oak (40% new). Medium to full-bodied with a wealth of blackcurrant, mulberry and cherry fruit. Oak is well and truly in play, as one might expect. The long, supple back-palate is very good. Cork. 14% alc. **Rating** 95 **To** 2038 $100

Steyning Coonawarra Cabernet Sauvignon 2017 Small open fermenters, part extended maceration, part completed primary fermentation in barrel (60% new). Very well made, no chasing of needless alcohol in a cool vintage. This is a delightfully ripened, medium-bodied cabernet, blackcurrant fruit to the fore, its balance faultless. Screwcap. 13.5% alc. **Rating** 95 **To** 2037 $45

Tolmer Coonawarra Cabernet Sauvignon 2018 Matured in French oak (35% new) for 12 months. A particularly pleasing Coonawarra cabernet from a very good vintage. The balance of fruit, oak and tannins is right on the money with cassis, Coonawarra mulberry and cedar. Screwcap. 14% alc. **Rating** 94 **To** 2038 $30 ○

ＹＹＹＹＹ **Chertsey 2017 Rating** 92 **To** 2027 $45

Penna Lane Wines ★★★★

Lot 51 Penna Lane, Penwortham via Clare, SA 5453 **Region** Clare Valley
T 0403 462 431 **www.**pennalanewines.com.au **Open** Fri–Sun 11–5
Winemaker Peter Treloar, Steve Baraglia **Est.** 1998 **Dozens** 4500 **Vyds** 4.37ha
Penna Lane is located in the beautiful Skilly Valley, 10km south of Clare. The estate vineyard (shiraz, cabernet sauvignon and semillon) is planted at an elevation of 450m, which allows a long, slow ripening period, usually resulting in wines with intense varietal fruit flavours.

ＹＹＹＹＹ **Skilly Valley Riesling 2019** Elegant, fresh and pulsating with lime and lemon on one side, apple blossom and flavours on the other; all up a classy, juicy mouthful. Screwcap. 11.5% alc. **Rating** 95 **To** 2029 $35 ○

ＹＹＹＹＹ **Watervale Riesling 2019 Rating** 90 **To** 2027 $28

Penny's Hill ★★★★★

281 Main Road, McLaren Vale, SA 5171 **Region** McLaren Vale
T (08) 8557 0800 **www.**pennyshill.com.au **Open** Mon–Sat 10–5, Sun 11–5
Winemaker Alexia Roberts **Est.** 1988 **Dozens** 60 000 **Vyds** 44ha
Founded in 1988 by Tony and Susie Parkinson, Penny's Hill produces high quality shiraz (Footprint and The Skeleton Key) from its close-planted McLaren Vale estate, also the source of the Edwards Road Cabernet Sauvignon and The Experiment Grenache. Malpas Road and Goss Corner vineyards complete the estate holdings, providing fruit for Cracking Black Shiraz and Malpas Road Merlot. White wines (The Agreement Sauvignon Blanc and The Minimalist Chardonnay) are sourced from 'estates of mates' in the Adelaide Hills. Also includes the Black Chook and Thomas Goss Brands. Penny's Hill cellars are located at the historic Ingleburne Farm, which also houses the award-winning The Kitchen Door restaurant and Red Dot Gallery. Noted for its distinctive 'red dot' packaging. Exports to all major markets.

ＹＹＹＹＹ **Cracking Black McLaren Vale Shiraz 2018** This offers exceptional value. Given 7–10 days on skins, before quality French oak (15% new) for 16 months. This is a plump rich red. The usual cavalcade of black fruit and spice, but what makes this a joy to drink is the effortless mouthfeel. A gentle sash of tannins. Floral scents. A trickle of acidity rather than a forcefield. The wine just sits there, buoyant, mellow and juicy. **Rating** 94 **To** 2024 $25 NG ○

ɟɟɟɟ♀ Skeleton Key McLaren Vale Shiraz 2018 Rating 93 To 2028 $40 NG
The Experiment Single Vineyard McLaren Vale Grenache 2018
Rating 93 To 2028 $40 NG
The Minimalist Single Vineyard Adelaide Hills Chardonnay 2018
Rating 92 $35 NG
Edwards Road McLaren Vale Cabernet Sauvignon 2018 Rating 92
To 2027 $25 NG ✪
The Agreement Single Vineyard Adelaide Hills Sauvignon Blanc 2019
Rating 91 To 2021 $22 NG ✪
Footprint McLaren Vale Shiraz 2018 Rating 90 To 2028 NG

Peos Estate   ★★★★★

1124 Graphite Road, Manjimup, WA 6258 **Region** Manjimup
T (08) 9772 1378 **www**.peosestate.com.au **Open** By appt
Winemaker Willow Bridge (Kim Horton) **Est.** 1996 **Dozens** 14000 **Vyds** 37.5ha
The Peos family has farmed in the west Manjimup district for over 50 years, the third
generation of four brothers developing the vineyard from 1996. There are over 37ha of vines
including shiraz, merlot, chardonnay, cabernet sauvignon, sauvignon blanc, pinot noir and
verdelho. Exports to China.

ɟɟɟɟɟ Four Aces Single Vineyard Manjimup Chardonnay 2018 Judiciously
proportioned in every way. The bouquet all floral, citrus and spicy with a hint of
flinty/struck-match. While the fuller palate takes its cue from stone fruit, leesy/
nutty flavours with seamlessly integrated oak. Just delicious. Screwcap. 13.5% alc.
Rating 95 To 2028 $35 JF ✪
Four Aces Single Vineyard Manjimup Pinot Noir 2019 There's plenty
of drinking pleasure to be had with this spot-on, ready-now wine. Full of ripe
cherries, rhubarb and raspberries sprinkled with baking spices. The unobtrusive
oak adds some depth, and plush tannins are gentle across the fuller-bodied palate
with tangy, sweet fruit to close. Screwcap. 14.5% alc. Rating 95 To 2028 $40 JF
Four Aces Single Vineyard Manjimup Shiraz 2018 This certainly struts its
stuff. It's laden with ripe fruit and spices. Oak has a part to play structurally plus
adding flavour and tannins, but it's in line. There's a succulence and such bright
raspberry-like acidity that another glass, or more, is not out of the question.
Screwcap. 14.5% alc. Rating 95 To 2028 $40 JF
Icon Manjimup Shiraz Cabernet 2018 Perhaps a new addition to Peos, but
information is sparse other than a blend of 71% shiraz, 29% cabernet sauvignon,
aged 18 months in French oak (70% new). Obvious quality fruit, obvious
quality oak, both working out the relationship. Time is needed. In the mix are
blackberries, cassis, plums, menthol/dried herbs with more interesting pencil
shavings and iron filings. Screwcap. 14.5% alc. Rating 95 To 2032 $70 JF
Four Aces Single Vineyard Manjimup Cabernet Sauvignon 2018 It smells
lovely and old-fashioned (in a good way) with cedar and cigar box aromas. Plenty
of varietal joy with cassis and blackberry essence, regional bracken–eucalyptus
acting more as a seasoning. Full-bodied, slightly terse tannins and the oak
impacting too. It needs time to settle and will do. Screwcap. 14.5% alc. Rating 95
To 2032 $40 JF
Four Kings Single Vineyard Manjimup Cabernet Sauvignon 2018 A
power house of flavour and intensity with a ball of sweet, ripe blackberries and
plums injected with cinnamon quills and woodsy spices à la oak. Full-bodied,
plump tannins and satisfaction guaranteed. Screwcap. 14.5% alc. Rating 94
To 2028 $32 JF

ɟɟɟɟ♀ Four Kings Single Vineyard Manjimup Chardonnay 2019 Rating 93
To 2027 $28 JF
Four Kings Single Vineyard Manjimup Pinot Noir 2019 Rating 92
To 2026 $32 JF
Four Kings Single Vineyard Manjimup Cabernet Sauvignon 2018
Rating 92 To 2030 $32 JF

Pepper Tree Wines

86 Halls Road, Pokolbin, NSW 2320 **Region** Hunter Valley
T (02) 4909 7100 **www.**peppertreewines.com.au **Open** Mon–Fri 9–5, w'ends 9.30–5
Winemaker Gwyn Olsen **Est.** 1991 **Dozens** 50 000 **Vyds** 172.1ha

Pepper Tree is owned by geologist Dr John Davis. It sources the majority of its Hunter Valley fruit from its Davis Family Vineyard at Mt View, but also has premium vineyards at Orange, Coonawarra and Wrattonbully. The highly credentialled Gwyn Olsen ('12 Dux, Advanced Wine Assessment course, AWRI; '14 Young Winemaker of the Year, *Gourmet Traveller WINE*;'15 Rising Star of the Year, Hunter Valley Legends Awards; and '15 Len Evans Tutorial Scholar) was appointed winemaker in '15. Exports to the UK, Canada, Denmark, Finland, Singapore and China.

Museum Release Single Vineyard Alluvius Hunter Valley Semillon 2009 It's a mature wine of power and precision. It offers texture, weight of flavour and quite gorgeous length. While complex, it has the energy and momentum to simply carry you along with it. Screwcap. 10.5% alc. **Rating** 96 **To** 2025 $65 CM ❂

Premium Reserve Single Vineyard 8R Wrattonbully Merlot 2018 Terrific merlot. Flavoursome, characterful, structured and sustained. The wealth of blackcurrant, the choc-mint notes, the wide spread of dusty tannin, the inherent juiciness. One sip and you're hooked. It will cellar like a charm but it offers irresistible drinking right now. Screwcap. 14.2% alc. **Rating** 96 **To** 2035 CM

Museum Release Single Vineyard Strandlines Wrattonbully Cabernet Shiraz 2009 Incredibly youthful and still bold with dark, sweet, berried fruit flavour. This is in terrific shape now and has another decade or 2 up its sleeve. Blackcurrant, graphite, peppercorn and choc-mint characters come infused with tobacco and leather. There's redcurrant here too. And a firm spread of tannin. Quite brilliant. Screwcap. 14.5% alc. **Rating** 96 **To** 2034 CM

Venus Block Single Vineyard Premium Reserve Orange Chardonnay 2018 Generous wine. Stone fruit, fig and apple are sewn together by citrussy acidity and a subtle waft of oak. Screwcap. 13.5% alc. **Rating** 95 **To** 2028 $45

Limited Release Coonawarra Rose 2019 Pale pink with no hint of salmon, the wine built on estate-grown merlot. It throbs with red berries – strawberry, raspberry and pomegranate – each reaching out to meet at the centre of the palate. This delivers real pleasure. Screwcap. 13.5% alc. **Rating** 95 **To** 2022 $30 ❂

Coquun Premium Shiraz Blend Hunter Valley Shiraz 2018 A medium to full-bodied blend of the best barrels of the vintage brings the great '18 vintage onto centre stage with luxuriant dark fruits on the bouquet and a palate that surges free on the lifted finish. Ticks all the boxes. Screwcap. 14.5% alc. **Rating** 95 **To** 2048 $90

Single Vineyard Tallavera Hunter Valley Shiraz 2009 Museum release. From 90yo vines. It's a mellow, fully integrated red with leather, plum, violet, malt and sweet earth characters pushing through to a convincing finish. It shows no signs of tiring but it is fully mature now. Screwcap. 14% alc. **Rating** 95 **To** 2028 $150 CM

Museum Release Single Vineyard Reserve Coquun Hunter Valley Shiraz 2009 The palate still boasts a sizeable ball of cherried, spicy fruit flavour; then the finish is smoky and meaty and generally savoury. It has mellowed without losing its shape; in short, its (significant) powers of persuasion are still intact. Screwcap. 14% alc. **Rating** 95 **To** 2035 $17 CM ❂

Single Vineyard Elderslee Road Reserve Wrattonbully Cabernet Sauvignon 2009 It was luscious in its youth and so it still is, even with 10+ years under its belt. Blackcurrant, vanilla-cream, choc-mint and tobacco characters sweep confidently through the palate. Pleasure, it provides plenty. In its drinking prime right now. Screwcap. 14.5% alc. **Rating** 95 **To** 2029 $75 CM

Museum Release Calcare Single Vineyard Coonawarra Cabernet Sauvignon 2009 Soft and well developed with leather, earth, choc-mint, currant and truffle flavours flowing sweetly through the palate. Fully mature but there's no hurry. Screwcap. 14.5% alc. **Rating** 94 **To** 2025 $75 CM

Single Vineyard Alluvius-TV Hunter Valley Semillon 2019 You'd rip into this right now. It's alive and kicking with pure fruit flavour but it still manages to carry well through the finish. Garden herbs, florals, a smoky note and, of course, citrus. Captivating in its youth. Screwcap. 11.9% alc. **Rating** 94 **To** 2029 $45 CM
Venator Limited Release Hunter Valley Shiraz 2018 Venator is said to be the Latin word for hunter of wine. Selected from estate blocks spread across the Lower Hunter, the name is clever, with multiple references to the places found in the region. It is medium-bodied with more red berry than Coquun. Screwcap. 13.8% alc. **Rating** 94 **To** 2033 $35
Single Vineyard Claude Hunter Valley Shiraz 2018 Machine-harvested, fermented as whole berries then into French oak (25% new), for 14 months. It feels svelte, it's well balanced and well fruited. Oak has been seductively applied and the finish is satisfying. We're in classy territory here. Screwcap. 14.4% alc. **Rating** 94 **To** 2030 $50 CM

ȲȲȲȲȲ **Museum Release Single Vineyard Reserve The Gravels Wrattonbully Shiraz Viognier 2009** Rating 93 To 2025 $75 CM
Single Vineyard Premium Reserve Alluvius-BM Hunter Valley Semillon 2019 Rating 93 To 2030 $38 CM
Limited Release Classics Wrattonbully Cabernet Sauvignon Merlot Petit Verdot 2017 Rating 93 To 2030 CM
Single Vineyard Reserve 14 Shores Coonawarra Merlot 2009 Rating 92 To 2026 $75 CM
Wrattonbully Cabernet Sauvignon 2017 Rating 92 To 2027 $20 CM ❂
Four Clones Orange Chardonnay 2018 Rating 91 To 2024 $30 CM
Wrattonbully Merlot 2017 Rating 91 To 2029 $20 ❂
Limited Release Classics Wrattonbully Cabernet Sauvignon Merlot Petit Verdot 2016 Rating 91 To 2028 $30 CM
Orange Chardonnay 2019 Rating 90 To 2025 $20 CM ❂
Single Vineyard Limited Release The Pebbles Wrattonbully Shiraz Viognier 2017 Rating 90 To 2026 $35 CM

Petaluma   ★★★★★

254 Pfeiffer Road, Woodside, SA 5244 **Region** Adelaide Hills
T (08) 8339 9300 **www.**petaluma.com.au **Open** 7 days 10–5
Winemaker Mike Mudge, Amy Hickling, Dave Horne **Est.** 1976 **Dozens** 130000
Vyds 240ha
The Petaluma range has been expanded beyond the core group of Croser sparkling, Clare Valley Riesling, Piccadilly Valley Chardonnay and Coonawarra Merlot. Newer arrivals of note include Adelaide Hills Viognier and Shiraz. The plantings in the Clare Valley, Coonawarra and Adelaide Hills provide a more than sufficient source of estate-grown grapes for the wines. A new winery and cellar door opened in 2015 on a greenfield site with views of Mt Lofty. In '17 Petaluma (along with all wine brands owned by Lion Nathan) was acquired by Accolade. Exports to all major markets.

ȲȲȲȲȲ **B&V Vineyard Adelaide Hills Shiraz 2017** While it has a core of juicy, tangy fruit and appealingly so, the clincher is the overall savouriness to this medium-bodied wine. Supple, ripe tannins smooth the way for the coating of sweet and charry oak. Screwcap. 14% alc. **Rating** 95 **To** 2030 $50 JF
Croser Piccadilly Valley Pinot Noir Chardonnay 2015 A 63/37% blend. Brioche, cashew cream, spice, strawberry, white flowers – where to start and where to finish? Immaculate length and balance courtesy 40 months on lees. Diam. 14% alc. **Rating** 95 $38

ȲȲȲȲȲ **Hanlin Hill Clare Valley Riesling 2019** Rating 92 To 2026 $36 JF
Piccadilly Valley Chardonnay 2018 Rating 92 To 2026 $46 JF
White Label Coonawarra Dry Rose 2019 Rating 92 To 2022 $27 JF

Peter Drayton Wines ★★★★☆

Ironbark Hill Vineyard, 694 Hermitage Road, Pokolbin, NSW 2321 **Region** Hunter Valley
T (02) 6574 7085 **www**.pdwines.com.au **Open** 7 days 10–5
Winemaker Damien Stevens, Peter Drayton **Est.** 2001 **Dozens** 20 000 **Vyds** 16.5ha
Owned by Peter and Leesa Drayton. The estate plantings include shiraz, chardonnay,
semillon, cabernet sauvignon, tempranillo, merlot, verdelho and tyrian. Peter is a commercial/
industrial builder, so constructing the cellar door was a busman's holiday. The vineyard
features an atmospheric function venue and wedding chapel set among the vines, with events
organised and catered for by Café Enzo. Exports to Vietnam, Hong Kong and China.

▼▼▼▼▼ **Wildstreak Hunter Valley Shiraz 2018** From the Ironbark Hill Vineyard;
crushed and destemmed, open-fermented, 6 days on skins, matured for 16 months
in 50% new American oak 2500l foudre (or similar) and 30% new American
puncheons. You can, of course, pick up the new American oak, but the fruit has
more than just proved it can stand up to that oak – it has devoured it. Tannins
might have been ready to jump in and take up the space, but they haven't. Great
bargain. Screwcap. 14% alc. **Rating** 95 **To** 2038 $32 **◐**

▼▼▼▼▽ **Wildstreak Hunter Valley Chardonnay 2019 Rating** 90 **To** 2023 $28
Anomaly Hunter Valley Vermentino 2019 Rating 90 **To** 2023 $30
Anomaly Hunter Valley Pinot Noir Shiraz 2018 Rating 90 **To** 2028 $36
Anomaly Hunter Valley Montepulciano 2018 Rating 90 **To** 2023 $36

Peter Lehmann ★★★★★

Para Road, Tanunda, SA 5352 **Region** Barossa Valley
T (08) 8565 9555 **www**.peterlehmannwines.com **Open** Mon–Fri 9.30–5, w'ends &
public hols 10.30–4.30
Winemaker Nigel Westblade **Est.** 1979 **Dozens** 750 000
The seemingly indestructible Peter Lehmann (the person) died in June 2013, laying the seeds
for what became the last step in the sale of the minority Lehmann family ownership in the
company. The Hess Group of California had acquired control in '03 (leaving part of the capital
with the Lehmann family) but a decade later it became apparent that Hess wished to quit its
holding. Various suitors put their case forward but Margaret Lehmann (Peter's widow) wanted
ongoing family, not corporate, ownership. Casella thus was able to make the successful bid in
November '14, followed by the acquisition of Brand's Laira in December '15. Exports to the
UK, the US and Canada.

▼▼▼▼▼ **Masterson Barossa Valley Shiraz 2015** From a single vineyard in Moppa;
the grapes crushed to a small fermenter with 14 days on skins, pressed to French
hogsheads for mlf, then to a 2500l oval foudre for 36 months after strict barrel
selection. It is a full-bodied shiraz of excellent quality, harmony and balance
perfectly expressed via seamless fruit, oak and tannin contributions. Only available
in magnum. Cork. 14.5% alc. **Rating** 97 **To** 2048 $2000

▼▼▼▼▼ **Wigan Eden Valley Riesling 2015** A wine equally split between its freshness
on the one hand and honeyed lime juice on the other. It's hard to see how it will
increase in complexity, yet it will, as every vintage of Wigan has demonstrated.
Screwcap. 11% alc. **Rating** 96 **To** 2035 $35 **◐**
Margaret Barossa Semillon 2013 Generations of Barossa Valley semillon were
made from grapes ripened to produce alcohol levels between 15% and 16.5%,
matured in used American oak and had no support outside of a hardy few until
winemaker Andrew Wigan decided to follow the Hunter Valley's lead and pick
early, cold ferment and bottle asap. It was an immediate success and continues to
this day: zesty citrus/lemongrass flavours and mouthfeel, and a 10–20 year life.
Screwcap. 10.9% alc. **Rating** 96 **To** 2035 $35 **◐**
Stonewell Barossa Shiraz 2016 Crushed and destemmed, fermented for
14 days on skins, 14 months in French oak (50% new). A serious shiraz with a
long life ahead. Screwcap. 14.5% alc. **Rating** 95 **To** 2036 $100

Mentor Barossa Cabernet 2015 Crushed and destemmed, static fermenter, cultured yeast, 14 days on skins, matured in French oak (50% new) for 14 months. Fresh and lively cassis fruit bears witness to the controlled alcohol and lack of extract. Screwcap. 14.4% alc. **Rating** 95 To 2030 $45

Black Queen Sparkling Shiraz 2014 Traditional method, 5 years on lees, disgorged '19. Skimpy facts supplied but the main facts of quality base wine and moderate dosage are all good. Diam. 14% alc. **Rating** 95 $45

H&V Eden Valley Riesling 2019 From an exceptional block in Springton and 3 vineyards in the High Eden. Lives up to expectations with an even-flowing stream of Rose's lime juice and lemon, acidity precisely balanced, the finish born of a spring day. Great value. Screwcap. 11% alc. **Rating** 94 To 2034 $25 ☼

♟♟♟♟♙ **8 Songs Shiraz 2016 Rating** 93 To 2029 $45
VSV Ruediger Cabernet Sauvignon 2018 Rating 93 To 2033 $60
H&V Shiraz 2018 Rating 92 To 2028 $25 ☼

Peter Teakle Wines ★★★★

PO Box 783, Clare SA 5453 **Region** Southern Eyre Peninsula
T 0412 213 136 www.peterteaklewines.com **Open** Not
Winemaker Liz Heidenreich **Est.** 2017 **Dozens** 2200 **Vyds** 12ha
Peter Teakle worked for over 40 years for his family company, Collotype Wine Labels, recipient of a number of industry awards. His first venture outside of label printing was managing a vineyard on Akuna Station in the Riverland for many years. In early 2016 he purchased the former Dellacolline Estate at Port Lincoln and has spent the intervening time in rehabilitating the rundown vineyard, doubling its size to 12ha. For the time being, the grapes are hand-picked and transported to O'Leary Walker Wines in the Clare Valley, where Liz Heidenreich makes the wines.

♟♟♟♟♟ **Estate Shiraz 2017** Hand-picked, crushed and destemmed, open-fermented, pressed to French and American oak (25% new) for 18 months. The medium to full-bodied palate offers dark/black fruits in profusion, then backs off on the airy finish. It all works well. Screwcap. 13.5% alc. **Rating** 94 To 2030 $30 ☼

♟♟♟♟♙ **Estate Merlot 2018 Rating** 93 To 2030 $30

Petrichor Wines ★★★★

41 Rosewood Lane, Tea Tree, Tas 7017 **Region** Tasmania
T 0422 437 449 www.petrichorwines.com.au **Open** Not
Winemaker Tim Hodgkinson, Justin Bubb **Est.** 2018 **Dozens** 130 **Vyds** 1.9ha
Petrichor is a noun meaning the scent of rain on dry soil. Kate Akmentins and Tim Hodgkinson visited Tasmania for their first wedding anniversary in 2006 and decided it was where their future lay. Three daughters, including twins, arrived, leading to the acceleration of their plans. In mid '14 they decamped from Sydney, three years later purchasing a 10ha property at Tea Tree in the Coal River Valley, with a north-facing slope and sunshine all day. One decision they made early on was to farm biodynamically, with a polyculture business in the future, but presently involves close-planting (1m × 1m) pinot noir, shiraz, gamay and gruner veltliner, buying a parcel of grapes from Tea Tree speaking of the Coal River Valley terroir – a purchase that will continue until their vineyard comes into production. Tim has created Masterclass 4 Business, running workshops for wine businesses. Kate manages the vineyard and assists in the winery.

♟♟♟♟♙ **Single Vineyard Coal River Valley Pinot Noir 30% Whole Bunch 2018** A mix of clones, cold-soaked and fermented in open stainless steel, 10 months in older French barriques. Aromas of cherry and sweet spice but also more earthy characters like beetroot. Sweet-fruited but tangy on the palate, quite mouthfilling and with good length. Screwcap. 13% alc. **Rating** 93 To 2025 $50 SC

Single Vineyard Coal River Valley Pinot Noir 50% Whole Bunch 2018 All clone 777, 50% whole bunch, cold-soaked, open-fermented with wild yeast. Oak handling as with the 30% release. Rather pale and lacking clarity in the glass.

Much stronger whole-bunch influence here; stemmy, green characters prevailing on the bouquet. Riper on the palate and again there's sweetness to the fruit, the flavours softening towards the finish. Screwcap. 13% alc. **Rating** 91 **To** 2025 $50 SC

Pewsey Vale Vineyard ★★★★★

Eden Valley Road, Eden Valley, SA 5353 **Region** Eden Valley
T (08) 8561 3200 **www**.pewseyvale.com **Open** By appt
Winemaker Louisa Rose **Est.** 1847 **Dozens** 20 000 **Vyds** 65ha
Pewsey Vale was a famous vineyard established in 1847 by Joseph Gilbert. It was appropriate that when the Hill-Smith family began the renaissance of the Eden Valley plantings in 1961, it should do so by purchasing Pewsey Vale and establishing 50ha of riesling. In '77 the Riesling also finally benefited from being the first wine to be bottled with a Stelvin screwcap. While public reaction forced the abandonment of the initiative for almost 20 years, Pewsey Vale never lost faith in the technical advantages of the closure. A quick taste (or better, a share of a bottle) of five to seven-year-old Contours Riesling will tell you why. Exports to all major markets.

🍷🍷🍷🍷🍷 **1961 Block Single Vineyard Estate Eden Valley Riesling 2019** It has all the hallmarks of a great riesling. Balance of citrus, spices and a mineral sensation to the acidity. It has a light raw silk texture and depth, yet is never showy. It's all class. Screwcap. 12% alc. **Rating** 95 **To** 2029 $32 JF ❂
The Contours Museum Reserve Single Vineyard Estate Eden Valley Riesling 2015 Pale straw-gold. Heady aromas reveal the added layers of age and it is all about complexity. Lime marmalade, baked ricotta topped with lemon zest and toasty too. It also has a line of acidity keeping this buoyant, tingling with freshness. Screwcap. 13% alc. **Rating** 95 **To** 2026 $38 JF
Prima 23GR Single Vineyard Estate Eden Valley Riesling 2019 An exquisite, off-dry style with its lemon blossom and chalky acidity. Flavours build, as does the texture and pleasure in drinking it. It never feels heavy-handed. A gorgeous wine. Screwcap. 9.5% alc. **Rating** 95 **To** 2028 $28 JF ❂

🍷🍷🍷🍷🍷 **Single Vineyard Estate Eden Valley Riesling 2019 Rating** 93 **To** 2028 $26 JF ❂
The Contours Museum Reserve Single Vineyard Estate Eden Valley Riesling 2014 Rating 92 **To** 2023 $38 JF

Phaedrus Estate ★★★★☆

220 Mornington-Tyabb Road, Moorooduc, Vic 3933 **Region** Mornington Peninsula
T (03) 5978 8134 **www**.phaedrus.com.au **Open** W'ends & public hols 11–5
Winemaker Ewan Campbell, Maitena Zantvoort **Est.** 1997 **Dozens** 3000 **Vyds** 2.5ha
Since Maitena Zantvoort and Ewan Campbell established Phaedrus Estate, they have gained a reputation for producing premium cool-climate wines. Their winemaking philosophy brings art and science together to produce wines showing regional and varietal character with minimal winemaking interference. The vineyard includes 1ha of pinot noir and 0.5ha each of pinot gris, chardonnay and shiraz.

🍷🍷🍷🍷🍷 **Single Vineyard Reserve Mornington Peninsula Pinot Noir 2018** Made similarly to the standard pinot noir but with longer post-ferment maceration, matured 18 months in 2 new/1yo used hogsheads. Altogether deeper, riper, richer and more intense than the estate pinot. Fruits are in red berry and dark plum mode with overlay of pomegranate and chocolate. Dense palate and super elegant. Screwcap. 13.9% alc. **Rating** 95 **To** 2026 $45 JP
Mornington Peninsula Pinot Noir 2018 A 3-days' cold soak, wild ferment, foot crushing, hand plunging, 11 months' maturation in French hogsheads (20% new). Phaedrus celebrated its 21st vintage in '18, a significant milestone on the Mornington Peninsula. Age of vines and experience speaks clearly in this estate pinot noir. A quiet energy in the glass to start: black cherry, macerated

plums, cranberry. Livens up with a few swooshes of air. Finely textured tannins lead to an elegant finish. Screwcap. 13.5% alc. **Rating** 94 **To** 2028 $28 JP ○

🍷🍷🍷🍷🍸 Mornington Peninsula Chardonnay 2019 **Rating** 93 **To** 2028 $26 JP ○
Mornington Peninsula Shiraz 2018 **Rating** 93 **To** 2030 $28 JP
Mornington Peninsula Pinot Gris 2019 **Rating** 90 **To** 2030 $24 JP

Philip Shaw Wines ★★★★★

100 Shiralee Road, Orange, NSW 2800 **Region** Orange
T (02) 6362 0710 **www**.philipshaw.com.au **Open** 7 days 11–5
Winemaker Daniel Shaw **Est.** 1989 **Dozens** 25 000 **Vyds** 47ha
Philip Shaw, former chief winemaker of Rosemount Estate and then Southcorp, first became interested in the Orange region in 1985. In '88 he purchased the Koomooloo Vineyard and began extensive plantings, the varieties included shiraz, merlot, pinot noir, sauvignon blanc, cabernet franc, cabernet sauvignon and viognier. Philip has handed the reins to sons Daniel and Damian to concentrate on his HOOSEGG wines. Exports to the UK, Norway, Finland, the Philippines, Indonesia, Hong Kong, China and NZ.

🍷🍷🍷🍷🍷 No. 89 Orange Shiraz 2018 Hand-picked and sorted, open-fermented with 60% whole bunches, 2% viognier co-fermented, matured in French barriques (30% new) for 11 months. Medium to full-bodied with black cherry/berry and strong spicy/savoury/earthy tannins. Overall very good length and balance. Screwcap. 13.8% alc. **Rating** 95 **To** 2038 $50
No. 11 Orange Chardonnay 2018 Absolutely identical vinification to its '19 sibling. Ironically, it does have intensity and focus to its grapefruit, Granny Smith apple and white peach fruit, 30% new French oak helping proceedings. Screwcap. 12.8% alc. **Rating** 94 **To** 2029 $35

🍷🍷🍷🍷🍸 No. 17 Orange Merlot Cabernet Franc Cabernet 2018 **Rating** 93
To 2038 $28
No. 19 Orange Sauvignon Blanc 2019 **Rating** 91 **To** 2021 $28
No. 11 Orange Chardonnay 2019 **Rating** 91 **To** 2029 $35
The Idiot Orange Shiraz 2018 **Rating** 90 **To** 2033 $22

Piano Piano ★★★★★

852 Beechworth-Wangaratta Road, Everton Upper, Vic 3678 **Region** Beechworth
T (03) 5727 0382 **www**.pianopiano.com.au **Open** By appt
Winemaker Marc Scalzo **Est.** 2001 **Dozens** 1500 **Vyds** 4.6ha
'Piano piano' means 'slowly slowly' in Italian, and this is how Marc Scalzo and wife Lisa Hernan have approached the development of their business. Marc has a degree in oenology from CSU, many years' practical experience as a winemaker with Brown Brothers and vintage experience with Giaconda, John Gehrig and in NZ with Seresin Estate and Delegat's. In 1997 they planted 2.6ha of merlot, cabernet sauvignon, tempranillo and touriga nacional on their Brangie Vineyard in the King Valley; they followed up with 1.2ha of chardonnay ('06) and 0.8ha of shiraz ('08) on their Beechworth property.

🍷🍷🍷🍷🍷 Henry's Block Beechworth Shiraz 2017 Hand-picked, 10% whole bunch, 90% whole berry, wild yeast–open fermented, matured in French oak (31% new) for 20 months. A lovely medium-bodied wine that follows in the footsteps of the '16. It's vibrant and juicy, yet also brings texture and structure into play. Effortless elegance. A long life beckons. Screwcap. 13.8% alc. **Rating** 97 **To** 2040 $42 ○

🍷🍷🍷🍷🍷 Reserve Beechworth Merlot 2017 The grapes were gently crushed with a high percentage of unbroken berries, wild yeast–open fermented, 14 days on skins, matured for 20 months in French hogsheads and puncheons (31% new). This is a really attractive merlot, with dark cherry/berry/plum fruit perfectly framed by the oak and polished tannins. Screwcap. 14.2% alc. **Rating** 95 **To** 2032 $35 ○

🍷🍷🍷🍷🍸 Sophie's Block Beechworth Chardonnay 2018 **Rating** 90 **To** 2021 $42

Pierro ★★★★★

Caves Road, Wilyabrup via Cowaramup, WA 6284 **Region** Margaret River
T (08) 9755 6220 **www**.pierro.com.au **Open** 7 days 10–5
Winemaker Dr Michael Peterkin **Est.** 1979 **Dozens** 10000 **Vyds** 7.85ha
Dr Michael Peterkin is another of the legion of Margaret River medical practitioner-vignerons; for good measure, he married into the Cullen family. Pierro is renowned for its stylish white wines, which often exhibit tremendous complexity; the Chardonnay can be monumental in its weight and texture. That said, its red wines from good vintages can be every bit as good. Exports to the UK, Denmark, Belgium, Russia, Malaysia, Indonesia, Hong Kong, Singapore and Japan.

🍷🍷🍷🍷🍷 **Semillon Sauvignon Blanc L.T.C. 2019** A refreshing take on the SBS partnership with a glug of chardonnay, mostly fermented in stainless steel, 25% goes into new French barriques. It's quite racy with lemon sorbet acidity keeping the sweet fruit in check. Smoky with delicious flavours of honeydew, sugar snap pea, limes and lemon juice with grapefruit pith texture. Screwcap. 13% alc. **Rating** 95 **To** 2024 $34 JF ✪
Margaret River Chardonnay 2018 Classic Pierro chardonnay with its power and drive thanks to spicy sweet vanillan oak and creamy butterscotch flavours from lees stirring and mlf. It's balanced and harmonised by neat acidity, grapefruit, white peach and some smoky sulphides. Screwcap. 13.5% alc. **Rating** 95 **To** 2028 $95 JF
Reserve Margaret River Cabernet Sauvignon Merlot 2016 Cabernet peaks at 70%, merlot 21% with splashes of petit verdot and cabernet franc, and it handles the 50% new French oak, but it does need more time to settle. The wine remains medium-bodied with a whorl of concentrated sweet red fruit, mulberries with a delightful Mister Lincoln rose fragrance and smoky tobacco. A composed, lithe wine with fine tannins and a gentleness across the palate. Screwcap. 14% alc. **Rating** 95 **To** 2030 $95 JF

🍷🍷🍷🍷🍷 **Cabernet Sauvignon Merlot L.T.Cf. 2016 Rating** 92 **To** 2023 $42 JF

Pike & Joyce ★★★★★

730 Mawson Road, Lenswood, SA 5240 **Region** Adelaide Hills
T (08) 8389 8102 **www**.pikeandjoyce.com.au **Open** Not
Winemaker Neil Pike, Steve Baraglia **Est.** 1998 **Dozens** 5000 **Vyds** 18.5ha
This is a partnership between the Pike family (of Clare Valley fame) and the Joyce family, related to Andrew Pike's wife, Cathy. The Joyce family have been orchardists at Lenswood for over 100 years and also have extensive operations in the Riverland. Together with Andrew they have established a vineyard planted to sauvignon blanc (5.9ha), pinot noir (5.73ha), pinot gris (3.22ha), chardonnay (3.18ha) and semillon (0.47ha). The wines are made at the Pikes' Clare Valley winery. Exports to the UK, China and other major markets.

🍷🍷🍷🍷🍷 **L'optimiste Adelaide Hills Shiraz 2018** As close to perfection in balance as an imperfect world will permit. It is so light on its feet that its varietal character is gloriously juicy, yet not even close to going over the top; polished acidity is an essential part of the balance. Screwcap. 14% alc. **Rating** 98 **To** 2043 $38 ✪

🍷🍷🍷🍷🍷 **W.J.J. Reserve Adelaide Hills Pinot Noir 2017** An excellent wine taking full advantage of the vintage. The bouquet and fine-woven tannins suggest some whole bunch, but not aggressively so. I really didn't want to spit out the rainbow of red and purple fruits, spices from a big cabinet and a trace of oak. Length too. Screwcap. 13.5% alc. **Rating** 96 **To** 2032 $58 ✪
Ceder Adelaide Hills Riesling 2019 The step across from the Clare Valley to the Adelaide Hills is repaid with this utterly delicious wine that is all about caressing the mouth with its range of citrus, passionfruit and apple flavours. The long palate will coast through 15 or so years, but it's no sin to share a bottle tonight or whenever. Screwcap. 12% alc. **Rating** 95 **To** 2034 $26 ✪

The Kay Reserve Adelaide Hills Chardonnay 2018 Purity, freshness and balance are the watchwords for this lovely Adelaide Hills chardonnay. A new level of excellence for Pike & Joyce. Screwcap. 13% alc. **Rating** 95 **To** 2029 $65

The Kay Reserve Adelaide Hills Chardonnay 2017 Incredibly youthful pale green-quartz. The obvious question is how, and the answer lies in the vintage, the grapefruit and apple flavours and the crisp acidity. Striking wine with a great future. Screwcap. 13% alc. **Rating** 95 **To** 2032 $58

W.J.J. Reserve Adelaide Hills Pinot Noir 2018 Deserves the Reserve tag: the colour clear and bright, the bouquet fragrant and spicy, the palate fresh and lively. Its red berry fruits at one with the messages of the bouquet. Screwcap. 13.5% alc. **Rating** 95 **To** 2030 $65

Les Saignees Adelaide Hills Dolcetto Pinot Noir Rose 2019 Vivid crimson; most attractive, juicy red cherry/pomegranate; and great length. A really impressive wine by any standard, every reason to buy it and drink it sooner rather than later. Screwcap. 12% alc. **Rating** 94 **To** 2023 $25 ✪

Innesti Adelaide Hills Nebbiolo 2018 Nebbiolo is a struggle all the way from the vineyard to the winery to the bottle. Most difficult of all is persuading anyone that they should enjoy it. On the international stage its red/sour/fresh cherry flavours are pretty good, especially when international pricing is taken into account. Screwcap. 13.5% alc. **Rating** 94 **To** 2023 $38

♟♟♟♟♟ **Beurre Bosc Adelaide Hills Pinot Gris 2019 Rating** 93 **To** 2026 $27 ✪
Separe Adelaide Hills Gruner Veltliner 2019 Rating 92 **To** 2029 $25 ✪
Rapide Adelaide Hills Pinot Noir 2018 Rating 92 **To** 2023 $20 ✪
Sirocco Adelaide Hills Chardonnay 2018 Rating 91 **To** 2023 $32
Epice Adelaide Hills Gewurztraminer 2019 Rating 90 **To** 2024 $26

Pikes

★★★★★

Polish Hill River Road, Sevenhill, SA 5453 **Region** Clare Valley
T (08) 8843 4370 **www**.pikeswines.com.au **Open** 7 days 10–4
Winemaker Steve Baraglia **Est.** 1984 **Dozens** 35 000 **Vyds** 73ha
There have been a number of major changes in recent years at Pikes. In late '17 Andrew Pike's son Jamie returned home with extensive marketing experience gained through six years with Fine Wine Partners and several years working with a NZ winery. In November '18 the snappy new tasting room and adjoining SLATE Restaurant were opened – slate is a building/structural material widely used in the Clare Valley for fermenters. (In August '16 Pikes had been given a $320 000 grant from the government's Regional Development Fund which helped pay for these improvements.) In April '19 the Family Succession Agreement saw changes that had long since been agreed, the most important being the retirement in September '19 of Neil Pike after 35 years as chief winemaker. Andrew Pike and wife Cathryn have acquired Neil's shareholding, sister Heather remains as a shareholder and Alister Pike came on board, alongside Jamie, to run the beer operation (the brewery opened in '14). The two brothers will be the sixth generation by direct descent from patriarch Henry Pike, who arrived from England in 1878.

♟♟♟♟♟ **The E.W.P. Clare Valley Shiraz 2017** This takes its '17 Eastside sibling and increases every metric without going over the top or out of balance. This is a special wine. The tannins have complexity within a silky exterior, the fruit flavours poised between dark cherry and opulent plum. Screwcap. 14% alc. **Rating** 97 **To** 2037 $75 ✪

♟♟♟♟♟ **The Merle Clare Valley Riesling 2019** This is Pike's top of the range riesling. The powerful, layered fruits roll along the mouth; acidity there of course, but well mannered. Previous vertical tastings have left no doubt about the ability of this wine to age with grace. Screwcap. 11% alc. **Rating** 96 **To** 2034 $48 ✪

Eastside Clare Valley Shiraz 2017 From the Polish Hill River. Exceptional length and focused intensity. Has immediate appeal that grows and grows each time it is retasted; cherry and blackberry with a fine skein of tannins providing structure. A great example of the cool vintage. Screwcap. 14% alc. **Rating** 95 To 2037 $32 ○

The Plantation Clare Valley Grenache 2018 Available only through cellar door. Grenache and the Clare Valley are making firm friends, the synergy coming from a reappraisal of the picking dates (and hence alcohol). The wine is only medium-bodied but the flavour is morning fresh, red fruits sustained by a filigree of fine tannins. Screwcap. 14% alc. **Rating** 95 To 2030 $25 ○

The Hill Block Clare Valley Cabernet 2017 This nails the vintage at its best: vibrant cassis has a mouth-watering bevy of bramble and cedar that are put in their place by the purity and power of the cabernet varietal fruit. The tannins are in a similar boat – they are exactly what cabernet needs if it is to fulfil expectations. Its balance will carry its long life. Screwcap. 14% alc. **Rating** 95 To 2037 $75

Homage Clare Valley Cabernet Malbec 2018 Over the decades some great cabernet malbec blends have been made by Wendouree (and Leasingham in '71). This has glorious colour and clarity. And it's no false dawn for an elegant, medium-bodied, juicy wine that calls out 'drink me, drink me'. Screwcap. 13.5% alc. **Rating** 95 To 2028 $25 ○

Traditionale Clare Valley Riesling 2019 Traditional by all means as it winds its way across the palate in typical Pikes style, offering as much today as it will in 5+ years' time. It has the full range of riesling flavour at a minimal alcohol level. Screwcap. 11% alc. **Rating** 94 To 2029 $26 ○

The E.W.P. Clare Valley Shiraz 2016 Plum, blackberry and spice fill the fruit profile; oak and gentle tannins doing the rest. It's a flagship red, but needs a bit of mongrel to grab attention. Screwcap. 13.5% alc. **Rating** 94 To 2031 $70

Los Companeros Clare Valley Shiraz Tempranillo 2017 Fragrant red and purple fruits on the bouquet and juicy, fresh palate. The '17 vintage aids the elegance of a most enjoyable wine. It will live, but an even better approach would be early consumption. Screwcap. 14.5% alc. **Rating** 94 To 2027 $22 ○

Premio Clare Valley Sangiovese 2017 A classy sangio with the full complement of cherry allsorts and matching spices. It's supple and long, the tannins well controlled. Screwcap. 13.5% alc. **Rating** 94 To 2030 $45

🍷🍷🍷🍷🍷 **Impostores Clare Valley Savignan 2019** Rating 93 To 2021 $22 ○
The Assemblage Clare Valley Shiraz Mourvedre Grenache 2017 Rating 93 To 2027 $26 ○
Wilfred's Block Clare Valley Cabernet Shiraz 2017 Rating 93 To 2032 $36
Luccio Clare Valley Sangiovese 2018 Rating 92 To 2023 $22 ○
Gill's Farm Clare Valley Mourvedre 2018 Rating 91 To 2024 $25
Rising Ground Clare Valley Cabernet Franc 2018 Rating 90 To 2027 $25

Pindarie ★★★★★

946 Rosedale Road, Gomersal, SA 5352 **Region** Barossa Valley
T (08) 8524 9019 **www.**pindarie.com.au **Open** Mon–Fri 11–4, w'ends 11–5
Winemaker Peter Leske **Est.** 2005 **Dozens** 8000 **Vyds** 32.4ha
Owners Tony Brooks and Wendy Allan met at Roseworthy College in 1985. Tony was the sixth generation of farmers in SA and WA, and was studying agriculture; NZ-born Wendy was studying viticulture. On graduation Tony worked overseas managing sheep feedlots in Saudi Arabia, Turkey and Jordan; Wendy worked for the next 12 years with Penfolds, commencing as a grower liaison officer and working her way up to become a senior viticulturist. She also found time to study viticulture in California, Israel, Italy, Germany, France, Portugal, Spain and Chile, working vintages and assessing vineyards for wine projects. In 2001 she completed a graduate diploma in wine business. The cellar door and the Grain Store cafe (winner of Australian tourism awards in '13 and '14 as well as Hall of fame for SA Tourism) has panoramic views. Exports to Taiwan and China.

🍷🍷🍷🍷🍷 **Western Ridge Barossa Valley Shiraz 2018** Made from the celebrated Barossa clone 1654; part fermented in tank, part open-fermented, 10 months in 95% French and 5% American oak (25% new). Inky deep purple; despite its colour, controlled extraction of an utterly delicious, utterly typical Barossa shiraz. Was awarded the intensely sought after trophy at the '19 Barossa Valley Wine Show for Best '18 Shiraz. The balance is flawless, the screwcap guaranteeing a nigh-on eternal life. 14% alc. **Rating** 97 **To** 2048 $28 **○**

Black Hinge Reserve Barossa Valley Shiraz 2017 A barely 20yo vineyard (planted to clone 1654) performing in a great vintage starts the discussion. Selected rows hand-picked, 6% saignee (juice run off), 8 days on skins, matured for 16 months in French oak (20% new). A brilliantly savoury, mouth-watering wine of dazzling length and complexity; 15% alcohol is just a number here. Cork. **Rating** 97 **To** 2047 $75 **○**

♥♥♥♥♥ **Schoff's Hill Barossa Valley Cabernet Sauvignon 2018** Planted '01; machine-harvested after midnight, whole-berry fermented. Deep colour. Supple, smooth — indeed succulent — layers of finely stitched velvet. Very good length, likewise balance. Masterly control of extract. Screwcap. 13.5% alc. **Rating** 95 **To** 2038 $35 **○**

♥♥♥♥♡ **Black Hinge Reserve Tempranillo 2017** **Rating** 91 **To** 2035 $50
Small Block Montepulciano 2018 **Rating** 90 **To** 2028 $30

Pipers Brook Vineyard   ★★★★★

1216 Pipers Brook Road, Pipers Brook, Tas 7254 **Region** Northern Tasmania
T (03) 6382 7555 **www.**kreglingerwineestates.com **Open** 7 days 10–5
Winemaker Luke Whittle **Est.** 1974 **Dozens** 70 000 **Vyds** 176.51ha

The Pipers Brook empire has almost 200ha of vineyard supporting the Ninth Island, Pipers Brook and Kreglinger labels with the major focus, of course, being on Pipers Brook. Fastidious viticulture and a passionate winemaking team along with immaculate packaging and enterprising marketing create a potent and effective blend. Pipers Brook operates a cellar door at the winery and is owned by Belgian-owned sheepskin business Kreglinger, which has also established the large Norfolk Rise Vineyard at Mount Benson in SA (see separate entry). Exports to the UK, the US and other major markets.

♥♥♥♥♥ **Rose 2019** Rose. Just like this. Delicious. It is dry and refreshing, textural and savoury thanks to barrel fermentation and incorporating a sprinkling of ginger spice over just-ripe red berries. Screwcap. 13.5% alc. **Rating** 95 **To** 2023 $50 JF

Reserve Pinot Noir 2018 A similar make-up to the straight pinot, just a tad more oak — 30% new French puncheons and barriques, aged 1 year. There's a bit more shape to the tannins, still plush and soft with requisite cherries and spice, hint of forest floor/humus. Again, a delicacy to this and very drinkable. Screwcap. 13.8% alc. **Rating** 95 **To** 2028 $65 JF

New Certan Pinot Noir 2018 A deceptive wine; it seems quite aloof with a flutter of fragrance, all lovely and restrained. Then the savouriness kicks in, abetted by the charry oak helping to bolster the tannins. It lingers. The acidity and the blood orange, zesty and juicy, all add to the pleasure. Screwcap. 13.2% alc. **Rating** 95 **To** 2030 $95 JF

Pinot Noir 2018 A pretty and surprisingly lighter-framed pinot with its delicate florals, cherries and spice. Still delicious though with supple, soft tannins, crunchy watermelon and tangy pomegranate-like acidity. Dangerously easy to drink. Screwcap. 13.5% alc. **Rating** 94 **To** 2026 $50 JF

♥♥♥♥♡ **Chardonnay 2018** **Rating** 93 **To** 2029 $45 JF
Kreglinger Vintage Brut 2015 **Rating** 93 $55 JF
Ninth Island Sparkling Rose NV **Rating** 93 $23 JF **○**
Ninth Island Riesling 2019 **Rating** 92 **To** 2028 $25 JF **○**
Gewurztraminer 2019 **Rating** 91 **To** 2025 $35 JF

Pirathon

979 Light Pass Road, Vine Vale, SA 5352 **Region** Barossa Valley
T (08) 7200 0129 **www**.pirathon.com **Open** By appt
Winemaker Adam Clay **Est.** 2005 **Dozens** 9000

Pirathon is a one-variety company that focuses on full-bodied Barossa Valley shiraz from the north-western Barossa area, encompassing Greenock, Moppa, Belvedere, Koonunga and Ebenezer; each district contributing to the complexity of the wine. Exports to all major markets.

ΥΥΥΥΥ **Gold Barossa Valley Shiraz 2016** Matured in French oak, 67% new. It's an incredibly smoky and an incredibly tannic wine with tar, salted caramel, licorice, coconut and spearmint flavours gushing through. The smokiness of this wine can't be emphasised enough; it makes for a distinctive profile. This wine's huge arms of tannin and big body of baked fruit will see it live and mature for a whopping long time. Screwcap. 15% alc. **Rating** 94 **To** 2045 $100 CM
Black Barossa Valley Shiraz 2016 Sweet, ripe, simple and warm but the volume of flavour and the swagger of tannin makes for a pretty convincing package. Porty blackberries with asphalt and wood smoke flavours drifting through. Nice and firm, which it needed to be. Screwcap. 15% alc. **Rating** 94 **To** 2032 $50 CM

ΥΥΥΥΥ **Blue Barossa Valley Shiraz 2017 Rating** 93 **To** 2027 $21 CM ○
Silver Barossa Valley Shiraz 2017 Rating 92 **To** 2026 $26 CM

Pirramimma

Johnston Road, McLaren Vale, SA 5171 **Region** McLaren Vale
T (08) 8323 8205 **www**.pirramimma.com.au **Open** Mon–Fri 10–4.30, w'ends & public hols 10.30–5
Winemaker Geoff Johnston **Est.** 1892 **Dozens** 50 000 **Vyds** 91.5ha

A long-established family-owned company with outstanding vineyard resources, which it is using to full effect. A series of intense old vine varietals includes semillon, sauvignon blanc, chardonnay, shiraz, grenache, cabernet sauvignon and petit verdot, all fashioned without over-embellishment. Wines are released in several ranges: Pirramimma, Stock's Hill, White Label, ACJ, Katunga, Eight Carat and Gilded Lilly. Exports to all major markets.

ΥΥΥΥΥ **Vineyard Select McLaren Vale Petit Verdot Shiraz 2015** A savvy move to meld such a late ripening variety as verdot with the excessive shiraz – a grape better grown in cooler zones than McLaren Vale or Barossa. As contentious as my view may be, I will voice it. Verdot's indomitable carapace of tannins holds court to shiraz's dark fruit tones. Shiraz wants to billow across the mouth and overwhelm everything in its path in a soporific claim to fame, however short-lived. Verdot has other ideas. For the better. Pulpy. Firm. Delicious. Screwcap. **Rating** 95 **To** 2030 $35 NG ○
Katunga McLaren Vale GTS 2016 An intelligent blend of grenache, providing the kirsch in the fore; shiraz, the plum midriff; and the ferrously grippy tannat, the seams across the aft. This is very Rhône-like, despite the uncanny make-up. The savoury tapenade, briar, bitter chocolate and thyme to rosemary scents splayed across the expansive finish are highly attractive. This rich red boasts exceptional value for money and frankly, could be twice the price. Screwcap. **Rating** 94 **To** 2025 $25 NG ○
Vineyard Select McLaren Vale GSM 2016 The grenache hails from an old plot dating from the '40s, the shiraz and mourvedre also from esteemed sites. The grenache was handled in 600l puncheons for brightness, the other varieties in older wood for texture and gentle tone. Again, strongly reminiscent of a wine from the southern Rhône, except for the tangy acidity. Sturdy, with a core of morello cherry, cranberry and raspberry bonbon, all slathered in dried herb, anise, scrub and black olive notes. Another value-add to the range. Screwcap. **Rating** 94 **To** 2026 $35 NG

McLaren Vale Cabernet Sauvignon 2017 These have always been unashamedly rich wines, exploiting the maritime cooling breezes and Mediterranean warmth of the Vale. But in the best sense. This is an amped-up, full-bodied dry red with cooler spearmint and herbal drifts of cabernet serving as a soprano of freshness juxtaposed against a phalanx of cherry, plum and darker fruit allusions. Long and quintessentially cabernet. Screwcap. **Rating** 94 **To** 2031 $22 NG⊙

ΥΥΥΥΥ **Stock's Hill Cabernet Merlot 2017 Rating** 93 **To** 2029 $22 NG⊙
Ironstone Petit Verdot 2015 Rating 92 **To** 2030 $70 NG
Limited Edition Petit Verdot 2016 Rating 91 **To** 2028 $50 NG

Pizzini   ★★★★★

175 King Valley Road, Whitfield, Vic 3768 **Region** King Valley
T (03) 5729 8278 **www**.pizzini.com.au **Open** 7 days 10–5
Winemaker Joel Pizzini **Est.** 1980 **Dozens** 30 000 **Vyds** 88.3ha
Fred and Katrina Pizzini have been grapegrowers in the King Valley for over 30 years. Originally much of the grape production was sold, but today it's retained for the Pizzini brand and the focus is on winemaking, which has been particularly successful. Indeed, Pizzini's success has resulted in an increase in its vineyard holdings to almost 90ha, and an increase in production (with more to come). The hectareage of its alternative varieties speaks for itself: 13.3ha of prosecco, 3.22ha brachetto, 2ha colorino, 2ha arneis, 1.5ha piccolit, 1.3ha verdicchio, 1.3ha verduzzo and 0.43ha trebbiano. Exports to the UK and Japan.

ΥΥΥΥΥ **King Valley Riesling 2019** Sourced from a young, hillside block. Machine-harvested at night, crushed, destemmed, pressed lightly, cool fermentation in stainless steel. Light lime-green. An array of florals – citrus blossom, honeysuckle, lavender – and so pretty. The touch of savouriness on the palate deserves your attention; this is a serious riesling with green apple, grapefruit, orange peel, preserved lemon spice. Steely too, in a tight and lean way. A wine to age. Screwcap. 11.7% alc. **Rating** 95 **To** 2030 $20 JP ⊙

Il Barone 2018 Made with 48/22/18/7/5% cabernet sauvignon/shiraz/sangiovese/nebbiolo/teroldego. Each variety fermented separately in a mix of stainless steel and oak, aged up to 12 months in a variety of French oak barrels (55% new), and then aged a further 6–12 months in bottle. A confident, expressive and delicious blend with each variety bringing something to the 5-member team. Earth, red and sour cherry clafoutis; anise, light herbals. A real Aussie blend – a mash-up of our favourite red grapes and some new chums. Round at heart and fine in figure. The five varieties would not be guessed. Teroldego? What are the chances? This is Pizzini's call to arms, to think differently, to challenge. Screwcap. 13.8% alc. **Rating** 95 **To** 2035 $45 JP

King Valley Nebbiolo 2015 Hand-harvested, crushed, destemmed, fermentation inoculated with yeast from Barolo, ferment finished in oak, mlf, matured in barrels for 20 months (20% new). Red with an orange hint. Utterly beguiling scent of Aussie bush, licorice, mandarin skin, sweet potpourri with a ferrous edge. Fine-lined throughout, angled nicely by tannin. Still a pup at 5yo. Give it 5 more, at least. Screwcap. 13.8% alc. **Rating** 95 **To** 2033 $55 JP

White Fields King Valley Pinot Grigio 2018 Pinot grigio gets deluxe treatment with 2 parcels of grapes from Whitlands – the highest, coolest part of the King Valley – hand-picked and placed in a cool room for 2 days, then pressed. One portion was fermented in oak with wild yeast, balance fermented in stainless steel with lees stirring for 5 months. Straw-green. Whitlands hits the mark with cool-climate fruit intensity and marked acidity. Concentrated and fine-edged apple, nettle, saline almost briny with acid crunch and just a little grassy sauvignon-like at times. Screwcap. 12.5% alc. **Rating** 94 **To** 2026 $28 JP ⊙

Pietra Rossa King Valley Sangiovese 2017 Machine-picked, fermented with Italian yeast, hot fermentation, mlf, barrel ageing for 14 months (20% new).

Pietra Rossa is Italian for red stone and makes perfect sense, the Valley's rock and iron oxide–rich soils is on display in both the appearance of the wine and effortless structure. It's all about bright red fruits – cherries, plums, cranberries – with balanced spicing, a gentle savouriness. Plush in the middle with a redcurrant tartness to close. Screwcap. 13.5% alc. **Rating** 94 **To** 2028 $28 JP ✪

Coronamento King Valley Nebbiolo 2015 Nebbiolo 230 clone; selected on grape bunches, crushed, destemmed into small fermentation vats, inoculated with Barolo yeast, 4–5 days' hot fermentation, aged in new French 500l oak barrels for 2 years. Shy not punchy. Delicate aroma of musk, roses, red fruits, Chinotto. Be patient. It invites you to look a little harder and see a nebbiolo that isn't immediately powerful but subtle. It's in building mode, just getting started, but the structure is there, as is the beauty. It's just going to take time. Screwcap. 13.8% alc. **Rating** 94 **To** 2035 $140 JP

♟♟♟♟♀ **Il Soffio Prosecco 2019 Rating** 93 $28 JP
Nonna Gisella Sangiovese 2018 Rating 92 **To** 2026 $22 JP ✪
King Valley Pinot Grigio 2019 Rating 91 **To** 2026 $21 JP ✪
King Valley Shiraz 2018 Rating 91 **To** 2026 $25 JP
La Volpe King Valley Nebbiolo 2018 Rating 91 **To** 2032 $28 JP
King Valley Rosetta 2019 Rating 90 **To** 2026 $19 JP ✪
Teroldego 2019 Rating 90 **To** 2027 $25 JP

Plan B Wines ★★★★★

Freshwater Drive, Margaret River, WA 6285 **Region** South West Australia zone
T 0413 759 030 **www.**planbwines.com **Open** Not
Winemaker Vanessa Carson **Est.** 2005 **Dozens** 40 000 **Vyds** 20ha
Founded by Terry Chellappah (wine consultant), Bill Crappsley (veteran winemaker/ consultant) and Andrew Blythe, Plan B is now owned and run by Terry 'between rocking the bass guitar and researching bars'. He says he is better at one than the other. Plan B has been notably successful, with significant increases in production. Winemaker Vanessa Carson has made wine in Margaret River and Frankland Valley, as well as in Italy and France, juggling winemaking and raising three children. Exports to all major markets.

♟♟♟♟♟ **DR Great Southern Riesling 2019** Includes 57% Frankland River, 43% Mount Barker; crushed and destemmed, only free-run juice used. A riveting young riesling with citrus, lime leaf and green apple driving the long palate and aftertaste. Screwcap. 12.5% alc. **Rating** 96 **To** 2032 $25 ✪
GT Gran Turismo 2018 Made from 60% cabernet sauvignon, 40% sangiovese. A very, very attractive regional and varietal blend. It is uncommon to strike synergy as bold and successful as this. Screwcap. 14% alc. **Rating** 95 **To** 2028 $25 ✪

♟♟♟♟♀ **The King Margaret River Chardonnay 2018 Rating** 93 **To** 2027 $30
TR Ferguson Valley Tempranillo Rose 2019 Rating 93 **To** 2021 $25 ✪
MB Frankland River Sauvignon Blanc 2018 Rating 92 **To** 2030 $20 ✪
OD Frankland River Riesling 2019 Rating 92 $25 ✪
ST Frankland River Shiraz 2017 Rating 91 **To** 2028 $25
CC Geographe Cabernet Sauvignon 2018 Rating 90 **To** 2030 $25
CC Geographe Cabernet Sauvignon 2017 Rating 90 **To** 2038 $25

Plantagenet ★★★★★

Albany Highway, Mount Barker, WA 6324 **Region** Mount Barker
T (08) 9851 3111 **www.**plantagenetwines.com **Open** 7 days 10–4.30
Winemaker Luke Eckerseley, Chris Murtha **Est.** 1968 **Dozens** 30 000 **Vyds** 130ha
Plantagenet was established by Tony Smith, who continues to be involved in its management over 45 years later, notwithstanding that it has been owned by Lionel Samson & Son for many years. He established five vineyards: Bouverie in 1968 (sold in 2017), Wyjup in '71,

Rocky Horror 1 in '88, Rocky Horror 2 in '97 and Rosetta in '99. These vineyards are the cornerstones of the substantial production of the consistently high quality wines that have always been the mark of Plantagenet: highly aromatic Riesling, tangy citrus-tinged Chardonnay, glorious Rhône-style Shiraz and ultra-stylish Cabernet Sauvignon. Exports to the UK, Canada, Japan, Hong Kong and China.

ҬҬҬҬҬ **Lancaster Great Southern Shiraz 2018** Great Southern shiraz (this wine is from Mount Barker) has a precision and a sense of inevitability about it: the depth and hue of the colour, the freshly picked fruit, the multi-spices, the cracked pepper, the persuasive tannins and the length. Screwcap. 14.5% alc. **Rating** 96 **To** 2033 $45 ✪

Wyjup Collection Mount Barker Shiraz 2017 Cool-climate shiraz at its best with a highly expressive mix of warm spices and cedar threaded through the medium-bodied array of dark cherry, plum and blackberry fruit flavours. The lithe mouthfeel and texture of the wine set it apart from its white siblings. Screwcap. 14% alc. **Rating** 96 **To** 2038 $80

Angevin Great Southern Riesling 2019 From 40+yo vines, fermented with cultured yeast. Hand of man or machine? It really doesn't matter. Place and variety do. Screwcap. 12.5% alc. **Rating** 95 **To** 2030 $32 ✪

Wyjup Collection Mount Barker Riesling 2018 The wine's display of lime, Meyer lemon and toast will build slowly but surely over the next 10 years. 'Surely' because the wine was born with perfect balance and great length, attesting to its ancestry. Screwcap. 12.5% alc. **Rating** 95 **To** 2030 $45

Wyjup Collection Mount Barker Chardonnay 2018 Gleaming straw-green. Pink grapefruit and white peach on the one hand, acidity and creamy cashew characters on the other. These coalesce on a continuous stream of flavour derived from fruit, not oak. Screwcap. 13% alc. **Rating** 94 **To** 2028 $70

ҬҬҬҬҬ **Aquitaine Cabernet Sauvignon 2018 Rating** 93 **To** 2030 $45
Three Lions Riesling 2019 Rating 92 **To** 2029 $23 ✪
Three Lions Chardonnay 2019 Rating 90 **To** 2028 $25
York Chardonnay 2019 Rating 90 **To** 2030 $40
Three Lions Pinot Noir 2019 Rating 90 **To** 2024 $40
Normand Pinot Noir 2019 Rating 90 **To** 2027 $40

Poacher's Ridge Vineyard   ★★★★★

1630 Spencer Road, Narrikup, WA 6326 **Region** Mount Barker
T (08) 9857 6066 **www.**poachersridge.com.au **Open** Fri–Sun 10–4
Winemaker Robert Diletti (Contract) **Est.** 2000 **Dozens** 1200 **Vyds** 6.9ha
Alex and Janet Taylor purchased the Poacher's Ridge property in 1999. It had previously been used for cattle grazing. The vineyard includes shiraz, cabernet sauvignon, merlot, riesling, marsanne, viognier and malbec. Winning the Tri Nations 2007 merlot class against the might of Australia, NZ and South Africa with its '05 Louis' Block Great Southern Merlot was a dream come true. And it wasn't a one-time success – Poacher's Ridge Merlot is always at, or near, the top of the tree. Exports to Malaysia and Singapore.

ҬҬҬҬҬ **Great Southern Riesling 2019** Only free-run juice is used, and cold-settled. The vinification has only one purpose: to produce the best quality wine from grapes picked at their optimum – between 11.5° and 12° baume and 9–10g/l of acid. However delicious now, wait 5 years for the flavours to gather pace and soar on the wings of the acidity. Screwcap. 12.5% alc. **Rating** 95 **To** 2029 $28 ✪

Great Southern Shiraz 2018 Crushed and destemmed, fermented with cultured yeast, 7 days' maturation post-ferment, matured in French barriques (30% new) for 15 months. Lovely wine. Abundant plum and blackberry fruit in a supple frame. Great balance. Screwcap. 13.8% alc. **Rating** 95 **To** 2033 $34 ✪

Great Southern Cabernet Sauvignon 2018 Hand-picked from selected low-yielding vines in Louis Block, crushed and destemmed, pumpovers post-fermentation, matured for 16 months in French oak (30% new). A high quality wine in every way: quality of fruit, winemaking skill, clear-cut varietal expression. Over-delivers. Screwcap. 13.7% alc. **Rating** 95 **To** 2038 $34 ✪

Great Southern Merlot 2018 Hand-picked, crushed and destemmed into overhead fermenters, 7 days' post-ferment maceration, matured in French oak (20% new) for 16 months. Elegant medium-bodied wine with very good varietal character on show. Purple and red berry fruits, good oak maturation. Screwcap. 12.5% alc. **Rating** 94 **To** 2032 $34

Great Southern Malbec 2018 From 19yo vines. The usual Poacher's Ridge fermentation method but maturation in new French barriques for 16 months imposes itself on the wine. Screwcap. 12.5% alc. **Rating** 94 **To** 2033 $46

Poachers Vineyard   ★★★★★

Marakei-Nanima Road, via Hall, NSW 2618 **Region** Canberra District
T (02) 6230 2487 **www.**poacherspantry.com.au **Open** 7 days 10–5
Winemaker Will Bruce **Est.** 1998 **Dozens** 3500 **Vyds** 18.5ha
Poachers Vineyard, owned by the Bruce family, shares its home with the Poachers Pantry, a renowned gourmet smokehouse. The quality of the wines is very good; they are a testament to the skills of the contract winemakers. The northeast-facing slopes, at an elevation of 720m, provide some air drainage and hence protection against spring frosts.

🍷🍷🍷🍷🍷 **Canberra District Riesling 2019** Hand-picked, whole bunches pressed straight into stainless steel tanks for fermentation, wine held on lees before bottling. Apples galore in this cool-climate, stylish riesling. Spring blossom and apple: Gala and Red Delicious with spiced baked apple to finish off the trifecta. Lemon and grapefruit mingle on the palate, acidity is keen and you have to love that touch of lime cordial and nougat confection notes to close. Refreshing and bright with ageing on its side. Screwcap. 11.5% alc. **Rating** 95 **To** 2041 $26 JP ✪

Canberra District Sauvignon Blanc 2019 Hand-picked, whole-bunch pressed to stainless steel, 10% fermented on skins in ceramic pots, held on lees until bottling. Enter the exciting new world of sauvignon blanc, toned down and exploring other facets to its personality. These are exciting times for the grape, so give wines like this another look. Complexity and focus are the keywords with pink grapefruit, preserved lemon, lime and a fresh, mineral lift. Honeysuckle, juicy apple, citrus flavours at the core with a kind of kulfi ice-cream, cardamom, pistachio input. Round in the middle, crunchy on the outside. Screwcap. 12% alc. **Rating** 95 **To** 2025 $25 JP ✪

Canberra District Syrah 2018 Hand-picked, fermented in 2t, open top fermenters, 30% whole bunches incorporated into the ferment and pumped over twice a day. Matured in French oak (15% new) for 11 months. Boasts all of Canberra's shiraz qualities: medium in weight, pleasing black fruit intensity, high spice, touch of pepper. Seems to be a lot more going on here than you might expect. There's also the fineness and slippery smooth palate with well balanced tannins. One to savour. Screwcap. 13% alc. **Rating** 94 **To** 2038 $29 JP ✪

🍷🍷🍷🍷🍷 **Canberra District Pinot Noir 2018 Rating** 93 **To** 2028 $28 JP

Pooley Wines   ★★★★★

Butcher's Hill Vineyard, 1431 Richmond Road, Richmond, Tas 7025
Region Southern Tasmania
T (03) 6260 2895 **www.**pooleywines.com.au **Open** 7 days 10–5
Winemaker Anna Pooley **Est.** 1985 **Dozens** 5000 **Vyds** 16ha
Three generations of the Pooley family have been involved in the development of Pooley Wines, although the winery was previously known as Cooinda Vale. Plantings have now reached 16ha in a region that is warmer and drier than most people realise. In 2003 the family planted pinot noir and pinot grigio (with more recent plantings of pinot noir and chardonnay) at Belmont Vineyard, a heritage property with an 1830s Georgian home and a (second) cellar door in the old sandstone barn and stables.

ⵂⵂⵂⵂⵂ **Butcher's Hill Single Vineyard Riesling 2019** The inaugural release from Pooley's highest site, facing northeast. The fruit is whole-bunch pressed to stainless steel, selected yeast and on fine lees for 6 months. It's a dynamo of a wine. Powerful with complex flavours; not overt citrus, although there's a flourish of lemony freshness. Expect quince paste, beeswax, hoya floral aromas and savoury nuances. Fabulous energy across the palate is at once textural yet finely tuned. 13.8% alc. **Rating** 96 **To** 2030 $65 JF ✪

Margaret Pooley Tribute Single Vineyard Riesling 2019 Fruit from Cooinda Vale planted in '85 and the DNA stamp is clear. While it has a backbone of fine acidity charging like an electric current, it's the slate-like, lemon-pith texture that sets it apart. A beautifully composed wine ready for the taking, but will reward the patient. Screwcap. 13.5% alc. **Rating** 96 **To** 2035 $75 JF ✪

Cooinda Vale Single Vineyard Chardonnay 2018 Now isn't this a funky number. It's flinty and fabulous. A balanced combo of stone fruit, citrus, kaffir lime with oak spices and a fluffy cream curd. So moreish, savoury and, while flavoursome, it is ethereal with a gossamer thread of acidity linking it all. Wow. Screwcap. 13.5% alc. **Rating** 96 **To** 2030 $65 JF ✪

Cooinda Vale Oronsay Single Vineyard Pinot Noir 2018 A new wine, named after the ship that brought Anna Pooley's father and grandparents to Australia after the Second World War. It was a brave step into the great unknown, as is this pinot. Pommard clone; 100% whole-bunches, wild fermented and aged in 2 French puncheons (one new) for a year; only 768 bottles. It's fabulous. Sapid as much as stemmy, but ripe, raspberry-rhubarb flavoured stems. Pepper and cardamom infuse the cherry fruit; structured but not dense because the acidity is refreshing and bright, the tannins precise and the finish long. Screwcap. 13% alc. **Rating** 96 **To** 2033 $110 JF

Jack Denis Pooley Single Vineyard Pinot Noir 2018 All about attention to detail here as apparently this is about fruit selection from 2 sites at Cooinda Vale, the tagged bunches identified as making the most powerful expression of the vineyard. Destemmed, whole berries, wild ferment and aged in French barriques (60% new) for 1 year. That oak is seamlessly integrated, the fruit deliciously succulent, the tannins pliant and shapely with a tang to the acidity, which merely sets you up for another sip. Screwcap. 13% alc. **Rating** 96 **To** 2033 $140 JF

Coal River Valley Riesling 2019 Fruit comes off Butcher's Hill 60% and Cooinda Vale 40%, whole-bunch pressed, selected yeast and into stainless steel. All rudimentary yet the wine performs; it has lovely florals, a citrus theme of kaffir lime leaves, lemon pith and juice. Nothing harsh about the palate. It has texture, flavour and fine, almost soft, acidity in the lead. A lovely drink. Screwcap. 13.9% alc. **Rating** 95 **To** 2029 $39 JF

Butcher's Hill Single Vineyard Chardonnay 2018 Poise and power in equal measure. Balanced flavours of white stone fruit sprinkled with lemon zest, ginger and oak spices. Finely tuned across the palate with texture from the lees influence, but still strikingly fine from its acidity. Screwcap. 13.5% alc. **Rating** 95 **To** 2028 $65 JF

Pinot Noir 2018 A perfect introduction to Tasmanian pinot noir generally and Pooley in particular. A core of succulent fruit, spiced black cherries and plums with a hint of forest floor and orange zest with oak imparting flavour and tannins. There's depth and complexity with supple tannins. Everything sits just right. Screwcap. 13.5% alc. **Rating** 95 **To** 2028 $46 JF

Cooinda Vale Single Vineyard Pinot Noir 2018 What a glorious wine. Immediately enticing with its heady aromas. Florals, humus, raspberries, cherries, bitter orange and no shortage of spices. It has an energy across the palate with a cooling menthol character and fine tannins. It seems at first delicate but it has plenty of definition. Screwcap. 13% alc. **Rating** 95 **To** 2030 $65 JF

Jack Denis Pooley Single Vineyard Pinot Noir 2017 Has the typically good depth and hue of Pooley. A very powerful pinot that has made light work of the 33% new French oak in which it was matured. Its red and purple fruits drive through a long palate and lingering aftertaste. This is Tasmania speaking. Screwcap. 13% alc. **Rating** 95 **To** 2027 $140

Clarence House Vineyard Single Vineyard Pinot Noir 2017 Purchased fruit off a 23yo vineyard, clone 777; destemmed whole berries, wild fermentation, aged in French barriques (35% new) for 14 months. This is no wallflower. It's a powerhouse of black cherries, mushrooms, earth and fresh herbs; lots of intense flavours and oak input. Full-bodied and grunt to the tannins – the sandpaper-textural type that leaves a mark. Obviously, this needs time. Screwcap. 14% alc. **Rating** 95 **To** 2032 $65 JF

J.R.D. Single Vineyard Syrah 2018 It's cool and cooling with its raspberry accents infused with black pepper and a touch of more exotic Sichuan pepper. But the highlight is the palate. Medium-bodied with a minerally sensation to the acidity. Prosciutto flavour, woodsy spices and the fine yet grainy tannins. It's a delicious drink and compelling at the same time. Screwcap. 14% alc. **Rating** 95 **To** 2028 $110 JF

Butcher's Hill Late Harvest Riesling 2019 This fruit comes in 5 weeks after the dry riesling is picked and put to bed. Crushed, destemmed and soaked overnight on skins, pressed to stainless steel tanks, wild fermentation and left on fine lees for 4 months. A heady elixir of poached stone fruit drizzled with honey and lemon curd, a touch of apricot compote too. The delicious sweetness tamed by the acidity. Screwcap. 13.8% alc. **Rating** 95 **To** 2028 $75 JF

ΨΨΨΨΨ **Butcher's Hill Single Vineyard Pinot Noir 2018 Rating** 93 **To** 2028 $65 JF
Cooinda Vale Pinot Noir Rose 2019 Rating 91 **To** 2020 $50 JF

Poonawatta   ★★★★★

1227 Eden Valley Road, Flaxman Valley, SA 5235 **Region** Eden Valley
T 0448 031 880 **www**.poonawatta.com.au **Open** By appt
Winemaker Andrew Holt, Christa Deans, Harry Mantzarapis **Est.** 1880 **Dozens** 1800
Vyds 4ha

The Poonawatta story is complex, stemming from 0.8ha of shiraz planted in 1880. When Andrew Holt's parents purchased the Poonawatta property, the vineyard had suffered decades of neglect and the slow process of restoration began. While that was underway, the strongest canes available from the winter pruning of the block were slowly and progressively dug into the stony soil, establishing the Cuttings Block over seven years, and the yield is even lower than that of the 1880 Block. The Riesling is produced from a separate vineyard planted by the Holts in the 1970s. Exports to Canada, France, Denmark, Malaysia, Taiwan and China.

ΨΨΨΨΨ **The Eden Riesling 2019** The near-50yo vineyard planted '72 typically yields 2t/a. This is a majestic wine, filling every corner of the mouth with layer upon layer of lime and Meyer lemon juice flavours. A great bargain, that could command twice its price. Screwcap. 12.2% alc. **Rating** 97 **To** 2034 $30 ✪

Museum Release The 1880 Eden Valley Shiraz 2010 From the 0.8ha of original vines; hand-picked, open-fermented, 18 months in very tight grain barriques. While this was tasted from a 750ml bottle, the principal release is in magnum. Last tasted in Mar '14; it is coasting along, its purple colour a flag of celebration. Cork. 14.7% alc. **Rating** 97 **To** 2035 $300

Museum Release The Cuttings Eden Valley Shiraz 2010 This has matured extremely well over the last 6 years. My original tasting note described the fruits as sombre, a word I would now extend to The 1880. Remarkably, this wine has revealed more primary black fruits and hence a more immediate welcome to the mouth. Screwcap. 14.8% alc. **Rating** 97 **To** 2035 $150 ✪

ΨΨΨΨΨ **Museum Release The Eden Riesling 2015** Bright straw-green. Its sibling relationship with the '19 is crystal clear – simply double the depth of the '19 and do no more, except rush to stock up with this very complex, perfectly balanced wine. Screwcap. 12% alc. **Rating** 96 **To** 2034 $35 ✪

The Cuttings Eden Valley Shiraz 2016 The cuttings were taken from the original 1880 plantings in the late '70s–early '80s. Open-fermented, matured for 18 months in French barriques (25% new). Deep crimson-purple. Full-bodied with no apologies for the level of fruit and oak extract that keeps the resentful tannins at bay. Screwcap. 14.5% alc. Rating 95 To 2036 $49

Museum Release The Four Corners of Eden Valley Grenache Shiraz 2012 This 52/48% blend comes from the wonderful '12 vintage. Moreover, the grenache comes from the utterly exceptional 1858 Stonegarden Vineyard. It's close to its peak now, but won't drop dead in its tracks for years to come. This is history made cheap. Screwcap. 14.2% alc. Rating 94 To 2029 $38

Museum Release The Four Corners of Eden Valley Cabernet Shiraz 2012 A 52/48% blend, the cabernet from Bob's Block in the Barossa Valley, the shiraz from the Four Corners Vineyard in the Eden Valley; matured for 18 months in French barriques. The power and youth of the wine is well beyond normal, as is the savoury length and finish. Needs more time. Screwcap. 13.9% alc. Rating 94 To 2032 $38

🍷🍷🍷🍷🍷 BS Barossa Shiraz 2017 Rating 93 To 2030 $23 ✪
Museum Release The Four Corners of Eden Valley Shiraz Cabernet 2011 Rating 92 To 2029 $38

Port Phillip Estate   ★★★★★

263 Red Hill Road, Red Hill, Vic 3937 **Region** Mornington Peninsula
T (03) 5989 4444 **www**.portphillipestate.com.au **Open** 7 days 11–5
Winemaker Glen Hayley **Est.** 1987 **Dozens** 7000 **Vyds** 9.3ha
Port Phillip Estate has been owned by Giorgio and Dianne Gjergja since 2000. The ability of the site to produce outstanding syrah, pinot noir and chardonnay, and very good sauvignon blanc, is something special. In July '15, following the departure of winemaker Sandro Mosele, his assistant of six years, Glen Hayley, was appointed to take his place. The futuristic, multimillion-dollar restaurant, cellar door and winery complex, designed by award-winning Wood/Marsh Architecture, overlooks the vineyards and Westernport Bay. Exports to Canada and China.

🍷🍷🍷🍷🍷 Single Vineyard Red Hill Chardonnay 2018 Full, bright yellow-gold. A very complex bouquet with some reduction. The palate takes over with drive and freshness courtesy of citrussy acidity, oak in the background. Excellent value. Screwcap. 13% alc. Rating 96 To 2032 $37 ✪

Morillon Single Block Mornington Peninsula Pinot Noir 2018 Wild-fermented in large oak foudres, 10 days on skins, pressed and racked into French barriques (20% new) for 14 months. Has succeeded handsomely, with a bright array of red and blue fruits, very good tannins and overall finesse. Screwcap. 13.5% alc. Rating 96 To 2033 $61 ✪

Mornington Peninsula Shiraz 2018 From a 0.5ha estate block, wild-fermented with a small amount of whole bunches in an open-top concrete fermenter for 17 days, matured for 13 months in old French barriques. Very deep colour. Mornington Peninsula and shiraz combine brilliantly in warm vintages, the fruit doing all the heavy lifting without any complaint. Satsuma plum, dark chocolate and blackberries are all there. Screwcap. 13.5% alc. Rating 96 To 2028 $39 ✪

Morillon Single Block Mornington Peninsula Chardonnay 2018 This is the inaugural vintage of the wine from the '88 planting hitherto not released as a single wine, previously used as a blend component. Whole-bunch pressed to French barriques, wild-fermented and matured for 11 months. Obvious colour development. It's easy to see why this should have been made as a single wine – it has greater depth and roundness than its siblings with stone fruit, melon and fig setting the pace, oak integrated. Screwcap. 13.5% alc. Rating 95 To 2028 $54

Salasso Mornington Peninsula Rose 2019 Estate shiraz and pinot, whole-bunch pressed, wild-fermented in used French barriques, then on lees for several months. Pink with a touch of salmon. The scented bouquet introduces a fruity/savoury mix on the track through to the finish. Screwcap. 13.5% alc. **Rating** 94 **To** 2023 $26 **✿**

ΨΨΨΨΨ **Single Vineyard Balnarring Chardonnay 2018 Rating** 93 **To** 2027 $37
Single Vineyard Red Hill Pinot Noir 2018 Rating 93 **To** 2028 $39
Mornington Peninsula Sauvignon 2019 Rating 90 **To** 2023 $27

Portsea Estate ★★★★★

7 Pembroke Place, Portsea, Vic 3944 **Region** Mornington Peninsula
T (03) 5984 3774 **www**.portseaestate.com **Open** By appt
Winemaker Tim Elphick **Est.** 2000 **Dozens** 3500 **Vyds** 4ha
Noted filmmaker Warwick Ross and sister (silent partner) Caron Wilson-Hawley have moved fast and successfully since the first vintage in 2004. Starting out with the luxury of having the first seven vintages made at Paringa Estate by Lindsay McCall and team, Portsea Estate has now built an onsite winery and hired Tim Elphick, who has a wealth of cool-climate winemaking experience. Warwick's film *Red Obsession* was given high ratings by film critics around the world. It takes an inside look at the Chinese fascination for the greatest wines of Bordeaux.

ΨΨΨΨΨ **Estate Syrah 2017** From a single vineyard at Tuerong, 5 days' cold soak, open-fermented, 10 days' post-ferment maceration, matured in French oak (35% new) and 675l ceramic egg. The bright, clear crimson-purple colour is a picture of the red cherry and strawberry fruits that close with superfine tannins. Screwcap. 12.3% alc. **Rating** 97 **To** 2032 $40 **✿**

ΨΨΨΨΨ **Birthday Hill Single Vineyard Pinot Noir 2018** A small parcel from a close-planted, low-yielding vineyard; fermented with 100% whole bunches, 900 bottles made. An exceptional pinot from an exceptional hatful of vines. Everything – fruit, tannins, oak and acidity – are in harmonious balance. Screwcap. 13.6% alc. **Rating** 96 **To** 2030 $60 **✿**
Estate Pinot Noir 2018 Excellent colour. By some distance the richest of the Portsea pinot noirs in this difficult vintage. It is crammed to the gills with dark berry fruit and ripe tannins. The vinification was the usual vigilant Portsea Estate approach, so this is a statement of place. It is very different from Birthday Hill but of similar quality – the choice is personal. Screwcap. 13.5% alc. **Rating** 96 **To** 2035 $45 **✿**
Stonecutters Block Single Vineyard Chardonnay 2018 Extremely complex: expressive aromas, layered flavours; flittering, never resting. If there are base notes, white peach, nectarine, fig and oak are among the candidates for recognition. Only 900 bottles made. Screwcap. 13.4% alc. **Rating** 95 **To** 2026 $60
Back Beach Chardonnay 2018 Hand-picked, whole-bunch pressed to new and used French oak for 3–5 weeks' fermentation and 10 months' maturation. An elegant wine, poised and balanced. White peach leads the flavour pack with a tinkle of grapefruit chiming in on the back-palate and aftertaste. Screwcap. 13.3% alc. **Rating** 95 **To** 2028 $30 **✿**
Estate Pinot Gris 2018 Whole-bunch pressed, free-run to barrel for fermentation on solids, 5% new oak, the remainder used. Distinct pale straw-pink. Florals and pears (nashi and otherwise) give the wine personality. Altogether serious vinification. Screwcap. 13.6% alc. **Rating** 94 **To** 2023 $31
Estate Pinot Noir Rose 2019 Treated as a serious wine: chilled, destemmed, 8 hours skin contact, wild-fermented in used barrels, matured for 5.5 months. Delicious small fruits, wild strawberry and crab-apple. Screwcap. 13.4% alc. **Rating** 94 **To** 2022 $31
Back Beach Pinot Noir 2018 Hand-picked, chilled, destemmed direct to open fermenters for a cold soak and wild ferment, 10 months in barrel (30% new). Spicy red berry aromas open the door for a fluid palate full to the brim with cherry and plum fruit. Screwcap. 13.4% alc. **Rating** 94 **To** 2028 $30 **✿**

ΨΨΨΨΨ **Estate Chardonnay 2018 Rating** 90 **To** 2022 $45

Prancing Horse Estate

39 Paringa Road, Red Hill South, Vic 3937 **Region** Mornington Peninsula
T (03) 5989 2602 **www**.prancinghorseestate.com **Open** W'ends 12–5
Winemaker Richard McIntyre, Jeremy Magyar **Est.** 1990 **Dozens** 1600 **Vyds** 6.5ha
Anthony and Catherine Hancy acquired the Lavender Bay Vineyard in early 2002, renaming
it Prancing Horse Estate and embarking on increasing the estate vineyards with 2ha each of
chardonnay and pinot noir, and 0.5ha of pinot gris. The vineyard moved to organic farming
in '03, progressing to biodynamic in '07. They appointed Sergio Carlei as winemaker and
the following year became joint owners with Sergio in Carlei Wines. (The wines are now
made by Richard McIntyre and Jeremy Magyar of Moorooduc Estate.) An additional
property 150m west of the existing vineyard was purchased and 2ha of vines planted. Prancing
Horse has become one of a small group of Australian wineries having wines made for them
in Burgundy. Pascal Marchand makes an annual release of Morey-St-Denis Clos des Ormes
Premier Cru and Meursault Premier Cru Blagny, while Patrick Piuze makes four Chablis
appellation wines. Exports to the UK, the US and France.

🍷🍷🍷🍷🍷 **Mornington Peninsula Chardonnay 2017** This wine is fresh, bright and tangy.
Grapefruit and white peach are given texture by balanced acidity and well handled
oak. To say it comes from the same stable as The Pony is factual, but nonetheless
still surprising. Screwcap. 13.6% alc. **Rating** 93 **To** 2027 $75

Pressing Matters

665 Middle Tea Tree Road, Tea Tree, Tas 7017 **Region** Southern Tasmania
T (03) 6268 1947, 0408 126 668 **www**.pressingmatters.com.au **Open** By appt
Winemaker Samantha Connew, Matt Connaughton **Est.** 2002 **Dozens** 2300 **Vyds** 7.3ha
Greg Melick wears more hats than most people manage in a lifetime. He is a major general
(the highest rank in the Australian Army Reserve) a top level barrister (senior counsel) and has
presided over a number of headline special commissions and enquiries into subjects as diverse
as cricket match–fixing and the Beaconsfield mine collapse. More recently he became deputy
president of the Administrative Appeals Tribunal and chief commissioner of the Tasmanian
Integrity Commission. Yet, if asked, he would probably nominate wine as his major focus
in life. Having built up an exceptional cellar of the great wines of Europe, he has turned his
attention to grapegrowing and winemaking, planting almost 3ha of riesling at his vineyard
in the Coal River Valley. It is on a perfect north-facing slope, and the Mosel-style rieslings
are making their mark. His multi-clone pinot noir block (just over 4ha) is also striking gold.
Exports to the US, Singapore and Hong Kong.

🍷🍷🍷🍷🍷 **R69 Riesling 2019** This cut of the cake has often emerged as the best in the
Tasmanian Wine Show and elsewhere. It retains its persona, its brightness of fruit,
when matched with savoury or sweet dishes. Screwcap. 10.2% alc. **Rating** 97
To 2044 $39 ✪

🍷🍷🍷🍷🍷 **Cuvee C Pinot Noir 2018** This is the superior Pressing Matters pinot. It is
more supple and has brighter fruit, the aromas more flowery (rose petals, violets,
spices, etc.), the palate perfectly balanced. Part of a tsunami of Tasmanian pinot
noirs offering new aspects to flavour, length, texture and structure. Screwcap.
13.9% alc. **Rating** 96 **To** 2028 $150
Cuvee C Pinot Noir 2017 A sharp move to the left with this wine. Smoky,
tobacco and whole bunch et al on the bouquet, the palate more juicy and
assertive, its length very good. Screwcap. 13.2% alc. **Rating** 96 **To** 2028 $150
R9 Riesling 2019 A 3-week cool ferment, then 6–8 weeks on lees. Shows that
9g/l of residual sugar should be baseline sweetness, which disappears after the fruit
and acidity click into place. Screwcap. 12.9% alc. **Rating** 95 **To** 2034 $39
Coal River Valley Pinot Noir 2017 Lower alcohol and slightly fresher, more
juicy red fruits than its '18 sibling. Finer too, although these distinctions are partly
personal preference. Once price is taken into account, a different ball game opens
up. Screwcap. 13.2% alc. **Rating** 95 **To** 2027 $65

R139 Riesling 2019 There's no doubting the quality and integrity of this wine, but it's in transition from youth to semi-maturity right now. Screwcap. 8.1% alc. Rating 95 To 2039 $39

Coal River Valley Pinot Noir 2018 Hand-picked and sorted, destemmed not crushed, 20% whole bunches included, 2–3 days' cold soak, hand-plunged, matured for 10 months in oak. The whole bunch is showing in this wine. Screwcap. 13.8% alc. Rating 94 To 2028 $65

ΥΥΥΥΥ **Cuvee C Pinot Noir 2016** Rating 93 To 2024 $150
R0 Riesling 2019 Rating 90 To 2029 $39

Primo Estate ★★★★★

McMurtrie Road, McLaren Vale, SA 5171 **Region** McLaren Vale
T (08) 8323 6800 **www.**primoestate.com.au **Open** 7 days 11–4
Winemaker Joseph Grilli, Daniel Grilli, Tom Garrett **Est.** 1979 **Dozens** 30000
Vyds 34ha
Joe Grilli has always produced innovative and excellent wines. The biennial release of the Joseph Sparkling Red (in its tall Italian glass bottle) is eagerly awaited, the wine immediately selling out. However, the core lies with the La Biondina, the Il Briccone Shiraz Sangiovese and the Joseph Moda Cabernet Merlot. The vineyard includes plantings of colombard, shiraz, cabernet sauvignon, riesling, merlot, sauvignon blanc, chardonnay, pinot gris, sangiovese, nebbiolo and merlot. Also highly regarded are the vintage-dated extra virgin olive oils. Exports to all major markets.

ΥΥΥΥΥ **Joseph Angel Gully Clarendon Shiraz 2017** Hand-picked from a single patch at the top of the rocky vineyard with very low yield, open-fermented, matured in French and American barriques for 18 months. The cool vintage has resulted in a medium-bodied wine with elegance and length. Finely ground tannins and spices complete the lovely palate. Screwcap. 14% alc. Rating 97 To 2040 $90 ✪

ΥΥΥΥΥ **Shale Stone McLaren Vale Shiraz 2018** From the McMurtrie Vineyard in the heart of McLaren Vale and the Angel Gully Vineyard in Clarendon; matured in French and American oak (40% new) for 15 months. Waves of spice, dark chocolate, black cherry and plum fill the bouquet and palate; the oak important but not over the top. Screwcap. 14.5% alc. Rating 95 To 2038 $35 ✪

La Biondina 2019 For many years this was made from 85% or more colombard, the balance sauvignon blanc. Daniel Grilli has made this from arneis, gruner veltliner and riesling, and given it bright new packaging. It's vibrant and juicy with a strikingly long palate stretching through to the fresh aftertaste. Screwcap. 12% alc. Rating 94 To 2022 $20 ✪

Joseph Clarendon Nebbiolo 2017 From the Angel Gully Vineyard; crushed to open fermenters, matured for 18 months on a mix of new and used French barriques. The very cool and wet spring was followed by a long, cool, dry summer/autumn. Not an easy wine to unravel, Joe Grilli's description of the flavour of the palate: Turkish delight and roses overlain with delicate spices and violets. Screwcap. 13% alc. Rating 94 To 2027 $90

ΥΥΥΥΥ **Merlesco McLaren Vale Merlot 2019** Rating 91 To 2022 $20 ✪

Principia ★★★★★

139 Main Creek Road, Red Hill, Vic 3937 (postal) **Region** Mornington Peninsula
T (03) 5931 0010 **www.**principiawines.com.au **Open** By appt
Winemaker Darrin Gaffy **Est.** 1995 **Dozens** 600 **Vyds** 3.5ha
Darrin Gaffy's guiding philosophy for Principia is minimal interference, thus the vines (2.7ha of pinot noir and 0.8ha of chardonnay) are not irrigated and yields are restricted to 3.75t/ha or less. All wine movements are by gravity or gas pressure, which in turn means there

is no filtration, and both primary and secondary fermentation are by wild yeast. 'Principia' comes from the word 'beginnings' in Latin. Exports to Hong Kong.

🍷🍷🍷🍷🍷 **Mornington Peninsula Chardonnay 2018** Fermented wild in quality French wood, a judicious percentage new. This is a delicious chardonnay that feels fresher, cooler and more mid-weighted than the labelled alcohol suggests. Truffles and hazelnut. Nougat. Stone fruit and yet, more important than this whimsy, is the wine's tenacity across the palate; the oak holding in the seams and the impeccably judged mineral freshness towing the flavours long. Class and poise are this wine's totem. Screwcap. **Rating** 95 **To** 2025 $45 NG
Kindred Hill Mornington Peninsula Pinot Noir 2018 This is a turbid mid to light ruby, indicative of the minimal interventionist policy: ambient yeast, no filtration nor fining. The skein of tannin, inflected with exotic Indian notes including turmeric and cardamom, suggests a higher percentage of bunches in the ferment; 18 months in classy French oak melds well, ably obviating the physiologically ripe fruit from an attenuated growing season. The overall impression is one of a svelte freshness, detail and intense succulence, despite the warmth of fruit. Truffled forest floor and crunchy red berry fruits sashay across maritime acid rails, towing the melee long. This is a delicious pinot. Screwcap. **Rating** 95 **To** 2026 $55 NG

🍷🍷🍷🍷🍷 **Mornington Peninsula Pinot Noir 2018** **Rating** 93 **To** 2024 $45 NG

Printhie Wines   ★★★★★

489 Yuranigh Road, Molong, NSW 2866 **Region** Orange
T (02) 6366 8422 **www**.printhiewines.com.au **Open** Mon–Sat 10–4
Winemaker Drew Tuckwell **Est.** 1996 **Dozens** 20 000 **Vyds** 30ha
Owned by the Swift family. The next generation, Edward and David, have taken over (from Ed Swift) to guide the business into its next era. In 2016 Printhie clocked up 10 years of commercial wine production and the vineyards are now reaching a good level of maturity at 20 years. The 30ha of estate vineyards are planted at lower elevations and supply all the red varieties and the pinot gris; other varieties are purchased from other growers in the region. Winemaker Drew Tuckwell has been at Printhie for a decade and has over 20 years of winemaking experience in Australia and Europe. Exports to Canada and China.

🍷🍷🍷🍷🍷 **Super-Duper Chardonnay 2018** Small-batch winemaking manifests as a medium-bodied wine of scintillating intensity with few obvious fruit references. For the better. Sourced from 2 sites at 900m and 1000m respectfully. A lees-inflected core of pungent mineral energy, toasted hazelnut, flint, oatmeal, cashew and nougat scents define the style. Wild yeast truffle too. The oak, clearly high quality, embedded into the fray. The finish infinitesimally long. A superlative chardonnay with all bells and whistles; seldom seen in these parts. Screwcap. **Rating** 96 **To** 2027 $85 NG
Swift Cuvee #7 NV A 2013 base, the third and final disgorgement; chardonnay 60%, pinot 40%; 72 months on lees. This is superlative. A juicy bead towing flavours of brioche, cinnamon spice, tarte tatin and quince long. Far! The acidity juicy, melded to the core of leesy nourishment. An impeccable balance between freshness and ampleur. A stunning domestic fizz. **Rating** 96 $40 NG ✪
Swift Blanc de Noirs 2016 Straight pinot noir, barrel fermented and minimally messed with, prizing the breadth of oak and cloudy juice as textural building blocks. Broad and buffered. A red berry tang and a swirl of tangy acid to mineral punch drives the dervish long. Fine. Powerful. Palate-staining of intensity. Cork. **Rating** 95 NG
Swift Vintage Brut 2012 This is exceptional fizz. The estate has it together by the taste of this. Chardonnay 73%, the remainder pinot. Leesy truffled scents to wild strawberry, loganberry and sour cherry. Long, detailed, taut and sapid. Refined, the 5g/l dosage nestled with aplomb. **Rating** 95 $50 NG

Swift Rose Brut #3 NV The first disgorgement of '12; chardonnay 58%, the rest pinot; 72 months on lees; 6g/l dosage. An easygoing, broader expression. Talc, musk stick, pink grapefruit and red plum. This is a floozy. Fresh enough, hanging everything out to ride across an early pleasure curve. Hedonistic, sure. But absolutely delicious. Cork. **Rating** 95 $40 NG

ŶŶŶŶŶ **Topography Riesling 2019 Rating** 93 To 2027 $26 NG ✪
Topography Pinot Gris 2019 Rating 93 To 2023 $26 NG ✪
Swift Rose Brut #4 NV Rating 93 NG
Topography Shiraz 2018 Rating 92 To 2024 $35 NG
Super-Duper Syrah 2018 Rating 92 To 2028 $85 NG
Swift Blanc de Blancs 2010 Rating 92 $85 NG
Mountain Range Orange Pinot Gris 2019 Rating 91 To 2023 $22 NG ✪
Snow Line Orange Three Pinots Rose 2019 Rating 90 To 2022 $26 NG
Topography Pinot Meunier 2019 Rating 90 To 2023 $35 NG

Project Wine ★★★★

83 Pioneer Road, Angas Plains, SA 5255 **Region** South Australia
T (08) 8537 0600 **www**.projectwine.com.au **Open** Not
Winemaker Peter Pollard **Est.** 2001 **Dozens** 155 000
Originally designed as a contract winemaking facility, Project Wine has developed a sales and distribution arm that has rapidly developed markets both domestic and overseas. Located in Langhorne Creek, it sources fruit from most key SA wine regions, including McLaren Vale, Barossa Valley and Adelaide Hills. The diversity of grape sourcing allows the winery to produce a wide range of products under the Tail Spin, Pioneer Road, Parson's Paddock, Bird's Eye View and Angas & Bremer labels. Exports to the UK, Canada, Japan and China.

ŶŶŶŶŶ **Angas & Bremer Langhorne Creek Shiraz Cabernet 2018** A classic blend that works very well in these parts. Cabernet the doughnut; shiraz, the fruit jam in the middle. The former's verdant make-up apparent across scents of spearmint and hedgerow. These segue to black and blueberry flavours, corralled by a phalanx of nicely wrought tannins at the finish. Rich, sumptuous and, in the context of the range, savoury all at once. Screwcap. 14.8% alc. **Rating** 92 To 2026 $20 NG ✪
Angas & Bremer Langhorne Creek Malbec 2016 A single vineyard expression massaged across 17 months in a combination of French and American oak. Rich, polished and driven as much by the piney oak tannins as it is by gushing dark fruit references, violet scents and clove. This will win many fans. Screwcap. 14% alc. **Rating** 91 To 2026 $40 NG
Bird's Eye View McLaren Vale Shiraz 2018 A fine value-driven shiraz. The reductive lilac lift of a contemporary take melds effortlessly with a juicy blueberry core, flecked with anise and iodine. Buoyant of fruit with just enough structure. Screwcap. **Rating** 90 To 2024 $18 NG ✪
Angas & Bremer Langhorne Creek Shiraz 2017 A dense crimson close to opaque, showing just a hint of maturity at the edges. A morass of dark fruits define the attack; some bramble, spice and woodsy scents across the finish. The oak, cedar-vanillan and plenty toasty, serves this sort of rich take-no-prisoners style well. One for the hedonists. **Rating** 90 To 2025 $25 NG
Angas & Bremer The Creek 2018 A multi-varietal, small parcel blend of grenache, malbec, touriga, dolcetto and shiraz, showcasing the region's capacity for diversity. A bit more grape tannin than other wines in the range, setting this up for versatility at the table. Hints of dark fruits, bitter chocolate, maraschino cherry and a whiff of apricot meld nicely, splaying across some coffee grind oak at the finish. Best drunk in its youth. Screwcap. 14.5% alc. **Rating** 90 To 2024 $20 NG ✪

ŶŶŶŶ **Angas & Bremer Langhorne Creek Pinot Grigio 2019 Rating** 89 To 2021 $18 NG ✪

Prosperitas Wines

156 Richmond Road, Marleston, SA 5263 (postal) **Region** Coonawarra
T (08) 8646 5604 **www.prosperitaswines.com** **Open** Not
Est. 2018 **Dozens** 8000 **Vyds** 324ha

Prosperitas wines are made from extensive estate plantings in South Australia. 'Our role is not to manipulate or construct taste, but to act as custodians of authenticity. Coonawarra should taste distinctly Coonawarra, McLaren Vale should taste distinctly McLaren Vale, and so forth.' Exports to the US and China.

ᵀᵀᵀᵀ **McLaren Vale Cabernet Sauvignon 2016** The best of the Prosperitas wines. It was grown organically and spent 22 months in French hogsheads. Medium-bodied and very well balanced, ditto length and aftertaste. Cork. 15% alc. **Rating** 92 **To** 2031 $59

ᵀᵀᵀᵀ **McLaren Vale Shiraz 2017** Cork. 15% alc. **Rating** 89 **To** 2022 $59

Provenance Wines

100 Lower Paper Mills Road, Fyansford, Vic 3221 **Region** Geelong
T (03) 5222 3422 **www.provenancewines.com.au** **Open** Summer 7 days 11–5, winter Thurs–Mon 11–5
Winemaker Scott Ireland, Sam Vogel **Est.** 1997 **Dozens** 6500 **Vyds** 14.2ha

In 1997 when Scott Ireland and partner Jan Lilburn established Provenance Wines, they knew it wouldn't be easy starting a winery with limited capital and no fixed abode. The one thing the business had was Scott's over 36 years' experience operating contract wine filtration and bottling services, moving from winery to winery in the Hunter Valley, Barossa, Coonawarra, Mudgee, Clare Valley, Yarra Valley and Tasmania regions. He says he met so many dedicated small winemakers that he was hooked for life. In 2004 he moved to Austins & Co, the largest winery in Geelong. Scott was Austins' winemaker, but with their knowledge and consent he continued to grow the much smaller Provenance business, developing key relationships with growers in Geelong, the ultra-cool Macedon, Ballarat and Henty. Scott took a long-term lease of 25% of the Fyansford Paper Mill, and refurbished the heritage-listed buildings. Built out of local bluestone on the banks of the Barwon River on the outskirts of Geelong, this 1870s industrial complex provides excellent wine cellar conditions. Sam Vogel is now a partner in the business. Exports to Malaysia and Hong Kong.

ᵀᵀᵀᵀᵀ **Henty Chardonnay 2018** It combines purity, power and finesse, and it does so while painting a complex picture. This is top drawer chardonnay if ever there was one, emphasised by both the wine's silken texture and excellent length. White peach, custard apples, shell grit, vanilla and cedar wood flavours are the workers of the magic. Screwcap. 13.2% alc. **Rating** 96 **To** 2029 $52 CM ❂

Ballarat Chardonnay 2018 Another terrific chardonnay from Provenance. There's fruit power but it's so controlled and so well maintained. Apples, white peach, smoked bacon, vanilla cream and cedar spice. It's one of those wines where you see something different every time you look at it. Screwcap. 13.2% alc. **Rating** 96 **To** 2028 $52 CM ❂

Geelong Chardonnay 2018 Quality chardonnay from start to finish. It commands the glass in the most effortless of ways. Stone fruit and flint, spice and toast. You'd think it was easy if you didn't know better. Buy with confidence. Screwcap. 13.2% alc. **Rating** 96 **To** 2029 $52 CM ❂

Golden Plains Chardonnay 2018 Geelong 50%, Ballarat 40%, Henty 10%. It puts on a cohesive display of stone fruit, fig, vanilla cream and oak-spice flavour. It's well powered and balanced, and lingers appreciably through the finish. Everything is in a good place. Factor in the price and you have an extremely attractive proposition. Screwcap. 13.2% alc. **Rating** 95 **To** 2026 $32 CM ❂

Regional Selection Macedon Pinot Noir 2017 Grown at 750m, fermented wild with 100% whole bunches, 11 days on skins. It starts off wild and then finishes taut and reserved. It's a bacony, bunchy, spicy pinot with fragrance aplenty and a solid bed of tangy fruit. Wood smoke and woodsy spice are key players.

It needs a couple of years in bottle but everything looks promising. Screwcap. 13% alc. **Rating** 95 **To** 2030 $52 CM

Henty Riesling 2019 The winemaking notes mention the wine's 'significant natural acid line' and they're not wrong. This cuts straight through to a dramatic finish. There are citrussy perfumes and flavours, slate notes, juicy green apples, punches of rind. There's an element of texture too, thankfully; a key complement to the pure acid line. It needs more time in bottle but we've got something impressive on the line here. Screwcap. 12.2% alc. **Rating** 94 **To** 2034 $30 CM ✪

Henty Pinot Gris 2019 It strikes a keen balance between richness of flavour and elegance. It's fruit-driven, egged on by acidity, shows inflections of seashells and honeysuckle, and lingers nicely on the finish. A year or two in bottle won't hurt it. Screwcap. 12.8% alc. **Rating** 94 **To** 2023 $30 CM ✪

Golden Plains Pinot Noir 2018 Ready to go now in the most pleasing of ways. This boasts an easygoing fruit-forward complexity, its pepper/twig/leaf notes slipped easily into cherried fruit. Spicy tannin completes a tasty picture. Value and quality in one. Screwcap. 13.5% alc. **Rating** 94 **To** 2026 $32 CM

Geelong Shiraz 2018 Single vineyard at Bannockburn; 2% viognier. Feels and tastes riper than its stated alcohol with its baked plum and licorice notes but there's plenty of floral and spice aspects to lighten the load. This is a complex shiraz, gently reductive, firm and dry to finish and with more than a little presence. Screwcap. 13.5% alc. **Rating** 94 **To** 2032 $34 CM

☙☙☙☙☙ **Western Districts Rose 2019** Rating 93 **To** 2022 $27 CM ✪
Regional Selection Geelong Pinot Noir 2017 Rating 93 **To** 2027 $52 CM
Ballarat Pinot Noir 2017 Rating 93 **To** 2027 $52 CM
Western Districts Shiraz 2018 Rating 93 **To** 2028 CM
Henty Pinot Gris 2018 Rating 90 **To** 2021 $30 CM

Punch   ★★★★★

10 Scott Street, St Andrews, Vic 3761 **Region** Yarra Valley
T 0424 074 234 www.punched.com.au **Open** W'ends 12–5
Winemaker James Lance **Est.** 2004 **Dozens** 1800 **Vyds** 3.45ha
In the wake of Graeme Rathbone taking over the brand (but not the real estate) of Diamond Valley, the Lances' son James and his wife Claire leased the vineyard and winery from David and Catherine Lance, including the 0.25ha block of close-planted pinot noir. In all, Punch has 2.25ha of pinot noir (including the close-planted), 0.8ha of chardonnay and 0.4ha of cabernet sauvignon. When the 2009 Black Saturday bushfires destroyed the crop, various grapegrowers wrote offering assistance, which led to the purchase of the grapes used for that dire year and the beginning of the 'Friends of Punch' wines. Exports to China

☙☙☙☙☙ **Lance's Vineyard Chardonnay 2017** Hand-picked, whole-bunch pressed direct to barrel, wild-fermented, matured for 10 months on lees in barrel. Fresh and bright grapefruit. Balance and length. All class. Screwcap. 13% alc. **Rating** 95 **To** 2027 $45

Lance's Vineyard Pinot Noir 2017 Hand-picked, wild-fermented with 20% whole bunches, 17 days on skins, 12 months in French oak (33% new); 259 dozen made. Most attractive. Here, even more than the Close Planted, the '17 vintage works its magic. More perfume, spice, forest fruits and some plum. Lovely wine. Screwcap. 13.5% alc. **Rating** 95 **To** 2027 $55

Lance's Vineyard Close Planted Pinot Noir 2017 Estate-grown MV6; fermented with 38% whole bunches, 18 days on skins, matured in French oak (75% new); 83 dozen made. The pH is 3.65 but looks much higher. Powerful, a lesson in plum (blood/satsuma). Good wine, great lineage. Screwcap. 13.5% alc. **Rating** 95 **To** 2027 $90

Lance's Vineyard Cabernet Sauvignon 2017 Hand-picked, 0.9t of 70g/l bunches, destemmed, wild-fermented, matured for 15 months; 65 dozen made. Very generous and will be irresistible to those who like high quality French oak, the more the better. Screwcap. 13.5% alc. **Rating** 94 **To** 2032 $45

Punt Road ★★★★★

10 St Huberts Road, Coldstream, Vic 3770 **Region** Yarra Valley
T (03) 9739 0666 **www**.puntroadwines.com.au **Open** 7 days 10–5
Winemaker Tim Shand, Travis Bush **Est.** 2000 **Dozens** 20 000 **Vyds** 65.61ha
Punt Road is owned by the Napoleone family, third-generation fruit growers in the Yarra
Valley. Their vineyard in Coldstream is one of the most historic sites in Victoria, first planted
to vines by Swiss immigrant Hubert De Castella in 1860. The Napoleone Vineyard was
established on the property in 1987. Chief winemaker Tim Shand joined the winery in 2014
and has established a reputation for consistent quality of all the Punt Road wines. The two
main ranges are Punt Road and Airlie Bank, plus a small production of single vineyard 'Block'
wines, only available at cellar door, made only in the best vintages. Exports to the US, the UK,
Canada, Sweden, Denmark, Singapore, China and Sri Lanka.

ꞮꞮꞮꞮꞮ Block 11 Napoleone Vineyard Yarra Valley Cabernet Sauvignon 2018
Cool-fermented after a long cold soak, 4 days on skins post ferment, matured
in French barriques (50% new). Block 11 must be special to achieve this deep
bright colour and cassis-accented fruit at 13.4% alcohol. Excellent length, line and
balance. Screwcap. **Rating** 95 **To** 2033 $85

ꞮꞮꞮꞮꞮ Napoleone Vineyard Block 3 Yarra Valley Cabernet Sauvignon 2018
Rating 93 **To** 2030 $32
Napoleone Vineyard Block 18 Yarra Valley Gamay 2019 **Rating** 90
To 2020 $27

Pure Vision Organic Wines ★★★☆

PO Box 258, Virginia, SA 5120 **Region** Adelaide Plains
T 0412 800 875 **www**.purevisionwines.com.au **Open** Not
Winemaker Joanne Irvine, Ken Carypidis **Est.** 2001 **Dozens** 18 000 **Vyds** 55ha
The Carypidis family runs two brands: Pure Vision and Nature's Step. The oldest vineyards
were planted in 1975; organic conversion began in 2009. Growing grapes under a certified
organic regime is much easier if the region is warm to hot and dry, conditions unsuitable for
botrytis and downy mildew. You are still left with weed growth (no herbicides are allowed)
and powdery mildew (sulphur sprays are permitted), but the overall task is much simpler.
The Adelaide Plains, where Pure Vision's vineyard is situated, is such a region. Ken Carypidis
has been clever enough to secure the services of Joanne Irvine as co-winemaker. Exports to
Singapore and China.

ꞮꞮꞮꞮꞮ Pure Vision Shiraz 2018 A dense, inky wine utilising ample whole-berry work
and the partial carbonic effect, to mitigate lower sulphite additions. Tarry violet
scents, bitter chocolate, mulberry and anise maraud across the palate. The finish,
chewy and pliant grape tannins. A simple, powerful red made to very good effect.
Best enjoyed imminently. Screwcap. 14.5% alc. **Rating** 90 **To** 2024 $17 NG ❂

ꞮꞮꞮꞮ Cabernet Sauvignon 2018 **Rating** 89 **To** 2023 $17 NG ❂

Purple Hands Wines ★★★★★

32 Brandreth Street, Tusmore, SA 5065 (postal) **Region** Barossa Valley
T 0401 988 185 **www**.purplehandswines.com.au **Open** Not
Winemaker Craig Stansborough **Est.** 2006 **Dozens** 3500 **Vyds** 14ha
This is a partnership between Craig Stansborough, who provides the winemaking know-how
and an 8ha vineyard of shiraz (northwest of Williamstown in a cooler corner of the southern
Barossa), and Mark Slade, who provides the passion. Don't ask me how this works – I don't
know – but I do know they are producing outstanding single vineyard wines (the grenache
is contract-grown) of quite remarkable elegance. The wines are made at Grant Burge, where
Craig is chief winemaker. Exports to the UK and China.

ꞮꞮꞮꞮꞮ After Five Wine Co. Single Vineyard Barossa Valley Shiraz 2017 Not
your ordinary Barossa Valley shiraz. It builds a complex, savoury palate with an
abundance of spices and notes of cedar. It's medium to full-bodied, yet the tannins

are subdued at all points along the way. Its large X-factor comes from the cool '17 vintage. Tasted in the early morning after breakfast, normally a death sentence, but rose to the challenge without hesitation. I really like this wine and its subdued alcohol. Screwcap. 14% alc. **Rating** 96 **To** 2032 $45 ✪

Colours of the South Pinot Gris 2019 Hand-picked, 10% tipped into open concrete fermenter and the balance was destemmed, crushed and placed on top, neutral cultured yeast, 8 days on skins, basket pressed and into mix of new (33%) and seasoned French oak, mlf, on light lees for 8 months, racked and returned to oak for 9 months, no fining. Another example of maximum effort winemaking from Craig Stansborough for a $25 wine that sings. Hits all the right gris chords from the honeysuckle, nougat and cut pear intro through to a smooth texture and warmth in the mouth. The touch of candied pineapple to close is so right. Screwcap. 12.5% alc. **Rating** 95 **To** 2024 JP ✪

Planta Circa Ancestor Vine Barossa Valley Shiraz 2018 Hand-picked, 10% of fruit was tipped into concrete open fermenter, balance was destemmed, lightly crushed, neutral yeast, 8 days on skins, basket pressed and into new (33%) and used French oak, mlf, left on lees to mature for 8 months, racked then back into oak for another 9 months. Old vines planted between 1880 and '90 shine, producing a multifaceted shiraz that is both humble and complex. Quiet to start, the perfume is almost faint but, yes, there is the sweet scent of violets and roses. Then all is revealed in a seamless and spectacular performance of a grape off old vines: florals, intense black fruits, full array of spices in a soothing synergy with background oak and supple tannin. Diam. 13.5% alc. **Rating** 95 **To** 2037 $80 JP

Planta Circa Ancestor Vine Barossa Valley Cabernet Sauvignon 2018 Fermented with indigenous yeast, hand-plunging 3–4 times daily, 12 days on skins, basket pressed and transferred into new (50%) and seasoned oak, mlf, left on lees for 6 months, racked and returned to oak for 9 months. Eye-catching deep purple for a wine that shows stylish winemaking at every step. Old vines may be the star but good winemaking brings added lustre. Aromas of loamy earth, ripe cassis, garden mint and dried leaves. A wealth of bright notes on the palate, sweetly spiced oak, supple tannins with tight finish. A keeper. Diam. 14% alc. **Rating** 95 **To** 2041 $80 JP

After Five Wine Co. Montepulciano 2018 A striking young Italian variety finding a home in the Barossa Valley. And what's not to like? It strikes a dramatic dense purple pose in the glass. The scent is pure La Dolce Vita with exotic spice, black cherry and enduring anise. It flows beautifully across the tongue, smooth, intense but with lively tannins. Screwcap. 14% alc. **Rating** 95 **To** 2031 $35 JP ✪

🍷🍷🍷🍷🍷 **After Five Wine Co. Single Vineyard Barossa Valley Shiraz 2018**
Rating 93 **To** 2034 $45 JP
Planta Circa Ancestor Vine Barossa Valley Grenache 2018 **Rating** 92 **To** 2028 $80 JP
After Five Wine Co. Aglianico 2018 **Rating** 92 **To** 2027 $35 JP
After Five Wine Co. Single Vineyard Barossa Valley Serata 2018
Rating 91 **To** 2041 $45 JP
Colours of the South Red 2018 **Rating** 91 **To** 2036 $28 JP

Pyren Vineyard   ★★★★☆

Glenlofty-Warrenmang Road, Warrenmang, Vic 3478 **Region** Pyrenees
T (03) 5467 2352 **www.**pyrenvineyard.com **Open** Not
Winemaker Leighton Joy, Brock Alford **Est.** 1999 **Dozens** 10 000 **Vyds** 28.3ha
Brian and Leighton Joy have 23ha of shiraz, 5ha of cabernet sauvignon and 1ha malbec, cabernet franc and petit verdot on the slopes of the Warrenmang Valley near Moonambel. Yield is restricted to between 3.7t and 6.1t/ha Exports to the UK and China.

🍷🍷🍷🍷🍷 **Union 2018** A union of 46/40/8/4/2% cabernet franc/cabernet sauvignon/petit verdot/malbec/shiraz. Five different components could make for a busy, unfocused wine, but not so here. Lifted aromas of rose, violets, mulberry, blueberry tart, boysenberry, potpourri and wild herbs. Agile on its feet and elegant, plump too, in sweet fruit. Star anise, red licorice, spice works well with earthy undertones and fine tannins. Diam. 14% alc. **Rating** 95 **To** 2032 $60 JP

Reserve Cabernet 2018 Whole-bunch (30%) fermentation, matured in 500l French oak (25% new), filtered. An ode to cabernet sauvignon in all of its floral beauty. Lifted aromas of roses, violets, wild berries and the almost always omnipresent Pyrenees bush mint, five-spice. Terroir speaking true. Dense. Alcohol definitely playing a role here in that comforting warm kind of way with stewed plums, rich chocolate and freshly turned earth. Oak-fuelled tannins have a way to go. Give it time. Diam. 14% alc. **Rating** 94 **To** 2030 $60 JP

♟♟♟♟♟ **Reserve Syrah 2018 Rating** 92 **To** 2032 $60 JP
Sauvignon 2018 Rating 90 **To** 2028 $35 JP

Quarisa Wines   ★★★★

743 Slopes Road, Tharbogang, NSW 2680 (postal) **Region** South Australia
T (02) 6963 6222 **www**.quarisa.com.au **Open** Not
Winemaker John Quarisa **Est.** 2005 **Dozens** NFP
John Quarisa has had a distinguished career as a winemaker spanning over 20 years, working for some of Australia's largest wineries including McWilliam's, Casella and Nugan Estate. He was also chiefly responsible in 2004 for winning the Jimmy Watson Trophy (Melbourne) and the Stodart Trophy (Adelaide). John and Josephine Quarisa have set up a very successful family business using grapes from various parts of NSW and SA, made in leased space. Production has risen in leaps and bounds, doubtless sustained by the exceptional value for money provided by the wines. Exports include the UK, the US, Canada, Sweden, Denmark, Finland, Poland, Russia, Malaysia, Indonesia, Thailand, Singapore, NZ, Japan, Hong Kong and China.

♟♟♟♟♟ **Johnny Q Shiraz Viognier 2017** Value here is pretty high. You get roasted plum and vanilla flavours and you get them served reasonably bright. There's some substance to the fruit, a bit of tannin, some dry/roasted spice notes and a floral aspect. It sits at the ripe/porty end of the flavour spectrum, but it has a whole lot going for it. Screwcap. 14.5% alc. **Rating** 92 **To** 2025 $18 CM ◐
Johnny Q Shiraz 2018 Straight up it pours on the flavour and it keeps it going pretty well through to the finish. If you like them big and bold then you've got a live one here. Black/red berries, violets and resiny vanilla. An aftertaste of mocha. Substantial. Screwcap. 15% alc. **Rating** 92 **To** 2026 $18 CM ◐
Mrs Q Cabernet Sauvignon 2016 Oak flavours dominate but grainy tannin and curranty fruit get a fair look in. It's toasty with a bit going for it, including value. Screwcap. 14.5% alc. **Rating** 90 **To** 2025 $18 CM ◐
Caravan Durif 2019 For hearty old-school fruit-and-oak flavour it'd be hard to find better value. This red is uncomplicated and heavy-handed, but it packs a big punch and has no rough edges. Screwcap. 14.5% alc. **Rating** 90 **To** 2025 $13 CM ◐

♟♟♟♟ **Mrs Q Shiraz 2016 Rating** 89 **To** 2024 $18 CM ◐
Mrs Q Cabernet Sauvignon 2015 Rating 89 **To** 2025 $18 CM ◐
Johnny Q Durif 2017 Rating 89 **To** 2025 $18 CM ◐

Quarry Hill Wines   ★★★★

2181 Barton Highway, Jeir, NSW 2582 **Region** Canberra District
T (02) 6223 7112 **www**.quarryhill.com.au **Open** Not
Winemaker Collector Wines (Alex McKay) **Est.** 1999 **Dozens** 650 **Vyds** 4.5ha
Dean Terrell is the ex-vice chancellor of the Australian National University and a professor of economics. The acquisition of the property, originally used as a quarry for the construction of the Barton Highway and thereafter as a grazing property, was the brainchild of his family, who wanted to keep him active in retirement. The vineyard was established in 1999, with further plantings in 2001 and '06. There are 2ha of shiraz, 1ha of sauvignon blanc and 0.25ha each of savagnin, sangiovese, tempranillo, grenache, pinot noir and sagrantino. Only part of the

production is released under the Quarry Hill label; grapes are also sold to wineries, including Clonakilla and Collector Wines.

TTTTT **Charcoal Gap Pinot Noir 2016** Fermented with whole bunches. Electric aromas of forest berries, red cherry, cranberry with dried flowers and herbs. There's an energy here, compelling and complex due to some stunning fruit that builds in the mouth aided and abetted by crunchy tannins. Screwcap. 13% alc. **Rating** 94 To 2024 $30 JP ✪

TTTTT **First Light Grenache Rose 2019** Rating 92 To 2022 $24 JF ✪
Five Rows Natural Sparkling 2018 Rating 92 $28 JP
Lost Acre Tempranillo 2019 Rating 91 To 2023 $25 JF
Canberra District Shiraz 2018 Rating 90 To 2028 $26 JF
Lost Acre Tempranillo 2016 Rating 90 To 2024 $25 JP

Quealy Winemakers ★★★★★

62 Bittern-Dromana Road, Balnarring, Vic 3926 **Region** Mornington Peninsula
T (03) 5983 2483 **www**.quealy.com.au **Open** 7 days 11–5
Winemaker Kathleen Quealy, Kevin McCarthy **Est.** 1982 **Dozens** 8000 **Vyds** 8ha
Kathleen Quealy and Kevin McCarthy were among the early waves of winemakers on the Mornington Peninsula. They challenged the status quo – most publicly by introducing Mornington Peninsula pinot gris/grigio (with great success). Behind this was improvement and diversification in site selection, plus viticulture and winemaking techniques that allowed their business to grow significantly. The estate plantings are 2ha each of pinot noir, pinot gris and friulano as well as smaller plots of riesling, chardonnay and moscato giallo. Their leased vineyards are established on what Kathleen and Kevin consider to be premium sites for pinot gris and pinot noir. These are now single vineyard wines: Musk Creek and the newer Tussie Mussie Vineyard. Kathleen and Kevin are assisted by winemaker Dan Calvert, who has worked with Quealy for 7 years. Their son Tom has joined the business, with a particular focus on natural wine, Turbul Friulano his first such wine. Exports to the UK and France.

TTTTT **Pinot Grigio 2019** Pitch-perfect pinot grigio. All ginger, spiced nashi pear, lemon zest and pith with fennel and crunchy daikon. Palate has texture with light phenolics and fine acidity plus a moreish saline hit. Delicious. Screwcap. 13.1% alc. **Rating** 95 To 2024 $35 JF ✪
Musk Creek Pinot Gris 2019 Texture sets this apart from its grigio sibling. It's also full of lemon balm, grapefruit pith and slightly crunchy pears laced with pepper and freshly cut herbs. Screwcap. 13.9% alc. **Rating** 95 To 2024 $35 JF ✪
Lina Lool 2018 Maybe there is someone called Lina Lool but the name is actually a terpene, the compound linalool found in aromatic varieties. Plenty in this wonderful blend of friulano, moscato giallo and riesling that spends 6 months on skins. Yes, it's an orange wine, although more straw-gold. Vibrant with lemon verbena, poached quince, pickled ginger and a dusting of Chinese five-spice. Refreshing with a squirt of lemon saline and neat tannins. Screwcap. 13.8% alc. **Rating** 95 To 2026 $30 JF ✪
Musk Creek Pinot Noir 2018 Quite ethereal, breezing through with a cherry glaze, bitter herbs and a dusting of spice. It's lighter framed but it is just so satisfying. Supple tannins, refreshing acidity and a pleasure to drink. Screwcap. 13.7% alc. **Rating** 94 To 2025 $45 JF
Seventeen Rows Pinot Noir 2018 Kathleen Quealy's son, Tom McCarthy, is charged with the winemaking and I like the result. This follows the lighter-framed format of the other pinot noirs, but still has plenty of flavour. All spiced cherries and a dash of kirsch, pepper and earth, black olives and juniper. Supple tannins, lithe and plenty of enjoyment. Screwcap. 13.2% alc. **Rating** 94 **To** 2027 $65 JF

TTTTT **Turbul Friulano 2018** Rating 93 To 2025 $35 JF
Campbell & Christine Pinot Noir 2018 Rating 90 To 2026 $40 JF

Quiet Mutiny

10 Elaine Cresecent, West Hobart, Tas, 7000 (postal) **Region** Tasmania
T 0410 552 317 **www**.quietmutiny.wine **Open** Not
Winemaker Greer Carland **Est.** 2017 **Dozens** 400

Owner and winemaker Greer Carland grew up on the Laurel Bank family property, learning to prune vines at an early age. She completed her oenology degree at the University of Adelaide in 2000 and, after a few years of international vintages in Chile, France and the US and a short stint in WA, she returned to Tasmania in '04. For the next 12 years she worked with Julian Alcorso at Winemaking Tasmania (now Tasmanian Vintners), also making the Laurel Bank wines. In '16 she left to focus on making the family wines at Laurel Bank and to start her own label. She intends to secure land and establish a vineyard for Quiet Mutiny with her viticulturist husband Paul Smart.

🍷🍷🍷🍷🍷 **Venus Rising Pinot Noir 2018** From the Coal River Valley, equal portions of clones 777, D2V6 and 115; wild-fermented with 20% whole bunches, matured for 10 months in oak (22% new). Attractive wine. Opens quietly, then rapid and major development of plum/dark cherry fruit on the long palate. Screwcap. 13.9% alc. Rating 96 To 2030 $48 ⚡

🍷🍷🍷🍷🍷 **Charlotte's Elusion Riesling 2019** Rating 92 To 2024 $38

R. Paulazzo

852 Oakes Road, Yoogali, NSW 2680 **Region** Riverina
T 0412 696 002 **www**.rpaulazzo.com.au **Open** Not
Winemaker Rob Paulazzo **Est.** 2013 **Dozens** NFP **Vyds** 12ha

Rob Paulazzo began winemaking in 2000 and covered a lot of ground before establishing his eponymous Riverina business. In Australia he worked for McWilliam's and Orlando, in NZ for Giesen. He also completed four vintages in Burgundy, plus vintages in Tuscany, the Napa Valley and Niagara Peninsula (Canada). In addition to the family's vineyard, established over 80 years ago, Rob also sources fruit from Hilltops, Tumbarumba, Orange and Canberra District.

🍷🍷🍷🍷🍷 **G-0501 Hilltops Shiraz 2017** Hand-picked, batches vinified separately, each with 15% whole bunches, matured for 12 months in French oak (25% new), then a barrel selection. This is a splendidly flavoured, textured and structured medium to full-bodied shiraz, ablaze with red and black fruits, spices, pepper and licorice. The tannin structure is impeccable. Exceptional value. Screwcap. 14% alc. Rating 97 To 2037 $30 ⚡

🍷🍷🍷🍷🍷 **V-8109 Canberra Syrah 2018** Canberra's total production may be small, but the percentage of high quality wines is impressive. Here each vineyard parcel is fermented separately with 25% whole bunches, matured separately for 12 months in French oak (20% new), culminating in a barrel selection. Classic medium-bodied syrah: red and black cherries sprinkled with cooking spices and pepper, the tannins present but not aggressive. Very smart wine. Screwcap. 14% alc. Rating 96 To 2031 $30 ⚡

S-3011 Hilltops Cabernet Sauvignon 2017 Hand-picked batches delivered separately to the winery and kept separate through the vinification process, matured in French oak (25% new) for 12 months. Deeply coloured. It is an extremely intense cabernet that keeps its line and shape through to the finish; cassis the engine, bay leaf and olive joining with strong but balanced tannins. Screwcap. 14% alc. Rating 96 To 2042 $30 ⚡

M-2305 Tumbarumba Chardonnay 2018 Hand-picked, whole-bunch pressed direct to barrel with full solids, wild-fermented, matured in French oak (25% new), then a barrel selection. Good wine, acidity a positive aspect, mlf having been prevented. Screwcap. 13% alc. Rating 94 To 2025 $30 ⚡

K-1707 Tumbarumba Pinot Noir 2018 Hand-picked, each vineyard parcel wild-fermented separately with 25–30% whole bunches, most pressed at dryness,

2 batches on skins for 5–6 weeks post fermentation, matured in French oak (20% new). An assemblage of cherry fruits, some confit on the bouquet, the palate adding savoury tannins. Screwcap. 13.5% alc. **Rating** 94 **To** 2023 $30 ✪

Ravensworth

312 Patemans Lane, Murrumbateman, ACT 2582 **Region** Canberra District
T (02) 6226 8368 **www**.ravensworthwines.com.au **Open** Not
Winemaker Bryan Martin **Est.** 2000 **Dozens** 2000 **Vyds** 2.6ha
Winemaker, vineyard manager and partner Bryan Martin (with dual wine science and winegrowing degrees from CSU) has a background in wine retail, food and beverage experience in the hospitality industry and teaches part-time. He is also assistant winemaker to Tim Kirk at Clonakilla, after seven years at Jeir Creek. Judging at wine shows is another string to his bow. Ravensworth's organically managed vineyard is mainly planted to shiraz (four clones, including Best's and Tahbilk), riesling (three Geisenheim clones) and sangiovese (three clones) with lesser amounts of white varieties.

🍷🍷🍷🍷🍷 **Murrumbateman Riesling 2019** Displays a vivid green–straw colour. It is a wine that reaffirms the symbiotic relationship between the Canberra District's terroir and riesling. The result is a cross between sheer intensity and fruit, acidity in second place. Screwcap. 12.5% alc. **Rating** 95 **To** 2032 $29 ✪
Estate Shiraz Viognier 2018 Everything is aligned here. Deep ruby hue, the 5% viognier co-ferment no doubt helping. It's fragrant with florals and red fruits and all the spicy-savoury elements that makes this so delicious. Fuller bodied, supple tannins and a succulence throughout. Screwcap. 13.5% alc. **Rating** 95 **To** 2029 $45 JF
Murrumbateman Sangiovese 2018 At first, this is reticent. It offers a hint of tangy cherries, raspberry-like acidity and spices. It unfurls, building in complexity as the raw-silk, textural tannins roll out. It surprises and delights in equal measure. Give it time to reveal its personality. Screwcap. 13% alc. **Rating** 95 **To** 2028 $38 JF

🍷🍷🍷🍷🍷 **Fiano & Friends 2019 Rating** 93 **To** 2024 $29 JF
Hilltops 2019 Rating 93 **To** 2026 $29 JF
Hilltops Nebbiolo 2018 Rating 93 **To** 2027 $42 JF
Regional Sangiovese 2019 Rating 92 **To** 2025 $29 JF
Seven Months 2019 Rating 90 **To** 2023 $38 JF
Tinto 2019 Rating 90 **To** 2024 $29 JF

Redesdale Estate Wines

PO Box 35, Redesdale Vic 3444 **Region** Heathcote
T 0408 407 108 **www**.redesdale.com **Open** By appt
Winemaker Alan Cooper **Est.** 1982 **Dozens** 1000 **Vyds** 4ha
Planting of the Redesdale Estate vines began in 1982 on the northeast slopes of a 25ha grazing property fronting the Campaspe River on one side. The rocky quartz and granite soil meant the vines had to struggle and the annual yield is little more than 1.2t/acre. The vineyard property has since been sold, allowing Peter and Suzanne Williams more time to market their wines.

🍷🍷🍷🍷🍷 **Heathcote Shiraz 2015** Deeply coloured. This is destined to be long-lived, all of its components coming forward with the same proposition. The only question is whether there is an errant note buried in the body of the wine. Screwcap. 14.5% alc. **Rating** 90 **To** 2028 $35

🍷🍷🍷🍷 **La Scassatina 2015 Rating** 89 **To** 2026 $35

RedHeads Wine

258 Angaston Road, Angaston, SA 5353 **Region** South Australia
T (08) 8562 2888 **www**.redheadswine.com **Open** Fri 12–7, w'ends 11–5
Winemaker Alex Trescowthick, Darren Harvey **Est.** 2003 **Dozens** 25 000 **Vyds** 8ha

RedHeads was established by Tony Laithwaite in McLaren Vale and has since moved to the Barossa Valley. The aim was to allow winemakers working under corporate banners to produce small-batch wines. The team 'liberates' premium parcels of grapes from large companies 'a few rows at a time, to give them the special treatment they deserve and to form wines of true individuality and character. It's all about creating wines with personality, that are made to be enjoyed.' Exports to most major markets.

ΤΤΤΤΤ **Esule McLaren Vale Cabernet Sauvignon Cabernet Franc 2018** A blend of 52/48% cabernet franc/cabernet sauvignon. Esule means exile in Italian. It's a bit of a harsh assessment of how drinkers see the cabernet franc/cabernet sauvignon blend, but more power to RedHeads for showing just how aromatic and elegant it can be. Intensely perfumed with dark berry aromas, violet floral tinges, cracked pepper and twists of licorice. Fine tannins persist. Cork. 14.5% alc. Rating 95 To 2032 $50 JP

ΤΤΤΤΥ **Rusty Roof Barbera 2019** Rating 92 To 2026 $25 JP **○**
Blue Belle Graciano 2018 Rating 91 To 2028 $25 JP
Night of the Living Red 2018 Rating 90 To 2034 $35 JP

Redman   ★★★★★

Main Road, Coonawarra, SA 5263 **Region** Coonawarra
T (08) 8736 3331 www.redman.com.au **Open** Mon–Fri 9–5, w'ends 10–4
Winemaker Bruce Redman, Malcolm Redman, Daniel Redman **Est.** 1966
Dozens 18000 **Vyds** 34ha
In March 2008 the Redman family celebrated 100 years of winemaking in Coonawarra. The '08 vintage also marked the arrival of Daniel, fourth-generation Redman winemaker. Daniel gained winemaking experience in Central Victoria, the Barossa Valley and the US before taking up his new position. It was felicitous timing because the '04 Cabernet Sauvignon and '04 Cabernet Merlot were each awarded a gold medal from the national wine show circuit in '07, the first such accolades for a considerable time. A major vineyard rejuvenation program is underway but there will be no change to the portfolio of wines. The quality has stabilised at a level in keeping with the long-term history of the winery and its mature vines.

ΤΤΤΤΤ **The Redman 2009** The prestige cuvee of the estate, demonstrating just how well these wines can age. Plush, yet not fat. Svelte, yet not anodyne. Vibrant, yet far from brittle. A pure stream of currant, mint, bitter chocolate, sage and mulched hints of middle age flow long and broad. The quality French oak melds with juicy grape tannins and a balanced acid line making for savoury, highly attractive drinking now and across a long future. Cork. Rating 96 To 2032 $70 NG **○**

ΤΤΤΤΥ **Coonawarra Cabernet Sauvignon 2017** Rating 91 To 2032 $30 NG

Reillys Wines   ★★★★☆

Cnr Leasingham Road/Hill Street, Mintaro, SA 5415 **Region** Clare Valley
T (08) 8843 9013 www.reillyswines.com.au **Open** 7 days 10–4
Winemaker Justin Ardill **Est.** 1994 **Dozens** 25000 **Vyds** 115ha
Established in 1993 by Justin and Julie Ardill. Justin handmade the first vintage in '94 on the verandah of the heritage-listed Reillys Cottage – built in 1856 by Irish shoemaker Hugh Reilly from local slate – which today serves as their cellar door and restaurant. Justin continues to use the same traditional winemaking techniques of prolonged open fermentation, hand-plunging and oak-barrel maturation. The wines are made from estate vineyards (the oldest planted in 1919). Exports to Canada, Malaysia, Singapore, NZ, Hong Kong and China.

ΤΤΤΤΤ **Museum Release Watervale Riesling 2016** Fruit from the low yielding St Clare Vineyard. It seems young to be a museum release but it's certainly showing some development, the varietal characters in the secondary phase with toast, beeswax, honey and straw more prominent than primary fruit. Importantly though, it retains freshness and vigour, the acidity pulling long and crisp through the finish. Screwcap. 12.5% alc. Rating 94 To 2026 $40 SC

The Dancer Limited Release Clare Valley Cabernet Sauvignon 2016
From the low cropping Smyth's 1945 block in Watervale. Traditional winemaking, maturation in French hogsheads for 24 months. A beautifully balanced wine. Blackcurrant and blackberry fruit seamlessly meshed with quality oak and fine tannin. It's Clare Valley cabernet presented in a smooth and well polished style, ready to drink now or cellar. Screwcap. 14.5% alc. **Rating** 94 **To** 2031 $70 SC

♥♥♥♥♀ Watervale Riesling 2019 Rating 93 To 2029 $25 SC ✪
Moon Vine Limited Release Barossa Valley Shiraz 2017 Rating 93 To 2027 $40 SC
Dry Land Clare Valley Cabernet Sauvignon 2017 Rating 93 To 2030 $38 SC
Dry Land Clare Valley Mataro 2017 Rating 93 To 2032 $32 SC
Dry Land Clare Valley Shiraz 2017 Rating 92 To 2030 $32 SC
Dry Land Clare Valley Tempranillo 2018 Rating 92 To 2025 $29 SC
Barking Mad Watervale Riesling 2019 Rating 91 To 2026 $20 SC ✪
Barking Mad Watervale Shiraz 2017 Rating 90 To 2027 $20 SC ✪

Renzaglia Wines   ★★★★☆

38 Bosworth Falls Road, O'Connell, NSW 2795 **Region** Central Ranges zone
T (02) 6337 5756 **www**.renzagliawines.com.au **Open** By appt
Winemaker Mark Renzaglia **Est.** 2011 **Dozens** 2000 **Vyds** 4.6ha
Mark Renzaglia is a second-generation vigneron, his father grows vines in southern Illinois, US. Mark and wife Sandy planted their first vineyard in 1997 (1ha of chardonnay, cabernet sauvignon and merlot), Mark making wine in small quantities while working as a grapegrower/winemaker at Winburndale Wines for 11 years. In 2011 he left Winburndale and he and Sandy started their own business. He also manages a vineyard in the middle of the famous Mount Panorama race circuit and has access to the grapes from the 4ha Mount Panorama Estate (another vineyard from which Brokenwood has purchased chardonnay for some years). This gives him access to shiraz, semillon, cabernet sauvignon and chardonnay. He also purchases grapes from other local growers. Exports to the US.

♥♥♥♥♥ Mount Panorama Estate Shiraz 2017 Hand-picked, 4 days' cold soak, wild-fermented with 15% whole bunches and 10% whole berries, pressed to French oak (25% new) after 14 days' open-top fermentation, matured for 15 months. Seriously good wine in an off-the-beaten-track (petrol heads not included) terroir. Exemplary balance and finesse for a shiraz that has taken all there is to offer in its swathe of black fruits. Screwcap. 13.9% alc. **Rating** 95 **To** 2032 $40
Bella Luna Chardonnay 2018 From the home vineyard; hand-picked by a team of volunteers on 4 Mar, crushed and pressed the same day, fermented in 1 new and 2 used French barriques. Well made, no oxidation, good stone fruit and melon flavours. Screwcap. 12.5% alc. **Rating** 94 **To** 2022 $40

♥♥♥♥♀ Shiraz 2017 Rating 90 To 2029 $22

Reynella   ★★★★★

Reynell Road, Reynella, SA 5161 **Region** McLaren Vale/Fleurieu Peninsula
T 1800 088 711 **www**.reynellawines.ocm.au **Open** Fri 11–4
Winemaker Paul Carpenter **Est.** 1838 **Dozens** NFP
John Reynell laid the foundations for Chateau Reynella in 1838; over the next 100 years the stone buildings, winery and underground cellars, with attractive gardens, were constructed. Thomas Hardy's first job in SA was with Reynella; he noted in his diary that he would be able to better himself soon. He did just that, becoming by far the largest producer in SA by the end of the 19th century; 150 or so years after Chateau Reynella's foundations were laid, CWA (now Accolade Wines) completed the circle by making it its corporate headquarters, while preserving the integrity of the Reynella brand in no uncertain fashion. Exports to all major markets.

🍷🍷🍷🍷🍷 **Basket Pressed McLaren Vale Grenache 2018** This delights because the flavours and complexity of the 45yo bushvines shine through, unencumbered by winemaking artefact or overripe fruit flavours. While there's a nutty, savoury overlay, there's also sweet raspberry, cherries and pips with grainy tannins working their way across the medium-bodied palate. Screwcap. 14% alc. **Rating** 95 To 2028 $71 JF

Ricca Terra ★★★★★

PO Box 305, Angaston, SA 5353 **Region** Riverland
T 0411 370 057 **www**.riccaterravintners.com.au **Open** Not
Winemaker Ashley Ratcliff **Est.** 2017 **Dozens** 6000 **Vyds** 80ha
The Ricca Terra venture of Ashley and Holly Ratcliff was decades in the making. Ashley began his journey in wine in 1992 when he joined Orlando as a viticulturist, thereafter moving to Yalumba where he remained until 2016. During this time he obtained a Bachelor of Applied Science, a masters degree in marketing and became a graduate of the AWRI sensory evaluation course. In his 15 years with Yalumba he was winery manager for the vast Riverland winery and technical manager (viticulture). He was the recipient of four major state and federal industry awards, all focusing on viticulture in drought-prone regions. So when he and Holly purchased an 8ha vineyard in the Riverland it presented the opportunity to plant varieties pushing the envelope, such as the rare planting of an ancient Balkan variety slankamenka bela. There are now 80ha of varieties, mainly selected for the climate, grown with surface mulches, soil moisture monitoring probes and smart viticultural practices. The wines are made using all of the cutting edge techniques, hand-picked into half-tonne bins and chilled for 12 hours before transfer to the winery in the Barossa Valley. Ricca Terra means rich earth in Italian. It was the first winery from the Riverland to receive a 5-star rating in the *Wine Companion*. Exports to the UK and the US.

🍷🍷🍷🍷🍷 **Soldiers' Land 90 Year Old Vines Grenache 2019** From 90yo vines; hand-pruned and hand-picked, wild yeast–open fermented, matured in 3yo barrels. Generosity and a strongly held belief and regard for history are the cream on the cake for this very good wine. Screwcap. 14.5% alc. **Rating** 95 To 2029 $30 ✪

🍷🍷🍷🍷🍷 **Bronco Buster 2019 Rating** 92 To 2021 $22 ✪
Small Batch Riverland Grenache Blanc 2019 Rating 91 To 2020 $27
Colour of Calmness Riverland Rose 2019 Rating 90 To 2020 $22

Richard Hamilton ★★★★★

Cnr Main Road/Johnston Road, McLaren Vale, SA 5171 **Region** McLaren Vale
T (08) 8323 8830 **www**.leconfieldwines.com **Open** Mon–Fri 10–5, w'ends & public hols 11–5
Winemaker Paul Gordon, Tim Bailey **Est.** 1972 **Dozens** 25 000 **Vyds** 71.6ha
Richard Hamilton has outstanding estate vineyards, some of great age, all fully mature. An experienced and skilled winemaking team has allowed the full potential of those vineyards to be realised. The quality, style and consistency of both red and white wines has reached a new level; being able to keep only the best parcels for the Richard Hamilton brand is an enormous advantage. Exports to the UK, the US, Canada, Denmark, Sweden, Germany, Belgium, Malaysia, Vietnam, Hong Kong, Singapore, Japan, China and NZ.

🍷🍷🍷🍷🍷 **Centurion McLaren Vale Shiraz 2018** The 126yo vines produce grapes of very high quality, fermentation in oak vats giving the grapes their due respect (followed by maturation in vats or hogsheads). It has finesse, length and balance, and will live for decades. Screwcap. 14.5% alc. **Rating** 96 To 2048 $75 ✪
Little Road McLaren Vale Shiraz 2018 While there's plenty of Vale charm in this – the juicy, red and black fruits, the choc-mint, the intensity of it all – there's a savoury overlay that keeps everything in check. Plenty of ripe tannins and intensity yet sits more on the medium spectrum. Screwcap. 14.5% alc. **Rating** 95 To 2028 $22 JF ✪

ŸŸŸŸŸ The Smuggler McLaren Vale Shiraz 2018 Rating 92 To 2027 $22 JF✪
Colton's McLaren Vale G.S.M. 2018 Rating 92 To 2027 $22 JF✪
Hut Block Cabernet Sauvignon 2017 Rating 92 To 2027 $21 ✪
Watervale Riesling 2019 Rating 90 To 2028 $20 JF✪

Ridgemill Estate ★★★★☆

218 Donges Road, Severnlea, Qld 4380 **Region** Granite Belt
T (07) 4683 5211 **www.**ridgemillestate.com **Open** Fri–Mon 10–5, Sun 10–3
Winemaker Martin Cooper, Peter McGlashan **Est.** 1998 **Dozens** 900 **Vyds** 2.1ha
Martin Cooper acquired what was then known as Emerald Hill Winery in 2004. In '05 he
reshaped the vineyards – which now have plantings of chardonnay, tempranillo, shiraz, merlot,
cabernet sauvignon, saperavi, verdelho and viognier – setting a course down the alternative
variety road. There is a quite spectacular winery and cellar door facility, and self-contained
cabins in the vineyard.

ŸŸŸŸŸ Ellie Blanc de Blanc 2018 A highly refreshing bottle of fizz, spending a year
on lees before being equipped with 6g/l dosage and a dollop of Cognac across
its liqueur d'expedition. Highly traditional in the world of Champagne, although
seldom practised any longer. The result is surprisingly subtle with green apple,
pear and a billow of dough across vibrant acid seams. Restrained. Understated.
Impeccably integrated. An apero style rather than a bombastic fizz, but long is the
linger. Poise is this wine's calling card. Very fine. Cork. Rating 95 $30 NG ✪

ŸŸŸŸŸ WYP Granite Belt Chardonnay 2018 Rating 93 To 2028 $35
Granite Belt Merlot 2017 Rating 93 To 2026 $28 NG
Granite Belt Pinot G 2019 Rating 92 To 2022 $28
The Lincoln Granite Belt Shiraz 2017 Rating 92 To 2027 $30
Malbec Mourvedre 2019 Rating 92 To 2027 $28 NG
Hungry Horse Granite Belt Semillon Viognier Riesling 2019 Rating 91
To 2023 $28 NG
Benny's Blend Merlot Malbec 2016 Rating 91 To 2028 $40 NG

RidgeView Wines ★★★★★

273 Sweetwater Road, Pokolbin, NSW 2320 **Region** Hunter Valley
T (02) 6574 7332 **www.**ridgeview.com.au **Open** Wed–Sun 10–5
Winemaker Darren Scott, Gary MacLean, Mark Woods **Est.** 2000 **Dozens** 3000
Vyds 9ha
Darren and Tracey Scott have transformed a 40ha timbered farm into a vineyard with self-
contained accommodation and a cellar door. The greater part of the plantings are 4.5ha of
shiraz; cabernet sauvignon, chambourcin, merlot, pinot gris, viognier and traminer making up
a somewhat eclectic selection of other varieties.

ŸŸŸŸŸ Museum Release Generations Reserve Hunter Valley Semillon 2009
From the great Braemore Vineyard on Hermitage Road. A wonderful semillon
that has entered the plateau of perfection that will last for decades to come. The
citrus flavours have a gently sweet, honeyed accent; toast to arrive over the next 5
years as an optional extra. Screwcap. 10.8% alc. Rating 97 To 2030 $60 ✪

ŸŸŸŸŸ Museum Release Generations Reserve Hunter Valley Semillon 2014
From 44yo vines on the Brokenback Vineyard. Still in the first stage of its
development, there has been an increase in the depth of its lemon/lemongrass/
citrus flavours. It's as fresh as a daisy. Screwcap. 11.2% alc. Rating 95 To 2029
$35 ✪
Impressions Effen Hill Vineyard Hunter Valley Shiraz 2018 Matured in
French barriques of varying ages (10% new) for 15 months. Said to have won
many gold medals already. Bright colour. A medium-bodied wine with bright
purple and black fruits, fine savoury tannins. Made at Leogate. Screwcap. 14.5% alc.
Rating 95 To 2043 $40

Museum Release Impressions Single Vineyard Hunter Valley Shiraz 2014 Some whole-bunch fermentation, matured in new and used French barriques for 15 months. Still a long way off maturity but is well worth waiting for 10 years minimum, with many years thereafter before it starts to show the first signs of tiredness. Red fruits, structure and texture are all on the same page. Screwcap. 13.5% alc. **Rating** 95 **To** 2040 $45

Generations Reserve Hunter Valley Semillon 2019 From the Brokenback Vineyard planted by Len Evans in '70. It immediately establishes its blue bloodlines with the already-apparent depth to its lemongrass and zesty/juicy acidity, the length excellent. Screwcap. 11% alc. **Rating** 94 **To** 2029 $30 ✪

♥♥♥♥♀ **Generations Single Vineyard Reserve Hunter Valley Shiraz 2017** **Rating** 93 **To** 2037 $45

Impressions Single Vineyard Hunter Valley Chardonnay 2017 Rating 90 **To** 2020 $35

Museum Release Impressions Single Vineyard Hunter Valley Chardonnay 2014 Rating 90 **To** 2020 $40

Rieslingfreak ★★★★★

103 Langmeil Road, Tanunda, SA 5352 **Region** Clare Valley
T 0439 336 250 **www**.rieslingfreak.com **Open** By appt
Winemaker John Hughes **Est.** 2009 **Dozens** 7500 **Vyds** 35ha
The name of John Hughes' winery leaves no doubt about his long-term ambition: to explore every avenue of riesling, whether bone-dry or sweet, coming from regions across the wine world, albeit with a strong focus on Australia. The wines made from his Clare Valley vineyard offer dry (No. 2, No. 3, No. 4 and No. 10), off-dry (No. 5 and No. 8), sparkling (No. 9) and fortified (No. 7) styles. Exports to the UK, the US, Canada, Denmark and Hong Kong.

♥♥♥♥♥ **No. 2 Riesling 2019** Winemaker John Hughes has adopted a numbering system for the styles of his wines. This has the quintessential bouquet and flavour of Polish Hill River, a delight now or in the years to come as notes of honey and toast join the citrus/green apple/white peach of today. Screwcap. 10.5% alc. **Rating** 96 **To** 2030 $37 ✪

No. 3 Riesling 2019 From the family vineyard at White Hut in the Clare Valley. It has enticing colour and an equally enticing palate with unusual but positive mandarin flavours that take pole position starting on the palate and continuing through the aftertaste. Screwcap. 11.5% alc. **Rating** 95 **To** 2030 $27 ✪

No. 4 Riesling 2019 It's taken time, but I've finally become used to John Hughes' brand name and label system. Here the Meyer lemon/lemongrass flavours of the Eden Valley are correct, even if they have hints of Hunter Valley semillon – a dreadful accusation for an SA riesling maker. While each of the 3 dry Rieslingfreak wines in this line-up has its own character, they are difficult to split on points. Screwcap. 11% alc. **Rating** 95 **To** 2032 $27 ✪

No. 5 Riesling 2019 From the family vineyard at White Hut. Bright, fresh and crisp, everything one should enjoy with this off-dry Clare riesling. As enjoyable tonight as it will be in the years to come. John Hughes continues to polish his skills. Screwcap. 10.5% alc. **Rating** 95 $27 ✪

No. 6 Riesling 2014 From the family White Hut Vineyard in the Clare Valley. Made to be held for later release. John Hughes believes it is still developing, and I think he may be right. Tart lemon juice might not please all. Screwcap. 10.5% alc. **Rating** 94 **To** 2023 $42

No. 8 Riesling 2019 From Polish Hill River, in Schatzkammer style. A high quality wine, appreciably richer and sweeter than its off-dry No. 5 sibling. The intense lime/lemon duo will outlive most consumers' patience – another 5 years could reveal a wine of startling quality. Screwcap. 6.5% alc. **Rating** 94 $37

♥♥♥♥♀ **No. 9 Riesling 2016 Rating** 90 $45

Rikard Wines   ★★★★★

140 McLachlan Street, Orange, NSW 2800 (postal) **Region** Orange
T 0428 633 320 **www**.rikardwines.com.au **Open** Not
Winemaker William Rikard-Bell **Est.** 2015 **Dozens** 700 **Vyds** 1ha
William Rikard-Bell's first job as winemaker was at Canobolas Smith in Orange. After
interludes in Bordeaux, Mudgee and the Hunter, he returned to Orange and purchased a
10ha block on Mt Canobolas with his wife Kimberley. They have planted 5000 pinot noir
and chardonnay vines at 850m above sea level. More chardonnay and pinot will be planted
in the future, and possibly some riesling and aligote. The vines are close-planted, with
narrow rows and a low cordon height. The grapes are hand-picked, the small batch wines
made using traditional Old World techniques. A winery and bottling line was completed in
December 2019, with pop-up cellar doors planned for '20 until the permanent cellar door
is constructed.

ΨΨΨΨΨ **Orange Riesling 2019** A lot of attention to winemaking detail involved here,
but to cut a long story short it was mostly (75%) fermented in old oak. Typically
pale young riesling in appearance and the varietal characters are pure, but the
barrel work has imparted an individual slant. It's not oaky, but there's a savoury,
textural feel. It's mouthfilling but also fresh, long and taut. Well done. Screwcap.
12.4% alc. **Rating** 95 **To** 2034 $30 SC ✿
Black Label Orange Pinot Noir 2018 Given 33% carbonic maceration,
25% whole bunches, wild ferment, soaked on skins for 18 days post ferment,
pressed to 40% new French barriques for 12 months' maturation. More 'sauvage'
than its sibling, with sour cherry and mulchy aromas and some tartness to the
flavours. More depth and complexity also, and the oak a little more prominent for
now. Give it time. Screwcap. 14% alc. **Rating** 95 **To** 2030 $65 SC
Black Label Orange Chardonnay 2018 The best 3 barrels of the '18 vintage.
Free-run juice wild-fermented in French barriques (65% new), full mlf with
monthly batonnage. The warm and ripe vintage and the time spent in new oak
has made its mark, and produced quite a full-on style. The batonnage seems to
have contributed some attractive matchstick characters and the length of flavour is
good. Screwcap. 12.8% alc. **Rating** 94 **To** 2025 $55 SC

ΨΨΨΨ♀ **Orange Pinot Noir 2018 Rating** 93 **To** 2028 $40 SC
Orange Chardonnay 2018 Rating 92 **To** 2023 $35 SC
Orange Shiraz 2018 Rating 92 **To** 2028 $50 SC
Orange Cabernet Franc 2018 Rating 92 **To** 2028 $45 SC

Rileys of Eden Valley   ★★★★

PO Box 71, Eden Valley, SA 5235 **Region** Eden Valley
T (08) 8564 1029 **www**.rileysofedenvalley.com.au **Open** Not
Winemaker Peter Riley, Jo Irvine (Consultant) **Est.** 2006 **Dozens** 2000 **Vyds** 11.24ha
Rileys of Eden Valley is owned by Terry and Jan Riley with son Peter, who, way back in
1982, purchased 32ha of a grazing property that they believed had potential for quality grape
production. The first vines were planted in that year and now extend to over 11ha. In '98
Terry retired from his position (professor of Mechanical Engineering) at the University of
South Australia, allowing him to concentrate on the vineyard and, more recently, winemaking
activities, but the whole family (including granddaughter Maddy) have been involved in the
development of the property. It had always been intended that the grapes would be sold, but
when not all the grapes were contracted in '06, the Rileys decided to produce some wine.

ΨΨΨΨ♀ **Jump Ship Shiraz 2017** Pulpier than the '16, with a whiff of reductive florals.
The oak is well appointed, the fruit blue and grapey. There seems to have been a
shift in the approach to crafting this vintage. For the better. Fresh, detailed, gently
peppery and long. Screwcap. **Rating** 92 **To** 2025 $30 NG
Maximus Premium Cabernet Sauvignon 2017 An unashamedly rich red
oozing blackcurrant, mint and bitter chocolate to vanillan oak scents. The tannins,

expansive and pliant, are impressive enough. A legacy of the extended maceration in lieu of a prodigious vintage. Screwcap. **Rating** 92 **To** 2027 $60 NG

Jump Ship Shiraz 2016 An avuncular shiraz, old-school and inviting. Violet scents. Black plum, boysenberry, anise and kirsch. Malty oak and an energetic skein of peppery acidity towing it long. Screwcap. **Rating** 91 **To** 2024 $30 NG

Rill House Vineyard ★★★★

O'Leary's Lane, Spring Hill, Vic 3444 **Region** Macedon Ranges
T 0414 235 062 **www.rillhouse.com Open** Not
Winemaker Matt Harrop, Loic Le Calvez **Est.** 1986 **Dozens** 400 **Vyds** 2.7ha
The Rill House Vineyard was planted in 1986 in a natural amphitheatre on the edge of the Wombat State Forest, with a natural spring (rill) that runs through the property. At 650m above sea level, it is one of the coolest sites in the region, and is managed using organic and biodynamic practices. Exports to France.

🍷🍷🍷🍷🍷 **My Deer Bride Chardonnay 2018** Made in similar fashion to the '17; the warmer vintage, a plus at this altitude (650m), giving the wine a little more mouthfeel and complexity. Natural acidity also a plus. Screwcap. 13% alc. **Rating** 94 **To** 2030 $60

Dashing Red Fox Pinot Noir 2018 From a 0.4ha planting; hand-picked, wild yeast–open fermented, matured in 3 barrels (old and new). A delicious pinot with pure red fruits that have freshness and considerable length. Screwcap. 13% alc. **Rating** 94 **To** 2027 $65

🍷🍷🍷🍷🍷 **My Deer Bride Chardonnay 2017 Rating** 93 **To** 2029 $60

Riposte Wines ★★★★★

PO Box 256, Lobethal, SA 5241 **Region** Adelaide Hills
T 0412 816 107 **www.timknappstein.com.au Open** Not
Winemaker Tim Knappstein **Est.** 2006 **Dozens** 11 000
Tim Knappstein is a third-generation vigneron, his winemaking lineage dating back to 1893 in the Clare Valley. He made his first wines at the family's Stanley Wine Company and established his own wine company in the Clare Valley in 1976. After the sale of that company in '81, Tim relocated to Lenswood in the Adelaide Hills to make cool-climate wines led by pinot noir and chardonnay. His quest has now been achieved with consistently excellent wines reflected in the winery's 5-star rating since the *Wine Companion 2012*. Exports to the UK, the US, Switzerland, Denmark, Indonesia and China.

🍷🍷🍷🍷🍷 **Museum Release Reserve Noble Traminer 2011** Abstemious yields and a painstaking hand-pick across different passes through a vineyard that had otherwise been left for dead. This was because of the cool, wet and subsequently, 'written off' vintage of '11. Yet moisture and humidity coalesce to deliver noble rot, the malevolent fungus responsible for phenomenal sweet wines. An immense clang of residual, concentrated and palate-staining viscosity, extract and spicy grapey exotic hubris. Long, intense and mind-spinning, finishing as savoury as it is sweet. Screwcap. **Rating** 98 **To** 2035 $35 NG ✪

🍷🍷🍷🍷🍷 **The Cutlass Single Vineyard Adelaide Hills Shiraz 2018** Fermented across 2 batches: 50% whole bunch with crushed fruit; the other, whole berries, to confer a partial carbonic softness and lifted lilac notes. The result is firm, aromatic and attractively rustic. The tannins, doused in black olive, pepper grind and iodine, are textural and moreish. This wine may not please effete technocrats but I am not one of them. The aromas are rewarding too: blueberry, salami and spice. A bit of a yeoman, this is nevertheless an expressive shiraz deserved of attention. Screwcap. **Rating** 94 **To** 2025 $28 NG ✪

🍷🍷🍷🍷🍷 **Reserve Adelaide Hills Pinot Noir 2018 Rating** 93 **To** 2026 $80 NG
The Stiletto Adelaide Hills Pinot Gris 2019 Rating 92 **To** 2022 $22 NG ✪
The Sabre Adelaide Hills Pinot Noir 2018 Rating 92 **To** 2022 $35 NG

The Scimitar Single Vineyard Clare Valley Riesling 2019 Rating 91
To 2029 $22 NG ✪
The Katana Single Vineyard Adelaide Hills Chardonnay 2018 Rating 91
To 2023 $28 NG

Risky Business Wines   ★★★★

PO Box 6015, East Perth, WA 6892 **Region** Various
T 0457 482 957 **www.**riskybusinesswines.com.au **Open** Not
Winemaker Andrew Vesey **Est.** 2013 **Dozens** 6500
The name Risky Business is decidedly tongue-in-cheek because the partnership headed by
Rob Quenby has neatly side-stepped any semblance of risk. The grapes come from vineyards
in Great Southern and Margaret River that are managed by Quenby Viticultural Services.
Since the batches of wine are small (140–2000 dozen), the partnership is able to select grapes
specifically suited to the wine style and price. So there is no capital tied up in vineyards, nor
in a winery – the wines are contract-made. In 2018 Risky Business expanded its operations
to Victoria's King Valley, making Italian-style prosecco, grigio and sangiovese. Exports to Japan
and China.

🍷🍷🍷🍷🍷 Luxe Mount Barker Riesling 2019 An off-dry style, so different in its way, but
shows the precision and poise we expect to see from riesling in this region. There's
the typical minerality underpinning the more floral, aromatic notes in the bouquet,
and the palate is built along a line of fine but firm acidity which flows into the
aftertaste. The sweetness, though obvious, is seamlessly integrated. Screwcap.
11% alc. **Rating** 94 $25 SC ✪

🍷🍷🍷🍷🍷 White Knuckle Margaret River Chardonnay 2019 Rating 91 To 2023
$25 NG
King Valley Pinot Gris 2019 Rating 91 To 2022 $25 SC
Malbec 2018 Rating 91 To 2022 $25 NG

RiverBank Estate   ★★★★★

126 Hamersley Road, Caversham, WA 6055 **Region** Swan Valley
T (08) 9377 1805 **www.**riverbankestate.com.au **Open** 7 days 10–5
Winemaker Digby Leddin **Est.** 1988 **Dozens** 4500 **Vyds** 12ha
RiverBank Estate was first planted on the fertile banks of the Swan River in 1988 and has
grown to encompass 12ha of mature, low-yielding vines (18 varieties), the wines made onsite.
The property was purchased by the Lembo family in 2017 and has been rebranded into three
wine ranges: On The Run, Rebellious and Eric Anthony. RiverBank was named Winery of
the Year 2019 by Ray Jordan and Best Small Cellar Door in the Swan Valley 2019 by Peter
Forrestal of *Gourmet Traveller*. Winemaker, Digby Leddin, spent two decades with Lamont's
Winery before joining RiverBank in '17. Exports to Azerbaijan, the Maldives and China.

🍷🍷🍷🍷🍷 Rebellious Swan Valley Vermentino 2019 Hand-picked, chilled overnight,
destemmed, pressed, only free-run juice fermented with X16 yeast and early
bottled. Mouth-puckering flavours and texture. Gold medal Wine Show of
WA '19. Screwcap. 12.5% alc. **Rating** 95 To 2023 $25 ✪
Rebellious Blackwood & Swan Valley Grenache 2017 A blend of
85% grenache and 15% shiraz from: the Blackwood Valley (55%), Swan Valley
(40%) and Donnybrook (5%). Made in small batches and matured in second-use
French and American hogsheads. Gold medals Hobart and Swan Valley. Very deep
and healthy colour. Remarkably good. Shades of Rhône Valley with both deep
fruits and persistent tannins. Screwcap. 13.6% alc. **Rating** 95 To 2027 $25 ✪
Eric Anthony Margaret River Chardonnay 2018 Hand-picked, whole-
bunch pressed to a new French puncheon, 8 months' maturation. Mouth-watering
intensity to grapefruit and company flavours, the oak barely noticeable. Trophy
Swan Valley Wine Show '19, gold medal Australian Small Winemakers Show '19.
Screwcap. 12.9% alc. **Rating** 94 To 2027 $35

Rebellious Swan Valley Fiano 2017 Fermented in French barriques. A scented bouquet of Australian wildflowers, then a palate of unexpected power and precision, citrus skin and pith. This is a good wine by any standard. Screwcap. 13.8% alc. **Rating** 94 **To** 2027 $25 ○

Rebellious Swan Valley Vermentino 2017 Two parcels picked early Mar, identical vinification to the '19. A small wine that throws a big punch; at once juicy, yet seashell dry. Crisp, long and expansive. Made for drinking anywhere, any time. Screwcap. 12.5% alc. **Rating** 94 **To** 2022 $25 ○

Rebellious Swan Valley Rose 2019 A field blend of shiraz, malbec, tempranillo and grenache. Chilled overnight, hand-sorted, destemmed, several hours on skins in the press, fermented with a specific yeast. The palate is driven by red cherry fruits and just the right amount of residual sugar. Small wonder it has had a great time in local/state wine shows, including a trophy at the Swan Valley Wine Show. Screwcap. 12.5% alc. **Rating** 94 **To** 2020 $25 ○

ҲҲҲҲҶ **Rebellious Swan Valley Verdelho 2018** Rating 93 **To** 2024 $25 ○
Rebellious Swan Valley Petit Verdot 2017 Rating 93 **To** 2030 $25 ○
Eric Anthony Margaret River Chardonnay 2017 Rating 91 **To** 2026 $35

Riversdale Estate   ★★★★★

222 Denholms Road, Cambridge, Tas 7170 **Region** Southern Tasmania
T (03) 6248 5555 www.riversdaleestate.com.au **Open** 7 days 10–5
Winemaker Nick Badrice **Est.** 1991 **Dozens** 9000 **Vyds** 37ha
Ian Roberts purchased the Riversdale property in 1980 while a university student. He says he paid a record price for the district. The unique feature of the property is its frontage to the Pittwater waterfront, which acts as a buffer against frost and also moderates the climate during the ripening phase. It is a large property with 37ha of vines and one of the largest olive groves in Tasmania, producing 50 olive-based products. Five families live permanently on the estate, providing all the labour for the various operations, which also include four 5-star French Provincial cottages overlooking the vines. A cellar door and French bistro opened in Jan '16. Wine quality is consistently good and can be outstanding.

ҲҲҲҲҲ **Coal River Valley Riesling 2019** The first thing you notice is the intense burst of cooked apple–like flavour, its tang intact, its flavours singing. The second is the texture, which is a step up on most young rieslings. This is a floral, spicy wine with excellent fruit concentration but with more than a little character to boot. Screwcap. 12.5% alc. **Rating** 95 **To** 2032 $35 CM ○
Crater Block 2 Chardonnay 2017 Custard apple and nectarine, white peach and vanilla cream, perhaps even a touch of fennel. It shoots straight and long and brings plenty along for the ride. Screwcap. 12.5% alc. **Rating** 94 **To** 2027 CM

ҲҲҲҲҶ **Crater Block 2 Chardonnay 2018** Rating 92 **To** 2026 CM
Blanc de Blancs NV Rating 92 $38 CM
Coal River Valley Rose 2019 Rating 91 **To** 2022 $28 CM
Coal River Valley Chardonnay 2019 Rating 90 **To** 2026 CM

Rob Dolan Wines   ★★★★★

21–23 Delaneys Road, South Warrandyte, Vic 3134 **Region** Yarra Valley
T (03) 9876 5885 www.robdolanwines.com.au **Open** 7 days 10–5
Winemaker Rob Dolan, Adrian Santolin **Est.** 2010 **Dozens** 30 000 **Vyds** 25ha
Rob Dolan has been making wine in the Yarra Valley for over 20 years and knows every nook and cranny there. In 2011 he was able to purchase the Hardys Yarra Burn winery at an enticing price. It is singularly well equipped and, in addition to making the excellent Rob Dolan wines there, he conducts an extensive contract winemaking business. Business is booming, production having doubled, with exports driving much of the increase. Exports to the UK, the US, Canada, Malaysia, Thailand, Singapore, Hong Kong and China.

White Label Yarra Valley Pinot Noir 2018 MV6 clone; whole-berry ferment, 7-day ferment on skins, 10 months in French oak (35% new). The bar has been lifted. Tightly focused. A raft of intoxicating scents of pomegranate, black olive, cherry compote, plum, vanilla pod. Deliciously irresistible. Underpinning succulent fruit is a warm savouriness filling the mid-palate accompanied by supple tannins that last right to the finish. Screwcap. 13% alc. **Rating** 95 **To** 2028 $35 JP ◆

White Label Yarra Valley Cabernet Sauvignon 2018 Destemmed, whole-berry ferment in open fermenters, mix of wild and cultured yeasts, pressed to oak barrels, maturation in French oak (35% new) for 16 months. A delicious taste of fruit and nothing but the fruit with a young cabernet that lifts and sings and excites. This is what we love to see in Yarra Valley cabernet: an elegance of line, of sweet cassis aromas and varietal intensity, of smart, modest tannins that go about their job with purpose in the background. And then, just a touch of oak – but only a touch. Screwcap. 13.5% alc. **Rating** 95 **To** 2032 $35 JP ◆

Signature Series Yarra Valley Cabernet Sauvignon 2017 SA125 clone; 7-day whole-berry ferment on skins, 16 months in French oak (35% new). From the Yarraland Vineyard and produced only in outstanding years, Signature keeps true to its Yarra address, lifted and polished with a touch of class. Deep garnet. An essay in letting fruit quality speak true. Pastille, crushed blackberry, clove. Fine on the palate with subtle forest floor earthiness laced with licorice, fennel. Lingers long. Screwcap. 13.2% alc. **Rating** 95 **To** 2032 $80 JP

White Label Yarra Valley Pinot Gris 2019 **Rating** 93 **To** 2025 $30 JP
White Label Yarra Valley Chardonnay 2018 **Rating** 92 **To** 2026 $30 JP
True Colours Yarra Valley Pinot Noir Rose 2019 **Rating** 92 **To** 2025 $24 JP◆
Black Label Yarra Valley Chardonnay 2018 **Rating** 91 **To** 2026 $27 JP
White Label Yarra Valley Shiraz 2018 **Rating** 90 **To** 2030 $35 JP

Robert Channon Wines ★★★★

32 Bradley Lane, Amiens, Qld 4352 **Region** Granite Belt
T (07) 4683 3260 **www.**robertchannonwines.com **Open** Mon, Tues & Fri 11–4, w'ends 10–5
Winemaker Paola Cabezas **Est.** 1998 **Dozens** 2500 **Vyds** 8ha
Peggy and Robert Channon have established verdelho, chardonnay, pinot gris, shiraz, cabernet sauvignon and pinot noir under permanent bird protection netting. The initial cost of installing permanent netting is high but in the long term it is well worth it: it excludes birds and protects the grapes against hail damage. Also, there is no pressure to pick the grapes before they are fully ripe.

Granite Belt Verdelho 2019 Perhaps it is a synergy with the granitic soils and altitude, but verdelho is always substantially more restrained here than its expressions elsewhere. Quince, grapefruit rind, bitter almond and less tropical fruit (thank goodness); some chew and a gentle flow of acidity melded with some leesy detail. Tastes like a Marchese verdicchio. Good gear. A highly versatile, dry mid-weight wine. Screwcap. **Rating** 92 **To** 2023 $28 NG

Granite Belt Cabernet Shiraz 2019 With 85% cabernet, this is a juicy, nicely tuned blend of the Australian heroes. Vivid. Pulpy. Cassis, vanilla pod, baking spice and dried sage to bay leaf scents. Yet there is nothing drying about it. Nothing forced. It simply flows from fore to aft following a judicious 9 months in American and French wood. A lovely drink. Screwcap. **Rating** 92 **To** 2025 $30 NG

Wild Ferment Granite Belt Verdelho 2019 Strung out across a longer ambient ferment in barrel, this is a glossier wine. Exudes ripe stone fruit notes with a riff of passionfruit and citrus glazed spice. There is something cool and herbal too, tucked behind the sheen. More of a crowd-pleaser. Screwcap. **Rating** 91 **To** 2023 $30 NG

Chardonnay Verdelho 2019 Not quite sure why one would blend these varieties but here we have it. It stands alone as a mealy, dry, medium-bodied table wine. Some oatmeal and curd from lees-handled chardonnay; some zip and citrus gloss, presumably from the verdelho. Whatever. Rather than examining each segment, the sum of the parts has turned out rather well. Screwcap. **Rating** 90 **To** 2023 $25 NG

Robert Oatley Margaret River   ★★★★★

3518 Caves Road, Wilyabrup, WA 6280 **Region** Margaret River
T (08) 9750 4000 **www**.robertoatley.com.au **Open** 7 days 10.30–4.30
Winemaker Larry Cherubino **Est.** 2006 **Dozens** NFP **Vyds** 155ha
Robert Oatley Wines, founded by the late Robert (Bob) Oatley AO BEM in 2006, is a family-owned winery led by his eldest son Sandy Oatley who, with his father, brother and sister, planted the first Oatley vineyards in the late 1960s. The trio of labels celebrates Bob Oatley's vision with the Signature Series, particular vineyard sites with Finisterre, and the best of the best barrels under The Pennant. Focusing on wines from Margaret River (and Great Southern) and McLaren Vale, the business now bases itself in the Margaret River, with a vineyard and cellar door on Caves Road in the heart of the region. Exports to the UK, the US, Canada and China.

ᵧᵧᵧᵧᵧ **The Pennant Margaret River Chardonnay 2018** Hand-picked from the 24 Karat Vineyard, whole-bunch pressed, wild-fermented in new and 1yo French oak, only 5 barriques made. Karridale gives the intensity and style, not keeping anyone guessing. Perfectly fine to open a bottle tonight as long as you have another to celebrate in '23. Screwcap. 13.5% alc. **Rating** 97 **To** 2028 $90 ✪

ᵧᵧᵧᵧᵧ **Signature Series Great Southern Riesling 2019** From Frankland River and Great Southern; 4 trophies (including Best White Wine of Show at the WA Wine Show), gold medal National Wine Show. High quality riesling, balancing lemon-lime fruit and youthful acidity like a highwire balancing act between 2 skyscrapers. Screwcap. 12.5% alc. **Rating** 96 **To** 2029 $23 ✪
Signature Series McLaren Vale Grenache G-18 2018 It has an elfin lightness and freshness, its 96-point gold medal one of 3 singled out from an additional eight golds on 95 points at the McLaren Vale Wine Show '19. It's one of those wines you just have to love to death (aka finish). Screwcap. 13.5% alc. **Rating** 96 **To** 2028 $23 ✪
The Pennant Frankland River Cabernet Sauvignon 2016 From the Justin Vineyard; hand-picked, berry-sorted, wild yeast–open fermented. Interesting wine. Autocratic cabernet with tannins, earth, black olive and savoury aromas and flavours ringing the bells; cassis/blackcurrant kept firmly in the back seat in company with oak. Screwcap. 13.5% alc. **Rating** 96 **To** 2040 $105
Finisterre Caves Road Red Blend 2017 This is some red blend: 43% cabernet sauvignon, 22% cabernet franc, 19% malbec and 8% each of merlot and petit verdot. It is truly delicious, the work of a master winemaker. Red and blue fruits frolic in the mouth, leaving it fresh. Deserves the extra point for its improbability. Screwcap. 14% alc. **Rating** 95 **To** 2030 $40
Finisterre Margaret River Chardonnay 2018 From Karridale and Wilyabrup; hand-picked, whole-bunch pressed to new oak, wild-fermented, matured for 10 months. Still ultra-pale, an almost delicate chardonnay, amazing given its age when tasted in Jan '20. No qualms for the future as it slowly opens its wings. Screwcap. 12% alc. **Rating** 94 **To** 2030 $38

ᵧᵧᵧᵧᵧ **Signature Series Margaret River Sauvignon Blanc 2019 Rating** 91 **To** 2021 $23 ✪
Signature Series McLaren Vale Shiraz 2018 Rating 90 **To** 2025 $23
Signature Series McLaren Vale Grenache G-19 2019 Rating 90 **To** 2022 $23
Signature Series McLaren Vale GSM Grenache Shiraz Mourvedre 2018 Rating 90 **To** 2025 $23

Robert Stein Vineyard ★★★★★

Pipeclay Lane, Mudgee, NSW 2850 **Region** Mudgee
T (02) 6373 3991 **www**.robertstein.com.au **Open** 7 days 10–4.30
Winemaker Jacob Stein, Lisa Bray **Est.** 1976 **Dozens** 20 000 **Vyds** 18.67ha
While three generations of the family have been involved since Robert (Bob) Stein began
the establishment of the vineyard, the chain stretches even further back, going to Bob's great-
great-grandfather, Johann Stein, who was brought to Australia in 1838 by the Macarthur
family to supervise the planting of the Camden Park Vineyard. Bob's son Drew and grandson
Jacob have now taken over winemaking responsibilities. Jacob has worked vintages in Italy,
Canada, Margaret River and Avoca and, more particularly, in the Rheingau and Rheinhessen
regions of Germany. Since his return, one success has followed another. Exports to Germany,
Hong Kong, Singapore and China.

ΨΨΨΨΨ **Dry Mudgee Riesling 2019** Six gold medals in the first year of its life is a
spectacular start (a seventh from a show with no credibility whatsoever). Jacob
Stein is a master winemaker of riesling, the grapes hand-picked from numerous
40+yo vineyards above 580m. The length and depth of the lime juice–driven fruit
is outstanding. Top drawer riesling. Screwcap. 12% alc. **Rating** 96 **To** 2032 $35 ✪
Reserve Mudgee Riesling 2018 From a 42yo estate block; hand-picked,
whole-bunch pressed, wild-fermented in 4yo French puncheons. Very good
texture and structure. Some phenolics ex the winemaking build the edifice for the
profusion of citrus flavours. The wine is ambling along the road to the first stage
of maturity. Screwcap. 12% alc. **Rating** 95 **To** 2038 $45
Reserve Mudgee Chardonnay 2018 Vines planted '76; hand-picked, whole-
bunch pressed, wild-fermented in French hogsheads (50% new), 10% mlf, matured
for 11 months. Two trophies, 3 gold medals. Has very good length, mouthfeel and
texture. Screwcap. 13% alc. **Rating** 95 **To** 2038 $40
Reserve Mudgee Shiraz 2017 From 2 vineyards planted '76; open-fermented
with 15% whole bunches, the remainder largely whole berry, a small part crushed,
14 days on skins, 12 months in French and American hogsheads (30% new).
More power and depth in every dimension. Screwcap. 14.5% alc. **Rating** 95
To 2037 $50
The Kinnear 2016 Hand-picked from the best rows of the oldest block of
estate shiraz. Open-fermented with 30% whole bunches, 70% whole berries. A
very good shiraz: plum/blackberry, supple, medium-bodied mouthfeel. Screwcap.
14% alc. **Rating** 95 **To** 2036 $80
Reserve Mudgee Cabernet Sauvignon 2017 Hand-picked from a single
estate vineyard planted '78, open-fermented, 15 days on skins, matured for
15 months in French hogsheads (40% new). Good wine – the oak needs time to
lower its lance, but will do so. Screwcap. 14.5% alc. **Rating** 95 **To** 2037 $50
Mudgee Gewurztraminer 2019 This is close to the real (Alsace) deal: musk,
rose petals, spice, lychee and more are in full volume, the bouquet and palate both
chiming in at various points. Screwcap. 11% alc. **Rating** 94 **To** 2023 $25 ✪
Half Dry Mudgee Riesling 2019 From J Block on the '76 vineyard; hand-
picked, whole-bunch pressed, free-run, fermented in stainless steel, the pressings
wild-fermented in 4yo French puncheons, blended and kept on lees with 15g/l of
residual sugar. Delicate and elegant, residual sugar and acidity in lockstep. Screwcap.
11.5% alc. **Rating** 94 $40

ΨΨΨΨΨ **Mudgee Shiraz 2017** **Rating** 93 **To** 2027 $30
Mudgee Cabernet Sauvignon 2017 **Rating** 93 **To** 2032 $30

Robin Brockett Wines ★★★★★

43 Woodville St, Drysdale, Vic 3222 (postal) **Region** Geelong
T 0418 112 223 **www**.robinbrockettwines.com **Open** Not
Winemaker Robin Brockett **Est.** 2013 **Dozens** 400

Robin Brockett is chief winemaker at Scotchmans Hill, a position he has held for over 30 years, making consistently very good wines through the ebbs and flows of climate. In 2013 he took the first steps towards the realisation of a 35-year dream of making and selling wines under his own label. He put in place an agreement to buy grapes from the Fenwick (2ha) and Swinburn (1ha) vineyards, and in '13 made the first wine, venturing into the unknown with the Amphora Syrah. In '14 he made pinots from each of the 2 vineyards, and a Fenwick Shiraz, but left it until January '16 to release, as it were, announcing the business and the wines available for sale.

🍷🍷🍷🍷🍷 **Fenwick Vineyard Bellarine Peninsula Pinot Noir 2017** Small open fermenters, 15% whole bunches on the bottom, the balance crushed on top, wild-fermented, matured for 12 months in used French oak. A smashing pinot making the most of '17, the purity of the red fruits on full display. Those who buy some will be hard-pressed not to drink it now, and that may be the way to go. Screwcap. **Rating** 98 **To** 2027 $38 ✪

🍷🍷🍷🍷🍷 **Swinburn Vineyard Bellarine Peninsula Chardonnay 2018** Pellenc Selectiv'-harvested, free-run juice to barrel for wild fermentation, 12 months on lees in used French oak. Has excellent drive and freshness; crisp citrussy acidity; white peach. Screwcap. 13.5% alc. **Rating** 95 **To** 2030 $35 ✪
Swinburn Vineyard Bellarine Peninsula Pinot Noir 2017 The vinification is identical in all respects to Fenwick, but the flavours, texture and mouthfeel all headed down a more complex/savoury path, trading this off for the freshness it loses. Screwcap. **Rating** 94 **To** 2024 $38

Rochford Wines ★★★★★

878–880 Maroondah Highway, Coldstream, Vic 3770 **Region** Yarra Valley
T (03) 5957 3333 **www.**rochfordwines.com.au **Open** 7 days 9–5
Winemaker Kaspar Hermann, Kelly Healey **Est.** 1988 **Dozens** 24 000 **Vyds** 34.2ha
This Yarra Valley property was purchased by Helmut Konecsny in 2002; he had already established a reputation for pinot noir and chardonnay from the family-owned Romsey Park Vineyard in the Macedon Ranges (sold in '10). Since '10, Helmut has focused on his Yarra Valley winery and vineyards. In addition to the cellar door, the property has two restaurants, a retail shop and an expansive natural amphitheatre and observation tower – a showpiece in the region. Exports to the US and China.

🍷🍷🍷🍷🍷 **Terre Single Vineyard Yarra Valley Pinot Noir 2019** From Swallowfield, the southernmost vineyard in the Yarra Valley. Hand-picked, wild-fermented with 60% whole bunches, pressed to French oak (25% new) for 10 months. Light, clear colour; has a perfumed bouquet. A supremely elegant and expressive wine that flows joyously along the palate and into the long aftertaste. Screwcap. 13% alc. **Rating** 98 **To** 2035 $70 ✪
Premier Single Vineyard Yarra Valley Chardonnay 2019 Swallowfield Vineyard, clones 76 and I10V5; hand-picked, crushed and pressed to French barriques (40% new) with juice solids, 40% mlf, 10 months on lees. The wine flows silently at first, then soars on the finish and aftertaste. The fruit is a seamless mix of white peach and grapefruit. Lovely, elegant chardonnay. Screwcap. 13% alc. **Rating** 97 **To** 2032 $100 ✪
Premier Single Vineyard Yarra Valley Pinot Noir 2019 MV6 from Block 4 of the estate Hill Road Vineyard; hand-picked, wild-fermented with 40% whole bunches, pressed to French oak (30% new). Takes Rochford's ability to combine complexity and drive with purity of varietal fruit expression onto another level, hence impeccable length. Screwcap. 13% alc. **Rating** 97 **To** 2033 $130 ✪

🍷🍷🍷🍷🍷 **Isabella's Single Vineyard Yarra Valley Chardonnay 2019** Estate-grown I10V5 clones; hand-picked, whole-bunch pressed with full juice solids to French barriques and puncheons (30% new) for fermentation, no mlf or stirring. The mouthfeel is very good, the balance between crisp youth and the measured complexity of maturity. Looked even better on retasting. Screwcap. 12.5% alc. **Rating** 96 **To** 2030 $75 ✪

Dans les Bois Single Vineyard Yarra Valley Chardonnay 2019 This is the chardonnay sibling to the beautiful pinot noir ex Swallowfield Vineyard. Clones 76, 96 and I10V3; hand-picked, whole-bunch pressed with juice solids to French oak, 10% mlf and 10 months' maturation. Exceptional complexity and length. Screwcap. 13% alc. **Rating** 96 **To** 2030 $49 ✪

Terre Single Vineyard Yarra Valley Chardonnay 2019 Swallowfield, single Block 1 planted with I10V3; whole-bunch pressed with full juice solids to French and Austrian barriques, no mlf, 10 months on lees with no stirring. The wine is vibrantly crisp and fresh; it's purity and, above all, it's length. That length is special, a single depiction of the Yarra Valley's ability to make great chardonnay. Screwcap. 12.8% alc. **Rating** 96 **To** 2030 $60 ✪

L'Enfant Unique Single Vineyard Yarra Valley Pinot Noir 2019 From 2 blocks on the Hill Road Vineyard; hand-picked clones MV6 and D5V2, wild-fermented with 60% whole bunches and 40% whole berries, 21 days on skins, matured for 10 months in French oak (20% new). A beautiful wine with drive, textural complexity and a pure stream of red fruits filling the centre of the palate. Screwcap. 13% alc. **Rating** 96 **To** 2033 $84

Dans les Bois Single Vineyard Yarra Valley Pinot Noir 2019 From Swallowfield. The hand-picked fruit is destemmed for a whole-berry ferment on skins for 12 days, matured in French oak (20% new) for 10 months. Bright, clear colour. A gloriously fragrant and flowery bouquet; the flavours of the palate precise replicas of the bouquet. Screwcap. 12.6% alc. **Rating** 96 **To** 2030 $54 ✪

Estate Yarra Valley Pinot Noir 2019 Clones 114, 155, MV6, 77 and Davis; hand-picked, whole berry–open fermented, 4 days' cold soak, plunged daily, 12 days on skins, racked to French barriques (10% new), matured for 10 months on lees. A complex wine with dark/foresty berries alongside dominant red berries. Screwcap. 13% alc. **Rating** 95 **To** 2032 $38

Isabella's Single Vineyard Yarra Valley Cabernet Sauvignon 2018 From the estate vineyard in Briarty Road; crushed and destemmed to large wooden vats, 4 days' cold soak, pressed to French oak (30% new). Intense varietal fruit of cassis/blackcurrant. The vinification was precisely framed to maximise the fruit but not extract too much, especially tannins. Screwcap. 13.7% alc. **Rating** 95 **To** 2038 $80

Estate Yarra Valley Chardonnay 2019 Four clones; hand-picked, crushed, pressed to French and Austrian barriques and puncheons (40% new) and a ceramic egg, matured for 10 months on lees. A vibrant and crisp palate sharing some faintly funky notes with Dans les Bois. Backs off slightly on the finish. Screwcap. 12.7% alc. **Rating** 94 **To** 2029 $38

Isabella's Single Vineyard Yarra Valley Pinot Noir 2019 Clone 144 from a south-facing slope in Rochford's vineyard on Briarty Road: hand-picked, 100% whole bunches, 4 weeks on skins, pressed to used French puncheons, matured for 10 months. Light colour. The 100% whole-bunch fermentation gives an entirely different mouthfeel and a foresty/spicy flavour spectrum. More tannins on display than its siblings, also more plum. Screwcap. 13.4% alc. **Rating** 94 **To** 2030 $48

RockBare ★★★★☆

62 Brooks Road, Clarendon, SA 5157 **Region** South Australia
T (08) 8388 7155 **www**.rockbare.com.au **Open** 7 days 11–5
Winemaker Shelley Torresan **Est.** 2000 **Dozens** 10 000 **Vyds** 29ha

The RockBare journey, which began in late 2000, took a new direction last year when two multi-generational wine families came together in partnership: the Jackson family from California and the Melbourne-based Valmorbida family. Their combined focus will create a distinctive expression on the diverse wine regions across SA and those varieties that make them famous. Winemaker Shelley Torresan heads a team that sources grapes from family owned vineyards and also well regarded growers. Many of these loyal growers have been involved with RockBare for the past 18 years, committed to representing the very best of SA and being part of the now bigger RockBare family. Exports to most major markets.

ҮҮҮҮҮ **Barossa Valley Shiraz 2017** Hailing from a single Marananga vineyard, concentrated grapes saw an extended maceration and a complex oak regime: all French, divvied across barrel formats of different sizes and ages. The result: full-bodied and plush, but beautifully fresh and boasting a stream of boysenberry, lilac, anise, Asian spice and satsuma plum scents, curtailed by oak tannins, nicely applied. Screwcap. **Rating** 94 **To** 2029 $50 NG

ҮҮҮҮҮ **McLaren Vale Shiraz 2018 Rating** 92 **To** 2026 $28 NG
McLaren Vale Grenache 2019 Rating 92 **To** 2023 $28 NG
The Clare Valley Riesling 2019 Rating 91 **To** 2025 $25 NG
Adelaide Hills Chardonnay 2019 Rating 91 **To** 2024 $28 NG
Wild Vine McLaren Vale Grenache Rose 2019 Rating 91 **To** 2020 $25 NG

Rockcliffe ★★★★★

18 Hamilton Road, Denmark, WA 6333 **Region** Great Southern
T (08) 9848 2622 **www.**rockcliffe.com.au **Open** 7 days 11–5
Winemaker Elysia Harrison **Est.** 1990 **Dozens** 30 000 **Vyds** 10ha
The Rockcliffe winery and vineyard business, formerly known as Matilda's Estate, is owned by citizen of the world Steve Hall. The wine ranges echo local surf place names, headed by Rockcliffe itself but extending to Third Reef, Forty Foot Drop and Quarram Rocks. Over the years, Rockcliffe has won more than its fair share of trophies and gold and silver medals in wine shows. Exports to the UK, Canada, Malaysia, Singapore, Thailand, Japan, Taiwan and China.

ҮҮҮҮҮ **Reserve Great Southern Cabernet Sauvignon 2018** Is 100% cabernet sauvignon; 35% new French oak. It starts and finishes beautifully. There's a slight dip to the mid-palate but there's so much stacked around it and you'd bet on it filling in over time. It tastes of blackcurrant, olive paste and gravel although dust, cedar wood, mint and wood smoke characters also play important roles. There's a significant spread of tannin here but fruit romps straight through it. It's excellent now but it has been built to be cellared. Screwcap. 14.6% alc. **Rating** 96 **To** 2045 $100 CM
Single Site Great Southern Chardonnay 2018 Struck-match characters introduce a powerful wine filled with stone fruit, melon and cedar. It has an almost exaggerated amount of texture; drinking it is like settling onto a velvet settee. The balance of fruit and oak is spot on and the finish, while still sorting itself out, lingers appreciably. Screwcap. 13.5% alc. **Rating** 94 **To** 2027 $60 CM
Reserve Great Southern Shiraz 2018 It's a svelte, plum-driven red with peppercorn, game and smoked cedar wood characters layered through. Tannin has been finessed so well through the back half of the wine that it almost steals the show. Peppercorn characters add lift to both the nose and the palate. It doesn't land any killer blows but there is a great deal to like about this wine and it has just been bottled. Screwcap. 14.8% alc. **Rating** 94 **To** 2040 $100 CM
Single Site Great Southern Shiraz 2018 Medium in weight (at most) with red and black cherry flavours running friskily through the palate. There's a dry, gamey edge to the finish along with honey soy and green, foresty herb notes. It's the kind of wine sometimes referred to as 'Burgundian shiraz'. Tannin dries the finish but also lends it a certain finesse. You could describe this wine as elegant and floral. It will be interesting to watch this wine develop. Screwcap. 14.9% alc. **Rating** 94 **To** 2034 $60 CM

ҮҮҮҮҮ **Third Reef Chardonnay 2019 Rating** 93 **To** 2027 $30 CM
Third Reef Rose 2019 Rating 93 **To** 2022 $28 CM
Limited Release Grenache Rose 2019 Rating 93 **To** 2022 $30 CM
Third Reef Cabernet Sauvignon 2018 Rating 93 **To** 2033 $35 CM
Single Site Cabernet Sauvignon 2018 Rating 92 **To** 2030 $60 CM
Quarram Rocks Chardonnay 2018 Rating 90 **To** 2024 $21 CM ✪

Rockford

131 Krondorf Road, Tanunda, SA 5352 **Region** Barossa Valley
T (08) 8563 2720 **www.**rockfordwines.com.au **Open** 7 days 11–5
Winemaker Robert O'Callaghan **Est.** 1984 **Dozens** NFP
Rockford can only be described as an icon, no matter how overused that word may be. It has a devoted band of customers who buy most of the wine through the cellar door or mail order (Robert O'Callaghan's entrancing annual newsletter is like no other). Some wine is sold through restaurants and there are two retailers in Sydney and one each in Melbourne, Brisbane and Perth. Whether they will have the Basket Press Shiraz available is another matter; it is as scarce as Henschke Hill of Grace (but less expensive). Exports to Canada, Switzerland, Vietnam, Singapore, Japan, Fiji, NZ, Thailand, Malaysia, Hong Kong and China.

Rogers & Rufus

PO Box 10, Angaston, SA 5353 **Region** Barossa Valley
T (08) 8561 3200 **www.**rogersandrufus.com **Open** Not
Winemaker Sam Wigan **Est.** 2009 **Dozens** NFP
This is a decidedly under the bedcover partnership between Robert Hill-Smith and his immediate family, and Rupert and Jo Clevely – Rupert is the former Veuve Clicquot director in Australia but now runs gastro pub group Geronimo Inns in London. Late in 2008 the Hill-Smiths and Clevelys decided (in their words) 'to do something fun together with a serious dip at Euro styled dry and savoury delicate rose using three site specific, old, low- yielding, dry-grown grenache sites from the Barossa floor'.

🍷🍷🍷🍷🍷 **Grenache of Barossa Rose 2019** Harvested in small bins, crushed and held in the press for 1–2 hours, wild-fermented, 50% in used oak 50% in tank, blended in tank, 1 month on lees with batonnage. Pale pink. Dry, crisp, fresh and with lots of small red-fruit flavours. Screwcap. 12% alc. **Rating** 93 **To** 2023 $23 ❂

Rogues Lane Vineyard

370 Lower Plenty Road, Viewbank, Vic 3084 (postal) **Region** Heathcote
T 0413 528 417 **www.**rogueslane.com.au **Open** Not
Winemaker Wild Duck Creek (Liam Anderson) **Est.** 1995 **Dozens** 240 **Vyds** 4ha
Philip Faure grew up in South Africa and studied agriculture at Stellenbosch University. After migrating to Australia and spending some time in the IT industry, Philip found his way to Heathcote, purchasing Rogues Lane Vineyard in 2015. The low-yielding vineyard, planted in 1995 and made up of 95% shiraz and 5% malbec, has seen 'an enormous amount of work'. Philip produced his first wine in '17.

🍷🍷🍷🍷🍷 **Heathcote Shiraz 2017** The yield from the estate vineyard was under 4t/ha (around 1.5t/acre). Hence the near-impenetrable colour and the full-bodied palate following on the path set by the colour and bouquet. It is not over-extracted, nor clumsy; the high quality tannins in balance with blackberry and soused plum flavours. Screwcap. 15% alc. **Rating** 94 **To** 2042 $55

Rojomoma ★★★★

16 Sturt Road, Nuriootpa, SA 5355 **Region** Barossa Valley
T 0421 272 336 **www.**rojomoma.com.au **Open** By appt
Winemaker Bernadette Kaeding, Sam Kurtz **Est.** 2004 **Dozens** 800 **Vyds** 5.44 ha
Winemaker Sam Kurtz left his position as chief winemaker within the Orlando group in 2015, where he had worked for over 20 years. He had in fact helped life partner Bernadette (Bernie) Kaeding with the care of Red Art since 1996, when Bernie purchased the nucleus of the vineyard. It had 1.49ha of 80-year-old dry-grown grenache, the remaining 3.95ha were planted over several years to shiraz, cabernet sauvignon, petit verdot and tempranillo. Until 2004 the grapes from the old and new plantings were sold to Rockford, Chateau Tanunda, Spinifex and David Franz. In that year Bernie decided to make a small batch of wine (with

advice from Sam) and continued to accumulate wine until '11, when she began selling wines under the Red Art label. Bernie is also an author and photographer, her art is displayed at the winery.

♀♀♀♀♀ Red Art Single Vineyard Barossa Valley Shiraz 2014 From a single vineyard at Ebenezer; 75% crushed and destemmed, 25% whole bunches wild yeast–open fermented. A mix of blue and purple fruits, touches of chocolate and forest. Holding on well. Screwcap. 14.2% alc. **Rating** 92 **To** 2028 $38

Red Art Vineyard Blend 2015 The components reflect the size of the planting of each variety: 41.3% shiraz, 22% grenache, 16.7% cabernet sauvignon, 11% petit Verdot, 9% tempranillo. Bernadette Kaeding creates a one-off label design that is imprinted on Japanese rice paper, both Bernadette and Sam Kurtz hand-coloured and signed each label with its bottle number (this 13/400). Each bottle comes in a printed cardboard box with an information card. Screwcap. 15% alc. **Rating** 90 **To** 2025 $185

♀♀♀♀ Red Art Amplify Cuvee I Shiraz NV Rating 89 **To** 2030 $395
Red Art Single Vineyard Barossa Valley Grenache 2018 Rating 89 **To** 2028 $38

Rolf Binder

Cnr Seppeltsfield Road/Stelzer Road, Tanunda, SA 5352 **Region** Barossa Valley
T (08) 8562 3300 **www.**rolfbinder.com **Open** Mon–Sat 10–4.30, Sun on long weekends
Winemaker Rolf Binder, Christa Deans, Harry Mantzarapis **Est.** 1955 **Dozens** 28 000
Vyds 90ha

A winery steeped in family tradition and Barossa history, Rolf Binder and sister Christa Deans are following their father's philosophy, using primarily estate-grown fruit from their own vineyards located in various districts of the Barossa. A vineyard acquisition in the Vine Vale area has provided the family with centenarian shiraz vines planted in the 1890s, in fact parent vines to the Hanisch Shiraz. In 2019 Rolf and Christa celebrated 25 consecutive vintages, surely a unique record achievement for a brother/sister winemaking team. The Vinify BV The Vineyard Architect wines are a joint venture between Rolf Binder and exporter Rob Turnbull, the wine named in honour of Barossa Valley viticulturist Vic Kraft. The wines are available through Rolf Binder's cellar door, wine clubs and export. Exports to all major markets.

♀♀♀♀♀ 1890's Vineyard Shiraz 2017 Take a moment, shelve those expectations of Barossa power – although power is undoubtedly present – and concentrate on the beauty and the almost deceptive elegance. Intense black fruits are a given, but the nuance delivered by blueberry, mulberry fruits and such pretty florals is an unexpected joy. Complex fruit is the sun and the winemaking revolves around it. Incredibly stylish. Screwcap. 14.5% alc. **Rating** 96 **To** 2040 $65 JP ✪

Heysen Barossa Valley Shiraz 2017 A wander on the Heysen walking trail on the western border of the Rolf Binder estate probably elicits the same Aussie bush scents as its namesake shiraz: pepperberry, briar, a touch of mint, eucalyptus. It beautifully encapsulates a sense of place. Stands tall in the glass with pronounced black plums, currants, nutmeg, cloves. Palate is velvety, tannins are plush and the oak shows care. Screwcap. 14% alc. **Rating** 95 **To** 2035 $70 JP

Hanisch Barossa Valley Shiraz 2017 Single vineyard, old vine Barossa shiraz heightens emotions, expectations. But first, a little air, please. Maybe one more swirl. It's tight, a touch closed and will definitely take its own sweet time to reveal more. Briar, loganberry, red fruits, dusty oak all coming together nicely in balance, and as one. Cork. 14.5% alc. **Rating** 95 **To** 2036 $125 JP

Homestead Cabernet Sauvignon 2018 Considerable charm with earth, sweet fruit aromas, Barossa violets and blackcurrants with just a touch of cedar. A steady hand lies behind the excellent balance displayed in this wine with polished tannins, a whisper of oak and lovely seductive flavours of smoky blackberries, bitter chocolate, toasted walnut, leafy fine herbs. A compelling wine for the price. Screwcap. 14% alc. **Rating** 94 **To** 2035 $25 JP ◐

♟♟♟♟♀ Heinrich Barossa Valley Shiraz Mataro Grenache 2017 **Rating** 93 **To** 2033 $40 JP
Eden Valley Riesling 2019 **Rating** 92 **To** 2030 $28 JP
JJ Hahn Western Ridge 1975 Planting Barossa Valley Shiraz 2017 **Rating** 92 **To** 2035 $40 JP
JJ Hahn Stockwell Barossa Valley Cabernet Sauvignon Shiraz 2017 **Rating** 92 **To** 2035 $35 JP
Veritas Winery Bull's Blood Barossa Valley Shiraz Mataro Pressings 2017 **Rating** 91 **To** 2035 $60 JP
The Vineyard Architect Barossa Valley Shiraz Mataro 2017 **Rating** 91 **To** 2034 $50 JP
JJ Hahn Stelzer Road Merlot 2018 **Rating** 91 **To** 2030 $25 JP
Hermann's Vineyard Shiraz 2017 **Rating** 90 **To** 2034 $25 JP
RHB Reserve Barossa Shiraz 2017 **Rating** 90 **To** 2027 $35 JP
Vinify BV The Vineyard Architect Barossa Valley Mataro Grenache 2017 **Rating** 90 **To** 2028 $45 JP

Ros Ritchie Wines

Magnolia House, 190 Mount Buller Road, Mansfield, Vic 3722 **Region** Upper Goulburn
T 0444 588 276 **www**.rosritchiewines.com **Open** Fri 5–8, w'ends & public hols 11–4
Winemaker Ros Ritchie **Est.** 2008 **Dozens** 2000 **Vyds** 7ha
Ros Ritchie was winemaker at the Ritchie family's Delatite winery from 1981 to 2006, but moved on to establish her own winery with husband John in '08 on a vineyard near Mansfield. They became shareholders in Barwite Vineyards in '12 (planted to chardonnay, pinot noir, riesling and pinot gris) and in '14 established their new winery there. Apart from gewurztraminer (grown at Dead Man's Hill Vineyard), they work with local growers, foremost the Kinlock, McFadden, Timbertop and Baxendale vineyards, the last planted by the very experienced viticulturist Jim Baxendale (and wife Ruth) high above the King River Valley. All vineyards are managed with minimal spray regimes. The cellar door is located at the historic Magnolia House at Mansfield, open on select weekends, hosting seasonal wine dinners and special events.

♟♟♟♟♟ Dead Man's Hill Vineyard Gewurztraminer 2018 It's a lovely wine. It balances the joy of the variety and all its flavours without going over the top. Of course it has lychee, musk, lavender and ginger spice fleshing out to a textural palate. It also has the acid lemony drive to keep it running along a straight line. Screwcap. 13.5% alc. **Rating** 95 **To** 2027 $29 JF ◐

♟♟♟♟♀ Barwite Vineyard Riesling 2018 **Rating** 93 **To** 2027 $27 JF ◐
McFadden's Vineyard Pinot Gris 2018 **Rating** 92 **To** 2023 $27 JF

Rosabrook Margaret River Wine

1390 Rosa Brook Road, Rosabrook, WA 6285 **Region** Margaret River
T (08) 9368 4555 **www**.rosabrook.com.au **Open** Not
Winemaker Severine Logan **Est.** 1980 **Dozens** 12000 **Vyds** 25ha
The original Rosabrook estate vineyards were established between 1984 and '96. In 2007 Rosabrook relocated its vineyard to the northwestern end of the Margaret River wine region, overlooking Geographe Bay and the Indian Ocean. Warm days and cool nights, influenced by the ocean, result in slow, mild-ripening conditions. Exports to Sweden, Dubai, Mongolia, Japan, Hong Kong and China.

♟♟♟♟♀ Single Vineyard Estate Cabernet Sauvignon 2016 Hand-picked fruit from 25yo vines, open-fermented and on dryness run into new barrels, 12 months in oak. Some toasty oak influence with this release, although the varietal and regional personalities are mainly calling the tune with redcurrant, mulberry, cedar and bay leaf playing a part. Rich and quite soft for the style but underpinned by firm tannin. Screwcap. 14.5% alc. **Rating** 93 **To** 2031 $45 SC

Sauvignon Blanc Semillon 2019 A roughly 50/50% blend, cold-fermented in stainless steel. It's a familiar theme as soon as you put your nose in the glass – pea pod and mown grass, passionfruit and mango or something similarly tropical. A well crafted example of the style, deft winemaking utilising good quality fruit. Chill it down and drink it, don't think long and hard about it. Screwcap. 12.5% alc. **Rating** 91 **To** 2022 $20 SC ✪

Chardonnay 2018 Line and length Margaret River chardonnay; not one to set the pulse racing, but ticks the requisite boxes. Peachy varietal aromas with some nutty/nougat character, presumably from oak, although the winemaker's notes describe it as 'lightly oak matured'. The flavours are fresh and the mouthfeel and finish show above average quality – it's a safe bet at the price. Screwcap. 13% alc. **Rating** 91 **To** 2025 $25 SC

Shiraz 2018 The gamey, slightly funky aromas pretty typical of shiraz from this region are prominent on the bouquet, but there's red berry, spice and oak in there as well. Medium-bodied and soft, the overall feel is quite savoury, but there's some sweetness to the fruit on the palate and it's an easily approachable style. A good match for something like chargrilled steak. Screwcap. 14.5% alc. **Rating** 91 **To** 2028 $25 SC

🍷🍷🍷🍷 **Cabernet Merlot 2018** **Rating** 89 **To** 2025 $20 SC

Rosby ★★★★

122 Strikes Lane, Mudgee, NSW 2850 **Region** Mudgee
T 0419 429 918 **www**.rosby.com.au **Open** Mon–Fri by appt, w'ends 10–4
Winemaker Tim Stevens **Est.** 1996 **Dozens** 1000 **Vyds** 9ha

Gerald and Kay Norton-Knight have shiraz and cabernet sauvignon established on what is a truly unique site in Mudgee. Many vignerons like to think that their vineyard has special qualities, but in this instance the belief is well based. The vineyard is situated in a small valley with unusual red basalt over a quartz gravel structure, encouraging deep root growth, making the use of water far less critical than normal. Tim Stevens of Huntington Estate has purchased some of the ample production and makes the Rosby wines.

🍷🍷🍷🍷🍷 **Mudgee Shiraz 2017** A little more tannic than it needs to be, especially given its medium-weight fruit, though a layer of oak and positive freshness help to sweep it along. It's good now but it will improve over the next handful of years. Screwcap. 14% alc. **Rating** 92 **To** 2030 $32 CM

Mudgee Cabernet Sauvignon 2017 An extractive style with assertive tannin, robust fruit and a slathering of coconutty oak. It feels creamy, it feels dry, it feels punchy. You might query the overall balance but you wouldn't query the effort; it does everything it can to deliver a mouthful of smooth-skinned flavour. Just watch those tannins. Screwcap. 14.1% alc. **Rating** 91 **To** 2034 CM

Rosenthal Wines ★★★★★

24 Rockford Street, Denmark, WA 6333 **Region** Great Southern
T 0432 312 918 **www**.rosenthalwines.com.au **Open** Not
Winemaker Luke Eckersley, Coby Ladwig **Est.** 2001 **Dozens** 35 000 **Vyds** 40ha

The original Rosenthal Vineyard (Springfield Park) was established in 1997 just north of Manjimup, by Dr John Rosenthal. In 2012 Coby Ladwig and Luke Eckersley acquired the business and relocated it to Mount Barker. Both have a sound knowledge of vineyards throughout the southwest of WA. The fruit for Rosenthal wines is sourced from their own leased vineyard in Mount Barker, plus growers in Frankland River and Pemberton. Coby and Luke have partnered with an importer/distributor in China and plan to open an office/showroom in Shanghai. Exports to the UK, India, the Philippines and China.

🍷🍷🍷🍷🍷 **The Collector Mount Barker Cabernet Sauvignon 2018** While a flagship wine seems to have more of everything, especially oak and time, in it – here French barrels (50% new), aged 17 months – winemaking can only do so much and there is an argument for less is better. However, quality fruit is key. Thankfully it is the foundation of this stunner. Built for ageing, it is finely tuned already. Cassis, currants, bitumen, licorice, beautifully shaped tannins and a length like no tomorrow. Screwcap. 14.2% alc. **Rating** 97 **To** 2038 $90 JF ✪

🍷🍷🍷🍷🍷 **Collector Mount Barker Chardonnay 2018** Gingin clone; hand-picked, whole bunches, wild fermentation in French oak (50% new), on full solids, lees stirring over 5 months and left in oak for 10 months. That's a worked over chardonnay. And yet the result is spectacular. No shortage of sulphides – bordering on too funky for some. The palate is tight with a gorgeous flavour of lemon fluff/ginger cream. Linear, savoury and moreish. A measly 800 bottles produced. Screwcap. 13.1% alc. **Rating** 96 **To** 2028 $90 JF

Richings Frankland River Shiraz 2018 There's a lot of polish and gloss partly from the 40% new French oak, aged 13 months, but mostly from the perfectly ripe fruit within. This has a depth of flavour without going over the top. Savoury with chiselled tannins and a vibrant acid line. Very stylish offering for now and years to come. Screwcap. 14.6% alc. **Rating** 96 **To** 2030 $60 JF ✪

Richings Frankland River Cabernet Sauvignon 2018 This is something special. Harmony through and through with everything in place from the cassis and spice flavours to the French oak (40% new) aged 14 months, seamlessly integrated and behaving. It's more mid-weighted, lithe, with beautifully shaped and savoury tannins. Screwcap. 14.5% alc. **Rating** 96 **To** 2033 $60 JF ✪

Richings Mount Barker Riesling 2019 Concentrated flavours of lime and grapefruit laced with ginger spice. The palate handles it all with a textural edge to its shape, fleshing out with more intensity. The acidity brilliantly keeping everything in check. Screwcap. 12.5% alc. **Rating** 95 **To** 2029 $35 JF ✪

The Marker Mount Barker Riesling 2019 Riesling from this region rarely disappoints. This makes its case with grapefruit and splashes of lemon juice; florals and the thread of minerally acidity its driving force. Lovely wine. Screwcap. 12.8% alc. **Rating** 95 **To** 2029 $35 JF ✪

Richings Pemberton Chardonnay 2019 While this has a real depth and plenty of flavour, elegance is included in the deal. Stone fruit, citrus, lemongrass and creamy leesy flavours. Razor-sharp acidity and a hint of flinty-sulphides keep the party going. Screwcap. 13.5% alc. **Rating** 95 **To** 2027 $60 JF

The Marker Frankland River Shiraz 2018 A lovely expression of the region with its dark fruits, squid ink and baking spices. It has depth, oak in check, savoury tannins and more besides, yet stays focused. Well composed and ready now. Screwcap. 14.5% alc. **Rating** 95 **To** 2028 $40 JF

The Marker Frankland River Cabernet Sauvignon 2018 This will make you stop and take time to smell the roses or rather the blackberries and licorice in the glass. It's so slinky and glossy with neat tannins. Refreshment all the way through and another reminder of how great cabernet is from this region. Screwcap. 14.5% alc. **Rating** 95 **To** 2030 $40 JF

🍷🍷🍷🍷🍷 **The Marker Pemberton Chardonnay 2019** **Rating** 93 **To** 2026 $40 JF
Garten Series Pemberton Cabernet Sauvignon 2018 **Rating** 93 **To** 2027 $28 JF
Garten Series Mount Barker Sauvignon Blanc 2019 **Rating** 92 **To** 2021 $28 JF
The Marker Pemberton Pinot Noir 2019 **Rating** 92 **To** 2027 $40 JF
Garten Series Pemberton Chardonnay 2019 **Rating** 90 **To** 2025 $28 JF
The Marker Blackwood Valley Shiraz Cabernet 2018 **Rating** 90 **To** 2027 $40 JF

Rosily Vineyard

871 Yelverton Road, Wilyabrup, WA 6284 **Region** Margaret River
T (08) 9755 6336 **www.**rosily.com.au **Open** Dec–Jan 7 days 11–5
Winemaker Mick Scott **Est.** 1994 **Dozens** 6000 **Vyds** 12.28ha
Ken Allan and Mick Scott acquired the Rosily Vineyard site in 1994 and the vineyard was
planted over three years to sauvignon blanc, semillon, chardonnay, cabernet sauvignon, merlot,
shiraz, grenache and cabernet franc. The first crops were sold to other makers in the region,
but by '99 Rosily had built a 120t capacity winery. It has gone from strength to strength, all of
its estate-grown grapes being vinified under the Rosily Vineyard label, the wines substantially
over-delivering for their prices. The vineyard was certified organic (ACO) in May 2017.

ŸŸŸŸŸ Margaret River Semillon Sauvignon Blanc 2019 An exotic blend of 61.4%
   semillon, 33% sauvignon blanc, 3% chardonnay and 2.6% muscadelle. It's fast out
   of the blocks with its array of fruits, mainly tropical ex the sauvignon blanc but
   also with a generous dose of lemon from the semillon. Its quality comes from the
   elegance and persistence of the finish and aftertaste. Screwcap. 13% alc. Rating 95
   To 2023 $22 ✪
   Margaret River Sauvignon Blanc 2019 From the newly certified organic
   estate vineyard, which has a long history of success; 94% tank-fermented
   sauvignon blanc, 6% semillon matured in new barrels for 6 weeks. Lemon sorbet,
   lemongrass, Meyer lemon juice and lively acidity; the oak handling curious.
   Screwcap. 12.5% alc. Rating 94 To 2021 $22 ✪
   Margaret River Chardonnay 2018 Bright straw-green. An ultra fresh wine.
   Grapefruit and white peach fruit has managed to hold sway over the theoretically
   obvious oak aroma and flavour – which aren't here. As ever, Rosily manages to
   turn normal economics of wine production on its head. Screwcap. 13.5% alc.
   Rating 94 To 2030 $28 ✪
   Reserve Margaret River Cabernet Sauvignon 2016 Only 55 dozen made
   from specific vine rows. Open and closed fermenters don't seem possible given
   the microscopic make, matured for 24 months in French oak (40% new). The oak
   is obvious but there is a commendable freshness to the overall flavour. Screwcap.
   14% alc. Rating 94 To 2029 $55

ŸŸŸŸ♀ Margaret River Merlot 2017 Rating 92 To 2029 $20 ✪

Ross Hill Wines

134 Wallace Lane, Orange, NSW 2800 **Region** Orange
T (02) 6365 3223 **www.**rosshillwines.com.au **Open** 7 days 10.30–5
Winemaker Scott Burke, Luke Steel **Est.** 1994 **Dozens** 27 000 **Vyds** 18.2ha
Peter and Terri Robson planted chardonnay, merlot, sauvignon blanc, cabernet franc, shiraz
and pinot noir on north-facing slopes of the Griffin Road Vineyard in 1994. In 2007 their
son James and his wife Chrissy joined the business and the Wallace Lane Vineyard (pinot
noir, sauvignon blanc and pinot gris) was planted. The vines are now mature and the winery
was NCOS Certified Carbon Neutral in '13. The Barrel & Larder School of Wine and
Food (WSET Levels 1 and 2) operates from the extended cellar door. Exports to Germany,
Singapore, Bali, Hong Kong and China.

ŸŸŸŸŸ Pinnacle Series Griffin Road Vineyard Orange Sauvignon Blanc 2018
   This is among the better renditions of what is too often an anaemic, overtly herbal
   expression of sauvignon on these shores. Seemingly inspired by the greatest source
   of sauvignon, France's Loire Valley, this is all pungent nettle, crushed chalk and
   greengage. Better, vibrant acid rails melded to reductive crunch and a lick of oak
   (surely?) pull the flavours from fore to aft, while pummelling the cheeks with
   some nourishing phenolics and wild-yeast funk. A textural coup d'état! Screwcap.
   12.8% alc. Rating 95 To 2023 $30 NG ✪
   Pinnacle Series Orange Chardonnay 2018 Whole-bunch pressed to high
   quality French oak before an ambient ferment had its way. The result is highly

impressive: toasted hazelnut, nougatine and a quotient of stone fruit aromas, all reminiscent of Meursault. Similarly oily too, with the oak absolutely buried. Nary a whiff. Rich of flavour, albeit restrained and fresh. A fine point of balance after pushing the envelope out for so long. This is the finest chardonnay tasted from this address. An example of what altitude melded to a sensitive hand can achieve. Screwcap. 13% alc. **Rating** 95 **To** 2026 $35 NG **⊙**

Orange Blanc de Blancs 2016 Matured on lees for 3 years, post-ambient fermentation of the base material. This is an impressive fizz. The dosage is extremely low to non-existent as cool-climate chardonnay's carriage of high acidity and chalky minerality has its way across a wisp of stone fruit flavours; yeast and hay pulling the flavours long with verve and true palate-staining authority. Cork. **Rating** 95 $35 NG **⊙**

♥♥♥♥♀ **Pinnacle Series Wallace Lane Vineyard Orange Pinot Gris 2019**
Rating 93 **To** 2023 $30 NG
Pinnacle Series Orange Pinot Noir 2018 Rating 93 **To** 2028 $45 NG
Maya and Max Orange Chardonnay 2018 Rating 92 **To** 2025 $25 **⊙**
Pinnacle Series Orange Shiraz 2018 Rating 92 **To** 2035 $40 NG
Lily Orange Sauvignon Blanc 2019 Rating 91 **To** 2021 $20 NG **⊙**
Lily Orange Sauvignon Blanc 2018 Rating 91 **To** 2020 $20 **⊙**
Maya and Max Orange Chardonnay 2019 Rating 91 **To** 2023 $25 NG
Jack's Lot Orange Shiraz 2018 Rating 91 **To** 2028 $25 NG
Orange Blanc de Blancs 2015 Rating 91 $35
Jessica Orange Rose 2019 Rating 90 **To** 2020 $20 NG **⊙**
Tom & Harry Orange Cabernet Sauvignon 2018 Rating 90 **To** 2028 $25 NG

Rouleur

150 Bank Street, South Melbourne, Vic 3205 (postal) **Region** Yarra Valley/McLaren Vale
T 0419 100 929 **www**.rouleurwine.com **Open** Not
Winemaker Matthew East **Est.** 2015 **Dozens** 2000
Owner Matt East's interest in wine began at an early age while he was growing up in the Yarra Valley and watching his father plant a vineyard in Coldstream. Between February 1999 and December 2015 his day job was in sales and marketing, culminating in his appointment in '11 as national sales manager for Wirra Wirra (which he had joined in '08). Following his retirement from that position, he set in motion the wheels of Rouleur. He lives in Melbourne, with the Yarra in easy striking distance, and together he and Rob Hall source fruit and make the wines. He makes some of the wine in McLaren Vale, using the facilities at Dennis Winery and drawing on the expertise/assistance of personal winemaking friends when needed. Back in Melbourne he is transforming a dilapidated milk bar in North Melbourne into the inner-city cellar door for Rouleur and he has leased an old vineyard in Wesburn.

Rowlee

19 Lake Canobolas Road, Nashdale, NSW 2800 **Region** Orange
T (02) 6365 3047 **www**.rowleewines.com.au **Open** 7 days 11–5
Winemaker Nicole Samodol, James Manny **Est.** 2000 **Dozens** 3000 **Vyds** 8ha
Rowlee's vineyard (chardonnay, pinot noir, pinot gris, riesling, sauvignon blanc, gewurztraminer and Italian varieties arneis and nebbiolo) was planted 20 years ago by Nik and Deonne Samodol in the high-altitude (950m) cool climate of Orange. Their daughter, Nicole Samodol, and her partner James Manny 'combine European wine growing heritage with new world practices' to make the wines in three ranges: By Rowlee, Single Vineyard and R-Series. The wines are available from the cellar door, specialist wine retailers and restaurants.

♥♥♥♥♥ **Orange Rose by Rowlee 2019** Very pale but bright pink. An exceptionally perfumed bouquet, then a crisply dry palate that pays full respect to the pinot noir origins of this great rose. Screwcap. 13% alc. **Rating** 95 **To** 2021 $28 **⊙**

Single Vineyard Orange Riesling 2019 The vineyard is at 950m, the grapes hand-picked. Lemon, apple and orange blossom aromas lead the way, the elegant light-bodied palate following the same path. Just a fraction light on. Screwcap. 12% alc. **Rating** 94 To 2030 $35

Single Vineyard Orange Arneis 2019 The variety shows itself to maximum advantage; it has excellent mouthfeel, providing gently savoury grip that prolongs the citrus zest/crushed lime leaf flavours. Screwcap. 13% alc. **Rating** 94 To 2028 $30 ○

♥♥♥♥♡ Single Vineyard Orange Chardonnay 2017 Rating 90 To 2023 $50

Rudderless

Victory Hotel, Main South Road, Sellicks Beach, SA 5174 **Region** McLaren Vale
T (08) 8556 3083 **www.**victoryhotel.com.au **Open** 7 days
Winemaker Peter Fraser **Est.** 2004 **Dozens** 550 **Vyds** 2ha

It's a long story how Doug Govan, owner of the Victory Hotel (circa 1858), came to choose the name Rudderless for his vineyard. The vineyard is planted on two levels (in 1999 and 2003) to a complex mix of shiraz, graciano, grenache, malbec, mataro and viognier. It surrounds the hotel, which is situated in the foothills of the Southern Willunga Escarpment as it falls into the sea. The wines are mostly sold through the Victory Hotel, where the laidback Doug keeps a low profile.

♥♥♥♥ Sellicks Hill McLaren Vale Grenache 2018 Hand-picked, with the berries abstemiously selected across a mechanical sorting table – still rare in this country. Destemmed and gently extracted, before 10 months in used French wood. Sour cherry, pomegranate and herb-clad, thirst-slaking tannins sandy and saline, corralling the show. Picked on the early side, yet nothing too green. The drinkability factor is high. Screwcap. **Rating** 95 To 2024 $35 NG ○

Sellicks Hill McLaren Vale Malbec 2018 Purple hue. Dense. Hand-picked. The nourishing, pulpy tannins reflect it, with the lilac florals reverberating across mulberry and boysenberry fruits, a whiff of dried nori imparting a sapid salinity. This is a joyous drink, demonstrating a lighter touch for the Vale while remonstrating with a culture of poor oak handling across the region. Here, it is a benchmark and it's about promoting joy, rather than obfuscating it. Screwcap. **Rating** 95 To 2025 $35 NG ○

Sellicks Hill McLaren Vale Shiraz 2018 Destemmed, with 50% whole berries across a 17-day fermentation. Rack and returned, before 11 months in oak (10% new). Floral. Violet. Blueberry, a gentle clench of seaweed reduction, salumi and a plume of clove to pepper-soused freshness. Long and effortless. Screwcap. **Rating** 94 To 2026 $35 NG

Rusty Mutt

PO Box 724 MSC, Torrens Park, SA 5062 **Region** McLaren Vale
T (08) 7228 6183 **www.**rustymutt.com.au **Open** Not
Winemaker Scott Heidrich **Est.** 2009 **Dozens** 1500

Scott Heidrich lived in the shadow of Geoff Merrill for 20 years, but has partially emerged into the sunlight with his virtual micro-winery. Back in 2006, close friends and family (Nicole and Alan Francis, Stuart Evans, David Lipman and Phil Cole) persuaded Scott to take advantage of the wonderful quality of the grapes that year and make a small batch of shiraz. The wines are made at a friend's micro-winery in McLaren Flat. The name Rusty Mutt comes from Scott's interest in Chinese astrology and feng shui; Scott was born in the year of the dog with the dominant element being metal, hence Rusty Mutt. What the ownership group doesn't drink is sold through fine wine retailers and selected restaurants, with a small amount exported to the UK and China.

♥♥♥♥♥ Rocky Ox McLaren Vale GSM 2018 A 61/27/12% blend of grenache, shiraz and mataro that is deliciously rich and fruity with equally seductive fresh raspberries and de-stoned cherries. There isn't even a glimpse of jam. Screwcap. 14.5% alc. **Rating** 95 To 2026 $35 ○

Vermilion Bird McLaren Vale Shiraz 2015 A dense, impenetrable wine, apparently in barrel and/or tank for 4 years. In Parkeresque bigger-is-best style, except for one thing: its tannins are now fully tamed without robbing the fruit. The quality cork was hand-inserted. 14.5% alc. **Rating** 94 **To** 2035 $88

ŸŸŸŸŸ **Original McLaren Vale Shiraz 2016 Rating** 91 **To** 2030 $35

Rymill Coonawarra ★★★★☆

Riddoch Highway, Coonawarra, SA 5263 **Region** Coonawarra
T (08) 8736 5001 **www**.rymill.com.au **Open** 7 days 11–5
Winemaker Shannon Sutherland **Est.** 1974 **Dozens** 50 000 **Vyds** 140ha
The Rymills are descendants of John Riddoch and have long owned some of the finest Coonawarra soil, upon which they have grown grapes since 1970. In 2016 the Rymill family sold the winery, vineyards and brand to a Chinese investor. The management, vineyard and winery teams have remained in place and new capital has financed moves to improve the vineyards and winery. Winemaker Shannon Sutherland has experience in the Napa Valley, Beaujolais, Canada and Marlborough, as well as Great Western and the Hunter Valley in Australia. The winery building also houses the cellar door and art exhibitions, which, together with viewing platforms over the winery, make it a must-see destination for tourists. Exports to all major markets.

ŸŸŸŸŸ **Sandstone Single Vineyard Cabernet Sauvignon 2018** Identical vinification to Block 6, but a radically different wine. It is full-bodied, full to overflowing with cassis/mulberry/plum fruit and a soft, plush texture. An ex tempore blend on my tasting table arguably produced the best wine, the points are for this wine, not Block 6. Screwcap. 14.8% alc. **Rating** 94 **To** 2038 $60

ŸŸŸŸŸ **Classic Release Shiraz 2018 Rating** 93 **To** 2028 $32
VI Viognier 2019 Rating 92 **To** 2022 $25 ❂
CF Cabernet Franc 2019 Rating 92 $25 ❂

Sailor Seeks Horse ★★★★★

Port Cygnet Winery, 60 Lymington Road, Cygnet, Tas 7112 **Region** Southern Tasmania
T 0418 471 120 **www**.sailorseekshorse.com.au **Open** W'ends 11–4 or by appt
Winemaker Paul Lipscombe, Gilli Lipscombe **Est.** 2010 **Dozens** 1500 **Vyds** 6.5ha
While I was given comprehensive information about the seriously interesting careers of Paul and Gilli Lipscombe, and about their vineyard, I am none the wiser about the highly unusual and very catchy name. The story began in 2005 when they resigned from their (unspecified) jobs in London, did a vintage in Languedoc and then headed to Margaret River to study oenology and viticulture. While combining study and work, their goal was to learn as much as possible about pinot noir. They worked in large, small, biodynamic, conventional, minimum and maximum intervention vineyards and wineries – Woodlands, Xanadu, Beaux Freres, Chehalem and Mt Difficulty, all household names. By '10 they were in Tasmania working for Julian Alcorso's Winemaking Tasmania (now Tasmanian Vintners) and found a derelict vineyard that had never cropped, having been abandoned not long after being planted in '05. It was in the Huon Valley, precisely where they had aimed to begin – the coolest district in Tasmania. They are working as winemakers for celebrated Home Hill Winery and manage Jim Chatto's vineyard in Glaziers Bay. Exports to the UK, the US and Singapore.

ŸŸŸŸŸ **Huon Valley Chardonnay 2017** The micro-print on the back label of this (and so many other labels) is irritating. No matter. A very complex Tasmanian chardonnay with notes of brioche and toast on the bouquet and fore-palate. It is there the game changes dramatically, for the wine has great intensity and length, acidity the spine, but with a lot of fancy dress around it. Lovely wine. Screwcap. 12% alc. **Rating** 97 **To** 2030 $55 ❂

ŸŸŸŸŸ **Huon Valley Chardonnay 2018** While this is ever so finely etched with acidity, like millefeuille it has layers of flavour. Expect lemon and zest, creamed honey and ginger curd with lightly buttered toast. It has power and a pulse yet runs along a linear path. Super chardonnay. Screwcap. 13.6% alc. **Rating** 96 **To** 2028 $55 JF ✪

Huldufolk Chardonnay 2018 The inaugural release turns out to be fruit sourced from clone 96. Aromatic and fruity, the wine was aged 12 months in a 1yo French hogshead, which is still imparting oak flavour and tannin. More obvious sulphides, savoury, flinty and pleasing, if drying. Good tension and a moreish wine. Screwcap. 13.6% alc. **Rating** 96 **To** 2029 $100 JF

Huldufolk Pinot Noir 2017 Crystal-bright crimson, so clear. It has the tannins that would make a Burgundian winemaker happy, and which are relatively rare on the Australian pinot scene. It's the ability of the tannins to disappear when they are not needed and reappear when they are. Its overall delicacy might make you believe this will have a short timeline but the opposite is the case. Screwcap. 12.3% alc. **Rating** 96 **To** 2030 $100

Huon Valley Pinot Noir 2018 An elegant wine that highlights its cool-climate credentials with cherry perfume spiked with pepper and juniper, all leading out onto a lean but not mean palate. Tannins supple, fine and savoury and the all important lively acidity. Feels effortless. Immediately delicious. Screwcap. 12.8% alc. **Rating** 95 **To** 2027 $55 JF

Huldufolk Pinot Noir 2018 The idea behind Huldufolk is to highlight something special in the winery that warrants its own bottling. A most unusual aroma of lavender-soap followed by rhubarb and ripe stems with oak spices. Raw silk–like tannins ensue and the palate reveals depth, but isn't expansive with more sweet cherry and pippy accents. Unfurls by the minute. Screwcap. 13.2% alc. **Rating** 95 **To** 2028 $100 JF

Huon Valley Pinot Noir 2017 A blend of clones 777, 115, 114, D5V12 and the trusty warrior MV6. Length is its calling card, the flavours lingering in the mouth long after the wine has been swallowed. The savoury/foresty background makes me wonder whether it might be at its best now, albeit with a lengthy window of opportunity going on from here. Screwcap. 12.9% alc. **Rating** 94 **To** 2025 $55

ŢŢŢŢŢ **Clone 76 Huon Valley Chardonnay 2018** **Rating** 93 **To** 2027 $55 JF

Saint and Scholar ★★★★★

Maximillian's Restaurant, 15 Onkaparinga Valley Road, Verdun, SA 5245
Region Adelaide Hills
T (08) 8388 7777 **www.**saintandscholar.com.au **Open** Wed–Sun 11–5
Winemaker Stephen Dew **Est.** 2018 **Dozens** 12 000 **Vyds** 50ha
Owned by Ed Peter, Dirk Wiedmann and Reid Bosward, Saint and Scholar is a substantial newcomer with 50ha of shiraz, pinot noir, pinot gris, chardonnay and sauvignon blanc. It has also recently opened a large cellar door in Maximilian's Restaurant in Verdun. Winemaker Stephen Dew is the Saint, Reid Bosward (winemaker at Kaesler) is the Scholar. Stephen Dew has worked vintages at Domaine Prieure-Roch owned by Henri Frederic Roch, a co-director of Domaine de la Romanée-Conti (by virtue of the Roch family ownership of 50% of Domaine). Henri Frederic is a natural winemaker and having tasted Roch's wines in his winery in Burgundy, I can attest that his wines reflect his beliefs. Reid Bosward has worked 30 harvests over 25 years in Bordeaux (the Lurton family), Minervois, Moldova, South Africa and Spain. He is the Scholar and absolutely not a natural winemaker, just a very good one. Exports to all major markets

ŢŢŢŢŢ **The Masters Series Adelaide Hills Chardonnay 2018** A somewhat worked style and yet it delivers. Injected with pineapple, stone fruit, oak spice and lots of creamy, leesy flavours and then super vibrant acidity comes along and boxes up the package. It's slick. Screwcap. 13.5% alc. **Rating** 95 **To** 2027 $80 JF

Holier Than Boz Adelaide Hills Chardonnay 2018 Now isn't this a glass of joy. It's pitch perfect with its flavours, structure, depth and drinkability. Expect lemon, just-ripe pear with ginger and the right amount of creamy-lees influence and oak spice too. Screwcap. 13% alc. **Rating** 95 **To** 2028 $40 JF

ŢŢŢŢŢ **Adelaide Hills Sauvignon Blanc 2019** **Rating** 90 **To** 2021 $25 JF

St Anne's Vineyards

Cnr Perricoota Road/24 Lane, Moama, NSW 2731 **Region** Perricoota
T (03) 5480 0099 **www.**stanneswinery.com.au **Open** 7 days 9–5
Winemaker Trent Eacott, Richard McLean **Est.** 1972 **Dozens** 20 000 **Vyds** 182ha
The McLean family has a multi-pronged grapegrowing and winemaking business with
182ha of vines on the Murray River. All the mainstream varieties are grown, the lion's share
to chardonnay, shiraz, cabernet sauvignon and merlot, with lesser quantities of semillon,
sauvignon blanc, durif and petit verdot. There is also a very small planting at Myrniong in the
Pentland Hills, a 50-minute drive from the heart of Melbourne, where the main cellar door
is situated. There are three other cellar doors: Moama (Cnr Perricoota Road and 24 Lane),
Lorne (150 Mount Joy Parade) and Echuca (53 Murray Esplanade). Exports to China.

St Hallett

St Hallett Road, Tanunda, SA 5352 **Region** Barossa
T (08) 8563 7000 **www.**sthallett.com.au **Open** 7 days 10–5
Winemaker Darin Kinzie, Jeremy Ottawa **Est.** 1944 **Dozens** 210 000
St Hallett sources all grapes from within the Barossa GI and is synonymous with the
region's icon variety – shiraz. Old Block is the ultra-premium leader of the band (using
old vine grapes from Lyndoch and Eden Valley), supported by Blackwell (Greenock,
Ebenezer and Seppeltsfield). The winemaking team continues to explore the geographical,
geological and climatic diversity of the Barossa, manifested through individual processing
of all vineyards and single vineyard releases. In 2017 St Hallett was acquired by Accolade.
Exports to all major markets.

♥♥♥♥♥ **Blackwell Barossa Shiraz 2017** If it follows in the footsteps of the '16, it was
crushed and destemmed, 10 days on skins and 14 months in oak (30% new). It
brings the energy, focus and finesse of '17 into high relief, making this a joy to
taste. Screwcap. 14.5% alc. **Rating** 97 **To** 2047 $42 ✪

Old Block Barossa Shiraz 2016 From 92yo vines; tank and open fermenters,
10 days on skins, matured in French hogsheads and puncheons (25% new) for
18 months. As magnificently rich and deeply flavoured as expected. Blackberry
and blackcurrant, then a move to licorice, onto cedary oak and supple tannin
providing texture and structure. Screwcap. 14.5% alc. **Rating** 97 **To** 2046 $148 ✪

♥♥♥♥♥ **Single Vineyard Mattschoss Eden Valley Shiraz 2017** From 58yo vines;
hand-picked, open-fermented, 14 days on skins, matured in 1–3yo French oak for
14 months. A luscious wine. Plum, chocolate, fine, ripe tannins. Very good line and
length. Screwcap. 14% alc. **Rating** 96 **To** 2042 $55 ✪

Single Vineyard Dawkins Eden Valley Shiraz 2017 From 23yo vines;
fermented with cultured yeast, 10 days on skins, 14 months in 1–3yo French oak.
Very good wine. Luscious red berry, plum and herb flavours, the tannins fine.
Screwcap. 14.5% alc. **Rating** 95 **To** 2042 $55

Old Vine Barossa Grenache 2018 The vines have an average age of 60 years.
Hand-picked, destemmed, open-fermented, matured in used French oak for
8 months. A powerful wine with layers of red fruits and time to go. Is full-bodied
in grenache terms. Screwcap. 13.5% alc. **Rating** 95 **To** 2028 $30 ✪

Black Barossa Sparkling Shiraz NV The base wine contains parcels from 60yo
vines. Traditional method, 18 months on lees pre-disgorgement in Feb '19 with
a dosage of 6.5g/l. As those details suggest, not only is this a very good sparkling
shiraz, it will repay extended cellaring. Diam. 13% alc. **Rating** 95 $50

Eden Valley Riesling 2019 Just as Eden Valley riesling should be: Meyer lemon
and Rose's lime juice embraced by enough acidity to carry the wine for years to
come. Screwcap. 11% alc. **Rating** 94 **To** 2029 $23 ✪

Blockhead Barossa Shiraz Grenache 2018 A blend of 75% shiraz,
20% grenache and 5% touriga; crushed and destemmed, 7 days on skins, matured
in 15% new French oak, the balance used American. The sophisticated approach
to the oak has paid dividends, the medium-bodied wine flowing along the palate
in an unbroken stream. Screwcap. 14% alc. **Rating** 94 **To** 2033 $27 ✪

ỊỊỊỊ̣ **Barossa Rose 2019** Rating 93 To 2021 $20 ◎
Lore of the Land Barossa Shiraz 2018 Rating 93 To 2032 $28
Garden of Eden Barossa Shiraz 2018 Rating 92 To 2030 $24 ◎

St Huberts   ★★★★☆

Cnr Maroondah Highway/St Huberts Road, Coldstream, Vic 3770 **Region** Yarra Valley
T (03) 5960 7096 **www.sthuberts.com.au Open** 7 days 10–5
Winemaker Greg Jarratt **Est.** 1966 **Dozens** NFP **Vyds** 20.49ha
The St Huberts of today has a rich 19th-century history, not least in its success at the 1881
Melbourne International Exhibition, which featured every type of agricultural and industrial
product. The wine section alone attracted 711 entries. The Emperor of Germany offered a
Grand Prize, a silver gilt epergne, for the most meritorious exhibit in the show. A St Huberts
wine won the wine section, then competed against objects as diverse as felt hats and steam
engines to win the Emperor's Prize, featured on its label for decades thereafter. Like other
Yarra Valley wineries, it dropped from sight at the start of the 20th century, was reborn in 1966
and, after several changes of ownership, became part of what today is TWE. The wines are
made at Coldstream Hills but have their own, very different, focus. St Huberts is dominated
by cabernet and the single vineyard roussanne. Its grapes come from warmer sites, particularly
the valley floor (part owned and part under contract).

ỊỊỊỊỊ **Yarra Valley Cabernet Sauvignon 2017** A classic medium-bodied cabernet in
the European sense, the cool vintage imposing leafy/black olive/savoury overtones
to the cassis at the core of the wine. Maturation for 14 months in French
barriques has added another layer to what is a complete and complex cabernet.
Screwcap. 13.5% alc. **Rating** 95 **To** 2032 $35 ◎

ỊỊỊỊ̣ **Yarra Valley Chardonnay 2018** Rating 90 To 2025 $27

St Hugo   ★★★★★

2141 Barossa Valley Way, Rowland Flat, SA 5352 **Region** Barossa Valley
T (08) 8115 9200 **www.sthugo.com Open** 7 days 10.30–4.30
Winemaker Daniel Swincer **Est.** 1983 **Dozens** 50000 **Vyds** 57ha
This is a stand-alone business within the giant bosom of Pernod Ricard, focused on the
premium and ultra-premium end of the market, thus differentiating it from Jacob's Creek. It
is presumably a substantial enterprise, even though little information about its size or modus
operandi is forthcoming. Exports to the UK, Singapore, NZ and China.

ỊỊỊỊỊ **Barossa Coonawarra Cabernet Shiraz 2017** Follows in the spirit, if not the
letter, of Penfolds Bin 60A. This 51/49% blend, 86% from the Barossa Valley and
14% from Coonawarra, was matured in French oak (33% new) for 18 months. An
exceptional wine that has taken the somewhat austere character of Coonawarra
and cabernet from a cool vintage into something rich and supple and overflowing
with fruit. As time goes by, elegance will start to appear, making a very good wine
into a great one. Screwcap. 14.7% alc. **Rating** 97 **To** 2047 $58 ◎

ỊỊỊỊỊ **Private Collection Seppeltsfield Shiraz 2015** This is a show-stopper with
spice, cedar and plum all playing a role in investing the blackberry and blueberry
fruits with another flavour dimension. A wine of real class. Cork. 14.6% alc.
Rating 96 **To** 2035 $100
Private Collection St Jakobi Shiraz 2015 Very intense savoury/earthy/briary
inflections give the wine a lightness of foot, an elegance its Private Collection
siblings don't have. Cork. 14.3% alc. **Rating** 96 **To** 2035 $100
Private Collection Rowland Flat Barossa Shiraz 2014 The difference in
vintage takes this wine off in another direction, with more savoury and even
darker fruit flavours. There are many very old vines in Rowland Flat and it may
be these vines were involved. This has a very particular appeal. Cork. 14.5% alc.
Rating 96 **To** 2035 $100

Eden Valley Riesling 2019 The bouquet is relatively quiet, the palate a deep pool of lime/lemon/apple flavour that gains character and structure every time it is retasted. Screwcap. 11% alc. **Rating** 95 **To** 2034 $40

Private Collection Greenock Shiraz 2015 This is full-bodied yet distinctly supple and round in the mouth. Blackberry with licorice and dark chocolate, the tannins embedded in the fruit and thus neutered to the right degree. French oak maturation for 18 months is an integral part. Cork. 14.8% alc. **Rating** 95 **To** 2035 $100

Coonawarra Cabernet Sauvignon 2017 The cool vintage has left its mark on this wine. There's plenty of room for disagreement, but I particularly like the elegance of this wine and am mightily pleased that it wasn't submerged in oak. It is savoury and spicy, the finish a tinker-bell of cassis. Screwcap. 13.8% alc. **Rating** 95 **To** 2030 $58

Barossa Grenache Shiraz Mataro 2018 You are given the bottle number (12175) but not the percentages of the varieties. Nor in the forest of words on the back label are you given any info on the vinification. Go figure. It's a pretty good wine with fresh, bright red and purple fruits, the overall balance excellent. Screwcap. 14.4% alc. **Rating** 94 **To** 2030 $58

Cellar Collection Coonawarra Cabernet Sauvignon 2016 Standard Cellar Collection vinification, matured in French oak for 18 months. Powerful and focused, Coonawarra and cabernet each calling their message with equal energy. Needs time to finally establish its station in life but it's promising. Screwcap. 14.2% alc. **Rating** 94 **To** 2036 $100

ϘϘϘϘϘ **Private Collection Barossa Grenache 2018 Rating** 93 **To** 2028 $100 SC
Eden Valley Chardonnay 2018 Rating 92 **To** 2023 $40 SC
Cellar Collection Barossa Shiraz 2016 Rating 90 **To** 2046 $100

St John's Road ★★★★☆

1468 Research Road, St Kitts, SA 5356 **Region** Barossa Valley
T (08) 8362 8622 **www.**stjohnsroad.com **Open** Not
Winemaker James Lienert, Andrew Hardy, Keeda Zilm **Est.** 2002 **Dozens** 20 000
Vyds 20ha
St John's Road, part of WD Wines Pty Ltd (which also owns Hesketh Wine Company, Parker Coonawarra Estate and Vickery Wines), brings together the highly experienced winemaking team of James Lienert (formerly of Penfolds, plus vintages in the US, Germany and NZ), Keeda Zilm (O'Leary Walker and Vickery Wines) and Andrew Hardy (over 35 years of winemaking in SA, plus Bordeaux and California; Andrew has recently launched the Ox Hardy label). Wines are sourced from the estate Resurrection Vineyard in Ebenezer, and from high quality local vineyards. Exports to all major markets.

ϘϘϘϘϘ **The Evangelist Old Vine Barossa Shiraz 2017** Made from 3 parcels of fruit from the Eden Valley, Stone Well and Ebenezer and coming as one to make this classic regional red. Core of ripe sweet fruit at once dense yet balanced, full-bodied but not overwhelming, the tannins detailed yet plush and pleasing right to the very end. Screwcap. 14.5% alc. **Rating** 95 **To** 2033 $58 JF

Prayer Garden Selection Barossa Valley Grenache 2018 It just sings with lovely, bright grenache flavours. It's not big, neither too sweet nor consumed by oak, but it has an array of tangy red fruits, musk, a dash of woodsy spices and red licorice. A delightful drink. Screwcap. 14.5% alc. **Rating** 94 **To** 2026 $30 JF ✪

St Leonards Vineyard ★★★★★

St Leonards Road, Wahgunyah, Vic 3687 **Region** Rutherglen
T 1800 021 621 **www.**stleonardswine.com.au **Open** Thurs–Sun 10–5
Winemaker Nick Brown, Chloe Earl **Est.** 1860 **Dozens** 5000 **Vyds** 12ha
An old favourite, relaunched in late 1997 with a range of premium wines cleverly marketed through an attractive cellar door and bistro at the historic winery on the banks of the Murray.

It is run by Eliza Brown (CEO), sister Angela (online communications manager) and brother Nick (vineyard and winery manager). They are perhaps better known as the trio who fulfil the same roles at All Saints Estate. Exports to the UK and the US.

Salomon Estate ★★★★★

Braeside Road, Finniss, SA 5255 **Region** Southern Fleurieu
T 0417 808 243 **www.**salomonwines.com **Open** Not
Winemaker Bert Salomon, Simon White **Est.** 1997 **Dozens** 7000 **Vyds** 12.1ha

Bert Salomon is an Austrian winemaker with a long-established family winery in the Kremstal region, not far from Vienna. He became acquainted with Australia during his time with import company Schlumberger in Vienna; he was the first to import Australian wines (Penfolds) into Austria, in the mid-1980s, and later became head of the Austrian Wine Bureau. He was so taken by Adelaide that he moved his family there for the first few months each year, sending his young children to school and setting in place an Australian red winemaking venture. He retired from the Bureau and is now a full-time travelling winemaker, running the family winery in the Northern Hemisphere vintage and overseeing the making of the Salomon Estate wines. Exports to all major markets.

ŸŸŸŸŸ **Finniss River Braeside Vineyard Fleurieu Peninsula Cabernet Sauvignon 2017** Matured in small French barrels (33% new) for 18 months. A very long palate with finesse and intensity, oak and fruit a single stream of flavour, tannins providing the banks. Screwcap. 14.5% alc. **Rating** 96 **To** 2037 $36 ✪
Finniss River Sea Eagle Vineyard Fleurieu Peninsula Shiraz 2017 Estate-grown, matured for 18 months in French barriques (33% new). A fragrant bouquet with the impact of the '17 vintage. Although medium to full-bodied, has retained poise and length, savoury nuances to the black fruits adding yet more complexity. Screwcap. 14.5% alc. **Rating** 95 **To** 2037 $40
Wildflower Fleurieu Peninsula Syrah-V 2018 Co-fermented with viognier. Full-bodied. Steps outside the usual elegant Salomon style, daring to reach for the top of the Rhône Valley. There are some exciting dark fruit flavours (despite the viognier) and well bred tannins. Screwcap. 14.5% alc. **Rating** 94 **To** 2038 $32

ŸŸŸŸŸ **The Verve Red 2018 Rating** 91 **To** 2038 $30
Norwood Adelaide Shiraz Cabernet 2018 Rating 90 **To** 2028 $27

Saltram ★★★★★

Murray Street, Angaston, SA 5353 **Region** Barossa Valley
T (08) 8561 0200 **www.**saltramwines.com.au **Open** 7 days 10–5
Winemaker Alex MacKenzie, Richard Mattner **Est.** 1859 **Dozens** 150 000

There is no doubt that Saltram has taken strides towards regaining the reputation it held 30 or so years ago. Grape sourcing has come back to the Barossa Valley for the flagship wines. The red wines, in particular, have enjoyed great show success over the past decade with No. 1 Shiraz and Mamre Brook leading the charge. Exports to all major markets.

ŸŸŸŸŸ **Mamre Brook Barossa Cabernet Sauvignon 2017** Matured in quality French oak for 15 months. There is ambition in these bones. And rightly so. The quality of the fruit is exemplary: cassis, black olive, bramble and a verdant whiff of herb. Bouquet garni soused tannins keep this full-bodied wine on the straight and narrow. Long. The poise of components auguring for a bright future. Screwcap. **Rating** 94 **To** 2032 $38 NG

ŸŸŸŸŸ **The Journal Centenarian Old Vine Barossa Shiraz 2016 Rating** 93 **To** 2033 $175 NG
No. 1 Barossa Shiraz 2016 Rating 93 **To** 2029 $100 NG
Pepperjack Premium Cut Barossa Cabernet Shiraz 2017 Rating 93 **To** 2029 $40 NG
Mr Pickwick's Limited Release Particular Tawny NV Rating 93 $75 NG
Mamre Brook Barossa Shiraz 2017 Rating 92 **To** 2029 NG

Angaston Road Barossa Valley Shiraz 2016 Rating 92 To 2028 $75 NG
Pepperjack Scotch Fillet Graded McLaren Vale Shiraz 2018 Rating 91
To 2030 $35 NG
Pepperjack Barossa Cabernet Sauvignon 2018 Rating 91 To 2025
$30 NG
Limited Release Winemaker's Selection Single Vineyard Barossa Valley
Fiano 2019 Rating 90 To 2023 $25 NG
Pepperjack Sparkling Shiraz NV Rating 90 $38 NG

Samson Tall ★★★★

219 Strout Road, McLaren Vale, SA 5171 **Region** McLaren Vale
T 0488 214 680 **www.**samsontall.com.au **Open** 7 days 10–5
Winemaker Paul Wilson **Est.** 2016 **Dozens** 500
Paul Wilson and Heather Budich purchase grapes from local growers, making the wine in a
small winery on their property. The cellar door is a small church built in 1854, the winery
and church (with a small historic cemetery) surrounded by gardens and a vineyard. Paul
has learned his craft as a winemaker well; all of the wines are well made and the grapes
well chosen.

🍷🍷🍷🍷🍷 Shiraz 2017 McLaren Vale and '17, that says it all. An elegant medium–bodied
wine with spices and balance from vintage, dark chocolate from the Vale. A most
attractive wine whichever way you look at it. Screwcap. 14.5% alc. **Rating** 94
To 2032 $30 ✪

🍷🍷🍷🍷🍷 Tempranillo 2017 **Rating** 92 To 2028 $30

Samuel's Gorge ★★★★★

193 Chaffeys Road, McLaren, SA 5171 **Region** McLaren Vale
T (08) 8323 8651 **www.**gorge.com.au **Open** 7 days 11–5
Winemaker Justin McNamee, Riley Harrison **Est.** 2003 **Dozens** 5000 **Vyds** 10ha
After a wandering winemaking career in various parts of the world, Justin McNamee became
a winemaker at Tatachilla in 1996, where he remained until 2003, leaving to found Samuel's
Gorge. He established his winery in a barn built in 1853, part of the old Seaview Homestead.
The historic property was owned by Sir Samuel Way, variously Chief Justice of the South
Australian Supreme Court and Lieutenant Governor of the state. The grapes come from small
contract growers spread across the ever-changing (unofficial) subregions of McLaren Vale and
are basket-pressed and fermented in old open slate fermenters lined with beeswax. Exports to
the UK, Canada, NZ and China.

🍷🍷🍷🍷🍷 Mosaic of Dreams Grenache Mourvedre Syrah 2017 I love this wine!
While the Kaleidoscope is the blockbuster, this is an infectious joy to drink.
Bramble (25% whole cluster), raspberry bonbon, damson plum and five-spice.
The tannins svelte; the oak (24 months in neutral French) a framework; the finish
long, herbal and crunchy, belying the wine's weight and vinosity. Cork. **Rating** 96
To 2027 $75 NG ✪
Kaleidoscope Horizons Grenache Graciano Tempranillo 2017 Grenache
(50%), graciano (35%) and tempranillo (15%); the graciano working wonders as it
splays peppery acidity, melding with tempranillo's classic tannin profile. A phalanx
of kirsch, blackberry and anise. A slurry of herb too, imparting further complexity:
thyme, rosemary and tomato skin. The finish is ferrous, nourishing and rich,
etched with a saline freshness. Bravo! Cork. **Rating** 95 To 2029 $75 NG
McLaren Vale Graciano 2018 This Spanish outlier performs far better than
tempranillo in this parched land. Almost a Mediterranean Beaujolais in terms
of the generosity of warm-climate fruit melded to a herb-doused paradigm of
effortlessness: juicy red to blue fruits and a ferrous meaty whiff teem along a pin
bone of peppery acidity. Juicy and long. Medium-weighted and savoury. This is an
exceptional graciano. Cork. **Rating** 95 To 2023 $40 NG

ΥΥΥΥ McLaren Vale Grenache 2018 Rating 93 To 2023 $40 NG
McLaren Vale Mourvedre 2018 Rating 93 To 2024 $40 NG
McLaren Vale Shiraz 2018 Rating 92 To 2026 $40 NG
McLaren Vale Tempranillo 2018 Rating 92 To 2026 $40 NG

Sandalford ★★★★★

3210 West Swan Road, Caversham, WA 6055 **Region** Margaret River
T (08) 9374 9374 **www**.sandalford.com **Open** 7 days 10–5
Winemaker Hope Metcalf **Est.** 1840 **Dozens** 60 000 **Vyds** 106.5ha
Sandalford is one of Australia's oldest and largest privately owned wineries. In 1970 it moved beyond its original Swan Valley base, purchasing a substantial property in Margaret River that is now the main source of its premium grapes. Wines are released under the 1840 (Swan Valley), Element, Winemakers, Margaret River and Estate Reserve ranges with Prendiville Reserve at the top. Exports to all major markets.

ΥΥΥΥΥ Prendiville Reserve Margaret River Cabernet Sauvignon 2017 Hand-picked, open-fermented, fermentation completed and 12 months' maturation in new French barriques, the best 15 barrels selected for this wine. Obviously, the 100% new French oak has had a major impact, both in flavour and texture. Screwcap. 14.5% alc. **Rating** 96 To 2047 $120

Estate Reserve Wilyabrup Vineyard Margaret River Chardonnay 2018 Sandalford works to a simple Margaret River chardonnay recipe: power and finesse with a savoury edge. Grapefruit pith, lemon delicious and melon alert the tastebuds. The follow through is effortless crushed honeycomb, lime, white peach, roasted hazelnuts and ultrafine oak leading to a fully integrated chardonnay experience. Screwcap. 13% alc. **Rating** 95 To 2032 $35 JP ✪

Prendiville Reserve Margaret River Shiraz 2017 The wine comes in one of those wrist-breaking heavy bottles. The grapes were from the best portions of the estate vineyard, crushed and taken to 100% new French barriques to finish fermentation and spend the next 12 months. It's got a lot going for it, but it begs for another couple of years – give it that and you'll be richly rewarded. Screwcap. 14.5% alc. **Rating** 95 To 2042 $120

Estate Reserve Wilyabrup Vineyard Margaret River Cabernet Sauvignon 2017 Open-fermented, matured in French oak. Very good cabernet with razor-sharp varietal definition. Overall, medium-bodied with juicy cassis fruit of striking purity. Screwcap. 14.5% alc. **Rating** 95 To 2037 $45

Prendiville Reserve Margaret River Chardonnay 2018 Pulls out all the stops with a richly textured ode to Margaret River's Gingin clone of chardonnay: forward, expressive with evocative oyster shell/rock pool salinity. Ostensibly camomile, peach and nectarine, beachy. A roasted almond, cashew, nashi pear and honeyed textural palate. Oak not totally absorbed. Big and beautiful. Screwcap. 13.5% alc. **Rating** 94 To 2020 $75 JP

Estate Reserve Wilyabrup Vineyard Margaret River Shiraz 2017 The good colour foretells a very fine and juicy palate that re-affirms all the good omens of the bouquet. It was matured in French oak, which certainly adds to the complexity. Screwcap. 14.5% alc. **Rating** 94 To 2032 $35

ΥΥΥΥ Margaret River Shiraz 2018 Rating 93 To 2030 $22 JP ✪
1840 Swan Valley Cabernet Merlot 2017 Rating 93 To 2030 $50 JP
Margaret River Sauvignon Blanc Semillon 2019 Rating 92 To 2026 $22 JP ✪
1840 Swan Valley Chenin Blanc 2019 Rating 92 To 2029 $30 SC
Estate Reserve Margaret River Verdelho 2019 Rating 92 To 2025 $25 JP ✪
1840 Swan Valley Shiraz 2017 Rating 92 To 2032 $50 JP
Estate Reserve Margaret River Sauvignon Blanc Semillon 2019 Rating 91 To 2022 $25 SC

Sandhurst Ridge

★★★★★

156 Forest Drive, Marong, Vic 3515 **Region** Bendigo
T (03) 5435 2534 **www.**sandhurstridge.com.au **Open** 7 days 11–5
Winemaker Paul Greblo **Est.** 1990 **Dozens** 3000 **Vyds** 7.3ha
The Greblo brothers (Paul is the winemaker, George the viticulturist) began the establishment of Sandhurst Ridge in 1990, planting the first 2ha of shiraz and cabernet sauvignon. Plantings have increased to over 7ha, principally cabernet and shiraz but also a little merlot, nebbiolo and sauvignon blanc. As the business has grown, the Greblos have supplemented their crush with grapes grown in the region. Exports to Malaysia, Taiwan and China.

🍷🍷🍷🍷 **Reserve Bendigo Shiraz 2017** Truly astonishing. The other Sandhurst Ridge shirazs vary between 14.7% and 15.5% alcohol, and are totally unbalanced. Here is a fresh, medium-bodied shiraz that has delicious red and purple fruits. Screwcap. 13.5% alc. **Rating** 95 **To** 2032 $50

🍷🍷🍷🍷 **Bendigo Nebbiolo 2018 Rating** 90 **To** 2033 $28

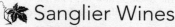 # Sanglier Wines

★★★★

99 Maud Street, Unley, SA 5061 (postal) **Region** South Australia
T (03) 9224 1914 **www.**sanglierwines.com **Open** Not
Winemaker Michael John Corbett **Est.** 2017 **Dozens** 1200
Sanglier shares the same winemaker as Vanguardist, Michael John Corbett, but more than that is decidedly unclear, simply because the short biography supplied by Sanglier is devoid of meaning (other than motherhood statements). Strange, because the quality of the wines is good.

🍷🍷🍷🍷 **Blewitt Springs Grenache Rose 2018** Single bushvine vineyard; wild ferment starts in tank before transfer to used French hogsheads and ceramic eggs. Five months maturation leaves the mouth high in red fruit flavours and fresh acidity on the finish. Screwcap. 12.1% alc. **Rating** 93 **To** 2022 $29
Adelaide Hills Chardonnay 2018 Hand-picked, whole bunch, foot-stomped/crushed then pressed into new foudres and a demi-muid. The bouquet is challenging, as is the medium to full-bodied palate, possibly the outcome of the very large foudres, demi-muid, puncheons and barriques. Screwcap. 12.7% alc. **Rating** 90 **To** 2024 $38
Grenache Shiraz Tannat 2017 A complex blend of McLaren Vale grenache (55%), Clare Valley shiraz (30%) and Adelaide Hills tannat (15%). Bright, clear red colour and upfront red fruits, slightly blurred finish the only issue. Fining and/or crossflow filtration might have made a special wine. Screwcap. 13.4% alc. **Rating** 90 **To** 2027 $32

🍷🍷🍷 **Light Dry Red 2018 Rating** 89 **To** 2027 $29

Sanguine Estate

★★★★★

77 Shurans Lane, Heathcote, Vic 3523 **Region** Heathcote
T (03) 5433 3111 **www.**sanguinewines.com.au **Open** W'ends & public hols 10–5
Winemaker Mark Hunter **Est.** 1997 **Dozens** 15000 **Vyds** 26ha
The Hunter family – parents Linda and Tony, their children Mark and Jodi and their respective partners Melissa and Brett – have 21.5ha of shiraz and a 'fruit salad block' of chardonnay, viognier, verdelho, merlot, tempranillo, petit verdot, lagrein, nebbiolo, grenache, cabernet sauvignon and cabernet franc. Low-yielding vines and the magic of the Heathcote region have produced Shiraz of exceptional intensity, which has received rave reviews in the US and led to the 'sold out' sign being posted almost immediately upon release. With the ever-expanding vineyard, Mark has become full-time vigneron and winemaker, and Jodi has taken over from her father as CEO and general manager. Exports to China.

🍷🍷🍷🍷 **Inception Heathcote Shiraz 2017** Shares the deep colour with D'Orsa. It has had a whole-bunch birth, matched with some parcels of extended maceration.

The wine's 2 extremes were brought to heel by 18 months in French oak (30% new). This allows the top class '17 vintage to spread its wings in graceful flight, evident from the first whiff of the bouquet through to the finish. Screwcap. 15% alc. **Rating** 96 **To** 2040 $40 ✪

Wine Club Heathcote Shiraz 2018 This is more medium-bodied than its siblings and may well have ended up with some viognier included. All 4 wines have 14.8% declared alcohol, and all except this wine seem to reflect full-bodied alcohol. Screwcap. **Rating** 95 **To** 2030 $30 ✪

D'Orsa Heathcote Shiraz 2017 70% on skins for 6 days with only 2–3 days fermentation before being pressed to new French oak at 4°baume for conclusion of fermentation in oak, ultimately spending 18 months in oak (70% new). I'll run with the belief that over the next 5+ years the oak will calm down – a lot – leaving a medium-bodied shiraz with fruit, oak and tannins in balance. Cork. 15% alc. **Rating** 95 **To** 2037 $70

Progeny Heathcote Shiraz 2018 Matured for 9 months in French oak (10% new). Intended to be approachable as a young wine. All things are relative but this medium to full-bodied wine will go the distance, however much it may be enjoyed now. It's supple, but the fruit still has to soften a little. Screwcap. 14.8% alc. **Rating** 94 **To** 2030 $25 ✪

Robo's Mob Heathcote Shiraz 2018 I don't have the faintest idea how much viognier, whole bunch, new French oak ended up in this wine. It's rich and bold, complex and, as with its siblings, body has come without a load of tannins (they are velvety). Screwcap. 14.8% alc. **Rating** 94 **To** 2030 $30 ✪

Music Festival Heathcote Shiraz 2018 A full-bodied shiraz that stays (just) within the borders of comfort. Fruit, oak and tannins are all in play. Screwcap. 14.8% alc. **Rating** 94 **To** 2030 $30 ✪

♟♟♟♟♟ **Special Release Heathcote Shiraz 2017 Rating** 93 **To** 2032 $50
Heathcote Cabernets 2018 Rating 93 **To** 2038 $25 ✪
Heathcote Tempranillo 2018 Rating 92 **To** 2028 $30
Heathcote Rose 2019 Rating 90 **To** 2021 $20 ✪

Santa & D'Sas   ★★★★

2 Pincott Street, Newtown, Vic 3220 **Region** Various
T 0417 384 272 **www**.santandsas.com.au **Open** Not
Winemaker Andrew Santarossa, Matthew Di Sciascio **Est.** 2014 **Dozens** 9000
Santa & D'Sas is a collaboration between the Santarossa and Di Sciascio families. Andrew Santarossa and Matthew Di Sciascio met while studying for a Bachelor of Applied Science (Wine Science). Wines are released under the Valentino label (fiano, sangiovese and shiraz), dedicated to Matthew's father; the remaining wines simply identify the region and variety. Exports to China.

♟♟♟♟♟ **Yarra Valley Chardonnay 2018** Has all the flavour, texture and – above all else – length one expects from quality Yarra Valley chardonnay. The oak handling has been light, leaving the way open for the chardonnay to gain more complexity over the coming years. Whether the gain in complexity is important is another question. Screwcap. 13.2% alc. **Rating** 94 **To** 2028 $45

...ish King Valley Pinot Beurot 2019 Free-run juice wild-fermented in used demi-muids, matured in oak on lees for 8 months. Quite luscious in the relative context of pinot gris. A pear and tropical fruit mix extends from the start to the aftertaste. Screwcap. 13.5% alc. **Rating** 94 **To** 2021 $25 ✪

Heathcote Shiraz 2017 The relatively light colour introduces a wine that fully reflects the cool vintage. It is very intense and long, red and purple fruits to the fore. Screwcap. 14.4% alc. **Rating** 94 **To** 2027 $45

♟♟♟♟♟ **Valentino King Valley Fiano 2018 Rating** 93 **To** 2022 $45
King Valley Pinot Grigio 2019 Rating 92 **To** 2021 $24 ✪
Yarra Valley Pinot Noir 2018 Rating 91 **To** 2024 $45
...ish King Valley Sangiovese 2018 Rating 90 **To** 2024 $25

Santarossa Wine Company ★★★★★

1 The Crescent, Yea, Vic 3717 (postal) **Region** Yarra Valley/Heathcote
T 0419 117 858 **www.**betterhalfwines.com.au **Open** Not
Winemaker Andrew Santarossa **Est.** 2007 **Dozens** NFP **Vyds** 16ha

Santarossa Vineyards, formerly known as Fratelli, started out as a virtual winery business owned and run by three brothers of Italian heritage. It is now solely owned by winemaker Andrew and wife Megan Santarossa. The Yarra Valley and Heathcote are the main focus of the business, while the Sea Glass range explores the many different terroirs of the Mornington Peninsula.

Sea Glass Single Vineyard Tuerong Mornington Peninsula Chardonnay 2018 The most elegant of the Single Vineyard quartet, its balance perfect, 40% new French oak barely evident. Supple fruits take on the trio of grapefruit, white peach and Granny Smith apple (and perhaps a touch of melon). These wines speak quietly, with no point of argument. Screwcap. 13.4% alc. **Rating** 95 To 2030 $70

Sea Glass Single Vineyard Red Hill Mornington Peninsula Chardonnay 2018 Vinification of the Santarossa Single Vineyard chardonnays is nigh on identical except for the vineyard and percentage of new oak. Here the fruit expression is more powerful than its siblings, pink grapefruit coming into play. The 35% new French oak doesn't upstage the fruit, simply providing context and structure. Screwcap. 13.4% alc. **Rating** 95 To 2033 $70

Sea Glass Single Vineyard Merricks Mornington Peninsula Chardonnay 2018 Richer and rounder than its siblings, the fruit balanced between stone fruit and white peach on one side, citrus and apple on the other; 35% new oak adding to the complexity. Screwcap. 13.4% alc. **Rating** 94 To 2030 $70

Sea Glass Mornington Peninsula Pinot Noir 2017 Multi-vineyard sources, hand-picked and sorted, whole-berry wild-yeast fermentation, 22 days on skins, matured in hogsheads for 11 months. Has that stamp of '17 all over it, allowing red berries and spicy/savoury nuances free play. Screwcap. 13.5% alc. **Rating** 94 To 2026 $50

Sea Glass Mornington Peninsula Chardonnay 2018 Rating 93 To 2028 $50

Sea Glass Single Vineyard Red Hill Mornington Peninsula Pinot Noir 2018 Rating 91 To 2023 $70

Sea Glass Single Vineyard Balnarring Mornington Peninsula Pinot Noir 2018 Rating 90 To 2023 $70

Santolin Wines ★★★★★

c/- 21–23 Delaneys Road, South Warrandyte, Vic 3134 **Region** Yarra Valley
T 0402 278 464 **www.**santolinwines.com.au **Open** Not
Winemaker Adrian Santolin **Est.** 2012 **Dozens** 1000

Adrian Santolin grew up in Griffith, NSW, and has worked in the wine industry since he was 15. He moved to the Yarra Valley in 2007 with wife Rebecca, who has worked in marketing roles at various wineries. Adrian's love of pinot noir led him to work at wineries such as Wedgetail Estate, Rochford, De Bortoli, Sticks and Rob Dolan Wines. In '12 his dream came true when he was able to buy 2t of pinot noir from the Syme-on-Yarra Vineyard, increasing production in '13 to 4t, split between chardonnay and pinot noir. The Boy Meets Girl wines are sold through www.nakedwines.com.au. Exports to the UK, the US and Hong Kong.

Cosa Nostra Alpine Valleys Friulano 2019 A mid to deep yellow hue portends what is to come: ripe apricot, bitter almond, lemon and some fennel to toasted nuttiness. Ripe and billowing across the mouth, this is at once a generous wine as much as it is a highly refined one. Richer than its alcohol suggests, this is by far the finest example crafted from this variety on these shores. Sheer deliciousness and ambition. Screwcap. **Rating** 95 To 2023 $25 NG ✪

Gladysdale Yarra Valley Chardonnay 2018 A small portion was skin-inflected, conferring a waft of phenolics and flavour intensity. Maturation: all French wood. Delicious. Long and intense, brimming with white nectarine, tatami, cedar-vanillan oak and truffled, wild yeast, nougat scents. This is tightly furled, nascent and virile. The smoky oak riding uber alles. I have little doubt that this will come good. Very. Screwcap. **Rating** 94 **To** 2026 $40 NG

Cosa Nostra Pinot Gris 2019 This is exceptional gris, attesting to just how this neutral variety has become among the more exciting idioms of the Australian vinous score card. Oxymoronic, perhaps, given its anodyne persuasion. And yet we have riffs of nashi pear gelato and cinnamon across a broad chord of baked apple pie pastry. A thrumming intensity and unbridled juiciness lifts this above most. Very well done. Screwcap. **Rating** 94 **To** 2023 $25 NG ✪

🍷🍷🍷🍷🍷 **Cosa Nostra Chardonnay 2018 Rating** 93 **To** 2023 $25 NG ✪
Cosa Nostra Alpine Valleys Vermentino 2019 Rating 93 **To** 2022 $25 NG ✪
Cosa Nostra Il Capo 2018 Rating 93 **To** 2023 $26 NG ✪
Gruyere Yarra Valley Pinot Noir 2018 Rating 92 **To** 2026 $45 NG
Gladysdale Yarra Valley Pinot Noir 2018 Rating 92 **To** 2027 $42 NG
Cosa Nostra Yarra Valley Arneis 2019 Rating 91 **To** 2023 $25 NG
Cosa Nostra Yarra Valley Pinot Syrah 2018 Rating 91 **To** 2023 $32 NG
Cosa Nostra Yarra Valley Pinot Noir 2018 Rating 90 **To** 2023 $32 NG

Sapling Yard Wines   ★★★★☆

56 Wallace Street, Braidwood, NSW 2622 **Region** Canberra District
T 0410 770 894 **www.**saplingyard.com.au **Open** Fri–Sat 11–5.30
Winemaker Carla Rodeghiero, Malcolm Burdett **Est.** 2008 **Dozens** 1800 **Vyds** 1.2ha
Carla Rodegheiro and Andrew Bennett work full-time in the pharmaceutical clinical research and building industries respectively. Carla started out as a microbiologist working as a locum in hospitals in Australia and London. While in London, she also worked evenings in a wine bar in Carnaby Street where she tasted a 1993 Mount Langi Ghiran Shiraz and vowed to one day make a wine of similar remarkable quality. In '97 she began a wine science degree at CSU, completing the last residential term in 2004 (with 9-week-old daughter Mia in tow), having worked vintages in the Hunter Valley, Orange, Macedon Ranges and Willamette Valley, Oregon. In '08 Carla and Andrew planted a 1.2ha vineyard at Braidwood to pinot noir, riesling, pinot blanc and tempranillo but they also continue to source their best grapes from the Canberra District.

🍷🍷🍷🍷🍷 **Braidwood Riesling 2019** Only 30 dozen made; fermented in stainless steel. Amazing – it's a powerhouse with intense unsweetened lime/lemon flavours. It's possible the level and nature of the acidity may upset some, but not me. Screwcap. 10.5% alc. **Rating** 94 **To** 2030 $32

Canberra Shiraz Viognier 2018 Includes 30% whole-bunch shiraz, 3% viognier; matured in new and used barriques. This is a pretty neat medium-bodied shiraz with a distinct cool-grown thrust to the cherry and plum fruit; integrated tannins another positive. Well done. Screwcap. 13.4% alc. **Rating** 94 **To** 2030 $32

🍷🍷🍷🍷🍷 **Bungendore Riesling 2019 Rating** 93 **To** 2030 $32
Entrechat 2017 Rating 92 $38
The Four Pinots 2019 Rating 90 **To** 2022 $27
Pinot Noir Gamay Rose 2019 Rating 90 **To** 2022 $27
Pinot Noir 2018 Rating 90 **To** 2021 $30

Sassafras Wines

20 Grylls Crescent, Cook, ACT 2614 (postal) **Region** Canberra District
T 0476 413 974 **www.**sassafraswines.com.au **Open** Not
Winemaker Paul Starr, Nick O'Leary **Est.** 2013 **Dozens** 720

Paul Starr and Tammy Braybrook brought unusual academic knowledge with them when they established Sassafras Wines. Tammy has a science degree, has worked as an economist and is now an IT professional and part-time florist. Paul has a PhD in cultural studies and intended to be an academic in humanities before a detour into environment work in government. Tammy knew Mark Terrell, of Quarry Hill, and the pair ended up working in the Terrell Vineyard with pruning and vintage work, leading to local college courses in winemaking. Paul worked at Eden Road cellar door on weekends for four years. History is an interest for both, and when thinking of heading in an altogether new wine direction, they read about what they describe as the ancestral method of making sparkling wine using the original yeast and fermentable sugar to create the mousse, bypassing disgorgement altogether.

🍷🍷🍷🍷 **Hilltops Fiano 2018** A little skin contact is used to add texture and structure to a variety that has its own textural markers. It would appear to be unwooded, and rightly so. The flavours of lemon drop, pear and honey/honeysuckle are delicious. If I had to nominate the best new white variety, it would be fiano. Screwcap. 12% alc. **Rating** 94 **To** 2025 $30 ✪

🍷🍷🍷🍷 **Salita Sagrantino 2017 Rating** 90 **To** 2023 $30
Chardonnay Savagnin Ancestral 2018 Rating 90 $30

Savaterre

929 Beechworth–Wangaratta Road, Everton Upper, Vic 3678 **Region** Beechworth
T (03) 5727 0551 **www.**savaterre.com **Open** By appt
Winemaker Keppell Smith **Est.** 1996 **Dozens** 2500 **Vyds** 8ha

Keppell Smith embarked on a career in wine in 1996, studying winemaking at CSU and (at a practical level) with Phillip Jones at Bass Phillip. He has established 8ha of chardonnay and pinot noir (close-planted at 7500 vines/ha), shiraz and sagrantino on the 40ha Savaterre property, at an elevation of 440m. Organic principles govern the viticulture and the winemaking techniques look to the Old World rather than the New. Smith's stated aim is to produce outstanding individualistic wines far removed from the mainstream. Exports to France, the UAE and Singapore.

🍷🍷🍷🍷 **Chardonnay 2018** An ambient fermentation had its way in classy French oak, where the wine sat unimpeded for 18 months, embedding a nourishing core of truffled curd, nougat and vanilla pod. Stone fruits, white fig and melon scents billow across the seams. Mid-weighted and juicy as is the wont at this address. Nothing hard. Nothing out of place. Softer than the prodigious '17, but this has a mellifluous almost gentle flow to it. Screwcap. **Rating** 95 **To** 2026 $75 NG
Shiraz 2017 A waft of dried seaweed, blueberry, lilac and salami are carried long by peppery acidity and a carriage of tannin, all detailed and succulent. Initially understated, this mid-weighted wine grows in stature with time in the glass or, ideally, in the cellar. Fermented wild and barely messed with, this is unadulterated winemaking at its best. Screwcap. 13.4% alc. **Rating** 95 **To** 2029 $70 NG
Pinot Noir 2017 A sandalwood and forest floor scent greets the first whiff. Candied orange rind, root beer and turmeric to clove, alluding to whole cluster in the mix. Woodsy red berry scents too, but the lead solo is the texture: spindly tannins, expansive and moreish. Akin to nebbiolo. Then the key riff of volatility conferring zest and lift, sensitively appointed to the style at hand. Screwcap. **Rating** 94 **To** 2024 $70 NG

🍷🍷🍷🍷 **Chardonnay Frere Cadet 2018 Rating** 92 **To** 2023 $45 NG
Sagrantino 2016 Rating 92 **To** 2024 $65 NG
Pinot Noir Frere Cadet 2015 Rating 91 **To** 2023 $45 NG

SC Pannell

60 Olivers Road, McLaren Vale, SA 5171 **Region** McLaren Vale
T (08) 8323 8000 **www**.pannell.com.au **Open** 7 days 11–5
Winemaker Stephen Pannell **Est.** 2004 **Dozens** 18 000 **Vyds** 22ha

The only surprising piece of background is that it took (an admittedly still reasonably youthful) Steve Pannell and wife Fiona so long to cut the painter from Constellation/ Hardys and establish their own winemaking and consulting business. Steve radiates intensity and his extended experience has resulted in wines of the highest quality, right from the first vintage. The Pannells have two vineyards in McLaren Vale, the first planted in 1891 with a precious 3.6ha of shiraz. The Koomilya Vineyard was purchased in 2012, lifting the total estate vineyards to 22ha (Steve first set foot on this viticultural jewel in 1994 and it was love at first sight). The future for the Pannells is limitless, the icon status of the label already well established. Exports to the UK, the US and China.

🍷🍷🍷🍷🍷 **Koomilya CP Block McLaren Vale Cabernet Sauvignon 2016** A block regenerated by the Pannells since they purchased it in '12, it produces small berries in small bunches of intensely flavoured grapes. Hand-picked, 10 days on skins, pressed to French puncheons for 19 months' maturation. It is the only unblended wine so far made and sold under the Koomilya banner; 4560 bottles made. It is a wine of beauty, effortless poise and flawless fruit that is medium to full-bodied at most. How long will it live? Try 40 years. Screwcap. 14% alc. **Rating** 99 **To** 2056 $110 ✪

Smart Clarendon Grenache 2018 Fruit comes off 63yo bushvines on a high, cool grenache vineyard in the Vale. It is beautifully composed. Bursting with cranberries and red cherries sprinkled with nutmeg and florals. Tending medium-bodied, yet structured and detailed with grainy, beautiful tannins and raspberry-sorbet acidity to close. Beguiling now and for years to come. Screwcap. 14.2% alc. **Rating** 97 **To** 2036 $60 JF ✪

Old McDonald McLaren Vale Grenache 2018 The provenance of the Old McDonald single vineyard comprises 76yo bushvines. This is heady with red fruits, florals, dried herbs/mint and a hint of green walnuts. There's a savoury overlay with very fine sandpaper tannins and neat acidity sashaying across the just medium-bodied palate. Detailed, complex yet ethereal. Screwcap. 14.5% alc. **Rating** 97 **To** 2032 $60 JF ✪

🍷🍷🍷🍷🍷 **Adelaide Hills Barbera 2017** Had 13 days on skins, gentle pressing, matured for 18 months in French puncheons (31% new). The high natural acidity of barbera has been putty in the hands of Steve Pannell. This is a luscious wine. The dark fruits are velvet-like, the acidity simply providing length and balance. Screwcap. 14% alc. **Rating** 96 **To** 2030 $40 ✪

Fi Fi McLaren Vale Fiano 2019 A superb fiano that straddles the crisp, citrussy, crunchy and zesty on the one hand and texture, layers of flavour and depth on the other. Lime juice, pink grapefruit and lemon blossom with lemon curd, saline and fresh herbs across the palate. Screwcap. 13% alc. **Rating** 95 **To** 2022 $28 JF ✪

Koomilya JC Block McLaren Vale Shiraz 2019 A pale dusty pink. Moreish with the requisite sprinkling of grenache spices and lively acidity. Really zesty with pomegranate and cranberry. Ultra-refreshing, almost thirst-quenching. Screwcap. 13% alc. **Rating** 95 **To** 2022 $25 JF ✪

Field Street McLaren Vale Shiraz 2018 This doesn't need cellaring, although it will last some distance, and it doesn't need hours in a decanter. Just enjoy it. It is lighter framed, laced with neat tannins, bright acidity and with a core of succulent fruit abetted by prosciutto and woodsy spices. Importantly, this has drinkability stamped all over it. Screwcap. 14% alc. **Rating** 95 **To** 2018 $28 JF ✪

The Vale 2017 Alternates between shiraz grenache and vice versa; this vintage the former. It certainly smells of the Vale – a whorl of dark fruit, the dash of menthol, the cocoa-dusting of tannins and the floral lift. Fuller bodied and richly flavoured, but not at all heavy; give it time to open up. Screwcap. 14% alc. **Rating** 95 **To** 2030 $40 JF

McLaren Vale Grenache Shiraz Touriga 2018 This trio has come together well to create a savoury, buoyant style. A core of tangy-tart, ripe fruit shines through with rose petal and red licorice aromatics. Layered with squid ink, mace and patchouli working across the medium-bodied palate; grainy tannins in tow. Screwcap. 14.5% alc. **Rating** 95 **To** 2026 $30 JF ✪

Tempranillo Touriga 2018 Sometimes partnerships just work. Like these 2 Iberian varieties. Comfortable together, complementing the qualities of each other to make an harmonious drink. Dark fruits, red and black licorice, roasted coffee beans, wood char and charcuterie, sarsaparilla and nutmeg. Medium-bodied, energetic and damn delicious. Screwcap. 14% alc. **Rating** 95 **To** 2028 $30 JF ✪

Dead End McLaren Vale Tempranillo 2018 This captures vibrant, primary flavours of sarsaparilla, juicy red plums, curry leaves and baking spices yet there's complexity too. Some meaty reduction, jamon and charry oak lend it a savoury outlook, as do the stealth-like tannins. Screwcap. 14% alc. **Rating** 95 **To** 2028 $28 JF ✪

McLaren Vale Aglianico 2018 This is one of the most important varieties to come out of Australia for quite some time; it is also very good. Dark blood-ruby. Amaro, woodsy spices such as cinnamon quills and star anise, with red licorice, sandalwood and juniper. Fuller bodied with all-encompassing tannins, yet a freshness throughout. The rest is magic. First vintage. Extraordinary. Bravo. Screwcap. 14% alc. **Rating** 95 **To** 2026 $40 JF

Koomilya McLaren Vale Tempranillo Touriga 2017 Stephen Pannell grafted 2 terraced blocks to tempranillo and touriga when he purchased Koomilya in '12. It's chock-full of black fruits, licorice, dark chocolate and multi-spices. Screwcap. 14% alc. **Rating** 94 **To** 2032 $50

🍷🍷🍷🍷🍷 **McLaren Vale Nero Diavola 2018 Rating** 93 **To** 2023 $28 JF
Basso McLaren Vale Garnacha 2018 Rating 92 **To** 2024 $28 JF
Langhorne Creek Montepulciano 2018 Rating 92 **To** 2024 $30 JF

Scarpantoni Estate ★★★★

Scarpantoni Drive, McLaren Flat, SA 5171 **Region** McLaren Vale
T (08) 8383 0186 **www**.scarpantoniwines.com **Open** Mon–Fri 9–5, w'ends & public hols 11.30–4.30
Winemaker Michael Scarpantoni, Filippo Scarpantoni, David Fleming **Est.** 1979
Dozens 37000 **Vyds** 40ha
Scarpantoni has come a long way since Domenico Scarpantoni purchased his first vineyard in 1958. He worked for Thomas Hardy at its Tintara winery, then as vineyard manager for Seaview Wines and soon became one of the largest private grapegrowers in the region. The winery was built in '79 with help from sons Michael and Filippo, who continue to manage the company. Michael and Filippo grew up on part of Oxenberry Farm, originally settled in 1840, and in 1998 were able to purchase part of that property. The Oxenberry wines are made in a different style from that of Scarpantoni and are available only from its cellar door at 24–26 Kangarilla Road, McLaren Flat. Exports to the UK and other major markets.

🍷🍷🍷🍷🍷 **Gamay 2018** Gamay is enjoying a moment. The Vale, with its Mediterranean climate, is a natural home for the variety and here it exudes a warmth and succulence. So inviting. Vibrant purple, confection and bright, just-picked red cherries rising from the glass succinctly reflects the prettiness of the grape. The hint of smoked smallgoods that was there on the aroma is more pronounced on the palate as the wine takes on a more serious flavour profile and weight. Screwcap. 13% alc. **Rating** 94 **To** 2028 $25 JP ✪

Brothers' Block McLaren Vale Cabernet Sauvignon 2016 Cast the high alcohol content from your mind, in the end it's present but the fruit is up for the dance. Indeed, the fruit is the star, a powerful, intense companion in this wine's journey – which will be a long one. Voluptuous wild berries, sweet aromatic spice, cedar with a herby trim. The palate is lush with an umami feel expressed through a series of savoury mushroom and roast game characters. Fine tannins all round. Screwcap. 15% alc. **Rating** 94 **To** 2046 JP

🍷🍷🍷🍷🍷 **McLaren Vale Rose 2019 Rating** 92 **To** 2026 $14 JP ✪

Schild Estate Wines   ★★★★★

1095 Barossa Valley Way, Lyndoch, SA 5351 **Region** Barossa Valley
T (08) 8524 5560 **www.**schildestate.com.au **Open** By appt
Winemaker Scott Hazeldine **Est.** 1998 **Dozens** 40 000 **Vyds** 163ha
Ed Schild is a Barossa Valley grapegrower who first planted a small vineyard at Rowland Flat
in 1952, steadily increasing his vineyard holdings over the next 50 years to their present level.
The flagship wine is made from 170+-year-old shiraz vines on the Moorooroo Vineyard.
Exports to all major markets.

♀♀♀♀♀ Moorooroo Barossa Valley Shiraz 2017 Four rows of vines planted by the
Jacob brothers in 1847 and saved from destruction by Ed Schild in 1984. Hand-
picked, bunch-sorted, berry-sorted by table post destemmer, open-fermented,
5–8 days' cold soak, 7–14 days' ferment, matured for 18–24 months in 90% French
and 10% American oak (30% new). A great wine; the oak handling exemplary,
keeping the cornucopia of purple and black fruits foremost. The mouthfeel
is supple, the alcohol also exemplary. It's history gives it an extra point. Cork.
14.5% alc. **Rating** 99 **To** 2057 $199 **۞**

♀♀♀♀♀ Narrow Road Vineyard Barossa Valley Shiraz Cabernet 2017 High
quality cork but the dumpy bottle doesn't impress. Estate-grown; 27 barrels made.
Succulently rich plum and blackberry jam fruit, the alcohol (just) under control,
the palate long and balanced. 14.9% alc. **Rating** 96 **To** 2042 $70 **۞**
Barossa Valley Shiraz 2018 From family vineyards in Lyndoch and Rowland
Flat; matured in a mix of French and American oak. It is medium-bodied and
fresh as a daisy with its shower of red and dark cherry fruits. It carries its modest
oak with ease, the tannins positive and balanced. Screwcap. 14.5% alc. **Rating** 95
To 2035 $24 **۞**
Pramie Narrow Road Vineyard Barossa Valley Shiraz 2017 Picked and
bunch-sorted by hand, berry-sorted by the destemmer, 3–5 days' cold soak,
7–14 days' ferment, matured for 21 months in French oak (30% new). It is very
full-bodied but the extract has been controlled with black and blue berries,
ripe plums and a hint of cream to the texture. Cork. 14.5% alc. **Rating** 95
To 2035 $50
Ben Schild Reserve Single Vineyard Barossa Valley Shiraz 2017 Picked
and bunch-sorted by hand, berry-sorted by the destemmer, open-fermented,
5–7 days' cold soak, 7–14 days' ferment, 18–24 months in French oak (30% new).
A high quality wine ticking all the boxes, especially length and balance. Screwcap.
14.5% alc. **Rating** 95 **To** 2042 $36
Edgar Schild Reserve Old Bush Vines Barossa Valley Grenache 2018
The vineyard was planted in 1916; hand-picked, destemmed, open-fermented,
15 days on skins, 13 months in large-format French oak. A distinguished Barossa
Valley grenache: red and purple fruits with clear integrity aided by a long, firm
finish. Screwcap. 14.5% alc. **Rating** 94 **To** 2031 $36

Schubert Estate   ★★★★★

26 Kensington Road, Rose Park, SA 5067 **Region** Barossa Valley
T (08) 8562 3375 **www.**schubertestate.com **Open** Mon–Fri 11–5
Winemaker Jason Barrette **Est.** 2000 **Dozens** 4200 **Vyds** 14ha
Founders Steve and Cecilia Schubert have sold their business to Mrs Sofia Yang and Mrs
Lin Tan, a sale that has been implemented over a three-year period. It was agreed that the
Schuberts would guide the new owners into the business as they came to grips with running
a small but ultra-successful high-end wine business. They aim to continue making the Goose-
yard Block and the Gander on the premises with plans for a larger winery and to have other
wines in an expanded portfolio contract-made elsewhere. In 2016 Schubert Estate opened a
cellar door in Adelaide in a renovated stone villa. Exports to Germany, Malaysia, Hong Kong
and China.

🍷🍷🍷🍷🍷 The Sentinel Single Vineyard Barossa Valley Shiraz 2017 Black fruits, licorice, forest tannins and French oak are well balanced, more so than its siblings. That said, less would have been better still if the grapes had been picked earlier and fresher. Diam. 15% alc. **Rating** 95 **To** 2037 $88

🍷🍷🍷🍷🍷 The Hatchling Barossa Valley Shiraz 2017 **Rating** 93 **To** 2029 $32 SC
The Lone Goose Barossa Valley Shiraz 2017 **Rating** 93 **To** 2032 $105
Goose-yard Block Barossa Valley Shiraz 2017 **Rating** 93 **To** 2029 $160
Le Jars Blanc Dry Viognier 2018 **Rating** 92 **To** 2023 $48 SC
The Gosling Single Vineyard Barossa Valley Shiraz 2017 **Rating** 91
To 2027 $55
The Hatchling Barossa Valley Shiraz 2015 **Rating** 91 **To** 2030 $32

Schwarz Wine Company ★★★★★

PO Box 779, Tanunda, SA 5352 **Region** Barossa Valley
T 0417 881 923 **www**.schwarzwineco.com.au **Open** At Vino Lokal
Winemaker Jason Schwarz **Est.** 2001 **Dozens** 5000
The economical name is appropriate for a business that started with 1t of grapes making two hogsheads of wine in 2001. Shiraz was purchased from Jason Schwarz's parents' vineyard in Bethany, the vines planted in 1968; the following year half a tonne of grenache was added, once again purchased from the parents. In '05, grape sale agreements with another (larger) winery were terminated, freeing up 1.8ha of shiraz and 0.8ha of grenache. From this point on things moved more quickly: in '06 Jason formed a partnership (Biscay Road Vintners) with Peter Schell of Spinifex, giving them total control over production. Exports to the UK, the US, France, Denmark, Singapore, Japan and China.

🍷🍷🍷🍷🍷 Nitschke Block Single Vineyard Barossa Valley Shiraz 2018 All the good stuff: dry-grown and fermented under the aegis of wild yeast; a smattering of whole-bunch seasoning (25%) and French oak (20% new) conferring poise, freshness and authority. As far as Barossa shiraz goes, this is benchmark. Plush but nicely taut. A stream of boysenberry fruit and violet scents sashay to a samba of thyme, tapenade and smoked meats, nicely avoiding any sense of reduction or clunky jam. This is smart. Screwcap. **Rating** 96 **To** 2026 $45 NG ✪
Barossa Valley Rose 2019 An astute blend of 64% grenache, the remainder the rewardingly ferrous mataro. This should be the archetypal Barossan blend. An exceptional rose in an age when it has usurped chardonnay's mantle as the most exciting category of Australian wine. Musk stick, watermelon and loganberry scents meander along a hinge of gentle acidity, but more impressive, a pillow of herbal phenolics. Sophisticated rose of great pleasure. A food wine akin to fine Tavel. Screwcap. **Rating** 95 **To** 2023 $25 NG ✪
Meta Barossa Shiraz 2018 Hand-picked, wild-fermented with a seasoning of 24% whole bunch. Neither fined, nor filtered. For the better. Purple opaque, sumptuous vermilion edges. Glossy. Gorgeous wine, thrumming the refreshment metre of pulpy tannin and dutiful acidity across a cage of violet, cocoa, blueberry and iodine. The tannins, svelte but chalky and present. So well extracted! Pay heed! This is liquid joy. Screwcap. **Rating** 95 **To** 2023 $35 NG ✪
Meta Barossa Valley Mataro 2019 A gorgeous, glossy purple hue. Saturated dark fruit scents melding with smoked meat and violet. The tannins, a ferrous timbre. This has no pretence. Just an honest mataro scented with fidelity, extracted appropriately and easy to drink. Delicious! Screwcap. **Rating** 95 **To** 2026 $35 NG ✪

🍷🍷🍷🍷🍷 The Schiller Single Vineyard Barossa Valley Shiraz 2017 **Rating** 93 **To** 2029 $75 NG
Barossa Valley GSM 2018 **Rating** 93 **To** 2024 $30 NG
Barossa Valley Shiraz 2018 **Rating** 92 **To** 2024 $30 NG
Thiele Road Single Vineyard Barossa Valley Grenache 2018 **Rating** 92 **To** 2024 $45 NG
Meta Barossa Valley Grenache 2019 **Rating** 91 **To** 2023 $35 NG

Scion ★★★★

74 Slaughterhouse Road, Rutherglen, Vic 3685 **Region** Rutherglen
T (02) 6032 8844 **www**.scionvineyard.com **Open** 7 days 10–5
Winemaker Rowly Milhinch **Est.** 2002 **Dozens** 2500 **Vyds** 3.2ha
Self-taught winemaker Rowly Milhinch is a descendant of GF Morris, one of Rutherglen's
most renowned vignerons of the mid-19th century. Rowly aspires to make contemporary
wines 'guided by a creative interpretation of traditional Rutherglen varietals, Durif a specialty'.
The wines are made from the estate Scion Vineyard and the revitalised 1.48ha Terravinia
Vineyard managed by Rowly.

🍷🍷🍷🍷🍷 **Fortrose Red 2017** An easygoing, fresh-faced durif with a burst of dark-berried
fruit flavour and an attractive floral element to boot. You get a bit more heft/
flavour than is usually the case with these fresh young things. Worth a punt.
Screwcap. 13.3% alc. **Rating** 92 **To** 2025 $32 CM
Stems Durif 2017 Estate-grown; hand-picked, crushed and fermented with
its stems courtesy of wild yeast. The result is a delicious, fresh and gently juicy
wine with flavours of wild red fruits and just a hint of licorice. Diam. 13.2% alc.
Rating 91 **To** 2025 $28

Scorpo Wines ★★★★★

23 Old Bittern-Dromana Road, Merricks North, Vic 3926 **Region** Mornington Peninsula
T (03) 5989 7697 **www**.scorpowines.com.au **Open** 1st w'end of each month or by appt
Winemaker Paul Scorpo **Est.** 1997 **Dozens** 6000 **Vyds** 17.3ha
Paul Scorpo has a background as a horticulturist/landscape architect, working on major
projects ranging from private gardens to golf courses in Australia, Europe and Asia. His family
has a love of food, wine and gardens, all of which led to them buying a derelict apple and
cherry orchard on gentle rolling hills between Port Phillip and Western Port bays. They have
established pinot noir (10.4ha), pinot gris and chardonnay (3.2ha each) and shiraz (0.5ha).
Exports to Japan.

🍷🍷🍷🍷🍷 **Mornington Peninsula Chardonnay 2019** Estate-grown clones P58,
I10V1, 76, 95; hand-picked, whole-bunch pressed to French oak (20% new),
wild-fermented, no stirring, no mlf, matured for 12 months. The fresh, vibrant
palate supports my suspicion that Mornington Peninsula chardonnay would be
better without mlf in most instances. Grapefruit provides the javelin of the fruit
expression, nothing more. Screwcap. 13.5% alc. **Rating** 95 **To** 2029 $48
Mornington Peninsula Pinot Noir 2018 MV6 and Abel clones; hand-picked
and vinified differently with some inclusion of whole bunches (10%), MV6 in
concrete, Abel in stainless steel. A perfumed bouquet leads into a spicy/savoury
palate with blood plum and black cherry fruits. Very good follow through on the
finish. Screwcap. 14% alc. **Rating** 95 **To** 2035 $55
Eocene High Density Vineyard Pinot Noir 2018 Abel clone vines were
close-planted in '13 at 10000 vines/ha. Hand-picked, wild yeast–open fermented
with 10% whole bunches, 20 days on skins, matured for 13 months in French
oak (20% new). The fruit is deep and complex, no surprise, but the savoury
tannin support has also been well managed. Watch this space. Screwcap. 14% alc.
Rating 95 **To** 2033 $90
Aubaine Mornington Peninsula Chardonnay 2018 Dijon clones 95 and 76;
hand-picked, whole-bunch pressed, wild-fermented in French barriques (5% new).
Here too, the fruit and mouthfeel have a sense of urgency as the fruit makes an
immediate impact. The flavours too, are different from the Estate version, white
peach and rock melon in the frame. Screwcap. 13.5% alc. **Rating** 94 **To** 2030 $32
Mornington Peninsula Rose 2018 Whole-bunch pressed (unusual for rose)
wild-fermented in used oak. Juicy red fruits but no hint of sweetness. Light-
bodied, but nonetheless a serious wine. Screwcap. 13% alc. **Rating** 94 **To** 2021
$28

🍷🍷🍷🍷♀ Noirien Mornington Peninsula Pinot Noir 2019 Rating 93 To 2025 $32
Pinsanto Mornington Peninsula Late Harvest Pinot Gris 2018 Rating 92
To 2021 $33

Scotchmans Hill   ★★★★★

190 Scotchmans Road, Drysdale, Vic 3222 **Region** Geelong
T (03) 5251 3176 **www**.scotchmans.com.au **Open** 7 days 10.30–4.30
Winemaker Robin Brockett, Marcus Holt **Est.** 1982 **Dozens** 50 000 **Vyds** 40ha
Established in 1982, Scotchmans Hill has been a consistent producer of well made wines
under the stewardship of long-term winemaker Robin Brockett and assistant Marcus Holt.
The wines are released under the Scotchmans Hill, Cornelius, Jack & Jill and Swan Bay
labels. A change of ownership in 2014 has resulted in significant vineyard investment. Exports
to Asia.

🍷🍷🍷🍷🍷 Cornelius Norfolk Vineyard Bellarine Peninsula Pinot Noir 2017 One
significant change to the otherwise fixed vinification was 25% whole bunch, the
balance destemmed on top. The aromas of the whole bunch translate as more new
oak (which isn't the case) and a long, fine and lingering finish. Trophies Best Pinot
Noir and Best Wine of Show from the Geelong Wine Show. Each time I return
to the wine it looks better. Screwcap. Rating 97 To 2030 $72 ✪

🍷🍷🍷🍷🍷 Cornelius Kincardine Vineyard Bellarine Peninsula Chardonnay 2017
Clones 76 and 95, otherwise identical vinification for the Scotchmans Hill
chardonnays in all regards. The 4 Dijon clones (these are 2 of them) are better
than the traditional clones. This wine has generous white peach fruit and a surge
of flavour on the finish. Screwcap. Rating 96 To 2028 $60 ✪
Cornelius Armitage Vineyard Bellarine Peninsula Pinot Noir 2017 This
wine and its Single Vineyard siblings have been identically vinified except 3 clones
here, MV6 the sole clone in the others. Destemmed, 5 days' cold soak, 10–day
ferment, matured in French oak (50% new) for 15 months. Complex bouquet;
very good mouthfeel and balance throughout the long, spicy red and purple fruits.
Screwcap. Rating 96 To 2027 $72 ✪
Cornelius Kirkcaldy Vineyard Bellarine Peninsula Pinot Noir 2017 The
wine has the drive and freshness that is so typical of the great '17 vintage. The
colour is bright and fresh, the palate long and lifted on the finish, red berries to
the fore. Screwcap. Rating 96 To 2027 $72 ✪
Cornelius Kirkcaldy Vineyard Bellarine Peninsula Pinot Noir 2013 Hand-
picked, destemmed, open-fermented, matured in French barriques (50% new)
for 15 months. It is, of course, complex and developed, but it has life, balance
and length. The more it is tasted, the more its quality shines through. Screwcap.
13.5% alc. Rating 96 To 2025 $66 ✪
Cornelius Strathallan Vineyard Bellarine Peninsula Syrah 2017 Identical
vinification in all respects to the Spray Farm Vineyard. Nonetheless, a slightly
richer wine. Screwcap. Rating 96 To 2035 $75 ✪
Cornelius Sutton Vineyard Bellarine Peninsula Chardonnay 2017 Penfolds
P58 clone, 33% mlf, 18 months on lees in French oak (33% new). The variables
here are too numerous to allow a line by line comparison but P58 is a far superior
clone to I10V1. This has richness but also retains natural acidity. Screwcap.
Rating 95 To 2028 $60
Cornelius Spray Farm Vineyard Bellarine Peninsula Syrah 2017
Destemmed on top of 25% whole bunches, 5 days' cold soak, 10–day ferment,
matured in French oak (50% new) for 18 months. Typical Spray Farm elegance
coupled with cool-climate complexity based on flavour, not tannin structure.
Drink tonight or in 10 years. Screwcap. Rating 95 To 2032 $75
Cornelius Spray Farm Vineyard Bellarine Peninsula Syrah 2014 Sourced
from the best small parcels ex Scotchmans Hill. Destemmed to small fermenters,
25% whole bunch, matured for 18 months in French oak (50% new, 50% 1yo).
Showing expected development approaching maturity, which will be sustained for
years to come. Screwcap. 14.5% alc. Rating 95 To 2029 $72

Cornelius Single Vineyard Bellarine Peninsula Sauvignon 2018 Whole-bunch pressed, wild-fermented, lees-stirred monthly for 6 months in used French oak, then racked for a further 6 months' maturation. Generous but controlled flavour, stone fruit and melon leading the way. Screwcap. **Rating** 94 **To** 2023 $35
Cornelius Airds Vineyard Bellarine Peninsula Chardonnay 2017 Clone I10V1, whole-bunch pressed, the first 500l of juice to French oak with medium solids (50/50% new/1yo), wild-fermented, 20% mlf, 15 months in oak on lees. The flavours are more intense than those of Mornington Peninsula but you can see the rationale for mlf in the 3 Scotchmans Hill chardonnays. Screwcap. **Rating** 94 **To** 2026 $60
Jack & Jill Bellarine Peninsula Pinot Noir Rose 2019 Whole berry pressed direct ex the vineyard (special harvester), fermented in used oak, matured on lees for 4–5 months. Lovely rose, available in restaurants for on-premise consumption. Strawberries on the top of the tongue are utterly seductive. Screwcap. 13% alc. **Rating** 94 **To** 2022

ŢŢŢŢŢ **Cornelius Single Vineyard Bellarine Peninsula Pinot Gris 2018** Rating 92 To 2026 $35
Bellarine Peninsula Chardonnay 2018 Rating 91 To 2024 $39

Seabrook Wines   ★★★★☆

1122 Light Pass Road, Tanunda, SA 5352 **Region** Barossa Valley
T 0427 224 353 www.seabrookwines.com.au **Open** Thurs–Mon 11–5
Winemaker Hamish Seabrook **Est.** 2004 **Dozens** 3000 **Vyds** 10.1ha
Hamish Seabrook is the youngest generation of a proud Melbourne wine family once involved in wholesale and retail distribution, and as leading show judges of their respective generations. Hamish too, is a wine show judge but was the first to venture into winemaking, working with Best's and Brown Brothers in Victoria before moving to SA with wife Joanne. In 2008 Hamish set up his own winery on the family property in Vine Vale, having previously made the wines at Dorrien Estate and elsewhere. Here they have shiraz (4.4ha), cabernet sauvignon (3.9ha) and mataro (1.8ha), and also continue to source small amounts of shiraz from the Barossa, Langhorne Creek and Pyrenees. Exports to Hong Kong and China.

ŢŢŢŢŢ **The Merchant Barossa Valley Shiraz 2016** Hand-picked, not crushed, open-fermented, 4 days' cold soak, 20 days on skins, matured for 22 months in half American/half French oak (35% new). A full-bodied shiraz but all the components are balanced. Blackberry fruit meshed with well handled oak and tannins. Screwcap. 14.5% alc. **Rating** 94 **To** 2030 $40

ŢŢŢŢŢ **The Broker Barossa Valley Grenache 2018** Rating 90 To 2024 $38
Tiger Moth Marshall Adelaide Hills Montepulciano 2018 Rating 90 To 2032 $29

See Saw   ★★★★

Annangrove Park, 4 Nanami Lane, Orange, NSW 2800 **Region** Orange
T (02) 6364 3118 www.seesawwine.com **Open** By appt
Winemaker Justin Jarrett **Est.** 1995 **Dozens** 6000 **Vyds** 171ha
Justin and Pip Jarrett have been growing grapes in Orange for over 25 years. Their approach to farming is sustainable with a focus on leaving a positive environmental legacy across their three high-elevation vineyards (between 700m and 900m). The wines are organically grown and made with as little intervention as possible. Fulcra is the ultra-premium label, made from small parcels of the best fruit. Exports to the UK and Taiwan.

ŢŢŢŢŢ **SAMM Orange Incubator Series Sauvignon Blanc Marsanne 2019** A pale orange-copper hue. Carbonic maceration and spent 18 days on skins so it is ever so gently phenolic, yet there's texture and tang. Creamed honey and ripe honeydew flavours. It's pulpy and very refreshing with cleansing lemony acidity to close. I like this a lot. Screwcap. 13% alc. **Rating** 93 **To** 2023 $35 JF

Semprevino

271 Kangarilla Road, McLaren Vale, SA 5171 **Region** McLaren Vale
T 0417 142 110 **www**.semprevino.com.au **Open** Not
Winemaker Russell Schroder **Est.** 2006 **Dozens** 800
Semprevino is the venture of Russell Schroder and Simon Doak, who became close friends while at Monash University in the early 1990s – studying mechanical engineering and science respectively. Russell is the prime mover, who, after working for CRA/Rio Tinto for five years, left on a four-month trip to Western Europe and became captivated by the life of a vigneron. Returning to Australia, he enrolled in part-time wine science at CSU, obtaining his wine science degree in 2005. Between '03 and '06 he worked vintages in Italy and Victoria, coming under the wing of Stephen Pannell at Tinlins (where the Semprevino wines are made).

♟♟♟♟♟ **McLaren Vale Shiraz 2018** Radiates regional charm with telltale dark fruits infused with black olive, dark chocolate and bay leaves. Works off a medium-bodied frame with cocoa-powder tannins and a savoury finish. Still glowing with youth, yet will age with certainty. Screwcap. 14.5% alc. **Rating** 95 **To** 2030 $35 JF ✪

♟♟♟♟♀ **McLaren Vale Grenache Rose 2019 Rating** 90 **To** 2021 $20 JF ✪

Sentio Wines

23 Priory Lane, Beechworth, Vic 3437 (postal) **Region** Various
T 0433 773 229 **www**.sentiowines.com.au **Open** Not
Winemaker Chris Catlow **Est.** 2013 **Dozens** 800
This is a winery to watch. Owner/winemaker Chris Catlow was born (1982) and raised in Beechworth and says, 'A passion for wine was inevitable'. He drew particular inspiration from Barry Morey of Sorrenberg, working there in his late teens. He completed a double-major in viticulture science and wine science at La Trobe University, working with Paringa Estate, Kooyong and Portsea Estate from 2006–13. Here Sandro Mosele led him to his fascination with the interaction between place and chardonnay; Chris in turn worked with Benjamin Leroux in Burgundy during vintage in '13, '14 and '16.

♟♟♟♟♟ **Tumbarumba Chardonnay 2018** Powerful chardonnay with length and more. Flint and stone fruit flavours are the wine's bedrock but cashew and honey notes hover throughout. One sniff/sip and you're convinced. Cracking wine. **Rating** 96 **To** 2028 CM
Beechworth Shiraz 2018 Perfumed expression of the variety. A velvety one too. Black cherry flavours tip just into ripe plum before swerving into anise and sweet spice. There's a floral lift to the nose and firm tannin to the finish. It's in tip-top shape. Screwcap. 13.2% alc. **Rating** 95 **To** 2034 CM
Macedon Ranges Chardonnay 2018 Long and elegant and, despite its relatively low alcohol, not short on flavour. Grapefruit, stone fruit, melon and toasty-spicy oak work in harmony to most pleasant effect. Will be better again in another year or 2. Screwcap. 12.5% alc. **Rating** 94 **To** 2027 CM
Beechworth Pinot Noir 2018 Sentio continues to defy the odds in terms of Beechworth and pinot noir. This is another complex, quality offering. It's sweet-sour and spicy, has both treble and bass well and truly covered, includes sappy/nutty characters and is firm-but-juicy to finish. Meat, smoke, tang, reduction; all play positive roles. Screwcap. 13.5% alc. **Rating** 94 **To** 2027 CM
Company Wine Beechworth Nebbiolo 2017 Firm, ripe and long. Feels authentic from go to whoa. Licorice and tar, dried herb and mint flavours. Builds appreciably as it rests in the glass. Will age well. Diam. 14% alc. **Rating** 94 **To** 2031 CM

♟♟♟♟♀ **Beechworth Chardonnay 2018 Rating** 93 **To** 2026 CM

Seppelt ★★★★★

36 Cemetery Road, Great Western, Vic 3377 **Region** Grampians
T (03) 5361 2239 **www**.seppelt.com.au **Open** 7 days 10–5
Winemaker Adam Carnaby **Est.** 1851 **Dozens** NFP **Vyds** 620ha

Seppelt once had dual, and very different, claims to fame. The first was as Australia's foremost producer of both white and red sparkling wine, the former led by Salinger, the latter by Show Sparkling and Original Sparkling Shiraz. The second claim, even more relevant to the Seppelt of today, was based on the small-volume superb red wines made by Colin Preece from the 1930s through to the early '60s. These were ostensibly Great Western–sourced but – as the laws of the time allowed – were often region, variety and vintage blends. Two of his labels (also of high quality) were Moyston and Chalambar, the latter recently revived. Preece would have been a child in a lolly shop if he'd had today's viticultural resources to draw on, and would have been quick to recognise the commitment of the winemakers and viticulturists to the supreme quality of today's portfolio. Ararat businessman Danial Ahchow has leased the cellar door and surrounds, including the underground drives.

🍷🍷🍷🍷🍷 **Drumborg Vineyard Riesling 2019** Seppelt came close to abandoning this vineyard in Henty 30 or so years ago due to variability of the crop, a problem no more. The perfumed fragrance is wonderful, at once light and intense. Citrus and apple blossom notes are quite special and illuminate the very long palate and aftertaste. Screwcap. 11.5% alc. **Rating** 98 **To** 2039 $40 ✪
St Peters Grampians Shiraz 2018 Some, if not all, of this wine comes from the vineyard adjacent to the winery. Small-batch open ferments facilitated gentle plunging, matured for 14 months in a combination of small and large-format French oak. The vintage wasn't a great one but the wine is. Screwcap. 14% alc. **Rating** 97 **To** 2048 $80 ✪

🍷🍷🍷🍷🍷 **Drumborg Vineyard Chardonnay 2018** Mature estate vines; hand-picked, whole-bunch pressed, barrel-fermented with full solids. A wine of striking purity and focus, minerally acidity the framework on which to display the classic ultra-cool grown fruit flavours with pink grapefruit and white peach leading the way. A long future. Screwcap. 12.5% alc. **Rating** 96 **To** 2030 $40 ✪
Henty Gruner Veltliner 2018 New to Henty. A perfumed bouquet delivers a full helping of white pepper, spice and pear picked up by the linear. It is long, intense, citrus-tinged and has real purpose. The very cool climate is the key to this exciting wine. Screwcap. 11% alc. **Rating** 95 **To** 2024 $27 ✪
Drumborg Vineyard Henty Pinot Meunier 2018 The second release from the Drumborg Vineyard. Brilliantly clear colour. The delicious palate of small red fruits and berries is perfectly framed by fine tannins and subtle, quality oak. Screwcap. 13.5% alc. **Rating** 95 **To** 2028 $36
Jaluka Henty Chardonnay 2018 Takes its name from the nearby Jaluka Forest. A very smart cool-grown chardonnay at any price, let alone this. Grapefruit, melon, apple are in play, ditto subtle French oak. Will have a long life. Screwcap. 12.5% alc. **Rating** 94 **To** 2030 $27✪

🍷🍷🍷🍷🍷 **Drumborg Vineyard Pinot Noir 2018 Rating** 93 **To** 2030 $45
Chalambar Grampians Heathcote Shiraz 2018 Rating 93 **To** 2033 $27✪
Original Sparkling Shiraz NV Rating 90 $27

Seppeltsfield ★★★★★

730 Seppeltsfield Road, Seppeltsfield, SA 5355 **Region** Barossa Valley
T (08) 8568 6200 **www**.seppeltsfield.com.au **Open** 7 days 10.30–5
Winemaker Fiona Donald, Matthew Pick **Est.** 1851 **Dozens** 10000 **Vyds** 1300ha

The historic Seppeltsfield property and its bounty of old fortified wines was originally established by the Seppelt family in 1851. Later acquired by Foster's Group (now Treasury Wine Estates), Seppeltsfield returned to private ownership in 2007 with Warren Randall now owning in excess of 90% of its capital. Randall, former sparkling winemaker for Seppelt Great Western in the 1980s, has led a revival of Seppeltsfield, gradually restoring the heritage-listed property. The estate's 1888 gravity cellar is back in full operation and a tourism village has been established. Randall has also slowly pieced together the largest premium, privately-owned vineyard holding in the Barossa – enabling Seppeltsfield to complement its treasure trove of fortifieds with table wine releases. Over the years I have tasted all the 100 Year Old Paras released, some singly, others both singly and as part of a vertical tasting. My tasting notes vary to a degree, but there are recurring themes and no vintage has stepped out of line. So it comes to this: either don't allot points; or try to pick holes and squeeze out a point higher here, drop a point there, knowing in my heart this was a charade; or say these wines have no parallel anywhere else in the world and the conjunction of 100 years of devoted stewardship (think former cellarmaster James Godfrey) and climate/terroir/varieties have had an outcome that can never, ever, be duplicated. Keywords: impenetrable colour, viscosity, searing intensity, endless finish, distillation of every spice known to humankind, bitter dark chocolate, burnt toffee, incisive acidity, rancio, supreme balance, aromas that not only remain in the glass but intensify, celestial anaesthesia. It is the only wine I give 100 points to; what's more, the points are already on the page as I pick up the glass of the next release. Exports to the UK, South East Asia, Hong Kong and China.

ΥΥΥΥΥ **100 Year Old Para Liqueur 1920** I describe this wine (not this vintage) at length in the winery summary but I have to tell you that the sheer intensity of the 1920 is breathtaking. Repetitious, but there it is. Cork. 21% alc. **Rating** 100 $700
Para Tawny 1999 There is no other fortified winemaker in the world able to match the range and sheer quality of the Seppeltsfield portfolio laid down in 1874 (and nourished each year thereafter), headed by the sublime 100 Year Old Para Vintage Tawny. This perfumed wine has wonderful texture and structure; a mesmerising array of perfumed shortbread, Christmas cake, raisins, butterscotch. Intensely rich and sweet until the edge of rancio simultaneously makes it even more complex, yet cleanses the finish. Screwcap. 20.9% alc. **Rating** 97 $88 ✪

ΥΥΥΥΥ **The Westing Barossa Shiraz 2018** Selectiv'-harvested and sorted, open-fermented with cultured yeast, 10 days on skins, matured for 14 months in French oak (30% new). Very different from the Easting. It's elegant and brings savoury notes into play. The light to medium-bodied palate is very long and brings in some red notes. Harmony is the take home message. Screwcap. 15.5% alc. **Rating** 95 **To** 2041 $70
Para Rare Tawny NV Slightly lighter and more developed colour than Para Grand Tawny but there's not much in it. The near doubling of age to an average of 18+ years sends a spear of intensity and complexity to the aromas and flavours courtesy of no-holds-barred rancio. Screwcap. 20.9% alc. **Rating** 95 $75
The Easting Barossa Shiraz 2018 Identical vinification to the Westing. Full-bodied, rich and layered; the blackberry, plum and licorice making tannins redundant; the oak obvious, but in the scheme of things is in balance. Screwcap. 14.5% alc. **Rating** 94 **To** 2038 $70

ΥΥΥΥΥ **Eden Valley Riesling 2019 Rating** 92 $25 ✪
Para Grand Tawny NV Rating 91 $38
Barossa Vermentino 2019 Rating 90 **To** 2021 $25
Barossa Shiraz 2018 Rating 90 **To** 2028 $25
Barossa Shiraz 2017 Rating 90 **To** 2027 $25
Barossa Grenache 2019 Rating 90 **To** 2023 $25
Barossa Nero d'Avola 2019 Rating 90 **To** 2030 $25

Serafino Wines   ★★★★★

Kangarilla Road, McLaren Vale, SA 5171 **Region** McLaren Vale
T (08) 8323 0157 **www.**serafinowines.com.au **Open** 7 days 10–4.30
Winemaker Charles Whish **Est.** 2000 **Dozens** 30 000 **Vyds** 121ha
After the sale of Maglieri Wines to Beringer Blass in 1998, Maglieri founder Serafino (Steve) Maglieri acquired the McLarens On The Lake complex originally established by Andrew Garrett. The operation draws upon over 120ha of shiraz, cabernet sauvignon, chardonnay,

merlot, semillon, barbera, nebbiolo, sangiovese and grenache; part of the grape production is sold. Serafino Wines has won a number of major trophies in Australia and the UK, Steve Maglieri awarded a Member of the Order of Australia in January 2018. Exports to the UK, the US, Canada, Hong Kong, Malaysia and NZ.

ΨΨΨΨΨ **Sharktooth McLaren Vale Shiraz 2017** Picked in 3 passes for varying levels of flavour and ripeness. Open and closed fermenters used for 8 days on skins, matured for 24 months in French oak (50% new). A lovely wine, capturing all that is good from the great vintage, weaving purple fruits into a fine, savoury finish. Screwcap. 14.5% alc. **Rating** 96 **To** 2040 $70 ◆

Magnitude McLaren Vale Shiraz 2017 From 4 estate vineyards; matured for 24 months in new American oak and used French barrels. It is very complex with a darker fruit play than expected from '17, but fills the mouth with all the vibrant flavours of the vintage. Screwcap. 14.5% alc. **Rating** 95 **To** 2037 $40

Reserve McLaren Vale Grenache 2016 Good colour, strong and clear. Classic modern interpretation of grenache, the emphasis on bright, fresh red fruits bolstered by fine-grained tannins and complexed by flowery spices. Ticks all the boxes. Screwcap. 14.5% alc. **Rating** 95 **To** 2026

McLaren Vale Cabernet Sauvignon 2018 From Serafino's best vineyards; closed fermenters with pumpovers, matured for 12 months in French and American hogsheads (25% new). The varietal expression of cabernet runs strong and pure in this wine, reaffirming the symbiotic connection with place. It's medium-bodied, cassis flows freely in its veins and the tannins are just as they should be. Screwcap. 14.5% alc. **Rating** 95 **To** 2038 $28 ◆

McLaren Vale Tawny NV A warming kaleidoscope of flavours and rancio energy attest to the long aged material in this elixir. Olive tinges at the rim of the glass, affirmative. Cheesecloth, tamari almond and toffeed walnuts doused in molasses. The volatility whiplashes the senses back into gear across a searingly long finish. Cork. 19% alc. **Rating** 95 $40 NG

Reserve McLaren Vale Grenache 2018 Dry-grown vines at Blewitt Springs planted in the 1930s. Hand-picked, 3 days' cold soak, destemmed to open fermenters, matured in used French oak for 7 months; only 12 barrels made. In the full-bodied spectrum, but impressive in that context. Screwcap. 14% alc. **Rating** 94 **To** 2033 $40

McLaren Vale GSM 2018 An 87/9/4% blend, which might equally have been simply labelled 'grenache' (85% is the legal minimum). The grapes were destemmed into small open fermenters for 1–2 weeks on skins to optimise colour-tannin extraction, then matured in neutral oak. A supple, round, medium-bodied wine offering pleasure at every turn. Screwcap. 14.5% alc. **Rating** 94 **To** 2033 $28 ◆

Bellissimo Nebbiolo 2018 Nebbiolo is famous around the world for its reluctance to make things easy for those who grow and/or make it (148 makers in Australia at the last count). This example has a strong perfume of violets, and the contradictions of sweet and sour cherries on the palate. The price is mouth-watering. Screwcap. 13% alc. **Rating** 94 **To** 2028 $25 ◆

ΨΨΨΨΨ **McLaren Vale BDX 2018 Rating** 93 **To** 2033 $28
Bellissimo Tempranillo 2019 Rating 92 **To** 2029 $25 ◆
Malpas Vineyard McLaren Vale Shiraz 2018 Rating 91 **To** 2030 $45
McLaren Vale Shiraz 2018 Rating 90 **To** 2033 $28

Serengale Vineyard   ★★★★★

1168 Beechworth-Wangaratta Road, Everton Upper, Vic 3678 **Region** Beechworth
T 0428 585 348 **www.**serengalebeechworth.com.au **Open** Second w'end each month or by appt
Winemaker Gayle Taylor **Est.** 1999 **Dozens** 1000 **Vyds** 7ha
Gayle Taylor and Serena Abbinga established their business in 1999. Gayle had worked in the wine industry for over 20 years, while Serena was seeking to return to North East Victoria

after many years living and working in Melbourne. A three-year search culminated in the acquisition of a 24ha property in the Everton Hills. In the first years they concentrated on planting the 7ha vineyard with 2.6ha of merlot, 1.2ha chardonnay, 1ha each of cabernet sauvignon, shiraz and pinot gris and 0.2ha of prosecco. In '15 the winery was completed and the first vintage made in it. While Gayle is winemaker and Serena estate manager, their hands-on approach means there's a fair degree of job sharing.

🍷🍷🍷🍷🍷 **Beechworth Chardonnay 2017** Hand-picked, wild yeast, 18 months in French oak. The top end of town for Beechworth: rich and opulent. It is very complex, with toasty oak and stone fruit and a grapefruit backdrop. Acidity is another plus. Screwcap. 12.6% alc. **Rating** 95 **To** 2026 $46

Serrat ★★★★★

PO Box 478, Yarra Glen, Vic 3775 **Region** Yarra Valley
T (03) 9730 1439 **www.**serrat.com.au **Open** Not
Winemaker Tom Carson **Est.** 2001 **Dozens** 1000 **Vyds** 3.1ha
Serrat is the family business of Tom Carson (after a 12-year reign at Yering Station, now running Yabby Lake and Heathcote Estate for the Kirby family) and wife Nadege Suné. They have close-planted (at 8800 vines/ha) 0.8ha each of pinot noir and chardonnay, 0.4ha of shiraz and a sprinkling of viognier. Most recent has been the establishment of an esoteric mix of 0.1ha each of malbec, nebbiolo, barbera and grenache. As well as being a consummate winemaker, Tom has one of the best palates in Australia and a deep understanding of the fine wines of the world, which he and Nadege drink at every opportunity (when they aren't drinking Serrat). Viticulture and winemaking hit new heights with the 2014 Yarra Valley Shiraz Viognier named *Wine Companion 2016* Wine of the Year (from a field of 8863 wines). Exports to Singapore.

🍷🍷🍷🍷🍷 **Yarra Valley Grenache Noir 2019** Hand-picked, bunch-sorted, open-fermented with 80% whole berry/20% whole bunch, 12 days on skins, matured in used French puncheons for 11 months. Clear and bright crimson. Gloriously pure varietal red fruits float across the mouth on a silken waft of red cherries and elfin spices. Meltingly beautiful wine. Screwcap. 13.5% alc. **Rating** 99 **To** 2029 $44 ✪
Yarra Valley Shiraz Viognier 2019 From 16yo vines; hand-picked, bunch-sorted, the varieties open-fermented together with 90% whole berries/10% whole bunches, 14 days on skins, matured for 11 months in French puncheons (25% new). The perfumed red fruit bouquet is enticing, but it's the palate that makes the wine with flavours of black cherry and texture woven together from start to finish, the aftertaste lingering for minutes. Screwcap. 13.5% alc. **Rating** 98 **To** 2039 $44 ✪

🍷🍷🍷🍷🍷 **Yarra Valley Pinot Noir 2019** Includes 90% MV6, 10% Pommard clones; hand-picked and sorted, open-fermented with 80% whole berry/10% whole bunch, matured in French puncheons (25% new) for 11 months. Crystal clear crimson colour. Dark cherry and spice scents float across the bouquet and drive the elegant, precisely balanced palate. Fine-spun tannins provide the full stop. Screwcap. 13.5% alc. **Rating** 96 **To** 2030 $44 ✪
Yarra Valley Chardonnay 2019 Has 100% Mendoza clone; whole-bunch pressed, wild-fermented in French oak (20% new), matured for 11 months. Very tight, intense and bound up. However the balance is faultless and the future of the wine is written in 24-carat gold. Screwcap. 12.5% alc. **Rating** 95 **To** 2032 $44
Fourre-Tout 2019 A co-fermented blend of barbera, malbec, pinot noir, nebbiolo and grenache. Hand-picked, bunch-sorted, open-fermented with 80% whole berry/20% whole bunch, 12 days on skins, matured for 11 months in used puncheons. Bright, full crimson-purple. A flower garden bouquet, then a palate of authority. It's a very good wine, as is expected from young vines – the future beckons. Screwcap. 13% alc. **Rating** 95 **To** 2030 $30 ✪
Yarra Valley Nebbiolo 2019 From 8yo vines; hand-picked and bunch-sorted, 100% whole berry–open fermented, 16 days on skins, matured in used puncheons.

Light, bright colour; superb fragrance. Savoury sunbeam tannins percolate the multifaceted cherry (fresh, sour, red) flavours. To top it all off, this is an old (Mudgee) clone. Screwcap. 13.5% alc. **Rating** 95 **To** 2029 $44

Sevenhill Cellars

111C College Road, Sevenhill, SA 5453 **Region** Clare Valley
T (08) 8843 5900 **www**.sevenhill.com.au **Open** 7 days 10–5
Winemaker Will Shields **Est.** 1851 **Dozens** 25 000 **Vyds** 96ha
One of the historical treasures of Australia; the oft-photographed stone wine cellars are the oldest in the Clare Valley and winemaking has been an enterprise within this Jesuit province of Australia since 1851. All the wines reflect the estate-grown grapes from old vines. Notwithstanding the difficult economic times, Sevenhill Cellars has increased its vineyard holdings from 74ha to 96ha and, naturally, production has risen. Exports to Switzerland, South Korea, Indonesia, Malaysia, Papua New Guinea, Singapore, NZ, Hong Kong and China.

St Francis Xavier Single Vineyard Riesling 2019 These wines have improved immensely since I last tasted them. Tightly furled upon opening. Quinine, tonic and lemon oil. It needs a work out in a decanter or time in the cellar. But as it opens, it impresses. Nothing hard. Just tension. A meld of chew and freshness drives the flavours long. Very! Impressive intensity that builds in the glass, auguring for a fine future. Screwcap. **Rating** 95 **To** 2031 $40 NG

Inigo Clare Valley Riesling 2019 Rating 93 **To** 2027 $22 NG ✪
Inigo Adelaide Hills Pinot Gris 2019 Rating 92 **To** 2023 $24 NG ✪
Inigo Clare Valley Shiraz 2018 Rating 92 **To** 2026 $28 NG
Inigo Clare Valley Cabernet Sauvignon 2017 Rating 92 **To** 2027 $28 NG
St Ignatius 2018 Rating 92 **To** 2032 $50 NG

Seville Estate

65 Linwood Road, Seville, Vic 3139 **Region** Yarra Valley
T (03) 5964 2622 **www**.sevilleestate.com.au **Open** 7 days 10–5
Winemaker Dylan McMahon **Est.** 1972 **Dozens** 8000 **Vyds** 12ha
Seville Estate was founded by Dr Peter and Margaret McMahon in 1972. After several changes of ownership, Yiping Wang purchased the property in early 2017. Yiping is a wine retailer in the Guangxi province of China. Yiping's supportive yet hands-off approach has allowed winemaker and general manager Dylan McMahon (grandson of founder Peter McMahon) to steer the ship. The estate has expanded to encompass the neighbouring vineyard and property (formerly Ainsworth Estate). This extra land has allowed for replanting original vine material grafted onto rootstock to preserve the original 1972 clones and safeguard the future of this unique property. Seville Estate also has luxury accommodation with the original homestead and three self-contained apartments. Exports to the US, Canada and China.

Old Vine Reserve Yarra Valley Shiraz 2018 Vines planted '72; hand-picked and sorted in the vineyard, wild yeast–open fermented with 70% whole berry/30% whole bunch, 28 days on skins, matured in used French hogsheads and puncheons for 10 months. The colour is deeper than its sibling and the medium to full-bodied palate has greater texture and structure. Red fruits are challenged by black, resolved by the very fine but persistent tannins. Screwcap. 13.5% alc. **Rating** 97 **To** 2041 $80 ✪
Dr McMahon Yarra Valley Shiraz 2017 Vines planted '72; sorted to only include perfect bunches, 100% whole bunch–open fermented in 2 new French puncheons, 60 days on skins. The oak is integrated courtesy of the barrel fermentation and, while obvious, provides the framework for the savoury, intense fruit courtesy of '17. Screwcap. 13.5% alc. **Rating** 97 **To** 2040 $150 ✪

Reserve Yarra Valley Chardonnay 2019 Clone I10V1; hand-picked, whole-bunch pressed, wild-fermented in French hogsheads and puncheons (25% new), matured for 10 months. That Yarra Valley grip and length takes a millisecond to assert itself. Grapefruit is an important ingredient, flanked by white-flesh stone fruit and, of course, acidity. Screwcap. 13% alc. **Rating** 96 **To** 2029 $80

Old Vine Reserve Yarra Valley Pinot Noir 2019 Vines planted '72; wild yeast–open fermented with 70% whole berry/30% whole bunch, 15 days on skins, matured in French oak (30% new) for 10 months. Old vines are the key to the deep colour, the intense red berry and spice flavours with a foresty undertow ex the whole-bunch use. Screwcap. 13.5% alc. **Rating** 96 **To** 2035 $80

Yarra Valley Chardonnay 2019 Identical vinification to the Reserve, except a 2200l foudre was also used. It's balanced and effortlessly long, the flavours those of a sibling with similar DNA. Screwcap. 13% alc. **Rating** 95 **To** 2027 $45

Yarra Valley Pinot Noir 2019 Identical vinification to the Old Vine Reserve, the vines for this wine planted '94. It all comes naturally – cherry/berry fruit, texture and structure. Screwcap. 13.5% alc. **Rating** 95 **To** 2032 $45

Yarra Valley Shiraz 2018 Vines planted '96; identical vinification to its Old Vine Reserve sibling except 65% whole berry/35% whole bunch. Bright colour. Juicy mouthfeel with red cherries/berries dominant; savoury nuances in the shadows of the finish. Lovely wine. Screwcap. 13.5% alc. **Rating** 95 **To** 2033 $45

Old Vine Reserve Yarra Valley Cabernet Sauvignon 2018 Vines planted '72; hand-picked, vineyard-sorted, 100% whole berry, 30 days on skins, matured in French hogsheads (20% new) for 10 months. Bright colour. Powerful attack by the wine in the mouth, as should be the case for a long-lived wine. Screwcap. 13% alc. **Rating** 95 **To** 2043 $80

ΨΨΨΨҰ **Yarra Valley Blanc de Blancs 2016 Rating** 92 $55

Sew & Sew Wines ★★★★

97 Pennys Hill Road, The Range, SA 5172 **Region** Adelaide Hills
T 0419 804 345 **www**.sewandsewwines.com.au **Open** By appt
Winemaker Jodie Armstrong **Est.** 2004 **Dozens** 3500
Winemaker and viticulturist Jodie Armstrong has worked in the wine industry for more than 20 years. She sources grapes from the vineyards that she manages, her in-depth knowledge of these vineyards allowing her to grow and select premium fruit. She makes the wines in friends' wineries 'where collaboration is a source of inspiration'. Exports to Denmark.

ΨΨΨΨҰ **McLaren Vale Grenache 2018** This mid-weighted juby red spent an admirable 21 days on skins across an ambient fermentation, before 18 months in French wood (presumably mostly used). Far longer an extraction regime than too many grenache. All the better for it. Kirsch, sandalwood and orange rind. I love the sheer joyousness of grenache and this is a solid one, boasting old vine vinosity and immense pleasure. Screwcap. **Rating** 93 **To** 2024 $40 NG

Adelaide Hills Syrah 2017 A lunchtime syrah, the nomenclature apt given the sort of sappy, light to mid-weighted drinking that this provides. Crunchy and spicy. Bergamot and blueberry. Iodine, olive and a skein of peppery acidity providing pulse and length. A very good drink. Screwcap. **Rating** 92 **To** 2024 $40 NG

Sashiko Series McLaren Vale Shiraz 2017 This is a lustrous crimson with all the postcode aromas in place. Delicious. Boysenberry, blueberry, anise and some Christmas cake spice billow across a juicy, rich palate. Not a prosaic wine but poised, plump and thoroughly of place. Made with a deft touch. Screwcap. **Rating** 92 **To** 2024 $25 NG ✪

Sashiko Series McLaren Vale GSM 2018 In this blend less shiraz is often better and here, grenache takes centre stage (70%), with syrah the underling (20%). Again, the extraction pedal is judiciously poised. Enough kirsch-like fruit; spindly tannins, gently edgy and fibrous. Balanced, crunchy and sappy. A solid drink. Screwcap. **Rating** 91 **To** 2023 $25 NG

ΨΨΨΨ **Sashiko Series Adelaide Hills Fiano 2018 Rating** 89 **To** 2022 $25 NG

Shadowfax

K Road, Werribee, Vic 3030 **Region** Geelong/Macedon Ranges
T (03) 9731 4420 **www**.shadowfax.com.au **Open** 7 days 11–5
Winemaker Alister Timms **Est.** 2000 **Dozens** 10000 **Vyds** 28ha
Once an offsping of Werribee Park and its grand mansion, Shadowfax is now very much its
own master. It has 10ha of mature vineyards at Werribee; plus 5ha of close-planted pinot noir,
5ha of chardonnay and 2ha of pinot gris at the Little Hampton Vineyard in Macedon; and 3ha
of pinot noir, 2ha of chardonnay and 1ha of gewurztraminer elsewhere in Macedon. Alister
Timms, with degrees in science (University of Melbourne) and oenology (University of
Adelaide) became chief winemaker in '17 (replacing long-serving winemaker Matt Harrop).
Exports to the UK, the US and China.

ŶŶŶŶŶ **Little Hampton Pinot Noir 2018** Hand-picked fruit carefully sorted and
destemmed so 100% whole berries in small open fermenters, wild fermentation
with daily plunging, 14 days on skins, pressed to used French hogsheads. A
beautifully detailed and harmonious palate with spice, rose petal and cedar run
through to a stunningly long finish and aftertaste. Screwcap. 13% alc. **Rating** 96
To 2030 $65 ❂
Macedon Ranges Pinot Gris 2019 Hand-picked, whole-bunch pressed, wild-
fermented in used French oak, matured for 9 months on lees. A very complex
gris, both bouquet and palate unfolding citrus, almonds and multi-spices moving
into a world of honeysuckle, poached pear and fig in the mouth. Screwcap.
13% alc. **Rating** 95 To 2025 $28 ❂
Minnow Roussanne 2019 From the estate vineyard at Werribee. Hand-picked,
whole-bunch pressed, cool-fermented in French hogsheads in the underground
cellar. Young roussanne is usually boring but this is the opposite with a plethora
of aromas and flavours in Southern Rhône style; honeycomb, fig, marzipan and
pear will do for a start, neatly corralled by just-in-time acidity. Screwcap. 13% alc.
Rating 95 To 2023 $26 ❂
K Road Shiraz 2018 Estate-grown, hand-picked, destemmed, open-fermented,
12 months in French puncheons. A lovely, medium-bodied, cool-grown shiraz
with a super fragrant bouquet. The supple palate brings red and blue forest fruit
salad and satsuma plum, fine-spun tannins harmoniously providing the finishing
touch. Screwcap. 14% alc. **Rating** 95 To 2033 $45
Midhill Chardonnay 2018 From Shadowfax's most powerful site in the
Macedon Ranges, and in another league. It takes flight with a mix of white and
pink grapefruit, juice and pith, plus a contrasting touch of nougat and cream. Fruit
thinning has paid its way too. Screwcap. 13% alc. **Rating** 94 To 2030 $45
Macedon Ranges Pinot Noir 2018 Near identical vinification to Little
Hampton Pinot Noir, except daily pumpovers and limited plunging and 28% new
oak. Its length is excellent, as is its harmony. Screwcap. 13% alc. **Rating** 94
To 2028 $34
Pyrenees Shiraz 2018 Hand-picked, destemmed, wild-fermented in small open
fermenters, matured in French oak (20% new). Good colour, hue and depth. The
bouquet has exotic spices that reshape themselves each time you return to the
glass. Medium to full bodied, it has an equally complex array of flavours before a
savoury finish. Screwcap. 14.5% alc. **Rating** 94 To 2035 $34

ŶŶŶŶŶ **Macedon Ranges Gewurztraminer 2019** **Rating** 93 To 2026 $28
Macedon Ranges Chardonnay 2018 **Rating** 90 To 2028 $28
Minnow Rose 2019 **Rating** 90 To 2022 $26

Sharmans

175 Glenwood Road, Relbia, Tas 7258 **Region** Northern Tasmania
T (03) 6343 0773 **www**.sharmanswines.com.au **Open** 7 days 10–4
Winemaker Jeremy Dineen, Ockie Myburgh **Est.** 1986 **Dozens** 2500 **Vyds** 7.25ha

When Mike Sharman planted the first vines at Relbia in 1986, he was the pioneer of the region and he did so in the face of a widespread belief that it was too far inland and frost-prone. He proved the doomsayers wrong, helped by the slope of the vineyard draining cold air away from the vines. In 2012 the property was acquired by local ophthalmologist Ian Murrell and his wife Melissa, a Launceston-based interor designer. The grounds and vineyards have been developed and renovated, the original residence now a cellar door and al fresco area, the picturesque grounds enhanced by award-winning landscaper Chris Calverly.

ŸŸŸŸŸ **Syrah 2018** Here you have the archetypal cool-climate syrah sporting an irrepressible vibrancy of fruit with fabulous line and length courtesy of super bright acidity/tannins. And did I mention the inviting black pepper intensity which does tend to indicate the presence of a cooler site? They're all here in this lively number. Makes you wonder why more producers don't plant shiraz in northern Tasmania. Screwcap. 14.3% alc. **Rating** 94 **To** 2028 $50 JP

ŸŸŸŸŸ **Chardonnay 2016 Rating** 93 **To** 2027 JP
Pinot Noir 2018 Rating 92 **To** 2028 $35 JP
Sparkling 2016 Rating 92 $45 JP
Cabernet Merlot 2018 Rating 90 **To** 2028 $35 JP

Shaw + Smith   ★★★★★

136 Jones Road, Balhannah, SA 5242 **Region** Adelaide Hills
T (08) 8398 0500 **www**.shawandsmith.com **Open** 7 days 11–5
Winemaker Martin Shaw, Adam Wadewitz **Est.** 1989 **Dozens** NFP **Vyds** 56ha
Cousins Martin Shaw and Michael Hill Smith MW already had unbeatable experience when they founded Shaw + Smith as a virtual winery in 1989. In '99 Martin and Michael purchased the 36ha Balhannah property, building the superbly designed winery in 2000 and planting more sauvignon blanc, shiraz, pinot noir and riesling. It is here that visitors can taste the wines in appropriately beautiful surroundings. The 20ha Lenswood Vineyard, 10km northwest of the winery, is mainly planted to chardonnay and pinot noir. Exports to all major markets.

ŸŸŸŸŸ **M3 Adelaide Hills Chardonnay 2018** Beautifully poised, balance and elegance inevitably part of the equation. There is a purity to the drive of the fruit that makes recitation of what are usual stages of vinification unnecessary. It's the quality of the fruit, the attention to detail and the cumulated decades of experience that make this wine so special. Screwcap. 13% alc. **Rating** 98 **To** 2033 $49 ✪
Lenswood Vineyard Adelaide Hills Chardonnay 2017 All 4 Bernard clones 76, 95, 96 and 277, then the usual winemaking techniques. However the quality of this wine is anything but usual. For the record: chilled overnight, whole-bunch pressed to new and used French puncheons. This is an utterly brilliant wine, elegant and intense, the fruit flavours reflecting the glorious vintage. Screwcap. 13% alc. **Rating** 98 **To** 2037 $90 ✪
Balhannah Vineyard Adelaide Hills Shiraz 2016 Hand-picked and sorted, open-fermented as whole berries and whole bunches, matured for 14 months in used French puncheons, then a further 14 months in bottle. The wine is still in its infancy: black fruits, spice, pepper and licorice in a Catherine wheel of flavours. It's a special wine that will have a very long life as the tannins are fully tamed. Screwcap. 14% alc. **Rating** 97 **To** 2046 $90 ✪

ŸŸŸŸŸ **Lenswood Vineyard Adelaide Hills Chardonnay 2018** From a propitiously situated vineyard at 500m, this plays a 'cool handed Luke' of reductive gun flint tension, a faint whiff of apricot and nectarine, alongside a rivet of creamed cashew and nougat. Tight and febrile of energy, yet far from severe. This is a streamlined chardonnay of the finest pedigree. Screwcap. **Rating** 96 **To** 2028 $88 NG
Adelaide Hills Riesling 2019 Riesling wasn't on the front burner when Shaw + Smith set up business, its Sauvignon Blanc was the cash cow funding other less popular varieties. Hand-picked, 50% whole-bunch pressed, 50% crushed, each fermented separately, blended and bottled after 4 months. The small crop meant the wine is intense and powerful, fine yet textured. Screwcap. 11.5% alc. **Rating** 95 **To** 2029 $32 ✪

Adelaide Hills Sauvignon Blanc 2019 Light straw-quartz hue. Not the easiest of vintages but you'd never know it given the intensity, the resonance and length of this vibrant, juicy wine. The 30th vintage, and I buy the back label comment: 'the wine is better now than at any time in our 30 years'. Screwcap. 12.5% alc. **Rating** 95 **To** 2022 $29 ❂

Lenswood Vineyard Adelaide Hills Pinot Noir 2018 From a vineyard planted in '99 at an altitude of 500m, pocked with loam over clay and a shale substrata. This is a richly flavoured pinot, belying the chiffonesque tannins and ethereal glide across the palate. Think root spice, generous red fruit references and forest floor to dill accents. Long and punchy with a carapace of gentle – but nicely pliant – tannins guiding it all long. Screwcap. **Rating** 95 **To** 2026 $88 NG

Adelaide Hills Pinot Noir 2019 A combination of whole berry and whole bunch, this richly flavoured, mid-weight pinot has spent 15 days on skins, ensuring a skirt of ripe, svelte tannin. These keep scents of bing cherry, raspberry, wood smoke and a carnal whiff of autumnal forest and whole cluster bristle focused and savoury. A spurt of juicy acidity pulls it all far and wide. This is the finest riff on this cuvee tasted in a long time. Screwcap. **Rating** 94 **To** 2027 $49 NG

Balhannah Vineyard Adelaide Hills Shiraz 2017 A mid-weighted shiraz with considerable perfume and class oozing across its ferrous tannic line. Think iodine, blueberry, mace, lilac and a whiplash of peppery acidity sweeping it all long. The mescaline and dill pepper aromas, a legacy of ample whole-bunch, will be absorbed with patience. For now, give an aggressive decant. Screwcap. **Rating** 94 **To** 2026 $88 NG

♥♥♥♥♡ **Adelaide Hills Shiraz 2018 Rating** 93 **To** 2026 $49 NG

Shaw Family Vintners ★★★★

369 Myrtle Grove Road, Currency Creek, SA 5214 **Region** Currency Creek/McLaren Vale **T** (08) 8555 4215 **www**.shawfamilyvintners.com **Open** Mon–Fri 10–5 **Winemaker** Brie Overcash, Brooke Blair **Est.** 2001 **Dozens** 60 000 **Vyds** 414ha Shaw Family Vintners was established in the early 1970s by Richard and Marie Shaw and sons Philip, Nathan and Mark when they planted shiraz at McLaren Flat. Extensive vineyards were acquired and developed in McLaren Vale (64ha) and Currency Creek (350ha), and a winery at Currency Creek. In April 2017 the winery, vineyards, stock and brands were purchased by Casella Family brands and are now managed by the next generation of Casella and Shaw families. Exports to the UK, the US, Canada and China.

♥♥♥♥♡ **The Ballaster McLaren Vale Cabernet Sauvignon 2016** A salubrious, fully amped regional red. A massage of French oak has toned billowing flavours of blackcurrant, saltbush, bouquet garni and black olive. The tannins, salty and oak inflected, easily weigh up by the rich extract. Hedonistic, but tucked in just enough for a mid-term ride in the cellar. Cork. **Rating** 92 **To** 2025 NG

Currency Creek Estate Reserve Brut Pinot Noir Chardonnay 2019 Pinot-dominant with a gentle coral hue to show for it, although the wine is not labelled a rose. For the price, this is delicious. Cooler Adelaide Hills climate fruit sought outside of the estate's Fleurieu base, delivers delicate crunchy red berry flavours, orange zest and tangerine scents, billowing across a frothy bead. Depth and lightness at once. Zork SPK. 12% alc. **Rating** 91 $18 NG ❂

The Cordelia Adelaide Hills Sauvignon Blanc 2019 This is solid poolside fare, far more intuitively tuned of grape spice, gooseberry and herb notes, melded to easygoing acidity, than many regional peers. An easy line of flavour, without any brittleness. Screwcap. **Rating** 90 **To** 2020 $17 NG ❂

Monster Pitch Windjammer McLaren Vale Shiraz 2018 A good effort at corralling shiraz's inherent richness in these parts, with some reductive tension and oak tannins. Violet, blueberry and some iodine. Saline, fresh enough and delivers some oomph for the price. Screwcap. **Rating** 90 **To** 2024 $22 NG

♥♥♥♥ **True Colours Clare Valley Riesling 2019 Rating** 89 **To** 2026 $17 NG ❂

Shaw Wines

34 Isabel Drive, Murrumbateman, NSW 2582 **Region** Canberra District
T (02) 6227 5827 **www.shawwines.com.au Open** 7 days 10–5
Winemaker Graeme Shaw, Jeremy Nascimben **Est.** 1999 **Dozens** 12000 **Vyds** 28ha
Graeme and Ann Shaw established their vineyard (cabernet sauvignon, merlot, shiraz, semillon and riesling) in 1998 on a 280ha fine wool–producing property established in the mid-1800s and known as Olleyville. It is one of the largest privately owned vineyard holdings in the Canberra area. Their children are fully employed in the family business, Michael as viticulturist and Tanya as cellar door manager. Shaw wines are available from a number of retail outlets in China including Suntay Wines in Hainan and 1919 wine stores in Shanghai and Guangzhou. Exports to Vietnam, Singapore, Thailand, the Philippines, South Korea, Hong Kong and China.

ΨΨΨΨΨ Estate Canberra Riesling 2019 Estate-grown, night-harvested. Packed with lime juice and largely concealed residual sugar (6.3g/l) that adds to the overall appeal. Drink any time from tonight through to 10+ years. Screwcap. 11% alc. **Rating** 94 **To** 2030 $30 ○

Reserve Canberra District Semillon 2019 Night-harvested, only free-run juice used. The essence of the wine comes from the lemon/lime sherbet and crisp acidity. The residual sugar can't be isolated, the balance coming from perfectly ripened fruit. Interesting wine. Screwcap. 11.5% alc. **Rating** 94 **To** 2034 $40

Estate Canberra Shiraz 2017 Machine-harvested at night, open-fermented, matured for 22 months in 80% French and 20% American oak (33% new). It's full-bodied, but the oak has not anaesthetised the fruit and is in fact of quality. For its part, the fruit has the typical dark cherry, licorice and pepper assemblage. Screwcap. 14% alc. **Rating** 94 **To** 2032 $34

ΨΨΨΨΨ Estate Canberra Merlot 2017 Rating 91 **To** 2030 $28
Canberra Rose 2019 Rating 90 **To** 2021 $20 ○

Sherrah Wines

19 St Marys Street, Willunga, SA 5172 (postal) **Region** McLaren Vale
T 0403 057 704 **www.sherrahwines.com.au Open** Not
Winemaker Alex Sherrah **Est.** 2016 **Dozens** 3000
Alex Sherrah's career started with a bachelor of science in organic chemistry and pharmacology, leading him to travel the world, returning home broke and in need of a job. He became a cellar rat at Tatachilla for the vintage and followed this by completing a graduate diploma in oenology at Waite University while working Fridays at Tatachilla, earning the nickname Boy Friday – turning up each Friday in time to do some work and then enjoy the weekly bbq. Two vintages of Tatachilla were followed by a job in the Napa Valley, where he worked at Kendall Jackson's crown jewel, Cardinale, making ultra-premium Bordeaux-blend wines. Before returning to Australia, he'd arranged a job with Knappstein in the Clare Valley, where he worked for two years before moving to O'Leary Walker. While there he was able to complete vintages in Burgundy and Austria. At the end of 2011 he moved to McLaren Vale and Coriole, where he became senior winemaker in '12, remaining there for six years, before moving on to head up winemaking at Haselgrove, his present day job. Along the way, his girlfriend became his wife and two children ensued. I cannot help but pass on some of his words of wisdom (and I'm not being sarcastic). 'Wine to me is not about tasting blackcurrant and cigar box but how the wine "feels" to drink. Flavour is obviously a big part of this, but how does the wine flow from the front to the back-palate? It should transition effortlessly from first smell and sip to swallow, aftertaste and lingering influence of tannin and acid. I believe in balance, a great wine should have no sharp edges, it should have beautiful smooth curves from front to back.' Small wonder he makes such wonderful wines. Exports to the US, Belgium, Singapore and China.

ΨΨΨΨΨ Reserve McLaren Vale Shiraz 2018 Selectiv'-harvested, transferred direct to open fermenters, pressed to a single new puncheon for 18 months' maturation,

not fined or filtered. Great balance and mouthfeel. Screwcap. 14.4% alc. **Rating** 97
To 2040 $60 **✪**

 McLaren Vale Grenache Rose 2019 From 60yo bushvines at Blewitt Springs,
picked early at 12°baume, kept in the press for 6 hours before draining juice.
Pale pink. This is as good as they come in rose. Full of spicy red fruits, yet fresh
and long. I don't recommend cellaring, but this will be around for several years.
Screwcap. 12.5% alc. **Rating** 95 To 2023 $20 **✪**

 Skin Party McLaren Vale Fiano 2019 **Rating** 91 To 2020 $30

Shingleback   ★★★★★
3 Stump Hill Road, McLaren Vale, SA 5171 **Region** McLaren Vale
T (08) 8323 7388 **www**.shingleback.com.au **Open** 7 days 10–5
Winemaker John Davey, Dan Hills **Est.** 1995 **Dozens** 150 000 **Vyds** 120ha
Brothers Kym and John Davey planted and nurture their family-owned and sustainably
managed vineyard on land purchased by their grandfather in the 1950s. Shingleback has been
a success story since its establishment. Its 120ha of estate vineyards are one of the keys to
that success, which includes winning the Jimmy Watson Trophy 2006 for the '05 D Block
Cabernet Sauvignon. The well made wines are rich and full-flavoured, but not overripe (and
hence, not excessively alcoholic). Exports to the UK, the US, Canada, Cambodia, Vietnam,
Singapore, NZ and China.

 McLaren Vale Vintage Fortified Shiraz 2018 A select few rows were allowed
to hang long, desiccating the fruit and concentrating the sugar levels, before
fortification. This is delicious. The varietal florals and blueberry fruits are buoyant
and transcendent across the rich throng; the spirit nestled in beautifully. Screwcap.
Rating 95 $20 NG **✪**
Davey Estate Single Vineyard McLaren Vale Shiraz 2018 Having spent
14 months in a combo of French and American oak, this is a curtain of toasty
vanillan, cedar and bourbon oak at this nascent stage. The florals and dark fruit
accents – anise and spice beyond – however, are dense and pure. This rich red
simply needs patience, a vigorous decant or robust food. Screwcap. **Rating** 94
To 2030 $25 NG **✪**
D Block Reserve McLaren Vale Shiraz 2016 The sort of bottle I wish I
had in a hotel without a gym. I could do bicep curls with it! Opaque wine. You
almost know what you are going to get based on the weight of the bottle alone.
Cherry bonbon aromas, bristling with intent. Fireworks across molten black fruit
allusions, bitter chocolate and black olive. Unashamedly bombastic, yet it pulls it
off with style, the charred oak tucking in the seams while the show goes on, long
and thick. Screwcap. **Rating** 94 To 2028 $55 NG
Davey & Browne Fellowship of Fine Wine Gordon and Bitner Block
Cabernet Sauvignon 2017 This is a brooding red. And yet, despite the
ambitious oak handling manifest as cedar and vanilla pod–clad tannins, there is
both regional mettle and ample varietal typicity: cassis, bouquet garni, sage, a
whiff of leaf and a skein of salty acidity. The finish is plush and long. **Rating** 94
To 2035 NG

 Local Heroes Shiraz Grenache 2018 **Rating** 93 To 2023 $25 NG **✪**
Davey & Browne Vortex McLaren Vale Cabernet Sauvignon 2017
Rating 93 To 2029 NG
Davey Estate McLaren Vale Fiano 2019 **Rating** 92 To 2023 $25 NG **✪**
Unedited Single Vineyard McLaren Vale Shiraz 2018 **Rating** 92
To 2030 NG
Davey Estate Single Vineyard McLaren Vale Cabernet Sauvignon 2018
Rating 92 To 2026 $25 NG **✪**
Haycutters Salmon McLaren Vale Adelaide Hills Rose 2019 **Rating** 90
To 2020 $18 NG **✪**

Shining Rock Vineyard

165 Jeffrey Street, Nairne, SA 5252 **Region** Adelaide Hills
T 0448 186 707 **www**.shiningrock.com.au **Open** By appt
Winemaker Con Moshos, Darren Arney **Est.** 2000 **Dozens** 1200 **Vyds** 14.4ha
Agronomist Darren Arney and psychologist wife Natalie Worth had the opportunity to
purchase the Shining Rock Vineyard from Lion Nathan in 2012. It had been established
by Petaluma in '00 and until '15 the grapes were sold to various premium wineries in the
Adelaide Hills. Darren graduated from Roseworthy Agricultural College in the late 1980s
and saw the vineyard as the opportunity of a lifetime to produce top quality grapes from a
very special vineyard. They hit the ground running with the inaugural vintage of '15 made
by Peter Leske (Revenir), but since '16 Con Moshos has taken over the task in conjunction
with Darren. It hardly need be said that the wines reflect the expertise of those involved, with
the eminence grise of Brian Croser in the background.

ŶŶŶŶŶ Adelaide Hills Gruner Veltliner 2018 Gruner veltliner's white pepper aromas
make their presence felt in no uncertain fashion on the bouquet, joining forces
with lemon and pear skin on the powerful, energetic palate. A very good gruner
that sweeps away anything impeding its progress. Only 350 dozen made. Screwcap.
13% alc. **Rating** 95 **To** 2030 $35 **۞**

ŶŶŶŶŶ Adelaide Hills Shiraz 2017 Rating 92 **To** 2030 $35

Shirvington

PO Box 220, McLaren Vale, SA 5171 **Region** McLaren Vale
T (08) 8323 7649 **www**.shirvington.com **Open** Not
Winemaker Kim Jackson **Est.** 1996 **Dozens** 950 **Vyds** 23.8ha
The Shirvington family began the development of their McLaren Vale vineyards in 1996
under the direction of viticulturist Peter Bolte and now have almost 24ha under vine, the
majority to shiraz and cabernet sauvignon, with small additional plantings of grenache
and mataro. A substantial part of the production is sold as grapes, the best reserved for the
Shirvington wines. Exports to the UK and the US.

ŶŶŶŶŶ Row X Row McLaren Vale Mataro 2018 Dark red hue and enticing. Excellent
varietal flavours laid bare from dark fruits, charcuterie, exotic spices plus licorice
to earthy-mushroom. It's full bodied but not too weighty with ripe, plush tannins.
A satisfying drink. Screwcap. 14.5% alc. **Rating** 93 **To** 2027 $25 JF **۞**
Row X Row McLaren Vale Rose 2019 Pale copper-pink. Made from grenache
so it's spicy with a tickle of musk, watermelon and red berries. It has a textural
element but the tangy, crunchy acidity leads this to a lingering finish. Screwcap.
12.5% alc. **Rating** 92 **To** 2021 $25 JF **۞**
The Redwind McLaren Vale Shiraz 2017 A fist full of flavour with ripe
black plums, blackberry essence, licorice blackstrap, molasses and plenty of oak
influence – it's aged for 20 months in 80% new French puncheons. Full-bodied
with powerful tannins, a bitter finish detracts but it has an intensity that fans of this
style will enjoy. Screwcap. 14.5% alc. **Rating** 92 **To** 2033 $45 JF
The Redwind McLaren Vale Cabernet Sauvignon 2017 Really fragrant
with cassis and rhubarb, oak char and licorice, eucalyptus and cedar with a hint of
violets. Yet there's a leanness across the palate with grippy tannins tapering off to a
drying finish. Screwcap. 13.8% alc. **Rating** 91 **To** 2028 $45 JF
Row X Row McLaren Vale Grenache 2019 A pretty and pleasant drink
without any fuss. It's very light and fresh with attractive raspberry and cherry fruits,
neat acidity with barely-there tannins. Screwcap. 13% alc. **Rating** 90 **To** 2024
$25 JF

Shoofly | Frisk

PO Box 119, Mooroolbark, Vic 3138 **Region** Various
T 0405 631 557 **www.**shooflywines.com **Open** Not
Winemaker Ben Riggs, Garry Wall, Mark O'Callaghan **Est.** 2003 **Dozens** 20 000
This is a far-flung, export-oriented, business. It purchases a little over 620t of grapes each
vintage, the lion's share (surprisingly) riesling (250t), followed by shiraz (200t) and chardonnay
(50t); the remainder is made up of pinot noir, gewurztraminer, merlot, dolcetto and muscat
gordo blanco. Ben Riggs makes Shoofly Shiraz and Chardonnay at Vintners McLaren Vale;
Frisk Riesling is made by Garry Wall at King Valley Wines, the Prickly Riesling by Garry Wall
of King Valley Wines. The bulk of exports go to the US, Canada, Ireland and South Korea.

Shottesbrooke   ★★★★★

Bagshaws Road, McLaren Flat, SA 5171 **Region** McLaren Vale
T (08) 8383 0002 **www.**shottesbrooke.com.au **Open** 7 days 11–5
Winemaker Hamish Maguire **Est.** 1984 **Dozens** 150 000 **Vyds** 30.64ha
Shottesbrooke is a proudly family-owned and managed business with second-generation
Hamish Maguire as chief winemaker and general manager. Before taking the reins at
Shottesbrooke, Hamish completed two vintages in France and one in Spain, giving him a
personal knowledge of the world of wine. The investment of time and money over the past
33 years have taken Shottesbrooke to the position where it can embark on the next major
step and undertake major improvements in the size and operation of its winery. The central
theme is the investment in state-of-the-art equipment allowing more gentle fermentation,
pressing, movement and maturation of the wines. Thus there has been a 25% increase in the
temperature-controlled main barrel storage areas, sufficient to hold an additional 600 barrels.
Once bottled and packaged, the wines are held in a purpose-built air-conditioned storage
facility until shipped to customers in refrigerated containers to ensure quality and consistency
throughout the entire process. Exports to all major markets, most importantly, China.

🍷🍷🍷🍷🍷 **Big Dreams McLaren Vale Grenache 2018** Among the big guns of the range,
this is by far the best wine. Kirsch, lavender, thyme and bergamot riffs ooze across
palpably fresh acidity and finely wrought Blewitt Springs tannins: sandy, nicely
pliant, gently herbal and attenuated. This rich red is exceptional, boasting real old
vine (80+ years) thrust and compelling length. Screwcap. **Rating** 96 **To** 2027
$95 NG

The Butchered Line McLaren Vale Shiraz 2018 A 4-day cold soak played a
small part in the elevage of a wine that is lively with juicy red fruits. It's delicious
and, while slightly off the McLaren Vale beaten track, needs no justification.
Screwcap. 14.5% alc. **Rating** 95 **To** 2033 $95

Reserve Series McLaren Vale The Proprietor 2018 A cabernet merlot
malbec of saline maritime freshness melded with the warm, densely rich fruit
of the Vale. Well appointed pillars of oak help guide the fray: bitter chocolate,
blackcurrant, damson plum, black olive and dried sage notes clad the finely tuned
tannic finish. Full-bodied. But sophisticated of structure and beautifully poised.
Will make old bones. Screwcap. 14.5% alc. **Rating** 95 **To** 2034 $60 NG

Measure Twice, Cut Once McLaren Vale Mataro 2018 A 9-day ferment
is the sole information provided, but it matters not. This is a high quality mataro
with exemplary varietal character. It's juicy, pliable red/purple fruits have a pleasing,
earthy substrate in place of drying tannins. Will live and love. Screwcap. 14.5% alc.
Rating 95 **To** 2040 $95

🍷🍷🍷🍷🍸 **Single Vineyard Bush Vine McLaren Vale Grenache 2018 Rating** 93
To 2024 $33 NG
Punch Reserve McLaren Vale Cabernet Sauvignon 2018 Rating 93
To 2033 $60 NG
Reserve Series Eliza McLaren Vale Shiraz 2018 Rating 91 **To** 2030
$60 NG
Estate Series McLaren Vale GSM 2018 Rating 91 **To** 2023 $20 NG ✪

Shut the Gate Wines

8453 Main North Road, Clare, SA 5453 **Region** Clare Valley
T 0488 243 200 **www.**shutthegate.com.au **Open** 7 days 10–4.30
Winemaker Contract **Est.** 2013 **Dozens** 6000

Shut the Gate is the venture of Richard Woods and Rasa Fabian, which took shape after five years' involvement in the rebranding of Crabtree Watervale Wines, followed by 18 months of juggling consultancy roles. During this time Richard and Rasa set the foundations for Shut the Gate; the striking and imaginative labels (and parables) catching the eye. The engine room of the business is the Clare Valley, where the wines are contract-made and the grapes for many of the wines are sourced. They have chosen their grape sources and contract winemakers with considerable care.

99999 **For Love Watervale Riesling 2019** Represents the best cut of the free-run juice, fermented dry, no pressings and all natural acid. Green-straw. A strong follow-up to the highly rated '18 with Watervale's concentrated lime again a feature. Pink grapefruit, citrus cut apple, jasmine, spring blossom leading to a lime core shows all the right riesling moves. Pretty smart on the palate too, with highish acidity. Screwcap. 12% alc. **Rating** 94 **To** 2034 $28 JP ✪

99999 **Rosie's Patch Watervale Riesling 2019 Rating** 93 **To** 2028 $22 JP ✪
For Hunger Single Site Adelaide Hills Pinot Noir 2018 Rating 93 **To** 2026 $32 JP
Fur Elise Clare Valley Grenache Rose 2019 Rating 92 **To** 2023 $22 JP ✪
For Love Clare Valley Fiano 2019 Rating 91 **To** 2026 $28 JP

Shy Susan Wines

Billy Button Wines, 11 Camp Street, Bright, Vic 3741 **Region** Tasmania
T 0434 635 510 **www.**shysusanwines.com.au **Open** 7 days 11–6
Winemaker Glenn James **Est.** 2015 **Dozens** 300

'Shy Susan (*Tetratheca gunnii*) is a critically endangered wildflower endemic to a tiny part of Tasmania. Her survival depends completely on a little native bee, who alone is capable of pollination. Their fate is forever entwined.' After working with Tasmanian fruit for nearly two decades Glenn James with his wife, Jo Marsh, have released a range of unique wines from some of Tasmania's most exciting vineyards. Their initial release includes Riesling, a Sylvaner Riesling blend, Gewurztraminer, Chardonnay, Pinot Noir and an Amphora Shiraz. Select small parcels of fruit are crafted to reflect variety, vineyard and the stylistic approach forged from Glenn's skill and experience. Jo Marsh is owner and winemaker of Billy Button Wines (see separate entry).

99999 **Pinot Noir 2018** From the Huon Valley (67%), Derwent Valley (21%) and Coal River Valley (12%). Hand-picked but from there on a significant number of vinification methods were used. Shy Susan says '18 was close to perfect for pinot noir. A quick sniff and sip brings instantaneous agreement, redoubling with every additional taste. The only pity is that the make was limited to 130 dozen. Screwcap. 13.5% alc. **Rating** 98 **To** 2033 $65 ✪

99999 **Chardonnay 2018** Is still indeed shy, but you can easily see the beauty now with more to come over the next 3+ years. The guarantee of its development is the length and harmony of the palate. Screwcap. 13% alc. **Rating** 95 **To** 2030 $55

Sidewood Estate

6 River Road, Hahndorf, SA 5245 **Region** Adelaide Hills
T (08) 8388 1673 **www.**sidewood.com.au **Open** Wed–Mon 11–5, Fri–Sat 11–8.30
Winemaker Darryl Catlin **Est.** 2004 **Dozens** NFP **Vyds** 90ha

Sidewood Estate was established in 2004. It is owned by Owen and Cassandra Inglis who operate it as a winery and cidery. Sidewood Estate lies in the Onkaparinga Valley, with the vines weathering the cool climate in the Adelaide Hills. Significant expenditure on regeneration of the vineyards was already well underway when Sidewood invested over $12 million in the expansion of the winery, increasing capacity from 500t to 2000t each vintage and implementing sustainable improvements including 100kW solar panels, water treatment works and insulation for the winery. The expansion includes new bottling and canning facilities capable of handling 6 million bottles of wine and cider annually. Wines are released under the Sidewood Estate, Stablemate and Mappinga labels. Exports to the UK, the US, Canada, the Netherlands, Malaysia, the Philippines, Norway, Denmark, Thailand, Vanuatu, Singapore, Japan and China.

ΨΨΨΨΨ **Ironstone Barrels The Tyre Fitter Adelaide Hills Syrah 2018** The inaugural release. Matured for 12 months in French oak (30% new), 1170 bottles made. I really like this wine, which has some of the savoury nuances of the best '17 vintage wines. It has energy and drive to its black fruit, and fine, savoury tannins. I'd never pick it as an '18. Screwcap. 14.5% alc. **Rating** 97 **To** 2037 $50 ◐

ΨΨΨΨΨ **Mappinga Fume Blanc 2018** Hand-picked, only free-run juice barrel-fermented in French barriques (30% new) and matured for 8 months. The bouquet is exceptionally fragrant (and complex), the palate equally long and intense. Tropical to herbal fruits on display. Screwcap. 11.5% alc. **Rating** 96 **To** 2023 $35 ◐

Adelaide Hills Chardonnay 2018 Clones 95 and 76; free-run juice direct to barrel, wild-yeast fermentation, matured for 10 months in French oak. An elegant, tightly focused wine built on grapefruit and white peach fruit flavours. The length and balance are very good. Screwcap. 12% alc. **Rating** 96 **To** 2030 $24 ◐

Stablemate Adelaide Hills Pinot Noir 2017 This has the tension and tight focus of the cool '17 vintage that the '18 lacks. It's not a question of richness, depth or even length. Go to the '17s and find the purity of the strawberries for example. It's a scent, a light breeze that blows briefly. Screwcap. 12.5% alc. **Rating** 96 **To** 2027 $22 ◐

Adelaide Hills Shiraz 2018 This is the complete package. Cold soak, wild-yeast ferment with partial whole bunch, partial whole berry, matured in French oak (25% new) for 18 months. The result is a wine of great complexity in both texture and flavour. Savoury black cherry, blackberry and forest notes. Skilled winemaking with 5-star success. Screwcap. 14.5% alc. **Rating** 96 **To** 2038 $26 ◐

Mappinga Shiraz 2017 Estate-grown; part hand-picked, part Selectiv'-harvested, wild-fermented with some whole bunches, matured in French oak (35% new), then a barrel selection. A richly robed wine. Blackberry, spice and cedar all weave their way harmoniously through the palate. It simply needs a decade. Screwcap. 14.5% alc. **Rating** 96 **To** 2032 $65 ◐

Adelaide Hills Pinot Noir Chardonnay NV A selection of Dijon clones for both the 60% pinot and 40% chardonnay components. Enormous care is taken for a non-vintage blend at a price of $22, following the trail of previous releases with a gold medal at the Hobart Wine Show '19. Fresh, lively, the balance excellent, ditto length. Diam. 11.5% alc. **Rating** 95 ◐

Adelaide Hills Sauvignon Blanc 2019 The low yield and row by row selective picking, has resulted in a wine that has effortless varietal expression. The flavours are captured in a citrus/tropical flavour range built on the power and structure of the fruit. Screwcap. 12.5% alc. **Rating** 94 **To** 2021 $22 ◐

Mappinga Chardonnay 2018 Hand-picked Dijon clones, partial whole-bunch pressed, wild-fermented, French oak (30% new), best barrel selection. Very powerful and complex. Reduction may be an issue for some – or is it early harvest? Screwcap. 12% alc. **Rating** 94 **To** 2027 $38

Adelaide Hills Pinot Blanc 2019 A limited release of 500 dozen. Hand-picked, low-yielding vines, whole-bunch pressed to French puncheons and hogsheads (10% new), matured for 6 months. A pinot blanc with flavour! Due in no small measure to skilled vinification, and a nod to its family with its pink grapefruit and white peach duo. Screwcap. 13% alc. **Rating** 94 **To** 2025 $22 ◐

Abel Adelaide Hills Pinot Noir 2018 Hand-picked, wild-fermented in small batches, 30% whole bunch, partial whole berry, matured in used French oak for

10 months, 400 dozen made. The colour is bright, although modest depth. A scented, spicy bouquet of cherry blossom leads the way into the light, but bright and finely structured palate. Screwcap. 13% alc. **Rating** 94 **To** 2030 $40

Adelaide Hills Pinot Noir 2018 MV6, Oberlin, Abel and 777 clones from the estate Mappinga Vineyard; each vinified separately but in the same fashion: chilled for 36 hours, wild-fermented with 30% whole bunches, 30% whole berries, the balance destemmed, matured in French oak (15% new) for 10 months. Light colour. Scented forest floor and berries, the palate fresh and juicy. Screwcap. 13% alc. **Rating** 94 **To** 2027 $32

Ironstone Barrels The Old China Hand Adelaide Hills Syrah 2018 Very powerful, it has plenty of ripe fruit flavours and tannins, and a depth to the wine that is wholly satisfying. Screwcap. 14% alc. **Rating** 94 **To** 2030 $50

Methode Traditionelle Adelaide Hills Chloe Cuvee 2015 A 60/40% blend of chardonnay and pinot noir, both Dijon clones; traditional method, minimum of 36 months on lees. Full on cherry and mandarin blossom, fresh vibrant finish. Gold medal National Cool Climate Wine Show. Diam. 12% alc. **Rating** 94 $32

ΨΨΨΨΩ **Adelaide Hills Pinot Gris 2019** Rating 93 To 2022 $22 ❂
Adelaide Hills Rose 2019 Rating 93 To 2021 $22 ❂
Methode Traditionelle Adelaide Hills Isabella Rose 2014 Rating 93 $32
Oberlin Adelaide Hills Pinot Noir 2018 Rating 92 To 2025 $40

Sieber Wines ★★★★

Sieber Road, Tanunda, SA 5352 **Region** Barossa Valley
T (08) 8562 8038 **www.**sieberwines.com **Open** 7 days 11–4
Winemaker Tony Carapetis **Est.** 1999 **Dozens** 7500 **Vyds** 18ha
Richard and Val Sieber are the third generation to run Redlands, the family property, traditionally a cropping/grazing farm. They have diversified into viticulture with shiraz (14ha) occupying the lion's share, the remainder split between viognier, grenache and mourvedre. Son Ben Sieber is the viticulturist. Exports to Canada and China.

ΨΨΨΨΨ **Reserve Barossa Valley Shiraz 2017** Matured for 22 months in French oak (80% new). The cork, the label with gold printing on black and the heavy bottle are all pointed in one direction. I hoped for much more, but it needed to be retasted several times for the heart of red and black cherry and satsuma plum to be drawn out. 14% alc. **Rating** 94 **To** 2033 $100

ΨΨΨΨΩ **Barossa Valley Shiraz Grenache 2016** Rating 92 To 2028 $20 JP ❂
Barossa Valley Shiraz Mataro 2017 Rating 90 To 2027 $20 ❂
Barossa Valley GSM 2017 Rating 90 To 2024 $20 ❂

Silent Noise ★★★☆

44 Hamilton Road, McLaren Flat **Region** McLaren Vale
T (08) 8383 0533 **www.**silentnoisewine.com **Open** By appt
Winemaker Charlie O'Brien **Est.** 2017 **Dozens** 2500 **Vyds** 4ha
Charlie O'Brien is the son of Helen and Kevin O'Brien, founders of Kangarilla Road. As a small child (a photo on the website says it all) he revelled in the noise of vintage, the 'silent noise' that of the wine when bottled. Since leaving school at the end of 2016 he worked vintages at Gemtree and Yangarra Estate in McLaren Vale, Pikes in the Clare Valley and Domaine Astruc (part of the Paul Mas group) in Provence in the south of France. He returns to France around the time of publication to work the vintage at Chateau Lafite; the world is his oyster. Exports to the UK, Denmark and NZ.

ΨΨΨΨΩ **Adelaide Hills Chardonnay 2019** A hipster expression of chardonnay with dried hay to tatami scents and a kernel of truffled yeasty nourishment. Nicely poised for easy gulpability. Cork. **Rating** 92 **To** 2025 NG

Silkman Wines

c/- The Small Winemakers Centre, McDonalds Road, Pokolbin, NSW 2320
Region Hunter Valley
T 0414 800 256 **www**.silkmanwines.com.au **Open** 7 days 10–5
Winemaker Shaun Silkman, Liz Silkman **Est.** 2013 **Dozens** 5000

Winemaking couple Shaun and Liz Silkman (one-time dux of the Len Evans Tutorial) were both born and raised in the Hunter Valley. They both worked many vintages (both in Australia and abroad) before joining forces at First Creek Wines, where Liz is senior winemaker. This gives them the opportunity to make small quantities of the three classic varieties of the Hunter Valley: semillon, chardonnay and shiraz. Unsurprisingly, the wines so far released have been of outstanding quality. Exports to the US.

ŸŸŸŸŸ Single Vineyard Blackberry Hunter Valley Semillon 2019 While it has the brashness of youth, there's also structure and depth. Requisite lemon juice and rind, ginger spice and fresh herbs mingle as one with superfine acidity taking hold of all and leading to a resounding finish. Screwcap. Rating 95 To 2029 $50 JF
Reserve Hunter Valley Shiraz 2018 No information forthcoming. A reductive whiff at first with some charcuterie, a whorl of dark fruits, baking spices and oak spice too. Very ripe fruit floods the full-bodied palate, tannins giving enough. There's also a juiciness throughout. Screwcap. Rating 94 To 2028 $50 JF

ŸŸŸŸ♀ Hunter Valley Shiraz 2018 Rating 93 To 2030 $35 JF
Hunter Valley Semillon 2019 Rating 92 To 2029 $30 JF
Reserve Hunter Valley Chardonnay 2019 Rating 92 To 2024 $50 JF
Reserve Hunter Valley Semillon 2019 Rating 91 To 2028 $50 JF

Silkwood Estate

2348 Channybearup Road, Pemberton, WA 6260 **Region** Pemberton
T (08) 9776 1584 **www**.silkwoodestate.com.au **Open** Fri–Mon & public hols 10–4
Winemaker Michael Ng **Est.** 1998 **Dozens** 20 000 **Vyds** 23.5ha

Silkwood Wines has been owned by the Bowman family since 2004. The vineyard is patrolled by a large flock of guinea fowl, eliminating most insect pests and reducing the use of chemicals. In '05 the adjoining vineyard was purchased, lifting the estate plantings to 23.5ha, which include shiraz, cabernet sauvignon, merlot, sauvignon blanc, chardonnay, pinot noir, riesling and zinfandel. The cellar door, restaurant and four luxury chalets overlook the large lake on the property. Exports to Malaysia, Singapore and China.

ŸŸŸŸŸ The Walcott Pemberton Riesling 2019 Tension is the thing. This holds its nerve through a taut palate, its flavours of lemon sorbet, mineral, slate and lime drilling straight through to a long finish. Electric riesling. Screwcap. 12.5% alc. Rating 94 To 2032 $28 CM ✪
The Walcott Pemberton Cabernet Sauvignon 2018 Pure blackcurrant, olive paste and peppercorn with well integrated cedar wood oak. This is as smooth as it is sure-footed, not to mention varietal. Tobacco notes pick out the finish. All the ducks are in a row. It's essentially medium-weight with just a bit extra. Screwcap. 14% alc. Rating 94 To 2020 $30 CM ✪

ŸŸŸŸ♀ The Bowman Pemberton Chardonnay 2019 Rating 93 To 2026 $55 CM
The Walcott Pemberton Shiraz 2018 Rating 92 To 2030 $30 CM
The Walcott Pemberton Malbec 2018 Rating 92 To 2032 $30 CM
The Walcott Pemberton Sauvignon Blanc 2019 Rating 91 To 2022 $28 CM
The Bowers Pemberton Shiraz 2018 Rating 91 To 2026 $21 CM ✪
The Bowers Autumn Riesling 2019 Rating 91 $21 CM ✪
The Walcott Pemberton Chardonnay 2019 Rating 90 To 2024 $30 CM

Silver Spoon Estate ★★★

503 Heathcote-Rochester Road, Heathcote, Mount Camel, Vic 3523 **Region** Heathcote
T 0412 868 236 **www**.silverspoonestate.com.au **Open** W'ends 11–5 or by appt
Winemaker Peter Young **Est.** 2008 **Dozens** 1500 **Vyds** 22ha
When Peter and Tracie Young purchased an existing shiraz vineyard on the top of the
Mt Camel Range in 2008, they did not waste any time. They immediately planted a second
vineyard, constructed a small winery and in '13 acquired a neighbouring vineyard. The estate
name comes from the Silver Spoon fault line that delineates the Cambrian volcanic rock from
the old silver mines on the property. Peter became familiar with vineyards when working
in the 1970s as a geologist in the Hunter Valley and he more recently completed the Master of
Wine Technology and Viticulture degree at the University of Melbourne. Exports to China.

Silverstream Wines ★★★★★

241 Scotsdale Road, Denmark, WA 6333 **Region** Denmark
T (08) 9848 2767 **www**.silverstreamwines.com **Open** Summer Tues–Sun 11–5, winter
by appt
Winemaker Michael Garland **Est.** 1997 **Dozens** 2500 **Vyds** 9ha
Tony and Felicity Ruse have 9ha of chardonnay, merlot, cabernet franc, pinot noir, riesling
and viognier in their vineyard 23km from Denmark. The wines are contract-made and, after
some hesitation, the Ruses decided their very pretty garden and orchard more than justified
opening a cellar door, a decision supported by the quality of the wines on offer at very
reasonable prices.

🍷🍷🍷🍷🍷 **Single Vineyard Denmark Riesling 2017** Offers a different experience; the
usual talc, spa salts, lime and pink grapefruit are punctuated with candied quince
and a grind of white pepper, almost reminiscent of gruner veltliner. This is a lovely
drink: nothing grating, nor excessive. Just a long transparent stream of flavour.
Screwcap. **Rating** 95 **To** 2029 $28 NG
Denmark Chardonnay 2016 This is a fine, pointed, single vineyard expression
of cool-climate chardonnay. The acidity is juicy, making one reach for another
sip while towing apricot, nectarine, toasted nuts and creamy nougat flavours long
and fresh. This melds ample flavour with a scintillating maritime freshness, while
tucking in high quality oak impeccably to curb the seams. Screwcap. **Rating** 95
To 2024 $30 NG

🍷🍷🍷🍷🍷 **Reserve Chardonnay 2013** **Rating** 93 NG
Single Vineyard Riesling 2015 **Rating** 92 **To** 2023 $30 NG
Sparkling Chardonnay 2012 **Rating** 92 $35 NG
Chardonnay 2015 **Rating** 91 **To** 2022 $30 NG
Reserve Chardonnay 2012 **Rating** 91 **To** 2022 NG
Single Vineyard Cabernet Franc 2014 **Rating** 91 **To** 2023 NG
Single Vineyard Pinot Noir 2016 **Rating** 90 **To** 2022 $32 NG
Single Vineyard Cabernet Franc 2011 **Rating** 90 **To** 2022 $30 NG

Sinapius ★★★★★

4232 Bridport Road, Pipers Brook, Tas 7254 **Region** Northern Tasmania
T 0418 998 665 **www**.sinapius.com.au **Open** Mon–Fri 11–5, w'ends 12–5
Winemaker Vaughn Dell **Est.** 2005 **Dozens** 1500 **Vyds** 4.07ha
Vaughn Dell and Linda Morice purchased the former Golders Vineyard in 2005 (planted
in 1994). More recent vineyard plantings include 13 clones of pinot noir and eight clones
of chardonnay, as well as a small amount of gruner veltliner. The vineyard is close-planted,
ranging from 5100 vines/ha for the gruner veltliner to 10250 vines/ha for the pinot noir and
chardonnay. The wines are made with a minimalist approach: natural ferments, basket pressing,
extended lees ageing and minimal fining and filtration. Tragically, Vaughn died suddenly, days
after celebrating his 39th birthday, in May 2020.

ŶŶŶŶŶ **The Enclave Single Vineyard Close Planted Pinot Noir 2017** The oldest high density block with 12 clones planted on red volcanic soils, the vinification the same as that for Le Clairiere. This is a majestic wine of great savoury complexity. It was 100% whole-berry fermented but, unless you know otherwise, whole-bunch involvement would come into calculations. Screwcap. 13.5% alc. **Rating** 99 To 2042 $80 **○**

La Clairiere Single Vineyard Close Planted Pinot Noir 2017 Wow. This is really something. The fruit comes from the newest high-density planting of 7 clones, each vine producing less than 1kg; hand-picked, 3-week whole berry–wild ferment, matured in French barriques for 18 months. Slightly lighter and with more juicy red fruit notes. Screwcap. 13.5% alc. **Rating** 97 To 2037 $68 **○**

ŶŶŶŶŶ **Single Vineyard Close Planted Chardonnay 2018** Eight clones; hand-picked, whole-bunch pressed, wild fermentation and mlf, matured in French oak (25% new) and a small portion (5%) in tank. An extremely powerful wine with structure ex the fruit, not oak. The length of the palate and aftertaste is striking. Screwcap. 13% alc. **Rating** 95 To 2033 $55

Sinclair of Scotsburn   ★★★☆

256 Wiggins Road, Scotsburn, Vic 3352 **Region** Ballarat
T 0419 885 717 **www.**sinclairofscotsburn.com.au **Open** W'ends by appt
Winemaker Scott Ireland **Est.** 1997 **Dozens** 150 **Vyds** 2ha
David and (the late) Barbara Sinclair purchased their property in 2001. At that time 1.2ha of chardonnay and 0.8ha of pinot noir had been planted but had struggled, the pinot noir yielding less than 0.25t in '02. With the aid of limited drip irrigation, cane pruning, low crop levels and bird netting, limited quantities of high quality chardonnay and pinot have since been produced. The vineyard has now been leased to Provenance Wines and the wine is distributed according to the terms of the lease agreement.

ŶŶŶŶŶ **Wallijak Chardonnay 2017** Mid-straw gold. Restrained style dabbing at lemon and curd, lavender and almost granular acidity with some phenolic grip on the finish. Screwcap. 13.4% alc. **Rating** 90 To 2026 $25 JF

Singlefile Wines   ★★★★★

90 Walter Road, Denmark, WA 6333 **Region** Great Southern
T 1300 885 807 **www.**singlefilewines.com **Open** 7 days 11–5
Winemaker Mike Garland, Coby Ladwig, Patrick Corbett **Est.** 2007 **Dozens** 10 000
Vyds 3.75ha
In 1986 geologist Phil Snowden and wife Viv moved from South Africa to Perth, where they developed their successful multinational mining and resource services company, Snowden Resources. Following the sale of the company in 2004, they turned their attention to their long-held desire to make and enjoy fine wine. In '07 they bought an established vineyard (planted in '89) in the beautiful Denmark subregion. They pulled out the old shiraz and merlot vines, kept and planted more chardonnay and retained Larry Cherubino to set up partnerships with established vineyards in Frankland River, Porongurup, Denmark, Pemberton and Margaret River. The cellar door, tasting room and restaurant are strongly recommended. The consistency of the quality of the Singlefile wines is outstanding, as is their value for money. Exports to the US, Singapore, Japan, Hong Kong and China.

ŶŶŶŶŶ **The Vivienne Denmark Chardonnay 2017** Only made in exceptional vintages. Infinite attention to detail across the full suite of vinification brings complexity together with an elegant focus on the varietal fruit of white peach, almond and excellent citrussy acidity. Singlefile's suggestion of cellaring for up to 20 years isn't fanciful. Screwcap. 12.2% alc. **Rating** 98 To 2040 $100 **○**

ŶŶŶŶŶ **Great Southern Riesling 2019** The scented bouquet is full of Granny Smith apple blossom aromas augmented by lemon/lime citrus fruit, the offer bound and packaged by minerally acidity – you will know this before it begins its journey along the palate to cleanse the aftertaste. Screwcap. 12.4% alc. **Rating** 96 To 2034 $25 **○**

Single Vineyard Mount Barker Riesling 2019 From the Blue Lake Vineyard, the second oldest in the Great Southern. Whole-bunch pressed to preserve maximum fruit expression and freshness; and passes with flying colours as it soars on the finish and aftertaste where its citrus heart is accompanied by bright acidity. Lovely wine with a great future. Screwcap. 12.7% alc. **Rating** 96 **To** 2034 $35 ✪

Single Vineyard Frankland River Shiraz 2018 Hand-picked, open-fermented, 25 days on skins, matured for 10 months in French barriques. Singlefile is a model of consistency, delivering aromas and flavours of purity and intensity yet very elegant. Black cherry, plum, blackberry, spice and pepper flavours with a negligee of fine tannins. Screwcap. 14.4% alc. **Rating** 96 **To** 2038 $39 ✪

Great Southern Cabernet Sauvignon Merlot 2018 A blend of 60% cabernet sauvignon, 25% merlot and 15% malbec (it varies from year to year), matured for 13 months in barriques (30% new). This has largely unbridled power courtesy of its medium to full-bodied palate, black fruits ex the cabernet first up, then red berries and a more succulent mid-palate ex the merlot and malbec. Exceptional value. Screwcap. 13.7% alc. **Rating** 96 **To** 2033 $25 ✪

Single Vineyard Frankland River Cabernet Sauvignon 2018 From the highly regarded Riversdale Vineyard planted in '97 on gravel and clay soils. Cold-soaked for 12 days, then fermented and macerated for 18 days, matured for 14 months in French barriques (30% new). The tannins are obvious but the wine will flourish in bottle for decades. Screwcap. 13.8% alc. **Rating** 96 **To** 2048 $39 ✪

The Philip Adrian Frankland River Cabernet Sauvignon 2017 Includes 3% malbec. Hand-picked, 2 weeks' cold soak, 6 weeks' maceration after fermentation, pressed to Bordeaux barrels (48% new) for 14 months' maturation. Very complex, rich and powerful. At the moment the oak is obvious and the wine needs another 3 or so years to settle, then its beauty will be there for all to see and admire. Screwcap. 14.2% alc. **Rating** 96 **To** 2047 $100

Single Vineyard Mount Barker Fume Blanc 2019 From St Werburgh's Vineyard; 50% stainless steel–fermented, the other 50% fermented in barriques (50% new), both parcels matured on lees for 4 months. A standout success, matching flavour and finesse, texture and varietal wild herb and lemon zest flavours. Screwcap. 12.8% alc. **Rating** 95 **To** 2022 $35 ✪

Small Batch Release Barrel Ferment Great Southern Fume Blanc 2018 The use of a cork to seal any white wine is hard to defend, even where the cost of the super heavy bottle, wax dipping and label design must have been greater than the cost of a screwcap. To this point of time, no oxidation is evident, so strike while the iron is hot. 12.7% alc. **Rating** 95 **To** 2021 $39

Clement V 2018 With 90% shiraz, 6% grenache, 4% mataro; each varietal batch fermented separately, in all 30% matured in new French barriques for 10 months. Deeply robed crimson-purple through to the rim of the glass. The wine is medium-bodied and the oak is more obvious than expected, but the 5-year outlook is for the oak to largely disappear, then a 10–20 year drinking window. Screwcap. 14.3% alc. **Rating** 94 **To** 2038 $32

🍷🍷🍷🍷 **Run Free Riesling 2019** **Rating** 93 **To** 2029 $25 ✪
Small Batch Pinot Noir 2018 **Rating** 93 **To** 2027 $59 JP
Tempranillo 2018 **Rating** 93 **To** 2028 $25 ✪
Run Free Sauvignon Blanc 2019 **Rating** 92 **To** 2021 $25 ✪
Run Free Pinot Noir 2019 **Rating** 92 **To** 2027 $25 JP ✪
Single Vineyard Pemberton Pinot Noir 2019 **Rating** 92 **To** 2025 $35 JP
Semillon Sauvignon Blanc 2019 **Rating** 91 **To** 2022 $25

Sir Paz Estate

54 Parker Road, Wandin East, Vic 3139 **Region** Yarra Valley
T (03) 5964 2339 **www.**sirpaz.com **Open** Sun 11–5 or by appt
Winemaker Rob Dolan **Est.** 1997 **Dozens** 5500 **Vyds** 22ha
The Zapris family established Sir Paz Estate in 1997, planting just under 6ha of shiraz; the first release of '01 scored an emphatic gold medal at the Victorian Wine Show '03 as the highest

scored entry. The success led to the planting of additional merlot, chardonnay and sauvignon blanc. It is not hard to see the anagrammatic derivation of the name. Exports to the US, Canada, Mexico, Germany, the UAE and China.

🍷🍷🍷🍷 **Bee Hive Yarra Valley Chardonnay 2014** The colour is within expectations for a 5yo chardonnay. Hand-picked, whole-bunch pressed, racked with light solids to oak for fermentation, which took place in a cool room, kept on lees for 9 months. It has softened with notes of honey, melon and fig alongside white peach fruit. Screwcap. 13.5% alc. **Rating** 92 **To** 2023 $32
Yarra Valley Sparkling Shiraz 2018 No info on vinification but certainly has shiraz varietal character and the residual sugar does not take away from the wine. The (very) patient might be rewarded. Diam. 13.5% alc. **Rating** 90 $52

Sister's Run ★★★★

PO Box 148, McLaren Vale, SA 5171 **Region** Barossa/McLaren Vale/Coonawarra
T (08) 8323 8979 **www.**sistersrun.com.au **Open** Not
Winemaker Elena Brooks **Est.** 2001 **Dozens** NFP
Sister's Run is now part of the Brooks family empire, the highly experienced Elena Brooks making the wines. The Stiletto and Boot on the label are those of Elena, and the motto 'The truth is in the vineyard, but the proof is in the glass' is, I would guess, the work of marketer extraordinaire husband Zar Brooks. Exports to all major markets.

🍷🍷🍷🍷 **St Petri's Eden Valley Riesling 2018** A wine from the Brooks stable going by the back label, so no surprise that it's clearly well made and indicative of variety and region. Aromas and flavours of citrus and honeysuckle are true to type and, while it's quite soft and approachable now for the style, that's a good fit for the price range. Screwcap. 11.5% alc. **Rating** 90 **To** 2025 $20 SC
St Ann's McLaren Vale Grenache 2018 Shows authentic grenache character in a soft and easy drinking sort of way. Perfume and spice on the bouquet. A medium-bodied palate with attractive red-fruited flavours edged with light astringency which doesn't intrude but lends some structure. To call it an ideal bbq wine might be selling it short, but it does have that kind of feel. Screwcap. 14.5% alc. **Rating** 90 **To** 2023 $22 SC

Sittella Wines ★★★★★

100 Barrett Street, Herne Hill, WA 6056 **Region** Swan Valley
T (08) 9296 2600 **www.**sittella.com.au **Open** Tues–Sun & public hols 11–5
Winemaker Colby Quirk, Yuri Berns **Est.** 1998 **Dozens** 15 000 **Vyds** 25ha
Simon and Maaike Berns acquired a 7ha block (with 5ha of vines) at Herne Hill, making the first wine in 1998 and opening a most attractive cellar door facility. They also own the Wildberry Estate Vineyard in Margaret River. Plantings in Margaret River have increased with new clones of cabernet sauvignon, cabernet franc, P95 chardonnay and malbec. New clones of tempranillo and touriga nacional have also been added to the Swan Valley plantings. Consistent and significant wine show success has brought well deserved recognition for the wines. Exports to Japan and China.

🍷🍷🍷🍷🍷 **A-G Rare Series Golden Mile Swan Valley Grenache 2019** Hand-picked, abstemiously selected fruit across ancient bushvines. This is exceptional grenache. An undercarriage of briary spice and fibrous tannins confers savouriness and a disposition far more typical of the southern Rhône (the grape's spiritual home) than typically fruity Australian expressions. For the better! Among the finest grenache in the country. No two ways about it. Cork. **Rating** 96 **To** 2025 $50 NG
Reserve Single Vineyard Margaret River Cabernet Malbec 2017 A 60/40% blend from the Sittella Vineyard in Wilyabrup; open-fermented, 22 days on skins, matured in French oak for 16 months. Very well made; an elegant medium-bodied wine with impeccable balance and length. Red fruits, blue

fruits and hints of forest floor all contribute, the mouthfeel right on the money. Screwcap. 14% alc. **Rating** 96 **To** 2042 $29 ✪

Museum Release Swan Valley Silk 2012 A confident move to release a blend that would otherwise risk perceptions of an early drinking meld of proprietary grape varieties thrown together as a dry white. While the wine is certainly dry, it is far more than that. It is long, mineral-inflected and thrumming with an effusive energy and juicy line of tangerine and lemon drop scents, making it hard to spit. Screwcap. **Rating** 95 **To** 2025 NG

Cuvee Rose NV Crafted in the traditional fashion, this is bolstered by an arsenal of reserves, considerably older than many. The lees-ageing too, is an attenuated 30 months. This is very smart. Subtle wild strawberry to rose petal accents define an attack that is ultimately sublimated by yeasty nourishment: baked bread, dried hay and iodine. The dosage finely managed by a juicy tail of acidity. Cork. **Rating** 95 $34 NG ✪

The Wild One Single Vineyard Margaret River Sauvignon Blanc 2018 Hand-picked, whole-bunch pressed, 50% to large-format barrels, 50% to stainless steel for wild-yeast fermentation, 3 months on lees. This is a seriously good wine, all about texture and structure, pushing overt tropical fruits off centre stage. It has a future too, although only Margaret River devotees would be likely to think about that. Screwcap. 12.5% alc. **Rating** 94 **To** 2023 $23 ✪

Avant-Garde Series Swan Valley Chardonnay 2019 A conflation of 3 clones; wild-fermented in Burgundian barrels and left on lees for 9 months for some tightening up. This is delicious. Mid-weighted and plump. Stone fruit accents, vanillan oak and some mineral pungency, yet nothing too tight or austere. This is a very slick chardonnay, generous and already drinking well. No need for additional age to loosen the bow. Screwcap. **Rating** 94 **To** 2024 NG

Reserve Wilyabrup Margaret River Chardonnay 2018 From the venerated alluvials of Wilyabrup, this is benchmark Margaret River chardonnay. Peaches and cream. Yet there is a winning tension from fore to aft; a maritime salinity and mineral presence driving it all long. The oak, impeccably placed. A whiff of reductive flint on the finish, to be resolved with an aggressive decant or a bit of patience. Screwcap. **Rating** 94 **To** 2026 $37 NG

Avant-Garde Series Swan Valley Grenache 2018 From 44yo bushvines; hand-picked, 10% whole bunches, 90% destemmed, 6–9 months in used hogsheads. It's a complex wine with savoury/bramble notes on the one hand, red cherry and pomegranate fruits on the other. A success. Screwcap. 14.5% alc. **Rating** 94 **To** 2025 $38

Marie Christien Lugten Methode Traditionnelle Grand Vintage 2014 The base wine is a 60/40% blend of pinot noir and chardonnay; 10% of the primary ferment in barriques, 4 months on lees, tiraged and held on lees for 52 months, disgorged with 6.5g/l dosage. Sittella has the game well under control, the quality of the wine unambiguously good. There's no shortage of stone fruit/ citrus/brioche flavours on the long palate. Diam. 12.5% alc. **Rating** 94 $42

ȳȳȳȳȳ **Avant-Garde Series Grenade Plot Pemberton Pinot Noir 2019** Rating 93 To 2023 NG

Berns Reserve 2018 Rating 92 To 2029 NG

Avant-Garde Series Swan Valley Tempranillo 2019 Rating 92 To 2023 $40 NG

Methode Traditionnelle Cuvee Blanc NV Rating 92 $32 NG

Show Reserve Liqueur Muscat NV Rating 92 $44 NG

Pedro Ximenez NV Rating 92 $50 NG

Chenin Blanc 2019 Rating 91 To 2023 $20 NG ✪

Avant-Garde Series Swan Valley Chardonnay 2018 Rating 90 To 2020 $28

Tinta Rouge 2018 Rating 90 To 2028 $20 ✪

Avant-Garde Series Methode Traditionnelle Blanc de Blancs NV Rating 90 $45

Methode Traditionnelle Sparkling Shiraz NV Rating 90 $32 NG

Skillogalee   ★★★★

Trevarrick Road, Sevenhill via Clare, SA 5453 **Region** Clare Valley
T (08) 8843 4311 www.skillogalee.com.au **Open** 7 days 8.30–5
Winemaker Dave Palmer, David King **Est.** 1970 **Dozens** 15000 **Vyds** 50.3ha
David and Diana Palmer have fully capitalised on the exceptional fruit quality of the
Skillogalee vineyards. All the wines are generous and full-flavoured, particularly the reds. In
2002 the Palmers purchased next-door neighbour Waninga Vineyard with 30ha of 30-year-
old vines, allowing an increase in production without any change in quality or style. Exports
to the UK, Switzerland, Malaysia, Vietnam, Thailand and Singapore.

🍷🍷🍷🍷🍷 **Basket Pressed Clare Valley The Cabernets 2016** Hand-picked fruit from a
40yo dry-grown vineyard. Includes 2% each of malbec and cabernet franc. Minty
varietal character is the first impression but there's a wave of ripe red fruit and a
touch of chocolate to follow. Medium-bodied and soft, it's gently mouthfilling
with the tannin surprisingly not too noticeable, really only asserting itself in the
aftertaste. Good drinking now. Screwcap. 14.5% alc. **Rating** 93 **To** 2028 $34 SC

Small Island Wines   ★★★★★

Drink Co, Shop 10, 33 Salamanca Place, Hobart, Tas 7004 **Region** Southern Tasmania
T 0414 896 930 www.smallislandwines.com **Open** Mon–Sat 10–8
Winemaker James Broinowski **Est.** 2015 **Dozens** 750 **Vyds** 4ha
Tasmanian-born James Broinowski completed his Bachelor of Viticulture and Oenology at
the University of Adelaide in 2013. He was faced with the same problem as many other young
graduates wanting to strike out on their own: cash. While others in his predicament may have
found the same solution, his is the first wine venture to successfully seek crowdfunding. The
first year ('15) allowed him to purchase pinot noir from Glengarry in the north of the island,
making 2100 bottles of pinot noir that won a gold medal at the Royal International Hobart
Wine Show '16; and 200 bottles of rose that sold out in four days at the Taste of Tasmania
Festival '15. In '16 he was able to buy pinot from the highly rated Gala Estate on the east
coast and back up the '15 purchase from the Glengarry Vineyard with a '16 purchase. It looks
very much like a potential acorn to oak story, for the quality of the wines is seriously good.

🍷🍷🍷🍷🍷 **Single Vineyard North Pinot Noir 2017** This really is quite wonderfully
complex. It tastes of forest berries and undergrowth, beetroot and sweet autumn
leaves, cranberry and woodsy, smoky spice. It's well weighted without being
overblown, strung with tannin without interrupting the flow. It will age well but
it's highly seductive right now. **Rating** 96 **To** 2030 $50 CM ✪
Patsie's Blush Rose 2019 A rose that stands out from the crowd. At no point
does it overstep the mark and yet it has texture, weight and impact. It's spicy and
jellied, sweet and savoury, juicy and stern at once. Yes it oozes drinkability but then
it oozes a lot of things. Screwcap. 13.5% alc. **Rating** 95 **To** 2022 $34 CM ✪
Single Vineyard Riesling 2019 Immediately impressive. Sweet citrussy flavours
of various description come infused with assorted herbs and florals. It feels weighty
even as it rushes through the mouth; it's a riesling of genuine presence and
irrefutable quality. Screwcap. 12.8% alc. **Rating** 94 **To** 2027 $34 CM
Single Site Gamay 2019 Fascinating wine. Crunchy with spice, floated with
fruit, a little smoky and quite a bit twiggy. Easy, energetic and complex at once.
Life-of-the-party style but a particularly sophisticated party. Sweet, smoky and sour.
Fundamentally delicious. Screwcap. 12.8% alc. **Rating** 94 **To** 2024 $39 CM
Black Label Pinot Noir 2018 Velvety and complex. Dark, foresty berry flavours
come laced with wood spice and undergrowth. It doesn't push for complexity, it
just seems to have it inherently. Tannin is firm, almost stringy, but the juicy wash
of flavour is its measure. It's a wine with a lot up its sleeve. Screwcap. 13.5% alc.
Rating 94 **To** 2030 $45 CM

🍷🍷🍷🍷🍷 **Saltwater River Chardonnay 2019 Rating** 93 **To** 2028 $34 CM

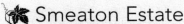 Smeaton Estate

Level 1, 206 Greenhill Road, Eastwood, SA 5063 (postal) **Region** Adelaide Hills
T 0429 109 537 **www**.smeaton.estate **Open** Not
Winemaker Con Moshos **Est.** 1996 **Dozens** 450 **Vyds** 25ha
This is the venture of Janice and John Smeaton who planted their Martin Hill Vineyard to
shiraz (6.5ha), sauvignon blanc (5.2ha), semillon (4.5ha), chardonnay (4ha), merlot (2.9ha),
riesling (1.3ha) and pinot gris (0.6ha). The intention was to sell the grapes to Adelaide Hills
wineries and this has been implemented. But in 2017 they teamed up with Con Moshos, an
Adelaide Hills veteran with longstanding close ties to Brian Croser, to make 450 dozen of
riesling. The wine is sold to retailers/wholesalers and if other wines are made in the future,
they would be marketed the same way.

TTTTT **Sienna Single Vineyard Adelaide Hills Riesling 2017** The cool vintage was
outstanding for Adelaide Hills riesling, the vibrancy of the mouthfeel fed by the
Rose's lime juice flavour, acidity joining the band. Each sip underlines the intensity
of this lovely wine. Screwcap. 13.2% alc. **Rating** 96 **To** 2032 $28 ✪
Sienna Single Vineyard Adelaide Hills Riesling 2019 The fruit comes from
Smeaton's Martin Hill Vineyard. Has a rich line of lime and Granny Smith apple
running through in an unbroken stream to the finish. A riesling of substance and
balance. Screwcap. 13.1% alc. **Rating** 94 **To** 2033 $28 ✪
Sienna Single Vineyard Adelaide Hills Riesling 2018 It has just taken the
first step towards maturity, as the fruit increases its footprint and the acidity seems
to be softening. In fact, the acidity doesn't alter at any point (true of all wines)
along the journey ahead. Screwcap. 13.5% alc. **Rating** 94 **To** 2030 $28 ✪

Smidge Wines

150 Tatachilla Road, McLaren Vale, SA 5171 **Region** McLaren Vale
T 0419 839 964 **www**.smidgewines.com **Open** By appt
Winemaker Matt Wenk **Est.** 2004 **Dozens** 5000 **Vyds** 4.1ha
Smidge Wines is owned by Matt Wenk and wife Trish Callaghan. It was for many years
an out-of-hours occupation for Matt; his day job was as winemaker for Two Hands Wines
(and Sandow's End). In 2013 he retired from Two Hands and plans to increase production
of Smidge to 8000 dozen over the next few years. His retirement meant the Smidge wines
could no longer be made at Two Hands and the winemaking operations have been moved to
McLaren Vale, where Smidge is currently leasing a small winery. Smidge owns the vineyard
in Willunga that provides the grapes for all the cabernet sauvignon releases and some of the
McLaren Vale shiraz. The vision is to build a modern customised facility on the Willunga
property in the not-too-distant future. The Magic Dirt shirazs are made in the same way, the
purpose to show the impact of terroir on each wine: 14–16 days in an open fermenter, then
after 10 months in barrel a selection of the best barrel is transferred to a single 2yo French
barrique and a further 14 months of maturation follows. Exports to the UK, the US, South
Korea and China.

TTTTT **Magic Dirt Greenock Barossa Valley Shiraz 2016** From a block of red-
brown clay loam with small pieces of ironstone and quartz. It is a wine of extreme
length – rich with black and blue fruits – yet it achieves this without any sign of
effort. Finesse on a high level. Screwcap. **Rating** 97 **To** 2046 $120 ✪
Magic Dirt Menglers Hill Eden Valley Shiraz 2016 The vines are grown by
the very highly regarded Peter and Joel Mattschoss on a west-facing vineyard at
480m with shallow red clay/loam full of quartz and ironstone. Very elegant. Red
fruits join in the fray along with ultrafine, but important, tannins providing the
length. Screwcap. **Rating** 97 **To** 2046 $120 ✪

TTTTT **S Barossa Valley Shiraz 2016** No fancy winemaking tricks; 16 days on skins,
barriques and 2 hogsheads, all 2yo French oak, 24 months in barrel. Yes, oak plays
a role, but it's the purity and freshness of the wine that makes it special. Screwcap.
Rating 96 **To** 2040 $65 ✪

Magic Dirt Willunga McLaren Vale Shiraz 2016 From Smidge's estate vineyard, the soil deep red clay/loam with small fragments of quartz and ironstone. Standard vinification. The result, like its McLaren Vale sibling, is a wine that explores every corner of the mouth; ripe, slightly fluffy tannins the standard bearers. Screwcap. **Rating** 96 **To** 2041 $120

Magic Dirt Strout Road McLaren Vale Shiraz 2016 Deep red clay/loam mottled with small pieces of quartz and ironstone. The wine expands on the back-palate and finish with ripe, persistent tannins. The shape of the wine in the mouth is wider than its Barossa siblings, but not as piercing. Dark chocolate makes a mark, but not to extremes. Screwcap. **Rating** 96 **To** 2041 $120

Adamo Barossa Valley Shiraz 2017 Grapes come from 91% Barossa Valley, 9% Eden Valley; 16 days on skins, 20 months in used French barriques and hogsheads. I cannot understand 15.5% alcohol in the context of '17, but the spice and texture can't be denied. Screwcap. **Rating** 95 **To** 2030 $38

The Ging McLaren Vale Shiraz 2016 Multiple batches vinified separately; 14 days on skins, 20 months in French barriques and hogsheads (8% new) plus further time in bottle before release. Its unusual cured pipe tobacco bouquet gives way to lush black fruits, licorice and a dab of chocolate on the palate. Screwcap. 14.9% alc. **Rating** 95 **To** 2036 $38

Pedra Branca McLaren Vale Saperavi 2018 Pedra Branca is an experimental range made in limited quantities – here a single hogshead. Saperavi is a Russian variety with red flesh, its intense colour giving the grape its name (in Russian saperavi means dyer). It's juicy and luscious, and gives no sense of elevated alcohol. Screwcap. 15% alc. **Rating** 95 **To** 2029 $45

La Grenouille McLaren Vale Cabernet Sauvignon 2016 No holds barred, in either fruit or tannins, both full force. Its real value will be understood in 10+ years. Screwcap. 14.5% alc. **Rating** 94 **To** 2036 $38

ɊɊɊɊɊ **Pedra Branca McLaren Vale Grenache 2018** **Rating** 92 **To** 2029 $45
Houdini McLaren Vale Shiraz 2018 **Rating** 90 **To** 2038 $28

Smith & Hooper

Caves Edward Road, Naracoorte, SA 5271 **Region** Wrattonbully
T (08) 8561 3200 **www**.smithandhooper.com **Open** By appt
Winemaker Natalie Cleghorn **Est.** 1994 **Dozens** 15000 **Vyds** 62ha

Smith & Hooper can be viewed as simply one of many brands within the Hill-Smith family financial/corporate structures. However, it is estate-based, with cabernet sauvignon and merlot planted on the Hooper Vineyard in 1994; and cabernet sauvignon and merlot planted on the Smith Vineyard in '98. Spread across both vineyards are 9ha of trial varieties. Exports to all major markets.

ɊɊɊɊɊ **Wrattonbully Pinot Grigio 2019** Just a little more textural and bodied than usual; almost, but not quite, into gris territory, which is no bad thing. Fruity but controlled. This is more like it. Screwcap. 13.5% alc. **Rating** 90 **To** 2021 CM

ɊɊɊɊ **Reserve Wrattonbully Merlot 2018** **Rating** 89 **To** 2028 $35
Wrattonbully Cabernet Sauvignon Merlot 2017 **Rating** 89 **To** 2023 $21

Smithbrook

Smithbrook Road, Pemberton, WA 6260 **Region** Pemberton
T (08) 9750 2150 **www**.smithbrookwines.com.au **Open** By appt
Winemaker Ben Rector **Est.** 1988 **Dozens** 10000 **Vyds** 57ha

The picturesque Smithbrook property is owned by Perth businessman Peter Fogarty and family, who also own Lake's Folly in the Hunter Valley, Deep Woods Estate in Margaret River and Millbrook in the Perth Hills. Originally planted in the 1980s and one of the first in the Pemberton region, the Smithbrook Vineyard covers over 57ha of the 110ha property and focuses on sauvignon blanc, chardonnay and merlot.

ŸŸŸŸŸ **Single Vineyard Pemberton Nebbiolo 2018** Hand-picked, crushed and destemmed into a small open fermenter, 4 weeks on skins. Special care to manage tannin extraction and promote fruit retention was an unqualified success. It's not full-bodied, but the flavours and wild forest fruits and red cherries come through well. And the price! Screwcap. 14% alc. **Rating** 94 **To** 2028 $25 ✪

ŸŸŸŸŸ **Single Vineyard Pemberton Chardonnay 2018 Rating** 92 **To** 2026 $25 ✪
Single Vineyard Pemberton Pinot Noir 2019 Rating 92 **To** 2027 $25 ✪
Single Vineyard Pemberton Chardonnay 2019 Rating 91 **To** 2025 $25
Single Vineyard Pemberton Merlot 2018 Rating 91 **To** 2028 $25
Single Vineyard Pemberton Pinot Noir 2018 Rating 90 **To** 2024 $25

Snake + Herring   ★★★★★

3763 Caves Road, Wilyabrup, WA 6284 **Region** South West Australia zone
T 0427 881 871 **www.**snakeandherring.com.au **Open** Summer 7 days 11–5, winter 7 days 11–4
Winemaker Tony Davis **Est.** 2010 **Dozens** 12 000
Tony (Snake) Davis and Redmond (Herring) Sweeny both started university degrees before finding that they were utterly unsuited to their respective courses. Having stumbled across Margaret River, Tony's life changed forever; he enrolled at the University of Adelaide, thereafter doing vintages in the Eden Valley, Oregon, Beaujolais and Tasmania, before three years at Plantagenet, next Brown Brothers, then a senior winemaking role at Yalumba, a six-year stint designing Millbrook Winery in the Perth Hills and four years with Howard Park in Margaret River. Redmond's circuitous course included a chartered accountancy degree and employment with an international accounting firm in Busselton, and the subsequent establishment of Forester Estate in 2001, in partnership with Kevin McKay. Back on home turf he is the marketing and financial controller of Snake + Herring. Exports to the US.

ŸŸŸŸŸ **Perfect Day Margaret River Sauvignon Blanc Semillon 2018** A 67/33% blend. A heap of work went into the vinification of this wine. The sauvignon blanc came from the cool Karridale district, the powerful semillon from Wilyabrup; pressed as cloudy juice to used puncheons, all components on lees for 8 months, 43% barrel-fermented. Its exuberance and complexity make it a great all-purpose white wine. Screwcap. 12.5% alc. **Rating** 95 **To** 2022 $25 ✪
Corduroy Karridale Chardonnay 2018 Still pale, bright straw-green. Everything has clicked into place, the boxes all ticked. It is an elegant display of varietal fruit outside the norm for Margaret River, Karridale in the very cool southern tip of the region. Screwcap. 13% alc. **Rating** 95 **To** 2028 $45
Dirty Boots Margaret River Cabernet Sauvignon 2018 Matured in French oak (21% new). It's beautifully ripened and therefore flavoured, the impact of oak mostly on the wine's soft, velvety texture. It's a creamy, curranty red with bay leaf and wood smoke notes lifting off. It's excellent buying/drinking. Screwcap. 14.5% alc. **Rating** 94 **To** 2029 $25 CM ✪
Dirty Boots Margaret River Cabernet Sauvignon 2016 First you take 3 small blocks from Yallingup in the north of the region, 3 from Wilyabrup in the centre and 3 from Karridale in the south. Then you turn up a side street, adding 13% merlot and 1% shiraz, the sources not disclosed. This is a seriously appealing, joyful even, cabernet at a juicy price. Balance is the key for early consumption. Screwcap. 14% alc. **Rating** 94 **To** 2029 $25 ✪
Cannonball Margaret River Cabernet Sauvignon Merlot Petit Verdot 2018 At 61% cabernet sauvignon (providing the grunt), 30% merlot (seduction), 9% petit verdot (the cannonball). It all comes together well and there's no argument about the grunt provided by the cabernet, or the overall length. The flavour descriptors, incidentally, are those of Snake + Herring. Screwcap. 14% alc. **Rating** 94 **To** 2038 $45

ŸŸŸŸŸ **Hallelujah Porongurup Chardonnay 2018 Rating** 93 **To** 2024 $45
Tough Love Chardonnay 2018 Rating 93 **To** 2024 $25 ✪

Tainted Love Margaret River Tempranillo Rose 2019 Rating 93 To 2021
$25 CM ❂
Tainted Love Margaret River Tempranillo Rose 2018 Rating 93 To 2020
$25 ❂
Business Time Syrah 2018 Rating 93 To 2030 $45 CM
Blue Monday Frankland River Grenache Mourvedre Syrah 2018
Rating 93 To 2027 $45 CM
Redemption Great Southern Syrah 2017 Rating 92 To 2032 $25 ❂
Vamos Margaret River Tempranillo 2017 Rating 92 To 2023 $25 ❂
High + Dry Porongurup Riesling 2018 Rating 91 To 2027 $33
Bizarre Love Triangle Frankland River Pinot Gris Gewurztraminer
Riesling 2019 Rating 91 To 2024 $29 CM
Stranded Margaret River Cabernet Sauvignon Merlot 2017 Rating 91
To 2030 $25
Extreme Ways Frankland River Tempranillo 2018 Rating 91 To 2026
$45 CM
Tough Love Chardonnay 2019 Rating 90 To 2024 $25 CM
Redemption Great Southern Syrah 2018 Rating 90 To 2030 $25
Dirty Boots Margaret River Cabernet Sauvignon 2017 Rating 90
To 2025 $25
The Distance Black Betty Yallingup Margaret River Cabernet Sauvignon
2017 Rating 90 To 2032 $80

Sons & Brothers Vineyard   ★★★★

Spring Terrace Road, Millthorpe, NSW 2798 **Region** Orange
T (02) 6366 5117 **www.**sonsandbrothers.com.au **Open** Not
Winemaker Dr Chris Bourke **Est.** 1978 **Dozens** 400 **Vyds** 2ha
Chris and Kathryn Bourke do not pull their punches when they say, 'Our vineyard
has had a chequered history, because in 1978 we were trying to establish ourselves in a
non-existent wine region with no local knowledge and limited personal knowledge of
grapegrowing and winemaking. It took us about 15 years of hit and miss before we started
producing regular supplies of appropriate grape varieties at appropriate ripeness levels for
sales to other NSW wineries.' Chris has published two fascinating papers on the origins
of savagnin in Europe; he has also traced its movements in Australia after it was one of
the varieties collected by James Busby – and moved just in time to save the last plantings
of Busby's importation in NSW. The 2018 Cabernet is the last made, Chris retired from
winemaking at the age of 70 in '19.

♀♀♀♀♀ Cabernet of Millthorpe 2018 Includes 85% cabernet sauvignon,
10% tempranillo and 5% savagnin; seemingly picked just a few days too early, but
the wine is bright and fresh with cassis to the fore. The site is theoretically too
cool for cabernet, the solution is far left field but clever: the vine is pruned to a
single head and 4 canes are tied vertically, resulting in a fan shape that maximises
sun penetration and consequent ripening. Crown seal. 13.5% alc. **Rating** 90
To 2025 $35

Sons of Eden   ★★★★★

Penrice Road, Angaston, SA 5353 **Region** Barossa
T (08) 8564 2363 **www.**sonsofeden.com **Open** 7 days 11–6
Winemaker Corey Ryan, Simon Cowham **Est.** 2000 **Dozens** 9000 **Vyds** 60ha
Corey Ryan and Simon Cowham both learnt and refined their skills in the vineyards and cellars
of Eden Valley. Corey is a trained oenologist with over 20 vintages under his belt, having cut
his teeth as a winemaker at Henschke. Thereafter he worked for Rouge Homme and Penfolds
in Coonawarra, backed up by winemaking stints in the Rhône Valley and in 2002 he took
the opportunity to work in NZ for Villa Maria Estates. In '07 he won the Institute of Masters
of Wine scholarship. Simon has had a similarly international career covering such diverse
organisations as Oddbins, UK and the Winemakers' Federation of Australia. Switching from

the business side to grapegrowing when he qualified as a viticulturist, he worked for Yalumba as technical manager of the Heggies and Pewsey Vale vineyards. With these backgrounds, it comes as no surprise to find that the estate-grown wines are of outstanding quality. Exports to the UK, the US, Germany, Switzerland, Hong Kong, the Philippines, Taiwan and China.

ΤΤΤΤΤ **Freya Eden Valley Riesling 2019** From 2 Eden Valley vineyards: 44yo vines at Craneford, the other at High Eden; both hand-picked and whole-bunch pressed. Intense, pure lime/lemon fruit hits the bullseye, juicy yet crisp/crunchy acidity on a long palate. Screwcap. 11.5% alc. **Rating** 96 **To** 2032 $28 ✪

Marschall Barossa Valley Shiraz 2018 An unashamed full-bodied shiraz that has perfect balance, a rare beast indeed. Blackberry, satsuma plum and polished cherries have unseen tannins and oak embedded in their core. This really is an exceptional wine. The one criticism is that the extensive print on the label remains unreadable even with a magnifying glass with an inbuilt torch. Screwcap. 14.5% alc. **Rating** 96 **To** 2038 $29 ✪

Zephyrus Barossa Shiraz 2018 From 14 parcels across the Eden (55%) and Barossa (45%) valleys; vinified with a multitude of techniques and an overarching 15 months' maturation in French hogsheads (40% new). The oak is obvious, but so too is the depth of the blackberry and licorice fruit. Screwcap. 14.5% alc. **Rating** 96 **To** 2037 $45 ✪

Cirrus Single Vineyard High Eden Valley Riesling 2019 Northeast aspect maximises morning sun, minimises sunburn. A very expressive bouquet with a mix of pear/apple/grapefruit. The fruit flavour intensity is mouthfilling, half suggesting there's some residual sugar but there isn't (1.1g/l of residual sugar can't be detected). Screwcap. 12% alc. **Rating** 95 **To** 2030 $56

Remus Old Vine Eden Valley Shiraz 2017 To qualify for inclusion in this wine all vines must be 50+yo and managed sustainably. This comes from 3 vineyards, two 60+yo, the third 80+yo, so there's no issue on that score. The palate of the wine tells you the vines are in good health. The tannins are polished and fine, the fruits sombre but composed, the balance good. Screwcap. 14.5% alc. **Rating** 95 **To** 2047 $70

Romulus Old Vine Barossa Valley Shiraz 2017 Two of the 3 vineyards used for this wine are over 80yo, the third over 60yo. Matured in new and used French oak for 18 months. It's an elegant wine, the structure and texture good, but the oak is currently too assertive and needs some years to settle down. The glass is three-quarters full. Screwcap. 14.5% alc. **Rating** 94 **To** 2037 $70

Kennedy Barossa Valley Grenache Shiraz Mourvedre 2018 A 46/36/18% blend from vines aged between 20–100+yo, picked between 9 Mar and 12 Apr, the vinification methods equally diverse. It is a rich, smooth, self-contained blend with rich red berry/red flesh wine. Screwcap. 14.5% alc. **Rating** 94 **To** 2038 $30 ✪

Pumpa Eden Valley Cabernet Sauvignon 2017 With 90% cabernet sauvignon 20–30yo vines, 10% shiraz. Named in tribute to Len Pumpa and his fellow Eden Valley winegrowing pioneers, Pumpa is one evocative wine, capturing the scent of the Australian bush – saltbush, briar, eucalyptus and sage – and generous warmth of ripe Australian cabernet. It's a plush wine with ripe tannins; length and ageability assured. Offers excellent value. Screwcap. 14.5% alc. **Rating** 94 **To** 2027 $30 JP ✪

Eurus Eden Valley Cabernet Sauvignon 2016 Mature vines, in this case 25yo, can bring a confident and mature set of flavours to a wine. Combined with a smart, cool-climate region like Eden Valley and a slightly warm vintage, the result is deliciously hedonistic. Robust black fruits, stewed plums, a world of spice and dried herbs on the nose. Seamless cabernet palate, cigar box, fine tannins, a touch of savoury to close. Screwcap. 14.5% alc. **Rating** 94 **To** 2028 $65 JP

ΤΤΤΤΦ **Pumpa Eden Valley Cabernet Sauvignon 2018 Rating** 90 **To** 2035 $30

Soul Growers

18 Krondorf Road, Tanunda, SA 5352 **Region** Barossa Valley
T (08) 8523 2691 **www**.soulgrowers.com **Open** By appt
Winemaker Paul Heinicke, Stuart Bourne **Est.** 1998 **Dozens** 10 000 **Vyds** 4.85ha
Owner Paul Heinicke now has additional partners: Stuart Bourne (ex Chateau Tanunda and
Barossa Valley Estate) as senior winemaker; Tom Fotheringham (ex Penfolds/Barossa Valley
Estate) and Leigh Underwood (ex Hentley Farm and Murray St Vineyards) both in sales and
marketing roles. Soul Growers source from multi-generational family growers (13 in total) in
Moppa, Ebenezer, Kalimna, Vine Vale, Eden Valley and Nuriootpa with pocket-handkerchief
vineyard blocks of mataro at Nuriootpa and grenache at Krondorf. Exports to the US, Canada,
Singapore, Hong Kong and China.

🍷🍷🍷🍷🍷 **Hampel Single Vineyard Barossa Valley Shiraz 2018** From 17+yo vines;
most of the vinification following Gobell, this with 50% new oak and 20 months'
maturation. This has a vibrant palate; the black and red fruits have a juicy quality
that sees them penetrate every corner of the mouth. Cork. 14.5% alc. **Rating** 97
To 2043 $160
Gobell Single Vineyard Barossa Valley Shiraz 2018 From 35–70yo vines in
Marananga; destemmed, open-fermented with 2 cultured yeasts, 10 days on skins,
21 months in new French hogsheads; 120 dozen made. An unqualified triumph
for the '18 vintage, the wine of grace, purity and balance. Yes, the new oak can
be seen but as the years pass it will slowly slide away. Cork. 14.5% alc. **Rating** 97
To 2048 $160
Hoffmann Single Vineyard Barossa Valley Shiraz 2018 From 100yo vines,
which is surely the reason for the fuller dark fruit profile. Matured for 21 months
in French hogsheads, 2 new, 1 used. Cork. 14.5% alc. **Rating** 97 **To** 2048 $160
Limb Single Vineyard Barossa Valley Cabernet Sauvignon 2018 From
25yo vines in Seppeltsfield; open-fermented, matured for 21 months in French
hogsheads (50% new). This ever so classy cabernet defies belief – the warm
vintage, the alcohol and the Seppeltsfield district should have conspired to make
this an impossible dream. It's positively juicy and elegant with cassis/blackcurrant,
bay leaf and sprightly tannins. Cork. 13.5% alc. **Rating** 97 **To** 2048 $160

🍷🍷🍷🍷🍷 **Eden Valley Riesling 2019** A wine that takes no prisoners at any stage along
the way from the bouquet to the unrelenting power of the back-palate, finish and
aftertaste. Citrus of all kinds and apples, led by Granny Smith, meet the depth of
the acidity and stare it down with ease. Great now, great later. Screwcap. 11% alc.
Rating 96 **To** 2034 $25 ✪
Slow Grown Barossa Valley Shiraz 2018 From vines 35–70yo. 'Slow Grown'
doesn't refer to any bonsai or similar technique, just the relationship between
the growers, their vines and this wine. Matured for 19 months in American and
French hogsheads (30% new), it has the same liveliness as its more complex (and
expensive) siblings; oak choice and handling one particular difference. Cork.
14.5% alc. **Rating** 95 **To** 2038 $60
Cellar Dweller Barossa Cabernet Sauvignon 2018 Matured for 19 months
in French hogsheads (15% new). Once again, Soul Growers has got the picking
spot on. This is cabernet to its boots in a warm vintage when so many others
let the alcohol rise to 15% or more. Earthy tannins and a firm profile to the
blackcurrant fruit provide exemplary varietal fruit. Cork. 14% alc. **Rating** 95
To 2040 $60
Barossa Valley El Mejor 2018 A quixotic blend of 70% cabernet sauvignon
and 15% each of mourvedre and shiraz; matured for 21 months in one each of
French and American hogsheads (both new). Positively vibrates with the intensity
of its ever-changing black, purple and red berry fruits; the tannins fine, the balance
impeccable. Cork. 14% alc. **Rating** 95 **To** 2038 $110
Persistence Barossa Valley Grenache 2018 From 50yo vines in Marananga;
7–10 days on skins, matured for 18 months in used French hogsheads. Very good
discipline; early (for grenache) picking in a very warm vintage; could have got out

doesn't feel it; such is its balance. It's not stretching things to call it stellar. Screwcap. 14.5% alc. **Rating** 96 **To** 2040 $70 CM **☉**

Garcon 2018 A grenache tour de force by Spinifex, holding the alcohol down yet taking its own stance with an array of totally supple and generous spices threaded through the red fruits at the heart of the palate; SWALK by fine tannins. Screwcap. 13.5% alc. **Rating** 96 **To** 2028 $28 **☉**

Miette Barossa Valley Grenache Mataro Cinsault 2017 Spinifex in best form. Tendrils of spice and wood smoke on the bouquet, ramping up the chorus of red and black cherries, raspberry and blackberry on the medium-bodied, juicy palate. This isn't simply a case of having fun with an esoteric blend, it's been carefully calibrated. Screwcap. 14.5% alc. **Rating** 96 **To** 2032 $25 **☉**

Barossa Valley Rose 2019 It's true that this displays juicy fruit and an element of texture, but it offers a lot more besides. It's spicy, slipped with pomegranate, pale salmon in colour and carries highlights of orange peel and fennel. It works simply as a refreshing drink but those who stop to contemplate will be rewarded. Screwcap. 13.1% alc. **Rating** 94 **To** 2022 $26 CM **☉**

Barossa Valley Syrah 2018 The entry point for Spinifex but it's in the heart of the mould of its more expensive siblings. There is a particular edge to the black fruit flavours akin to a mix of spice, licorice and dried citrus peel (omitting the sugar). Screwcap. 13.5% alc. **Rating** 94 **To** 2033 $30 **☉**

Miette Barossa Valley Grenache Shiraz Mataro 2018 Exotic scents and flavours. Florals, fragrant herbs, meats and delicious summer berries. Smoky reduction put to positive effect. Raspberry and port wine jelly characters and then all that woodsy/earthen goodness. It's gamey too, but the wine carries it beautifully. Screwcap. 14% alc. **Rating** 94 **To** 2026 $22 CM **☉**

Esprit 2018 Has 56% grenache, 40% mataro, 4% shiraz. A distinctly spicy bouquet and the medium-bodied palate play follow-the-leader. Plush and welcoming, neither tannin nor oak doing anything more – this leaves the spicy, juicy fruit free to roam across the palate. Screwcap. 14.5% alc. **Rating** 94 **To** 2033 $35

ＹＹＹＹＹ **Adelaide Hills Aglianico 2018** Rating 93 To 2023 $35 SC
Lola 2018 Rating 92 To 2022 $30 SC
Miette Barossa Valley Vermentino 2018 Rating 91 To 2022 $24 SC

Spring Spur ★★★★☆

52 Fredas Lane, Tawonga Vic 3697 **Region** Alpine Valleys
T (03) 5754 4849 **www.**springspur.com.au **Open** Thurs–Mon 8–6
Winemaker Alex Phillips **Est.** 2017 **Dozens** 80
Alex Phillips was born and raised in South Africa; one of the most vibrant and diverse wine-producing countries in the world. She graduated cum laude from the University of Stellenbosch in 2013, where she was awarded the prestigious Prof PA van der Bijl medal and crowned Best Academic Student: Viticulture and Oenology. After mentoring under celebrated winemaker Adam Mason at Mulderbosch Vineyards, she launched into vintages across the world before finding her feet as assistant winemaker at Billy Button Wines in the Alpine Valleys of North East Victoria. It is here she found love; not only in the picturesque winemaking region itself but in her fiancé, Lin. The pair lives on Spring Spur – a beautiful working horse property in the Kiewa Valley where Alex is free to spread her wings and do what she does best – bringing Spring Spur wines to life.

Spring Vale Vineyards ★★★★

130 Spring Vale Road, Cranbrook, Tas 7190 **Region** East Coast Tasmania
T (03) 6257 8208 **www.**springvalewines.com **Open** 7 days 11–4
Winemaker Matt Wood **Est.** 1986 **Dozens** 8000 **Vyds** 17.6ha
Rodney Lyne has progressively established pinot noir (6.5ha), chardonnay (2ha), gewurztraminer (1.6ha), pinot gris and sauvignon blanc (1ha each). Spring Vale also owns the Melrose Vineyard, which is planted to pinot noir (3ha), sauvignon blanc and riesling (1ha each) and chardonnay (0.5ha). Exports to Singapore and Hong Kong.

ΨΨΨΨΨ **Estate Chardonnay 2018** Hand-picked, whole-bunch pressed, barrel-fermented matured for 9 months. Tasmanian acidity is exactly where it's needed to provide length and balance, supporting the white peach, nectarine and grapefruit palate. Screwcap. 13% alc. **Rating** 94 **To** 2032 $40

Pinot Gris 2019 Hand-picked, whole-bunch pressed, fermented in stainless steel with cultured yeast, transferred at 6°baume to old puncheons to complete fermentation. Has terrific mouthfeel courtesy of the barrel ferment, and also more depth than most pinot gris. Screwcap. 13.5% alc. **Rating** 94 **To** 2022 $30 ✪

Estate Pinot Noir 2018 Machine-harvested, open-fermented, 10–12 days on skins incorporating 3 days' cold soak, matured in old French oak for 3 months. A very powerful, intense and focused wine that utterly belies its cheap vinification. Screwcap. 13.6% alc. **Rating** 94 **To** 2029 $48

ΨΨΨΨΫ **Gewurztraminer 2019 Rating** 93 **To** 2025 $30
Melrose Pinot Noir 2019 Rating 93 **To** 2027 $30
Sauvignon Blanc 2019 Rating 91 $28
Rose 2019 Rating 90 **To** 2022 $30

Squitchy Lane Vineyard ★★★★★

Medhurst Road, Coldstream, Vic 3770 **Region** Yarra Valley
T (03) 5964 9114 **www**.squitchylane.com.au **Open** W'ends 11–5
Winemaker Medhurst Wines **Est.** 1982 **Dozens** 2000 **Vyds** 5.75ha
Mike Fitzpatrick acquired a taste for fine wine while a Rhodes scholar at Oxford University in the 1970s. Returning to Australia he guided Carlton Football Club to two premierships as captain, then established Melbourne-based finance company Squitchy Lane Holdings. The wines of Mount Mary inspired him to look for his own vineyard and in '96 he found a vineyard of sauvignon blanc, chardonnay, pinot noir, merlot, cabernet franc and cabernet sauvignon, planted in '82, just around the corner from Coldstream Hills and Yarra Yering.

ΨΨΨΨΨ **Yarra Valley Cabernet Sauvignon 2018** A wine with a very good track record, surpassing itself with this vintage. It's a classic medium-bodied, cool-climate cabernet giving rise to many words adding up to the same thing: elegant and harmonious, long in the mouth, then cassis and fine tannins. Four trophies, including Best Wine of Show at the Yarra Valley Wine Show '19. Screwcap. 13.5% alc. **Rating** 97 **To** 2038 $80 ✪

ΨΨΨΨΨ **The Key Single Vineyard Yarra Valley Chardonnay 2016** Estate-grown; hand-picked, whole-bunch pressed direct to French oak for fermentation. The less-is-more winemaking philosophy saw no stirring during the maturation. A low yield 5t/ha and bottling in Dec also contribute to a long-lived, grapefruit-accented, slow-developing wine. Screwcap. 13% alc. **Rating** 96 **To** 2025 $40 ✪

ΨΨΨΨΫ **Yarra Valley Cabernet Sauvignon 2017 Rating** 93 **To** 2024 $65 NG
Peter's Block Yarra Valley Pinot Noir 2018 Rating 92 **To** 2026 $70 NG
Peter's Block Yarra Valley Pinot Noir 2017 Rating 92 **To** 2027 $70

Stage Door Wine Co ★★★★★

22 Whibley Street, Henley Beach, SA 5022 **Region** Eden Valley
T 0400 991 968 **www**.stagedoorwineco.com.au **Open** At Taste Eden Valley
Winemaker Graeme Thredgold, Phil Lehmann **Est.** 2013 **Dozens** 5000 **Vyds** 32.3ha
It took a long time for Graeme Thredgold to establish Stage Door Wine Co. Having been a successful professional musician for 15 years during the 1980s and '90s, he developed vocal nodules in the early '90s, putting an end to his musical career. Having spent so much time working in hotels and night clubs, a new occupation stared him in the face: the liquor industry. In '92 he began working for Lion Nathan as a sales representative, then spent five years with SA Brewing and in '98 ventured into the world of wine as national sales manager for Andrew Garrett. Around 2000 he moved on to the more fertile pasture of Tucker Seabrook as state sales manager for SA. Further roles with Barossa Valley Estate and as general manager of

Chain of Ponds Wines added to an impressive career in sales and marketing, before he made his final move – to general manager of Eden Hall Wines, which just happens to be owned by his sister and brother-in-law, Mardi and David Hall. Grapes are sourced mainly from the family vineyard, plus contract-grown fruit. Exports to Canada

White Note Wild Ferment Eden Valley Gruner Veltliner 2019 Hand-picked, fermented wild and unusually, at least for a lighter tensile white, aged briefly in French barriques. The colour, a resinous yellow. The palate, a seamless sheath of apricot, sugar snap pea and quince notes. The finish, a curl of white pepper–grind acidity. This is as good as any gruner in this country. Screwcap. **Rating** 92 **To** 2023 $25 NG ✪

Eden Valley Shiraz 2018 A sumptuous, satinesque red that hits all the right buttons: a floral nose and a bumptiously smooth palate. Rich, without any angles or creases aside from some well positioned French oak, curtailing any excess. Dark to blue fruit allusions, a whiff of iodine and a lingering finish of creamy vanilla. Screwcap. **Rating** 92 **To** 2030 $50 NG

Eden Valley Cabernet Sauvignon 2018 Spending almost 24 months in French barriques (40% new) to bolster the fruit while toning the tannins, this is a smooth operator. Think crushed rock, blackcurrant, anise, floral scents and a sachet of bouquet garni. Cedar oak seams tuck it all into a nourishing enough whole. Screwcap. **Rating** 92 **To** 2030 $50 NG

The Green Room Eden Valley Riesling 2019 I like this riesling because it is more relaxed than the tangy regional norm. Almost supine. There is, nevertheless, enough acidity to carry riffs of lime cordial, green apple and nashi pear long. But it is palpably juicy and natural, conferring poise and an effortless drinkability. Screwcap. **Rating** 91 **To** 2025 $25 NG

Full House Barossa Cabernet Sauvignon 2018 A lustrous crimson, this rich red hits the jackpot of value, intensity and sheer amplitude of fruit. Think blackcurrant, plum and a waft of sage-clad tannins, bound to some vanillan oak. Far from complex. But a lot of wine. Screwcap. **Rating** 91 **To** 2024 $25 NG

Front and Centre Barossa Shiraz 2018 This is a buxom red, melding a contemporary sash of reductive floral scents with the sort of plush palate and lavish oak of yesteryear. While only 15% new French was used, the nature of its application and cooperage, perhaps, means it stands out. Liquid blueberry pie with vanillan oak cream. Screwcap. **Rating** 90 **To** 2023 $25 NG

Three Piece Barossa Grenache Shiraz Mataro 2019 A 4-square richer red, reliant on a spindle of reductive tension for a modicum of freshness. Think violet aromas and a core of dark fruit aspersions, punctuated by licorice allsorts. Some real tannins would be welcome, but otherwise satisfying enough. Screwcap. **Rating** 90 **To** 2023 $25 NG

Staindl Wines ★★★☆

63 Shoreham Road, Red Hill South, Vic 3937 (postal) **Region** Mornington Peninsula
T 0419 553 299 **www.**staindlwines.com.au **Open** By appt
Winemaker Rollo Crittenden (Contract) **Est.** 1982 **Dozens** 350 **Vyds** 3.1ha
As often happens, the establishment date for a wine producer can mean many things. In this instance it harks back to the planting of the vineyard by the Ayton family and the establishment of what was thereafter called St Neots. Juliet and Paul Staindl acquired the property in 2002 and have extended the plantings to 2.6ha of pinot noir, 0.4ha of chardonnay and 0.1ha of riesling; the vineyard is run biodynamically.

Mornington Peninsula Chardonnay 2019 Somewhat reticent and taut yet there is a charm to this. Merely a flutter of stone fruit and citrus with ginger spice. The palate linear, almost lean, with good tension to the acidity. Screwcap. 13% alc. **Rating** 90 **To** 2026 $40 JF

Staniford Wine Co ★★★★★

20 Jackson Street, Mount Barker, WA 6324 **Region** Great Southern
T 0405 157 687 **www**.stanifordwineco.com.au **Open** By appt
Winemaker Michael Staniford **Est.** 2010 **Dozens** 500

Michael Staniford has been making wine in Great Southern since 1995, principally as senior winemaker for Alkoomi at Frankland River, with additional experience as a contract maker for other wineries. The business is built around single vineyard wines; a Chardonnay from a 20+-year-old vineyard in Albany and a Cabernet Sauvignon from a 15+-year-old vineyard in Mount Barker. The quality of these two wines is every bit as one would expect. Michael plans to introduce a Riesling and a Shiraz with a similar individual vineyard origin, quality being the first requirement.

🍷🍷🍷🍷🍷 **Great Southern Reserve Chardonnay 2016** A clonal blend of Mendoza (80%) and the 4 Dijon/Bernard clones (20%); fermented and matured in French oak (33% new) for 11 months. Bright, light straw-green. It is lively, fresh and lingers long on the finish and aftertaste. Screwcap. 13.5% alc. **Rating** 95 **To** 2026
Great Southern Reserve Cabernet Sauvignon 2014 Includes small amounts of merlot, cabernet franc and petit verdot; matured for 20 months in French hogsheads (40% new). The tannin framework is appropriate for the long haul involved in bringing the wine onto the market, still evident but matched by the fruit with black and redcurrant to the fore. Screwcap. 13.5% alc. **Rating** 95 **To** 2034

Stanton & Killeen Wines ★★★★★

440 Jacks Road, Murray Valley Highway, Rutherglen, Vic 3685 **Region** Rutherglen
T (02) 6032 9457 **www**.stantonandkilleen.com.au **Open** Mon–Sat 9–5, Sun 10–5
Winemaker Nick Bulleid, Steven O'Callaghan **Est.** 1875 **Dozens** 10000 **Vyds** 34ha

In 2020 Stanton & Killeen celebrated its 145th anniversary. The business is owned and run by seventh-generation vigneron Natasha Killeen and her mother and CEO, Wendy Killeen. Fortifieds are a strong focus for the winery with around half of its production dedicated to this style. Their vineyards comprise 14 varieties, including seven Portuguese cultivars used for both fortified and table wine production – two additional Portuguese varieties are planned for future planting. A vineyard rejuvenation program has been implemented since 2014, focusing on sustainable and environmentally friendly practices. Exports to the UK, Switzerland, Taiwan, Hong Kong and China.

🍷🍷🍷🍷🍷 **Rutherglen Vintage Fortified 2017** Buoyant with youth from its dark red and purple tinged hue to its primary fruit and fragrance. Violets and lavender, cassis and musk, fennel and wood spices create a heady combination. The spirit is neatly balanced alongside the sweetness and grainy tannins. This has all the hallmarks of being a great aged wine, if its cork holds up; this one was badly stained. 17.8% alc. **Rating** 95 $42 JF
Rutherglen Vintage Fortified 2007 While this is beautifully fresh, it has morphed into a very fine aged fortified. Woodsy, earthy tones with coffee and vanilla, blackberry essence and brandy-esque flavours to the spirit. Lovely balance, clean with tannins adding a raw-silk texture. A lot of emotion infused into this: a fitting tribute to Chris Killeen's skill as a fortified winemaker. Cork. 18% alc. **Rating** 95 $90 JF
Rutherglen Arinto 2019 Arinto is a high-acid Portuguese white that is quite at home in Rutherglen – it retains its acidity in warmer climes. This is super dry with lemon-lime juice mixing it with green apple, grapefruit and a sprinkling of fresh herb. Moreish and savoury. Screwcap. 13.5% alc. **Rating** 95 **To** 2022 $30 JF ✪
The Prince Iberian Blend 2018 Comprising 42% tinta roriz, 30% touriga nacional, 22% tinta cao and 6% tinta barroca for the newly named Iberian blend, once known as the Reserva but still the tribute wine to Chris Killeen. While it has plenty of fragrance and flavour from red fruits, licorice, tar and a dusting of

warm earth, it has composure – it's not too big. A pleasure to drink. Screwcap. 14% alc. **Rating** 95 **To** 2028 $50 JF

♀♀♀♀♀ **Rutherglen Alvarinho 2019 Rating** 93 **To** 2021 $30 JF
Fortitude Rutherglen Durif 2018 Rating 93 **To** 2029 $38 JF
Rutherglen Shiraz Durif 2017 Rating 92 **To** 2034 $24 JP ✪
Reserve Rutherglen Tinta Roriz 2018 Rating 92 **To** 2023 $38 JF
Classic Rutherglen Muscat NV Rating 92 $38 JP
Methode Traditionnelle Rutherglen Tempranillo 2017 Rating 91 $38 JP
Methode Traditionelle Sparkling Shiraz 2018 Rating 90 $38 JF

Star Lane ★★★

51 Star Lane, Beechworth, Vic 3747 **Region** Beechworth
T 0427 287 278 **www**.starlanewinery.com.au **Open** By appt
Winemaker Liz Barnes **Est.** 1996 **Dozens** 1500 **Vyds** 9ha
Star Lane is the venture of Brett and Liz Barnes, and Kate and Rex Lucas. Both families have small vineyards, the Barnes's with merlot and shiraz, and the Lucas's with sangiovese and nebbiolo. Liz is the winemaker and has received encouragement and assistance from Rick Kinzbrunner; Brett is overall vineyard manager.

Stargazer Wine ★★★★★

37 Rosewood Lane, Tea Tree, Tas 7017 **Region** Tasmania
T 0408 173 335 **www**.stargazerwine.com.au **Open** By appt
Winemaker Samantha Connew **Est.** 2012 **Dozens** 1700 **Vyds** 3ha
Samantha (Sam) Connew has racked up a series of exceptional achievements, commencing with Bachelor of Law and Bachelor of Arts degrees, majoring in political science and English literature, from the University of Canterbury, Christchurch, NZ, then deciding her future direction by obtaining a Postgraduate Diploma of Oenology and Viticulture from Lincoln University, Canterbury, NZ. Sam moved to Australia, undertaking the Advanced Wine Assessment course at the Australian Wine Research Institute in 2000, being chosen as a scholar at the '02 Len Evans Tutorial, winning the George Mackey Award for the best wine exported from Australia in '04 and was awarded International Red Winemaker of the Year at the International Wine Challenge, London in '07. After a highly successful and lengthy position as chief winemaker at Wirra Wirra, Sam moved to Tasmania (via the Hunter Valley) to make the first wines for her own business, something she said she would never do. The emotive name (and label) is in part a tribute to Abel Tasman, the first European to sight Tasmania before proceeding to the South Island of NZ, navigating by the stars. Exports to the UK, Singapore and Japan.

♀♀♀♀♀ **Tupelo 2019** An ode to an Alsatian Edelzwicker, this is a magical potpourri of flavours and textures. In fact, it is the best blend of this ilk tasted from these shores. Limpid in the glass, the nose is an autumnal fruit bowl with gewurtz's hedonism nicely contained and folded into the meld. Hints of frangipani, lychee and spice, though, are lingering in the background. Mellifluous. The texture is a rich tapestry, unfolding in layers across the mouth. This deserves to be expensive. A profound white. Screwcap. **Rating** 97 **To** 2025 $35 NG ✪

♀♀♀♀♀ **Coal River Valley Riesling 2019** A single vineyard sourcing; fermented wild: the wont of this estate which, to be frank, is no longer an up and coming address but a freight train on express mode. The wines are beautiful. This is no exception. The decision to assuage riesling's high voltage acidity with a dollop of residual sugar was a brave one, as much as it was sensible. Talc, citrus allusions, ripe apple. Nothing sweet and sour. The wine sits in the glass knowing that it is going to stun: limpid, gently viscous and strident across the mouth, expanding across every crevice, bud and pore. An Australian benchmark with longing glimpses towards the variety's soulful Germanic home. Screwcap. **Rating** 96 **To** 2030 $38 NG ✪
Coal River Valley Riesling 2018 Fermented wild with fruit hailing from the Palisander Vineyard. This is a cracking riesling due to a finely tuned balance

between fruit ripeness, a tiny dollop of residual and the grape's febrile natural acidity. The nose is a joy as quince, pink grapefruit pulp, yuzu and a slate to chalky whiff of fealty to place meander from fore to a long aft. Seamless and engagingly energetic, this is very fine. Screwcap. Rating 95 To 2030 $32 NG ✪

Rada 2019 More juice, middle, sap and crunch than the straight Pinot, this is a delicious blend. Light, but the middle fattens with air and the effect is one of generosity: succulent red forest fruits, a whiff of whole-cluster spice and an effortless, tapered finish. Sort of like a Cru Beaujolais in Tasmanian mode. Screwcap. Rating 94 To 2023 $35 NG

♟♟♟♟♟ **Coal River Valley Pinot Noir 2018** Rating 92 To 2023 $55 NG

Steels Creek Estate   ★★★★

1 Sewell Road, Steels Creek, Vic 3775 **Region** Yarra Valley
T (03) 5965 2448 www.steelscreekestate.com.au **Open** Fri–Mon & public hols 10–6
Winemaker Simon Peirce **Est.** 1981 **Dozens** 400 **Vyds** 1.7ha
The Steels Creek Vineyard (chardonnay, shiraz, cabernet sauvignon, cabernet franc and colombard), family-operated since 1981, is located in the picturesque Steels Creek Valley with views towards Kinglake National Park. All the wines are made onsite by winemaker and owner Simon Peirce following renovations to the winery.

♟♟♟♟♟ **Single Vineyard Yarra Valley Cabernet Franc 2018** A bonanza of red fruits – raspberries, cherries, plums – with some discreet violets and licorice allsorts poking through. Runs smooth across the palate with a pinch of pleasant tartness from sour cherries and cranberries; some deeper bitter chocolate richness adding another layer. Delicious with juicy tannins working hard. Diam. 13% alc. Rating 93 To 2026 JP

Stefani Estate   ★★★★★

735 Old Healesville Road, Healesville, Vic 3777 **Region** Yarra Valley
T (03) 9570 8750 www.stefaniwines.com.au **Open** By appt
Winemaker Peter Mackey **Est.** 1998 **Dozens** 10 000 **Vyds** 30ha
Stefano Stefani came to Australia in 1985. Business success has allowed Stefano and wife Rina to follow in the footsteps of Stefano's grandfather, who had a vineyard and was an avid wine collector. The first property they acquired was at Long Gully Road in the Yarra Valley, planted to pinot grigio, cabernet sauvignon, chardonnay and pinot noir. The next was in Heathcote, where they acquired a property adjoining that of Mario Marson (ex Mount Mary), built a winery and established 14.4ha of shiraz, cabernet sauvignon, merlot, cabernet franc, malbec and petit verdot. In 2003 a second Yarra Valley property, named The View, reflecting its high altitude, was acquired and Dijon clones of chardonnay and pinot noir were planted. In addition, 1.6ha of sangiovese have been established, using scion material from the original Stefani Vineyard in Tuscany. Exports to China.

♟♟♟♟♟ **The View Yarra Valley Vineyard Chardonnay 2017** Frustratingly no information supplied. A rich style that has ripe stone fruit and melons, oak flavour and a creamy-leesy fullness across the palate. It also has a lovely line of acidity, threading all the richness together, resulting in a balanced wine. Diam. 14% alc. Rating 94 To 2027 $65 JF

♟♟♟♟♟ **Barrel Selection Heathcote Shiraz 2018** Rating 93 To 2030 $65 JF
Riserva Yarra Valley Sangiovese 2017 Rating 92 To 2027 $85 JF
Heathcote Shiraz 2018 Rating 91 To 2028 $50 JF
Vigna Stefani Yarra Valley Chardonnay 2019 Rating 90 To 2024 $30 JF
The Gate Yarra Valley Shiraz 2017 Rating 90 To 2026 $65 JF

Stefano Lubiana

60 Rowbottoms Road, Granton, Tas 7030 **Region** Southern Tasmania
T (03) 6263 7457 **www.**slw.com.au **Open** Wed–Sun 11–4
Winemaker Steve Lubiana **Est.** 1990 **Dozens** NFP **Vyds** 25ha

Monique and Steve Lubiana moved from the hot inland of a brown Australia to the beautiful banks of the Derwent River in 1990 to pursue Steve's dream of making high quality sparkling wine. The sloping site allowed them to build a gravity-fed winery and his whole winemaking approach since that time has been based on attention to detail within a biodynamic environment. The first sparkling wines were made in 1993 from the initial plantings of chardonnay and pinot noir. Over the years they have added riesling, sauvignon blanc, pinot gris and merlot. The Italian-inspired Osteria restaurant is based on their own biodynamically produced vegetables and herbs, the meats (all free-range) are from local farmers and the seafood is wild-caught. In 2016 the Lubianas purchased the Panorama Vineyard, first planted in 1974, in the Huon Valley. Exports to the UK, Sweden, Singapore, Indonesia, South Korea, Japan, Taiwan, Hong Kong and China.

Ruscello Pinot Noir 2018 A wine rich in a profound complexity, seamless and dark. It moves, it glides with fruit intensity deep in dark fruits and savoury spice, bitter chocolate, pomegranate. Smooth across the middle with beautifully crafted tannins. The next step up in Australian pinot noir is here. Cork. 13.5% alc. **Rating** 96 **To** 2031 $90 JP

La Roccia Pinot Noir 2018 Another in the single block series of pinots and this time drinkers are in for a spice-fuelled treat. What an exhilarating wine with energy to burn. The scent of licorice, nutmeg, musk and pepper are joined in the glass by black fruits and forest floor. Smooth and even with nicely defined tannins, the middle palate's lift and long goodbye provides a starring role for dark spices. Cork. 13.5% alc. **Rating** 96 **To** 2030 $80 JP

Riesling 2018 Captures the reason why so many wine lovers are turning to Tasmanian riesling. It's at once buoyant and intense, wild and spicy. It's a complex youngster with ripe lime, grapefruit pith and stony notes to charming Earl Grey tea spice aromas. Concentrated with a super dry snap of acidity that starts the gastric juices working overtime. Taut and tidy. Screwcap. 12.5% alc. **Rating** 95 **To** 2030 $33 JP ✪

Estate Chardonnay 2018 A wine with strong Tasmanian credentials including an inner energy, steely reserve and powerful acidity. That's the groundwork for a long-lived chardonnay, right there. Immediately reserved and still youthful with grapefruit pith, lemon curd, cut pear, fleshy mango. Good, strong backbone in play with a line of citrus infusion. A waiting-game kind of wine, be patient. Screwcap. 13% alc. **Rating** 95 **To** 2033 $58 JP

Estate Pinot Noir 2018 A rocking, rolling, fruit pastille–charged, filigree-fine pinot noir from a winemaker who always delivers. An upbeat entry with small red berries, toasted spice, orange rind aromas. Class act throughout from the tight coils of concentrated fruit and supple, even-handed tannins to smooth-knit oak. With texture and presence. Screwcap. 13% alc. **Rating** 95 **To** 2028 $62 JP

Sasso Pinot Noir 2017 From a fab year in Tasmania comes a pinot noir that beautifully exemplifies the meaning of a 'brooding' young red. It's a challenge to describe, you drink it in large gulps of verbiage. Dark, dense, back-to-back black fruits, stewed rhubarb, truffle and leather, violets. It's both savoury and fruit-focused; red licorice mixes it up with smoky clove and cigar box. Tannins run and run. And still so young. Cork. 13.5% alc. **Rating** 95 **To** 2032 $120 JP

Syrah 2018 The first syrah produced under this label and what elegance! Takes a leaf straight out of the Lubiana winemaking school of pinot noir with great lift and expansive, pretty fruit and spice. Highly articulate approach to the grape allowing drinkers to see the Rhône-side of the variety with full 5-spice, nutmeg, pepper and Aussie bush notes sitting under blueberries, stewed plums. Clean, lithe and juicy to taste with spice to the fore, accompanied by soft, cedary oak. Screwcap. 13.5% alc. **Rating** 95 **To** 2028 $62 JP

Brut Rose 2015 Fine bead with good yeasty complexity and flavour. Time on lees has certainly provided a delicate but noticeable touch of savoury autolysis too, which all adds up to some mighty fine drinking. Aromas of acacia, cherry and dried cranberry with watermelon inflection throughout. The palate has excellent layering of flavour and texture with poached quince, spiced apple, shortbread, stone fruits and tart cranberries. Long and brisk. Cork. 12.5% alc. **Rating** 94 $58 JP

ȚȚȚȚ̦ **Il Giardino Pinot Noir 2018 Rating** 93 To 2030 $80 JP
Primavera Chardonnay 2019 Rating 92 To 2026 $33 JP

Stella Bella Wines ★★★★★

205 Rosabrook Road, Margaret River, WA 6285 **Region** Margaret River
T (08) 9758 8611 **www**.stellabella.com.au **Open** 7 days 10–5
Winemaker Luke Jolliffe, Jarrad Olsen **Est.** 1997 **Dozens** 40 000 **Vyds** 55.7ha
This enormously successful winemaking business produces wines of true regional expression with fruit sourced from the central and southern parts of Margaret River. The company owns and operates six vineyards, and also purchases fruit from small contract growers. Substantial quantities of wine covering all styles and price points make this an important producer for Margaret River. Exports Stella Bella, Suckfizzle and Skuttlebutt wines to all major markets.

ȚȚȚȚȚ **Suckfizzle Margaret River Sauvignon Blanc Semillon 2018** An intense yet classy SBS. It's riff is savoury thanks to oak inputs and some flinty funk, but its beat is delicious fruit. Tangy, vibrant, citrussy with basil, lemongrass and more besides. It has length. It has definition. It has the X-factor. Screwcap. 13.5% alc. **Rating** 96 To 2028 $45 JF ✪
Luminosa Margaret River Chardonnay 2018 Hand-picked, whole-bunch pressed, wild-fermented in French barriques. The wine is supple and full of delicious pink grapefruit, white peach and a quite beautiful touch of wild honey. Screwcap. 13.4% alc. **Rating** 96 To 2032 $70 ✪
Margaret River Sauvignon Blanc 2019 This is good. Really good. It's the chalky acidity and lemon sorbet–like texture. Punchy tropical flavours, but not so overt that you'll fall over. Lemon-lime bitters, crunchy daikon. Absurdly refreshing to the very last drop. Screwcap. 13.2% alc. **Rating** 95 To 2025 $25 JF ✪
Margaret River Semillon Sauvignon Blanc 2019 A happy combo bringing out the best in each other. Feijoa, grapefruit and pith, a squirt of lime juice plus basil with a shot of natural acidity acting as the pulse to this delicious drink. Screwcap. 12.5% alc. **Rating** 95 To 2025 $25 JF ✪
Suckfizzle Margaret River Chardonnay 2018 It's tightly wound and not ready to reveal its potential. Lemon/grapefruit juice and zest with brisk acidity and then a waft of savoury chicken stock. Sweet oak inputs with some nutty leesy influence and sulphides adding other layers. Screwcap. 13.5% alc. **Rating** 95 To 2028 $70 JF
Skuttlebutt Margaret River Rose 2019 Fresh and vibrant from the first whiff through to the long finish. Red berries hold centre stage, acidity providing balance and brightness. Totally, ravishingly juicy red berries are the drivers. Screwcap. 13.1% alc. **Rating** 95 To 2023 $19 ✪
Luminosa Margaret River Cabernet Sauvignon 2017 While some of the '17 Stella Bella reds have been disappointing, thankfully the flagship isn't one of them. A concentrated, rich style with cassis, currants and violets plus spicy, toasty oak inputs. Perky acidity alongside the firm tannins acts as a buffer and freshens the palate. It's a keeper. Come back to this in a few years. Screwcap. 14.5% alc. **Rating** 95 To 2037 $90 JF

ȚȚȚȚ̦ **Margaret River Chardonnay 2018 Rating** 93 To 2028 $38 JF
Otro Vino Chardonnay 2018 Rating 92 To 2025 $26 JF
Suckfizzle Cabernet Sauvignon 2017 Rating 92 To 2032 $65 JF
Otro Vino Pinot Gris 2019 Rating 90 To 2022 $24 JF

Otro Vino Rose 2019 Rating 90 To 2020 $26 JF
Margaret River Cabernet Merlot 2018 Rating 90 To 2028 $25 JF
Otro Vino Tempranillo Shiraz Malbec 2018 Rating 90 To 2028 $35 JF

Steve Wiblin's Erin Eyes ★★★★★

58 Old Road, Leasingham, SA 5452 **Region** Clare Valley
T (08) 8843 0023 **www.**erineyes.com.au **Open** Not
Winemaker Steve Wiblin **Est.** 2009 **Dozens** 2500
Steve Wiblin became a winemaker accidentally when he was encouraged by his mentor
at Tooheys Brewery who had a love of fine art and fine wine. This was 40 years ago and
because Tooheys owned Wynns and Seaview, the change in career from beer to wine was
easy. He watched the acquisition of Wynns and Seaview by Penfolds and then Seppelt, before
moving to Orlando. He moved from the world of big wineries to small when he co-founded
Neagles Rock in 1997. In 2009 he left Neagles Rock and established Erin Eyes explaining,
'In 1842 my English convict forebear John Wiblin gazed into a pair of Erin eyes. That gaze
changed our family make-up and history forever. In the Irish-influenced Clare Valley, what
else would I call my wines but Erin Eyes?'

♀♀♀♀♀ **Emerald Isle Clare Valley Riesling 2019** A bullseye depiction of Clare riesling,
the varietal expression spot-on, the balance of citrus fruits and slatey acidity taking
the flavours on a never-never path of rare beauty. Screwcap. 11.5% alc. **Rating** 95
To 2030 $25 ✪
Pride of Erin Single Vineyard Reserve Clare Valley Riesling 2019 The
grapes come from a single vineyard in Penwortham. The wine is focused and
powerful, all its dimensions scaled up to maximum. It won't change its spots, the
only question its likely longevity. Screwcap. 11.5% alc. **Rating** 94 To 2029 $35

Sticks | Rising ★★★★

Yow Yow Rising, St Andrews, Vic 3761 **Region** Yarra Valley
T (03) 9224 1911 **www.**sticks.com.au **Open** Not
Winemaker Anthony Fikkers **Est.** 2000 **Dozens** 25 000
Anthony Fikkers crafts wines that express the power of the Rising Vineyard, while also
coaxing out the elegance that the Yarra Valley is renowned for. Anthony's philosophy of
minimal intervention but maximum attention to detail allows each of the wines to fully
express its origins.

♀♀♀♀♀ **Rising Pinot Noir 2018** The grapes were split into 2 parcels, one whole-
bunch fermented, the grapes crushed by hand and finally by foot, the other
parcel destemmed and fermented, in each case with wild yeast. The parcels
were combined and taken to French oak (40% new) for maturation. Screwcap.
12.5% alc. **Rating** 94 To 2028 $30 ✪

♀♀♀♀♀ **Rising Pinot Noir 2019** Rating 93 To 2026 $30 CM
Rising Gamay 2019 Rating 92 To 2024 $35 SC
Rising Pinot Noir 2019 Rating 91 To 2026 $30 CM

Stomp Wine ★★★★★

504 Wilderness Road, Lovedale, NSW 2330 **Region** Hunter Valley
T 0409 774 280 **www.**stompwines.com.au **Open** Thurs–Mon 10–5
Winemaker Michael McManus **Est.** 2004 **Dozens** 1000
After a seeming lifetime in the food and beverage industry, Michael and Meredith McManus
moved to full-time winemaking. They have set up Stomp Winemaking, a contract winemaker
designed to keep small and larger parcels of grapes separate through the fermentation and
maturation process, thus meeting the needs of boutique wine producers in the Hunter Valley.
The addition of their own Stomp label is a small but important part of their business.

ⵙⵙⵙⵙⵙ **Hunter Valley Semillon 2019** All free-run juice, this is archetypal '19: ample dry extract manifest as lemongrass, thyme and fennel, careening along dutiful rails of acid freshness with a citrus twist. A bit tangy, but eminently drinkable. This will show toasty complexity with patience. Screwcap. **Rating** 91 **To** 2027 $23 NG ✪

Limited Release Hunter Valley Fiano 2019 Fiano is a great hope across this parched landscape, be it the Hunter or otherwise. Quintessentially deep Mediterranean of birth and far from thirsty, the future is surely bright for the grape. In this case, the free-run was separated and fermented cool with a smidgeon (10%) barrel-treated for amplitude. A bit more barrel; a bit more of the variety's inherent viscosity and paradoxical freshness, welcome. But good, nevertheless. Mandarin, cumquat, fennel and citrus. Again, the pH tweaks a bit aggressive. Long and satisfying, either way. Screwcap. **Rating** 91 **To** 2023 $29 NG

Hunter Valley Verdelho 2019 Tropical exuberance and scents of bath salts run riot across gentle beams of support. This fits the mould for many and is well done. Palpably softer than the rest of the range, without forfeiting freshness. Screwcap. **Rating** 90 **To** 2022 $23 NG

Sparkling Chambourcin 2017 Fermented warm in tank, before being transferred to older oak for malolactic conversion. Matured for 20 months, the wine then underwent secondary fermentation in tank (Charmat), a more economical approach than bottle. Dark berry fruit, some twiggy oak and a riff of licorice and violet. A rich, bumptious fizz. Plenty of fun in the bones. Cork. **Rating** 90 $55 NG

Hunter Valley Tawny NV A smart bottle. This is comprised of shiraz across a multitude of vintages that has been fortified and aged oxidatively for an extended period. Plenty of molasses, dried walnut and Moroccan souk allusions of date and spice. The spirit, a tad harsh. 18% alc. **Rating** 90 $55 NG

Stone Bridge Wines ★★★★

20 Gillentown Road, Clare, SA 5453 **Region** Clare Valley
T (08) 8843 4143 **www**.stonebridgewines.com.au **Open** Thurs–Mon 11–4
Winemaker Craig Thomson, Angela Meaney **Est.** 2005 **Dozens** 3500 **Vyds** 85ha
'From little things, big things grow' is certainly true for Craig and Lisa Thomson, who planted 0.6ha of shiraz in 1997 and now own 85ha in three locations across the Clare Valley. They crush around 150t, more than 10 times their first batch in '05 when they launched the Stone Bridge Wines label and cellar door. They make grenache, riesling, shiraz, malbec, pinot gris and sangiovese, along with sparkling wines made in the traditional method. Their winery is also a contract processing plant for local and interstate wine labels. Visitors to the rammed earth cellar door can enjoy pizza from the wood-fired oven made by Craig, a baker by trade. Exports to Canada, Denmark, Singapore and China.

ⵙⵙⵙⵙ **Reserve Shiraz 2014** The first release of a Reserve shiraz in Stone Bridge's 15 years of operation, sourced from the iconic Armagh Vineyard. It's a mountainous wine with opulent fruits, but also with grippy tannins that take hold of the flesh of the upper lip and demand food. Screwcap. 14.8% alc. **Rating** 89 **To** 2034 $58

Clare Valley Sangiovese 2017 Looks backward rather than forward. The line of the palate wobbles and wanders, throwing out come-hither propositions, then moving on before an answer is given. Screwcap. 13.5% alc. **Rating** 89 **To** 2022 $22

Stonefish ★★★★★

24 Kangarilla Road, McLaren Vale, SA 5171 **Region** Various
T (02) 9668 9930 **www**.stonefish.wine **Open** Not
Winemaker Contract, Peter Papanikitas **Est.** 2000 **Dozens** 20 000 **Vyds** 58ha
Peter Papanikitas has been involved in various facets of the wine industry for the past 30+ years. Initially his contact was with companies that included Penfolds, Lindemans and Leo Buring, then he spent five years working for Cinzano, gaining experience in worldwide sales

and marketing. In 2000 he established Stonefish, a virtual winery operation, in partnership with various grapegrowers and winemakers, principally in the Barossa Valley and Margaret River, who provide the wines. The value for money has never been in doubt but Stonefish has moved to another level with its Icon and Reserve Barossa wines. Exports to Thailand, Vietnam, Indonesia, the Philippines, the Maldives, Singapore, Fiji, Hong Kong and China.

ΨΨΨΨΨ **Reserve Barossa Valley Shiraz 2018** From 30+yo vines; open-fermented, 7 days' cold soak, 12 months in French oak (50% new). Well balanced blackberry fruit, cedary oak and warm spices. Screwcap. 14.8% alc. **Rating** 95 **To** 2033 $30 ✪
Nero Old Vines Barossa Valley Shiraz 2017 From 50yo vines; hand-picked and sorted, crushed, open-fermented, 18 months in French oak (30% new). An elegant, medium-bodied wine with a fresh mix of red and black fruits, fine tannins and restrained cedary oak. Cork. 14.7% alc. **Rating** 95 **To** 2032 $48
Reserve Margaret River Cabernet Sauvignon 2017 Machine-harvested, crushed and destemmed, 124 days on skins with pumpovers, matured in French barriques (45% new). Has all the restraint, elegance and length '17 can bestow. Screwcap. 14.2% alc. **Rating** 95 **To** 2032 $30 ✪

ΨΨΨΨΨ **Nero Old Vines Barossa Valley Shiraz 2016** **Rating** 93 **To** 2036 $48

Stoney Rise ★★★★★
96 Hendersons Lane, Gravelly Beach, Tas 7276 **Region** Northern Tasmania
T (03) 6394 3678 **www**.stoneyrise.com **Open** Thurs–Mon 11–5
Winemaker Joe Holyman **Est.** 2000 **Dozens** 2000 **Vyds** 7.2ha
The Holyman family had been involved in vineyards in Tasmania for 20 years, but Joe Holyman's career in the wine industry – first as a sales rep, then as a wine buyer and more recently working in wineries in NZ, Portugal, France, Mount Benson and Coonawarra – gave him an exceptionally broad-based understanding of wine. In 2004 Joe and wife Lou purchased the former Rotherhythe Vineyard, which had been established in 1986, and set about restoring it to its former glory. There are two ranges: the Stoney Rise wines, focusing on fruit and early drinkability; and the Holyman wines, with more structure, more new oak and the best grapes, here the focus is on length and potential longevity. Exports to the UK, the Netherlands, Singapore and Japan.

ΨΨΨΨΨ **Holyman Pinot Noir 2017** If the wine didn't come from Tasmania, you'd be transfixed by its vivid hue and clarity, likewise the brightness and purity of its aromas and flavours, built within a citadel of dark cherry and satsuma plum, the certainty of spices and flowers around the corner. A very, very seductive pinot. Screwcap. 12% alc. **Rating** 96 **To** 2032 $55 ✪
Holyman Chardonnay 2018 Immaculately made and balanced. Fleshy peach and pink grapefruit, acidity just so, oak simply a vehicle. Screwcap. 13% alc. **Rating** 95 **To** 2025 $55
Pinot Noir 2018 There's no doubting the variety, nor the place (Tasmania's Tamar Valley), but this has an uncommon elegance and finesse to its light to medium-bodied palate. Its length and balance are first class. Freshness is another major virtue. Screwcap. 12.5% alc. **Rating** 95 **To** 2030 $29 ✪
Holyman Project X Pinot Noir 2017 Whole-bunch complexity on the bouquet and palate alike. A polarising style. It's 100% whole bunch from the same small block (1t of fruit, 55 dozen), matured in new French oak. The maker's thumbprint is all over the wine and it needs time to sort itself out. It'll be all duck or no dinner when that happens. Screwcap. 12% alc. **Rating** 94 **To** 2029 $90

Stonier Wines ★★★★★
Cnr Thompson's Lane/Frankston-Flinders Road, Merricks, Vic 3916
Region Mornington Peninsula
T (03) 5989 8300 **www**.stonier.com.au **Open** 7 days 11–5
Winemaker Michael Symons, Will Byron, Luke Buckley **Est.** 1978 **Dozens** 35 000
Vyds 17.6ha

This may be one of the most senior wineries on the Mornington Peninsula but that does not stop it moving with the times. It has embarked on a serious sustainability program that touches on all aspects of its operations. It is one of the few wineries in Australia to measure its carbon footprint in detail, using the officially recognised system of the Winemaker's Federation of Australia. It is steadily reducing its consumption of electricity; it uses rainwater, collected from the winery roof, for rinsing and washing in the winery, as well as for supplying the winery in general; it has created a balanced ecosystem in the vineyard by strategic planting of cover crops and reduction of sprays; and it has reduced its need to irrigate. All the Stonier wines are estate-grown and made with a mix of wild yeast (from initiation of fermentation) and cultured yeast (added towards the end of fermentation to ensure that no residual sugar remains), and almost all are destemmed to open fermenters. All have a two-stage maturation – always French oak and variable use of barriques and puncheons for the first stage. Exports to all major markets.

ΨΨΨΨΨ **Reserve Mornington Peninsula Pinot Noir 2019** A best barrel selection from all vineyards, focusing on structural strength and fruit depth (rather than fruit purity). This release included the Windmill, KBS, Merrons and Gainsborough vineyards plus 40% whole bunch ex W-WB. This has depth and structure to its red and dark berry fruits backed by balanced and integrated tannins, the oak absorbed. Screwcap. 13.6% alc. **Rating** 97 **To** 2034 $60 ✪

ΨΨΨΨΨ **KBS Vineyard Mornington Peninsula Chardonnay 2019** Fermented in French puncheons (33% new), 17% mlf, matured on gross lees for 8 months with some stirring. Has more energy and bite than the Reserve, even if (possibly) a little less complex. Screwcap. 13.7% alc. **Rating** 96 **To** 2030 $50 ✪

KBS Vineyard Mornington Peninsula Pinot Noir 2019 MV6; hand-picked, destemmed, chilled for a 5-day cold soak, after a total of 15 days on skins pressed to French puncheons (25% new) for 9 months' maturation. Across the Peninsula '19 was a very good vintage for pinot noir. Bright, clear crimson. The east-facing block has produced a wine of intense red cherry/berry fruits with excellent structure and length. Screwcap. 13.5% alc. **Rating** 96 **To** 2029 $65 ✪

Merron's Vineyard Mornington Peninsula Pinot Noir 2019 A vineyard with a strong personality. Identical vinification to KBS. Texture, structure and varietal fruit are all high class, the red fruits with a particularly attractive mouthfeel as they provide a gloss over the entire palate. Screwcap. 13% alc. **Rating** 96 **To** 2030 $55 ✪

W-WB Mornington Peninsula Pinot Noir 2019 100% whole bunch, matured in French puncheons (50% new); 92 dozen bottles made. Unsurprisingly radically different from its siblings. New oak first up on the bouquet, closely pursued by spices, the particular tannins ex whole-bunch ferment building as the wine is re-tasted. Screwcap. 13.8% alc. **Rating** 96 **To** 2029 $90

KBS Vineyard Mornington Peninsula Pinot Noir 2018 Two pickings 12 days apart, both vinified much the same way – as indeed are many of the Stonier Wines: 100% destemmed into 2t fermenters, gentle pumpovers and plunging, 24 days on skins. Spicy/savoury notes are the leaders of the flavour pack, interleaved with small red and blue fruits. Screwcap. 13.5% alc. **Rating** 96 **To** 2035 $75 ✪

Windmill Vineyard Mornington Peninsula Pinot Noir 2018 An enviable site on a projected north-facing slope on deep red basalt soils. Decided to only use destemmed fruit. Apart from that, the usual approach (with 19 days total maceration). Fragrant to the point of perfume, rosehip and violets, the fluid contact caressing the tongue, tannins seen but not heard. Screwcap. 13.8% alc. **Rating** 96 **To** 2038 $65 ✪

Reserve Mornington Peninsula Pinot Noir 2018 Has always been a blend of Stonier's highest quality and most distinctive vineyards, all single releases in their own right. When selecting barrels from all vineyards on the southern part of the Peninsula, the search is for structural strength and depth, not fruit purity. That strength, texture and structure are all here in high relief. Screwcap. 13.8% alc. **Rating** 96 **To** 2033 $60 ✪

Reserve Mornington Peninsula Chardonnay 2019 With 67% from the KBS Vineyard, 16% Thompson Vineyard and 17% Gainsborough Vineyard. Each component was whole-bunch pressed and fermented separately in French puncheons (34% new), 66% mlf, blended after 9 months on lees in barrel. Typical suave Stonier style, impeccably groomed. The eternal question is do they need more balance? Screwcap. 13.5% alc. **Rating** 95 **To** 2029 $50

Reserve Mornington Peninsula Chardonnay 2018 No single vineyard releases from '18, but a synergistic blend of 3 vineyards emerged from protracted tasting sessions. The final blend had 50% mlf, 8 months in oak (30% new). The wine has that Mornington Peninsula flavour and texture combination that no other part of Australia produces: a deceptive softness of stone fruit, apple, cream and fig. Screwcap. 13.5% alc. **Rating** 95 **To** 2030 $50

Windmill Vineyard Mornington Peninsula Pinot Noir 2019 The Windmill Vineyard is planted on a steep north-facing red soil slope, the lower trellis fermented as whole bunches, the higher trellis destemmed. The combination of whole bunch and destemmed fruit is especially synergistic with very impressive structure and length. Will richly repay 5 years in bottle. Screwcap. 13.5% alc. **Rating** 95 **To** 2034 $65

Merron's Vineyard Mornington Peninsula Pinot Noir 2018 Grown on a steep northeast-facing block. Unusually, chilled to well below 10°C for a 5-day cold soak, then the usual approach, pumped to French puncheons (15% new). A fragrant bouquet; sweet red berry fruits of every description flood across the bouquet and palate alike. Screwcap. 13.8% alc. **Rating** 95 **To** 2031 $55

Mornington Peninsula Chardonnay 2018 Sourced from growers with long-term supply contracts; fermented and matured in barriques and puncheons (10% new) for 10 months, 50% mlf. The grape supply and winemaking result in a first class entry-point wine for Stonier. Screwcap. 13% alc. **Rating** 94 **To** 2025 $25 ✪

♟♟♟♟♙ **Gainsborough Park Vineyard Mornington Peninsula Chardonnay 2019** **Rating** 90 **To** 2024 $45
Mornington Peninsula Pinot Noir 2018 **Rating** 90 **To** 2025 $28

Stormflower Vineyard ★★★★☆

3503 Caves Road, Wilyabrup, WA 6280 **Region** Margaret River
T (08) 9755 6211 **www.**stormflower.com.au **Open** 7 days 11–5
Winemaker Stuart Pym **Est.** 2007 **Dozens** 2800 **Vyds** 9ha

Stormflower Vineyard was founded by David Martin, Howard Cearns and Nic Trimboli, three friends better known as co-founders of Little Creatures Brewery in Fremantle. They thought the location of the property (and the vineyard on it that had been planted in the mid-1990s) was ideal for producing high quality wines. Whether they knew that storms hit the property on a regular basis, with hail and wind impacting the crop in most seasons, isn't known. What is known is the investment they have made in the vineyard by pulling out one-third of the vines planted in the wrong way, in the wrong place, leaving the present 9ha of cabernet sauvignon, shiraz, chardonnay, sauvignon blanc, semillon and chenin blanc in place. Now the sole owner, David Martin is the driving force in the vineyard, with a family background in agriculture. The vineyard, certified organic by NASAA in 2016, is managed using natural soil biology and organic compost.

♟♟♟♟♟ **Wilyabrup Cabernet Sauvignon 2017** You pick up clues from the technical background notes: 'three barrels were filled at the start of fermentation … after completion of fermentation, remaining wines spent a further 20 days on skins until the tannins softened … mlf completed in barrel to soften the acidity of the wine'. QED. A cabernet with wonderful texture and structure, the varietal fruit in awe of the flavour profile it has been given. Screwcap. 14.5% alc. **Rating** 96 **To** 2037 $60 ✪

Wilyabrup Shiraz 2017 Certified organic, open-fermented with 15% whole bunches, 20% completing primary ferment in French oak (30% new), matured

for 20 months. Abundant character given the cool/wet Feb/Mar, saved by the
dry Apr. Hard to quarrel with the handling. Screwcap. 14% alc. **Rating** 94
To 2030 $35

ŸŸŸŸŸ Wilyabrup Sauvignon Blanc 2019 Rating 92 To 2025 $25 ○
Wilyabrup Cabernet Shiraz 2018 Rating 92 To 2028 $27

Studley Park Vineyard

5 Garden Terrace, Kew, Vic 3101 (postal) **Region** Port Phillip zone
T 9852 8483 **www**.studleypark.com.au **Open** Not
Winemaker Llew Knight (Contract) **Est.** 1994 **Dozens** 500 **Vyds** 0.5ha
Geoff Pryor's Studley Park Vineyard is one of Melbourne's best kept secrets. It is on a bend
of the Yarra River barely 4km from the Melbourne CBD, on a 0.5ha block once planted to
vines, but for a century used for market gardening, then replanted with cabernet sauvignon. A
spectacular aerial photograph shows that immediately across the river, and looking directly to
the CBD, is the epicentre of Melbourne's light industrial development, while on the northern
and eastern boundaries are suburban residential blocks.

Stumpy Gully   ★★★★

1247 Stumpy Gully Road, Moorooduc, Vic 3933 **Region** Mornington Peninsula
T 1800 STUMPY (788 679) **www**.stumpygully.com.au **Open** 7 days 10–5
Winemaker Michael Zantvoort **Est.** 1988 **Dozens** 15 000 **Vyds** 30ha
Frank and Wendy Zantvoort began developing the family vineyard in 1988, planting it
solely to red varieties, predominantly cabernet sauvignon, merlot, shiraz and sangiovese. They
believed that ripening should present no problems for late-ripening varieties such as shiraz and
sangiovese as the vineyard is one of the warmest sites on the Peninsula. Son Michael Zantvoort
and wife Liz now own and run the business after Frank and Wendy retired, continuing to
produce both mainstream and alternative varieties from the original vines; the cellar door and
restaurant have been updated.

ŸŸŸŸŸ Mornington Peninsula Sauvignon Blanc 2018 Given a chord of textural
intrigue by partial barrel fermentation (20%), this is fully ramped with gooseberry,
blackcurrant, nettle and greengage. Aside from the lower acidity (kudos for
not jamming it with tartaric) and the stream of fruit as a result, this boasts a
harmonious synergy with better wines from the Loire. Very encouraging to taste
something like this on these shores. Screwcap. **Rating** 93 To 2023 $20 NG ○
Mornington Peninsula Chardonnay 2018 60% of this was fermented in
French hogsheads and left on lees for 10 months; the remainder, on lees for 9. This
goes for the knockout punch across the first whiff: creamed corn, white peach,
vanillan oak and cashew. Truffled leesiness imparts a creamy centre. The oak nestles
nicely, but this is a rich chardonnay that plays a gentle hand of tension to keep the
cavalcade of further stone fruit references all on the straight and narrow. Screwcap.
Rating 91 To 2024 $30 NG
Encore Mornington Peninsula Chardonnay 2018 It was 100% barrel
fermented before spending 9 months in oak. The result: honeydew melon
and white fig. Plenty of vanillan-cedar-clad oak and a creamy nougatine core.
Loosely knit. Lots of amp, but not quiet the right wattage. Screwcap. **Rating** 90
To 2024 $50 NG
Shark Point Mornington Peninsula Pinot Gris 2019 This was partly barrel
fermented (30%) in used French hogsheads, issuing a textural deliverance of nashi
pear, baking spice and apple scents. Mid-weighted and poised, it could use a little
more mid-palate richness. A minor gripe. Screwcap. **Rating** 90 To 2024 $35 NG

ŸŸŸŸ Magic Black Zantvoort Reserve Pinot Noir 2018 Rating 89 To 2025
$50 NG
Mornington Peninsula Sangiovese 2018 Rating 89 To 2024 $28 NG

SubRosa ★★★★★

PO Box 181, Ararat, Vic 3377 **Region** Grampians/Pyrenees
T 0478 072 259 **www**.subrosawine.com **Open** Not
Winemaker Adam Louder **Est.** 2013 **Dozens** 400

SubRosa, one of the best new wineries in the *Wine Companion 2019*, was created by two high performing partners in life and in this exceptional new winery. Adam Louder had completed 31 vintages in the Grampians, Pyrenees, Margaret River, Bordeaux and the Napa Valley, most with famous names. He met Gold Coast–born partner Nancy Panter in the Napa Valley in '11 while she was working for Visa on projects that included the Olympic Games, FIFA World Cup and NFL. After the '12 London Olympics, she and Adam moved between the US and Australia, returning permanently to Australia in '15, having laid the ground work for SubRosa in '13. This is a business that will win gold medals galore should it enter wine shows.

🍷🍷🍷🍷🍷 **Grampians Viognier 2018** Natural ferment, 15 months in French oak, no fining. Good winemaking presents the attractive characters of the variety and avoids those less so. Apricot and pear provide the fruit driven input with some almond-like nuttiness which is probably an oak/varietal synergy. It's silky and textural but retains a feeling of crispness through the palate and finish. Screwcap. 14.2% alc. **Rating** 94 **To** 2023 $30 SC ✪
Pyrenees Nebbiolo 2017 Hand-picked fruit from the Malakoff Estate. Matured for 16 months in French oak. Authentically pale in colour, the bouquet offers aromas of cherry, floral perfume, licorice and woody spice. The palate only just medium-weighted, quite supple in texture although edged with fine, savoury tannin, the flavours mostly in a slightly tart red berry vein, persisting through the finish. Screwcap. 13.5% alc. **Rating** 94 **To** 2029 $45 SC

🍷🍷🍷🍷🍾 **Grampians Shiraz 2017 Rating** 92 **To** 2027 $30 SC
Monseigneur Grampians Cabernet Sauvignon 2017 Rating 92 **To** 2030 $45 SC

Summerfield ★★★★★

5967 Stawell-Avoca Road, Moonambel, Vic 3478 **Region** Pyrenees
T (03) 5467 2264 **www**.summerfieldwines.com **Open** Mon–Sat 10–5, Sun 10–3
Winemaker Mark Summerfield **Est.** 1979 **Dozens** 7000 **Vyds** 18.2ha

Founder Ian Summerfield handed over the winemaker reins to son Mark several years ago. Mark has significantly refined the style of the wines with the introduction of French oak and by reducing the alcohol without compromising the intensity and concentration of the wines. If anything, the longevity of the wines produced by Mark will be even greater than that of the American-oaked wines of bygone years. Exports to Japan and China.

🍷🍷🍷🍷🍷 **Jo Shiraz 2018** Hand-picked, open-fermented with 30% whole bunches, 7 days on skins, matured for 18 months in French oak, only 2 barrels selected. Resplendently and unapologetically full-bodied, the balance keeping the flow of the wine in the mouth moving through to the long finish; 50yo vines and skilled winemaking are the drivers. Screwcap. 14.6% alc. **Rating** 97 **To** 2043 $150 ✪

🍷🍷🍷🍷🍷 **Sahsah Shiraz 2018** A single block of shiraz planted '70; hand-picked, open-fermented with 30% whole bunches, 18 months in French oak (20% new). A return to normality with high quality fruit picked while the bunches were still tight. It coasts along without effort, its plum/blackberry/cherry fruits not allowing your attention to wander. Screwcap. 14.2% alc. **Rating** 96 **To** 2038 $75 ✪
Taiyo Cabernet Sauvignon 2018 From the '70 block; hand-picked, 50% whole bunches, 7 days on skins, 18 months in French oak (30% new). Very interesting use of whole bunches, especially given the source of the grapes; I wouldn't have expected the outcome to be as successful as it is – this is a pretty smart wine. Screwcap. 14.2% alc. **Rating** 96 **To** 2038 $75 ✪
Jo Cabernet Sauvignon 2018 From a 1.8ha block on the Moonambel Vineyard, a 2-barrel selection of the best. Hand-picked, 30% whole bunch,

the remainder crushed (as with all the Summerfield reds), likewise stalk return. Tannins outweigh the fruit, although not by much. All it needs is 5 of its projected 30 years. Screwcap. 15% alc. **Rating** 96 $150

Reserve Pyrenees Shiraz 2018 Hand-picked, open-fermented with 30% whole bunches, matured in 15% new French oak, the balance used French and American, for 18 months. Densely coloured. The texture is so velvety and soft that you blink before it settles down thanks to the balance between the components of blackberry jam, dark chocolate and ripe tannins. This will bring smiles to the faces of most who taste it. Screwcap. 15% alc. **Rating** 95 **To** 2043 $63

Tradition 2018 Has 66% shiraz, 27% merlot, 7% cabernet sauvignon; hand-picked, 30% whole bunches, the remainder crushed and destemmed, 7 days on skins, matured for 18 months in oak (15% new). A very different flavour set, the cabernet and merlot introducing a savoury, dark chocolate edge; alcohol warmth not involved. Screwcap. 14.6% alc. **Rating** 95 **To** 2033 $36

Rose 2019 Pale salmon; rose petal/powder puff perfume. Elegant, fresh and long. Merlot strikes in an unexpected fashion. Screwcap. 13.5% alc. **Rating** 94 **To** 2021 $27 ✪

Pyrenees Shiraz 2018 Hand-picked, open-fermented with 30% whole bunches, 7 days on skins, matured for 18 months in French and American oak (15% new). Superabundant flavour, the fruit and tannins overflowing. Put it in a dark place for 5+ years. Screwcap. 15.2% alc. **Rating** 94 **To** 2033 $39

Reserve Pyrenees Cabernet Sauvignon 2018 Another wine in the line-up that (relatively speaking) has a degree of restraint, partly due to the demotion of new oak, although the fruit is so powerful (and pure) that oak was never going to play a lead role. Screwcap. 14.7% alc. **Rating** 94 **To** 2038 $63

♥♥♥♥♡ Saieh Shiraz 2018 **Rating** 93 **To** 2030 $75
Pyrenees Cabernet Sauvignon 2018 **Rating** 91 $39

Sunshine Creek   ★★★★

350 Yarraview Road, Yarra Glen, Vic 3775 **Region** Yarra Valley
T (03) 9882 1800 **www**.sunshinecreek.com.au **Open** Not
Winemaker Chris Lawrence **Est.** 2009 **Dozens** 7000 **Vyds** 20ha

Packaging magnate James Zhou has a wine business in China and, over the years, has worked with an A–Z of distinguished Australian winemakers, including Grant Burge, Philip Shaw, Phillip Jones, Pat Carmody and Geoff Hardy, to bring their wines to China. It was a logical extension to produce Australian wine of similar quality and James commissioned Mario Marson to find an appropriate existing vineyard. They discovered Martha's Vineyard, which was planted in the 1980s by Olga Szymiczek. The site was a particularly good one, which compensated for the need to change the existing spur-pruned vineyard (for mechanisation) to vertical shoot position (VSP) for increased quality and hand-picking. At the same time, an extensive program of grafting was undertaken and new clones were planted. In 2011 Andrew Smith (formerly of Lusatia Park Vineyard) was appointed vineyard manager to change the focus of management to sustainability and minimal interference. In '14 winemaker Chris Lawrence joined the team and an onsite winery (capable of handling 275t) was completed prior to the '16 vintage. In '17 there was a changing of the guard in the winery as Mario decided to concentrate solely on his Vinea Marson brand and Chris took on the role of chief winemaker. Exports to Hong Kong, Japan and China.

♥♥♥♥♡ Yarra Valley Pinot Noir 2017 There's an unusual first impression on the bouquet here, almost like dried or glace fruit, but not quite. Cherry and strawberry aromas are there when you look for them. Generous in flavour on the palate – ripeness bordering on sweetness – but fresh despite that, some tangy acidity helping out to that end. Light tannin firms up the finish. Better in time perhaps. Diam. 13.5% alc. **Rating** 91 **To** 2027 $45 SC

Yarra Valley Cabernets 2016 Cabernet sauvignon is the dominant variety at 79%, then in descending order merlot, cabernet franc, malbec and petit verdot. A really typical Yarra Bordeaux variety bouquet with blackcurrant and mulberry prominent, and a touch of the earthy/truffle character we often see. Medium-bodied and rather sweet-fruited, it's an attractive wine to drink now. Diam. 14.5% alc. **Rating** 91 **To** 2025 $45 SC

Yarra Valley Chardonnay 2017 Five clones, fermented and aged for 8 months in French barriques. A cool vintage but a ripe, quite sweet-fruited wine in style. Aromas predominantly of juicy yellow peaches with some spicy oak seasoning; the same sort of feel on the palate. Plenty of flavour and fullness in the mouth. Just a little uncertain on the finish which has acidity but somehow lacks crispness. Screwcap. 13.5% alc. **Rating** 90 **To** 2025 $45 SC

Surveyor's Hill Vineyards

215 Brooklands Road, Wallaroo, NSW 2618 **Region** Canberra District
T (02) 6230 2046 **www.**survhill.com.au **Open** W'ends & public hols
Winemaker Brindabella Hills (Dr Roger Harris), Greg Gallagher (sparkling) **Est.** 1986
Dozens 1000 **Vyds** 10ha
Surveyor's Hill Vineyards is on the slopes of the eponymous hill, at 550m–680m above sea level. It is an ancient volcano, producing granite-derived, coarse-structured (and hence well drained) sandy soils of low fertility. This has to be the ultimate patchwork-quilt vineyard with 1ha each of chardonnay, shiraz and viognier; 0.5ha each of roussanne, marsanne, aglianico, nero d'Avola, mourvedre, grenache, muscadelle, moscato giallo, cabernet franc, riesling, semillon, sauvignon blanc, touriga nacional and cabernet sauvignon.

Sussex Squire Wines

293–295 Spring Gully Road, Gillentown, SA 5453 **Region** Clare Valley
T 0458 141 169 **www.**sussexsquire.com.au **Open** 7 days 11–5
Winemaker Daniel Wilson, Mark Bollen **Est.** 2014 **Dozens** 1200 **Vyds** 6ha
There's a long family history attached to this wine business. The history began with Walter Hackett (1827–1914), a Sussex farmer; next came Joseph Hackett (1880–1958), followed by Joseph Robert Hackett (1911–98) and now fourth-generation Mark and Skye Bollen. Over the generations, the family worked in a successful major grain and seed business, then established the Nyora grazing property near Mintaro and Wyndham Park near Sevenhill, which is still farmed today with herds of black and red Angus cattle. Mark and Skye returned to the Clare Valley after spending 25 years working in other pursuits: Mark in wine sales and marketing; Skye in 5-star hotels for a decade before embarking on a successful career in recruitment. In 2014 Mark and Skye purchased 6ha of shiraz (planted '98), which is now dry-grown and organically managed. In lieu of Angus cattle, they have a flock of Black Suffolk sheep that roam the vineyard during winter to provide natural weed control and fertilise the soil.

Sutherland Estate ★★★★★

2010 Melba Highway, Dixons Creek, Vic 3775 **Region** Yarra Valley
T 0402 052 287 **www.**sutherlandestate.com.au **Open** W'ends & public hols 10–5
Winemaker Cathy Phelan, Angus Ridley, Rob Hall, Phil Kelly **Est.** 2000 **Dozens** 1500 **Vyds** 4ha
The Phelan family established Sutherland Estate in 2000 when they purchased a mature 2ha vineyard at Dixons Creek. Further plantings followed: the vineyard now consists of 1ha each of chardonnay and pinot noir, and 0.5ha each of gewurztraminer, cabernet sauvignon, tempranillo and shiraz. Ron Phelan designed and built the cellar door, which enjoys stunning views over the Yarra Valley, while daughter Cathy studied Wine Science at CSU. The sparkling wines are made by Phil Kelly, the reds by Cathy and partner Angus Ridley (who worked at Coldstream Hills for a decade) and the Chardonnay by Rob Hall.

ȲȲȲȲȲ **Daniel's Hill Vineyard Yarra Valley Chardonnay 2019** Hand-picked, whole-bunch pressed straight to barrel (with the pressings), 75% cultured yeast, 25% wild. Made for the long haul but sufficiently juicy – grapefruit and citrussy acidity making a coherent style. A good wine from a year with some heat-related issues. Screwcap. 13.9% alc. **Rating** 95 **To** 2032 $32 ✪

ŶŶŶŶŶ Daniel's Hill Vineyard Yarra Valley Pinot Noir 2019 Rating 93 To 2030 $32
Daniel's Hill Vineyard Yarra Valley Gewurztraminer 2019 Rating 92
To 2026 $26
Daniel's Hill Vineyard Yarra Valley Shiraz 2019 Rating 92 To 2039 $32
Yarra Valley Blanc de Blancs 2015 Rating 92 $36

Sutton Grange Winery   ★★★★★

Carnochans Road, Sutton Grange, Vic 3448 **Region** Bendigo
T (03) 8672 1478 **www**.suttongrange.com.au **Open** Sun 11–5
Winemaker Melanie Chester **Est.** 1998 **Dozens** 6000 **Vyds** 12ha
The 400ha Sutton Grange property is a horse training facility acquired in 1996 by Peter
Sidwell, a Melbourne businessman with horseracing and breeding interests. A lunch visit to
the property by long-term friends Alec Epis and Stuart Anderson led to the decision to plant
shiraz, merlot, cabernet sauvignon, viognier and sangiovese. The winery is built from WA
limestone. Exports to the UK, the US, Canada, Switzerland and China.

ŶŶŶŶŶ Estate Syrah 2018 Hand-picked in small batches from the best sections of
the vineyard; fermented separately, building a wine with 15% whole bunch,
85% whole berry. Open-fermented, with an average of 9 days on skins, matured
for 18 months in French oak (25% new). It's medium-bodied but offers a
multiplicity of flavours, texture and structure; the fruit ripened à point, filling the
mouth and very long palate. Screwcap. 14% alc. **Rating** 97 To 2043 $50 ✪

ŶŶŶŶŶ Fairbank Syrah 2018 Hand-picked and sorted, one batch with 100% whole-
bunch carbonic maceration contributed 35% of the blend, the balance whole-
berry fermented, matured in French oak (16% new) for 9 months. An impressive
support role to the Estate Syrah, vinified totally differently and reflecting skilled
winemaking. It's light to medium-bodied with the juicy carbonic contribution
tickling the tongue, black cherry and plum to the fore. Screwcap. 14% alc.
Rating 95 To 2033 $27 ✪
Fairbank Rose 2019 Includes 35% cabernet sauvignon, 30% shiraz,
25% sangiovese and 10% viognier. Hand-picked, cold-fermented in old French
oak, 3 months on lees. A complex wine with spicy glimpses of red berries, the
palate seamlessly tracking the bouquet. It has length and a lingering dry finish.
A match for virtually any cuisine. Screwcap. 12.5% alc. **Rating** 94 To 2021 $27 ✪
Fairbank Cabernet Merlot 2018 A 90/10% blend; vinified separately,
100% whole berry–open fermented, 8 days on skins, matured for 18 months in
French oak (10% new). Bright, full crimson-purple; an object lesson in ripeness
fully realised at 13.5% alcohol, the brightness of the fruit flavours and mouthfeel
the result. Screwcap. **Rating** 94 To 2032 $27 ✪

ŶŶŶŶŶ Estate Viognier 2019 Rating 92 To 2021 $50
Estate Fiano 2019 Rating 92 To 2024 $50

Swan Wine Group   ★★★★☆

218 Murray Street, Tanunda, SA 5352 **Region** Barossa Valley
T 0451 849 887 **www**.auswancreek.com.au **Open** Mon–Fri 10–5
Winemaker Ben Riggs, Paul Heinicke, Matt Jackman **Est.** 2010 **Dozens** 235 000
Vyds 20ha
Swan Wine Group was formed through the merger of Inspire Vintage and Australia Swan
Vintage. The jewel in the business is a 10ha vineyard in Angaston that includes shiraz (a small
patch of which was planted in 1908), cabernet sauvignon and grenache. The 2ha cellar door
and winery vineyard in Tanunda provide the home base. The major part of the production
comes from grapes purchased from growers across SA and the wines are released under the
Auswan Creek, Discovery, Red Deer Station, Finders & Keepers and Inspire Estate labels. The
focus is on exports to Canada, Sweden, Singapore, Sri Lanka, Nigeria, South Korea, Indonesia,
Malaysia and China.

ŸŸŸŸŸ **Finders & Seekers Unique Vat 98 McLaren Vale Shiraz 2015** Over-cooked and overdone but the texture is soft and the fruit, aided by creamy oak, feels plush. It tastes of asphalt, Christmas cake, cooked plum, coconut and vanilla, and while the finish shows alcohol warmth it's both well structured and still manages to feel neat. Diam. 15% alc. **Rating** 92 **To** 2032 $60 CM

Red Deer Station 100 Royal Reserve Cabernet Sauvignon 2017 A substantial, warm, sweet, mellow red, not necessarily varietal but certainly powerful, with dusty tannin and an even finish. It never really hits any high notes but nor does it put a foot wrong. Refreshing acidity is one of its key aspects. Cork. 14.5% alc. **Rating** 92 **To** 2030 CM

Red Deer Station 50 Barossa Valley Vineyards Cabernet Sauvignon 2017 The fruit feels slightly over-cooked but there's enough red-berried flavour here and a decent framework of tannin. It catches slightly but there's a robust edge to this full-throttle Barossan red. Cork. 14.5% alc. **Rating** 92 **To** 2030 CM

Red Deer Station 70 Antiquities Barossa Valley Shiraz 2015 From 70yo vines. It's a porty wine with cream and resin-like oak slathered over flavours of plum and redcurrant. It's all about richness and smoothness and, while it's both those things, there's more oak and alcohol warmth than there is fruit. Tannin has been well handled though and it certainly has volume on its side. Cork. 14.5% alc. **Rating** 91 **To** 2029 CM

Red Deer Station Iconic South Australia Shiraz Cabernet 2017 A firm, solid red with red licorice, blackberry, saltbush and musk flavours rollicking through the palate. The finish doesn't seal the deal as well at it could but it's by no means short; it's pretty good drinking. Cork. 14% alc. **Rating** 90 **To** 2026 CM

Inspire Estate Premium Reserve Barossa Valley Cabernet Shiraz 2016 Cork stained all the way through. Sweet, soft-centred and offering plum/redcurrant flavours for the most part, though it also dips briefly into deeper blackcurrant notes. Not a lot of oak flavour though it's slipped with creamy vanilla and resin. Tannin is present but well integrated so that the overall impression remains one of softness. 15% alc. **Rating** 90 **To** 2026 $69 CM

ŸŸŸŸ **Auswan Creek Minister Selection 50 Langhorne Creek Shiraz 2018** **Rating** 89 **To** 2027 $29 CM

Red Deer Station 30 Coonawarra Shiraz 2017 **Rating** 89 **To** 2026 CM

Finders & Seekers Respect Vat 93 Coonawarra Shiraz 2016 **Rating** 89 **To** 2026 $29 CM

Inspire Estate 218 Selection McLaren Vale Shiraz Cabernet 2017 **Rating** 89 **To** 2025 $29 CM

Inspire Estate Limited Edition Barossa Valley Shiraz Cabernet 2016 **Rating** 89 **To** 2024 $69 CM

Auswan Creek Peacock V60 Cabernet Shiraz 2017 **Rating** 89 **To** 2025 $39 CM

Sweetwater Wines ★★★★☆

117 Sweetwater Road, Belford, NSW 2335 **Region** Hunter Valley
T (02) 4998 7666 **www.**sweetwaterwines.com.au **Open** Not
Winemaker Bryan Currie **Est.** 1998 **Dozens** NFP **Vyds** 16ha

Sweetwater Wines is in the same ownership as Hungerford Hill and wouldn't normally have a separate winery entry in the *Wine Companion*. But it's a single vineyard winery making only two wines, shiraz and cabernet sauvignon, the wines made by Andrew Thomas from 2003 to '16 and all stored in a temperature-controlled underground wine cellar that is part of the very large ornate house and separate guest accommodation built on the property. The reason for the seemingly unusual focus on cabernet sauvignon (true, second to shiraz) is the famed red volcanic soil over limestone. Exports to Hong Kong and China.

ŸŸŸŸŸ **Hunter Valley Shiraz 2018** A contemporary parlance of Hunter shiraz: blueberry pie, violet and iodine. Floral. Very. Mid-weighted and sassy. An easy ride across early to mid-term drinking. Screwcap. **Rating** 92 **To** 2024 $65 NG

Swinging Bridge

701 The Escort Way, Orange, NSW 2800 **Region** Orange
T 0409 246 609 **www**.swingingbridge.com.au **Open** By appt Tues–Wed
Winemaker Tom Ward **Est.** 1995 **Dozens** NFP **Vyds** 6ha

Swinging Bridge Estate was established in 1995 by the Ward and Payten families. In 2008, having been involved from the start, Tom and Georgie Ward took the helm and have since evolved Swinging Bridge into a premium supplier of cool-climate wines from Orange. The label had its founding in Canowindra with initial plantings of chardonnay and shiraz, named after the historic wooden pedestrian bridge that traverses the Belubula River at the foot of the vineyard. Today, Swinging Bridge has a variety of ranges on offer, including a number of Reserve wines, the Experimental Series, Winemaker Series and Estate Series. Tom and Georgie searched for a number of years for the perfect place to call home in Orange, both for their family and Swinging Bridge. Tom's pursuit of premium grapes resulted in a number of wines made from grapes grown on Peter and Lee Hedberg's Park Hill Vineyard (planted in 1998). Hill Park Vineyard is now the permanent home of Swinging Bridge; Tom and Georgie were able to realise their move when this outstanding property became available. Tom was a Len Evans scholar in 2012 and has been president of NSW Wine since '13

ŸŸŸŸŸ **Tom Ward Block A Orange Chardonnay 2018** Hand-picked at first light in the morning, chilled, whole-bunch pressed, matured for 8 months in French oak (20% new). Two years after vintage it is still elegant and understated, and will meander along at its own pace towards full maturity. Screwcap. 13.2% alc. **Rating** 95 **To** 2028 $58

Tom Ward Hill Park Orange Chardonnay 2018 Identical vinification to Block A, the fruit a little richer and a little more on show in Mar '20. The accent is on white peach and melon but grapefruit is also there to provide balance. Screwcap. 13.4% alc. **Rating** 95 **To** 2026 $80

Tom Ward M.A.W. Orange Pinot Noir 2018 Three clones, shoot and fruit-thinned, cold soak, 10% whole bunch, 20% new oak. Fragrant/perfumed strawberry and red cherry fruit soars out of the glass, the elegant and long palate, with multi-spice, lending enthusiastic support. Screwcap. 13.4% alc. **Rating** 95 **To** 2028 $35 ✪

Tom Ward William J. Orange Shiraz 2018 Open-fermented, pressed to barrel, matured in French puncheons (20% new) for 9 months, then a barrel selection. Particularly well made. Generous black cherry/berry fruit with excellent balance and length. The warm vintage suited Orange's red wines down to a T. Screwcap. 14.1% alc. **Rating** 95 **To** 2038 $35 ✪

Tom Ward Mrs Payten Orange Chardonnay 2019 Hand-picked in the early morning, whole-bunch pressed, 8 months in French oak (20% new). Very good depth and definition of white peach/grapefruit/apple flavours. Screwcap. 13.6% alc. **Rating** 94 **To** 2029 $30 ✪

Tom Ward #006 Orange Tempinot 2018 With 72% tempranillo, 28% pinot; the varieties handled separately, matured for 9 months in old puncheons. Fragrant, fresh cherry/blood plum aromas are replicated on the lively, light-bodied palate. Screwcap. 13.6% alc. **Rating** 94 **To** 2026 $35

ŸŸŸŸŸ **Tom Ward #004 Rose 2019 Rating** 92 **To** 2023 $30
Tom Ward Mrs Payten Chardonnay 2017 Rating 90 **To** 2024 $32 JP

Swings & Roundabouts

2807 Caves Road, Yallingup, WA 6232 **Region** Margaret River
T (08) 9756 6640 **www**.swings.com.au **Open** 7 days 10–5
Winemaker Brian Fletcher **Est.** 2004 **Dozens** 20 000 **Vyds** 5ha

The Swings & Roundabouts name comes from the expression used to encapsulate the eternal balancing act between the various aspects of grape and wine production. Swings aims to balance the serious side with a touch of fun. The wines are released under the Swings & Roundabouts and Backyard Stories labels. The arrival of Brian Fletcher as winemaker has underwritten the quality of the wines. He has never been far from the wine headlines, with over 35 years of experience making wine all over the world. Exports to the US, Canada, Japan and China.

🍷🍷🍷🍷🍷 **Backyard Stories Wildwood Cabernet Sauvignon 2017** From Wildwood Vineyard, planted almost 40 years ago; close-planted and dry-grown, it became very neglected until its purchase by Swings & Roundabouts in '04 and has been progressively rehabilitated. This is a selection of the best barrels. It's only light to medium-bodied – will it fill out with time in bottle? Its elegance may assist it. Screwcap. 14.3% alc. **Rating** 94 **To** 2037 $100

🍷🍷🍷🍷🍷 **Margaret River Rose 2019 Rating** 90 **To** 2020 $24
Margaret River Shiraz 2017 Rating 90 **To** 2022 $24
Margaret River Cabernet Merlot 2017 Rating 90 **To** 2027 $24

Swinney ★★★★★

325 Frankland-Kojonup Road, Frankland River, WA 6396 **Region** Frankland River
T (08) 9200 4483 **www.**swinney.com.au **Open** Not
Winemaker Robert Mann **Est.** 1998 **Dozens** 2500 **Vyds** 160ha
The Swinney family (currently parents Graham and Kaye, and son and daughter Matt and Janelle) has been resident on their 2500ha property since it was settled by George Swinney in 1922. In the '90s they decided to diversify and now have 160ha of vines across four vineyards, including the Powderbark Ridge Vineyard in Frankland River (planted in '98, purchased in partnership with former Hardys winemaker Peter Dawson). The lion's share goes to shiraz (67ha) and cabernet sauvignon (48ha), followed by riesling, semillon, pinot gris, gewurztraminer, viognier, vermentino and malbec. They also pushed the envelope by establishing grenache, tempranillo and mourvedre as bushvines, a rarity in this part of the world. Exports to the UK, Singapore and Hong Kong.

🍷🍷🍷🍷🍷 **Frankland River Riesling 2019** The intensity of the citrus fruit, with grapefruit swimming beside lime, builds before the acid-based structure swings into play. It has that racy Frankland River flavour and a brilliantly clean, mouth-watering finish. Screwcap. 12% alc. **Rating** 96 **To** 2028 $33 ✪
Frankland River Syrah 2018 The Frankland River never fails to create a sense of urgency with its shiraz, amplified here by the contributions of (some) new oak and whole-berry fermentation. It has a complex tannin structure from start to finish, a framework for the fruit to establish dominance somewhere down the track. Screwcap. 14% alc. **Rating** 95 **To** 2043 $42
Farvie Frankland River Grenache 2018 Estate bushvines; hand-picked and berry-sorted direct to French oak vat, 15% whole bunches and 5% mourvedre, wild-fermented, 10 days on skins, basket-pressed to large-format French oak for 11 months' maturation. This is a full-bodied grenache with forest fruits, manicured tannins and a long future. Screwcap. 14% alc. **Rating** 95 **To** 2038 $150
Farvie Frankland River Syrah 2018 Two hand-picked parcels from 21yo vines, berry-sorted, open-fermented with 55% whole bunches, pressed to large-format French oak, matured for 11 months. Elegant, savoury and long with sour and black cherry fruit. Was there enough extraction? A curious question in the context of reverence of fruit flavours in current practises. Time may answer an emphatic yes. Screwcap. 14% alc. **Rating** 94 **To** 2035 $150
Frankland River Syrah Mourvedre Grenache 2018 No surprise that the zesty/zippy Frankland River blend performs very differently to the Barossa Valley or McLaren Vale; it's closer to the middle/Northern Rhône Valley. This is a very enjoyable mouthful of spicy red and black fruits. Screwcap. 14% alc. **Rating** 94 **To** 2033 $42

🍷🍷🍷🍷🍷 **Frankland River Grenache 2018 Rating** 90 **To** 2023 $42

Symphonia Wines

1699 Boggy Creek Road, Myrrhee, Vic 3732 **Region** King Valley
T (02) 4952 5117 **www**.symphoniafinewines.com.au **Open** By appt
Winemaker Lilian Carter **Est.** 1998 **Dozens** 1500 **Vyds** 28ha
Peter Read and his family are veterans of the King Valley, commencing the development
of their vineyard in 1981. After extensive trips to both Western and Eastern Europe, Peter
embarked on an ambitious project to trial a series of grape varieties little known in this
country. Current owners Peter and Suzanne Evans are committed to continuing Peter Read's
pioneering legacy, making arneis, petit manseng, pinot grigio, savagnin, tannat, tempranillo and
saperavi. Exports to the UK.

King Valley Arneis 2019 Cool fermentation aimed to protect the textural
persona of arneis — and it does. Screwcap. 12.3% alc. **Rating** 90 **To** 2022 $24
King Valley Saperavi 2017 Picking was left until very late in the season for
the tannins to soften, fermented in small pots to limit extraction, matured for
16 months in mainly French oak. Tannin management was very good. For the
wine nerd. Screwcap. 14.8% alc. **Rating** 90 **To** 2025 $30

Pinot Trois King Valley Rose 2019 **Rating** 89 **To** 2023 $24

Symphony Hill Wines

2017 Eukey Road, Ballandean, Qld 4382 **Region** Granite Belt
T (07) 4684 1388 **www**.symphonyhill.com.au **Open** 7 days 10–4
Winemaker Abraham de Klerk **Est.** 1999 **Dozens** 6000 **Vyds** 3.5ha
Ewen Macpherson purchased an old table grape and orchard property in 1996. A partnership
with his parents, Bob and Jill Macpherson, led to development of the vineyard while Ewen
completed his Bachelor of Applied Science in viticulture (2003). The vineyard (now much
expanded) was established using state-of-the-art technology. Exports to China.

Reserve Granite Belt Cabernet Sauvignon 2017 This has received an
extended maceration, at least by Australian standards, across 3 weeks of pre-
fermentation cold soak and the fermentation period in addition, before being
pressed to barrel (30% new, 12 months, all French). This is an exceptional cabernet.
Long, detailed and almost supine across entry to finish. Incredibly long. The oak,
a cedar harness to the cassis, mulch and graphite scents. Akin to a riper vintage of
high quality Bordeaux with tannins tuned to a soprano detail. A privilege to taste.
Screwcap. **Rating** 96 **To** 2031 $95 NG
Reserve Granite Belt Petit Verdot 2017 A highly savoury wine that is mid-
weighted on the lower side and yet impeccably ripe. Verdant herb scents but the
sashay of dark cherry, licorice and bitter chocolate tannins service an impression
of richness and balance. This is delicious wine. A variety too that we should
increasingly get our heads around. Its tannic mettle and high natural acidity will
see it survive way after the effete classics are dead and dusted, at least in this
parched land. Screwcap. **Rating** 94 **To** 2027 $65 NG

Gewurztraminer 2019 **Rating** 93 **To** 2023 $45 NG
Granite Belt Vermentino 2019 **Rating** 93 **To** 2021 $30 NG
Inspiration Range Reserve Barossa Shiraz 2017 **Rating** 93 **To** 2029
$95 NG
Albarino 2019 **Rating** 92 **To** 2023 $65 NG
Granite Belt Shiraz 2018 **Rating** 92 **To** 2023 $30 NG
Reserve Organic Montepulciano 2017 **Rating** 92 **To** 2024 $65 NG
Fiano 2019 **Rating** 91 **To** 2022 $45 NG
Tempranillo 2017 **Rating** 90 **To** 2022 $30 NG

T'Gallant

1385 Mornington-Flinders Road, Main Ridge, Vic 3928 **Region** Mornington Peninsula
T (03) 5931 1300 **www.**tgallant.com.au **Open** 7 days 9–5
Winemaker Clare Dry **Est.** 1990 **Dozens** NFP **Vyds** 8ha

Husband and wife winemakers Kevin McCarthy and Kathleen Quealy carved out such an important niche market for the T'Gallant label that in 2003, after protracted negotiations, it was acquired by Beringer Blass (now part of TWE). The acquisition of a 15ha property and the planting of 8ha of pinot gris gave the business a firm geographic base, as well as providing increased resources for its signature wine.

ΨΨΨΨΨ **Tribute Pinot Gris 2019** A different fork on the same road, this more generous wine, a 'gris'. All the better for it. Plump and reliant on a billow of phenolics as guiding pillars for a flow of Asian pear, baked apple, quince, honeysuckle and cinnamon spice; similarly reliant on its gentler acidity for freshness. Balanced, intense of flavour and long. This is impressive and dangerously easy to drink. Screwcap. **Rating** 93 **To** 2024 $25 NG ✪

Cyrano Pinot Noir 2019 A pallid to mid-ruby. Beaming bright aromas of rhubarb, raspberry and cranberry across a mid-weighted palate. A carriage of gentle astringency keeps everything on the straight and narrow. Of good sappy length. The oak well appointed. Screwcap. **Rating** 91 **To** 2023 $28 NG

Prosecco NV A sort of 'don't think, just drink' proposal. A bubble bath of spiced apple, pear and orange blossom frothing across the palate. Juicy. Effusive in its parade of generous flavour. What's not to like? Cork. **Rating** 90 $20 NG ✪

ΨΨΨΨ **Cape Schanck Pinot Grigio 2019** **Rating** 89 **To** 2021 $20 NG

Tahbilk

254 O'Neils Road, Tabilk, Vic 3608 **Region** Nagambie Lakes
T (03) 5794 2555 **www.**tahbilk.com.au **Open** Mon–Sat 9–5, Sun 11–5
Winemaker Alister Purbrick, Neil Larson, Alan George **Est.** 1860 **Dozens** 120 000
Vyds 221.5ha

A winery steeped in tradition (with National Trust classification) and which should be visited at least once by every wine-conscious Australian. It makes wines – particularly red wines – utterly in keeping with that tradition. The essence of that heritage comes in the form of their tiny quantities of shiraz made from vines planted in 1860. A founding member of Australia's First Families of Wine. *Wine Companion 2016* Winery of the Year. Exports to all major markets.

ΨΨΨΨΨ **1860 Vines Shiraz 2016** It is amazing how this unfurls in the glass. As if those old vines have a point to make – not so much 'look at me' rather, 'I am all about grace'. Everything is just so. The red and blue fruits, the dash of spices and the cedary oak that's tucked in well. It's medium-bodied yet there's length once the supple tannins finish gliding across the palate. Screwcap. 13.7% alc. **Rating** 96 **To** 2042 $325 JF

1860 Vines Shiraz 2015 The youthful colour, the flavours, tannins and acidity all come from a small sandy rise immune to the ravages of phylloxera. The inclusion of a small amount of new French oak has lifted the opening stanza and the vintage conditions were considered to be among the best for many years. Its value cannot be adequately measured in points. Screwcap. 14% alc. **Rating** 96 **To** 2045 $350

Grenache Mourvedre Rose 2019 Light, bright pink. A pleasing tussle between lively red fruits on the bouquet and mid-palate, complexity arriving on the finish with some spicy/savoury notes. Tahbilk is rightly establishing a reputation for this rose style. Screwcap. 13% alc. **Rating** 95 **To** 2023 $22 ✪

Eric Stevens Purbrick Shiraz 2016 While the sweet, cedary oak needs more time to settle, there's a gloss to this. Ripe fruit, woodsy spices and eucalyptus to the fore. It's full of flavour and is a rich, but not a humongous wine. Grip to the tannins and freshness throughout. Will be better with more time. Screwcap. 14.7% alc. **Rating** 95 **To** 2033 $72 JF

Eric Stevens Purbrick Cabernet Sauvignon 2016 This needed a jump start, as in air to rev it into action. After that it cruises along. It'll offer cassis, woodsy spices, dried herbs and some gritty texture. What surprises, it is medium-bodied with fine tannins. Screwcap. 13.9% alc. **Rating** 95 **To** 2030 $72 JF

Old Vines Cabernet Shiraz 2017 This has morphed into a harmonious wine. Expect dark sweet plums and cherries doused in cinnamon and star anise with some herbal tones. A savoury overlay, all earthy and ferrous with lovely, supple tannins. Screwcap. 14.4% alc. **Rating** 95 **To** 2032 $46 JF

Eric Stevens Purbrick Cabernet Sauvignon 2015 Has retained remarkably fresh colour, its freshness on the palate repeating the message. Indeed, it speaks of elegance, not normally a feature of the Tahbilk style. The only question is how long will it take to flesh out? Screwcap. 14% alc. **Rating** 94 **To** 2030 $72

ŶŶŶŶŶ **Marsanne 2019 Rating** 93 **To** 2039 $20 ✪
1927 Vines Marsanne 2014 Rating 92 **To** 2024 $46 JF
Shiraz 2018 Rating 92 **To** 2026 $26 JF
Cane Cut Marsanne 2017 Rating 92 **To** 2023 $25 JF ✪
Roussanne Marsanne Viognier 2018 Rating 91 **To** 2024 $26 JF
Museum Release Marsanne 2014 Rating 90 **To** 2024 $26 JF
Grenache Shiraz Mourvedre 2018 Rating 90 **To** 2023 $26 JF
Grenache Shiraz Mourvedre 2017 Rating 90 **To** 2023 $26

Talbots Block Wines ★★★★☆

62 Possingham Pit Road, Sevenhill, SA 5453 **Region** Clare Valley
T 0403 517 401 **www**.talbotsblock.com.au **Open** By appt
Winemaker Contract **Est.** 2011 **Dozens** 1000 **Vyds** 5ha

Thanks to careers in government and the oil industry, Alex and Bill Talbot started their journey to wine in 1997 while working and living at Woomera in the SA desert. They purchased land in the Sevenhill area of the Clare Valley, having fallen in love with the place, and dreamed of some day making wine for their friends. They then moved to various places in Asia, including Kuala Lumpur, Jakarta and Singapore, their minds always returning to their Sevenhill vineyard. They now live in the house they built high on the block, with views across the vineyard, and have the opportunity to tend the vines whenever they please. Initially the grapes were sold but since 2012 they have kept enough of the production to have around 1000 dozen made across their two distinctly different shiraz styles. The labels are striking and evocative.

ŶŶŶŶŶ **The Prince Clare Valley Shiraz 2018** Designed as an earlier drinking option, having spent 10 months in an assortment of American and French oak. Of postcode with a breeze of black cherry, violet, tapenade, smoked meat and mint blowing across well appointed oaky seams. As is seldom the case, this wine achieves exactly what the back label blurb suggests. Screwcap. **Rating** 93 **To** 2026 $28 NG

The Sultan Clare Valley Shiraz 2017 The flagship. Aged for 18 months in hogsheads (35% new), a whiff of coconut and bourbon suggesting a good portion American. Cherry cola, a potpourri of green herb and tapenade. This surely has a fan club but The Prince is by far the more poised and attractive wine. Both fullbodied. One simply far more drinkable. Screwcap. **Rating** 91 **To** 2029 $38 NG

Talisman Wines ★★★★☆

Wheelman Road, Wellington Mill, WA 6236 **Region** Geographe
T 0401 559 266 **www**.talismanwines.com.au **Open** By appt
Winemaker Peter Stanlake **Est.** 2009 **Dozens** 3000 **Vyds** 9ha

Kim Robinson (and wife Jenny) began the development of their vineyard in 2000 and now have cabernet, shiraz, malbec, zinfandel, chardonnay, riesling and sauvignon blanc. Kim says that 'after eight frustrating years of selling grapes to Evans & Tate and Wolf Blass, we decided to optimise the vineyard and attempt to make quality wines'. The measure of their success has been consistent gold medal performance (and some trophies) at the Geographe Wine Show. They say this could not have been achieved without the assistance of vineyard manager Victor Bertola and winemaker Peter Stanlake.

ŸŸŸŸŸ **Gabrielle Ferguson Valley Chardonnay 2018** Wild-fermented in new and 1yo French barriques, matured for 9 months. This has real character, starting well and finishing with a surge of grapefruit and stone fruit flavours. Oak has been taken on board, but is then lost in the fruit. Seriously impressive. Screwcap. 14.3% alc. **Rating** 95 **To** 2030 $40
Ferguson Valley Cabernet Malbec 2014 Shows that the balance and flavour of its '18 sibling will richly repay cellaring. This is so still full of life and, if anything, is still on an upward trajectory. It's elegant, yet also juicy. Screwcap. 14.1% alc. **Rating** 94 **To** 2030 $30 ✪

ŸŸŸŸŸ **Cellar Release Ferguson Valley Riesling 2012 Rating** 93 $35
Ferguson Valley Malbec 2018 Rating 93 **To** 2030 $35
Ferguson Valley Zinfandel 2017 Rating 93 **To** 2027 $45
Ferguson Valley Riesling 2019 Rating 92 $25 ✪
Ferguson Valley Sauvignon Blanc Fume 2019 Rating 92 **To** 2021 $30
Arida 2019 Rating 92 **To** 2021 $25 ✪
Ferguson Valley Malbec 2013 Rating 92 **To** 2028 $35
Ferguson Valley Cabernet Malbec 2018 Rating 91 **To** 2028 $30

Talits Estate   ★★★☆

722 Milbrodale Road, Broke, NSW 2321 **Region** Hunter Valley
T 0404 841 700 **www**.talitsestate.com.au **Open** Thurs–Mon 10–6
Winemaker Daniel Binet **Est.** 2008 **Dozens** 400 **Vyds** 4ha
Gayle Meredith is the owner of this 4ha vineyard in the Broke Fordwich subregion of the Hunter Valley. The prime function of the property is luxury accommodation and the house sits on 20ha of meticulously maintained gardens with olive trees and the estate merlot and shiraz vines. Winemaker Daniel Binet has had a distinguished career in the region over the past two decades. I'm not at all sure I understand why the wines should not be better than they are, perhaps it's just early days.

ŸŸŸŸŸ **Hunter Valley Merlot 2018** From the estate vineyard on the red volcanic soils of the Broke Fordwich subregion. Open-fermented, 10 days on skins, 10 months' maturation in French oak. Bright and crisp. There is a shadow of a question on full ripeness. Time will tell. Screwcap. 13.5% alc. **Rating** 92 **To** 2028 $30

ŸŸŸŸ **The Forbidden Fruit Pinot Noir Syrah 2018 Rating** 87 **To** 2024 $48

Tallarook   ★★★★

140 Evans Road, Tallarook, Vic 3569 **Region** Central Victoria
T 0423 205 370 **www**.tallarookwines.com.au **Open** By appt
Winemaker Martin Williams MW **Est.** 1980 **Dozens** 7000 **Vyds** 12ha
Martin Williams collects degrees like those who collect postage stamps, his Master of Wine almost incidental to his wine career. His academic career started with chemistry and biochemistry at the University of Sydney, moving to the US to complete his masters at the University of California in 1991. By this time he had worked in Burgundy ('88–89) with Domaine Tollot-Beaut and Domaine Anne Gros. He arrived in the Yarra Valley for the '92 vintage with a deep love and respect for pinot noir and chardonnay. Between then and 2000 he worked for Tarrawarra, Hardys, Rosemount, Petaluma and Virgin Hills. In '00 he became a partner and director of Master Winemakers, a significant contract winemaking business in the Yarra Valley. In early '07 Master Winemakers was acquired by Hardys/Accolade and Martin returned to academia and obtained a doctorate in medicinal chemistry from Monash University in '12. He returned to the wine world in '15 and is now chief winemaker for Tallarook, a winery that has had a chequered existence after the vineyard was planted in

1980. It was intended to be a feature of a Porsche racing event centre, the track on the 475ha property on which the vineyard is planted. In '17 it was acquired by the Yang family. Only a token amount of wine is sold in Australia, China taking the lion's share.

♀♀♀♀♀ Marsanne 2018 Hand-picked, crushed, chilled, wild fermentation of cloudy juice, 9 months' lees contact, sterile-filtered. The ability of marsanne to respond to maturation in tank has been proved many times by Tahbilk and will occur here. Lemon curd, spice and citrus will come together, providing a complex, long-lived wine. Screwcap. 13.5% alc. **Rating** 94 **To** 2030 $30 ✪

Roussanne 2018 The vinification is precisely the same as that of the Marsanne. This wine has slightly more mouthfeel and may reach its peak slightly earlier. It's all a game of pluses and minuses. Screwcap. 14.5% alc. **Rating** 94 **To** 2028 $30 ✪

♀♀♀♀♀ Chardonnay 2018 Rating 90 **To** 2025 $25

Taltarni   ★★★★★

339 Taltarni Road, Moonambel, Vic 3478 **Region** Pyrenees
T (03) 5459 7900 **www.**taltarni.com.au **Open** 7 days 11–5
Winemaker Robert Heywood, Peter Warr, Ben Howell **Est.** 1969 **Dozens** 80 000
Vyds 78.5ha

The American owner and founder of Clos du Val (Napa Valley), Taltarni and Clover Hill (see separate entry) has brought the management of these three businesses and Domaine de Nizas (Languedoc) under the one roof, the group known as Goelet Wine Estates. Taltarni is the largest of the Australian ventures, its estate vineyards of great value and underpinning the substantial annual production. Insectariums are established in permanent vegetation corridors, each containing around 2000 native plants that provide a pollen and nectar source for the beneficial insects, reducing the need for chemicals and other controls of the vineyards. In recent years Taltarni has updated its winemaking techniques and in '17 celebrated 40 years of winemaking. Exports to all major markets.

♀♀♀♀♀ Pyrenees Shiraz 2016 Fermented in small batches, whole bunch, 18 months in French oak barriques. Taltarni regards '16 as a 'great' vintage and the winemakers' labours have not been in vain. Aromas sing in a chorus that includes intense, saturated fruit and smart, well balanced oak. There's a savoury element lurking in the background of the palate, a bit of a tease really, that lifts on the finish. Enticing. Screwcap. 14% alc. **Rating** 97 **To** 2030 $40 JP ✪

♀♀♀♀♀ Old Vine Estate Pyrenees Cabernet Sauvignon 2017 From the initial block of cabernet planted in the late '60s. Fruit and shoot thinned to reduce yield, 15% whole bunches, the remainder crushed on top, 9 days on skins, 18 months in French barriques. Every decision from vine to wine exact. It has the concentration, depth and layered blackcurrant/black olive power that is typical of the Pyrenees. Screwcap. 13.5% alc. **Rating** 96 **To** 2042 $45 ✪

Old Vine Estate Pyrenees Shiraz 2018 Crushed into small open fermenters with a small percentage of whole bunches, 8 days on skins with pumpovers and header boards, matured for 18 months in French barriques (30% new). Deep colour and full-on black fruits plus a slice of licorice all contribute to this full-bodied wine from a small block of the first planting in the late '60s. Screwcap. 14.5% alc. **Rating** 95 **To** 2040 $45

Reserve Pyrenees Shiraz Cabernet 2016 Given 15 months in 40% new French oak barriques. Classic Aussie red blend comes up a treat with a bit of extra new oak attention. It's energising. Shiraz grabs the attention to start: blackcurrant, blueberry, sage, aniseed, chocolate rum ball. Cabernet smoothes the way on the palate with a leafy greenness and dusty, tobacco tones. Slight dip to close. Cork. 14.5% alc. **Rating** 95 **To** 2031 $75 JP

Pyrenees Shiraz 2018 Picked over 5 weeks, each parcel vinified separately. The inclusion of 11% mourvedre and 1% viognier adds an extra flow of aromas and flavours, as does fermentation and maturation in a mix of new and used barriques. Screwcap. 14.5% alc. **Rating** 94 **To** 2038 $40

Cabernets 2018 An open-fermented blend of 55% cabernet sauvignon, 40% merlot and 5% petit verdot, 85% taken to tank at the conclusion of fermentation, 15% held on skins for 6 weeks and finished in French oak (10% new). It's medium to full-bodied, but supple and well weighted with fruit; underlining the renaissance underway at Taltarni. Screwcap. 14.5% alc. **Rating** 94 **To** 2038 $26 ✪

Pyrenees Cabernet Sauvignon 2018 Rating 92 To 2038 $40
Cabernet Merlot Petit Verdot 2017 Rating 92 To 2027 $26
Methode Traditionnelle Sparkling Shiraz 2017 Rating 92 $26
Reserve Pyrenees Shiraz Cabernet 2018 Rating 91 To 2040 $75
Sangiovese 2017 Rating 91 To 2025 $26
Methode Traditionnelle Brut 2014 Rating 90 $26

Tamar Ridge | Pirie ★★★★★

1A Waldhorn Drive, Rosevears, Tas 7277 **Region** Northern Tasmania
T (03) 6330 0300 **www**.tamarridge.com.au **Open** 7 days 10–5
Winemaker Tom Wallace, Anthony De Amicas **Est.** 1994 **Dozens** 14 000 **Vyds** 130ha
Tamar Ridge has been owned by Brown Brothers since 2010, its vineyards of inestimable value on an island unable to meet more than a small part of demand from the Australian mainland. It is focusing its attention on pinot noir for table wine and – along with chardonnay – sparkling wine. It goes without saying that the 14 000 dozen production only accounts for a small part of the annual crop from 130ha. Exports to all major markets.

Tamar Ridge Single Block Pinot Noir 2017 Clone D4V2, destemmed, cold-soaked, matured for 12 months in French barriques (16% new). A very smart pinot that effortlessly ticks all the boxes. It's very complex, yet it's the fruit that emerges on top of the tannins and oak, which are relegated to support roles. Screwcap. 14% alc. **Rating** 97 **To** 2037 $100 ✪

Pirie Traditional Method 2013 With 57% chardonnay, 43% pinot noir; the blend spending 5 years on yeast lees. Still pale straw-green, which sends all the right signals of a beautifully fresh and elegant wine selling at a price that would give a cost accountant's mind lasting distress. Cork. 12% alc. **Rating** 95 $40

Pirie Traditional Method Rose 2016 Rating 93 $48
Tamar Ridge Sauvignon Blanc 2019 Rating 92 To 2021 $28
Tamar Ridge Reserve Pinot Noir 2018 Rating 92 To 2033 $65
Pirie Traditional Method NV Rating 92 $30
Tamar Ridge Pinot Gris 2018 Rating 90 To 2021 $28
Tamar Ridge Pinot Noir 2018 Rating 90 To 2030 $34
Tamar Ridge Research Series Pinot Noir 2017 Rating 90 To 2027 $50

Tapanappa ★★★★★

15 Spring Gully Road, Piccadilly, SA 5151 **Region** Adelaide Hills
T (08) 7324 5301 **www**.tapanappa.com.au **Open** Thurs–Mon 11–4
Winemaker Brian Croser **Est.** 2002 **Dozens** 2500 **Vyds** 16.7ha
Tapanappa was founded by Brian Croser in 2002. The word Tapanappa is probably derived from the local Aboriginal language and likely translates to 'stick to the path'. Through Tapanappa, Brian is continuing a career-long mission of matching the climate, soil and geology of distinguished sites to the right varieties, and then developing and managing the vineyards to optimise quality. Tapanappa is dedicated to producing unique 'wines of terroir' from its three distinguished sites in SA with its winery located in the heart of the Piccadilly Valley. The brand's components are the Whalebone Vineyard at Wrattonbully (planted to cabernet sauvignon, shiraz and merlot over 30 years ago), the Tiers Vineyard at Piccadilly in the Adelaide Hills (chardonnay) and the Foggy Hill Vineyard on the southern tip of the Fleurieu Peninsula (pinot noir). Exports to the UK, France, Sweden, the UAE, South Korea, Singapore, Hong Kong and China.

ㅜㅜㅜㅜㅜ **Tiers Vineyard Piccadilly Valley Chardonnay 2018** This is a spectacular chardonnay, eschewing malolactic in the name of precision and freshness, while sacrificing nothing in the way of flavour and textural detail by doing so. A reductive riff of gunflint segues to notes of white fig, honeydew melon, nectarine and creamed cashew. A chassis of mineral and bright acidity carry the flavours long and broad, chaperoned by high class oak that is nestled into the fray. This will age beautifully over the coming decade but oozes class and such poise already that it is difficult to refrain from opening a bottle. Screwcap. 13.6% alc. **Rating** 97 To 2030 $90 NG ✪

ㅜㅜㅜㅜ **Definitus Foggy Hill Parawa-Fleurieu Peninsula Pinot Noir 2018** I prefer this to the '17. More integrated, compact, layered and detailed. The tension, curtailing the ripe and inherently sweet fruit. The oak, tannic extract and judicious whole bunch amalgamating as a finely tuned structural skein, corralling the billowing sweet berry fruit, root spice and undergrowth scents. The finish long and generous, yet nothing overt. Cork. **Rating** 96 To 2030 $90 NG

Whalebone Vineyard Wrattonbully Cabernet Shiraz 2016 A very good example of the union between place and variety, the richness of the fruit flavours bringing blackcurrant and blackberry together. Then cigar box and polished tannins come into play on the perfectly balanced palate. Cork. 14.7% alc. **Rating** 96 To 2036 $55 ✪

Single Vineyard Eden Valley Riesling 2018 Pink grapefruit pulp, bath salts and lemon rind notes cascade along a gentle phenolic waft and juicy acid rails. This is ripe and luscious, eschewing contemporary trends towards earlier harvest windows and brittle acidity. At once pointed and richly flavoured. Finessed too, while boasting a real propulsion of flavours and textures. Mouthfilling, gratifying and very long. Screwcap. **Rating** 95 To 2027 $29 NG ✪

Whalebone Vineyard Wrattonbully Merlot Cabernet Franc 2016 A full-bodied red based on the quintessential Bordeaux Right Bank prototype, this is rich yet fresh, forceful yet somehow savoury. And while reflective of a warm, dry year manifest as salubrious dark fruit tones, bitter chocolate, mocha oak (20 months, 50% French) and thicker framed tannins than the norm, perhaps, they drag the flavours long. Textural. Delicious. **Rating** 95 To 2035 $90 NG

Piccadilly Valley Chardonnay 2018 The warm season is certainly reflected in this wine with honey, fig and even brulee, all finely balanced by citrussy acidity. Enjoyable drink-now style. Screwcap. 13.5% alc. **Rating** 94 To 2024 $39

Tiers Vineyard 1.5m Piccadilly Valley Chardonnay 2018 Brian Croser's ode to his halcyon youth when California first convinced him that high quality chardonnay was indeed possible outside of Burgundy. Mid-weighted with seams of toasty oak corralling ample stone fruit allusions, scents of toasted hazelnut and praline. This needs patience for the shins and elbows to settle. When they do, it will stun. **Rating** 94 To 2026 $55 NG

Foggy Hill Vineyard Fleurieu Peninsula Pinot Noir 2017 A broad patina of sous-bois, pickled cherry and fecund strawberry, aged judiciously in French oak (30%). Silky with a gentle rasp of herb-inflected tannins and saline maritime acidity. Cork. **Rating** 94 To 2024 $55 NG

Tar & Roses   ★★★★★

61 Vickers Lane, Nagambie, Vic 3608 **Region** Heathcote
T (03) 5794 1811 **www.tarandroses.com.au Open** 1st w'end each month 10–4
Winemaker Narelle King **Est.** 2006 **Dozens** 40 000

Tar & Roses produces wines inspired by the classic Mediterranean varietals and was named after the signature characteristics of nebbiolo. The name also ties back to the winemaking team behind the venture, the legendary Don Lewis and his winemaking partner Narelle King. Narelle is carrying on the Tar & Roses tradition after Don's passing in 2017. Exports to the UK, the US, Canada, Switzerland, Singapore, Japan, China and NZ.

 ♟♟♟♟♟ **Lewis Riesling 2019** The late Don Lewis was a superlative maker of riesling and in his time at Mitchelton fashioned some of Australia's best. His winemaking partner, Narelle King, produces a fine wine in homage with his signature-style striking aromatics: lime skin, spring blossom, grapefruit, leatherwood honey. A solid riesling profile drives the palate with citrus pith and peel, finishing with a ping of zingy acidity. Concentrated, yes, but there is a developing savouriness which is moreish. A keeper. Screwcap. 13% alc. **Rating** 95 **To** 2030 $24 JP ○

The Rose Heathcote Shiraz 2018 Poised yet powerful, The Rose goes for minimalist labelling, letting the wine do the talking. It speaks of the Heathcote soil, of blackberry concentrate but also of Central Victorian warmth and generosity. Dense and bold, sweet-fruited but with a dried herb, Aussie bush character – and just a smidge of eucalyptus – it sings with a strong voice. Screwcap. 14.5% alc. **Rating** 95 **To** 2032 $55 JP

Heathcote Tempranillo 2018 From a master tempranillo maker comes a wine that is very well suited to the dry summers of Heathcote. No problem with colour – deepest purple, almost black. No problem either with distinctive varietal indicators – dark cherries, red licorice, dried herbs. Fruit powers through the palate; fabulous balance and what lingering length. Screwcap. 14.2% alc. **Rating** 95 **To** 2030 $24 JP ○

 ♟♟♟♟♀ **Heathcote Sangiovese 2018 Rating** 93 **To** 2028 $24 JP ○
Heathcote Nebbiolo 2017 Rating 93 **To** 2032 $50 JP
Pinot Grigio 2019 Rating 90 **To** 2025 $18 JP ○
Heathcote Rose 2019 Rating 90 **To** 2025 $30 JP
Heathcote Shiraz 2018 Rating 90 **To** 2026 $22 JP
Prosecco NV Rating 90 $25 JP

Tarrahill.   ★★★★★

340 Old Healesville Road, Yarra Glen, Vic 3775 **Region** Yarra Valley
T (03) 9730 1152 **www**.tarrahill.com **Open** By appt
Winemaker Jonathan Hamer, Geof Fethers **Est.** 1992 **Dozens** 700 **Vyds** 6.5ha
Owned by former Mallesons Lawyers partner Jonathan Hamer and wife Andrea, a former doctor and daughter of Ian Hanson, who made wine for many years under the Hanson-Tarrahill label. Ian had a 0.8ha vineyard at Lower Plenty but needed 2ha to obtain a vigneron's licence. In 1990 the Hamers purchased a property in the Yarra Valley and planted the requisite vines (pinot noir – ultimately destroyed by the 2009 bushfires). Jonathan and company director friend Geof Fethers worked weekends in the vineyard and in '04 decided that they would undertake a wine science degree (at CSU); they graduated in '11. In '12 Jonathan retired from law and planted more vines (cabernet sauvignon, cabernet franc, merlot, malbec and petit verdot) and Ian (aged 86) retired from winemaking. Andrea has also contributed with a second degree (horticulture); she is a biodynamics advocate.

 ♟♟♟♟♟ **Le Savant Cabernets 2017** Despite the label, this is in fact 100% cabernet sauvignon. Despite the lower price of its '18 sibling, this has better mouthfeel and flavour, the fruit fractionally riper. Screwcap. 13.8% alc. **Rating** 94 **To** 2040 $42

 ♟♟♟♟♀ **Chardonnay 2018 Rating** 92 **To** 2026 $30
Le Savant Cabernets 2018 Rating 91 **To** 2038 $50
Le Batard 2017 Rating 90 **To** 2047 $30

TarraWarra Estate   ★★★★★

311 Healesville-Yarra Glen Road, Yarra Glen, Vic 3775 **Region** Yarra Valley
T (03) 5962 3311 **www**.tarrawarra.com.au **Open** Tues–Sun 11–5
Winemaker Clare Halloran, Adam McCallum **Est.** 1983 **Dozens** 12000 **Vyds** 26.42ha
TarraWarra is, and always has been, one of the top-tier wineries in the Yarra Valley. Founded by Marc Besen AO and wife Eva, it has operated on the basis that quality is paramount, cost a secondary concern. The creation of the TarraWarra Museum of Art (twma.com.au) in a

purpose-built building provides another reason to visit; indeed, many visitors come specifically to look at the ever-changing displays in the Museum. Changes in the vineyard include the planting of shiraz and merlot, and in the winery, the creation of a four-tier range: a deluxe MDB label made in tiny quantities and only when the vintage permits; the single vineyard range; a Reserve range; and the 100% estate-grown varietal range. Exports to France, Vietnam and China.

ŢŢŢŢŢ Reserve Yarra Valley Pinot Noir 2018 H Block MV6 planted in '83 and I Block D5V12 planted in '89; matured for 10 months in French oak (10% new). By some length, the most convincing and complex of the Tarrawarra pinots. Screwcap. 13.8% alc. **Rating** 96 **To** 2029 $70 ◐

Yarra Valley Chardonnay 2018 An eclectic mix of clones; hand-picked, whole-bunch pressed, 50% fermented in tank, 50% in oak of various sizes, forests and toasts, no mlf. Good mouthfeel; balance of stone fruits, apple and grapefruit; oak subtly balanced. Screwcap. 13.2% alc. **Rating** 95 **To** 2028 $30 ◐

Yarra Valley Barbera 2018 A single clone of barbera was grafted in '11 onto vines planted in '89. Well, well. I'm surprised and, even more, impressed by the quality and sheer drinkability of this wine. Crossflow filtration has made the colour and clarity a pleasure to behold and also freshened the flavours. Screwcap. 14% alc. **Rating** 95 **To** 2030 $30 ◐

Reserve Yarra Valley Chardonnay 2018 Hand-picked, whole-bunch pressed, wild-fermented in French oak (25% new), no additions of any kind except SO_2. Not as fresh as the Estate but has complexity and depth. Screwcap. 13% alc. **Rating** 94 **To** 2030 $50

I Block Yarra Valley Pinot Noir 2018 I Block was planted in '89 to D5V12 clone; matured for 10 months in French oak (10% new). Bright, clear crimson; as fresh as a daisy, long finish. Screwcap. 13.7% alc. **Rating** 94 **To** 2032 $45

ŢŢŢŢŢ Yarra Valley Roussanne Marsanne Viognier 2019 Rating 93 **To** 2022 $35
Yarra Valley Pinot Noir 2018 Rating 93 **To** 2030 $30
J Block Yarra Valley Shiraz 2017 Rating 92 **To** 2025 $40

 # Tasmanian Vintners

PO Box 1085, Rosny Park, Tas 7018 **Region** Southern Tasmania
T (03) 6232 9400 **www.**tasvintners.wine **Open** Not
Winemaker Liam McElhinney, Pat Colombo **Est.** 2019 **Dozens** NFP
Tasmanian Vintners (TV) is a joint company owned 50/50% by Tasmanian businessman Rod Roberts and the Fogarty Wine Group which acquired the assets of Winemaking Tasmania from the administrator of that business. TV will continue to process grapes and wine for a broad range of smaller Tasmanian producers, and also buy their excess fruit and assist them to market their wines. TV is well set up for small-batch production with Liam McElhinney as winemaker and responsible for business operation. Fogarty Wine Group (in its own right) has a number of other rapidly developing major projects in Tasmania.

ŢŢŢŢŢ Terra Verde Chardonnay 2018 Hand-picked, each vineyard parcel whole-berry pressed, sequentially filled into French oak and wild-fermented. The breadth of the individual components, and further maturation on lees for 9 months, has made a fine and elegant wine. It is incredibly youthful now but with years to go to reach its best. Screwcap. 13% alc. **Rating** 95 **To** 2030 $50

Pinot Noir Rose 2018 The semi-cryptic background notes disclose the pinot noir base but gave little else away. The depth of the colour underlines skin contact and the wine is bone-dry. It's in another league from mainstream rose, deliberately built from the word go. Screwcap. 12.5% alc. **Rating** 95 **To** 2022 $25 ◐

Anon Riesling 2018 Mainstream Tasmanian acidity provides the structure and texture for the intense, unsweetened citrus juice, pith and zest flavours. 'Refreshing' doesn't pay the wine its dues. Screwcap. 12.5% alc. **Rating** 94 **To** 2028 $25 ◐

Terra Verde Pinot Noir 2017 From 11 different vineyards in 6 distinct districts. A complex bouquet with wisps of wood and meat morphing into spice. Has good

length and balance, the varietal portrait precise. Screwcap. 13.5% alc. **Rating** 94
To 2027 $50

⚟ **Anon Pinot Gris 2018** Rating 90 To 2021 $25

Tatachilla   ★★★★

151 Main Road, McLaren Vale, SA 5171 **Region** McLaren Vale
T (08) 8563 7000 **www.**tatachillawines.com.au **Open** Not
Winemaker Jeremy Ottawa **Est.** 1903 **Dozens** 43000 **Vyds** 12.4ha
Tatachilla was reborn in 1995 but has had a tumultuous history going back to 1903. Between
then and '61 the winery was owned by Penfolds; it was closed in '61 and reopened in '65 as
the Southern Vales Co-operative. In the late '80s it was purchased and renamed The Vales but
did not flourish; in '93 it was purchased by local grower Vic Zerella and former Kaiser Stuhl
chief executive Keith Smith. After extensive renovations, the winery was officially reopened
in '95 and won a number of tourist awards and accolades. It became part of Banksia Wines in
2001, in turn acquired by Lion Nathan in '02. In '17 it (along with all wine brands owned by
Lion Nathan) was acquired by Accolade. Exports to all major markets.

Taylor Ferguson   ★★★★☆

Level 1, 62 Albert Street, Preston, Vic 3072 (postal) **Region** South Eastern Australia
T (03) 9487 2599 **www.**alepat.com.au **Open** Not
Winemaker Nick Conolly **Est.** 1996 **Dozens** 40000
Taylor Ferguson is the indirect descendant of a business of that name established in Melbourne
in 1892. A connecting web joined it with Alexander & Paterson in '92 and the much more
recent distribution business of Alepat Taylor formed in 1996. The Taylor Ferguson wines
use grapes sourced from various regions around Australia, predominantly from Coonawarra,
Langhorne Creek, Riverina and McLaren Vale. Exports to Germany, Iraq, Singapore, Malaysia,
Vietnam, Taiwan and China.

⚟ **Fernando the First Barossa Cabernet Sauvignon 2016** A medium-bodied
cabernet with positive varietal character courtesy of cassis/blackcurrant flavours
complexed by oak. The tannins expected of the variety are soft but do extend the
finish. Drink sooner than later. Cork. 14% alc. **Rating** 90 **To** 2026 $45

Taylors   ★★★★★

Taylors Road, Auburn, SA 5451 **Region** Clare Valley
T (08) 8849 1111 **www.**taylorswines.com.au **Open** Mon–Fri 9–5, w'ends 10–4
Winemaker Adam Eggins, Phillip Reschke, Chad Bowman **Est.** 1969 **Dozens** 250000
Vyds 400ha
The family-founded and owned Taylors continues to flourish and expand – its vineyards are
now by far the largest holding in the Clare Valley. There have also been changes in terms of
the winemaking team and the wine style and quality, particularly through the outstanding
St Andrews range. With each passing vintage, Taylors is managing to do for the Clare Valley
what Peter Lehmann did for the Barossa Valley. Recent entries in international wine shows
have resulted in a rich haul of trophies and gold medals for wines at all price points. A
founding member of Australia's First Families of Wine. Exports (under the Wakefield brand
due to trademark reasons) to all major markets.

⚟ **The Visionary Exceptional Parcel Release Clare Valley Cabernet
Sauvignon 2015** The extraction regime here is apt given the varietal code
we are dealing with: cabernet and its unfettered structural mettle. Extended skin
contact and malolactic in barrel evinces both authority and a creamy palate-feel.
Then, cabernet's potpourri of herb-doused tannins mingle with currant, olive and
graphite to pencil lead scents. Following 12 months in new French wood, a barrel-
by-barrel selection was made. The result is both salubrious and persuasive. More so
than the shiraz. Screwcap. **Rating** 94 **To** 2033 $200 NG

ŸŸŸŸŸ St Andrews Clare Valley Chardonnay 2018 Rating 93 To 2024 $40 NG
Jaraman Clare Valley McLaren Vale Shiraz 2018 Rating 93 To 2026
$30 NG
The Pioneer Exceptional Parcel Release Clare Valley Shiraz 2015
Rating 93 To 2033 $200 NG
St Andrews Clare Valley Cabernet Sauvignon 2017 Rating 93 To 2028
$70 NG
St Andrews Clare Valley Shiraz 2017 Rating 92 To 2025 $70 NG
St Andrews Clare Valley Riesling 2019 Rating 91 To 2027 $40 NG
Clare Valley Riesling 2019 Rating 91 To 2025 $20 NG ✪
Adelaide Hills Sauvignon Blanc 2019 Rating 91 To 2020 $20 NG ✪
Reserve Parcel Clare Valley Shiraz 2018 Rating 91 To 2024 $25 NG
Clare Valley Pinot Gris 2019 Rating 90 To 2021 $20 NG ✪
Clare Valley Shiraz 2018 Rating 90 To 2023 $19 NG ✪
Clare Valley McLaren Vale Tempranillo 2018 Rating 90 To 2022
$19 NG ✪

Telera

PO Box 299, Red Hill South, Vic 3937 **Region** Mornington Peninsula
T 0407 041 719 **www.**telera.com.au **Open** By appt
Winemaker Michael Telera **Est.** 2006 **Dozens** 45 **Vyds** 0.4ha
Michael Telera learnt his trade from nine vintages at Dr George Mihaly's Paradigm Hill
winery at Merricks. He makes pinot noir and sauvignon blanc from a small leased vineyard
at Red Hill, and shiraz sourced from other growers on the Peninsula. He plans to plant more
pinot noir at the leased property, making the total 20 rows of pinot noir and nine rows of
sauvignon blanc; production is increased with small amounts of contract-grown fruit.

ŸŸŸŸŸ Su Mar Mornington Peninsula Pinot Noir 2018 Clones 115 and 777, wild
yeast–open fermented, matured for 18 months in French barriques (25% new).
Light-bodied but fresh, juicy red fruits lead to a spicy finish. Screwcap. 14% alc.
Rating 93 To 2026 $50

ŸŸŸŸ Pernella Fume Sauvignon Blanc 2019 Rating 89 To 2020 $25
Itana Fume Sauvignon Blanc 2018 Rating 89 To 2020 $35
Pernella Fume Sauvignon Blanc 2018 Rating 89 To 2020 $25

Tellurian

408 Tranter Road, Toolleen, Vic 3551 **Region** Heathcote
T 0431 004 766 **www.**tellurianwines.com.au **Open** W'ends 11–4.30 or by appt
Winemaker Tobias Ansted **Est.** 2002 **Dozens** 7000 **Vyds** 21.87ha
The vineyard is situated on the western side of Mt Camel at Toolleen, on the red Cambrian
soil that has made Heathcote one of the foremost regions in Australia for the production of
shiraz (Tellurian means 'of the earth'). Viticultural consultant Tim Brown not only supervises
the Tellurian estate plantings, but also works closely with the growers of grapes purchased
under contract for Tellurian. Further Rhône red and white varieties were planted on the
Tellurian property in 2011. Exports to Canada, Singapore and China.

ŸŸŸŸŸ Block 3 SR Heathcote Shiraz 2017 Destemmed and fermented in used 5000l
French oak vats, 14 days on skins with pneumatic plunging twice daily, matured
for 18 months in barriques and demi-muids (40% new). The 3 short rows of the
vineyard produce an elegant, well balanced wine. There is little or no oak and/
or tannin dive-bombing the palate, as some of the Tellurian wines seek to do.
Screwcap. 14.5% alc. Rating 95 To 2030 $44
Tranter Heathcote Shiraz 2017 Destemmed, fermented in stainless steel and
plastic fermenters, wild-fermented, 12–15 days on skins, with hand or pneumatic
plunging, matured in French oak (25% new) for 18 months. The supple, medium-
bodied wine delivers its message of purple and black fruits. Totally delicious,

its length and aftertaste wholly impressive. Screwcap. 14.5% alc. Rating 95
To 2030 $42

Block 3 TLR Heathcote Shiraz 2016 Top of the Long Rows (TLR);
destemmed and fermented in stainless steel–lined concrete, matured for 18 months
in larger format French oak (30% new). A rich, layered medium to full-bodied
palate with sufficient balance to warrant the extended cellaring needed to soften
its expressions. Screwcap. 14.5% alc. Rating 94 To 2036 $44

GSM Heathcote Grenache Shiraz Mourvedre 2018 A 46/36/18% blend,
each variety vinified separately. The colour is excellent. Like all the Tellurian reds,
it takes no prisoners, but the numbers (14.5% alcohol, 5.8g/l acidity, 3.65 pH)
suggest the incisive fruit flavours will settle down well. Screwcap. Rating 94
To 2030 $29 ⊙

🍷🍷🍷🍷🍷 **Heathcote Marsanne 2018** Rating 93 To 2028 $29
Block 3 TLR Heathcote Shiraz 2017 Rating 93 To 2030 $44
Heathcote Nero d'Avola 2018 Rating 93 To 2028 $29
Tranter Heathcote Shiraz 2016 Rating 92 To 2030 $40
Heathcote Fiano 2019 Rating 91 To 2023 $29
Pastiche Heathcote Shiraz 2018 Rating 90 To 2038 $29

Temple Bruer   ★★★★

689 Milang Road, Angas Plains, SA 5255 **Region** Langhorne Creek
T (08) 8537 0203 **www.**templebruer.com.au **Open** Mon–Fri 9.30–4.30
Winemaker Kate Wall, Verity Cowley **Est.** 1980 **Dozens** 35 000 **Vyds** 123ha
Temple Bruer was in the vanguard of the organic movement in Australia and was the focal
point for the formation of Organic Vignerons Australia. Part of the production from its estate
vineyards is used for its own label, part sold. Owner David Bruer also has a vine propagation
nursery, likewise run on an organic basis. Temple Bruer has 40ha of vineyards in Langhorne
Creek, 59ha in Eden Valley, and 24ha in the Riverland (Loxton and Moorook). Exports to the
UK, the US, Canada, Sweden, Japan and China.

🍷🍷🍷🍷🍷 **Organic Preservative Free Shiraz 2019** Riverland/Fleurieu. The best wine
they've produced under this label. It's sweet, soft and seductive but it has good
oomph, plush mouthfeel and tastes downright delicious. Screwcap. 14.5% alc.
Rating 92 To 2022 $22 CM ⊙

The Agonist Shiraz Mataro 2018 A supple red with choc-orange, peppercorn
and plum flavours swinging both amiably and confidently through the palate.
Concentration is good, so too is mouthfeel. Indeed the soft creaminess of this
wine will be enjoyed by many. Screwcap. 14% alc. Rating 91 To 2024 $35 CM

Organic Preservative Free Grenache Shiraz 2019 Licorice and redcurrant,
hay and a sweet tobacco–like character. It has volume and personality. It's not
particularly long-flavoured but it's not short, and it has much going for it.
Screwcap. 13.6% alc. Rating 91 To 2023 $20 CM ⊙

Eden Valley Riesling 2019 There's a smidgen of sweetness to this release and it
works a treat. Orange and sweet lime flavours rush attractively through the palate.
Not hard to like. Screwcap. 11% alc. Rating 90 To 2024 $22 CM

🍷🍷🍷🍷 **Organic Preservative Free Cabernet Sauvignon Merlot 2019** Rating 89
To 2025 $22 CM

Tempus Two Wines   ★★★★

Cnr Broke Road/McDonalds Road, Pokolbin, NSW 2320 **Region** Hunter Valley
T (02) 4993 3999 **www.**tempustwo.com.au **Open** 7 days 10–5
Winemaker Andrew Duff **Est.** 1997 **Dozens** 270 000 **Vyds** 120ha
Tempus Two is a mix of Latin (Tempus means time) and English. It has been a major success
story: production was just 6000 dozen in 1997 with sales increasing by over 140% in the
last 5 years. Its cellar door and restaurant complex (including the Oishii Japanese restaurant)

are situated in a striking building. The design polarises opinion; I like it. Exports to all major markets.

🍷🍷🍷🍷🍷 **Pewter Barossa Valley Shiraz 2018** This has flow. Some bourbon-vanillan scented oak melds effortlessly with the mulberry, tapenade and peppery notes. Lilac florals too. The acidity, juicy rather than hard, cleans up the back end. Screwcap. **Rating** 91 **To** 2028 NG

Pewter Coonawarra Cabernet Sauvignon 2017 Single vineyard, matured in unspecified oak for 15 months. Light but bright colour. A fresh, fruit forward style with cassis and dried herbs. The tannins are fine, the oak likewise (it is likely all used). Screwcap. 13.5% alc. **Rating** 91 **To** 2027 $45

Ten Minutes by Tractor ★★★★★

1333 Mornington-Flinders Road, Main Ridge, Vic 3928 **Region** Mornington Peninsula
T (03) 5989 6455 **www**.tenminutesbytractor.com.au **Open** 7 days 11–5
Winemaker Imogen Dillon, Martin Spedding **Est.** 1999 **Dozens** 12 000 **Vyds** 38.3ha

Ten Minutes by Tractor is owned by Martin and Karen Spedding. It was established in 1997 with three Main Ridge vineyards – McCutcheon, Judd and Wallis – all located within a ten-minute tractor ride from each other. Three vineyards have been added since: a recently replanted high-density vineyard at the cellar door and restaurant site (organically certified in 2004), the Coolart Road Vineyard in the north of the Peninsula, and the Main Ridge Spedding Vineyard, a high-density (12 120 vines/ha) pinot noir vineyard planted in '16. The wines are released in three ranges: 10X, made from a number of estate-managed vineyards on the Mornington Peninsula; Estate, a reserve level blend; and Single Vineyard, from the best performing vineyard sites, usually a single block. In February 2018, a fire destroyed the main storage facility at the cellar door and restaurant site, with over 16 000 bottles of wine lost (including a treasured collection acquired across 20 years for the restaurant cellar). The site was rebuilt, including a new private dining room and underground cellar for the restaurant, as well as a private cellar door tasting room and wine gallery. The gallery (due to open in late '20) will include many items from the Speddings' wine history collection and will tell the story of the development of the wine industry in the Mornington Peninsula and the rest of Victoria. Exports to the UK, Canada, Scandinavia, Eastern Europe, Hong Kong and China.

🍷🍷🍷🍷🍷 **McCutcheon Mornington Peninsula Chardonnay 2018** Hand-picked 18 Mar, standard wild-yeast fermentation of unsettled juice, 91% mlf (effectively total), 40% new French oak. Stands out for the energy and drive of the fruit: grapefruit in the lead, towing white peach and Granny Smith apple fruit flavours. Has made light work of the oak. Screwcap. 13% alc. **Rating** 96 **To** 2033 $68 ✪

Wallis Mornington Peninsula Chardonnay 2018 Hand-picked 8 Mar, standard fermentation procedure, 64% mlf, 38% new French oak. All the single vineyard wines were bottled 18 Dec. This has both depth and weight, white peach/nectarine first up, citrussy acidity drawing out the long finish. Screwcap. 13% alc. **Rating** 96 **To** 2033 $68 ✪

10X Mornington Peninsula Pinot Gris 2017 Pinot gris loves the Peninsula and the feeling is mutual in wines such as this which explore a finer, quieter, deeper side to the grape's personality. It demands attention. Oyster grit, rock pool maritime influences, green apple, nougat. So delicate on the palate, almost talcy, honeysuckle, pear compote and that bright acidity – so cleansing. Complexity rising and ready to go on a bit of a journey in the bottle. Screwcap. 13.5% alc. **Rating** 96 **To** 2028 $28 JP ✪

Coolart Road Mornington Peninsula Pinot Noir 2018 Standard Ten Minutes by Tractor vinification: hand-picked, 15% whole bunches, the balance destemmed, wild yeast, 25–30 days on skins, matured in French barriques (17% new) for 11 months, the shortest ever hang time (budbust-harvest) of 179 days against an average of 203. The colour is bright and clear; highly aromatic red fruits and spices on the bouquet and palate. Screwcap. 14% alc. **Rating** 96 **To** 2030 $78

Wallis Mornington Peninsula Pinot Noir 2018 Standard vinification, but here the impact of 25% new oak is obvious on both the bouquet and palate. Throughout the 4 pinots it's clear that the shortest ever time between budburst and harvest has cut back the amount of core fruit flavours, increasing savoury nuances across the range. Screwcap. 13.5% alc. **Rating** 96 **To** 2030 $78

Judd Mornington Peninsula Chardonnay 2018 Hand-picked 20 Mar, whole-bunch pressed, wild-fermented, 37% mlf, matured in French oak (25% new). As with all the Ten Minutes by Tractor wines, higher alcohol than the '17s is reflected in the initial mouthfeel, changing gears to gather pace on the finish. Screwcap. 14% alc. **Rating** 95 **To** 2030 $68

10X Mornington Peninsula Chardonnay 2017 Excellent vintage conditions in '17 certainly delivered some super smart Peninsula chardonnay. In the hands of a trusted maker, quality soared offering a regional chardonnay masterclass. Nectarines, white peach, melon, grapefruit, citrus and background oak all hum. Rounded, seamless division of fruit and oak, fine-textured all the way. Screwcap. 13% alc. **Rating** 95 **To** 2031 $30 JP ✪

Judd Mornington Peninsula Pinot Noir 2018 Nearly identical vinification to its siblings except this has 17% new oak and 10% whole bunches. Spice and wild strawberry. Oak contributes more to the mouthfeel and flow, rather than distracting. Screwcap. 13.5% alc. **Rating** 95 **To** 2028 $78

Estate Mornington Peninsula Chardonnay 2018 Incorporated parts from all vineyards. Hand-picked, whole-bunch pressed, unsettled juice wild-fermented, 9 months' maturation in barrel, a significant variation in the percentage of new oak. The 62% mlf lays the foundation for fleshy stone fruit/melon flavours. Screwcap. 13.5% alc. **Rating** 94 **To** 2026 $48

Estate Mornington Peninsula Pinot Noir 2018 Comprises 70% from Coolart Road, 12% Wallis, 7% Spedding, 6% Judd and 5% McCutcheon vineyards. Hand-picked, 0–20% whole bunches depending on the batch, 25–30 days on skins, 21% new oak for 11 months. An aromatic bouquet with plum joining red berries. Screwcap. 13.5% alc. **Rating** 94 **To** 2027 $48

10X Mornington Peninsula Pinot Noir 2017 Belies the cooler '17 vintage to deliver a well rounded wine of some panache. Tomato leaf and gently sappy on the nose opening to a chorus of earthy, dusty beets and red berries that fills the mouth. Fine, chalky tannins bring a savoury edge. Screwcap. 13% alc. **Rating** 94 **To** 2025 $34 JP

🍷🍷🍷🍷🍷 **10X Mornington Peninsula Rose 2018** **Rating** 91 **To** 2023 $28 JP

Terra Felix ★★★★☆

52 Paringa Road, Red Hill South, Vic 3937 (postal) **Region** Central Victoria zone **T** 0419 539 108 **www.terrafelix.com.au** **Open** Not

Winemaker Willy Lunn **Est.** 2001 **Dozens** 12 000 **Vyds** 8ha

Long-term industry stalwart Peter Simon has built on the estate plantings of pinot noir (5ha) and chardonnay (2ha) through purchases from Coonawarra, McLaren Vale, Barossa Valley, Langhorne Creek, Yarra Valley and Strathbogie Ranges. Terra Felix exports 70% of its production to the US, Nepal, Hong Kong and China.

🍷🍷🍷🍷🍷 **Reserve Mornington Peninsula Pinot Noir 2018** While the bouquet promises sweet cherries, cedar/menthol, orange peel and crushed coriander, the palate doesn't follow through convincingly. Sweet-sour fruits, especially cranberry and pomegranate with lemony acidity, but it opens up to offer some refreshment. Screwcap. 13.4% alc. **Rating** 92 **To** 2026 $60 JF

🍷🍷🍷🍷 **Yarra Valley Cabernet Sauvignon 2017** **Rating** 89 **To** 2027 $50 JF

Terra Riche

153 Jones Road, Mount Barker, WA 6234 **Region** Mount Barker
T 0432 312 918 **www.**terrarichewines.com.au **Open** Not
Winemaker Coby Ladwig, Luke Eckersley **Est.** 2017 **Dozens** 10000 **Vyds** 15ha
Luke Eckersley and Coby Ladwig are two of the most experienced winemakers in the
Great Southern. In various ways, and for various businesses, they have demonstrated their
winemaking skills again and again. Terra Riche brings a third partner into the structure of
this new business – Hong Chenggen (known as Ken) owns a Shanghai-based wine importing
business, supplying to all cities throughout mainland China. Hitherto, his business has been
focused on WA wines. Becoming a partner in Terra Riche puts the business in an enviable
position. The quality of the wines made for the first releases is excellent, typical of Coby and
Luke's skills. The wines come in four ranges: Birds of Paint, Endgame, War of the Roses
and Southern Navigator. Exports to Vietnam, Taiwan and China.

🍷🍷🍷🍷🍷 **Endgame the Rook Great Southern Riesling 2019** Strange that there
was no Terra Riche riesling tasted last year, possibly the Chinese shareholder
influence – riesling is yet to gain a significant hold in China. Either way, this is a
high class riesling with effortless power and length to the pure lime juice flavours.
Screwcap. 12.8% alc. **Rating** 96 **To** 2034 $35 ✪
Birds of Paint Catcher Series Pemberton Chardonnay 2018 Chilled
before vinification, fermented in French oak (30% new), 15% wild yeast,
85% cultured yeast, matured for 9 months. Elegant, but with power and
complexity to the waves of fruit on the palate. Screwcap. 13.6% alc. **Rating** 95
To 2027 $40
Endgame The Rook Great Southern Shiraz 2018 60% from Mount Barker,
40% Frankland River. Destemmed whole berries open-fermented, 5 days' cold
soak, 19-day ferment, matured in French oak (30% new) for 12 months. Unusually
rich and plush black fruits, cedar, dark chocolate. Will flourish with extended
cellaring. Screwcap. 14.5% alc. **Rating** 95 **To** 2043 $40
Birds of Paint Catcher Series Mount Barker Shiraz 2017 Machine-
harvested, whole berry–open fermented, 5 days' cold soak, 17-day ferment,
matured in French oak (35% new) for 14 months. High class wine, juicy red and
black cherry fruits with a sprinkling of spice and cracked pepper, the tannins fine
and balanced. Screwcap. 14% alc. **Rating** 95 **To** 2047 $40
Endgame the Rook Great Southern Cabernet Sauvignon 2018 Whole-
berry fermented, 42 days on skins, (6 cold soak, 22 fermentation, 14 post-ferment).
The extreme length of the time on skins can come back to bite you, but not
here. It's still a masculine cabernet and will match best with maximum protein.
Screwcap. 14.5% alc. **Rating** 94 **To** 2038 $40

🍷🍷🍷🍷🍸 **Endgame the Rook Pemberton Chardonnay 2019 Rating** 93 **To** 2030 $40
Endgame Victory Frankland River Cabernet Sauvignon 2018 Rating 93
To 2043 $60
Birds of Paint Catcher Series Mount Barker Cabernet Sauvignon 2017
Rating 92 **To** 2040 $40
Endgame Victory Pemberton Pinot Noir 2019 Rating 90 **To** 2029 $60

Terre à Terre

PO Box 273, Crafers, SA 5152 **Region** Wrattonbully/Adelaide Hills
T 0400 700 447 **www.**terreaterre.com.au **Open** At Tapanappa
Winemaker Xavier Bizot **Est.** 2008 **Dozens** 4000 **Vyds** 16ha
It would be hard to imagine two better credentialled owners than Xavier Bizot (son of the
late Christian Bizot of Bollinger fame) and wife Lucy Croser (daughter of Brian and Ann
Croser). 'Terre à terre' is a French expression meaning down to earth. The close-planted
vineyard is on a limestone ridge, adjacent to Tapanappa's Whalebone Vineyard. The vineyard
area has increased, leading to increased production (the plantings include cabernet sauvignon,
sauvignon blanc, cabernet franc and shiraz). In 2015, Terre à Terre secured the fruit from

one of the oldest vineyards in the Adelaide Hills, the Summertown Vineyard, which will see greater quantities of Daosa and a Piccadilly Valley pinot noir. Wines are released under the Terre à Terre, Down to Earth, Sacrebleu and Daosa labels. Exports to the UK, Singapore, Taiwan and Hong Kong.

Daosa Blanc de Blancs 2015 From the Bizot Vineyard planted '95–96; hand-picked, whole-bunch pressed, primary ferment and mlf carried out in 'old' French barriques, matured for 23 months. Tiraged in bottle for 30 months before disgorged Aug '19 with a dosage of 7g/l. Bright straw-green. It's very elegant, very long and superbly balanced. Xavier Bizot says, 'This is by far the best vintage of our Blanc de Blancs'. Diam. 12.5% alc. **Rating** 97 $90 ❂

Down to Earth Sauvignon Blanc 2019 Hand-picked, part whole-bunch pressed, 40% fermented in large foudres and demi-muids, the balance crushed and destemmed and cool-fermented in stainless steel. The bouquet and palate hunt together as one; stone fruit and citrus neatly trimmed by fresh acidity. Distinctive style. Screwcap. 13.5% alc. **Rating** 96 **To** 2024 $26 ❂

Crayeres Vineyard Wrattonbully Sauvignon Blanc 2018 Hand-picked, whole-bunch pressed, cool-fermented in 600l demi-muids for 10 days, then left on lees for 10 months. It is all about texture and structure, and emphatically not about tropical fruit. Made to be consumed with food. Screwcap. 13.1% alc. **Rating** 95 **To** 2025 $40

Crayeres Vineyard Wrattonbully Sauvignon Blanc 2017 Hand-picked, the juice cold-settled for 2 months (others might use 4 days or less), fermented in large old demi-muids before 8 months' maturation. It's way left of centre but has undoubted complexity and personality. I enjoyed it. Screwcap. 12.9% alc. **Rating** 95 **To** 2025 $40

Crayeres Vineyard Reserve 2016 Made with 68% cabernet sauvignon, 16% each of shiraz and cabernet franc. Fermented in closed (Potter) fermenters, thence to French barriques (44% new) for 11 months, the varieties then blended and matured for a further 17 months in 4000l French foudres. A highly textured wine with a cedary subtext to the polished mix of purple and black fruits. Cork. 14.5% alc. **Rating** 95 **To** 2036 $90

Piccadilly Rose 2019 Uses 70% pinot noir/30% chardonnay made from the pressings ex a sparkling wine – a reverse saignee that had a very complex elevage and more than fulfilled the expectations had for it. Seriously good rose. Screwcap. 12.5% alc. **Rating** 94 **To** 2021 $32

Daosa Piccadilly Valley Natural Reserve NV Rating 93 $45

Tertini Wines ★★★★★

Kells Creek Road, Mittagong, NSW 2575 **Region** Southern Highlands
T (02) 4878 5213 **www.**tertiniwines.com.au **Open** 7 days 10–5
Winemaker Jonathan Holgate **Est.** 2000 **Dozens** 5500 **Vyds** 7.9ha

When Julian Tertini began the development of Tertini Wines in 2000, he followed in the footsteps of Joseph Vogt 145 years earlier. History does not relate the degree of success that Joseph had, but the site he chose then was, as it is now, a good one. Tertini has pinot noir and riesling (1.8ha each), cabernet sauvignon and chardonnay (1ha each), arneis (0.9ha), pinot gris (0.8ha), merlot (0.4ha) and lagrein (0.2ha). Winemaker Jonathan Holgate, who is responsible for the outstanding results achieved at Tertini, presides over High Range Vintners, a contract winemaking business also owned by Julian Tertini. Exports to Asia.

Tasmania Pinot Noir 2018 Clear crimson-purple; the bouquet is fragrant and filled with red fruits and spices; the light to medium-bodied palate supple and pure. The oak is subdued, red and black cherries framed by fine tannins. Trophies for Best Tasmanian Pinot Noir and Best Australian Pinot Noir at the Australian Pinot Noir Challenge '19. Screwcap. 13.5% alc. **Rating** 97 **To** 2030 $60 ❂

ŶŶŶŶŶ Yaraandoo Vineyard Riesling 2018 Wastes no time in establishing its lime and
Meyer lemon fruit, which are fleshy but dry. Acidity of 7.8g/l is the engine room
of a wine with power and elegance and a lingering finish. Screwcap. 12.4% alc.
Rating 95 To 2030 $33 ✪

Tasmania Chardonnay 2018 A bracing wine with minerally acidity more
obvious than the chemical analysis would suggest. Picked in the early morning,
pressed direct to barrel, no mlf or batonnage. Its purity won it the top gold medal
at the International Cool Climate Wine Show '19. I think it needs to loosen its
purse strings a little. Screwcap. 13% alc. **Rating** 94 **To** 2028 $60

Hilltops Cabernet Sauvignon 2018 Open-fermented, plunged twice-daily,
matured in French oak (20% new) for 9 months. A juicy, cassis-filled cabernet
with ripe tannins and cedary oak adding texture and structure to an already good
wine. Screwcap. 13.7% alc. **Rating** 94 **To** 2030 $29 ✪

ŶŶŶŶŶ Yaraandoo Vineyard Pinot Noir 2018 **Rating** 93 **To** 2030 $40
**Private Cellar Collection Southern Highlands Refosco dal Peduncolo
Rosso 2018 Rating** 93 **To** 2028 $50
Southern Highlands Blanc de Blancs 2017 Rating 93 $35
Private Cellar Collection Southern Highlands Arneis 2018 Rating 91
To 2028 $38
Prosecco 2019 Rating 90 **To** 2021 $24

Teusner   ★★★★★

95 Samuel Road, Nuriootpa, SA 5355 **Region** Barossa Valley
T (08) 8562 4147 **www**.teusner.com.au **Open** By appt
Winemaker Kym Teusner, Matt Reynolds **Est.** 2001 **Dozens** 30 000
Teusner is a partnership between former Torbreck winemaker Kym Teusner and Javier Moll,
and is typical of the new wave of winemakers determined to protect very old, low-yielding,
dry-grown Barossa vines. The winery approach is based on lees ageing, little racking, no fining
or filtration and no new American oak. As each year passes, the consistency, quality (and range)
of the wines increases; there must be an end point, but it's not easy to guess when, or even if,
it will be reached. Exports to the UK, the US, Canada, the Netherlands, Malaysia, Singapore,
Japan, Hong Kong and China.

ŶŶŶŶŶ Avatar 2018 Old vine grenache, mataro and shiraz. Firm, bold, fresh and
characterful. A terrific release. Plum, redcurrant, campfire and sweet spice. Ribs of
velvety tannin. Somehow manages to feel both generous and controlled. Super.
Screwcap. 14.5% alc. **Rating** 96 **To** 2030 $40 CM ✪

Teusner & Page Barossa Cabernet Sauvignon 2017 So svelte. This is a
gorgeous Barossa red. As much redcurrant as black, dusted with just the right
amount of herbs, seductively oaked and lifted with mint. It glides persuasively
through the palate and then spreads out impressively on the finish. A ripper.
Screwcap. 14.5% alc. **Rating** 96 **To** 2036 $65 CM ✪

Bilmore Barossa Valley Shiraz 2018 The flavours pop up like the plastic
clowns at the Easter Show, either to be shot or stunned and lie flat at the end of
the moving belt. There is a persistent tune with spicy/savoury/preserve flavours
that works very well for me, even if it's left field. Screwcap. 14.5% alc. **Rating** 95
To 2035 $25 ✪

Big Jim Barossa Valley Shiraz 2018 Oodles of sweet, blueberried fruit flavour,
an appropriately lavish swoosh of smoky oak and just the right volume of fine-
grained tannin. Every box here has been ticked with a flourish. Satiny smoothness
is a key feature, as indeed is balance. Screwcap. 14.5% alc. **Rating** 95 **To** 2033
$65 CM

Big Jim Barossa Valley Shiraz 2017 The colour is showing development
consistent with the spicy/savoury overtones to the blackberry fruit at the core of
the wine. The oak contribution is in balance, as is that of the tannins. Screwcap.
14.5% alc. **Rating** 95 **To** 2032 $65

MC Barossa Valley Sparkling Shiraz 2013 There's volume and there's softness but most of all there's a wide array of flavours. This ramps up the complexity a step or 3. Mushroom, sweet plum, earth, spice and leather flavours combine to beautiful effect. Throughout, it remains fresh. Upper echelon in its style. Crown seal. **Rating** 95 $65 CM

Albert Shiraz 2018 A fragrant, medium weight red with boysenberry and fresh plum flavours tempered by spice. Fine-grained tannin and a subtle meatiness complete an elegant, fine-boned picture. Screwcap. 14.5% alc. **Rating** 94 **To** 2028 $65 CM

Righteous FG Barossa Valley Shiraz 2016 Beefy shiraz with asphalt, blackcurrant and vanilla flavours pressing through the palate. A wave of tannin continues the sturdy, big-bodied theme. Indeed out of the big heavy bottle pours a big heavy wine. Cork. 15% alc. **Rating** 94 **To** 2032 $160 CM

The G Grenache 2018 Lovely expression of grenache. It has meat on its bones yet it remains delicate; everything here feels as though it's been etched into place. It tastes of red licorice and asphalt, twiggy spices and cedar, and at all times it's the Barossa and grenache doing the talking, oak in a supporting role only. It's another winner from the Teusner team. Screwcap. 14.5% alc. **Rating** 94 **To** 2027 $32 CM

ŸŸŸŸ♀ **The Wark Family Shiraz 2018 Rating** 93 **To** 2030 $30 CM
The Gentleman Barossa Cabernet Sauvignon 2018 Rating 93 **To** 2027 $27 CM ❂
The Riebke Barossa Valley Shiraz 2018 Rating 92 **To** 2028 $27 CM
The Independent Barossa Valley Shiraz Mataro 2018 Rating 92 **To** 2027 $27 CM
Righteous Barossa Valley Grenache 2018 Rating 92 **To** 2025 $95 CM
Joshua 2019 Rating 92 **To** 2029 $32
Salsa Barossa Valley Rose 2019 Rating 91 **To** 2021 $23 CM ❂

The Bridge Vineyard ★★★★

Shurans Lane, Heathcote, Vic 3552 **Region** Heathcote
T 0417 391 622 **www.**thebridgevineyard.com.au **Open** Select w'ends
Winemaker Lindsay Ross **Est.** 1997 **Dozens** 1000 **Vyds** 4.75ha
This venture of former Balgownie winemaker Lindsay Ross and wife Noeline is part of a broader business known as Winedrops, which acts as a wine production and distribution network for the Bendigo wine industry. The wines are sourced from long-established vineyards, providing shiraz (3.5ha), malbec and viognier (0.5ha each) and sangiovese (0.25ha). The viticultural accent is on low cropping and thus concentrated flavours, the winemaking emphasis on finesse and varietal expression.

ŸŸŸŸ **Shurans Lane Heathcote Rose 2019** A tangerine-coral hue, on the deeper side. Squashed red fruits, orange zest, cumquat and musk scents meander across an intensely flavoured palate, corralled by gentle acidity and a waft of well placed phenolics. Gently oxidative, but not in a bad way. Richer than the norm and destined to parry with food. Screwcap. **Rating** 89 **To** 2020 $20 NG

Shurans Lane Heathcote Shiraz Malbec 2016 A mid-ruby. Violet, wood smoke, licorice, sandalwood and dark fruit allusions. The palate, mid to full-weighted, is bound to some twiggy oak that somehow works, integrating with and binding the intense fruit sweetness as it expands in the glass. This is an enjoyable drink, auguring well into a mid-term future. Cork. **Rating** 89 **To** 2026 $30 NG

The Hairy Arm ★★★★★

18 Plant Street, Northcote, Vic 3070 **Region** Sunbury/Heathcote
T 0409 110 462 **www.**hairyarm.com **Open** By appt
Winemaker Steven Worley **Est.** 2004 **Dozens** 1000 **Vyds** 3ha
Steven Worley graduated as an exploration geologist, then added a Master of Geology degree, followed by a Postgraduate Diploma in Oenology and Viticulture. Until December 2009 he

was general manager of Galli Estate Winery. The Hairy Arm started as a university project in '04. It has grown from a labour of love to a commercial undertaking. Steven has an informal lease of 2ha of shiraz at Galli's Sunbury vineyard, which he manages, and procures 1ha of nebbiolo from the Galli vineyard in Heathcote. Exports to the UK, Canada and Hong Kong.

⟡⟡⟡⟡⟡ **Merri. Sunbury Shiraz 2018** 100% whole-bunch fermented in 2 batches, one wrapped and undisturbed for 5 weeks, the other foot-stomped after 3 days, thereafter with pumpovers and hand-plunging, matured for 18 months in French puncheons (50% new). Highly fragrant, showing no sign of high alcohol. Screwcap. 14.9% alc. **Rating** 95 **To** 2036 $50

Sunbury Shiraz 2016 Hand-picked, 70% destemmed whole berries, 30% whole bunches, matured in French puncheons (30% new) for 18 months. The bouquet is delicious with highly perfumed spicy red berry fruits, the savoury palate is elegant and fresh. Time in barrel and bottle has preserved a lovely wine. Screwcap. 14.9% alc. **Rating** 95 **To** 2030 $35 ○

Heathcote Nebbiolo 2017 The most striking bouquet of any wine I can remember. Gingerbread cake and ginger biscuits with icing of rose petals. The flavours follow along a similarly striking path. Not easy to pinpoint, but its interest is compelling. Screwcap. 14.7% alc. **Rating** 95 **To** 2029 $45

Sunbury Shiraz 2018 Was 60% destemmed, 40% whole bunch, fermented in 2 batches, both wild yeast, one given 14 days post-ferment maceration, matured in French puncheons for 11 months. A combination of power and delicacy, high-toned berry fruit with spices to burn. Screwcap. 14.9% alc. **Rating** 94 **To** 2030 $35

🌿 The Happy Winemaker   ★★★★

16 Maddern Street, Black Hill, Vic 3350 **Region** Ballarat/Heathcote/Bendigo
T 0431 252 015 **www**.thehappywinemaker.com.au **Open** Not
Winemaker Jean-Paul Trijsburg **Est.** 2015 **Dozens** 700 **Vyds** 1ha

Jean-Paul Trijsburg graduated with an agronomy degree from the Wageningen University in the Netherlands and followed this with a joint MSc in Viticulture and Oenology in Montpellier, France and Geisenheim, Germany. In between degrees he headed to Burgundy in 2007 and says, 'I started out picking grapes in Nuits-Saint-Georges, but somehow I ended up in the winery within a week'. The experience left him with a love of all things French, but he went on to work in wineries in Pomerol, the Rheingau, Rioja, Chile and South Africa. Since '12, he has called Australia home, having worked for Hanging Rock Winery in the Macedon Ranges and Lethbridge Wines in Geelong. He and wife Jessica live in Ballarat and, following the arrival of their second son, Jean-Paul runs a nearby 1ha vineyard of pinot noir and is an at-home dad for their children, Jessica working at a local health service. Jean-Paul moved from his garage-cum-winery to Hanging Rock for the '19 vintage (and ongoing thereafter). Additional grapes come from Heathcote, Bendigo and Ballarat.

⟡⟡⟡⟡⟡ **Mount Alexander Pinot Gris by Jean-Paul 2019** Hand-picked, fermented and matured in French barriques. The removal of the screwcap suggested a release of CO_2. Bright colour. Jean-Paul has managed to bring stone fruit flavours into the wine and happily not the green olive Jean-Paul mentions on the back label. Screwcap. 12.7% alc. **Rating** 91 **To** 2024 $25

Ballarat Syrah by Jean-Paul 2018 Single vineyard; destemmed, wild-fermented, plunged daily, hand-operated basket press, 12 months in French barriques (fourth use), not filtered; 46 dozen made. A strong sense of place; what is a hot vintage for others is a good vintage for Ballarat. Screwcap. 12.8% alc. **Rating** 91 **To** 2033 $35

Heathcote Carmenere by Jean-Paul 2017 Single vineyard; destemmed, wild-fermented, 21 days on skins, matured for 12 months in fourth-used French barriques. A powerful wine with dark berry fruits, savoury tannins and green (not black) olive nuances. Screwcap. 13.1% alc. **Rating** 91 **To** 2030 $35

Bendigo Ballarat BDX II by Jean-Paul 2018 The light to medium-bodied blend of 70% merlot from Bendigo, 20% cabernet sauvignon from Ballarat and

10% carmenere from Heathcote has good overall balance between fruit, oak and tannins. One of the very few plantings of carmenere in Australia. Cork. 13.2% alc. **Rating** 90 **To** 2025 $38

ΨΨΨΨ **Mount Alexander Ballarat Rose by Jean-Paul 2019 Rating** 89 **To** 2020 $25
Ballarat BDX I by Jean-Paul 2018 Rating 89 **To** 2038 $38

The Islander Estate Vineyards ★★★★★

78 Gum Creek Road, Cygnet River, SA 5223 **Region** Kangaroo Island
T (08) 8553 9008 **www**.iev.com.au **Open** Thurs–Tues 12–5
Winemaker Jacques Lurton, Yale Norris **Est.** 2000 **Dozens** 6000 **Vyds** 10ha
Established by one of the most famous Flying Winemakers in the world, Bordeaux-born and trained and part-time Australian resident Jacques Lurton. He has established a close-planted vineyard. The principal varieties are cabernet franc, shiraz and sangiovese, with lesser amounts of grenache, malbec, semillon and viognier. The wines are made and bottled at the onsite winery in true estate style. The property was ravaged by the terrible bushfire that devastated many (not all) parts of the island in January 2020. The fire consumed the entire vineyard and its infrastructure, the house, the laboratory and the office, which became the sacrificial lamb slowing the fire sufficiently to allow the protection of the winery and its stock of bottled wine, and the wines still in barrel and tank. Long-time friend and business partner Yale Norris has cut back every vine down to 20cm hoping that shoots would appear – many have done so, but far from all. If the regeneration ceases, the entire vineyard will be pulled out and replanted. Jacques Lurton has been in step with every move since and has formulated a contingency plan for the '21 vintage. Jeni Port's tasting notes for the *Wine Companion 2021* should encourage those wishing to buy the wines online. Exports to the UK, the US, Canada, France, Switzerland, Germany, Malta, Hong Kong, Taiwan and China.

ΨΨΨΨΨ **The Wally White Kangaroo Island Semillon 2018** Semillon on Kangaroo Island clearly has a future. Wally White responds to the terroir with generosity, offering up an intriguing complexity that attacks all the senses. Eye-catching, medium-deep yellow in hue. Aromas of honeysuckle, beeswax and baked pear. Waves of flavour ride the mouth; concentrated, intense with abiding texture and acidity. As a 2yo it comes across as developed, but the acidity ensures a long life. Screwcap. 13.5% alc. **Rating** 95 **To** 2027 $38 JP

Viognier 2019 Archetypal viognier with the scent of honey-drizzled peaches and pears, orange blossom and fruit peel. Intoxicating stuff. Golden and creamy style with a slightly nutty demeanour that lasts to the finish; the apricot stone and dried fruit savouriness complete the textbook example. A wine of many parts and with many years ahead. Screwcap. 12.5% alc. **Rating** 95 **To** 2027 JP

Old Rowley 2019 A brilliant purple sheen is an enticing introduction to this smart, young shiraz grenache. Softness is the key here, together with a discreet, still emerging personality. It has a way to go. Pepper, spice, blackberries and red earth aromas. Deliciously ripe palate with dark cherry, black fruits and grenache violets and confection. Tannins are firm. Bottle age is a must. Screwcap. 14% alc. **Rating** 95 **To** 2032 $38 JP

Sangiovese 2019 The Islander produces wines that are often more European than Australian. Note the degree of savouriness in its wines and the use of fruit as a conduit for complexity, and not necessarily an end in itself. Sangiovese is such a wine. Fragrant with black cherries, capers, anise, bitter chocolate. It runs smooth across the palate, supple oak playing its part and imparting sweet mocha. Cherry pip, chalky tannins still melding. Screwcap. 14% alc. **Rating** 95 **To** 2030 $28 JP ✪

Tempranillo 2019 From a winery founded by a Frenchman comes a wine made by an American and featuring a Spanish grape from an up-and-coming Aussie wine region, is it any wonder there is so much happening in this unusually savoury and complex tempranillo? Layer upon layer of black fruits, spice, vanillan oak with chocolate mocha overtones, saline brightness and sturdy tannin lines all add up to an exciting wine. The charcuterie, smoked meat savouriness on the back-palate adds a special touch. Screwcap. 14% alc. **Rating** 94 **To** 2028 $28 JP ✪

ꝐꝐꝐꝐꝐ Bark Hut Rd 2019 Rating 93 To 2032 $30 JP
Petiyante NV Rating 92 $38 JP
SoFar SoGood Kangaroo Island Shiraz 2019 Rating 90 To 2023 $28 JP

The Lake House Denmark ★★★★★

106 Turner Road, Denmark, WA 6333 **Region** Denmark
T (08) 9848 2444 **www**.lakehousedenmark.com.au **Open** 7 days 10–5
Winemaker Harewood Estate (James Kellie) **Est.** 1995 **Dozens** 8000 **Vyds** 5.2ha
Garry Capelli and Leanne Rogers purchased the property in 2005 and have restructured
the vineyard to grow varieties suited to the climate – chardonnay, pinot noir, semillon and
sauvignon blanc – incorporating biodynamic principles. They also manage a couple of small
family-owned vineyards in Frankland River and Mount Barker with a similar ethos. Wines are
released in three tiers: the flagship Premium Reserve range, the Premium Block range and the
quirky He Said, She Said easy-drinking wines. The combined cellar door, restaurant and
gourmet food emporium is a popular destination. Exports to Singapore and China.

ꝐꝐꝐꝐꝐ **Premium Reserve Single Vineyard Porongurup Riesling 2019** Delicate-
but-flavoursome riesling with talc, passionfruit, green apple and lemon-blossom
characters tripping their way through to a lengthy finish. Perfume and persistence
are well in this wine's favour. The flavours are robust but the mouthfeel is light and
intricate. Screwcap. 12.5% alc. **Rating** 94 To 2028 $40 CM
Premium Reserve Premium Selection Cabernet Sauvignon 2017 Given
4 weeks on skins post ferment, all French oak (40% new). It sits at the upper end
of the ripeness spectrum but it feels well balanced and indeed seamless. Dark
chocolate, blackcurrant, gravel, toast and mint characters swoop convincingly
through the palate and on through the finish. Built to age, but it's good now.
Screwcap. 14.5% alc. **Rating** 94 To 2033 $55 CM

ꝐꝐꝐꝐꝐ **Premium Block Selection Cabernet Sauvignon 2016** Rating 93 To 2025
$28 SC
Premium Reserve Single Vineyard Chardonnay 2018 Rating 92 To 2024
$40 CM
Premium Reserve Frankland River Shiraz 2017 Rating 92 To 2028 $45 CM
Postcard Series Shiraz 2017 Rating 92 To 2027 $25 CM ○
Postcard Series Merlot 2017 Rating 92 To 2026 $25 CM ○
Postcard Series Cabernet Sauvignon 2017 Rating 91 To 2026 $28 CM
Single Vineyard Selection Sauvignon Blanc 2018 Rating 90 To 2021 $25
Single Vineyard Selection Semillon Sauvignon Blanc 2018 Rating 90
To 2022 $25
Postcard Series Pinot Noir 2018 Rating 90 To 2024 $25 CM

The Lane Vineyard ★★★★★

Ravenswood Lane, Hahndorf, SA 5245 **Region** Adelaide Hills
T (08) 8388 1250 **www**.thelane.com.au **Open** 7 days 10–4.30
Winemaker Michael Schreurs, Martyn Edwards **Est.** 1993 **Dozens** 25 000 **Vyds** 75ha
After 15 years at The Lane Vineyard, Helen and John Edwards, and sons Marty and Ben, took
an important step towards realising their long-held dream – to grow, make and sell estate-based
wines that have a true sense of place. In 2005, at the end of the (now discontinued) Starvedog
Lane joint venture with Hardys, they commissioned a state-of-the-art 500t winery, bistro and
cellar door overlooking their vineyards on picturesque Ravenswood Lane. Having previously
invested in Delatite and much earlier established Coombe Farm in the Yarra Valley, the Vestey
Group (UK) has acquired a significant shareholding in The Lane Vineyard. The remaining
shares are owned by Martyn Edwards and Ben Tolstoshev. Exports to the UK, the US, Canada,
the Netherlands, Belgium, the UAE, Hong Kong and China.

ꝐꝐꝐꝐꝐ **Reginald Germein Single Vineyard Adelaide Hills Chardonnay 2017**
Hand-picked, whole-bunch pressed to new 350l French barrels, wild-fermented,
no mlf, matured in oak for 9 months. Long, intense, Granny Smith apple. A very

good example of what '17 had to offer for those who understand the song. Screwcap. 12.5% alc. **Rating** 97 **To** 2030 $100 ✪

𝟃𝟃𝟃𝟃𝟃 **Block 14 Single Vineyard Basket Press Adelaide Hills Shiraz 2018** A very good estate-grown shiraz, building intensity and depth on modest alcohol that enlivens and lengthens the palate. Delicious stuff. Screwcap. 13.5% alc. **Rating** 95 **To** 2038 $40

Reunion Single Vineyard Adelaide Hills Shiraz 2017 Given 16 months' maturation in French oak (30% new) of various shapes and sizes. 'Mine is bigger than yours' type of stuff, yet not swamped by oak. The '17 vintage and moderate alcohol have combined to produce a challenging and stimulating wine. Screwcap. 13.5% alc. **Rating** 95 **To** 2037 $65

19th Meeting Single Vineyard Adelaide Hills Cabernet Sauvignon 2017 Destemmed whole berries static-fermented 10–14 days, pumped over twice daily, some parcels given up to 3 months' post-ferment maceration, matured in French barriques (30% new) for 16 months. As complex as its vinification would suggest. Screwcap. 13.5% alc. **Rating** 95 **To** 2032 $65

𝟃𝟃𝟃𝟃𝟃 **Beginning Single Vineyard Chardonnay 2018 Rating** 93 **To** 2024 $50
Cuvee Helen Blanc de Blancs 2013 Rating 93 $65
Block 5 Shiraz 2018 Rating 92 **To** 2028 $30
Single Vineyard Pinot Noir 2018 Rating 90 **To** 2027 $40

The Other Wine Co ★★★★

136 Jones Road, Balhannah, SA 5242 **Region** South Australia
T (08) 8398 0500 **www**.theotherwineco.com **Open** At Shaw + Smith
Winemaker Martin Shaw, Adam Wadewitz **Est.** 2015 **Dozens** 1000
This is the venture of Michael Hill Smith and Martin Shaw, established in the shadow of Shaw + Smith but with an entirely different focus and separate marketing. The name reflects the wines, which are intended for casual consumption; the whole focus being freshness combined with seductive mouthfeel. The concept of matching variety and place is one without any particular limits and there may well be other wines made by The Other Wine Co in years to come. Exports to the UK, Canada and Germany.

𝟃𝟃𝟃𝟃𝟃 **Adelaide Hills Pinot Gris 2019** Exceptional gris with the textural pedal hitting all the right notes. A chalky breeze of phenolics and the breadth of older oak melds with gentle acidity, pulling nashi pear, cinnamon, blossom and toffee apple scents long and broad. This expands, staining the cheeks with flavour. Drinkability factor melded with a pointed intensity of flavour. Bravo! Screwcap. **Rating** 93 **To** 2023 $26 NG ✪

Kangaroo Island Cabernet Franc 2019 I hate to imagine the future for viticulture on the island after the torrid '19/20 summer so many of us have experienced. With this in mind, I raise a glass: a sumptuous franc, reminiscent of a Chinon with mettle of fruit and amplitude. Ripe, but crunchy. Mid-weighted and sassy. Lilac florals. Bitter chocolate–chilli, blackcurrant, cherry and a swathe of herb, barely detectable amid the riot of fruit. Long and sappy. A delicious wine and a homage to all that can be. Screwcap. **Rating** 93 **To** 2024 $35 NG

Shiraz Pinot Noir 2019 It is rewarding that this archetypal Aussie blend is seeing a resurgence. A blend of Adelaide Hills (shiraz) and Tasmanian fruit. This is delicious. Surely a whole berry/cluster ferment. Partial carbonic influence having sway across a pulpy and juicy mid-weighted frame, gentle tannins and a spurt of acidity. Otherwise, violet and ripe cherry. A whiff of reductive tension. Screwcap. **Rating** 92 **To** 2023 $26 NG

McLaren Vale Grenache 2019 Hand-picked across parcels, some less ripe than others. The result is certainly fresh but lacking the pulpy, hedonistic prerequisite joy of grenache. Gently reductive with a whiff of orange rind, tomatillo and sour cherry to raspberry scents, careening along a beam of herbal acidity and gently bunchy (10% cluster) tannins, palpable just enough. Screwcap. 13.5% alc. **Rating** 90 **To** 2024 $27 NG

The Remarkable State   ★★★★☆

GPO Box 1001, Adelaide, SA 5001 **Region** South Australia
T 0437 267 881 **www**.remarkablestate.com.au **Open** Not
Winemaker Various **Est.** 2018 **Dozens** 10000

Owner Rob Turnbull moved to Australia from the UK in 1997, at that stage without any experience in the wine industry other than drinking it — and landed a vintage start with Peter Lehmann. One thing led to another in every part of the business, including study at the University of Adelaide. Fifteen years later he took the plunge and started his own business, calling on many of his friends as he built a portfolio of wines made by various winemakers using grapes grown in SA. His brief to those winemakers was simple: to make wines they'd want to take to dinner themselves. No capital cost, just working capital — then he went and spoilt it by purchasing tanks and equipment for the '19 vintage. But he does have an admirable marketing plan: make alternative varieties for Dan Murphy and mainstream varieties for export. The wine quality and value for money is good, the labels cleverly designed. Exports to the UK, Canada, NZ and China.

🍷🍷🍷🍷🍷 One Remarkable Barrel Barossa Valley Shiraz 2018 From a single old vine vineyard near Greenock; open-fermented, basket-pressed, the best hogshead (from a total of 21) bottled Nov '19; bottle no. 113/365. The juicy flavours and fine tannins are easy to like, signifying a gentle hand in the winery. Cork. 14.5% alc. Rating 95 To 2033 $85

🍷🍷🍷🍷🍷 Captain Hayes Eden Valley Riesling 2018 Rating 92 To 2028 $25 SC ❂
The Proclamation Single Vineyard Adelaide Hills Chardonnay 2017
Rating 90 To 2021 $30

The Ridge North Lilydale   ★★★★☆

106 Browns Road, North Lilydale, Tas, 7268 **Region** Northern Tasmania
T 0408 192 000 **Open** Sun 10.30–5
Winemaker Harry Rigney, Susan Denny **Est.** 2008 **Dozens** NFP **Vyds** 2ha

This venture marks the return to Tasmania of husband and wife Harry Rigney and Susan Denny after more than 30 years on the east coast of the mainland. In his mid-20s Harry was the sole recipient of the prized Menzies Scholarship to undertake his master's degree at Harvard, becoming a highly acclaimed specialist in taxation law (while continuing to this day to play his electric guitar in a rock band). Susan completed a fine arts degree in the '70s (dux of her year) then moving into Applied Arts inter alia mastering oxy and electric welding. She also saw her father Tim's scientific, engineering and agricultural innovations trail-blaze the world's lavender industry. So, they were equipped to purchase a 20ha property with north-facing slopes at an altitude of 350m and planted a 2ha close-planted 6000 vine vineyard in 2013/14. It earned them the title of Best Small Vineyard Tasmania '17.

🍷🍷🍷🍷🍷 Pinot Noir 2017 Highly aromatic, small red flowers and petals fill the bouquet; the colour bright, clear and deep; the palate living up to all the promises. It's a wine of distinction, its texture and structure seriously good. Screwcap. 13.5% alc. Rating 96 To 2037 $45 ❂
Pinot Noir 2018 This is very well made. It is deeply coloured and supple with predominantly red fruits, cherries and pomegranate all contributing to a palate that is a reprise of the bouquet. Screwcap. 13.5% alc. **Rating** 94 To 2030 $45

🍷🍷🍷🍷🍷 Chardonnay 2019 Rating 90 To 2023 $35

The Stoke Wines   ★★★★

98 Sneyd Road, Mount Jagged, SA 5211 **Region** Kangaroo Island/Adelaide Hills
T 0407 389 130 **www**.thestokewines.com **Open** Summer w'ends
Winemaker Nick Dugmore, Rebecca Dugmore **Est.** 2016 **Dozens** 600

The Stoke Wines was born of a six-month conversation that spanned Australia, Bali, Scotland, France and India. Wishing to escape their jobs in commercial winemaking, Nick and Rebecca Dugmore set off for a sea-change in Bordeaux. Arriving in France, they realised that their half-baked attempt to learn French on the road was seriously insufficient. While left out of the conversation at their own party, the idea of The Stoke Wines was born. Nick's love affair with Kangaroo Island had begun on a surf trip around Australia in a banana-yellow Ford Falcon in 2008. Kangaroo Island was the first stop, the rest of the itinerary is still awaiting completion. Making wine from Kangaroo Island is all about a connection to a place where Nick and Rebecca love to be and this is reflected in their winemaking. The '20 bushfires came as a terrible blow for those with vineyards, none more so than Jacques Lurton's The Islander Estate, which provided The Stoke Wines with some of its best grapes. But the Island is much larger than most people realise and large parts were left untouched (and the vineyards in those parts). Nick and Rebecca produce the wines in a collective space in Mount Jagged where they have started a collective called Southern Artisans (SA) with another small producer, SKEW Wines. Their goal is to promote the Southern Fleurieu and Kangaroo Island. Nick is a winemaker at Wirra Wirra but with their support has gone part-time in '20 to be able to focus on the Island. Rebecca is the part-time brand manager at Terre à Terre in the Adelaide Hills and full-time mum of their 17-month-old boy, Finlay.

ΨΨΨΨΨ **KIN Far From Home Adelaide Hills Pinot Gris 2018** Hand-picked, destemmed, gently pressed, 10% barrel-fermented for mouthfeel, matured for 6 months on lees. Granny Smith apple and nashi pear flavours. Only 195 dozen made. Screwcap. 12.5% alc. **Rating** 93 **To** 2022 $30
Kangaroo Island Pinot Gris 2019 From the False Cape Vineyard; hand-picked, 20% fermented warm on solids in French oak, 80% cold-settled and fermented in stainless steel, then on lees for 4 months, no additives. Soars and dips between small ripe fruits and citrussy acidity. Screwcap. 12.5% alc. **Rating** 92 **To** 2025 $30
Kangaroo Island Syrah 2019 From the False Cape Vineyard; hand-picked, wild-fermented, 50% whole bunch, 50% crushed, matured in used French oak, no additives, not fined or filtered. Very savoury/spicy/meaty on the bouquet and medium-bodied palate, tannins joining fruits with equal enthusiasm. Screwcap. 13.3% alc. **Rating** 92 **To** 2029 $35
Kangaroo Island Sangiovese Rose 2018 Hand-picked, whole-bunch pressed, a low extraction of 500l/t, batonnage. Bright pale pink. Opens with gently sweet cherry fruit, then moves to a savoury finish. Easy to enjoy; good food style. Screwcap. 13% alc. **Rating** 91 **To** 2022 $30

The Story Wines   ★★★★★

170 Riverend Road, Hangholme, Vic 3175 **Region** Grampians
T 0411 697 912 **www**.thestory.com.au **Open** Not
Winemaker Rory Lane **Est.** 2004 **Dozens** 2500
Over the years I have come across winemakers with degrees in atomic science, doctors with specialties spanning every human condition, town-planners, sculptors and painters; Rory Lane adds yet another to the list: a degree in ancient Greek literature. He says that after completing his degree and 'desperately wanting to delay an entry into the real world, I stumbled across and enrolled in a postgraduate wine technology and marketing course at Monash University, where I soon became hooked on ... the wondrous connection between land, human and liquid'. Vintages in Australia and Oregon germinated the seed and he zeroed in on the Grampians, where he purchases small parcels of high quality grapes. He makes the wines in a small factory where he has assembled a basket press, a few open fermenters, a mono pump and some decent French oak. Exports to the UK.

ΨΨΨΨΨ **R. Lane Vintners Henty Pinot Noir 2018** Wild-fermented with 100% whole bunches. Highly fragrant and floral, the palate of similar complexity, utterly seductive, every cadence carefully built. Screwcap. 13.5% alc. **Rating** 97 **To** 2028 $50 ✪
R. Lane Vintners Westgate Vineyard Grampians Syrah 2017 Before anyone gets too excited, let me tell you there were only 65 dozen bottles made, and Rory Lane had just enough room to move in deciding how to handle options normally too small to contemplate. The upshot is a wine made with endless patience from great parcels of grapes. Spicy, zesty black cherry, berry and

plum fruits plus numerous secondary aromas and flavours. Screwcap. 13.5% alc. Rating 97 To 2037 $75 ○

ŶŶŶŶŶ **Once Upon a Clime Grampians Syrah 2017** I'm mystified by the amazingly low price, which caused me to check twice to verify. It's spicy, peppery, juicy, and a whole lot more tied in with its multi-berry fruits and supportive tannins. Screwcap. 13.5% alc. **Rating** 96 To 2040 $30 ○
Whitlands Close Planted Riesling 2018 From the Croucher Vineyard at 800m at Whitlands. The bouquet was closed for business at the beginning of '20, but the palate more than compensated with thrilling acidity and length. It all makes sense when you find the residual sugar and titratable acidity are in balance at 7.6g/l and 7.5g/l. Screwcap. 12% alc. **Rating** 94 To 2033 $30 ○
Whitlands Close Planted Riesling 2017 This is the first vintage from the close-planted vineyard, but balanced oenologically by 9g/l of residual sugar. It's elegant to the point of ethereal. It beguiles you into relaxing to the point of not focusing on all that's there. Screwcap. 12% alc. **Rating** 94 To 2033 $30 ○

ŶŶŶŶ **Marsanne Roussanne Viognier 2017** Rating 93 To 2027 $30

The Vintner's Daughter   ★★★★☆

5 Crisps Lane, Murrumbateman, NSW 2582 **Region** Canberra District
T (02) 6227 5592 **www**.thevintnersdaughter.com.au **Open** W'ends 10–4
Winemaker Stephanie Helm **Est.** 2014 **Dozens** 1000 **Vyds** 3ha
The Vintner's Daughter is Stephanie Helm, daughter of Ken Helm, who made her first wine when she was nine and won her first trophy when she was 14. On finishing school she enrolled in an arts/law degree at the Australian National University, thereafter pursuing a career outside the wine industry until 2011, when she began the wine science degree at CSU. Along the way, while she was at ANU, she met a young bloke from Lightning Ridge at a pub and introduced him to the world of wine. It wasn't too long before he (Benjamin Osborne) was vineyard manager (with his background as a qualified horticulturist and landscaper) for Ken Helm. In late '14 all the wheels came full circle when a vineyard, originally planted in 1978 with traminer, crouchen and riesling, extended to 3ha in '99, came on the market. It was in an immaculate position between Clonakilla and Eden Road, and they purchased it in a flash and set about some urgently need rejuvenation. Stephanie (and Ben) waltzed into the trophy arena at the Canberra International Riesling Challenge '15, winning the trophy for Best Canberra District Riesling and, for good measure, winning the trophy for Best Riesling at the Winewise Small Vignerons Awards '15. Gewurztraminer, pinot noir and shiraz are also part of the estate-based portfolio. And yes, they are life partners.

ŶŶŶŶŶ **Shiraz Viognier 2017** It spreads impressively through the palate and on through the finish. Indeed structure and length are this wine's strongest points. Viognier is only 4% of the blend but it's effect is overt; there are stone fruit characters on both the nose and palate. Clove, meat, plum and toffee-apple characters keep things rolling, with pepper lifting out through the aftertaste. It's good now and it will mature well. Screwcap. 13.5% alc. **Rating** 94 To 2034 $55 CM

ŶŶŶŶ **Riesling 2019** Rating 93 To 2029 $35 CM
Gewurztraminer 2019 Rating 93 To 2025 $30 CM
Pinot Noir 2018 Rating 90 To 2026 $35 CM

The Wanderer   ★★★★★

2850 Launching Place Road, Gembrook, Vic 3783 **Region** Yarra Valley
T 0415 529 639 **www**.wandererwines.com **Open** By appt
Winemaker Andrew Marks **Est.** 2005 **Dozens** 500
The Wanderer Wines are a series of single vineyard wines made by Andrew Marks, winemaker and viticulturalist at Gembrook Hill Vineyard. Andrew spent 6 years as a winemaker with Penfolds before returning to Gembrook Hill in 2005. He has worked numerous vintages in France and Spain including Etienne Sauzet in Puligny Montrachet in '06 and more recently

over 10 vintages in the Costa Brava, Spain. Andrew seeks to achieve the best expression of his vineyards through minimal handling in the winery. In '12 he founded The Melbourne Gin Company.

ŸŸŸŸŸ **Upper Yarra Valley Chardonnay 2018** A very easy wine to enjoy, with balance the key. Ripe stone fruit aromas on the bouquet, citrus as well, cashew and oatmeal characters – presumably from the oak handling – seamlessly integrated. It glides along the palate, flavoursome but elegant, a light wash of acidity providing freshness but not intruding. It should age well, but no need to wait, it's great drinking now. Diam. 12% alc. **Rating** 95 **To** 2025 $35 SC ✪

Upper Yarra Valley Pinot Noir 2018 It looks like a delicate sort of wine in the glass and for the most part, that's what it is. The bouquet is subtle with aromas of cherry and tart red berries mingling with earthy, mulchy, slightly reductive characters. The first impression on the palate is of lightness of weight, but it gradually builds in flavour and mouthfeel and finishes with a flourish. Elegant and refined. Diam. 13.5% alc. **Rating** 95 **To** 2030 $55 SC

Yarra Valley Shiraz 2016 A wealth of savoury and spice type aromas on the bouquet with green stems, licorice, shoe polish and sandalwood all among it. You can find some dark cherry notes if you look hard. It holds your interest. It opens up on the palate, the slightly sweet-tinged red berry fruit developing more depth as it rolls along; light but firm astringency the counterpoint. Diam. 13.5% alc. **Rating** 94 **To** 2025 $35 SC

ŸŸŸŸŸ **Yarra Valley Pinot Noir 2018 Rating** 93 **To** 2028 $35 SC
Yarra Valley Syrah 2017 Rating 93 **To** 2027 $55 SC

The Willows Vineyard ★★★★☆

310 Light Pass Road, Light Pass, Barossa Valley, SA 5355 **Region** Barossa Valley
T (08) 8562 1080 **www**.thewillowsvineyard.com.au **Open** Wed–Mon 10.30–4.30
Winemaker Peter Scholz **Est.** 1989 **Dozens** 6000 **Vyds** 42.74ha
The Scholz family have been grapegrowers for generations and they have over 40ha of vineyards, selling part of the crop. Current-generation winemaker Peter Scholz makes rich, ripe, velvety wines, some marketed with some bottle age. Exports to the UK, Canada, Switzerland, China and NZ.

ŸŸŸŸŸ **Bonesetter Barossa Valley Shiraz 2017** Archetypal with its flush of black and blue fruits, licorice and oak spices with swathes of powerful, gritty tannins working across a structured palate. However, this is built to last and has come together with nothing out of place. Cork. 14.7% alc. **Rating** 95 **To** 2035 $70 JF

ŸŸŸŸŸ **Barossa Valley Shiraz 2017 Rating** 92 **To** 2027 $28 JF
The Doctor Sparkling Red NV Rating 92 $40 JF
Barossa Valley Riesling 2019 Rating 90 **To** 2028 $20 JF ✪

Thick as Thieves Wines ★★★★★

355 Healesville-Kooweerup Road, Badger Creek, Vic 3777 **Region** Yarra Valley
T 0417 184 690 **www**.tatwines.com.au **Open** By appt
Winemaker Syd Bradford **Est.** 2009 **Dozens** 2000 **Vyds** 1.5ha
Syd Bradford is living proof that small can be beautiful and, equally, that an old dog can learn new tricks. A growing interest in good food and wine might have come to nothing had it not been for Pfeiffer Wines giving him a vintage job in 2003. In that year he enrolled in the wine science course at CSU; he moved to the Yarra Valley in '05. He gained experience at Coldstream Hills (vintage cellar hand), Rochford (assistant winemaker), Domaine Chandon (cellar hand) and Giant Steps/Innocent Bystander (assistant winemaker). In '06 Syd achieved the Dean's Award of Academic Excellence at CSU and in '07 was the sole recipient of the A&G Engineering Scholarship. Aged 35, he was desperate to have a go at crafting his own 'babies' and in '09 came across a small parcel of arneis from the Hoddles Creek area, and Thick as Thieves was born. The techniques

used to make his babies could only come from someone who has spent a long time observing and thinking about what he might do if he were calling the shots. Exports to Singapore, Japan and China.

ŸŸŸŸŸ **The Aloof Alpaca Yarra Valley Arneis 2019** Sits comfortably as a ripper example of Australian arneis. Delicate aromas of citrus blossom and ginger flowers with all the action on the palate. Lemon salts, grapefruit pith with crunchy acidity and the right amount of texture, the merest hint of neat phenolics. So appealing. Screwcap. 12% alc. **Rating** 95 **To** 2023 $25 JF ✪

Plump Yarra Valley Pinot Noir 2019 Actually, the wine isn't plump at all. Certainly it's flavoursome with cherries and pips, humus-warm earth and orange zest, yet altogether buoyant and bloody delicious. Medium-bodied, just, with raw-silk tannins and squirts of refreshing acidity all the way through. Screwcap. 13.1% alc. **Rating** 95 **To** 2028 $37 JF

Driftwood Yarra King Valley Pinot Noir Gamay 2019 An even split between varieties, 100% whole bunches with a delightful carbonic prickle and tease across the palate. It's juicy, refreshing, vibrant even energising, which makes it so easy to drink. Love it. Screwcap. 13.1% alc. **Rating** 95 **To** 2025 $32 JF ✪

ŸŸŸŸŸ **Another Bloody Yarra Valley Chardonnay 2019** **Rating** 92 **To** 2028 $37 JF
Left-Field Blend 2018 **Rating** 92 **To** 2030 $25 JP ✪
Left-Field Blend 2019 **Rating** 92 **To** 2025 $26 JF
King Valley Nebbiolo Rose 2019 **Rating** 92 **To** 2022 $25 JF ✪
Purple Prose King Valley Gamay 2019 **Rating** 92 **To** 2025 $37 JF
Purple Prose King Valley Gamay 2018 **Rating** 92 **To** 2025 $35 JP

Thistledown Wines   ★★★★★

c/- Revenir, Peacock Road North, Lenswood, SA 5240 **Region** South Australia
T 0405 038 757 **www**.thistledownwines.com **Open** Not
Winemaker Giles Cooke MW **Est.** 2010 **Dozens** 5000
Giles Cooke and Fergal Tynan are based in Scotland and have a collective 40+ years' experience in buying and selling Australian wines. They have been friends since 1998, when they met over a pint of beer on the evening before the first Master of Wine course they were about to embark on. In 2006 they established Alliance Wine Australia, which purchases Australian wines for distribution in the UK; they took the process one step further when Alliance began the Thistledown Wines venture. This focuses on Barossa Valley shiraz, McLaren Vale grenache, and smaller amounts of chardonnay from the Adelaide Hills. The wines are made under Peter Leske's direction at his Revenir small-batch winery in the Adelaide Hills. Giles says he has particular affection for grenache and is precisely right (in my view) when he says, 'McLaren Vale grenache is world class, and it best expresses itself when made in the mould of pinot noir'. Exports to the UK, the US, Canada, Ireland, the Netherlands, Denmark, Czech Republic, Poland, Malta, South Korea, Singapore, China and NZ.

ŸŸŸŸŸ **Advance Release Mengler Hill Eden Valley Grenache 2019** An amalgam of quartz, sandy loams and ironstone soils. Young dry-grown vines, propitiously sited at 550m and articulated across a wild-yeast fermentation, incorporating 22% whole-bunch. And versed winemaking nous. Kirsch, sandalwood, pomegranate, wood smoke, clove and the rasp of real tannic mettle. This flows long with an attractive brittle weave for savouriness and the next glass. The alcohol sits right for this late ripener. Screwcap. **Rating** 97 **To** 2025 $60 NG ✪

ŸŸŸŸŸ **Our Fathers Barossa Shiraz 2018** This rich, pulpy shiraz is dichotomously as dense as it is finessed. Seasoned with some whole-bunch spice and ensuing herbal seams, the gentle extraction is the gear that allows the fruit to flow. And it does. Long. Blue, black and mulberry. Anise, charcuterie, five-spice, bergamot. Floral aromas. The skein of pepper-grind acidity and detailed tannins, the clutch. Cork. 14% alc. **Rating** 96 **To** 2030 $50 NG ✪

She's Electric Old Vine Single Vineyard McLaren Vale Grenache 2019
Dry-grown on stingy soils in Seaview. This smells like Turkish delight, tomato,

wild raspberry, bergamot, sour cherry and something rocky. The tannins, sand-etched and beautifully detailed. A pliant density. This set of wines is so on the pulse! I am astounded, smitten and swooning, all at once. Screwcap. **Rating** 96 To 2025 $60 NG ✪

Bachelor's Block Ebenezer Barossa Valley Shiraz 2018 I like this. A lot! A twine of peppery acidity serves to galvanise teeming blue and black fruit flavours with a sense of restraint. No shortage of richness, soaring violet aromas and the heft desired by many. Barossa, after all. But the overall sense is of a wine from somewhere cooler; a hand with a deft touch. Vinous density juxtaposed against an uncanny lightness and thrumming intensity. Kudos! Cork. 14% alc. **Rating** 95 To 2028 $80 NG

The Vagabond Old Vine Blewitt Springs Grenache 2019 A delicious full-bodied wine that seems, despite it all, barely mid-weighted. This is due to the maritime salinity, pointed acidity and fishbone tannins, etching the flow of fruit with a detailed edge that confers savouriness and a sense of freshness while corralling persimmon, pomegranate, fecund strawberry and cranberry scents. This is looser knit than the other top cuvees, but no less delicious. Screwcap. **Rating** 95 To 2024 $60 NG

The Vagabond Old Vine Blewitt Springs Grenache 2018 Hand-picked, wild-fermented, 33% layered passive whole bunch, half in a concrete pyramid egg, the remainder with 20% whole bunches, then a barrel selection. Delicious grenache, fresh and juicy, with a skein of fruit and oak tannins. Screwcap. 14.5% alc. **Rating** 95 To 2024 $60

Sands of Time Old Vine Single Vineyard Blewitt Springs McLaren Vale Grenache 2018 Dry-grown 80yo bushvines, fermented with 33% whole bunches, part in a concrete egg, matured in French puncheons (25% new). A rich grenache with superabundant blood plum fruit and tannins to provide structure and longevity. Diam. 14.5% alc. **Rating** 95 To 2026 $75

This Charming Man Single Vineyard Clarendon McLaren Vale Grenache 2018 Wild-fermented with 20% whole bunches, matured in French puncheons (20% new). Full-bodied and demanding time, but there's a power of varietal fruit to reward those with patience. The tannins are the key to a wine of character – and an undoubted future. Diam. 14.5% alc. **Rating** 94 To 2028 $75

🍷🍷🍷🍷🍷 **Thorny Devil Barossa Valley Grenache 2018** Rating 93 To 2026 $32
Suilven Adelaide Hills Chardonnay 2018 Rating 91 To 2025 $80 NG
Cloud Cuckoo Land Fiano Greco di Tufo Zibibbo 2019 Rating 91 To 2021 $24 NG
Silken Beastie Nor'wester Barossa Valley Shiraz 2018 Rating 91 To 2028 $60 NG
Cunning Plan McLaren Vale Shiraz 2018 Rating 90 To 2033 $30

🍃 Thomas St Vincent   ★★★★★

PO Box 633, McLaren Vale, SA 5171 **Region** McLaren Vale
T 0438 605 694 **www.**thomasstvincent.com **Open** Not
Winemaker Gary Thomas **Est.** 2016 **Dozens** 240
Owner-winemaker Gary Thomas is the only vigneron I know of who is a ruthless critic of his own wines. He explains he has come from a writing background in the (unspecified) media and has had a passion for Rhône wines since the mid-1980s. He made his way 'to the cool heart of McLaren Vale's Blewitt Springs, and its old vines, dry-grown on sand for flavour and purity. Wines in small batches, extended ferments, subtle blends, reflecting the terroir and the season. Bottled without fining or filtration. As wines used to be made.' He makes his wines at McLaren Vale winery La Curio.

🍷🍷🍷🍷🍷 **Blewitt Springs Fleurieu Provencale Rose 2018** The generous yields of '18 meant access to a good spread of varieties, leading to this blend of mourvedre, cinsaut, counoise and grenache. The pale salmon colour gives no warning of the power and grip of the wine, nor of the war dance between the fruit components on the one hand and savoury/earthy notes on the other. Extremely aromatic. Cork. 13% alc. **Rating** 95 **To** 2021 $27 ✪

Blewitt Springs Fleurieu Meridionale Rouge 2017 'Lacks concentration and complexity' is the Thomas St Vincent verdict. All things are relative and I take leave to disagree. Excellent colour; it's lighter than the '18s and shows most on the mid-palate with bright, small berry fruits before a savoury finish. The best of the '17s. Cork. 14.5% alc. **Rating** 95 **To** 2027 $39

Blewitt Springs Fleurieu Provencale Rouge 2016 This deeply coloured blend is nigh on identical to its '17 sibling, but the wine is massively different, the fruit deep, rich and assertive. It has some newer oak; this will join hands with the fruit through the next decade. Cork. 14.5% alc. **Rating** 95 **To** 2036 $39

Blewitt Springs Fleurieu Provencale Rose 2019 A blend of mourvedre, grenache, cinsaut and counoise. Pale pink. It's a pretty wine with rose petals, crab-apple and bath powder aromas. It offers all sorts of flavours, with fruit skins as important as fruit flesh. Diam. 13% alc. **Rating** 94 **To** 2021 $27 ✪

Blewitt Springs Fleurieu Septentrionale Rouge 2018 A well balanced outcome for the vintage. A blend of 90% shiraz and 10% old vine cabernet sauvignon; matured in used oak. A relaxed and elegant wine, fresh and generous. Diam. 14.5% alc. **Rating** 94 **To** 2028 $39

Blewitt Springs Fleurieu Provencale Rouge 2017 Gary Thomas is a hard taskmaster when he comments that in this cooler year the wine lacks concentration and complexity. Elegance is a word that might be equally applicable. Either way, the wine will grow another leg over the next 3–5 years. Cork. 14.5% alc. **Rating** 94 **To** 2027 $39

🍷🍷🍷🍷🍷 **Blewitt Springs Fleurieu Provencale Rouge 2018** Rating 93 To 2033 $39
Blewitt Springs Fleurieu Septentrionale Rouge 2017 Rating 92 To 2027 $39

Thomas Wines   ★★★★★

28 Mistletoe Lane, Pokolbin, NSW 2320 **Region** Hunter Valley
T (02) 4998 7134 **www**.thomaswines.com.au **Open** 7 days 10–5
Winemaker Andrew Thomas, Eden Walpole **Est.** 1997 **Dozens** 10 000 **Vyds** 6ha

Andrew Thomas came to the Hunter Valley from McLaren Vale to join the winemaking team at Tyrrell's Wines. After 13 years, he left to undertake contract work and to continue the development of his own label. He makes individual-vineyard wines, underlining the subtle differences between the various subregions of the Hunter. Plans for the construction of an estate winery have been abandoned for the time being; for the foreseeable future he will continue to lease the James Estate winery on Hermitage Road. The major part of the production comes from long-term arrangements with growers of semillon (15ha) and shiraz (25ha); an additional 3ha of shiraz is leased. The quality of the wines and the reputation of Andrew Thomas have never been higher. The acquisition of Braemore Vineyard in December 2017 was significant, giving Thomas Wines a long-term supply of grapes from one of the Hunter Valley's most distinguished semillon vineyards. Exports to Japan and China.

🍷🍷🍷🍷🍷 **Braemore Cellar Reserve Hunter Valley Semillon 2014** A classic example of a wine that is still only part of the way on the journey to full development. The colour is still quartz-green, the mouthfeel in perfect balance and the fruit with a sweetness (not residual sugar) that is totally seductive. Screwcap. 10.6% alc. **Rating** 97 **To** 2034 $65 ✪

🍷🍷🍷🍷🍷 **Belford Shiraz 2018** A gorgeous colour as the wine pours: mid-ruby with glossy crimson edges. Quintessentially Hunter with leather polish tannins curtailing violet, blueberry, satsuma plum and Asian spice scents. A rich wine, but drinking like a mid-weighted luncheon claret; the sturdy tannins a bulwark against the teeming fruit. Structural authority. The most Hunteresque of these single sites. Pointed drive and intensity. **Rating** 96 **To** 2035 NG

The Cote Shiraz 2018 This is a different voltage aromatically than the Dam Block. Lilac, Turkish delight and Middle Eastern souk. Thoroughly exotic. Less pulpy, less earthy and tannic-authoritative than the Belford. A nice splay of differentiation across these single site wines; with this, a stream of expanding sweet fruit. This is the belly dancer. Screwcap. **Rating** 96 **To** 2033 $35 NG ✪

Sweetwater Individual Vineyard Hunter Valley Shiraz 2018 Definitively medium-bodied. Cherry Ripe. Succulent. Violet and salumi too. The acidity melded with a well proportioned swathe of tannin. Beautifully long and effortless. This is the wine I would choose over the others. A succulence of fruit, a curb of tannin and juicy thoroughbred acidity. Screwcap. **Rating** 96 **To** 2023 $35 NG ✪

Braemore Individual Vineyard Hunter Valley Semillon 2019 The forcefield of the range. The most reticent and yet paradoxically, as with many fine wines, the longest driver of flavour, intensity and ageability. Lemongrass, lanolin and grapefruit zest. Pulpy. Fleshy. Strident length. Athletic. Crunchy and laden with '19-esque slatiness. Screwcap. **Rating** 95 **To** 2029 $35 NG ✪

The Dam Block Individual Vineyard Hunter Valley Shiraz 2018 This is a sumptuous shiraz. Pulpy, joyous, floral and energetic. Almost ethereal as far as the region goes. The extraction metre is right on the drinkability pulse. Mid to full-weighted, but buoyant. Iodine, blue fruits and tapenade. Effortless. Screwcap. **Rating** 95 **To** 2033 $45 NG

Kiss Limited Release Hunter Valley Shiraz 2018 This was once a standout based on extract and bombast of oak alone. It was made to a code. Today, the tannin management, intensity of flavour, complexity and integration evince an authority and mellifluousness unlike before. Blue to dark fruit accents, five-spice, iodine and charcuterie. The pH metre a little shrill, but the tanginess will be massaged into the melee in time. Screwcap. **Rating** 95 **To** 2033 $85 NG

Synergy Vineyard Selection Hunter Valley Semillon 2019 A blend of small parcels from a number of old vineyards. It has an extra flourish from its fruit, which tends to ameliorate the impact of the high tensile wire of the Hunter Valley's semillon acidity. Five years will transform the wine. Screwcap. 10.8% alc. **Rating** 94 **To** 2029 $20 ✪

The Cote Shiraz 2017 Far more reliant on a sash of reductive tension – wet neoprene to lilac scents – than the sumptuous '18. More obvious density of sweet fruit too. This has eons left in the tank but may be just on the sweet-angular side in comparison. An adolescent as opposed to the strident juvenile. Screwcap. **Rating** 94 **To** 2031 $35 NG

🍷🍷🍷🍷🍷 **Fordwich Hill Individual Vineyard Hunter Valley Semillon 2019** **Rating** 93 **To** 2026 $26 NG ✪

The O.C. Individual Vineyard Hunter Valley Semillon 2019 **Rating** 93 **To** 2029 $26 NG ✪

Elenay Barrel Selection Hunter Valley Shiraz 2018 **Rating** 93 **To** 2026 $55 NG

DJV Individual Vineyard Hunter Valley Shiraz 2018 **Rating** 93 **To** 2026 $35 NG

Six Degrees Vineyard Selection Hunter Valley Semillon 2019 **Rating** 91 $25 NG

Thompson Estate ★★★★★

Tom Cullity Drive, Wilyabrup, WA 6284 **Region** Margaret River
T (08) 9755 6406 **www**.thompsonestate.com **Open** 7 days 10.30–4.30
Winemaker Paul Dixon **Est.** 1994 **Dozens** 14000 **Vyds** 40ha
Cardiologist Peter Thompson planted the first vines at Thompson Estate in 1997, inspired by his and his family's shareholdings in the Pierro and Fire Gully vineyards and by visits to many of the world's premium wine regions. Two more vineyards (both planted in '97) have been purchased, varieties include cabernet sauvignon, cabernet franc, merlot, chardonnay, sauvignon blanc, semillon, pinot noir and malbec. Thompson Estate wines are made onsite at

its state-of-the-art winery. Exports to the UK, Canada, Belgium, the Netherlands, Denmark, Finland, Singapore, Hong Kong and China.

🍷🍷🍷🍷 **Margaret River Chardonnay 2018** I sometimes describe cabernet (and its tannins) as autocratic. This is the chardonnay counterpart; its mouth-watering charge of grapefruit, white peach and white nectarine putting maturation in 30% new French oak into observer status. For the number nerds, its pH of 3.18 and titratable acidity of 8.2g/l are the measures. Screwcap. 13.3% alc. **Rating** 97 To 2033 $50 ✪

🍷🍷🍷🍷 **The Specialist Margaret River Chardonnay 2016** Hand-picked from selected rows and conventionally vinified. The result is impressive. The wine has conviction and drive thanks to its acidity and low pH. Grapefruit is the leader of the flavour pack but white stone fruit, cashew and melon all contribute. Screwcap. 12.5% alc. **Rating** 96 To 2028 $80

SSB Margaret River Semillon Sauvignon Blanc 2019 This moves up and away from the Estate Sauvignon Blanc with a 60/40% split, putting semillon in the driver's seat, but we don't know if 2 wild-fermented barrels were semillon or sauvignon blanc. Whichever, it's a complex assembly of tastes and textures, Thompson Estate suggesting a 10+-year cellaring potential. Screwcap. 12% alc. **Rating** 95 To 2029 $35 ✪

Margaret River Cabernet Sauvignon 2017 An altogether serious wine that includes 5% each of malbec and cabernet franc plus 2% merlot. Despite suggestions of tenderly doing this or that in the vinification, this is Wilyabrup's answer to Bordeaux. While there are some delicious red/cassis/purple flavours, it is the stern mouthfeel that makes you stand up and salute. It is still in its first flush of youth. Screwcap. 14.2% alc. **Rating** 95 To 2037 $50

Four Chambers Margaret River Shiraz 2018 Includes 2% each of malbec and cabernet franc. The minimal extract during vinification fully justified given the full-bodied, powerful wine that emerged. As it is, will develop slowly and with certainty. The 11 months in used oak was also a plus factor. Screwcap. 14.5% alc. **Rating** 94 To 2038 $25 ✪

Zero Dosage Margaret River Pinot Noir Chardonnay 2010 An 80/20% blend made in the traditional method, 9 years on tirage with no sugar added to the dosage wine. There's a trade off, but I think it's a winner. Diam. 11.3% alc. **Rating** 94 $48

🍷🍷🍷🍷 **Four Chambers Sauvignon Blanc 2019** Rating 93 To 2024 $25 ✪
Four Chambers Chardonnay 2019 Rating 93 To 2028 $25 ✪
Cabernet Merlot 2018 Rating 93 To 2036 $35
The Specialist Cabernet Sauvignon 2016 Rating 93 To 2041 $90

Thorn-Clarke Wines   ★★★★★

Milton Park, 266 Gawler Park Road, Angaston, SA 5353 **Region** Barossa Valley **T** (08) 8564 3036 **www.**thornclarkewines.com.au **Open** Mon–Fri 9–5, w'ends 11–4 **Winemaker** Peter Kelly **Est.** 1987 **Dozens** 80 000 **Vyds** 222ha
Established by David and Cheryl Clarke (née Thorn), and son Sam, Thorn-Clarke is one of the largest family-owned estate-based businesses in the Barossa. Their winery is close to the border between the Barossa and Eden valleys and three of their four vineyards are in the Eden Valley: the Mt Crawford Vineyard is at the southern end of the Eden Valley, while the Milton Park and Sandpiper vineyards are further north in the Eden Valley. The fourth vineyard is at St Kitts, at the northern end of the Barossa Ranges. In all four vineyards careful soil mapping has resulted in matching of variety and site, with all the major varieties represented. The quality of grapes retained for the Thorn-Clarke label has resulted in a succession of trophy and gold medal–winning wines at very competitive prices. Exports to all major markets.

🍷🍷🍷🍷 **William Randell Eden Valley Cabernet Sauvignon 2017** From the Milton Park and St Kitts vineyards. Destemmed, open-fermented, 10 days on skins, matured for 16 months in French hogsheads (35% new). The vintage was made to measure for cabernet in this district, the wine revelling in its full-bodied guise. Blackcurrant, black olive, dark chocolate and cedar sweep you along – relax and enjoy it. Cork. 14.5% alc. **Rating** 96 **To** 2047 $60 ✪

Sandpiper Eden Valley Riesling 2019 An exercise in purity and elegance: the perfumed bouquet trailing through florals, powder puff and a touch of spice; the delicately engineered palate keeping all the components in their place. Terrific balance and length to an all-out bargain. Screwcap. 11% alc. **Rating** 95 **To** 2029 $20 ✪

William Randell Barossa Shiraz 2017 From the estate St Kitts and Milton Park vineyards. Matured for 18 months in American oak (40% new). A powerful, full-bodied shiraz with blackberry fruit, tannins and oak all driving the long palate. The absorption of the oak into the fabric of the wine is particularly impressive. Cork. 14.5% alc. **Rating** 95 **To** 2037 $60

Single Vineyard Selection Saleyards Road Old Vine Block Barossa Grenache 2018 From 60yo vines, partial whole-bunch fermentation, 10 days on skins, pressed to French oak (15% new) for 18 months' maturation. A medley of forest floor fruits (wild strawberry, raspberry) with very good length and balance. Screwcap. 14.5% alc. **Rating** 95 **To** 2038 $40

Single Vineyard Selection Mt Crawford Block 5 Eden Valley Riesling 2019 Night-harvested, free-run juice only, minimal fining and filtration. Seriously good wine, with even more goodness to come over the next 5 years. Screwcap. 11% alc. **Rating** 94 **To** 2029 $26 ✪

Ron Thorn Single Vineyard Barossa Shiraz 2016 The best of the 40 batches of grapes vinified in the vintage, from Block 7 of the St Kitts Vineyard. Matured for 20 months in 100% new American oak, which combines with the tannins to thickly coat the mouth. Needs many years to soften the overall impact of the wine. Cork. 15.5% alc. **Rating** 94 **To** 2051 $95

🍷🍷🍷🍷🍷 **Single Vineyard Selection Mt Crawford Block 1 Eden Valley Chardonnay 2018 Rating** 93 **To** 2025 $32
Sandpiper Eden Valley Pinot Gris 2019 Rating 92 **To** 2022 $20 ✪
Shotfire Barossa Shiraz 2018 Rating 92 **To** 2032 $28
Sandpiper Barossa Shiraz 2018 Rating 91 **To** 2028 $20 ✪
Sandpiper Barossa Cabernet Sauvignon 2018 Rating 90 **To** 2028 $20 ✪
Single Vineyard Selection St Kitts Block 226 Barossa Malbec 2018 Rating 90 **To** 2028 $40

Three Dark Horses ★★★★★

49 Fraser Avenue, Happy Valley, SA 5159 **Region** McLaren Vale
T 0405 294 500 **www.**3dh.com.au **Open** Not
Winemaker Matt Broomhead **Est.** 2009 **Dozens** 5000 **Vyds** 8.9ha

Three Dark Horses is the project of former Coriole winemaker Matt Broomhead. After vintages in southern Italy (2007) and the Rhône Valley, he returned to McLaren Vale in late 2009 and, with his father Alan, buys quality grapes, thanks to the many years of experience they both have in the region. The third dark horse is Matt's grandfather, a vintage regular. But things are changing. In Nov '17 the business acquired a vineyard in McLaren Vale and will build an onsite winery. They are expanding the plantings with grenache blanc, clairette and touriga nacional, and reworking some of the shiraz vines planted in 1964. Part of the vineyard is sand soil–based interspersed with ironstone, a highly desirable mix for shiraz and cabernet sauvignon. Exports to NZ and China.

🍷🍷🍷🍷🍷 **Frank Ernest McLaren Vale Shiraz 2016** 70yo vines, wild-fermented with 20% whole bunches, matured in French oak (50% new) for 24 months. Multi-horsepower but delivers its message in a controlled and balanced fashion. The sole question is whether less new oak (or a shorter maturation) might have made a better wine. Screwcap. 14.5% alc. **Rating** 96 **To** 2036 $50 ✪

McLaren Vale Shiraz 2018 With 10% whole bunches. Flavoursome shiraz with personality to burn and good persistence too. In short, it's a ripper shiraz to drink.

It's slightly meaty, plum-drenched, lively, juicy and herbal. Lots going on but, most importantly, it's inherently harmonious. Screwcap. 14.5% alc. **Rating** 94 **To** 2030 $25 CM ✪

McLaren Vale Shiraz 2017 Estate-grown, the vines 20–50yo; wild-fermented with 10% whole bunches, matured in French oak (30% new). Considerable power and drive; savoury, spicy. The freshness and zip of '17 is on full display. Will mature well. Screwcap. 14.5% alc. **Rating** 94 **To** 2032 $25 ✪

McLaren Vale Grenache 2018 From 70yo bushvines; fermented with 30% whole bunches, matured for 11 months in used French puncheons. The components of the palate slide seamlessly together, allowing equal space and time for each other to have their say. Great value. Screwcap. 14.5% alc. **Rating** 94 **To** 2023 $25 ✪

♥♥♥♥♀ **McLaren Vale Shiraz Touriga 2019 Rating** 92 **To** 2026 $25 CM ✪
McLaren Vale Shiraz Grenache Touriga 2017 Rating 92 **To** 2029 $22 ✪
Langhorne Creek Touriga 2018 Rating 92 **To** 2025 $25 ✪
McLaren Vale Fiano 2018 Rating 91 **To** 2022 $22 CM ✪

3 Drops   ★★★★★

PO Box 1828, Applecross, WA 6953 **Region** Mount Barker
T (08) 9315 4721 **www**.3drops.com **Open** Not
Winemaker Contract (Robert Diletti) **Est.** 1998 **Dozens** 3500 **Vyds** 21.5ha
3 Drops is the name given to the Bradbury family vineyard at Mount Barker. The name reflects three elements: wine, olive oil and water – all of which come from the substantial property. The vineyard is planted to riesling, sauvignon blanc, semillon, chardonnay, cabernet sauvignon, merlot, shiraz and cabernet franc, and irrigated by a large wetland on the property. 3 Drops also owns the 14.7ha Patterson's Vineyard, planted in 1982 to pinot noir, chardonnay and shiraz. Exports to South Korea, Hong Kong and China.

♥♥♥♥♥ **Great Southern Riesling 2019** Pale quartz-green. A single vineyard wine from Mount Barker made by Rob Diletti that is an exercise in purity. Starts with lime/lemon/Granny Smith apple, then a necklace of crisp, crunchy acidity to close. Screwcap. 12% alc. **Rating** 95 **To** 2029 $26 ✪

Great Southern Cabernets 2018 Eye-catching colour. Rich but restrained, the bouquet offers notes of blackcurrant, red berries, bay leaf, green herb and toasty oak; the flavours follow in similar vein. It flows effortlessly through the palate, fine tannin pulling it along and culminating with a gently mouth-puckering aftertaste. Screwcap. 14% alc. **Rating** 95 **To** 2030 $26 SC ✪

Great Southern Shiraz 2018 As always, this presents the unequivocally cool-climate character of Great Southern shiraz in a very approachable, juicy style. It's a seamless combination of peppery spice, red fruits and cedary, chocolatey oak. Well measured astringency provides balance and structure. Great drinking. Screwcap. 14% alc. **Rating** 94 **To** 2028 $26 SC ✪

Great Southern Merlot 2018 As good an invitation as any for those seeking merlot that has texture and structure to red and blackcurrant fruit – not residual sugar – that drives the palate with precision and balance. Screwcap. 14% alc. **Rating** 94 **To** 2028 $26 ✪

♥♥♥♥♀ **Great Southern Shiraz 2017 Rating** 92 **To** 2025 $26
Great Southern Cabernet Franc 2018 Rating 92 **To** 2025 $26 SC
Great Southern Pinot Noir 2018 Rating 91 **To** 2024 $32 JF
Great Southern Cabernets 2017 Rating 91 **To** 2027 $26
Great Southern Chardonnay 2018 Rating 90 **To** 2023 $28
Great Southern Nebbiolo Rose 2019 Rating 90 **To** 2021 $26

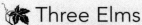 # Three Elms   ★★★★☆

82 Riversdale Road, Frankland River, WA 6396 **Region** Frankland River
T 0458 877 734 **www**.threeelms.com.au **Open** Not
Winemaker Laura Hallett **Est.** 2017 **Dozens** 8000 **Vyds** 44ha
This venture is succession planning at its best. Merv and Judy Lange had a 1200ha wool and grain farm when, in 1971, they decided to plant a few vines as a possible diversification. They were the first to take this step in the Frankland River region and Alkoomi was born. My first visit in '81 was illuminating. They had all the viticultural equipment required, and needed no outside help in creating and progressively expanding the size of the vineyard or building an initially small winery. Roll forward to 2014 and Alkoomi is one of the Top 100 Australian Wineries in my book published that year, with 104ha of estate vineyards and annual production of 60000 dozen. Four years earlier (in '10) they had handed ownership to daughter Sandy and husband Rod Hallett, who had been an integral part of the business for many years as they raised their three daughters Emily, Laura and Molly. In '17 Three Elms was established, its name taking the first letter of the name of each daughter. Laura obtained a Bachelor of Agribusiness, majoring in viticulture, from Curtin University in '15. Her sisters both have admin/marketing roles in the business and are both part of decision making in the management group of Three Elms. Exports to the US, Denmark, Singapore, Taiwan and China.

🍷🍷🍷🍷🍷 **Mount Frankland Shiraz 2018** Single vineyard, single block, single batch. Destemmed, open-fermented, 15 days on skins, matured for 18 months in French oak (30% new). Intense and powerful black fruits of the Frankland River. Has the balance and length to repay prolonged cellaring. Screwcap. 14.5% alc. **Rating** 95 To 2038 $55
Mount Frankland Shiraz 2017 Those fresh red cherries, those sweet, saturated plums, those floral overtones. Throw black pepper spice, clove and malty oak into the mix, add sheets of fine-grained tannin and you have yourself a lovely medium-weighted wine of genuine quality. Creamy mouthfeel too, which never hurts. Screwcap. 14.5% alc. **Rating** 94 To 2032 $55 CM

🍷🍷🍷🍷♀ **Timbertops Great Southern Riesling 2019** Rating 92 To 2025 $30
Timbertops Frankland River Shiraz 2017 Rating 92 To 2025 $35 CM
Timbertops Great Southern Cabernet Sauvignon 2017 Rating 92 To 2028 $35 CM
Timbertops Frankland River Shiraz 2018 Rating 90 To 2025 $35
Timbertops Great Southern Cabernet Sauvignon 2018 Rating 90 To 2026 $35

Three Kangaroos   ★★★★☆

Level 3, 242–244 Franklin Street, Adelaide, SA 5000 **Region** Barossa Valley
T (08) 8212 0459 **www**.threekangaroos.com.au **Open** Not
Winemaker Janelle Badrice (Consultant) **Est.** 2014 **Dozens** NFP **Vyds** 30.4ha
What a surprise, and what a pleasure. Three Kangaroos began as a virtual wine business that owned neither vineyard nor winery, its primary business exporting wines to Vietnam, Japan and China. There is nothing unusual in this business strategy but it's rare for such wines to be of high quality. Owners Easan Liu and Tally Gao had previous successful business ventures in real estate and telecommunications and in 2012 they began an international wine distribution business, expanding this by establishing Three Kangaroos; they now own just over 30ha of vines in Stockwell. Exports to Vietnam, Japan and China.

🍷🍷🍷🍷🍷 **Double Barrels Barossa Valley Shiraz 2017** Matured for 30 months in oak. Bright, deep crimson-purple. This has so much vibrant black cherry/berry fruit that the oak is irrelevant to its quality. The vintage has played a far more important role, giving the wine a sense of precision and a finish that is exceptionally long. Cork. 14.5% alc. **Rating** 96 To 2037 $60 ⊙

Citrus Flowers Eden Valley Riesling 2019 Appropriately named as aromas of citrus flowers are easily found in the bouquet, along with lemon zest and honeysuckle. The flavours are yet to fully develop on the palate, but there's an excellent framework in place for them to do so with a tight line of acidity as the spine and a chalky, minerally finish with some real persistence in the aftertaste. Worth cellaring. Screwcap. 12.5% alc. **Rating** 94 **To** 2034 $35 SC

ΨΨΨΨ **Hill Side Barossa Valley Cabernet Sauvignon Shiraz 2018** Rating 93 **To** 2033 $60
Only Yesterday Barossa Valley Grenache Shiraz Mataro 2019 Rating 91 **To** 2022 $45 SC
Elegant Knight Barossa Valley Grenache 2019 Rating 90 **To** 2022 $45 SC

3 Willows Vineyard   ★★★★

46 Montana Road, Red Hills, Tas 7304 **Region** Northern Tasmania
T 0488 417 980 **www.3willows.com.au Open** See www
Winemaker Shane Holloway **Est.** 2002 **Dozens** 270 **Vyds** 1.6ha
Peter and Susan Stokes relocated from Sydney's northern beaches to 3 Willows Vineyard in Tasmania in late 2017. Peter was a senior manager in local council and has now studied viticulture at Launceston TAFE and Susan was a senior ancient history teacher. They look after the vines together (expanding the vineyard with recent plantings of pinot noir and chardonnay) and Susan runs the cellar door, boutique B&B, weddings and events. The wines are made by Shane Holloway at Delamere.

ΨΨΨΨ **Pinot Gris 2019** Pinot gris performs best in cool climates, although its ubiquitous presence is on the mainland. This has a much richer palate for the winemaker to experiment with: pear supported by tropical and citrus fruits alike. Screwcap. 13.8% alc. **Rating** 93 **To** 2026 $28
Old Block Pinot Noir 2019 From the estate vineyard in the northwest corner of Tasmania. Bright, clear colour. A statement of variety and place that adds up to a light-bodied wine, juicy red/purple fruits with a salt and pepper touch of forest/forest floor. Screwcap. 13% alc. **Rating** 93 **To** 2028 $40

🍇 Tillie J   ★★★★☆

305 68B Gadd Street, Northcote, Vic 3070 (postal) **Region** Yarra Valley
T 0428 554 311 **Open** Not
Winemaker Tillie Johnston **Est.** 2019 **Dozens** 200
Mark my words. Tillie Johnston is going to become a great winemaker. She began her career in 2012, one of the vintage crew at Coldstream Hills, and says her love for pinot noir began there. She then spent four of the next eight years 'gypsying' between the Northern and Southern hemispheres unerringly picking the eyes out of an all-star cast of wineries: Leeuwin Estate, Brokenwood, Cristom (Oregon), Keller (Rheinhessen), Framingham (Marlborough) and Yarra Yering. Since then, she's been Assistant Winemaker at Giant Steps to Steve Flamsteed and Jess Clark. In '19 she was offered the opportunity to buy 2t of grapes from Helen's Hill of whatever variety she chose which was, of course, pinot noir. It came in two parcels: one Pommard and 943, hand-picked, whole bunches and destemmed; the second 777, Selectiv' harvested, 100% whole berries. Seven barriques: one new, six used.

ΨΨΨΨ **Yarra Valley Pinot Noir 2019** Pommard, 943 and 777 clones from Helen's Hill; open-fermented, daily pumpovers, matured for 9 months in barriques. Tillie Johnston's exposure to great makers of pinot around the world is the soul of this elegant, very long pinot. It is perfumed and, while light-bodied, has great mouthfeel from emery-board tannins. Screwcap. 13% alc. **Rating** 95 **To** 2029 $35 ✪

Tim Adams ★★★★★

156 Warenda Road, Clare, SA 5453 **Region** Clare Valley
T (08) 8842 2429 **www**.timadamswines.com.au **Open** Mon–Fri 10.30–5, w'ends 11–5
Winemaker Tim Adams, Brett Schutz **Est.** 1986 **Dozens** 60 000 **Vyds** 145ha
Tim Adams and partner Pam Goldsack preside over a highly successful business. Having expanded the range of estate plantings with tempranillo, pinot gris and viognier, in 2009 the business took a giant step forward with the acquisition of the 80ha Leasingham Rogers Vineyard from CWA, followed in '11 by the purchase of the Leasingham winery and winemaking equipment (for less than replacement cost). The winery is now a major contract winemaking facility for the region. Exports to the UK, the Netherlands, Sweden, South Korea, Hong Kong, China and NZ.

🍷🍷🍷🍷🍷 **Skilly Ridge Clare Valley Riesling 2018** Dazzling quartz-green. This has a purity and restraint that is in the fountainhead of all great rieslings. It is as much about what it doesn't have (overt acidity, extract, etc.) as it is about its many high points. Free-run juice from high quality grapes has its own reward. Part of this wine has been held back for release in 8–10 years' time (at a very different price no doubt). Screwcap. 11% alc. **Rating** 97 **To** 2043 $30 ✪

🍷🍷🍷🍷🍷 **Clare Valley Riesling 2019** In one sense there's nothing much to say about this wine, simply because its persona is classic Clare. Lemon, lemongrass and lime fruit are fused together by acidity that doesn't jar on the finish, simply provides the all-important length and crisp finish. Screwcap. 11.5% alc. **Rating** 95 **To** 2034 $24 ✪
Clare Valley Cabernet Malbec 2016 In excellent form. Fluid, characterful and soft but with the inherent structure to last. Red and black berries, gum leaf, vanilla and violets. Leathery, leafy characters too. As soon as you open it you know you're onto something good. Terrific value. Screwcap. 14.5% alc. **Rating** 94 **To** 2028 $26 CM ✪

🍷🍷🍷🍷🍷 **Clare Valley Semillon 2017** Rating 92 **To** 2025 $25 CM ✪
The Fergus 2015 Rating 91 **To** 2026 $25
Clare Valley Shiraz 2016 Rating 90 **To** 2026 $26

Tim McNeil Wines ★★★★☆

71 Springvale Road, Watervale, SA 5452 **Region** Clare Valley
T (08) 8843 0040 **www**.timmcneilwines.com.au **Open** Fri–Sun & public hols 11–5
Winemaker Tim McNeil **Est.** 2004 **Dozens** 1500 **Vyds** 2ha
When Tim and Cass McNeil established Tim McNeil Wines, Tim had long since given up his teaching career, graduating with a degree in oenology from the University of Adelaide in 1999. He then spent 11 years honing his craft at important wineries in the Barossa and Clare valleys. In Aug 2010 Tim McNeil Wines became his full-time job. The McNeils' 16ha property at Watervale includes mature dry-grown riesling. The cellar door overlooks the riesling vineyard, with panoramic views of Watervale and beyond. Exports to Canada.

🍷🍷🍷🍷🍷 **Reserve Watervale Riesling 2018** On an altogether different level to the '19: 1 year older, the better vintage and the Reserve designation. Meyer lemon and Rose's lime juice are Bib and Bub, caressed by life-giving acidity that also provides length. Screwcap. 13% alc. **Rating** 95 **To** 2028 $32 ✪

🍷🍷🍷🍷🍷 **Watervale Riesling 2019** Rating 92 **To** 2030 $24 ✪

Tim Smith Wines ★★★★★

PO Box 446, Tanunda, SA 5352 **Region** Barossa Valley
T 0416 396 730 **www**.timsmithwines.com.au **Open** Not
Winemaker Tim Smith **Est.** 2002 **Dozens** 5000 **Vyds** 1ha
With a talent for sourcing exceptional old vine fruit from the Barossa floor, Tim Smith has created a small but credible portfolio of wines, currently including mataro, grenache, shiraz, viognier and, more recently, Eden Valley Riesling and Viognier. Tim left his full-time

winemaking role with a large Barossa company in 2011, allowing him to concentrate 100% of his energy on his own brand. In '12 Tim joined forces with the team from First Drop (see separate entry), and has moved winemaking operations to a brand-new winery fondly named 'Home of the Brave', in Nuriootpa. Exports to the UK, the US, Canada, Denmark, Taiwan and Singapore.

ŸŸŸŸŸ **Eden Valley Riesling 2019** This is blazing with freshness and attractive grip. The acidity snakes along the citrus/apple fruit line in classic mouth-watering fashion. To be enjoyed on command. Screwcap. 11% alc. **Rating** 95 **To** 2029 $28 ○

Reserve Barossa Shiraz 2018 From 4 of Tim Smith Wines' favourite vineyards in the Eden and Barossa valleys. Deep crimson-purple. A constellation of sombre black fruits, spice, pepper and licorice opening up layer upon layer as the wine is retasted, yet the tannins and oak are neatly controlled. You could drink more than a glass of this. Screwcap. 14.5% alc. **Rating** 95 **To** 2038 $125

Barossa Shiraz 2017 From vineyards in the Barossa and Eden valleys, matured on lees in French oak for 20 months. Has the '17 vintage drive and intensity to its black fruits that will underwrite very long development in bottle. Screwcap. 14.5% alc. **Rating** 94 **To** 2042 $40

ŸŸŸŸŸ **Barossa Valley Mataro 2018 Rating** 92 **To** 2032 $40

Tinklers Vineyard   ★★★★★

Pokolbin Mountains Road, Pokolbin, NSW 2320 **Region** Hunter Valley
T (02) 4998 7435 **www**.tinklers.com.au **Open** 7 days 10–5
Winemaker Usher Tinkler **Est.** 1946 **Dozens** 7000 **Vyds** 41ha
Three generations of the Tinkler family have been involved with the property since 1942. Originally a beef and dairy farm, vines have been both pulled out and replanted at various stages and part of the adjoining 80+-year-old Ben Ean Vineyard has been acquired. Plantings include semillon (14ha), shiraz (11.5ha), chardonnay (6.5ha) and smaller areas of merlot, muscat and viognier. The majority of the grape production is sold to McWilliam's and Tyrrell's. Usher has resigned his roles as chief winemaker at Poole's Rock and Cockfighter's Ghost to take on full-time responsibility at Tinklers, and production has been increased to meet demand. Exports to Sweden, Singapore and China.

ŸŸŸŸŸ **Museum Release School Block Hunter Valley Semillon 2014** A museum release. The '14s are delicious. Suave. Cool. Transparent with a serious pulse towing the flavours long: grapefruit pulp, citrus zest, Asian pear, lemongrass and tatami. A hint of buttered toast and lanolin emerging, auguring well for more as the wine matures. Bags of life left. Screwcap. **Rating** 95 **To** 2028 $25 NG ○

Old Vines Hunter Valley Shiraz 2018 Given 10 months in French wood. So on the money! This is how contemporary Hunter shiraz should be made. Frisky and mid-weighted, the extraction partial whole-berry gentle; a skein of juicy acidity and gentle tannins placating the seams. This is a lovely drink. Bravo! Not intellectual. But poised, relaxed and absolutely thirst-quenching and delicious. Screwcap. **Rating** 95 **To** 2024 $35 NG ○

School Block Hunter Valley Semillon 2019 I like the '19 Hunter semillon. The wines, while lightweighted, are a bit more bumptious. Forward. There is a waxy sheen of chalky phenolics that is very attractive, usurping the role of the tart acid norm. More pucker over sour rasp. This, from sandy gravel, exudes hay, lemon-drop candy and quince notes. A delicious wine that will fatten with mid-term cellaring, but is already delicious. Screwcap. **Rating** 94 **To** 2028 $25 NG ○

U and I Hunter Valley Shiraz 2018 The name is suggestive of the partnership between brothers Usher and Ian. Get it? Very good. Full-bodied, despite the clench of reduction and confluence with quality oak tightening up the seams. Mottled blueberry, iodine, salumi and tapenade. The freshness is not forced; the finish long and pulpy. A delicious wine. Screwcap. **Rating** 94 **To** 2030 $45 NG

🍷🍷🍷🍷⚲ Museum Release Reserve Hunter Valley Semillon 2015 Rating 93
To 2025 $35 NG
Museum Release School Block Hunter Valley Semillon 2015 Rating 93
To 2025 $25 NG ⊘
Hill Chardonnay 2019 Rating 92 To 2024 $25 NG ⊘
PMR Merlot 2018 Rating 92 To 2023 $25 NG ⊘
Mount Bright Semillon 2019 Rating 91 To 2027 $22 NG ⊘
Poppys Hunter Valley Chardonnay 2019 Rating 91 To 2024 $35 NG

Tokar Estate   ★★★★★

6 Maddens Lane, Coldstream, Vic 3770 **Region** Yarra Valley
T (03) 5964 9585 **www**.tokarestate.com.au **Open** 7 days 10.30–5
Winemaker Martin Siebert **Est.** 1996 **Dozens** 5000 **Vyds** 12ha
Leon Tokar, a very successful businessman, and wife Rita dreamed of a weekender and hobby
farm and it was largely by chance that in 1995 they found a scruffy paddock fronting onto
Maddens Lane. By the end of the day they had signed a contract to buy the property, following
in the footsteps of myself, and wife Suzanne, ten years earlier when we also signed a contract
to purchase what became Coldstream Hills on the day we first set foot on it (albeit several
years after we first saw it). The Tokars wasted no time and by '99 had planted their 12ha
vineyard and built a Mediterranean-inspired cellar door and restaurant. Martin Siebert has
been winemaker for many years, making consistently good wines and, with son Daniel Tokar
as general manager, has full responsibility for the day-to-day management of the business.
Exports to the UK, Canada, Malaysia and China.

🍷🍷🍷🍷🍷 Coldstream Vineyard Yarra Valley Pinot Noir 2018 Hand-picked, wild-
fermented with 30% whole bunches and a long post-ferment maceration. Ablaze
with spices and flowery nuances on the bouquet; the palate long and silky smooth,
red berries through to the finish. Delicious. Screwcap. 13.5% alc. **Rating** 95
To 2029 $50
Coldstream Vineyard Yarra Valley Cabernet Sauvignon 2018 The same
vinification as the 'white label' cabernet, but rigourous barrel selection and
maturation in French hogsheads (30% new). More fruit, more oak, the same
balance and texture. Screwcap. 13.6% alc. **Rating** 95 To 2038 $50
Yarra Valley Cabernet Sauvignon 2018 Hand-picked, destemmed and
crushed, wild-fermented, matured in French hogsheads for 10 months. Pure
varietal expression through the bouquet and medium-bodied palate. Balance and
length also tick the boxes. Screwcap. 13.5% alc. **Rating** 94 To 2030 $30 ⊘

🍷🍷🍷🍷⚲ Yarra Valley Shiraz 2018 Rating 92 To 2025 $30 CM
Yarra Valley Tempranillo 2018 Rating 91 To 2024 $30 CM
Coldstream Vineyard Tempranillo 2018 Rating 91 To 2026 $50

Tolpuddle Vineyard   ★★★★★

37 Back Tea Tree Road, Richmond, Tas 7025 **Region** Southern Tasmania
T (08) 8155 6003 **www**.tolpuddlevineyard.com **Open** At Shaw + Smith
Winemaker Martin Shaw, Adam Wadewitz **Est.** 1988 **Dozens** 1800 **Vyds** 20ha
If ever a winery was born with blue blood in its veins, Tolpuddle would have to be it. The
vineyard was established in 1988 on a continuous downhill slope facing northeast; in '06 it
won the inaugural Tasmanian Vineyard of the Year Award. Michael Hill Smith MW and
Martin Shaw are joint managing directors. David LeMire looks after sales and marketing;
Adam Wadewitz, one of Australia's brightest winemaking talents, is senior winemaker.
Vineyard manager Carlos Souris loses nothing in comparison, with over 30 years of
grapegrowing in Tasmania under his belt and an absolutely fearless approach to making a
great vineyard even greater. Exports to the US, the UK, Canada, Denmark, China, Japan
and Singapore.

🍷🍷🍷🍷🍷 Chardonnay 2018 Hand-picked, whole-bunch pressed, fermented in French oak
barrels with limited stirring. The bouquet and palate send the same message of

perfectly captured white stone fruits, then apple and grapefruit. An irresistible wine with spectacular length. Screwcap. 13% alc. **Rating** 98 **To** 2033 $75 ✪
Pinot Noir 2018 Hand-picked, a combination of whole bunch and whole berry in open fermenters, matured in French oak (33% new) for 9 months. It is a portrait of top end Tasmanian pinot noir. Intensely aromatic, it achieves complexity and depth to its spice-laden berry aromas and flavours. Beautiful. Screwcap. 13.5% alc. **Rating** 97 **To** 2030 $85 ✪

Tomboy Hill   ★★★★★

204 Sim Street, Ballarat, Vic 3350 (postal) **Region** Ballarat
T (03) 5331 3785 **Open** Not
Winemaker Scott Ireland, Sam Vogel (Contract) **Est.** 1984 **Dozens** 500 **Vyds** 3.6ha
Former schoolteacher Ian Watson seems to be following the same path as Lindsay McCall of Paringa Estate (also a former schoolteacher) in extracting greater quality and style than any other winery in their respective regions. Since 1984 Ian has patiently built up a patchwork quilt of small plantings of chardonnay and pinot noir. In the better years, single vineyard Chardonnay and/or Pinot Noir are released; Rebellion Chardonnay and Pinot Noir are multi-vineyard blends, but all 100% Ballarat. After difficult vintages in 2011 and '12, Tomboy Hill has been in top form since '15.

🍷🍷🍷🍷🍷 **Jude's Picking Chardonnay 2018** While the focus is more stone fruit than citrus, more creamy leesy than funky sulphides, it makes a convincing case. A hint of toffee-nutty oak adds another layer of flavour. It's by no means a big wine but it does have a certain power thanks to a fine line of natural acidity. Only 50 dozen made. Screwcap. 13.5% alc. **Rating** 95 **To** 2028 $55 JF
Jude's Picking Pinot Noir 2018 Yes it has the mint DNA attached but there's so much in this that the mint just acts as another seasoning. Like the exotic spices and licorice across flavours of blood orange and dark cherries. Full-bodied, determined tannins and oak neatly etched. Only 50 dozen made. Ouch. Screwcap. 13.2% alc. **Rating** 95 **To** 2028 $75 JF

🍷🍷🍷🍷🍷 **Rebellion Ballarat Pinot Noir 2018 Rating** 90 **To** 2026 $35 JF

Tomich Wines   ★★★★★

87 King William Road, Unley, SA 5061 **Region** Adelaide Hills
T (08) 8299 7500 **www**.tomich.com.au **Open** Mon–Sat 11–4
Winemaker Randal Tomich **Est.** 2002 **Dozens** 40 000 **Vyds** 85ha
Patriarch John Tomich was born on a vineyard near Mildura, where he learnt firsthand the skills and knowledge required for premium grapegrowing. He went on to become a well known Adelaide ear, nose and throat specialist. Taking the wheel full circle, he completed postgraduate studies in winemaking at the University of Adelaide in 2002 and embarked on the Master of Wine revision course from the Institute of Masters of Wine. His son Randal is a cutting from the old vine (metaphorically speaking), having invented new equipment and techniques for tending the family's vineyard in the Adelaide Hills, resulting in a 60% saving in time and fuel costs. Exports to the US, Singapore and China.

🍷🍷🍷🍷🍷 **Woodside Vineyard I777 Adelaide Hills Pinot Noir 2018** The nomenclature refers to Block I and straight 777 clone, an earlier ripening Dijon clone. This is an exceptional Adelaide Hills pinot. As good as the region gives us. Nothing root-spiced sarsaparilla about this. Thankfully. Truffled underbrush, red and black cherry and, most joyously, fibrous svelte tannins and natural-feeling acidity propelling this long. Very. The tannins growing in stature across the mouth. Bravo! Cork. **Rating** 96 **To** 2025 $60 NG ✪
Woodside Vineyard Q96 Adelaide Hills Chardonnay 2018 This tastes expensive and rightly so: ambient barrel fermentation, judicious lees work and classy French barrique, Burgundian and Bordeaux cooperage (30%, 18 months). Stone fruit accents aplenty. But the best bit is the confluence of mealy oatmeal notes and toasted hazelnut scents, care of the barrel work. A mineral thread

plies the components, towing them impressively long. This will age well. Cork.
Rating 95 To 2028 $60 NG

Woodside Vineyard Adelaide Hills Pinot Noir 2018 A pallid to mid-ruby.
Bing cherry and fecund strawberry notes are strung across a herbal carapace of
spiced tannins. Think clove, cardamom and turmeric. And yet there is nothing
green. Zilch! Fibrous, energetic and long. Lightweight and ethereal. A lovely pinot,
so well appointed across its varied constituents, tasting far more expensive than
what it is. Screwcap. Rating 95 To 2023 $30 NG ✪

H888 Adelaide Hills Shiraz 2018 A single block offering, this is opaque of hue,
belied by the fireworks of floral aromas: violet, iodine, smoked meat and anise. The
overall impression is one of lift and pulpy blue fruits. The finish is juicy. Long and
succulent. Nothing drying. A little American oak–coffee bean nestled beautifully.
I dig this. Cork. Rating 95 To 2025 NG

Tomich Hill Hilltop Adelaide Hills Pinot Noir 2018 This is solid estate pinot;
hand-picked and given the love of wild fermentation, a smidgeon of whole bunch
(10%) for aromatic lift and spike, and 100% quality French oak. It remonstrates
too, against the medicinal notes that too often define the region. Firm. Juicy. Dark
cherry. The oak seams are classy, tucking it all in. Excellent. Screwcap. Rating 94
To $25 NG ✪

♟♟♟♟♟ **Woodside Vineyard Adelaide Hills Shiraz 2018** Rating 93 To 2023
$30 NG

Tomich Hill McLaren Vale Shiraz 2018 Rating 93 To 2024 $25 NG ✪

Woodside Vineyard Adelaide Hills Pinot Gris 2019 Rating 92 To 2022
$25 NG ✪

Tomich Hill Barossa Valley Shiraz 2018 Rating 91 To 2024 $25 NG

Tomich Hill Adelaide Hills Sauvignon Blanc 2019 Rating 90 To 2020
$22 NG

Woodside Vineyard Adelaide Hills Sauvignon Blanc 2019 Rating 90
To 2021 $25 NG

Tomich Hill Adelaide Hills Pinot Grigio 2019 Rating 90 To 2021 $22 NG

Toolangi Vineyards   ★★★★★

Rochford, 878–880 Maroondah Highway, Coldstream, Vic 3770 **Region** Yarra Valley
T (03) 5947 3388 **www**.toolangi.com **Open** At Rochford Wines
Winemaker Kaspar Hermann, Kelly Healey **Est.** 1995 **Dozens** 7500 **Vyds** 12.2ha
Helmut Konecsny, owner of Rochford Wines, purchased Toolangi Vineyards in 2018 and
immediately started ringing in the changes. Apart from new-look packaging, Konecsny and
his winemaking and vineyard team also set about rejuvenating and upgrading the vineyard
and introducing new winemaking practises. Exports to Fiji and China.

♟♟♟♟♟ **F Block Yarra Valley Chardonnay 2019** Hand-picked Gingin clone, the 18yo
vines considered to be the best on the property. Whole-bunch pressed with solids
to French barriques and puncheons (35% new) for fermentation and maturation.
With layered fruit of the highest quality, it is as long as it is complex, oak merely a
whisper. Screwcap. 13.5% alc. Rating 97 To 2032 $100 ✪

♟♟♟♟♟ **Pauls Lane Yarra Valley Chardonnay 2019** From 24yo vines, I10V3
and Gingin clones; crushed and pressed with juice solids to French barriques
(20% new). Again the drive is exceptional, the fruit range the classic cool-grown
duo of grapefruit and white peach. Screwcap. 13.5% alc. Rating 96 To 2030
$44 ✪

E Block Yarra Valley Pinot Noir 2019 From 18yo MV6 clones; hand-picked,
destemmed whole berries, cold soak, 12 days on skins, matured in French oak
(10% new) for 10 months. Very well made to throw all of the attention onto
flavour and texture. Screwcap. 13% alc. Rating 96 To 2029 $100

Yarra Valley Chardonnay 2019 From 18yo vines, clones I10V3 and Mendoza;
hand-picked, crushed and pressed with juice solids to French puncheons

(10% new), no mlf, 10 months on lees. Has unexpected drive and intensity of pink grapefruit flavour. Screwcap. 13.5% alc. **Rating** 95 **To** 2027 $30
Pauls Lane Yarra Valley Pinot Noir 2019 From 18yo MV6 vines; hand-picked, 80% wholes berries, 20% whole bunches wild-fermented in French oak (20% new), matured for 10 months. The vinification provides a forest floor/funk complexity to both the texture and wild-berry flavour. Screwcap. 13% alc. **Rating** 95 **To** 2029 $44

🍷🍷🍷🍷 **Yarra Valley Pinot Noir 2019 Rating** 91 **To** 2024 $30

Toorak Winery ★★★☆

Vineyard 279 Toorak Road, Leeton, NSW 2705 **Region** Riverina
T (02) 6953 2333 **www**.toorakwines.com.au **Open** Mon–Fri 10–5, w'ends by appt
Winemaker Robert Bruno, Martin Wozniak **Est.** 1965 **Dozens** 200000 **Vyds** 145ha
A traditional, long-established Riverina producer with a strong Italian-based clientele. Production has increased significantly, utilising substantial estate plantings and grapes purchased from other growers in the Riverina and elsewhere. Wines are released under the Willandra Estate, Willandra Leeton Selection, Amesbury Estate and Toorak Road labels. There has been a shift in emphasis away from bulk and buyers-own-brand sales and towards improving quality of Toorak's own brands. Exports to the US, China and other major markets.

🍷🍷🍷🍷 **Toorak Road Tumbarumba Pinot Noir 2018** Good colour and quality; fresh mouthfeel and dark cherry aromas and flavours. At its best now and is a credit to Toorak. Screwcap. 13.5% alc. **Rating** 90 **To** 2025

Top Note ★★★★

546 Peters Creek Road, Kuitpo, SA 5172 **Region** Adelaide Hills
T 0406 291 136 **www**.topnote.com.au **Open** W'ends 11–4 (closed Jun–Jul)
Winemaker Nick Foskett **Est.** 2011 **Dozens** 800 **Vyds** 17ha
Computer chip designer Nick and opera singer Cate Foskett were looking for a lifestyle property in the Adelaide Hills after full-on careers in their very different occupations. By chance they came across a 24ha property planted to five varieties, all mainstream except for 0.5ha of a rare mutation of semillon that turns the skin red. They say, 'Despite the small hurdles of our not knowing much about anything and none of the grapes being under contract, we sold our city house, enrolled in postgraduate viticulture and winemaking at the Waite Campus, University of Adelaide, and became grapegrowers'. Two years on, Cate became possibly the only qualified operatic viticulturist in the world and still works as a singer between harvests, managing the vineyard and sales.

🍷🍷🍷🍷 **Adelaide Hills Cabernet Sauvignon 2017** The potential of the vintage was challenged again and again; incessant rain made mildew a trial, spraying by helicopter was the only solution, the ground too wet for the tractor. Normally picked in early Apr, the grapes were picked on 10 May. The wine is light-bodied, but does have enough sweet cassis fruit to save the day. Screwcap. 13.5% alc. **Rating** 90 **To** 2026 $35

Topper's Mountain Wines ★★★★

13420 Guyra Road, Tingha, NSW 2369 **Region** New England
T 0411 880 580 **www**.toppers.com.au **Open** By appt
Winemaker Mike Hayes, Jared Dixon, Glen Robert **Est.** 2000 **Dozens** 1000 **Vyds** 9.79ha
Topper's Mountain is named after brothers Edward and William Topper, who were employees of George Jr and Alwyn Wyndham (sons of George Wyndham, founder of Wyndham Estate). They previously owned 'New Valley Station', which included the present day 'Topper's Mountain'. These days, Topper's Mountain is owned by Mark Kirkby. Planting began in the spring of 2000 with the ultimate fruit salad trial of 15 rows each of innumerable varieties and clones. The total area planted was made up of 28 separate plantings, many of these with only 200 vines in a block. As varieties proved unsuitable, they were grafted over to those that held

the most promise. Thus far, gewurztraminer and sauvignon blanc hold most promise among the white wines, the Mediterranean reds doing better than their French cousins. The original 28 varieties are now down to 16; chardonnay, gewurztraminer, sauvignon blanc, tempranillo, shiraz and merlot are the commercial varieties, the remainder in the fruit salad block still under evaluation. In February '19 a bushfire destroyed 90% of the vineyard hours before harvest was due to begin. Exports to Germany, Singapore and Japan.

ŸŸŸŸŸ **Vintage Tinta Roriz 2010** A rare find, a New England fortified tinta roriz (aka tempranillo) with 10 years' bottle age. No wonder the number of bottles produced is so small (987). And it's good. This is indicated not only by the youthful colour (red) and fruit development and expression (chocolate, currants, licorice with lovely spice) but also its super fresh spirit. It's delicious now but it's bound for greater riches with way more time in bottle. Screwcap. 18.5% alc. **Rating** 92 $35 JP

Torbreck Vintners ★★★★★

Roennfeldt Road, Marananga, SA 5352 **Region** Barossa Valley
T (08) 8562 4155 **www**.torbreck.com **Open** 7 days 10–6
Winemaker Ian Hongell, Scott McDonald **Est.** 1994 **Dozens** 55 000 **Vyds** 150ha
Torbreck Vintners was already one of Australia's best known high quality red wine makers when, in Sept 2013, wealthy Californian entrepreneur and vintner Peter Kight (of Quivira Vineyards) acquired 100% ownership of the business. The brand structure remains as before: the top quartet led by The Laird (single vineyard shiraz), RunRig (shiraz/viognier), The Factor (shiraz) and Descendant (shiraz/viognier). Exports to all major markets.

ŸŸŸŸŸ **The Factor 2016** Deep and densely coloured. Full-bodied and rich in Torbreck style. On the first assessment the wine is indeed impressive, then impact ex tannins and alcohol hit, then a mouthful of soda water recalibrates all and the black cherry, blackberry, licorice and charcuterie flavours come striding through on the mid-palate and on to the finish. Cork. 15% alc. **Rating** 97 **To** 2046 $125 ✪

ŸŸŸŸŸ **The Gask 2017** Several winemakers over the years at Torbreck have managed to make the alcohol irrelevant. It's certainly the case here, the palate fresh and elegant, the winemaker's thumbprint all but invisible. Good now, still better later. Cork. 15% alc. **Rating** 95 **To** 2032 $75
Hillside Vineyard Barossa Valley Shiraz and Roussanne 2018 Very good colour. The bouquet overflows with spices/garam marsala, some of those flavours adopted in the complex/textured palate, juices running one way, tannins the other. There's some whole-bunch influence. Screwcap. 14.5% alc. **Rating** 95 **To** 2033 $32 ✪
Hillside Vineyard Barossa Valley Grenache 2017 Only Torbreck could construct a grenache as awesome – monolithic – as this. Despite its power, it is balanced and varietal. All you have to decide is whether there can be too much of a good thing. Cork. 15% alc. **Rating** 95 **To** 2027 $75
Barossa Valley Marsanne 2018 Barrel fermentation in used oak has helped broaden the base for long-term development. You can taste the wild honey that will intensify with age and feel the acidity that will remain the key to the future. Screwcap. 13% alc. **Rating** 94 **To** 2028 $49

ŸŸŸŸŸ **Woodcutter's Barossa Valley Shiraz 2018 Rating** 90 **To** 2029 $29

🍇 Tornielli Family Wines ★★★

450 Spring Gully Road, Emu Flat, SA 5453 **Region** Langhorne Creek/Barossa Valley
T 0424 801 590 **www**.tfwines.com **Open** By appt
Winemaker Ed Tornielli **Est.** 2015 **Dozens** 8000
The Tornielli family traces its winemaking roots in Italy back to 1500, albeit with gaps during wars and relocations within Italy. The last vintage in Italy was in 1966, and another gap to 2014 when Eduardo (Ed) Torniello migrated to Australia with a Bachelor of Science in Law,

and a post-graduate course in Food and Beverage Logistics gained in China. The extensive website is full of grand plans and statements such as 'The wines are the resultant (sic) blend of Italian tradition and Australia viniculture, with notes of each country's cultures, marking for a strong yet refined finish' or 'Our vineyards are Langhorne Creek and Barossa Valley', and there is no winery mentioned. Exports to China.

ŸŸŸŸ **Langhorne Creek Shiraz 2015** Very good colour. The best value of the Torinelli range with bright red fruits to open and some structure to the finish. Screwcap. 15% alc. **Rating** 89 **To** 2022 $29
500 Series Barossa Valley Shiraz 2015 Massively extractive and heavily alcoholic. It's a wine that points to the past, not the future. Cork. 15.5% alc. **Rating** 89 **To** 2023 $75

Torzi Matthews Vintners ★★★★★

Cnr Eden Valley Road/Sugarloaf Hill Road, Mt McKenzie, SA 5353 **Region** Eden Valley **T** 0412 323 486 **www.torzimatthews.com.au Open** By appt **Winemaker** Domenic Torzi **Est.** 1996 **Dozens** 3000 **Vyds** 10ha
Domenic Torzi and Tracy Matthews, former Adelaide Plains residents, searched for a number of years before finding a block at Mt McKenzie in the Eden Valley. The block they chose is in a hollow; the soil is meagre but they were in no way deterred by the knowledge that it would be frost-prone. The result is predictably low yields, concentrated further by drying the grapes on racks, thus reducing the weight by around 30% (the Appassimento method is used in Italy to produce Amarone-style wines). Newer plantings of sangiovese and negro amaro, and an extension of the original plantings of shiraz and riesling, have seen the wine range increase. Exports to the UK and Denmark.

ŸŸŸŸŸ **Frost Dodger Eden Valley Riesling 2019** Such energy with this that starts with florals and lemon bath salts. Its acidity finely tuned across the palate. It has depth, texture and is deliciously dry. It finishes with great composure. Screwcap. 12.5% alc. **Rating** 95 **To** 2030 $28 JF ❂
Frost Dodger Single Vineyard Eden Valley Shiraz 2018 There is something rather compelling about this, starting with its inky, crimson hue. Heady with florals, dark fruit and lots of oak and Mediterranean herbs. Glossy rich palate, ripe but not overwhelming. It's savoury, tarry and cries out for chargrilled meat. Screwcap. 14.5% alc. **Rating** 95 **To** 2033 $48 JF

ŸŸŸŸŸ **Schist Rock Barossa Shiraz 2018 Rating** 93 **To** 2028 $25 JF ❂
Terraced Hills Adelaide Hills Chardonnay 2018 Rating 92 **To** 2026 $28 JF
Terraced Hills Adelaide Hills Pinot Noir 2018 Rating 92 **To** 2027 $28 JF

Towerhill Estate ★★★★★

32288 Albany Highway, Mount Barker, WA 6324 **Region** Mount Barker **T** 0427 323 073 **www.towerhillwine.com.au Open** Not **Winemaker** Mike Garland, Andrew Hoadley **Est.** 1993 **Dozens** 350 **Vyds** 5ha
Towerhill Estate was established in 1993 by the Williams family, who began the planting of the (now) 5ha vineyard of cabernet sauvignon, merlot, riesling and chardonnay. The venture was acquired by former sheep farmer Julian Hanna in 2007; he runs the estate vineyard in partnership with Leith Schmidt. The first vintage was in '08, its Riesling from that year winning the Best Riesling trophy at the Perth Wine Show '12; yet another testament to the skills of Robert Diletti at Castle Rock Estate. Since then winemaking has shifted to the nearer Mount Shadforth contract winemaking facility run by Mike Garland and Andrew Hoadley. Their wines are held back for release when mature. Exports to Singapore.

ŸŸŸŸŸ **Aged Release Mount Barker Dry Riesling 2008** A delicate, fine, beautifully mature riesling that is on a plateau of perfection that will hold for years yet. Screwcap. 12.4% alc. **Rating** 95 **To** 2028 $38
Mount Barker Cabernet Sauvignon 2013 The bright, clear crimson-purple hue runs right through to the rim. It's a truly delicious medium-bodied cabernet,

still as fresh as a daisy, still with years to run, yet absolutely open for business tonight. Screwcap. 14.4% alc. **Rating** 95 **To** 2033 $36

Mount Barker Riesling Royale 2015 A small percentage of the wine was fermented in old French oak. Towerhill says the wine is dry – fascinating because it tastes fruit-sweet with Meyer lemon and Tahitian lime, the acidity a guy rope. Screwcap. 12.8% alc. **Rating** 94 **To** 2025 $29 ✪

Aged Release Mount Barker Dry Riesling 2012 Gleaming straw-green. Citrus/Granny Smith apple/lime fruit changes its spots from penetrating to mouth-watering; delicacy on the final read of the mouth map. Screwcap. 13% alc. **Rating** 94 **To** 2025 $30 ✪

ҴҴҴҴҵ **Mount Barker Cabernet Merlot 2014 Rating** 92 **To** 2030 $32
Mount Barker Chardonnay 2013 Rating 90 **To** 2022 $30
Aged Release Mount Barker Cabernet Sauvignon 2009 Rating 90 **To** 2023 $45

Travertine Wines ★★★

78 Old North Road, Pokolbin, NSW 2320 **Region** Hunter Valley
T (02) 6574 7329 **www.**travertinewines.com.au **Open** Wed–Sun 10–4
Winemaker Liz Silkman **Est.** 1988 **Dozens** 3000 **Vyds** 10.73ha
This is the reincarnation of Pendarves Estate, originally planted by medico-cum-wine historian-cum-wine health activist Dr Phillip Norrie. It was purchased by Graham Burns in January 2008 and vineyard manager Chris Dibley, who had previously worked in the vineyard, was brought back to 'get the place back up to scratch'. There is a Joseph's coat of plantings including pinot noir (2.35ha), verdelho (2.25ha), chardonnay (1.25ha) and chambourcin (1.7ha) and lesser plantings of tannat, semillon, shiraz and merlot.

Traviarti ★★★★★

39 Elgin Road, Beechworth, Vic 3747 **Region** Beechworth
T 0439 994 075 **www.**traviarti.com **Open** By appt
Winemaker Simon Grant **Est.** 2011 **Dozens** 650 **Vyds** 0.43ha
After 15 years in the wine trade, first as a buyer in retail, followed by sales and marketing roles for producers, Simon Grant and partner Helen Murray spent several years looking for the right place to grow nebbiolo, the wine which had the greatest appeal to them. They found a site at around 600m on red decomposed shale and mudstone soils just above the town of Beechworth. They planted multiple clones of nebbiolo and tempranillo on their own rootstocks in 2011.

ҴҴҴҴҴ **Beechworth Nebbiolo 2018** The '17 was an exciting release and the '18 is at least its equal, if not better. There's genuine tar here, genuine licorice root and woodsy spice, and the potent shelf of ferrous-like tannin sits within the wine rather than as an addendum. The Traviarti Vineyard and onsite winery is tiny, but this release suggests that it's a star in the making. Screwcap. 14.2% alc. **Rating** 97 **To** 2033 $65 CM ✪

ҴҴҴҴҴ **Beechworth Rosso 2018** The blend of 42% each of nebbiolo and barbera plus 16% cabernet sauvignon provides a look back at the 100% nebbiolo that Campbell Mattinson enjoyed so much. This has enough high quality nebbiolo input to dig its blend mates in the ribs and come up with a wine full of character and uninhibited fleshy enjoyment. Screwcap. 13.8% alc. **Rating** 95 **To** 2030 $30 ✪

Beechworth Chardonnay 2018 Hand-picked, basket-pressed, matured in French barriques (33% new). Very attractive wine, the white peach/pink grapefruit duo at work, supported by subtle oak. Balance is the keyword. One-third mlf worked well. Screwcap. 12.8% alc. **Rating** 94 **To** 2027 $40

ҴҴҴҴҵ **Beechworth Chardonnay 2019 Rating** 93 **To** 2029 $40 CM

Trentham Estate

6531 Sturt Highway, Trentham Cliffs, NSW 2738 **Region** Murray Darling
T (03) 5024 8888 **www.**trenthamestate.com.au **Open** 7 days 10–5
Winemaker Anthony Murphy, Shane Kerr, Kerry Morrison **Est.** 1988 **Dozens** 70 000
Vyds 50.17ha

Remarkably consistent tasting notes across all wine styles from all vintages attest to the expertise of ex-Mildara winemaker Tony Murphy, a well known and highly regarded producer. The estate vineyards are on the Murray Darling. With an eye to the future, but also to broadening the range of the wines on offer, Trentham Estate is selectively buying grapes from other regions with a track record for the chosen varieties. The value for money is unfailingly excellent. In 2018 Trentham Estate celebrated its 30th anniversary. Exports to the UK, China and other major markets.

🍷🍷🍷🍷🍷 **Family Reserve Coonawarra Cabernet Sauvignon 2018** This is a very good cabernet, exhibiting none of the green astringency and cooked fruit too often a postage stamp. The flow of blackcurrant, mint and bitter chocolate is transparent, clad by refined gentle sage-brushed tannins and impeccably appointed oak. Highly refined. Will age. However the smooth tannin management facilitates imminent enjoyment. Screwcap. **Rating** 94 To 2027 $28 NG ☺

🍷🍷🍷🍷🍷 **Reserve Tumbarumba Chardonnay 2018** Rating 93 To 2024 $28 NG
Estate Pinot Gris 2019 Rating 93 To 2024 $18 NG ☺
The Family Nero d'Avola 2018 Rating 93 To 2024 $18 ☺
Estate Chardonnay 2018 Rating 92 To 2022 $18 NG ☺
The Family Vermentino 2019 Rating 92 To 2021 $18 ☺
Reserve Heathcote Shiraz 2016 Rating 92 To 2029 $28
Estate Noble Taminga 2014 Rating 90 To 2024 $18 NG ☺

Trevelen Farm

506 Weir Road, Cranbrook, WA 6321 **Region** Great Southern
T 0418 361 052 **www.**trevelenfarm.com.au **Open** By appt
Winemaker Harewood Estate (James Kellie) **Est.** 1993 **Dozens** 3000 **Vyds** 6.5ha

In 2008 John and Katie Sprigg decided to pass ownership of their 1300ha wool, meat and grain producing farm to son Ben and wife Louise. However, they have kept control of the 6.5ha of sauvignon blanc, riesling, chardonnay, cabernet sauvignon and merlot planted in 1993. When demand requires, they increase production by purchasing grapes from growers in the Frankland River subregion. Riesling remains the centrepiece of the range. Exports to the US and China.

🍷🍷🍷🍷🍷 **The Tunney Cabernet Sauvignon 2017** A medium-weighted red with dusty blackcurrant and bay leaf notes floating through. It doesn't have a lot of stuffing but it has style, structure and length. It should mature charmingly. Screwcap. 14% alc. **Rating** 93 To 2032 $25 CM ☺
Estate Aged Release Riesling 2009 Smoky reductive-like notes with kerosene, honey and lime. Personality on full show. Surprising amount of texture too. Screwcap. 12.5% alc. **Rating** 90 To 2024 CM ☺
506 Frankland Reserve Shiraz 2017 It hasn't soaked up the oak as well as you might hope, but it's quality oak and it's matched to quality fruit. Smooth blueberry, plum and black cherry flavours meet earth, spice and round after round of creamy/chocolatey/resiny oak. If the balance wasn't off it would be beautiful. Screwcap. 14.7% alc. **Rating** 90 To 2036 $40 CM

🍷🍷🍷🍷 **Estate Riesling 2019** Rating 89 To 2025 $25 CM

Trinchini Estate Wines

6 Noble Street, Anglesea, Vic 3230 (postal) **Region** Geelong
T 0411 205 044 **www**.trinchini.com.au **Open** Not
Winemaker Marcus Trinchini **Est.** 2014 **Dozens** 1500

Marcus Trinchini was born in December 1975, after his father came from Italy to Australia when he was 21 years old. He had always made wine, like his father and his grandfather before him. From a childhood interest in everything about wine, in 2006 Marcus started working with wines and wineries. He moved to Victoria with his wife and in '12 started working with a small winery on the surf coast. This allowed him to begin the search for the perfect location for his first vineyard, which he found in Heathcote. He also found the old Pettavel winery in Geelong. He was underway making his own wine by '14, sourcing fruit from Heathcote, Geelong and the Yarra Valley. No machinery is used at any stage and while this is no doubt true of the crushing and pressing of the grapes, one assumes pumps are used to move the wine around the winery. Marcus certainly learnt his craft well. The wines submitted so far have all been of good quality. Marcus says, 'I continue to enjoy my craft, strive to master it, making a better piece of art each time so that one day I craft a Mona Lisa of wine'. Exports to China.

Limited Edition White S Heathcote Shiraz 2016 Identical vinification to that of Black S. It may be the power of suggestion, but this is slightly more savoury and lighter bodied than its sibling. Bottle no. 255/800. Screwcap. 13.8% alc. **Rating** 91 **To** 2027

Limited Edition Black S Heathcote Shiraz 2016 Two clones hand-picked and sorted, 80% destemmed and foot-stomped, 20% whole bunches, open-fermented, 15 days on skins, matured for 24 months in French and American oak (20% new). The impact of oak is somewhat more obvious than expected, American oak most obvious. Bottle no. 731/2000. Screwcap. 14% alc. **Rating** 90 **To** 2026

tripe.Iscariot

20 McDowell Road, Witchcliffe, WA 6286 **Region** Margaret River
T 0414 817 808 **www**.tripeiscariot.com **Open** Not
Winemaker Remi Guise **Est.** 2013 **Dozens** 800

This has to be the most way out winery name of the century. It prompted me to email South African–born and trained winemaker/owner Remi Guise asking to explain its derivation and/or meaning. He courteously responded with a reference to Judas as 'the greatest black sheep of all time', and a non-specific explanation of 'tripe' as 'challenging in style'. He added, 'I hope this sheds some light, or dark, on the brand'. The wines provide a better answer, managing to successfully harness highly unusual techniques at various points of their elevage. His day job as winemaker at Naturaliste Vintners, the large Margaret River contract winemaking venture of Bruce Dukes, provides the technical grounding, allowing him to throw the 'how to' manual out of the window when the urge arises. His final words on his Marrow Syrah Malbec are: 'So, suck the marrow from the bone, fry the fat, and savour the warm, wobbly bits'.

Stygian Bloom Margaret River Cabernet Sauvignon 2018 From Wilyabrup, Houghton clone; open-fermented, 50% pressed to oak after 14 days, the other half kept on skins in a topped up and sealed fermenter for just under 100 days, aged in French barriques (60% new) for 15 months after blending. This has worked to perfection, giving the best of both worlds: flowery, fragrant, juicy cassis dances around the basement of ripe tannins and other fruit-based extract. Screwcap. 13.8% alc. **Rating** 97 **To** 2043 $52 ○

Aspic Margaret River Grenache Rose 2019 Pale bright fuchsia-pink. This is a serious rose, not just some juice run off the real wine. Grenache from Karridale is crushed and drained, settled, part fermented with whole bunches in tank, the ferment finished in used puncheons, likewise 9 months' maturation. Remarkable intensity and balance with small red fruits, spice and the finest possible tannins. Screwcap. 13% alc. **Rating** 96 **To** 2025 $32 ○

Brawn Margaret River Chardonnay 2018 Gingin clone, grown in Karridale; hand-picked, 25% submerged under 75% whole-bunch pressed juice, fermented semi-carbonically, then pressed and the fermentation completed in French barriques (40% new) and matured for 10 months. Succeeds where others have not, their wines submerged in phenolics. Screwcap. 13% alc. **Rating** 94 **To** 2028 $42
Marrow Margaret River Syrah 2018 Hand-picked, 25% whole bunches under cold destemmed berries, 2–3 days cold soak, fermented with gentle punch downs, basket-pressed to French puncheons (35% new), kept on full solids for 10 months. Very interesting mouthfeel with a creamy, almost velvety, display of black and purple fruits. Time needed for full expression as a mature wine. Screwcap. 13.8% alc. **Rating** 94 **To** 2033 $42

Trofeo Estate   ★★★★★

85 Harrisons Road, Dromana, Vic 3936 **Region** Mornington Peninsula
T (03) 5981 8688 **www**.trofeoestate.com **Open** Thurs–Sun 10–5
Winemaker Richard Darby **Est.** 2012 **Dozens** 7500 **Vyds** 18.5ha
This property has had a chequered history. In the 1930s Passiflora Plantations Company was set up to become Australia's leading exporter of passionfruit and associated products. By '37, 120ha was covered with 70000 passionfruit vines and a processing factory was in operation. The following year a disease devastated the passionfruit and the company went into receivership, never to be seen again. In '48 a member of the Seppelt family planted a vineyard on the exact site of Trofeo Estate and it was thereafter acquired by leading Melbourne wine retailer and wine judge, the late Doug Seabrook, who maintained the vineyard and made the wine until the vines were destroyed in a bushfire in '67. In '98 it was replanted but passed through several hands and fell into and out of neglect until the latest owner, Jim Manolios, developed the property as a cafe restaurant, vineyard and winery with pinot noir (8.2ha), chardonnay (5ha), shiraz (2.5ha), pinot gris (1.6ha) and cabernet sauvignon (1.2ha). Trofeo Estate is the exclusive Australian distributor of terracotta amphorae made in Italy, hence the involvement of amphorae in the making of a number of the wines. Exports to China.

♟♟♟♟♟ **Aged in Terracotta Single Block Shiraz 2017** Terrific wine. Complex, well fruited and beautifully long. Dark cherries, slightly stewed with chicory, salted chocolate and white pepper notes. The palate is good but it's the finish that really emphasises the quality. Cork. 14% alc. **Rating** 95 **To** 2029 CM
The Chosen Few Mornington Peninsula Chardonnay 2018 There's no shortage of flavour but there's a delicacy to this wine. It's a mellifluous chardonnay, but it's also a complex one. It tastes of cider apples and white peach, dry pear and honeysuckle with spice notes almost adding a grain but not quite. It has excellent extension through the finish, always a good sign. It'll be an interesting wine to follow over the next few years. Cork. 13% alc. **Rating** 94 **To** 2027 $49 CM
The Chosen Few Pinot Noir 2018 Seriously savoury, meaty, complex pinot with chicory and stewed cherry, undergrowth and woodsy spice notes charging through. A pinot to blow your hair back. It's firm, dry, sturdy and earnest; well prepared to take on the future. Cork. 13.5% alc. **Rating** 94 **To** 2028 CM
Aged in Terracotta Single Block Pinot Noir 2018 Carbon copy of the standard Aged in Terracotta release though showing just a little extra length. Firmly in the dry, spicy, structural style but with decent fruit power and an impressive finish. Cork. 13.5% alc. **Rating** 94 **To** 2028 CM

♟♟♟♟♟ **Aged in Terracotta Mornington Peninsula Pinot Gris 2019** **Rating** 93 **To** 2022 CM
The Chosen Few Pinot Gris 2019 **Rating** 93 **To** 2022 $36 CM
Aged in Terracotta Rose 2019 **Rating** 93 **To** 2022 $28 CM
The Chosen Few Shiraz 2017 **Rating** 93 **To** 2030 $45 CM
Skin Contact Pinot Noir 2018 **Rating** 92 **To** 2025 $35 CM
Aged in Terracotta Pinot Noir 2018 **Rating** 92 **To** 2027 $36 CM
Aged in Terracotta Shiraz 2017 **Rating** 91 **To** 2026 $34 CM
Skin Contact Pinot Gris 2018 **Rating** 90 **To** 2021 $29 CM

Trove Estate ★★★★★

19 Villers Street, Cowaramup, WA 6284 **Region** Margaret River
T 0412 412 192 **www**.troveestate.com.au **Open** Not
Winemaker Laura Bowler **Est.** 2017 **Dozens** 8500 **Vyds** 16.03ha
The slick website could do with a spell and fact check here and there, and elsewhere agreement
on the establishment date ('16 or '17) and ownership (two or four people). But that's arguably
beside the point, for its range of wines at three price points is well made and priced to sell.
The key players are business partners Paul Byron and Ralph Dunning, with decades of sales
and marketing in and around the wine industry. While Margaret River is (understandably)
the focus, the entry-point Secret Squirrel range of wines come from the Great Southern.
Next up the ladder is the Forest Grand group of Margaret River wines, and at the top is The
Laurels trio of Chardonnay, Shiraz and Cabernet. Part of the production comes from the estate
vineyards of 9.5ha cabernet sauvignon, 2.12ha shiraz and 4.41ha sauvignon blanc.

🍷🍷🍷🍷🍷 **The Laurels Margaret River Chardonnay 2018** Selectiv'-harvested Gingin
    clone; whole berry–wild fermentation in French oak (35% new), matured for
    9 months. Lovely wine; the vibrancy of the fruit, its freshness, the acidity all on
    song. Screwcap. 12.5% alc. **Rating** 96 **To** 2028 $40 ○
    The Laurels Margaret River Cabernet Sauvignon 2018 Includes 7% merlot,
    crushed and destemmed, 14–30 days on skins, matured for 19 months in French
    oak (29% new). A full-bodied, high quality cabernet; varietal purity of expression
    its major strength; length and balance also in the game. Screwcap. 14.8% alc.
    Rating 95 **To** 2033 $40

🍷🍷🍷🍷🍷 **Forest Grand Sauvignon Blanc 2019 Rating** 92 **To** 2020 $28
    The Laurels Cabernet Sauvignon 2017 Rating 92 **To** 2037 $40
    Forest Grand Chardonnay 2018 Rating 90 **To** 2023 $28
    Forest Grand Cabernet Sauvignon 2018 Rating 90 **To** 2028 $28

Trust Wines ★★★★

PO Box 8015, Seymour, Vic 3660 **Region** Central Victoria zone
T (03) 5794 1811 **www**.trustwines.com.au **Open** Not
Winemaker Narelle King **Est.** 2004 **Dozens** 500 **Vyds** 5ha
Partners Don Lewis and Narelle King had been making wine together for many years at
Mitchelton and Priorat, Spain. Don came from a grapegrowing family in Red Cliffs, near
Mildura and in his youth was press-ganged into working in the vineyard. When he left home
he swore never to be involved in vineyards again, but in 1973 found himself accepting the
position of assistant winemaker to Colin Preece at Mitchelton, where he remained until his
retirement 32 years later. Narelle, having qualified as a chartered accountant, set off to travel,
and while in South America met a young Australian winemaker who had just completed
a vintage in Argentina and who lived in France. The lifestyle appealed greatly, so on her
return to Australia she obtained her winemaking degree from CSU and was offered work by
Mitchelton as a bookkeeper and cellar hand. The estate-based wines are a reflection of Central
Victorian style. They also make the Tar & Roses wines. Don passed away in 2017, causing
much sadness for his innumerable friends. Narelle continues to make the Trust Wines from
the Crystal Hill Vineyard. Exports to Canada.

🍷🍷🍷🍷🍷 **Shiraz 2018** An expressive, well structured wine worthy of extended ageing. The
    '18 keeps its cards close to its chest: reserved and coiled, but already revealing dark
    fruits and fine-lined tannins. A long journey ahead is assured. Screwcap. 13.8% alc.
    Rating 93 **To** 2032 $35 JP
    Crystal Hill White 2015 A coming together of like-minded aromatic grapes:
    riesling, gewurztraminer, savagnin and viognier. Gewurztraminer takes an assertive
    lead on the bouquet with a high-toned musk spiciness. From then on, it's a
    melding of flavours – baked apple, honeysuckle, apricot – against a lanolin-smooth
    mouthfeel. Screwcap. 13% alc. **Rating** 92 **To** 2027 $20 JP ○

🍷🍷🍷🍷 **Riesling 2019 Rating** 89 **To** 2025 $25 JP

Tuck's

37 Shoreham Road, Red Hill South, Vic 3937 **Region** Mornington Peninsula
T (03) 5989 8660 **www.tuckswine.com.au** **Open** Wed–Sun 11–5
Winemaker Simon Black **Est.** 1985 **Dozens** 2000 **Vyds** 3.4ha
Tuck's Ridge has changed focus significantly since selling its large Red Hill vineyard, but it
has retained the Buckle Vineyard with chardonnay and pinot noir that consistently provide
outstanding grapes (and wine). In late 2017 Tuck's Ridge was purchased by John and Wendy
Mitchell of neighbouring Montalto. They have revamped the cellar door and restaurant,
keeping Tuck's as a separate operation.

ŢŢŢŢŢ **Mornington Peninsula Savagnin 2019** Has varietal presence in flavour and, to
a lesser degree, texture. Screwcap. 14.1% alc. **Rating** 90 **To** 2022 $32

Tulloch ★★★★★

Glen Elgin, 638 De Beyers Road, Pokolbin, NSW 2321 **Region** Hunter Valley
T (02) 4998 7580 **www.tullochwines.com** **Open** 7 days 10–5
Winemaker Jay Tulloch, First Creek **Est.** 1895 **Dozens** 40 000 **Vyds** 80ha
The Tulloch brand continues to build success on success. Its primary grape source is estate
vines owned by part-shareholder Inglewood Vineyard in the Upper Hunter Valley. It also
owns the JYT Vineyard, which was established by Jay Tulloch in the mid-1980s at the foot of
the Brokenback Range, right in the heart of Pokolbin. Contract-grown fruit is also sourced
from other growers in the Hunter Valley and futher afield. With Christina Tulloch a livewire
marketer, skilled winemaking by First Creek Winemaking Services has put the icing on the
winemaking cake. Exports to Belgium, the Philippines, Singapore, Hong Kong, Malaysia,
Thailand, Japan and China.

ŢŢŢŢŢ **Cellar Door Release Orange Vermentino 2018** The Sardinian star is making
a name for itself in Australia because it holds its acidity in the heat. In a cooler
region like Orange, its acidity becomes more of a feature. This is not a bad thing.
Green apple, grapefruit, lantana florals, honeysuckle. Savoury overtones and herbals
operate on the palate, but the acidity is key to enjoyment. Screwcap. 13% alc.
Rating 93 **To** 2024 $22 JP ✪
Cellar Door Release Orange Cabernet Sauvignon 2017 The higher, cooler
climes of Orange are usually reserved for pinot noir but Tulloch takes a chance
and delivers a superfine cabernet that is bound to be a revelation to some. Aromas
range from high spice and wild berries to a pleasant leafiness with no overt
herbaceous greenness. Flavours are fruit-filled all the way with stewed plums and
blackberry. Fine, with good line and length throughout, sinewy tannins to close.
Screwcap. 13.5% alc. **Rating** 93 **To** 2027 $50 JP
Cellar Door Release Hilltops Sangiovese 2018 Young, juicy dry red in
vogue and moving up the sommelier charts. This is the kind of sangiovese starring
in smart wine bars. Honest in fruit, it's not fancied up in the least. Starts with
sangio-style cherry, then raspberry bright appeal on the bouquet and reveals an
attractive herbal edge in the glass. Feel free to chill. Screwcap. 13% alc. **Rating** 93
To 2023 $26 JP ✪
Cellar Door Release Orange Pinot Gris 2018 Easy, well made entry-level
kind of pinot gris here. Spiced apple, pear compote and honeysuckle freshness.
Medium weight, laidback acidity, smooth with a solid, sustained finish. Screwcap.
14% alc. **Rating** 90 **To** 2023 $22 JP

ŢŢŢŢ **Cellar Door Release Hilltops Zinfandel 2018 Rating** 89 **To** 2027 $26 JP
Creme de Vin NV Rating 89 $35 JP

Tumblong Hills ★★★★☆

PO Box 38, Gundagai, NSW 2722 **Region** Gundagai
T 0408 684 577 **www.tumblonghills.com** **Open** Not
Winemaker Michael Hatcher **Est.** 2009 **Dozens** 10 000 **Vyds** 202ha

This large vineyard was established by Southcorp Wines in the 1990s, as part of 'Project Max', an initiative to honour Max Schubert of Penfolds Grange fame. In 2009 it was acquired by business partners Danny Gilbert, Peter Leonard and Peter Waters. They were able to secure the services of viticulturist and general manager Simon Robertson, who knew the vineyard like the back of his hand, his experience stretching across the wine regions of Southern New South Wales. In '11, investors Wang Junfeng and Handel Lee came onboard to strengthen Tumblong Hills' presence in Australia and China. While shiraz and cabernet sauvignon remain the two most significant varieties, nebbiolo, barbera, sangiovese and fiano are increasingly important. Exports to China.

ŶŶŶŶŶ **Premiere Cuvee Gundagai Shiraz 2017** Open-fermented, matured in French oak (30% new) for 18 months. A first class shiraz, medium-bodied but filling the mouth with supple, juicy fruit neatly dovetailed with fine-grained tannins. Lingers in the mouth long after the last sip. Screwcap. 14% alc. **Rating** 95 **To** 2037 $30 ✪

ŶŶŶŶŶ **Table of Plenty Fiano 2019 Rating** 93 **To** 2023 $20 ✪
Table of Plenty Sangiovese Rose 2019 Rating 90 **To** 2021 $20 ✪

Turkey Flat   ★★★★★
Bethany Road, Tanunda, SA 5352 **Region** Barossa Valley
T (08) 8563 2851 **www**.turkeyflat.com.au **Open** 7 days 11–5
Winemaker Mark Bulman **Est.** 1990 **Dozens** 20 000 **Vyds** 47.83ha
The establishment date of Turkey Flat is given as 1990 but it might equally have been 1870 (or thereabouts), when the Schulz family purchased the Turkey Flat Vineyard; or 1847, when the vineyard was first planted – to the very old shiraz that still grows there today and the 8ha of equally old grenache. Plantings have since expanded significantly, now comprising shiraz (24ha), grenache (10.5ha), cabernet sauvignon (5.9ha), mourvedre (3.7ha) and smaller plantings of marsanne, viognier and dolcetto. The business is run by sole proprietor Christie Schulz. Exports to the UK, the US, China and other major markets.

ŶŶŶŶŶ **The Ancestor Barossa Valley Shiraz 2016** Estate-grown; open-fermented, matured for 12 months in French hogsheads (50% new), plus a further 12 months in bottle. A beautiful wine made with all the respect the vines' fruit deserves. Impeccable length and balance. Screwcap. 14% alc. **Rating** 98 **To** 2046 $200 ✪
Barossa Valley Grenache 2018 Predominantly sourced from estate vines planted over 100 years ago. It's been treated with total respect in the winery, matured in used oak without any additions other than SO_2. Extraordinary value for a wine with decades ahead of it. Screwcap. 15% alc. **Rating** 97 **To** 2043 $40 ✪

ŶŶŶŶŶ **Barossa Valley Rose 2019** Pale salmon-pink. The red cherry bouquet sets the scene for the wholly seductive palate, candy floss never tasting better, the finish as bright as a spring day. Screwcap. 12.5% alc. **Rating** 95 **To** 2022 $22 ✪
Barossa Valley Shiraz 2018 Ground coffee, ripe plum/redcurrant and blackberry flavours sweep confidently through the palate, chicory and sweet earth characters carried along for the ride. It's not flashy or necessarily seductive, but it's the most impeccable Barossa shiraz you could ever hope to find. It will mature beautifully. Screwcap. 14.1% alc. **Rating** 95 **To** 2040 $50 CM
Butchers Block Barossa Valley Shiraz 2018 Total disassociation from all previous Turkey Flat labels is hard to fathom. It's an entry-point wine, but that still doesn't answer the question. And it's not as if the quality of this reflects adversely upon that of its peers. It's complex, relaxed, medium-bodied; its black fruits playing the game. Screwcap. 13.7% alc. **Rating** 94 **To** 2028 $25 ✪
Barossa Valley Mataro 2019 Given 25% whole bunches, 50% new French oak. It's a wine in complete command of matters. It's balanced, svelte, well powered and exceptionally well finished. Sweet fruit, top notes of spice, a suede leather aspect and (dark) chocolate-infused tannin. It's very good. Screwcap. 13.8% alc. **Rating** 94 **To** 2032 $32 CM

ŶŶŶŶŶ **Butchers Block Red Blend 2018 Rating** 93 **To** 2027 $22 CM ✪

Turner's Crossing Vineyard

747 Old Bridgewater-Serpentine Road, Serpentine, Vic 3517 **Region** Bendigo
T 0427 843 528 **www.turnerscrossing.com.au Open** Not
Winemaker Various **Est.** 1999 **Dozens** 4000 **Vyds** 42ha

This outstanding, mature vineyard was named to remember the original landholder, Thomas Turner. During the 1800s, farmers and gold rush prospectors crossed the Loddon River beside the property, at what became known as Turners Crossing. During the Gold Rush period European settlers in the area started to plant vineyards, trusting that Bendigo's terroir would reveal itself as a suitable site on which to grow grapes. And they were right to be so confident. Its alluvial composition of rich limestone soils and Mediterranean climate make it a happy home for viticulture in particular. Turners Crossing Vineyard now spans 42ha of mature vines. The vineyard is virtually pesticide and chemical free; warm days and cool nights allow the grapes to ripen during the day and the vines to recover overnight. The vineyard bears shiraz, cabernet sauvignon, viognier and picolit (a rare white Italian variety). Exports to the UK, Canada, Vietnam and China.

ℙℙℙℙℙ **Bendigo Shiraz 2016** Machine-harvested at night, destemmed to open fermenters, co-fermented with 5% viognier, aged for 20 months in French oak. Very good retention of colour, not the least forward. Medium-bodied with plum, spice and a touch of Central Victoria mint. The gentle tannins are resolved, the only question is whether a shorter time in oak (or different handling) would have made an even better wine. Good value and ready now. Screwcap. 14.5% alc. **Rating** 92 **To** 2026 $27
Bendigo Viognier 2019 Turner's Crossing has chosen the path of full varietal flavour, accepting the downside of oily phenolics. *Chacun à son gout* (to each his own). Screwcap. 13.5% alc. **Rating** 90 **To** 2021 $25

ℙℙℙℙ **Bendigo Rose 2019 Rating** 89 **To** 2020 $22

Turon Wines

1760 Lobethal Road, Lobethal, SA 5241 **Region** Adelaide Hills
T 0423 956 480 **www.turonwines.com.au Open** Not
Winemaker Turon White **Est.** 2013 **Dozens** 600 **Vyds** 5ha

This is the thoroughly impressive venture of newlyweds Turon and Alex White. Working for several small wineries while studying at university, Turon realised the potential of the ever-varying site climates within the Adelaide Hills. His overseas winemaking experience while completing his degree was appropriately lateral, with vintage winemaking at Argyle in Oregon and at Kovac Nimrod in Eger, Hungary. Out of this has come a minimal intervention approach to winemaking, being confident enough to stand back and let the wine develop and be itself, but equally being prepared to intervene if needs must. Selecting the right site, soil and meso climate within the region is, Turon believes, crucial in allowing the wines to reach their full potential. That said, experimentation of method is also of prime importance in understanding the potential of terroir and variety. One could go on with the philosophical side, but there is also a practical element. They have built a winery at their property in Lenswood and turned it into a cooperative winery from the outset, where young winemakers can work together, share equipment, resources and knowledge. They called the venture the Hills Handcrafted Collective, with wines to be released from the Collective a bit further down the track. Given the quality of the wines released under the Turon Wines label, one is tempted to say the sky's the limit. As it is, it was one of the top new wineries in the *Wine Companion 2019*.

ℙℙℙℙℙ **Artist Series Lenswood Adelaide Hills Chardonnay 2019** Whole-bunch pressed, fermented in French puncheons and barriques (20% new), matured for 9 months. There's a hint of perfume to the expressive bouquet, while the palate opens graciously before suddenly accelerating to find every corner of the mouth with bittersweet sorbet flavours. Screwcap. 12.9% alc. **Rating** 96 **To** 2029 $32 ✪
Artist Series Lenswood Adelaide Hills Pinot Noir 2019 MV6; 70% destemmed, 30% whole bunch, matured in French oak (20% new)

for 9 months. Good mouthfeel and varietal expression – cherry is in the driver's seat – plus hints of rose petal and spice. Good grapes here. Screwcap. 13.2% alc. **Rating** 95 **To** 2028 $32 **⭘**

Single Vineyard Single Barrel Lenswood Adelaide Hills Pinot Noir 2018 Destemmed, wild-fermented, 15 months in second-use French oak, minimal intervention in the vinification. Spicy, savoury nuances add greatly to the wine, yet it's not easy to see where they come from. Doing less is harder than doing more. Screwcap. 13.7% alc. **Rating** 95 **To** 2028 $45

Artist Series Balhannah Adelaide Hills Syrah 2018 Wild-fermented with 80% whole berries and 20% whole bunches, matured in French puncheons (33% new) for 18 months. More magic from Turon White with perfumed rose petal and foresty aromas and flavours. The wine is at the gentle end of medium-bodied but its balance and length will serve it well for decades. Screwcap. 14.4% alc. **Rating** 95 **To** 2033 $32 **⭘**

Artist Series Adelaide Hills Field Blend 2019 Sauvignon blanc, pinot gris, chardonnay and viognier; 43% fermented on skins, 25% in French oak, 32% in tank. An unlikely background for a wine that leaps out of the glass in a boisterous burst of juicy flavour. Screwcap. 12.6% alc. **Rating** 94 **To** 2021 $25 **⭘**

Single Vineyard Single Barrel Lobethal Adelaide Hills Syrah 2018 Majestic full-bodied power – to be respected, not loved. Depending on the size of the barrel, 22 or 40 dozen made. Screwcap. 15.5% alc. **Rating** 94 **To** 2038 $40

Twinwoods Estate ★★★★★

Brockman Road, Cowaramup, WA 6284 **Region** Margaret River
T 0419 833 122 **www.**twinwoodsestate.com **Open** Not
Winemaker Deep Woods Estate (Julian Langworthy), Aldo Bratovic **Est.** 2005
Dozens 2500 **Vyds** 8.5ha
This is a winery that was bound to succeed. It is owned by the Jebsen family, for many years a major player in the importation and distribution of fine wine in Hong Kong, more recently expanded into China. Jebsen invested in a NZ winery, following that with the acquisition of this vineyard in Margaret River in 2005. It brings together senior Jebsen managing director Gavin Jones, and peripatetic winemaker Aldo Bratovic, who began his career decades ago under the tutelage of Brian Croser. Its widespread distribution is interesting, not all the eggs being put in the Hong Kong/China markets. The quality of the wines I have tasted fully lives up to what one would expect. (I tasted the wines without any knowledge of the background of Twinwoods.) It commenced selling wine in Australia in '14, with Terroir Selections its Australian partner, another intersection with Brian Croser. Exports to Denmark, Germany, Singapore, Taiwan, Hong Kong, China and NZ.

🍷🍷🍷🍷🍷 **Margaret River Cabernet Sauvignon 2016** Three parcels harvested on different days: Old Lane, Old Spur and Young. The old vines provide the structure, the young fresher/fruitier cabernet blackcurrant flavours. It all comes together very well indeed. Screwcap. 13.5% alc. **Rating** 96 **To** 2036

Margaret River Shiraz 2016 Given 3 days' cold soak, 6-day ferment, pressed off before dryness to 300l French casks (30% new), matured for 14 months. Rich and measured, the mouthfeel supple and deep, the accent on satsuma plum bolstered by soft tannins. Screwcap. 14% alc. **Rating** 95 **To** 2036

Two Hands Wines ★★★★★

273 Neldner Road, Marananga, SA 5355 **Region** Barossa Valley
T (08) 8562 4566 **www.**twohandswines.com **Open** 7 days 10–5
Winemaker Ben Perkins **Est.** 2000 **Dozens** 55 000 **Vyds** 15ha
The 'hands' in question are those of SA businessmen Michael Twelftree and Richard Mintz, Michael in particular having extensive experience in marketing Australian wine in the US (for other producers). On the principle that if big is good, bigger is better, the style of the wines has been aimed squarely at the palate of Robert Parker Jr and *Wine Spectator*'s Harvey Steiman. Grapes are sourced from the Barossa Valley (where the business has 15ha of shiraz), McLaren

Vale, Clare Valley, Langhorne Creek and Padthaway. The emphasis is on sweet fruit and soft tannin structure, all signifying the precise marketing strategy of what is a very successful business. At the end of 2015 Two Hands embarked on an extensive planting programme using vines propagated from a number of vineyards (including Prouse Eden Valley, Wendouree 1893, Kaelser Alte Reben, Penfolds Modbury, Kays Block 6, Kalimna 3C), as well as a high-density 1.4ha clos (a walled vineyard) with the vines trained in the goblet style of the Northern Rhône Valley. Exports to all major markets.

ŸŸŸŸŸ Twelftree Moritz Road Blewitt Springs McLaren Vale Grenache 2017
Hand-picked from dry-grown bushvines, destemmed, not crushed, wild-fermented with 15% whole bunches. An utterly delicious grenache with only one problem: the total production was 50 dozen. Supple, fine, silky – tastes more like 13.5% alcohol than 14.5%. Screwcap. **Rating** 97 **To** 2032 $45 ✪

ŸŸŸŸŸ Gnarly Dudes Barossa Valley Shiraz 2018 Everything is right with this wine. The colour is full but clear, the bouquet composed and welcoming, the medium-bodied palate continuing the theme. Dark berry fruits do all the lifting (this is only medium-bodied, in any event), the mouthfeel is juicy, the tannins fine-spun, the length exemplary. Screwcap. 13.8% alc. **Rating** 95 **To** 2028 $30 ✪

Bella's Garden Barossa Valley Shiraz 2018 Matured for 17 months in French oak (14% new). The bouquet is fragrant, the wine no more than medium-bodied and well balanced courtesy of fresh red and dark fruits. It's not often that tannins decide the all-up quality of a Barossa Valley shiraz but they do in this instance. Diam. 14.2% alc. **Rating** 95 **To** 2038 $60

Yacca Block Single Vineyard Menglers Hill Eden Valley Shiraz 2018 Fermented with 20% whole bunches, the remainder whole berry, the free-run and pressings combined after fermentation and racked off gross lees, matured for 18 months in French barriques and hogsheads (15% new). Spicy/textured whole bunch delivers. Diam. 14.3% alc. **Rating** 95 **To** 2043 $100

Waterfall Block Single Vineyard Waterfall Gully Road Burnside Adelaide Shiraz 2018 A tiny parcel from a vineyard on the urban edge of the Adelaide CBD. Destemmed into a single 5t open fermenter, 10 days on skins, pressed to French puncheons (20% new). A no-holds-barred full-bodied wine, not yet ready, but promises much through its balance and tapestry of ripe fruit flavours. Diam. 13.9% alc. **Rating** 95 **To** 2043 $100

Ares Barossa Valley Shiraz 2017 The grapes are destemmed/crushed into open fermenters, pumped over, after 15 days on skins the must is part free-run/part pressed, part of each included in the blend, matured in French oak (20% new) for 25 months, bottled with minimal fining, no filtration. Wine for Dummies. Even the '17 vintage and only French oak didn't cause somersaults. Diam. 14.5% alc. **Rating** 95 **To** 2042 $165

Samantha's Garden Clare Valley Shiraz 2018 Enjoyed 18 months in used French oak Has that black fruit power of the Clare Valley that can seem impenetrable, but this has its best years in front of it. A complex bouquet, the palate locked up with its tar and roses flavour base. Diam. 14.2% alc. **Rating** 94 **To** 2038 $60

Holy Grail Single Vineyard Seppeltsfield Road Barossa Valley Shiraz 2018 The lethal weight of the bottles used for this wine can create mayhem in a tasting. Couriers through to sommeliers and tasters groan in protest. The wine lives up to the package – at the far end of full-bodied, saved to a degree by its moderate alcohol. Diam. 14.1% alc. **Rating** 94 **To** 2043 $100

Twelftree Schuller Road Blewitt Springs McLaren Vale Grenache 2017 From 89yo dry-grown bushvines, destemmed, not crushed, fermented with 15% whole bunches, matured in French and stainless steel puncheons. A little more Barossa Valley–like than Blewitt Springs, more like '18 than '17. Nonetheless, a high quality grenache. Screwcap. 14.5% alc. **Rating** 94 **To** 2029 $45

ŸŸŸŸŸ Lily's Garden McLaren Vale Shiraz 2018 Rating 93 To 2038 $60
Holy Grail Single Vineyard Seppeltsfield Road Barossa Valley Shiraz
2017 Rating 90 To 2032 $100

2 Mates

160 Main Road, McLaren Vale, SA 5171 **Region** McLaren Vale
T 0411 111 198 **www.**2mates.com.au **Open** Not
Winemaker Mark Venable, David Minear, Matt Rechner, **Est.** 2003 **Dozens** 300
Vyds 20ha
The two mates are Mark Venable and David Minear, who say, 'Over a big drink in a small
bar in Italy a few years back, we talked about making "our perfect Australian Shiraz". When
we got back, we decided to have a go.' The wine ('05) was duly made and won a silver medal
at the Decanter World Wine Awards in London, in some exalted company. Eleven years on,
they hit the rarefied heights of 97 points for their $35 The Perfect Ten McLaren Vale Shiraz.

ŸŸŸŸŸ The First Eleven McLaren Vale Shiraz 2017 The 11th vintage, still crushing
grapes from the original growers, including one patch of 140+yo vines. All grapes
hand-picked, open-fermented, hand-plunged. Full-bodied and very complex, it
revels in the spicy/savoury injections of the cool vintage. Screwcap. 14.9% alc.
Rating 95 To 2047 $35 ✪
And Then There Were Twelve McLaren Vale Shiraz 2018 Marks the
12th vintage by the two mates, taking grapes from the original vineyards they
started with in '05, the vines aged 30–145yo, matured in used French oak for
23 months. The wine is fascinating: full-bodied, dark fruits, tannins – yet borders
on outright elegance. Screwcap. 14.9% alc. Rating 94 To 2040 $35

Two Rivers

2 Yarrawa Road, Denman, NSW 2328 **Region** Hunter Valley
T (02) 6547 2556 **www.**tworivers.com.au **Open** 7 days 11–4
Winemaker Liz Silkman **Est.** 1988 **Dozens** 10 000 **Vyds** 67.5ha
A significant part of the viticultural scene in the Upper Hunter Valley with 67.5ha of
vineyards, involving an investment of several million dollars. Part of the fruit is sold under
long-term contracts and part is kept for Two Rivers. The emphasis is on chardonnay and
semillon, most rated 95 or 96 points. Two Rivers is also a partner in the Tulloch business,
together with the Tulloch and Angove families, and supplies grapes for the Tulloch label. A
contemporary cellar door adds significantly to the appeal of the Upper Hunter Valley as a
wine-tourist destination. The appointment of immensely talented winemaker Liz Silkman has
had an immediate impact.

ŸŸŸŸŸ Vigneron's Reserve Hunter Valley Chardonnay 2018 The use of 'Reserve'
in this instance indicates fruit taken from the best block in the vineyard with the
aim of highlighting regional character. There is Hunter generosity from the aromas
of melon, fig and cashew through to a palate defined by stone fruits, citrus and
subtle oak. With less alcohol than some chardonnays, perhaps the real story here
is the structure and bright acidity that keeps things tight and delicious. Screwcap.
12.8% alc. Rating 91 To 2028 $26 JP

ŸŸŸŸ Lightning Strike Chardonnay 2018 Rating 89 To 2023 $20 JP
Hidden Hive Verdelho 2018 Rating 89 To 2023 $16 JP ✪

Tynan Road Wines

185 Tynan Road, Kuitpo, SA 5172 (postal) **Region** Adelaide Hills
T 0413 004 829 **www.**tynanroadwines.com.au **Open** Not
Winemaker Duane Coates **Est.** 2015 **Dozens** 150 **Vyds** 10.25ha
This is the venture of Heidi, a lawyer who wanted a pretty outlook and tolerates the folly
of her gastroenterologist husband, Sandy Craig. Living in Kuitpo made the folly eminently

reasonable and they have gone the whole way with building an onsite winery and securing the services of the experienced and very good winemaker Duane Coates.

ŢŢŢŢŢ **Kuitpo Adelaide Hills Chardonnay 2018** This is an opulent medium-bodied wine in an age when expressions of this variety can tend towards the anaemic. Broad and creamy, the mid-palate suggestive of oatmeal and a reductive fleck of struck match. Well handled vanillan oak tucks in further flavours of apricot, white fig, peach and nougat. Screwcap. **Rating** 91 **To** 2024 $40 NG

ŢŢŢŢ **Kuitpo Adelaide Hills Nebbiolo 2017 Rating** 89 **To** 2024 $40 NG

Tyrrell's Wines ★★★★★

1838 Broke Road, Pokolbin, NSW 2321 **Region** Hunter Valley
T (02) 4993 7000 **www**.tyrrells.com.au **Open** Mon–Sat 9–5, Sun 10–4
Winemaker Andrew Spinaze, Mark Richardson **Est.** 1858 **Dozens** 220 000 **Vyds** 364ha
One of the most successful family wineries, a humble operation for the first 110 years of its life that has grown out of all recognition over the past 40 years. Vat 1 Semillon is one of the most dominant wines in the Australian show system and Vat 47 Chardonnay is one of the pacesetters for this variety. Tyrrell's has an awesome portfolio of single vineyard semillons released when 5–6 years old. Its estate plantings include over 100ha in the Hunter Valley and 26ha in Heathcote. In December '17 Tyrrell's purchased the 13.5ha Stevens Old Hillside Vineyard on Marrowbone Road; 6.11ha are planted to shiraz, including a 1.1ha block planted in 1867, the balance planted in 1963, notably to shiraz and semillon. There are 11 blocks of vines older than 100 years in the Hunter Valley and the Tyrrell family owns seven of those blocks. A founding member of Australia's First Families of Wine. Exports to all major markets.

ŢŢŢŢŢ **Old Patch Hunter Valley Shiraz 2018** Planted in 1867 on the mid-slope of the Stevens Vineyard, the oldest vineyard in NSW. Hand-picked, vineyard-sorted, open-fermented, matured in 1yo 2700l French casks. This is the most beautiful wine of the '18 releases; it is supple with a silk and velvet mouthfeel – it defies normal standards. Screwcap. 13.5% alc. **Rating** 98 **To** 2057 $108 ❂
Museum Release Vat 1 Hunter Semillon 2015 Hand-picked in the early morning, lightly pressed before relatively cool fermentation. This is still in its infancy but is gloriously well balanced, which guarantees youth at 10yo, maturity at 20 and age yet further down the track. When to drink? Your choice. Screwcap. 11% alc. **Rating** 97 **To** 2030 $90 ❂
4 Acres Hunter Valley Shiraz 2018 Planted in 1879 on a precious patch of volcanic soil. Hand-picked, vineyard-sorted, wild yeast–open fermented, matured in a single 4yo French 2500l cask for 15 months. This is the heart of the Ashman's Vineyard. This is quintessential, medium-bodied Hunter Valley shiraz from an exceptional vintage, framed by the freshness of the alcohol, in turn presenting gently earthy red and purple fruits and the gentle throb of acidity. Screwcap. 13.8% alc. **Rating** 97 **To** 2048 $108 ❂

ŢŢŢŢŢ **Vat 47 Hunter Chardonnay 2018** From the Short Flat Vineyard that produced the grapes for the first Vat 47 in '71. The barrel fermentation protocols have long been set in stone, giving this wine a sense of variety, not of place. It often upstages cool-climate chardonnays in wine shows. Screwcap. 13.5% alc. **Rating** 96 **To** 2023 $80
Johnno's Hunter Valley Shiraz 2018 From the HVD Block planted 1908 on all alluvial soils (in contrast to the red volcanic soils of 4 Acres). Wild-fermented, matured in a single new 2700l French cask. Very different in its attack to its siblings, a wine that will always attract consumers thanks to its shimmering freshness and length. Screwcap. 13.8% alc. **Rating** 96 **To** 2043 $108
Vat 9 Winemaker's Selection Hunter Valley Shiraz 2018 From the oldest and best blocks on the Ashman property; hand-picked and vineyard-sorted, each block vinified separately in open vats, maturation in new and 1yo 2700l French casks until the blend assembled in Dec '19, then given a further 5 months before

bottling. This is a woven tapestry of black fruits studded with sparks of red. Soars after a challenging bouquet. Screwcap. 13.5% alc. **Rating** 95 **To** 2048 $100

Single Vineyard HVD Hunter Semillon 2015 This wine is only sourced from the vineyard planted by the Hunter Valley Distillery in 1908 on very sandy soil, the legacy of creek beds countless years before. It's stacked with flavour to the point of space invasion and doesn't need more time for muscle building. Screwcap. 10.5% alc. **Rating** 94 **To** 2025 $35

HVD Hunter Valley Chardonnay 2019 The vineyard planted in 1908 is believed to be the oldest producing chardonnay vineyard in the world. Hand-picked, basket-pressed, fermentation initiated in stainless steel tanks thence to French barriques for 8 months' maturation. Screwcap. 12% alc. **Rating** 94 **To** 2027 $56

Old Hillside Vineyard Hunter Valley Shiraz 2018 Previously known as Stevens Vineyard, purchased by Tyrrell's in Dec '17. The vines for this wine average 50yo and sit on darker, richer soils. Matured in used 2500l French casks for 15 months. Very good wine, sharing freshness with its siblings, but needs to mature and expand around its acidity. Screwcap. 13.4% alc. **Rating** 94 **To** 2038 $54

Hunter Valley Shiraz 2018 From dry-grown estate blocks averaging 40yo; fermented in large 2700l used casks. It is spectacular value and more obvious in all aspects: depth, colour, richness (plum to the fore), tannins (for balance and longevity). There's no sin in drinking this now but it will still be on the up 20 years from now. Screwcap. 13.5% alc. **Rating** 94 **To** 2040 $25 ✪

🍷🍷🍷🍷 **Vat 8 Winemaker's Selection Hunter Valley Shiraz Cabernet 2018** **Rating** 93 **To** 2038 $80

Ubertas Wines ★★★★

790 Research Road, Light Pass, SA 5355 **Region** Barossa Valley
T (08) 8565 7820 **www**.ubertaswines.com.au **Open** Wed–Sun 12–5
Winemaker Wine Wise, Philip Liu **Est.** 2013 **Dozens** 3800 **Vyds** 13.8ha

Brothers Phil and Kevin Liu followed their father from Taiwan to mainland China, working for their father's car component factory. In 2006 they made a life-changing decision to migrate to Australia and saw an opportunity to start a wine export business to China. They named their business Rytor. It succeeded and over the following years they both obtained masters degrees – Phil in oenology from the University of Adelaide, Kevin in marketing from the University of South Australia. By '14 they had taken another major step: building and managing their own winery at Light Pass in the Barossa Valley. Exports to Malaysia, Japan, Taiwan, Hong Kong and China.

Ulithorne ★★★★★

85 Kays Road, Blewitt Springs, SA 5171 **Region** McLaren Vale
T 0406 336 282 **www**.ulithorne.com.au **Open** By appt
Winemaker Matthew Copping **Est.** 1971 **Dozens** 2500 **Vyds** 7.2ha

Ulithorne produces small quantities of red wines from selected parcels of grapes from its estate vineyard in McLaren Vale, planted in 1950 by Bob Whiting. The small batch, high quality wines are influenced by Ulithorne's associate Laurence Feraud, owner of Domaine du Pegau of Chateauneuf du Pape. Exports to the UK, Canada, Sweden, Malaysia, Hong Kong and China.

🍷🍷🍷🍷🍷 **Avitus McLaren Vale Shiraz 2017** Concentration of blackberried fruit flavour. This strikes a blow in a positive way. It's chocolatey, rich and satiny, and feels substantial all the way through the palate. It pushes ripeness all the way to the edge but the payoff is such beautiful flavour and such impressive length. Screwcap. 14.5% alc. **Rating** 95 **To** 2040 $85 CM

Frux Frugis McLaren Vale Shiraz 2017 It's rich and porty but it doesn't feel unbalanced, and while there's some alcohol warmth it's not excessive.

This is a powerhouse shiraz with smooth texture and flavours of saturated plums, nuts-coated-in-toffee, choc-orange and malt. It's a bomb of flavour but juicy/flavour-infused acidity and noteworthy length take its quality to higher realms. Cork. 15.5% alc. **Rating** 95 **To** 2037 $125 CM

Chi McLaren Vale Shiraz Grenache 2018 A 52/48% blend from Blewitt Springs. French oak, most of it used. It's a lifted, pretty, interesting red. Not your standard fare. Orange rind and juice tossed through redcurrant, violets, chocolate powder and malt. Tannin is ultrafine-grained and length is decent. Much to recommend it. Screwcap. 14.5% alc. **Rating** 94 **To** 2028 $50 CM

Nova Duo McLaren Vale Grenache Shiraz 2018 Hand-picked from Ulithorne's vineyard planted in the '50s; filled a single 1t fermenter, hand-plunged, pressed to French oak for completion of fermentation and 3 months' maturation. A superabundance of flavours are carefully balanced by tannins, oak not really in play. Screwcap. 14.5% alc. **Rating** 94 **To** 2038 $35

Specialis McLaren Vale Tempranillo Grenache Graciano 2018 Tempranillo 52%, grenache 37%, graciano 10% (1% unstated). It's a spicy, meaty, iodine-inflected red with redcurrant, campfire, earth and leather characters bursting through. It has weight and impact without overly relying on either sweet fruit or oak. Lovely wine to drink. Screwcap. 14.1% alc. **Rating** 94 **To** 2027 $35 CM

ŶŶŶŶŶ **Unicus McLaren Vale Shiraz 2017** Rating 93 To 2034 $85 CM
Nova Duo McLaren Vale Grenache Shiraz 2019 Rating 93 To 2029 $35 CM
Dona Blanc 2019 Rating 92 To 2023 $27 CM
Epoch McLaren Vale Rose 2019 Rating 92 To 2022 $30 CM
Dona McLaren Vale Grenache Shiraz Mourvedre 2018 Rating 92 To 2026 $27 CM
Dona McLaren Vale Shiraz 2018 Rating 91 To 2027 $27 CM

Ulupna Winery   ★★★☆

159 Crawfords Road, Strathmerton, Vic 3641 **Region** Goulburn Valley
T (03) 9533 8831 **www**.ulupnawinery.com.au **Open** By appt
Winemaker Vio Buga, Viviana Ferrari **Est.** 1999 **Dozens** 35 000 **Vyds** 22ha
Ulupna started out as a retirement activity for Nick and Kathy Bogdan. The vineyard on the banks of the Murray River is planted to shiraz (50%), cabernet sauvignon (30%) and chardonnay (20%); the plantings allowing for expansion in the years ahead. The wines are made under the direction of Vio Buga, who also designed and planted the vineyard. Exports are primarily directed to China, followed by Hong Kong, South Korea and Singapore.

ŶŶŶŶŶ **Royal Phoenix Single Vineyard Shiraz 2018** Pre-ferment maceration 2–3 days, matured in French oak (15% new) for 18 months. Deep red hue. A solid shiraz with Central Victorian earthiness as a constant - and attractive - thread. Black cherry, fruit pastille, white pepper and dusty oak aromas. Builds a strong case for further ageing on the palate, adding bright fruit and freshness to the earthiness with fine tannins. Well structured. Cork. 14.5% alc. **Rating** 91 **To** 2027 $55 JP

Umamu Estate   ★★★★★

PO Box 1269, Margaret River, WA 6285 **Region** Margaret River
T (08) 9757 5058 **www**.umamuestate.com **Open** Not
Winemaker Bruce Dukes (Contract) **Est.** 2005 **Dozens** 1000 **Vyds** 16.8ha
Chief executive Charmaine Saw explains, 'My life has been a journey towards Umamu. An upbringing in both eastern and western cultures, graduating in natural science, training as a chef combined with a passion for the arts and experience as a management consultant have all contributed to my building the business creatively yet professionally.' The palindrome 'Umamu', says Charmaine, is inspired by balance and contentment. In practical terms this means an organic approach to viticulture and a deep respect for the terroir. The plantings,

dating back to 1978, include cabernet sauvignon, chardonnay, shiraz, semillon, sauvignon blanc, merlot and cabernet franc. Exports to Canada, Malaysia, Indonesia, the Philippines, Singapore and Hong Kong.

🍷🍷🍷🍷🍷 **Margaret River Cabernet Sauvignon 2018** Made with the usual attention to detail by Bruce Dukes. It is elegant, balanced, very long and a perfect vinous picture of cabernet sauvignon picked at the right moment. Supple and round, it fills the mouth, cassis/blackcurrant providing the structure and texture needed. Screwcap. 13.5% alc. **Rating** 96 **To** 2038

Margaret River Chardonnay 2018 Gleaming straw-green. A lusciously rich chardonnay, all its wares laid out before you. It needs food, but will happily accompany every dish. Screwcap. 13.8% alc. **Rating** 94 **To** 2025 $60

🍷🍷🍷🍷🍷 **Margaret River Cabernet Merlot 2017 Rating** 92 **To** 2032 $35
Margaret River Sauvignon Blanc Semillon 2019 Rating 90 **To** 2024 $28

Upper Reach ★★★★★

77 Memorial Avenue, Baskerville, WA 6056 **Region** Swan Valley
T (08) 9296 0078 **www.**upperreach.com.au **Open** 7 days 11–5
Winemaker Derek Pearse **Est.** 1996 **Dozens** 4000 **Vyds** 8.45ha
This 10ha property on the banks of the upper reaches of the Swan River was purchased by Laura Rowe and Derek Pearse in 1996. The original 4ha vineyard was expanded and plantings now include chardonnay, shiraz, cabernet sauvignon, verdelho, semillon, merlot, petit verdot and muscat. All wines are estate-grown. The Broads Restaurant is encased by full-length glass doors and surrounded by a deck overlooking the vineyard. The cellar door is integrated with the restaurant, and they have constructed a deck where visitors can relax and enjoy a glass or two, resulting in *Gourmet Traveller WINE* choosing Upper Reach as the Star Cellar Door in the Swan Valley.

🍷🍷🍷🍷🍷 **Reserve Margaret River Cabernet Sauvignon 2017** Dry-grown grapes from Wilyabrup; hand-picked, crushed and (surprisingly) the juice concentrated, 7 days on skins, matured in French hogsheads (50% new). Good line, length and balance – the juice concentration worked. Screwcap. 14% alc. **Rating** 95 **To** 2042

🍷🍷🍷🍷 **Swan Valley Muscat NV Rating** 89 $45

Utopos ★★★★★

PO Box 764, Tanunda, SA 5352 **Region** Barossa Valley
T 0409 351 166 **www.**utopos.com.au **Open** Not
Winemaker Kym Teusner **Est.** 2015 **Dozens** 1500 **Vyds** 20ha
The fates were kind when Neil Panuja, a friend of Kym Teusner's from 'the big smoke', said he had the wish (and the cash) to get into fine wine production and asked that Kym keep an eye out for something special. Shortly thereafter a vineyard that Kym had coveted from his beginnings in the Barossa Valley came onto the market. The 20ha vineyard was duly acquired, Kym investing in a small share that he couldn't really afford but had to have. The vineyard is perched on Roenfeldt Road at one of the highest points of the boundary between Greenock and Marananga. The depleted stoney soils consistently produce low yields of high quality grapes that loudly proclaim their Barossan origin. The X-factor is the site-driven savoury balance that Kym says he always longs for. The name they have given the business is the root word of Utopia. Everything is just so right: great vineyard, great winemaker, great story, great packaging. Exports to China.

🍷🍷🍷🍷🍷 **Shiraz 2017** The fragrant bouquet serves notice that this is no ordinary wine. There is a vibrant elegance to its array of red and black fruits and a slinky, juicy mouthfeel to the very long palate. A totally seductive wine of rare quality and style. Cork. 14.5% alc. **Rating** 97 **To** 2037 $65 ✪

ŢŢŢŢŢ Mataro Shiraz Grenache 2018 A full-bodied opening with peels of thunder, then licorice black fruits, tar and fruit conserve; tannins and oak presently hidden in the rolls of fleshy fruits. Cork. 14.5% alc. Rating 95 To 2043 $65

Cabernet Sauvignon 2017 A full-bodied cabernet that relished the vintage, not so much the place – which is a warm spot in the (naturally warm) Barossa Valley. This is a pretty good Barossa cabernet, luscious and rich (not cooked). Cork. 14.5% alc. Rating 94 To 2042 $65

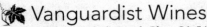 ## Vanguardist Wines   ★★★★☆

203 Main North Road, Clare, SA 5453 **Region** South Australia
T 0487 193 053 **www.vanguardistwines.com Open** Not
Winemaker Michael John Corbett **Est.** 2014 **Dozens** 1500 **Vyds** 7.5ha

The Wine Companion has always encouraged its panel of tasters to speak with their own voices and subtly or overtly express their opinions on wine style. Because natural wines represent less than 1% (in volume) of Australia's wines, and because most natural winemakers are content to work in a closed environment, they seldom submit wines. Vanguardist has done so and Ned Goodwin has found much to be enjoyed in these wines. Winemaker Michael John Corbett has the last (explanatory) word: 'Driven by a passion for creating wines with intrigue, structure and substance, "V" is about pushing the boundaries of status quo in winemaking and viticulture. Each glass of wine produced is a reflection of the knowledge, considered techniques and deep passion for telling the complete story from soil, vine, handcrafted through to the wine.' Exports to France and NZ.

ŢŢŢŢŢ McLaren Vale Grenache 2018 This does not stray from the variety's sweet spot of physiological ripeness in an endeavour to be overtly light and because the wine has real tannins: the sort of cardamom and bergamot-doused tannins that assuage grenache's hedonistic tendencies while curtailing them into a stream of anise, chipotle and raspberry-infused goodness. Fermented with 40% whole bunches. Right on the money! Cork. 13.9% alc. Rating 95 To 2023 $50 NG

Adelaide Hills Blanc 2018 An intriguing white once one gets their head around it, as it is completely unconventional in its make-up. A result of foot stomping, cold soaking and partial further maceration on skins in egg; the rest in barriques; ambient fermentation sans fining or filtration. Reminiscent of a wine from the Jura with oxidation its calling card; a slinky rail of tatami, mountain herb, camomile and apricot notes, all its signature. A versatile style at the table. Screwcap. 11.9% alc. Rating 94 To 2022 $40 NG

Adelaide Hills Chardonnay 2018 This delicious light to mid-weighted chardonnay bursts with licks of oatmeal, peach and curd rummaging along rails of juicy natural acidity and cedar. A combination of whole-bunch pressed and foot-crushed fruit, fermented wild in 2200l foudre with controlled oxidation the key to the wine's detailed complexity. Screwcap. 12.2% alc. Rating 94 To 2023 $50 NG

ŢŢŢŢŢ Clare Valley Riesling 2018 Rating 93 To 2024 $40 NG
Petillant Naturel Chardonnay Musque 2018 Rating 92 $50 NG
La Petite Vanguard Riesling 2018 Rating 90 To 2022 $30 NG
La Petite Vanguard Bistro Rouge 2018 Rating 90 $30 NG

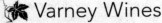 ## Varney Wines   ★★★★★

62 Victor Harbor Road, Old Noarlunga, SA 5168 **Region** McLaren Vale
T 0450 414 570 **www.varneywines.com.au Open** Thurs–Mon 11–5
Winemaker Alan Varney **Est.** 2017 **Dozens** 1050

Alan Varney's Australian career (based on an oenology degree from the University of Melbourne) grew out of a vintage stint with d'Arenberg into an 11-year employment, much of it as senior winemaker. He says that this period meant he came to be friends with many of the best local growers in McLaren Vale, the Adelaide Hills and Langhorne Creek. The d'Arenberg vintage typically included making nine varieties, some mainstream, some alternative. He is a brilliant winemaker, saying, 'I am not afraid to step out of the box and go with my intuition … I only use old seasoned oak with no fining or filtration.' His ability to draw the varietal heart of each wine he makes with alcohol levels between 12% and 14% is extraordinary. He has built an environmentally sensitive winery alongside wife Kathrin's restaurant, Victor's Place, overlooking the rolling hills of the Onkaparinga Gorge. The unspoken question is whether he will increase the small amounts of each wine he makes; my guess is not by much. Varney Wines are the *Wine Companion 2021* Best New Winery.

🍷🍷🍷🍷🍷 **GSM 2017** A 38/32/30% grenache/shiraz/mourvedre blend. Multiply the '17 vintage with Alan Varney's vinous beliefs and the quality of each piece in the jigsaw puzzle has been put in place. Its complexity knows no bounds; savoury yet sweet, the mouth-watering flavours leading me close to drooling. Screwcap. 13.9% alc. **Rating** 97 **To** 2027 $30 ❂

🍷🍷🍷🍷🍷 **Shiraz 2017** From vineyards in Clarendon, Tatachilla and Macclesfield; fermented with custom-made headed down open top fermenters, pressed to mature barrels for 10 months; 84 dozen made. Everything to love about the wine: the spicy/savoury input of '17, the mouth-watering texture, the evocative call of a wine blended with such skill, yet keeping the blend undercover. Screwcap. 14.2% alc. **Rating** 96 **To** 2047 $42 ❂

Chardonnay 2018 From a single block planted '99 at 390m at Echunga; hand-picked, whole-bunch pressed, wild-fermented in 2–3yo French barriques, matured for 7 months with frequent stirring; 85 dozen made. This is no pushover. It has considerable attitude and push-back on the long, tenacious oak and finish. Screwcap. 12.9% alc. **Rating** 95 **To** 2028 $32 ❂

Entrada McLaren Vale Rose of Grenache 2019 From 60yo bushvines in Blewitt Springs; crushed and destemmed, 90% cool-fermented in tank, 10% wild-fermented in used French barriques to add palate weight. Bright, clear puce. It is fresh, fruity and finishes bone dry. This means – à la Spanish manzanilla – it can be served with literally anything. Can't be faulted. Screwcap. 12.1% alc. **Rating** 95 **To** 2022 $25 ❂

Grenache 2019 From a 60yo bushvine vineyard, picked slightly early to retain natural acidity and vibrancy. Partial whole-bunch carbonic maceration, 14 days on skins in the open fermenter with gentle plunging, pressed to one used French hogshead, matured for 8 months; 33 dozen made. Message to all grenache growers: this is from another planet. Screwcap. 13.9% alc. **Rating** 95 **To** 2039 $35 ❂

Entrada McLaren Vale Grenache Mourvedre Touriga 2018 The 60/30/10% blend was cold-soaked for 3–5 days, partial whole-bunch fermentation, thence to used French barriques for a short maturation. It's light-bodied but that counterintuitively serves to highlight the rainbow of red, purple, blue and black fruit flavours. Screwcap. 13.1% alc. **Rating** 95 **To** 2024 $25 ❂

Semillon Fiano 2018 Includes 60% semillon from Kuitpo in the Adelaide Hills, cool-fermented in tank, 40% fiano from Langhorne Creek; cold-soaked for 24 hours, the juice hyper-oxidised to soften phenolics prior to fermentation in used barriques. Just as you think another taste is needed, the combination of flavour and texture makes you realise it's already there. Screwcap. 12.4% alc. **Rating** 94 **To** 2028 $28 ❂

🍷🍷🍷🍷🍷 **Entrada Adelaide Hills Verdelho 2019** **Rating** 90 **To** 2022 $25

Vasse Felix   ★★★★★

Cnr Tom Cullity Drive/Caves Road, Cowaramup, WA 6284 **Region** Margaret River
T (08) 9756 5000 **www.**vassefelix.com.au **Open** 7 days 10–5
Winemaker Virginia Willcock **Est.** 1967 **Dozens** 150 000 **Vyds** 232ha
Vasse Felix is Margaret River's founding wine estate, established in 1967 by regional pioneer Dr Tom Cullity. Owned and operated by the Holmes à Court family since 1987, Paul Holmes à Court has brought the focus to Margaret River's key varieties of cabernet sauvignon and chardonnay. Chief Winemaker Virginia Willcock has energised the winemaking and viticultural team with her no-nonsense approach and fierce commitment to quality. Vasse

Felix has four scrupulously managed vineyards throughout Margaret River that contribute all but a small part of the annual production. Wines include icons Tom Cullity (cabernet blend) and Heytesbury Chardonnay as well as Cabernet Sauvignon, Chardonnay, Sauvignon Blanc Semillon and Shiraz; Filius Chardonnay and Filius Cabernet Sauvignon; Classic Dry White and Classic Dry Red, plus limited quantities of Cane Cut Semillon and Blanc de Blancs. Exports to all major markets.

ŸŸŸŸŸ **Heytesbury Margaret River Chardonnay 2018** Heytesbury has always been a yin and yang wine. It has power, structure and depth, yet can appear reticent in its youth. The fruit is fabulous. Wafts of lemon balm, ginger cream and spicy oak too, but it is all about the palate – linear, long, superfine, a tight acid line, it has a crushed rock character with moreish flinty sulphides – the list goes on. Everything in sync. It's one heck of a classy chardonnay. Screwcap. 13% alc. **Rating** 98 To 2030 $92 JF ✪

Tom Cullity Margaret River Cabernet Sauvignon Malbec 2016 It's a pleasure to spend time with Tom Cullity. This is all about refinement. It has a presence and a whole lot of detail. The fruit is savoury and sweet, the iodine and graphite character of the malbec infused into the DNA. There are also finely chiselled tannins, lively acidity and a length like no tomorrow. Sure there's a power and energy but the wine's defining feature is elegance. Screwcap. 14% alc. **Rating** 97 To 2036 $180 JF

ŸŸŸŸŸ **Margaret River Chardonnay 2018** This is a bit of rock 'n' roll that performs brilliantly in Vasse Felix's chardonnay hierarchy. Perfect balance of flavours from grapefruit, lemon pith and delicate leesy-nutty characters with plenty of flint and saline. It's linear, long and pure, with a riff of acidity that keeps the band together. Screwcap. 13% alc. **Rating** 96 To 2027 $39 JF ✪

Filius Margaret River Cabernet Sauvignon 2017 Bright crimson-purple; this has provenance written large across its visage, likewise purity. Restructuring of the Vasse Felix offers to the market has lifted, not compromised, this dark, fruit-filled cabernet. Screwcap. 14% alc. **Rating** 96 To 2032 $28 ✪

Margaret River Cabernet Sauvignon 2016 Fits more or less into the middle of the Vasse Felix cabernet sauvignon range with no mention of a dash of this or that common with many Margaret River cabernets, and I would argue all the better for that. Its balance and structure ex bramble-like tannins fits neatly in the midpoint of cabernet with blackcurrant, bay leaf and dried herbs. Screwcap. 14% alc. **Rating** 96 To 2046 $47 ✪

Margaret River Sauvignon Blanc Semillon 2018 Sauvignon blanc leads this duet at 82% with almost half the blend spending time in a mix of French oak for 6 or so months. It's a classy outcome. Superb balance of flavours; it has precision, length and line. A crisp, dry finish quite savoury with a phenolic edge adding another layer of complexity. Screwcap. 13% alc. **Rating** 95 To 2025 $26 JF ✪

Margaret River Shiraz 2018 Cabernet sauvignon might be the regional red darling, but sometimes shiraz stands proudly. Still in a restrained style with excellent fruit at its heart, a dusting of woodsy spices, black pepper with an iodine/ferrous note. Sandpaper tannins and poppy acidity go hand-in-hand. Screwcap. 14% alc. **Rating** 95 To 2030 $37 JF

Margaret River Cabernet Sauvignon 2017 Sure it has the exuberance of youth, but this will age gracefully. Full of raspberries and currants with a cranberry tang alongside menthol; oak playing a part but not a lead role. Fine and poised tannins, although acidity is very much a driver this vintage, it's refreshing and lively. And like seasoning in cooking, the glug of malbec and petit verdot adds another dimension. Screwcap. 14.5% alc. **Rating** 95 To 2037 $47 JF

ŸŸŸŸŸ **Margaret River Classic Dry White 2019 Rating** 92 To 2021 $19 JF ✪
Filius Margaret River Chardonnay 2018 Rating 92 To 2028 $28
Margaret River Classic Dry Red 2018 Rating 91 To 2019 $19 JF ✪
Margaret River Classic Dry Rose 2019 Rating 90 To 2021 $19 ✪

Vickery Wines

28 The Parade, Norwood, SA 5067 **Region** Clare Valley/Eden Valley
T (08) 8362 8622 **www**.vickerywines.com.au **Open** Not
Winemaker John Vickery, Keeda Zilm **Est.** 2014 **Dozens** 4000 **Vyds** 12ha

It must have been a strange feeling for John Vickery to begin at the beginning again, 60 years after his first vintage in 1951. His interest in, love of and exceptional skills with riesling began with Leo Buring in '55 at Chateau Leonay. Over the intervening years he became the uncrowned but absolute monarch of riesling makers in Australia until, in his semi-retirement, he passed the mantle on to Jeffrey Grosset. Along the way he had (unsurprisingly) won the Wolf Blass Riesling Award at the Canberra International Riesling Challenge 2007 and had been judged by his peers as Australia's Greatest Living Winemaker in a survey conducted by *The Age Epicure* in '03. His new venture has been undertaken in conjunction with Phil Lehmann, with 12ha of Clare and Eden valley riesling involved and wine marketer Jonathon Hesketh moving largely invisibly in the background. The Da Vinci code letters and numerals are easy when it comes to EVR (Eden Valley Riesling) and WVR (Watervale Riesling), but thereafter the code strikes. The numerics are the dates of harvest, thus '103' is 10 March, '172' is 17 February. The initials that follow are even more delphic, standing for the name of the vineyard or those of the multiple owners. Exports to the UK, the EU and Canada.

🍷🍷🍷🍷🍷 **The Reserve Koerner G6 Block Watervale Riesling 2017** WVR 603 K.
The Koerner G6 Block stood out when the time came to bottle the main release, so this small parcel was retained and released separately. Add another 3+ years and you'll have something to celebrate for your wisdom and patience. Screwcap. 12.5% alc. **Rating** 96 **To** 2037 $32 ✪
The Reserve Zander Kosi Block Eden Valley Riesling 2017 EVR 704 Z.
This is the least advanced of Vickery's '16 and '17 releases; '16 is the most pure, the most relaxed and the most certain about its future. Screwcap. 11.5% alc.
Rating 96 **To** 2037 $32 ✪
Watervale Riesling 2019 WVR 262 CK. There's a generosity to this wine.
Opens with lime, lemon and apple blossom, then throwing in hints of spice and lemon zest. The palate picks up the pace with flavours from here, there and everywhere. Lovely wine for early consumption. Screwcap. 12.5% alc. **Rating** 95 **To** 2034 $23 ✪
Eden Valley Riesling 2019 EVR 703 MZ. A precise portrait of Eden Valley riesling achieved despite a torrid growing season: the downside the miserable size of the yield, the upside its floral lime/lemon aromas. The palate has marvellous juicy flavours framed by mouth-watering acidity. Screwcap. 12% alc. **Rating** 95 **To** 2036 $23 ✪
Eden Valley Riesling 2017 Sourced from the high-altitude 500m 'Kosi Block' which stood out early for its potential for ageing. The Vickery riesling 'recipe' is maintained here with the aim of a pure start and extended bottle ageing. It delivers a fresh, vibrant lemon-delicious aroma and mounts a persuasive argument for aged riesling such is its complexity and confident display of vitality, of lime zest, grapefruit pith, developing brioche. Screwcap. 11.5% alc. **Rating** 95 **To** 2039 $32 JP ✪

Victory Point Wines

★★★★★

92 Holben Road, Cowaramup, WA 6284 **Region** Margaret River
T 0417 954 655 **www**.victorypointwines.com **Open** Thurs–Sun 11–4
Winemaker Mark Messenger (Contract) **Est.** 1997 **Dozens** 2000 **Vyds** 12.9ha

Judith and Gary Berson have set their sights high. They established their vineyard without irrigation, emulating those of the Margaret River pioneers (including Moss Wood). The fully mature plantings comprise 4.2ha chardonnay and 0.5ha of pinot noir; the remainder Bordeaux varieties with cabernet sauvignon (6.2ha), cabernet franc (0.5ha), malbec (0.8ha) and petit verdot (0.7ha). The cellar door overlooks the 20+-year-old vineyard.

ŶŶŶŶŶ **Margaret River Chardonnay 2017** Peaches and cream references fealty to the Margaret River postcode; this is unashamedly rich. Yet the oak is nestled in, the maritime acidity febrile; a hint of reductive flint evincing authority and energy amid truffled wild–yeast influence. Delicious! Screwcap. **Rating** 96 **To** 2025 $45 NG

Margaret River Rose 2019 A blend of malbec, pinot noir and cabernet franc. It is a striking wine with strong allspice, vanilla pod and red fruits on the bouquet, promptly built on by the finish of the palate. Estate-grown, the winemaking skills of Mark Messenger on display. Screwcap. 13.5% alc. **Rating** 95 **To** 2022 $23 ✪

The Mallee Root Margaret River Cabernet Sauvignon Malbec Petit Verdot 2017 A 56/34/10% estate blend; open-fermented, 7–14 days on skins, pressed to French oak (25% new) for 16 months, the components managed separately before blending. In the seductive, generous and soft style that is the hallmark of Victory Point. Screwcap. 14% alc. **Rating** 95 **To** 2029 $28 ✪

Margaret River Cabernet Sauvignon 2017 Exceptional wine from the stellar '17 vintage. This is 91% cabernet, 6% malbec and a dollop of petit verdot. Cassis, dried sage, a smear of tapenade and bouquet garni run riot across finely hewn tannins, well appointed oak and saline acidity, a bit trop. The finish, a gentle flourish of pyrazine to reassure one of the varietal makeup. Screwcap. **Rating** 94 **To** 2029 $45 NG

ŶŶŶŶŶ **Margaret River Cabernet Franc 2018 Rating** 92 **To** 2031 $35
Margaret River Pinot Noir 2018 Rating 91 **To** 2027 $55

View Road Wines ★★★★★

Peacocks Road, Lenswood, SA 5240 **Region** Adelaide Hills
T 0402 180 383 www.viewroadwines.com.au **Open** Not
Winemaker Josh Tuckfield **Est.** 2011 **Dozens** 3000
View Road Wines sources prosecco, arneis, chardonnay, sangiovese, merlot, sagrantino and syrah from Adelaide Hills vineyards; shiraz, aglianico and sagrantino from McLaren Vale vineyards; and nero d'Avola and fiano from the Riverland. All of the wines are wild-yeast fermented and matured in used oak.

ŶŶŶŶŶ **McLaren Vale Shiraz 2016** This is beautifully crafted. A ricochet of violet, iodine, salami and blueberry, towed long by a whiplash of pepper-doused acidity, give an impression of crunch, energy and palate-staining intensity. Wines like this are making naysayers such as myself pay closer attention to a newer, fresher zeitgeist in SA's warmer areas. Take advantage of the buoyant fruit and drink on the younger side. Screwcap. 14.2% alc. **Rating** 96 **To** 2025 $37 NG ✪

Barossa Shiraz 2016 Even in a Barossan context '16 was a warm year. Yet physiologically ripe fruit was brought in early. The result is impressive: moreishly chewy, dense and devoid of excessively sweet fruit, fortressed by a phalanx of reassuring natural tannins seldom seen in these parts. Almost ferruginous. Pulpy too. The nose, while restrained, offers licorice, smoked meat, bitter chocolate and a violet lilt. Screwcap. 14.2% alc. **Rating** 95 **To** 2031 $80 NG

Vigena Wines ★★★★★

210 Main Road, Willunga, SA 5172 **Region** McLaren Vale
T 0433 966 011 **Open** Not
Winemaker Ben Heide **Est.** 2010 **Dozens** 20 000 **Vyds** 15.8ha
The principal business of Vigena Wines is exporting to Singapore, Hong Kong and China. In recent years the vineyard has been revitalised, with one significant change: chardonnay has been grafted to shiraz, giving the business a 100% red wine focus.

ŶŶŶŶŶ **Limited Edition McLaren Vale Shiraz 2018** As with all the Vigena wines, they are built with intention, so you have to be a fan of mammoth, tannic reds. This is a powerhouse of flavour, ripeness and oak and yet, there's a freshness, a life to the palate. Cork. 14.8% alc. **Rating** 95 **To** 2034 $79 JF

McLaren Vale Cabernet Sauvignon 2018 There's often a scorched earth/just-baked blackberry pie character to McLaren Vale cabernet, and this is awash with it. Plenty of currants, bracken, leafy freshness too, with decisive tannins. The palate is fuller-bodied yet there is, thankfully, a freshness throughout. Cork. 14.5% alc. Rating 95 To 2033 $65 JF

McLaren Vale Cabernet Sauvignon Shiraz 2018 Despite winemaking artefact – the extraction, the lashings of oak and slightly brutish tannins as a result – this has been stitched together well. Intense ripe blackberries and essence flecked with cocoa, woodsy spices and plenty of dried herbs for good measure. As with all the Vigena wines, in an absurdly heavy bottle. Cork. 14.5% alc. **Rating** 95 To 2034 $55 JF

ΨΨΨΨΨ **McLaren Vale Shiraz Grenache 2018** Rating 93 To 2032 $50 JF
Gran Reserve McLaren Vale Shiraz 2017 Rating 92 To 2032 JF

Vignerons Schmölzer & Brown ★★★★★

39 Thorley Road, Stanley, Vic 3747 **Region** Beechworth
T 0411 053 487 **www.**vsandb.com.au **Open** By appt
Winemaker Tessa Brown, Jeremy Schmölzer **Est.** 2014 **Dozens** 500 **Vyds** 2ha
Winemaker/viticulturist Tessa Brown graduated from CSU with a degree in viticulture in the late 1990s and undertook postgraduate winemaking studies at the University of Adelaide in the mid-2000s. Her self-description of being 'reasonably peripatetic' covers her winemaking in Orange in '99 and also in Canberra, SA, Strathbogie Ranges, Rioja and Central Otago before joining Kooyong and Port Phillip Estate in '08. In '09 Mark Walpole showed Tess and architect partner Jeremy Schmölzer a property that he described as 'the jewel in the crown of Beechworth'. When it came onto the market unexpectedly in '12, they were in a position to jump. The property (named Thorley) was 20ha and cleared; they have planted chardonnay, shiraz, riesling and nebbiolo. By sheer chance, just across the road from Thorley was a tiny vineyard, a bit over 0.4ha, with dry-grown pinot and chardonnay around 20 years old. When they realised it was not being managed for production, they struck up a working relationship with the owners, getting the vineyard into shape and making their first (very good) wines in '14. The Obstgarten wines come from a small, high-altitude riesling vineyard in the King Valley.

ΨΨΨΨΨ **Obstgarten T King Valley Riesling 2019** From the Croucher Vineyard at Whitlands; 50/50% fermented in tank and barrel; 140 dozen made. It's essentially dry in style though the fruit has both power and punch. This stops you in your tracks; it's not your standard riesling fare. It tastes of grapefruit, lemon, sweet lime and more. The intensity of this, both on the palate and through the finish, is quite something. Screwcap. 11.5% alc. **Rating** 95 To 2026 $35 CM ✪

Thorley Shiraz 2018 Two barrels only. Second shiraz harvest from the estate vineyard, planted at 820m. Bottled unfined and unfiltered. Incredible purity of fruit complemented by significant peppery/stemmy complexities. Apart from anything else it smells absolutely beautiful. Cherry-plum with emphasis on the latter; graphite notes; wood smoke. Cool-climate at every turn, but ripe. It's a wine of impeccable balance and life. Screwcap. 13.5% alc. **Rating** 95 To 2028 $40 CM

Pret-a-Rose 2019 Made with sangiovese and pinot noir, all non-estate but Beechworth origin. Fermented in old oak. There's a softness to the palate but the finish cuts long. It has the tartness of a cranberried wine but there's enough cherry-plum to make it feel juicy and fruity, savoury and pale-dry as its overall style may be. In short it's absolutely delicious to drink. Screwcap. 13% alc. **Rating** 94 To 2022 $28 CM ✪

ΨΨΨΨΨ **Selection King Valley Riesling 2018** Rating 93 To 2026 $45 CM

Vinaceous Wines

49 Bennett Street, East Perth, WA 6004 (postal) **Region** Various
T (08) 9221 4666 **www**.vinaceous.com.au **Open** Not
Winemaker Gavin Berry, Michael Kerrigan **Est.** 2007 **Dozens** 25000
This is the somewhat quirky venture of wine marketer Nick Stacy, Michael Kerrigan (winemaker/partner Hay Shed Hill) and Gavin Berry (winemaker/partner West Cape Howe). The fast-moving and fast-growing brand was originally directed at the US market, but has changed direction due to the domestic demand engendered (one might guess) by the decidedly exotic/erotic labels and, more importantly, by the fact that the wines are of seriously good quality and equally good value. Margaret River provides over half of the production, the remainder comes from Frankland River, Mount Barker, McLaren Vale and the Adelaide Hills. Yet more labels, ranges and wines are in the pipeline; the website is the best method of keeping up to date. Exports to the UK, the US, Canada, South America, Denmark, Finland, Indonesia, the Philippines, Thailand, Singapore and Hong Kong.

🍷🍷🍷🍷🍷 **Reverend V Cabernet Sauvignon 2018** Comprises 60% from Margaret River, 40% from Frankland River. Elegant, although medium-bodied. Good handling of oak more than pays its way. Red fruits keep the wine on its feet, although black fruits are also in attendance. Complicated logistics have been made to look simple. Screwcap. 14.5% alc. Rating 95 To 2033 $25 ✪
Voodoo Moon Margaret River Malbec 2018 Hand-picked, open-fermented, basket-pressed, 16 months in French barriques (25% new). Although there is no obvious reason why, this is far lighter and brighter on its feet than its Reverend V sibling. Screwcap. 14.5% alc. **Rating** 94 To 2025 $22 ✪

🍷🍷🍷🍷🍷 **Divine Light Mount Barker Riesling 2019** Rating 93 To 2029 $22 ✪
Reverend V Syrah 2018 Rating 93 To 2033 $25 ✪
Reverend V Chardonnay 2018 Rating 92 To 2027 $25 ✪
Reverend V Vermentino 2019 Rating 92 To 2020 $25 ✪
Red Right Hand Margaret River Shiraz Grenache Tempranillo 2018
Rating 92 To 2038 $22 ✪
Clandestine Vineyards #3 Margaret River Cabernet Franc 2018
Rating 92 To 2022 $30
Snake Charmer Frankland River Shiraz 2018 Rating 91 To 2035 $22 ✪
Reverend V Malbec 2018 Rating 90 To 2024 $25

🌿 Vindana Wines

PO Box 705, Lyndoch, SA 5351 **Region** Barossa Valley
T 0437 175 437 **www**.vindanawines.com.au **Open** Not
Winemaker Scott Higginson **Est.** 1968 **Dozens** 350 **Vyds** 1ha
Scott Higginson is a seventh-generation vigneron, whose family history starts in 1846 on the banks of Jacobs Creek and continues there for 111 years until an ill-fated decision to sell and move to the Riverland where a series of Peter Lehmann–like moves to protect growers from collapses in the wine-grape market turned sour. Scott has returned to the Barossa Valley, completing the wine marketing degree at Roseworthy Agricultural College and adding extensive work with medium to large (Foster's group) wineries. In 2013 he purchased a housing block at Lyndoch with enough room for 1ha of vines. He also purchases small parcels of premium fruit, making wine on a minimum-intervention basis. With a couple of eighth-generation feet on the ground, some very good wines have materialised overnight. Exports to China.

🍷🍷🍷🍷🍷 **Keeper of the Stones Limited Release Barossa Valley Shiraz 2015** From 40yo vines; open-fermented, 12 days on skins in used American hogsheads with the heads knocked out, 18 months in American hogsheads (50% new). It is full-bodied and held in a corset of oak. The oak handling has been very skilful – time could produce a revolution. Cork. 15% alc. **Rating** 95 To 2040 $70
Keeper of the Stones Limited Release Barossa Valley Grenache 2018
Hand-picked from 100yo vines at Williamstown in the cool southern tip of the

Barossa Valley. Open-fermented with 20% whole bunches in hogsheads with the tops knocked out, matured in used French barriques for 18 months. It breaks all the rules and expectations on my part. It is a beautifully structured grenache with fresh colour and fruit, showing little development so far, thus offering cellaring if you so wish. Screwcap. 14% alc. **Rating** 95 **To** 2033 $30 ✪

Vinden Wines ★★★★★

138 Gillards Road, Pokolbin, NSW 2320 **Region** Hunter Valley
T 0488 777 493 **www**.vindenwines.com.au **Open** Wed–Sun 10–5
Winemaker Angus Vinden, Daniel Binet **Est.** 1998 **Dozens** 4000 **Vyds** 5ha
Vinden Estate is under the guidance of second-generation winemaker Angus Vinden, who took over the business from parents Sandra and Guy in 2015. He has maintained the original traditional Hunter wines as well as introducing newer styles. All wines are Hunter Valley–sourced, mainly from the estate vineyard (2ha alicante bouschet, 1.25ha shiraz, 1ha mourvedre, 0.75ha gamay) and local old vines sites, in particular the Somerset Vineyard in Pokolbin where Angus was mentored under eighth-generation grower Glen Howard.

🍷🍷🍷🍷🍷 **Somerset Vineyard Hunter Valley Semillon 2019** Vines planted '69 on fine clay-loam soil, the juice fermented with fine solids, extended lees contact before bottling. Full to the brim with flavours in a lemon circle – zest, grass, mineral. Screwcap. 10.5% alc. **Rating** 96 **To** 2034 $30 ✪
The Vinden Headcase Somerset Vineyard Single Barrel #1 Eastern Slope Hunter Valley Shiraz 2018 From the eastern slope planted '66 on red volcanic soil. Open-fermented, cold soak, wild-fermented in open concrete fermenter, matured in French oak for 14 months, not fined or filtered, gravity bottled. More black fruits and more tannins than Fountainhead. Will be very long-lived. Diam. 13.7% alc. **Rating** 96 **To** 2043 $60 ✪
The Vinden Headcase Somerset Vineyard Single Barrel #3 Western Slope Hunter Valley Shiraz 2018 Identical vinification to its siblings. Slightly richer/firmer mouthfeel. Diam. 13.9% alc. **Rating** 96 **To** 2043 $60 ✪
Somerset Vineyard Hunter Valley Chardonnay 2019 Vines planted '73, '80 and '87; basket-pressed juice direct to French oak (30% new) for fermentation and 8 months' maturation with stirring every 2 weeks. Angus Vinden says this is 'a modern chardonnay balanced fruit and minerally with texture and lees weight'. I'm in 2 minds about the bouquet but the varietal expression is pure Hunter with its inbuilt acidity. Screwcap. 12.5% alc. **Rating** 95 **To** 2026 $40
Somerset Vineyard Fountainhead Hunter Valley Shiraz 2018 From 3 blocks planted '66, '68 and '70 on red volcanic clay soils. Open-fermented, cold soak, hand-plunged, matured in French oak (25% new) for 16 months. Fine, fragrant red fruits are as obvious as black. An elegant, light to medium-bodied, superfine wine that didn't chase extract. I really like this wine. Screwcap. 13.9% alc. **Rating** 95 **To** 2038 $60
The Vinden Headcase Somerset Vineyard Single Barrel #2 Northern Slope Hunter Valley Shiraz 2018 Vines planted '68, identical vinification to its siblings. Deeply coloured. Slightly more velvety sweet-plum flavour corresponding to the 50yo vines. Diam. 13.9% alc. **Rating** 95 **To** 2038 $60
The Vinden Headcase Somerset Vineyard Hunter Valley Tempranillo 2018 A very, very good tempranillo with a clarity of colour and of red cherry flavour. It's juicy, supple and has tannins where needed, no more, no less. Screwcap. 14% alc. **Rating** 95 **To** 2022 $40

🍷🍷🍷🍷🍷 **The Vinden Headcase Somerset Vineyard Single Barrel 73 Block Hunter Valley Chardonnay 2019 Rating** 93 **To** 2027 $50
The Vinden Headcase Somerset Vineyard Single Barrel 87 Block Hunter Valley Chardonnay 2019 Rating 92 **To** 2027 $50
Aged Release Hunter Valley Semillon 2014 Rating 91 **To** 2022 $50

Vinea Marson

411 Heathcote-Rochester Road, Heathcote, Vic 3523 **Region** Heathcote
T 0430 312 165 **www**.vineamarson.com **Open** W'ends
Winemaker Mario Marson **Est.** 2000 **Dozens** 2500 **Vyds** 7.12ha

Owner-winemaker Mario Marson spent many years as the winemaker/viticulturist with the late Dr John Middleton at the celebrated Mount Mary. Mario has over 35 years of experience in Australia and overseas, having undertaken vintages at Isole e Olena in Tuscany and Piedmont and at Domaine de la Pousse d'Or in Burgundy, where he was inspired to emulate the multi-clonal wines favoured by these producers, pioneered in Australia by John Middleton. In 1999 he and his wife, Helen, purchased the Vinea Marson property on the eastern slopes of the Mt Camel Range. They have planted shiraz and viognier, plus Italian varieties of sangiovese, nebbiolo, barbera and refosco dal peduncolo. Marson also sources northeastern Italian varietals from Porepunkah in the Alpine Valleys. Exports to China.

Nebbiolo 2015 Twelve clones contribute to this wine and combine with the cool growing season to produce an accomplished and complex nebbiolo. There's incredible depth of fruit flavour and layers of winemaking on show. But first to the perfume: rose petal, musk, sour cherry, anise and tobacco leaf. Tannins and acidity under control but lurking, a sheen of herbs and spice-infused red berries. Come back to it and it has changed in the glass, a chameleon. Diam. 13.5% alc. Rating 96 To 2035 $46 JP ✪

Sangiovese 2016 An astonishing number of clones employed here – 13 altogether – which bring an extraordinary degree of complexity and savouriness to the finished wine. Feel the sun and the earth, the black cherries, charcuterie and leather. Sour cherry, cherry pip resonates on the palate which is taut, savoury and wild. An Italian-Australian's glorious ode to sangiovese. Diam. 14% alc. Rating 95 To 2032 $42 JP

Shiraz Viognier 2016 Comprises 96% shiraz, 4% viognier. If drinkers ever wonder what dark and brooding means in a tasting note, here is a perfect example. There is a darkness in fruit colour – dark plums, black fruits, brown spices, pastille – and even the florals of violet and cherry/orange blossom are underplayed. The tone is sophisticated, savoury and a bit of a slow burn as the wine reveals itself. Further ageing required. Diam. 14% alc. **Rating** 94 **To** 2029 $42 JP

Col Fondo Prosecco 2018 You will never view prosecco the same way again after tasting it col fondo (with the bottom), which is old-school winemaking with the second fermentation in the bottle on lees and no disgorgement. The lees are where the flavour resides, and what flavour! Delightfully cloudy with aromas of honeysuckle, lemon drop, peach skin and gingersnap biscuit. The mouth fills with white peach, lemon pith, barley sugar and a subtle dryness. Remember to swirl. Crown seal. 11.5% alc. **Rating** 94 $32 JP

Reserve Viognier 2017 Rating 93 To 2027 $50 JP
Friulano #7 2016 Rating 93 To 2026 $34 JP
Viognier 2017 Rating 92 To 2028 $34 JP
Grazia 2017 Rating 92 To 2027 $34 JP
Pinot Noir 2018 Rating 92 To 2028 $34 JP
Picolit 2018 Rating 92 To 2025 $34 JP

Vineyard Road ★★★★☆

697 Langhorne Creek Road, Belvidere, SA 5255 **Region** Langhorne Creek
T (08) 85368 334 **www**.fabalwines.com.au **Open** Wed–Mon 10–5
Winemaker Project Wine (Peter Pollard) **Est.** 2016 **Dozens** 10 000 **Vyds** 1500ha

This business is owned by Fabal Wines Pty Ltd. Fabal has been growing grapes and managing vineyards Australia-wide for over 30 years and decided to venture into wine production in 2016. It currently has 13 wines on offer at the cellar door, half the Vineyard Road business is dedicated to Vasse Virgin Natural Olive Oil skin products. The majority of the estate vineyards are situated in Langhorne Creek, with 565ha of the major varieties. There are also outlying vineyards in the Clare Valley (riesling) and Heathcote (tempranillo). Exports to the US, Singapore and China.

♨♨♨♨♨ **Belvidere Estate Block 9 Langhorne Creek Shiraz 2015** Open-fermented, 11 days on skins, 21 months in American hogsheads. Excellent colour. A well structured and balanced wine, bordering on outright elegance, the oak and tannin particularly well handled. Blackberry, plum and spice fill the flavour profile. Cork. 14.5% alc. **Rating** 95 To 2030 $55

♨♨♨♨♨ **Moppa Springs Estate Barossa Valley Shiraz 2016** Rating 93 To 2030 $48
Belvidere Estate Langhorne Creek Shiraz 2015 Rating 93 To 2028 $35
The Edge Barossa Valley Shiraz 2017 Rating 91 To 2037 $75
Reserve Barossa Valley Shiraz 2017 Rating 90 To 2029 $30

Vintners Ridge Estate ★★★

Lot 18 Veraison Place, Yallingup, Margaret River, WA 6285 **Region** Margaret River
T 0417 956 943 **www.**vintnersridge.com.au **Open** By appt
Winemaker Flying Fish Cove (Simon Ding) **Est.** 2001 **Dozens** 250 **Vyds** 2.1ha
When Maree and Robin Adair purchased the Vintners Ridge Vineyard in 2006 (cabernet sauvignon), it had already produced three crops, having been planted in November '01. The vineyard overlooks the picturesque Geographe Bay.

♨♨♨♨ **Margaret River Cabernet Sauvignon 2018** Relatively light-bodied with purple/black fruits and some texture and structure. Screwcap. 14.2% alc. **Rating** 89 To 2025

Virago Nebbiolo ★★★★

5A Ford Street, Beechworth, Vic 3747 **Region** Beechworth
T 0411 718 369 **www.**viragobeechworth.com.au **Open** By appt
Winemaker Karen Coats, Rick Kinzbrunner **Est.** 2007 **Dozens** 175 **Vyds** 1ha
Karen Coats was a tax accountant but has now completed the Bachelor of Wine Science at CSU. It was her love of nebbiolo and the Beechworth region that made Virago Vineyard her new office of choice. Prue Keith is an orthopaedic surgeon but devotes her free time (whatever is not occupied by mountain biking, skiing and trekking to the peaks of mountains) to Virago Vineyard. The vines had been removed from the property long before Karen and Prue purchased it, but the existing terracing, old posts and broken wires laid down a challenge that was easily accepted, although the planting of nebbiolo was not so easy. The one and only Rick Kinzbrunner has a more than passing interest in nebbiolo, so it was inevitable that he would be the consultant winemaker.

♨♨♨♨♨ **Beechworth Nebbiolo 2016** You had me with Rick Kinzbrunner (winemaker), nebbiolo and Beechworth. It's a powerful trio, one not to be ignored. Evocative and complex aromas of cranberry, pomegranate, spice, violets, rose petal. No mistaking the variety when tasted, it launches into earth, smoked meat, leather, chocolate, tobacco. And then the big finish where concentrated, quality tannins mingle with panforte and glace cherry. It's some wine. Diam. 14% alc. **Rating** 96 To 2036 $45 JP

Virgara Wines ★★★★☆

143 Heaslip Road, Angle Vale, SA 5117 **Region** Adelaide Plains
T (08) 8284 7688 **www.**virgarawines.com.au **Open** Mon–Fri 9–5, w'ends 11–4
Winemaker Tony Carapetis **Est.** 2001 **Dozens** 50 000 **Vyds** 118ha
In 1962 the Virgara family – father Michael, mother Maria and 10 children – migrated to Australia from southern Italy. Through the hard work so typical of many such families, in due course they became market gardeners on land purchased at Angle Vale (1967) and in the early '90s acquired an existing vineyard in Angle Vale. The plantings have since been expanded to almost 120ha of shiraz, cabernet sauvignon, grenache, malbec, merlot, riesling, sangiovese,

sauvignon blanc, pinot grigio and alicante bouschet. In 2001 the Virgara brothers purchased the former Barossa Valley Estates winery but used it only for storage and maturation. The death of Domenic Virgara in a road accident led to the employment of former Palandri (and before that, Tahbilk) winemaker Tony Carapetis and the full re-commissioning of the winery. Exports to the US, Canada, China, Thailand, Malaysia and Japan.

ŸŸŸŸŸ **Allure Single Vineyard Pinot Noir Rose 2017** Deep, pink-red hue introduces a rose with more colour and flavour than most. Raspberries, fresh-cut strawberries and spice. Dusty, earthy dryness on the palate is more dry red than pretty, lifted rose and, as such, offers a different rose voice. Dry, grippy and food-friendly. Screwcap. 12.5% alc. **Rating** 92 **To** 2024 $21 JP ✪

ŸŸŸŸ **Legacy Adelaide Pinot Grigio 2018 Rating** 89 **To** 2023 JP

Voyager Estate   ★★★★★

Lot 1 Stevens Road, Margaret River, WA 6285 **Region** Margaret River
T (08) 9757 6354 **www.**voyagerestate.com.au **Open** 7 days 10–5
Winemaker Steve James, Travis Lemm **Est.** 1978 **Dozens** 40 000 **Vyds** 112ha
The late mining magnate Michael Wright pursued several avenues of business and agriculture before setting his sights on owning a vineyard and winery. It was thus an easy decision when he was able to buy what was then called Freycinet Estate from founder and leading viticulturist Peter Gherardi in 1991. Peter had established the vineyard in '78 and it was significantly expanded by Michael over the ensuing years. Apart from the Cape Dutch–style tasting room and vast rose garden, the signpost for the estate is the massive Australian flagpole – after Parliament House in Canberra, it's the largest flagpole in Australia. Michael's daughter, Alexandra Burt, has been at the helm of Voyager Estate for many years, supported by general manager Chris Furtado and a long-serving and committed staff. Michael is remembered as a larger-than-life character, more at home in his favourite work pants and boots than a suit, and never happier than when trundling around the estate on a four-wheeler or fixing a piece of machinery. Exports to all major markets.

ŸŸŸŸŸ **Broadvale Block 6 Margaret River Chardonnay 2018** The hand-picked fruit had higher than normal acidity so it was pressed to tank overnight to diminish it and to prompt wild fermentation in barrique. White peach, plus notes of malt and croissant, join with spices to make an attractive wine. Screwcap. 12.5% alc. **Rating** 96 **To** 2030 $65 ✪
MJW Margaret River Chardonnay 2017 Pale straw-green. A most attractive wine from start to finish. The palate opens with a flourish, but does so without bombast. Rock melon, white peach and an echo of grapefruit lay down the path for the long journey ahead. Screwcap. 13.5% alc. **Rating** 96 **To** 2029 $110
Margaret River Shiraz 2018 The jury is still out in deciding just how far Margaret River shiraz has to travel before drawing the proverbial line in the sand. Yes, it's more elegant and arguably less complex than cabernet or cabernet with little tricks in the wrapping of its parcel. But is that a bad thing? The answer is emphatically no for this whole berry–vinified wine. Its savoury characters are, quite simply, brilliant. Screwcap. 14% alc. **Rating** 96 **To** 2033 $38 ✪
Margaret River Chardonnay 2018 Four clones, 4 estate blocks, 4 tonnelleries and innumerable vinification approaches. This lends substance to the number of newly created labels; here the acidity sends a farewell lift to the finish and aftertaste. Length, life and grace. Screwcap. 13.5% alc. **Rating** 95 **To** 2027 $50
Broadvale Block 5 Margaret River Chardonnay 2018 Has paid little or no attention to the wet conditions, and with lateral thinking, the grapes were hand-picked over 3 days in Feb, good acidity maintained. Batonnage had to be conducted monthly during the maturation process, however mlf was blocked. The result is a chardonnay with a creamy cashew and melon note, and excellent length. Screwcap. 14% alc. **Rating** 95 **To** 2028 $65

Margaret River Chenin Blanc 2019 Sow's ears and silk purses. Shows what can be achieved with a variety usually reserved for bank managers' Christmas parties. Screwcap. 14% alc. **Rating** 95 **To** 2029 $20 ✪

Project Margaret River Rose 2019 From designated shiraz and merlot vineyards, plus a handful of co-fermented viognier. Ticks all the boxes, including a universe of food matches. Has texture, length and a twist of the tiger's tail to keep everything moving. Screwcap. 13.5% alc. **Rating** 94 **To** 2022 $24 ✪

ŦŦŦŦŦ **Project U10 Margaret River Semillon 2016 Rating** 93 **To** 2036
Margaret River Sauvignon Blanc Semillon 2019 Rating 93 **To** 2023 $24 ✪
Girt by Sea Margaret River Chardonnay 2018 Rating 93 **To** 2023 $28
Girt by Sea Margaret River Cabernet Merlot 2018 Rating 93 **To** 2030 $28
Margaret River Cabernet Sauvignon 2016 Rating 93 **To** 2024 $85
North Block U12 Margaret River Cabernet Sauvignon 2016 Rating 93 **To** 2030 $105
Old Block V9 Margaret River Cabernet Sauvignon 2016 Rating 92 **To** 2026 $105
Project Margaret River Sparkling Chenin Blanc 2019 Rating 90 $30

Walsh & Sons ★★★★★

4/5962 Caves Road, Margaret River, WA 6285 **Region** Margaret River
T (08) 9758 8023 **www**.walshandsons.com.au **Open** Not
Winemaker Ryan Walsh, Freya Hohnen **Est.** 2014 **Dozens** 1500 **Vyds** 20ha
The name Walsh & Sons has a Burgundian twist, the only difference is that Walsh & Sons would be Walsh et Fils. The analogy continues: the sons Roi and Hamish (Ryan Walsh and Freya Hohnen their parents) are in turn from McHenry Hohnen, of Margaret River blue blood wine aristocracy. Ryan and Freya have had a Burgundian family association making wine for McHenry Hohnen from 2004 to '12, and over that time visiting/working for wineries in France, Spain, Switzerland and the US. At present, part of the crop from their 11ha Burnside Vineyard (where they base themselves) and the Walsh 7ha Osmington Vineyard is sold to McHenry Hohnen, Yalumba and Domain & Vineyards. The Burnside Vineyard is managed biodynamically. Exports to the US.

ŦŦŦŦŦ **Burnside Margaret River Chardonnay 2018** A very good chardonnay, rich and layered in classic Margaret River style, but not overdone. White peach, nectarine, cashew. Good oak balance/integration. Screwcap. 13.5% alc. **Rating** 95 **To** 2027 $50
Roi Margaret River Cabernet Sauvignon 2017 This is as pure an expression of cabernet sauvignon as you are ever likely to come across. Every single box has been ticked, crossed and locked. Walsh & Sons don't bother to supply any vinification notes because the wine has risen above all that nonsense. Cork. 13.5% alc. **Rating** 95 **To** 2037 $45
Felix Margaret River Syrah 2017 From a single vineyard. Red and black fruits have a freshness and spiciness derived from early picking, and achieved without diluting the core of varietal fruit and tannins. Cork. 13.5% alc. **Rating** 94 **To** 2027 $30 ✪

ŦŦŦŦŦ **Lola Red 2018 Rating** 93 **To** 2028 $26 SC ✪
Remi Margaret River Rose 2019 Rating 90 **To** 2022 $26 SC
Remi Margaret River Rose 2018 Rating 90 **To** 2020 $26
Roi Margaret River Cabernet Sauvignon 2018 Rating 90 **To** 2029 $45

Walter ★★★

179 Tinja Lane, Mudgee, NSW 2850 **Region** Mudgee
T 0419 251 208 **www**.walterwines.com.au **Open** Thurs–Mon & public hols 10.30–4.30
Winemaker Lisa Bray (Contract) **Est.** 2005 **Dozens** 750 **Vyds** 17ha
Lynn and Paul Walter had been keen observers of Mudgee and its wines for 15 years before deciding to take the plunge and plant a 17ha vineyard. It was the mid-1990s and all the

portents were good. As competition increased and prices for grapes decreased, they realised that their original business plan of simply being growers was not going to be financially viable, even though they thought the downturn would prove to be a temporary one.

Wangolina ★★★★★

8 Limestone Coast Road, Mount Benson, SA 5275 **Region** Mount Benson
T (08) 8768 6187 **www**.wangolina.com.au **Open** 7 days 10–4
Winemaker Anita Goode **Est.** 2001 **Dozens** 4000 **Vyds** 11ha
Four generations of the Goode family have been graziers at Wangolina Station, but Anita Goode has broken with tradition by becoming a vigneron. She has planted sauvignon blanc, shiraz, cabernet sauvignon, semillon and pinot gris.

ŶŶŶŶŶ **The Originals Semillon 2019** Estate-grown, hand-picked, whole-bunch pressed, 50% to a ceramic egg, 50% to used French oak for fermentation. Impressive winemaking has subtly shaped the texture and length of the wine. The length and finish and, above all, the balance are superb. This wine owes nothing to the Hunter Valley or Adelaide Hills. Screwcap. 12% alc. **Rating** 95 **To** 2029 $32 ✪
Gruner Veltliner 2019 Although '19 was a hot, windy vintage, the vines paid no attention. Two-thirds of the whole-bunch pressed juice was cool-fermented in stainless steel, one-third in 'Egor' – a ceramic egg, its slightly porous nature creating texture. This is a very high quality gruner. The texture on the back-palate is outstanding. Screwcap. 12.5% alc. **Rating** 95 **To** 2029 $28 ✪
Spectrum Syrah 2016 Sets the standard from the get-go with bright colour, an expressive dark berry bouquet, then a carefully constructed medium-bodied palate. It has a treasure trove of cherry/plum fruits girdled by fine tannins and French oak. It is the result of a preliminary selection of barrels placed in the spectrum nursery for individual attention through to the final selection. Screwcap. 14% alc. **Rating** 95 **To** 2030 $50

ŶŶŶŶŶ **Single Vineyard Mt Benson Syrah 2019** **Rating** 93 **To** 2034 $32
Single Vineyard Mt Benson Cabernet 2018 **Rating** 92 **To** 2030 $34
Tempranillo 2018 **Rating** 91 **To** 2028 $25
Lagrein 2018 **Rating** 91 **To** 2039 $28
Montepulciano 2019 **Rating** 90 **To** 2025 $28

Wanted Man ★★★★

School House Lane, Heathcote, Vic 3523 **Region** Heathcote
T (03) 9639 6100 **www**.wantedman.com.au **Open** Not
Winemaker Shadowfax, Adrian Rodda, Mark Walpole **Est.** 1996 **Dozens** 2000
Vyds 8.19ha
The Wanted Man Vineyard was planted in 1996 and was managed by Andrew Clarke, producing Jinks Creek's Heathcote Shiraz. That wine was sufficiently impressive to lead Andrew and partner Peter Bartholomew (a Melbourne restaurateur) to purchase the vineyard in 2006 and give it its own identity. The vineyard, now managed by Callan Randall, is planted to shiraz (4ha), marsanne, viognier, grenache, roussanne and mourvedre. The quirky Ned Kelly label is the work of Mark Knight, cartoonist for the *Herald Sun*. Exports to the UK.

ŶŶŶŶŶ **Grenache Mataro 2017** Heathcote's ancient, iron-clad Cambrian soils confer a herbal loamy scent to what is otherwise, a quintessential southern French–Mediterranean blend. Mint, pulpy red fruit suggestions and a whiff of smoked charcuterie are hauled across a carapace of gently ferrous tannins. Delivers abundant pleasure and joy at the table. Screwcap. **Rating** 92 **To** 2022 $27 NG
Single Vineyard Heathcote Mataro 2016 Ferruginous tannins could be extracted more. But perhaps, that is not the point. Particularly at this price point. This is mataro for easy drinking. Then again, easy drinking is not mataro's opus. So what is the point? Put it this way, this is a sassy, easy drinking, medium-bodied red of ample red to dark fruit aspersions, a meaty core of salumi scents and a bright flourish to the finish. Screwcap. **Rating** 90 **To** 2023 $27 NG

Wantirna Estate

10 Bushy Park Lane, Wantirna South, Vic 3152 **Region** Yarra Valley
T (03) 9801 2367 **www**.wantirnaestate.com.au **Open** Not
Winemaker Maryann Egan, Reg Egan **Est.** 1963 **Dozens** 700 **Vyds** 4.2ha
Reg and Tina Egan were among the early movers in the rebirth of the Yarra Valley. The
vineyard surrounds the house they live in, which also incorporates the winery. These days
Reg describes himself as the interfering winemaker but in the early years he did everything,
dashing from his legal practice to the winery to check on the ferments. Today much of the
winemaking responsibility has been transferred to daughter Maryann, who has a degree in
wine science from CSU. Both have honed their practical skills among the small domaines
and chateaux of Burgundy and Bordeaux, inspired by single vineyard, terroir-driven wines.
Maryann was also winemaker for many years in Domaine Chandon's infancy. Exports to
Thailand, Hong Kong and China.

🍷🍷🍷🍷🍷 Lily Yarra Valley Pinot Noir 2018 Good depth and hue. Inevitably not as
striking as the sold out '16 and '17 vintages, but does have conviction and a strong
sense of place. Cherry and crab-apple blossom are anchored with the flavours and
a long finish. Well done. Screwcap. 13.5% alc. **Rating** 96 **To** 2029 $78
Isabella Yarra Valley Chardonnay 2018 Light straw-green. Lively and
particularly well balanced. Subtle, but does provide texture and structure. Will
develop slowly but surely. Screwcap. 13.5% alc. **Rating** 94 **To** 2026 $78

🍷🍷🍷🍷🍷 Amelia Cabernet Sauvignon Merlot 2017 **Rating** 92 **To** 2027 $78

Warner Glen Estate

PO Box 383, Mount Barker, WA 6324 **Region** Margaret River
T 0457 482 957 **www**.warnerglenwines.com.au **Open** Not
Winemaker Various **Est.** 1993 **Dozens** 6000 **Vyds** 34.6ha
Warner Glen Estate is a partnership of five WA families, led by viticulturist Glen Harding.
The Jindawarra Vineyard, just south of Karridale, is only 6km from the Southern Ocean and
4km from the Indian Ocean; it avoids extreme high temperatures as a result of the cooling
sea breezes. It is planted to shiraz, chardonnay, sauvignon blanc, pinot noir, viognier and pinot
gris. Cabernet sauvignon is sourced from the Warner Glen–managed vineyard at Wilyabrup.
Wines are released under the Warner Glen Estate, Frog Belly and Smokin' Gun labels. Exports
to Switzerland and China.

🍷🍷🍷🍷🍷 Margaret River Chardonnay 2019 Dijon and Gingin clones; destemmed not
crushed, fermented in French oak (45% new), matured on lees for 9 months. It's
difficult to believe the price of the wine given the use of new oak, but it was the
same last year – don't look this astonishing gift horse in the mouth. Screwcap.
13% alc. **Rating** 94 **To** 2027 $20 😊

🍷🍷🍷🍷🍷 Margaret River Cabernet Sauvignon 2018 **Rating** 93 **To** 2033 $20 😊
**Smokin' Gun Margaret River Great Southern Shiraz Cabernet Merlot
2017 Rating** 91 **To** 2025 $10 JP 😊

Warramate

27 Maddens Lane, Gruyere, Vic 3770 **Region** Yarra Valley
T (03) 5964 9267 **www**.warramatewines.com.au **Open** Not
Winemaker Sarah Crowe **Est.** 1970 **Dozens** 3000 **Vyds** 6.6ha
A long-established and perfectly situated winery reaping the full benefits of its 50-year-old
vines; recent plantings have increased production. All the wines are well made, the Shiraz
providing further proof (if such be needed) of the suitability of the variety to the region. In
2011 Warramate was purchased by the partnership that owns the adjoining Yarra Yering; the
Warramate brand is kept as a separate operation, using the existing vineyards. Exports to
the UK, the US, Singapore, Hong Kong and China.

🍷🍷🍷🍷🍷 Yarra Valley Cabernet Sauvignon 2018 Destemmed, small open ferments,
fermented on skins, a percentage of post ferment maceration. Medium-bodied,

★ ★ ★ ★ ★ firm, great balance with immediate impact. A spicy, leafy, elegant cabernet with distinctive rosemary, dried herb and Minties confection. Grippy tannins hold promise on the ageing front. Screwcap. 13.5% alc. **Rating** 95 **To** 2035 $32 JP ✪

🍷🍷🍷🍷♀ **Yarra Valley Chardonnay 2019 Rating** 91 **To** 2026 $32 JP
Yarra Valley Pinot Noir 2019 Rating 90 **To** 2028 $32 JP

Warramunda Estate ★ ★ ★ ★ ☆

860 Maroondah Highway, Coldstream, Vic 3770 **Region** Yarra Valley
T 0412 694 394 **www**.warramundaestate.com.au **Open** Fri–Sun 10–6
Winemaker Brendan Hawker, Ben Haines **Est.** 1998 **Dozens** 6500 **Vyds** 25ha
Ted Vogt purchased the original Warramunda property, on which a cattle and sheep stud known as 'Warramunda Station' was run, in 1975. He then extended the property by 320 acres in '80. A large dam was built in '81 and the property now supports three vineyards and some grazing land. The Magdziarz family acquired Warramunda from the Vogt family in 2007. The Magdziarz family have built on the existing solid foundations with a deep respect for the surrounding landscape and a vision for terroir-driven wines. Exports to the UK, the US, Japan and China.

🍷🍷🍷🍷🍷 **Coldstream Yarra Valley Pinot Noir 2018** Hand-picked, complex vinification: first 7–19 days on skins for critical carbonic maceration, the second period of 5–7 days for completion of primary ferment, these 2 stages linked by digging out the fermenter at the end of the carbonic maceration; destemmed and returned to the fermenter for the last stage, the process invented by Simon Black of Montalto. A perfumed bouquet and elegant palate. The impact of the whole bunch is obvious but does not obscure the varietal red berry/spicy/savoury flavours. Diam. 12.5% alc. **Rating** 95 **To** 2028 $50

🍷🍷🍷🍷♀ **Liv Zak Yarra Valley Chardonnay 2019 Rating** 92 **To** 2023 $35
Liv Zak Yarra Valley Pinot Noir 2018 Rating 92 **To** 2029 $35
Liv Zak Yarra Valley Malbec 2018 Rating 91 **To** 2032 $45
Coldstream Yarra Valley Syrah 2018 Rating 90 **To** 2030 $50
Liv Zak Yarra Valley Syrah 2018 Rating 90 **To** 2030 $35

Warwick Billings ★ ★ ★ ★

c/- Post Office, Lenswood, SA 5240 (postal) **Region** Adelaide Hills
T 0405 437 864 **www**.wowique.com.au **Open** Not
Winemaker Warwick Billings **Est.** 2009 **Dozens** 250
This is the venture of Warwick Billings and partner Rose Kemp. Warwick was a cider maker in the UK who came to study at Roseworthy and got diverted into the wine world. He completed a postgraduate oenology degree at the University of Adelaide in 1995 and worked for Miranda Wine, Orlando and Angove Family Winemakers from 2002 to '08, along the way moonlighting in France and Spain for 12 vintages. Warwick's approach to his eponymous label is self-deprecating, beginning with the name Wowique and saying, 'Occasionally a vineyard sings to the winemaker. [We] have taken one of these songs and put it into a bottle'. The vineyard in question is planted to an unusual clone of chardonnay and nurtured on a sloping hilltop site in Mt Torrens. Warwick's final word on all of this is, 'The winemaking is unashamedly inspired by Burgundy, but care is taken to acknowledge that the soil is different, the clones are often different, the climate is definitely different, and the end consumer is usually different'.

🍷🍷🍷🍷🍷 **Wowique Single Vineyard Adelaide Hills Chardonnay 2018** Warwick Billings says, 'A full winemaker influence wine, whole bunch, full solids, full barrel ferment, gentle French oak, 25% new'. All no issue. 'Full malo' – now here I wonder why. However, it's not for me to argue. This is an elegant wine. Screwcap. **Rating** 94 **To** 2027 $35

🍷🍷🍷🍷♀ **Wowique Adelaide Hills Sauvignon Semillon 2019 Rating** 92 **To** 2023 $26

Water Wheel

Bridgewater-Raywood Road, Bridgewater-on-Loddon, Vic 3516 **Region** Bendigo
T (03) 5437 3060 **www**.waterwheelwine.com **Open** Mon–Fri 9–5, w'ends 12–4
Winemaker Bill Trevaskis, Amy Cumming **Est.** 1972 **Dozens** 35 000 **Vyds** 136ha
Peter Cumming, with more than two decades of winemaking under his belt, has quietly
built on the reputation of Water Wheel year by year. The winery is owned by the Cumming
family, which has farmed in the Bendigo region for more than 50 years, with horticulture
and viticulture special areas of interest. Over half the vineyard area is planted to shiraz (75ha),
followed by chardonnay and sauvignon blanc (15ha each), cabernet sauvignon and malbec
(10ha each) and smaller plantings of petit verdot, semillon, roussanne and grenache. Water
Wheel continues to make wines that over-deliver at their modest prices. Exports to the UK,
the US, Canada and China.

ŶŶŶŶŶ **Bendigo Grenache 2018** Whole-bunch fermented and matured in a single
natural French puncheon; this is a recipe for nourishment. Crunchy and effusively
energetic, yet not bereft of the weight that this hedonistic variety requires to
push the pedal of joy. Raspberry bonbon, crushed rock and Mediterranean herb,
garrigue-like and dousing the gritty tannins, serves to galvanise the spice and
fruit as one. Such poise and savouriness! This is a winner and for the price, an
outstanding wine. Screwcap. **Rating** 95 To 2024 $18 NG ✪

ŶŶŶŶŶ **Bendigo Viognier 2018 Rating** 93 To 2022 $20 NG ✪
Bendigo Shiraz Cabernet 2006 Rating 93 To 2024 $80 NG
Baringhup Bendigo Shiraz 2018 Rating 92 To 2030 $25 NG ✪
Museum Release Baringhup Single Vineyard Shiraz 2012 Rating 92
To 2025 $45 NG
Kettle of Fish Grenache Primitivo Rose 2019 Rating 91 To 2021 $18
NG ✪
Bendigo Shiraz 2018 Rating 91 To 2026 $18 NG ✪
Bendigo Cabernet Sauvignon 2018 Rating 91 To 2028 $18 NG ✪
Bendigo Chardonnay 2018 Rating 90 To 2023 $18 NG ✪

Waterton Hall Wines

61 Waterton Hall Road, Rowella, Tas 7270 **Region** Northern Tasmania
T 0417 834 781 **www**.watertonhall.com.au **Open** By appt
Winemaker Tasmanian Vintners **Est.** 2006 **Dozens** 1500 **Vyds** 2.5ha
The homestead that today is the home of Waterton Hall Wines was built in the 1850s.
Originally a private residence, it was modified extensively in 1901 by well known neo-gothic
architect Alexander North and ultimately passed into the ownership of the Catholic church
from '49–96. Together with various outbuildings it was variously used as a school, a boys'
home and a retreat. In 2002 it was purchased by Jennifer Baird and Peter Cameron and in
'15 passed into the family ownership of 'one architect, one farmer, one interior designer, one
finance director and one labradoodle'. Their real names are David and Susan Shannon (based
in SA) and John Carter and Belinda Evans (based in Sydney). Susan and John are sister and
brother. Planting is underway and will see the current 2.5ha progressively extended to 10ha.

ŶŶŶŶŶ **Tamar Valley Riesling 2018** Vines planted in '99; 389 dozen produced. It's a
searing riesling, all cut and thrust, but blossomy aromatics and a punchy aspect to
its orange/citrussy flavours make you sit up and take notice. It doesn't lack texture
either. Indeed, the more you look at this wine the more impressive it seems.
Screwcap. 11.8% alc. **Rating** 94 To 2029 $29 CM ✪

ŶŶŶŶŶ **20-Year-Old Vines Tamar Valley Shiraz 2018 Rating** 93 To 2029 $46 CM
Tamar Valley Viognier 2018 Rating 92 To 2024 $42 CM

WayWood Wines

67 Kays Road, McLaren Vale, SA 5171 **Region** McLaren Vale
T (08) 8323 8468 **www.**waywoodwines.com **Open** At Vale Cru
Winemaker Andrew Wood **Est.** 2005 **Dozens** 2000 **Vyds** 3ha
This is the culmination of Andrew Wood and Lisa Robertson's wayward odyssey. Andrew left his career as a sommelier in London and retrained as a winemaker, working in Portugal, the UK, Italy and the Granite Belt (an eclectic selection), settling in McLaren Vale in early 2004. Working with Kangarilla Road winery for the next six years, while making small quantities of shiraz, cabernets and tempranillo from purchased grapes, led them to nebbiolo, montepulciano and shiraz. The wines are available from Vale Cru at the McLaren Vale Visitors Centre, Main Road, McLaren Vale; private tastings by appointment at WayWood. Exports to Canada and China.

🍷🍷🍷🍷 **97 Years Shiraz Cabernet 2017** A barrel selection, the parcels made in similar fashion in new French (shiraz) and new European oak (cabernet), blended and spent a further year in French oak. That's a lot of oak and the wine shows it, yet says 'so what'. It's integrated, the mouthfeel is good and the fruit hasn't been annihilated. Screwcap. 14.9% alc. **Rating** 94 **To** 2032 $50

🍷🍷🍷🍷 **McLaren Vale PX NV Rating** 91 $75
McLaren Vale Shiraz 2017 Rating 90 **To** 2027 $25

Weathercraft Wines

1241 Beechworth-Wangaratta Road, Everton Upper, Vic 3678 **Region** Beechworth
T (03) 5727 0518 **www.**weathercraft.com.au **Open** Fri–Sat 11–4
Winemaker Raquel Jones, Mark O'Callaghan **Est.** 1998 **Dozens** 1800 **Vyds** 4ha
After two years of searching, Hugh and Raquel Jones discovered a vineyard 10 minutes out of Beechworth. It had an immaculate 20-year-old vineyard, set up by Roland Wahlquist, the ex-CEO of Brown Brothers. For years the fruit had only ever been sold to Yalumba for a single vineyard shiraz and it had the best possible address with nearby neighbours Giaconda, Sorrenberg, Golden Ball, Savaterre, Castagna and Fighting Gully Road. So it was that Hugh and Raquel followed their own advice and surrounded themselves with the best advisors possible. They retained Mark Walpole for the vineyard and Mark O'Callaghan for winemaking advice to Raquel, helping her on her winemaking journey. Dr Mary Cole, an academic from Melbourne and Monash universities and a renowned scientist, has advised on their move to organic certification. The Weathercraft winery was built in 2019, and while Raquel runs the winery and vineyard production, Hugh continues to run their property advisory practice Garcia & Jones.

🍷🍷🍷🍷 **Beechworth Rose 2019** Shiraz base; plenty of vinification steps, but why, after cool fermentation in tank, would you put the wine in used oak for a short maturation time? Screwcap. 12.5% alc. **Rating** 90 **To** 2021 $25

🍷🍷🍷🍷 **Beechworth Shiraz 2018 Rating** 89 **To** 2023 $35

Wendouree ★★★★★

Wendouree Road, Clare, SA 5453 **Region** Clare Valley
T (08) 8842 2896 **Open** Not
Winemaker Tony Brady **Est.** 1895 **Dozens** 2000 **Vyds** 12ha
An iron fist in a velvet glove best describes these extraordinary wines. They are fashioned with commitment from the very old vineyard (shiraz, cabernet sauvignon, malbec, mataro and muscat of Alexandria), with its unique terroir, by Tony and Lita Brady, who rightly see themselves as custodians of a priceless treasure. The 100+-year-old stone winery is virtually unchanged from the day it was built; this is in every sense a treasure beyond price. Wendouree has never made any comment about its wines, but the subtle shift from the lighter end of full- bodied to the fuller end of medium-bodied seems to be a permanent one (always subject to the dictates of the vintage). The best news of all is that I will get to drink some of the Wendourees I have bought over the past 10 years before I die and not have to rely on my few remaining bottles from the 1970s (and rather more from the '80s and '90s).

West Cape Howe Wines ★★★★★

Lot 14923 Muir Highway, Mount Barker, WA 6324 **Region** Mount Barker
T (08) 9892 1444 **www**.westcapehowewines.com.au **Open** 7 days (various hours)
Winemaker Gavin Berry, Andrew Vasey, Caitlin Gazey **Est.** 1997 **Dozens** 60 000
Vyds 310ha

West Cape Howe is owned by a partnership of four WA families, including winemaker/
managing partner Gavin Berry and viticulturist/partner Rob Quenby. Grapes are sourced
from estate vineyards in Mount Barker and Frankland River. The Langton Vineyard (Mount
Barker) has 100ha planted to cabernet sauvignon, shiraz, riesling, sauvignon blanc, chardonnay
and semillon; the Russell Road Vineyard (Frankland River) has 210ha. West Cape Howe
also sources select parcels of fruit from valued contract growers. Best Value Winery *Wine
Companion 2016.* Exports to the UK, the US, Denmark, Switzerland, South Korea, Singapore,
Japan, Hong Kong and China.

🍷🍷🍷🍷🍷 **King Billy Mount Barker Cabernet Sauvignon 2014** Only 93 dozen
bottles were made, the wine matured for 42 months in French oak (50% new).
Mesmerising flavours. A full-bodied cabernet of exceptional varietal character
cocooned in ripe tannins. A 50-year wine, yet its purity and balance mean it can
be enjoyed now. Screwcap. 14.5% alc. **Rating** 98 **To** 2064 $50 ✪

🍷🍷🍷🍷🍷 **Porongurup Riesling 2019** From a small, well established vineyard. Shows
varietal purity and delicacy, but some slatey minerality in the spine as well.
Sweet citrus and floral aromas; flavours of lime juice and zest. Tautly strung and
elegant. Enjoy it now or with bottle age. Screwcap. 12% alc. **Rating** 95 **To** 2029
$30 SC ✪

Mount Barker Sauvignon Blanc 2019 From the Langton Vineyard that stamps
the bouquet with a smoky/toasty edge, the flavours shifting on the palate towards
a mix of grassy/herbal notes and contrasting juicy citrus/gooseberry flavours.
A cut above much of the sauvignon blanc from east or west Australia. Screwcap.
12% alc. **Rating** 95 **To** 2023 $22 ✪

Frankland River Shiraz 2018 From West Cape Howe's Langton Vineyard that
provides high quality shiraz at self-grown cost and making expenditure on new
French oak superfluous and the price great value. This is juicy, fresh and full of red
and black cherry fruit; the medium-bodied palate singing happily. Ready now (or
in 10+ years). Screwcap. 14.5% alc. **Rating** 94 **To** 2028 $22 ✪

🍷🍷🍷🍷🍷 **Styx Gully Mount Barker Chardonnay 2018 Rating** 93 **To** 2026 $30 NG
Rose 2019 Rating 93 **To** 2021 $17 SC ✪
Two Steps Mount Barker Shiraz 2017 Rating 93 **To** 2024 $30 NG
Semillon Sauvignon Blanc 2019 Rating 92 **To** 2021 $17 SC ✪
Book Ends Mount Barker Cabernet Sauvignon 2017 Rating 92 **To** 2027
$30 NG
Shiraz 2018 Rating 91 **To** 2023 $17 NG ✪
Frankland River Malbec 2018 Rating 91 **To** 2023 $22 NG ✪
Hanna's Hill Frankland River Cabernet Malbec 2018 Rating 90 **To** 2024
$22 NG

Whicher Ridge ★★★★☆

200 Chapman Hill East Road, Busselton, WA 6280 **Region** Geographe
T (08) 9753 1394 **www**.whicherridge.com.au **Open** Thurs–Mon 11–5
Winemaker Cathy Howard **Est.** 2004 **Dozens** 2000 **Vyds** 5ha

It is hard to imagine a founding husband and wife team with such an ideal blend of viticultural
and winemaking experience accumulated over a combined 40+ years. Cathy Howard (nee
Spratt) was a winemaker for 16 years at Orlando and St Hallett in the Barossa Valley, and at
Watershed Wines in Margaret River. She now has her own winemaking consulting business
covering the southwest regions of WA, as well as making the Whicher Ridge wines. Neil
Howard's career as a viticulturist began in the Pyrenees region with Taltarni and Blue
Pyrenees Estate, then he moved to Mount Avoca as vineyard manager for 12 years. When he

moved to the west, he managed the Sandalford vineyard in Margaret River for several years, then developed and managed a number of smaller vineyards throughout the region. Whicher Ridge's Odyssey Creek Vineyard at Chapman Hill has sauvignon blanc, cabernet sauvignon and viognier. The Howards have chosen the Frankland River subregion of the Great Southern to supply shiraz and riesling; they also buy grapes from Margaret River.

ŸŸŸŸŸ **Long Road Frankland River Shiraz 2016** Wonderfully intense, complex and long. The spicy/peppery bouquet is an indirect introduction to the red and black cherry flavours of the palate. It's only medium-bodied, and the tannins aren't the least bit aggressive. The vinification is AAA in attention to detail. Screwcap. 14% alc. **Rating** 96 To 2041 $34 ✪

ŸŸŸŸŸ **Elevation Geographe Cabernet Sauvignon 2016 Rating** 93 To 2031 $44
Une Rangee Geographe Petit Verdot 2016 Rating 93 To 2030 $45
The Jetty Geographe Cabernet Shiraz 2019 Rating 92 To 2030 $22 ✪
The Jetty Geographe Sauvignon Blanc Semillon 2018 Rating 90 To 2021 $20 ✪
Pretty Flamingo Margaret River Rose 2019 Rating 90 To 2022 $23

Whispering Brook ★★★★★

Rodd Street, Broke, NSW 2330 **Region** Hunter Valley
T (02) 6579 1386 **www**.whispering-brook.com **Open** Fri by appt, w'ends 11–5,
Winemaker Susan Frazier, Adam Bell **Est.** 2000 **Dozens** 1000 **Vyds** 3ha
It took some time for partners Susan Frazier and Adam Bell to find the property on which they established their vineyard 20 years ago. It has a combination of terra rossa loam soils on which the reds are planted, and sandy flats for the white grapes. The partners have also established an olive grove and accommodation for 10–18 guests in the large house set in the vineyard, offering vineyard and winery tours. Exports to Canada and Japan.

ŸŸŸŸŸ **Single Vineyard Hunter Valley Semillon 2019** Produced from 50+yo dry-grown vines on sandy soils at Broke. Aromas and flavours of citrus and flowering herbs are underpinned by a slatey minerality in the bouquet and on the palate; fine, lingering acidity is the structural buttress. Feels like a complete wine already, although, of course, bottle age will impart further richness and complexity. Screwcap. 10.5% alc. **Rating** 95 To 2031 $28 SC ✪
Single Vineyard Hunter Valley Shiraz 2018 From 21yo vines growing in red volcanic clay loam soils. Aged for 17 months in French barriques, hogsheads (30% new) and a puncheon. There's a sense of polish and precision about this wine; Hunter shiraz with regional and varietal identity, but a touch of gloss as well. Medium weight, ripe red fruit, earth, spice and balanced astringency are the key ingredients. Screwcap. 14.5% alc. **Rating** 95 To 2033 $40 SC
Museum Release Single Vineyard Hunter Valley Shiraz 2014 Interesting to taste this with the '18 and see the similarities and differences. The bottle-aged, leathery, waxed cedar wood complexity on the bouquet is most noticeable, the red-berry aromas more toasty now than fresh in character. The distinctive Hunter earthiness is coming through quite clearly on the palate, while the depth of flavour and energy are undiminished. Screwcap. 14% alc. **Rating** 95 To 2030 $100 SC

ŸŸŸŸŸ **Basket Pressed Hunter Valley Touriga Nacional 2018 Rating** 92 To 2025 $45 SC

Whispering Hills ★★★☆

580 Warburton Highway, Seville, Vic 3139 **Region** Yarra Valley
T (03) 5964 2822 **www**.whisperinghills.com.au **Open** 7 days 10–6
Winemaker Murray Lyons, Darcy Lyons **Est.** 1985 **Dozens** 800 **Vyds** 3.2ha
Whispering Hills is owned and operated by the Lyons family (Murray, Audrey and Darcy Lyons). Murray and Darcy are responsible for the winemaking, while Audrey takes care of the cellar door and distribution. The vineyard was established in 1985 with further plantings

in '96 and some grafting in 2003. It now consists of cabernet sauvignon, riesling, chardonnay and pinot noir.

♀♀♀♀♀ **Seville Yarra Valley Riesling 2018** This brings into question the idea that the Yarra Valley can't produce good riesling, but admits the wine has its limitations. It has balance and length, and the label design and printing is of high quality. Screwcap. 11% alc. **Rating** 90 **To** 2027 $25

Whistle Post

PO Box 340, Coonawarra, SA 5263 **Region** Coonawarra
T 0408 708 093 **www**.whistlepost.com.au **Open** Not
Winemaker Contract **Est.** 2012 **Dozens** 5000 **Vyds** 80ha
Brian and Jennifer Smibert, together with son Angus, established Whistle Post in 2012, following 40 years of grapegrowing and winery experience. It takes its name from the railway that ran alongside the Home Block, specifically the signpost requiring trains to let off a warning whistle as they approached the nearby V&A Lane crossing. In 2016, the family purchased the remaining B Seppelt & Sons' assets in Coonawarra: two 20ha vineyards which incorporated the Coonawarra Wine Gallery sales outlet. The Whistle Post cellar door opened in 2017 following renovations, and the wines are now made onsite in the newly constructed winery. The substantial estate vineyard comprises cabernet sauvignon, chardonnay, merlot, cabernet franc and pinot noir. Exports to Asia and the Pacific.

♀♀♀♀♀ **Coonawarra Cabernet Franc 2017** Gentle extraction platforms a mid-weighted, plush red. Aromas of redcurrant, sarsaparilla, chilli, bitter chocolate and spearmint are bound to nourishing, loamy tannins. This has plenty of pulpy give. A good drink. Screwcap. **Rating** 91 **To** 2022 $28 NG

Whistler Wines

241 Seppeltsfield Road, Stone Well, SA 5352 **Region** Barossa Valley
T (08) 8562 4942 **www**.whistlerwines.com **Open** 7 days 10.30–5
Winemaker Josh Pfeiffer, Adam Hay **Est.** 1999 **Dozens** 6500 **Vyds** 14.2ha
Whistler was established in 1999 by brothers Martin and Chris Pfeiffer but is now in the hands of the next generation, brothers Josh and Sam Pfeiffer. Josh took over the winemaking and viticulture in 2013 and has incorporated the sustainable approach of organic and biodynamic techniques. Sam has stepped into the general manager role, largely focused on sales and marketing. Whistler maintains the traditional Estate range of wines as well as the fun, easy drinking 'next gen' range, which has more adventurous labelling and names. Exports to the UK, Canada, Denmark, Mauritius, Singapore, Hong Kong and China.

♀♀♀♀♀ **Barossa Rose 2019** This is a very smart rose. Crunchy red berry flavours jitterbug across the palate, boasting real intensity and thrust. It is driven by a thirst-slaking skein of herb-soused acidity, pulling the flavours long, dry and fresh. While many of us still talk about chardonnay being the most exciting idiom in the country, for me it is by far and away rose. A savvy blend of grenache and mataro, with shiraz a minor back-burner. Screwcap. **Rating** 95 **To** 2020 $28 NG ✪

Estate Barossa Valley Shiraz 2017 Blue fruits, nori and salami are woven by a thread of peppery acidity, tying fore to aft. The mid-palate could use a little more stuffing. Just a bit. Otherwise, this is a delicious wine of aromatic complexity and textural intrigue; the 20 months in 70% American and 30% French oak righteous and just, all in service of pleasure. **Rating** 95 **To** 2028 $60 NG

Estate Cabernet Sauvignon 2017 This is a pulpy and soft cabernet, exuding currant, spearmint, a fleck of sage and bouquet garni; all driven long, fresh, pure and compellingly intense by a skein of gentle acidity melded to delicate, compact tannins. Medium-bodied and highly savoury, it is a far cry from the regional norm. And all the better for it. I would be hedging my bets on earlier, rather than later drinking. Delicious. **Rating** 94 **To** 2025 $40 NG

🍷🍷🍷🍷🍷 **Estate Barossa Shiraz Cabernet 2017** **Rating** 93 **To** 2029 **$40** NG
Shock Value Barossa SMG 2018 **Rating** 93 **To** 2021 **$25** NG ✪
Estate Riesling 2019 **Rating** 92 **To** 2024 **$28** NG
Thank God It's Friday Barossa Shiraz 2018 **Rating** 92 **To** 2023 **$28** NG
Shiver Down My Spine Barossa Shiraz 2018 **Rating** 91 **To** 2022 **$40** NG

Whistling Kite Wines ★★★★☆

73 Freundt Road, New Residence via Loxton, SA 5333 **Region** Riverland
T (08) 8584 9014 **www**.whistlingkitewines.com.au **Open** By appt
Winemaker 919 Wines (Eric Semmler, Jenny Semmler) **Est.** 2010 **Dozens** 360
Vyds 16ha

Owners Pam and Tony Barich have established their vineyard and house on the banks of the Murray River, which is a haven for wildlife. They believe custodians of the land have a duty to maintain its health and vitality – their vineyard has had organic certification for over 2 decades, and biodynamic certification since 2008.

🍷🍷🍷🍷🍷 **Classic Petit Manseng NV** A tawny-amber hue with a flash of red. Smells of butterscotch, toffee brittle and candied pears. The palate is rich, warming with more flavours of salted caramel and fruitcake. Luscious and sweet, the spirit is fresh and integrated while petit manseng's natural high acidity keeps this lively. Fabulous. 500ml. Screwcap. 18% alc. **Rating** 95 **$50** JF

🍷🍷🍷🍷🍷 **Biodynamic Shiraz 2019** **Rating** 90 **To** 2025 **$30** JF
Biodynamic Mencia 2019 **Rating** 90 **To** 2025 **$30** JF

Whitlocks Vineyard ★★★★☆

PO Box 467, Maldon, Vic 3463 **Region** Bendigo
T 0439 031 075 **www**.whitlocksvineyard.com.au **Open** Not
Winemaker Cameron Leith **Est.** 2012 **Dozens** 380 **Vyds** 1ha

Emily Girdwood and partner Simon Smith moved from Melbourne to the country in 2011 so that their children could enjoy the freedom, space and safety of country life. The property they purchased overlooks Lake Cairn Curran and Mt Tarrengower to the east. The historic township of Maldon is the closest habitation. It just so happened the property had a 1ha vineyard of largely 20yo shiraz, and they cleverly gained the services of Cameron Leith to make the wines. Emily and Simon are in charge of the vineyard, although at times vineyards are in charge of their carers. Good luck!

🍷🍷🍷🍷🍷 **Smiths Paddock Shiraz 2018** A deft hand on the winemaking tiller sees a medium-bodied shiraz that blends Bendigo fruit, in a sympathetic fashion, with cherry, satsuma plum and a brocade of mint; the tannins almost silky they are so soft. Screwcap. 13.6% alc. **Rating** 92 **To** 2030 **$30**

Wicks Estate Wines ★★★★☆

21 Franklin Street, Adelaide, SA 5000 (postal) **Region** Adelaide Hills
T (08) 8212 0004 **www**.wicksestate.com.au **Open** Not
Winemaker Leigh Ratzmer **Est.** 2000 **Dozens** 20 000 **Vyds** 53.96ha

Tim and Simon Wicks had a long-term involvement with orchard and nursery operations at Highbury in the Adelaide Hills prior to purchasing their property at Woodside in 1999. They planted fractionally less than 54ha of sauvignon blanc, shiraz, chardonnay, pinot noir, cabernet sauvignon, tempranillo and riesling. Wicks Estate has won more than its fair share of wine show medals over the years, the wines priced well below their full worth. Exports to the US, Singapore, Hong Kong and China.

🍷🍷🍷🍷🍷 **Adelaide Hills Pinot Gris 2019** This gris is good. Very. Especially at this price. Asian pear gelato and a sluice of green apple slushy. Broad and billowing with textural warmth, cushioned by gentle phenolics. The acidity is soft and palpably natural. Well done! Screwcap. **Rating** 93 **To** 2022 **$20** NG ✪

C.J. Wicks Adelaide Hills Chardonnay 2018 A discreet chardonnay. Very subtle. Dried hay, toasted cashew, nougat, toasted hazelnut and a beam of leesy curd notes. This is almost bereft of obvious fruit references and all for the better, as far as I am concerned. Micro-vinifications in fine French oak constitute a chardonnay that should fill out over time. Screwcap. **Rating** 92 **To** 2026 $45 NG

Adelaide Hills Pinot Rose 2019 A gentle coral. This plays Provençale meets Adelaide Hills pretty well. Very well, in fact. Musk, strawberry, a sash of herb squeezed across a burst of intensity through the midriff and a plume of gentle acidity. A fine rose. Screwcap. **Rating** 92 **To** 2020 $20 NG ♦

Adelaide Hills Sauvignon Blanc 2019 A solid sauvignon that avoids the sweet/sour meld of so many. Soapy across the midriff, imparting some textural intrigue. Guava, gooseberry and greengage. Fresh without being brittle. Screwcap. **Rating** 91 **To** 2020 $20 NG ♦

ΨΨΨΨ **Adelaide Hills Chardonnay Pinot Noir 2019 Rating** 89 $20 NG

Wignalls Wines ★★★★★

448 Chester Pass Road (Highway 1), Albany, WA 6330 **Region** Albany
T (08) 9841 2848 **www**.wignallswines.com.au **Open** Thurs–Mon 11–4
Winemaker Rob Wignall, Michael Perkins **Est.** 1982 **Dozens** 7000 **Vyds** 18.5ha
While the estate vineyards have a diverse range of sauvignon blanc, semillon, chardonnay, pinot noir, merlot, shiraz, cabernet franc and cabernet sauvignon, founder Bill Wignall was one of the early movers with pinot noir, producing wines that, by the standards of their time, were well in front of anything else coming out of WA (and up with the then limited amounts being made in Victoria and Tasmania). The establishment of an onsite winery and the assumption of the winemaking role by son Rob, with significant input from Michael Perkins, saw the quality and range of wines increase. Exports to Denmark, Japan, Singapore and China.

ΨΨΨΨΨ **Great Southern Shiraz 2018** The tightrope between Rhône-like florals, freshness and overt reduction is fine; this mid-weighted and wholly savoury shiraz treads it with aplomb. Bergamot, iodine, spiced plum and dried nori scents captivate. A skein of peppery acidity and carriage of gentle astringency tow it all long. Screwcap. **Rating** 93 **To** 2025 $29 NG

Single Vineyard Albany Pinot Noir 2018 There was a day when this address was considered cutting edge for this fickle grape. Perhaps it is time to re-evaluate. In an age of anorexic hipster expressions, there is plenty of flavour in these bones. Great Southern's medicinal stamp, to boot. Stewed cherry, raspberry and cinnamon oak, guiding the fray nicely. Screwcap. **Rating** 92 **To** 2025 $34 NG

Great Southern Cabernet Merlot 2018 While I try to assess wine irrespective of price, given the price-point here I can strongly suggest that this is very good value. Dried sage, redcurrant, tobacco and olive. The tannins are firm, as they should be, but expansive, while coating the mouth with a sense of savouriness. Moreish. Screwcap. **Rating** 91 **To** 2025 $19 NG ♦

ΨΨΨΨ **Single Vineyard Albany Chardonnay 2019 Rating** 89 **To** 2022 $19 NG ♦

Willem Kurt Wines ★★★★☆

365 Buckland Gap Road, Beechworth, Vic 3747 **Region** Beechworth
T 0428 400 522 **www**.willemkurtwines.com.au **Open** Not
Winemaker Daniel Balzer **Est.** 2014 **Dozens** 600 **Vyds** 1.6ha
This is the venture of Daniel Balzer and Marije van Epenhuijsen; he with a German background, she Dutch. The name of the winery is drawn from the middle names of their two children: Willem (Dutch) and Kurt (German), in each instance reflecting long usage in the two families. Daniel moved into the wine industry in 1998 having already obtained a science degree, working first at Yarra Ridge (including a vintage in Germany) before moving to Gapsted Wines in 2003, then completing his Bachelor of Wine Science at CSU the following year. Seven years were given over to contract winemaking for smaller producers and it was inevitable that sooner or later they would start making wine for their own brand.

They currently lease a vineyard in Beechworth and buy select parcels of fruit. Beechworth is the region they know and love best, and they began planting their own vineyard in '17 with 0.6ha of chardonnay, 0.6ha of shiraz following in '18. The quality of the wines made to date suggests it should succeed.

ⵣⵣⵣⵣⵣ **Beechworth Chardonnay 2018** It has the depth and ripe flavour that this region achieves with chardonnay. It's powerful, yet the acidity keeps a firm hold on ensuring it's not too much. Citrus and stone fruit together, spice and cedary sweet oak in balance, creamy lees/curd and lemon tang on the finish; the combo makes this spot on. Screwcap. 13% alc. **Rating** 95 **To** 2028 $38 JF

ⵣⵣⵣⵣⵣ **Alpine Valleys Vermentino 2018 Rating** 91 **To** 2022 $23 JF ⚫

Willoughby Park ★★★★★

678 South Coast Highway, Denmark, WA 6333 **Region** Great Southern
T (08) 9848 1555 **www**.willoughbypark.com.au **Open** 7 days 10–5
Winemaker Elysia Harrison **Est.** 2010 **Dozens** 13 000 **Vyds** 19ha
Bob Fowler, who comes from a rural background and had always hankered for a farming life, stumbled across the opportunity to achieve this in early 2010. Together with wife Marilyn, he purchased the former West Cape Howe winery and surrounding vineyard that became available when West Cape Howe moved into the far larger Goundrey winery. In '11 Willoughby Park purchased the Kalgan River Vineyard and business name, and winemaking operations have been transferred to Willoughby Park. There are now three labels: Kalgan River single vineyard range (Kalgan River Ironrock from single sites within the Kalgan River Vineyard); Willoughby Park, the Great Southern brand for estate and purchased grapes; and Jamie & Charli, a sub-$20 Great Southern range of wines. Exports to China.

ⵣⵣⵣⵣⵣ **Ironrock Kalgan River Albany Riesling 2019** Intensity and length. The purity and power of the fruit here is quite glorious and yet it's not a searing wine; it has body, softness and flavour, all of which are perhaps aided by a touch of fruit sweetness. The short story is that it offers quite wonderful drinking. Screwcap. 13.5% alc. **Rating** 95 **To** 2029 CM

Ironrock Kalgan River Albany Cabernet Sauvignon 2018 Curranty fruit flavour has just started to mellow but it still feels authoritative. This impression is aided by a sturdy framework of peppercorn-studded tannin. Though the fruit is not overt, it continues to flow seamlessly out through the finish. A pretty classy wine, made to endure. Screwcap. 14.5% alc. **Rating** 95 **To** 2035 $55 CM

Kalgan River Albany Riesling 2019 A mellifluous riesling. It has excellent intensity but it ushers softly through the mouth; its citrussy, slatey, apple-like flavours whispered with talc and florals. It's tempting to call it pretty but it has more power than that implies. Screwcap. 13% alc. **Rating** 94 **To** 2027 CM

Kalgan River Albany Pinot Noir 2018 Undergrowthy complexity, bright fruit and sturdy tannin. Sweet-sour and tangy with earth, root vegetable and lively fruit flavour. Twig and herb notes too. There's a lot here to keep you interested. Screwcap. 14% alc. **Rating** 94 **To** 2026 $32 CM

Kalgan River Albany Shiraz 2017 Ripe, berried fruit flavour is served with a complex savoury overlay. Peppercorn, wood smoke and twiggy herb notes make a clear and positive impression, the finish then firm but juicy and flowing. Admirable from all angles. Screwcap. 14.5% alc. **Rating** 94 **To** 2030 $32 CM

Ironrock Albany Shiraz 2017 A polished shiraz with excellent volume of flavour, effectively into plush territory and more than enough savoury/peppery nuance to keep things interesting. It's neither short nor abbreviated and my only query would be on the wine's length; is it a little rounded? It is without question a lovely style of wine. Screwcap. 14.5% alc. **Rating** 94 **To** 2032 CM

ⵣⵣⵣⵣⵣ **Ironrock Kalgan River Albany Chardonnay 2019 Rating** 93 **To** 2025 CM
Kalgan River Albany Great Southern Cabernet Sauvignon 2017
Rating 93 **To** 2029 $32 CM
Great Southern Shiraz 2017 Rating 91 **To** 2026 $22 CM ⚫

Great Southern Shiraz 2016 Rating 90 To 2024 $22 JP
Albany Cabernet Sauvignon 2017 Rating 90 To 2026 $22 CM
Cabernet Sauvignon 2016 Rating 90 To 2024 $22 JP

Willow Bridge Estate ★★★★★

178 Gardin Court Drive, Dardanup, WA 6236 **Region** Geographe
T (08) 9728 0055 **www**.willowbridge.com.au **Open** 7 days 11–5
Winemaker Kim Horton **Est.** 1997 **Dozens** 25 000 **Vyds** 59ha

Jeff and Vicky Dewar have followed a fast track in developing Willow Bridge Estate since acquiring the spectacular 180ha hillside property in the Ferguson Valley. Chardonnay, semillon, sauvignon blanc, shiraz and cabernet sauvignon were planted, with merlot, tempranillo, chenin blanc and viognier following. Many of its wines offer exceptional value for money. Kim Horton, with 25 years of winemaking in WA, believes that wines are made in the vineyard; the better the understanding of the vineyard and its unique characteristics, the better the wines reflect the soil and the climate. Exports to the UK, China and other major markets.

ᵠᵠᵠᵠᵠ **Black Dog Geographe Shiraz 2015** There is something about this wine. It's deep and resonates with the aromas of the vineyard: all florals, warm gravel and gorgeous fruit. Usual oak flavours abound but are not obtrusive as silky rivulets of tannin glide across the plush palate. Screwcap. 14.7% alc. **Rating** 96 To 2030 $65 JF ○

G1-10 Geographe Chardonnay 2018 Hand-picked, whole-bunch pressed, fermented in new and 1yo French oak. Interesting wine. As you start assembling the fruit and oak components in the mouth, you come across the bridge of fresh, tingling acidity that extends the length and aftertaste to an unexpected degree. Screwcap. 13.5% alc. **Rating** 95 To 2033 $30 ○

Gravel Pit Geographe Shiraz 2018 Has greater body than its Dragonfly sibling. It is remarkable that there's so little difference in the price of this wine ($30) and Dragnofly ($22). This is a classy and restrained medium-bodied wine, the headline balance between fruit, oak and tannin irreproachable. Screwcap. 14.5% alc. **Rating** 95 To 2038 $30 ○

Dragonfly Geographe Sauvignon Blanc Semillon 2019 Willow Bridge nailed this blend many years ago. Not only do the varietal flavours always present themselves very well, but they do so with a grand gesture. They are really intense. Screwcap. 13.4% alc. **Rating** 94 To 2022 $22 ○

G.S.M Geographe Grenache Shiraz Mataro 2019 An enticing spicy and peppery blend – percentages not known. It's really perfumed with florals, musk and a meaty-charcuterie note. Juicy and vibrant on the palate and while not simple, it's not overly complex either. The end result is a really good drink. Screwcap. 14.5% alc. **Rating** 94 To 2025 $25 JF ○

ᵠᵠᵠᵠᵠ **Bookends Fume Geographe Sauvignon Blanc Semillon 2019** Rating 93 To 2026 $25 JF ○
Dragonfly Geographe Shiraz 2018 Rating 93 To 2025 $22 ○
Coat of Arms Cabernet Sauvignon 2018 Rating 92 To 2028 $30 JF
Dragonfly Geographe Chardonnay 2019 Rating 91 To 2024 $22 JF ○
Dragonfly Cabernet Sauvignon Merlot 2018 Rating 90 To 2028 $22

Willow Creek Vineyard ★★★★★

166 Balnarring Road, Merricks North, Vic 3926 **Region** Mornington Peninsula
T (03) 5931 2502 **www**.rarehare.com.au **Open** 7 days 11–5
Winemaker Geraldine McFaul **Est.** 1989 **Dozens** 6000 **Vyds** 11ha

Significant changes have transformed Willow Creek. In 2008, winemaker Geraldine McFaul, with many years of winemaking in the Mornington Peninsula under her belt, was appointed and worked with viticulturist Robbie O'Leary to focus on minimal intervention in the winery; in other words, to produce grapes in perfect condition. In '13 the Li family arrived from China and expanded its portfolio of hotel and resort properties in Australia by purchasing Willow Creek, developing the luxury 46-room Jackalope Hotel, the Rare Hare and Doot Doot Doot restaurants, a cocktail bar and tasting room.

🍷🍷🍷🍷 **Mornington Peninsula Chardonnay 2018** Clones I10V1, 95 and 96; hand-picked, whole-bunch pressed, wild-fermented in French oak (20% new), matured for 10 months. A delicate chardonnay, but has focus and length. No mlf may be the reason for its character. Screwcap. 13% alc. **Rating** 95 **To** 2028 $45

O'Leary Block Mornington Peninsula Pinot Noir 2018 Hand-picked and bunch-sorted, 100% whole-bunch fermented, 26 days on skins, matured for 15 months in French oak (20% new). Very light, clear crimson. An attractive light-bodied pinot with fresh, bright flavours. It's very pretty and is tailor-made for early consumption. Screwcap. 13.5% alc. **Rating** 94 **To** 2023 $80

🍷🍷🍷🍷♀ **Mornington Peninsula Pinot Gris 2019** Rating 92 To 2021 $35
Rare Hare Fume Blanc 2018 Rating 90 To 2022 $30
Rare Hare Pinot Noir Rose 2019 Rating 90 To 2021 $30

Wills Domain   ★★★★★

Cnr Abbeys Farm Road/Brash Road, Yallingup, WA 6281 **Region** Margaret River
T (08) 9755 2327 **www**.willsdomain.com.au **Open** 7 days 10–5
Winemaker Richard Rowe **Est.** 1985 **Dozens** 12500 **Vyds** 22ha
When the Haunold family purchased the original Wills Domain Vineyard in 2000, they were adding another chapter to a family history of winemaking stretching back to 1383 in what is now Austria. Remarkable though that may be, more remarkable is that Darren, who lost the use of his legs in an accident in 1989, runs the estate (including part of the pruning) from his wheelchair. The vineyard is planted to shiraz, semillon, cabernet sauvignon, sauvignon blanc, chardonnay, merlot, petit verdot, malbec, cabernet franc and viognier. Exports to Indonesia, Hong Kong and China.

🍷🍷🍷🍷🍷 **Paladin Hill Margaret River Matrix 2018** A very complex 4-variety Bordeaux blend that includes 5.7% cabernet from '19. A high quality wine with soft tannins, good balance and length. Screwcap. 14% alc. **Rating** 95 **To** 2030 $115

Eightfold Margaret River Cabernet Sauvignon 2018 Includes 12% malbec; hand-picked, destemmed, 13 days on skins, pressed to French barriques (33% new) for 9 months' maturation. Is still on the road to maturity but the juicy cassis fruit and quality French oak have come together well. It will be a medium-bodied cabernet that will drink well for many years. Screwcap. 14% alc. **Rating** 94 **To** 2038 $39

🍷🍷🍷🍷♀ **Paladin Hill Margaret River Chardonnay 2019** Rating 92 To 2027 $85
Mystic Spring Margaret River Sauvignon Blanc 2019 Rating 90 To 2021 $25
Eightfold Margaret River Shiraz 2018 Rating 90 To 2026 $39
Mystic Spring Margaret River Cabernet Sauvignon 2018 Rating 90 To 2028 $25

Willunga 100 Wines

PO Box 2239, McLaren Vale, SA 5171 **Region** McLaren Vale
T 0417 401 856 **www**.willunga100.com **Open** Not
Winemaker Tim James, Mike Farmilo, Skye Salter **Est.** 2005 **Dozens** 9500 **Vyds** 19ha
Willunga 100 is owned by Liberty Wines (UK), sourcing its grapes from McLaren Vale (it owns a 19ha vineyard in Blewitt Springs). The winemaking team is decidedly high powered with the hugely experienced Tim James and Mike Farmilo the conductors of the band. The focus is on the diverse districts within McLaren Vale and dry-grown bushvine grenache. Exports to the UK, Canada, Singapore, Hong Kong and NZ.

🍷🍷🍷🍷 **The Hundred Blewitt Springs Grenache 2018** The Hundred range shows off the diversity in style of Vale grenache with Blewitt Springs bringing its sunniness and spice to the grape. A real crowd-pleaser with exceptional fruit concentration, all the while remaining light on its toes. Black cherries, lifted florals, high spice, licorice blackstrap, pastille. That pastille jubeyness follows on the palate, adding just a touch of sweetness. On song. Screwcap. 14.5% alc. **Rating** 94 **To** 2031 $45 JP

❦❦❦❦❦ McLaren Vale Shiraz Viognier 2018 **Rating** 92 **To** 2030 $25 JP ✪
The Hundred McLaren Vale Grenache 2018 **Rating** 91 **To** 2027 $45 JP

Wilson Vineyard ★★★★★

Polish Hill River, Sevenhill via Clare, SA 5453 **Region** Clare Valley
T (08) 8822 4050 **www**.wilsonvineyard.com.au **Open** W'ends 10–4
Winemaker Daniel Wilson **Est.** 1974 **Dozens** 3000 **Vyds** 11.9ha
In 2009 the winery and general operations were passed on to son Daniel Wilson, the second generation. Daniel, a graduate of CSU, spent three years in the Barossa with some of Australia's largest winemakers before returning to Clare in '03. Parents John and Pat Wilson still contribute in a limited way, content to watch developments in the business they created. Daniel continues to follow John's beliefs about keeping quality high, often at the expense of volume, and rather than talk about it, believes the proof is in the bottle.

❦❦❦❦❦ Polish Hill River Riesling 2019 From 40yo vines planted by John and Pat Wilson in heavy clay soil that routinely produces a miniscule crop. It's fruity and moreish, the line of steely acidity giving shape and balance to a very good riesling that has an outstanding finish. Screwcap. 12.5% alc. **Rating** 96 **To** 2032 $29 ✪
DJW Polish Hill River Riesling 2019 Hand-picked, chilled and whole-bunch pressed. Has citrus blossom and crushed tangerine aromas, backed by hints of spice that also materialise on the palate. The overall clarity of the wine and its acidity are exemplary. Screwcap. 12% alc. **Rating** 95 **To** 2030 $24 ✪

❦❦❦❦❦ Watervale Riesling 2019 **Rating** 93 $19 ✪

Windance Wines ★★★★★

2764 Caves Road, Yallingup, WA 6282 **Region** Margaret River
T (08) 9755 2293 **www**.windance.com.au **Open** 7 days 10–5
Winemaker Tyke Wheatley **Est.** 1998 **Dozens** 5000 **Vyds** 7.25ha
Drew and Rosemary Brent-White founded this family business, situated 5km south of Yallingup. Cabernet sauvignon, shiraz, sauvignon blanc, semillon and merlot have been established, incorporating sustainable land management and organic farming practices where possible. The wines are exclusively estate-grown. Daughter Billie and husband Tyke Wheatley now own the business: Billie, a qualified accountant, was raised at Windance and manages the business and the cellar door; and Tyke (with winemaking experience at Picardy, Happs and Burgundy) has taken over the winemaking and manages the vineyard.

❦❦❦❦❦ Margaret River Shiraz 2018 From 2 estate blocks, both batches fermented with 10% whole bunches, one pumped over, the other hand-plunged, 11 months before blending and bottling. Full, deep crimson-purple. A medium-bodied shiraz that has black cherry as its flavour base and exemplary texture, balance and length. Trophies Best Shiraz Queensland and WA wine shows, 5 gold medals. Screwcap. 14% alc. **Rating** 98 **To** 2038 $29 ✪

❦❦❦❦❦ Margaret River Cabernet Merlot 2018 Includes 85% cabernet sauvignon, 10% merlot and 5% malbec, vinified separately; matured for 10 months in French oak (25% new). The wine establishes its credentials with its complex dark berry aromas. Very good fruit flavours to one side, the texture and structure are exceptionally good, woven through the fabric of the fruit. Gold medals WA and WA Boutique wine shows. Screwcap. 14.2% alc. **Rating** 96 **To** 2032 $26 ✪
Glen Valley Mount Barker Riesling 2019 Machine-harvested at night, trucked to Margaret River for pressing and fermentation at 11°C in stainless steel. Intensely fruited with a blaze of citrus centred on lime and lemon, acidity also

a positive contributor to the overall flavour and mouthfeel. Screwcap. 12.5% alc.
Rating 95 To 2029 $28 ✪

Margaret River Sauvignon Blanc Semillon 2019 A 70/30% blend. Has the vibrancy that is so special to Margaret River. Pea pod, lemon and lime give a dressing of passionfruit. It has spectacular length and flawless balance. Screwcap. 12% alc. Rating 95 To 2022 $21 ✪

Glen Valley Margaret River Shiraz 2017 A radical new label design for Windance is attractive for its upper level wines; this wine also has 9% malbec. Immaculately balanced, the influence of the malbec adding another dimension of red fruits to join the darker berry flavours. Screwcap. 14.5% alc. Rating 95 To 2032 $42

Glen Valley Margaret River Cabernet Sauvignon 2018 SA126 clone grown on an estate site that creates some stress, hence smaller berries, smaller bunches and intense colour. Several days cold soak pre-fermentation, matured for 12 months in French barriques (70% new). The oak is inevitably very obvious but the intensity of the medium-bodied blackcurrant fruit will overtake the oak in time. Trophy Best Cabernet Sauvignon Australian and NZ Boutique Wine Show. Screwcap. 14.5% alc. Rating 95 To 2038 $55

Glen Valley Margaret River Chardonnay 2018 Hand-picked, whole-bunch pressed, matured for 10 months in French oak. The oak is subtle in flavour, although helps the texture and structure of a wine just negotiating the ripeness bar. Made with courage of conviction. Screwcap. 12.8% alc. Rating 94 To 2026 $38

ŸŸŸŸŸ **Margaret River Cabernet Sauvignon 2018** Rating 93 To 2033 $34
Glen Valley Margaret River Blanc de Blancs 2017 Rating 90 $35

Windfall Wine Estate ★★★★

7 Dardanup West Road, North Boyanup, WA 6237 **Region** Geographe
T 0408 930 332 **www.windfallwine.com.au Open** Not
Winemaker Luke Eckersley **Est.** 1996 **Dozens** 3000 **Vyds** 3ha
Julie and Phil Hutton put their money where their hearts are, electing to plant a merlot-only vineyard in 1996. Presumably knowing the unpredictable habits of merlot when planted on its own roots, they began by planting 3500 Schwartzman rootstock vines and then 12 months later field-grafted the merlot scion material. Small wonder their backs are still aching. I don't doubt for a millisecond the sincerity of their enthusiasm for the variety when they say, 'Fruity, plummy, smooth and velvety. Hints of chocolate too. If you're new to wine and all things merlot, this is a wonderful variety to explore.' The previous name, Bonking Frog, was fun but became wildly unsuited to what has become a serious player in the Geographe region.

ŸŸŸŸŸ **Ivor Reserve Geographe Merlot 2017** A complex blend of 85.2% merlot, 13.6% shiraz and 1.2% cabernet sauvignon. The outcome is very good indeed. Merlot varietal character of dark plum/blackcurrant balanced with a modest amount of shiraz and cabernet sauvignon. The regional play including 14.9% fruit from Great Southern also a success. Screwcap. 14% alc. Rating 95 To 2042 $40

ŸŸŸŸŸ **Single-Handed Geographe Rose 2018** Rating 90 To 2020 $24

Windows Estate ★★★★★

4 Quininup Road, Yallingup, WA 6282 **Region** Margaret River
T (08) 9756 6655 **www.windowsestate.com Open** 7 days 10–5
Winemaker Chris Davies **Est.** 1996 **Dozens** 2500 **Vyds** 6.3ha
Chris Davies planted the Windows Estate Vineyard (cabernet sauvignon, shiraz, chenin blanc, chardonnay, semillon, sauvignon blanc and merlot) in 1996, at the age of 19, and has tended the vines ever since. Initially selling the grapes, Chris moved into winemaking in 2006 and has had considerable show success for the consistently outstanding wines.

ŸŸŸŸŸ **Petit Lot Basket Pressed Cabernet Sauvignon 2017** Includes 3% petit verdot; hand-picked, destemmed, cold-soaked, open-fermented, 28 days on skins, matured in French oak (40% new) for 18 months. A distinctly elegant wine, its best years in front of it as the cedary oak and dusty tannins are absorbed by the fruit. Screwcap. 14% alc. **Rating** 96 **To** 2040 $49 ✪

Petit Lot Chardonnay 2018 Bottle number 5828/7100. The luscious, rich array of white peach and pink grapefruit isn't always as convincing and seductive as it is here. Screwcap. 13% alc. **Rating** 95 **To** 2033 $48

Petit Lot Chardonnay 2017 Whole-bunch pressed direct to French oak for wild ferment. Notwithstanding the low yield from 15yo dry-grown vines, picked early, this is a wine highly charged with natural acidity and grapefruit married with white peach flavours. Screwcap. 12.5% alc. **Rating** 95 **To** 2027 $65

Petit Lot Semillon Sauvignon Blanc 2018 A 70/30% blend. It's got to the point where Margaret River SBS/SSB blends can be relied on, sight unseen, to provide a complex, mouthfilling wine with a basket of fruit and fresh herbs/green vegetables that are irresistible. Screwcap. 12% alc. **Rating** 94 **To** 2028 $27 ✪

Petit Lot Malbec 2016 From 19yo estate vines; hand-picked, destemmed, cold soak in 1t fermenters, 14 days on skins, matured for 18 months in French oak (45% new). A pretty wine: soft red and purple fruits, minimal tannins, the oak integrated. Screwcap. 13.8% alc. **Rating** 94 **To** 2029 $49

Wine x Sam

69–71 Anzac Avenue, Seymour, Vic 3660 **Region** Strathbogie Ranges
T 0403 059 423 **www**.winebysam.com.au **Open** 7 days 9–4
Winemaker Sam Plunkett, Matt Froude **Est.** 2012 **Dozens** 70 000 **Vyds** 10.2ha
Since 1991 Sam Plunkett and partner Bron Dunwoodie have changed shells as often as a lively hermit crab: 1991, first estate vineyard established and mudbrick winery built; 2001, created a new winery at Avenel; 2004, purchased the large Dominion Wines in partnership with the Fowles family; 2011, Fowles purchased the Plunkett family's shareholding, except 7ha of shiraz and 3.2ha of chardonnay. Winemaking moved to the Taresch family's Elgo Estate winery. Within two years the Plunkett interests had leased the entire Elgo winery, now making the Elgo wines as well as their own brands. A large contract make for Naked Wines saw production increase and a few blinks of the eye later production is now 70 000 dozen. Exports to the UK, the US and China.

🍷🍷🍷🍷🍷 **The Victorian Strathbogie Ranges Riesling 2018** Sourced from the Antcliff's Chase Vineyard in the Strathbogies, one of the highest and coolest in the region, and made by seriously underrated riesling maker Sam Plunkett. It starts a little quiet on the nose and then, wham! What intensity. Lime cordial, preserved lemon, apple, orange peel and pear. Generous mouthfeel. A seamless beauty. Screwcap. 12.3% alc. **Rating** 95 **To** 2032 $24 JP ✪

Single Vineyard Series Forest Hut Vineyard Pyrenees Shiraz 2018 Sourced from the Forest Hut Vineyard at Moonambel which has no irrigation. Here is a lesson in dealing with small berries which gives a high concentration of skins compared to juice, and therefore abundant tannins. Deep garnet. A wine of serious cred, detailed and plush with the fruit-to-tannin ratio just right. Nicely subdued introduction of fine aromas: blackcurrant, bramble, plum, cinnamon, brioche and violets. More concentrated and plush on the palate, weaving a spell. Screwcap. 14.9% alc. **Rating** 95 **To** 2032 $41 JP

The Halo Effect Strathbogie Ranges Late Harvest Viognier 2018 Many wine producers are withdrawing from sweet wines due to lack of interest. So, it's great to see someone still in the game and pursuing excellence. The Halo Effect uses late harvest viognier to its best advantage by balancing high residual sugar with refreshing acidity. Orange blossom, musk, spiced apple and white peach captivate with a honeyed mouthfeel. Intense sweetness is delicious. Perfect balance. Screwcap. 12.5% alc. **Rating** 94 **To** 2032 $28 JP ✪

🍷🍷🍷🍷🍷 **Single Vineyard Series Whitegate Vineyard Strathbogie Ranges Cabernet Sauvignon 2017 Rating** 93 **To** 2027 $38 JP
The Victorian Primitivo 2018 Rating 92 **To** 2025 $24 JP ✪

Stardust & Muscle Shiraz 2018 Rating 91 **To** 2028 $32 JP
Single Vineyard Series Tait Hamilton Vineyard Heathcote Shiraz 2018 Rating 91 **To** 2031 $41 JP
The Victorian Heathcote Shiraz 2018 Rating 90 **To** 2025 $24 JP

Wines by Geoff Hardy ★★★★★

327 Hunt Road, McLaren Vale, SA 5171 **Region** South Australia
T (08) 8383 2700 **www**.winesbygeoffhardy.com.au **Open** 7 days 11–5
Winemaker Geoff Hardy, Shane Harris **Est.** 1980 **Dozens** 122 000 **Vyds** 43ha

Geoff Hardy's great-great-grandfather, the original Thomas Hardy, first planted grapes in SA in the 1850s and was one of the founding fathers of the Australian wine industry. In 1980, Geoff left the then family company, Thomas Hardy & Sons, to make his own way with wife Fiona. Wines by Geoff Hardy is made up of three ventures/brands founded by Geoff: Pertaringa in McLaren Vale, K1 by Geoff Hardy in the Adelaide Hills (Tynan Road, Kuitpo) and Hand Crafted by Geoff Hardy sourced from a variety of premium regions across SA. Exports to Canada, Sweden, Finland, India, Malaysia, South Korea, Indonesia, Thailand, Vietnam, Japan, Taiwan and China.

🍷🍷🍷🍷🍷 **Pertaringa Tipsy Hill Single Vineyard McLaren Vale Cabernet Sauvignon 2017** From a single vineyard in Blewitt Springs, for me the foremost district of McLaren Vale, planted on an easterly slope in '99 by sixth-generation owner Bec Hardy. Destemmed, open-fermented, 14 days on skins, pressed to barrel (50% new French hogsheads) on gross lees for 9 months, further rackings over the second 9 months of its maturation. Marvellous wine, fluid, juicy and vibrant. Very long finish, the tannins a gossamer web. Diam. 15% alc. **Rating** 99 **To** 2047 $295 ✪

Pertaringa Yeoman McLaren Vale Shiraz 2017 Four blocks (130yo, 80yo, the balance 20–30yo) whole berry–open fermented separately. Ultra-full-bodied but juicy black fruits/dark chocolate and tannins all bear witness to its bloodline and heritage. Diam. 15% alc. **Rating** 97 **To** 2047 $250

🍷🍷🍷🍷🍷 **Pertaringa Over The Top McLaren Vale Shiraz 2017** Small-batch whole berry–open fermented, 7–10 days on skins (block dependant, each kept separate), 30 months in French oak. A very powerful wine that carries the burden of its extract without complaint. Diam. 15% alc. **Rating** 95 **To** 2032 $40

K1 by Geoff Hardy Adelaide Hills Shiraz 2017 Comprises 80% hand-picked, 20% hand-picked for whole-bunch inclusion plus a small percentage of viognier co-fermented, matured in French oak (15% new) for 18 months. Very fragrant, on the light side of medium-bodied, excellent balance and length. My personal prejudice at work here. Diam. 13.5% alc. **Rating** 95 **To** 2027 $45

K1 by Geoff Hardy Adelaide Hills Cabernet Sauvignon 2017 From 30yo vines; whole berries open-fermented, matured for 18 months in French oak (30% new). Very neat medium to full-bodied cabernet with supple tannins and oak support. Overall length and balance ditto. Blackberry-accented berries/flashes of red fruit and spice. Diam. 13.5% alc. **Rating** 95 **To** 2032 $45

K1 by Geoff Hardy Adelaide Hills Tzimmukin 2017 Comprises 60% shiraz, 40% cabernet sauvignon. The grapes are partially dried in an earth-floored shed in the vineyard, crushed into small fermenters, matured in used French hogsheads for 20 months. The alcohol is far from fierce and a question that Geoff Hardy might consider irrelevant is what would the alcohol have been without dehydration? Diam. 15% alc. **Rating** 94 **To** 2037 $295

🍷🍷🍷🍷 **Pertaringa Understudy McLaren Vale Cabernet Sauvignon 2018 Rating** 92 **To** 2030 $22 ✪
Pertaringa Rifle & Hunt McLaren Vale Cabernet Sauvignon 2017 Rating 92 **To** 2032 $40
K1 by Geoff Hardy Adelaide Hills Sauvignon Blanc 2019 Rating 91 **To** 2021 $25
K1 by Geoff Hardy Adelaide Hills Gruner Veltliner 2019 Rating 91 **To** 2026 $25

GMH Winemaker's Reserve Shiraz 2018 Rating 90 To 2026 $20 JP ✪
Pertaringa Undercover McLaren Vale Shiraz 2018 Rating 90 To 2033 $22

Wines of Merritt ★★★

PO Box 1122, Margaret River, WA 6285 **Region** Margaret River
T 0438 284 561 **www**.winesofmerritt.com.au **Open** Not
Winemaker Nick James-Martin **Est.** 2017 **Dozens** 600
Nick James-Martin grew up in a tiny Riverland town, spending his early working life in
some of Adelaide's better restaurants, helping his family establish a vineyard in McLaren Vale.
Two years working for *WINE Magazine* in London offered him the opportunity of travelling
through France, Spain, Portugal and Italy, immersing himself in wine in those countries.
He then studied wine marketing and oenology at the University of Adelaide, sitting for a
masters degree. He worked at Rosemount, Vasse Felix and Stella Bella, plus overseas vintages
in Hawke's Bay, NZ and Languedoc, France. Sarah James-Martin is a hospitality professional
and prior to moving to Margaret River she ran the acclaimed Salopian Inn in McLaren
Vale and worked for other wineries in the region. She's currently mastering the art of
cheesemaking at Yallingup Cheese Company.

Wirra Wirra ★★★★★

463 McMurtrie Road, McLaren Vale, SA 5171 **Region** McLaren Vale
T (08) 8323 8414 **www**.wirrawirra.com **Open** Mon–Sat 10–5, Sun & public hols 11–5
Winemaker Paul Smith, Tom Ravech, Kelly Wellington **Est.** 1894 **Dozens** 140 000
Vyds 45.26ha
Long respected for the consistency of its white wines, Wirra Wirra has now established an
equally formidable reputation for its reds. The wines are of exemplary character, quality and
style; The Angelus Cabernet Sauvignon and RWS Shiraz battling each other for supremacy,
with The Absconder Grenache one to watch. Long may the battle continue under managing
director Andrew Kay and the winemaking team of Paul Smith and Tom Ravech, who forge
along the path of excellence first trod by the late (and much loved) Greg Trott, the pioneering
founder of modern-day Wirra Wirra. Its acquisition of Ashton Hills in 2015 added a major
string to its top quality bow. Exports to all major markets.

🍷🍷🍷🍷🍷 **Mrs Wigley McLaren Vale Rose 2019** Vivid, light lipstick–pink. Its
100% grenache red fruit composition comes through loud and clear; the variety,
region and winemaker each singing in harmony and joy. Fantastic value. Crush,
press and ferment cool is a simple but unbeatable approach. Screwcap. 13.5% alc.
Rating 95 To 2022 $20 ✪
Original Blend McLaren Vale Grenache Shiraz 2018 Named in honour of
the first such blend established decades ago. It has a fragrant violet and rose petal
bouquet, then a juicy, flowery palate with red fruits providing all that is needed. A
spectacular success for '18, beseeching you to drink copious amounts over the next
few years. Screwcap. 14.5% alc. Rating 95 To 2025 $25 ✪
**Hiding Champion Select Vineyards Adelaide Hills Sauvignon Blanc
2019** A wine of effortless attitude generated by a foundation of Meyer lemon that
absolutely refuses to hide any of its many attributes on the mid-palate or lingering
finish. Screwcap. 13% alc. Rating 94 To 2022 $24 ✪
Scrubby Rise McLaren Vale Shiraz 2018 It's remarkable how many boxes can
be ticked for an $18 wine. It is quintessential McLaren Vale with dark chocolate
whipped into black fruits, leaving a sense of freshness on the long palate and
aftertaste. There is a raft of black fruits that are also lively and fresh. Screwcap.
14.5% alc. Rating 94 To 2028 $18 ✪

🍷🍷🍷🍷 **The 12th Man Adelaide Hills Chardonnay 2019** Rating 93 To 2026
$35 SC
The Holy Thirst McLaren Vale Cabernet Sauvignon Shiraz 2017
Rating 93 To 2034 $35
Amator Biodynamic Vineyards McLaren Vale Tempranillo Touriga 2018
Rating 93 To 2033 $35

Catapult Elevated Vineyards Shiraz 2018 Rating 92 To 2028 $26
Amator Biodynamic Vineyards McLaren Vale Shiraz Cabernet
Sauvignon 2018 Rating 92 To 2028 $35
The Absconder McLaren Vale Grenache 2018 Rating 92 To 2028 $70
Scrubby Rise Sauvignon Blanc 2019 Rating 91 To 2021 $18 ⊙
Sparrow's Lodge McLaren Vale Shiraz 2018 Rating 91 To 2030
The Lost Watch Adelaide Hills Riesling 2019 Rating 90 To 2029 $26
Scrubby Rise Adelaide Hills Chardonnay 2019 Rating 90 To 2023 $18 ⊙

Wirrega Vineyards   ★★★☆

PO Box 94, Mundulla, SA 5270 **Region** Limestone Coast zone
T (08) 8743 4167 **www**.wirregavineyards.com **Open** Not
Winemaker Tom O'Donnell **Est.** 1993 **Dozens** 4500 **Vyds** 163ha
This is the venture of what might kindly be called wine village elders or, less kindly, likely
suspects, as they have an awesome amount of knowledge about every aspect of the wine
industry. In 1993 they formed a partnership to develop this large vineyard which, until 2013,
was content to stick to supplying grapes for some of the partners' own enterprises and to
businesses as large as Pernod Ricard. For the record, the partners are Scott Collett, Rocco
Melino, Roger Oakeshott, Grant Tilbrook, John Younger and Guido Zuccoli. The Lilliputian
production will skyrocket if the partners so wish, for the quality is obvious. Exports to the
UK, Ireland, Switzerland, Malaysia and China.

🍷🍷🍷🍷🍷 **Sfera Limestone Coast Shiraz 2016** Blackberry, plum and gum leaf characters
are served smooth and soft. This offers pretty decent volume of flavour, good
texture and is satisfying enough through the finish. Ready to drink now. Screwcap.
14% alc. **Rating** 90 **To** 2024 $20 CM ⊙

🍷🍷🍷🍷 **Sfera Limestone Coast Pinot Gris 2018** Rating 89 To 2020 $20 CM

Wise Wine   ★★★★★

237 Eagle Bay Road, Eagle Bay, WA 6281 **Region** Margaret River
T (08) 9750 3100 **www**.wisewine.com.au **Open** 7 days 11–5
Winemaker Andrew Siddell, Matt Buchan, Larry Cherubino (Consultant) **Est.** 1986
Dozens 10 000 **Vyds** 2.5ha
Wise Wine, headed by Perth entrepreneur Ron Wise, has been a remarkably consistent
producer of high quality wine. The vineyard adjacent to the winery (2ha of cabernet
sauvignon and shiraz, and 0.5ha of zinfandel) in the Margaret River is supplemented by
contract-grown grapes from Pemberton, Manjimup and Frankland River. The value for
money of many of the wines is extraordinarily good. Exports to Switzerland, the Philippines
and Singapore.

🍷🍷🍷🍷🍷 Eagle Bay Margaret River Chardonnay 2018 Sourced from Dijon clones
grown in the cool Karridale district at the southern end of Margaret River. Hand-
picked, whole-bunch pressed, fermented and matured in new French barriques.
This is a wine of exceptional intensity, length and freshness; white peach/grapefruit
duo have absorbed the oak and relished its acidity. Screwcap. 13.2% alc. **Rating** 97
To 2035 $50 ⊙
Eagle Bay Wilyabrup Margaret River Cabernet Sauvignon 2017 Matured
for 18 months in French barriques. While it is medium to full-bodied, the balance
is such that many will be unable to resist the temptation of drinking some tonight.
It is full of luscious cassis fruit, the contrast – and the balance – soft, almost
chocolatey, tannins. Screwcap. 14% alc. **Rating** 97 **To** 2047 $75 ⊙

🍷🍷🍷🍷🍷 **Reserve Margaret River Chardonnay 2018** A strange juxtaposition of prices
between this and its Eagle Bay sibling. This is a nice Margaret River chardonnay
with abundant, textured, ripe fruits; the only question being a slightly reductive
bouquet. Screwcap. 13.5% alc. **Rating** 94 **To** 2023 $30 ⊙

🍷🍷🍷🍷🍷 Eagle Bay Wilyabrup Margaret River Shiraz 2017 Rating 90 To 2027 $75

Witches Falls Winery

79 Main Western Road, Tamborine Mountain, Qld 4272 **Region** Queensland
T (07) 5545 2609 **www.**witchesfalls.com.au **Open** Mon–Thurs 10–4, Fri–Sun 10–5
Winemaker Jon Heslop **Est.** 2004 **Dozens** 12 000 **Vyds** 10.5ha
Witches Falls is the venture of Jon and Kim Heslop. Jon has a deep interest in experimenting with progressive vinification methods in order to achieve exceptional and interesting results. He has a degree in applied science (oenology) from CSU and experience working in the Barossa and Hunter valleys, as well as at Domaine Chantal Lescure in Burgundy and with a Napa-based winegrower. Witches Falls' grapes are sourced from the Granite Belt (in addition to its 0.4ha of estate durif) and it is one of the consistently good performers in that context. Exports to Taiwan and China.

🍷🍷🍷🍷🍷 **Wild Ferment Granite Belt Malbec 2019** Fabulous dark purple hue. Super bright cherry fruit, spicy as anything with bitumen and earthy aromas. Some grip to the grainy tannins but not out of place. Crank up the bbq and pour this for everyone. Screwcap. 13.2% alc. **Rating** 92 **To** 2027 $40 JF

Wolf Blass ★★★★★

97 Sturt Highway, Nuriootpa, SA 5355 **Region** Barossa Valley
T (08) 8568 7311 **www.**wolfblass.com **Open** 7 days 10–4.30
Winemaker Chris Hatcher, Steve Frost, Marie Clay, Clare Dry, John Ashwell **Est.** 1966
Dozens NFP
The Wolf Blass wines are made at all price points, ranging through Red, Yellow, Gold, Brown, Grey, Black, White and Platinum labels covering every one of the main varietals. In 2016 a new range of wines labelled BLASS was introduced. The style and range of the wines continue to subtly evolve under the leadership of chief winemaker Chris Hatcher. Exports to all major markets.

🍷🍷🍷🍷🍷 **Platinum Label Medlands Vineyard Barossa Cabernet Sauvignon 2018** A paucity of information other than this is aged in French oak (28% new), for 16 months. Still there's no denying the strength and appeal here. It's neatly composed with cassis, pepper, licorice blackstrap and savoury elements – bitumen, squid ink and cedary woodsy spices. It's full-bodied and structured, yet the fruit is ripe not sweet and the tannins are supple and detailed. Cork. 14.5% alc. **Rating** 96 **To** 2038 $200 JF
Black Label Cabernet Sauvignon Shiraz 2017 With 51% cabernet sauvignon, 44% shiraz and 5% malbec for good measure. It's big, ripe and concentrated in a Wolf Blass way, yet not so humongous that it can't be appreciated. The tannins are plush and appealing with ingrained savouriness among the fruit and spice. It holds its own. Screwcap. 14.5% alc. **Rating** 95 **To** 2035 $130 JF

🍷🍷🍷🍷🍷 **Brown Label Classic Shiraz 2017 Rating** 93 **To** 2030 $50 JF
Grey Label Adelaide Hills Chardonnay 2018 Rating 92 **To** 2028 $34 JF
Grey Label Langhorne Creek Cabernet Shiraz 2018 Rating 92 **To** 2033 $45 JF
Altitude Shiraz 2018 Rating 90 **To** 2026 $20 JF ✪

Wood Park

263 Kneebones Gap Road, Markwood, Vic 3678 **Region** King Valley
T (03) 5727 3778 **www.**woodparkwines.com.au **Open** At Milawa Cheese Factory
Winemaker John Stokes **Est.** 1989 **Dozens** 7000 **Vyds** 16ha
John Stokes planted the first vines at Wood Park in 1989 as part of a diversification program for his property at Bobinawarrah, in the hills of the Lower King Valley, east of Milawa. The vineyard is managed with minimal chemical use and a mix of modern and traditional winemaking techniques are used (wild yeast–open fermentation and hand-plunging). The reach of Wood Park has been expanded with Beechworth Pinot Noir and Chardonnay, the mix of mainstream and alternative varieties all well made.

ŦŦŦŦ♀ **Whitlands King Valley Pinot Gris 2018** From vineyards at 800m, whole-bunch pressed, stainless steel–fermented. Is very much in gris (not grigio) style, this coming without elaboration in the winery. Good length, acidity a feature. Screwcap. 13.6% alc. **Rating** 90 **To** 2020 $24

ŦŦŦŦ **Forgotten Patch King Valley Sangiovese 2018 Rating** 89 **To** 2025 $24

Woodhaven Vineyard   ★★★★

87 Main Creek Road, Red Hill, Vic 3937 **Region** Mornington Peninsula
T 0421 612 178 **www.**woodhavenvineyard.com.au **Open** By appt
Winemaker Lee Ward, Neil Ward **Est.** 2003 **Dozens** 250 **Vyds** 1.6ha
Woodhaven is the venture of Lee and Neil Ward, both qualified accountants for 30 years in Melbourne, albeit working in different industries. They spent two years looking for a suitable site on the Mornington Peninsula, ultimately finding one high on Red Hill. Bringing the venture to the point of production has been a slow and, at times, frustrating business. They decided from the outset to be personally responsible for all aspects of growing the grapes and making the wines, relying on the advice readily given to them by George and Ruth Mihaly of Paradigm, David and (the late) Wendy Lloyd of Eldridge, John and Julie Trueman of Myrtaceae and Nat and Rose White, formerly of Main Ridge. They also decided to grow the vines organically and biodynamically; it took eight years to produce their first two barrels of wine in 2010. In '13 the 0.8ha each of pinot noir and chardonnay finally produced more than one barrel of each wine.

ŦŦŦŦ♀ **Chardonnay 2018** This is a nutty, mealy and nourishing chardonnay with ample stone fruit aromas glossing the nose. The palate is at once rich at the attack, while tapering to a taut skein of mineral tang, maritime acidity and well applied oak. Could use a bit more mid-palate weight. Screwcap. **Rating** 92 **To** 2025 $40 NG
Pinot Noir 2017 A pallid ruby segueing to notes of extremely ripe strawberry, rhubarb, cumquat, sarsaparilla and twig. This is attractively medicinal in a light to mid-weighted typical Australian fashion. Sappy. Modest length. Savoury and gently astringent. An attractive pinot. Screwcap. **Rating** 91 **To** 2024 $50 NG

Woodlands   ★★★★★

3948 Caves Road, Wilyabrup, WA 6284 **Region** Margaret River
T (08) 9755 6226 **www.**woodlandswines.com **Open** 7 days 10–5
Winemaker Stuart Watson **Est.** 1973 **Dozens** 18 000 **Vyds** 26.58ha
Founders David Watson and wife Heather had spectacular success with the cabernets he made in 1979 and the early '80s. Commuting from Perth on weekends and holidays, as well as raising a family, became all too much and for some years the grapes from Woodlands were sold to other Margaret River producers. With the advent of sons Stuart and Andrew (Stuart primarily responsible for winemaking), the estate has bounced back to pre-eminence. The wines come in four price bands, the bulk of the production under the Chardonnay and Cabernet Merlot varietals, then a series of Reserve and Special Reserves, then Reserve de la Cave and finally Cabernet Sauvignon. The top end wines primarily come from the original Woodlands Vineyard, where the vines are almost 50 years old. Exports to the UK, the US, Sweden, Denmark, Finland, South Korea, Mauritius, Indonesia, Malaysia, the Philippines, Singapore, Japan and China.

ŦŦŦŦŦ **Chloe 2018** This is an immense chardonnay, a barometer for a style defined by ample oak, albeit, used sensitively to curb a cavalcade of nougatine, toasted hazelnut and stone fruit flavours barreling across the mouth. Far from shy. And yet, beautifully fresh. A paradoxical meld of sheer richness and fine-boned tension. Rating 95 **To** 2030 NG
Margaret 2017 Includes 87% cabernet, 8% merlot and 5% malbec. Tobacco and graphite are the first scents. Currant too, red and black. Authoritative. Fine-boned. Well melded tannins, juicy and moreish. This pushes long with an overall feeling of mid-weighted confidence in the glass and across a table. Screwcap. **Rating** 95 **To** 2036 $70 NG

Emily 2018 Comprises 45% franc, 44% merlot, 7% malbec and a smattering of cabernet and petit verdot. I love this wine. A vibrant arc of blackcurrant, hedgerow, olive and sage fill every nook and cranny of the mouth, pummelling it with ripe and precisely tuned, yet looser knit, tannins that fall, thankfully, on the savoury side. This delivers. Screwcap. **Rating** 95 **To** 2034 $39 NG

Reserve de la Cave Margaret River Cabernet Franc 2018 Given 14 months in quality new French wood. This is very fine. Ripe. Herbal-savoury. Attenuated sage-crusted tannins, juicy and moreish. Long. Precise and noble. Violet, chilli, spearmint, currant. Exceptional. Screwcap. **Rating** 95 **To** 2033 NG

Reserve de la Cave Margaret River Malbec 2018 Hand-picked and macerated for 26 days including the fermentation period, 14 months in oak. The '18s at this address are sumptuous. Impeccably ripe. Nothing sweet. Violet, pulpy blue fruit. Lovely astringency. Long, sappy and fine to drink now or over the medium term. Screwcap. **Rating** 95 **To** 2030 NG

♥♥♥♥♡ **Wilyabrup Valley Margaret River Cabernet Sauvignon Merlot 2018** **Rating** 92 **To** 2030 $28 NG
Malbec 2018 Rating 92 **To** 2027 $39 NG
Wilyabrup Valley Margaret River Chardonnay 2018 Rating 91 **To** 2024 $28 NG
Margaret River Cabernet Sauvignon 2016 Rating 90 **To** 2028 $165 NG

Woods Crampton   ★★★★★

PO Box 417, Hamilton, NSW 2303 **Region** Barossa Valley
T 0417 670 655 **www.**woods-crampton.com.au **Open** Not
Winemaker Nicholas Crampton, Aaron Woods **Est.** 2010 **Dozens** 11 000
This is one of the most impressive ventures of Nicholas Crampton (his association with McWilliam's is on a consultancy basis) and winemaking friend Aaron Woods. The two make the wines at the Sons of Eden winery with advice from Igor Kucic. The quality of the wines and the enticing prices have seen production soar from 1500 to 11 000 dozen, with every expectation of continued success. Exports to the UK, Canada, Denmark, Switzerland, Russia, Singapore, Hong Kong, China and NZ.

♥♥♥♥♥ **Frances & Nicole Old Vine Single Vineyard Eden Valley Shiraz 2017** This address deserves more attention. A striking wine! Despite coming from a relatively warm place in the grand scheme of things, this rich red manages to encapsulate an ethereal, gentle and virtual medium-bodied gait. It embraces ripe fruit endowed by place, without under-extracting and relying on oak, as is too often the case. Conversely, blueberry, anise, tapenade, iodine and a morass of violet scents flow across a beam of gentle tannic detail and bright peppery acidity. Nothing forced. Nothing sloppy. Nothing reductive-hard. A wondrous flow of length, precision and honesty. Screwcap. **Rating** 97 **To** 2026 NG

♥♥♥♥♥ **Old Vine Single Vineyard Eden Valley Shiraz 2018** The vineyard is at Craneford; hand-picked, fermented with 15% whole bunches, minimal handling in the winery, near to natural winemaking. Complex and rich with dark fruit flavours, the tannins soft, spice and pepper up front. Only 333 dozen made. Screwcap. 14.5% alc. **Rating** 95 **To** 2038 $28 ❂

Mengler Hill Old Vine Barossa Shiraz 2018 A more intense expression than its brethren, boasting a vinous drive of mocha, coffee bean and bitter chocolate melded with the assorted dark berry fruits across the palate. Long and sumptuous. I prefer the juiciness of the regular Barossa wine but this wins based on its intrinsic qualitative make-up: tenacity and intensity of flavour. Screwcap. **Rating** 95 **To** 2026 NG

Old Vine Barossa Valley Cabernet Sauvignon 2017 This is a rich red but, as is the wont at this address, it is extracted righteously. With purpose. The result is a marauding wave of earthy tannins tucking in billowing seams of blackcurrant, graphite, bouquet garni and loamy scents. The oak is buried, serving as an adjunct to the fluidity of the whole. This is a new contemporary benchmark for Barossa cabernet. Screwcap. **Rating** 95 **To** 2029 NG

High Eden Single Vineyard Riesling 2019 There's a sense of place about this wine; you can almost smell and taste the rocky soil of High Eden. It shows varietal aromatics and the familiar citrus qualities (along with some herbal character) typical of the region, but in a subtle way; and it's really the chalky texture and fine-boned acid structure that lingers long on the finish that draws you in. Screwcap. 12% alc. **Rating** 94 **To** 2029 $28 SC ☉

Take it to the Grave Pale & Dry Barossa Valley Rose 2019 This is a joyous rose. Made by somebody with the knowledge of what 'thirst-slaking' means, guiding crunchy red fruit and musk stick scents across a pale coral hue. Rose-101 to advanced level. This is delicious and should be a strong consideration as a glass-pour across every restaurant in the country. **Rating** 94 **To** 2020 $18 NG ☉

Old Vine Barossa Shiraz 2018 Cool-fermented, hand plunged and matured in oak (30% new) of assorted formats, neither fined nor filtered. A glossy opaque. This is a delicious wine, strongly of place and yet a confidence, poise and almost savoury mid-weighted feel belying such a warm zone. Fruitcake spice, violet scents and cherry-bitter-chocolate notes bound by a gentle sash of reductive tension and a juicy stream of acidity. This goes down very easily due to the sheer succulence of fruit and integration of structural pillars. Screwcap. **Rating** 94 **To** 2024 $21 NG ☉

ⵣⵣⵣⵣⵣ **Single Vineyard Eden Valley Riesling 2019 Rating** 93 **To** 2027 $28 NG
Take it to the Grave Clare Valley Riesling 2018 Rating 93 **To** 2026 $18 NG ☉
Eden Valley Dry Riesling 2019 Rating 92 **To** 2029 $21 SC ☉
Little Giant Coonawarra Cabernet Sauvignon 2018 Rating 92 **To** 2025 $22 NG ☉
Take it to the Grave Langhorne Creek Shiraz 2018 Rating 91 **To** 2024 $18 NG ☉
Take it to the Grave Langhorne Creek Barossa Valley Grenache 2019 Rating 91 **To** 2024 $18 CM ☉
Take it to the Grave McLaren Vale Grenache 2018 Rating 91 **To** 2023 $18 NG ☉
Take it to the Grave Coonawarra Cabernet Sauvignon 2019 Rating 91 **To** 2023 $18 NG ☉
Little Giant McLaren Vale Grenache 2019 Rating 90 **To** 2024 $22 CM

Woodside Park Vineyards ★★★★

27 Croydon Road, Keswick, SA 5035 **Region** Adelaide Hills
T (08) 7070 1401 **www**.cloudbreakwines.com.au **Open** Not
Winemaker Simon Greenleaf, Randal Tomich **Est.** 1998 **Dozens** 10 000 **Vyds** 17ha
Woodside Park Vineyards is a joint venture between Randal Tomich and Simon Greenleaf, who share a friendship of over 20 years. Woodside specialises in cool-climate wines (released under the Cloudbreak label), grown on the Tomich family's Woodside Park Vineyard. Simon has been producing wines from the Tomich vineyards since 2005 and has a strong understanding of the site and fruit quality. Randal has had more than 20 years' experience in winemaking, specialising in vineyard development and establishes vineyards for brands across Australia and California, US. The Woodside Park vineyards include chardonnay, sauvignon blanc, pinot noir, gruner veltliner, riesling, gewurztraminer and shiraz. Exports to the US, South-East Asia and China.

ⵣⵣⵣⵣⵣ **Cloudbreak Adelaide Hills Chardonnay 2019** The packaging, label, Diam cork and old-fashioned dumpy bottle are distracting. The wine is focused with Meyer lemon and pink grapefruit, oak having little skin in the game. 13% alc. **Rating** 90 **To** 2025 $35

Adelaide Hills Pinot Noir 2018 The creation of winemaker Ben Riggs and viticulturist Randal Tomich. At this price, over-delivers. Varietal character is there, as are some textural and structural garnishes. Screwcap. **Rating** 90 **To** 2023 $20 ☉

Woodstock

215 Douglas Gully Road, McLaren Flat, SA 5171 **Region** McLaren Vale
T (08) 8383 0156 **www**.woodstockwine.com.au **Open** 7 days 10–5
Winemaker Ben Glaetzer **Est.** 1905 **Dozens** 22000 **Vyds** 18.44ha
The Collett family is among the best known in McLaren Vale, the late Doug Collett AM was known for his World War II exploits flying Spitfires and Hurricanes with the RAF and RAAF, returning to study oenology at Roseworthy Agricultural College and rapidly promoted to take charge of SA's largest winery, Berri Co-operative. In 1973 he purchased the Woodstock estate, built a winery and in '74 he crushed its first vintage. Son Scott Collett, once noted for his fearless exploits in cars and on motorcycles, became winemaker in '82 and has won numerous accolades; equally importantly, he purchased an adjoining shiraz vineyard planted circa 1900 (now the source of The Stocks Shiraz) and a bushvine grenache vineyard planted in '30. In '99 he joined forces with Ben Glaetzer, passing responsibility for winemaking to Ben, but retaining responsibility for the estate vineyards. Exports to most major markets.

⦿⦿⦿⦿⦿ **McLaren Vale Very Old Fortified NV** Winemaker Scott Collett recently found some old barrels at the back of a shed containing an ambrosia his late father, Doug, had made. Age unknown, the thick elixir had long morphed into a tawny style yet very much alive, just a special pump was needed to extract it. Dark walnut hue. Heady with flavours of balsamic, menthol, coffee, cracked pepper and baking spices. Incredibly concentrated, silky rich and almost molasses-like, but key is its freshness. Serendipitous find. Stylishly packaged in a 150ml pottery bottle. Cork. 20% alc. **Rating** 95 $450 JF

⦿⦿⦿⦿⦿ **Adelaide Hills Sauvignon Blanc 2019 Rating** 93 To 2022 $19 CM ○
The Stocks Single Vineyard McLaren Vale Shiraz 2017 Rating 93 To 2035 $95 CM
The OCTOgenarian McLaren Vale Grenache 2016 Rating 93 To 2029 $32 CM
Scott Collett McLaren Vale Shiraz Cabernet Sauvignon 2015 Rating 92 To 2030 $180 JF
Collett Lane Single Vineyard McLaren Vale Cabernet Sauvignon 2016 Rating 92 To 2030 $45 JF
Naughty Monte Montepulciano 2016 Rating 92 To 2027 $30 CM
The Stocks Single Vineyard McLaren Vale Shiraz 2016 Rating 91 To 2028 $95 JF
Deep Sands McLaren Vale Shiraz 2017 Rating 90 To 2026 $19 CM ○

Woodvale

PO Box 54, Watervale, SA 5453 **Region** Clare Valley
T 0417 829 204 **Open** Not
Winemaker Kevin Mitchell **Est.** 2014 **Dozens** 3000 **Vyds** 7ha
This is the personal venture of Kevin Mitchell and wife Kathleen Bourne, not an offshoot of Kilikanoon (see separate entry). The main targets are what Kevin describes as 'modest, sustainable growth, working with the varieties that Clare does so well: riesling, shiraz, cabernet sauvignon, mataro, semillon, pinot gris, and of course, grenache'. Given he is a third-generation Clare Valley grapegrower, procuring grapes from mates to supplement the estate shiraz, pinot gris and riesling should not be a problem.

⦿⦿⦿⦿⦿ **Cellar Release Skilly Clare Valley Riesling 2011** Encapsulates what the Woodvale wines have to offer the patient, winning trophies for Best Aged Riesling, Best Riesling and Best Wine of Show at the Clare Valley Wine Show '18. It's the depth and length of the structure that is the beating heart of these Woodvale rieslings. Screwcap. 12% alc. **Rating** 97 To 2029 $30 ○

⦿⦿⦿⦿⦿ **Watervale Riesling 2017** From the 57yo Churinga Vineyard in Watervale at 450m; hand-picked, lightly crushed, only free-run used. The power and concentration of this wine immediately manifests itself, Meyer and standard lemon flavours with hints of herb fill the mouth. A great future. Screwcap. 12.5% alc. Rating 96 To 2032 $25 ○

The Khileyre Clare Valley Riesling 2018 From the high altitude (450m) Churinga and adjacent Milburn vineyards north of Watervale. Its bouquet is clean, not saying much at this stage; the palate a completely different story: crisp, intense with lime and mineral notes the most intense. If you are tempted to cellar any of these Woodvale wines, choose one of the 500 six-packs available. Screwcap. 12.5% alc. Rating 95 To 2028 $35 ○

Cellar Release Skilly Clare Valley Riesling 2014 Developing slowly but surely, the fruit yet to move onto the next stage of toast and/or spice. The balance of fruit and acid is excellent. Screwcap. 12.5% alc. Rating 95 To 2030 $30 ○

Cellar Release Watervale Riesling 2014 Gleaming pale green. A perfectly beautiful riesling in every respect, still very youthful, delicate even. It did come from a classic vintage but this nailed it. It will steadily build on what is already in the bottle. The price is absurd. Screwcap. 12.5% alc. Rating 95 To 2025 $30 ○

Cellar Release Watervale Riesling 2013 Some slight deepening of the colour, albeit still light. The bouquet and palate are moving with the fruit softening and filling the palate courtesy of touches of passionfruit alongside the citrus base. Screwcap. 12.5% alc. Rating 95 To 2029 $30 ○

Woodberry Clare Valley Shiraz 2017 A reserve shiraz from the 70yo contoured Churinga Vineyard, last made in '14, matured in new and used French hogsheads. The finesse and freshness of the cherry and plum fruit is a celebration of the '17 vintage. Screwcap. 14.5% alc. Rating 95 To 2032 $45

Skilly Clare Valley Riesling 2018 From the estate vineyard in the Skilly Valley in Penwortham; 250 dozen bottles made. It is completely dry, a full-blown riesling with ripe citrus providing all the flavours now, with more to come as the wine ages. Very pure and precise. Screwcap. 12% alc. Rating 94 To 2033 $25 ○

M.C.D. Clare Valley Grenache 2016 Named after Kevin Mitchell's maternal grandfather, Maurice Charles Duke of Penwortham who, among other things, grew grapes. From 2 vineyards planted '50 and '52; hand-picked, matured in used French hogsheads for 15 months; 250 dozen made. Bright, clear crimson. It's got great perfume and the varietal fruit is in full song with red fruits of every description. Screwcap. 14.5% alc. Rating 94 To 2031 $30 ○

Woody Nook   ★★★★★

506 Metricup Road, Wilyabrup, WA 6280 **Region** Margaret River
T (08) 9755 7547 **www.**woodynook.com.au **Open** 7 days 10–4.30
Winemaker Neil Gallagher, Craig Dunkerton **Est.** 1982 **Dozens** 7500 **Vyds** 14.23ha
Woody Nook, with a backdrop of 18ha of majestic marri and jarrah forest, doesn't have the high profile of the biggest names in Margaret River but it has had major success in wine shows over the years. It was purchased by Peter and Jane Bailey in 2000 and major renovations have transformed it, with a new winery, a gallery tasting room for larger groups and an alfresco dining area by the pond. A link with the past is Neil Gallagher's continuing role as winemaker, viticulturist and minority shareholder (Neil is the son of founders Jeff and Wynn Gallagher). Exports to the UK, the US, Canada, Bermuda, Hong Kong and China.

♀♀♀♀♀ **Single Vineyard Margaret River Cabernet Merlot 2017** An older school regional expression boasting currant, bouquet garni, tapenade, bitter chocolate and a firm spurt of twiggy tannins that, with little doubt, will mould into something harmonious over time. A long time. Rating 93 To 2029 NG

♀♀♀♀ **Single Vineyard Margaret River Shiraz 2018** Rating 89 To 2024 NG

Word of Mouth Wines ★★★★☆

42 Wallace Lane, Orange, NSW 2800 **Region** Orange
T 0429 533 316 **www**.wordofmouthwines.com.au **Open** 7 days 10.30–5
Winemaker David Lowe, Liam Heslop, Will Rikard-Bell **Est.** 1999 **Dozens** 1100
Vyds 2.5ha

Peter Gibson has been the one constant figure in Word of Mouth, his involvement dating back to 1999, when he established Pinnacle Wines with an early planting of pinot gris. Word of Mouth was formed when Pinnacle amalgamated with neighbouring Donnington Vineyard. In 2013 the Donnington parcel was sold and has since become Colmar Estate. Peter retained his original block and continues under the Word of Mouth label.

ϘϘϘϘϘ **Orange Pinot Gris 2018** This is exceptional gris, a testament to just how exciting this idiom has become domestically. A billowing quilt of a skinsy weave and substantial detail, subtle acidity and a diplomatic spool of volatility. Nashi pear, baking spice and tarte tatin. Riding broad and very long, this is among the country's finer expressions. Screwcap. **Rating** 95 **To** 2024 $30 NG ✪

ϘϘϘϘϙ **1K High Chardonnay 2018 Rating** 93 **To** 2024 $40 NG
Orange Petit Manseng 2018 Rating 91 **To** 2023 NG
Fluffy 2013 Rating 91 $70 NG
Orange Riesling 2019 Rating 90 **To** 2027 $30 NG
Orange Pinot Noir 2018 Rating 90 **To** 2023 $45 NG

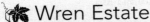 Wren Estate ★★★★★

389 Heathcote-Rochester Road, Mount Camel, Vic 3523 **Region** Heathcote
T (03) 9972 9638 **www**.wrenestate.com.au **Open** W'ends & public hols 10–5
Winemaker Michael Wren **Est.** 2017 **Dozens** 10 000 **Vyds** 14.5ha

Michael Wren, winemaker and owner of Wren Estate, has been making wine for over 15 years across multiple continents. For 10 years he was a Flying Winemaker for one of Portugal's top wineries, Esporao, and was particularly struck by the use of lagares for top quality wines. Lagares are low, wide, open red-wine fermenters that allow foot treading (or stomping) with the level of must little more than knee deep. The consequence is the very soft, yet high extraction of colour, flavour and soft tannins. The red wine fermenters in the Wren winery are replicas of the traditional lagares. The vineyard (of 14.5ha) sits in a 52ha property and was planted in 2002, the shiraz with 16 different clone and rootstock combinations, giving Michael priceless information on the vagaries of the site. Each block is picked, fermented and aged separately, the best in a limited release single block series. All the premium wines are individually barrel selected. Exports to the US and China.

ϘϘϘϘϘ **Elementary Heathcote Shiraz 2018** The blend of 3 single blocks all saw new or second-use French puncheons, 25–50% whole bunches, foot-trodden, then cool-fermented. A distinct change of pace to a supple, medium-bodied palate, still in the overarching savoury style of the Wren shirazs. Red and black fruits are woven through a wine that carries its alcohol well. Screwcap. 15.5% alc. **Rating** 96 **To** 2043 $65 ✪
I'm So Ronely Heathcote Shiraz 2018 From a single block that Wren says produced the prettiest wine of all the shiraz blocks in '18, a view I entirely agree with. Picked mid-Mar, foot-trodden, cool-fermented, 2 weeks on skins post-ferment. It's spicy and borderline juicy, the mouthfeel welcoming. No use looking for oak – it didn't see any. Screwcap. 14% alc. **Rating** 95 **To** 2038 $35 ✪
The Plot Thickens Heathcote Shiraz 2018 Fermented with 20–25% whole bunches, 2 weeks on skins post-ferment, 12 months in a mix of new and predominantly old American barrels. An energetic wine with one foot in the big end of town. The mix of red and dark fruits and supple tannins makes the plot work well. Not sure I understand the pricing of this wine. Screwcap. 14% alc. **Rating** 95 **To** 2038 $32 ✪
Block 14 Heathcote Shiraz 2018 Fermented in beeswax-lined concrete vats, 30% whole bunch, foot-trodden, 3 weeks on skins post-ferment. Maturation

for 12 months in French puncheons has produced significant oak influence. Trenchantly full-bodied, it has a savoury (more than tannic) make-up to the layers of black fruits. It's impossible not to give these 2 Wren Estate single block wines their due. Cork. 15.5% alc. **Rating** 95 **To** 2048 $159

Block 6 Heathcote Shiraz 2018 Single block; picked late Mar, 3 weeks on skins post-ferment, matured for 12 months in American hogsheads. The texture and structure are good, the bouquet and palate singing the same part of the same song. Briary, brambly, black fruits, integrated tannins on a long journey; the outcome, decades away. Cork. 15.8% alc. **Rating** 95 **To** 2048 $198

ŸŸŸŸŸ **Heathcote Marsanne 2018 Rating** 92 **To** 2038 $24 ✪

Wynns Coonawarra Estate ★★★★★

Memorial Drive, Coonawarra, SA 5263 **Region** Coonawarra
T (08) 8736 2225 **www**.wynns.com.au **Open** 7 days 10–5
Winemaker Sue Hodder, Sarah Pidgeon **Est.** 1897 **Dozens** NFP
Large-scale production has not prevented Wynns (an important part of TWE) from producing excellent wines covering the full price spectrum from the bargain-basement Riesling and Shiraz through to the deluxe John Riddoch Cabernet Sauvignon and Michael Shiraz. Even with steady price increases, Wynns offers extraordinary value for money. Investments in rejuvenating and replanting key blocks, under the direction of Allen Jenkins and skilled winemaking by Sue Hodder, have resulted in wines of far greater finesse and elegance than many of their predecessors. Exports to the UK, the US, Canada and Asia.

ŸŸŸŸŸ **John Riddoch Limited Release Cabernet Sauvignon 2016** From a tiny fraction (about 1%) of Wynns' cabernet crush, handled with kid gloves in the specialised winery. Densely coloured. Its amalgam of cassis and bay leaf is held within a fine web of ripe tannins. The excellent vintage also helping shape a cabernet of the highest class. Screwcap. 13.7% alc. **Rating** 98 **To** 2046 $150 ✪

Michael Limited Release Shiraz 2016 The apex of Wynns' shiraz releases. It is still too young to enjoy; the oak, and tannins, are very obvious. A mere 5 more years will give you a wine to be enjoyed for the next 30+ years. In the meantime French oak and glorious black fruits (with modest alcohol) may be too much for some. Screwcap. 13.8% alc. **Rating** 97 **To** 2056 $150 ✪

ŸŸŸŸŸ **Black Label Cabernet Sauvignon 2018** One sip, you're in. Excellent vintage conditions have no doubt helped, but this Australian icon doesn't need a lot of assistance outside its trio of long-time 'curators' Sue Hodder, Allen Jenkins and Sarah Pidgeon. Masses of blackberry fruits, a touch of black olive savouriness, stewed rhubarb, violets. Casts a wide net across the palate with sustained black fruits and spice, but also notes of coffee grounds, bay leaf and vanilla. Oak enhances yet keeps itself in the background. Screwcap. 13.7% alc. **Rating** 96 **To** 2041 $45 JP ✪

V&A Lane Shiraz 2018 The V&A story is all about fineness, grace and beauty, but there is an underlying power too. Oozes class from this outstanding vintage with blackcurrants, mulberry, cinnamon, crushed violets and faint notes of the Aussie bush. Skimming the depths that it has yet to reach. Nevertheless, mighty fine drinking in its youth. Screwcap. 12.4% alc. **Rating** 95 **To** 2038 $60 JP

The Siding Cabernet Sauvignon 2017 I'm seldom impressed by redesigns of labels that have history on their side. This is an exception. It also hits home runs in the mouth notwithstanding a challenging vintage. It is a pure rendition of blackcurrant varietal fruit; hints of mulberry and mint attesting to its region. Screwcap. 13.4% alc. **Rating** 95 **To** 2032 $25 ✪

Old Vines Shiraz 2018 Old vine? Most definitely. The vines responsible for this complex youngster were planted in the 1890s and 1920s and are the reason for the concentration and fruit development. It will wriggle into your affections with its bright purple hue and tightly focused blackberry, black cherry, clove, saltbush and turned earth. Focused, tight with a developing full spectrum of black fruit intensity, licorice bullets, cigar box and fine tannins. It was newly bottled when tasted and yet so very persuasive. Has a way to go. Screwcap. 13.8% alc. Rating 94 To 2032 $45 JP

ŶŶŶŶႳ Cabernet Shiraz Merlot 2017 Rating 92 To 2035 $25 JP ◐
V&A Lane Cabernet Shiraz 2018 Rating 92 To 2031 $60 JP
Riesling 2019 Rating 91 To 2036 $20 JP ◐
The Gables Limited Release Cabernet Sauvignon 2018 Rating 91 To 2032 $25 JP
The Gables Limited Release Cabernet Sauvignon 2017 Rating 91 To 2032 $25

Xabregas ★★★★★
Spencer Road, Mount Barker, WA 6324 **Region** Mount Barker
T (08) 9200 2267 **www.xabregas.com.au Open** Not
Winemaker Luke Eckersley **Est.** 1996 **Dozens** 16 000 **Vyds** 80ha
The Hogan family have five generations of WA history and family interests in sheep grazing and forestry in the Great Southern, dating back to the 1860s. Terry Hogan AM (1939–2018), founding Xabregas chairman, felt the Mount Barker region was 'far too good a dirt to waste on blue gums', and vines were planted in 1996. The Hogan family concentrates on the region's strengths – shiraz and riesling. Exports to China.

ŶŶŶŶŶ X by Xabregas Terence Syrah 2018 I would put this wine among the country's most exemplary cool-climate expressions. A benchmark! Feels more mid-weighted due to the savoury concourse of salumi, nori, blue fruit allusions and anise. The pepper grind acidity, juicy and towing the fray infinitesimally long. Miraculously, no overt reduction! An Aussie Cornas. Absolutely delicious syrah. Screwcap. 14.4% alc. Rating 97 To 2028 $55 NG ◐

ŶŶŶŶŶ Mount Barker Shiraz 2018 Super cool-climate aromas of mace, lilac, damson plum, iodine, five-spice, olive and fennel salami. Spot on! Taut, refined and towed long by a skein of juicy peppery acidity. By the same token, strutting and sumptuous of fruit. Superb estate shiraz! Screwcap. 14.5% alc. Rating 95 To 2026 $25 NG ◐
Mount Barker Shiraz Cabernet 2018 A great spectrum of vivid purple hues, verging on opaque. The tannin management across the range is the signature and masterstroke: taut, palpable and highly refined. Some baby back-rib smokehouse aromas, evidencing barrel ferment chicanery. In the best sense. Dark brooding fruit. Anise, mocha and strewn herb too. This is a superlative meld of these 2 varieties, yet far from the SA norm. Cork. Rating 95 To 2028 $55 NG
Mount Barker Riesling 2019 I wish there was more riesling like this, especially at such a diplomatic price point. Dry and mid-weighted with a forcefield of talcy granitic acidity typical of the Spencer site. This is placated by the sheer extract of impeccably poised essences: candied citrus zest, pink grapefruit pulp and orange blossom. There is nothing hard or angular here. Just an expanse of flavour and scintillating length. Screwcap. 12.5% alc. Rating 94 To 2028 $25 NG ◐

ŶŶŶŶႳ Mount Barker Rose 2019 Rating 92 To 2020 $25 NG ◐
X 280 Mount Barker Shiraz Cabernet 2018 Rating 92 To 2024 $25 NG ◐
Mount Barker Sauvignon Blanc 2019 Rating 91 $25 NG
Mount Barker Cabernet Sauvignon 2018 Rating 91 To 2028 $25 NG

Xanadu Wines ★★★★★
316 Boodjidup Road, Margaret River, WA 6285 **Region** Margaret River
T (08) 9758 9500 **www.xanaduwines.com Open** 7 days 10–5
Winemaker Glenn Goodall, Brendan Carr, Steve Kyme, Darren Rathbone **Est.** 1977
Dozens 70 000 **Vyds** 82.8ha

Xanadu Wines was established in 1977 by Dr John Lagan. In 2005 it was purchased by the Rathbone family and together with Glenn Goodall's winemaking team they have significantly improved the quality of the wines. The vineyard has been revamped via soil profiling, improved drainage, precision viticulture and reduced yields. The quality of the wines made since the acquisition of the Stevens Road Vineyard in '08 has been consistently outstanding. Exports to most major markets.

Reserve Margaret River Chardonnay 2018 Fruit from the oldest chardonnay vines on the property; fermented wild in barrel, no mlf at all. It puts a fresh face on power, it puts succulence into length, it puts botanical nuances into pristine varietal flavour. The X-factor here is quite pronounced. Screwcap. 13% alc. **Rating** 97 **To** 2032 $110 CM ✪

Reserve Margaret River Cabernet Sauvignon 2017 With 95% cabernet sauvignon, 5% malbec. It's a best barrels selection with the final blend seeing 45% new French oak. This takes quality by the scruff of the neck. It's seriously good cabernet: firm, flavoursome, tidy, balanced and long. It has excellent concentration, a thick mesh of tannin and enough nuance for you to know that more is to come. You could build a cellar around a wine like this. Screwcap. 14% alc. **Rating** 97 **To** 2050 $110 CM ✪

DJL Margaret River Sauvignon Blanc Semillon 2019 Takes on the power, hitting on where others fall by the wayside. The flavours are conventional enough but their density is in a league of its own. Apple, herbs, citrus and tropical fruits are all there in abundance. Partial barrel ferment is the key to its complexity and texture. Screwcap. 12.5% alc. **Rating** 96 **To** 2022 $25 ✪

Stevens Road Margaret River Cabernet Sauvignon 2017 The combination here is one of coiled power and medium-weighted fruit. That's almost a contradiction in terms but it feels natural here. Bay leaf, blackcurrant, juicy boysenberry and clove flavours come drifted with wood smoke and dark chocolate. It warms to its task beautifully as it breathes in the glass, but remains a cool, elegant cabernet of genuine quality. Screwcap. 14% alc. **Rating** 96 **To** 2045 $80 CM

Margaret River Chardonnay 2018 Excellent intensity and length. Green pineapple, stone fruit, steel and cedar wood flavours crash authoritatively through the mouth. No doubting its variety, no doubting its region. There's a piercing aspect to the finish but it brings flavour right along with it. Screwcap. 13% alc. **Rating** 95 **To** 2030 $40 CM

Stevens Road Margaret River Malbec 2018 From 11 rows of malbec on the Stevens Road Vineyard. Most of it goes to the Reserve Cabernet, but 100 dozen was kept as a varietal release. It sees 40% new French oak for 14 months. It tastes of cocoa and leather, jubey black cherries and bay leaves, and its filigreed tannins and wonderful length are about as clear quality sighters as anyone could hope to find. Screwcap. 14% alc. **Rating** 95 **To** 2036 $80 CM

Stevens Road Margaret River Chardonnay 2018 An elegant chardonnay showing freshness first and foremost. Although there's flint and there's funk, there's also flavour and there's a clip of quality oak. It moves confidently across all areas of the dance floor, the effect entertaining and satisfying. Linger of citrus-and-grapefruit-driven flavour on the finish is a particular highlight. Screwcap. 13% alc. **Rating** 94 **To** 2026 $80 CM

Margaret River Cabernet Sauvignon 2018 Includes 92% cabernet sauvignon, 5% petit verdot, 3% malbec; 4 weeks on skins, 40% new French oak for 14 months. Olive paste, gum leaf and blackcurrant flavours flow slowly into cedar wood and vanilla cream, the latter more texture than overt flavour. It sits at the upper end of medium weight, the flavours cruising through the mouth with confident ease. Screwcap. 14.5% alc. **Rating** 94 **To** 2036 $40 CM

Exmoor Cabernet Sauvignon 2018 Rating 93 **To** 2027 $20 CM ✪
DJL Cabernet Sauvignon 2018 Rating 93 **To** 2029 $25 CM ✪
DJL Shiraz Graciano Rose 2019 Rating 91 **To** 2021 $25 SC

DJL Shiraz 2018 Rating 91 To 2026 $25 CM
Exmoor Chardonnay 2018 Rating 90 To 2023 $18 ✪
Exmoor Cabernet Sauvignon 2017 Rating 90 To 2027 $18 ✪

XO Wine Co

13 Wicks Road, Kuitpo, SA 5172 **Region** Adelaide Hills
T 0402 120 680 **www**.xowineco.com.au **Open** Not
Winemaker Greg Clack, Kate Horstmann **Est.** 2015 **Dozens** 1000
Clackers is dead, long-live XO Wine Co. Greg Clack spent 11 years in McLaren Vale
with Haselgrove Wines. In 2014 he took himself to the Adelaide Hills as chief winemaker
at Chain of Ponds – this remains his day job, nights and days here and there devoted to
the then Clackers Wine Co. But when he met Kate Horstmann in mid-'16, its name, its
owners and its mission statement all changed to a lesser or greater degree, the name change
to XO Wine Co the most obvious. Its raison d'être still revolves around small batch, single
vineyard wines chiefly made from grenache, barbera, chardonnay and gamay. The winemaking
minimises wine movements, protecting freshness.

♟♟♟♟♟ **Single Vineyard Small Batch Adelaide Hills Barbera 2018** Hand-picked,
10% added to half-tonne open fermenters, 3 days' cold soak, matured for 6 months
in second-use French hogsheads. Plump and juicy, it reflects astute winemaking to
accent the hedonistic nature of the variety. Drink whenever the mood takes you.
Screwcap. 14% alc. **Rating** 93 To 2022 $32
Single Vineyard Small Batch Adelaide Hills Tempranillo 2018 Hand-
picked from a single vineyard at Kuitpo, fermented with 10% whole bunches,
90% destemmed fruit on top. A neatly fashioned medium-bodied wine with
tempranillo's red cherry calling card nestled in a mix of spice and bramble
providing texture. Screwcap. 14% alc. **Rating** 93 To 2023 $32
Single Vineyard Small Batch Adelaide Hills Chardonnay 2018 From a
vineyard at Kenton Valley; bunch-pressed into new and 1yo French hogsheads,
50% mlf, aged on lees for 9 months. Notes of cashew and butterscotch mingle
with ripe stone fruit aromas in the bouquet, the palate showing richness of texture
and sweetness of fruit. Well integrated acidity provides freshness on the finish.
Good drinking now. Screwcap. 13% alc. **Rating** 92 To 2025 $32 SC
Small Batch Adelaide Hills Pinot Noir 2019 Grown at Kuitpo; carbonic
maceration and whole bunch employed with different parcels, 8 months'
maturation in 3yo and 4yo French oak. Some spicy, bunchy, stemmy action
happening here, but the wine's built around a core of varietal cherry character
both in aroma and flavour. Lightly sappy astringency provides a foil for the
youthful, soft fruit on the palate. Screwcap. 13.5% alc. **Rating** 92 To 2029 $32 SC
Single Vineyard Small Batch Adelaide Hills Barbera 2019 From Kuitpo;
some whole bunch but mainly destemmed berries, 3 days' cold soak, inoculated
with a varietal enhancing yeast, matured on lees for 6 months in French oak. The
winemaking approach has been very effective in capturing the essential appeal of
barbera, here with abundant soft cherry and berry fruit and a savoury twist on the
finish. Screwcap. 14% alc. **Rating** 92 To 2024 $32 SC
Single Vineyard Small Batch Adelaide Hills Tempranillo 2019 Hand
picked, 10% whole bunch, the balance destemmed only. Open-fermented and
pressed off skins to 3yo French oak for 6 months' maturation. Typical varietal
cherry-cola aromas prominent on the bouquet, some vanillan spice and herb
lurking in the background. Juicy, plummy flavours on the palate balanced
nicely with dry but not overwhelming tannin. Well made. Screwcap. 13.5% alc.
Rating 92 To 2026 $32 SC
Single Vineyard Games Night McLaren Vale Shiraz Grenache 2018
Comprises 55% shiraz, 45% grenache from Willunga. Aged in seasoned French
oak. The bright, deep colour in the glass is eye-catching. Perfumed grenache
aromas dominate the bouquet with ripe shiraz flavour coming through as you
taste, marred slightly by very drying tannins and a little warmth on the finish.
Screwcap. 14.5% alc. **Rating** 91 To 2028 $27 SC

ŸŸŸŸ **Single Vineyard Small Batch McLaren Vale Shiraz 2018 Rating** 89
To 2030 $32 SC

Yabby Lake Vineyard ★★★★★

86–112 Tuerong Road, Tuerong, Vic 3937 **Region** Mornington Peninsula
T (03) 5974 3729 **www**.yabbylake.com **Open** 7 days 10–5
Winemaker Tom Carson, Chris Forge, Luke Lomax **Est.** 1998 **Dozens** 3350 **Vyds** 50ha
This high-profile wine business was established by Robert and Mem Kirby (of Village
Roadshow), who had been landowners in the Mornington Peninsula for decades. In 1998
they established Yabby Lake Vineyard, under the direction of vineyard manager Keith Harris;
the vineyard is on a north-facing slope, capturing maximum sunshine while also receiving sea
breezes. The main focus is the 25ha of pinot noir, 14ha of chardonnay and 8ha of pinot gris;
3ha of shiraz, merlot and sauvignon blanc take a back seat. The arrival of the hugely talented
Tom Carson as group winemaker has added lustre to the winery and its wines, making the first
Jimmy Watson Trophy–winning Pinot Noir in 2014 and continuing to blitz the Australian
wine show circuit with Single Block pinots. Exports to the UK, Canada, Sweden, Hong Kong
and China.

ŸŸŸŸŸ **Single Vineyard Mornington Peninsula Pinot Noir 2018** Multiple clones
hand-picked and sorted, 25% whole bunches, gentle destemming, 13–15 days
on skins, matured in French puncheons (25% new) for 11 months. Perfectly
balanced. Has developed into an entrancing, delicately framed and poised wine
with a silky mouthfeel and lingering aftertaste. Gold medal and runner up for the
James Halliday Trophy for Best Pinot Noir Melbourne Wine Awards, gold medal
Australian Pinot Noir Challenge. Screwcap. 13.5% alc. **Rating** 97 **To** 2029 $64 ✪

ŸŸŸŸŸ **20th Anniversary Mornington Peninsula Pinot Noir 2018** MV6 from
Blocks 1 and 2 planted in '98; wild-fermented with 30% whole bunches, 15 days
on skins, matured in 1yo French puncheons, 600 magnums made. Combines
richness with elegance, texture with freshness; its ultimate quality quietly defined
by its length. Screwcap. 13.5% alc. **Rating** 96 **To** 2033 $250

Single Block Release Block 1 Mornington Peninsula Pinot Noir 2018
Hand-picked and sorted, gently destemmed leaving 25% whole bunches in
traditional oak ferment, 3–4 days' cold soak, 14 days on skins, pressed to French
puncheons for 11 months' maturation. Exceptional colour, super supple mouthfeel,
a velvety mid-palate balanced by savoury/foresty glimpses on the finish. Tasted
again in '20: vibrant and still in primary mode with juicy pinot fruit. A drink-to
date is largely irrelevant. Screwcap. 13.5% alc. **Rating** 96 **To** 2035 $100

Single Block Release Block 5 Mornington Peninsula Pinot Noir 2018
Hand-picked and sorted, gently destemmed, partial whole-berry adherence for
stems, 4 days' cold soak, wild-fermented, 14 days on skins, pressed to tight-grain
puncheons for 8 months' maturation. A layered palate interleaving velvety fruit
and hints of forest on the long, medium-bodied palate. Trophy Best Pinot Noir
Mornington Peninsula Wine Show. Screwcap. 13.5% alc. **Rating** 96 **To** 2035 $100

Single Vineyard Mornington Peninsula Syrah 2018 It takes a microsecond
for the wine to establish this part of the Mornington Peninsula's ability to deliver
full-bodied shiraz that hasn't been over-extracted or otherwise forced to provide
its layered purple and black fruits. The oak and tannin contributions have been
calculated with the usual attention to detail. Screwcap. 14% alc. **Rating** 96
To 2033 $36 ✪

Red Claw Mornington Peninsula Pinot Noir 2018 Whole-bunch ferments
and matured in used French puncheons. There are very few entry pinot noirs
with value such as this. An utterly delicious tapestry of red and purple fruits sewn
through a fine web of tannins, the finish long and convincing. Screwcap. 14% alc.
Rating 95 **To** 2029 $30 ✪

Single Vineyard Mornington Peninsula Cuvee Nina 2013 Traditional
method. Disgorged Sept '19, dosage 4.5g/l, 9% reserve wine from '12. Very fine
and elegant, the low dosage perfectly judged. Diam. 12.5% alc. **Rating** 95 $45

Single Vineyard Mornington Peninsula Pinot Gris 2019 Hand-picked, whole-bunch pressed, cold-settled, wild-fermented, 50% in stainless steel, 50% in used French puncheons. Has aromas of stone fruit and a gently creamy palate. Screwcap. 13% alc. **Rating** 94 **To** 2023 $33
Single Vineyard Mornington Peninsula Pinot Noir Rose 2019 Made from a small parcel of clone 115 from Block 3. A rose petal and spice bouquet, and a fresh palate with wild fruits (strawberry/raspberry). The bone-dry finish adds to the appeal. Screwcap. 12.5% alc. **Rating** 94 **To** 2021 $30 ✪

ΨΨΨΨ **Red Claw Mornington Peninsula Pinot Gris 2019 Rating** 93 **To** 2022 $28
Red Claw Mornington Peninsula Sauvignon Blanc 2019 Rating 90 **To** 2021 $28

Yal Yal Estate

15 Wynnstay Road, Prahran, Vic 3181 (postal) **Region** Mornington Peninsula
T 0416 112 703 **www.**yalyal.com.au **Open** Not
Winemaker Rollo Crittenden **Est.** 1997 **Dozens** 2500 **Vyds** 7ha
In 2008 Liz and Simon Gillies acquired a vineyard in Merricks, planted in 1997 to 1.6ha of chardonnay and a little over 1ha of pinot noir. It has since been expanded to 7ha, half devoted to chardonnay, half to pinot noir.

ΨΨΨΨ **Edith Mornington Peninsula Chardonnay 2018** Sourced from a propitious single vineyard well signposted across an intensity of flavour, belied by aromatic restraint. Subdued but confident. A workout in the glass delivers riffs of oatmeal, white peach and praline, bound to well appointed vanillan oak (20% new, 11 months). A classy, medium-bodied wine auguring well for mid-term cellaring. Screwcap. **Rating** 93 **To** 2026 $45 NG
Winifred Mornington Peninsula Pinot Noir 2018 As with the rest of the range, this mid-weighted pinot was fermented wild. Red cherry, raspberry and plum. A portion of whole bunch in the mix, imparting a spicy brood of forested scents, turmeric and sandalwood. Plenty of snap to the tannins, lithe but firm. This should fill out nicely with a little patience. Screwcap. **Rating** 93 **To** 2026 $45 NG
Yal Yal Rd Mornington Peninsula Pinot Noir 2018 A light ruby. Luminescent. Made by Rollo Crittenden, his gentle touch manifest in the wine's detail. A nice drink. Sappy. Chalky. Light and fresh, but a purity of fruit on display that neither overreaches, nor strays into New World sweetness: bing cherry, satsuma plum and root spice, corralled by well appointed French oak tannins. Screwcap. **Rating** 92 **To** 2023 $32 NG
Yal Yal Rd Mornington Peninsula Chardonnay 2018 A zesty, mid-weighted wine, as reliant on a gentle swathe of cedary oak as it is on zesty acidity for structure. And yet the wine's opus is its breezy fruit: nashi pear, apple, citrus and stone fruit allusions wound around a creamy core of nougat. Screwcap. **Rating** 91 **To** 2024 $30 NG
Yal Yal Rd Mornington Peninsula Rose 2018 I like this straight out of the gate. A gorgeous pale coral hue. Some unresolved CO_2 for lift. Scents of mandarin, orange zest and red berries careen along a carriage of crunchy acidity given some breadth by barrel fermentation. Very easy to drink in large draughts. Screwcap. **Rating** 91 **To** 2020 $23 NG ✪

Yalumba

40 Eden Valley Road, Angaston, SA 5353 **Region** Eden Valley
T (08) 8561 3200 **www.**yalumba.com **Open** 7 days 10–5
Winemaker Louisa Rose (chief), Kevin Glastonbury, Natalie Cleghorn, Sam Wigan, Heather Fraser, Will John, Teresa Heuzenroeder **Est.** 1849 **Dozens** 930 000 **Vyds** 180ha
Owned and run by the Hill-Smith family, Yalumba has a long commitment to quality and great vision in its selection of vineyard sites, new varieties and brands. It has always been a serious player at the top end of full-bodied Australian reds and was a pioneer in the use of

screwcaps. It has a proud history of lateral thinking and rapid decision making by a small group led by Robert Hill-Smith. The synergy of the range of brands, varieties and prices is obvious, but it received added lustre with the creation of The Caley. A founding member of Australia's First Families of Wine. Exports to all major markets.

ТТТТТ **The Virgilius Eden Valley Viognier 2018** A stellar viognier. A wine that fans of the Northern Rhône, such as myself, increasingly hold in great esteem. A complete understanding of the physiological tendencies of the variety is apparent: a salubrious texture. Unafraid of viscosity, weight and phenolics. Then, the aroma! Apricot, orange blossom, cumquat, honeysuckle and crystalline ginger. Long, slippery and yet not out of hand. Impeccable oak management reining it all in across the seams. Very fine. Screwcap. **Rating** 97 **To** 2025 $50 NG ✪
The Octavius Old Vine Barossa Shiraz 2017 For long an Australian icon, this has really lightened up its act. For the better. The sort of exotic perfume – lifted lilac floral – that is seldom seen across shiraz from such a warm zone. Pulpy and juicy in the mouth, rather than over-extracted and desiccated. A beautiful sash of oak, directing a cavalcade of clove, five-spice and ample blue to dark fruit references along a skein of peppery acidity. Riveting complexity. This is a thrilling wine. Cork. **Rating** 97 **To** 2033 $150 NG ✪

ТТТТТ **The Caley Coonawarra Barossa Cabernet Shiraz 2018** This is an impressive wine and an expensive one, clear of purpose, clarity, power, intensity and detail. A benchmark cabernet and shiraz meld – a blend that many Australians perceive as the homegrown quintessence. The oak cladding is salubrious. Well applied. Apparent, but not too much in lieu of the pummelling fruit: currant, dark cherry, satsuma plum and blue fruit references brushed with five-spice, cinnamon and a gentle swathe of verdant herb before a finish marked by graphite and iodine. This is polished. The tannins nicely wrought. But fresh, eminently drinkable and firmly of place with a confident swagger and undeniable impact. Cork. **Rating** 96 **To** 2038 $365 NG
Eden Valley Viognier 2018 This address has always played a deft hand with viognier and it is only getting better. This is exemplary. Poached apricot, custard lees, orange blossom and ginger spice. The finish is gentle but far from shirking the pillow of phenolics inherent to the physiology. Nothing pushed, shrill or out of whack. Screwcap. **Rating** 95 **To** 2022 $28 NG ✪
The Menzies Coonawarra Cabernet Sauvignon 2016 Long an icon across my memory bank from my early days in retail to time as a sommelier in Paris where it appeared momentarily on the list at Willie's. A seminal moment when Australian wine got a look in. And now? Classic. In an Australian sense. Lightened up over the years in terms of the oak, but the forcefield of graphite-bitter-chocolate-bouquet grain tannins is the driver. Long. Mulch, red and blackcurrant scents and a swab of olive linger. This is very good, auguring for a long life. Cork. **Rating** 95 **To** 2031 $60 NG
The Menzies Coonawarra Cabernet Sauvignon 2014 Matured for 20 months in French oak (30% new). Thirty months after the first tasting, it is evolving as hoped, my tasting note still totally valid: elegance is the key to this wine. It is Old World in its restraint, with an earthy/savoury background to the blackcurrant and mulberry fruit; bay leaf and black olive adding their bit. The oak is restrained, the fine tannins likewise. Cork. 14% alc. **Rating** 95 **To** 2034 $60
Block 44 Eden Valley Riesling 2019 This boasts a restraint light years away from many zonal rieslings. A waft of talc, lemon oil and bath salt, but a resinous stream of texture, tension and easygoing freshness is the winning hand. Screwcap. **Rating** 94 **To** 2031 $40 NG
Samuel's Collection Barossa Grenache Shiraz Mataro 2017 Light, clear, bright crimson. There's nothing ostentatious about the wine, it offers maximum enjoyment from the sparkling red fruits given freshness by the cool vintage. Terrific value. Screwcap. 13.5% alc. **Rating** 94 **To** 2025 $28 ✪
Sanctum The Menzies Estate Vineyard Coonawarra Cabernet Sauvignon 2017 Deep colour. The 13% alcohol and a cool Coonawarra vintage

might lead to expectations of a leaner style of cabernet, whereas this is the reverse. The bouquet is the first to announce the quality and style of the wine, although the palate is in close pursuit with its plum, cassis and mulberry fruits wrapped in soft tannins and French oak. Screwcap. **Rating** 94 **To** 2030 $26 ✪

The Signature Barossa Cabernet Sauvignon Shiraz 2016 The first impression is that of an ethereal nose: floral scents, bitter chocolate, graphite and iodine. Beguiling. While each of these traits is true to form, they float across the organoleptics like a carpet ride. The tannins are very finely managed: granular and precise; almost pixelated. The finish, long. A bit tangy but I'll turn a blind eye. Cork. **Rating** 94 **To** 2031 $65 NG

♥♥♥♥♡ Samuel's Garden Collection Eden Valley Roussanne 2019 Rating 93 To 2024 $28 NG

Paradox Northern Barossa Shiraz 2018 Rating 93 To 2026 $50 NG
Steeple Vineyard Light Pass Barossa Valley Shiraz 2016 Rating 93 To 2031 $80 NG
Hand Picked Eden Valley Shiraz + Viognier 2017 Rating 93 To 2025 $40 NG
Carriage Block Dry Grown Barossa Valley Grenache 2018 Rating 93 To 2025 $50 NG
Vine Vale Barossa Valley Grenache 2018 Rating 93 To 2024 $40 NG
FSW8B Wrattonbully Botrytis Viognier 2019 Rating 93 To 2027 $30 NG
Samuel's Garden Collection Eden Valley Chardonnay 2019 Rating 92 To 2024 $28 NG
Samuel's Collection Bush Vine Barossa Grenache 2019 Rating 92 To 2022 $28 NG
The Cigar The Menzies Vineyard Cabernet Sauvignon 2017 Rating 92 To 2029 $35 NG
FDR1A Cabernet Shiraz 2015 Rating 92 To 2024 $50 NG
Running With Bulls Barossa Tempranillo 2018 Rating 92 To 2023 $23 CM ✪
Organic Viognier 2019 Rating 91 To 2023 $22 NG ✪
Block 2 Barossa Valley Grenache Rose 2019 Rating 91 To 2021 $40 NG
Samuel's Collection Barossa Grenache Shiraz Mataro 2018 Rating 91 To 2023 $28 NG
Ringbolt Margaret River Cabernet Sauvignon 2018 Rating 91 To 2028 $29
The Tri-Centenary Barossa Grenache 2016 Rating 90 To 2021 $60 NG

Yangarra Estate Vineyard ★★★★★

809 McLaren Flat Road, Kangarilla SA 5171 **Region** McLaren Vale
T (08) 8383 7459 **www**.yangarra.com.au **Open** Mon–Sat 10–5
Winemaker Peter Fraser, Guillaume Camougrand **Est.** 2000 **Dozens** 15 000 **Vyds** 89.3ha
This is the Australian operation of Jackson Family Wines, one of the leading premium wine producers in California, which in 2000 acquired the 172ha Eringa Park Vineyard from Normans Wines (the oldest vines dated back to 1923). The renamed Yangarra Estate Vineyard is the estate base for the operation and has moved to certified biodynamic status with its vineyards. Peter Fraser has taken Yangarra Estate to another level altogether with his innovative winemaking and desire to explore all the possibilities of the Rhône Valley red and white styles. Thus you will find grenache, shiraz, mourvedre, cinsaut, carignan, tempranillo and graciano planted, and picpoul noir, terret noir, muscardin and vaccarese around the corner. The white varieties are roussanne and viognier, with grenache blanc, bourboulenc and picpoul blanc planned. Then you see ceramic eggs being used in parallel with conventional fermenters. In 2015 Peter was named Winemaker of the Year at the launch of the *Wine Companion 2016*. Exports to the UK, the US, China and other major markets.

♥♥♥♥♥ High Sands McLaren Vale Grenache 2017 From Block 31, the highest elevation at 210m, with the deepest sand. Hand-picked, mechanically sorted,

50% whole berries, open-fermented, 21 days on skins, 11 months on lees in French oak. A rainbow of aromas leading me to abort my first mental description because I'd already run out of breath. Screwcap. 14% alc. **Rating** 99 To 2047 $150 ✪

Ironheart McLaren Vale Shiraz 2017 Hand-picked, 75% destemmed and berry-sorted, 25% whole bunches, wild-fermented, on lees in French oak (35% new) for 15 months, then a barrel selection to showcase the characteristic ironstone it grows in. A magnificent wine with length to its stride and a lightness of foot. Screwcap. 14.5% alc. **Rating** 99 To 2047 $110 ✪

King's Wood McLaren Vale Shiraz 2018 From the 12.3ha east-facing Block 12 on an ironstone sandy outcrop. Hand-picked, open-fermented with 25% whole bunches, matured in a 2500l French foudre for 15 months. Vivid crimson-purple through to the rim. An incredibly fresh wine that literally dances in the mouth, juicy streams of bright red flavours – this from '18, not a vintage known for delicacy. Fantastic bargain. Screwcap. 14.5% alc. **Rating** 98 To 2040 $55 ✪

ŸŸŸŸŸ **McLaren Vale Shiraz 2018** From 6 estate blocks, 50% on sand, 50% ironstone; destemmed and mechanically sorted whole berries and 20% whole bunches open-fermented with a splash of viognier, 10 months in French oak (20% new). Dark fruits with earth, chocolate and licorice nuances. Sensational price. Screwcap. 14% alc. **Rating** 96 To 2038 $35 ✪

Old Vine McLaren Vale Grenache 2018 Hand-picked from vines planted in '46; wild yeast–open fermented. It only takes a millisecond in the mouth for the wine to establish its varietal purity and generosity. It is supple, round and deeply satisfying. Red and purple fruits to the fore, fine-grained tannins bringing up the rear. Screwcap. 14.5% alc. **Rating** 96 To 2033 $35 ✪

Ovitelli McLaren Vale Grenache 2018 From Block 20 planted '46; hand-picked, mechanically berry-sorted, crushed, fermented in 675l ceramic eggs, remaining on skins for 158 days post-ferment, no oak used, the wine pressed and matured in eggs for another 6 months. Brilliant colour. Perfumed. The late Len Evans' description for a bouquet such as this was 'old lady's handbag'. Arrestingly fresh and vibrant. Screwcap. 14.5% alc. **Rating** 96 To 2029 $55 ✪

McLaren Vale Noir 2019 Noir indeed. This lovely light-bodied, juicy wine is a voyage of discovery by the intrepid Peter Fraser. The grapes were mechanically sorted 50% whole berries, wild-fermented, 14–16 days on skins, matured for 6 months in used French oak. A wonderfully different wine, welcoming investigation, not hiding anything. Comprises 62% grenache, 15% shiraz, 12% mourvedre, 6% carignan, 3% cinsaut and 2% counoise. Screwcap. 14% alc. **Rating** 95 To 2026 $25 ✪

McLaren Vale Noir 2018 It's impossible to bypass the southern Rhône Valley in writing about this wine with its blend of grenache, mourvedre, shiraz, cinsaut, carignan and counoise. Auto-suggestion of course, but its ultra-fragrant bouquet crosses into that of the garrigue, the juicy palate bubbling with similar flavours. Such value. Screwcap. 14% alc. **Rating** 95 To 2030 $25 ✪

McLaren Vale Roussanne 2019 Hand-picked, whole-bunch pressed using a basket press, wild-fermented in used French oak, 7 months in barrel with lees stirring. The wine has wonderful texture and enjoyable fruits that suggest some brioche may be around the corner. Screwcap. 14.5% alc. **Rating** 94 To 2029 $35

ŸŸŸŸŸ **McLaren Vale Blanc 2019 Rating** 93 To 2024 $25 ✪
McLaren Vale Rose 2019 Rating 93 To 2022 $25 ✪
Roux Beaute McLaren Vale Roussanne 2018 Rating 92 To 2029 $55

Yarra Burn   ★★★☆

4/19 Geddes Street, Mulgrave, Vic 3170 **Region** Yarra Valley
T 1800 088 711 **www.yarraburn.com.au** **Open** Not
Winemaker Nic Bowen **Est.** 1975 **Dozens** NFP

At least in terms of name, this is the focal point of Accolade's Yarra Valley operations. However, the winery was sold and the wines are now made elsewhere. The Upper Yarra vineyard largely remains.

ᵀᵀᵀᵀᵀ **King Valley Prosecco 2019** An assured prosecco sourced from Australia's pioneering prosecco wine region, the King Valley. The grape simply loves the area. Neutral pale colour. Tight, percussive bubble. Aromas of dusty lemon, citrus blossom, jasmine. Almond meal, pear skin, crunchy apple wind their way through the palate. Bright and sunny. Cork. 12% alc. **Rating** 92 JP

ᵀᵀᵀᵀ **Non Vintage Prosecco NV Rating** 89 CM
Methode Champenoise 2016 Rating 89 JP

Yarra Edge ★★★★★

455 Edward Road, Chirnside Park, Vic 3116 **Region** Yarra Valley
T 0428 301 517 **www**.yarraedge.com.au **Open** Not
Winemaker Dylan McMahon **Est.** 1983 **Dozens** 3500 **Vyds** 12.73ha
Yarra Edge was established by the Bingeman family in 1983, who were advised and guided by John Middleton (of Mount Mary). The advice was, of course, good and Yarra Edge has always been able to produce high quality fruit if the vineyard was properly managed. Up to '98 the wines were made onsite under the Yarra Edge label, but in that year the vineyard was leased by Yering Station, which used the grapes for their own wines. Subsequently the vineyard received minimal care until it was purchased by a Chinese-owned company, which set about restoring it to its full glory. This has been achieved with Lucas Hoorn (formerly of Hoddles Creek Estate and Levantine Hill) as full-time vineyard manager and Dylan McMahon as contract winemaker, the wines made at Seville Estate. The quality of the wines speaks for itself. Exports to China.

ᵀᵀᵀᵀᵀ **Premium Single Vineyard Chardonnay 2016** Fine and intense, still with the power of youth. A delicious array of white flowers and a fully laden basket of stone fruits, citrus and nougat/cream. Screwcap. 13.5% alc. **Rating** 95 To 2026 $49

Single Vineyard Chardonnay 2016 A substantial chardonnay that has made light of its time in bottle and has the base to build on. Oak is obvious but not obstreperous. Screwcap. 13.5% alc. **Rating** 94 To 2026 $29 ✪
Edward Single Vineyard Cabernet Sauvignon Cabernet Franc Merlot 2016 Here the blend of 65% cabernet sauvignon, 20% cabernet franc, 14% merlot and 1% malbec has knitted with a generous supply of soft tannins and enough new oak to extend the length of the palate. Screwcap. 14.5% alc. **Rating** 94 To 2041 $39

ᵀᵀᵀᵀᵀ **Edward Single Vineyard Cabernet Sauvignon Cabernet Franc Merlot 2018 Rating** 93 To 2028 $49
Premium Single Vineyard Chardonnay 2018 Rating 91 To 2025 $59
Single Vineyard Pinot Noir 2016 Rating 91 To 2026 $29
Ally Single Vineyard Cabernet Sauvignon Merlot Cabernet Franc Malbec 2018 Rating 90 To 2038 $59

Yarra Yering ★★★★★

Briarty Road, Coldstream, Vic 3770 **Region** Yarra Valley
T (03) 5964 9267 **www**.yarrayering.com **Open** 7 days 10–5
Winemaker Sarah Crowe **Est.** 1969 **Dozens** 5000 **Vyds** 26.37ha
In September 2008, founder Bailey Carrodus died and in April '09 Yarra Yering was on the market. It was Bailey Carrodus's clear wish and expectation that any purchaser would continue to manage the vineyard and winery, and hence the wine style, in much the same way as he had done for the previous 40 years. Its acquisition in June '09 by a small group of investment bankers has fulfilled that wish. The low-yielding, unirrigated vineyards have always produced wines of extraordinary depth and intensity. Dry Red No. 1 is a cabernet blend; Dry Red No. 2 is a shiraz blend; Dry Red No. 3 is a blend of touriga nacional, tinta cao, tinta roriz,

tinta amarela, alvarelhao and souzao; Pinot Noir and Chardonnay are not hidden behind delphic numbers; Underhill Shiraz (planted in 1973) is from an adjacent vineyard purchased by Yarra Yering in '87. Sarah Crowe was appointed winemaker after the 2013 vintage. She has made red wines of the highest imaginable quality right from her first vintage in '14 and, to the delight of many, myself included, has offered all the wines with screwcaps. For good measure, she introduced the '14 Light Dry Red Pinot Shiraz as a foretaste of that vintage and an affirmation of the exceptional talent recognised by her being named Winemaker of the Year in the *Wine Companion 2017*. Exports to the UK, the US, Singapore, Hong Kong, China and NZ.

ℙℙℙℙℙ **Light Dry Red Pinot Shiraz 2019** A 50/50% blend. It's a medium-weight wine (at most) but it's in rude good health; its complex flavours are like flowing robes, all silk and fine stitching. Red cherry and plum, garden herbs and twigs, nuts and bowls of wet flowers. Tannin, spicy, is laced exquisitely through the finish. If an elegant, mid-weight wine can be a humdinger, this is it. Screwcap. 13.5% alc. **Rating** 97 **To** 2037 $95 CM ✪

Pinot Noir 2018 Sarah Crowe continues to find new features to the Yarra Yering wines. This is a subtle expression with no thumping of drums; intensely pleasing. The bouquet fills all the senses with red fruits, the palate seamlessly taking on the theme. The length and balance mean this wine will seem ageless as the years go by. All this from a year in which many Yarra Valley pinot makers had to work hard. Screwcap. 13% alc. **Rating** 97 **To** 2030 $105 ✪

Carrodus Shiraz 2018 Vines planted in '69; 100 dozen made; 50% new French oak. It's 100% shiraz. Intense black cherry and plum flavours run headlong into graphite, cedar wood and wood smoke. Peppery notes hum in the background but the drill of smoke–infused fruit flavour is where the major shots are fired. It's tight, complex, dramatic and intense. Screwcap. 14% alc. **Rating** 97 **To** 2040 $275 CM

Carrodus Cabernet Sauvignon 2018 An exceptional wine. Blackcurrant and redcurrant flavours come soaked in milk chocolate, bay leaves, pencil and tobacco; the end result is seamless, classy and majestically long. It's not a big wine but it lives life entirely on its own terms; every step is firm, sure and considered. Screwcap. 13% alc. **Rating** 97 **To** 2045 $275 CM

ℙℙℙℙℙ **Chardonnay 2018** Whole-bunch pressed, matured in French oak. The highly expressive bouquet is quickly followed by an equally loquacious palate, white stone fruit, oak and natural acidity. Screwcap. 13% alc. **Rating** 96 **To** 2030 $105

Underhill 2018 A wine with long fingers and arms. It was grown on a single block of shiraz, planted in '73. It eats elegance for breakfast, berried fruit for lunch, herb and wood spice notes for afters. Plum, char, smoked herbs, fresh red cherries, a slip of creamy/smoky oak. The balance of this wine is an experience in itself. Best of all: it pushes out gloriously through the finish. Screwcap. 13.5% alc. **Rating** 96 **To** 2036 $120 CM

Dry Red No. 1 2018 Comprises 55% cabernet sauvignon, 28% merlot, 12% malbec, 5% petit verdot. Essence of blackcurrant with a boysenberried freshness, almost into forest berry territory, with polished cedar wood oak and drifts of fragrant herbs. Pure, complete, svelte; all these words apply. Has a long run ahead of it. Screwcap. 13.5% alc. **Rating** 96 **To** 2040 $120 CM

Carrodus Viognier 2018 Vines planted in '82. Viognier juice is run to barrel – without any clarification – where it's fermented and matured for 10 months. Two barrels produced. Lifted aromatics, crunch and power, pretty blossomy notes, crackles of spice. It flexes its quality throughout; an authoritative wine. Screwcap. 14% alc. **Rating** 95 **To** 2025 $160 CM

Carrodus Pinot Noir 2018 Highly textural and to a degree tannic, though it's impeccably well balanced throughout. This comes riddled with dry, meaty, woodsy spice notes, though crushed rose petal, red/black cherry and toasty oak notes keep the palate purring along. It's well fruited and powered but 2 keywords spring to mind: structural integrity. Screwcap. 13% alc. **Rating** 95 **To** 2034 $275 CM

Dry Red No. 2 2018 Shiraz 95%, mataro 3%, viognier 1%, marsanne 1%. Impeccable form. There's a sweetness to the fruit and a savouriness to the finish, redcurrant and twists of herbs, with floral overtones and oak as garnish. It's smooth-skinned but not syrupy; it's a wine in complete control. Not a question mark in sight. Screwcap. 13.5% alc. **Rating** 95 **To** 2036 $120 CM

Agincourt Cabernet Malbec 2018 A wine of absolute charm. It's a 75/25% blend in cabernet's favour though it presents as a seamless whole. Blackcurrant, mulberry, roasted nut and fresh briar flavours come brightened by redcurrant. Tannin has melted in, clean acidity keeps it all fresh and true, the finish feels assured. It will age gracefully and (very) well. Screwcap. 13.5% alc. **Rating** 95 **To** 2035 $105 CM

Dry Red No. 3 2018 Made from '90 plantings of touriga nacional, tinta cao, tinta roriz, tinta amarela, avarelhao and sousao. Excellent winemaking, the varieties embracing each other on the medium-bodied palate. The texture of the purple and black fruits is perfect. Screwcap. 13% alc. **Rating** 95 **To** 2028 $105

Dry White No. 2 2018 Marsanne, viognier and roussanne. Pale straw-green. There is contrasting phenolic weight ex the viognier, chalky notes from the roussanne and floral notes ex the marsanne. Screwcap. 13.5% alc. **Rating** 94 **To** 2025 $55

New Territories Shiraz Touriga 2018 A 55/45% blend. It's fleshy and sweet-fruited upfront but it soon turns sinewy and stern. Plump plum and red cherry move over to seaweed, woody spice, cedar wood and twigs. It's not unbalanced but the structure here has a force to it. The 'interest' factor is high. Screwcap. 13% alc. **Rating** 94 **To** 2034 $55 CM

ȲȲȲȲȲ **Dry White No. 1 2018 Rating** 91 **To** 2029 $55

Yarrabank   ★★★★★

38 Melba Highway, Yarra Glen, Vic 3775 **Region** Yarra Valley
T (03) 9730 0100 **www.**yering.com **Open** 7 days 10–5
Winemaker Willy Lunn, James Oliver, Darren Rathbone **Est.** 1993 **Dozens** 5000
Vyds 4ha

The highly successful Yarrabank was established as a joint venture between the French Champagne house Devaux and Yering Station in 1993. Until '97 the Yarrabank Cuvee Brut was made under Claude Thibaut's direction at Domaine Chandon, but thereafter the entire operation has been conducted at Yarrabank and the venture is now owned solely by Yering Station. There are 4ha of dedicated vineyards at Yering Station planted to pinot noir and chardonnay, the balance of the intake comes from growers in the Yarra Valley and southern Victoria. Exports to all major markets.

ȲȲȲȲȲ **Cuvee 2013** Traditional method, prolonged tirage, not disgorged until Jul '19. The blend is 56% chardonnay and 44% pinot noir, the latter seemingly more influential. Absolutely ready now, its fruit woven through the yeasty/bready development. Diam. 13% alc. **Rating** 95 $38 ✪

Brut Rose 2013 Has 44% pinot noir, 1% pinot noir as a red wine, 55% chardonnay; traditional method. Red fruits to the fore, the length and balance are very good and the wine is very fresh. Exceptional value. Cork. 13% alc. **Rating** 95 $38 ✪

Yarradindi Wines   ★★★★

1018 Murrindindi Road, Murrindindi, Vic 3717 **Region** Upper Goulburn
T 0438 305 314 **www.**mrhughwine.com **Open** Not
Winemaker Hugh Cuthbertson **Est.** 1979 **Dozens** 90 000 **Vyds** 70ha

Murrindindi Vineyards was established by Alan and Jan Cutherbertson as a minor diversification from their cattle property. Son Hugh Cutherbertson (with a long and high-profile wine career) took over the venture and in 2015 folded the business into his largest customers to create Yarradindi Wines. The main focus now is export to China with distribution organisations in Hangzhou, shipping 1 million bottles annually. Exports to the UK and China.

ΨΨΨΨΨ **Mr Hugh Sipping Bliss Digestif NV** As with its aperitif sibling, this is old Seabrook stock apparently from the Talavera port solera believed to have an average age of 80yo, give or take. A mahogany-brown hue. Complex and rich with burnt toffee, licorice blackstrap with a hint of baking spices and pomander. Super fresh with brandy-esque spirit balanced, luscious yet a sensation of warmth and dryness on the finish. The half bottles are sealed in wax, seemingly by goblins – quite unappealing, unlike the wine within. Cork. 18% alc. **Rating** 95 $40 JF

ΨΨΨΨΨ **Mr Hugh Sipping Bliss Aperitif NV Rating** 92 $40 JF

YarraLoch   ★★★★

11 Range Road, Gruyere, Vic 3770 **Region** Yarra Valley
T 0407 376 587 **www**.yarraloch.com.au **Open** By appt
Winemaker Contract **Est.** 1998 **Dozens** 2000 **Vyds** 6ha
This is the ambitious project of successful investment banker Stephen Wood. He has taken the best possible advice and has not hesitated to provide appropriate financial resources to a venture that has no exact parallel in the Yarra Valley or anywhere else in Australia. Six hectares of vineyards may not seem so unusual, but in fact he has assembled three entirely different sites, 70km apart, each matched to the needs of the variety/varieties planted on that site. Pinot noir is planted on the Steep Hill Vineyard with a northeast orientation and a shaley rock and ironstone soil. Cabernet sauvignon has been planted at Kangaroo Ground with a dry, steep northwest-facing site and abundant sun exposure in the warmest part of the day, ensuring full ripeness. Merlot, shiraz, chardonnay and viognier are planted at Upper Plenty, 50km from Kangaroo Ground. This has an average temperature 2°C cooler and a ripening period 2–3 weeks later than the warmest parts of the Yarra Valley.

ΨΨΨΨΨ **Stephanie's Dream Whole Bunch Pinot Noir 2016** The fruit was chilled and tipped into small open fermenters, 6 days' cold soak, wild ferment. Whole-bunch tannins are in one person's view too obvious, the next person has no problem with it. Screwcap. 13% alc. **Rating** 94 **To** 2029 $50
Stephanie's Dream LC Block Pinot Noir 2016 Has 90% MV6, 10% D (Davis) clones; the usual slow, cool fermentation, 21 days on skins, matured in French oak (18% new). Very good colour, depth and hue. The flavours are a mix of savoury, spicy and fruity. Screwcap. 13% alc. **Rating** 94 **To** 2024 $50
Stephanie's Dream Whole Bunch Pinot Noir 2015 Chilled fruit into open fermenters for wild fermentation, foot stomping every 2 days, 25 days on skins, pressed to French barriques (25% new). Fine tannins permeate the scented bouquet and convincingly long palate. Screwcap. 13% alc. **Rating** 94 **To** 2030 $50

ΨΨΨΨΨ **Single Vineyard Pinot Noir 2016 Rating** 93 **To** 2026 $35
La Cosette Chardonnay 2017 Rating 92 **To** 2027 $30
La Cosette Pinot Noir 2018 Rating 91 **To** 2023 $30

Yarran Wines

178 Myall Park Road, Yenda, NSW 2681 **Region** Riverina
T (02) 6968 1125 **www**.yarranwines.com.au **Open** Mon–Sat 10–5
Winemaker Sam Brewer **Est.** 2000 **Dozens** 8000 **Vyds** 30ha
Lorraine Brewer (and late husband John) were grapegrowers for over 30 years and when son Sam completed a degree in wine science at CSU, they celebrated his graduation by crushing 1t of shiraz, fermenting the grapes in a milk vat. The majority of the grapes from the estate plantings are sold but each year a little more has been made under the Yarran banner; along the way a winery with a crush capacity of 150t has been built. Sam worked for Southcorp and De Bortoli in Australia, and overseas (in the US and China), but in 2009 decided to take the plunge and concentrate on the family winery with his parents. The majority of the grapes come from the family vineyard but some parcels are sourced from growers, including Lake Cooper Estate in the Heathcote region. Over the past three years Sam has focused on improving the quality of the estate-grown grapes, moving to organic conversion. Yarran is the *Wine Companion 2021* Dark Horse of the Year. Exports to Singapore and China.

ΥΥΥΥΥ A Few Words... Whole Bunch Heathcote Shiraz 2018 From Colbinabbin
Estate, whole bunches tipped straight into open fermenters, matured for
12 months in French oak. Gold medal Great Australian Shiraz Challenge '19. Very
astute winemaking has produced a seductively soft shiraz. Screwcap. 14.2% alc.
Rating 95 To 2025 $32 ✪
Shiraz 2018 A Bendigo, Hilltops and Heathcote blend based on availability and
price. Made with equipment that can handle substantial volumes of grapes which
means (for example) there is no pumping of skins post fermentation. Medium-
bodied, supple and balanced. Gold medal Cowra Wine Show '19. Screwcap.
14.2% alc. Rating 95 To 2026 $15 ✪
Limited Release Block Series Riverina Durif 2018 Sam Brewer set out to
make a durif just under 14% alcohol, and succeeded. The bouquet is strikingly
floral, the palate dipped in dark chocolate (more please) and the tannins support
rather than intrude. Richly deserved its 2 silver medals, especially from the
Melbourne Wine Show. Screwcap. 14% alc. Rating 94 To 2030 $28 ✪

ΥΥΥΥΥ Limited Release Block Series Heathcote Shiraz 2018 Rating 92
To 2022 $32
Limited Release Block Series Riverina Petit Verdot 2018 Rating 92
To 2028 $28
Sauvignon Blanc 2019 Rating 90 To 2020 $15 ✪

Yarrh Wines   ★★★★

440 Greenwood Road, Murrumbateman, NSW 2582 **Region** Canberra District
T (02) 6227 1474 **www.**yarrhwines.com.au **Open** Fri–Sun 11–5
Winemaker Fiona Wholohan **Est.** 1997 **Dozens** 2000 **Vyds** 6ha
Fiona Wholohan and Neil McGregor are IT refugees; both now work full-time running
the Yarrh Wines Vineyard and making the wines. Fiona undertook the oenology and
viticulture course at CSU and has also spent time as an associate judge at wine shows. They
spent five years moving to a hybrid organic vineyard with composting, mulching, biological
controls and careful vineyard floor management. The vineyard includes cabernet sauvignon,
shiraz, sauvignon blanc, riesling, pinot noir and sangiovese. They have recently tripled their
sangiovese plantings with two new clones. Yarrh was the original Aboriginal name for the
Yass district.

ΥΥΥΥΥ Canberra District Riesling 2019 Just enough fruit generosity and very good
length. Style, quality and value are all well in the buyer's favour here. Lime
and lime leaf, bath salts and (almost peppery) spice. Lovely. Screwcap. 11% alc.
Rating 94 To 2030 $25 CM ✪

ΥΥΥΥΥ Canberra District Shiraz 2018 Rating 93 To 2032 $30 CM
Canberra District Sangiovese 2018 Rating 92 To 2025 $30 CM
Canberra District Pinot Noir 2018 Rating 91 To 2027 $35 CM
Canberra District Cabernet Sauvignon 2018 Rating 91 To 2032 $35 CM

🍇 Year Wines   ★★★★☆

PO Box 638, Willunga, SA 5172 **Region** McLaren Vale
T 0434 970 162 **www.**yearwines.com.au **Open** Not
Winemaker Luke Growden, Caleigh Hunt **Est.** 2012 **Dozens** 600
Luke Growden and Caleigh Hunt live with their two children on a small farm in the Whites
Valley district of McLaren Vale. The name of their winery is very clever. Luke and Caleigh tell
it this way: 'Through a mixture of serendipity and blind faith, we started Year Wines in 2012.
Amidst the chaos of a new baby, sleep deprivation, house renovations and juggling day jobs,
the lure of fruit from a block of old vine grenache was too much to resist. It was a crazy life-
changing year.' The wines are made with minimal intervention (notably no fining or filtration)
in small quantities. Attention to detail is the panacea. Exports to the US and Singapore.

♟♟♟♟♟ Serge McLaren Vale Mataro Syrah Grenache 2017 A 42/38/20% blend
from 2 vineyards in Whites Valley; the shiraz picked early, 100% whole bunches,
4 weeks on skins, matured in old oak for 9 months. A very attractive wine,
fresh and juicy vibrant red fruits; balance, line and length. Screwcap. 13.9% alc.
Rating 95 To 2029 $30 ✪

McLaren Vale Fiano 2018 A very striking, full-flavoured fiano with a rich fruit
spectrum and a distinct touch of honey to add further interest. Paradoxically, the
texture fiano often has isn't obvious here, but who's to argue? Screwcap. 12.9% alc.
Rating 94 To 2023 $28 ✪

♟♟♟♟♟ McLaren Vale Cinsault 2017 Rating 91 To 2023 $30
McLaren Vale Grenache 2017 Rating 90 To 2024 $32

Yeates Wines   ★★★★

138 Craigmoor Road, Mudgee, NSW 2850 **Region** Mudgee
T 0427 791 264 **www.**yeateswines.com.au **Open** By appt
Winemaker Jacob Stein **Est.** 2010 **Dozens** 750 **Vyds** 11ha
In 2010 the Yeates family purchased the 16ha Mountain Blue Vineyard in Mudgee from
Foster's, planted in 1968 by the late Robert (Bob) Oatley. The vines have since been
reinvigorated and cane-pruned, with the grapes now being hand-picked. In 2013 the use
of chemicals and inorganic fertiliser were eliminated and organic management practices
introduced in an effort to achieve a more sustainable ecological footprint. The vines and wines
have flourished under this new management regimen.

♟♟♟♟♟ Reserve Shiraz Cabernet 2018 A flood of silken flavour. Plum and creamy
vanilla, as smooth as they come. It hits, runs and continues through to a satisfying
finish. Tannin has melted straight in. You can't help but be seduced. Screwcap.
14.5% alc. **Rating** 92 To 2029 CM

♟♟♟♟ Jack Roth Mudgee Shiraz 2018 Rating 89 To 2026 CM

Yelland & Papps   ★★★★★

279 Nuraip Road, Nuriootpa, SA 5355 **Region** Barossa Valley
T 0408 628 494 **www.**yellandandpapps.com **Open** By appt
Winemaker Michael Papps, Susan Papps **Est.** 2005 **Dozens** 4000 **Vyds** 2ha
Michael and Susan Papps (nee Yelland) set up this venture after their marriage in 2005. It
is easy for them to regard the Barossa Valley as their home because Michael has lived and
worked in the wine industry in the Barossa Valley for more than 20 years. He has a rare
touch, producing consistently excellent wines, but also pushing the envelope; as well as using
a sustainable approach to winemaking with minimal inputs, he has not hesitated to challenge
orthodox approaches to a number of aspects of conventional fermentation methods. Exports
to Norway and China.

♟♟♟♟♟ Second Take Barossa Valley Shiraz 2018 Hand-picked, whole bunches
wild-fermented, matured in French oak (15% new) for 10 months. 'Old World
techniques', say Yelland & Papps, but I think they are well and truly embodied
in Australia as a primary option. This wine has delicious flavour and mouthfeel
that can quickly mesmerise the unwary. Totally delicious. Screwcap. 12.8% alc.
Rating 96 To 2038 $45 ✪

Devote Greenock Barossa Valley Shiraz 2017 Wild yeast–open fermented,
14 days on skins, matured in 76% French, 24% American oak (47% new) for
23 months. This has everything its standard Barossa Valley sibling lacks: it's
gloriously intense and rich, focused and balanced. The more it is tasted, the better
it is. Only 1675 bottles made. Screwcap. 13.5% alc. **Rating** 96 To 2042 $45 ✪

Second Take Barossa Valley Grenache 2018 From 61yo vines; 56% whole
bunch, 22% foot-stomped, fermented in puncheons. It is, quite simply, a beautiful
wine; all the focus is on raspberry/cherry/plum fruit; only 4% of the oak used was
new. Only 1675 bottles made. Screwcap. 13.7% alc. **Rating** 96 To 2030 $45 ✪

Vin de Soif 2017 A blend of 70.1% grenache, 24.9% mataro, 5% carignan from multiple vineyards with an average age of 87yo. Matured for 20 months in used French oak. The cool vintage is reflected in the savoury intensity that permeates every part of a (very) complex wine. Food matches? A hundred or so. Screwcap. 13.9% alc. **Rating** 95 **To** 2032 $30 ✪

Second Take Barossa Valley Mataro 2018 Hand-picked, wild yeast, open and barrel fermentation with 85% whole bunches, 21 days on skins, matured in old French oak for 10 months. Wonderfully fragrant, elegant and – above all else – literally floats across the palate. The antithesis of so much stodgy mataro. Screwcap. 12.8% alc. **Rating** 95 **To** 2030 $45

Second Take Barossa Valley Vermentino 2018 Wild-fermented, 310 days on skins in tank. Full gold. The wine plays cat and mouse in the mouth, momentarily settled, then up and running. And no, it's not the taint called mousy (pronounced mowzee). Just 974 bottles made. Screwcap. 11.2% alc. **Rating** 94 **To** 2028 $45

🍷🍷🍷🍷♀ **Barossa Valley Vermentino 2018** **Rating** 92 **To** 2021 $30
Second Take Barossa Valley Roussanne 2018 **Rating** 90 **To** 2026 $45
Barossa Valley Shiraz 2017 **Rating** 90 **To** 2028 $30

Yering Station ★★★★★

38 Melba Highway, Yarra Glen, Vic 3775 **Region** Yarra Valley
T (03) 9730 0100 **www.**yering.com **Open** 7 days 10–5
Winemaker Willy Lunn, James Oliver, Darren Rathbone **Est.** 1988 **Dozens** 60 000
Vyds 112ha

The historic Yering Station (or at least the portion of the property on which the cellar door and vineyard are established) was purchased by the Rathbone family in 1996; it is also the site of Yarrabank (see separate entry). A spectacular and very large winery was built, handling the Yarrabank sparkling and the Yering Station table wines, immediately becoming one of the focal points of the Yarra Valley – particularly as the historic Chateau Yering, where luxury accommodation and fine dining are available, is next door. Winemaker Willy Lunn, a graduate of the University of Adelaide, has more than 25 years' cool-climate winemaking experience around the world, including at Petaluma, Shaw + Smith and Argyle Winery (Oregon). Exports to all major markets.

🍷🍷🍷🍷🍷 **Reserve Yarra Valley Shiraz Viognier 2018** The only reserve from '18. A gothic dark purple hue. It's deep, fleshy and very ripe and brooding. Blood plums dipped in chocolate and a dusting of cinnamon, full-bodied with sumptuous tannins and the cedary oak flavour neatly in place. Screwcap. **Rating** 96 **To** 2030 $130 JF

Reserve Yarra Valley Shiraz Viognier 2017 There is slightly less than 2% co-fermented viognier but it plays an important role in creating the highly fragrant and expressive bouquet. Yes, it's vintage-driven with a riot of red and purple fruits, but the perfect structure and balance goes way beyond normal wines. Screwcap. 12.5% alc. **Rating** 96 **To** 2037 $130

Yarra Valley Chardonnay 2018 Tightly coiled, just hinting at how this might unfurl in time. A savouriness overall, yet hints of lemon balm, grapefruit, flinty with perky acidity, so this is quite moreish. Oak adds an extra dimension and is seamlessly integrated. Screwcap. 12.5% alc. **Rating** 95 **To** 2028 $40 JF

Laura Barnes Pinot Noir 2018 Surprisingly open and plush rather than structured and deep. That's OK. It is ready to be enjoyed now with its core of spicy red berries, cherries and some pomegranate tartness. The merest nod to oak, a subtle implementation of 10 months with 30% new French puncheons, yet it adds a touch of spice and smooths out the tannins. Medium-bodied, soft and supple; and a lovely drink. Screwcap. 13.5% alc. **Rating** 95 **To** 2029 $70 JF

Yarra Valley Shiraz Viognier 2018 Silky, slinky and sexy. Everything in harmony from the dark fruits and spices to the cedary French oak adding another complexing layer; some deli meats also in the mix. Juicy across the palate with velvety tannins adding to the pleasure. Screwcap. 14.5% alc. **Rating** 95 **To** 2030 $40 JF

Reserve Yarra Valley Cabernet Sauvignon 2017 Savoury and oaky with wafts of cedar, menthol, tobacco and the merest touch of cassis. The palate is tight, austere even, but has refreshing acidity, textural tannins and length. There's just a hardness on the finish but I'm giving this the benefit of doubt or rather, more time. Screwcap. 14% alc. **Rating** 95 **To** 2033 $130 JF

Yarra Valley Pinot Noir 2018 Rating 93 **To** 2026 $40 JF
Village Yarra Valley Rose 2019 Rating 91 **To** 2021 $26 JF
Village Yarra Valley Chardonnay 2018 Rating 90 **To** 2024 $26 JF
Little Yering Pinot Noir 2018 Rating 90 **To** 2025 $18 ⊘

Yeringberg ★★★★★

Maroondah Highway, Coldstream, Vic 3770 **Region** Yarra Valley
T (03) 9739 0240 **www.yeringberg.com.au Open** By appt
Winemaker Sandra de Pury **Est.** 1863 **Dozens** 1500 **Vyds** 3.66ha
Guill de Pury and daughter Sandra, with Guill's wife Katherine in the background, make wines for the new millennium from the low-yielding vines re-established in the heart of what was one of the most famous (and infinitely larger) vineyards of the 19th century. In the riper years, the red wines have a velvety generosity of flavour rarely encountered, while never losing varietal character; the long-lived Marsanne Roussanne takes students of history back to Yeringberg's fame in the 19th century. Exports to the UK, the US, Switzerland, Hong Kong and China.

Yarra Valley Viognier 2018 This is exceptional viognier. Benchmark. Be it Australian or French. This level of warmth is necessitated to showcase the exuberance of the variety: honeysuckle, apricot and ginger glaze. The billowing phenolic chew beautifully melded to a gentle wash of acidity. A plume of flavour brushing the cheeks. This could do with more phenolic pucker, but is still very fine. Screwcap. **Rating** 95 **To** 2023 NG
2017 Yeringberg A quintessential Bordeaux blend of cabernet, cabernet franc, petit verdot and merlot. Currant red and black. Mid-weighted and soused with bouquet garni, a swab of green olive and sage crusted tannins. A bit shins and elbows and unresolved at this point. The track record of this wine is such, however, that I have no doubt that the astringency will meld with patience. Screwcap. **Rating** 95 **To** 2032 NG

Yarra Valley Pinot Noir 2017 Rating 93 **To** 2024 NG
Yarra Valley Chardonnay 2018 Rating 92 **To** 2024 NG

Yes said the Seal ★★★★★

1251–1269 Bellarine Highway, Wallington, Vic 3221 **Region** Geelong
T (03) 5250 6577 **www.yessaidtheseal.com.au Open** 7 days 10–5
Winemaker Darren Burke **Est.** 2014 **Dozens** 1200 **Vyds** 8ha
This is the newest venture of David and Lyndsay Sharp, long-term vintners on Geelong's Bellarine Peninsula. It is situated onsite at the Flying Brick Cider Co's Cider House in Wallington. The estate vineyard includes 3ha of pinot noir, 2ha each of chardonnay and shiraz and 1ha of sauvignon blanc.

The Bellarine Sauvignon Blanc 2018 A mid-weighted, barrel-fermented sauvignon that is as much about aromas of quince, cumquat and lemon oil, as it is about a slippery, textural palate of considerable complexity and chew. Stirred occasionally and left on lees for some tightening up, this is a refreshing gust of change amid a breeze of monochromatic sameness. Screwcap. 13.5% alc. **Rating** 93 **To** 2023 $38 NG
The Bellarine Shiraz 2017 In the name of a cool fermentation to promote aromatic exuberance – think blackberry, iodine, coppa and violet – this richly flavoured wine was inoculated across a whole-berry fermentation and given 10 months in French wood (10% new). Reduction imparts tension, while a sluice

of pepper grind acidity tows the wine long and fresh. I'd decant this. Aggressively. Screwcap. 14% alc. **Rating** 93 **To** 2024 $42 NG

The Bellarine Chardonnay 2018 A fruit-forward bumptious chardonnay exuding notes of white fig and stone fruits with gentle rails of quality French oak (25% new, 10 months) imparting vanillan spice, nougat and creamed cashew scents, while keeping everything in check. This billows along nicely. Screwcap. 14% alc. **Rating** 92 **To** 2024 $38 NG

The Bellarine Pinot Noir 2018 A pallid ruby, this is quintessential Bellarine pinot, marked strongly with the stamp of place: a waft of sarsaparilla, wood smoke and decadently ripe strawberry. Maritime acidity and tannins, spindly and moreish, confer pulse, sap and good linger. Screwcap. 13.5% alc. **Rating** 92 **To** 2024 $42 NG

Reserve Blanc de Blanc 2011 With a whopping 8 years on lees, this is a creamy swirl of yeasty nourishment across the palate: brioche and toasted nuts. A generous fizz that is at an optimal drinking window. Cork. 11.5% alc. **Rating** 92 $42 NG

Z Wine

Shop 3, 109–111 Murray Street, Tanunda, SA 5352 **Region** Barossa Valley **T** (08) 8563 3637 **www**.zwine.com.au **Open** Mon–Wed 10–5, Thurs–Sun 10–late **Winemaker** Janelle Zerk **Est.** 1999 **Dozens** 10000

Z Wine is the partnership of sisters Janelle and Kristen Zerk, whose heritage dates back five generations at the Zerk Vineyard in Lyndoch. Vineyard resources include growers that supply old vine shiraz, old bushvine grenache and High Eden Valley riesling. Both women have completed degrees at the University of Adelaide (Janelle winemaking and Kristen wine marketing). Janelle also has vintage experience in Puligny Montrachet, Tuscany and Sonoma Valley. Wines are released under the Z Wine, Rustica and Section 3146 labels. In 2017 Z Wine opened a cellar door in the main street of Tanunda. Exports to the US, Singapore, NZ, Taiwan, Hong Kong and China.

Rustica Barossa Valley Grenache 2019 Fragrant, flowery red fruit aromas are as beautiful as they are striking, and the silky, supple palate adds even more to the wine. It takes Barossa Valley grenache in a direction all of its own with a fine flick of tannins on the finish. Very high winemaking skills; a mind boggling bargain. Screwcap. 14.5% alc. **Rating** 97 **To** 2029 $20 ✪

Hein Ancestor Vine Barossa Valley Shiraz 2018 Sourced from a plot of ancestor vines in Langmeil, over 140yo, this glossy red was hand-picked and plunged across a cap of whole-berry fruit, spiced with a skerrick of 10% whole cluster and judicious oak. Extremely limited … yadda yadda. Most impressive is the pulpy flow. The winning vinosity. Real drive, precision and length to the cavalcade of lilac, peppery red berry and blue fruit references. Lovely texture and rewardingly, NOT overdone. Cork. **Rating** 96 **To** 2035 NG

Saul Eden Valley Riesling 2019 An impressive wine with a full measure of mouth-watering acidity travelling alongside the predominantly citrus palate, some crunchy green apple also in the party. How these wines, from the hot vintage and its heat spikes, kept acidity and balance, time alone will tell. Screwcap. **Rating** 95 **To** 2030 $32 ✪

Roman Old Vine Barossa Valley GSM 2018 A conflation of 90yo grenache, 140yo mataro and 65yo shiraz. Impressive. Drinking history, here. Kirsch. A finely sculpted rail of tannin, more reliant on extraction and neutral oak texture than whole bunch. A lovely juicy natural feel to the wine across the gums; a ferrous pulse growing with time in the glass. Nicely grippy. More mataro would be nice. GMS should be the acronym in descending order of importance. Screwcap. **Rating** 95 **To** 2026 $38 NG

Section 3146 Barossa Valley Cabernet Sauvignon 2017 The vintage was responsible for this excellent evocation of cabernet. Bay leaf, dried herb and black olive nuances join with the blackcurrant fruit that is the heart of good cabernet. Screwcap. **Rating** 95 To 2037 $35 **✪**

Hilder Ancestor Vine Barossa Valley Mataro 2019 From 145yo biodynamic vines. While I am unsure of any official certification, I will sort of believe this trope. Mid–ruby. Wild-fermented, 8 months in oak (20% new). Blueberry. Meaty. Ferruginous. Great, expansive tannins that pummel the gums, rendering them eager for the next sip while providing a platform for age. A bit too tangy, but otherwise very good. Cork. **Rating** 95 To 2029 $300 NG

August Old Vine Barossa Valley Grenache 2019 A light ruby suggesting good things in store. The nose, initially subdued, unravels across finely tuned tannins derived from sensitive extraction across 6 months in neutral wood. Anise, thyme, marjoram. A potpourri. Raspberry aplenty too. This is a delicious mid-weighted grenache that plies imminent drinkability and immense charm alongside a structural seriousness. Very fine. Screwcap. **Rating** 94 To 2024 $30 NG **✪**

ΨΨΨΨ♀ **Julius Barossa Valley Shiraz 2018** Rating 93 To 2030 $70 NG
Plowman Dry Grown Barossa Valley Shiraz 2017 Rating 93 To 2032 $120 NG
Audrey Barossa Valley Cabernet Sauvignon 2017 Rating 93 To 2029 $35 NG
Rohrlach Survivor Vine Barossa Valley Grenache 2018 Rating 92 To 2025 $120 NG
Section 3146 Barossa Valley Shiraz 2017 Rating 91 To 2025 $35 NG
Hedley Barossa Valley Shiraz 2017 Rating 91 To 2029 $35 NG
Franz Cabernet Shiraz 2018 Rating 91 To 2026 $60 NG
Xave Late Harvest 2019 Rating 91 To 2029 $20 NG **✪**
Rustica Barossa Valley Shiraz 2016 Rating 90 To 2024 $20 NG **✪**

Zema Estate   ★★★★★

14944 Riddoch Highway, Coonawarra, SA 5263 **Region** Coonawarra
T (08) 8736 3219 **www.**zema.com.au **Open** Mon–Fri 9–5, w'ends & public hols 10–4
Winemaker Joe Cory **Est.** 1982 **Dozens** 15 000 **Vyds** 61ha
Zema is one of the last outposts of hand-pruning in Coonawarra; members of the Zema family tend the vineyard set in the heart of Coonawarra's terra rossa soil. Winemaking practices are straightforward; if ever there was an example of great wines being made in the vineyard, this is it. Exports to Hong Kong, Singapore, China and NZ.

ΨΨΨΨΨ **Family Selection Coonawarra Shiraz 2016** It's a joy to see a 4yo shiraz being released from one of the country's unsung shiraz regions, Coonawarra. It's a wake-up call, if one was needed, to the excitement that the region and the grape can deliver. A youthful 4yo built to last a long time with tight, close-knitted black fruits, high spice and toasted vanillan oak. Coonawarra earth, a mineral clarity of the soil, resides throughout. A beauty in the making. Screwcap. 14.8% alc. Rating 95 To 2042 $50 JP

Coonawarra Cabernet Sauvignon 2017 Has the Coonawarra signature written all over it from the unforced balance, medium-bodied stance and blackberry concentration to the bright flourish of bay leaf, sage and menthol. Savoury tannins and oak work a treat in creating extra layers of interest. It can only get better from here. Screwcap. 14% alc. Rating 95 To 2038 $33 JP **✪**

Family Selection Coonawarra Cabernet Sauvignon 2016 It's hard to argue against the beauty, the vibrancy of fruit, the buoyant mood this wine puts you in; the concentrated cabernet blackberry and spice, the whiff of Coonawarra bay leaf, white pepper and the defining tannins that draw in tight. So I won't. Screwcap. 14.5% alc. Rating 95 To 2038 $50 JP

Zerella Wines

182 Olivers Rd, McLaren Vale, SA 5171 **Region** McLaren Vale
T (08) 8323 8288/0488 929 202 **www.zerellawines.com.au Open** Thurs–Mon 11–4
Winemaker Jim Zerella **Est.** 2006 **Dozens** 2500 **Vyds** 58ha

In 1950 Ercole Zerella left his native Campania in southern Italy to seek a better life in SA. With a lifetime of farming and grapegrowing, the transition was seamless. Ercole's son Vic followed in his father's footsteps, becoming an icon of the SA farming and wine industries. He founded Tatachilla, where his son Jim began as a cellar hand, eventually controlling all grape purchases. While working there, Jim purchased land in McLaren Vale and, with help from family and friends, established what is now the flagship vineyard of Zerella Wines. He also established a vineyard management business catering to the needs of absentee owners. When Tatachilla was purchased by Lion Nathan in 2000 he declined the opportunity of continuing his role there and by '06 had purchased two more vineyards, and become a shareholder in a third. These all now come under the umbrella of Zerella Wines, with its 58ha of vines. The winemaking techniques used are thoroughly à la mode and definitely not traditional Italian. Exports to the UK and Canada.

ŶŶŶŶŶ **Workhorse McLaren Vale Shiraz 2017** Part machine, part hand-picked, 90% destemmed, 10% whole bunches, wild yeast–open fermented, 5 days' cold soak, 21 days on skins in total, pressed to French hogsheads (50% new) for 18 months' maturation. Big wine; has used the '17 vintage well. Screwcap. 14.5% alc. **Rating** 95 **To** 2037 $30 ☉

La Gita McLaren Vale Barbera 2017 Hand-picked, destemmed, wild yeast– open fermented with 10% whole bunches, 18 days on skins, matured for 12 months in French oak (30% new). A lively, juicy, medium-bodied palate, its spicy blood plum flavours following precisely the same path of the bouquet. A totally delicious example of the variety. Screwcap. 14% alc. **Rating** 95 **To** 2030 $35 ☉

Home Block Single Vineyard McLaren Vale Shiraz 2016 Hand-picked, destemmed, 10% whole bunches, wild yeast–open fermented, 5 days' cold soak, 15 days on skins in total, pressed to French oak (65% new) for 18 months. Very potent and powerful, and positively cries out for more time in bottle. Screwcap. 13.5% alc. **Rating** 94 **To** 2035 $60

ŶŶŶŶŶ **La Gita McLaren Vale Arneis 2017 Rating** 90 **To** 2024 $30
Workhorse McLaren Vale Shiraz 2018 Rating 90 **To** 2028 $30

Zilzie Wines

544 Kulkyne Way, Karadoc, Vic 3496 **Region** Murray Darling
T (03) 5025 8100 **www.zilziewines.com Open** Not
Winemaker Jonathan Creek **Est.** 1999 **Dozens** NFP **Vyds** 800ha

The Forbes family has been farming since the early 1900s. Zilzie is currently run by Roslyn Forbes and sons Steven and Andrew, the diverse range of farming activities now solely focused on grapegrowing from substantial vineyards. Having established a dominant position as a supplier of grapes to Southcorp, Zilzie formed a wine company in '99 and built a winery in 2000, expanding it to its current capacity of 60000t. The wines consistently far exceed expectations, given their enticing prices, that consistency driving the substantial production volume in an extremely competitive market. The business includes contract processing, winemaking and storage. Exports to the UK, Canada, Hong Kong and China.

ŶŶŶŶŶ **Regional Collection Coonawarra Cabernet Sauvignon 2018** The very good Coonawarra vintage allowed Zilzie to purchase very good wine/grapes and use French barrels for maturation. The wine is medium-bodied, blackcurrant cabernet fruit matched with a splash of merlot. It's balanced, ready to enjoy now. Screwcap. 14% alc. **Rating** 91 **To** 2028 $20 ☉

Regional Collection Adelaide Hills Pinot Gris 2019 Majority cool-fermented in tank with a yeast to enhance varietal character, a small portion fermented in oak. Light bronze colour; highly aromatic and a strongly fruited palate takes this out of the pack. Screwcap. 13.5% alc. **Rating** 90 **To** 2021 $20 ☉

Regional Collection Clare Valley Rose 2019 Full rose colour. An ultra-expressive and fragrant red berry bouquet, the palate following suit. Sangiovese was in top form in the Clare Valley in '19, albeit in short supply ex low yields. Screwcap. 12% alc. **Rating** 90 **To** 2022 $20 ✪

ŶŶŶŶ **Regional Collection Yarra Valley Chardonnay 2019 Rating** 89 **To** 2024 $20
MCMXI Cabernet Sauvignon 2018 Rating 89 **To** 2023 $50

Zonte's Footstep   ★★★★★

The General Wine Bar, 55A Main Road, McLaren Flat, SA 5171 **Region** McLaren Vale
T (08) 7286 3088 **www.zontesfootstep.com.au Open** Fri–Sat 11–6, Mon–Thurs by appt
Winemaker Brad Rey **Est.** 2003 **Dozens** 20 000 **Vyds** 214.72ha
Zonte's Footstep has been very successful since a group of long-standing friends, collectively
with deep knowledge of every aspect of the wine business, decided it was time to do
something together. Along the way there has been some shuffling of the deck chairs but all
achieved without any ill feeling from those who moved sideways or backwards. The major
change has been a broadening of the regions (Langhorne Creek, McLaren Vale, the Barossa
and Clare valleys and elsewhere) from which the grapes are sourced. Even here, however, most
of the vineyards supplying grapes are owned by members of the Zonte's Footstep partnership.
Exports to the UK, the US, Canada, Ireland, Belgium, Finland, Sweden, Denmark, Thailand,
Singapore, South Korea, Hong Kong and China.

ŶŶŶŶŶ **Z-Force McLaren Vale Shiraz 2017** Cherry-chocolate cake in a glass,
smothered in vanillan oak sprinkles. Thickly textured, without being jammy.
A smooth piste of well massaged tannins corals the party. Rich and manicured.
Screwcap. **Rating** 92 **To** 2026 $70 NG
Canto Fleurieu Sangiovese Lagrein 2018 This blend sounds so good on
paper. And thankfully it is pretty good in the glass too. Sangiovese's spurt of
sour cherry, amaro and skein of frisky tannin is allowed to unravel, reeling in the
malty oak accents, darker fruit notes and bitter chocolate to a point of palpable
savouriness and imminent drinkability. Screwcap. **Rating** 92 **To** 2028 $28 NG
Blackberry Patch Fleurieu Cabernet 2018 A welcome step away from the
fruity exuberance that serves as this address' calling card. Nothing wrong with that.
However, frankly, I needed some tannin. Real tannin. This delivers. Just. Tapenade,
cassis, bay leaf and bitter chocolate. The usual morass of oak. But a line of
nourishing tannins serves the drinker and the wine well. At times like these, thank
God for cabernet! Screwcap. **Rating** 91 **To** 2026 $28 NG
Baron Von Nemesis Barossa Shiraz 2018 After pulling this out of styrofoam
I was greeted by a slurpy, slick full-bodied red. Plenty of polish. Root beer, violet,
five-spice and dark fruit references are gently tucked in by some oaky pillars and a
trickle of saline acidity. This is a winning formula for many. Screwcap. **Rating** 90
To 2026 $35 NG
Love Symbol McLaren Vale Grenache 2018 I love grenache and McLaren
Vale holds great promise for the variety. Kirsch, damson plum, candied orange zest
and Asian spice. Oak allusions and some fuzzy tannins hold in the seams. Screwcap.
Rating 90 **To** 2023 $28 NG
Violet Beauregard Langhorne Creek Malbec 2018 One of the few
times when the back label blurb serves as an accurate description of the wine:
rich. Blueberry, mulberry and violet aromas. Mint–bitter chocolate tannins sew
the seams of faint restraint. No real point in ageing this given the exuberance.
Screwcap. **Rating** 90 **To** 2024 $28 NG

ŶŶŶŶ **Shades of Gris Adelaide Hills Pinot Grigio 2019 Rating** 89 **To** 2020
$22 NG
Dawn Patrol Adelaide Hills Pinot Noir 2018 Rating 89 **To** 2023 $35 NG
Chocolate Factory McLaren Vale Shiraz 2018 Rating 89 **To** 2026 $28 NG

Zyrah

4 Grey Box Drive, Strathtulloh, Vic 3338 **Region** Sunbury
T 0403 321 417 **www**.zyrahwinery.com.au **Open** By appt
Winemaker Brett Gatt **Est.** 2007 **Dozens** NFP

Brett Gatt began winemaking as a hobby in 2005 with his parents and his wife's parents, keeping the European family tradition, and in '07 he planted 328 vines to make wine for family consumption. His ambition to grow and make better wines is laudable, but the lack of formal training is fraught with danger, bacterial issues appear to be a particular issue with the '18 vintage wines.

Basket Pressed Shiraz 2016 The back label isn't easy to read but it does say the wine was matured for 18 months in puncheons. It is medium-bodied with blackberry fruit doing the heavy lifting in a wine that has been well made. Screwcap. 14.5% alc. **Rating** 89 **To** 2029 $45

Index

Wineries are arranged alphabetically under geographical indications (states, zones, regions and subregions as outlined on pages 50–3), to help you find a wine or winery if you're looking locally or on the road. If you are hoping to visit, the following key symbols will be of assistance.

♀   **Cellar door sales**

❚❚   **Food:** lunch platters to à la carte restaurants

⊢⊣   **Accommodation:** B&B cottages to luxury vineyard apartments

♪   **Music events:** monthly jazz in the vineyard to spectacular yearly concerts

Beechworth (Vic)

Bendigo (Vic)

Coonawarra (SA)

Currency Creek (SA)

Denmark (WA)

Eden Valley (SA)

Manjimup (WA)

Mornington Peninsula (Vic)

Mount Barker (WA)